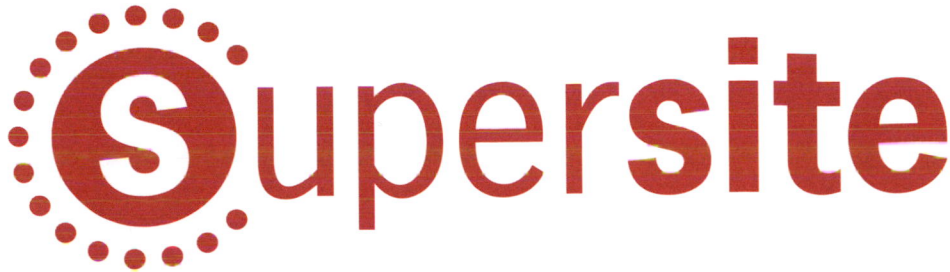

LEARNING IS JUST A CLICK AWAY

The **Vistas Supersite**—everything you need to motivate students and support language learning.

- Engages and focuses students
- Improves student performance
- Saves you time with auto-grading, quick setup, and reporting tools
- Provides flexibility to personalize your course
- Offers cost-saving digital options
- Includes vText—the online, interactive Student Edition

 Go to vhlcentral.com to get started

INSTRUCTOR'S ANNOTATED EDITION   SIXTH EDITION

VISTAS

INTRODUCCIÓN A LA LENGUA ESPAÑOLA

José A. Blanco

Philip Redwine Donley, late
Austin Community College

VISTA®
HIGHER LEARNING

Boston, Massachusetts

On the cover:
Machu Picchu, Peru

Creative Director: José A. Blanco
Publisher: Sharla Zwirek
Editorial Development: Judith Bach, Camilo Cerpa, María Victoria Echeverri, Jo Hanna Kurth
Project Management: Tiffany Kayes, Faith Ryan
Rights Management: Annie Pickert Fuller, Ashley Poreda
Technology Production: Jamie Kostecki, Paola Ríos Schaaf
Design: Radoslav Mateev, Gabriel Noreña, Andrés Vanegas
Production: Oscar Díez, Sebastián Díez, Alejandro Rojas

Student Text (Casebound) ISBN: 978-1-54330-129-8
Instructor's Annotated Edition ISBN: 978-1-54330-131-1

Library of Congress Control Number: 2018934157

1 2 3 4 5 6 7 8 9 TC 23 22 21 20 19 18

Printed in Canada.

Instructor's Annotated Edition
Table of Contents

THE VISTA HIGHER LEARNING STORY
Your Specialized World Language Publisher

Independent, specialized, and privately owned, Vista Higher Learning was founded in 2000 with one mission: to raise the teaching and learning of world languages to a higher level. This mission is based on the following beliefs:

- It is essential to prepare students for a world in which learning another language is a necessity, not a luxury.
- Language learning should be fun and rewarding, and all students should have the tools necessary for achieving success.
- Students who experience success learning a language will be more likely to continue their language studies both inside and outside the classroom.

With this in mind, we decided to take a fresh look at all aspects of language instructional materials. Because we are specialized, we dedicate 100 percent of our resources to this goal and base every decision on how well it supports language learning.

That is where you come in. Since our founding in 2000, we have relied on the continuous and invaluable feedback from language instructors and students nationwide. This partnership has proved to be the cornerstone of our success by allowing us to constantly improve our programs to meet your instructional needs.

The result? Programs that make language learning exciting, relevant, and effective through:

- an unprecedented access to resources
- a wide variety of contemporary, authentic materials
- the integration of text, technology, and media, and
- a bold and engaging textbook design

By focusing on our singular passion, we let you focus on yours.

The Vista Higher Learning Team

VISTA
HIGHER LEARNING

500 Boylston Street, Suite 620, Boston, MA 02116-3736 TOLL-FREE: 800-618-7375
TELEPHONE: 617-426-4910 FAX: 617-426-5209 www.vistahigherlearning.com

Getting to Know Vistas

Now in its Sixth Edition, **Vistas** is better than ever. Its fresh, student-friendly approach to introductory Spanish makes both teaching and learning easier, more enjoyable, and more successful. The pedagogical approach of **Vistas** continues to be communicative. It presents vocabulary and grammar as tools for effective personalized communication as it develops students' listening, reading, writing, and speaking skills. Moreover, because cultural knowledge is an integral part of both language learning and successful communication, **Vistas** introduces students to all of the countries in the Spanish-speaking world and the everyday lives of Spanish speakers.

Vistas offers features that make it truly different from other textbooks based on these same principles. Here are a few of our distinguishing features:

- **Vistas** was the first textbook to cohesively integrate a dramatic video into the student text to model target structures. The goal of the **Fotonovela** is to motivate and inspire the next generation of Spanish students.

- **Vistas** was also the first introductory college Spanish textbook to incorporate graphic design—page layout, use of colors, typefaces, and other graphic elements—as an integral part of the learning process. To enhance learning and make navigation easy, lesson sections are color-coded and appear either completely on one page or on spreads of two facing pages.

- **Vistas** offers student sidebars with on-the-spot linguistic, cultural, and language-learning information, as well as **recursos** boxes with on-page correlations of student supplements.

- **Vistas** provides a unique four-part practice sequence for virtually every grammar point. It moves from form-focused **¡Inténtalo!** exercises to directed, yet meaningful, **Práctica** exercises to communicative, interactive **Comunicación** activities, and lastly to cumulative, open-ended **Síntesis** activities.

- **Vistas** also offers two cultural videos, **Flash cultura** and **Panorama cultural**, as well as authentic TV clips and short films in **En pantalla**.

- vText—the interactive, online text—in an iPad®-friendly* format.

NEW! to the Sixth Edition

- New **Contextos** illustrations and activity art
- Revised audio activities
- Video Virtual Chats
- 7 new **En pantalla** videos
- 3 new literary readings in **Lectura**
- Pronunciation tutorials with speech recognition
- New **Panorama cultural** videos
- New **Panorama** activities
- Illustration bank for use with instructor-created activities
- Oral Testing Suggestions now available online as chat activities
- Redesigned textbook icons, including easy-to-identify chat activities

*Students must use a computer for audio recording and select presentations.

table of contents

	contextos	**fotonovela**

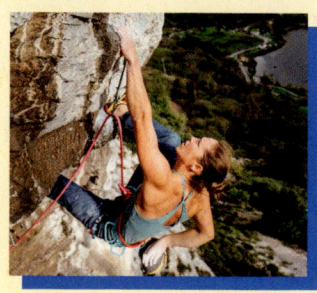

cultura	estructura	adelante

	contextos	**fotonovela**

cultura	estructura	adelante

	contexts	fotonovela

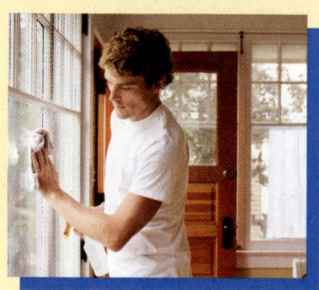

cultura	estructura	adelante

	contextos	fotonovela

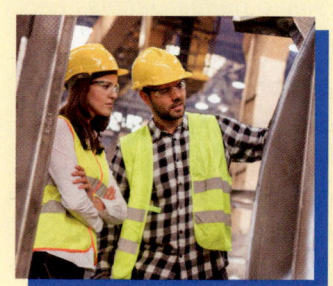

cultura	estructura	adelante

contextos	fotonovela

Lección 17
Un festival de arte

Lección 18
Las actualidades

Consulta (*Reference*)

cultura

estructura

adelante

Icons

Familiarize yourself with these icons that appear throughout **Vistas**.

(S) Presentational content for this section available online

Textbook activity available online

Partner Chat or Video Virtual Chat activity available online

Pair activity

Group activity

Activity with handout

Listening activity/section

Video available for this paragraph of **Panorama**

More activities			
(S) vhlcentral	LM p. 0	WB pp. 00–00	Online activities

The **More activities** box indicates additional
print and online activities.

The Vistas, Sixth Edition, Supersite

The **Vistas** Supersite is your online source for integrating text and technology resources. The Supersite enhances language learning and facilitates simple course management. With powerful functionality, a focus on language learning, and a simplified user experience, the Supersite offers features based directly on feedback from thousands of users.

- **Student Friendly:** Make it a cinch for students to track due dates, save work, and access all assignments and resources.
- **Set-Up Ease:** Customize your course and section settings, create your own grading categories, plus copy previous settings to save time.
- **All-in-One Gradebook:** Add your own activities or use the grade adjustment tool for a true, cumulative grade.
- **Grading Options:** Choose to grade student-by-student, question-by-question, or spot check. Plus, give targeted feedback via in-line editing and voice comments.
- **Accessible Student Data:** Conveniently share information one-on-one, or issue class reports in the formats that best fit you and your department.

For Instructors

- A gradebook to manage classes, view rosters, set assignments, and manage grades
- Time-saving auto-graded activities, plus question-by-question and automated spot-checking
- A communication center for announcements and notifications
- Pre-made sample syllabus and sample lesson plan in customizable DOCX format
- Testing Program in editable DOCX format
- Answer keys, audioscripts, Spanish and English videoscripts, grammar presentation slides, and digital image bank
- Online administration of quizzes and exams, now with time limits and password protection
- Assessments that are customizable by adding, removing, or editing questions and providing section references
- Tools to add your own content to the Supersite
  - Create and assign Partner Chat and open-ended activities
  - Upload and assign videos and outside resources
- Single sign-on feature for integration with your school's LMS
- Activity Pack (PDF) with additional activities for every lesson
- MP3 files of the complete Textbook, Lab, and Testing Audio Programs
- Live Chat for video chat, audio chat, and instant messaging
- Forums for oral assignments, group discussions, and projects

Each section of your textbook comes with activities on the **Vistas** Supersite, many of which are auto-graded for immediate feedback. Plus, the Supersite is iPad®-friendly*, so it can be accessed on the go! Visit **vhlcentral.com** to explore this wealth of exciting resources.

CONTEXTOS
- Vocabulary hotspots with audio
- Textbook activities and additional activities for extra practice
- Audio activities
- Chat activities for conversational skill-building and oral practice

FOTONOVELA
- Streaming video of **Fotonovela**, with instructor-managed options for subtitles and transcripts in Spanish and English
- Pronunciation tutorials with speech recognition
- Textbook activities and additional activities for extra practice
- Audio files for **Pronunciación**
- Record-compare practice

CULTURA
- **Con ritmo hispano** information and activities
- **Conexión Internet** activity
- Textbook activities and additional activities for extra practice
- Additional reading

ESTRUCTURA
- Interactive grammar tutorials
- Textbook activities and additional activities for extra practice
- Chat activities for conversational skill-building and oral practice
- Diagnostics in **Recapitulación** section

ADELANTE
- Audio-sync reading in **Lectura**
- Additional reading
- Writing activity in **Escritura** with composition engine
- Audio files for listening activity in **Escuchar**
- Textbook activities and additional activities for extra practice
- Streaming **En pantalla** TV clips or short films, with instructor-managed options for subtitles and transcripts in Spanish and English
- Streaming video of **Flash cultura** series, with instructor-managed options for subtitles and transcripts in Spanish and English

PANORAMA
- Textbook activities and additional activities for extra practice
- **Conexión Internet** activity
- Streaming video of **Panorama cultural** series, with instructor-managed options for subtitles and transcripts in Spanish and English

VOCABULARIO
- Vocabulary list with audio
- Customizable study lists

Plus! Also found on the Supersite:
- All textbook and lab audio MP3 files
- Communication center for instructor notifications and feedback
- Live Chat tool for video chat, audio chat, and instant messaging without leaving your browser
- A single gradebook for all Supersite activities
- WebSAM online Workbook/Video Manual/Lab Manual

*Students must use a computer for audio recording and select presentations.

New Features and Technology

Illustrations and Photos

New **Contextos** drawings are bright and colorful; they clearly depict the lesson vocabulary. Each large illustration includes at least one humorous element. All activity art is also new. Photos have been updated for the Sixth Edition.

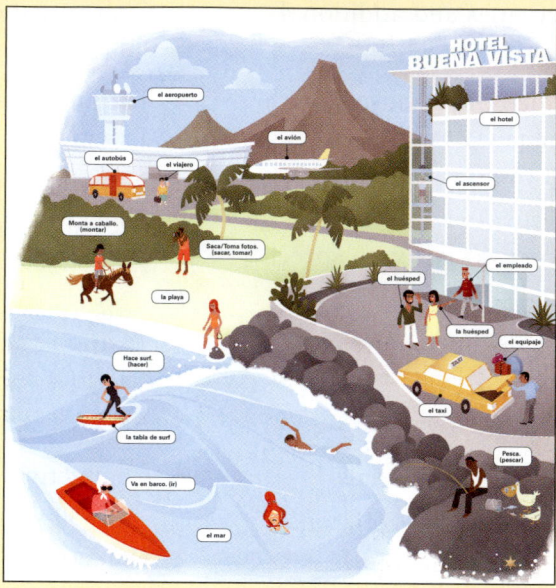

There is also a new Illustration Bank you can use to create your own activities.

Activities

Audio activities in the **Contextos** section have been revised for the Sixth Edition. The audio input for the first activity progresses from word to phrase to sentence. The audio input for the second activity progresses from sentences to short descriptions, dialogues, radio ads, etc. The activities are mostly true/false, multiple-choice, matching, or fill-in-the-blank.

There are also new activities on the **Práctica** and **Comunicación** pages of the **Contextos** and **Estructura** sections. In the **Panorama** section there are new comprehension and pair/group activities. The activities are related to the lesson's vocabulary, grammar, and/or theme.

Con ritmo hispano

This new feature in the **Cultura** section profiles musicians from the Spanish-speaking world. A box on the textbook page gives the birthdate, the birthplace, and a sentence or two about the artist. There is more information as well as activities on the Supersite.

CON RITMO HISPANO

Lin-Manuel Miranda (1980–)
Birthplace: New York City, New York

He won two Tony Awards for his musical *Hamilton* (2016) and one for *In the Heights* (2008), his musical about the predominantly Latino New York neighborhood of Washington Heights.

Go to **vhlcentral.com** to find out more about **Lin-Manuel Miranda** and his music.

Panorama cultural

There are 42 new **Panorama cultural** videos. They provide interesting visuals for two of the paragraphs on every **Panorama** spread.

Recapitulación de vocabulario

The vocabulary quiz has been moved from the **Repaso** section to the **Recapitulación** section of the Supersite and now includes diagnostics.

Refuerzo de vocabulario

There is a new summative vocabulary activity in the **Repaso** section of the Supersite in which students identify and say the terms illustrated by photos. Speech recognition lets students know if they are correct.

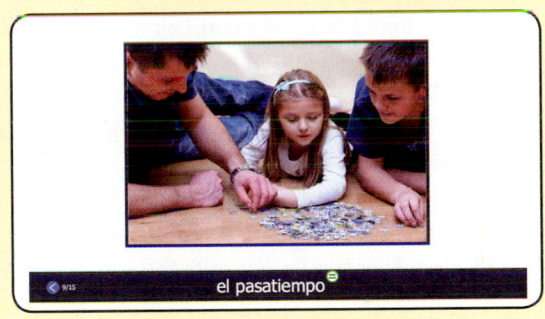

Video Virtual Chats

Video Virtual Chat activities provide students with opportunities to develop their listening and speaking skills and to build confidence as they practice with video recordings of native speakers. Unlike other listening activities where students can easily pause and repeat, Video Virtual Chats require them to answer questions in real time—just as they do when they engage in conversations with fluent speakers in the target language. Students also benefit from nonverbal and articulatory cues that are essential for production and pronunciation.

Video Virtual Chats are available in the **Comunicación** section of half of the **Contextos** and **Estructura** strands.

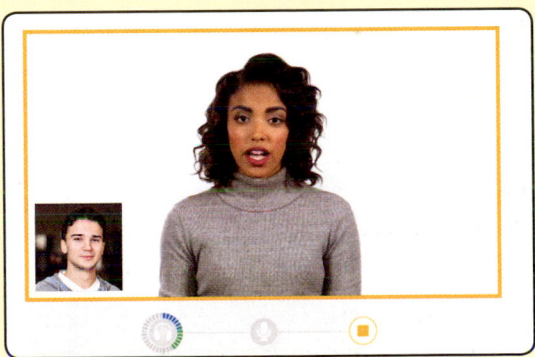

Pronunciation Tutorials with Speech Recognition

Pronunciation tutorials allow students to engage with the material via interactive quick checks throughout each tutorial.

Interactive feedback via embedded Speech Recognition gives students an opportunity to reflect on their language patterns and increases their awareness of pronunciation through low-stakes production practice.

STUDENT

▶ **Student Edition (SE)**
The SE is available in print and digital (online vText or downloadable eBook) formats.

▶ **Supersite**
Student access to the Supersite (**vhlcentral.com**) is provided with the purchase of a new student text. See page IAE-17 for all Supersite resources available to students.

▶ **Student Activities Manual (Workbook/Video Manual/Lab Manual) (SAM)**
The Workbook contains the workbook activities for each textbook lesson.

The Video Manual contains activities for the **Fotonovela** Video, and pre-, while-, and post-viewing activities for the **Flash cultura** Video.

The Lab Manual contains lab activities for each textbook lesson for use with the Lab Audio Program.

INSTRUCTOR

▶ **Instructor's Annotated Edition (IAE)**
The IAE contains a wealth of teaching information. The expanded trim size and enhanced design of **Vistas 6/e** make the annotations and facsimile student pages easy to read and reference in the classroom.

▶ **Activity Pack**
The **Vistas** Activity Pack offers discrete and communicative practice for individuals, pairs, and groups. It is organized by type of activity: information gap, survey, task-based, role-play, directed practice, and board game.

▶ **Supersite**
The password-protected Instructor Supersite allows instructors to assign and track student progress through its course management system. Instructors have full access to the Student Supersite, and seamless integration with the **Vistas 6/e WebSAM** and **vText**, and access to the **Vistas 6/e eBook**. Instructor Resources for easy access and download include:

- Classroom handouts for the textbook
- Audioscripts
- Video program transcripts and translations
- Workbook/Lab Manual/Video Manual Answer Keys
- Digital Image Bank
- Grammar Presentation Slides

▶ **Testing Program**
The Testing Program is provided in DOCX files.

- There are quizzes for each **Contextos** presentation and each **Estructura** grammar point. There are two versions of each quiz.
- There are six versions of each lesson test.
- There are also quarter exams, semester exams, listening scripts, answer keys for the tests, and optional test items for culture, video, and reading sections.

Lesson Openers
outline the content and features of each lesson.

A primera vista activities jump-start the lessons, allowing you to use the Spanish you know to talk about the photos.

Communicative goals highlight the real-life tasks you will be able to carry out in Spanish by the end of each lesson.

Supersite

- Supersite resources are available for every section of the lesson at **vhlcentral.com**. Icons show you which textbook activities are also available online, and where additional practice activities are available. The description next to the ⓢ icon indicates what additional resources are available for each section: videos, recordings, tutorials, and more!

- Textbook activity

Supersite features vary by access level.

Contextos
presents vocabulary in meaningful contexts.

Más vocabulario boxes call out other important theme-related vocabulary in easy-to-reference Spanish-English lists.

Variación léxica presents alternate words and expressions used throughout the Spanish-speaking world.

Illustrations High-frequency vocabulary is introduced through expansive, full-color illustrations.

More activities The icons in the **More activities** boxes let you know exactly which print and technology components you can use to reinforce and expand on every section of every lesson.

Práctica This section always begins with two listening exercises and continues with activities that practice the new vocabulary in meaningful contexts.

Comunicación activities allow you to use the vocabulary creatively in interactions with a partner, a small group, or the entire class.

Supersite

- Audio support for vocabulary presentation
- Textbook activities
- Additional online-only practice activities
- Chat activities for conversational skill-building and oral practice
- Vocabulary activities in Activity Pack

Supersite features vary by access level.

Fotonovela
follows the adventures of a group of students living and traveling in Mexico.

Personajes The photo-based conversations take place among a cast of recurring characters—a Mexican family with two college-age children, and their group of friends.

Icons signal activities by type (pair, group, audio, handout) and let you know which activities can be completed online.

Fotonovela Video The video episodes that correspond to this section are available for viewing online.

Expresiones útiles These expressions organize new, active structures by language function so you can focus on using them for real-life, practical purposes.

Conversations Taken from the **Fotonovela** Video, the conversations reinforce vocabulary from **Contextos**. They also preview structures from the upcoming **Estructura** section in context and in a comprehensible way.

Supersite

- Streaming video of the **Fotonovela** episode
- Additional online-only practice activities
- Textbook activities

Supersite features vary by access level.

Pronunciación & Ortografía
present the rules of Spanish pronunciation and spelling.

Pronunciación explains the sounds and pronunciation of Spanish in Lessons 1–9.

Ortografía focuses on topics related to Spanish spelling in Lessons 10–18.

Supersite

- Pronunciation tutorials with speech recognition
- Spelling tutorials
- Record-compare textbook activities

Supersite features vary by access level.

Cultura
exposes you to different aspects of Hispanic culture tied to the lesson theme.

En detalle & Perfil Two articles on the lesson theme focus on a specific place, custom, person, group, or tradition in the Spanish-speaking world. In Spanish starting in Lesson 7, these features also provide reading practice.

Coverage While the **Panorama** section takes a regional approach to cultural coverage, **Cultura** is theme-driven, covering several Spanish-speaking regions in every lesson.

Así se dice & El mundo hispano Lexical and comparative features expand cultural coverage to people, traditions, customs, trends, and vocabulary throughout the Spanish-speaking world.

Con ritmo hispano This new feature profiles musicians of the Spanish-speaking world.

Ⓢupersite

- **Con ritmo hispano** information and activities
- Textbook activities
- Additional online-only practice activities
- **Conexión Internet** activity with questions and keywords related to lesson theme
- Additional cultural reading

Supersite features vary by access level.

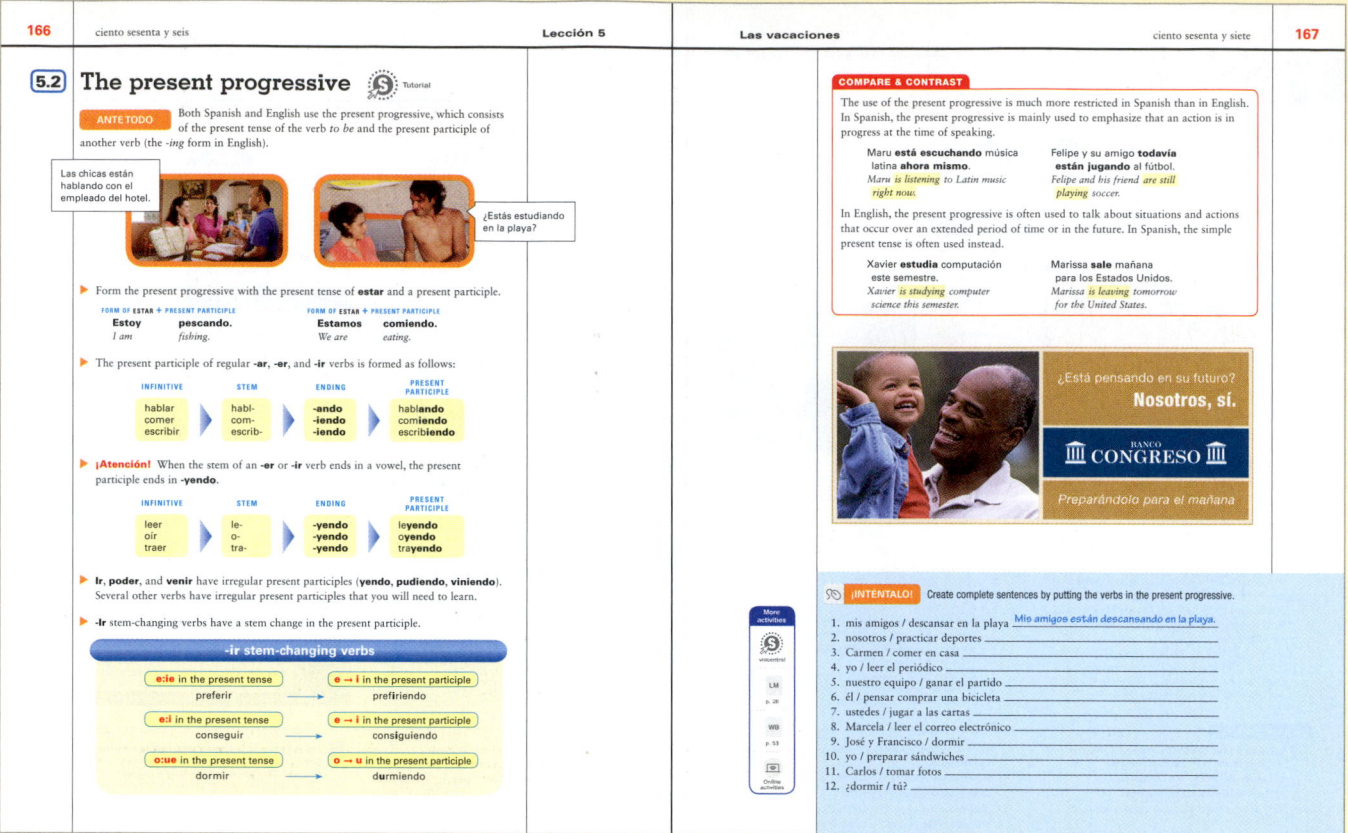

Estructura
presents Spanish grammar in a graphic-intensive format.

Ante todo Ease into grammar with definitions of grammatical terms, reminders about what you already know of English grammar, and Spanish grammar you have learned in earlier lessons.

Charts To help you learn, colorful, easy-to-use charts call out key grammatical structures and forms, as well as important related vocabulary.

Compare & Contrast This feature focuses on aspects of grammar that native speakers of English may find difficult, clarifying similarities and differences between Spanish and English.

Student sidebars provide you with on-the-spot linguistic, cultural, or language-learning information directly related to the materials in front of you.

Diagrams Clear and easy-to-grasp grammar explanations are reinforced by colorful diagrams that present sample words, phrases, and sentences.

¡Inténtalo! offers an easy first step into each grammar point.

Supersite

- Interactive, animated grammar tutorials with quick checks
- Textbook activities

Supersite features vary by access level.

Estructura
provides directed and communicative practice.

Práctica Guided, yet meaningful exercises weave current and previously learned vocabulary together with the current grammar point.

Activities with handouts In information gap activities, you and your partner each have only half of the information you need, so you must work together to accomplish the task at hand. Other activities with handouts include surveys.

Comunicación Opportunities for creative expression use the lesson's grammar and vocabulary.

Sidebars The **Notas culturales** expand coverage of the cultures of Spanish-speaking peoples and countries, while the other sidebars provide on-the-spot language support.

Síntesis activities integrate the current grammar point with previously learned points, providing built-in, consistent review.

Supersite

- Textbook activities
- Additional online-only practice activities
- Chat activities for conversational skill-building and oral practice
- Grammar activities in Activity Pack

Supersite features vary by access level.

Estructura

Recapitulación reviews the grammar of each lesson and provides a short quiz, available with auto-grading on the Supersite.

Resumen gramatical This review panel provides you with an easy-to-study summary of the basic concepts of the lesson's grammar, with page references to the full explanations.

Points Each activity is assigned a point value to help you track your progress. All **Recapitulación** sections add up to one hundred points, plus four additional points for successfully completing the bonus activity.

Activities A series of activities, moving from directed to open-ended, systematically test your mastery of the lesson's grammar. The section ends with a riddle or puzzle using the grammar from the lesson.

Supersite

- Textbook activity with diagnostics
- Additional online-only review activities
- Review activities in Activity Pack
- Vocabulary practice quiz with diagnostics

Supersite features vary by access level.

Adelante
Lectura develops reading skills in the context of the lesson theme.

Antes de leer Valuable reading strategies and pre-reading activities strengthen your reading abilities in Spanish.

Readings Selections related to the lesson theme recycle vocabulary and grammar you have learned. The selections in Lessons 1–12 are cultural texts, while those in Lessons 13–18 are literary pieces.

Después de leer Activities include post-reading exercises that review and check your comprehension of the reading as well as expansion activities.

Supersite

- Audio-sync reading that highlights text as it is being read
- Textbook activities
- Additional reading

Supersite features vary by access level.

Adelante

Escritura develops writing skills while *Escuchar* practices listening skills in the context of the lesson theme.

Estrategia Strategies help you prepare for the writing and listening tasks to come.

Escritura The **Tema** describes the writing topic and includes suggestions for approaching it.

Escuchar A recorded conversation or narration develops your listening skills in Spanish. **Preparación** prepares you for listening to the recorded passage.

Ahora escucha walks you through the passage, and **Comprensión** checks your listening comprehension.

Supersite

- Composition engine for writing activity in **Escritura**
- Audio for listening activity in **Escuchar**
- Textbook activities

Supersite features vary by access level.

Adelante

En pantalla and *Flash cultura* present additional video tied to the lesson theme.

En pantalla TV clips, many **NEW!** to this edition, give you additional exposure to authentic language. The clips include commercials, documentaries, public service announcements, and short films that feature the language, vocabulary, and theme of the lesson.

Presentation Cultural notes, video stills with captions, and vocabulary support all prepare you to view the clips. Activities check your comprehension and expand on the ideas presented.

Flash cultura An icon lets you know that the enormously successful **Flash cultura** Video offers specially shot content tied to the lesson theme.

Activities Due to the overwhelming popularity of the **Flash cultura** Video, previewing support and comprehension activities are integrated into the student text.

Supersite

- Streaming video of **En pantalla** and **Flash cultura**
- Textbook activities
- Additional online-only practice activities

Supersite features vary by access level.

Panorama
presents the nations of the Spanish-speaking world.

El país en cifras presents interesting key facts about the featured country.

Maps point out major cities, rivers, and geographical features and situate the country in the context of its immediate surroundings and the world.

Readings A series of brief paragraphs explores facets of the country's culture such as history, places, fine arts, literature, and aspects of everyday life.

¡Increíble pero cierto! highlights an intriguing fact about the country or its people.

Activities Three activities related to the lesson's vocabulary, grammar, and/or theme check your comprehension.

***Panorama cultural* Video** This video provides an exciting visual companion for two of the **Panorama** paragraphs about the featured country.

Supersite

- Streaming video of the **Panorama cultural** program
- Textbook activities
- Additional online-only practice activities
- **Conexión Internet** activity with questions and keywords related to lesson theme

Supersite features vary by access level.

Vocabulario
summarizes all the active vocabulary of the lesson.

Vocabulario The end-of-lesson page lists the active vocabulary from each lesson. This is the vocabulary that may appear on quizzes or tests.

Supersite

- Audio for all vocabulary items
- Customizable study lists
- Summative vocabulary activity with speech recognition
- Practice test with diagnostics
- Oral practice

Supersite features vary by access level.

Fotonovela Video Program

The cast

Here are the main characters you will meet in the **Fotonovela** Video:

 From Mexico,
Jimena Díaz Velázquez

 From Argentina,
Juan Carlos Rossi

 From Mexico,
Felipe Díaz Velázquez

 From the U.S.,
Marissa Wagner

 From Mexico,
María Eugenia (Maru)
Castaño Ricaurte

 From Spain,
Miguel Ángel
Lagasca Martínez

The **Vistas 6/e Fotonovela** Video is a dynamic and contemporary window into the Spanish language. The video centers around the Díaz family, whose household includes two college-aged children and a visiting student from the U.S. Over the course of an academic year, Jimena, Felipe, Marissa, and their friends explore **Mexico City** and other parts of Mexico as they make plans for their futures. Their adventures take them through some of the greatest natural and cultural treasures of the Spanish-speaking world, as well as the highs and lows of everyday life.

The **Fotonovela** section in each textbook lesson is actually an abbreviated version of the dramatic episode featured in the video. Therefore, each **Fotonovela** section can be done before you see the corresponding video episode, after it, or as a section that stands alone.

In each dramatic segment, the characters interact using the vocabulary and grammar you are studying. As the storyline unfolds, the episodes combine new vocabulary and grammar with previously taught language, exposing you to a variety of authentic accents along the way. At the end of each episode, the **Resumen** section highlights the grammar and vocabulary you are studying.

We hope you find the **Fotonovela** Video to be an engaging and useful tool for learning Spanish!

En pantalla Video Program

The **Vistas** Supersite features an authentic video clip for each lesson. Clip formats include commercials, documentaries, and even short films. These clips, many **NEW!** to the Sixth Edition, have been carefully chosen to be comprehensible for students learning Spanish, and are accompanied by activities and vocabulary lists to facilitate understanding. More importantly, though, these clips are a fun and motivating way to improve your Spanish!

Here are the countries represented in each lesson in **En pantalla**:

Lesson 1 U.S.	Lesson 7 Argentina	Lesson 13 Spain
Lesson 2 Chile	Lesson 8 Colombia	Lesson 14 Honduras
Lesson 3 Argentina	Lesson 9 Chile	Lesson 15 Mexico
Lesson 4 Spain	Lesson 10 Spain	Lesson 16 Spain
Lesson 5 Panama	Lesson 11 Spain	Lesson 17 Spain
Lesson 6 Spain	Lesson 12 Spain	Lesson 18 Chile

Flash cultura Video Program

In the dynamic **Flash cultura** Video, young people from all over the Spanish-speaking world share aspects of life in their countries with you. The similarities and differences among Spanish-speaking countries that come up through their adventures will challenge you to think about your own cultural practices and values. The segments provide valuable cultural insights as well as linguistic input; the episodes will introduce you to a variety of accents and vocabulary as they gradually move into Spanish.

Panorama cultural Video Program

The **Panorama cultural** Video provides visuals for two of the **Panorama** paragraphs about the featured country.

Vistas and the *World-Readiness Standards for Learning Languages*

Since 1982, when the *ACTFL Proficiency Guidelines* were first published, that seminal document and its subsequent revisions have influenced the teaching of modern languages in the United States. **Vistas** was written with the concerns and philosophy of the *ACTFL Proficiency Guidelines* in mind, incorporating a proficiency-oriented approach from its planning stages.

The pedagogy of **Vistas** was also informed from its inception by the *Standards for Foreign Language Learning in the 21st Century*. First published in 1996 under the auspices of the National Standards in Foreign Language Education Project, the Standards are organized into five goal areas, often called the Five Cs: Communication, Cultures, Connections, Comparisons, and Communities.

Since **Vistas** takes a communicative approach to the teaching and learning of Spanish, the Communication goal is central to the student text. For example, the diverse formats used in **Comunicación** and **Síntesis** activities—pair work, small group work, class circulation, information gap, task-based, and so forth—engage students in communicative exchanges, providing and obtaining information, and expressing feelings and emotions.

The Cultures goal is most evident in the lessons' **Cultura** sections, **Nota cultural** student sidebars, and **En pantalla**, **Flash cultura**, and **Panorama** sections, but **Vistas** also weaves culture into virtually every page, exposing students to the multiple facets of practices, products, and perspectives of the Spanish-speaking world. In keeping with the Connections goal, students can connect with other disciplines such as geography, history, fine arts, and science in the **Panorama** section; they can acquire information and recognize distinctive cultural viewpoints in the non-literary and literary texts of the **Lectura** sections.

The **Estructura** sections, with their clear explanations and special *Compare & Contrast* features, reflect the Comparisons goal. Students can work toward the Connections and Communities goal when they do the **Cultura** and **Panorama** sections' **Conexión Internet** activities, as well as the activities and information on the **Vistas** Supersite. In addition, special Standards icons appear on the student text pages of your IAE to call out sections that have a particularly strong relationship with the Standards. These are a few examples of how **Vistas** was written with the Standards firmly in mind, but you will find many more as you use the textbook and its ancillaries.

Communication Understand and be understood: read and listen to understand the Spanish-speaking world, converse with others, and share your thoughts clearly through speaking and writing.

Cultures Experience Spanish-speaking cultures through their own viewpoints, in the places, objects, behaviors, and beliefs important to the people who live them.

Connections Apply what you learn in your Spanish course to your other studies; apply what you know from other courses to your Spanish studies.

Comparisons Discover in which ways the Spanish language and Spanish-speaking cultures are like your own—and how they differ.

Communities Engage with Spanish-speaking communities locally, nationally, and internationally both in your courses and beyond—for life.

Your Instructor's Annotated Edition

Vistas, Sixth Edition, offers you the most thoroughly developed Instructor's Annotated Edition ever written for introductory college Spanish. The IAE features reduced student text pages, overprinted with answers, and a wealth of teaching resources in the side and bottom panels. The annotations complement and support varied teaching styles, extending the already rich content of the student textbook and saving you time in class preparation and course management.

This section is designed as a quick orientation to the principal types of instructor annotations you will find in the **Vistas 6/e** IAE. As you familiarize yourself with them, it is important to keep in mind that the annotations are merely suggestions. Any Spanish questions, or simulated instructor-student exchanges are not meant to be prescriptive. You are encouraged to view these suggested "scripts" as flexible points of departure that will help you achieve your instructional goals.

Icons

For your convenience, the suggestions in the side and bottom channels have been tagged with icons if they engage one of the three different modes of communication.

- **Interpretive communication** Suggestions for exercises that target students' reading or listening skills and assess their comprehension

- **Presentational communication** Ideas and contexts that require students to produce a written or verbal presentation in the target language

- **Interpersonal communication** Activities that provide students with opportunities to carry out language functions in simulated real-life contexts or engage in personalized communication with others

    For an annotation to merit one of these icons, it must use the target language at a discourse level in a sustained context. As with the activities in the student text, many of these annotations employ more than one mode of communication; in these cases the mode that is best represented in the "product" of the activity is the one that is reflected in the icon. For example, if students are asked to talk to a classmate (interpersonal) and write a summary of the conversation (presentational), the written summary is the product, and the icon will therefore reflect the presentational mode of communication.

On the Lesson Opener Pages

- **Lesson Goals** A list of the lexical, grammatical, and socio-cultural goals of the lesson, including language-learning strategies and skill-building techniques

- **A primera vista** Questions related to the photograph for jump-starting the lesson

- **Instructional Resources** A correlation to all student and instructor supplements available to reinforce the lesson

---

The **Vistas** Supersite provides additional instructor materials for each lesson. Visit **vhlcentral.com** for extra activities, supplemental vocabulary, assessment materials, and more!

In the Side Panels

- **Section Goals** A list of the goals of the corresponding section
- **Instructional Resources** A correlation to student and instructor ancillaries
- **Teaching Tips** Suggestions for recycling language, leading into the corresponding section, working with materials, and carrying out specific activities
- **Expansion** Expansions and variations for the activities in the student textbook
- **Script** Transcripts of the audio and video recordings
- **Possible Conversation** Answers based on known vocabulary, grammar, and language functions that students might produce
- **Video Recap** Questions to help students recall the events of the previous lesson's **Fotonovela** episode
- **Video Synopsis** A summary of each lesson's **Fotonovela** episode
- **Expresiones útiles** Suggestions for introducing upcoming **Estructura** grammar points incorporated into the **Fotonovela** episode
- **Estrategia** Suggestions for working with the reading, writing, and listening strategies presented in the **Lectura, Escritura,** and **Escuchar** sections, respectively
- **Tema** Ideas for presenting and expanding the writing assignment topic in **Escritura**
- **El país cn cifras** Additional information expanding on the data presented for each Spanish-speaking country featured in the **Panorama** sections
- **¡Increíble pero cierto!** Curious facts about a lesser-known aspect of the country featured in the **Panorama** sections
- **Section-specific Annotations** Suggestions for presenting, expanding, varying, and reinforcing individual instructional elements, including the sidebars in the student text (**¡Atención!, Ayuda, Nota cultural,** etc.)
- **Successful Language Learning** Strategies to enhance students' language-learning experience
- **The Affective Dimension** Suggestions for reducing students' language-learning anxieties

In the *Teaching Options* Boxes

- **Extra Practice, Pairs, Small Groups,** and **Large Groups** Additional activities intended to supplement those in the student textbook
- **Game** Games that practice the language of the section and/or recycle previously learned language
- **TPR** Total Physical Response activities that engage students physically in learning Spanish
- **Variación léxica** Extra information related to the **Variación léxica** boxes in **Contextos,** terms that come up in **Lectura,** and terms from the Spanish-speaking countries featured in **Panorama**
- **Worth Noting** More detailed information about an interesting aspect of the history, geography, culture, or people of the Spanish-speaking countries in **Panorama**
- **Heritage Speakers** Suggestions and activities tailored to heritage speakers, who in many colleges and universities are enrolled in the same introductory courses as non-heritage speakers
- **Video** Techniques and activities for using the **Vistas** video program with **Fotonovela** and other lesson sections
- **Evaluation** Rubrics for grading students' work in **Escritura**

Teaching with Vistas

Orienting Students to the Student Textbook

Because **Vistas 6/e** treats graphic design as an integral part of students' language-learning experience, you may want to take a few minutes to orient students to the student textbook. Have them flip through one lesson, and point out that all lessons are organized exactly the same way. Also point out how the major sections of each lesson are color-coded for easy navigation: red for **Contextos**, purple for **Fotonovela**, orange for **Cultura**, blue for **Estructura**, green for **Adelante**, and gold for **Vocabulario**. Let them know that, because of these design elements, they can be confident that they will always know "where they are" in their textbook.

Emphasize that sections are self-contained, occupying either a full page or a spread of two facing pages, thereby eliminating "bad breaks" and the need to flip back and forth to do activities or to work with explanatory material. Finally, call students' attention to the use of color to highlight key information in elements such as charts, diagrams, word lists, and activity **modelos**, titles, and sidebars.

Flexible Lesson Organization

Vistas 6/e uses a flexible lesson organization designed to accommodate diverse teaching styles, institutions, and instructional goals. For example, you can begin with the lesson opener page and progress sequentially through a lesson. If you do not want to devote class time to grammar, you can assign the **Estructura** explanations for outside study, freeing up class time for other purposes like developing oral communication skills; building listening, reading, or writing skills; learning more about the Spanish-speaking world; or working with the video program. You might decide to work extensively with the **Cultura** and **Adelante** sections in order to focus on students' reading, writing, and listening skills and their knowledge of the Spanish-speaking world. Or, you might prefer to use these sections periodically in response to your students' interests as the opportunity arises. If you plan on using the **Vistas** Testing Program, however, be aware that the quizzes, tests, and exams check language presented in **Contextos**, **Estructura**, and the **Expresiones útiles** boxes of **Fotonovela**.

Identifying Active Vocabulary

All words and expressions taught in the illustrations and **Más vocabulario** lists in **Contextos** are considered active, testable vocabulary. Any items in the **Variación léxica** or **Así se dice** boxes, however, are intended for receptive learning and are presented for enrichment only. The words and expressions in the **Expresiones útiles** boxes in **Fotonovela**, as well as words in charts, word lists, ¡**Atención!** sidebars, and sample sentences in **Estructura** are also part of the active vocabulary load. At the end of each lesson, **Vocabulario** provides a convenient one-page summary of the items students should know and that may appear on tests and exams. Point this out to students and tell them that an easy way to study from **Vocabulario** is to cover up the Spanish half of each section, leaving only the English equivalents exposed. They can then quiz themselves on the Spanish items. To focus on the English equivalents of the Spanish entries, they simply reverse this process.

Taking into Account the Affective Dimension

While many factors contribute to the quality and success rate of learning experiences, two factors are particularly germane to language learning. One is students' beliefs about how language is learned; the other is language-learning anxiety.

As studies show and experienced instructors know, students often come to modern language courses either with a lack of knowledge about how to approach language learning or with mistaken notions about how to do so. For example, many students believe that making mistakes when speaking the target language must be avoided because doing so will lead to permanent errors. Others are convinced that learning another language is like learning any other academic subject. In other words, they believe that success is guaranteed, provided they attend class regularly, learn the assigned vocabulary words and grammar rules, and study for exams. In fact, in a study of college-level beginning language learners in the United States, over one-third of the participants thought that they could become fluent if they studied the language for only one hour a day for two years or less. Mistaken and unrealistic beliefs such as these can cause frustration and ultimately demotivation, thereby significantly undermining students' ability to achieve a successful language-learning experience.

Another factor that can negatively impact students' language-learning experience is language-learning anxiety. As Professor Elaine K. Horwitz of The University of Texas at Austin and Senior Consulting Editor of **Vistas 1/e** wrote, "Surveys indicate that up to one-third of American foreign language students feel moderately to highly anxious about studying another language. Physical symptoms of foreign language anxiety can include heart-pounding or palpitations, sweating, trembling, fast breathing, and general feelings of unease." The late Dr. Philip Redwine Donley, **Vistas** co-author and author of articles on language-learning anxiety, spoke with many students who reported feeling nervous or apprehensive in their classes. They mentioned freezing when called on by their instructors or going inexplicably blank when taking tests. Some so dreaded their classes that they skipped them or dropped the course.

Vistas contains several features aimed at reducing students' language anxiety and supporting successful language-learning. Its highly structured, visually dramatic design was conceived as a learning tool to make students feel comfortable with the content and confident about navigating the lessons. The Instructor's Annotated Edition includes *Affective Dimension* annotations with suggestions for managing and/or reducing language-learning anxieties, as well as *Successful Language Learning* annotations with learning strategies for enhancing students' learning experiences. In addition, the student text provides a wealth of helpful sidebars that assist students by making relevant connections with new information or reminding them of previously learned concepts.

Student Sidebars

¡Atención! Provides active, testable information about the vocabulary or grammar point

Ayuda Offers specific grammar and vocabulary reminders related to a particular activity or suggests pertinent language-learning strategies

Consulta References related material introduced in previous or upcoming lessons

¡Lengua viva! Presents relevant information on everyday language use

Nota cultural Provides a wide range of cultural information relevant to the topic of an activity or section

Suggestions for Using the Vistas
Fotonovela Video

The **Fotonovela** section in each lesson of the student textbook and the **Vistas Fotonovela** Video were created as interlocking pieces. All photos in this section are images from the corresponding video module, while the printed conversations are abbreviated versions of the video module's dramatic segment. Both the **Fotonovela** conversations and their expanded video versions represent comprehensible input at the discourse level; they were purposely written to use language from the corresponding lesson's **Contextos** and **Estructura** sections. Thus, as of **Lección 2,** they recycle known language, preview grammar points students will study later in the lesson, and, in keeping with the concept of "i + 1," contain a small amount of unknown language.

You can use the **Fotonovela** Video and corresponding textbook section in many ways. For instance, you can use the **Fotonovela** spread as an advance organizer, presenting it before showing the video module. You can also show the video module first. You can even use **Fotonovela** as a stand-alone, video-independent section. You might decide to show all video modules in class or to assign them solely for viewing outside of the classroom. You could begin by showing the first one or two episodes in class to gain familiarity with the characters, storyline, style, and **Resumen** sections. After that, you could work in class only with

Fotonovela pages and have students view the remaining episodes outside of class. For each episode, there are **¿Qué pasó?** activities in the **Fotonovela** section of the corresponding textbook lesson and video activities in the Video Manual section of the **Vistas 6/e** Student Activities Manual and on the Supersite.

You might also want to use the **Fotonovela** Video in class when working with **Estructura**. You could play parts of the dramatic episode that demonstrate the grammar point you are teaching or show selected scenes that review old grammar points and ask students to identify them. In class, you could play the parts of the **Resumen** section that exemplify individual grammar points as you progress through each **Estructura** section. You could also wait until you complete an **Estructura** section and review it by showing the corresponding **Resumen** section in its entirety.

No matter which approach you choose, students have ample materials to support viewing the video independently and processing it in a meaningful way. We hope you and your students will continue to find the **Fotonovela** Video and corresponding materials to be an engaging and effective tool for language-learning.

Suggestions for Using the Vistas
Flash cultura Videos

The **Flash cultura** Video expands on an aspect of the lesson theme in the format of a news broadcast. Like the conversations in the **Fotonovela** Video, these video segments deliver comprehensible input. Each was written to make the most of the vocabulary and grammar students learned in the corresponding and previous lessons, while still providing a controlled amount of unknown language.

Activities for the **Flash cultura** Videos are located in the Video Manual section of the **Vistas 6/e** Student Activities Manual and on the Supersite. They follow a process approach of pre-viewing, while-viewing, and post-viewing and use a variety of formats to prepare students for watching the video segments, to focus them while watching, and to check comprehension after they have watched the footage.

When showing the **videos** in class, you might also want to implement a process approach. You could start with an activity that prepares students for the video segment by taking advantage of what they learned in previous lessons. This could be followed by an activity that students do while you play certain parts or all of the video segment. The final activity, done in the same class period or in the next one as warm-up, could recap what students saw and heard and expand on the video segment's topic. The following suggestions for working with the **Flash cultura** Video in class can be carried out as described or expanded upon in any number of ways.

Before viewing

- After students have practiced the lesson's vocabulary and grammar and worked through the **Cultura** section of the student textbook, mention the video segment's title and ask them to guess what the segment might be about.

- Have pairs make a list of the lesson vocabulary they expect to hear in the video segment.

- Read the class a list of true/false or multiple-choice questions about the video. Students must use what they learned in the **Cultura** section to guess the answers. Confirm their guesses after watching the segment.

While viewing

- Show the video segment with the audio turned off and ask students to use lesson vocabulary and structures to describe what is happening. Have them confirm their guesses by showing the segment again with the audio on.

- Have students refer to the list of words they brainstormed before viewing the video and put a check mark in front of any words they actually see in the segment.

- First, have students simply watch the video. Then, show it again and ask students to take notes on what they see and hear. Finally, have them compare their notes in pairs or groups for confirmation.

- Photocopy the segment's Videoscript from the Supersite and white out words and expressions related to the lesson theme, in order to create cloze paragraphs. Distribute the scripts for pairs or groups to complete the sentences.

After viewing

- Have students say what aspects of the cultural information presented in their textbook appear in the video segment.

- Ask groups to write a brief summary of the content of the video segment. Have them exchange papers with another group for peer editing.

- Ask students to discuss any aspects of the featured country and topic of which they were unaware before watching. Encourage them to explain why they did not expect those aspects to be true of the country in question.

- Have students pick one characteristic about the country and topic that they learned from watching the video segment. Have them research additional information about that topic and write a brief composition that expands on it.

Suggestions for Using the Vistas *Panorama cultural* Videos

You may choose to use the new **Panorama cultural** videos to present two of the culture paragraphs on each **Panorama** spread. Here are a few suggestions.

- Play the video without sound and have students comment on the images.

- Play the video with the sound on. Point out the pronunciation of certain words.

- Have students raise their hand every time they hear a familiar word as they watch the video.

acknowledgments

On behalf of its authors and editors, Vista Higher Learning expresses its sincere appreciation to the many instructors and college professors across the U.S. and Canada who contributed their ideas and suggestions.

Vistas, Sixth Edition, is the direct result of extensive reviews and ongoing input from both students and instructors using the Fifth Edition. Accordingly, we gratefully acknowledge those who shared their suggestions, recommendations, and ideas as we prepared this Sixth Edition.

We express our sincere appreciation to the instructors who completed our online review.

Reviewers

Elizabeth Aguilar
University of Illinois at Chicago

Soraya Alamdari, PhD
Glendale Community College, CA

Pilar Alcalde, PhD
University of Memphis, TN

Tim Altanero, PhD
Austin Community College, TX

Felipe Amaro
University of Illinois at Chicago

Isabel Anievas-Gamallo
San Joaquin Delta College, CA

Rosalind Arthur
Clark Atlanta University, GA

Collin Ashmore
Washington College, MD

Inge R. Baird
Anderson University, IN

Tim Barnett
St. Mary's University, TX

Wanda Baumgartel
Somerset Community College, KY

Kevin Beard
Richland College, TX

Sarah Beeman
University of St. Thomas, MN

Janet Bell
Tarleton State University, TX

Martha Black de Frías
University of Alaska Anchorage

Tom Blodget
Butte College, CA

Jeanne A. Boettcher
Madison Area Technical College, WI

Stella M. Boghosian
Queens College, CUNY

Teresa L. Borden
Columbia College, CA

Sara Blossom Bostwick
Lansing Community College, MI

Teresa Buzo Salas
Georgia Southern University

Silvia Castellini-Patel
West Valley College, CA

Lisa Celona
Tunxis Community College, CT

Gabriela Cerghedean
Beloit College, WI

Dr. Silvia Choi
Georgia Gwinnett College

Sonia Ciccarelli
San Joaquin Delta College, CA

Carrie Y. Clay
Anderson University, IN

Scott Cooper
Anne Arundel Community College, MD

Fina Coronel
Fresno City College, CA

Miryam Criado, PhD
Hanover College, IN

José V. Cruz
Fayetteville Technical Community College, NC

Walberto Diaz
San Diego City College, CA

Dr. Karen Dollinger
University of Pikeville, KY

Danion L. Doman
Truman State University, MO

Mark A. Dowell
St. Charles Community College, MO

Scott Estes
North Idaho College

Kim Faber
Oberlin College, OH

Kelly Montijo Fink
Kirkwood Community College, IA

Catherine Fountain
Appalachian State University, NC

Lloyd J. Frias
Loyola University Maryland

Lucas Fricke
Bethany Lutheran College, MN

Dr. Vasant Gadre
Richland College, TX

Angélica Galván
Tennessee Tech University

Dr. Eduardo Garcia
Drake University, IA

Raquel Gaytán
Rice University, TX

Hasmik Gharaghazaryan
Richland College, TX

Michael Gismondi
University of Illinois at Chicago

Jill R. Gomez
Miami University Hamilton, OH

Lucila González Cirre
Cerro Coso Community College, CA

Ana González-Gómez
Northern Arizona University

Kate Grovergrys
Madison Area Technical College, WI

Cassandra Gulam
Washington State University Vancouver

Kenneth Habecker, MA
Columbia College, CA

Michael Harrison
San Diego Mesa College, CA

Richard A. Heath
Kirkwood Community College, IA

Valerie Hecht
College of Southern Nevada

Dawn Heston
University of Missouri

Matt Hoch
Northern Arizona University

Lourdes Huici Clever, MA
Community College of Aurora, CO

Rene Iraheta
West Hills College Lemoore, CA

Becky S. Jaimes
Austin Community College, TX

Stacy Jazán, PhD
Glendale Community College, CA

Aggie Johnson
Flagler College, FL

Stephanie H. Langston
Perimeter College at Georgia State
University

Katie MacLean, PhD
Kalamazoo College, MI

María José Maguire
Flagler College, FL

Donna Marqués
MiraCosta College, CA

Dr. Cecilia Marrugo
Tarleton State University, TX

Dr. Mark McGraw
Ouachita Baptist University, AR

José Mendoza
Beaufort County Community
College, NC

Dr. Joshua Mora
Wayland Baptist University, TX

Arturo Morales
LeTourneau University, TX

Anna Moreno
West Hills Community College, CA

Antonio Olivas
East Los Angeles College, CA

Ruth Ore' Giron
Pima Community College, AZ

Lucía Osa-Melero
Duquesne University, PA

Lulú De Panbehchi
Virginia Commonwealth University

George Pappas
Pace University, NY

Jeana Paul-Ureña
Stephen F. Austin State University, TX

Chachi Perez
Richland College, TX

Susana Pérez Castillejo
University of St. Thomas, MN

Mary Perley
Cairn University, PA

Zorayda H. Pina
Owens Community College, OH

Karry Putzy
Kirkwood Community College, IA

Micaela Ramos
University of San Diego, CA

Aida Ramos-Sellman
Goucher College, MD

Liz Rangel Arriola
Pima Community College, AZ

Dr. John W. Reed
Saint Mary's University of Minnesota

Timothy Reed
Ripon College, WI

Jesus Reyes
Hartnell College, CA

Steve Richman
Mercer County Community
College, NJ

Vanessa Rocha
San Joaquin Delta College, CA

Monica Pilar Rodriguez
Lyon College, AR

Linda A. Roy
Tarrant County College - South
Campus, TX

Marilin Sarria
Fairfield University, CT

Eduardo Santa Cruz, PhD
Hanover College, IN

Dora Schoenbrun-Fernandez
San Diego Mesa College, CA

Mariana R. Segovia
Palomar College, CA

Albert Shank
Scottsdale Community College, AZ

Angeles Solana
SUNY Cortland

Stacy Spears
Texarkana College, TX

Abbey Stell
Butte College, CA

Cristina Szterensus
Rock Valley College, IL

Karen Tharrington, PhD
Sandhills Community College, NC

Daniel G. Tight
University of St. Thomas, MN

Dr. Ivelisse Urbán
Tarleton State University, TX

Silvia Vazquez
MiraCosta College, CA

Alexandra Vinarov, PhD
LIM College, NY

F. Vivar
University of Memphis, TN

Dr. Lynn Vogel-Zuiderweg
East Los Angeles College, CA

Montana Walsh
Northern New Mexico College

Dr. Wesley J. Weaver III
SUNY Cortland

Sarah Willoughby
Everett Community College, WA

James R. Wilson
Madison Area Technical College, WI

Aurora Wold-Krogmann
Temple College, TX

Mikela Zhezha-Thaumanavar
Kalamazoo College, MI

Hola, ¿qué tal?

1

Communicative Goals

You will learn how to:
- Greet people in Spanish
- Say goodbye
- Identify yourself and others
- Talk about the time of day

Lesson Goals

In **Lección 1**, students will be introduced to the following:
- terms for greetings and goodbyes
- identifying where one is from
- courtesy expressions
- greetings in the Spanish-speaking world
- the **plaza principal**
- nouns and articles (definite and indefinite)
- numbers 0–30
- present tense of **ser**
- telling time
- recognizing cognates
- reading a comic strip
- writing a telephone/address list in Spanish
- listening for known vocabulary
- a television commercial for MasterCard
- a video about **plazas** and greetings
- demographic and cultural information about Hispanics in the United States and Canada

A primera vista Have students look at the photo, and ask them what they think the young people are doing. Explain that it is common in Hispanic cultures for friends to greet each other with one or two kisses on the cheek. As a class, discuss how friends typically greet each other in North America.

Teaching Tip You will see a series of icons pointing out communicative expansions, activities, and teaching tips in the instructor annotations. Follow this key:

→🔺	**Interpretive communication**
↔🔺	**Presentational communication**
🔺↔🔺	**Interpersonal communication**

👀 A PRIMERA VISTA
- Guess what the people on the photo are saying:
  a. Adiós. b. Hola. c. salsa
- Most likely they would also say:
  a. Gracias. b. fiesta c. Buenos días.
- The women are:
  a. amigas b. chicos c. señores

INSTRUCTIONAL RESOURCES

Supersite (vhlcentral.com)
Video: *Fotonovela, Flash cultura, En pantalla, Panorama cultural*
Audio: Textbook and Lab MP3 Files

Activity Pack: Information Gap Activities, games, additional activity handouts
Resources: SAM Answer Key, Scripts, Translations, **Vocabulario adicional**, sample lesson plan, Grammar Presentation Slides, Digital Image Bank

Testing Program: Quizzes, Tests, Exams, MP3s
Student Activities Manual: Workbook/Video Manual/Lab Manual
WebSAM (online Student Activities Manual)

Section Goals

In **Contextos**, students will learn and practice:
- basic greetings
- introductions
- courtesy expressions

Instructional Resources

Supersite: Audio (Textbook and Lab MP3 Files); Resources (Digital Image Bank, **Vocabulario adicional**, Activity Pack, Scripts, Answer Keys); Testing Program (Quizzes)
WebSAM
Workbook
Lab Manual

Teaching Tips

- To familiarize students with lesson headings and vocabulary for classroom interactions, hand out *Vocabulario adicional: Más vocabulario para la clase de español* from the Supersite.
- For a sample lesson plan, go to **vhlcentral.com** to access the instructor's part of the **Vistas** Supersite.
- Use the **Lección 1 Contextos** digital images to assist with this presentation.
- Write a few greetings, farewells, and courtesy expressions on the board, explain their meaning, and model their pronunciation. Circulate around the class, greeting students, making introductions, and encouraging responses. Then have students open to pages 2–3, and ask them to identify which conversations seem to be exchanges between friends and which seem more formal. Draw attention to the use of **usted** vs. **tú** in these conversations. Explain situations in which each form is appropriate.

Hola, ¿qué tal?

Más vocabulario

Hola.	*Hi.*
Buenos días.	*Good morning.*
Buenas noches.	*Good evening; Good night.*
Hasta la vista.	*See you later.*
Hasta pronto.	*See you soon.*
¿Cómo se llama usted?	*What's your name? (form.)*
Le presento a…	*I would like to introduce you to (name). (form.)*
Te presento a…	*I would like to introduce you to (name). (fam.)*
el nombre	*name*
¿Cómo estás?	*How are you? (fam.)*
No muy bien.	*Not very well.*
¿Qué pasa?	*What's happening?; What's going on?*
por favor	*please*
De nada.	*You're welcome.*
No hay de qué.	*You're welcome.*
Lo siento.	*I'm sorry.*
Gracias.	*Thank you; Thanks.*
Muchas gracias.	*Thank you very much; Thanks a lot.*

Variación léxica

Items are presented for recognition purposes only.

Buenos días.	⟷	Buenas.
De nada.	⟷	A la orden.
Lo siento.	⟷	Perdón.
¿Qué tal?	⟷	¿Qué hubo? (*Col.*)
Chau.	⟷	Ciao; Chao.

More activities

 vhlcentral   LM p. 1   WB pp. 1–2   Online activities

1
ELENA Patricia, le presento a Jorge Perales.
PATRICIA Encantada.
SEÑOR PERALES Igualmente. ¿De dónde es usted, señorita?
PATRICIA Soy de México. ¿Y usted?
SEÑOR PERALES De Puerto Rico.

3
SEÑOR VARGAS Buenas tardes, señora Wong. ¿Cómo está usted?
SEÑORA WONG Muy bien, gracias. ¿Y usted, señor Vargas?
SEÑOR VARGAS Bien, gracias.
SEÑORA WONG Hasta mañana, señor Vargas. Saludos a la señora Vargas.
SEÑOR VARGAS Adiós.

5
CARMEN Buenas tardes. Me llamo Carmen. ¿Cómo te llamas tú?
ANTONIO Buenas tardes. Me llamo Antonio. Mucho gusto.
CARMEN El gusto es mío. ¿De dónde eres?
ANTONIO Soy de los Estados Unidos, de California.

TEACHING OPTIONS

Extra Practice Bring in photos or magazine images of people greeting each other or saying goodbye. Ask pairs to write dialogue captions for each photo. Remind students to use formal and informal expressions as appropriate.
Groups Write questions and possible answers from the new set of expressions in **Contextos** on separate note cards. Give each student one note card and have them find the student with the matching card that completes their question/answer. Then have students work with other pairs to see if they can create a longer dialogue with their expressions.
Extra Practice Prepare name tags with a variety of different names, titles, and ages. Ex: **señora Lopez, 63; Carlos de la Vega, 22**, etc. Each student should wear a name tag and greet their peers according to the information on their tags.

②
> **TOMÁS** ¿Qué tal, Alberto?
> **ALBERTO** Regular. ¿Y tú?
> **TOMÁS** Bien. ¿Qué hay de nuevo?
> **ALBERTO** Nada.

④
> **BERTA** Hasta luego, Tere.
> **TERESA** Chau, Berta. Nos vemos mañana.

AYUDA

In Spanish, people can be addressed either formally or informally. Dialogues 1 and 3 are formal exchanges and use **usted** (*you*) forms. Dialogues 2, 4, and 5 are informal and use the familiar **tú** (*you*) form or other informal expressions. You will learn more about this in **Estructura 1.3.**

Práctica

1 **Indicar** Check **sí** if you might use the expression you hear to greet someone or **no** if you would not.

	Sí	No			Sí	No
1.	✓	○		5.	✓	○
2.	○	✓		6.	○	✓
3.	○	✓		7.	✓	○
4.	✓	○		8.	○	✓

2 **Escuchar** Choose the correct response for each question or statement you hear.

1. a. Muy bien, gracias. b. Me llamo Graciela. **b**
2. a. Lo siento. b. Mucho gusto. **b**
3. a. Soy de Puerto Rico. b. No muy bien. **a**
4. a. No hay de qué. b. Regular. **a**
5. a. Mucho gusto. b. Hasta pronto. **b**
6. a. Nada. b. Igualmente. **a**
7. a. Me llamo Guillermo Montero. b. Muy bien, gracias. **b**
8. a. Buenas tardes. ¿Cómo estás? b. El gusto es mío. **a**

3 **Escoger** For each expression, write another word or phrase that expresses a similar idea.

> **modelo**
> ¿Cómo estás? ¿Qué tal?

1. De nada. No hay de qué.
2. Encantado. Mucho gusto.
3. Adiós. Chau o Hasta luego/ mañana/pronto.
4. Mucho gusto. El gusto es mío.
5. Hasta la vista. Hasta luego.

4 **Ordenar** Work with a partner to put this scrambled conversation in order. Then act it out.

—Soy de México. ¿Y tú?
—Muy bien, gracias. Soy Rosabel.
—Mucho gusto, Rosabel.
—Hola. Me llamo Carlos. ¿Cómo estás?
—Soy de Argentina.
—Igualmente. ¿De dónde eres, Carlos?

CARLOS	Hola. Me llamo Carlos. ¿Cómo estás?
ROSABEL	Muy bien, gracias. Soy Rosabel.
CARLOS	Mucho gusto, Rosabel.
ROSABEL	Igualmente. ¿De dónde eres, Carlos?
CARLOS	Soy de México. ¿Y tú?
ROSABEL	Soy de Argentina.

1 Teaching Tip You may want to do this activity as a TPR exercise. Have students give a thumbs-up for **sí** and a thumbs-down for **no**.

1 Script 1. ¿Qué hay de nuevo? 2. Nos vemos. 3. Chau. 4. Hola. 5. Buenas tardes. 6. Hasta luego. 7. ¿Qué tal? 8. De nada.
Textbook MP3s

2 Teaching Tip Before students listen, ask them to read through the items and write down the questions or statements they think would elicit those responses.

2 Script 1. ¿Cómo te llamas? 2. Te presento a Juan Pablo. 3. ¿De dónde es usted? 4. Muchas gracias. 5. Nos vemos. 6. ¿Qué pasa? 7. ¿Cómo está usted? 8. Buenas tardes, señor Fernández.
Textbook MP3s

3 Expansion To challenge students, have them provide the question or statement that would elicit each item. Ex: **1.** —Gracias. —De nada.

4 Teaching Tip 👤↔👤 Have volunteers role-play the finished conversations for the class. Encourage students to add to the conversations by ad-libbing additional phrases they've learned in **Contextos.**

4 Expansion ←👤→ In small groups, ask students to write a new conversation and then to scramble the order of the dialogue. Have groups exchange papers and put the conversations in order.

TEACHING OPTIONS

Game Divide the class into two teams. Point to a team member and call out an original statement or question based on **Contextos**. If the student responds appropriately, his or her team earns one point. The team with the most points at the end wins.
Pairs Write several times on the board. Ex: **9:00 a.m., 4:00 p.m., 10:30 p.m.** Have students work in pairs to greet each other according to the time of day.

Heritage Speakers Ask heritage speakers to mention other greetings and courtesy expressions that are used in their families' countries of origin. Have them indicate if the expressions are used in formal or informal situations, and write the phrases on the board in these categories. Then ask volunteers to state who in the **Contextos** illustration would use each expression.

5 Expansion Challenge students to create two-line exchanges using the incorrect answers from each item.

5 Seleccionar Choose the best word or phrase to complete each mini-conversation.

1. —Nos vemos mañana.

   —_____

   a. Gracias.   b. ¡Chau!   c. ¿Y usted?

2. —¿Qué tal?

   —_____

   a. Lo siento.   b. Igualmente.   c. Regular.

3. —Mucho gusto, señora Ochoa.

   —_____

   a. Muy bien.   b. No hay de qué.   c. Encantada, señor Rubio.

4. —¿De dónde eres?

   —_____

   a. De California.   b. El gusto es mío.   c. De nada.

5. —_____

   —No muy bien.

   a. ¿Qué pasa?   b. Hasta la vista.   c. ¿Cómo está usted?

6 Teaching Tip Have pairs share their responses with the class.

6 Expansion
👤↔👤 Have pairs or small groups create conversations that include the expressions used in **Actividad 5**. Ask volunteers to present their conversations to the class.

6 Completar Work with a partner to complete these dialogues. Some answers will vary. Suggested answers:

modelo
Estudiante 1: ¿Cómo estás?
Estudiante 2: Muy bien, gracias._____

1. **Estudiante 1:** Buenos días._____
   Estudiante 2: Buenos días. ¿Qué tal?
2. **Estudiante 1:** ¿Cómo te llamas?_____
   Estudiante 2: Me llamo Carmen Sánchez.
3. **Estudiante 1:** ¿De dónde eres?_____
   Estudiante 2: De Canadá.
4. **Estudiante 1:** Te presento a Marisol.
   Estudiante 2: Encantado/a._____
5. **Estudiante 1:** Gracias.
   Estudiante 2: De nada._____
6. **Estudiante 1:** ¿Qué pasa?_____
   Estudiante 2: Nada.

7 Teaching Tips
• Discuss the **modelo** before assigning the activity to pairs.
• 👤↔👤 After students have completed the activity, have pairs role-play the corrected mini-conversations. Ask them to substitute their own names and personal information where possible.
• Have volunteers write each mini-conversation on the board. Work as a class to identify and explain any errors.

7 Cambiar Work with a partner and correct the second part of each conversation to make it logical. Answers will vary.

modelo
Estudiante 1: ¿Qué tal?
Estudiante 2: ~~No hay de qué.~~ Bien. ¿Y tú?

1. **Estudiante 1:** Hasta mañana, señora Ramírez. Saludos al señor Ramírez.
   Estudiante 2: *Muy bien, gracias.*
2. **Estudiante 1:** ¿Qué hay de nuevo, Alberto?
   Estudiante 2: *Sí, me llamo Alberto. ¿Cómo te llamas tú?*
3. **Estudiante 1:** Gracias, Tomás.
   Estudiante 2: *Regular. ¿Y tú?*
4. **Estudiante 1:** Miguel, te presento a la señorita Perales.
   Estudiante 2: *No hay de qué, señorita.*
5. **Estudiante 1:** ¿De dónde eres, Antonio?
   Estudiante 2: *Muy bien, gracias. ¿Y tú?*
6. **Estudiante 1:** ¿Cómo se llama usted?
   Estudiante 2: *El gusto es mío.*

¡Lengua viva! Have students locate examples of the titles in **Actividad 7**. Then ask them to create short sentences in which they use the titles with people they know.

¡LENGUA VIVA!

The titles **señor, señora,** and **señorita** are abbreviated **Sr., Sra.,** and **Srta.** Note that these abbreviations are capitalized, while the titles themselves are not.

•••

There is no Spanish equivalent for the English title *Ms.;* women are addressed as **señora** or **señorita.**

TEACHING OPTIONS

Extra Practice Add an auditory exercise to this vocabulary practice. Read some phrases aloud and ask if students would use them with a person of the same age or someone older. Ex: **1. Te presento a Luis.** (same age) **2. ¿Cómo estás?** (same age) **3. Buenos días, doctor Soto.** (older) **4. ¿De dónde es usted, señora?** (older) **5. Chau, Teresa.** (same age) **6. No hay de qué, señor Perales.** (older)

Game Prepare a series of response statements using language in **Contextos.** Divide the class into two teams and invite students to guess the question or statement that would have elicited each of your responses. Read one statement at a time. The first team to correctly guess the question or statement earns a point. Ex: **Me llamo Lupe Torres Garza. (¿Cómo se llama usted? / ¿Cómo te llamas?)** The team with the most points at the end wins.

Comunicación

8 **Diálogos** With a partner, complete and act out these conversations.   Answers will vary.

Conversación 1

—Hola. Me llamo Teresa. ¿Cómo te llamas tú?

—_____

—Soy de Puerto Rico. ¿Y tú?

—_____

Conversación 2

—_____

—Muy bien, gracias. ¿Y usted, señora López?

—_____

—Hasta luego, señora. Saludos al señor López.

—_____

Conversación 3

—_____

—Regular. ¿Y tú?

—_____

—Nada.

9 **Conversaciones** Write four short conversations based on what the people would say.
Answers will vary.

10 **Situaciones** In groups of three, write and act out these situations.   Answers will vary.

1. On your way out of class on the first day of school, you strike up a conversation with the two students who were sitting next to you. You find out each student's name and where he or she is from before you say goodbye and go to your next class.
2. At the next class you meet up with a friend and find out how he or she is doing. As you are talking, your friend Elena enters. Introduce her to your friend.
3. As you're leaving the bookstore, you meet your parents' friends Mrs. Sánchez and Mr. Rodríguez. You greet them and ask how each person is. As you say goodbye, you send greetings to Mrs. Rodríguez.
4. Make up and act out a real-life situation that you and your classmates can role-play with the language you've learned.

---

8 Expansion
- ⬤ Have students work in small groups to write a few mini-conversations modeled on this activity. Then ask them to copy the dialogues, omitting a few words or phrases. Have groups exchange papers and fill in the blanks.
- Have students rewrite **Conversaciones 1** and **3** in the formal register and **Conversación 2** in the informal register.

9 Teaching Tip To simplify, have students brainstorm who the people in the illustration are and what they are talking about. Ask students which groups would be speaking to each other in the **usted** form, and which would be using the **tú** form.

9 Expansion
⬤ In pairs, have students take turns selecting a person from the drawing and providing 2-3 statements that he or she might be saying. The partner will try to guess who it is.

10 Teaching Tip
⬤ To challenge students, have each group pick a situation to write and perform. Tell groups not to memorize every word of the conversation, but rather to re-create it.

The Affective Dimension
Have students rehearse the situations a few times, so that they will feel more comfortable with the material and less anxious when presenting it before the class.

Bienvenida, Marissa

Marissa llega a México para pasar un año con la familia Díaz.

PERSONAJES MARISSA SRA. DÍAZ

 Video

1

MARISSA ¿Usted es de Cuba?

SRA. DÍAZ Sí, de La Habana. Y Roberto es de Mérida. Tú eres de Wisconsin, ¿verdad?

MARISSA Sí, de Appleton, Wisconsin.

2

MARISSA ¿Quiénes son los dos chicos de las fotos? ¿Jimena y Felipe?

SRA. DÍAZ Sí. Ellos son estudiantes.

DON DIEGO ¿Cómo está usted hoy, señora Carolina?

SRA. DÍAZ Muy bien, gracias. ¿Y usted?

DON DIEGO Bien, gracias.

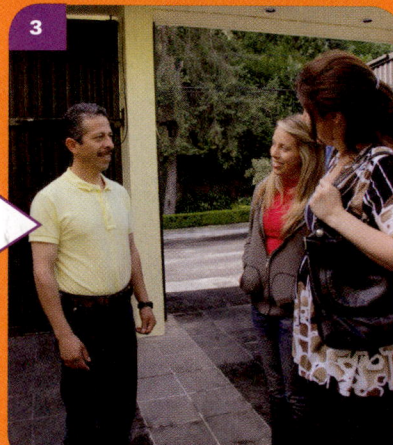

3

DON DIEGO Buenas tardes, señora. Señorita, bienvenida a la Ciudad de México.

MARISSA ¡Muchas gracias!

5

4

MARISSA ¿Cómo se llama usted?

DON DIEGO Yo soy Diego. Mucho gusto.

MARISSA El gusto es mío, don Diego.

6

SRA. DÍAZ Ahí hay dos maletas. Son de Marissa.

DON DIEGO Con permiso.

Section Goals

In **Fotonovela**, students will:
- receive comprehensible input from free-flowing discourse
- learn functional phrases that preview lesson grammatical structures

Instructional Resources
Supersite: Video (*Fotonovela*); Resources (Scripts, Translations, Answer Keys)
WebSAM
Video Manual

Video Synopsis **Marissa**, an American college student, arrives in Mexico City for a year abroad. She meets her Mexican hosts, **Carolina** and **Roberto Díaz**, and their doorman, **don Diego**. As **Marissa** unpacks, the **Díaz** children, **Felipe** and **Jimena**, take away her English-Spanish dictionary as a joke. **Marissa** accepts the challenge and leaves the dictionary with **Carolina**.

Teaching Tips
- In small groups, have students cover the captions and guess the plot based on the video stills. Write their predictions on the board. After students have watched the video, compare their predictions to what actually happened in the episode.
- Point out that **don** is a title of respect and neither equivalent nor related to the English name *Don*. Ask if students think **Diego** is the doorman's first or last name. (It is his first name.) Students will learn more about the titles **don** and **doña** on page 8.
- Tell students that all items in **Expresiones útiles** on page 7 are active vocabulary. Model the pronunciation of each item and have the class repeat.
- ⬥↔⬥ You can also practice the **Expresiones útiles** by using them in short conversations with individual students.

TEACHING OPTIONS

Video Tips General suggestions for using video clips in the classroom can be found in the front matter of this Instructor's Annotated Edition.
Bienvenida, Marissa →⬥← Have students make a three-column chart with these headings: *Greetings*, *Self-Identification*, and *Courtesy Expressions*. Have students suggest two or three possible phrases for each category. Then play the **Bienvenida, Marissa** episode once and ask students to fill in the first column with the basic greetings that they hear. Repeat this process for the second column, where they should list the expressions the characters use to identify themselves. Play the video a third time for students to jot down courtesy expressions, such as ways to say "pleased to meet you" and "pardon me."

DON DIEGO **SR. DÍAZ** **FELIPE** **JIMENA**

SR. DÍAZ ¿Qué hora es?

FELIPE Son las cuatro y veinticinco.

SRA. DÍAZ Marissa, te presento a Roberto, mi esposo.

SR. DÍAZ Bienvenida, Marissa.

MARISSA Gracias, señor Díaz.

JIMENA ¿Qué hay en esta cosa?

MARISSA Bueno, a ver, hay tres cuadernos, un mapa... ¡Y un diccionario!

JIMENA ¿Cómo se dice mediodía en inglés?

FELIPE "Noon".

FELIPE Estás en México, ¿verdad?

MARISSA ¿Sí?

FELIPE Nosotros somos tu diccionario.

More activities

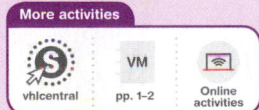

vhlcentral | VM pp. 1–2 | Online activities

Expresiones útiles

Identifying yourself and others

¿Cómo se llama usted?
What's your name?
Yo soy Diego, el portero. Mucho gusto.
I'm Diego, the doorman. Nice to meet you.
¿Cómo te llamas?
What's your name?
Me llamo Marissa.
My name is Marissa.
¿Quién es...? / ¿Quiénes son...?
Who is...? / Who are...?
Es mi esposo.
He's my husband.
Tú eres..., ¿verdad?/¿cierto?/¿no?
You are..., right?

Identifying objects

¿Qué hay en esta cosa?
What's in this thing?
Bueno, a ver, aquí hay tres cuadernos...
Well, let's see, here are three notebooks...
Oye/Oiga, ¿cómo se dice *suitcase* en español?
Hey, how do you say suitcase in Spanish?
Se dice *maleta*.
You say maleta.

Saying what time it is

¿Qué hora es?
What time is it?
Es la una. / Son las dos.
It's one o'clock. / It's two o'clock.
Son las cuatro y veinticinco.
It's four twenty-five.

Polite expressions

Con permiso.
Pardon me; Excuse me. (to request permission)
Perdón.
Pardon me; Excuse me. (to get someone's attention or excuse yourself)
¡Bienvenido/a! *Welcome!*

Expresiones útiles Identify forms of the verb **ser** and point out some subject pronouns. Identify time-telling expressions. Point out the verb form **hay** and explain that it means *there is/are*. Tell students that they will learn more about these concepts in **Estructura**.

Teaching Tip
👥↔👤 Have volunteers read individual parts of the **Fotonovela** captions aloud. Then have students work in groups of six to role-play the episode, ad-libbing when possible. Have one or two groups present the episode to the class.

Successful Language Learning Tell students that their conversational skills will grow more quickly as they learn each lesson's **Expresiones útiles**. This feature is designed to teach phrases that will be useful in conversation, and it will also help students understand key phrases in each **Fotonovela**.

Nota cultural Mexico City's metropolitan area is the largest in the hemisphere, with about 21 million people. This number is still only a fraction of Mexico's total population of 125 million. It is the most highly populated Spanish-speaking country in the world.

TEACHING OPTIONS

Extra Practice →👤← Photocopy pages 6–7 or the **Fotonovela** Videoscript (Supersite) and white out some key words. Play the episode once, and then distribute the photocopied scripts. Play the video a second time and ask students to fill in the missing words. Go over the answers as a class.
Extra Practice Write questions and phrases from **Expresiones útiles** on the board. Ex: **Es la una. Con permiso. ¿Cómo te llamas?**

With their books closed, have students describe a context in which each question or phrase could be used.
Pairs In pairs, have students predict whom **Marissa** will get along with better: **Felipe** or **Jimena**. Have them support their opinions with specific scenes from the episode.

¿Qué pasó?

1 ¿Cierto o falso? Indicate if each statement is **cierto** or **falso.** Then correct the false statements.

	Cierto	Falso	
1. La Sra. Díaz es de Caracas.	○	✓	La Sra. Díaz es de La Habana.
2. El Sr. Díaz es de Mérida.	✓	○	
3. Marissa es de Los Ángeles, California.	○	✓	Marissa es de Appleton, Wisconsin.
4. Jimena y Felipe son profesores.	○	✓	Jimena y Felipe son estudiantes.
5. Las dos maletas son de Jimena.	○	✓	Las dos maletas son de Marissa.
6. El Sr. Díaz pregunta "¿qué hora es?".	✓	○	
7. Hay un diccionario en la mochila (*backpack*) de Marissa.	✓	○	

2 Identificar Indicate which person says the equivalent of each statement.

1. Son las cuatro y veinticinco, papá. Felipe
2. Roberto es mi esposo. Sra. Díaz
3. Igualmente, don Diego. Marissa
4. ¿Qué hay de nuevo, doña Carolina? don Diego
5. Yo soy de Cuba. Sra. Díaz
6. ¿Qué hay en la mochila, Marissa? Jimena

MARISSA   FELIPE   SRA. DÍAZ

DON DIEGO   JIMENA

3 Completar Complete this new version of the conversation between Don Diego and Marissa.

DON DIEGO Hola, (1)___señorita___.
MARISSA Hola, señor. ¿Cómo se (2)___llama___ usted?
DON DIEGO Yo me llamo Diego, ¿y (3)___usted___?
MARISSA Yo me llamo Marissa. (4)_Encantada_.
DON DIEGO (5)_Igualmente_, señorita Marissa.
MARISSA Nos (6)___vemos___, don Diego.
DON DIEGO Hasta (7)_luego/pronto/_ señorita Marissa.
la vista

4 Conversar With a partner, prepare a conversation between two travelers at an airport.
Some answers will vary.

Estudiante 1	**Estudiante 2**
Say "good afternoon" to your partner and ask for his or her name.	→ Say hello and what your name is. Then ask what your partner's name is.
Say what your name is and that you are glad to meet your partner.	→ Say that the pleasure is yours.
Ask how your partner is.	→ Say that you're doing well, thank you.
Ask where your partner is from.	→ Say where you're from.
Say it's one o'clock and say goodbye.	→ Say goodbye.

TEACHING OPTIONS

Small Groups Ask students to work in small groups to ad-lib the exchanges between **Marissa** and **Sra. Díaz, Marissa** and **don Diego,** and **Marissa, Felipe,** and **Jimena.** Tell them to convey the general meaning using vocabulary and expressions they know, and assure them that they do not have to stick to the original dialogues word for word. Then, ask volunteers to present their exchanges to the class.

Extra Practice Choose four or five lines of the **Fotonovela** to use as a dictation. Read the lines twice slowly to give students sufficient time to write. Then read them again at normal speed to allow students to correct any errors or fill in any gaps. You may have students correct their own work by checking it against the **Fotonovela** text and ask follow-up questions to test comprehension.

Pronunciación

 Tutorial

The Spanish alphabet

The Spanish and English alphabets are almost identical, with a few exceptions. For example, the Spanish letter **ñ (eñe)** doesn't occur in the English alphabet. Furthermore, the letters **k (ka)** and **w (doble ve)** are used only in words of foreign origin. Examine the chart below to find other differences.

Letra	Nombre(s)	Ejemplos	Letra	Nombre(s)	Ejemplos
a	a	adiós	m	eme	mapa
b	be	bien, problema	n	ene	nacionalidad
c	ce	cosa, cero	ñ	eñe	mañana
ch	che	chico	o	o	once
d	de	diario, nada	p	pe	profesor
e	e	estudiante	q	cu	qué
f	efe	foto	r	ere	regular, señora
g	ge	gracias, Gerardo, regular	s	ese	señor
h	hache	hola	t	te	tú
i	i	igualmente	u	u	usted
j	jota	Javier	v	ve	vista, nuevo
k	ka, ca	kilómetro	w	doble ve	walkman
l	ele	lápiz	x	equis	existir, México
ll	elle	llave	y	i griega, ye	yo
			z	zeta, ceta	zona

El alfabeto Repeat the Spanish alphabet and example words after your instructor.

Práctica Spell these words aloud in Spanish.

1. nada
2. maleta
3. quince
4. muy
5. hombre
6. por favor
7. San Fernando
8. Estados Unidos
9. Puerto Rico
10. España
11. Javier
12. Ecuador
13. Maite
14. gracias
15. Nueva York

Refranes Read these sayings aloud.

Ver es creer.[1]

En boca cerrada no entran moscas.[2]

[1] Seeing is believing. [2] Silence is golden.

More activities

vhlcentral · LM p. 2

¡LENGUA VIVA!

Note that **ch** and **ll** are digraphs, or two letters that together produce one sound. Conventionally they have been considered part of the alphabet, but **ch** and **ll** do not have their own entries when placing words in alphabetical order, as in a glossary.

AYUDA

The letter combination **rr** produces a strong trilled sound that does not have an English equivalent. English speakers commonly make this sound when imitating the sound of a motor. This sound occurs with the **rr** between vowels and with the **r** at the beginning of a word: **puertorriqueño**, **terrible**, **Roberto**, etc. See **Lección 7**, p. 233 for more information.

Section Goals

In **Pronunciación**, students will be introduced to:
• the Spanish alphabet
• the names of the letters

Instructional Resources
Supersite: Audio (Textbook and Lab MP3 Files); Resources (Scripts, Answer Keys)
WebSAM
Lab Manual

Teaching Tip Point out that the **Real Academia Española** has decided that **ch** and **ll** are no longer letters. In 2010 the **Real Academia** recommended the use of a unified naming convention for the alphabet. The suggested names for **r, v, w,** and **y** are **erre, uve, doble uve,** and **ye**. However, most Spanish speakers tend to use the traditional naming conventions followed in their countries.

TEACHING OPTIONS

Extra Practice Do a dictation activity in which you spell aloud Spanish words (e.g., world capitals and countries). Spell each word twice to allow students sufficient time to write. After you have finished, write your list on the board or project it and have students check their work. You can also have students spell their names in Spanish.

Extra Practice Here are four additional **refranes** to practice the alphabet: **De tal palo, tal astilla** (*A chip off the old block*); **Los ojos son el espejo del alma** (*Eyes are the window to the soul*); **El rayo nunca cae dos veces en el mismo lugar** (*Lightning never strikes twice in the same place*); **No dejes para mañana lo que puedas hacer hoy** (*Don't put off until tomorrow what you can do today*).

Section Goals

In **Cultura**, students will:
- read about greetings in Spanish-speaking countries
- learn informal greetings and farewells
- read about the **plaza principal**
- read about famous friends and couples

Instructional Resource
Supersite

En detalle

Antes de leer Ask students to share how they would normally greet a friend or family member.

Lectura
- Linguists have determined that, in the U.S., friends generally remain at least eighteen inches apart while chatting. Friends in Spanish-speaking countries would probably deem eighteen inches to be excessive.
- Show students the locations mentioned here by referring them to the maps in their textbooks. Explain that there may be regional variations within each country.
- Explain that an "air kiss" is limited to a grazing of cheeks.

Después de leer Call on two volunteers to stand in front of the class. Point out the natural distance between them. Then demonstrate reduced personal space in Hispanic cultures by having the volunteers face each other with their toes touching and start a conversation. Tell the rest of the class to do the same. Ask students to share their feelings on this change in personal space.

1 Expansion Ask students to write three more true/false statements for a classmate to complete.

EN DETALLE

Saludos y besos en los países hispanos

In Spanish-speaking countries, kissing on the cheek is a customary way to greet friends and family members. Even when people are introduced for the first time, it is common for them to kiss, particularly in non-business settings. Whereas North Americans maintain considerable personal space when greeting, Spaniards and Latin Americans tend to decrease their personal space and give one or two kisses (**besos**) on the cheek, sometimes accompanied by a handshake or a hug. In formal business settings, where associates do not know one another on a personal level, a simple handshake is appropriate.

Greeting someone with a **beso** varies according to gender and region. Men generally greet each other with a hug or warm handshake, with the exception of Argentina, where male friends and relatives lightly kiss on the cheek. Greetings between men and women, and between women, generally include kissing, but can differ depending on the country and context. In Spain, it is customary to give **dos besos**, starting with the right cheek first. In Latin American countries, including Mexico, Costa Rica, Colombia, and Chile, a greeting consists of a single "air kiss" on the right cheek. Peruvians also "air kiss," but strangers will simply shake hands. In Colombia, female acquaintances tend to simply pat each other on the right forearm or shoulder.

Tendencias

País	Beso	País	Beso
Argentina	💋	**España**	💋💋
Bolivia	💋	**México**	💋
Chile	💋	**Paraguay**	💋💋
Colombia	💋	**Puerto Rico**	💋
El Salvador	💋	**Venezuela**	💋 / 💋💋

ACTIVIDADES

1 **¿Cierto o falso?** Indicate whether these statements are true (**cierto**) or false (**falso**). Correct the false statements.

1. In Spanish-speaking countries, people use less personal space when greeting than in the U.S. **Cierto.**
2. Men never greet with a kiss in Spanish-speaking countries. **Falso.** Argentine men can greet with a light kiss.
3. Shaking hands is not appropriate for a business setting in Latin America. **Falso.** In most business settings, people greet one another by shaking hands.
4. Spaniards greet with one kiss on the right cheek. **Falso.** They greet with one kiss on each cheek.
5. In Mexico, people greet with an "air kiss." **Cierto.**
6. Gender can play a role in the type of greeting given. **Cierto.**
7. If two women acquaintances meet in Colombia, they should exchange two kisses on the cheek. **Falso.** They pat one another on the right forearm or shoulder.
8. In Peru, a man and a woman meeting for the first time would probably greet each other with an "air kiss." **Falso.** They would probably shake hands.

TEACHING OPTIONS

Game Divide the class into two teams. Give situations in which people greet one another, and have one member from each team identify the appropriate way to greet. Ex: Two male friends in Argentina. (light kiss on the cheek) Give one point for each correct answer. The team with the most points at the end wins.

Un beso Kisses are not only a form of greeting in Spanish-speaking countries. It is also common to end phone conversations and close letters or e-mails with the words **un beso** or **besos**. Additionally, friends may use **un abrazo** to end a written message. In a more formal e-mail, one can write **un saludo (cordial)** or **saludos**.

ASÍ SE DICE

Saludos y despedidas

¿Cómo te/le va?	How are things going (for you)?
¡Cuánto tiempo!	It's been a long time!
Hasta ahora.	See you soon.
¿Qué hay?	What's new?
¿Qué onda? (Méx., Arg., Chi.); ¿Qué más? (Ven., Col.)	What's going on?

EL MUNDO HISPANO

Parejas y amigos famosos

Here are some famous couples and friends from the Spanish-speaking world.

- **Penélope Cruz** (España) y **Javier Bardem** (España) Both Oscar-winning actors, the couple married in 2010. They starred together in *Vicky Cristina Barcelona* (2008) and *Loving Pablo* (2017).

- **Gael García Bernal** (México) y **Diego Luna** (México) These lifelong friends became famous when they starred in the 2001 Mexican film *Y tu mamá también*. They continue to work together on projects, such as the 2012 film *Casa de mi padre*.

- **Salma Hayek** (México) y **Penélope Cruz** (España) These two close friends developed their acting skills in their home countries before meeting in Hollywood.

PERFIL

La plaza principal

In the Spanish-speaking world, public space is treasured. Small city and town life revolves around the **plaza principal**. Often surrounded by cathedrals or municipal buildings like the **ayuntamiento** (*city hall*), the pedestrian **plaza** is designated as a central meeting place for family and friends. During warmer months, when outdoor cafés usually line the **plaza**, it is a popular spot to have a leisurely cup of coffee, chat, and people watch. Many town festivals, or **ferias**, also take place in this space. One of the most famous

La Plaza Mayor de Salamanca

La Plaza de Armas, Lima, Perú

town squares is the **Plaza Mayor** in the university town of Salamanca, Spain. Students gather underneath its famous clock tower to meet up with friends or simply take a coffee break.

CON RITMO HISPANO

Lin-Manuel Miranda (1980–)
Birthplace: New York City, New York

He won two Tony Awards for his musical *Hamilton* (2016) and one for *In the Heights* (2008), his musical about the predominantly Latino New York neighborhood of Washington Heights.

Go to **vhlcentral.com** to find out more about **Lin-Manuel Miranda** and his music.

ACTIVIDADES

2 Comprensión Answer these questions. *Some answers may vary. Suggested answers:*

1. What are two types of buildings found on the **plaza principal**? *municipal buildings and cathedrals*
2. What two types of events or activities are common at a **plaza principal**? *meeting with friends and festivals*
3. How would Diego Luna greet his friends? *¿Qué onda?*
4. Would Salma Hayek and Gael García Bernal greet each other with one kiss or two? *one*

3 Saludos Role-play these greetings with a partner. Include a verbal greeting as well as a kiss or handshake, as appropriate. *Role-plays will vary according to student gender.*

1. friends in Mexico
2. business associates at a conference in Chile
3. friends meeting in Madrid's Plaza Mayor
4. Peruvians meeting for the first time
5. relatives in Argentina

More activities

vhlcentral | Online activities

Así se dice

- Ask students to identify situations in which these expressions can be used.
- To challenge students, add these phrases to the list: **Hasta siempre** (*Farewell*), **Que te/le vaya bien** (*Have a nice day/time*).
- Explain that greetings frequently are pronounced in a shortened way. Ex: **Hasta ahora** → Stahora.

Perfil

- Construction on Salamanca's **Plaza Mayor** began in 1729, led by **Alberto Churriguera**. Silhouettes of prominent Spaniards are carved between the stone arches that border the square. City Hall is situated at the north end of the plaza.
- Lima's **Plaza de Armas** is flanked on three sides by three-story arcades. On the east end of the square lies the massive **Catedral**, begun in 1535.

El mundo hispano

Have pairs choose any two people from **El mundo hispano**. Ask them to write a brief dialogue in which they meet for the first time. Encourage them to use phrases from **Así se dice**. Have volunteers role-play their dialogues for the class.

Con ritmo hispano
Point out to students that they will find supporting activities and information at **vhlcentral.com**.

2 Expansion Ask students to write two additional questions for a classmate to answer.

3 Teaching Tip Before beginning this activity, ask students if they would use **tú** or **usted** in each situation.

TEACHING OPTIONS

Cultural Activity For homework, have students use the Internet to research a famous **plaza principal** in a Spanish-speaking city or town. They should find out the **plaza**'s location in the city, when it was built, current uses, and other significant information. Encourage them to bring in a photo. Then have the students present their findings to the class.

Heritage Speakers Ask heritage speakers to describe cities and towns in their families' countries of origin. Is there a **plaza principal**? How is it used? Ask the class to think of analogous public spaces in the U.S. (Ex: a common or "town green" in small New England towns)

1.1 Nouns and articles   Tutorial

Spanish nouns

ANTE TODO A noun is a word used to identify people, animals, places, things, or ideas. Unlike English, all Spanish nouns, even those that refer to non-living things, have gender; that is, they are considered either masculine or feminine. As in English, nouns in Spanish also have number, meaning that they are either singular or plural.

Nouns that refer to living things			
Masculine nouns		**Feminine nouns**	
el hombre	*the man*	la mujer	*the woman*
ending in –o		**ending in –a**	
el chico	*the boy*	la chica	*the girl*
el pasajero	*the (male) passenger*	la pasajera	*the (female) passenger*
ending in –or		**ending in –ora**	
el conductor	*the (male) driver*	la conductora	*the (female) driver*
el profesor	*the (male) teacher*	la profesora	*the (female) teacher*
ending in –ista		**ending in –ista**	
el turista	*the (male) tourist*	la turista	*the (female) tourist*

▶ Generally, nouns that refer to males, like **el hombre**, are masculine, while nouns that refer to females, like **la mujer**, are feminine.

▶ Many nouns that refer to male beings end in **–o** or **–or**. Their corresponding feminine forms end in **–a** and **–ora**, respectively.

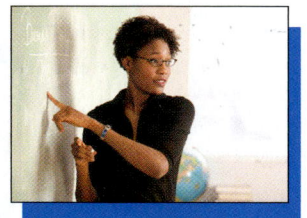

el conductor   la profesora

▶ The masculine and feminine forms of nouns that end in **–ista**, like **turista**, are the same, so gender is indicated by the article **el** (masculine) or **la** (feminine). Some other nouns have identical masculine and feminine forms.

el joven	**la** joven
the young man	*the young woman*
el estudiante	**la** estudiante
the (male) student	*the (female) student*

Nouns that refer to non-living things

Masculine nouns		**Feminine nouns**	
ending in –o		**ending in –a**	
el cuaderno	*the notebook*	la computadora	*the computer*
el diario	*the diary*	la cosa	*the thing*
el diccionario	*the dictionary*	la escuela	*the school*
el número	*the number*	la maleta	*the suitcase*
el video	*the video*	la palabra	*the word*
ending in –ma		**ending in –ción**	
el problema	*the problem*	la lección	*the lesson*
el programa	*the program*	la conversación	*the conversation*
ending in –s		**ending in –dad**	
el autobús	*the bus*	la nacionalidad	*the nationality*
el país	*the country*	la comunidad	*the community*

¡LENGUA VIVA!

The Spanish word for *video* can be pronounced with the stress on the **i** or the **e**. For that reason, you might see the word written with or without an accent: **video** or **vídeo**.

▶ As shown above, certain noun endings are strongly associated with a specific gender, so you can use them to determine if a noun is masculine or feminine.

▶ Because the gender of nouns that refer to non-living things cannot be determined by foolproof rules, you should memorize the gender of each noun you learn. It is helpful to learn each noun with its corresponding article, **el** for masculine and **la** for feminine.

▶ Another reason to memorize the gender of every noun is that there are common exceptions to the rules of gender. For example, **el mapa** (*map*) and **el día** (*day*) end in **-a**, but are masculine. **La mano** (*hand*) ends in **-o**, but is feminine.

Plural of nouns

▶ To form the plural, add **–s** to nouns that end in a vowel. For nouns that end in a consonant, add **–es**. For nouns that end in **z**, change the **z** to **c**, then add **–es**.

el chic**o** ⟶ los chic**os**   la nacionalida**d** ⟶ las nacionalida**des**

el diari**o** ⟶ los diari**os**   el paí**s** ⟶ los paí**ses**

el problem**a** ⟶ los problem**as**   el lápi**z** (*pencil*) ⟶ los lápi**ces**

CONSULTA

You will learn more about accent marks in **Lección 4, Pronunciación**, p. 123.

▶ In general, when a singular noun has an accent mark on the last syllable, the accent is dropped from the plural form.

la lecci**ón** ⟶ las lecci**ones**   el autob**ús** ⟶ los autob**uses**

▶ Use the masculine plural form to refer to a group that includes both males and females.

1 pasajer**o** + 2 pasajer**as** = 3 pasajer**os**   2 chic**os** + 2 chic**as** = 4 chic**os**

Teaching Tips
• Work through the list of nouns, modeling their pronunciation. Point out patterns of gender, including word endings **–ma**, **–ción**, and **–dad**. Give cognate nouns with these endings and ask students to indicate the gender. Ex: **diagrama**, **acción**, **personalidad**. Point out common exceptions to gender agreement rules for **el mapa**, **el día**, and **la mano**.
• Stress the addition of **–s** to nouns that end in vowels and **–es** to nouns that end in consonants. Write ten nouns on the board and ask volunteers to give the plural forms, along with the appropriate articles.
• Point to three male students and ask if the group is **los** or **las estudiantes** (**los**). Next, point to three female students and ask the same question (**las**). Then indicate a group of males and females and ask for the correct term to refer to them (**los estudiantes**). Stress that even if a group contains 100 women and one man, the masculine plural form and article are used.
• Point out that words like **lección** and **autobús** lose the written accent in the plural form in order to keep the stress on the same syllable as in the singular noun.

The Affective Dimension
Tell students that many people feel anxious when learning grammar. Tell them that grammar will seem less intimidating if they think of it as a description of how the language works instead of a list of strict rules.

TEACHING OPTIONS

TPR Give four students each a card with a different definite article. Give the other students each a card with a noun (include a mix of masculine, feminine, singular, and plural). Have students form a circle; each student's card should be visible to others. Call out one of the nouns; that student must step forward. The student with the corresponding article has five seconds to join the noun student.

Game Divide the class into two teams, A and B. Point to a member of team A and say a singular noun. The student repeats the noun with the definite article, and then spells it. Then point to a team B member, who will supply the plural form and spell it. Award one point per correct answer and deduct one point for each wrong answer. Make sure to give each team a variety of both plural and singular nouns. The team with the most points wins.

Spanish articles

ANTE TODO   As you know, English often uses definite articles (*the*) and indefinite articles (*a, an*) before nouns. Spanish also has definite and indefinite articles. Unlike English, Spanish articles vary in form because they agree in gender and number with the nouns they modify.

Definite articles

▶ Spanish has four forms that are equivalent to the English definite article *the*. Use definite articles to refer to specific nouns.

Masculine		**Feminine**	
SINGULAR	PLURAL	SINGULAR	PLURAL
el diccionario	**los** diccionarios	**la** computadora	**las** computadoras
the dictionary	*the dictionaries*	*the computer*	*the computers*

Indefinite articles

▶ Spanish has four forms that are equivalent to the English indefinite article, which according to context may mean *a*, *an*, or *some*. Use indefinite articles to refer to unspecified persons or things.

Masculine		**Feminine**	
SINGULAR	PLURAL	SINGULAR	PLURAL
un pasajero	**unos** pasajeros	**una** fotografía	**unas** fotografías
a (one) passenger	*some passengers*	*a (one) photograph*	*some photographs*

¡INTÉNTALO!   Provide a definite article for each noun in the first column and an indefinite article for each noun in the second column.

¿el, la, los o las?	¿un, una, unos o unas?
1. **la** chica	1. **un** autobús
2. **el** chico	2. **unos** hombres
3. **los** cuadernos	3. **una** computadora
4. **la** maleta	4. **unas** escuelas
5. **el** lápiz	5. **una** señora
6. **las** mujeres	6. **unos** lápices

More activities

vhlcentral

LM
p. 3

WB
p. 3

Online activities

Práctica

1 **¿Singular o plural?** If the word is singular, make it plural. If it is plural, make it singular.

> **modelo**
>
> el hombre   los hombres
> unas señoritas   una señorita

1. el número
   los números
2. un diario
   unos diarios
3. la estudiante
   las estudiantes
4. el conductor
   los conductores

5. el país
   los países
6. las cosas
   la cosa
7. unos turistas
   un turista
8. las nacionalidades
   la nacionalidad

9. unas computadoras
   una computadora
10. los problemas
    el problema
11. los profesores
    el profesor
12. la señora
    las señoras

2 **Identificar** Provide the nouns with their corresponding definite and indefinite articles.

> **modelo**
>
> las computadoras, unas computadoras

1. la maleta,
   una maleta

2. las mujeres,
   unas mujeres

3. los cuadernos,
   unos cuadernos

4. el diario, un diario

5. los hombres,
   unos hombres

6. los lápices,
   unos lápices

7. el chico, un chico

8. los autobuses,
   unos autobuses

Comunicación

NATIONAL communication STANDARDS

3 **Charadas** In groups, play a game of charades. Individually, think of two nouns for each charade, for example, a boy using a computer (**un chico; una computadora**). The first person to guess correctly acts out the next charade. Answers will vary.

---

1 **Expansion** Reverse the activity by reading the on-page answers and having students convert the singular to plural and vice versa. Make sure they close their books. Give the nouns in random order.

2 **Expansion** As an additional visual exercise, bring in photos or magazine pictures that illustrate items whose names students know. Ask students to indicate the definite article and the noun. Include a mix of singular and plural nouns. Repeat the exercise with indefinite articles.

3 **Teaching Tip** Model the game of charades by writing some new cognates on the board (Ex: **la guitarra, el teléfono, la televisión**). Act out sitting on a couch and flipping channels on a remote and invite students to guess. Emphasize that the student acting out the charade must not speak and that he or she may show the number of syllables by using fingers.

3 **Expansion** Split the class into two teams, with volunteers from each team acting out the charades. Give a point to each team for correctly guessing the charade. The team with the most points wins.

Section Goals

In **Estructura 1.2**, students will be introduced to:
• numbers 0–30
• the verb form **hay**

Instructional Resources
Supersite: Audio (Lab MP3 Files); Resources (Grammar Presentation Slides, Activity Pack, Scripts, Answer Keys); Testing Program (Quizzes)
WebSAM
Workbook
Lab Manual

Teaching Tips
• Introduce numbers by asking students if they can count to ten in Spanish. Model the pronunciation of each number. Write individual numbers on the board and call on students at random to say the number.
• Say numbers aloud at random and have students hold up the appropriate number of fingers. Then reverse the drill; hold up varying numbers of fingers at random and ask students to shout out the corresponding number in Spanish.
• Emphasize the variable forms of **uno** and **veintiuno**, giving examples of each. Ex: **veintiún profesores, veintiuna profesoras.**
• Ask questions like these: **¿Cuántos estudiantes hay en la clase? (Hay _____ estudiantes en la clase.)**

1.2 # Numbers 0–30 Tutorial

0	cero				
1	uno	**11**	once	**21**	veintiuno
2	dos	**12**	doce	**22**	veintidós
3	tres	**13**	trece	**23**	veintitrés
4	cuatro	**14**	catorce	**24**	veinticuatro
5	cinco	**15**	quince	**25**	veinticinco
6	seis	**16**	dieciséis	**26**	veintiséis
7	siete	**17**	diecisiete	**27**	veintisiete
8	ocho	**18**	dieciocho	**28**	veintiocho
9	nueve	**19**	diecinueve	**29**	veintinueve
10	diez	**20**	veinte	**30**	treinta

AYUDA

Though it is less common, the numbers 16 through 29 (except 20) can also be written as three words: **diez y seis, diez y siete…**

▶ The number **uno** (*one*) and numbers ending in **–uno**, such as **veintiuno**, have more than one form. Before masculine nouns, **uno** shortens to **un**. Before feminine nouns, **uno** changes to **una**.

un hombre → veinti**ún** hombres   **una** mujer → veinti**una** mujeres

▶ **¡Atención!** The forms **uno** and **veintiuno** are used when counting (**uno, dos, tres… veinte, veintiuno, veintidós…**). They are also used when the number *follows* a noun, even if the noun is feminine: **la lección uno**.

▶ To ask *how many people* or *things* there are, use **cuántos** before masculine nouns and **cuántas** before feminine nouns.

▶ The Spanish equivalent of both *there is* and *there are* is **hay**. Use **¿Hay…?** to ask *Is there…?* or *Are there…?* Use **no hay** to express *there is not* or *there are not*.

—**¿Cuántos** estudiantes **hay**?
How many students are there?

—**Hay** seis estudiantes en la foto.
There are six students in the photo.

—**¿Hay** chicos en la fotografía?
Are there guys in the picture?

—**Hay** tres chicas y **no hay** chicos.
There are three girls, and there are no guys.

More activities

vhlcentral

LM
p. 4

WB
pp. 4

Online activities

🔊 **¡INTÉNTALO!** Provide the Spanish words for these numbers.

1. **7** ___siete___
2. **15** ___quince___
3. **29** ___veintinueve___
4. **1** ___uno___
5. **0** ___cero___
6. **16** ___dieciséis___
7. **21** ___veintiuno___
8. **9** ___nueve___
9. **23** ___veintitrés___
10. **11** ___once___
11. **10** ___diez___
12. **4** ___cuatro___
13. **12** ___doce___
14. **28** ___veintiocho___
15. **14** ___catorce___
16. **30** ___treinta___

TEACHING OPTIONS

TPR Assign ten students a number from 0–30 and line them up in front of the class. Call out one of the numbers at random, and have the student assigned that number step forward. When two students have stepped forward, ask them to repeat their numbers. Then ask individuals to add (Say: **Suma**) or subtract (Say: **Resta**) the two numbers, giving the result in Spanish.

Game Ask students to write B-I-N-G-O across the top of a blank piece of paper. Have them draw five squares vertically under each letter and randomly fill in the squares with numbers from 0–30, without repeating any numbers. Draw numbers from a hat and call them out in Spanish. The first student to mark five in a row (horizontally, vertically, or diagonally) yells **¡Bingo!** and wins. Have the winner confirm the numbers for you in Spanish.

Práctica

1 **Contar** Following the pattern, write out the missing numbers in Spanish.

1. 1, 3, 5, ..., 29　　7, 9, 11, 13, 15, 17, 19, 21, 23, 25, 27
2. 2, 4, 6, ..., 30　　8, 10, 12, 14, 16, 18, 20, 22, 24, 26, 28
3. 3, 6, 9, ..., 30　　12, 15, 18, 21, 24, 27
4. 30, 28, 26, ..., 0　　24, 22, 20, 18, 16, 14, 12, 10, 8, 6, 4, 2
5. 28, 24, 20, ..., 0　　16, 12, 8, 4
6. 30, 25, 20, ..., 0　　15, 10, 5

2 **Resolver** Solve these math problems with a partner.

> **modelo**
> 5 + 3 =
> **Estudiante 1:** cinco más tres son...
> **Estudiante 2:** ocho

AYUDA

+	→	más
−	→	menos
=	→	son

1. **2 + 15 =** Dos más quince son diecisiete.
2. **5 + 7 =** Cinco más siete son doce.
3. **20 − 1 =** Veinte menos uno son diecinueve.
4. **18 + 12 =** Dieciocho más doce son treinta.
5. **3 + 22 =** Tres más veintidós son veinticinco.
6. **6 − 3 =** Seis menos tres son tres.
7. **11 + 12 =** Once más doce son veintitrés.
8. **8 + 5 =** Ocho más cinco son trece.
9. **7 − 2 =** Siete menos dos son cinco.
10. **23 − 14 =** Veintitrés menos catorce son nueve.

3 **¿Cuántos hay?** How many persons or things are there in these drawings?

> **modelo**
> Hay tres maletas.

1. _Hay veinte lápices._　　　2. _Hay un mapa._

3. _Hay cuatro fotos._　4. _Hay una chica._　5. _Hay diecisiete hombres._

6. _Hay seis turistas._　7. _Hay veinticuatro mujeres._　8. _Hay treinta cuadernos._

---

1 Teaching Tips
• Before beginning the activity, make sure students know each pattern: odds (**los números impares**), evens (**los números pares**), count by threes (**contar de tres en tres**).
• To simplify, write complete patterns out on the board.
• Have students say all of the numbers out loud.

1 Expansion Explain that a prime number (**un número primo**) is any number that can only be divided by itself and 1. To challenge students, ask the class to list the prime numbers up to 30. (They are: 1, 2, 3, 5, 7, 11, 13, 17, 19, 23, 29.)

2 Expansion Do simple multiplication problems. Introduce the phrases **multiplicado por** and **dividido por**. Ex: **Cinco multiplicado por cinco son... (veinticinco). Veinte dividido por cuatro son... (cinco).**

3 Teaching Tip Have students read the directions and the model. Cue student responses by asking questions related to the drawings. Ex: **¿Cuántos lápices hay? (Hay veinte lápices.)**

3 Expansion Add an additional visual aspect to this activity. Hold up or point to classroom objects and ask how many there are. Since students will not know the names of many items, a simple number or **hay** + the number will suffice to signal comprehension. Ex:
—**¿Cuántas plumas hay aquí?**
—**(Hay) Dos.**

TEACHING OPTIONS

TPR Give ten students each a card that contains a different number from 0–30. The cards should be visible to the other students. Then call out simple math problems (addition or subtraction) involving the assigned numbers. When the first two numbers are called, each student steps forward. The student whose assigned number completes the math problem then has five seconds to join them.

Extra Practice Ask questions about your university and the town or city in which it is located. Ex: **¿Cuántos profesores hay en el departamento de español? ¿Cuántas universidades hay en _____? ¿Cuántas pizzerías hay en _____?** Encourage students to guess the number. If a number exceeds 30, write that number on the board and model its pronunciation.

Comunicación

4

En la clase With a partner, take turns asking and answering these questions about your classroom. Answers will vary.

1. ¿Cuántos estudiantes hay?
2. ¿Cuántos profesores hay?
3. ¿Hay una computadora?
4. ¿Hay una maleta?
5. ¿Cuántos mapas hay?

6. ¿Cuántos lápices hay?
7. ¿Hay cuadernos?
8. ¿Cuántos diccionarios hay?
9. ¿Hay hombres?
10. ¿Cuántas mujeres hay?

5

Preguntas With a partner, take turns asking and answering questions about the drawing. Talk about: Answers will vary.

1. how many children there are
2. how many women there are
3. if there are some photographs
4. if there is a boy
5. how many notebooks there are

6. if there is a bus
7. if there are tourists
8. how many pencils there are
9. if there is a man
10. how many computers there are

---

4 Teaching Tip For items 3, 4, 7, and 9, ask students: **¿Cuántos/as hay?** If there are no examples of the item listed, students should say: **No hay ____.**

4 Expansion After completing the activity, call on individuals to give rapid responses for the same items. To challenge students, mix up the order of items.

5 Teaching Tip Remind students that they will be forming sentences with **hay** and a number. Give them four minutes to do the activity. You might also have students write out their answers.

5 Expansion After pairs have finished analyzing the drawing, call on individuals to respond. Convert the statements into questions in Spanish. Ask: **¿Cuántos chicos hay? ¿Cuántas mujeres hay?**

5 Expansion Have students work in pairs to role-play conversations between one of the family members in the drawing and an exchange student that has come to live with them. Encourage students to use phrases they learned in **Contextos**, as well as simple questions about the host family, such as **¿Cuántas personas hay en la casa?**

TEACHING OPTIONS

Pairs Have each student draw a scene similar to the one on this page. Of course, stick figures are perfectly acceptable! Give them three minutes to draw the scene. Encourage students to include multiple numbers of particular items (**cuadernos, maletas, lápices**). Then have pairs take turns describing what is in their partner's picture. The student who created the drawing should ask questions to verify the accuracy of the description.

Pairs Divide the class into pairs. Give half of the pairs magazine pictures that contain images of familiar words or cognates. Give the other half written descriptions of the pictures, using **hay**. Ex: **En la foto hay dos mujeres, un chico y una chica.** Have pairs circulate around the room to match the descriptions with the corresponding pictures.

1.3 Present tense of ser Tutorial

Subject pronouns

ANTE TODO In order to use verbs, you will need to learn about subject pronouns. A subject pronoun replaces the name or title of a person and acts as the subject of a verb.

Subject pronouns

SINGULAR		PLURAL	
yo	*I*	nosotros	*we* (masculine)
		nosotras	*we* (feminine)
tú	*you* (familiar)	vosotros	*you* (masc., fam.)
usted (Ud.)	*you* (formal)	vosotras	*you* (fem., fam.)
		ustedes (Uds.)	*you*
él	*he*	ellos	*they* (masc.)
ella	*she*	ellas	*they* (fem.)

¡LENGUA VIVA!

In Latin America, **ustedes** is used as the plural for both **tú** and **usted**. In Spain, however, **vosotros** and **vosotras** are used as the plural of **tú**, and **ustedes** is used only as the plural of **usted**.

• • •

Usted and **ustedes** are abbreviated as **Ud.** and **Uds.**, or occasionally as **Vd.** and **Vds.**

▶ Spanish has two subject pronouns that mean *you* (singular). Use **tú** when addressing a friend, a family member, or a child you know well. Use **usted** to address a person with whom you have a formal or more distant relationship, such as a superior at work, a professor, or an older person.

Tú eres de Canadá, ¿verdad, David?
You are from Canada, right, David?

¿Usted es la profesora de español?
Are you the Spanish professor?

▶ The masculine plural forms **nosotros**, **vosotros**, and **ellos** refer to a group of males or to a group of males and females. The feminine plural forms **nosotras**, **vosotras**, and **ellas** can refer only to groups made up exclusively of females.

nosotros, vosotros, ellos

nosotros, vosotros, ellos

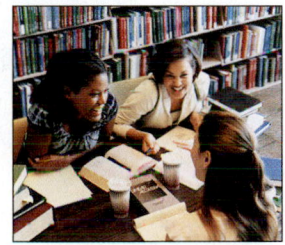
nosotras, vosotras, ellas

▶ There is no Spanish equivalent of the English subject pronoun *it*. Generally *it* is not expressed in Spanish.

Es un problema.
It's a problem.

Es una computadora.
It's a computer.

Section Goals

In **Estructura 1.3**, students will be introduced to:
• subject pronouns
• the present tense of the verb **ser**
• the uses of **ser** (to identify, to indicate possession, to describe origin, and to talk about professions or occupations)

Instructional Resources

Supersite: Audio (Lab MP3 Files); Resources (Grammar Presentation Slides, Activity Pack, Scripts, Answer Keys); Testing Program (Quizzes)
WebSAM
Workbook
Lab Manual

Teaching Tips

• Point to yourself and say: **Yo soy profesor(a).** Then point to a student and ask: **¿Tú eres profesor(a) o estudiante?** (estudiante) Say: **Sí, tú eres estudiante.** Indicate the whole class and tell them: **Ustedes son estudiantes.** Once the pattern has been established, include other subject pronouns and forms of **ser** while indicating other students. Ex: **Él es…, Ella es…, Ellos son…**

• Review familiar and formal forms of address students learned in **Contextos**.

• You may want to point out that while **usted** and **ustedes** are second person forms of address equivalent to the English *you*, they take third person verb forms.

Note: While the **vosotros/as** forms are listed in verb paradigms in **Vistas,** they will not be actively practiced.

TEACHING OPTIONS

Extra Practice Indicate people in the classroom and have students give subject pronouns based on their point of view. Ex: Point to yourself (**usted**), a female student (**ella**), everyone in the class (**nosotros**).
Extra Practice Ask students to indicate whether certain people would be addressed as **tú** or **usted**. Ex: A roommate, a friend's grandfather, a doctor, a neighbor's child.

Heritage Speakers Ask heritage speakers how they address elder members of their family, such as parents, grandparents, aunts, and uncles—whether they use **tú** or **usted**. Also ask them if they use **vosotros/as** (they typically will not unless they or their family are from Spain) or **voseo**. Explain that **voseo** is the use of the second-person subject pronoun **vos** instead of **tú**. It is used extensively in much of Latin America, including Argentina, Uruguay, and Costa Rica.

Teaching Tips

- Work through the explanation and the forms of **ser** in the chart. Emphasize that **es** is used for **usted**, **él**, and **ella**, and that **son** is used for **ustedes**, **ellos**, and **ellas**. Context, subject pronouns, or names will determine who is being addressed or talked about.

- Explain that **ser** is used to identify people and things. At this point there is no need to explain that **estar** also means *to be*; it will be introduced in **Lección 2**.

- Explain the meaning of **¿quién?** and ask questions about students. Ex: _____, **¿quién es ella? Sí, es _____. ¿Quién soy yo? Sí, soy el/la profesor(a) _____**. Introduce **¿qué?** and ask questions about items in the class. Ex: (*Pointing to a map*) **¿Qué es? Sí, es un mapa**.

- Point out the construction of **ser + de** to indicate possession. Stress that the construction [*apostrophe + s*] does not exist in Spanish. Pick up objects belonging to students and ask questions. Ex: **¿De quién es el cuaderno? (Es de _____.) ¿De quién son los libros? (Son de _____.)** Then hold up items from two different students and ask: **¿De quiénes son las plumas? Son de _____ y _____**.

- Introduce the contraction **de + el = del**. Emphasize that **de** does not make contractions with other definite articles, and provide examples. Ex: **Soy del estado de _____. El diccionario no es de la profesora de _____**. Also use examples of possession to illustrate the contraction. Ex: **¿Es el mapa del profesor?**

The present tense of ser

ANTE TODO In **Contextos** and **Fotonovela**, you have already used several present-tense forms of **ser** (*to be*) to identify yourself and others, and to talk about where you and others are from. **Ser** is an irregular verb; its forms do not follow the regular patterns that most verbs follow. You need to memorize the forms, which appear in this chart.

The verb ser (*to be*)			
SINGULAR FORMS	yo	**soy**	*I am*
	tú	**eres**	*you are* (fam.)
	Ud./él/ella	**es**	*you are* (form.); *he/she is*
PLURAL FORMS	nosotros/as	**somos**	*we are*
	vosotros/as	**sois**	*you are* (fam.)
	Uds./ellos/ellas	**son**	*you are; they are*

Uses of *ser*

▶ Use **ser** to identify people and things.

—¿Quién **es** él?
Who is he?

—**Es** Felipe Díaz Velázquez.
He's Felipe Díaz Velázquez.

—¿Qué **es**?
What is it?

—**Es** un mapa de España.
It's a map of Spain.

Es Marissa.

Es una maleta.

▶ **Ser** also expresses possession, with the preposition **de**. There is no Spanish equivalent of the English construction [*noun*] + 's (*Maru's*). In its place, Spanish uses [*noun*] + **de** + [*owner*].

—¿**De** quién **es**?
Whose is it?

—**Es** el diario **de** Maru.
It's Maru's diary.

—¿**De** quién **son**?
Whose are they?

—**Son** los lápices **de** la chica.
They are the girl's pencils.

▶ When **de** is followed by the article **el**, the two combine to form the contraction **del**. **De** does *not* contract with **la**, **las**, or **los**.

—**Es** la computadora **del** conductor.
It's the driver's computer.

—**Son** las maletas **del** chico.
They are the boy's suitcases.

TEACHING OPTIONS

Extra Practice As a rapid-response drill, call out subject pronouns and have students answer with the correct form of **ser**. Ex: **tú (eres)**, **ustedes (son)**. Reverse the drill by starting with forms of **ser**. Students must give the subject pronouns. Accept multiple answers for **es** and **son**.

TPR Have students form a circle. Toss a ball to individual students. When a student catches it, call on another to state whose ball it is. Ex: **Es de _____**. Take two balls and toss them to different students to elicit **Son de _____ y _____**.

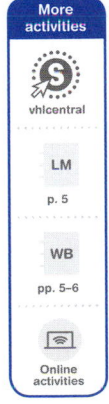
▶ **Ser** also uses the preposition **de** to express origin.

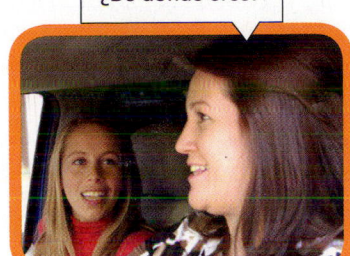

¿De dónde eres?

¿De dónde es usted?

Yo soy de Cuba.

Yo soy de Wisconsin.

—¿**De** dónde **es** Juan Carlos?
Where is Juan Carlos from?

—Es **de** Argentina.
He's from Argentina.

—¿**De** dónde **es** Maru?
Where is Maru from?

—**Es de** Costa Rica.
She's from Costa Rica.

▶ Use **ser** to express profession or occupation.

Don Francisco **es conductor**.
Don Francisco is a driver.

Yo **soy estudiante**.
I am a student.

▶ Unlike English, Spanish does not use the indefinite article (**un, una**) after **ser** when referring to professions, unless accompanied by an adjective or other description.

Marta **es** profesora.
Marta is a teacher.

Marta **es una** profesora excelente.
Marta is an excellent teacher.

Somos Perú

LATAMPerú

¡INTÉNTALO! Provide the correct subject pronouns and the present forms of **ser**.

1. Gabriel — él — es
2. Óscar y Flora — ellos — son
3. Juan y yo — nosotros — somos
4. Adriana — ella — es
5. las turistas — ellas — son
6. los conductores — ellos — son
7. el chico — él — es
8. los señores Ruiz — ellos — son

Práctica

1 Pronombres

Pronombres What subject pronouns would you use to (a) talk *to* these people directly and (b) talk *about* them to others?

> **modelo**
> un joven tú, él

1. una chica tú, ella
2. el presidente de México Ud., él
3. tres chicas y un chico Uds., ellos
4. la señora Ochoa Ud., ella
5. un estudiante tú, él
6. dos profesoras Uds., ellas

2 Identidad y origen

Identidad y origen With a partner, take turns asking and answering these questions about the people indicated: **¿Quién es?/¿Quiénes son?** and **¿De dónde es?/¿De dónde son?**

> **modelo**
> Selena Gomez (Estados Unidos)
> **Estudiante 1:** *¿Quién es?* **Estudiante 1:** *¿De dónde es?*
> **Estudiante 2:** *Es Selena Gomez.* **Estudiante 2:** *Es de los Estados Unidos.*

1. Enrique Iglesias (España)
   E1: ¿Quién es? E2: Es Enrique Iglesias. E1: ¿De dónde es? E2: Es de España.
2. Gustavo Dudamel (Venezuela)
   E2: ¿Quién es? E1: Es Gustavo Dudamel. E2: ¿De dónde es? E1: Es de Venezuela.
3. America Ferrera y Marc Anthony (Estados Unidos) E1: ¿Quiénes son?
   E2: Son America Ferrera y Marc Anthony. E1: ¿De dónde son? E2: Son de (los) Estados Unidos.
4. Carlos Santana y Salma Hayek (México) E2: ¿Quiénes son? E1: Son Carlos Santana y
   Salma Hayek. E2: ¿De dónde son? E1: Son de México.
5. Shakira (Colombia)
   E1: ¿Quién es? E2: Es Shakira. E1: ¿De dónde es? E2: Es de Colombia.
6. Sergio García y Penélope Cruz (España) E2: ¿Quiénes son? E1: Son Sergio García
   y Penélope Cruz. E2: ¿De dónde son? E1: Son de España.
7. Ariana Grande y Michael Peña (Estados Unidos) E1: ¿Quiénes son? E2: Son Ariana Grande
   y Michael Peña. E1: ¿De dónde son? E2: Son de (los) Estados Unidos.
8. José Abreu (Cuba) E2: ¿Quién es? E1: Es José Abreu. E2: ¿De dónde es? E1: Es de Cuba.

3 ¿Qué es?

¿Qué es? Ask your partner what each object is and to whom it belongs.

> **modelo**
> **Estudiante 1:** *¿Qué es?* **Estudiante 1:** *¿De quién es?*
> **Estudiante 2:** *Es un diccionario.* **Estudiante 2:** *Es del profesor Núñez.*

1. 2. 3. 4.

1. E1: ¿Qué es?
   E2: Es una maleta.
   E1: ¿De quién es?
   E2: Es de la Sra. Torres.

2. E1: ¿Qué es?
   E2: Es un diario.
   E1: ¿De quién es?
   E2: Es de Natalia.

3. E1: ¿Qué es?
   E2: Es una computadora.
   E1: ¿De quién es?
   E2: Es del Sr. Acosta.

4. E1: ¿Qué es?
   E2: Es un cuaderno.
   E1: ¿De quién es?
   E2: Es de Mauricio.

Teaching notes (left margin)

1 Teaching Tip Review **tú** and **usted**, asking students which pronoun they would use in a formal situation and which they would use in an informal situation.

1 Expansion Once students have identified the correct subject pronouns, ask them to give the form of **ser** they would use when *addressing* each person and when *talking about* each person.

2 Expansion Give additional names of well-known Spanish speakers and ask students to tell where they are from. Have students give the country names in English if they do not know the Spanish equivalent. Ex: **¿De dónde es Javier Bardem? (Es de España.)**

3 Teaching Tips
• To simplify, before beginning the activity, guide students in identifying the objects.
• You might tell students to answer the second part of the question (**¿De quién es?**) with any answer they wish. Have students take turns asking and answering questions.

TEACHING OPTIONS

Video Replay the **Fotonovela**, having students focus on subject pronouns and the verb **ser**. Ask them to copy down as many examples of sentences that use forms of **ser** as they can. Stop the video where appropriate to ask comprehension questions on what the characters said.

Heritage Speakers Encourage heritage speakers to describe themselves and their family briefly. Make sure they use the cognates **familia**, **mamá**, and **papá**. Call on students to report the information given. Ex: **Francisco es de la Florida. La mamá de Francisco es de España. Ella es profesora. El papá de Francisco es de Cuba. Él es dentista.**

Comunicación

4 **Preguntas** Ask your partner questions about the ad. Be imaginative in your responses.

Answers will vary.

¿Cuántas?	¿De dónde?	¿Qué?
¿Cuántos?	¿De quién?	¿Quién?

SOMOS ECOTURISTA, S.A.
Los autobuses oficiales de la Ruta Maya

• 25 autobuses en total
• 30 conductores del área
• pasajeros internacionales
• mapas de la región

¡Todos a bordo!

5 **¿Quién es?** In small groups, take turns pretending to be a famous person from a Spanish-speaking country. Use the list of professions to think of people from a variety of backgrounds. Your partners will ask you questions and try to guess who you are. Answers will vary.

actor *actor*	cantante *singer*	escritor(a) *writer*
actriz *actress*	deportista *athlete*	músico/a *musician*

modelo
> **Estudiante 3:** ¿Eres de Puerto Rico?
> **Estudiante 1:** No. Soy de Colombia.
> **Estudiante 2:** ¿Eres hombre?
> **Estudiante 1:** Sí. Soy hombre.
> **Estudiante 3:** ¿Eres escritor?
> **Estudiante 1:** No. Soy actor.
> **Estudiante 2:** ¿Eres John Leguizamo?
> **Estudiante 1:** ¡Sí! ¡Sí!

TEACHING OPTIONS

Small Groups Bring in personal photos or magazine pictures that show people. In small groups, have students invent stories about the people: who they are, where they are from, and what they do. Circulate around the room and assist with unfamiliar vocabulary as necessary, but encourage students to use terms they already know.

Game Hand out individual strips of paper with names of famous people on them. There should be several duplicates of each name. Then give descriptions of one of the famous people (**Es de _____. Es** [*profession*].), including cognate adjectives if you wish (**inteligente, pesimista**). The first person to stand and indicate that the name they have is the one you are describing (**¡Yo lo tengo!**) wins that round.

---

4 **Teaching Tip** If students ask, explain that the abbreviation **S.A.** in the ad stands for **Sociedad Anónima** and is equivalent to the English abbreviation *Inc.* (*Incorporated*).

4 **Expansion** Ask pairs to write four true/false statements about the ad. Call on volunteers to read their sentences. The class will indicate whether the statements are true (**cierto**) or false (**falso**) and correct the false statements.

5 **Teaching Tips**
• To simplify, have students brainstorm a list of names in the categories suggested.
• Have three students read the **modelo** aloud.

5 **Expansion** Have each group select a famous person that was mentioned during the activity and write a description of him or her. Before they begin writing, brainstorm some useful cognate adjectives that students can use, and tell them to be sure not to use the person's name in their description. Then have groups take turns reading their descriptions aloud for the class to guess the person's identity. If this guessing proves too difficult, allow the class to ask for a hint (**una pista**), such as a song or movie title.

1.4 **Telling time** Tutorial

Section Goals

In **Estructura 1.4**, students will be introduced to:
• asking and telling time
• times of day

Instructional Resources

Supersite: Audio (Lab MP3 Files); Resources (Grammar Presentation Slides, Digital Image Bank, Activity Pack, Scripts, Answer Keys); Testing Program (Quizzes)
WebSAM
Workbook
Lab Manual

Teaching Tips

• To prepare students for telling time, review **es** and **son** and numbers 0–30.
• Use the **Lección 1** digital images to assist with this presentation.
• Introduce **es la una** and **son las dos (tres, cuatro…)**. Remind students that **las** in time constructions refers to **las horas**. Introduce **y cinco (diez, veinte…)**, **y quince/ cuarto**, and **y treinta/media**.
• Draw three clocks on the board, each displaying a different time. Ask the class: **¿Qué hora es?** and have students correctly identify the time for each one. Concentrate on this until students are relatively comfortable with expressing the time in Spanish.
• Introduce **menos diez (cuarto, veinte…)** and explain this method of telling time in Spanish. It typically takes students longer to master this aspect of telling time. Spend about five minutes with your moveable-hands clock and ask students to state the times shown.

ANTE TODO In both English and Spanish, the verb *to be* (**ser**) and numbers are used to tell time.

▶ To ask what time it is, use **¿Qué hora es?** When telling time, use **es + la** with **una** and **son + las** with all other hours.

Es la una.   **Son las** dos.   **Son las** seis.

▶ As in English, you express time in Spanish from the hour to the half hour by adding minutes.

Son las cuatro **y cinco**.   Son las once **y veinte**.

▶ You may use either **y cuarto** or **y quince** to express fifteen minutes or quarter past the hour. For thirty minutes or half past the hour, you may use either **y media** or **y treinta**.

Es la una **y cuarto**.   Son las nueve **y quince**.   Son las doce **y media**.   Son las siete **y treinta**.

▶ You express time from the half hour to the hour in Spanish by subtracting minutes or a portion of an hour from the next hour.

Es la una **menos cuarto**.   Son las tres **menos quince**.   Son las ocho **menos veinte**.   Son las tres **menos diez**.

TEACHING OPTIONS

Extra Practice Draw a large clock face on the board with numbers but without hands. Say a time and ask a volunteer to come up to the board and draw the hands to indicate that time. The rest of the class verifies that their classmate has written the correct time. Continue until several volunteers have participated.

Pairs 👤↔👤 Tell the class **tengo** means *I have*. Have pairs take turns telling each other what time their classes are this semester/ quarter. (Ex: **Tengo una clase a las…**) For each time given, the other student draws a clock face with the corresponding time. The first student verifies the time. To challenge students, give a list of course names (**las matemáticas**, **la biología**, etc.).

▶ To ask at what time a particular event takes place, use the phrase **¿A qué hora (...)?**
To state at what time something takes place, use the construction **a la(s)** + *time*.

¿A qué hora es la clase de biología?
(At) what time is biology class?

La clase es **a las dos**.
The class is at two o'clock.

¿A qué hora es la fiesta?
(At) what time is the party?

A las ocho.
At eight.

▶ Here are some useful words and phrases associated with telling time.

Son las ocho **en punto**.
It's 8 o'clock on the dot/sharp.

Son las nueve **de la mañana**.
It's 9 a.m./in the morning.

Es **el mediodía**.
It's noon.

Son las cuatro y cuarto **de la tarde**.
It's 4:15 p.m./in the afternoon.

Es **la medianoche**.
It's midnight.

Son las diez y media **de la noche**.
It's 10:30 p.m./at night.

¡LENGUA VIVA!

Other useful expressions for telling time:

Son las doce (del día).
It is twelve o'clock (p.m.).

Son las doce (de la noche).
It is twelve o'clock (a.m.).

¿Qué hora es?

Son las cuatro menos diez.

¿Qué hora es?

Son las cuatro y veinticinco.

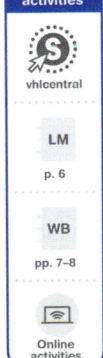

More activities

vhlcentral

LM
p. 6

WB
pp. 7–8

Online activities

¡INTÉNTALO!   Practice telling time by completing these sentences.

1. (1:00 a.m.) Es la _____una_____ de la mañana.
2. (4:15 p.m.) Son las cuatro y _____cuarto/quince_____ de la tarde.
3. (2:50 a.m.) Son las tres _____menos_____ diez de la mañana.
4. (8:30 p.m.) Son las ocho y _____media/treinta_____ de la noche.
5. (9:15 a.m.) Son las nueve y quince de la _____mañana_____.
6. (12:00 p.m.) Es el _____mediodia_____.
7. (6:00 a.m.) Son las seis de la _____mañana_____.
8. (4:05 p.m.) Son las cuatro y cinco de la _____tarde_____.
9. (12:00 a.m.) Es la _____medianoche_____.
10. (2:15 a.m.) Son las _____dos_____ y cuarto de la mañana.
11. (3:45 a.m.) Son las cuatro menos _____cuarto/quince_____ de la mañana.
12. (1:25 p.m.) Es la una y _____veinticinco_____ de la tarde.
13. (6:50 a.m.) Son las _____siete_____ menos diez de la mañana.
14. (10:40 p.m.) Son las once menos veinte de la _____noche_____.

Teaching Tips

• Review **¿Qué hora es?** and introduce **¿A qué hora?** and make sure students know the difference between them. Ask a few questions to contrast the constructions. Ex: **¿Qué hora es? ¿A qué hora es la clase de español?** Emphasize the difference between the questions by looking at your watch as you ask **¿Qué hora es?** and shrugging your shoulders with a quizzical look when asking **¿A qué hora es?**

• Go over **en punto, mediodía,** and **medianoche.** Explain that **medio/a** means *half.*

• Go over **de la mañana/tarde/noche.** Ask students what time it is now.

• You may wish to explain that Spanish speakers tend to view times of day differently than English speakers do. In many countries, only after someone has eaten lunch does one say **Buenas tardes.** Similarly, with the evening, Spanish speakers tend to view 6:00 and even 7:00 as **de la tarde,** not **de la noche.**

¡Lengua viva! Introduce the Spanish equivalents for noon (**las doce del día**) and midnight (**las doce de la noche**).

TEACHING OPTIONS

Extra Practice Give half of the class slips of paper with clock faces depicting certain times. Give the corresponding times written out in Spanish to the other half of the class. Have students circulate around the room to match their times. To increase difficulty, include duplicates of each time with **de la mañana** or **de la tarde/noche** on the written-out times and a sun or a moon on the clock faces.

Heritage Speakers Ask heritage speakers if they generally tell time as presented in the text. If they use different constructions, ask them to share these with the class. Some ways Hispanics use time constructions include (1) stating the hour and the minute (**Son las diez cuarenta**) rather than using **menos,** and (2) asking the question **¿Qué horas son?** Stress, however, that the constructions presented in the text are the ones students should focus on.

Práctica

1 **Ordenar** Put these times in order, from the earliest to the latest.

a. Son las dos de la tarde. **4**
b. Son las once de la mañana. **2**
c. Son las siete y media de la noche. **6**
d. Son las seis menos cuarto de la tarde. **5**
e. Son las ocho y veintidós de la mañana. **1**
f. Son las dos menos diez de la tarde. **3**

2 **¿Qué hora es?** Give the times shown.

modelo

Son las cuatro y cuarto/quince de la tarde.

1. Son las nueve y cinco de la mañana.

2. Es la una de la tarde.

3. Son las doce menos diez de la noche.

4. Son las tres menos cuarto/quince de la tarde.

5. Son las seis y media/treinta de la mañana.
6. Son las once menos veinticinco de la noche.
7. Son las siete y cuarto/quince de la mañana.

8. Son las cinco y veinte de la tarde.

NOTA CULTURAL

Many Spanish-speaking countries use both the 12-hour clock and the 24-hour clock (that is, military time). The 24-hour clock is commonly used in written form on signs and schedules. For example, 1 p.m. is **13h**, 2 p.m. is **14h** and so on. See the photo on p. 33 for a sample schedule.

3 **¿A qué hora?** Ask your partner at what time these events take place. Your partner will answer according to the cues provided.

modelo
la clase de matemáticas (2:30 p.m.)
Estudiante 1: ¿A qué hora es la clase de matemáticas?
Estudiante 2: Es a las dos y media de la tarde.

1. el programa *Las cuatro amigas* (11:30 a.m.)
2. el drama *La casa de Bernarda Alba* (7:00 p.m.)
3. el programa *Las computadoras* (8:30 a.m.)
4. la clase de español (10:30 a.m.)
5. la clase de biología (9:40 a.m.)
6. la clase de historia (10:50 a.m.)
7. el partido (*game*) de béisbol (5:15 p.m.)
8. el partido de tenis (12:45 p.m.)
9. el partido de baloncesto (*basketball*) (7:45 p.m.)

1. E1: ¿A qué hora es el programa *Las cuatro amigas*?
   E2: Es a las once y media/treinta de la mañana.
2. E1: ¿A qué hora es el drama *La casa de Bernarda Alba*?
   E2: Es a las siete de la noche.
3. E1: ¿A qué hora es el programa *Las computadoras*?
   E2: Es a las ocho y media/treinta de la mañana.
4. E1: ¿A qué hora es la clase de español?
   E2: Es a las diez y media/treinta de la mañana.
5. E1: ¿A qué hora es la clase de biología?
   E2: Es a las diez menos veinte de la mañana.
6. E1: ¿A qué hora es la clase de historia?
   E2: Es a las once menos diez de la mañana.
7. E1: ¿A qué hora es el partido de béisbol?
   E2: Es a las cinco y cuarto/quince de la tarde.
8. E1: ¿A qué hora es el partido de tenis?
   E2: Es a la una menos cuarto/quince de la tarde.
9. E1: ¿A qué hora es el partido de baloncesto?
   E2: Es a las ocho menos cuarto/quince de la noche.

NOTA CULTURAL

La casa de Bernarda Alba is a famous play by Spanish poet and playwright **Federico García Lorca** (1898–1936). Lorca was one of the most famous writers of the 20th century and a close friend of Spain's most talented artists, including the painter Salvador Dalí and the filmmaker Luis Buñuel.

## Sidebar (left margin)

1 **Teaching Tip** To add a visual aspect to this activity, have students draw clock faces showing the times presented in the activity. Have them compare drawings with a partner to verify accuracy.

2 **Teaching Tip** Read aloud the two ways of saying *4:15* in the model sentence. Point out that the clocks and watches indicate the part of day (morning, afternoon, or evening) as well as the hour. Have students include this information in their responses.

2 **Expansion** At random, say aloud times shown in the activity. Students must give the number of the clock or watch you describe. Ex: **Es la una de la tarde.** (**Es el número 2.**)

3 **Teaching Tips**
• To simplify, go over new vocabulary introduced in this activity and model pronunciation. Have students repeat the items after you to build confidence.
• Have partners switch roles and ask and answer the questions again.

3 **Expansion** Have students come up with three additional items to ask their partner, who should respond with actual times. Ex: —¿A qué hora es el programa *Modern Family*? —**Es a las nueve de la noche.**

TEACHING OPTIONS

Pairs Have students work with a partner to create an original conversation in which they: (1) greet each other appropriately, (2) ask for the time, (3) ask what time a particular class is, and (4) say goodbye. Have pairs role-play their conversations for the class.
Game Divide the class into two teams and have each team form a line. Write two city names on the board. (Ex: **Los Ángeles** and **Miami**) Check that students know the time difference and then list a time underneath the first city. (Ex: **10:30 a.m.**) Point to the first member of each team and ask: **En Los Ángeles son las diez y media de la mañana. ¿Qué hora es en Miami?** The first student to write the correct time in Spanish under the second column earns a point for their team. Vary the game with different times and cities. The team with the most points wins.

Comunicación

4   **En la televisión** With a partner, take turns asking questions about these television listings.

Answers will vary.

> **modelo**
>
> **Estudiante 1:** ¿A qué hora es el documental *Las computadoras*?
> **Estudiante 2:** Es a las nueve en punto de la noche.

TV Hoy - Programación

11:00 am	Telenovela: *La casa de la familia Díaz*
12:00 pm	Película: *El cóndor* (drama)
2:00 pm	Telenovela: *Dos mujeres y dos hombres*
3:00 pm	Programa juvenil: *Fiesta*
3:30 pm	Telenovela: *¡Sí, sí, sí!*
4:00 pm	Telenovela: *El diario de la Sra. González*
5:00 pm	Telenovela: *Tres mujeres*
6:00 pm	Noticias
7:00 pm	Especial musical: *Música folklórica de México*
7:30 pm	La naturaleza: *Jardín secreto*
8:00 pm	Noticiero: *Veinticuatro horas*
9:00 pm	Documental: *Las computadoras*

5   **Preguntas** With a partner, answer these questions based on your own knowledge. Some answers will vary.

1. Son las tres de la tarde en Nueva York. ¿Qué hora es en Los Ángeles?
   Es el mediodía./ Son las doce.
2. Son las ocho y media en Chicago. ¿Qué hora es en Miami?
   Son las nueve y media/treinta.
3. Son las dos menos cinco en San Francisco. ¿Qué hora es en San Antonio?
   Son las cuatro menos cinco.
4. ¿A qué hora es el programa *Saturday Night Live*? Es a las once y media/treinta de la noche.

Síntesis

6   **Situación** With a partner, play the roles of a journalism student interviewing a visiting literature professor (**profesor(a) de literatura**) from Venezuela. Be prepared to act out the conversation for your classmates. Answers will vary.

Estudiante	**Profesor(a) de literatura**
Ask the professor his/her name.	→ Ask the student his/her name.
Ask the professor what time his/her literature class is.	→ Ask the student where he/she is from.
Ask how many students are in his/her class.	→ Ask to whom the notebook belongs.
Say thank you and goodbye.	→ Say thank you and you are pleased to meet him/her.

4 Teaching Tip Before beginning the activity, have students scan the schedule for cognates and predict their meanings. Guide them in understanding the meanings of other programming categories: **película, programa juvenil, noticias/noticiero**.

4 Expansion Ask students what time popular TV programs are shown. Ex: —¿**A qué hora es el programa** *The Daily Show with Trevor Noah*? —**Es a las once**.

5 Teaching Tip Remind students that there are four time zones in the continental United States, and that when it is noon in the Eastern Time zone, it is three hours earlier in the Pacific Time zone.

5 Expansion Have students make up four questions of their own for a partner to answer.

6 Teaching Tip Point out that this activity synthesizes everything students have learned in this lesson: greetings and farewells, nouns and articles, numbers 0–30 and **hay**, the verb **ser**, and telling time. Spend a few moments reviewing these topics.

TEACHING OPTIONS

Small Groups Have small groups prepare skits. Students can choose any situation they wish, provided that they use material presented in the **Contextos** and **Estructura** sections. Possible situations include: meeting to go on an excursion, meeting between classes, and introducing friends to professors.

Heritage Speakers Ask heritage speakers to describe popular shows that are currently featured on Spanish-language television, noting the type of show (**telenovela, reality,** etc.), the channel (**canal**), and time when they are shown. As a class, try to think of English-language versions or similar programs. Examples may include *American Idol, Big Brother, Dancing with the Stars,* and their respective Latin American counterparts.

Section Goal

In **Recapitulación**, students will review the grammar concepts from this lesson.

Instructional Resource
Supersite

Teaching Tip You may want to assign this **Recapitulación** activity on the Supersite because it has diagnostics. There is an online-only review activity for each grammar point. The Supersite also has a **Repaso de vocabulario** activity with diagnostics.

1 Teaching Tips
- Before beginning the activity, remind students that nouns ending in **-ma** tend to be masculine, despite ending in an **-a**.
- To add an auditory aspect to this activity, read aloud a masculine or feminine noun, then call on individuals to supply the other form. Do the same for plural and singular nouns. Keep a brisk pace.

1 Expansion Have students identify the corresponding definite and indefinite articles in both singular and plural forms for all of the nouns.

2 Teaching Tips
- Have students explain why they chose their answers. Ex: 1. **Cuántas** is feminine and modifies **chicas**.
- Ask students to explain the difference between **¿Tienes un diccionario?** and **¿Tienes el diccionario?** (general versus specific).

2 Expansion
- 👥 Ask students to rewrite the dialogue with information from one of their own classes.
- 👥 Have volunteers ask classmates questions using possessives with **ser**. Ex:
  —¿De quién es esta mochila?
  —Es de ella.

Recapitulación

Review the grammar concepts you have learned in this lesson by completing these activities.

1 **Completar** Complete the charts according to the models. **28 pts.**

Masculino	Femenino
el chico	la chica
el profesor	la profesora
el amigo	la amiga
el señor	la señora
el pasajero	la pasajera
el estudiante	la estudiante
el turista	la turista
el joven	la joven

Singular	Plural
una cosa	unas cosas
un libro	unos libros
una clase	unas clases
una lección	unas lecciones
un conductor	unos conductores
un país	unos países
un lápiz	unos lápices
un problema	unos problemas

2 **En la clase** Complete each conversation with the correct word. **22 pts.**

 César   Beatriz

CÉSAR ¿(1) _Cuántas_ (Cuántos/Cuántas) chicas hay en la (2) _clase_ (maleta/clase)?

BEATRIZ Hay (3) _catorce_ (catorce/cuatro) [14] chicas.

CÉSAR Y, ¿(4) _cuántos_ (cuántos/cuántas) chicos hay?

BEATRIZ Hay (5) _trece_ (tres/trece) [13] chicos.

CÉSAR Entonces (*Then*), en total hay (6) _veintisiete_ (veintiséis/veintisiete) (7) _estudiantes_ (estudiantes/chicas) en la clase.

ARIANA ¿Tienes (*Do you have*) (8) _un_ (un/una) diccionario?

 Ariana   Daniel

DANIEL No, pero (*but*) aquí (9) _hay_ (es/hay) uno.

ARIANA ¿De quién (10) _es_ (son/es)?

DANIEL (11) _Es_ (Son/Es) de Carlos.

RESUMEN GRAMATICAL

1.1 **Nouns and articles** *pp. 12–14*

Gender of nouns

Nouns that refer to living things

	Masculine		Feminine
-o	el chico	-a	la chica
-or	el profesor	-ora	la profesora
-ista	el turista	-ista	la turista

Nouns that refer to non-living things

	Masculine		Feminine
-o	el libro	-a	la cosa
-ma	el programa	-ción	la lección
-s	el autobús	-dad	la nacionalidad

Plural of nouns

▶ ending in vowel + *-s*   la chica → las chicas

▶ ending in consonant + *-es*   el señor → los señores
(-z → -ces un lápiz → unos lápices)

▶ Definite articles: el, la, los, las

▶ Indefinite articles: un, una, unos, unas

1.2 **Numbers 0–30** *p. 16*

0	cero	8	ocho	16	dieciséis
1	uno	9	nueve	17	diecisiete
2	dos	10	diez	18	dieciocho
3	tres	11	once	19	diecinueve
4	cuatro	12	doce	20	veinte
5	cinco	13	trece	21	veintiuno
6	seis	14	catorce	22	veintidós
7	siete	15	quince	30	treinta

1.3 **Present tense of *ser*** *pp. 19–21*

yo	soy	nosotros/as	somos
tú	eres	vosotros/as	sois
Ud./él/ella	es	Uds./ellos/ellas	son

TEACHING OPTIONS

Extra Practice To add a visual aspect to this grammar review, bring in pictures from newspapers, magazines, or the Internet illustrating nouns that students have learned. Ask them to identify the people or objects using **ser**. As a variation, ask students questions about the photos, using **hay**. Ex: ¿Cuántos/as _____ hay en la foto?

TPR Give certain times of day and night and ask students to identify who would be awake: **vigilante** (*night watchman*), **estudiante**, or **los dos**. Have students raise their left hand for the **vigilante**, right hand for the **estudiante**, and both hands for **los dos**. Ex: **Son las cinco menos veinte de la mañana.** (left hand) **Es la medianoche.** (both hands)

1.4   Telling time   *pp. 24–25*

Es la una.	*It's 1:00.*
Son las dos.	*It's 2:00.*
Son las tres y diez.	*It's 3:10.*
Es la una **y cuarto/ quince.**	*It's 1:15.*
Son las siete **y media/ treinta.**	*It's 7:30.*
Es la una **menos cuarto/quince.**	*It's 12:45.*
Son las once **menos veinte.**	*It's 10:40.*
Es **el mediodía.**	*It's noon.*
Es **la medianoche.**	*It's midnight.*

3   **Presentaciones** Complete this conversation with the correct form of the verb **ser**. 【12 pts.】

JUAN   ¡Hola! Me llamo Juan. (1) _____Soy_____ estudiante en la clase de español.

DANIELA   ¡Hola! Mucho gusto. Yo (2) _____soy_____ Daniela y ella (3) _____es_____ Mónica. ¿De dónde (4) _____eres_____ (tú), Juan?

JUAN   De California. Y ustedes, ¿de dónde (5) _____son_____ ?

MÓNICA   Nosotras (6) _____somos_____ de Florida.

4   **¿Qué hora es?** Write out in words the following times, indicating whether it's morning, noon, afternoon, or night. 【10 pts.】

1. It's 12:00 p.m.
Es el mediodía./Son las doce del día.

2. It's 7:05 a.m.
Son las siete y cinco de la mañana.

3. It's 9:35 p.m.
Son las diez menos veinticinco de la noche.

4. It's 5:15 p.m.
Son las cinco y cuarto/quince de la tarde.

5. It's 1:30 p.m.
Es la una y media/treinta de la tarde.

5   **¡Hola!** Write five sentences introducing yourself and talking about your classes. You may want to include your name, where you are from, who your Spanish teacher is, the time of your Spanish class, how many students are in the class, etc. 【28 pts.】 Answers will vary.

_____

_____

_____

_____

6   **Canción** Choose the appropriate words to complete this children's song. 【4 EXTRA points!】

cinco	cuántas	cuatro	media	quiénes

"_____Cuántas_____ patas° tiene un gato°? Una, dos, tres y _____cuatro_____ ."

patas legs   tiene un gato does a cat have

Section Goals

In **Lectura**, students will:
- learn to recognize cognates
- use prefixes and suffixes to recognize cognates
- read a biography on **Joaquín Salvador Lavado (Quino)**
- read a comic strip

Instructional Resource
Supersite

Estrategia Have students look at the cognates in the **Estrategia** box. Write some of the common suffix correspondences between Spanish and English on the board: **–ción/–sión** = *–tion/–sion* (**nación, decisión**); **–ante/–ente** = *–ant/–ent* (**importante, inteligente, elegante**); **–ia/–ía** = *–y* (**farmacia, sociología, historia**); **–dad** = *–ty* (**oportunidad, universidad**).

The Affective Dimension Tell students that reading in Spanish will be less anxiety-provoking if they follow the advice in the **Estrategia** sections, which are designed to reinforce and improve reading comprehension skills.

Examinar el texto Ask students to tell you what type of text this is and how they can tell. *(It is a comic strip and it consists of a series of drawings with speech bubbles.)*

Cognados Ask students to mention any cognates that they see in the author's biography or the comic strip. Discuss the cognates and ask students to look for other examples of words with suffixes that have correspondence to English. Ex: **protagonista; -ista** = *-ist*

Lectura

Antes de leer

Estrategia
Recognizing cognates

As you learned earlier in this lesson, cognates are words that share similar meanings and spellings in two or more languages. When reading in Spanish, it's helpful to look for cognates and use them to guess the meaning of what you're reading. But watch out for false cognates. For example, **librería** means *bookstore*, not *library*, and **embarazada** means *pregnant*, not *embarrassed*. Look at this list of Spanish words, paying special attention to prefixes and suffixes. Can you guess the meaning of each word?

importante	oportunidad
farmacia	cultura
inteligente	activo
dentista	sociología
decisión	espectacular
televisión	restaurante
médico	policía

Examinar el texto
Glance quickly at the reading selection and guess what type of document it is. Explain your answer.

Cognados
Read the document and make a list of the cognates you find. Guess their English equivalents, then compare your answers with those of a partner.

More activities
vhlcentral | Online activities

Joaquín Salvador Lavado nació (*was born*) en Argentina en 1932 (mil novecientos treinta y dos). Su nombre profesional es **Quino**. Es muy popular en Latinoamérica, Europa y Canadá por sus tiras cómicas (*comic strips*). Mafalda es su serie más famosa. La protagonista, Mafalda, es una chica muy inteligente de seis años (*years*). La tira cómica ilustra las aventuras de ella y su grupo de amigos. Las anécdotas de Mafalda y los chicos también presentan temas (*themes*) importantes como la paz (*peace*) y los derechos humanos (*human rights*).

Después de leer

Preguntas
Answer these questions. *Some answers may vary. Suggested answers:*

1. What is Joaquín Salvador Lavado's pen name?
   Quino
2. What is Mafalda like?
   She is a precocious six-year-old.
3. Where is Mafalda in panel 1? What is she doing?
   She is in bed, counting sheep in order to fall asleep.
4. What happens to the sheep in panel 3? Why?
   It is left balancing on the hurdle because Mafalda falls asleep.
5. Why does Mafalda wake up?
   The sheep says ¡Béeee!
6. What number corresponds to the sheep in panel 5?
   veintiséis
7. In panel 6, what is Mafalda doing? How do you know?
   She is sleeping; the Zs indicate this.

TEACHING OPTIONS

Extra Practice If time and resources permit, bring in a few more **Mafalda** comics for students to read. If possible, bring in examples of another Spanish-language comic, such as **Baldo**, which deals with topics particular to the experience of growing up as a Latino in the U.S. Have students compare and contrast the comic strips.

Extra Practice Write some Spanish words on the board and have students name the English cognate: **democracia, actor, eficiente, nacionalidad, diferencia, guitarrista, artista, doctora, dificultad, exploración.**

Preguntas Have students work in pairs to answer the questions. Then check the answers as a class.

Los animales

This comic strip uses a device called onomatopoeia: a word that represents the sound that it stands for. Did you know that many common instances of onomatopoeia are different from language to language? The noise a sheep makes is *baaaah* in English, but in Mafalda's language it is **béeeee**.

Do you think you can match these animals with their Spanish sounds? First, practice saying aloud each animal sound in group B. Then, match each animal with its sound in Spanish. If you need help remembering the sounds the alphabet makes in Spanish, see p. 9.

A

1. _f_ **gato**   2. _d_ **perro**   3. _b_ **vaca**   4. _a_ **gallo**

5. _c_ **rana**   6. _e_ **pato**   7. _g_ **cerdo**

B

a. kikirikí   b. muuu   c. croac   d. guau

e. cuac cuac   f. miau   g. oinc

Los animales

- Have a volunteer read aloud the animal names in group A.
- Model the animal sounds in group B and have students repeat them so that they become comfortable making these sounds.
- Review the answers as a class. Then, ask students if any of the animal/sound combinations were surprising to them and why.
- Write the names of a few more animals (Ex: **pollito, búho, pavo**) accompanied by simple drawings on the board and have students try to guess what the sound would be in Spanish (**pío pío, uu uu, gluglú**).

TEACHING OPTIONS

Small Groups In small groups, have students create an alternate ending for the *Mafalda* comic above. Ask them to create new content for panels 3 through 6. When they are finished, have groups share their comic strips, and have the class vote for the funniest or most creative.

Heritage Speakers Ask heritage speakers if they are familiar with any other classic Spanish-language comic strips, such as *Condorito*. Have them describe the general characteristics of the main character. As a class, compare this character to *Mafalda*.

Escritura

Estrategia
Writing in Spanish

Why do we write? All writing has a purpose. For example, we may write an e-mail to share important information or compose an essay to persuade others to accept a point of view. Proficient writers are not born, however. Writing requires time, thought, effort, and a lot of practice. Here are some tips to help you write more effectively in Spanish.

DO

▸ Try to write your ideas in Spanish

▸ Use the grammar and vocabulary that you know

▸ Use your textbook for examples of style, format, and expression in Spanish

▸ Use your imagination and creativity

▸ Put yourself in your reader's place to determine if your writing is interesting

AVOID

▸ Translating your ideas from English to Spanish

▸ Simply repeating what is in the textbook or on a web page

▸ Using a dictionary until you have learned how to use foreign language dictionaries

Tema
Hacer una lista

Create a telephone/address list that includes important names, numbers, and websites that will be helpful to you in your study of Spanish. Make whatever entries you can in Spanish without using a dictionary. You might want to include this information:

▸ The names, phone numbers, and e-mail addresses of at least four other students

▸ Your professor's name, e-mail address, and office hours

▸ Three phone numbers and e-mail addresses of campus offices or locations related to your study of Spanish

▸ Five electronic resources for students of Spanish, such as chat rooms and sites dedicated to the study of Spanish as a second language

Nombre *Sally (la chica de Indiana)* ☎
Teléfono 655-8888
Dirección electrónica *sally@uru.edu* ✉

Nombre *Profesor José Ramón Casas*
Teléfono 655-8090
Dirección electrónica *jrcasas@uru.edu*
Horas de oficina 12 a 12:30

Nombre *Biblioteca* 655-7000
Dirección electrónica *library@uru.edu*

EVALUATION: Lista

Criteria	Scale
Content	1 2 3 4 5
Organization	1 2 3 4 5
Accuracy	1 2 3 4 5
Creativity	1 2 3 4 5

Scoring	
Excellent	18–20 points
Good	14–17 points
Satisfactory	10–13 points
Unsatisfactory	< 10 points

Escuchar

Antes de escuchar

Estrategia
Listening for words you know

You can get the gist of a conversation by listening for words and phrases you already know.

 To help you practice this strategy, listen to the following sentence and make a list of the words you have already learned.

Preparación

Based on the photograph, what do you think Dr. Cavazos and Srta. Martínez are talking about? How would you get the gist of their conversation, based on what you know about Spanish? *Answers will vary.*

Ahora escucha

Palabras y frases

Now you are going to hear Dr. Cavazos's conversation with Srta. Martínez. List the familiar words and phrases each person says. *Answers will vary.*

Dr. Cavazos	Srta. Martínez
1. _____	9. _____
2. _____	10. _____
3. _____	11. _____
4. _____	12. _____
5. _____	13. _____
6. _____	14. _____
7. _____	15. _____
8. _____	16. _____

With a partner, use your lists of familiar words as a guide to come up with a summary of what happened in the conversation. *Answers will vary.*

Comprensión

Identificar

Who would say the following things, Dr. Cavazos or Srta. Martínez?

1. Me llamo… *Dr. Cavazos*
2. De nada. *Srta. Martínez*
3. Gracias. Muchas gracias. *Dr. Cavazos*
4. Aquí tiene usted los documentos de viaje (*trip*), señor. *Srta. Martínez*
5. Usted tiene tres maletas, ¿no? *Srta. Martínez*
6. Tengo dos maletas. *Dr. Cavazos*
7. Hola, señor. *Srta. Martínez*
8. ¿Viaja usted a Buenos Aires? *Srta. Martínez*

Contestar

1. Does this scene take place in the morning, afternoon, or evening? How do you know? *The scene takes place in the morning, as indicated by* **Buenos días**.
2. How many suitcases does Dr. Cavazos have? *two*
3. Using the words you already know to determine the context, what might the following words and expressions mean? *Answers will vary.*
   - boleto
   - pasaporte
   - un viaje de ida y vuelta
   - ¡Buen viaje!

Section Goals

In **Escuchar**, students will:
- listen to sentences containing familiar and unfamiliar vocabulary
- learn the strategy of listening for known vocabulary
- answer questions based on the content of a recorded conversation

Instructional Resources
Supersite: Audio (Textbook MP3s); Resources (Scripts)

Estrategia
Script Creo que hay… este… treinta pasajeros en el autobús que va a Guayaquil.

The Affective Dimension
Tell students that many people feel nervous about their ability to comprehend what they hear in a foreign language. Tell them that they will probably feel less anxious if they follow the advice for increasing listening comprehension in the **Estrategia** sections.

Teaching Tip
Have students look at the photo. Guide them to guess where **Dr. Cavazos** and **Srta. Martínez** are and what they are talking about.

Ahora escucha
Teaching Tip To simplify, give students a list of the familiar words and phrases from the conversation. As you play the audio, have students indicate who says each one.

Script DR. CAVAZOS: Buenos días.
SRTA. MARTÍNEZ: Buenos días, señor. ¿En qué le puedo servir?
C: Yo soy el doctor Alejandro Cavazos. Voy a Quito. Aquí tiene mi boleto. Deseo facturar mis maletas.
M: ¿Alejandro Cavazos? ¿C-A-V-A-Z-O-S?
C: Sí.

M: ¿Un viaje de ida y vuelta a Quito?
C: Sí.
M: ¿Cuántas maletas tiene usted? ¿Tres?
C: Dos.

M: Bueno, aquí tiene usted su boleto.
C: Muchas gracias.
M: No hay de qué, doctor Cavazos. ¡Buen viaje!
C: Gracias. ¡Adiós!

(Script continues at far left in the bottom panels.)

En pantalla Video

Latinos form the largest minority group in the United States. The Census Bureau projects that by the year 2060, the Latino population will grow to 30 percent. Viewership of the two major Spanish-language TV stations, **Univisión** and **Telemundo**, has skyrocketed, at times surpassing that of the four major English-language networks. With Latino purchasing power estimated at 1.5 trillion dollars a year, many companies have responded by adapting successful marketing campaigns to target a Spanish-speaking audience. Turn on a Spanish-language channel, and you'll see ads for the world's biggest consumer brands, from soft drinks to car makers; many of these advertisements are adaptations of their English-language counterparts.

Vocabulario útil

carne en salsa	*beef with sauce*
copa de helado	*cup of ice cream*
no tiene precio	*priceless*
plato principal	*main course*
un domingo en familia	*Sunday with the family*

Preparación

Have you seen any Spanish versions of English-language commercials? If so, which ones? How are they different from the originals? Have you seen any bilingual ads? If so, when did they air and what did they advertise? Answers will vary.

Emparejar

Match each item with its price. **¡Ojo!** (*Careful!*) One of the responses will not be used.

b 1. aperitivo   a. quince dólares
a 2. plato principal   b. ocho dólares
d 3. postre   c. treinta dólares
          d. seis dólares

Un comercial

With a partner, brainstorm and write a MasterCard-like TV ad about something you consider priceless. Then read it to the class. Use as much Spanish as you can. Answers will vary.

Aperitivo *Appetizer* Postre *Dessert*

Anuncio de MasterCard

Aperitivo°...

copa de helado: $6

Postre°...

un domingo en familia: no tiene precio

Un domingo en familia...

More activities

vhlcentral   Online activities

NATIONAL communication cultures STANDARDS

Video

The **Plaza de Mayo** in Buenos Aires, Argentina, is perhaps best known as a place of political protest. Aptly nicknamed **Plaza de Protestas** by the locals, it is the site of weekly demonstrations. Despite this reputation, for many it is also a traditional **plaza**, a spot to escape from the hustle of city life. In warmer months, office workers from neighboring buildings flock to the plaza during lunch hour. **Plaza de Mayo** is also a favorite spot for families, couples, and friends to gather, stroll, or simply sit and chat. Tourists come year-round to take in the iconic surroundings: **Plaza de Mayo** is flanked by the rose-colored presidential palace (**Casa Rosada**), city hall (**municipalidad**), a colonial-era museum (**Cabildo**), and a spectacular cathedral (**Catedral Metropolitana**).

Vocabulario útil

abrazo	hug
¡Cuánto tiempo!	It's been a long time!
encuentro	encounter
plaza	city or town square
¡Qué bueno verte!	It's great to see you!
¡Qué suerte verlos!	How lucky to see you!

Preparación

Where do you and your friends usually meet? Are there public places where you get together? What activities do you take part in there? Answers will vary.

Identificar

Identify the person or people who make(s) each of these statements.

1. ¿Cómo están ustedes? d   a. Gonzalo
2. ¡Qué bueno verte! b   b. Mariana
3. Bien, ¿y vos? a   c. Mark
4. Hola. a, b, c, d   d. Silvina
5. ¡Qué suerte verlos! d

Encuentros en la plaza

Today we are at the Plaza de Mayo.

People come to walk and get some fresh air...

And children come to play...

More activities

vhlcentral | VM pp. 37–38 | Online activities

Section Goal

In **Panorama**, students will read demographic and cultural information about Hispanics in the United States and Canada.

Instructional Resources

Supersite: Video (*Panorama cultural*); Resources (Scripts, Translations, Digital Image Bank, Answer Keys)
WebSAM
Workbook

Teaching Tips

• Use **Lección 1 Panorama** digital images to assist with this presentation.

• Have students look at the map. Have volunteers read aloud the labeled cities and geographic features. Model Spanish pronunciation of names as necessary. Have students jot down as many names of places and geographic features with Spanish origins as they can.

El país en cifras Have volunteers read the bulleted headings in **El país en cifras**. Point out cognates and clarify unfamiliar words. Explain that numerals in Spanish have a comma where English would use a decimal point (**3,7%**) and have a period where English would use a comma (**14.800.000**). Explain that **EE.UU.** is the abbreviation of **Estados Unidos**, and the doubling of the initial letters indicates plural. Model the pronunciation of **Florida** (accent on the second syllable) and point out that it is often used with an article (**la Florida**) by Spanish speakers. For perspective, give the total populations for the five states: California, 39,144,818; Texas, 27,469,114; Florida, 20,271,272; New York, 19,745,289; Illinois, 12,801,539.

Estados Unidos

El país en cifras°

▶ **Población° de los EE.UU.:** 326 millones
▶ **Población de origen hispano:** 57 millones
▶ **País de origen de hispanos en los EE.UU.:**

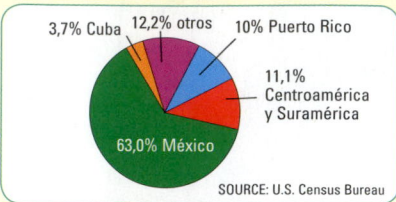

3,7% Cuba — 12,2% otros — 10% Puerto Rico
11,1% Centroamérica y Suramérica
63,0% México

SOURCE: U.S. Census Bureau

▶ **Estados con la mayor° población hispana:**

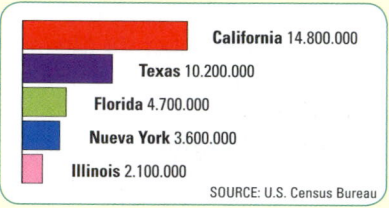

California 14.800.000
Texas 10.200.000
Florida 4.700.000
Nueva York 3.600.000
Illinois 2.100.000

SOURCE: U.S. Census Bureau

Canadá

El país en cifras

▶ **Población de Canadá:** 36 millones
▶ **Población de origen hispano:** 461.000
▶ **País de origen de hispanos en Canadá:**

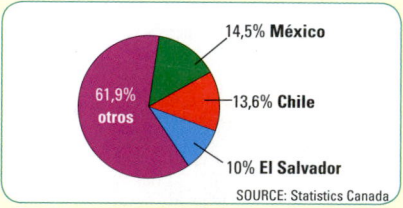

14,5% **México**
13,6% **Chile**
10% **El Salvador**
61,9% **otros**

SOURCE: Statistics Canada

▶ **Ciudades° con la mayor población hispana:**
Montreal, Toronto, Vancouver

en cifras by the numbers **Población** *Population* **mayor** *largest* **Ciudades** *Cities*

Mission District, en San Francisco

CANADÁ
Vancouver · Calgary
Ottawa ★ · Mon
Toronto
San Francisco
Chicago · Nueva York
Las Vegas
EE.UU.
Los Ángeles
San Diego
Washington, D.C. ★
San Antonio
MÉXICO
Océano Atlántico
Miami
Golfo de México
Mar Caribe

El Álamo, en San Antonio, Texas

AK HI

More activities

vhlcentral · WB pp. 9–10 · Online activities

ACTIVIDADES

1 **Escoger** Elige la opción correcta.

1. ¿Cuántos millones de personas de origen hispano hay en los Estados Unidos? **a**
   a. 57   b. 45   c. 36

2. ¿Cuántos millones de hispanos hay en Illinois? **c**
   a. cuatro   b. tres   c. dos

3. ¿De dónde son las enchiladas y los tacos? **b**
   a. Puerto Rico   b. México   c. Cuba

4. ¿Cómo se llama el barrio cubano de Miami? **a**
   a. La Pequeña Habana   b. El Álamo
   c. Mission District

5. ¿Qué hacen (do) los puertorriqueños en junio? **b**
   a. una conversación   b. un desfile
   c. una comida

6. ¿Cuántos millones de personas hablan español en los Estados Unidos? **c**
   a. 60   b. 13   c. 43

TEACHING OPTIONS

Heritage Speakers Ask heritage speakers to describe the celebrations that are held in their families' countries of origin. Ask them to tell the date when the celebration takes place, the event it commemorates, and some of the particulars of celebration. Possible celebrations: **Cinco de Mayo, Día de la Raza, Día de los Muertos, Fiesta de San Juan, Carnaval.**

Game Divide the class into teams of five. Give teams five minutes to brainstorm place names (cities, states, lakes, rivers, mountain ranges) in the United States that have Spanish origins. One team member should jot down the names in a numbered list. After five minutes, go over the names with the class, confirming the accuracy of each name. The team with the greatest number wins.

Comida • La comida mexicana

La comida° mexicana es muy popular en los Estados Unidos. Los tacos, las enchiladas, las quesadillas y los frijoles frecuentemente forman parte de las comidas de muchos norteamericanos. También° son populares las variaciones de la comida mexicana en los Estados Unidos: el tex-mex y el cali-mex.

⊙ Lugares • La Pequeña Habana

La Pequeña Habana° es un barrio° de Miami, Florida, donde viven° muchos cubanoamericanos. Es un lugar° donde se encuentran° las costumbres° de la cultura cubana, los aromas y sabores° de su comida y la música salsa. La Pequeña Habana es una parte de Cuba en los Estados Unidos.

Costumbres • Desfile puertorriqueño

Cada junio, desde° 1958 (mil novecientos cincuenta y ocho), los puertorriqueños celebran su cultura con un desfile° en Nueva York. Es un gran espectáculo con carrozas° y música salsa, merengue y hip-hop. Muchos espectadores llevan° la bandera° de Puerto Rico en su ropa° o pintada en la cara°.

⊙ Comunidad • Hispanos en Canadá

En Canadá viven° muchos hispanos. Toronto y Montreal son las ciudades con mayor población hispana. Muchos de ellos tienen estudios universitarios° y hablan° una de las lenguas° oficiales: inglés o francés°. Los hispanos participan activamente en la vida cotidiana° y profesional de Canadá.

comida *food* También *Also* La Pequeña Habana *Little Havana* barrio *neighborhood* viven *live* lugar *place* se encuentran *are found* costumbres *customs* sabores *flavors* Cada junio desde *Each June since* desfile *parade* con carrozas *with floats* llevan *wear* bandera *flag* ropa *clothing* cara *face* viven *live* tienen estudios universitarios *have a degree* hablan *speak* lenguas *languages* inglés o francés *English or French* vida cotidiana *daily life*

¡Increíble pero cierto!

Después° del inglés, el español es la lengua más hablada° en los EE.UU. Aproximadamente 40 millones de hispanos y 3 millones de personas no hispanas hablan esta lengua en los EE.UU. Hoy, 13% de la población habla español en sus hogares°.

Después *After* hablada *spoken* hogares *homes*

---

2 **¿Qué aprendiste?** Completa las oraciones.

1. Los cuatro estados con las poblaciones hispanas más grandes son California, Texas, Florida y <u>Nueva York</u>.
2. Toronto, Montreal y <u>Vancouver</u> son las ciudades con más población hispana de Canadá.
3. La Pequeña <u>Habana</u> es un barrio de Miami.
4. Muchos hispanos en Canadá hablan <u>inglés</u> o francés.

3 **Describir** En parejas, describan la población de origen hispano en los Estados Unidos y en Canadá.

> **modelo**
> Hay quince millones de hispanos en California.

TEACHING OPTIONS

Variación léxica Hispanic groups in the United States refer to themselves with various names. The most common of these terms, **hispano** and **latino**, refer to all people who come from Hispanic backgrounds, regardless of the country of origin of their ancestors. **Puertorriqueño, cubanoamericano**, and **mexicoamericano** refer to Hispanics whose ancestors came from Puerto Rico, Cuba, and Mexico, respectively.

Many Mexican Americans also refer to themselves as **chicanos**. This word has stronger socio-political connotations than **mexicoamericano**. Use of the word **chicano** implies identification with Mexican Americans' struggle for civil rights and equal opportunity in the United States. It also suggests an appreciation of the indigenous aspects of Mexican and Mexican-American culture.

Instructional Resources
Supersite: Audio (Textbook & Lab MP3s); Testing Program (Tests, MP3s)
WebSAM
Lab Manual

Teaching Tip Tell students that this is active vocabulary for which they are responsible and that it will appear on tests and exams.

Teaching Tip You may want to assign the **Prueba de práctica**, with its diagnostics and review activities, in the online-only **Repaso** section on the Supersite. There is also a **Repaso oral** in this section. For the Sixth Edition, a new summative vocabulary activity with speech recognition has been added to the **Repaso** section.

Saludos

Hola.	*Hi.*
Buenos días.	*Good morning.*
Buenas tardes.	*Good afternoon.*
Buenas noches.	*Good evening; Good night.*

Despedidas

Adiós.	*Goodbye.*
Nos vemos.	*See you.*
Hasta luego.	*See you later.*
Hasta la vista.	*See you later.*
Hasta pronto.	*See you soon.*
Hasta mañana.	*See you tomorrow.*
Saludos a...	*Greetings to…*
Chau.	*Bye.*

¿Cómo está?

¿Cómo está usted?	*How are you? (form.)*
¿Cómo estás?	*How are you? (fam.)*
¿Qué hay de nuevo?	*What's new?*
¿Qué pasa?	*What's happening?; What's going on?*
¿Qué tal?	*How are you?; How is it going?*
(Muy) bien, gracias.	*(Very) well, thanks.*
Nada.	*Nothing.*
No muy bien.	*Not very well.*
Regular.	*So-so; OK.*

Expresiones de cortesía

Con permiso.	*Pardon me; Excuse me.*
De nada.	*You're welcome.*
Lo siento.	*I'm sorry.*
(Muchas) gracias.	*Thank you (very much); Thanks (a lot).*
No hay de qué.	*You're welcome.*
Perdón.	*Pardon me; Excuse me.*
por favor	*please*

Títulos

señor (Sr.); don	*Mr.; sir*
señora (Sra.); doña	*Mrs.; ma'am*
señorita (Srta.)	*Miss*

Presentaciones

¿Cómo se llama usted?	*What's your name? (form.)*
¿Cómo te llamas?	*What's your name? (fam.)*
Me llamo...	*My name is…*
¿Y usted?	*And you? (form.)*
¿Y tú?	*And you? (fam.)*
Mucho gusto.	*Pleased to meet you.*
El gusto es mío.	*The pleasure is mine.*
Encantado/a.	*Delighted; Pleased to meet you.*
Igualmente.	*Likewise.*
Le presento a...	*I would like to introduce you to (name). (form.)*
Te presento a...	*I would like to introduce you to (name). (fam.)*
el nombre	*name*

¿De dónde es?

¿De dónde es usted?	*Where are you from? (form.)*
¿De dónde eres?	*Where are you from? (fam.)*
Soy de...	*I'm from…*

Palabras adicionales

¿cuánto(s)/a(s)?	*how much/many?*
¿de quién...?	*whose…? (sing.)*
¿de quiénes...?	*whose…? (plural)*
(no) hay	*there is (not); there are (not)*

Sustantivos

el autobús	*bus*
el chico	*boy*
la chica	*girl*
la computadora	*computer*
la comunidad	*community*
el/la conductor(a)	*driver*
la conversación	*conversation*
la cosa	*thing*
el cuaderno	*notebook*
el día	*day*
el diario	*diary*
el diccionario	*dictionary*
la escuela	*school*
el/la estudiante	*student*
la foto(grafía)	*photograph*
el hombre	*man*
el/la joven	*young person*
el lápiz	*pencil*
la lección	*lesson*
la maleta	*suitcase*
la mano	*hand*
el mapa	*map*
la mujer	*woman*
la nacionalidad	*nationality*
el número	*number*
el país	*country*
la palabra	*word*
el/la pasajero/a	*passenger*
el problema	*problem*
el/la profesor(a)	*teacher*
el programa	*program*
el/la turista	*tourist*
el video	*video*

Verbo

ser	*to be*

Numbers 0–30	*See page 16.*
Telling time	*See pages 24–25.*
Expresiones útiles	*See page 7.*

More activities

vhlcentral   LM p. 6

En la universidad 2

Communicative Goals

You will learn how to:

- Talk about your classes and school life
- Discuss everyday activities
- Ask questions in Spanish
- Describe the location of people and things

A PRIMERA VISTA
- ¿Hay un chico y una chica en la foto?
- ¿Hay una computadora o dos?
- ¿Son turistas o estudiantes?
- ¿Qué hora es, la una de la mañana o de la tarde?

Lesson Goals

In **Lección 2**, students will be introduced to the following:
- classroom- and university-related words
- names of academic courses and fields of study
- class schedules
- days of the week
- universities and majors in the Spanish-speaking world
- the **Universidad de Salamanca**
- present tense of regular **–ar** verbs
- forming negative sentences
- the verb **gustar**
- forming questions
- the present tense of **estar**
- prepositions of location
- numbers 31 and higher
- using text formats to predict content
- brainstorming and organizing ideas for writing
- writing descriptions of themselves
- listening for cognates
- a television commercial for **Jumbo**, a Chilean superstore chain
- a video about the **Universidad Nacional Autónoma de México (UNAM)**
- cultural, geographic, and economic information about Spain

A primera vista Have students look at the photo. Say: **Es una foto de dos jóvenes en la universidad.** Then ask: **¿Qué son los jóvenes? (Son estudiantes.) ¿Qué hay en la mano del chico? (Hay una computadora.)**

Teaching Tip Look for these icons for additional communicative practice:

Icon	Description
→👥	**Interpretive communication**
←👤	**Presentational communication**
👤↔👤	**Interpersonal communication**

INSTRUCTIONAL RESOURCES

Supersite (vhlcentral.com)
Video: **Fotonovela, Flash cultura, En pantalla, Panorama cultural**
Audio: Textbook and Lab MP3 Files

Activity Pack: Information Gap Activities, games, additional activity handouts
Resources: SAM Answer Key, Scripts, Translations, **Vocabulario adicional**, sample lesson plan, Grammar Presentation Slides, Digital Image Bank

Testing Program: Quizzes, Tests, Exams, MP3s
Student Activities Manual: Workbook/Video Manual/Lab Manual
WebSAM (online Student Activities Manual)

En la universidad

Más vocabulario

la biblioteca	library
la cafetería	cafeteria
la casa	house; home
el estadio	stadium
el laboratorio	laboratory
la librería	bookstore
la residencia estudiantil	dormitory
la universidad	university; college
el/la compañero/a de clase	classmate
el/la compañero/a de cuarto	roommate
la clase	class
el curso	course
la especialización	major
el examen	test; exam
el horario	schedule
la prueba	test; quiz
el semestre	semester
la tarea	homework
el trimestre	trimester; quarter
la administración de empresas	business administration
el arte	art
la biología	biology
las ciencias	sciences
la computación	computer science
la contabilidad	accounting
la economía	economics
el español	Spanish
la física	physics
la geografía	geography
la música	music

LAS MATERIAS	COURSES
la historia	history
las humanidades	humanities
el inglés	English
las lenguas extranjeras	foreign languages
la literatura	literature
las matemáticas	mathematics
el periodismo	journalism
la psicología	psychology
la química	chemistry
la sociología	sociology

la pizarra
la ventana
la profesora
el marcador
el borrador
la mesa
la estudiante
la pluma
la mochila
el estudiante
el papel

Variación léxica

pluma ⟷ bolígrafo
pizarra ⟷ pizarrón (*Amér. L.*); tablero (*Col.*)

More activities

vhlcentral	LM p. 7	WB pp. 11–12	Online activities

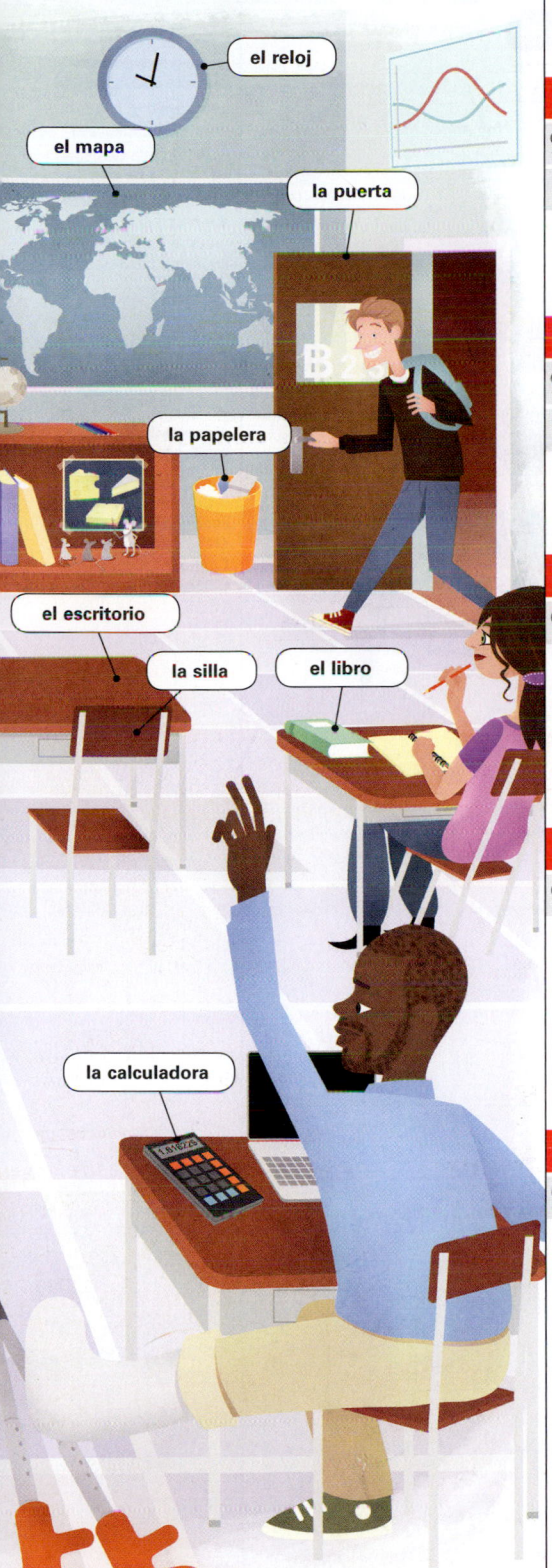

el reloj
el mapa
la puerta
la papelera
el escritorio
la silla
el libro
la calculadora

Práctica

1 **Indicar** Check **sí** if the word you hear is an academic subject or **no** if it's not.

	Sí	No		Sí	No
1.	○	☑	5.	○	☑
2.	○	☑	6.	☑	○
3.	☑	○	7.	○	☑
4.	☑	○	8.	☑	○

2 **¿Cierto o falso?** Indicate whether each statement about the drawing is **cierto** or **falso**.

1. _cierto_   5. _cierto_
2. _falso_   6. _cierto_
3. _cierto_   7. _falso_
4. _falso_   8. _cierto_

3 **Identificar** Identify the word that does not belong in each group.

1. examen • casa • tarea • prueba   casa
2. pizarra • marcador • borrador • librería   librería
3. economía • matemáticas • biblioteca • contabilidad   biblioteca
4. lápiz • cafetería • papel • cuaderno   cafetería
5. veinte • diez • pluma • treinta   pluma
6. conductor • laboratorio • autobús • pasajero   laboratorio

4 **Emparejar** Match each question with its most logical response.

1. ¿Qué clase es?   d
2. ¿Quiénes son?   g
3. ¿Quién es?   e
4. ¿De dónde es?   c
5. ¿Cuántos estudiantes hay?   a
6. ¿A qué hora es la clase de inglés?   f

a. Hay veinticinco.
b. Es un reloj.
c. Es de Perú.
d. Es la clase de química.
e. Es el señor Bastos.
f. Es a las nueve en punto.
g. Son los profesores.

5 **¿Qué clase es?** Name the class associated with the subject matter.

> **modelo**
>
> los elementos, los átomos   Es la clase de química.

1. Abraham Lincoln, Winston Churchill   Es la clase de historia.
2. África, el océano Pacífico   Es la clase de geografía.
3. Freud, Jung   Es la clase de psicología.
4. Picasso, Leonardo da Vinci   Es la clase de arte.
5. la cultura de España, verbos   Es la clase de español.
6. Hemingway, Shakespeare   Es la clase de literatura.
7. geometría, calculadora   Es la clase de matemáticas.

1 **Teaching Tip** You may want to do this activity as a TPR exercise. Have students give a thumbs-up for **sí** and a thumbs-down for **no**.

1 **Script** 1. la mochila 2. el escritorio 3. la química 4. las matemáticas 5. la ventana 6. la historia 7. el horario 8. la sociología *Textbook MP3s*

2 **Expansion** Have students indicate whether the statements are true or false about your class.

2 **Script** 1. Hay una profesora. 2. Hay cuatro estudiantes. 3. Hay escritorios y sillas. 4. Es una clase de arte. 5. Hay una calculadora. 6. Hay mochilas. 7. Hay dos borradores. 8. Hay una papelera. *Textbook MP3s*

3 **Expansion** Have students write four additional items for a partner to complete.

4 **Expansion** Have student pairs ask each other the questions and answer truthfully, based on your class. Ex: 1. **¿Qué clase es? (Es la clase de español.)** For items 2–4, the questioner should indicate specific people in the classroom.

5 **Expansion** Have the class associate famous people with these fields: **periodismo, computación, humanidades**. Then have them guess the fields associated with these people: Albert Einstein (**física**), Charles Darwin (**biología**).

TEACHING OPTIONS

Extra Practice Ask students what phrases or vocabulary words they associate with these items: **1. la pizarra** (Ex: **el marcador, el borrador**), **2. la residencia estudiantil** (Ex: **el/la compañero(a) de cuarto, el/la estudiante**), **3. el reloj** (Ex: **¿Qué hora es?, Son las…, Es la…**), **4. la biblioteca** (Ex: **los libros, los exámenes, las materias**).

Extra Practice On the board, write **¿Qué clases tomas?** and **Tomo…** Explain the meaning of these phrases and ask students to circulate around the classroom and imagine that they are meeting their classmates for the first time. Tell them to introduce themselves, find out where each person is from, and ask what classes they are taking. Follow up by asking individual students what their classmates are taking.

Teaching Tips

• Write these questions and answers on the board, explaining their meaning as you do so:
—**¿Qué día es hoy?**
—**Hoy es _____.**
—**¿Qué día es mañana?**
(Students learned **mañana** in **Lección 1.**)
—**Mañana es _____.**
—**¿Cuándo es la prueba?**
—**Es el _____.**
Then ask students the questions on the board.

• Explain that Monday is considered the first day of the week in the Spanish-speaking world and usually appears as such on calendars.

6 Expansion To challenge students, ask them questions such as: **Mañana es viernes… ¿qué día fue ayer? (miércoles); Ayer fue domingo… ¿qué día es mañana? (martes)**

7 Teaching Tip To simplify, before doing this activity, have students review the numbers 0–30 on page 16, the present tense of **ser** on page 20, and telling time on page 24.

Los días de la semana

¡LENGUA VIVA!

The days of the week are never capitalized in Spanish.

• • •

Monday is considered the first day of the week in Spanish-speaking countries.

CONSULTA

Note that September in Spanish is **septiembre.** For all of the months of the year, go to **Contextos, Lección 5,** p. 154.

6

¿Qué día es hoy? Complete each statement.

1. Hoy es martes. Mañana es __miércoles__. Ayer fue (*Yesterday was*) __lunes__.
2. Ayer fue sábado. Mañana es __lunes__. Hoy es __domingo__.
3. Mañana es viernes. Hoy es __jueves__. Ayer fue __miércoles__.
4. Hoy es jueves. Ayer fue __miércoles__. Mañana es __viernes__.
5. Ayer fue domingo. Hoy es __lunes__. Mañana es __martes__.
6. Mañana es lunes. Hoy es __domingo__. Ayer fue __sábado__.

7

Preguntas Answer the questions.

ciencias	geografía	residencia estudiantil
domingo	lenguas extranjeras	siete
especialización	libros	veinticuatro

1. ¿Cuántas horas hay en un día? __veinticuatro__
2. ¿Cuántos días hay en una semana? __siete__
3. ¿Qué día no hay clases? __domingo__
4. ¿En qué clase hay mapas de Asia y Europa? __geografía__
5. ¿Qué es la administración de empresas? __especialización__
6. ¿Qué son el español y el italiano? __lenguas extranjeras__
7. ¿Qué hay en una mochila? __libros__
8. ¿Qué son la física y la biología? __ciencias__

TEACHING OPTIONS

Extra Practice Have students prepare a day-planner for the upcoming week. Tell them to list each day of the week and the things they expect to do each day, including classes, homework, tests, appointments, and social events. Provide unfamiliar vocabulary as needed. Tell them to include the time each activity takes place. Have them exchange their day-planners with a partner and check each other's work for accuracy.

Game Have groups of five or six play a "word-chain" game in which the first group member says a word in Spanish (e.g., **estudiante**). The next student has to say a word that begins with the last letter of the first person's word (e.g., **español**). If a student cannot think of a word, he or she is eliminated and it is the next student's turn. The last student left in the game is the winner.

Comunicación

8　Horario Choose three courses from the chart to create your own class schedule, then discuss it with a classmate. *Answers will vary.*

materia	horas	días	profesor(a)
historia	9–10	lunes, miércoles	Prof. Ordóñez
biología	12–1	lunes, jueves	Profa. Dávila
periodismo	2–3	martes, jueves	Profa. Quiñones
matemáticas	2–3	miércoles, jueves	Prof. Jiménez
arte	12–1:30	lunes, miércoles	Prof. Molina

modelo

Estudiante 1: Tomo biología los lunes y jueves, de 12 a 1, con la profesora Dávila.
Estudiante 2: ¿Sí? Yo no tomo biología. Yo tomo arte los lunes y miércoles, de 12 a 1:30, con el profesor Molina.

9　Memoria Take a good look around your Spanish classroom and then close your eyes. Your partner will ask you questions about the classroom, using these words and other vocabulary. Each person should answer six questions and switch roles every three questions. *Answers will vary.*

escritorio	mapa	pizarra	reloj
estudiante	mesa	profesor(a)	ventana
libro	mochila	puerta	silla

modelo

Estudiante 1: ¿Cuántas ventanas hay?
Estudiante 2: Hay cuatro ventanas.

10　Nuevos amigos With a partner, prepare a conversation between two students meeting for the first time. Then act it out for the class. *Answers will vary.*

Estudiante 1	**Estudiante 2**
Greet your new acquaintance.	→ Introduce yourself.
Find out about him or her.	→ Tell him or her about yourself.
Ask about your partner's class schedule.	→ Compare your schedule to your partner's.
Say nice to meet you and goodbye.	→ Say nice to meet you and goodbye.

8　Teaching Tip Point out the professors' names in the chart and the use of the abbreviations **Prof.** and **Profa.**

8　Expansion Tell students to write their name at the top of their schedules, and have pairs exchange papers with another pair. Then have them repeat the activity with the new schedules, asking and answering questions in the third person. Ex: —¿Qué clases toma _____? —Los lunes y jueves _____ toma biología con la profesora Dávila.

9　Expansion Repeat the activity with campus-related vocabulary.

Successful Language Learning Remind the class that errors are a natural part of language learning. Point out that it is impossible to speak "perfectly" in any language. Emphasize that their spoken and written Spanish will improve if they make the effort to practice.

10　Teaching Tip To simplify, quickly review the basic greetings, courtesy expressions, and introductions taught in **Lección 1, Contextos,** pages 2–3.

10　Expansion ←→ Ask volunteers to introduce their new acquaintances to the class and present any new information they learned about their partners.

TEACHING OPTIONS

Groups ←→ Have students do **Actividad 10** in groups, imagining that they meet several new students in the cafeteria. Have the groups present this activity as a skit for the class. Give the groups time to prepare and rehearse, and tell them that they will be presenting it without a script or any other kind of notes.

Game Point out the **modelo** in **Actividad 8**. Have students write a few simple sentences that describe their own course schedules. Ex: **Tomo dos clases. Los lunes, miércoles y viernes, de 10 a 11, tomo español con la profesora Morales. Los martes y jueves, de 2:30 a 4, tomo arte con el profesor Casas.** Then collect the descriptions, shuffle them, and read them aloud. The class should guess who wrote each description.

Section Goals

In **Fotonovela**, students will:
- receive comprehensible input from free-flowing discourse
- learn functional phrases that preview lesson grammatical structures

Instructional Resources
Supersite: Video (*Fotonovela*); Resources (Scripts, Translations, Answer Keys)
WebSAM
Video Manual

Video Recap: Lección 1

Before doing this **Fotonovela** section, review the previous episode with these questions:
1. En la familia Díaz, ¿quiénes son estudiantes? (Felipe y Jimena son estudiantes.)
2. ¿Quién es Roberto? (Es el esposo de Carolina.) **3. ¿De dónde es Marissa?** (Es de Wisconsin.) **4. ¿De dónde es la señora Díaz?** (Es de Cuba.) **5. ¿Es de Felipe el diccionario?** (No, es de Marissa.)

Video Synopsis
Felipe takes **Marissa** around Mexico City. Along the way, they meet some friends, **Juan Carlos** and **Miguel. Felipe, Marissa,** and **Juan Carlos** compare schedules for the upcoming semester, while **Miguel** rushes off to meet **Maru.**

Teaching Tips
- Have students cover up the **Expresiones útiles.** Have them scan the **Fotonovela** captions to find phrases about classes and then phrases that express what people like.
- Ask a few basic questions that use the **Expresiones útiles.** Ex: **¿Cuántas clases tomas? ¿Te gusta la clase de _____?**

¿Qué estudias?

Felipe, Marissa, Juan Carlos y Miguel visitan Chapultepec y hablan de las clases.

 Video

PERSONAJES

 MARISSA

 FELIPE

1

FELIPE Dos boletos, por favor.

2

EMPLEADO Dos boletos son 64 pesos.
FELIPE Aquí están 100 pesos.
EMPLEADO 100 menos 64 son 36 pesos de cambio.

MIGUEL Marissa, hablas muy bien el español... ¿Y dónde está tu diccionario?
MARISSA En casa de los Díaz. Felipe necesita practicar inglés.
MIGUEL ¡Ay, Maru! Chicos, nos vemos más tarde.

3

FELIPE Ésta es la Ciudad de México.

5

4

FELIPE Oye, Marissa, ¿cuántas clases tomas?
MARISSA Tomo cuatro clases: español, historia, literatura y también geografía. Me gusta mucho la cultura mexicana.

6

FELIPE Juan Carlos, ¿quién enseña la clase de química este semestre?
JUAN CARLOS El profesor Morales. Ah, ¿por qué tomo química y computación?
FELIPE Porque te gusta la tarea.

TEACHING OPTIONS

Video Tips General suggestions for using video clips in the classroom can be found in the front matter of this Instructor's Annotated Edition.
¿Qué estudias? 👥↔👥 Play the **¿Qué estudias?** episode of the **Fotonovela** and have students give you a "play-by-play" description of the action. Write their descriptions on the board.

Give the class a moment to read the descriptions you have written and then play the episode a second time so that students can add more details to the descriptions or consolidate information. Finally, discuss the material on the board with the class and call attention to any incorrect information. Help students prepare a brief plot summary.

JUAN CARLOS   **MIGUEL**   **EMPLEADO**   **MARU**

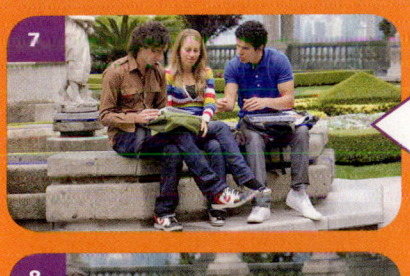

FELIPE Los lunes y los miércoles, economía a las 2:30. Tú tomas computación los martes en la tarde, y química, a ver... Los lunes, los miércoles y los viernes ¿a las 10? ¡Uf!

FELIPE Y Miguel, ¿cuándo regresa?

JUAN CARLOS Hoy estudia con Maru.

MARISSA ¿Quién es Maru?

MIGUEL ¿Hablas con tu mamá?

MARU Mamá habla. Yo escucho. Es la 1:30.

MIGUEL Ay, lo siento. Juan Carlos y Felipe...

MARU Ay, Felipe.

MARU Y ahora, ¿adónde? ¿A la biblioteca?

MIGUEL Sí, pero primero a la librería. Necesito comprar unos libros.

More activities

vhlcentral   VM pp. 3–4   Online activities

Expresiones útiles

Talking about classes

¿Cuántas clases tomas?
How many classes are you taking?
Tomo cuatro clases.
I'm taking four classes.
Mi especialización es en arqueología.
My major is archeology.
Este año, espero sacar buenas notas y, por supuesto, viajar por el país.
This year, I hope / I'm hoping to get good grades. And, of course, travel through the country.

Talking about likes/dislikes

Me gusta mucho la cultura mexicana.
I like Mexican culture a lot.
Me gustan las ciencias ambientales.
I like environmental science.
Me gusta dibujar.
I like to draw.
¿Te gusta este lugar?
Do you like this place?

Paying for tickets

Dos boletos, por favor.
Two tickets, please.
Dos boletos son sesenta y cuatro pesos.
Two tickets are sixty-four pesos.
Aquí están cien pesos.
Here's a hundred pesos.
Son treinta y seis pesos de cambio.
That's thirty-six pesos change.

Talking about location and direction

¿Dónde está tu diccionario?
Where is your dictionary?
Está en casa de los Díaz.
It's at the Díaz house.
Y ahora, ¿adónde? ¿A la biblioteca?
And now, where to? To the library?
Sí, pero primero a la librería.
Está al lado.
Yes, but first to the bookstore.
It's next door.

¿Qué pasó?

1

Escoger Choose the answer that best completes each sentence.

1. Marissa toma (*is taking*) _____c_____ en la universidad.
   a. español, psicología, economía y música   b. historia, inglés, sociología y periodismo
   c. español, historia, literatura y geografía
2. El profesor Morales enseña (*teaches*) _____a_____.
   a. química   b. matemáticas   c. historia
3. Juan Carlos toma química _____b_____.
   a. los miércoles, jueves y viernes   b. los lunes, miércoles y viernes
   c. los lunes, martes y jueves
4. Miguel necesita ir a (*needs to go to*) _____c_____.
   a. la biblioteca   b. la residencia estudiantil   c. la librería

2

Identificar Indicate which person made each statement.

1. ¿Quién es Maru? ___Marissa___
2. Mamá habla. Yo escucho. ___Maru___
3. Sí, tomo química con el profesor Morales.
   ___Juan Carlos___
4. En clase, me gusta estar cerca de la ventana.
   ___Marissa___
5. Necesito comprar unos libros. ___Miguel___
6. Dos boletos, por favor. ___Felipe___

 MARISSA   **MARU**

 JUAN CARLOS

 MIGUEL   **FELIPE**

> **NOTA CULTURAL**
>
> **Maru** is a shortened version of the name **María Eugenia**. Other popular "combination names" in Spanish are **Juanjo** (**Juan José**) and **Maite** (**María Teresa**).

3

Completar Complete each sentence that is similar to one in the **Fotonovela** with the correct word(s).

| Castillo de Chapultepec | estudiar | miércoles |
| clase | inglés | tarea |

1. Marissa, éste es el ___Castillo de Chapultepec___.
2. Felipe tiene (*has*) el diccionario porque (*because*) necesita practicar ___inglés___.
3. A Juan Carlos le gusta mucho la ___tarea___.
4. Hay clase de economía los lunes y ___miércoles___.
5. Miguel está con Maru para ___estudiar___.

> **NOTA CULTURAL**
>
> The **Castillo de Chapultepec** is one of Mexico City's most historic landmarks. Constructed in 1785, it was the residence of emperors and presidents. It has been open to the public since 1944 and now houses the National Museum of History.

4

Preguntas personales Interview a partner. Answers will vary.

1. ¿Qué clases tomas en la universidad?
2. ¿Qué clases tomas los martes?
3. ¿Qué clases tomas los viernes?
4. ¿En qué clase hay más chicos?
5. ¿En qué clase hay más chicas?
6. ¿Te gusta la clase de español?

 NATIONAL communication STANDARDS

TEACHING OPTIONS

Small Groups Have students work in small groups to create a skit in which a radio reporter asks local university students where they are from, which classes they are taking, and which classes they like. Encourage students to use the phrases in **Expresiones útiles** as much as possible. Have one or two groups role-play their skit for the class.

Extra Practice Have students close their books and complete these statements with information from the **Fotonovela**. You may slowly read aloud the sentences or write them on the board. Ex: **1. Tomo cuatro ____:** español, historia, literatura y geografía. (clases) **2. Y Miguel, ¿cuándo ____?** (regresa) **3. Dos ____ son 64 pesos. (boletos) 4. ¿Dónde ____ tu diccionario? (está)**

Pronunciación
Spanish vowels

 Tutorial

a   **e**   **i**   **o**   **u**

Spanish vowels are never silent; they are always pronounced in a short, crisp way without the glide sounds used in English.

Álex	**clase**	**nada**	**encantada**

The letter **a** is pronounced like the *a* in *father*, but shorter.

el	**ene**	**mesa**	**elefante**

The letter **e** is pronounced like the *e* in *they*, but shorter.

Inés	**chica**	**tiza**	**señorita**

The letter **i** sounds like the *ee* in *beet*, but shorter.

hola	**con**	**libro**	**don Francisco**

The letter **o** is pronounced like the *o* in *tone*, but shorter.

uno	**regular**	**saludos**	**gusto**

The letter **u** sounds like the *oo* in *room*, but shorter.

Práctica Practice the vowels by saying the names of these places in Spain.

1. Madrid
2. Alicante
3. Tenerife
4. Toledo
5. Barcelona
6. Granada
7. Burgos
8. La Coruña

Oraciones Read the sentences aloud, focusing on the vowels.

1. Hola. Me llamo Ramiro Morgado.
2. Estudio arte en la Universidad de Salamanca.
3. Tomo también literatura y contabilidad.
4. Ay, tengo clase en cinco minutos. ¡Nos vemos!

Refranes Practice the vowels by reading these sayings aloud.

Cada loco con su tema.²

Del dicho al hecho hay un gran trecho.¹

More activities

 vhlcentral   LM p. 8

Section Goal

In **Pronunciación**, students will be introduced to Spanish vowels and how they are pronounced.

Instructional Resources
Supersite: Audio (Textbook and Lab MP3 Files); Resources (Scripts, Answer Keys)
WebSAM
Lab Manual

Teaching Tips

- Point out that the drawings above the vowels on this page indicate the approximate position of the mouth as the vowels are pronounced.
- Model the pronunciation of each vowel and have students pay attention to the shape of your mouth. Have them repeat the vowel after you. Then go through the example words.
- To practice pure vowel sounds, teach students this chant: **A-E-I-O-U, ¡el burro sabe más que tú!**
- Pronounce a few of the example words and have the students write them on the board with their books closed.

Práctica/Oraciones/Refranes

These exercises are recorded on the *Textbook MP3s*. You may want to play the audio so that students practice listening to Spanish spoken by speakers other than yourself.

AYUDA

Although **hay** and **ay** are pronounced identically, they do not have the same meaning. As you learned in **Lección 1**, **hay** is a verb form that means *there is/are*. **Hay veinte libros**. (*There are twenty books.*) **¡Ay!** is an exclamation expressing pain, shock, or affliction: *Oh!; Oh, dear!*

TEACHING OPTIONS

Extra Practice Provide additional names of places in Spain. Have students spell each name aloud in Spanish; then ask them to pronounce each one. Avoid names that contain diphthongs. Ex: **Sevilla, Salamanca, Santander, Albacete, Gerona, Lugo, Badajoz, Tarragona, Logroño, Valladolid, Orense, Pamplona, Ibiza**.

Small Groups Have the class turn to the **Fotonovela**, pages 44–45, and work in groups of four to read all or part of the **Fotonovela** aloud, focusing on the correct pronunciation of the vowels. Circulate among the groups and, as needed, model the correct pronunciation and intonation of words and phrases.

EN DETALLE

La elección de una carrera universitaria

Since higher education in the Spanish-speaking world is heavily state-subsidized, tuition is almost free. As a result, public universities see large enrollments. Spanish and Latin American students generally choose their **carrera universitaria** (major) when they're eighteen—which is either the year they enter the university or the year before. In order to enroll, all students must complete a high school degree, known as the **bachillerato**. In countries like Bolivia, Mexico, and Peru, the last year of high school (**colegio***) tends to be specialized in an area of study, such as the arts or natural sciences.

Universidad Central de Venezuela en Caracas

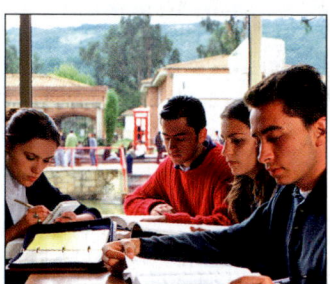

Students then choose their major according to their area of specialization. Similarly, university-bound students in Argentina focus their studies on specific fields, such as the humanities and social sciences, natural sciences, communication, art and design, and economics and business, during their five years of high school. Based on this coursework, Argentine students choose their **carrera**. Finally, in Spain, students choose their major according to the score they receive on the **prueba de aptitud** (skills test or entrance exam).

University graduates receive a **licenciatura**, or bachelor's degree. In Argentina and Chile, a **licenciatura** takes four to six years to complete, and may be considered equivalent to a master's degree. In Peru and Venezuela, a bachelor's degree is a five-year process. Spanish and Colombian **licenciaturas** take four to five years, although some fields, such as medicine, require six or more.

Estudiantes hispanos en los EE.UU.

In the 2015–16 academic year, over 16,500 Mexican students (2% of all international students) studied at U.S. universities. Venezuelans were the second-largest Spanish-speaking group, with over 8,000 students.

*¡Ojo! El **colegio** is a false cognate. In most countries, it means *high school*, but in some regions it refers to an elementary school. All undergraduate study takes place at **la universidad**.

ACTIVIDADES

1 **¿Cierto o falso?** Indicate whether these statements are **cierto** or **falso**. Correct the false statements.

1. Students in Spanish-speaking countries must pay large amounts of money toward their college tuition. **Falso**. At public universities tuition is almost free.
2. **Carrera** refers to any undergraduate or graduate program that students enroll in to obtain a professional degree. **Cierto**.
3. After studying at a **colegio**, students receive their **bachillerato**. **Cierto**.
4. Undergraduates study at a **colegio** or an **universidad**. **Falso**. An undergraduate student takes classes at an **universidad**.
5. In Latin America and Spain, students usually choose their majors in their second year at the university. **Falso**. They choose their majors either upon entering the university or the year before.
6. In Argentina, students focus their studies in their high school years. **Cierto**.
7. In Mexico, the **bachillerato** involves specialized study. **Cierto**.
8. In Spain, majors depend on entrance exam scores. **Cierto**.
9. Venezuelans complete a **licenciatura** in five years. **Cierto**.
10. According to statistics, Venezuelans constitute the third-largest Latin American group studying at U.S. universities. **Falso**. Venezuelans are the second-largest group.

ASÍ SE DICE

Clases y exámenes

aprobar	*to pass*
la asignatura (Esp.)	la clase, la materia
la clase anual	*year-long course*
el examen parcial	*midterm exam*
la facultad	*department, school*
la investigación	*research*
el profesorado	*faculty*
reprobar; suspender (Esp.)	*to fail*
sacar buenas/ malas notas	*to get good/ bad grades*
tomar apuntes	*to take notes*

EL MUNDO HISPANO

Las universidades hispanas

It is not uncommon for universities in Spain and Latin America to have extremely large student body populations.

- **Universidad de Buenos Aires** (Argentina) 316.000 estudiantes
- **Universidad Autónoma de Santo Domingo** (República Dominicana) 200.000 estudiantes
- **Universidad Complutense de Madrid** (España) 83.000 estudiantes
- **Universidad Central de Venezuela** (Venezuela) 62.600 estudiantes

PERFIL

La Universidad de Salamanca

The University of Salamanca, established in 1218, is the oldest university in Spain. It is located in Salamanca, one of the most spectacular Renaissance cities in Europe. Salamanca is nicknamed **La Ciudad Dorada** (*The Golden City*) for the golden glow of its famous sandstone buildings, and it was declared a UNESCO World Heritage Site in 1988.

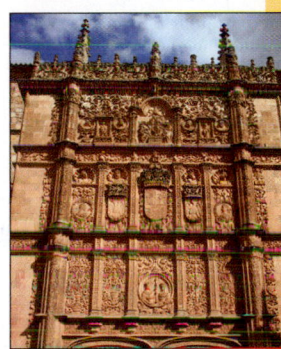

Salamanca is a true college town, as its prosperity and city life depend on and revolve around the university population. Over 32,000 students from all over Spain, as well as abroad, come to study here each year. The school offers over 250 academic programs, as well as renowned Spanish courses

for foreign students. To walk through the university's historic grounds is to follow the footsteps of immortal writers like Miguel de Cervantes and Miguel de Unamuno.

CON RITMO HISPANO

Enrique Iglesias (1975–)
Birthplace: Madrid, Spain

He used the name **Enrique Martínez** on demos to get his first record contract; he wanted to succeed without the help or influence of his famous father, Spanish pop singer Julio Iglesias.

Go to **vhlcentral.com** to find out more about **Enrique Iglesias** and his music.

ACTIVIDADES

2   **Comprensión**   Complete these sentences.

1. The University of Salamanca was established in the year ___**1218**___.
2. A ___**clase anual**___ is a year-long course.
3. Salamanca is called ___**La Ciudad Dorada**___.
4. Over 300,000 students attend the ___**Universidad de Buenos Aires**___.
5. An ___**examen parcial**___ occurs about halfway through a course.

3   **La universidad en cifras**   With a partner, research a Spanish or Latin American university online and find five statistics about that institution (for instance, the total enrollment, majors offered, year it was founded, etc.). Using the information you found, create a dialogue between a prospective student and a university representative. Present your dialogue to the clas.
Answers will vary.

More activities

 vhlcentral   Online activities

TEACHING OPTIONS

Extra Practice   Tell students to imagine they have the opportunity to study abroad at one of the universities listed in **El mundo hispano** or **Perfil**. Have them choose a location and explain why they would like to attend that particular school. You may want to assign this as homework, and ask students to research the universities on the Internet in order to reach their decision.

Game   Play a Pictionary-style game. Divide the class into two teams, A and B. Have one member from each team go to the board, and hand each one an index card with a university-related vocabulary word. The member from team A has one minute to draw a representation of that word, while the rest of team A guesses what the word is. Alternate between teams and award one point for each correct answer. The team with the most points wins.

Así se dice
- Model the pronunciation of each term and have students repeat it.
- To challenge students, add these words to the list: **la beca** (*scholarship*); **el préstamo educativo** (*student loan*); **el/la profe** (*professor, colloquial*).
- Ask simple questions using the terms. Ex: **¿Hay un examen parcial en esta clase?**

Perfil   Perhaps the most iconic of the **Universidad de Salamanca's** buildings is the **Escuelas Mayores**, which was completed in 1533. Hidden among the hundreds of items on its ornately carved façade is the figure of a small frog. According to tradition, being able to find the frog brings success.

El mundo hispano   Have students read the enrollment numbers. Ask a volunteer to state your university's enrollment. Then have students discuss the advantages and disadvantages of studying at a large university.

Con ritmo hispano   Point out to students that they will find supporting activities and information at **vhlcentral.com**.

2 **Expansion**   Give students these sentences as items 6–8:
6. About _____ students take classes at the **Universidad de Salamanca**. (32,000)
7. A _____ is a university department or school. (**facultad**)
8. The _____ is located in the Dominican Republic. (**Universidad Autónoma de Santo Domingo**)

3 **Expansion**   To add a visual aspect to this exercise, have the same pairs design a university brochure to attract prospective students. Encourage students to highlight the university's strengths and unique traits.

2.1 **Present tense of -ar verbs** Tutorial

ANTE TODO In order to talk about activities, you need to use verbs. Verbs express actions or states of being. In English and Spanish, the infinitive is the base form of the verb. In English, the infinitive is preceded by the word *to: to study, to be.* The infinitive in Spanish is a one-word form and can be recognized by its endings: **-ar**, **-er**, or **-ir**.

-ar verb		*-er* verb		*-ir* verb	
estudiar	*to study*	**comer**	*to eat*	**escribir**	*to write*

▶ In this lesson, you will learn the forms of regular **-ar** verbs.

The verb estudiar (*to study*)

SINGULAR FORMS	yo	estudi**o**	*I study*
	tú	estudi**as**	*you* (fam.) *study*
	Ud./él/ella	estudi**a**	*you* (form.) *study; he/she studies*
PLURAL FORMS	nosotros/as	estudi**amos**	*we study*
	vosotros/as	estudi**áis**	*you* (fam.) *study*
	Uds./ellos/ellas	estudi**an**	*you study; they study*

Juan Carlos estudia ciencias ambientales.

Y tú, ¿qué estudias, Miguel?

▶ To create the forms of most regular verbs in Spanish, drop the infinitive endings (**-ar**, **-er**, **-ir**). You then add to the stem the endings that correspond to the different subject pronouns. This diagram will help you visualize verb conjugation.

Conjugation of *-ar* verbs

INFINITIVE	VERB STEM	CONJUGATED FORM
estudi**ar**	estudi-	yo estudi**o**
bail**ar**	bail-	tú bail**as**
trabaj**ar**	trabaj-	nosotros trabaj**amos**

Section Goals

In **Estructura 2.1**, students will learn:
- the present tense of regular **-ar** verbs
- the formation of negative sentences
- the verb **gustar**

Instructional Resources
Supersite: Audio (Lab MP3 Files); Resources (Grammar Presentation Slides, Activity Pack, Scripts, Answer Keys); Testing Program (Quizzes)
WebSAM
Workbook
Lab Manual

Teaching Tips
- Check students' progress through comprehensible input. Point out that students have been using verbs and verb constructions from the start: **¿Cómo te llamas?**, **hay**, **ser**, and so forth. Ask a student: **¿Qué clases tomas?** Model student answer as **Yo tomo…** Then ask another student: **¿Qué clases toma _____?** (**Toma _____.**)
- Explain that, since the verb endings indicate the person speaking or spoken about, subject pronouns are usually optional in Spanish.
- To drill verb conjugation, divide the class into groups of three. Hand each group a small bag in which you have placed strips of paper containing subject pronouns or names. Assign each group member one of the following verbs: **bailar**, **estudiar**, or **trabajar**. Students should take turns drawing out a strip of paper and reading aloud the subject pronoun or name(s). Each group member then writes on a separate sheet of paper the correct conjugation for their assigned verb. As a follow-up, you may want students that were assigned the same infinitive to form new groups and compare their lists.

TEACHING OPTIONS

Extra Practice Do a pattern practice drill. Write an infinitive from the list of common –ar verbs on page 51 on the board and ask individual students to provide conjugations for the subject pronouns and names you suggest. Reverse the activity by saying a conjugated form and asking students to give the corresponding subject pronoun. Allow multiple answers for the third-person singular and plural.

Extra Practice Ask questions using **estudiar**, **bailar**, and **trabajar**. Students should answer in complete sentences. Ask additional questions to get more information. Ex: —_____, ¿trabajas? —Sí, trabajo. —¿Dónde trabajas? —Trabajo en _____. • —¿Quién baila los sábados? —Yo bailo los sábados. —¿Bailas merengue? • —¿Estudian mucho ustedes? —¿Quién estudia más? —¿Cuántas horas estudias los lunes? ¿Y los sábados?

Common -ar verbs

bailar	to dance	**estudiar**	to study
buscar	to look for	**explicar**	to explain
caminar	to walk	**hablar**	to talk; to speak
cantar	to sing	**llegar**	to arrive
cenar	to have dinner	**llevar**	to carry
comprar	to buy	**mirar**	to look (at); to watch
contestar	to answer	**necesitar (+ inf.)**	to need
conversar	to converse, to chat	**practicar**	to practice
desayunar	to have breakfast	**preguntar**	to ask (a question)
descansar	to rest	**preparar**	to prepare
desear (+ inf.)	to desire; to wish	**regresar**	to return
dibujar	to draw	**terminar**	to end; to finish
enseñar	to teach	**tomar**	to take; to drink
escuchar	to listen (to)	**trabajar**	to work
esperar (+ inf.)	to wait (for); to hope	**viajar**	to travel

▶ **¡Atención!** Unless referring to a person, the Spanish verbs **buscar, escuchar, esperar,** and **mirar** do not need to be followed by prepositions as they do in English.

Busco la tarea.
I'm looking for the homework.

Escucho la música.
I'm listening to the music.

Espero el autobús.
I'm waiting for the bus.

Miro la pizarra.
I'm looking at the board.

COMPARE & CONTRAST

English uses three sets of forms to talk about the present: (1) the simple present (*Paco works*), (2) the present progressive (*Paco is working*), and (3) the emphatic present (*Paco does work*). In Spanish, the simple present can be used in all three cases.

Paco **trabaja** en la cafetería.
1. *Paco works in the cafeteria.*
2. *Paco is working in the cafeteria.*
3. *Paco does work in the cafeteria.*

In Spanish and English, the present tense is also sometimes used to express future action.

Marina **viaja** a Madrid mañana.
1. *Marina travels to Madrid tomorrow.*
2. *Marina will travel to Madrid tomorrow.*
3. *Marina is traveling to Madrid tomorrow.*

▶ When two verbs are used together with no change of subject, the second verb is generally in the infinitive. To make a sentence negative in Spanish, the word **no** is placed before the conjugated verb. In this case, **no** means *not*.

Deseo hablar con el señor Díaz.
I want to speak with Mr. Díaz.

Alicia **no** desea bailar ahora.
Alicia doesn't want to dance now.

Spanish speakers often omit subject pronouns because the verb endings indicate who the subject is. In Spanish, subject pronouns are used for emphasis, clarification, or contrast.

—¿Qué enseñan?
What do they teach?

—**Ella** enseña arte y **él** enseña física.
She teaches art, and he teaches physics.

—¿Quién desea trabajar hoy?
Who wants to work today?

—**Yo** no deseo trabajar hoy.
I don't want to work today.

The verb gustar

▶ **Gustar** is different from other **-ar** verbs. To express your likes and dislikes, use the expression **(no) me gusta** + **el/la** + [*singular noun*] or **(no) me gustan** + **los/las** + [*plural noun*]. Note: You may use the phrase **a mí** for emphasis, but never the subject pronoun **yo**.

Me gusta la música clásica.
I like classical music.

Me gustan las clases de español y biología.
I like Spanish and biology classes.

A mí me gustan las artes.
I like the arts.

A mí no me gusta el programa.
I don't like the program.

▶ To talk about what you like and don't like to do, use **(no) me gusta** + [*infinitive(s)*]. Note that the singular **gusta** is always used, even with more than one infinitive.

No me gusta viajar en autobús.
I don't like to travel by bus.

Me gusta cantar y **bailar**.
I like to sing and dance.

▶ To ask a friend about likes and dislikes, use the pronoun **te** instead of **me**. Note: You may use **a ti** for emphasis, but never the subject pronoun **tú**.

—**¿Te gusta la geografía?**
Do you like geography?

—**Sí, me gusta. Y a ti, ¿te gusta el inglés?**
Yes, I like it. And you, do you like English?

▶ You can use this same structure to talk about other people by using the pronouns **nos**, **le**, and **les**. Unless your instructor tells you otherwise, only the **me** and **te** forms will appear on test materials until **Lección 7**.

Nos gusta dibujar. (nosotros)
We like to draw.

Nos gustan las clases de español e inglés. (nosotros)
We like Spanish class and English class.

No le gusta trabajar. (usted, él, ella)
You don't like to work. He/She doesn't like to work.

Les gusta el arte. (ustedes, ellos, ellas)
You like art. They like art.

¡ATENCIÓN!

Note that **gustar** does not behave like other **-ar** verbs. You must study its use carefully and pay attention to prepositions, pronouns, and agreement.

AYUDA

Use the construction **a** + [*name/pronoun*] to clarify to whom you are referring. This construction is not always necessary.
A Gabriela le gusta bailar.
A Sara y a él les gustan los animales.
A mí me gusta viajar.
¿A ti te gustan las clases?

CONSULTA

For more on **gustar** and other verbs like it, see **Estructura 7.4**, pp. 246–247.

More activities

vhlcentral

LM
p. 9

WB
pp. 13–14

Online activities

¡INTÉNTALO! Provide the present tense forms of these verbs.

hablar

1. Yo ___hablo___ español.
2. Ellos ___hablan___ español.
3. Inés ___habla___ español.
4. Tú ___hablas___ español.
5. Nosotras ___hablamos___ español.

gustar

1. ___Me gusta___ el café. (a mí)
2. ¿___Te gustan___ las clases? (a ti)
3. No ___te gusta___ el café. (a ti)
4. No ___me gusta___ el café. (a mí)
5. No ___me gustan___ las clases. (a mí)

Práctica

1 **Completar** Complete the conversation with the appropriate forms of the verbs.

JUAN   ¡Hola, Linda! ¿Qué tal las clases?

LINDA   Bien. (1)___Tomo___ (tomar) tres clases… química, biología y computación.
Y tú, ¿cuántas clases (2)___tomas___ (tomar)?

JUAN   (3)___Tomo___ (tomar) tres también… biología, arte y literatura. El doctor
Cárdenas (4)___enseña___ (enseñar) la clase de biología.

LINDA   ¿Ah, sí? Lily, Alberto y yo (5)___tomamos___ (tomar) biología a las diez con la
profesora Garza.

JUAN   ¿(6)___Estudian___ (estudiar) mucho ustedes?

LINDA   Sí, nosotros (7)___necesitamos___ (necesitar) estudiar dos horas todos los días (*every day*).

---

2 **Oraciones** Form sentences. Remember to conjugate the verbs and add any other necessary words.

> **modelo**
> ustedes / practicar / vocabulario   Ustedes practican el vocabulario.

1. ¿preparar (tú) / tarea? ¿Preparas la tarea?
2. clase de español / terminar / once La clase de español termina a las once.
3. ¿qué / buscar / ustedes? ¿Qué buscan ustedes?
4. (yo) comprar / calculadora Compro una calculadora.
5. (nosotros) buscar / pluma Buscamos una pluma.

---

3 **Gustos** Use the information in parentheses to tell what the people like.

> **modelo**
> Yo enseño en la universidad. (las clases)   Me gustan las clases.

1. Tú deseas mirar cuadros (*paintings*) de Picasso. (el arte) Te gusta el arte.
2. Busco una computadora. (la computación) Me gusta la computación.
3. Tú estudias italiano y español. (las lenguas extranjeras) Te gustan las lenguas extranjeras.
4. No descansas los sábados. (cantar y bailar) Te gusta cantar y bailar.
5. Soy estudiante de economía. (estudiar) Me gusta estudiar.

---

4 **Actividades** Get together with a partner and take turns asking each other if you do these activities.
Which activities does your partner like? Which do you both like? Answers will vary.

> **modelo**
> tomar el autobús
> **Estudiante 1:** ¿Tomas el autobús?
> **Estudiante 2:** Sí, tomo el autobús, pero (*but*) no me gusta./ No, no tomo el autobús.

bailar merengue	escuchar música rock	practicar el español
cantar bien	estudiar física	trabajar en la universidad
dibujar en clase	mirar la televisión	viajar a Europa

AYUDA

The Spanish **no** translates to both *no* and *not* in English. In negative answers to questions, you will need to use **no** twice:
¿Estudias geografía?
No, no estudio geografía.

---

1 **Teaching Tip** To simplify, guide the class to first identify the subject and verb ending for each item.

1 **Expansion** Go over the answers quickly as a class. Then ask volunteers to role-play the dialogue.

2 **Teaching Tip** Point out that students will need to conjugate the verbs and add missing articles and other words to complete these dehydrated sentences. Tell them that subject pronouns in parentheses are not necessary in the completed sentences. Model completion of the first sentence for the class.

2 **Expansion** Give these dehydrated sentences to the class as items 7–10: **7. (yo) desear / practicar / verbos / hoy** (Deseo practicar los verbos hoy.) **8. mi compañero de cuarto / regresar / lunes** (Mi compañero de cuarto regresa el lunes.) **9. ella / cantar / y / bailar / muy bien** (Ella canta y baila muy bien.) **10. jóvenes / necesitar / descansar / ahora** (Los jóvenes necesitan descansar ahora.)

3 **Teaching Tip** To simplify, start by reading the model aloud. Then ask students why **me** is used in the answer (the first-person singular is used in the example sentence) and why **gustan** is needed (**las clases** is plural). Have students identify the indirect object pronoun and choose **gusta** or **gustan** for each item, then complete the activity.

3 **Expansion** If you wish to practice the third-person forms, repeat the activity, providing different subjects for each item. Ex: **1. Deseamos mirar cuadros de Picasso.** (Nos gusta el arte.)

4 **Teaching Tip** Before beginning the activity, give a two- to three-minute oral rapid-response drill. Provide infinitives and subjects, and call on students to give the conjugated form.

TEACHING OPTIONS

Pairs Have individual students write five dehydrated sentences and exchange them with a partner, who will complete them. After pairs have completed their sentences, ask volunteers to share some of their dehydrated sentences. Write them on the board and have the class "hydrate" them.

Game Divide the class into two teams. Prepare brief descriptions of easily recognizable people, using –ar verbs. Write each name on a card, and give each team a set of names. Then read the descriptions aloud. The first team to hold up the correct name earns a point. Ex: **Ella canta, baila y viaja a muchos países.** (Jennifer López)

Comunicación

5 Teaching Tip To challenge students, make copies of this activity with the text removed so that students can only see the illustrations. Pass out the copies and have students close their books. Write all the verbs of the activity in one list on the board. Tell students to complete the activity using three of the verbs from the board for each drawing.

5 Expansion Ask students to write additional descriptions of the drawings. Ex: **La chica estudia arte. Dibuja una casa.** Have volunteers share their descriptions with the class.

5 Describir With a partner, describe what you see using the given verbs. Also ask your partner whether or not he/she likes one of the activities.   Answers will vary.

modelo
dibujar, escuchar
Estudiante 1: La chica dibuja y escucha música. ¿Te gusta dibujar?
Estudiante 2: Sí, me gusta dibujar.

1. desayunar, estudiar, conversar

2. llegar, cantar, bailar

3. trabajar, viajar, llevar

4. mirar, esperar, cenar

6 Teaching Tip You may want to split the class into two teams with volunteers from each team acting out the charades. Give points for correct guesses. The team with the most points at the end wins.

6 Charadas In groups of three, play a game of charades using the verbs. For example, if someone is studying, you say "**Estudias.**" The first person to guess correctly acts out the next charade.   Answers will vary.

bailar	cantar	descansar	enseñar	mirar
caminar	conversar	dibujar	escuchar	preguntar

Síntesis

7 Teaching Tip Point out that, in addition to practicing **-ar** verbs, this activity recycles and reviews material from **Lección 1**: greetings, farewells, and telling time. Allow students several minutes to plan their conversation before they begin speaking.

7 Conversación With a partner, prepare a conversation between two friends who have not seen each other on campus lately and want to catch up on things. Mention how you're feeling, what classes you're taking, what days and times you have classes, and which classes you like and don't like.   Answers will vary.

TEACHING OPTIONS

Extra Practice Have students write a description of themselves made up of activities they like or do not like to do, using sentences containing **(no) me gusta…** Collect the descriptions and read them aloud. Have the class guess who wrote each description.
Game To add a visual aspect to this grammar practice, play **Concentración**. Choose eight infinitives taught in this section, and write each one on a separate card. On another eight cards, draw or paste a picture that illustrates the action of each infinitive. Randomly place the cards facedown in four rows of four. Play with even-numbered groups of students. In pairs, students select two cards. If the two cards match, the pair keeps them. If the cards do not match, students return them to their original position. The pair that finishes with the most cards wins.

2.2 Forming questions in Spanish Tutorial

ANTE TODO   There are three basic ways to ask questions in Spanish. Can you guess what they are by looking at the photos and photo captions on this page?

Te gusta mucho la tarea, ¿no?

¿Hablas con tu mamá?

¿Estudia Maru?

▶ One way to form a question is to raise the pitch of your voice at the end of a declarative sentence. When writing any question in Spanish, be sure to use an upside-down question mark (¿) at the beginning and a regular question mark (?) at the end of the sentence.

Statement	Question
Ustedes trabajan los sábados.	¿Ustedes trabajan los sábados?
You work on Saturdays.	*Do you work on Saturdays?*
Carlota busca un mapa.	¿Carlota busca un mapa?
Carlota is looking for a map.	*Is Carlota looking for a map?*

▶ You can also form a question by inverting the order of the subject and the verb of a declarative statement. The subject may even be placed at the end of the sentence.

Statement	Question
SUBJECT VERB	VERB SUBJECT
Ustedes trabajan los sábados.	¿**Trabajan ustedes** los sábados?
You work on Saturdays.	*Do you work on Saturdays?*
SUBJECT VERB	VERB SUBJECT
Carlota regresa a las seis.	¿**Regresa** a las seis **Carlota**?
Carlota returns at six.	*Does Carlota return at six?*

▶ Questions can also be formed by adding the tags **¿no?** or **¿verdad?** at the end of a statement.

Statement	Question
Ustedes trabajan los sábados.	Ustedes trabajan los sábados, **¿no?**
You work on Saturdays.	*You work on Saturdays, don't you?*
Carlota regresa a las seis.	Carlota regresa a las seis, **¿verdad?**
Carlota returns at six.	*Carlota returns at six, right?*

Question words

Interrogative words

¿Adónde?	Where (to)?	**¿De dónde?**	From where?
¿Cómo?	How?	**¿Dónde?**	Where?
¿Cuál?, ¿Cuáles?	Which?; Which one(s)?	**¿Por qué?**	Why?
¿Cuándo?	When?	**¿Qué?**	What?; Which?
¿Cuánto/a?	How much?	**¿Quién?**	Who?
¿Cuántos/as?	How many?	**¿Quiénes?**	Who (plural)?

▶ To ask a question that requires more than a *yes* or *no* answer, use an interrogative word.

¿Cuál de ellos estudia en la biblioteca?
Which of them studies in the library?

¿Cuántos estudiantes hablan español?
How many students speak Spanish?

¿Dónde trabaja Ricardo?
Where does Ricardo work?

¿Qué clases tomas?
What classes are you taking?

¿Adónde caminamos?
Where are we walking (to)?

¿Por qué necesitas hablar con ella?
Why do you need to talk to her?

¿Quién enseña la clase de arte?
Who teaches the art class?

¿Cuánta tarea hay?
How much homework is there?

CONSULTA

You will learn more about the difference between **qué** and **cuál** in **Estructura 9.3**, p. 316.

▶ When you pronounce this type of question, the pitch of your voice falls at the end of the sentence.

¿Cómo llegas a clase?
How do you get to class?

¿Por qué necesitas estudiar?
Why do you need to study?

▶ Notice the difference between **¿por qué?**, which is written as two words and has an accent, and **porque**, which is written as one word without an accent.

¿Por qué estudias español?
Why do you study Spanish?

¡Porque es divertido!
Because it's fun!

▶ In Spanish **no** can mean both *no* and *not*. Therefore, when answering a yes/no question in the negative, you need to use **no** twice.

¿Caminan a la universidad?
Do you walk to the university?

No, **no** caminamos a la universidad.
No, we do not walk to the university.

¡INTÉNTALO!

Make questions out of these statements. Use the intonation method and the tag **¿no?** method.

Statement	Intonation	Tag questions
1. Hablas inglés.	¿Hablas inglés?	Hablas inglés, ¿no?
2. Trabajamos mañana.	¿Trabajamos mañana?	Trabajamos mañana, ¿no?
3. Raúl estudia mucho.	¿Raúl estudia mucho?	Raúl estudia mucho, ¿no?
4. Ustedes desean bailar.	¿Ustedes desean bailar?	Ustedes desean bailar, ¿no?
5. Enseño a las nueve.	¿Enseño a las nueve?	Enseño a las nueve, ¿no?
6. Luz mira la televisión.	¿Luz mira la televisión?	Luz mira la televisión, ¿no?

More activities

vhlcentral

LM p. 10

WB pp. 15–16

Online activities

TEACHING OPTIONS

Video Show the **Fotonovela** again to give students more input on forming questions. Stop the video where appropriate to discuss how certain questions, including tag questions, are formed. Have students focus on characters' rising and falling intonation in questions and statements.

Heritage Speakers Ask heritage speakers to give original statements and questions at random. Have the rest of the class determine whether each sentence is a statement or a question.

Pairs Give pairs of students five minutes to write original questions using as many interrogative words as they can. Can any pair come up with questions using all interrogative words?

Práctica

1

Preguntas Change these sentences into questions by inverting the word order.

> **modelo**
>
> Ernesto habla con su compañero de clase.
>
> **¿Habla Ernesto con su compañero de clase? /**
>
> **¿Habla con su compañero de clase Ernesto?**

1. La profesora Cruz prepara la prueba.
   ¿Prepara la profesora Cruz la prueba? / ¿Prepara la prueba la profesora Cruz?
2. Sandra y yo necesitamos estudiar.
   ¿Necesitamos Sandra y yo estudiar? / ¿Necesitamos estudiar Sandra y yo?
3. Los chicos practican el vocabulario.
   ¿Practican los chicos el vocabulario? / ¿Practican el vocabulario los chicos?
4. Tú trabajas en la biblioteca.
   ¿Trabajas tú en la biblioteca? / ¿Trabajas en la biblioteca tú?
5. Jaime termina la tarea.
   ¿Termina Jaime la tarea? / ¿Termina la tarea Jaime?

2

Preguntas Change each statement into two questions, using the interrogative words given.
Answers may vary. Suggested answers:

> **modelo**
>
> Ernesto habla bien en la clase de español. (¿quién? ¿dónde?)
>
> **¿Quién habla bien en la clase de español? /**
>
> **¿Dónde habla bien Ernesto?**

1. Ignacio estudia hoy porque hay un examen el jueves. (¿cuándo? ¿por qué?)
   ¿Cuándo estudia Ignacio? ¿Por qué estudia Ignacio hoy?
2. Tú trabajas seis horas en la librería. (¿cuántas? ¿dónde?)
   ¿Cuántas horas trabajas en la librería? ¿Dónde trabajas?
3. Los chicos practican el vocabulario en clase. (¿quiénes? ¿qué?)
   ¿Quiénes practican el vocabulario en clase? ¿Qué practican los chicos?
4. Valeria y Sergio viajan a Barcelona en autobús. (¿adónde? ¿cómo?)
   ¿Adónde viajan Valeria y Sergio? ¿Cómo viajan Valeria y Sergio a Barcelona?
5. Catalina y Susana cenan en la cafetería. (¿quiénes? ¿dónde?)
   ¿Quiénes cenan en la cafetería? ¿Dónde cenan Catalina y Susana?

3

Completar Complete the conversation with the appropriate questions. Answers will vary.

IRENE   Hola, Manolo. (1) ¿Cómo estás?/¿Qué tal?

MANOLO   Bien, gracias. (2) ¿Y tú?

IRENE   Muy bien. (3) ¿Qué hora es?

MANOLO   Son las nueve.

IRENE   (4) ¿Qué estudias?

MANOLO   Estudio historia.

IRENE   (5) ¿Por qué?

MANOLO   Porque hay un examen mañana.

IRENE   (6) ¿Te gusta la clase?

MANOLO   Sí, me gusta mucho la clase.

IRENE   (7) ¿Quién enseña la clase?

MANOLO   El profesor Padilla enseña la clase.

IRENE   (8) ¿Tomas psicología este semestre?

MANOLO   No, no tomo psicología este (*this*) semestre.

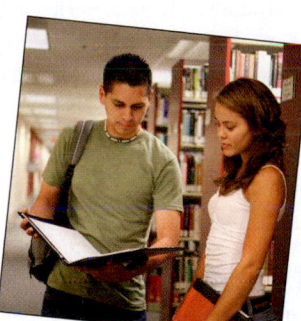

1 Teaching Tip Ask students to give both ways of forming questions for each item. Then have student pairs take turns making the statements and converting them into questions.

1 Expansion Have students add tag questions to the statements.

2 Teaching Tip Remind students that the subject of a question can go after the verb or at the end of the sentence.

2 Expansion Have students ask an additional question about each statement using a different interrogative word.

3 Expansion
👥↔👤 Have pairs of students create a similar conversation, replacing Manolo's answers with information that is true for them. Then ask volunteers to role-play their conversations for the class.

TEACHING OPTIONS

Heritage Speakers Ask students to interview heritage speakers, whether in the class or outside. Students should prepare questions about who the person is, if he or she works and when/where, what he or she studies and why, and so forth. Have students use the information they gather in the interviews to write a brief profile of the person.

Large Groups Divide the class into two groups, A and B. To each member of group A give a strip of paper with a question on it. Ex: **¿Cuántos estudiantes hay en la clase?** Give an answer to each member of group B. Ex: **Hay treinta estudiantes en la clase.** Have students find their partners. Be sure that each question has only one possible answer.

Comunicación

4

Encuesta Your instructor will give you a worksheet. Change the categories in the first column into questions, then use them to survey your classmates. Find at least one person for each category. Be prepared to report the results of your survey to the class. *Answers will vary.*

5

Un juego In groups of four or five, play a game (**un juego**) of Jeopardy®. Each person has to write two clues. Then take turns reading the clues and guessing the questions. The person who guesses correctly reads the next clue. *Answers will vary.*

Es algo que...	**Es un lugar donde...**	**Es una persona que...**
It's something that...	*It's a place where...*	*It's a person that...*

modelo

Estudiante 1: Es un lugar donde estudiamos.
Estudiante 2: ¿Qué es la biblioteca?

Estudiante 1: Es algo que escuchamos.
Estudiante 2: ¿Qué es la música?

Estudiante 1: Es un director de España.
Estudiante 2: ¿Quién es Pedro Almodóvar?

6

El nuevo estudiante You are a transfer student and today is your first day of Spanish class. Ask your partner questions to find out all you can about the class, your classmates, and the university. Use the list for ideas. Then switch roles. *Answers will vary.*

biblioteca	curso	librería
cafetería	especialización	residencia estudiantil
clase	examen	tarea

modelo

Estudiante 1: Hola, me llamo Samuel. ¿Cómo te llamas?
Estudiante 2: Me llamo Laura.
Estudiante 1: En la universidad hay cursos de ciencias, ¿verdad?
Estudiante 2: Sí, hay clases de biología, química y física.
Estudiante 1: ¿Cuántos exámenes hay en esta clase?
Estudiante 2: Hay dos.

Síntesis

7

Entrevista You are a reporter for the school newspaper. Write five questions about student life at your school and use them to interview two classmates. Be prepared to report your findings to the class. *Answers will vary.*

Instructor's Annotated Edition notes (left margin)

4 Teaching Tips
- If this is the first time students are completing an activity from the Activity Pack, explain that they need a handout.
- Distribute the *Hojas de actividades* (Activity Pack/ Supersite) and explain that students must actively approach their classmates with their *Hoja* in hand. When they find someone who answers affirmatively, that student signs his or her name.
- For survey-type activities, encourage students to ask one question per person and move on. This will promote circulation throughout the room and prevent students from remaining in clusters.

4 Expansion
Ask students to say the name of someone who signed their *Hoja*. Then ask that student for more information. Ex: ¿Quién estudia computación? Ah, ¿sí? _____ estudia computación. ¿Dónde estudias computación, _____? ¿Quién es el/la profesor(a)?

5 Expansion Play this game with the entire class. Select a few students to play the contestants and to "buzz in" their answers.

6 Teaching Tip Write **la clase, los compañeros de clase,** and **la universidad** on the board. Guide students in brainstorming questions and write each one in the appropriate column.

7 Teaching Tip Brainstorm ideas for interview questions and write them on the board, or have students prepare their questions as homework for an in-class interview session.

TEACHING OPTIONS

Extra Practice Have students go back to the **Fotonovela** on pages 44–45 and write as many questions as they can about what they see in the photos. Ask volunteers to share their questions as you write them on the board. Then call on individual students to answer them.

Extra Practice Prepare eight questions and answers. Write only the answers on the board in random order. Then read the questions aloud and have students identify the appropriate answer. Ex: ¿Cuándo es la clase de español? (Es los lunes, miércoles y viernes.)

2.3 Present tense of estar Tutorial

CONSULTA

To review the forms of **ser**, see **Estructura 1.3**, pp. 19–21.

ANTE TODO   In **Lección 1**, you learned how to conjugate and use the verb **ser** (*to be*). You will now learn a second verb which means *to be*, the verb **estar**. Although **estar** ends in **-ar**, it does not follow the pattern of regular **-ar** verbs. The **yo** form (**estoy**) is irregular. Also, all forms have an accented **á** except the **yo** and **nosotros/as** forms.

The verb estar (*to be*)

SINGULAR FORMS	yo	est**oy**	*I am*
	tú	est**ás**	*you* (fam.) *are*
	Ud./él/ella	est**á**	*you* (form.) *are; he/she is*
PLURAL FORMS	nosotros/as	est**amos**	*we are*
	vosotros/as	est**áis**	*you* (fam.) *are*
	Uds./ellos/ellas	est**án**	*you are; they are*

¡Estamos en Perú!

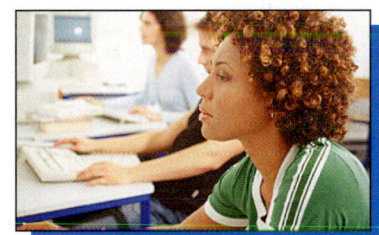

María está en la biblioteca.

AYUDA

Use **la casa** to express *the house*, but **en casa** to express *at home*.

CONSULTA

To learn more about the difference between **ser** and **estar**, see **Estructura 5.3**, pp. 170–171.

COMPARE & CONTRAST

Compare the uses of the verb **estar** to those of the verb **ser**.

Uses of *estar*

Location
Estoy en casa.
I am at home.

Marissa **está** al lado de Felipe.
Marissa is next to Felipe.

Health
Juan Carlos **está** enfermo hoy.
Juan Carlos is sick today.

Well-being
—¿Cómo **estás**, Jimena?
How are you, Jimena?

—**Estoy** muy bien, gracias.
I'm very well, thank you.

Uses of *ser*

Identity
Hola, **soy** Maru.
Hello, I'm Maru.

Occupation
Soy estudiante.
I'm a student.

Origin
—¿**Eres** de México?
Are you from Mexico?

—Sí, **soy** de México.
Yes, I'm from Mexico.

Telling time
Son las cuatro.
It's four o'clock.

Section Goals

In **Estructura 2.3**, students will be introduced to:
- the present tense of **estar**
- contrasts between **ser** and **estar**
- prepositions and adverbs of location used with **estar**

Instructional Resources
Supersite: Audio (Lab MP3 Files); Resources (Grammar Presentation Slides, Digital Image Bank, Activity Pack, Scripts, Answer Keys); Testing Program (Quizzes)
WebSAM
Workbook
Lab Manual

Teaching Tips
- Point out that only the **yo** and **nosotros/as** forms do not have a written accent.
- Emphasize that the principal distinction between **estar** and **ser** is that **estar** is generally used to express temporary conditions (**Juan Carlos está enfermo hoy**) and **ser** is generally used to express inherent qualities (**Juan Carlos es inteligente**).
- On the board, make a chart similar to the one in **Compare & Contrast**, but create sample sentences using the names of your students and information about them.
- Students will learn to compare **ser** and **estar** formally in **Estructura 5.3**.

TEACHING OPTIONS

TPR Have students write **ser** and **estar** on separate sheets of paper. Give statements in English and have students indicate if they would use **ser** or **estar** in each by holding up the appropriate paper. Ex: *I'm at home.* (**estar**) *I'm a student.* (**ser**) *I'm tired.* (**estar**) *I'm glad.* (**estar**) *I'm generous.* (**ser**)
Extra Practice Ask students to tell where certain people are or probably are at this moment. Ex: **¿Dónde estás? (Estoy en la**

clase.) **¿Dónde está el presidente? (Está en Washington, D.C.)**
Heritage Speakers Ask heritage speakers to name instances where either **ser** or **estar** may be used. They may point out more advanced uses, such as with certain adjectives: **Es aburrido** vs. **Está aburrido**. This may help to compare and contrast inherent qualities and temporary conditions.

Teaching Tips
- Explain that prepositions typically indicate where one thing or person is in relation to another thing or person: *near, far, on, between, below.*
- Point out that **estar** is used in the model sentences to indicate presence or existence in a place.
- Take a book or some other object and place it in various locations in relation to your desk or a student's. Ask individual students about its location. Ex: **¿Dónde está el libro? ¿Está cerca o lejos del escritorio de ____? ¿Qué objeto está al lado del libro?** Work through various locations, eliciting all of the prepositions of location.
- Ask where students are in relation to one another. Ex: **____, ¿dónde está ____? Está al lado (a la derecha/ izquierda, delante, detrás) de ____.**
- Describe students' locations in relation to each other. Ex: **Esta persona está lejos de ____. Está delante de ____. Está al lado de ____** … Have the class call out the student you identify. Ex: **Es ____.** Then have students describe other students' locations for a partner to guess.

▶ **Estar** is often used with certain prepositions and adverbs to describe the location of a person or an object.

Prepositions and adverbs often used with estar

al lado de	*next to*	**delante de**	*in front of*
a la derecha de	*to the right of*	**detrás de**	*behind*
a la izquierda de	*to the left of*	**en**	*in; on*
allá	*over there*	**encima de**	*on top of*
allí	*there*	**entre**	*between*
cerca de	*near*	**lejos de**	*far from*
con	*with*	**sin**	*without*
debajo de	*below*	**sobre**	*on; over*

El marcador **está al lado de** la pluma.
The marker is next to the pen.

Los libros **están encima del** escritorio.
The books are on top of the desk.

El laboratorio **está cerca de** la clase.
The lab is near the classroom.

Maribel **está delante de** José.
Maribel is in front of José.

La maleta **está allí**.
The suitcase is there.

El estadio no **está lejos de** la librería.
The stadium isn't far from the bookstore.

El mapa **está entre** la pizarra y la puerta.
The map is between the board and the door.

Los estudiantes **están en** la clase.
The students are in class.

La calculadora **está sobre** la mesa.
The calculator is on the table.

Los turistas **están allá**.
The tourists are over there.

Estamos lejos de casa.

La biblioteca está al lado de la librería.

More activities

vhlcentral

LM
p. 11

WB
pp. 17–18

Online activities

¡INTÉNTALO! Provide the present tense forms of **estar**.

1. Ustedes _**están**_ en la clase.
2. José _**está**_ en la biblioteca.
3. Yo _**estoy**_ bien, gracias.
4. Nosotras _**estamos**_ en la cafetería.
5. Tú _**estás**_ en el laboratorio.
6. Ellas _**están**_ en la clase.
7. Elena _**está**_ en la librería.
8. Ana y yo _**estamos**_ en la clase.
9. Javier y Maribel _**están**_ en el estadio.
10. ¿Cómo _**está**_ usted?
11. Nosotros _**estamos**_ en la cafetería.
12. Yo _**estoy**_ en el laboratorio.
13. Carmen y María _**están**_ enfermas.
14. Tú _**estás**_ en la clase.

TEACHING OPTIONS

Extra Practice Name well-known campus buildings and ask students to describe their location in relation to other buildings. Model sample sentences so students will know how to answer. You may wish to write **la Facultad de…** on the board and explain its meaning. Ex: —**¿Dónde está la biblioteca? —Está al lado de la Facultad de Química y detrás de la librería.**

TPR Have students remain seated. One student starts with a ball. Identify another student by his or her location with reference to other students. Ex: **Es la persona a la derecha de ____.** The student with the ball has to throw it to the student you described. The latter student must then toss the ball to the next person you identify.

Práctica

1 **Completar** Complete the conversation with the appropriate forms of **ser** or **estar**.

MAMÁ   Hola, Daniela. ¿Cómo (1)___estás___?

▶ DANIELA   Hola, mamá. (2)___Estoy___ bien. ¿Dónde (3)___está___ papá?
     ¡Ya (*Already*) (4)___son___ las ocho de la noche!

MAMÁ   No (5)___está___ aquí. (6)___Está___ en la oficina.

DANIELA   Y Andrés y Margarita, ¿dónde (7)___están___ ellos?

MAMÁ   (8)___Están___ en el restaurante La Palma con Martín.

DANIELA   ¿Quién (9)___es___ Martín?

MAMÁ   (10)___Es___ un compañero de clase. (11)___Es___ de México.

DANIELA   Ah. Y el restaurante La Palma, ¿dónde (12)___está___?

MAMÁ   (13)___Está___ cerca de la Plaza Mayor, en San Modesto.

DANIELA   Gracias, mamá. Voy (*I'm going*) al restaurante. ¡Hasta pronto!

2 **Escoger** Choose the preposition that best completes each sentence.

1. La pluma está (encima de / detrás de) la mesa.   encima de
2. La ventana está (a la izquierda de / debajo de) la puerta.   a la izquierda de
3. La pizarra está (debajo de / delante de) los estudiantes.   delante de
4. Los estudiantes llevan los libros (en / sobre) la mochila.   en
5. España está (cerca de / lejos de) Puerto Rico.   lejos de
6. La biblioteca está (sobre / al lado de) la residencia estudiantil.   al lado de
7. Las sillas están (encima de / detrás de) los escritorios.   detrás de
8. México está (cerca de / lejos de) los Estados Unidos.   cerca de

3 **La librería** Ask the school bookstore clerk (your partner) the location of items in the drawing.   Answers will vary.

modelo
Estudiante 1: ¿Dónde están las computadoras?
Estudiante 2: Las computadoras están encima de la mesa.

Comunicación

4 **¿Dónde estás...?** Get together with a partner and take turns asking each other where you normally are at these times. *Answers will vary.*

> **modelo**
> lunes / 10:00 a.m.
> **Estudiante 1:** *¿Dónde estás los lunes a las diez de la mañana?*
> **Estudiante 2:** *Estoy en la clase de español.*

1. sábados / 6:00 a.m.
2. miércoles / 9:15 a.m.
3. lunes / 11:10 a.m.
4. jueves / 12:30 a.m.

5. viernes / 2:25 p.m.
6. martes / 3:50 p.m.
7. jueves / 5:45 p.m.
8. miércoles / 8:20 p.m.

5 **La ciudad universitaria** You are an exchange student at a Spanish university. Ask a classmate to identify the people for you. *Answers will vary.*

> **modelo**
> **Estudiante 1:** *¿Quién es Valeria? ¿Está a la izquierda de la facultad?*
> **Estudiante 2:** *Sí, está a la izquierda de la facultad. Está al lado de David.*

Facultad de Filosofía y Letras

David • Valeria • Isabel • Prof. Rojas • Luis • Andrea • Víctor

Síntesis

6 **Entrevista** With a partner, take turns asking and answering these questions. *Answers will vary.*

1. ¿Cómo estás?
2. ¿Dónde tomas la clase de inglés/periodismo/física/computación?
3. ¿Dónde está tu (*your*) compañero/a de cuarto ahora?
4. ¿Cuántos estudiantes hay en tu clase de historia/literatura/química/matemáticas?
5. ¿Quién(es) no está(n) en la clase hoy?
6. ¿A qué hora terminan tus clases los lunes?
7. ¿Estudias mucho?
8. ¿Cuántas horas estudias para (*for*) una prueba?

---

4 **Teaching Tips**
- Ask two volunteers to read the model aloud.
- Have students scan the days and times and ask you for any additional vocabulary.

4 **Expansion** After students have completed the activity, ask the same questions of selected individuals. Then expand on their answers by asking additional questions. Ex: —**¿Dónde estás los sábados a las seis de la mañana?** —**Estoy en la residencia estudiantil.** —**¿Dónde está la residencia?**

5 **Expansion**
- Have students choose a new location in the drawing and repeat the activity.
- Make copies of your campus map and distribute them to the class. Ask questions about where particular buildings are. Give yourself a starting point so that you can ask questions with as many prepositions as possible. Ex: **Estoy en la biblioteca. ¿Está lejos la librería?**
- Have students form groups of three and take turns describing the location of different places on your campus. Ex: —**Está lejos de la cafetería y la biblioteca. Está al lado de la librería.** —**¿Es el estadio?**

6 **Expansion** Call on students to share the information they obtained with the class.

2.4 Numbers 31 and higher Tutorial

ANTE TODO You have already learned numbers 0–30. Now you will learn the rest of the numbers.

Numbers 31–100

▶ Numbers 31–99 follow the same basic pattern as 21–29.

Numbers 31–100					
31	treinta y uno	40	cuarenta	50	cincuenta
32	treinta y dos	41	cuarenta y uno	51	cincuenta y uno
33	treinta y tres	42	cuarenta y dos	52	cincuenta y dos
34	treinta y cuatro	43	cuarenta y tres	60	sesenta
35	treinta y cinco	44	cuarenta y cuatro	63	sesenta y tres
36	treinta y seis	45	cuarenta y cinco	64	sesenta y cuatro
37	treinta y siete	46	cuarenta y seis	70	setenta
38	treinta y ocho	47	cuarenta y siete	80	ochenta
39	treinta y nueve	48	cuarenta y ocho	90	noventa
		49	cuarenta y nueve	100	cien, ciento

▶ **Y** is used in most numbers from **31** through **99**. Unlike numbers 21–29, these numbers must be written as three separate words.

Hay **noventa y dos** exámenes.
There are ninety-two exams.

Hay **cuarenta y dos** estudiantes.
There are forty-two students.

Hay cuarenta y siete estudiantes en la clase de geografía.

Cien menos sesenta y cuatro son treinta y seis pesos de cambio.

▶ With numbers that end in **uno** (31, 41, etc.), **uno** becomes **un** before a masculine noun and **una** before a feminine noun.

Hay **treinta y un** chicos.
There are thirty-one guys.

Hay **treinta y una** chicas.
There are thirty-one girls.

▶ **Cien** is used before nouns and in counting. The words **un**, **una**, and **uno** are never used before **cien** in Spanish. Use **cientos** to say *hundreds*.

Hay **cien** libros y **cien** sillas.
There are one hundred books and one hundred chairs.

¿Cuántos libros hay? **Cientos.**
How many books are there? Hundreds.

Numbers 101 and higher

▶ As shown in the chart, Spanish uses a period to indicate thousands and millions, rather than a comma, as is used in English.

Numbers 101 and higher			
101	ciento uno	**1.000**	mil
200	doscientos/as	**1.100**	mil cien
300	trescientos/as	**2.000**	dos mil
400	cuatrocientos/as	**5.000**	cinco mil
500	quinientos/as	**100.000**	cien mil
600	seiscientos/as	**200.000**	doscientos/as mil
700	setecientos/as	**550.000**	quinientos/as cincuenta mil
800	ochocientos/as	**1.000.000**	un millón (de)
900	novecientos/as	**8.000.000**	ocho millones (de)

▶ Notice that you should use **ciento**, not **cien**, to count numbers over 100.

110 = **ciento diez**   118 = **ciento dieciocho**   150 = **ciento cincuenta**

▶ The numbers 200 through 999 agree in gender with the nouns they modify.

324 plum**as**   3.505 libr**os**
trescient**as** veinticuatro plum**as**   tres mil quinient**os** cinco libr**os**

▶ The word **mil**, which can mean *a thousand* and *one thousand*, is not usually used in the plural form to refer to an exact number, but it can be used to express the idea of *a lot, many,* or *thousands.* **Cientos** can also be used to express *hundreds* in this manner.

¡Hay **miles** de personas en el estadio!   Hay **cientos** de libros en la biblioteca.
There are thousands of people   *There are hundreds of books*
in the stadium!   *in the library.*

▶ To express a complex number (including years), string together all of its components.

55.422   cincuenta y cinco mil cuatrocientos veintidós

¡LENGUA VIVA!
In parts of Latin America, you will see a comma instead of a period to indicate thousands and millions.

¡LENGUA VIVA!
In Spanish, years are not expressed as pairs of two-digit numbers as they are in English (1979, *nineteen seventy-nine*): **1776, mil setecientos setenta y seis; 1945, mil novecientos cuarenta y cinco; 2016, dos mil dieciséis.**

¡ATENCIÓN!
When **millón** or **millones** is used before a noun, the word **de** is placed between the two: **1.000.000 hombres = un millón de hombres 12.000.000 casas = doce millones de casas.**

More activities

vhlcentral

LM
p. 12

WB
pp. 19–20

Online activities

¡INTÉNTALO! Write out the Spanish equivalent of each number.

1. **102** _ciento dos_
2. **5.000.000** _cinco millones_
3. **76** _setenta y seis_
4. **201** _doscientos uno_
5. **92** _noventa y dos_
6. **550.300** _quinientos cincuenta mil trescientos_
7. **113** _ciento trece_
8. **79** _setenta y nueve_
9. **235** _doscientos treinta y cinco_
10. **88** _ochenta y ocho_
11. **17.123** _diecisiete mil ciento veintitrés_
12. **497** _cuatrocientos noventa y siete_

Práctica y Comunicación

1 **Baloncesto** Provide these basketball scores in Spanish.

1. Ohio State 76, Michigan 65
2. Florida 92, Florida State 104
3. Stanford 83, UCLA 89
4. Duke 115, Virginia 121
5. Princeton 67, Harvard 55
6. Purdue 81, Indiana 78

1. setenta y seis, sesenta y cinco   3. ochenta y tres, ochenta y nueve   5. sesenta y siete, cincuenta y cinco
2. noventa y dos, ciento cuatro   4. ciento quince, ciento veintiuno   6. ochenta y uno, setenta y ocho

2 **Completar** Following the pattern, write out the missing numbers in Spanish.

1. 50, 150, 250 ... 1.050   trescientos cincuenta, cuatrocientos cincuenta, quinientos cincuenta, seiscientos cincuenta, setecientos cincuenta, ochocientos cincuenta, novecientos cincuenta
2. 5.000, 20.000, 35.000 ... 95.000
   cincuenta mil, sesenta y cinco mil, ochenta mil
3. 100.000.000, 90.000.000, 80.000.000 ... 0   setenta millones, sesenta millones, cincuenta millones, cuarenta millones, treinta millones, veinte millones, diez millones
4. 100.000, 200.000, 300.000 ... 1.000.000
   cuatrocientos mil, quinientos mil, seiscientos mil, setecientos mil, ochocientos mil, novecientos mil

3 **Resolver** In pairs, take turns reading the math problems aloud for your partner to solve.

AYUDA

+	→	más
−	→	menos
=	→	son

> **modelo**
>
> 200 + 300 =
>
> **Estudiante 1:** Doscientos más trescientos son...
> **Estudiante 2:** ...quinientos.

1. 1.000 + 753 =   Mil más setecientos cincuenta y tres son mil setecientos cincuenta y tres.
2. 1.000.000 − 30.000 =   Un millón menos treinta mil son novecientos setenta mil.
3. 10.000 + 555 =   Diez mil más quinientos cincuenta y cinco son diez mil quinientos cincuenta y cinco.
4. 15 + 150 =   Quince más ciento cincuenta son ciento sesenta y cinco.
5. 100.000 + 205.000 =   Cien mil más doscientos cinco mil son trescientos cinco mil.
6. 29.000 − 10.000 =   Veintinueve mil menos diez mil son diecinueve mil.

4 **Entrevista** Find out the phone numbers and e-mail addresses of four classmates.   Answers will vary.

> **modelo**
>
> **Estudiante 1:** ¿Cuál es tu (your) número de teléfono?
> **Estudiante 2:** Es el 635-19-51.
> **Estudiante 1:** ¿Y tu dirección de correo electrónico?
> **Estudiante 2:** Es a-Smith-arroba-pe-ele-punto-e-de-u. (asmith@pl.edu)

AYUDA

arroba *at* (@)
punto *dot* (.)

Síntesis

5 **¿A qué distancia...?** Your instructor will give you and a partner incomplete charts that indicate the distances between Madrid and various locations. Fill in the missing information on your chart by asking your partner questions.   Answers will vary.

> **modelo**
>
> **Estudiante 1:** ¿A qué distancia está Arganda del Rey?
> **Estudiante 2:** Está a veintisiete kilómetros de Madrid.

1 **Expansion** In pairs, have each student write three additional basketball scores and dictate them to his or her partner, who writes them down.

2 **Teaching Tip** To simplify, have students identify the pattern of each sequence. Ex: 1. Add one hundred.

3 **Expansion** To challenge students, have them create four additional math problems for a partner to solve.

4 **Teaching Tips**
- Write your own e-mail address on the board as you pronounce it.
- Point out that **el correo electrónico** means *e-mail.*
- Reassure students that, if they are uncomfortable revealing their personal information, they can invent a number and address.
- Ask volunteers to share their phone numbers and e-mail addresses. Other students write them on the board.

5 **Teaching Tips**
- If this is the first time students are completing an activity from the Activity Pack, explain that they will need a handout.
- Divide the class into pairs and distribute the handouts associated with this Information Gap activity (Activity Pack/Supersite). Explain that in this type of exercise, each partner has information that the other needs, and the only way to get this information is by asking the partner questions.
- Point out and model **está a _____ de...** to express distance.
- Give students ten minutes to complete this activity.

TEACHING OPTIONS

Small Groups In groups of three or four, ask students to think of a city or town within a 100-mile radius of the university. Have them find out the distance in miles (**Está a _____ millas de la universidad.**) and what other cities or towns are nearby (**Está cerca de…**). Then have groups read their descriptions for the class to guess.

Game Ask for two volunteers and station them at opposite ends of the board so neither one can see what the other is writing. Say a number for them to write on the board. If both students are correct, continue to give numbers until one writes an incorrect number. The winner continues on to play against another student.

Section Goal

In **Recapitulación**, students will review the grammar concepts from this lesson.

Instructional Resource
Supersite

Teaching Tip You may want to assign this **Recapitulación** activity on the Supersite because it has diagnostics. There is an online-only review activity for each grammar point. The Supersite also has a **Repaso de vocabulario** activity with diagnostics.

1 Teaching Tips
- To simplify, ask students to identify the infinitive of the verb in each row.
- Complete this activity orally as a class. Write each form on the board as students call them out.

1 Expansion Ask students to provide the third-person singular (**Ud./él/ella**) conjugations.

2 Expansion
- Ask students to write five more numbers above 31. Have them read the numbers to a partner, who will jot them down. Remind students to check each other's answers.
- To challenge students, have them complete the activity and then say what they can buy with that amount of money. Model the first item for the class. Ex: **Con 49 dólares, compro una mochila.**

3 Teaching Tips
- Remind students that all question words should carry accent marks.
- Remind students that verbs in Spanish do not require subject pronouns; they are used for emphasis or clarification.

Recapitulación

Review the grammar concepts you have learned in this lesson by completing these activities.

1 **Completar** Complete the chart with the correct verb forms. **24 pts.**

yo	tú	nosotros	ellas
compro	compras	compramos	compran
deseo	**deseas**	deseamos	desean
miro	miras	**miramos**	miran
pregunto	preguntas	preguntamos	**preguntan**

2 **Números** Write these numbers in Spanish. **16 pts.**

modelo
645: *seiscientos cuarenta y cinco*

1. **49:** cuarenta y nueve
2. **97:** noventa y siete
3. **113:** ciento trece
4. **632:** seiscientos treinta y dos
5. **1.781:** mil setecientos ochenta y uno
6. **3.558:** tres mil quinientos cincuenta y ocho
7. **1.006.015:** un millón seis mil quince
8. **67.224.370:** sesenta y siete millones doscientos veinticuatro mil trescientos setenta

3 **Preguntas** Write questions for these answers. **12 pts.**

1. —¿ De dónde es _____ Patricia?
   —Patricia es de Colombia.
2. —¿ Quién es _____ él?
   —Él es mi amigo (*friend*).
3. —¿ Cuántos idiomas hablas _____ (tú)?
   —Hablo dos idiomas (*languages*).
4. —¿ Qué desean (tomar) _____ (ustedes)?
   —Deseamos tomar café.
5. —¿ Por qué tomas biología _____ ?
   —Tomo biología porque me gustan las ciencias.
6. —¿ Cuándo descansa Camilo _____ ?
   —Camilo descansa por las mañanas.

RESUMEN GRAMATICAL

2.1 Present tense of -ar verbs *pp. 50–52*

estudiar	
estudio	estudiamos
estudias	estudiáis
estudia	estudian

The verb gustar

(no) me gusta + el/la + [*singular noun*]

(no) me gustan + los/las + [*plural noun*]

(no) me gusta + [*infinitive(s)*]

Note: You may use a mí for emphasis, but never yo.

To ask a friend about likes and dislikes, use te instead of me, but never tú.

¿Te gusta la historia?

2.2 Forming questions in Spanish *pp. 55–56*

▸ ¿Ustedes trabajan los sábados?
▸ ¿Trabajan ustedes los sábados?
▸ Ustedes trabajan los sábados, ¿verdad?/¿no?

Interrogative words		
¿Adónde?	¿Cuánto/a?	¿Por qué?
¿Cómo?	¿Cuántos/as?	¿Qué?
¿Cuál(es)?	¿De dónde?	¿Quién(es)?
¿Cuándo?	¿Dónde?	

2.3 Present tense of estar *pp. 59–60*

▸ estar: estoy, estás, está, estamos, estáis, están

2.4 Numbers 31 and higher *pp. 63–64*

31	treinta y uno	101	ciento uno
32	treinta y dos	200	doscientos/as
	(and so on)	500	quinientos/as
40	cuarenta	700	setecientos/as
50	cincuenta	900	novecientos/as
60	sesenta	1.000	mil
70	setenta	2.000	dos mil
80	ochenta	5.100	cinco mil cien
90	noventa	100.000	cien mil
100	cien, ciento	1.000.000	un millón (de)

TEACHING OPTIONS

Pairs Have students write ten questions using the interrogative words from **Estructura 2.2** to ask their partner about his/her family, house, friends, etc. Remind students that ¿**Cuánto/a?** and ¿**Cuántos/as?** should agree with their corresponding nouns. Then have students exchange papers with a classmate and answer the questions. Finally, have pairs work together to review the answers. Have them write sentences using

nosotros/as about any items they have in common.
Extra Practice On the board, write a list of landmarks (libraries, parks, churches, restaurants, hotels, and so forth) in the community. Have students choose a landmark and write a short paragraph describing its location. Ex: **El Hotel Plaza está al lado de la biblioteca. Está cerca de la catedral y delante de Sebastian's Café. Está lejos de mi casa.**

4 **Al teléfono** Complete this phone conversation with the correct forms of the verb **estar**.   `16 pts.`

MARÍA TERESA Hola, señora López. (1) ¿ ___Está___ Elisa en casa?

SRA. LÓPEZ Hola, ¿quién es?

MARÍA TERESA Soy María Teresa. Elisa y yo (2) ___estamos___ en la misma (*same*) clase de literatura.

SRA. LÓPEZ ¡Ah, María Teresa! ¿Cómo (3) ___estás___ ?

MARÍA TERESA (4) ___Estoy___ muy bien, gracias. Y usted, ¿cómo (5) ___está___ ?

SRA. LÓPEZ Bien, gracias. Pues, no, Elisa no (6) ___está___ en casa. Ella y su hermano (*her brother*) (7) ___están___ en la Biblioteca Cervantes.

MARÍA TERESA ¿Cervantes?

SRA. LÓPEZ Es la biblioteca que (8) ___está___ al lado del café Bambú.

MARÍA TERESA ¡Ah, sí! Gracias, señora López.

SRA. LÓPEZ Hasta luego, María Teresa.

5 **¿Qué te gusta?** Write a paragraph of at least five sentences stating what you like and don't like about your university. If possible, explain your likes and dislikes.   `32 pts.`   Answers will vary.

> *Me gusta la clase de música porque no hay muchos exámenes. No me gusta cenar en la cafetería...*

6 **Canción** Use the appropriate forms of the verb **gustar** to complete the beginning of a popular song by Manu Chao.   `4 EXTRA points!`

“Me ___gustan___ los aviones°,
me gustas tú,
me ___gusta___ viajar,
me gustas tú,
me gusta la mañana,
me gustas tú. ”

aviones *airplanes*

Section Goals

In **Lectura**, students will:
• learn to use text formats to predict content
• read documents in Spanish

Instructional Resource
Supersite

Estrategia Introduce the strategy. Point out that many documents have easily identifiable formats that can help readers predict content. Have students look at the document in the **Estrategia** box, and ask them to name the recognizable elements: (days of the week, time, classes). Ask what kind of document it is (a student's weekly schedule).

Cognados Have pairs of students scan **¡Español en Madrid!** and identify cognates and guess their meanings.

Examinar el texto Ask students what type of information is contained in **¡Español en Madrid!** (It is a brochure for an intensive Spanish-language summer program.) Discuss elements of the recognizable format that helped them predict the content, such as the headings, the lists of courses, and the course schedule with dates.

Lectura

Antes de leer

Estrategia
Predicting content through formats

Recognizing the format of a document can help you to predict its content. For instance, invitations, greeting cards, and classified ads follow an easily identifiable format, which usually gives you a general idea of the information they contain. Look at the text and identify it based on its format.

	lunes	martes	miércoles	jueves	viernes
8:30	biología		biología		biología
9:00		historia		historia	
9:30	inglés		inglés		inglés
10:00					
10:30					
11:00					
12:00					
12:30					
1:00					
2:00	arte		arte		arte

If you guessed that this is a page from a student's schedule, you are correct. You can now infer that the document contains information about a student's weekly schedule, including days, times, and activities.

Cognados

Make a list of the cognates in the text and guess their English meanings. What do cognates reveal about the content of the document?

Examinar el texto

Look at the format of the document entitled **¡Español en Madrid!** What type of text is it? What information do you expect to find in this type of document?

More activities

vhlcentral

Online activities

¡ESPAÑOL EN MADRID!

UAE

Programa de Cursos Intensivos de Español
Universidad Autónoma de España

Después de leer

Correspondencias

Provide the letter of each item in Column B that matches the words in Column A.

 A   **B**

1. profesores f
2. vivienda h
3. Madrid d
4. número de teléfono a
5. Español 2B c
6. número de fax g

a. (34) 91 523 4500
b. (34) 91 524 0210
c. 23 junio–30 julio
d. capital cultural de Europa
e. 16 junio–22 julio
f. especializados en enseñar español como lengua extranjera
g. (34) 91 523 4623
h. familias españolas

TEACHING OPTIONS

Extra Practice For homework, ask students to write a weekly schedule (**horario semanal**) of a friend or family member. Ask them to label the days of the week in Spanish and add notes for that person's appointments and activities as well. In class, ask students questions about the schedules they wrote.
Ex: **¿Qué clase toma _____ hoy? ¿Trabaja _____ manaña?**
¿Cuántos días trabaja _____ esta semana?

Heritage Speakers Ask heritage speakers who have attended a school in the Spanish-speaking world to describe their schedule there, comparing and contrasting it with their schedule now. Invite them to make other comparisons between U.S. or Canadian institutions and those in the Spanish-speaking world.

Universidad Autónoma de España

Madrid, la capital cultural de Europa, y la UAE te ofrecen cursos intensivos de verano° para aprender° español como nunca antes°.

¿Dónde?
En el campus de la UAE, edificio° de la Facultad de Filosofía y Letras.

¿Quiénes son los profesores?
Son todos hablantes nativos del español y catedráticos° de la UAE especializados en enseñar el español como lengua extranjera.

¿Qué niveles se ofrecen?
Se ofrecen tres niveles° básicos:
1. Español Elemental, A, B y C
2. Español Intermedio, A y B
3. Español Avanzado, A y B

Viviendas
Para estudiantes extranjeros se ofrece vivienda° con familias españolas.

¿Cuándo?
Este verano desde° el 16 de junio hasta el 10 de agosto. Los cursos tienen una duración de 6 semanas.

Cursos	Empieza°	Termina
Español 1A	16 junio	22 julio
Español 1B	23 junio	30 julio
Español 1C	30 junio	10 agosto
Español 2A	16 junio	22 julio
Español 2B	23 junio	30 julio
Español 3A	16 junio	22 julio
Español 3B	23 junio	30 julio

Información
Para mayor información, sirvan comunicarse con la siguiente° oficina:

Universidad Autónoma de España
Programa de Español como Lengua Extranjera
Calle del Valle de Mena 95, 28039 Madrid, España
Tel. (34) 91 523 4500, **Fax** (34) 91 523 4623
www.uae.es

verano *summer* aprender *to learn* nunca antes *never before* edificio *building* catedráticos *professors* niveles *levels* vivienda *housing* desde *from* Empieza *Begins* siguiente *following*

¿Cierto o falso?
Indicate whether each statement is **cierto** or **falso**. Then correct the false statements.

	Cierto	Falso
1. La Universidad Autónoma de España ofrece (*offers*) cursos intensivos de italiano. Ofrece cursos intensivos de español.	○	⊘
2. La lengua nativa de los profesores del programa es el inglés. La lengua nativa de los profesores es el español.	○	⊘
3. Los cursos de español son en la Facultad de Ciencias. Son en el edificio de la Facultad de Filosofía y Letras.	○	⊘
4. Los estudiantes pueden vivir (*can live*) con familias españolas.	⊘	○

	Cierto	Falso
5. La universidad que ofrece los cursos intensivos está en Salamanca. Está en Madrid.	○	⊘
6. Español 3B termina en agosto. Termina en julio.	○	⊘
7. Si deseas información sobre (*about*) los cursos intensivos de español, es posible llamar al (34) 91 523 4500.	⊘	○
8. Español 1A empieza en julio. Empieza en junio.	○	⊘

TEACHING OPTIONS

Language Notes Explain that in Spanish dates are usually written in the order of day/month/year rather than month/day/year, as they are in the United States and Canada. Someone from Mexico with a birthdate of July 5, 1998, would write his or her birthdate as 5/7/98.

Pairs Provide pairs of students with Spanish-language magazines and newspapers. Ask them to look for documents with easily recognizable formats, such as classified ads or advertisements. Ask them to use cognates and other context clues to predict the content. Then have partners present their examples and findings to the class.

Escritura

Estrategia
Brainstorming

How do you find ideas to write about? In the early stages of writing, brainstorming can help you generate ideas on a specific topic. You should spend ten to fifteen minutes brainstorming and jotting down any ideas about the topic. Whenever possible, try to write your ideas in Spanish. Express your ideas in single words or phrases, and jot them down in any order. While brainstorming, don't worry about whether your ideas are good or bad. Selecting and organizing ideas should be the second stage of your writing. Remember that the more ideas you write down while you're brainstorming, the more options you'll have to choose from later when you start to organize your ideas.

Me gusta
- bailar
- viajar
- mirar la televisión
- la clase de español
- la clase de psicología

No me gusta
- cantar
- dibujar
- trabajar
- la clase de química
- la clase de biología

Tema
Una descripción

Write a description of yourself to post in a chat room on a website in order to meet Spanish-speaking people. Include this information in your description:

- your name and where you are from, and a photo (optional) of yourself
- your major and where you go to school
- the courses you are taking
- where you work (if you have a job)
- some of your likes and dislikes

ON   **inicio**   **perfil**

Hola! Me llamo Alicia Roberts. Estudio matemáticas en la Universidad de Toronto.

EVALUATION: Descripción

Criteria	Scale
Content	1 2 3 4 5
Organization	1 2 3 4 5
Use of vocabulary	1 2 3 4 5
Grammatical accuracy	1 2 3 4 5

Scoring	
Excellent	18–20 points
Good	14–17 points
Satisfactory	10–13 points
Unsatisfactory	< 10 points

Escuchar

Antes de escuchar

Estrategia

Listening for cognates

You already know that cognates are words that have similar spellings and meanings in two or more languages: for example, *group* and **grupo** or *stereo* and **estéreo**. Listen for cognates to increase your comprehension of spoken Spanish.

 To help you practice this strategy, you will now listen to two sentences. Make a list of all the cognates you hear.

Preparación

Based on the photograph, who do you think Armando and Julia are? What do you think they are talking about? *Answers will vary.*

Ahora escucha

Armando y Julia

Now you are going to hear Armando and Julia's conversation. Make a list of the cognates they use.

Armando	Julia
clases, biología	semestre, astronomía
antropología, filosofía	geología, italiano
japonés, italiano	cálculo, clase
cálculo, profesora	profesora

Based on your knowledge of cognates, decide whether the following statements are **cierto** or **falso**.

	Cierto	Falso
1. Armando y Julia hablan de la familia.	○	◉
2. Armando y Julia toman una clase de matemáticas.	◉	○
3. Julia toma clases de ciencias.	◉	○
4. Armando estudia lenguas extranjeras.	◉	○
5. Julia toma una clase de religión.	○	◉

democracia
gobierno
gustar
concierto
obra
danza

Comprensión

Seleccionar

Choose the answer that best completes each sentence.

1. Armando toma ____b____ clases en la universidad.
   a. cuatro   b. cinco   c. seis
2. Julia toma dos clases de ____c____.
   a. matemáticas   b. lengua   c. ciencias
3. Armando toma italiano y ____b____.
   a. astronomía   b. japonés   c. geología
4. Armando y Julia estudian ____c____ los martes y jueves.
   a. filosofía   b. antropología   c. italiano

Preguntas

Answer the questions.

1. ¿Qué clases toma Armando?
   Toma antropología, filosofía, japonés, italiano y cálculo.

2. ¿Qué clases toma Julia?
   Toma astronomía, geología, italiano y cálculo.

Preguntas personales   *Answers will vary.*

1. ¿Cuántas clases tomas tú este semestre?
2. ¿Qué clases tomas este semestre?
3. ¿Qué clases te gustan y qué clases no te gustan?

Section Goals

In **Escuchar**, students will:
• listen for cognates in a short paragraph
• answer questions based on the content of a recorded conversation

Instructional Resources
Supersite: Audio (Textbook MP3s); Resources (Scripts)

Estrategia
Script 1. La democracia es una forma de gobierno. 2. A mí me gustan los conciertos, las obras de teatro y la danza.

Teaching Tip
Invite students to look at the photo and describe what they see. Guide them to guess where they think **Julia** and **Armando** are and what they are talking about.

Ahora escucha
Script ARMANDO: ¡Hola, Julia! ¿Cómo estás?
JULIA: Bien. ¿Y tú, Armando?
A: Bien, gracias. ¿Qué tal tus clases?
J: Van bien.
A: ¿Tomas biología?
J: Este semestre no. Pero sí tomo astronomía y geología… los lunes, miércoles y viernes.
A: ¿Sólo dos? ¿Qué otras clases tomas?
J: Italiano y cálculo, los martes y jueves. ¿Y tú?
A: Los lunes, miércoles y viernes tomo antropología, filosofía y japonés. Los martes y jueves tomo italiano y cálculo.
J: ¿A qué hora es tu clase de italiano?
A: A las nueve, con la profesora Menotti.
J: Yo también tomo italiano los martes y jueves con la profesora Menotti, pero a las once.

En pantalla Video

Christmas isn't always in winter. During the months of cold weather and snow in North America, the southern hemisphere enjoys warm weather and longer days. Since Chile's summer lasts from December to February, school vacation coincides with these months. In Chile, the school year starts in early March and finishes toward the end of December.

Vocabulario útil

quería	*I wanted*
pedirte	*to ask you*
te preocupa	*it worries you*
ahorrar	*to save (money)*
Navidad	*Christmas*
aprovecha	*take advantage of*
nuestras	*our*
ofertas	*offers, deals*
calidad	*quality*
no cuesta	*doesn't cost*

Preparación

Think about occasions when you normally receive gifts. How do you let your family and friends know what you want? Do you usually get what you want?

¿Qué hay?

For each item, write **sí** if it appears in the TV clip or **no** if it does not.

- <u>no</u> 1. papelera
- <u>sí</u> 2. lápiz
- <u>sí</u> 3. mesa
- <u>no</u> 4. computadora
- <u>no</u> 5. diccionario
- <u>sí</u> 6. cuaderno
- <u>no</u> 7. tiza
- <u>sí</u> 8. ventana

¿Qué quieres?

Write a list of things that you want for your next birthday. Then read it to the class so they know what to get you. Use as much Spanish as you can. Answers will vary.

Lista de cumpleaños°
Quiero°...

cumpleaños *birthday* Quiero *I want* Viejito Pascuero *Santa Claus (Chile)*

Anuncio de Jumbo

Viejito Pascuero°...

¿Cómo se escribe *mountain bike*?

M... O...

More activities
vhlcentral / Online activities

NATIONAL STANDARDS / communication cultures

Video

Mexican author and diplomat Octavio Paz (March 31, 1914–April 19, 1998) studied both law and literature at the **Universidad Nacional Autónoma de México** (**UNAM**), but after graduating he immersed himself in the art of writing. An incredibly prolific writer of poetry and essays, Paz solidified his prestige as Mexico's preeminent author with his 1950 book ***El laberinto de la soledad***, a fundamental study of Mexican identity. Among the many awards he received in his lifetime are the **Premio Miguel de Cervantes** (1981) and Nobel Prize for Literature (1990). Paz foremost considered himself a poet and affirmed that poetry constitutes "**la religión secreta de la edad° moderna**".

Vocabulario útil

¿Cuál es tu materia favorita?	*What is your favorite subject?*
¿Cuántos años tienes?	*How old are you?*
¿Qué estudias?	*What do you study?*
el/la alumno/a	*student*
la carrera (de medicina)	*(medical) degree program, major*
derecho	*law*
reconocido	*well-known*

Preparación

What is the name of your school or university? What degree program are you in? What classes are you taking this semester? *Answers will vary.*

Emparejar

Match the first part of the sentence with the appropriate ending.

1. En la UNAM no hay **c**
2. México, D.F. es **d**
3. La UNAM es **a**
4. La UNAM ofrece **b**

   a. una universidad muy grande.
   b. 74 carreras de estudio.
   c. residencias estudiantiles.
   d. la ciudad más grande (*biggest*) de Hispanoamérica.

edad age   *¿Conoces a algún...? Do you know any...?*   *que dé that teaches*

Los estudios

—¿Qué estudias?
—Ciencias de la comunicación.

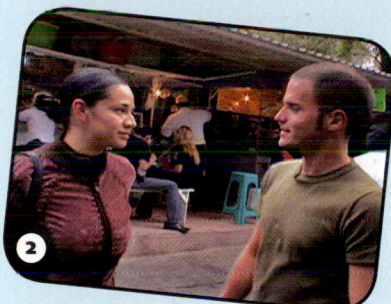

Estudio derecho en la UNAM.

¿Conoces a algún° profesor famoso que dé° clases... en la UNAM?

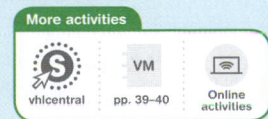

More activities

vhlcentral   VM pp. 39–40   Online activities

Section Goals

In **Flash cultura**, students will:
• read about **Octavio Paz**
• watch a video about the **Universidad Nacional Autónoma de México (UNAM)**

Instructional Resources
Supersite: Video (*Flash cultura*); Resources (Scripts, Translations, Answer Keys)
WebSAM
Video Manual

Introduction Ask students these comprehension questions: 1. Where and what did Octavio Paz study? 2. What is *El laberinto de la soledad* and what does it deal with? 3. What type of literature did Paz prefer, and why?

Antes de ver

• Read through the **Vocabulario útil** with students. Explain that **¿Qué (carrera) estudias?** is a common way of asking someone's major (**especialización**). Also explain that **tienes** means *you have* and **tener... años** means *to be... years old*.

• Assure students that they do not need to understand every Spanish word they hear in the video. Tell them to rely on visual cues and to listen for cognates and words from **Vocabulario útil**.

Preparación

👤↔👤 Have students write down the answers in Spanish using complete sentences. Then, using words and phrases from **Vocabulario útil** and **Contextos**, have them interview a partner. Ask a few volunteers to report their findings.

Emparejar After completing the activity, ask students to share their impressions of the **UNAM**. Have them name some advantages and disadvantages of studying at such a large university.

TEACHING OPTIONS

Extra Practice Tell students to imagine that their family is moving to Mexico City and they will be transfer students at the **UNAM**. Have them research their major at the **UNAM** and write about the department, requirements, length of the program, etc. Then have them compare this information to their experience at their own university and share the differences with the class.
Extra Practice Ask students to research one of the alumni mentioned in the video (other than Octavio Paz) and prepare a brief report. If possible, have them bring in a photo of the person. Have a few volunteers present their reports to the class. After each presentation, have the presenter play the role of the famous person. Encourage the class to ask the student questions about his or her likes, dislikes, and activities. Ex: **¿Trabajas en un laboratorio? ¿Te gustan las ciencias?**

Section Goal

In **Panorama**, students will read about the geography, culture, and economy of Spain.

Instructional Resources
Supersite: Video (*Panorama cultural*); Resources (Scripts, Translations, Digital Image Bank, Answer Keys)
WebSAM
Workbook

Teaching Tips
• Have students use the map in their books to find the places mentioned. Explain that the Canary Islands are located in the Atlantic Ocean, off the northwestern coast of Africa. Point out the photos that accompany the map on this page.
• Use the **Lección 2** digital images to assist with this presentation.

El país en cifras After students have read **Idiomas**, associate the regional languages with the larger map by asking questions. Ex: **¿Hablan catalán en Barcelona?** (sí) **¿Qué idioma hablan en Madrid?** (español) Point out that the names of languages may be capitalized as map labels, but are not capitalized when they appear in running text.

España

NATIONAL connections cultures STANDARDS

El país en cifras

▶ **Área:** 505.370 km² (kilómetros cuadrados) o 195.124 millas cuadradas°, incluyendo las islas Baleares y las islas Canarias
▶ **Población:** 48.958.000
▶ **Capital:** Madrid—6.199.000
▶ **Ciudades° principales:** Barcelona—5.258.000, Valencia—810.000, Sevilla, Zaragoza
▶ **Moneda°:** euro
▶ **Idiomas°:** español o castellano, catalán, gallego, valenciano, euskera

Regiones lingüísticas

Bandera de España

Españoles célebres
▶ **Miguel de Cervantes,** escritor° (1547–1616)
▶ **Pedro Almodóvar,** director de cine° (1949–)
▶ **Rosa Montero,** escritora y periodista° (1951–)
▶ **Fernando Alonso,** corredor de autos° (1981–)
▶ **Paz Vega,** actriz° (1976–)
▶ **Severo Ochoa,** Premio Nobel de Medicina, 1959; doctor y científico (1905–1993)

millas cuadradas *square miles* Ciudades *Cities* Moneda *Currency*
Idiomas *Languages* escritor *writer* cine *film* periodista *reporter*
corredor de autos *race car driver* actriz *actress*

Plaza Mayor en Madrid

La Sagrada Familia en Barcelona

La costa de Ibiza
El baile flamenco
Islas Canarias
La Palma · Tenerife · Gran Canaria · Lanzarote · Gomera · Hierro

More activities
vhlcentral · WB pp. 21–22 · Online activities

ACTIVIDADES

3 **Escoger** Elige las respuestas correctas.

1. ¿Qué celebran las personas cada año en Buñol, Valencia? **b**
   a. el día de la lengua española   b. el festival de *La Tomatina*

2. ¿Quién es Rosa Montero? **b**
   a. una actriz   b. una escritora

3. ¿Cuál es la moneda de España? **b**
   a. el peso   b. el euro

4. ¿Cuáles son algunas de las ciudades más importantes de España? **a**
   a. Barcelona y Valencia   b. Barcelona y La Coruña

5. ¿Quién es el pintor de *Las meninas*? **b**
   a. El Greco   b. Velázquez

6. ¿Quién es un pintor español famoso? **a**
   a. Goya   b. Andrés

TEACHING OPTIONS

Heritage Speakers **Paella,** the national dish of Spain, is the ancestor of the popular Latin American dish **arroz con pollo**. Ask heritage speakers if they know of any traditional dishes in their families that have their roots in Spanish cuisine. Invite them to describe the dish(es) to the class.

Variación léxica Tell students that they may also see the word **euskera** spelled **euskara** and **eusquera**. The letter **k** is used in Spanish only in words of foreign origin. **Euskara** is the Basque name of the Basque language, which linguists believe is unrelated to any other known language. The Spanish name for *Basque* is **vascuence** or **vasco**.

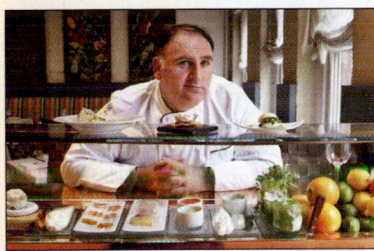

Gastronomía • José Andrés

José Andrés es un chef español famoso internacionalmente°. Le gusta combinar platos° tradicionales de España con las técnicas de cocina más innovadoras°. Andrés vive° en Washington, DC, y es dueño° de varios restaurantes en los EE.UU. En 2012 la revista° *Time* lo incluyó° en su lista de las "100 personas más influyentes° del mundo". También° ha estado° en el programa *Top Chef*.

Cultura • La diversidad

La riqueza° cultural y lingüística de España refleja la combinación de las diversas culturas que han habitado° en su territorio durante siglos°. El español es la lengua oficial del país, pero también son oficiales el catalán, el gallego, el euskera y el valenciano.

Póster en catalán

> Sóc molt fan de la pàgina 335.
>
> Ajuntament de Barcelona

Artes • Velázquez y el Prado

El Prado, en Madrid, es uno de los museos más famosos del mundo°. En el Prado hay pinturas° importantes de Botticelli, de El Greco y de los españoles Goya y Velázquez. *Las meninas* es la obra° más conocida° de Diego Velázquez, pintor° oficial de la corte real° durante el siglo° XVII.

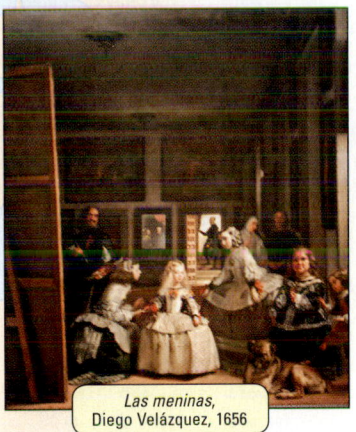

Las meninas, Diego Velázquez, 1656

Comida • La paella

La paella es uno de los platos más típicos de España. Siempre se prepara° con arroz° y azafrán°, pero hay diferentes recetas°. La paella valenciana, por ejemplo, es de pollo° y conejo°, y la paella marinera es de mariscos°.

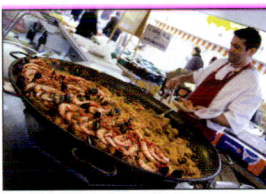

internacionalmente *internationally* platos *dishes* más innovadoras *most innovative* vive *lives* dueño *owner* revista *magazine* lo incluyó *included him*
influyentes *influential* También *Also* ha estado *has been* riqueza *richness* han habitado *have lived* durante siglos *for centuries* mundo *world* pinturas *paintings*
obra *work* más conocida *best-known* pintor *painter* corte real *royal court* siglo *century* Siempre se prepara *It is always prepared* arroz *rice* azafrán *saffron*
recetas *recipes* pollo *chicken* conejo *rabbit* mariscos *seafood*

¡Increíble pero cierto!

En Buñol, un pueblo° de Valencia, la producción de tomates es un recurso económico muy importante. Cada año° se celebra el festival de *La Tomatina*. Durante todo un día°, miles de personas se tiran° tomates. Llegan turistas de todo el país, y se usan varias toneladas° de tomates.

pueblo *town* Cada año *Every year* Durante todo un día *All day long* se tiran *throw at each other*
varias toneladas *many tons*

---

2 **¿Qué aprendiste?** Completa las oraciones.

1. El chef español ___José Andrés___ es muy famoso.
2. El arroz y el azafrán son ingredientes básicos de la ___paella___.
3. El Prado está en ___Madrid___.
4. José Andrés vive en ___Washington, DC/EE.UU.___
5. El gallego es una de las lenguas oficiales de ___España___.

3 **Preguntas** En parejas, formen y contesten preguntas sobre las personas y los lugares de la sección **Panorama**.

> **modelo**
> **Estudiante 1:** ¿Dónde está el Prado?
> **Estudiante 2:** Está en Madrid.

TEACHING OPTIONS

Variación léxica Regional cultures and languages have remained strong in Spain, despite efforts made in the past to suppress them in the name of national unity. The language that has come to be called *Spanish*, **español,** is the language of the region of north central Spain called **Castilla.** Because Spain was unified under the Kingdom of Castile at the end of the Middle Ages, the language of Castile, **castellano**, became the principal language of government, business, and literature. Even today one is likely to hear Spanish speakers refer to Spanish as **castellano** or **español.** Efforts to suppress the regional languages, though often harsh, were ineffective, and after the death of the dictator **Francisco Franco** and the return of power to regional governing bodies, the regional languages of Spain were given co-official status.

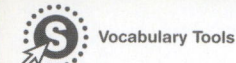
Instructional Resources

Supersite: Audio (Textbook & Lab MP3s); Testing Program (Tests, MP3s)

WebSAM

Lab Manual

Teaching Tip You may want to assign the **Prueba de práctica**, with its diagnostics and review activities, in the online-only **Repaso** section on the Supersite. There is also a **Repaso oral** in this section. For the Sixth Edition, a new summative vocabulary activity with speech recognition has been added to the **Repaso** section.

La clase y la universidad

el/la compañero/a de clase	classmate
el/la compañero/a de cuarto	roommate
el/la estudiante	student
el/la profesor(a)	teacher
el borrador	eraser
la calculadora	calculator
el escritorio	desk
el libro	book
el mapa	map
el marcador	marker
la mesa	table
la mochila	backpack
el papel	paper
la papelera	wastebasket
la pizarra	whiteboard
la pluma	pen
la puerta	door
el reloj	clock; watch
la silla	seat
la ventana	window
la biblioteca	library
la cafetería	cafeteria
la casa	house; home
el estadio	stadium
el laboratorio	laboratory
la librería	bookstore
la residencia estudiantil	dormitory
la universidad	university; college
la clase	class
el curso, la materia	course
la especialización	major
el examen	test; exam
el horario	schedule
la prueba	test; quiz
el semestre	semester
la tarea	homework
el trimestre	trimester; quarter

Las materias

la administración de empresas	business administration
la arqueología	archeology
el arte	art
la biología	biology
las ciencias	sciences
la computación	computer science
la contabilidad	accounting
la economía	economics
el español	Spanish
la física	physics
la geografía	geography
la historia	history
las humanidades	humanities
el inglés	English
las lenguas extranjeras	foreign languages
la literatura	literature
las matemáticas	mathematics
la música	music
el periodismo	journalism
la psicología	psychology
la química	chemistry
la sociología	sociology

Preposiciones y adverbios

al lado de	next to
a la derecha de	to the right of
a la izquierda de	to the left of
allá	over there
allí	there
cerca de	near
con	with
debajo de	below
delante de	in front of
detrás de	behind
en	in; on
encima de	on top of
entre	between
lejos de	far from
sin	without
sobre	on; over

Palabras adicionales

¿Adónde?	Where (to)?
ahora	now
¿Cuál?, ¿Cuáles?	Which?; Which one(s)?
¿Por qué?	Why?
porque	because

Verbos

bailar	to dance
buscar	to look for
caminar	to walk
cantar	to sing
cenar	to have dinner
comprar	to buy
contestar	to answer
conversar	to converse, to chat
desayunar	to have breakfast
descansar	to rest
desear	to wish; to desire
dibujar	to draw
enseñar	to teach
escuchar la radio/ música	to listen (to) the radio/music
esperar (+ *inf.*)	to wait (for); to hope
estar	to be
estudiar	to study
explicar	to explain
gustar	to like
hablar	to talk; to speak
llegar	to arrive
llevar	to carry
mirar	to look (at); to watch
necesitar (+ *inf.*)	to need
practicar	to practice
preguntar	to ask (a question)
preparar	to prepare
regresar	to return
terminar	to end; to finish
tomar	to take; to drink
trabajar	to work
viajar	to travel

Los días de la semana

¿Cuándo?	When?
¿Qué día es hoy?	What day is it?
Hoy es…	Today is…
la semana	week
lunes	Monday
martes	Tuesday
miércoles	Wednesday
jueves	Thursday
viernes	Friday
sábado	Saturday
domingo	Sunday

Numbers 31 and higher	See pages 63–64.
Expresiones útiles	See page 45.

More activities

vhlcentral

LM p. 12

La familia

3

Communicative Goals

You will learn how to:
- Talk about your family and friends
- Describe people and things
- Express possession

A PRIMERA VISTA
- ¿Cuántos chicos hay en la foto?
- ¿Hay una mujer detrás de la chica? ¿Y a la izquierda?
- ¿Hay una cosa en la mano del chico?
- ¿Conversan ellos? ¿Trabajan? ¿Descansan?
- ¿Están en su casa?

Lesson Goals

In **Lección 3**, students will be introduced to the following:
- terms for family relationships
- names of various professions
- surnames and families in the Spanish-speaking world
- talented families in the Spanish-speaking world
- descriptive adjectives
- possessive adjectives
- the present tense of common regular –er and –ir verbs
- the present tense of **tener** and **venir**
- context clues to unlock meaning of unfamiliar words
- using idea maps when writing
- how to write a friendly letter
- strategies for asking clarification in oral communication
- a television commercial for **Banco Galicia**, an Argentinian bank
- a video about two Ecuadorian families
- geographical and cultural information about Ecuador

A primera vista Here are some additional questions you can ask to personalize the photo: **¿Cuántas personas hay en tu familia? ¿De qué conversas con ellos? ¿Estudias lejos o cerca de la casa de tu familia? ¿Viajas mucho con ellos?**

Teaching Tip Look for these icons for additional communicative practice:

→👤←	Interpretive communication
←👤→	Presentational communication
👤↔👤	Interpersonal communication

INSTRUCTIONAL RESOURCES

Supersite (vhlcentral.com)
Video: *Fotonovela, Flash cultura, En pantalla, Panorama cultural*
Audio: Textbook and Lab MP3 Files

Activity Pack: Information Gap Activities, games, additional activity handouts
Resources: SAM Answer Key, Scripts, Translations, **Vocabulario adicional**, sample lesson plan, Grammar Presentation Slides, Digital Image Bank

Testing Program: Quizzes, Tests, Exams, MP3s, Oral Testing Suggestions
Student Activities Manual: Workbook/Video Manual/Lab Manual
WebSAM (online Student Activities Manual)

La familia

Más vocabulario

los abuelos	grandparents
el/la bisabuelo/a	great-grandfather/ great-grandmother
el/la gemelo/a	twin
el/la hermanastro/a	stepbrother/stepsister
el/la hijastro/a	stepson/stepdaughter
la madrastra	stepmother
el medio hermano/ la media hermana	half-brother/ half-sister
el padrastro	stepfather
los padres	parents
los parientes	relatives
el/la cuñado/a	brother-in-law/ sister-in-law
la nuera	daughter-in-law
el/la suegro/a	father-in-law/ mother-in-law
el yerno	son-in-law
el/la amigo/a	friend
el apellido	last name
la gente	people
el/la muchacho/a	boy/girl
el/la niño/a	child
el/la novio/a	boyfriend/girlfriend
la persona	person
el/la artista	artist
el/la ingeniero/a	engineer
el/la doctor(a), el/la médico/a	doctor; physician
el/la periodista	journalist
el/la programador(a)	computer programmer

Variación léxica

madre ⟷ mamá, mami (*colloquial*)
padre ⟷ papá, papi (*colloquial*)
muchacho/a ⟷ chico/a

More activities

vhlcentral | LM p. 13 | WB pp. 23–24 | Online activities

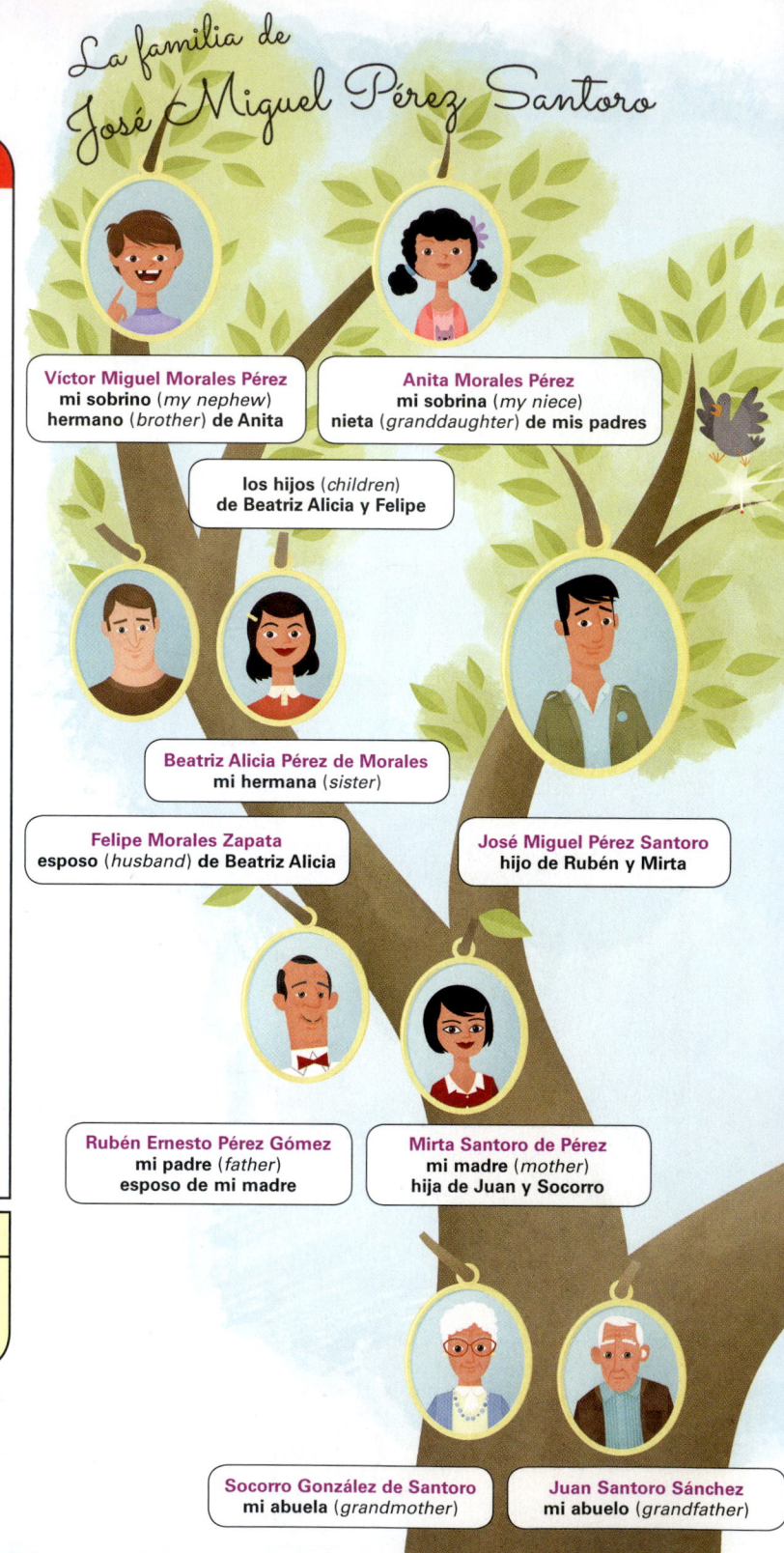

La familia de José Miguel Pérez Santoro

Víctor Miguel Morales Pérez
mi sobrino (*my nephew*) hermano (*brother*) **de Anita**

Anita Morales Pérez
mi sobrina (*my niece*) nieta (*granddaughter*) **de mis padres**

los hijos (*children*) de Beatriz Alicia y Felipe

Beatriz Alicia Pérez de Morales
mi hermana (*sister*)

José Miguel Pérez Santoro
hijo de Rubén y Mirta

Felipe Morales Zapata
esposo (*husband*) **de Beatriz Alicia**

Rubén Ernesto Pérez Gómez
mi padre (*father*) esposo de mi madre

Mirta Santoro de Pérez
mi madre (*mother*) hija de Juan y Socorro

Socorro González de Santoro
mi abuela (*grandmother*)

Juan Santoro Sánchez
mi abuelo (*grandfather*)

Práctica

Héctor Manuel Santoro Gutiérrez
mi primo (*cousin*)
nieto (*grandson*) **de Juan y Socorro**

Carmen Santoro Gutiérrez
mi prima
hija de Ernesto y Marina

Silvia Socorro Santoro Gutiérrez
mi prima (*cousin*)
hija (*daughter*) **de Ernesto y Marina**

Marina Gutiérrez de Santoro
mi tía (*aunt*)
esposa (*wife*) **de Ernesto**

Ernesto Santoro González
mi tío (*uncle*)
hijo (*son*) **de Juan y Socorro**

¡LENGUA VIVA!

In Spanish-speaking countries, it is common for people to go by both their first name and middle name, such as **José Miguel** or **Juan Carlos**. You will learn more about names and naming conventions on p. 86.

1 **Indicar** Write **sí** if the word you hear indicates a family member or **no** if it does not.

1. ___sí___
2. ___no___
3. ___no___
4. ___sí___
5. ___sí___
6. ___no___
7. ___no___
8. ___sí___

2 **Escuchar** Indicate whether each statement you hear made by José Miguel Pérez Santoro is **cierto** or **falso**, based on his family tree.

	Cierto	Falso		Cierto	Falso
1.	●	○	5.	○	●
2.	●	○	6.	●	○
3.	○	●	7.	●	○
4.	●	○	8.	○	●

3 **Emparejar** Match the phrase to the description.

1. Mi hermano programa las computadoras. **c**
2. Son los padres de mi esposo. **e**
3. Es el hijo de mi hermana. **k**
4. Mi tía trabaja en un hospital. **a**
5. Es el hijo de mi madrastra y el hijastro de mi padre. **b**
6. Son los hijos de mis (*my*) tíos. **h**
7. Mi hermanastra enseña en la universidad. **j**
8. Mi primo dibuja y pinta mucho. **i**
9. Es el esposo de mi hija. **l**
10. Mi padre trabaja con planos (*blueprints*). **d**

a. Es médica.
b. Es mi hermanastro.
c. Es programador.
d. Es ingeniero.
e. Son mis suegros.
f. Es mi novio.
g. Es mi padrastro.
h. Son mis primos.
i. Es artista.
j. Es profesora.
k. Es mi sobrino.
l. Es mi yerno.

4 **Oraciones** Complete each sentence.

abuelo	cuñado	madrastra	nuera
apellidos	gemelas	novia	tío

1. Mi ___nuera___ es la esposa de mi hijo.
2. Las muchachas son idénticas porque son ___gemelas___.
3. El esposo de mi hermana es mi ___cuñado___.
4. La periodista usa dos ___apellidos___: Norma *Pardo Alonso*.
5. Es la esposa de mi padre, pero no es mi madre; es mi ___madrastra___.
6. El padre de mi madre es mi ___abuelo___.

TEACHING OPTIONS

TPR Make a "living" family tree. Assign students different roles as family members and have students write down the term assigned to them on a sheet of paper. Arrange students as in a family tree and ask questions about relationships. Ex: **¿Quién es la madre de ____? ¿Cómo se llama el tío de ____?**

Game Have students state the relationship between people on **José Miguel's** family tree; have their classmates guess which person they are describing. Ex: **Es la hermana de Ernesto y su padre es Juan. (Mirta) Héctor Manuel es su hermano y Beatriz Alicia es su prima. (Carmen o Silvia)** Take turns until each member of the class or group has stated a relationship.

5 Escoger Complete the description of each photo.
Some answers will vary. Possible answers:

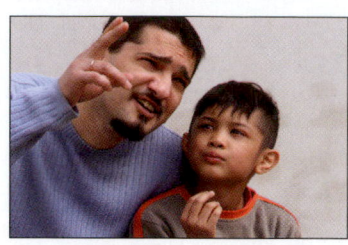

1. La ___familia___ de Sara es grande. 2. Rubén habla con su ___hijo/padre___.

3. Maira Díaz es ___periodista___. 4. Héctor y Lupita son ___novios___.

5. Irene es ___ingeniera___. 6. Elena Vargas Soto es ___artista___.

6 Definiciones Define these family terms. Some answers may vary.

modelo
hijastro *Es el hijo de mi esposo/a, pero no es mi hijo.*

1. abuela 5. tío
2. cuñado 6. bisabuelo
3. suegra 7. nietos
4. primas 8. medio hermano

1. la madre de mi madre/padre 5. el hermano de mi madre/padre
2. el esposo de mi hermana 6. el abuelo de mi madre/padre
3. la madre de mi esposo/a 7. los hijos de mis hijos
4. las hijas de mis tíos/as 8. el hijo de mi padre pero no de mi madre

Comunicación

7 **Una familia** With a classmate, ask each other questions about how each family member is related to Graciela Vargas García.

modelo

Estudiante 1: ¿Quién es Beatriz Pardo de Vargas?
Estudiante 2: Es la abuela de Graciela.

CONSULTA

To see the cities where these family members live, look at the map in **Panorama** on p. 112.

David Vargas Olmedo — de Quito — abuelo
Beatriz Pardo de Vargas — de Ibarra — abuela
Carlos Antonio López Ríos — de Cuenca — tío
Lupe Vargas de López — de Quito — tía
Juan Vargas Pardo — de Quito — padre
María Susana García de Vargas — de Guayaquil — madre
Ernesto López Vargas — de Loja — primo
Ramón Vargas García — de Machala — hermano
Graciela Vargas García — de Machala

Now take turns asking each other these questions. Then invent three original questions.

1. ¿Cómo se llama el primo de Graciela? Se llama Ernesto López Vargas.
2. ¿Cómo se llama la hija de David y de Beatriz? Se llama Lupe Vargas de López.
3. ¿De dónde es María Susana? Es de Guayaquil.
4. ¿De dónde son Ramón y Graciela? Son de Machala.
5. ¿Cómo se llama el yerno de David y de Beatriz? Se llama Carlos Antonio López Ríos.
6. ¿De dónde es Carlos Antonio? Es de Cuenca.
7. ¿De dónde es Ernesto? Es de Loja.
8. ¿Cuáles son los apellidos del sobrino de Lupe? Son Vargas García.

8 **Preguntas personales** With a classmate, take turns asking each other these questions.

Answers will vary.

1. ¿Cuántas personas hay en tu familia?
2. ¿Cómo se llaman tus padres? ¿De dónde son? ¿Dónde trabajan?
3. ¿Cuántos hermanos tienes? ¿Cómo se llaman? ¿Dónde estudian o trabajan?
4. ¿Cuántos primos tienes? ¿Cuáles son los apellidos de ellos? ¿Cuántos son niños y cuántos son adultos? ¿Hay más chicos o más chicas en tu familia?
5. ¿Eres tío/a? ¿Cómo se llaman tus sobrinos/as? ¿Dónde estudian o trabajan?
6. ¿Quién es tu pariente favorito?
7. ¿Tienes novio/a? ¿Tienes esposo/a? ¿Cómo se llama?

AYUDA

tu, tus *your* (sing., pl.)
mi, mis *my* (sing., pl.)
tienes *you have*
tengo *I have*

---

7 Teaching Tip Remind students that it is common for Spanish speakers to go by two names (like **Carlos Antonio** in this chart). Students will learn about surnames on page 86; however, you may want to preview that information by pointing out how **Graciela** and her brother got their last names.

7 Expansion
- Ask students to write five statements about people in the chart (Ex: **Es la prima de Ernesto; Es una mujer de Quito.**). Then, in pairs, have them take turns reading their statements aloud. The other student should identify the person (**Es Graciela; Es Lupe**).
- Model the pronunciation of the Ecuadorian cities mentioned. Ask students to locate each on the map of Ecuador, page 112. Ask students to talk about each city based on the map. Ex: **Guayaquil y Machala son ciudades de la costa del Pacífico. Quito, Loja y Cuenca son ciudades de la cordillera de los Andes. Quito es la capital de Ecuador.**

8 Teaching Tips
- Tell students to take notes on their partner's responses. When they are finished, ask students questions about their partner's answers.
- As an alternative, first read through the questions as a class. Tell students to select a partner that they have not worked with before. Individually, have them jot down guesses to their partner's responses for a few of the questions. Students can write down any other predictions they may have about their partner's family. Then have pairs get together and complete the activity. Survey the class to find out the accuracy of the predictions.

TEACHING OPTIONS

Extra Practice For homework, ask students to draw their own family tree or that of a fictional family. Have them label each position on the tree with the appropriate family term and the name of their family member. In class, ask students questions about their families. Ex: **¿Cómo se llama tu prima? ¿Cómo es ella? ¿Ella es estudiante? ¿Cómo se llama tu madre? ¿Quién es tu cuñado?**

Pairs Tell students to imagine that they have the opportunity to interview a famous person from a Spanish-speaking country. In pairs, using the questions in **Actividad 8** as a guide, have one student play the role of the famous person and the other student conduct the interview. Have volunteers perform their dialogues for the class to guess the famous person's identity.

Un domingo en familia

Marissa pasa el día en Xochimilco con la familia Díaz.

PERSONAJES

 FELIPE

 TÍA NAYELI

 Video

1

JIMENA Hola, tía Nayeli.

TÍA NAYELI ¡Hola, Jimena! ¿Cómo estás?

JIMENA Bien, gracias. Y, ¿dónde están mis primas?

TÍA NAYELI No sé. ¿Dónde están mis hijas? ¡Ah!

MARISSA ¡Qué bonitas son tus hijas! Y ¡qué simpáticas!

2

MARISSA La verdad, mi familia es pequeña.

SRA. DÍAZ ¿Pequeña? Yo soy hija única. Bueno, y ¿qué más? ¿Tienes novio?

MARISSA No. Tengo mala suerte con los novios.

3

FELIPE Soy guapo y delgado.

JIMENA Ay, ¡por favor! Eres gordo, antipático y muy feo.

5

6

TÍO RAMÓN ¿Tienes una familia grande, Marissa?

MARISSA Tengo dos hermanos mayores, Zack y Jennifer, y un hermano menor, Adam.

4

MARISSA Tía Nayeli, ¿cuántos años tienen tus hijas?

TÍA NAYELI Marta tiene ocho años y Valentina doce.

Section Goals

In **Fotonovela**, students will:
- receive comprehensible input from free-flowing discourse
- learn functional phrases for talking about their families

Instructional Resources

Supersite: Video (*Fotonovela*); Resources (Scripts, Translations, Answer Keys)
WebSAM
Video Manual

Video Recap: Lección 2

Before doing this **Fotonovela** section, review the previous episode with these questions:
1. **¿Quién estudia historia del arte?** (Miguel estudia historia del arte.) 2. **¿Quién toma cuatro clases?** (Marissa toma cuatro clases.) 3. **¿Qué necesita comprar Miguel?** (Necesita comprar unos libros.) 4. **¿Qué enseña el profesor Morales?** (Enseña la clase de química.)

Video Synopsis

The **Díaz** family spends Sunday afternoon in **Xochimilco. Marissa** meets some of the extended family and answers questions about her own family. The group has a picnic and the women take a boat ride through the canals. **Carolina** makes arrangements for **Marissa** and her friends to travel to **Mérida.**

Teaching Tips

- Ask students to read the title, glance at the video stills, and predict what they think the episode will be about.
- 👥↔👥 Work through the **Expresiones útiles** by asking students about their families. React to their responses and ask other students questions about their classmates' answers. Ex: **¿Tienes hermanos?** (Sí, tengo una hermana menor.) Ask another student: **¿Tiene hermanos _____?** (Sí, tiene una hermana menor.)

TEACHING OPTIONS

Video Tips General suggestions for using video clips in the classroom can be found in the front matter of this Instructor's Annotated Edition.

Un domingo en familia →👥← Before viewing the **Un domingo en familia** episode of the **Fotonovela**, ask students to brainstorm a list of what they might see and hear in an episode in which the characters find out about each other's families. Then play the video once without sound and have the class create a plot summary based on visual clues. Next, show the episode with sound and have the class correct any mistaken guesses and fill in any gaps in the plot summary. Ask comprehension questions as a follow-up.

JIMENA   **MARTA**   **VALENTINA**   **SRA. DÍAZ**   **TÍO RAMÓN**   **SR. DÍAZ** **MARISSA**

7

SRA. DÍAZ Chicas, ¿compartimos una trajinera?

MARISSA ¡Claro que sí! ¡Qué bonitas son!

SRA. DÍAZ ¿Vienes, Jimena?

JIMENA No, gracias. Tengo que leer.

8

MARISSA Me gusta mucho este sitio. Tengo ganas de visitar otros lugares en México.

SRA. DÍAZ ¡Debes viajar a Mérida!

TÍA NAYELI ¡Sí, con tus amigos! Debes visitar a Ana María, la hermana de Roberto y de Ramón.

9

(La Sra. Díaz habla por teléfono con la tía Ana María.)

SRA. DÍAZ ¡Qué bien! Excelente. Sí, la próxima semana. Muchísimas gracias.

10

MARISSA ¡Gracias, Sra. Díaz!

SRA. DÍAZ Tía Ana María.

MARISSA Tía Ana María.

SRA. DÍAZ ¡Un beso, chau!

MARISSA *Bye!*

More activities

vhlcentral | VM pp. 5–6 | Online activities

Expresiones útiles

Talking about your family

¿Tienes una familia grande?
Do you have a big family?
Tengo dos hermanos mayores y un hermano menor.
I have two older siblings and a younger brother.
La verdad, mi familia es pequeña.
The truth is, my family is small.
¿Pequeña? Yo soy hija única.
Small? I'm an only child.

Describing people

¡Qué bonitas son tus hijas!
Y ¡qué simpáticas!
Your daughters are so pretty!
And so nice!
Soy guapo y delgado.
I'm handsome and slim.
¡Por favor! Eres gordo, antipático y muy feo.
Please! You're fat, unpleasant, and very ugly.

Talking about plans

¿Compartimos una trajinera?
Shall we share a trajinera?
¡Claro que sí! ¡Qué bonitas son!
Of course! They're so pretty!
¿Vienes, Jimena?
Are you coming, Jimena?
No, gracias. Tengo que leer.
No, thanks. I have to read.

Saying how old people are

¿Cuántos años tienen tus hijas?
How old are your daughters?
Marta tiene ocho años y Valentina doce.
Marta is eight and Valentina twelve.

Additional vocabulary

ensayo *essay*
pobrecito/a *poor thing*
próxima *next*
sitio *place*
todavía *still*
trajinera *type of barge*

¿Qué pasó?

1 ¿Cierto o falso?
Indicate whether each sentence is **cierto** or **falso**. Correct the false statements.

	Cierto	Falso	
1. Marissa dice que (*says that*) tiene una familia grande.	○	☑	Marissa dice que tiene una familia pequeña.
2. La Sra. Díaz tiene dos hermanos.	○	☑	La señora Díaz es hija única.
3. Marissa no tiene novio.	☑	○	
4. Valentina tiene veinte años.	○	☑	Valentina tiene doce años.
5. Marissa comparte una trajinera con la Sra. Díaz y la tía Nayeli.	☑	○	
6. A Marissa le gusta mucho Xochimilco.	☑	○	◄

2 Identificar
Indicate which person says the equivalent of each statement.

1. Felipe es antipático y feo. Jimena
2. Mis hermanos se llaman Jennifer, Adam y Zack. Marissa
3. ¡Soy un joven muy guapo! Felipe
4. Mis hijas tienen ocho y doce años. tía Nayeli
5. Me gusta Xochimilco. Marissa
6. Ana María es la hermana de Ramón y Roberto. tía Nayeli
7. No puedo (*I can't*) compartir una trajinera porque tengo que leer. Jimena
8. Tus hijas son bonitas y simpáticas, tía Nayeli. Marissa

SRA. DÍAZ

JIMENA

MARISSA

FELIPE

TÍA NAYELI

◄

3 Escribir
In pairs, choose Marissa, Sra. Díaz, or tía Nayeli and write a brief description of her family. Be creative! Answers will vary.

MARISSA

Marissa es de los EE.UU. ¿Cómo es su familia?

SRA. DÍAZ

La Sra. Díaz es de Cuba. ¿Cómo es su familia?

TÍA NAYELI

La tía Nayeli es de México. ¿Cómo es su familia?

4 Conversar
With a partner, use these questions to talk about your families. Answers will vary.

1. ¿Cuántos años tienes?
2. ¿Tienes una familia grande?
3. ¿Tienes hermanos o hermanas?
4. ¿Cuántos años tiene tu abuelo (tu hermana, tu primo, etc.)?
5. ¿De dónde son tus padres?

◄

---

1 **Expansion** Give these true/false statements to the class as items 7–10: **7. Jimena dice que Felipe es feo. (Cierto.) 8. Marissa tiene un novio. (Falso. Tiene mala suerte con los novios.) 9. Valentina tiene una hermana menor. (Cierto.) 10. Jimena no comparte la trajinera porque tiene que asistir a clase. (Falso. Tiene que leer.)**

2 **Expansion** **Sra. Díaz** is the only person not associated with a statement. Ask students to look at the **Fotonovela** captions and **Expresiones útiles** on pages 82–83 and invent a statement for her. Remind them not to use her exact words. Ex: **Necesitas viajar a Mérida.**

Nota cultural In the 19th century, the **chinampas** fulfilled agricultural purposes. At that time, **trajineras** were used to transport crops from the islands of **Xochimilco** to markets in Mexico City.

3 **Expansion** Have pairs who wrote about the same family exchange papers and compare their descriptions. Ask them to share the differences with the class.

4 **Teaching Tip** Model the activity by providing answers based on your own family.

4 **Expansion** Ask volunteers to share their partners' answers with the rest of the class.

TEACHING OPTIONS

Extra Practice Ask volunteers to ad-lib the **Fotonovela** episode for the class. Assure them that it is not necessary to memorize the script or stick strictly to its content. They should try to get the general meaning across with the vocabulary and expressions they know, and they also should feel free to be creative. Give students time to prepare.

Small Groups Have groups of three interview each other about their families. Assign one person as the interviewer, one the interviewee, and the third person as the note taker. At three-minute intervals, have students switch roles. When everyone has been interviewed, have students report back to the class.

Pronunciación
 Tutorial
Diphthongs and linking

hermano   **niña**   **cuñado**

In Spanish, **a**, **e**, and **o** are considered strong vowels. The weak vowels are **i** and **u**.

ruido   **parientes**   **periodista**

A diphthong is a combination of two weak vowels or of a strong vowel and a weak vowel. Diphthongs are pronounced as a single syllable.

mi hijo   **una clase excelente**

Two identical vowel sounds that appear together are pronounced like one long vowel.

la abuela

con Natalia   **sus sobrinos**   **las sillas**

Two identical consonants together sound like a single consonant.

es ingeniera   **mis abuelos**   **sus hijos**

A consonant at the end of a word is linked with the vowel sound at the beginning of the next word.

mi hermano   **su esposa**   **nuestro amigo**

A vowel at the end of a word is linked with the vowel sound at the beginning of the next word.

Práctica Say these words aloud, focusing on the diphthongs.

1. historia
2. nieto
3. parientes
4. novia
5. residencia
6. prueba
7. puerta
8. ciencias
9. lenguas
10. estudiar
11. izquierda
12. ecuatoriano

Oraciones Read these sentences aloud to practice diphthongs and linking words.

1. Hola. Me llamo Anita Amaral. Soy del Ecuador.
2. Somos seis en mi familia.
3. Tengo dos hermanos y una hermana.
4. Mi papá es del Ecuador y mi mamá es de España.

Refranes Read these sayings aloud to practice diphthongs and linking sounds.

Cuando una puerta se cierra, otra se abre.[1]

Hablando del rey de Roma, por la puerta se asoma.[2]

 More activities
vhlcentral   LM p. 14

1 When one door closes, another opens. 2 Speak of the devil and he will appear.

Section Goals

In **Pronunciación**, students will be introduced to:
- the strong and weak vowels
- common diphthongs
- linking in pronunciation

Instructional Resources
Supersite: Audio (Textbook and Lab MP3 Files); Resources (Scripts, Answer Keys)
WebSAM
Lab Manual

Teaching Tips
- Write **hermano, niña**, and **cuñado** on the board. Ask students to identify the strong and weak vowels.
- Pronounce **ruido, parientes,** and **periodista**, and have students identify the diphthong in each word. Point out that the strong vowels (**a, e, o**) do not combine with each other to form diphthongs. When two strong vowels come together, they are in different syllables.
- Pronounce **mi hermano** and **su esposa** and ask volunteers to write them on the board. Point out that the linked vowels form a diphthong and are pronounced as one syllable.
- Follow the same procedure with **es ingeniera** and **mis abuelos**. You may want to introduce linking involving the other final consonants (**l, n, r, z**). Ex: **Son hermanos. El hermano mayor está aquí. ¿Cuál es tu hermana?**
- Ask students to provide words they learned in **Lecciones 1** and **2** and **Contextos** and **Fotonovela** of this lesson that exemplify each point.

Práctica/Oraciones/Refranes
These exercises are recorded on the *Textbook MP3s*. Play the audio so that students practice listening to Spanish spoken by speakers other than yourself.

EN DETALLE

¿Cómo te llamas?

In the Spanish-speaking world, it is common to have two last names: one paternal and one maternal. In some cases, the conjunctions **de** or **y** are used to connect the two. For example, in the name **Juan Martínez de Velasco**, *Martínez* is the paternal surname (**el apellido paterno**), and *Velasco* is the maternal surname (**el apellido materno**); **de** simply links the two. This convention of using two last names (**doble apellido**) is a European tradition that Spaniards brought to the Americas. It continues to be practiced in many countries, including Chile, Colombia, Mexico, Peru, and Venezuela. There are exceptions, however. In Argentina, the prevailing custom is for children to inherit only the father's last name.

When a woman marries in a country where two last names are used, legally she retains her two maiden surnames. However, socially she may take her husband's paternal surname in place of her inherited maternal surname. For example, **Mercedes**

Gabriel García Márquez

Mercedes Barcha Pardo

Rodrigo García Barcha

Barcha Pardo, widow of Colombian writer **Gabriel García Márquez**, might use the names **Mercedes Barcha García** or **Mercedes Barcha de García** in social situations (although officially her name remains **Mercedes Barcha Pardo**). Adopting a husband's last name for social purposes, though widespread, is only legally recognized in Ecuador and Peru.

Most parents do not break tradition upon naming their children; regardless of the surnames the mother uses, they use the father's first surname followed by the mother's first surname, as in the name **Rodrigo García Barcha**. However, one should note that both surnames come from the grandfathers, and therefore all **apellidos** are effectively paternal.

> ### Hijos en la casa
>
> In Spanish-speaking countries, family and society place very little pressure on young adults to live on their own (**independizarse**), and children often live with their parents well into their thirties. For example, about 60% of Spaniards under 34 years of age live at home with their parents. This delay in moving out is both cultural and economic—lack of job security or low wages coupled with a high cost of living may make it impractical for young adults to live independently before they marry.

ACTIVIDADES

1 **¿Cierto o falso?** Indicate whether these statements are **cierto** or **falso**. Correct the false statements.

1. Most Spanish-speaking people have three last names. **Falso.** Most people have two last names.
2. Hispanic last names generally consist of the paternal last name followed by the maternal last name. **Cierto.**
3. It is common to see **de** or **y** used in a Hispanic last name. **Cierto.**
4. Someone from Argentina would most likely have two last names. **Falso.** They would use only the father's last name.
5. Generally, married women legally retain two maiden surnames. **Cierto.**
6. In social situations, a married woman often uses her husband's last name in place of her inherited paternal surname. **Falso.** She often uses it in place of her inherited maternal surname.
7. Adopting a husband's surname is only legally recognized in Peru and Ecuador. **Cierto.**
8. Hispanic last names are effectively a combination of the maternal surnames from the previous generation. **Falso.** They are a combination of the paternal surnames from the previous generation.

ASÍ SE DICE

Familia y amigos

el/la bisnieto/a	great-grandson/daughter
el/la chamaco/a (Méx.); el/la chamo/a (Ven.); el/la chaval(a) (Esp.); el/la pibe/a (Arg.)	el/la muchacho/a
mi colega (Esp.); mi cuate (Méx.); mi parcero/a (Col.); mi pana (Ven., P. Rico, Rep. Dom.)	my pal; my buddy
la madrina	godmother
el padrino	godfather
el/la tatarabuelo/a	great-great-grandfather/ great-great-grandmother

EL MUNDO HISPANO

Las familias

Although worldwide population trends show a decrease in average family size, households in many Spanish-speaking countries are still larger than their U.S. counterparts.

- **México** 4,0 personas
- **Colombia** 3,4 personas
- **Argentina** 3,6 personas
- **Uruguay** 3,0 personas
- **España** 2,9 personas
- **Estados Unidos** 2,6 personas

PERFIL

Parientes talentosos

Jesse & Joy

Many families have more than one "star" in their midst. **Jesse & Joy** are a brother-and-sister pop music duo from Mexico City. They won a Grammy for Best Latin Pop Album in 2017 for their album *Un besito más.*

One of the world's most famous families has made music a real family affair. Legendary Spanish singer **Julio Iglesias** has recorded albums in 14 different languages and has sold more than 350 million records in a career that spans decades. Following his lead are his sons **Julio Jr.** and **Enrique**, both popular singers in Spain and around the world.

Julio Iglesias

Enrique Iglesias

Julio Iglesias Jr.

CON RITMO HISPANO

Mirella Cesa (1984–)
Birthplace: Guayaquil, Ecuador

Mirella Cesa is known as the "mother of Andipop." Her music is a mix of Latin percussion, Andean instruments, and pop.

Go to **vhlcentral.com** to find out more about **Mirella Cesa** and her music.

ACTIVIDADES

2 Comprensión Complete these sentences.

1. Joy is the _____sister_____ of Jesse.
2. In Spanish, your godmother is called _____la madrina_____.
3. Enrique Iglesias is the _____brother_____ of Julio Jr.
4. Uruguay's average household has _____3.0_____ people.
5. If a Venezuelan calls you **mi pana**, you are that person's _____friend_____.

3 Una familia famosa Create a genealogical tree of a famous family, using photos or drawings labeled with names and ages. Present the family tree to a classmate and explain who the people are and their relationships to each other. Answers will vary.

More activities

vhlcentral   Online activities

3.1 Descriptive adjectives Tutorial

ANTE TODO Adjectives are words that describe people, places, and things. In Spanish, descriptive adjectives are used with the verb **ser** to point out characteristics such as nationality, size, color, shape, personality, and appearance.

Forms and agreement of adjectives

> **COMPARE & CONTRAST**
>
> In English, the forms of descriptive adjectives do not change to reflect the gender (masculine/feminine) and number (singular/plural) of the noun or pronoun they describe.
>
> | | | |
> |---|---|---|
> | *Juan is **nice**.* | *Elena is **nice**.* | *They are **nice**.* |
>
> In Spanish, the forms of descriptive adjectives agree in gender and/or number with the nouns or pronouns they describe.
>
> | | | |
> |---|---|---|
> | Juan es simpátic**o**. | Elena es simpátic**a**. | Ellos son simpátic**os**. |

▶ Adjectives that end in **-o** have four different forms. The feminine singular is formed by changing the **-o** to **-a**. The plural is formed by adding **-s** to the singular forms.

Masculine		Feminine	
SINGULAR	PLURAL	SINGULAR	PLURAL
el muchach**o** alt**o**	los muchach**os** alt**os**	la muchach**a** alt**a**	las muchach**as** alt**as**

¡Qué bonitas son tus hijas, tía Nayeli!

Felipe es gordo, antipático y muy feo.

▶ Adjectives that end in **-e** or a consonant have the same masculine and feminine forms.

Masculine		Feminine	
SINGULAR	PLURAL	SINGULAR	PLURAL
el chico inteligent**e**	los chicos inteligent**es**	la chica inteligent**e**	las chicas inteligent**es**
el examen difíci**l**	los exámenes difíci**les**	la clase difíci**l**	las clases difíci**les**

▶ Adjectives that end in **-or** are variable in both gender and number.

Masculine		Feminine	
SINGULAR	PLURAL	SINGULAR	PLURAL
el hombre trabajad**or**	los hombres trabajad**ores**	la mujer trabajad**ora**	las mujeres trabajad**oras**

Use the masculine plural form to refer to groups that include males and females.

Manuel es alt**o**. Lola es alt**a**. Manuel y Lola son alt**os**.

AYUDA

Many adjectives are cognates, that is, words that share similar spellings and meanings in Spanish and English. A cognate can be a noun like **profesor** or a descriptive adjective like **interesante**.

Common adjectives

alto/a	tall	**gordo/a**	fat	**mucho/a**	much; many; a lot of
antipático/a	unpleasant	**grande**	big		
bajo/a	short (in height)	**guapo/a**	good-looking	**pelirrojo/a**	red-haired
		importante	important	**pequeño/a**	small
bonito/a	pretty	**inteligente**	intelligent	**rubio/a**	blond(e)
bueno/a	good	**interesante**	interesting	**simpático/a**	nice; likeable
delgado/a	thin	**joven**	young	**tonto/a**	foolish
difícil	difficult	**malo/a**	bad	**trabajador(a)**	hard-working
fácil	easy	**mismo/a**	same	**viejo/a**	old
feo/a	ugly	**moreno/a**	brunet(te)		

¡ATENCIÓN!

Note that **joven** takes an accent in its plural form. **Los jóvenes estudian mucho.**

Adjectives of nationality

▶ Unlike in English, Spanish adjectives of nationality are **not** capitalized. Proper names of countries, however, are capitalized.

Some adjectives of nationality

alemán, alemana	German	**francés, francesa**	French
argentino/a	Argentine	**inglés, inglesa**	English
canadiense	Canadian	**italiano/a**	Italian
chino/a	Chinese	**japonés, japonesa**	Japanese
costarricense	Costa Rican	**mexicano/a**	Mexican
cubano/a	Cuban	**norteamericano/a**	(North) American
ecuatoriano/a	Ecuadorian	**puertorriqueño/a**	Puerto Rican
español(a)	Spanish	**ruso/a**	Russian
estadounidense	from the U.S.		

▶ Adjectives of nationality are formed like other descriptive adjectives. Those that end in **-o** change to **-a** when forming the feminine.

chin**o** ⟶ chin**a** mexican**o** ⟶ mexican**a**

The plural is formed by adding an **-s** to the masculine or feminine form.

argentin**o** ⟶ argentin**os** cuban**a** ⟶ cuban**as**

▶ Adjectives of nationality that end in **-e** have only two forms, singular and plural.

canadiens**e** ⟶ canadiens**es** estadounidens**e** ⟶ estadounidens**es**

▶ To form the feminine of adjectives of nationality that end in a consonant, add **–a**.

alemá**n** ⟶ alema**na** españo**l** ⟶ españo**la**
japoné**s** ⟶ japone**sa** inglé**s** ⟶ ingle**sa**

¡ATENCIÓN!

Note that adjectives with an accent on the last syllable drop the accent in the feminine and plural forms.
inglés ⟶ inglesa
alemán ⟶ alemanes

Teaching Tips

• Point out that when referring to people, **bonito/a** can only be used for females, but **guapo/a** can be used for both males and females. Some heritage speakers may use **moreno/a** to refer to someone with dark skin, and **rubio/a** for someone with light brown hair.

• You may want to introduce **tiene el pelo negro/castaño/rubio** as a way to say that someone has black/brown/blond hair.

• Use pictures or names of celebrities to teach descriptive adjectives in semantic pairs. Ex: **¿Marc Gasol es alto o bajo? (Es alto.) ¿Salma Hayek es fea? (No, es bonita.)**

• Use names of celebrities to practice adjectives of nationality. Ex: **Daniel Craig, ¿es canadiense? (No, es inglés.) Taylor Swift, ¿es francesa? (No, es norteamericana.)**

• Point out that adjectives with an accent mark on the last syllable drop the accent mark in the feminine and plural forms. Ex: **inglés, inglesa, ingleses, inglesas**

• Point out that adjectives of nationality also can be used as nouns. Ex: **La chica rusa es guapa. La rusa es guapa.** Like adjectives, nouns of nationality are not capitalized.

• At this point you may want to present *Vocabulario adicional: Más adjetivos* and *Más vocabulario relacionado con las nacionalidades y las mascotas* from the Supersite.

• You may want to add to the list of nationalities. Ex: **¿Rebel Wilson es australiana? (Sí, es australiana.) ¿Cuáles son las formas plurales de *australiano*? (australianos/australianas)**

TEACHING OPTIONS

Pairs If the majority of your students are **norteamericanos**, have pairs ask each other their family's origin. Write **¿Cuál es el origen de tu familia?** and **Mi familia es de origen…** on the board. Brainstorm other adjectives of nationality as necessary (Ex: **galés, indígena, nigeriano, polaco**). Point out that since **el origen** is masculine and singular, any adjectives they use will be as well.

TPR Create two sets of note cards with a city and a corresponding adjective of nationality. Shuffle the cards and distribute them. Have students circulate around the room to find the person who shares their nationality. Ex: **¿De dónde eres? Soy de Toronto. Soy canadiense.** Then students should arrange themselves in a "map," finding their place by asking other pairs' nationality (**¿De dónde son ustedes? Somos cubanos.**).

Position of adjectives

▶ Descriptive adjectives and adjectives of nationality generally follow the nouns they modify.

El niño **rubio** es de España.
The blond boy is from Spain.

La mujer **española** habla inglés.
The Spanish woman speaks English.

▶ Unlike descriptive adjectives, adjectives of quantity precede the modified noun.

Hay **muchos** libros en la biblioteca.
There are many books in the library.

Hablo con **dos** turistas puertorriqueños.
I am talking with two Puerto Rican tourists.

▶ **Bueno/a** and **malo/a** can appear before or after a noun. When placed before a masculine singular noun, the forms are shortened: **bueno → buen; malo → mal**.

Joaquín es un **buen** amigo.
Joaquín es un amigo **bueno**. → *Joaquín is a good friend.*

Hoy es un **mal** día.
Hoy es un día **malo**. → *Today is a bad day.*

▶ When **grande** appears before a singular noun, it is shortened to **gran**, and the meaning of the word changes: **gran** = *great* and **grande** = *big, large.*

Don Francisco es un **gran** hombre.
Don Francisco is a great man.

La familia de Inés es **grande**.
Inés' family is large.

◉ **¡INTÉNTALO!** Provide the appropriate forms of the adjectives.

simpático

1. Mi hermano es _simpático_.
2. La profesora Martínez es _simpática_.
3. Nosotros somos _simpáticos_.
4. Rosa y Teresa son _simpáticas_.

difícil

1. La química es _difícil_.
2. El curso es _difícil_.
3. Las pruebas son _difíciles_.
4. Los libros son _difíciles_.

alemán

1. Hans es _alemán_.
2. Marcus y yo somos _alemanes_.
3. Mis primas son _alemanas_.
4. Mi tía es _alemana_.

guapo

1. Su esposo es _guapo_.
2. Mis sobrinas son _guapas_.
3. Los padres de ella son _guapos_.
4. Marta es _guapa_.

More activities

vhlcentral

LM
p. 15

WB
pp. 25–26

Online activities

Práctica

1 **Emparejar** Match the opposites.

Jorge   Marcos

A		**B**
1. guapo	d	a. delgado
2. alto	h	b. pequeño
3. joven	e	c. malo
4. gordo	a	d. feo
5. moreno	f	e. viejo
6. grande	b	f. rubio
7. simpático	g	g. antipático
		h. bajo

2 **Completar** Indicate the nationalities of these people.

1. Penélope Cruz es ___española___.
2. Alfonso Cuarón es un gran director de cine de México; es ___mexicano___.
3. Emma Watson y Daniel Radcliffe son actores ___ingleses___.
4. Serena Williams y Stephen Curry son ___estadounidenses___.
5. Ana de Armas es de La Habana, Cuba; ella es ___cubana___.
6. Giorgio Armani es un diseñador de modas (*fashion designer*) ___italiano___.
7. Heidi Klum y Michael Fassbender son ___alemanes___.
8. Ellen Page y Avril Lavigne son ___canadienses___.

3 **Describir** Describe the family members using as many adjectives as possible.
Some answers will vary. Possible answers:

Josefina Barcos de Romero
Carlos Romero Sandoval
Susana Romero Barcos
Tomás Romero Barcos
Alberto Romero Pereda

1. Susana Romero Barcos es ___delgada, rubia, alta___.
2. Tomás Romero Barcos es ___pelirrojo, inteligente, gordo___.
3. Los dos hermanos son ___jóvenes___.
4. Alberto Romero Pereda es ___viejo, bajo, gordo___.
5. Carlos Romero Sandoval es ___bajo, gordo, pelirrojo___.
6. Josefina Barcos de Romero es ___alta, bonita, rubia___.
7. Susana y su (*her*) madre son ___altas, delgadas, rubias___.
8. Tomás y su (*his*) padre son ___pelirrojos, gordos___.

---

1 **Expansion**
- Ask volunteers to create sentences describing famous people, using an adjective from column A and its opposite from B. Ex: **Barack Obama no es gordo; es delgado. Jennifer Lawrence no es morena; es rubia.**
- Have students describe **Jorge** and **Marcos** using as many of the antonyms as they can. Ex: **Jorge es muy simpático, pero Marcos es antipático.**

2 **Teaching Tip** To simplify, guide students in first identifying the gender and number of the subject for each sentence.

2 **Expansion** Ask pairs of students to write four original statements modeled on the activity. Have them leave a blank where the adjectives of nationality should go. Ask each pair to exchange its sentences with another pair, who will fill in the adjectives.

3 **Teaching Tip** To challenge students, ask them to provide all possible answers for each item. Ex: **1. joven, alta, bonita, guapa**

3 **Expansion**
- Have students say what each person in the drawing is not. Ex: **Susana no es vieja. Tomás no es moreno.**
- Have students ask each other questions about the family relationships shown in the illustration. Ex: — **Tomás Romero Barcos es el hijo de Alberto Romero Pereda, ¿verdad? —No, Tomás es el hijo de Carlos Romero Sandoval.**

TEACHING OPTIONS

Extra Practice Have students write brief descriptions of themselves. Ask them to mention where they are from and what they study, as well as describe their personalities and what they look like. Collect the descriptions, shuffle them, and read a few of them to the class. Have the class guess who wrote each description.
Heritage Speakers Ask heritage speakers to use adjectives of nationality to describe their family's origin.
Extra Practice Add an auditory aspect to this grammar practice. Prepare descriptions of easily recognizable people. Write their names on the board in random order. Then read your descriptions and have students match each one to the appropriate name. Ex: **Son hermanas. Son jóvenes y atléticas. Practican el tenis todos los días. (Venus & Serena Williams)**

Comunicación

4 🔗👥 **¿Cómo es?** With a partner, take turns describing each item on the list. Tell your partner whether you agree (**Estoy de acuerdo**) or disagree (**No estoy de acuerdo**) with their descriptions. *Answers will vary.*

> **modelo**
> San Francisco
> **Estudiante 1:** San Francisco es una ciudad (*city*) muy bonita.
> **Estudiante 2:** No estoy de acuerdo. Es muy fea.

1. Nueva York
2. Ryan Gosling
3. las canciones (*songs*) de Taylor Swift
4. el presidente de los Estados Unidos
5. Christopher Nolan
6. la primera dama (*first lady*) de los Estados Unidos
7. el/la profesor(a) de español
8. las personas de Los Ángeles
9. las residencias de mi universidad
10. mi clase de español

5 👥 **Anuncio personal** Write a personal ad that describes yourself and your ideal boyfriend, girlfriend, or mate. Then compare your ad with a classmate's. How are you similar and how are you different? Are you looking for the same things in a romantic partner? *Answers will vary.*

★ **SOY ALTA** y bonita.

Soy cubana, de Holguín.
Estudio arte en la universidad.
Busco un chico similar.
Mi novio ideal es alto, inteligente
y muy simpático.

Síntesis

6 👥✍️ **Diferencias** Your instructor will give you and a partner each a drawing of a family. Describe your version of the drawing to your partner in order to find at least five differences between your picture and your partner's. *Answers will vary.*

> **modelo**
> **Estudiante 1:** Susana, la madre, es rubia.
> **Estudiante 2:** No, la madre es morena.

3.2 Possessive adjectives Tutorial

ANTE TODO   Possessive adjectives, like descriptive adjectives, are words that are used to qualify people, places, or things. Possessive adjectives express the quality of ownership or possession.

Forms of possessive adjectives

SINGULAR FORMS	PLURAL FORMS	
mi	mis	*my*
tu	tus	*your* (fam.)
su	sus	*his, her, its, your* (form.)
nuestro/a	nuestros/as	*our*
vuestro/a	vuestros/as	*your* (fam.)
su	sus	*their, your*

COMPARE & CONTRAST

In English, possessive adjectives are invariable; that is, they do not agree in gender and number with the nouns they modify. Spanish possessive adjectives, however, do agree in number with the nouns they modify.

my cousin	*my cousins*	*my aunt*	*my aunts*
mi primo	**mis** primos	**mi** tía	**mis** tías

The forms **nuestro** and **vuestro** agree in both gender and number with the nouns they modify.

nuestr**o** prim**o**	nuestr**os** prim**os**	nuestr**a** tía	nuestr**as** tí**as**

▶ Possessive adjectives are always placed before the nouns they modify.

—¿Está **tu novio** aquí?   —No, **mi novio** está en la biblioteca.
Is your boyfriend here?   *No, my boyfriend is in the library.*

▶ Because **su** and **sus** have multiple meanings (*your, his, her, their, its*), you can avoid confusion by using this construction instead: [*article*] + [*noun*] + **de** + [*subject pronoun*].

	los parientes **de él/ella**	*his/her relatives*
sus parientes ◀	los parientes **de Ud./Uds.**	*your relatives*
	los parientes **de ellos/ellas**	*their relatives*

 ¡INTÉNTALO!   Provide the appropriate form of each possessive adjective.

1. Es ___mi___ (*my*) libro.
2. ___Mi___ (*My*) familia es ecuatoriana.
3. ___Tu___ (*Your,* fam.) esposo es italiano.
4. Es ___su___ (*her*) reloj.
5. ___Nuestro___ (*Our*) profesor es español.
6. Es ___tu___ (*your,* fam.) mochila.
7. Es ___su___ (*your,* form.) maleta.
8. ___Su___ (*Their*) sobrina es alemana.

1. ___Sus___ (*Her*) primos son franceses.
2. ___Nuestros___ (*Our*) primos son canadienses.
3. Son ___sus___ (*their*) lápices.
4. ___Mis___ (*My*) amigas son inglesas.
5. Son ___nuestras___ (*our*) plumas.
6. Son ___mis___ (*my*) papeles.
7. ___Sus___ (*Their*) nietos son japoneses.
8. Son ___sus___ (*his*) cuadernos.

Práctica

1 La familia de Manolo Complete each sentence with the correct possessive adjective. Use the subject of each sentence as a guide.

1. Me llamo Manolo, y ____mi____ (nuestro, mi, sus) hermano es Federico.
2. ____Nuestra____ (Nuestra, Sus, Mis) madre Silvia es profesora y enseña química.
3. Ella admira a ____sus____ (tu, nuestro, sus) estudiantes porque trabajan mucho.
4. Yo estudio en la misma universidad, pero no tomo clases con ____mi____ (mi, nuestras, tus) madre.
5. Federico trabaja en una oficina con ____nuestro____ (mis, tu, nuestro) padre.
6. ____Su____ (Mi, Su, Tu) oficina está en el centro de la Ciudad de México.
7. Javier y Óscar son ____mis____ (mis, mi, sus) tíos de Oaxaca.
8. ¿Y tú? ¿Cómo es ____tu____ (mi, su, tu) familia?

2 Clarificar Clarify each sentence with a prepositional phrase. Follow the model.

> **modelo**
> Su hermana es muy bonita. (ella)
> *La hermana de ella es muy bonita.*

1. Su casa es muy grande. (ellos) ____ La casa de ellos es muy grande.
2. Sus padres trabajan en el centro. (ella) ____ Los padres de ella trabajan en el centro.
3. ¿Cómo se llama su hermano? (ellas) ____ ¿Cómo se llama el hermano de ellas?
4. Su primo lee los libros. (ellos) ____ El primo de ellos lee los libros.
5. Maribel es su prima. (ella) ____ Maribel es la prima de ella.
6. Sus abuelos son muy simpáticos. (él) ____ Los abuelos de él son muy simpáticos.

3 ¿Dónde está? With a partner, take turns asking where your belongings are. Answers will vary.

> **modelo**
> **Estudiante 1:** *¿Dónde está mi mochila?*
> **Estudiante 2:** *Tu mochila está encima del escritorio.*

1.   2.   3.

4.   5.   6.

Comunicación

4 **Describir** With a partner, describe the people and places listed. Make note of any similarities.

Answers will vary.

> **modelo**
>
> la biblioteca de su universidad
> La biblioteca de nuestra universidad es muy grande. Hay muchos libros
> en la biblioteca. Mis amigos y yo estudiamos en la biblioteca.

1. tu profesor favorito
2. tu profesora favorita
3. su clase de español
4. la librería de su universidad
5. tus padres
6. tus abuelos
7. tu mejor (*best*) amigo
8. tu mejor amiga
9. su universidad
10. tu país de origen

5 **Una familia famosa** Assume the identity of a member of a famous family, real or fictional, and write a description of "your" family. Be sure not to use any names! Then, in small groups, take turns reading the descriptions aloud. The other group members may ask follow-up questions to help them identify the famous person. Answers will vary.

> **modelo**
>
> **Estudiante 1:** Soy cantante. Mi padre y mi hermano se llaman Julio.
> **Estudiante 2:** ¿Eres español?
> **Estudiante 1:** Sí.
> **Estudiante 3:** ¿Eres Enrique Iglesias?
> **Estudiante 1:** Sí.

Síntesis

6 **Describe a tu familia** Describe your family in several sentences to two classmates (**Mi padre es alto y moreno. Mi madre es delgada y muy bonita. Mis hermanos son…**). They will work together to try to repeat your description (**Su padre es alto y moreno. Su madre…**). If they forget any details, they can ask you questions (**¿Es alto tu hermano?**). Alternate roles until all of you have described your families. Answers will vary.

Teaching Tips & Sidebar

4 Teaching Tips
- Ask students to suggest a few more details to add to the **modelo**.
- Have students report on any similarities to the class. Remind students to use **nuestro/a** and **nuestros/as** when reporting on the similarities they found.

5 Teaching Tips
- Quickly review the descriptive adjectives on page 89. You can do this by saying an adjective and having a volunteer give its antonym (**antónimo**).
- Before dividing the class into groups, have students edit their paragraphs for subject-verb and noun-adjective agreement. First, have them underline each subject, circle its corresponding verb, and then verify the correct conjugation. Then have students draw an arrow from each adjective to the word it modifies and make sure that they agree in gender and/or number.

5 Expansion Have each group choose their favorite description and share it with the class.

6 Teaching Tips
- Review the family vocabulary on pages 78–79.
- Explain that the class will be divided into groups of three. One student will describe his or her own family (using **mi**), and then the other two will describe the first student's family to one another (using **su**) and ask for clarification as necessary (using **tu**).
- You may want to model this for the class. Before beginning, ask students to list the family members they plan to describe.

TEACHING OPTIONS

Extra Practice ⟵👥⟶ Have students work in small groups to prepare a description of a famous person, such as a politician, a movie star, or a sports figure, and his or her extended family. Tell them to feel free to invent family members as necessary. Have groups present their descriptions to the class.

Heritage Speakers ⟵👥⟶ Ask heritage speakers to describe their families' home countries (**países de origen**) to the class. As they are giving their descriptions, ask them questions that elicit more information. Clarify for the class any unfamiliar words and expressions they may use.

Section Goals

In **Estructura 3.3**, students will learn:

- the present-tense forms of regular –er and –ir verbs
- some high-frequency regular –er and –ir verbs

Instructional Resources

Supersite: Audio (Lab MP3 Files); Resources (Grammar Presentation Slides, Activity Pack, Scripts, Answer Keys); Testing Program (Quizzes)
WebSAM
Workbook
Lab Manual

Teaching Tips

- Review the present tense of –ar verbs. Write **trabajo** on the board and ask for the corresponding subject pronoun. (**yo**) Continue until you have the entire paradigm. Underline the endings, pointing out the characteristic vowel (–a–) where it appears and the personal endings.
- Ask questions and make statements that use the verb **comer** to elicit all the present-tense forms.
Ex: **¿Comes en la cafetería o en un restaurante? Yo no como en la cafetería. ¿Come _____ en casa o en un bar?**
As you elicit responses, write just the verbs on the board until you have the complete conjugation. Repeat the process with **escribir**.
Ex: **¿Quién escribe muchos mensajes electrónicos? ¿A quién escribes?** When you have a complete paradigm of both verbs, contrast it with the paradigm of **trabajar**. Help students identify the ending that is the same in all three conjugations. **yo = (–o)**

3.3 Present tense of -er and -ir verbs Tutorial

ANTE TODO   In **Lección 2,** you learned how to form the present tense of regular -ar verbs. You also learned about the importance of verb forms, which change to show who is performing the action. The chart below shows the forms from two other important groups, **-er** verbs and **-ir** verbs.

Present tense of -er and -ir verbs

		comer (to eat)	**escribir** (to write)
SINGULAR FORMS	yo	com**o**	escrib**o**
	tú	com**es**	escrib**es**
	Ud./él/ella	com**e**	escrib**e**
PLURAL FORMS	nosotros/as	com**emos**	escrib**imos**
	vosotros/as	com**éis**	escrib**ís**
	Uds./ellos/ellas	com**en**	escrib**en**

▶ **-Er** and **-ir** verbs have very similar endings. Study the preceding chart to detect the patterns that make it easier for you to use them to communicate in Spanish.

Felipe y su tío comen.

Jimena lee.

▶ Like **-ar** verbs, the **yo** forms of **-er** and **-ir** verbs end in **-o.**

Yo com**o**.   Yo escrib**o**.

▶ Except for the **yo** form, all of the verb endings for **-er** verbs begin with **-e.**

-es	-emos	-en
-e	-éis	

▶ **-Er** and **-ir** verbs have the exact same endings, except in the **nosotros/as** and **vosotros/as** forms.

nosotros ◀ com**emos** / escrib**imos**   vosotros ◀ com**éis** / escrib**ís**

CONSULTA

To review the conjugation of **-ar** verbs, see **Estructura 2.1**, p. 50.

AYUDA

Here are some tips on learning Spanish verbs:
1) Learn to identify the verb's stem, to which all endings attach.
2) Memorize the endings that go with each verb and verb tense.
3) As often as possible, practice using different forms of each verb in speech and writing.
4) Devote extra time to learning irregular verbs, such as **ser** and **estar**.

TEACHING OPTIONS

Heritage Speakers ←👤→ Have heritage speakers make statements about themselves or their family members, using different verbs from the chart on page 97. Some statements should be true and others should be false. Have the class guess which statements they think are true, and encourage them to ask any follow-up questions.

Game Divide the class into two teams. Name an infinitive and a subject pronoun (Ex: **creer/yo**) and have a member of team A give the appropriate conjugation. If the student answers correctly, team A gets one point. If he or she is incorrect, give a member of team B the same items. If that student doesn't know the answer, say the correct form and start over with a new infinitive and subject pronoun. The team with the most points at the end wins.

Common -er and -ir verbs

-er verbs		-ir verbs	
aprender (a + *inf.*)	to learn	abrir	to open
beber	to drink	asistir (a)	to attend
comer	to eat	compartir	to share
comprender	to understand	decidir (+ *inf.*)	to decide
correr	to run	describir	to describe
creer (en)	to believe (in)	escribir	to write
deber (+ *inf.*)	should	recibir	to receive
leer	to read	vivir	to live

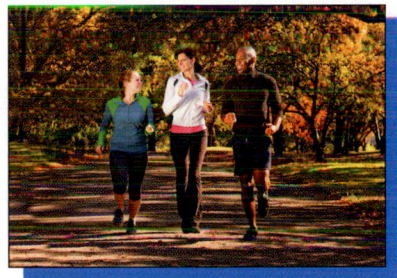

Ellos **corren** en el parque.

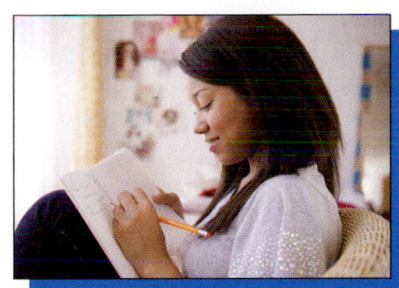

Ella **escribe** en su diario.

More activities

vhlcentral

LM
p. 17

WB
pp. 29–30

Online activities

¡INTÉNTALO!   Provide the appropriate present tense forms of these verbs.

correr

1. Graciela _corre_.
2. Tú _corres_.
3. Yo _corro_.
4. Sara y Ana _corren_.
5. Usted _corre_.
6. Marcos y yo _corremos_.
7. La gente _corre_.
8. Ustedes _corren_.

abrir

1. Ellos _abren_ la puerta.
2. Carolina _abre_ la maleta.
3. Yo _abro_ las ventanas.
4. Usted _abre_ el cuaderno.
5. Nosotras _abrimos_ los libros.
6. Tú _abres_ la ventana.
7. Ustedes _abren_ las maletas.
8. Los muchachos _abren_ los cuadernos.

aprender

1. Él _aprende_ español.
2. Maribel y yo _aprendemos_ inglés.
3. Tú _aprendes_ japonés.
4. Mi hijo _aprende_ chino.
5. Tú y tu hermanastra _aprenden_ francés.
6. Yo _aprendo_ alemán.
7. Usted _aprende_ inglés.
8. Nosotros _aprendemos_ italiano.

Teaching Tips

- Point out the characteristic vowel (–**e**–) of –**er** verbs. Help students see that all the present-tense endings of regular –**er/–ir** verbs are the same except for the **nosotros/as** and **vosotros/as** forms.
- Reinforce –**er/–ir** endings and introduce the verbs by asking the class questions. First, ask a series of questions with a single verb until you have elicited all of its present-tense forms. Have students answer with complete sentences. Ex: **¿Aprenden ustedes historia en nuestra clase? ¿Aprendes álgebra en tu clase de matemáticas? ¿Qué aprenden _____ y _____ en la clase de computación? Aprendo mucho cuando leo, ¿verdad?** Then, ask questions using all the verbs at random.
- Prepare a series of sentences about students and professors using the verbs on this page, but do not include the subjects. Have students write **estudiante** and **profesor** on separate sheets of paper. Read each sentence aloud and have students hold up **estudiante** if it refers to a student, **profesor** if it refers to a professor, or both pieces of paper if it can relate to either person. Ex: **No vive en una residencia estudiantil.** (students hold up **profesor**) **Aprende los verbos.** (students hold up **estudiante**) **Hoy decide comer en la cafetería.** (students hold up both papers)
- Ask questions based on the photos. Ex: **¿Quiénes corren en el parque en la foto? ¿Ustedes corren? ¿Dónde corren? ¿Qué creen que escribe la chica? ¿Ustedes escriben en un diario? ¿Qué escriben?**
- Ask students to write a description of things they routinely do in Spanish class or in any of their other classes. Encourage them to use as many of the –**er/–ir** verbs as they can.

TEACHING OPTIONS

Video Replay the **Fotonovela**. Have students listen for –**er/–ir** verbs and write down those they hear. Afterward, write the verbs on the board and ask their meanings. Have students write original sentences using each verb.
Extra Practice Have students answer questions about their Spanish class. Have them answer in complete sentences. Ex: **¿Ustedes estudian mucho para la clase de español o**
deben estudiar más? ¿Leen las lecciones? Escriben mucho en clase, ¿verdad? ¿Abren los libros? Asisten al laboratorio de lenguas, ¿verdad? ¿Comen sándwiches en la clase? ¿Beben café? Comprenden el libro, ¿no? Pairs may ask each other these questions by changing the verbs to the **tú** form.

Práctica

1 Expansion
- As a class, come up with the questions that would elicit the statements in this activity. Ex: **¿Dónde viven tú y tu familia? ¿Cuántos libros tienes? ¿Por qué tienes muchos libros? ¿Cómo es tu hermano Alfredo? ¿Cuándo asiste Alfredo a sus clases? ¿Cuándo corren ustedes? ¿Qué comen tus padres los domingos? ¿Cuánto deben comer tus padres?**
- ↤👤→ Have small groups describe the family pictured here. Ask the groups to invent each person's name, using Hispanic naming conventions, and include a physical description, place of origin, and the family relationship to the other people in the photo.

2 Teaching Tip To simplify, guide students in classifying the infinitives as **–er** or **–ir**. Then help them identify the subject for each verb and the appropriate verb ending. Finally, aid students in identifying any missing words.

2 Expansion Have pairs create two additional dehydrated sentences for another pair to write out.

3 Teaching Tip To challenge students, add these words to the list: **aprender historia japonesa, comer más *sushi*, describir sus experiencias.**

3 Expansion
↤👤→ Have students imagine that they are studying abroad in a Spanish-speaking country. Using the verbs in the word bank as a guide, have them write an e-mail to a friend back home. Tell students to state four things they are doing, three things they and their classmates are doing, and two things that they should be doing.

1 **Completar** Complete Susana's sentences about her family with the correct forms of the verbs. One of the verbs will remain in the infinitive.

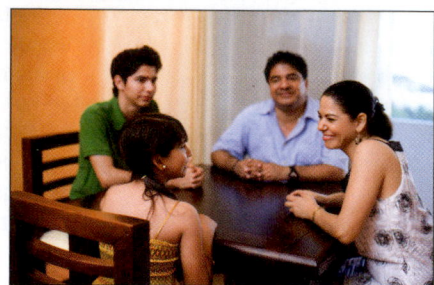

1. Mi familia y yo _____vivimos_____ (vivir) en Mérida, Yucatán.
2. Tengo muchos libros. Me gusta _____leer_____ (leer).
3. Mi hermano Alfredo es muy inteligente. Alfredo _____asiste_____ (asistir) a clases los lunes, miércoles y viernes.
4. Los martes y jueves Alfredo y yo _____corremos_____ (correr) en el Parque del Centenario.
5. Mis padres _____comen_____ (comer) mucha lasaña los domingos y se quedan dormidos (*they fall asleep*).
6. Yo _____creo_____ (creer) que (*that*) mis padres deben comer menos (*less*).

2 **Oraciones** Form complete sentences by adding any other necessary elements.

> **modelo**
> yo / correr / amigos / lunes y miércoles
> *Yo corro con mis amigos los lunes y miércoles.*

1. Manuela / asistir / clase / yoga   Manuela asiste a la clase de yoga.
2. Isabel y yo / leer / biblioteca   Isabel y yo leemos en la biblioteca.
3. Sofía y Roberto / aprender / hablar / inglés   Sofía y Roberto aprenden a hablar inglés.
4. Eugenio / abrir / correo electrónico (*e-mail*)   Eugenio abre su correo electrónico.
5. tú / comer / cafetería / universidad   Tú comes en la cafetería de la universidad.
6. mi novia y yo / compartir / libro de historia   Mi novia y yo compartimos el libro de historia.

3 **Consejos** In pairs, say what Mario and/or his family members are doing or should do to adjust to living in Japan for a year to learn Japanese. Then, create one more sentence using a verb not on the list.

Answers will vary.

> **modelo**
> recibir libros / deber practicar japonés
> **Estudiante 1:** *Mario y su esposa reciben muchos libros en japonés.*
> **Estudiante 2:** *Los hijos deben practicar japonés.*

aprender japonés	decidir explorar el país
asistir a clases	escribir listas de palabras en japonés
beber sake	leer novelas japonesas
deber comer cosas nuevas	vivir con una familia japonesa

TEACHING OPTIONS

Pairs 👤↔👤 Have pairs of students role-play an interview with a movie star. Allow sufficient time to plan and practice; they can review previous lesson vocabulary if needed. After completing the activity ask a few of them to introduce their characters and perform the interview for the class.
TPR Create a list of phrases similar to those in **Actividad 3**, but change the context to a Spanish-speaking country. In groups of three, have students act out the activities for their classmates to guess.
Heritage Speakers ↤👤→ Have heritage speakers brainstorm a list of things that a study-abroad student in a Spanish-speaking country might want to do. Have them base their list on **Actividad 3** using as many **–er/–ir** verbs as they can. Then have the rest of the class write complete sentences based on the list.

Comunicación

4   **Entrevista** In pairs, use these questions to interview each other.   *Answers will vary.*

1. ¿Dónde comes al mediodía? ¿Comes mucho?
2. ¿Cuándo asistes a tus clases?
3. ¿Cuál es tu clase favorita? ¿Por qué?
4. ¿Dónde vives?
5. ¿Con quién vives?
6. ¿Qué cursos debes tomar el próximo (*next*) semestre?
7. ¿Recibes muchos mensajes de texto (*text messages*)? ¿De quién(es)?
8. ¿Crees en fantasmas (*ghosts*)?

5   **¿Acción o descripción?** In small groups, take turns choosing a verb. Then choose to act out the verb or give a description. The other members of the group will say what you are doing. Be creative!

Answers will vary.

abrir (un libro, una puerta, una mochila)	correr (en el parque, en un maratón)
aprender (a bailar, a hablar francés, a dibujar)	escribir (una composición, un mensaje de texto [*text message*], con lápiz)
asistir (a una clase de yoga, a un concierto de rock, a una clase interesante)	leer (una carta [*letter*] de amor, un mensaje electrónico [*e-mail message*], un periódico [*newspaper*])
beber (agua, Coca-Cola)	recibir un regalo (*gift*)
comer (pasta, un sándwich, pizza)	¿?
compartir (un libro, un sándwich)	

modelo

Estudiante 1: (*pantomimes typing on a keyboard*)
Estudiante 2: ¿Escribes un mensaje electrónico?
Estudiante 1: Sí.

modelo

Estudiante 1: Soy estudiante y tomo muchas clases. Vivo en Roma.
Estudiante 2: ¿Comes pasta?
Estudiante 1: No, no como pasta.
Estudiante 3: ¿Aprendes a hablar italiano?
Estudiante 1: ¡Sí!

Síntesis

6   **Horario** Your instructor will give you and a partner incomplete versions of Alicia's schedule. Fill in the missing information on the schedule by talking to your partner.   *Answers will vary.*

Small Groups Have small groups talk about their favorite classes and teachers. They should describe the classes and the teachers and indicate why they like them. They should also mention what days and times they attend each class. Ask a few volunteers to present a summary of their conversations.

Extra Practice Add an auditory aspect to this grammar practice. Use these sentences as a dictation. Read each twice, pausing after each time for students to write. **1. Mi hermana Juana y yo asistimos a la Universidad de Quito. 2. Ella vive en la casa de mis padres y yo vivo en una residencia. 3. Juana es estudiante de literatura y lee mucho. 4. Yo estudio computación y aprendo a programar computadoras.**

---

4 Teaching Tips
- Tell students that one of them should complete their interview before switching roles.
- This activity is also suited to a group of three students, one of whom acts as note taker. They should switch roles at the end of each interview until each student has played all three roles.

5 Teaching Tip Make sure that students understand that they have the option of acting out an activity or describing it in a creative way. Write a verb phrase on the board and model both methods. Ex: Write on the board **beber té** (*tea*). First, act out sitting primly in a chair, serving tea from a teapot, stirring in sugar, and holding the cup daintily while taking small sips. Then give a description: **Estoy en Londres. Son las cuatro de la tarde. Deseo tomar algo** (*something*).

5 Expansion Write **asociación** on the board. Have students repeat the activity, but this time they must make associations with the verbs instead of acting them out or describing them. Ex: **Santa Claus/Papá Noel (recibir un regalo); clases de tango (aprender a bailar)**

6 Teaching Tip Divide the class into pairs and distribute the handouts from the Activity Pack that correspond to this Information Gap Activity (Activity Pack/Supersite). Give students ten minutes to complete this activity.

6 Expansion
- Ask questions based on **Alicia's** schedule. Ex: **¿Qué hace Alicia a las nueve? (Ella desayuna.)**
- Have volunteers take turns reading aloud **Alicia's** schedule. Then have them write their own schedules using as many **–er/–ir** verbs as they can.

3.4 Present tense of **tener** and **venir** Tutorial

ANTE TODO The verbs **tener** (*to have*) and **venir** (*to come*) are among the most frequently used in Spanish. Because most of their forms are irregular, you will have to learn each one individually.

The verbs tener and venir

		tener	**venir**
SINGULAR FORMS	yo	ten**go**	ven**go**
	tú	tien**es**	vien**es**
	Ud./él/ella	tien**e**	vien**e**
PLURAL FORMS	nosotros/as	ten**emos**	ven**imos**
	vosotros/as	ten**éis**	ven**ís**
	Uds./ellos/ellas	tien**en**	vien**en**

▶ The endings are the same as those of regular **-er** and **-ir** verbs, except for the **yo** forms, which are irregular: **tengo, vengo.**

▶ In the **tú, Ud.,** and **Uds.** forms, the **e** of the stem changes to **ie,** as shown below.

INFINITIVE	VERB STEM	VERB FORM
tener →	ten- →	tú ti**e**nes
		Ud./él/ella ti**e**ne
		Uds./ellos/ellas ti**e**nen
venir →	ven- →	tú vi**e**nes
		Ud./él/ella vi**e**ne
		Uds./ellos/ellas vi**e**nen

¿Tienes una familia grande, Marissa?

No, tengo una familia pequeña.

▶ Only the **nosotros** and **vosotros** forms are regular. Compare them to the forms of **comer** and **escribir** that you learned on page 96.

	tener	**comer**	**venir**	**escribir**
nosotros/as	ten**emos**	com**emos**	ven**imos**	escrib**imos**
vosotros/as	ten**éis**	com**éis**	ven**ís**	escrib**ís**

▶ In certain idiomatic or set expressions in Spanish, you use the construction **tener** + [*noun*] to express *to be* + [*adjective*]. This chart contains a list of the most common expressions with **tener**.

Expressions with tener

tener... años	*to be... years old*	**tener (mucha) prisa**	*to be in a (big) hurry*
tener (mucho) calor	*to be (very) hot*	**tener razón**	*to be right*
tener (mucho) cuidado	*to be (very) careful*	**no tener razón**	*to be wrong*
tener (mucho) frío	*to be (very) cold*	**tener (mucha) sed**	*to be (very) thirsty*
tener (mucha) hambre	*to be (very) hungry*	**tener (mucho) sueño**	*to be (very) sleepy*
tener (mucho) miedo (de)	*to be (very) afraid/ scared (of)*	**tener (mucha) suerte**	*to be (very) lucky*

—¿**Tienen** hambre ustedes?
Are you hungry?

—Sí, y **tenemos** sed también.
Yes, and we're thirsty, too.

▶ To express an obligation, use **tener que** (*to have to*) + [*infinitive*].

—¿Qué **tienes que** estudiar hoy?
What do you have to study today?

—**Tengo que** estudiar biología.
I have to study biology.

▶ To ask people if they feel like doing something, use **tener ganas de** (*to feel like*) + [*infinitive*].

—¿**Tienes ganas de** comer?
Do you feel like eating?

—No, **tengo ganas de** dormir.
No, I feel like sleeping.

miciudad.com
Usted tiene que visitarnos.

 ¡INTÉNTALO! Provide the appropriate forms of **tener** and **venir**.

tener	venir
1. Ellos ___tienen___ dos hermanos.	1. Mis padres ___vienen___ de México.
2. Nosotros ___tenemos___ diez tíos.	2. Yo ___vengo___ de Francia.
3. El artista ___tiene___ tres primos.	3. Nosotras ___venimos___ de Cuba.
4. Yo ___tengo___ una hermana.	4. Pepe ___viene___ de Italia.
5. Eva y Diana ___tienen___ un sobrino.	5. Tú ___vienes___ de España.
6. Usted ___tiene___ cinco nietos.	6. Ustedes ___vienen___ de Canadá.
7. Tú ___tienes___ dos hermanastras.	7. Alfonso y yo ___venimos___ de Portugal.
8. Ustedes ___tienen___ cuatro hijos.	8. Ellos ___vienen___ de Alemania.
9. Ella ___tiene___ una hija.	9. Usted ___viene___ de Venezuela.

More activities

vhlcentral

LM
p. 18

WB
pp. 31–32

Online activities

Teaching Tips

• Remind the class that Spanish uses **tener** + [*noun*] in many cases where English uses *to be* + [*adjective*].

• Model the use of the expressions by talking about yourself and asking students questions about themselves. Ex: **Tengo ____ años. Y tú, ¿cuántos años tienes? Esta mañana tengo frío. ¿Tienen frío ustedes? Y tú, ____, ¿tienes frío también o tienes calor? Yo no tengo sueño esta mañana. Me gusta enseñar por la mañana.**

• Present **tener que** + [*infinitive*] and **tener ganas de** + [*infinitive*] together. Go around the class asking questions that use the expressions, having students answer in complete sentences. Ex: **____, ¿tienes que estudiar más para la clase de español? ¿Tienes ganas de ir a la biblioteca ahora?**

• Give locations and have students name the **tener** expressions that they associate with those places. Accept all possible responses. Ex: **el desierto del Sahara (tener calor, tener sed); un debate político en Washington D.C. (tener razón, no tener razón)**

TEACHING OPTIONS

TPR Assign gestures to each expression with **tener**. Ex: **tener calor:** *wipe brow;* **tener cuidado:** *look around suspiciously;* **tener frío:** *wrap arms around oneself and shiver;* **tener miedo:** *hold hand over mouth in fear.* Have students stand. Say an expression at random (Ex: **Tienes sueño**) and point at a student, who should perform the appropriate gesture. Vary by pointing to more than one student (Ex: **Ustedes tienen hambre**).

Variación léxica Point out that **tener que** + [*infinitive*] not only expresses obligation, but also need. **Tengo que estudiar más** can mean either *I have to (am obligated to) study more* or *I need to study more.* Another way of expressing need is with the regular –ar verb **necesitar** + [*infinitive*]. Ex: **Necesito estudiar más.** This can also be said with **deber** + [*infinitive*]. Ex: **Debo estudiar más.**

Práctica

1

Emparejar Match the items to the most appropriate expressions with **tener**. Then, come up with a new item that corresponds with the leftover expression in column B.

A		B
1. el Polo Norte	c	a. tener calor
2. una sauna	a	b. tener sed
3. una dieta	f	c. tener frío
4. un abuelo	g	d. tener razón
5. la comida salada (*salty food*)	b	e. tener ganas de
6. una persona muy inteligente	d	f. tener hambre
		g. tener 75 años

2

Completar Complete the sentences with the correct forms of **tener** or **venir**.

1. Hoy nosotros ___tenemos___ una reunión familiar (*family reunion*).
2. Todos mis parientes ___vienen___, excepto mi tío Manolo y su esposa.
3. Ellos no ___tienen___ ganas de venir porque viven en Portoviejo.
4. Yo ___vengo___ en autobús de la Universidad de Quito.
5. Mi prima Susana y su novio no ___vienen___ hasta las ocho porque ella ___tiene___ que trabajar.
6. En las fiestas, mi hermana siempre (*always*) ___viene___ muy tarde (*late*).
7. Nosotros ___tenemos___ mucha suerte porque las reuniones son divertidas (*fun*).
8. Mi madre cree que mis sobrinos son muy simpáticos. Creo que ella ___tiene___ razón.

3

Describir Describe what these people are doing or feeling using an expression with **tener**.

1. ___Tiene (mucho) calor.___

2. ___Tienen (mucho) frío.___

3. ___Tiene (mucha) prisa.___

4. ___Tienen (mucha) hambre.___

5. ___Tiene diez años.___

6. ___Tiene (mucho) sueño.___

Comunicación

4 **¿Sí o no?** Indicate whether these statements apply to you by checking either **Sí** or **No**.

Answers will vary.

	Sí	No
1. Mi padre tiene 50 años.	○	○
2. Mis amigos vienen a mi casa todos los días (*every day*).	○	○
3. Vengo a la universidad los martes.	○	○
4. Tengo hambre.	○	○
5. Tengo dos computadoras.	○	○
6. Tengo sed.	○	○
7. Tengo que estudiar los domingos.	○	○
8. Tengo una familia grande.	○	○

Now interview a classmate by transforming each statement into a question. Answers will vary.

modelo

Estudiante 1: ¿Tiene tu padre 50 años?
Estudiante 2: No, no tiene 50 años. Tiene 65.

5 **Preguntas** Get together with a classmate and ask each other these questions. Answers will vary.

1. ¿Tienes que estudiar hoy?
2. ¿Cuántos años tienes? ¿Y tus hermanos/as?
3. ¿Cuándo vienes a la clase de español?
4. ¿Cuándo vienen tus amigos a tu casa, apartamento o residencia estudiantil?
5. ¿De qué tienes miedo? ¿Por qué?
6. ¿Qué tienes ganas de hacer esta noche (*tonight*)?

6 **Conversación** Use an expression with **tener** to hint at what's on your mind. Your partner will ask questions to find out why you feel that way. If your partner cannot guess what's on your mind after three attempts, tell him/her. Then switch roles. Answers will vary.

estar cerca/lejos de la ventana	no beber/desayunar/descansar
hablar/cantar en público	tener una clase/un examen/buenos amigos

modelo

Estudiante 1: Tengo miedo.
Estudiante 2: ¿Tienes que hablar en público?
Estudiante 1: No.
Estudiante 2: ¿Tienes un examen hoy?
Estudiante 1: Sí, y no tengo tiempo para estudiar.

Síntesis

7 **Minidrama** Act out this situation with a partner: you are introducing your boyfriend/girlfriend to your extended family. To avoid any surprises before you go, talk about who is coming and what each family member is like. Switch roles. Answers will vary.

---

4 Teaching Tip Give students two minutes to read the statements and mark their answers. Then form pairs and model question formation. Encourage students to answer with complete sentences. Have students report the results of their interview to the class.

5 Teaching Tips
• You may want to provide additional vocabulary for item 5.
• Ask volunteers to summarize the responses. Record these responses on the board as a survey about the class's characteristics.

6 Teaching Tip Model the activity by giving an expression with **tener**. Ex: **Tengo mucha prisa.** Encourage students to guess the reason, using **tener** and **venir**. If they guess incorrectly, give them more specific clues. Ex: **Tengo mucho que hacer hoy. Es un día especial. (Viene un amigo a la casa.)**

7 Teaching Tip Before doing **Síntesis**, have students quickly review this material: family vocabulary on pages 78–79; descriptive adjectives on pages 88–90; possessive adjectives on page 93; and the forms of **tener** and **venir** on pages 100–101.

TEACHING OPTIONS

Small Groups Have small groups prepare skits in which one person takes a few friends to a family reunion. The introducer should make polite introductions and tell the people he or she is introducing a few facts about each other. All the people involved should attempt to make small talk.

Pairs Give pairs of students five minutes to write a conversation in which they use as many **tener** expressions as they can in a logical manner. Have the top three pairs perform their conversations for the class.

Recapitulación

Review the grammar concepts you have learned in this lesson by completing these activities.

1 Adjetivos Complete each phrase with the appropriate adjective. Make all necessary changes. **12 pts.**

antipático	interesante	mexicano
difícil	joven	moreno

1. Mi tía es __mexicana__. Vive en Guadalajara.
2. Mi primo no es rubio, es __moreno__.
3. Mi novio cree que la clase no es fácil; es __difícil__.
4. Los libros son __interesantes__; me gustan mucho.
5. Mis hermanos son __antipáticos__; no tienen muchos amigos.
6. Las gemelas tienen quince años. Son __jóvenes__.

2 Completar For each set of sentences, provide the appropriate form of the verb **tener** and the possessive adjective. Follow the model. **24 pts.**

modelo
Él **tiene** un libro. Es **su** libro.

1. Esteban y Julio __tienen__ una tía. Es __su__ tía.
2. Yo __tengo__ muchos amigos. Son __mis__ amigos.
3. Tú __tienes__ tres primas. Son __tus__ primas.
4. María y tú __tienen__ un hermano. Es __su__ hermano.
5. Nosotras __tenemos__ unas mochilas. Son __nuestras__ mochilas.
6. Usted __tiene__ dos sobrinos. Son __sus__ sobrinos.

3 Oraciones Arrange the words in the correct order to form complete logical sentences. ¡Ojo! Don't forget to conjugate the verbs. **10 pts.**

1. libros / unos / tener / interesantes / tú / muy
   Tú tienes unos libros muy interesantes.
2. dos / leer / fáciles / compañera / tu / lecciones
   Tu compañera lee dos lecciones fáciles.
3. mi / francés / ser / amigo / buen / Hugo
   Hugo es mi buen amigo francés./Mi buen amigo francés es Hugo.
4. ser / simpáticas / dos / personas / nosotras
   Nosotras somos dos personas simpáticas.
5. a / clases / menores / mismas / sus / asistir / hermanos / las
   Sus hermanos menores asisten a las mismas clases.

RESUMEN GRAMATICAL

3.1 Descriptive adjectives *pp. 88–90*

Forms and agreement of adjectives

Masculine		Feminine	
Singular	Plural	Singular	Plural
alto	altos	alta	altas
inteligente	inteligentes	inteligente	inteligentes
trabajador	trabajadores	trabajadora	trabajadoras

► Descriptive adjectives follow the noun: **el chico rubio**
► Adjectives of nationality also follow the noun: **la mujer española**
► Adjectives of quantity precede the noun: **muchos libros, dos turistas**
► When placed before a masculine singular noun, these adjectives are shortened.
  bueno → buen   malo → mal
► When placed before a singular noun, **grande** is shortened to **gran**.

3.2 Possessive adjectives *p. 93*

Singular		Plural	
mi	nuestro/a	mis	nuestros/as
tu	vuestro/a	tus	vuestros/as
su	su	sus	sus

3.3 Present tense of -er and -ir verbs *pp. 96–97*

comer		escribir	
como	comemos	escribo	escribimos
comes	coméis	escribes	escribís
come	comen	escribe	escriben

3.4 Present tense of tener and venir *pp. 100–101*

tener		venir	
tengo	tenemos	vengo	venimos
tienes	tenéis	vienes	venís
tiene	tienen	viene	vienen

4 **Carta** Complete this letter with the correct forms of the appropriate verbs. `20 pts.`

abrir	correr	recibir
asistir	creer	tener
compartir	escribir	venir
comprender	leer	vivir

Hola, Ángel:

¿Qué tal? (Yo) (1) _Escribo_ esta carta (this letter) en la biblioteca. Todos los días (2) _vengo_ aquí y (3) _leo_ un buen libro. Yo (4) _creo_ que es importante leer por diversión. Mi compañero de apartamento no (5) _comprende_ por qué me gusta leer. Él sólo (6) _abre/lee_ los libros de texto. Pero nosotros (7) _compartimos_ unos intereses. Por ejemplo, los dos somos atléticos; por las mañanas nosotros (8) _corremos_. También nos gustan las ciencias; por las tardes (9) _asistimos_ a nuestra clase de biología. Y tú, ¿cómo estás? ¿(Tú) (10) _Tienes_ mucho trabajo (work)?

5 **Su familia** Write a brief description of a friend's family. Describe the family members using vocabulary and structures from this lesson. Write at least five sentences. `34 pts.`

Answers will vary.

modelo

La familia de mi amiga Gabriela es grande. Ella tiene tres hermanos y una hermana. Su hermana mayor es periodista...

6 **Proverbio** Complete this proverb with the correct forms of the verbs. `4 EXTRA points!`

❝ Dos andares° _tiene_ (tener) el dinero°,
viene (venir) despacio°
y se va° ligero°. ❞

andares *speeds* dinero *money* despacio *slowly*
se va *it leaves* ligero *quickly*

Section Goals

In **Lectura**, students will:
- learn to use context clues in reading
- read context-rich selections about Hispanic families

Instructional Resource
Supersite

Estrategia Tell students that they can often infer the meaning of an unfamiliar Spanish word by looking at the word's context and by using common sense. Five types of context clues are:
- synonyms
- antonyms
- clarifications
- definitions
- additional details

Have students read the sentence **Ayer fui a ver a mi tía abuela, la hermana de mi abuela** from the letter. Point out that the meaning of **tía abuela** can be inferred from its similarity to the known word **abuela** and from the clarification that follows (**la hermana de mi abuela**).

Examinar el texto Have students read Paragraph 1 silently, without looking up the glossed words. Point out the phrase **salgo a pasear** and ask a volunteer to explain how the context might give clues to the meaning. Afterward, point out that **salgo** is the first-person singular form of **salir** (*to go out*). Tell students they will learn all the forms of **salir** in **Lección 4**.

Examinar el formato Guide students to see that the photos and captions reveal that the paragraphs are about several different families.

Lectura

 NATIONAL STANDARDS · communication cultures

Antes de leer

Estrategia
Guessing meaning from context

As you read in Spanish, you'll often come across words you haven't learned. You can guess what they mean by looking at the surrounding words and sentences. Look at the following text and guess what **tía abuela** means, based on the context.

> ¡Hola, Claudia!
> ¿Qué hay de nuevo?
> ¿Sabes qué? Ayer fui a ver a mi tía abuela, la hermana de mi abuela. Tiene 85 años, pero es muy independiente. Vive en un apartamento en Quito con su prima Lorena, quien también tiene 85 años.

If you guessed *great-aunt*, you are correct, and you can conclude from this word and the format clues that this is a letter about someone's visit with his or her great-aunt.

Examinar el texto

Quickly read through the paragraphs and find two or three words you don't know. Using the context as your guide, guess what these words mean. Then glance at the paragraphs where these words appear and try to predict what the paragraphs are about.

Examinar el formato

Look at the format of the reading. What clues do the captions, photos, and layout give you about its content?

More activities

vhlcentral | Online activities

Gente... Las familias

1. Me llamo Armando y tengo setenta años, pero no me considero viejo. Tengo seis nietas y un nieto. Vivo con mi hija y tengo la oportunidad de pasar mucho tiempo con ella y con mi nieto. Por las tardes salgo a pasear° por el parque con él y por la noche le leo cuentos°.

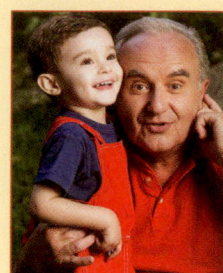

Armando. Tiene seis nietas y un nieto.

2. Mi prima Victoria y yo nos llevamos muy bien. Estudiamos juntas° en la universidad y compartimos un apartamento. Ella es muy inteligente y me ayuda° con los estudios. Además°, es muy simpática y generosa. Si necesito cualquier° cosa, ¡ella me la compra!

Diana. Vive con su prima.

3. Me llamo Ramona y soy paraguaya, aunque° ahora vivo en los Estados Unidos. Tengo tres hijos, uno de nueve años, uno de doce y el mayor de quince. Es difícil a veces, pero mi esposo y yo tratamos° de ayudarlos y comprenderlos siempre°.

Ramona. Sus hijos son muy importantes para ella.

TEACHING OPTIONS

Extra Practice Ask students to use the paragraphs in **Gente… Las familias** as models for writing paragraphs about their families, but from the perspective of another family member (e.g., their mother). Have volunteers read their paragraphs aloud.

Extra Practice Use these items, each of which contains an unfamiliar word or phrase, to practice using context clues. **1. Mi tío Daniel es maestro en una escuela secundaria; enseña ciencias. 2. No, Daniel no es antipático, ¡es un cariño! 3. Por favor, ¿tienes un boli o un lápiz? Te escribo su número de teléfono.**

4. Tengo mucha suerte. Aunque mis padres están divorciados, tengo una familia muy unida. Tengo dos hermanos y dos hermanas. Me gusta hablar y salir a fiestas con ellos. Ahora tengo novio en la universidad y él no conoce a mis hermanos. ¡Espero que se lleven bien!

Ana María. Su familia es muy unida.

5. Antes quería° tener hermanos, pero ya no° es tan importante. Ser hijo único tiene muchas ventajas°: no tengo que compartir mis cosas con hermanos, no hay discusiones° y, como soy nieto único también, ¡mis abuelos piensan° que soy perfecto!

Fernando. Es hijo único.

6. Como soy joven todavía°, no tengo ni esposa ni hijos. Pero tengo un sobrino, el hijo de mi hermano, que es muy especial para mí. Se llama Benjamín y tiene diez años. Es un muchacho muy simpático. Siempre tiene hambre y por lo tanto vamos° frecuentemente a comer hamburguesas. Nos gusta también ir al cine° a ver películas de acción. Hablamos de todo. ¡Creo que ser tío es mejor que ser padre!

Santiago. Cree que ser tío es divertido.

salgo a pasear *I go take a walk* cuentos *stories* juntas *together* me ayuda *she helps me* Además *Besides* cualquier *any* aunque *although* tratamos *we try* siempre *always* quería *I wanted* ya no *no longer* ventajas *advantages* discusiones *arguments* piensan *think* todavía *still* vamos *we go* ir al cine *to go to the movies*

Después de leer

Emparejar

Glance at the paragraphs and see how these words and phrases are used in context. Then find their English equivalents.

A		B
1. me la compra	d	a. the oldest
2. nos llevamos bien	h	b. movies
3. no conoce	g	c. the youngest
4. películas	b	d. buys it for me
5. mejor que	j	e. borrows it from me
6. el mayor	a	f. we see each other
		g. doesn't know
		h. we get along
		i. portraits
		j. better than

Seleccionar

Choose the sentence that best summarizes each paragraph.

1. Párrafo 1 a
   a. Me gusta mucho ser abuelo.
   b. No hablo mucho con mi nieto.
   c. No tengo nietos.

2. Párrafo 2 c
   a. Mi prima es antipática.
   b. Mi prima no es muy trabajadora.
   c. Mi prima y yo somos muy buenas amigas.

3. Párrafo 3 a
   a. Tener hijos es un gran sacrificio, pero es muy bonito también.
   b. No comprendo a mis hijos.
   c. Mi esposo y yo no tenemos hijos.

4. Párrafo 4 c
   a. No hablo mucho con mis hermanos.
   b. Comparto mis cosas con mis hermanos.
   c. Mis hermanos y yo somos como (*like*) amigos.

5. Párrafo 5 a
   a. Me gusta ser hijo único.
   b. Tengo hermanos y hermanas.
   c. Vivo con mis abuelos.

6. Párrafo 6 b
   a. Mi sobrino tiene diez años.
   b. Me gusta mucho ser tío.
   c. Mi esposa y yo no tenemos hijos.

Escritura

Estrategia

Using idea maps

How do you organize ideas for a first draft? Often, the organization of ideas represents the most challenging part of the process. Idea maps are useful for organizing pertinent information. Here is an example of an idea map you can use:

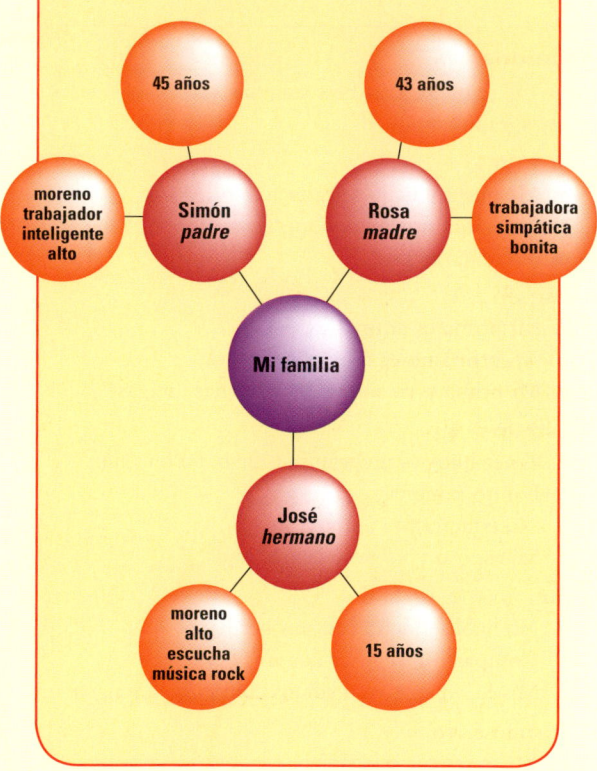

MAPA DE IDEAS

- 45 años
- 43 años
- moreno trabajador inteligente alto
- **Simón** *padre*
- **Rosa** *madre*
- trabajadora simpática bonita
- **Mi familia**
- **José** *hermano*
- moreno alto escucha música rock
- 15 años

Tema

Escribir un mensaje electrónico

A friend you met in a chat room for Spanish speakers wants to know about your family. Using some of the verbs and adjectives you have learned in this lesson, write a brief e-mail describing your family or an imaginary family, including:

▶ Names and relationships

▶ Physical characteristics

▶ Hobbies and interests

Here are some useful expressions for writing an e-mail or letter in Spanish:

Salutations

Estimado/a Julio/Julia:	*Dear Julio/Julia,*
Querido/a Miguel/Ana María:	*Dear Miguel/Ana María,*

Closings

Un abrazo,	*A hug,*
Abrazos,	*Hugs,*
Cariños,	*Much love,*
¡Hasta pronto!	*See you soon!*
¡Hasta la próxima semana!	*See you next week!*

Section Goals

In **Escritura**, students will:
- learn to write a friendly letter in Spanish
- integrate vocabulary and structures taught in **Lección 3** and before

Instructional Resource
Supersite

Estrategia Have students create their idea maps in Spanish. Some students may find it helpful to create their idea maps with note cards. They can write each detail that would be contained in a circle on a separate card to facilitate rearrangement.

Tema
- Introduce students to the common salutations (**saludos**) and closings (**despedidas**) used in friendly letters in Spanish. Point out that the salutation **Estimado/a** is more formal than **Querido/a**, which is rather familiar. Also point out that **Un abrazo** is less familiar in Spanish than its translation *A hug* would be in English.
- Point out that **Estimado/a** and **Querido/a** are adjectives and therefore agree in gender and number with the nouns they modify. Write these salutations on the board and have students supply the correct form:

_____ **Señora Martínez: (Estimada)**
_____ **Allison: (Querida)**
_____ **padres: (Queridos)**

- Point out the use of the colon (**dos puntos**). Tell students that a colon is used instead of a comma in letter salutations.

EVALUATION: Mensaje electrónico

Criteria	Scale
Appropriate salutations/closings	1 2 3 4 5
Appropriate details	1 2 3 4 5
Organization	1 2 3 4 5
Accuracy	1 2 3 4 5

Scoring	
Excellent	18–20 points
Good	14–17 points
Satisfactory	10–13 points
Unsatisfactory	< 10 points

Escuchar
Antes de escuchar

Estrategia
Asking for repetition/
Replaying the recording

Sometimes it is difficult to understand what people say, especially in a noisy environment. During a conversation, you can ask someone to repeat by saying **¿Cómo?** (*What?*) or **¿Perdón?** (*Pardon me?*). In class, you can ask your teacher to repeat by saying **Repita, por favor** (*Repeat, please*). If you don't understand a recorded activity, you can simply replay it.

To help you practice this strategy, you will listen to a short paragraph. Ask your professor to repeat it or replay the recording, and then summarize what you heard.

Preparación
Based on the photograph, where do you think Cristina and Laura are?

Ahora escucha

Adjetivos
Now you are going to hear Laura and Cristina's conversation. Use **R** to indicate which adjectives describe Cristina's boyfriend, Rafael. Use **E** for adjectives that describe Laura's boyfriend, Esteban. Some adjectives will not be used.

____	rubio	E	interesante
____	feo	____	antipático
R	alto	R	inteligente
E	trabajador	R	moreno
E	un poco gordo	____	viejo

Comprensión

Identificar
Which person would make each statement: Cristina or Laura?

	Cristina	Laura
1. Mi novio habla sólo de fútbol y de béisbol.	⊙	○
2. Tengo un novio muy interesante y simpático.	○	⊙
3. Mi novio es alto y moreno.	⊙	○
4. Mi novio trabaja mucho.	○	⊙
5. Mi amiga no tiene buena suerte con los muchachos.	○	⊙
6. El novio de mi amiga es un poco gordo, pero guapo.	⊙	○

¿Cierto o falso?
Indicate whether each sentence is **cierto** or **falso**, then correct the false statements.

	Cierto	Falso
1. Esteban es un chico interesante y simpático.	⊙	○
2. Laura tiene mala suerte con los chicos. *Cristina tiene mala suerte con los chicos.*	○	⊙
3. Rafael es muy interesante. *Esteban es muy interesante.*	○	⊙
4. Laura y su novio hablan de muchas cosas.	⊙	○

Section Goals
In **Escuchar**, students will:
- listen to and summarize a short paragraph
- learn strategies for asking for clarification in oral communication
- answer questions based on the content of a recorded conversation

Instructional Resources
Supersite: Audio (Textbook MP3s); Resources (Scripts)

Estrategia
Script La familia de María Dolores es muy grande. Tiene dos hermanos y tres hermanas. Su familia vive en España. Pero la familia de Alberto es muy pequeña. No tiene hermanos ni hermanas. Alberto y sus padres viven en el Ecuador.

Ahora escucha
Script LAURA: ¿Qué hay de nuevo, Cristina?
CRISTINA: No mucho… sólo problemas con mi novio.
L: ¿Perdón?
C: No hay mucho de nuevo… sólo problemas con mi novio, Rafael.
L: ¿Qué les pasa?
C: Bueno, Rafael es alto y moreno… es muy guapo. Y es buena gente. Es inteligente también… pero es que no lo encuentro muy interesante.
L: ¿Cómo?
C: No es muy interesante. Sólo habla del fútbol y del béisbol. No me gusta hablar del fútbol las veinticuatro horas al día. No comprendo a los muchachos. ¿Cómo es tu novio, Laura?
L: Esteban es muy simpático. Es un poco gordo, pero creo que es muy guapo. También es muy trabajador.
C: ¿Es interesante?
L: Sí. Hablamos dos o tres horas cada día. Hablamos de muchas cosas… las clases, los amigos… de todo.
C: ¡Qué bien! Siempre tengo mala suerte con los novios.

En pantalla Video

With over 440 million native Spanish speakers worldwide and the number growing due to an increasing popularity in learning Spanish, it is not uncommon to hear words that end in **-ito(a)** used not only to denote small size (for example, **niñita** and **pequeñito**), but also to express affection (for example, **abuelita** and **papito**). These words are called diminutives. The use of diminutives can vary by country and region; in some places the diminutive endings **-ico(a)**, **-illo(a)**, and **-uelo(a)** are more commonly used than **-ito(a)**.

Vocabulario útil	
cerraremos	*we will close*
conjuntito	*little outfit*
par de zapatitos	*little pair of shoes*
piecitos	*little feet*
saquito	*little coat*
¿Te falta mucho?	*Are you almost done?*

Preparación

Do you like shopping or spending time in malls? Do you prefer buying things for yourself or for others? Answers will vary.

 ### Completar

Complete the sentences.

comprar	hija	regresar
esposo	prisa	zapatitos

1. Marcos es el ___esposo___ de Claudia.
2. Claudia compra ___zapatitos___ y otras cosas.
3. Marcos y Claudia tienen una ___hija___.
4. Claudia tiene ___prisa___ porque debe ___regresar___ pronto a casa.
5. Claudia necesita ___comprar___ algo para la beba en diez minutos.

 ### Descripción

Write descriptions of the characters. Then compare your descriptions with a partner's. Answers will vary.

compró *bought* algo *something* me mata *is going to kill me*

¡Un saquito te compró° mamá!

Un par de zapatitos...

Tengo que buscar algo° para la beba, si no, Marcos me mata°.

vhlcentral   Online activities

More activities

communication cultures
NATIONAL STANDARDS

TEACHING OPTIONS

Large Group Ask students to think of a time when a word or a phrase led to a misunderstanding and share their story with class. Could the same misunderstanding have happened in Spanish? What are some similarities and differences in language usage?
Extra Practice Have students imagine other situations in Spanish in which diminutives cause humorous misunderstandings.

Heritage Speakers Ask heritage speakers to talk about how they and their families use diminutives. Have them mention the purposes (to express affection, to denote size or lack of importance, to soften a request, etc.) and the endings of the diminutives they use.
Language Note This Argentinian commercial features **vos** forms: **morís**, **apurás**. Students will learn about these forms in the **En pantalla** section of Lesson 14.

Video

If a Spanish-speaking friend told you he was going to a **reunión familiar,** what type of event would you picture? Most likely, your friend would not be referring to an annual event reuniting family members from far-flung cities. In Hispanic culture, family gatherings are much more frequent and relaxed, and thus do not require intensive planning or juggling of schedules. Some families gather every Sunday afternoon to enjoy a leisurely meal; others may prefer to hold get-togethers on a Saturday evening, with food, music, and dancing. In any case, gatherings tend to be laid-back events in which family members spend hours chatting, sharing stories, and telling jokes.

Vocabulario útil

el Día de la Madre	*Mother's Day*
estamos celebrando	*we are celebrating*
familia grande y feliz	*a big, happy family*
familia numerosa	*a large family*
hacer (algo) juntos	*to do (something) together*
el patio interior	*courtyard*
pelear	*to fight*
reuniones familiares	*family gatherings, reunions*

Preparación

What is a "typical family" like where you live? Is there such a thing? What members of a family usually live together?

Answers will vary.

Completar

Complete this paragraph with the correct options.

Los Valdivieso y los Bolaños son dos ejemplos de familias en Ecuador. Los Valdivieso son una familia (1) __numerosa__ (difícil/numerosa). Viven en una casa (2) __grande__ (grande/buena). En el patio, hacen (*they do*) muchas reuniones (3) __familiares__ (familiares/con amigos). Los Bolaños son una familia pequeña. Ellos comen (4) __juntos__ (separados/juntos) y preparan canelazo, una bebida (*drink*) típica ecuatoriana.

tan *so*

La familia

—Érica, ¿y cómo se llaman tus padres?
—Mi mamá, Lorena y mi papá, Miguel.

¡Qué familia tan° grande tiene!

Te presento a la familia Bolaños.

More activities

vhlcentral · VM pp. 41–42 · Online activities

Section Goals

In **Flash cultura**, students will:
- read about **reuniones familiares**
- watch a video about two Ecuadorian families

Instructional Resources
Supersite: Video (*Flash cultura*); Resources (Scripts, Translations, Answer Keys)
WebSAM
Video Manual

Introduction To check comprehension, ask these questions. 1. How do you say **reunión familiar** in English? (*family gathering*) 2. In Hispanic culture, what are family gatherings like and how often do they occur? (*They are relaxed and happen frequently, perhaps once a week.*) 3. What might a Saturday evening gathering involve? (*food, music, dancing*)

Antes de ver
- Have students look at the video stills, read the captions, and predict the content of the video.
- Read through **Vocabulario útil** with students. Model the pronunciation.
- Explain to students that they do not need to understand every word they hear. Tell them to rely on visual cues, cognates, and words from **Vocabulario útil**.

Preparación Survey the class. Ask students if they think there is such a thing as a "typical" family. If so, what does it look like?

Completar To challenge students, make copies of this activity with the options in parentheses removed. Pass out the copies and have students close their books. Write all the possible options on the board. Tell students to complete the activity using one word from the board for each item.

TEACHING OPTIONS

Heritage Speakers Ask heritage speakers if they know of any traditions in Spanish-speaking countries involving Mother's Day or Father's Day. As a class, compare and contrast the traditions with what is usually done in the U.S. (e.g., flowers, cards, brunch or a meal in a restaurant).

Extra Practice Tell students to imagine that they recently attended a family reunion at which there were several family members that they had never met before. Since their brother or sister was unable to attend, have students write their sibling an e-mail, describing the "new" family members. You may want to provide a few key phrases, such as **Conocí a...**

Section Goal

In **Panorama**, students will receive comprehensible input by reading about the geography and culture of Ecuador.

Instructional Resources

Supersite: Video (*Panorama cultural*); Resources (Scripts, Translations, Digital Image Bank, Answer Keys)
WebSAM
Workbook

Teaching Tip

• Have students examine the map of Ecuador and look at the call-out photos and read the captions. Encourage students to mention anything they may know about Ecuador.
• Use the **Lección 3 Panorama** digital images to assist with this presentation.

El país en cifras

• Ask students to glance at the headings. Establish the kind of information contained in each and clarify unfamiliar words. Point out that most words in the headings have an English cognate.
• Point out that in September 2000, the U.S. dollar became the official currency of Ecuador.

Ecuador

connections cultures / *NATIONAL STANDARDS*

El país en cifras

▶ **Área:** 283.560 km² (109.483 millas²), *incluyendo las islas Galápagos, aproximadamente el área de Colorado*
▶ **Población:** 16.290.00
▶ **Capital:** Quito—1.726.000
▶ **Ciudades° principales:** Guayaquil—2.709.000, Cuenca, Machala, Portoviejo
▶ **Moneda:** dólar estadounidense
▶ **Idiomas:** español (oficial), quichua
La lengua oficial de Ecuador es el español, pero también se hablan° otras° lenguas en el país. Aproximadamente unos 4.000.000 de ecuatorianos hablan lenguas indígenas; la mayoría° de ellos habla quichua. El quichua es el dialecto ecuatoriano del quechua, la lengua de los incas.

Bandera de Ecuador

Ecuatorianos célebres

▶ **Francisco Eugenio de Santa Cruz y Espejo,** médico, periodista y patriota (1747–1795)
▶ **Juan León Mera,** novelista (1832–1894)
▶ **Eduardo Kingman,** pintor° (1913–1997)
▶ **Rosalía Arteaga,** abogada°, política y ex vicepresidenta (1956–)
▶ **Iván Vallejo Ricaurte,** montañista (1959–)

Ciudades cities se hablan are spoken otras other mayoría majority pintor painter abogada lawyer

Las islas Galápagos

ESTADOS UNIDOS
OCÉANO ATLÁNTICO
OCÉANO PACÍFICO
ECUADOR
AMÉRICA DEL SUR

COLOMBIA
Indígena del Amazonas

Río Esmeraldas
• Ibarra
Quito ★
Volcán Cotopaxi ▲ Río Napo
Portoviejo •
Río Daule
Volcán Tungurahua ▲
Río Pastaza
Guayaquil •
Cordillera de los Andes
Volcán Chimborazo ▲
Océano Pacífico
• Cuenca
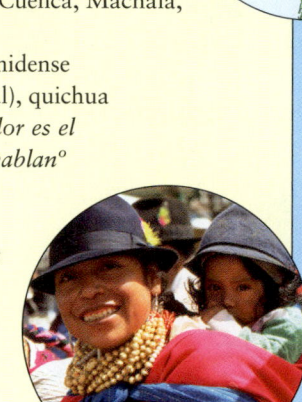
Muchos indígenas de Ecuador hablan quichua.
Machala •
• Loja

La ciudad de Quito y la cordillera de los Andes

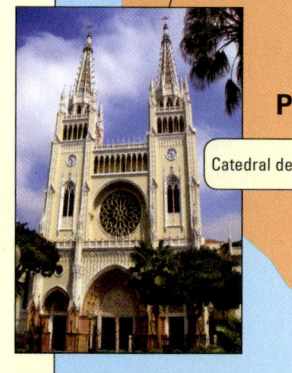
Catedral de Guayaquil

PERÚ

More activities
 vhlcentral | WB pp. 33–34 | Online activities

ACTIVIDADES

1 **Seleccionar** Escoge la respuesta correcta.

1. ¿Por qué es famoso Oswaldo Guayasamín? a
   a. por ser escultor y muralista
   b. por estudiar la evolución de las especies

2. ¿Por qué son famosas las islas Galápagos? b
   a. por el monumento la Mitad del Mundo
   b. por las tortugas gigantes

3. ¿Quién es Juan León Mera? b
   a. un ingeniero
   b. un novelista

4. Además del español, ¿cuál es la lengua más popular en Ecuador? b
   a. el alemán
   b. el quichua

5. ¿Cuál es la moneda oficial de Ecuador? a
   a. el dólar estadounidense
   b. el peso ecuatoriano

TEACHING OPTIONS

Heritage Speakers If a heritage speaker is of Ecuadorian origin or has visited Ecuador, ask him or her to share some of his or her favorite experiences there. Encourage the rest of the class to ask follow-up questions, and if a particular topic piques their interest, to find out more online.

Language Notes Remind students that **km²** is the abbreviation for **kilómetros cuadrados** and that **millas²** is the abbreviation for **millas cuadradas**. Ask a volunteer to explain why **kilómetros** takes **cuadrados** and **millas** takes **cuadradas**.

▷ **Lugares** • **Las islas Galápagos**

Muchas personas vienen de lejos a visitar las islas Galápagos porque son un verdadero tesoro° ecológico. Aquí Charles Darwin estudió° las especies que inspiraron° sus ideas sobre la evolución. Como las Galápagos están lejos del continente, sus plantas y animales son únicos. Las islas son famosas por sus tortugas° gigantes.

Artes • **Oswaldo Guayasamín**

Oswaldo Guayasamín fue° uno de los artistas latinoamericanos más famosos del mundo. Fue escultor° y muralista. Su expresivo estilo viene del cubismo y sus temas preferidos son la injusticia y la pobreza° sufridas° por los indígenas de su país.

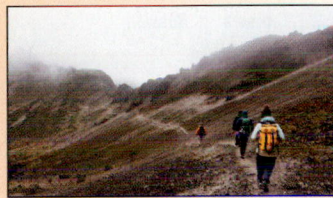

Deportes • **El *trekking***

El sistema montañoso de los Andes cruza° y divide Ecuador en varias regiones. La Sierra, que tiene volcanes, grandes valles y una variedad increíble de plantas y animales, es perfecta para el *trekking*. Muchos turistas visitan Ecuador cada° año para hacer° *trekking* y escalar montañas°.

▷ **Lugares** • **Latitud 0**

Hay un monumento en Ecuador, a unos 22 kilómetros (14 millas) de Quito, donde los visitantes están en el hemisferio norte y el hemisferio sur a la vez°. Este monumento se llama la Mitad del Mundo° y es un destino turístico muy popular.

verdadero tesoro *true treasure* estudió *studied* inspiraron *inspired* tortugas *tortoises* fue *was* escultor *sculptor* pobreza *poverty* sufridas *suffered* cruza *crosses* cada *every* hacer *to do* escalar montañas *to climb mountains* a la vez *at the same time* Mitad del Mundo *Equatorial Line Monument (lit. Midpoint of the World)*

¡Increíble pero cierto!

El volcán Cotopaxi, situado a unos 50 kilómetros al sur° de Quito, es considerado uno de los volcanes activos más altos del mundo°. Tiene una altura de 5.897 metros (19.340 pies°). Es dos veces más alto que° el monte Santa Elena (2.550 metros o 9.215 pies) en el estado de Washington.

sur *south* mundo *world* pies *feet* dos veces más alto que *twice as tall as*

---

2 **¿Qué aprendiste?** Completa las oraciones.

1. La ciudad más grande (*biggest*) de Ecuador es ___Guayaquil___.
2. La capital de Ecuador es ___Quito___.
3. Unos 4.000.000 de ecuatorianos hablan ___lenguas indígenas___.
4. Un monumento muy popular es ___la Mitad del Mundo___.
5. La Sierra es un lugar perfecto para el ___trekking___.

3 **Conversar** En parejas, describan uno de los lugares más importantes de Ecuador y expliquen por qué creen que es interesante.

> **modelo**
> La Mitad del Mundo es un lugar fantástico. Es interesante porque...

Las islas Galápagos
→👤← Bring in books, magazines, or Internet articles about the Galapagos Islands for students to read. You may want to play the **Panorama cultural** video for this paragraph.

Oswaldo Guayasamín
The name **Guayasamín** means *white bird* in Quichua. The artist took this name out of solidarity with his Incan ancestors. If possible, bring reproductions of some of **Guayasamín's** work to class. Show a variety of his paintings and encourage students to talk about what the artist's social and political stance might be.

El *trekking* Although the word **senderismo** is widely used, *trekking* is one of many English words that have been incorporated into Spanish. Generally, these are words for phenomena whose popularity originated in the English-speaking world. Some words enter Spanish without much change: **camping**, **marketing**. Others are modified to match Spanish spelling patterns, as **líder** (*leader*) or **mítin** (*meeting*).

Latitud 0 Bring in a globe and have students find Ecuador and point out its location on the equator. You may want to play the **Panorama cultural** video for this paragraph.

¡Increíble pero cierto!
Mt. St. Helens in Washington and **Cotopaxi** in Ecuador are just two of a chain of volcanoes that stretches along the entire Pacific coast of North and South America, from Mt. Denali in Alaska to **Monte Sarmiento** in the **Tierra del Fuego** of southern Chile.

TEACHING OPTIONS

Variación léxica A word that the Quichua language has contributed to English is *jerky* (salted, dried meat), which comes from the Quichua word **charqui**. The Quichua-speaking peoples of the Andean highlands had perfected techniques for "freeze-drying" both vegetable tubers and meat before the first Spaniards arrived in the region. (Freeze-dried potatoes, called **chuño**, are a staple in the diet of the inhabitants of the Andes.)

In Ecuador and throughout the rest of South America, **charqui** is the word used to name meat preserved by drying. **Charqui** is an important component in the national cuisines of South America, and in Argentina, Uruguay, and Brazil, its production is a major industry. In other parts of the Spanish-speaking world, you may hear the terms **tasajo** or **carne seca** used instead of **charqui**.

Instructional Resources
Supersite: Audio (Textbook & Lab MP3s); Testing Program (Tests, MP3s, Oral Testing Suggestions)
WebSAM
Lab Manual

Teaching Tip You may want to assign the **Prueba de práctica**, with its diagnostics and review activities, in the online-only **Repaso** section on the Supersite. There is also a **Repaso oral** in this section. For the Sixth Edition, a new summative vocabulary activity with speech recognition has been added to the **Repaso** section.

La familia

el/la abuelo/a	grandfather/grandmother
los abuelos	grandparents
el apellido	last name
el/la bisabuelo/a	great-grandfather/great-grandmother
el/la cuñado/a	brother-in-law/sister-in-law
el/la esposo/a	husband/wife; spouse
la familia	family
el/la gemelo/a	twin
el/la hermanastro/a	stepbrother/stepsister
el/la hermano/a	brother/sister
el/la hijastro/a	stepson/stepdaughter
el/la hijo/a	son/daughter
los hijos	children
la madrastra	stepmother
la madre	mother
el/la medio/a hermano/a	half-brother/half-sister
el/la nieto/a	grandson/granddaughter
la nuera	daughter-in-law
el padrastro	stepfather
el padre	father
los padres	parents
los parientes	relatives
el/la primo/a	cousin
el/la sobrino/a	nephew/niece
el/la suegro/a	father-in-law/mother-in-law
el/la tío/a	uncle/aunt
el yerno	son-in-law

Otras personas

el/la amigo/a	friend
la gente	people
el/la muchacho/a	boy/girl
el/la niño/a	child
el/la novio/a	boyfriend/girlfriend
la persona	person

Profesiones

el/la artista	artist
el/la doctor(a), el/la médico/a	doctor; physician
el/la ingeniero/a	engineer
el/la periodista	journalist
el/la programador(a)	computer programmer

Nacionalidades

alemán, alemana	German
argentino/a	Argentine
canadiense	Canadian
chino/a	Chinese
costarricense	Costa Rican
cubano/a	Cuban
ecuatoriano/a	Ecuadorian
español(a)	Spanish
estadounidense	from the U.S.
francés, francesa	French
inglés, inglesa	English
italiano/a	Italian
japonés, japonesa	Japanese
mexicano/a	Mexican
norteamericano/a	(North) American
puertorriqueño/a	Puerto Rican
ruso/a	Russian

Adjetivos

alto/a	tall
antipático/a	unpleasant
bajo/a	short (in height)
bonito/a	pretty
buen, bueno/a	good
delgado/a	thin
difícil	difficult
fácil	easy
feo/a	ugly
gordo/a	fat
grande	big
guapo/a	good-looking
importante	important
inteligente	intelligent
interesante	interesting
joven (sing.), jóvenes (pl.)	young
mal, malo/a	bad
mismo/a	same
moreno/a	brunet(te)
mucho/a	much; many; a lot of
pelirrojo/a	red-haired
pequeño/a	small
rubio/a	blond(e)
simpático/a	nice; likeable
tonto/a	foolish
trabajador(a)	hard-working
viejo/a	old

Verbos

abrir	to open
aprender (a + *inf.*)	to learn
asistir (a)	to attend
beber	to drink
comer	to eat
compartir	to share
comprender	to understand
correr	to run
creer (en)	to believe (in)
deber (+ *inf.*)	should
decidir (+ *inf.*)	to decide
describir	to describe
escribir	to write
leer	to read
recibir	to receive
tener	to have
venir	to come
vivir	to live

Possessive adjectives	See page 93.
Expressions with *tener*	See page 101.
Expresiones útiles	See page 83.

More activities

vhlcentral | LM p. 18

Los pasatiempos

4

Communicative Goals

You will learn how to:

- Talk about pastimes, weekend activities, and sports
- Make plans and invitations

Lesson Goals

In **Lección 4**, students will be introduced to the following:
- names of sports and other pastimes
- names of places in a city
- soccer rivalries
- Mexican diver **Paola Espinosa** and Venezuelan baseball player **Miguel Cabrera**
- present tense of **ir**
- the contraction **al**
- **ir a** + [*infinitive*]
- present tense of common stem-changing verbs
- verbs with irregular **yo** forms
- predicting content from visual elements
- using a Spanish-English dictionary
- writing an events pamphlet
- listening for the gist
- an excerpt of a documentary about skateboarding and BMX
- a video about soccer in Spain
- cultural, historical, economic, and geographic information about Mexico

A primera vista Ask these additional questions to personalize the photo: **¿Te gusta practicar los deportes? ¿Crees que son importantes los pasatiempos? ¿Estudias mucho los sábados y domingos? ¿Bailas? ¿Lees? ¿Escuchas música?**

Teaching Tip Look for these icons for additional communicative practice:

→👤←	Interpretive communication
←👤→	Presentational communication
👤↔👤	Interpersonal communication

🔊 A PRIMERA VISTA
- ¿Es esta persona una atleta o una artista?
- ¿Tiene cuidado?
- ¿Es vieja? ¿Es delgada?
- ¿Tiene frío o calor?

INSTRUCTIONAL RESOURCES

Supersite (vhlcentral.com)
Video: *Fotonovela, Flash cultura, En pantalla, Panorama cultural*
Audio: Textbook and Lab MP3 Files

Activity Pack: Information Gap Activities, games, additional activity handouts
Resources: SAM Answer Key, Scripts, Translations, **Vocabulario adicional**, sample lesson plan, Grammar Presentation Slides, Digital Image Bank

Testing Program: Quizzes, Tests, Exams, MP3s
Student Activities Manual: Workbook/Video Manual/Lab Manual
WebSAM (online Student Activities Manual)

Section Goals

In **Contextos**, students will learn and practice:
- names of sports and other pastimes
- names of places in a city

Instructional Resources
Supersite: Audio (Textbook and Lab MP3 Files); Resources (Digital Image Bank, **Vocabulario adicional,** Activity Pack, Scripts, Answer Keys); Testing Program (Quizzes)
WebSAM
Workbook
Lab Manual

Teaching Tips

- Write **practicar un deporte** on the board and explain what it means. Ask: **¿Qué deportes practicas?** Offer some cognates as suggestions: **¿Practicas el béisbol? ¿El vóleibol? ¿El tenis? ¿El golf?** After the student answers, ask another student: **¿Qué deporte practica _____?**
- Use the **Lección 4 Contextos** digital images to assist with this presentation.
- Ask true/false questions about the illustration. Ex: **¿Cierto o falso? Una chica anda en patineta. (Falso. Es un chico.)** Next, name famous athletes and have students give the sports they play. Ex: **¿Qué deporte practica LeBron James?**
- Point out that, except for the **nosotros/as** and **vosotros/as** forms, all present tense forms of **esquiar** carry an accent over the **i**: **esquío, esquías, esquía, esquían.**

Note: At this point you may want to present *Vocabulario adicional: Más vocabulario para el fin de semana* from the Supersite.

Los pasatiempos

Más vocabulario

el baloncesto	basketball
el béisbol	baseball
el ciclismo	cycling
el esquí (acuático)	(water) skiing
el fútbol americano	football
el hockey	hockey
la natación	swimming
el equipo	team
el parque	park
el partido	game; match
la piscina	swimming pool
la plaza	city or town square
bucear	to scuba dive
escalar montañas (f., pl.)	to climb mountains
esquiar	to ski
ganar	to win
ir de excursión	to go on a hike
nadar	to swim
patinar	to skate
practicar deportes (m., pl.)	to play sports
visitar monumentos (m., pl.)	to visit monuments
escribir una carta/ un mensaje electrónico	to write a letter/ an e-mail
leer el correo electrónico	to read e-mail
leer el periódico	to read the newspaper
deportivo/a	sports-related

Variación léxica

piscina	⟷	pileta (*Arg.*); alberca (*Méx.*)
baloncesto	⟷	básquetbol (*Amér. L.*)
béisbol	⟷	pelota (*P. Rico, Rep. Dom.*)

More activities

vhlcentral	LM p. 19	WB pp. 37–38	Online activities

PARQUE MUNICIPAL

Pasean. (pasear)

Pasea en bicicleta. (pasear)

Lee una revista. (leer)

el fútbol

el vóleibol

la pelota

el jugador

la jugadora

el tenis

TEACHING OPTIONS

Pairs 👤↔👤 Ask students to write down in Spanish their three favorite sports or leisure activities. Have students pair up and share the information using complete sentences. Ex: **Me gusta practicar la natación. Es un deporte divertido. Nado en mi piscina. ¿Qué deportes practicas?** As a class, call on individuals to report their partners' favorite pastimes. Partners will confirm or correct the information.

Variación léxica Point out that many sports in Spanish are referred to by names derived from English (**básquetbol, béisbol, fútbol**), including **el golf, el hockey, el vóleibol.** Ask students to guess the meaning of these activities (be sure to use Spanish pronunciation): **el footing** (*jogging*), **el camping, el surf(ing), el windsurf.**

Práctica

1 **Indicar** Write **sí** if each activity your hear requires a ball or **no** If does not.

1. _no_
2. _sí_
3. _no_
4. _sí_

5. _sí_
6. _sí_
7. _no_
8. _sí_

2 **Escuchar** Indicate the activity that best corresponds to each statement you hear.

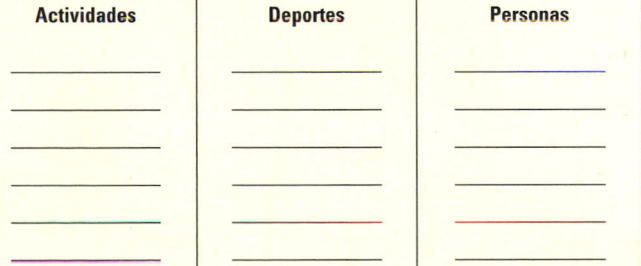

A	B
1. _b_	a. leer el correo electrónico
2. _d_	b. tomar el sol
3. _f_	c. ir de excursión
4. _h_	d. ir a un partido de fútbol americano
5. _g_	e. escribir una carta
6. _c_	f. practicar muchos deportes
	g. nadar
	h. pasear en bicicleta

3 **¿Cierto o falso?** Indicate whether each statement is **cierto** or **falso** based on the illustration.

	Cierto	Falso
1. Una persona pasea en bicicleta.	●	○
2. Hay un partido de baloncesto.	○	●
3. Las personas viejas esquían.	○	●
4. Hay dos jugadores de vóleibol.	●	○
5. Dos niñas tienen una pelota.	●	○
6. Una mujer lee el periódico.	○	●
7. Hay un equipo de hockey.	○	●
8. Un chico anda en patineta.	●	○

4 **Clasificar** Fill in the chart with as many terms from **Contextos** as you can. Answers will vary.

Actividades	Deportes	Personas

el golf

Anda en patineta. (andar)

Toma el sol. (tomar)

1 **Teaching Tip** You may want to do this activity as a TPR exercise. Have students give a thumbs-up for **sí** and a thumbs-down for **no**.

1 **Script** 1. la natación 2. el vóleibol 3. el esquí 4. el baloncesto 5. el béisbol 6. el golf 7. el ciclismo 8. el fútbol *Textbook MP3s*

2 **Teaching Tip** Have students check their answers with a partner before going over **Actividad 2** with the class.

2 **Script** 1. No me gusta nadar, pero paso mucho tiempo al lado de la piscina. 2. Alicia y yo vamos al estadio a las cuatro. 3. Me gusta patinar, esquiar y practicar el tenis. 4. El ciclismo es mi deporte favorito. 5. Me gusta mucho la natación. 6. Mi hermana camina mucho. *Textbook MP3s*

3 **Expansion** Ask students to write three additional true/false sentences based on the illustration. Have volunteers read sentences aloud for the rest of the class to answer.

4 **Expansion** Ask students to write three sentences using the words they listed in each category. You can cue students to elicit more responses. Ex: **¿Qué es la natación? (La natación es un deporte.)**

TEACHING OPTIONS

Extra Practice →🔴← Add an auditory aspect to this vocabulary practice. Prepare short descriptions of different places you need to visit using the vocabulary from the lesson. Read each description aloud and have students name an appropriate location. Ex: **Necesito estudiar en un lugar tranquilo. También deseo leer una revista y unos periódicos. Aquí la gente no debe comer ni beber ni hablar por teléfono. (la biblioteca)**

Game 🔴↔🔴 Play a modified version of **20 Preguntas**. Ask a volunteer to choose an activity, person, or place from the illustration or **Más vocabulario** that other students will take turns guessing by asking yes/no questions. Limit the attempts to ten questions, after which the volunteer will reveal the item. You may need to provide some phrases on the board.

Teaching Tip Ask brief yes/no questions to review vocabulary in **En el centro** and **Más vocabulario**. Ex: **¿Hay muchas diversiones en el centro? No tienen ratos libres los fines de semana, ¿verdad? ¿Pasan ustedes los ratos libres en el museo?**

5 **Expansion**
• Have students read each item aloud, and ask individuals to respond. After each answer is given, ask a different student to verify whether the answer is correct, using a complete sentence. Do the first verification yourself to model possible student responses. Ex: —**Tomamos una limonada.** —**Es un café/restaurante.** —**Sí. En un café/restaurante tomamos una limonada.**
• To challenge students, ask them to convert items into yes/no questions. Ex: **¿Tomamos una limonada en el café? (Sí.) ¿Vemos una película en el restaurante? (No.)** Have pairs take turns answering questions.

6 **Teaching Tip** Quickly review the verbs in the list. Make sure that students understand the meaning of **¿Qué haces…?** Tell them that they will use this phrase throughout the activity.

6 **Expansion**
• Ask additional questions and have volunteers answer. Ex: **¿Qué haces en la residencia estudiantil?** Suggested places: **un apartamento, la casa de un amigo/una amiga, el centro, un gimnasio**
• Write a new list of places on the board. Then, in pairs, have students perform the activity again, this time including information specific to a Spanish-speaking country. Their partner will guess where they are. Ex: —**¿Qué haces cuando estás en un restaurante?** —**Como paella.** —**¿Estás en España?** —**Sí.**

En el centro

el gimnasio
el museo
el café
el restaurante
el cine

Más vocabulario

la diversión	fun activity; entertainment; recreation
el fin de semana	weekend
el pasatiempo	pastime; hobby
los ratos libres	spare (free) time
el videojuego	video game
la iglesia	church
el lugar	place
ver películas (f., pl.)	to watch movies
favorito/a	favorite

5 **Identificar** Identify the place where these activities would take place.

modelo
Esquiamos. **Es una montaña.**

1. Tomamos una limonada. **Es un café./Es un restaurante.**
2. Vemos una película. **Es un cine.**
3. Practicamos deportes. **Es un gimnasio./Es un parque.**
4. Hay muchos monumentos. **Es un parque./Es una plaza.**
5. Comemos tacos y fajitas. **Es un restaurante.**
6. Nadamos y tomamos el sol. **Es una piscina./Es un parque.**
7. Hay mucho tráfico. **Es el centro.**
8. Miramos pinturas (*paintings*) de Diego Rivera y Frida Kahlo. **Es un museo.**

6 **Preguntar** Ask a classmate what he or she does in the places mentioned. Your classmate will respond using one of the verbs. **Answers will vary.**

modelo
una plaza
Estudiante 1: ¿Qué haces (*do you do*) cuando estás en una plaza?
Estudiante 2: Camino por la plaza y miro a las personas.

beber	escalar	mirar	practicar
caminar	escribir	nadar	tomar
correr	leer	patinar	visitar

1. una biblioteca
2. las montañas
3. un café
4. una piscina
5. un estadio
6. un parque
7. una plaza
8. un museo

TEACHING OPTIONS

Extra Practice Give students five minutes to write a short description of three to five sentences about a typical weekend: what they do and where, and with whom they spend time. Circulate through the class and help with unfamiliar vocabulary. Have volunteers share their paragraphs with the class. Then have the class discuss what a "typical weekend" consists of; compose a description on the board.

Game Have students tell a chain story. For example, one student begins with: **Es el sábado por la mañana y voy [al café].** The next student continues with: **Estoy en el café y tomo una *Coca-Cola*.** You may need to provide some phrases on the board: **voy a/al/a la…, luego, después.** The story may change location; set a time limit for each response. The game ends after ten minutes or when all students have participated.

Comunicación

7 **Crucigrama** Your instructor will give you and your partner an incomplete crossword puzzle. Yours has the words your partner needs and vice versa. In order to complete the puzzle, take turns giving each other clues, using definitions, examples, and phrases. Answers will vary.

> **modelo**
>
> **2 horizontal:** Es un deporte que practicamos en la piscina.
> **6 vertical:** Es un mensaje que escribimos con lápiz o con pluma.

8 **Entrevista** In pairs, take turns asking and answering these questions. Answers will vary.

1. ¿Hay un café cerca de la universidad? ¿Dónde está?
2. ¿Cuál es tu restaurante favorito?
3. ¿Te gusta viajar y visitar monumentos? ¿Por qué?
4. ¿Te gusta ir al cine los fines de semana?
5. ¿Cuáles son tus películas favoritas?
6. ¿Te gusta practicar deportes?
7. ¿Cuáles son tus deportes favoritos? ¿Por qué?
8. ¿Cuáles son tus pasatiempos favoritos?

CONSULTA

To review expressions with **gustar**, see **Estructura 2.1**, p. 52.

9 **Conversación** Work with a partner to prepare a short conversation about pastimes. Answers will vary.

| ¿a qué hora? | ¿con quién(es)? | ¿dónde? |
| ¿cómo? | ¿cuándo? | ¿qué? |

> **modelo**
>
> **Estudiante 1:** ¿Cuándo patinas?
> **Estudiante 2:** Patino los domingos. Y tú, ¿patinas?
> **Estudiante 1:** No, no me gusta patinar. Me gusta practicar el béisbol.

10 **Pasatiempos** In pairs, tell each other what pastimes three of your friends and family members enjoy. Be prepared to share with the class any pastimes you noticed they have in common. Answers will vary.

> **modelo**
>
> **Estudiante 1:** Mi hermana pasea mucho en bicicleta, pero mis padres practican la natación. Mi hermano no nada, pero visita muchos museos.
> **Estudiante 2:** Mi primo lee muchas revistas, pero no practica muchos deportes. Mis tíos esquían y practican el golf...

TEACHING OPTIONS

Large Group Have students write down six activities they enjoy and then circulate around the room to collect signatures from others who enjoy the same activities (**¿Te gusta…? Firma aquí, por favor.**). Ask volunteers to report back to the class.

Game Ask students to take out a piece of paper and write anonymously a set of activities that best corresponds to them. Collect and shuffle the slips of paper. Divide the class into two teams. Pull out and read aloud each slip of paper, and have the teams take turns guessing the student's identity.

---

7 **Teaching Tip** Model the different ways that students can give clues. Write **el gimnasio** on the board. Then write: **Es un lugar donde la gente corre. (definición) / En nuestra universidad se llama The Plex. (ejemplo) / un lugar para practicar deportes (frase)** Explain that while the definition and phrase could apply to other places, the person receiving the clue should use the empty letter spaces to figure out the answer.

7 **Expansion** In pairs, have students create another type of word puzzle, such as a word search. Tell them to use vocabulary related to sports and pastimes.

8 **Teaching Tip** Before beginning the activity, review the verb **gustar**.

8 **Expansion** Have the same pairs ask each other additional questions. Then ask volunteers to share their mini-conversations with the class.

9 **Teaching Tip** After students have asked and answered questions, ask volunteers to report their partners' activities back to the class. The partners should verify the information and provide at least one additional detail.

10 **Expansion**
- Ask volunteers to share any pastimes they and their partners, friends, and families have in common.
- In pairs, have students write sentences about the pastimes of a famous person without using their name. Encourage them to also recycle the descriptive adjectives and adjectives of nationality they learned in Lesson 3. Then have them work with another pair, asking questions as necessary, to guess the identity of the person being described.

Section Goals

In **Fotonovela**, students will:
• receive comprehensible input from free-flowing discourse
• learn functional phrases that preview lesson grammatical structures

Instructional Resources
Supersite: Video (*Fotonovela*); Resources (Scripts, Translations, Answer Keys)
WebSAM
Video Manual

Video Recap: Lección 3
Before doing this **Fotonovela** section, review the previous episode with these fill-in-the-blank sentences:
1. Marta y Valentina son las ____ de Jimena y Felipe. (primas) 2. Marissa tiene ____ hermanos y una hermana. (dos) 3. ____ es hija única. (la Sra. Díaz) 4. Las mujeres comparten una ____. (trajinera) 5. Marissa tiene planes para visitar a ____. (tía Ana María)

Video Synopsis The friends have arrived at **tía Ana María's** house in **Mérida**. Juan Carlos and Felipe head off to play soccer with **Felipe's** cousins, **Eduardo** and **Pablo**. Meanwhile, **Maru, Miguel,** and **Jimena** take **Marissa** to explore a **cenote**.

Teaching Tips
• Have students quickly glance over the **Fotonovela** captions and make a list of the cognates they find. Then, ask them to predict what this episode is about.
• Have students look for a few expressions used to talk about pastimes. Then ask a few questions. Ex: **¿Qué te gusta hacer en tus ratos libres? ¿Te gusta el fútbol?**

Fútbol, cenotes y mole

Maru, Miguel, Jimena y Marissa visitan un cenote, mientras Felipe y Juan Carlos van a un partido de fútbol.

PERSONAJES   MIGUEL   PABLO

 Video

MIGUEL Buenos días a todos.

TÍA ANA MARÍA Hola, Miguel. Maru, ¿qué van a hacer hoy?

MARU Miguel y yo vamos a llevar a Marissa a un cenote.

MARISSA ¿No vamos a nadar? ¿Qué es un cenote?

MIGUEL Sí, sí vamos a nadar. Un cenote... difícil de explicar. Es una piscina natural en un hueco profundo.

MARU ¡Ya vas a ver! Seguro que te va a gustar.

(*unos minutos después*)

EDUARDO Hay un partido de fútbol en el parque. ¿Quieren ir conmigo?

PABLO Y conmigo. Si no consigo más jugadores, nuestro equipo va a perder.

ANA MARÍA Marissa, ¿qué te gusta hacer? ¿Escalar montañas? ¿Ir de excursión?

MARISSA Sí, me gusta ir de excursión y practicar el esquí acuático. Y usted, ¿qué prefiere hacer en sus ratos libres?

PABLO Mi mamá tiene muchos pasatiempos y actividades.

EDUARDO Sí. Ella nada y juega al tenis y al golf.

PABLO Va al cine y a los museos.

ANA MARÍA Sí, salgo mucho los fines de semana.

FELIPE ¿Recuerdas el restaurante del mole?

EDUARDO ¿Qué restaurante?

JIMENA El mole de mi tía Ana María es mi favorito.

MARU Chicos, ya es hora. ¡Vamos!

TEACHING OPTIONS

Video Tips General suggestions for using video clips in the classroom can be found in the front matter of this Instructor's Annotated Edition.
Fútbol, cenotes y mole →👥← Play the last half of the **Fútbol, cenotes y mole** episode and have the class give you a description of what they saw. Write their observations on the board, pointing out any incorrect information. Repeat this process to allow the class to pick up more details of the plot. Then ask students to use the information they have accumulated to guess what happened at the beginning of the episode. Write their guesses on the board. Then play the entire episode and, through discussion, help the class summarize the plot.

ANA MARÍA **MARU** **MARISSA** **EDUARDO** **FELIPE** **JUAN CARLOS** **JIMENA** **DON GUILLERMO**

(más tarde, en el parque)

PABLO No puede ser. ¡Cinco a uno!

FELIPE ¡Vamos a jugar! Si perdemos, compramos el almuerzo. Y si ganamos...

EDUARDO ¡Empezamos!

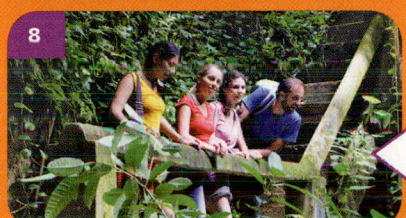

(mientras tanto, en el cenote)

MARISSA ¿Hay muchos cenotes en México?

MIGUEL Sólo en la península de Yucatán.

MARISSA ¡Vamos a nadar!

(Los chicos visitan a don Guillermo, un vendedor de paletas heladas.)

JUAN CARLOS Don Guillermo, ¿dónde podemos conseguir un buen mole?

FELIPE Eduardo y Pablo van a pagar el almuerzo. Y yo voy a pedir un montón de comida.

FELIPE Sí, éste es el restaurante. Recuerdo la comida.

EDUARDO Oye, Pablo... No tengo...

PABLO No te preocupes, hermanito.

FELIPE ¿Qué buscas? *(muestra la cartera de Pablo)* ¿Esto?

More activities

 vhlcentral   VM pp. 7–8   Online activities

Expresiones útiles

Making invitations

Hay un partido de fútbol en el parque. ¿Quieren ir conmigo?
There's a soccer game in the park. Do you want to come with me?

¡Yo puedo jugar!
I can play!

Mmm... no quiero.
Hmm... I don't want to.

Lo siento, pero no puedo.
I'm sorry, but I can't.

¡Vamos a nadar!
Let's go swimming!

Sí, vamos.
Yes, let's go.

Making plans

¿Qué van a hacer hoy?
What are you going to do today?

Vamos a llevar a Marissa a un cenote.
We are taking Marissa to a cenote.

Vamos a comprar unas paletas heladas.
We're going to buy some popsicles.

Vamos a jugar. Si perdemos, compramos el almuerzo.
Let's play. If we lose, we'll buy lunch.

Talking about pastimes

¿Qué te gusta hacer? ¿Escalar montañas? ¿Ir de excursión?
What do you like to do? Mountain climbing? Hiking?

Sí, me gusta ir de excursión y practicar esquí acuático.
Yes, I like hiking and water skiing.

Y usted, ¿qué prefiere hacer en sus ratos libres?
And you, what do you like to do in your free time?

Salgo mucho los fines de semana.
I go out a lot on the weekends.

Voy al cine y a los museos.
I go to the movies and to museums.

Additional vocabulary

el/la aficionado/a *fan*
la cartera *wallet*   el hueco *hole*
un montón de *a lot of*

¿Qué pasó?

1 **Escoger** Choose the answer that best completes each sentence.

1. Marissa, Maru y Miguel desean _____a_____.
   a. nadar b. correr por el parque c. leer el periódico

2. A Marissa le gusta _____c_____.
   a. el tenis b. el vóleibol c. ir de excursión y practicar esquí acuático

3. A la tía Ana María le gusta _____b_____.
   a. jugar al hockey b. nadar y jugar al tenis y al golf c. hacer ciclismo

4. Pablo y Eduardo pierden el partido de _____a_____.
   a. fútbol b. béisbol c. baloncesto

5. Juan Carlos y Felipe desean _____c_____.
   a. patinar b. esquiar c. comer mole ◀

NOTA CULTURAL

Mole is a typical sauce in Mexican cuisine. It is made from pumpkin seeds, chile, and chocolate, and it is usually served with chicken, beef, or pork. To learn more about **mole**, go to page 272.

2 **Identificar** Identify the person who made each statement.

1. ¿Qué es un cenote? _____Marissa_____

2. Mi mamá tiene muchos pasatiempos y actividades. _____Pablo_____

3. Yo voy a pedir un montón de comida. _____Felipe_____

4. Hay un partido de fútbol en el parque. ¿Quieren ir conmigo? _____Eduardo_____

5. Sí, salgo mucho los fines de semana. _____tía Ana María_____

MARISSA

FELIPE

PABLO

EDUARDO

TÍA ANA MARÍA ◀

NOTA CULTURAL

Cenotes are deep, freshwater sinkholes found in caves throughout the Yucatán peninsula.

They were formed in prehistoric times by the erosion and collapse of cave walls. The Mayan civilization considered the **cenotes** sacred, and performed rituals there. Today, they are popular destinations for swimming and diving.

3 **Preguntas** Answer the questions.

1. ¿Qué van a hacer Miguel y Maru?
   Miguel y Maru van a llevar a Marissa a un cenote.

2. ¿Adónde van Felipe y Juan Carlos mientras sus amigos van al cenote?
   Felipe y Juan Carlos van a jugar al fútbol con Pablo y Eduardo.

3. ¿Quién gana el partido de fútbol?
   Felipe y Juan Carlos ganan el partido de fútbol.

4. ¿Quiénes van al cenote con Maru y Miguel?
   Marissa y Jimena van al cenote con Maru y Miguel.

4 **Conversación** With a partner, prepare a conversation in which you talk about pastimes and invite each other to do some activity together. Use these expressions and also look at **Expresiones útiles** on the previous page. Answers will vary.

¿A qué hora? *(At) What time?* **contigo** *with you*	**¿Dónde?** *Where?* **No puedo porque...** *I can't because...*	**Nos vemos a las siete.** *See you at seven.*

▶ ¿Eres aficionado/a a...?
▶ ¿Te gusta...?

▶ ¿Por qué no...?
▶ ¿Quieres... conmigo?

▶ ¿Qué vas a hacer esta noche?

NATIONAL communication STANDARDS

---

1 **Teaching Tip** Read the activity items to the class as true/false sentences. Ask students to correct the false statements. Ex: **Marissa, Maru y Miguel desean correr por el parque. (Falso. Desean nadar.)**

2 **Expansion** Tell the class to add **Jimena** to the list of possible answers. Then give students these statements as items 6–8: **6. Recuerdo la comida. (Felipe) 7. No te preocupes, hermanito. (Pablo) 8. El mole de mi tía Ana María es mi favorito. (Jimena)**

Nota cultural Since the **Yucatán** peninsula does not have any rivers, **cenotes** were an important source of potable water for the pre-Hispanic Maya. One of the peninsula's most famous **cenotes** is the **Cenote Sagrado**, located near **Chichén Itzá**. It was used by Mayans in pre-Hispanic times for worship of the rain god **Chaac**.

3 **Expansion** Give these questions to the class as items 5–6: **5. ¿Qué le pregunta Juan Carlos a don Guillermo? (Le pregunta dónde pueden conseguir un buen mole.) 6. ¿Quiénes pierden dos partidos? (Eduardo y Pablo pierden dos partidos.)**

4 **Possible Conversation**
E1: ¿Qué prefieres hacer en tus ratos libres?
E2: Me gustan los deportes.
E1: ¿Te gusta el fútbol?
E2: Sí, mucho. Me gusta también nadar y correr. Oye, ¿qué vas a hacer esta noche?
E1: No tengo planes.
E2: ¿Quieres ir a correr conmigo?
E1: Lo siento, pero no me gusta correr. ¿Te gusta patinar? ¿Por qué no vamos al parque a patinar?
E2: Sí, vamos.

TEACHING OPTIONS

Small Groups Have the class quickly glance at frames 7, 8, and 10 of the **Fotonovela**. Then have students work in groups of three to ad-lib what transpires between the friends. Assure them that it is not necessary to follow the **Fotonovela** word for word. Students should be creative while getting the general meaning across with the vocabulary and expressions they know.

Extra Practice Have students close their books and complete these statements with words from the **Fotonovela**. 1. ¿Qué prefiere _____ usted en sus ratos libres? (hacer) 2. ¿Dónde _____ conseguir un buen mole? (podemos) 3. ¿Nosotros _____ a nadar? (vamos) 4. Eduardo y Pablo _____ a pagar el almuerzo. (van) 5. ¿Ustedes _____ ir conmigo al partido de fútbol? (quieren)

Pronunciación
Word stress and accent marks

 Tutorial

pe-**lí**-cu-la   e-di-**fi**-cio   **ver**   **yo**

Every Spanish syllable contains at least one vowel. When two vowels are joined in the same syllable they form a **diphthong***. A **monosyllable** is a word formed by a single syllable.

bi-blio-**te**-ca   vi-si-**tar**   **par**-que   **fút**-bol

The syllable of a Spanish word that is pronounced most emphatically is the "stressed" syllable.

pe-**lo**-ta   pis-**ci**-na   **ra**-tos   **ha**-blan

Words that end in **n**, **s**, or a **vowel** are usually stressed on the next-to-last syllable.

na-ta-**ción**   pa-**pá**   in-**glés**   Jo-**sé**

If words that end in **n**, **s**, or a **vowel** are stressed on the last syllable, they must carry an accent mark on the stressed syllable.

bai-**lar**   es-pa-**ñol**   u-ni-ver-si-**dad**   tra-ba-ja-**dor**

Words that do not end in **n**, **s**, or a **vowel** are usually stressed on the last syllable.

béis-bol   **lá**-piz   **ár**-bol   **Gó**-mez

If words that do not end in **n**, **s**, or a **vowel** are stressed on the next-to-last syllable, they must carry an accent mark on the stressed syllable.

*The two vowels that form a diphthong are either both weak or one is weak and the other is strong.

En la unión
está la fuerza.[2]

Práctica   Pronounce each word, stressing the correct syllable. Then give the word stress rule for each word.

1. profesor
2. Puebla
3. ¿Cuántos?
4. Mazatlán
5. examen
6. ¿Cómo?
7. niños
8. Guadalajara
9. programador
10. México
11. están
12. geografía

Oraciones   Read the conversation aloud to practice word stress.

MARINA   Hola, Carlos. ¿Qué tal?
CARLOS   Bien. Oye, ¿a qué hora es el partido de fútbol?
MARINA   Creo que es a las siete.
CARLOS   ¿Quieres ir?
MARINA   Lo siento, pero no puedo. Tengo que estudiar biología.

Quien ríe
de último, ríe mejor.[1]

Refranes   Read these sayings aloud to practice word stress.

1 He who laughs last, laughs best.
2 United we stand.

More activities

 vhlcentral   LM p. 20

In **Cultura**, students will:
• read about soccer rivalries
• learn sports-related terms
• read about **Miguel Cabrera** and **Paola Espinosa**
• read about renowned athletes

Instructional Resource
Supersite

En detalle

Antes de leer Ask students to predict the content of this reading based on the title and photos. Have them share what they know about these teams or about other sports rivalries.

Lectura

• Use the map on page 74 to point out the locations of Barcelona and Madrid. Briefly explain that Spain's regional cultures (Basque, Catalan, Galician, etc.) were at odds with the authoritarian, centralized approach of **Franco's** regime, which banned the public use of regional languages. Point out that the nickname **Barça** is Catalan, which is why it has a cedilla to indicate a soft **c**.

• Describe the stadiums: **Camp Nou** (Catalan for *new field*) holds about 100,000 spectators and is the largest soccer stadium in Europe. Madrid's **Estadio Santiago Bernabéu**, named after an ex-player and club president, can seat about 80,000.

• Remind students that **el fútbol** is *soccer* and **el fútbol americano** is *football*.

Después de leer Ask students what facts in this reading are new or surprising to them.

1 **Expansion** To challenge students, ask them to write two additional items. Then have them exchange papers with a classmate and complete the activity.

EN DETALLE

Real Madrid y Barça: rivalidad total

Soccer in Spain is a force to be reckoned with, and no two teams draw more attention than **Real Madrid** and the **Fútbol Club Barcelona**. Whether the venue is Madrid's **Santiago Bernabéu** or Barcelona's **Camp Nou**, the two cities shut down for the showdown,

paralyzed by **fútbol** fever. A ticket to the actual game is always the hottest ticket in town.

The rivalry between **Real Madrid** and **Barça** is about more than soccer. As the two biggest, most powerful cities in Spain, Barcelona and Madrid are constantly compared to one another and have a natural rivalry. There is also a political component to the dynamic. Barcelona, with its distinct language and culture, has long struggled for increased autonomy from Madrid's centralized government. Under Francisco Franco's rule (1939–1975), when repression of the Catalan identity was at its height, a game between **Real Madrid** and **FC Barcelona** was wrapped up with all the symbolism of the regime versus the resistance, even though both teams suffered casualties in Spain's civil war and the subsequent Franco dictatorship.

Although the dictatorship is long over, the momentum of all those decades of competition still transforms both cities into a frenzied, tense panic leading up to the game. Once the final score is announced, one of those cities is transformed again, this time into the best party in the country.

Rivalidades del fútbol

Argentina: Boca Juniors vs. River Plate
México: Águilas del América vs. Chivas del Guadalajara
Chile: Colo Colo vs. Universidad de Chile
Guatemala: Comunicaciones vs. Municipal
Uruguay: Peñarol vs. Nacional
Colombia: Millonarios vs. Independiente Santa Fe

ACTIVIDADES

1 **¿Cierto o falso?** Indicate whether each statement is **cierto** or **falso**. Correct the false statements.

1. People from Spain don't like soccer. **Falso**. People from Spain like soccer very much.
2. Madrid and Barcelona are the most important cities in Spain. **Cierto.**
3. Santiago Bernabéu is a stadium in Barcelona. **Falso**. It is a stadium in Madrid.
4. The rivalry between Real Madrid and FC Barcelona is not only in soccer. **Cierto.**
5. Barcelona has resisted Madrid's centralized government. **Cierto.**
6. Only the FC Barcelona team was affected by the civil war. **Falso**. Both teams were affected by the civil war.
7. During Franco's regime, the Catalan culture thrived. **Falso**. Catalan culture was repressed during Franco's regime.
8. There are many famous rivalries between soccer teams in the Spanish-speaking world. **Cierto.**
9. River Plate is a popular team from Argentina. **Cierto.**
10. Comunicaciones and Peñarol are famous rivals in Guatemala. **Falso**. Comunicaciones and Municipal are important rivals in Guatemala.

TEACHING OPTIONS

Project Have small groups choose famous soccer rivalries, then split up to research and create a web page for each of the rival teams. The pages should feature each team's colors, players, home stadium, official song, and other significant or interesting information. Have the groups present their rivals' web pages to the class.

¡Gooooooool! Explain that sportscasters in the Spanish-speaking world are famous for their theatrical commentaries. One example is **Andrés Cantor**, who provides commentary for soccer matches on Spanish-language stations in the U.S. Each time a goal is scored, fans know they can hear a drawn-out bellow of **¡Gooooooool! Cantor's** call, which can last for nearly thirty seconds, was made into a ringtone for cell phones in the U.S.

ASÍ SE DICE

Los deportes

el/la árbitro/a	*referee*
el/la atleta	*athlete*
la bola; el balón	la pelota
el campeón/ la campeona	*champion*
la carrera	*race*
competir	*to compete*
empatar	*to tie*
la medalla	*medal*
el/la mejor	*the best*
mundial	*worldwide*
el torneo	*tournament*

EL MUNDO HISPANO

Atletas importantes

World-renowned Hispanic athletes:

- **Rafael Nadal** (España) has won 16 Grand Slam singles titles and the 2008 Olympic gold medal in singles tennis.

- **Lionel Andrés Messi** (Argentina) is one of the world's top soccer players. He plays for **FC Barcelona** and for the Argentine national team.

- **Mireia Belmonte García** (España) won two silver medals in swimming at the 2012 Olympics. She also won a gold and a bronze at the 2016 Olympics.

- **Lorena Ochoa** (México) was the top-ranked female golfer in the world when she retired in 2010 at the age of 28. She still hosts an LPGA golf tournament every year.

PERFIL

Miguel Cabrera y Paola Espinosa

Miguel Cabrera, considered one of the best hitters in baseball, now plays first base for the Detroit Tigers. Born in Venezuela in 1983, he made his Major League debut at the age of 20. Cabrera has been selected for both the National League and American League All-Star Teams. In 2012, he became the first player since 1967 to win the Triple Crown.

Mexican diver **Paola Milagros Espinosa Sánchez**, born in 1986, has competed in four Olympics (2004, 2008, 2012, and 2016). She and her partner Tatiana Ortiz took home a bronze medal in 2008. In 2012, she won a silver medal with partner Alejandra Orozco. She won three gold medals at the Pan American Games in 2007 and again in 2011; in 2015 she won two.

CON RITMO HISPANO

Maná (1987–)
Place of origin: Guadalajara, Mexico

Maná has sold over 40 million copies of its 21 albums worldwide, which makes it the most successful and one of the most influential Latin American rock bands of all time.

Go to **vhlcentral.com** to find out more about **Maná**.

ACTIVIDADES

2 Comprensión Write the name of the athlete described in each sentence.

1. Es un jugador de fútbol de Argentina. Lionel Messi
2. Es una mujer que practica el golf. Lorena Ochoa
3. Es un jugador de béisbol de Venezuela. Miguel Cabrera
4. Es una mujer mexicana que practica un deporte en la piscina. Paola Milagros Espinosa Sánchez

3 ¿Quién es? Write a short paragraph describing an athlete that you like, but do not mention his/her name. What does he/she look like? What sport does he/she play? Where does he/she live? Read your description to the class to see if they can guess who it is. Answers will vary.

More activities

 vhlcentral
 Online activities

Section Goals

In **Estructura 4.1**, students will learn:
- the present tense of **ir**
- the contraction **al**
- **ir a** + [*infinitive*] to express future events
- **vamos a** to express *let's…*

Instructional Resources

Supersite: Audio (Lab MP3 Files); Resources (Grammar Presentation Slides, Activity Pack, Scripts, Answer Keys); Testing Program (Quizzes)
WebSAM
Workbook
Lab Manual

Teaching Tips

- Write your next day's schedule on the board. Ex: **8:00— la biblioteca; 12:00—comer**. Explain where you are going or what you are going to do, using the verb **ir**. Ask volunteers about their schedules, using forms of **ir**.
- Add a visual aspect to this grammar presentation. Write names of Spanish-speaking countries on construction paper, and pin up the papers at different points around the classroom in order to make a "map." Point to your destination "country," and as you pantomime flying there, ask students: **¿Adónde voy? (Vas a Chile.)** Once there, act out an activity, asking: **¿Qué voy a hacer? (Vas a esquiar.)**
- Practice **vamos a** to express the idea of *let's* by asking volunteers to suggest things to do. Ex: **Tengo hambre. (Vamos a la cafetería.)**

Ayuda Point out the difference in usage between **dónde** and **adónde**. Ask: **¿Adónde va el presidente de los Estados Unidos para descansar? (Va a Camp David.) ¿Dónde está Camp David? (Está en Maryland.)**

4.1 Present tense of ir Tutorial

ANTE TODO The verb **ir** (*to go*) is irregular in the present tense. Note that, except for the **yo** form (**voy**) and the lack of a written accent on the **vosotros** form (**vais**), the endings are the same as those for regular present tense **-ar** verbs.

The verb ir (to go)

Singular forms		Plural forms	
yo	**voy**	nosotros/as	**vamos**
tú	**vas**	vosotros/as	**vais**
Ud./él/ella	**va**	Uds./ellos/ellas	**van**

▶ **Ir** is often used with the preposition **a** (*to*). If **a** is followed by the definite article **el**, they combine to form the contraction **al**. If **a** is followed by the other definite articles (**la, las, los**), there is no contraction.

a + el = al

Voy **al** parque con Juan.
I'm going to the park with Juan.

Mis amigos van **a las** montañas.
My friends are going to the mountains.

▶ The construction **ir a** + [*infinitive*] is used to talk about actions that are going to happen in the future. It is equivalent to the English *to be going* + [*infinitive*].

Va a leer el periódico.
He is going to read the newspaper.

Van a pasear por el pueblo.
They are going to walk around town.

¡Voy a ir con ellos!

Ella va al cine y a los museos.

▶ **Vamos a** + [*infinitive*] can also express the idea of *let's (do something)*.

Vamos a pasear.
Let's take a walk.

¡Vamos a comer!
Let's eat!

CONSULTA

To review the contraction **de** + **el**, see **Estructura 1.3**, pp. 20–21.

AYUDA

When asking a question that contains a form of the verb **ir**, remember to use **adónde**:
¿Adónde vas?
(To) Where are you going?

More activities

vhlcentral

LM
p. 21

WB
pp. 39–40

Online activities

∞ **¡INTÉNTALO!** Provide the present tense forms of **ir**.

1. Ellos ___van___.
2. Yo ___voy___.
3. Tu novio ___va___.
4. Tú ___vas___.
5. Mi prima y yo ___vamos___.
6. Adela ___va___.
7. Ustedes ___van___.
8. Nosotros ___vamos___.
9. Usted ___va___.
10. Ellas ___van___.
11. Miguel ___va___.
12. Nosotras ___vamos___.

TEACHING OPTIONS

TPR Invent gestures to act out the activities mentioned in **Lección 4**. Ex: **leer el periódico** (act out reading and holding a newspaper), **patinar** (skate), **nadar** (move arms as if swimming). Signal individuals to gesture appropriately as you cue activities with **Vamos a**. Keep a brisk pace.
Pairs Have students form pairs, and tell them they are going somewhere with a friend. On paper strips, write varying dollar amounts, ranging from three dollars to five thousand. Have each pair draw out a dollar amount at random and tell the class where they will go and what they will do with the money they've drawn. Encourage creativity. Ex: **Tenemos seis dólares. Vamos a McDonald's para comer. Ella va a cenar, pero yo voy a beber agua porque no tenemos más dinero./Tenemos cinco mil dólares. Vamos a cenar en París…**

Práctica

1

¿Adónde van? Tell where the people are going.

> **modelo**
> los chicos / el parque **Los chicos van al parque.**

1. la señora Castillo / el centro **La señora Castillo va al centro.**
2. las hermanas Gómez / la piscina **Las hermanas Gómez van a la piscina.**
3. yo / el Museo de Arte Moderno **(Yo) Voy al Museo de Arte Moderno.**
4. tu tío y tu papá / el partido de fútbol **Tu tío y tu papá van al partido de fútbol.**
5. nosotros / el restaurante Miramar **(Nosotros) Vamos al restaurante Miramar.**

2

¿Qué van a hacer? Use **ir a** + [*infinitive*] to say that these people are also going to do the same activities tomorrow.

> **modelo**
> Ellas nadan en la piscina. **Van a nadar en la piscina mañana también.**

1. Sara lee una revista. **Va a leer una revista mañana también.**
2. Yo practico deportes. **Voy a practicar deportes mañana también.**
3. Paseamos con nuestros amigos. **Vamos a pasear con nuestros amigos mañana también.**
4. Tú tomas el sol. **Vas a tomar el sol mañana también.**
5. Ustedes van de excursión. **Van a ir de excursión mañana también.**

3

Preguntas With a partner, take turns asking and answering questions about where the people are going and what they are going to do there. **Some answers will vary.**

> **modelo**
> **Estudiante 1:** *¿Adónde va Estela?*
> **Estudiante 2:** *Va a la librería.*
> **Estudiante 1:** *Va a comprar un libro.*

Estela

1. ustedes **¿Adónde van ustedes? Vamos a la piscina. Vamos a…**

2. mi amigo **¿Adónde va mi amigo? Va al cine. Va a…**

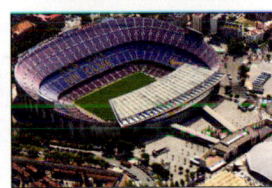
3. los estudiantes **¿Adónde van los estudiantes? Van al estadio. Van a…**

4. tú **¿Adónde vas? Voy al restaurante. Voy a…**

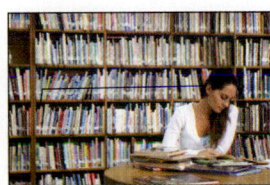
5. la profesora Torres **¿Adónde va la profesora Torres? Va a la biblioteca. Va a…**

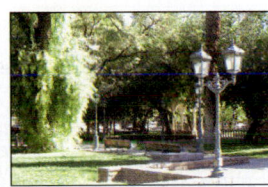
6. Álex y Miguel **¿Adónde van Álex y Miguel? Van al parque. Van a…**

---

1 Teaching Tip To add a visual aspect to this exercise, bring in photos of people dressed for a particular activity. As you hold up each photo, have the class say where they are going, using the verb **ir**. Ex: Show a photo of a basketball player. (**Va al gimnasio./Va a un partido.**)

1 Expansion After completing the activity, extend each answer with **pero** and a different name or pronoun, and have students complete the sentence. Ex: **La señora Castillo va al centro, pero el señor Castillo…** (**va al trabajo**).

2 Expansion
- Show the same photos you used for **Actividad 1** and ask students to describe what the people are going to do. Ex: **Va a jugar al baloncesto.**
- Ask students about tomorrow's activities. Ex: **¿Qué van a hacer tus amigos mañana? ¿Qué va a hacer tu compañero/a mañana?**

3 Expansion
Ask pairs to write a riddle using **ir a** + [*infinitive*]. Ex: **Ángela, Laura, Tomás y Manuel van a hacer cosas diferentes. Tomás va a nadar y Laura va a comer, pero no en casa. Uno de los chicos y una de las chicas van a ver una película. ¿Adónde van todos?** Then have pairs exchange papers to solve the riddles.

TEACHING OPTIONS

Heritage Speakers Ask heritage speakers to write six sentences with the verb **ir** indicating places they go on weekends either by themselves or with friends and family. Ex: **Mi familia y yo vamos a visitar a mi abuela los domingos…** Share the descriptions with the class and ask comprehension questions.
Game Have students work in teams to write a brief description of a well-known fictional character's activities for tomorrow, using the verb **ir**. Ex: **Mañana va a dormir de día. Va a caminar de noche. Va a buscar una muchacha bonita. La muchacha va a tener mucho miedo.** Have each team read their description aloud without naming the character. Teams can ask for and share more details about the person as needed. The first team to correctly identify the person (**Es Drácula.**) receives a point. The team with the most points at the end wins.

Comunicación

4 **Situaciones** Work with a partner and say where you and your friends go in these situations. Answers will vary.

1. Cuando deseo descansar…
2. Cuando mi novio/a tiene que estudiar…
3. Si deseo hablar con mis amigos…
4. Cuando mis amigos y yo tenemos hambre…
5. En mis ratos libres…
6. Cuando mis amigos desean esquiar…
7. Si estoy de vacaciones…
8. Si tengo ganas de leer…

5 **Encuesta** Your instructor will give you a worksheet. Walk around the class and ask your classmates if they are going to do these activities today. Find one person to answer **Sí** and one to answer **No** for each item and note their names on the worksheet in the appropriate column. Answers will vary.

modelo
Tú: ¿Vas a leer el periódico hoy?
Ana: Sí, voy a leer el periódico hoy.
Luis: No, no voy a leer el periódico hoy.

Actividades	Sí	No
1. comer en un restaurante chino		
2. leer el periódico	Ana	Luis
3. escribir un mensaje electrónico		
4. correr 20 kilómetros		
5. ver una película de terror		
6. pasear en bicicleta		

6 **Entrevista** Talk to two classmates in order to find out where they are going and what they are going to do on their next vacation. Answers will vary.

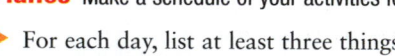
modelo
Estudiante 1: ¿Adónde vas de vacaciones (*on vacation*)?
Estudiante 2: Voy a Guadalajara con mis amigos.
Estudiante 3: ¿Y qué van a hacer (*to do*) ustedes en Guadalajara?
Estudiante 2: Vamos a visitar unos monumentos y museos. ¿Y tú?

Síntesis

7 **Planes** Make a schedule of your activities for the weekend. Then, share with a partner. Answers will vary.

▶ For each day, list at least three things you have to do.
▶ For each day, list at least two things you will do for fun.
▶ Tell a classmate what your weekend schedule is like. He or she will write down what you say.
▶ Switch roles to see if you have any plans in common.
▶ Take turns asking each other to participate in some of the activities you listed.

TEACHING OPTIONS

Pairs Write these times on the board: **8:00 a.m., 12:00 p.m., 12:45 p.m., 4:00 p.m., 6:00 p.m., 10:00 p.m.** Have student pairs take turns reading a time and suggesting an appropriate activity or place. Ex: E1: Son las ocho de la mañana. E2: Vamos a correr./Vamos al gimnasio.
Game Divide the class into teams. Name a category (Ex: **lugares públicos**) and set a time limit of two minutes. The first team

member will write down one answer on a piece of paper and pass it to the next person. The paper will continue to be passed from student to student until the two minutes are up. The team with the most words wins.
Video →👤← Show the **Fotonovela** episode again to give students more input containing the verb **ir**. Stop the video where appropriate to discuss how **ir** is used to express different ideas.

---

## Sidebar (left margin)

4 **Expansion** Have students make the phrases negative and then provide a new appropriate ending. Ex: **Cuando no deseo descansar, voy al gimnasio.**

5 **Teaching Tip** Model question formation. Ex: **1. ¿Vas a comer en un restaurante chino hoy?** Then distribute the *Hojas de actividades* (Activity Pack/ Supersite) that correspond to this activity. Allow students five minutes to fill out the surveys. Have students report their findings to the class.

5 **Expansion** After collecting the surveys, ask individuals about their plans. Ex: If someone's name appears by **ver una película de terror**, ask him or her: **¿Qué película vas a ver hoy?**

6 **Teaching Tip** Add a visual aspect to this activity. Ask students to use an idea map to brainstorm a trip they would like to take. Have them write **lugar** in the central circle, and in the surrounding ones: **visitar, deportes, otras actividades, comida, compañeros/as.**

7 **Teaching Tips**
• To simplify, have students make two columns on a sheet of paper. The first one should be headed **El fin de semana tengo que…** and the other **El fin de semana tengo ganas de…** Give students a few minutes to brainstorm about their activities for the weekend.
• Before students begin the last step, brainstorm a list of expressions as a class. Ex: **—¿Quieres jugar al tenis conmigo? —Lo siento, pero no puedo./Sí, vamos.**

4.2 Stem-changing verbs: Tutorial
e→ie, o→ue

ANTE TODO Stem-changing verbs deviate from the normal pattern of regular verbs. When stem-changing verbs are conjugated, they have a vowel change in the last syllable of the stem.

CONSULTA

To review the present tense of regular **-ar** verbs, see **Estructura 2.1**, p. 50.

•••

To review the present tense of regular **-er** and **-ir** verbs, see **Estructura 3.3**, p. 96.

INFINITIVE	VERB STEM	STEM CHANGE	CONJUGATED FORM
empezar	empez-	empiez-	empiezo
volver	volv-	vuelv-	vuelvo

▶ In many verbs, such as **empezar** (*to begin*), the stem vowel changes from **e** to **ie**. Note that the **nosotros/as** and **vosotros/as** forms don't have a stem change.

The verb empezar (e:ie) (*to begin*)

Singular forms		Plural forms	
yo	emp**ie**zo	nosotros/as	empezamos
tú	emp**ie**zas	vosotros/as	empezáis
Ud./él/ella	emp**ie**za	Uds./ellos/ellas	emp**ie**zan

Los chicos empiezan a hablar de su visita al cenote.

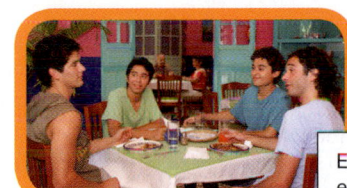

Ellos vuelven a comer en el restaurante.

▶ In many other verbs, such as **volver** (*to return*), the stem vowel changes from **o** to **ue**. The **nosotros/as** and **vosotros/as** forms have no stem change.

The verb volver (o:ue) (*to return*)

Singular forms		Plural forms	
yo	v**ue**lvo	nosotros/as	volvemos
tú	v**ue**lves	vosotros/as	volvéis
Ud./él/ella	v**ue**lve	Uds./ellos/ellas	v**ue**lven

▶ To help you identify stem-changing verbs, they will appear as follows throughout the text:

empezar (e:ie), volver (o:ue)

Section Goals

In **Estructura 4.2**, students will be introduced to:
• present tense of stem-changing verbs: e → ie; o → ue
• common stem-changing verbs

Instructional Resources
Supersite: Audio (Lab MP3 Files); Resources (Grammar Presentation Slides, Activity Pack, Scripts, Answer Keys); Testing Program (Quizzes)
WebSAM
Workbook
Lab Manual

Teaching Tips
• Take a survey of students' habits. Ask: **¿Quiénes empiezan las clases a las ocho?** Make a chart with students' names on the board. Ask: **¿Quiénes vuelven a casa a las seis?** Then create sentences based on the chart. Ex: **Tú vuelves a casa a las siete, pero Amanda vuelve a las seis. Daniel y yo volvemos a las cinco.**
• Copy the forms of **empezar** and **volver** on the board. Reiterate that the personal endings for the present tense of all the verbs listed in **Estructura 4.2** are the same as those for the present tense of regular −ar, −er, and −ir verbs.
• Explain that an easy way to remember which forms of these verbs have stem changes is to think of them as boot verbs. Draw a line around the stem-changing forms in each paradigm to show the boot-like shape.

Teaching Tips

- Write **e:ie** and **o:ue** on the board and explain that some very common verbs have these types of stem changes. Point out that all the verbs listed are conjugated like **empezar** or **volver**, except that **preferir** and **dormir** are **-ir** verbs. Model the pronunciation of the verbs and ask students a few questions using verbs of each type. Have them answer in complete sentences. Ex: **¿A qué hora cierra la biblioteca? ¿Duermen los estudiantes hasta tarde, por lo general? ¿Qué piensan hacer este fin de semana? ¿Quién quiere comer en un restaurante esta noche?**

- Point out the structure **jugar al** used with sports. Practice it by asking students about the sports they play. Have them answer in complete sentences. Ex: ____, **¿te gusta jugar al fútbol? Y tú, ____, ¿juegas al fútbol? ¿Prefieres jugar al fútbol o ver un partido en el estadio? ¿Cuántos juegan al tenis? ¿Qué prefieres, ____, jugar al tenis o jugar al fútbol?**

- Prepare a few dehydrated sentences. Ex: **Raúl / empezar / la lección; ustedes / mostrar / los trabajos; nosotros / jugar / al fútbol** Write them on the board one at a time, and ask students to form complete sentences based on the cues.

Common stem-changing verbs

e:ie		o:ue	
cerrar	to close	almorzar	to have lunch
comenzar (a + *inf.*)	to begin	contar	to count; to tell
empezar (a + *inf.*)	to begin	dormir	to sleep
entender	to understand	encontrar	to find
pensar	to think	mostrar	to show
perder	to lose; to miss	poder (+ *inf.*)	to be able to; can
preferir (+ *inf.*)	to prefer	recordar	to remember
querer (+ *inf.*)	to want; to love	volver	to return

¡LENGUA VIVA!

The verb **perder** can mean *to lose* or *to miss*, in the sense of "to miss a train."
Siempre pierdo mis llaves.
I always lose my keys.
Es importante no perder el autobús.
It's important not to miss the bus.

▶ **Jugar** (*to play a sport or a game*) is the only Spanish verb that has a **u:ue** stem change. **Jugar** is followed by **a** + [*definite article*] when the name of a sport or game is mentioned.

Ella juega al tenis y al golf.

Los chicos juegan al fútbol.

▶ **Comenzar** and **empezar** require the preposition **a** when they are followed by an infinitive.

Comienzan a jugar a las siete.
They begin playing at seven.

Ana **empieza a** escribir una postal.
Ana is starting to write a postcard.

▶ **Pensar** + [*infinitive*] means *to plan* or *to intend to do something*. **Pensar en** means *to think about someone* or *something*.

¿Piensan ir al gimnasio?
Are you planning to go to the gym?

¿En qué **piensas**?
What are you thinking about?

¡INTÉNTALO! Provide the present tense forms of these verbs.

cerrar (e:ie)
1. Ustedes _cierran_.
2. Ella _cierra_.
3. Nosotras _cerramos_.
4. Mi hermano _cierra_.
5. Yo _cierro_.
6. Usted _cierra_.
7. Los chicos _cierran_.
8. Tú _cierras_.

dormir (o:ue)
1. Mi abuela no _duerme_.
2. Yo no _duermo_.
3. Mis hijos no _duermen_.
4. Tú no _duermes_.
5. Usted no _duerme_.
6. Nosotros no _dormimos_.
7. Él no _duerme_.
8. Ustedes no _duermen_.

More activities

vhlcentral

LM
p. 22

WB
pp. 41–42

Online activities

TEACHING OPTIONS

TPR Add an auditory aspect to this grammar presentation. At random, call out infinitives of regular and **e:ie** stem-changing verbs. Have students raise their hands if the verb has a stem change. Repeat for **o:ue** stem-changing verbs.
Extra Practice For additional drills of stem-changing verbs, do the **¡Inténtalo!** activity orally using infinitives other than **cerrar** and **dormir**. Keep a brisk pace.

TPR Have the class stand in a circle. As you toss a ball to a student, call out the infinitive of a stem-changing verb, followed by a pronoun. (Ex: **querer, tú**) The student should say the appropriate verb form (**quieres**), then name a different pronoun (Ex: **usted**) and throw the ball to another student. When all subject pronouns have been covered, start over with another infinitive.

Práctica

1 **Completar** Complete this conversation with the appropriate forms of the verbs. Then act it out with a partner.

PABLO Óscar, voy al centro ahora.
ÓSCAR ¿A qué hora (1)_____*piensas*_____ (pensar) volver? El partido de fútbol
(2)_____*empieza*_____ (empezar) a las dos.
PABLO (3)_____*Vuelvo*_____ (volver) a la una. (4)_____*Quiero*_____ (querer) ver el partido.
ÓSCAR (5)¿_____*Recuerdas*_____ (recordar) que (*that*) nuestro equipo es muy bueno?
(6)¡_____*Puede*_____ (poder) ganar!
PABLO No, (7)_____*pienso*_____ (pensar) que va a (8)_____*perder*_____ (perder). Los jugadores de Guadalajara son salvajes (*wild*) cuando (9)_____*juegan*_____ (jugar).

2 **Preferencias** With a partner, take turns asking and answering questions about what these people want to do.

> **modelo**
> Guillermo: estudiar / pasear en bicicleta
> **Estudiante 1:** ¿Quiere estudiar Guillermo?
> **Estudiante 2:** No, prefiere pasear en bicicleta.

1. tú: trabajar / dormir
   ¿Quieres trabajar? No, prefiero dormir.
2. ustedes: mirar la televisión / jugar al dominó
   ¿Quieren ustedes mirar la televisión? No, preferimos jugar al dominó.
3. Elisa: ver una película / leer una revista
   ¿Quiere ver una película Elisa? No, prefiere leer una revista.
4. tú: comer en la cafetería / ir a un restaurante
   ¿Quieres comer en la cafetería? No, prefiero ir a un restaurante.
5. tus amigos: ir de excursión / descansar
   ¿Quieren ir de excursión tus amigos? No, mis amigos prefieren descansar.
6. María y su hermana: tomar el sol / practicar el esquí acuático
   ¿Quieren tomar el sol María y su hermana? No, prefieren practicar el esquí acuático.

3 **Describir** Use the verbs to describe what these people are doing.

almorzar   cerrar   contar   dormir   jugar   mostrar

1. yo (Yo) Cierro la ventana.
2. las niñas Las niñas duermen.
3. Pedro Pedro muestra una foto.
4. tú (Tú) Juegas al golf.
5. nosotros (Nosotros) Almorzamos.
6. Teresa Teresa cuenta.

Left margin notes

4 Teaching Tip Model the activity by asking questions about famous people. Ex: **¿Con qué frecuencia juega al fútbol americano Aaron Rodgers?** Write the answers on the board.

4 Expansion After tallying results on the board, have students work in pairs to graph them. Have them refer to **Lectura,** pages 142–143, for models.

5 Teaching Tips
• Model the activity by stating two programs from the listing that you want to watch and asking the class to react.
• Remind students that the 24-hour clock is often used for schedules. Model a few of the program times. Then ask: **Quiero ver *Héroes* y mi amigo prefiere ver *Elsa y Fred*. ¿Hay un conflicto? (No.) ¿Por qué? (Porque *Héroes* es a las 15:00 y *Elsa y Fred* es a las 22:00.)** Give students the option of answering with the 12-hour clock.

5 Expansion First, guide students in identifying the shows and movies that have versions in English: **Yo soy Betty, la fea; Héroes; Hermanos y hermanas; El padrastro; 60 Minutos.** Then, have students personalize the activity by choosing their favorite programs from the list. Divide the class into pairs and have them compare and contrast their reasons for their choices.

6 Teaching Tip Divide the class into pairs and distribute the handouts from the Activity Pack (Activity Pack/Supersite) that correspond to this Information Gap Activity.

6 Expansion Have volunteers take turns completing the information in the puzzle. Then have students invent their own stories, using stem-changing verbs, about what happens to the same group of tourists.

Comunicación

4 Frecuencia In pairs, take turns using the verbs from the list and other stem-changing verbs you know to tell your partner which activities you do daily (**todos los días**), which you do once a month (**una vez al mes**), and which you do once a year (**una vez al año**). Record your partner's responses in the chart so that you can report back to the class. Answers will vary.

> **modelo**
> **Estudiante 1:** Yo recuerdo a mi familia todos los días.
> **Estudiante 2:** Yo pierdo uno de mis libros una vez al año.

cerrar perder
dormir poder
empezar preferir
encontrar querer
jugar recordar
¿? ¿?

todos los días	una vez al mes	una vez al año

5 En la televisión In pairs, write a conversation between two siblings arguing about what to watch on TV. Be creative and be prepared to act out your conversation for the class. Answers will vary.

> **modelo**
> **Hermano:** Podemos ver la Copa Mundial.
> **Hermana:** ¡No, no quiero ver la Copa Mundial! Prefiero ver...

Síntesis

6 Situación Your instructor will give you and your partner each a partially illustrated itinerary of a city tour. Complete the itineraries by asking each other questions using the verbs in the captions and vocabulary you have learned. Answers will vary.

> **modelo**
> **Estudiante 1:** Por la mañana, empiezan en el café.
> **Estudiante 2:** Y luego...

NOTA CULTURAL
Iker Casillas Fernández was a famous goalkeeper for **Real Madrid**. A native of Madrid, he is among the best goalkeepers of his generation.

TEACHING OPTIONS

Small Groups Have students choose their favorite pastime and work in small groups with other students who have chosen that same activity. Have each group write six sentences about the activity, using a different stem-changing verb in each.

Pairs Ask students to write incomplete dehydrated sentences (only subjects and infinitives) about people and groups at the university. Ex: **el equipo de béisbol / perder / ¿?** Then have them exchange papers with a classmate, who will form a complete sentence by conjugating the verb and inventing an appropriate ending. Ask volunteers to write sentences on the board.

4.3 Stem-changing verbs: e→i Tutorial

ANTE TODO You've already seen that many verbs in Spanish change their stem vowel when conjugated. There is a third kind of stem-vowel change in some verbs, such as **pedir** (*to ask for; to request*). In these verbs, the stressed vowel in the stem changes from **e** to **i**, as shown in the diagram.

INFINITIVE	VERB STEM	STEM CHANGE	CONJUGATED FORM
pedir	ped-	pid-	pido

▶ As with other stem-changing verbs you have learned, there is no stem change in the **nosotros/as** or **vosotros/as** forms in the present tense.

The verb pedir (e:i) (to ask for; to request)

Singular forms		Plural forms	
yo	pido	nosotros/as	pedimos
tú	pides	vosotros/as	pedís
Ud./él/ella	pide	Uds./ellos/ellas	piden

▶ To help you identify verbs with the **e:i** stem change, they will appear as follows throughout the text:

pedir (e:i)

▶ These are the most common **e:i** stem-changing verbs:

conseguir	**decir**	**repetir**	**seguir**
to get; to obtain	*to say; to tell*	*to repeat*	*to follow; to continue; to keep (doing something)*

Pido favores cuando es necesario.
I ask for favors when it's necessary.

Javier **dice** la verdad.
Javier is telling the truth.

Sigue con su tarea.
He continues with his homework.

Consiguen ver buenas películas.
They get to see good movies.

▶ **¡Atención!** The verb **decir** is irregular in its **yo** form: **yo digo**.

▶ The **yo** forms of **seguir** and **conseguir** have a spelling change in addition to the stem change **e:i**.

Sigo su plan.
I'm following their plan.

Consigo novelas en la librería.
I get novels at the bookstore.

¡INTÉNTALO! Provide the correct forms of the verbs.

repetir (e:i)	decir (e:i)	seguir (e:i)
1. Arturo y Eva _repiten_.	1. Yo _digo_.	1. Yo _sigo_.
2. Nosotros _repetimos_.	2. Él _dice_.	2. Los chicos _siguen_.
3. Yo _repito_.	3. Tú _dices_.	3. Tú _sigues_.
4. Julia _repite_.	4. Ellas _dicen_.	4. Nosotros _seguimos_.
5. Sofía y yo _repetimos_.	5. Usted _dice_.	5. Usted _sigue_.

More activities

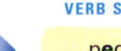
vhlcentral

LM
p. 23

WB
pp. 43–44

Online activities

Práctica

1 Expansion
←■→ Have students use **conseguir, decir, pedir, repetir,** and **seguir** to write sentences about their own family members. Then have them exchange papers with a partner for peer editing.

Nota cultural
→■← Have students read about **El Bosque de Chapultepec** in Spanish in either the library or on the Internet and bring a photo of the park to class. Ask them to share one new fact they learned about the park.

2 Teaching Tips
• Before beginning the activity, point out that not all verbs in column B have an **e:i** stem change. Have students identify those that do not (**poder, dormir, perder**).
• In pairs, have students decide which activities in column B are characteristic of a good student. Ex: **Un buen estudiante repite el vocabulario.**

2 Expansion In pairs, have students read their sentences aloud. Their partner must decide if they are true or false.

3 Teaching Tip Remind students that their partners may guess information that is true, but not necessarily what they wrote for **Actividad 2.**

4 Teaching Tip As you check answers, ask follow-up questions so that students provide more details.

1 Completar Complete these sentences with the correct form of the verb.

1. Cuando mi familia pasea por la ciudad, mi madre siempre (*always*) va a un café y _____ **pide** _____ (pedir) una soda.
2. Pero mi padre _____ **dice** _____ (decir) que perdemos mucho tiempo. Tiene prisa por llegar al Bosque de Chapultepec.
3. Mi padre tiene suerte, porque él siempre _____ **consigue** _____ (conseguir) lo que (*that which*) desea.
4. Cuando llegamos al parque, mis hermanos y yo _____ **seguimos** _____ (seguir) conversando (*talking*) con nuestros padres.
5. Mis padres siempre _____ **repiten** _____ (repetir) la misma cosa: "Nosotros tomamos el sol aquí sin ustedes".
6. Yo siempre _____ **pido** _____ (pedir) permiso para volver a casa un poco más tarde porque me gusta mucho el parque.

NOTA CULTURAL
A popular weekend destination for residents and tourists, **el Bosque de Chapultepec** is a beautiful park located in Mexico City. It occupies over 1.5 square miles and includes lakes, wooded areas, several museums, and a botanical garden. You may recognize this park from **Fotonovela, Lección 2.**

2 Combinar Combine words from the two columns to create sentences about yourself and people you know. Answers will vary.

modelo
> Mi hermana consigue libros en Internet.

A	B
yo	nunca (*never*) pedir perdón
mi compañero/a de cuarto	(no) pedir muchos favores
mi mejor (*best*) amigo/a	nunca seguir las instrucciones
mi familia	siempre seguir las instrucciones
mis amigos/as	repetir el vocabulario
mis amigos/as y yo	conseguir libros en Internet
mis padres	poder hablar dos lenguas
mi hermano/a	dormir hasta el mediodía
mi profesor(a) de español	siempre perder sus libros

3 Opiniones In pairs, take turns guessing how your partner completed the sentences from **Actividad 2**. If you guess incorrectly, your partner must supply the correct answer. Answers will vary.

modelo
> **Estudiante 1:** Creo que tus padres consiguen libros en Internet.
> **Estudiante 2:** ¡No! Mi hermana consigue libros en Internet.

CONSULTA
To review possessive adjectives, see **Estructura 3.2**, p. 93.

4 ¿Quién? Your instructor will give you a worksheet. Talk to your classmates until you find one person who does each of the activities. Use **e:ie, o:ue,** and **e:i** stem-changing verbs.

modelo
> **Tú:** ¿Pides consejos con frecuencia?
> **Maira:** No, no pido consejos con frecuencia.
> **Tú:** ¿Pides consejos con frecuencia?
> **Lucas:** Sí, pido consejos con frecuencia.

TEACHING OPTIONS

Pairs Ask students to write four simple statements using **e:i** verbs. Then have them read their sentences to a partner, who will guess where the situation takes place. Ex: **Consigo libros para las clases. (Estás en la biblioteca.)** Then reverse the activity, allowing them to answer with verbs from **Estructura 4.2.**

Small Groups Explain to students that movie titles for English-language films are frequently not directly translated into Spanish and that titles may vary from country to country. Bring in a list of movie titles in Spanish. Ex: *La guerra de las galaxias* (*Star Wars*); *Lo que el viento se llevó* (*Gone with the Wind*). In groups, have students guess the movies based on the Spanish titles. Then ask them to state which movies they'd prefer to watch.

Comunicación

5 **Las películas** Use these questions to interview a classmate. *Answers will vary.*

1. ¿Prefieres las películas románticas, las películas de acción o las películas de terror? ¿Por qué?
2. ¿Dónde consigues información sobre (*about*) cine y televisión?
3. ¿Dónde consigues las entradas (*tickets*) para ver una película?
4. Para decidir qué películas vas a ver, ¿sigues las recomendaciones de los críticos de cine? ¿Qué dicen los críticos en general?
5. ¿Qué cines en tu comunidad muestran las mejores (*best*) películas?
6. ¿Vas a ver una película esta semana? ¿A qué hora empieza la película?

Síntesis

6 **El cine** In pairs, first scan the ad and jot down all the stem-changing verbs. Then answer the questions. *Answers will vary.*

1. ¿Qué palabras indican que *Dunkirk* es una película dramática?
2. ¿Cómo está el personaje (*character*) del póster? ¿Qué quiere hacer?
3. ¿Te gustan las películas como ésta (*this one*)? ¿Por qué?
4. Describe tu película favorita con los verbos de la **Lección 4**. *Answers will vary.*

★★★★★

Una de las mejores películas del año

Dunkerque: un momento decisivo de la Segunda Guerra Mundial

Cuando los nazis comienzan a controlar toda Francia, las fuerzas aliadas no pierden la esperanza. Sólo quieren cumplir su misión: evacuar las tropas de Dunkerque y seguir luchando por la libertad de Europa.

¿Consiguen escapar? ¿Vuelven a Inglaterra?

Una película dramática de acción histórica, con actuación y efectos especiales espectaculares. Escrita y dirigida por Christopher Nolan.

4.4 Verbs with irregular **yo** forms

 Tutorial

ANTE TODO In Spanish, several verbs have irregular **yo** forms in the present tense. You have already seen three verbs with the **-go** ending in the **yo** form: **decir → digo, tener → tengo,** and **venir → vengo.**

▶ Here are some common expressions with **decir.**

decir la verdad *to tell the truth*	**decir mentiras** *to tell lies*
decir que *to say that*	**decir la respuesta** *to say the answer*

▶ The verb **hacer** is often used to ask questions about what someone does. Note that when answering, **hacer** is frequently replaced with another, more specific action verb.

Verbs with irregular yo forms

	hacer (to do; to make)	poner (to put; to place)	salir (to leave)	suponer (to suppose)	traer (to bring)
SINGULAR FORMS	**hago**	**pongo**	**salgo**	**supongo**	**traigo**
	haces	pones	sales	supones	traes
	hace	pone	sale	supone	trae
PLURAL FORMS	hacemos	ponemos	salimos	suponemos	traemos
	hacéis	ponéis	salís	suponéis	traéis
	hacen	ponen	salen	suponen	traen

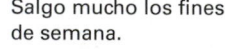

Salgo mucho los fines de semana.

Yo no salgo, yo hago la tarea y veo películas en la televisión.

▶ **Poner** can also mean *to turn on* a household appliance.

Carlos **pone** la radio. *Carlos turns on the radio.*	María **pone** la televisión. *María turns on the television.*

▶ **Salir de** is used to indicate that someone is leaving a particular place.

Hoy **salgo del** hospital. *Today I leave the hospital.*	**Sale de** la clase a las cuatro. *He leaves class at four.*

▶ **Salir para** is used to indicate someone's destination.

Mañana **salgo para** México. Hoy **salen para** España.
Tomorrow I leave for Mexico. *Today they leave for Spain.*

▶ **Salir con** means *to leave with someone* or *something*, or *to date someone.*

Alberto **sale con** su mochila. Margarita **sale con** Guillermo.
Alberto is leaving with his backpack. *Margarita is going out with Guillermo.*

The verbs ver and oír

▶ The verb **ver** (*to see*) has an irregular **yo** form. The other forms of **ver** are regular.

The verb **ver** (*to see*)			
Singular forms		**Plural forms**	
yo	**veo**	nosotros/as	vemos
tú	ves	vosotros/as	veis
Ud./él/ella	ve	Uds./ellos/ellas	ven

▶ The verb **oír** (*to hear*) has an irregular **yo** form and the spelling change **i:y** in the **tú**, **usted/él/ella**, and **ustedes/ellos/ellas** forms. The **nosotros/as** and **vosotros/as** forms have an accent mark.

The verb **oír** (*to hear*)			
Singular forms		**Plural forms**	
yo	**oigo**	nosotros/as	oímos
tú	oyes	vosotros/as	oís
Ud./él/ella	oye	Uds./ellos/ellas	oyen

▶ While most commonly translated as *to hear*, **oír** is also used in contexts where the verb *to listen* would be used in English.

Oigo a unas personas en la otra sala. ¿**Oyes** la radio por la mañana?
I hear some people in the other room. *Do you listen to the radio in the morning?*

More activities

vhlcentral

LM
p. 24

WB
pp. 45–46

Online activities

¡INTÉNTALO! Provide the correct forms of these verbs.

1. salir Isabel ___sale___. Nosotros ___salimos___. Yo ___salgo___.
2. ver Yo ___veo___. Ustedes ___ven___. Tú ___ves___.
3. poner Rita y yo ___ponemos___. Yo ___pongo___. Los niños ___ponen___.
4. traer Ellas ___traen___. Yo ___traigo___. Tú ___traes___.
5. oír Él ___oye___. Nosotros ___oímos___. Yo ___oigo___.
6. hacer Yo ___hago___. Tú ___haces___. Usted ___hace___.
7. suponer Yo ___supongo___. Mi amigo ___supone___. Nosotras ___suponemos___.

Teaching Tips

• Point out that **oír** is irregular in all forms. Write a model sentence on the board. Ex: **Ustedes oyen el programa de radio todos los viernes.** Then change the subject, and have students give the new sentence. Ex: **tú (Tú oyes el programa de radio todos los viernes.)**

• Call out different forms of the verbs in **Estructura 4.4** and have volunteers say the infinitive. Ex: **oyen (oír).** Keep a brisk pace.

• Do a chain drill. Start by writing **¿Qué haces los sábados?** on the board. Model an appropriate answer, such as **Salgo con mis amigos.** Ask one student to respond (Ex: **Veo una película.**). The next student you call on should repeat what the first said and add on (Ex: **Cindy ve una película y yo salgo con…**). Continue until the chain becomes too long; then start with a new question. Keep a brisk pace.

• Write these phrases on the board: **ver la tele, traer un sándwich a la universidad, salir con amigos,** and **hacer yoga.** Model the question and possible answers for each phrase. Then elicit follow-up questions (Ex: **¿Dónde ves la tele?**). Have student pairs take turns asking and answering the questions. They should be prepared to report to the class about their partners' habits.

• Explain to students that the i → y spelling change strengthens the **i** sound between vowels, which clarifies to the ear that the verb is **oír.**

• Explain the difference between **escuchar** (*to listen*) and **oír** (*to hear*). Ex: **Escucho la radio. No oigo el perro.**

TEACHING OPTIONS

Extra Practice Add an auditory aspect to this grammar presentation. Call out subject pronouns and titles of songs or movies (Ex: **ustedes,** *Dunkerque*). Have students respond with a complete sentence, using **ver** or **oír.** (Ex: **Ustedes ven** *Dunkerque.***)**

Pairs Have pairs create questions using the vocabulary of the lesson to ask each other about their habits. Ex: **¿Sales a comer a restaurantes con tus amigos? ¿Ves la televisión en español? ¿Supones que una clase de matemáticas es muy difícil?** Have students record their partner's answers and be prepared to share the information with the class.

Práctica

1 Completar Complete this conversation with the correct forms of the verbs. Then act it out with a partner.

ERNESTO David, ¿qué (1)_____ *haces* _____ (hacer) hoy?

DAVID Ahora estudio biología, pero esta noche (2)_____ *salgo* _____ (salir) con Luisa. Vamos al cine. Los críticos (3)_____ *dicen* _____ (decir) que la nueva (*new*) película de Almodóvar es buena.

ERNESTO ¿Y Diana? ¿Qué (4)_____ *hace* _____ (hacer) ella?

DAVID (5)_____ *Sale* _____ (salir) a comer con sus padres.

ERNESTO ¿Qué (6)_____ *hacen* _____ (hacer) Andrés y Javier?

DAVID Tienen que (7)_____ *hacer* _____ (hacer) las maletas. (8)_____ *Salen* _____ (salir) para Monterrey mañana.

ERNESTO Pues, ¿qué (9)_____ *hago* _____ (hacer) yo?

DAVID Yo (10)_____ *supongo* _____ (suponer) que puedes estudiar o (11)_____ *ver* _____ (ver) la televisión.

ERNESTO No quiero estudiar. Mejor (12)_____ *pongo* _____ (poner) la televisión. Mi programa favorito empieza en unos minutos.

2 Oraciones Form sentences using verbs from **Estructura 4.4**.

> **modelo**
> tú / _____ / cosas / en / su lugar / antes de (*before*) / salir
> Tú *pones las cosas en su lugar antes de salir.*

1. mis amigos / _____ / conmigo / centro *Mis amigos salen conmigo al centro.*
2. yo / no / _____ / muchas películas *Yo no veo muchas películas.*
3. Alberto / _____ / música del café Pasatiempos *Alberto oye la música del café Pasatiempos.*
4. tú / _____ / mentiras / pero / yo _____ / verdad *Tú dices mentiras, pero yo digo la verdad.*
5. domingo / nosotros / _____ / mucha / tarea *El domingo nosotros hacemos mucha tarea.*
6. si / yo / _____ / que / yo querer / ir / cine / mis amigos / ir / también *Si yo digo que quiero ir al cine, mis amigos van también.*

3 Describir Use the verbs from **Estructura 4.4** to describe what these people are doing.

1. Fernán *Fernán pone/ve la televisión.*

2. el estudiante *El estudiante hace su tarea.*

3. los aficionados *Los aficionados salen del estadio/para sus casas.*

4. nosotros *Nosotros vemos una película.*

5. la señora Vargas *La señora Vargas no oye bien.*

6. yo *Yo traigo/salgo con una pelota.*

Comunicación

4　　**Tu rutina** In pairs, take turns asking each other these questions.　Answers will vary.

1. ¿Qué traes a clase?
2. ¿A qué hora sales de tu residencia estudiantil o de tu casa por la mañana? ¿A qué hora sale tu compañero/a de cuarto?
3. ¿Dónde pones tus libros cuando regresas de clase? ¿Siempre (*Always*) pones tus cosas en su lugar?
4. ¿Oyes música cuando estudias?
5. ¿Ves películas en casa o prefieres ir al cine?
6. ¿Haces mucha tarea los fines de semana?
7. ¿Sales con tus amigos los fines de semana? ¿A qué hora? ¿Qué hacen?
8. ¿Te gusta ver deportes en la televisión o prefieres ver otros programas? ¿Cuáles?

5　**Charadas** In groups, play a game of charades. Each person should think of two phrases containing the verbs **hacer, oír, poner, salir, traer,** or **ver**. The first person to guess correctly acts out the next charade.　Answers will vary.

6　**Entrevista** You are doing a market research report on lifestyles. Interview a classmate to find out when he or she goes out with these people and what they do for entertainment.　Answers will vary.

▶ los/las amigos/as
▶ el/la novio/a
▶ el/la esposo/a
▶ la familia

Síntesis

7　**Situación** With a partner, prepare a conversation between two roommates.　Answers will vary.

Estudiante 1	Estudiante 2
Ask your partner what he or she is doing. →	Tell your partner that you are watching TV.
Say what you suppose he or she is watching. →	Say that you like the show _____. Ask if he or she wants to watch.
Say no, because you are going out with friends, and tell where you are going. →	Say you think it's a good idea, and ask what your partner and his or her friends are doing there.
Say what you are going to do, and ask your partner whether he or she wants to come along. →	Say no and tell your partner what you prefer to do.

TEACHING OPTIONS

Pairs ▪↔▪ Have pairs of students role-play an awful first date. Students should write their script first, then present it to the class. Encourage students to use descriptive adjectives as well as the new verbs learned in **Estructura 4.4**.

Heritage Speakers ▪→ Ask heritage speakers to talk about a social custom in their cultural community. Remind them to use familiar vocabulary and simple sentences.

4 Teaching Tip Model the activity by having volunteers answer the first two items.

4 Expansion
▪↔▪ Ask volunteers to call out some of their answers. The class should speculate about the reason behind each answer and offer more information. Have the volunteer confirm or deny the speculation.
Ex: —**Traigo mi tarea a clase.**
—**Eres un(a) buen(a) estudiante.**
—**Sí, soy un(a) buen(a) estudiante porque hago mi tarea.**

5 Teaching Tips
• Model the activity by doing a charade for the class to guess. Ex: **Pongo un lápiz en la mesa.** Then divide the class into small groups.
• Ask each group to choose the best **charada**. Then have students present them to the class, who will guess the activities.

6 Teaching Tip Model the activity by giving a report on your lifestyle. Ex: **Salgo al cine con mis amigas. Me gusta comer en restaurantes con mi esposo. En familia vemos deportes en la televisión.** Remind students that a market researcher and the interviewee would address each other with the **usted** form of verbs.

7 Possible Conversation
E1: **¿Qué haces?**
E2: **Veo la tele.**
E1: **Supongo que ves** *Los Simpson.*
E2: **Sí. Me gusta el programa. ¿Quieres ver la tele conmigo?**
E1: **No puedo. Salgo con mis amigos a la plaza.**
E2: **Buena idea. ¿Qué hacen en la plaza?**
E1: **Vamos a escuchar música y a pasear. ¿Quieres venir?**
E2: **No. Prefiero descansar.**

Recapitulación

Review the grammar concepts you have learned in this lesson by completing these activities.

1 **Completar** Complete the chart with the correct verb forms. **30 pts.**

Infinitive	yo	nosotros/as	ellos/as
volver	**vuelvo**	volvemos	vuelven
comenzar	comienzo	**comenzamos**	comienzan
hacer	hago	**hacemos**	**hacen**
ir	voy	vamos	van
jugar	**juego**	jugamos	juegan
repetir	repito	repetimos	**repiten**

2 **Un día típico** Complete the paragraph with the correct forms of the appropriate verbs. **20 pts.**

almorzar	ir	salir
cerrar	jugar	seguir
empezar	mostrar	ver
hacer	querer	volver

¡Hola! Me llamo Cecilia y vivo en Puerto Vallarta, México. ¿Cómo es un día típico en mi vida (*life*)? Por la mañana bebo café con mis padres y juntos (*together*) (1) _vemos_ las noticias (*news*) en la televisión. A las siete y media, (*yo*) (2) _salgo_ de mi casa y tomo el autobús. Me gusta llegar temprano (*early*) a la universidad porque siempre (*always*) (3) _veo_ a mis amigos en la cafetería. Tomamos café y planeamos lo que (4) _queremos_ hacer cada (*each*) día. A las ocho y cuarto, mi amiga Sandra y yo (5) _vamos_ al laboratorio de lenguas. La clase de francés (6) _empieza_ a las ocho y media. ¡Es mi clase favorita! A las doce y media (*yo*) (7) _almuerzo_ en la cafetería con mis amigos. Después (*Afterward*), yo (8) _sigo_ con mis clases. Por las tardes, mis amigos (9) _vuelven_ a sus casas, pero yo (10) _juego_ al vóleibol con mi amigo Tomás.

RESUMEN GRAMATICAL

4.1 Present tense of ir *p. 126*

yo	**voy**	nos.	**vamos**
tú	**vas**	vos.	**vais**
él	**va**	ellas	**van**

▶ ir a + [*infinitive*] = to be going + [*infinitive*]
▶ a + el = al
▶ vamos a + [*infinitive*] = let's (*do something*)

4.2 Stem-changing verbs e:ie, o:ue, u:ue *pp. 129–130*

	empezar	volver	jugar
yo	emp**ie**zo	v**ue**lvo	j**ue**go
tú	emp**ie**zas	v**ue**lves	j**ue**gas
él	emp**ie**za	v**ue**lve	j**ue**ga
nos.	empezamos	volvemos	jugamos
vos.	empezáis	volvéis	jugáis
ellas	emp**ie**zan	v**ue**lven	j**ue**gan

▶ Other e:ie verbs: cerrar, comenzar, entender, pensar, perder, preferir, querer
▶ Other o:ue verbs: almorzar, contar, dormir, encontrar, mostrar, poder, recordar

4.3 Stem-changing verbs e:i *p. 133*

	pedir		
yo	p**i**do	nos.	pedimos
tú	p**i**des	vos.	pedís
él	p**i**de	ellas	p**i**den

▶ Other e:i verbs: conseguir, decir, repetir, seguir

4.4 Verbs with irregular yo forms *pp. 136–137*

hacer	poner	salir	suponer	traer
hago	pongo	salgo	supongo	traigo

▶ ver: **veo**, ves, ve, vemos, veis, ven
▶ oír: o**i**go, o**y**es, o**y**e, oímos, oís, o**y**en

3 **Oraciones** Arrange the cues in the correct order to form complete sentences. Make all necessary changes. `14 pts.`

1. tarea / los / hacer / sábados / nosotros / la
Los sábados nosotros hacemos la tarea./Nosotros hacemos la tarea los sábados.

2. en / pizza / Andrés / una / restaurante / el / pedir
Andrés pide una pizza en el restaurante.

3. a / ? / museo / ir / ¿ / el / (tú)
¿(Tú) Vas al museo?

4. de / oír / amigos / bien / los / no / Elena
Los amigos de Elena no oyen bien.

5. libros / traer / yo / clase / mis / a
Yo traigo mis libros a clase.

6. película / ver / en / Jorge y Carlos / pensar / cine / una / el
Jorge y Carlos piensan ver una película en el cine.

7. unos / escribir / Mariana / electrónicos / querer / mensajes
Mariana quiere escribir unos mensajes electrónicos.

4 **Escribir** Write a short paragraph about what you do on a typical day. Use at least six of the verbs you have learned in this lesson. You can use the paragraph on the opposite page (**Actividad 2**) as a model. `36 pts.`   Answers will vary.

> *Un día típico*
>
> *Hola, me llamo Julia y vivo en Vancouver, Canadá. Por la mañana, yo...*

5 **Rima** Complete the rhyme with the correct forms of the appropriate verbs. `4 EXTRA points!`

contar	poder
oír	suponer

66 Si no ___puedes___ dormir
y el sueño deseas,
lo vas a conseguir
si ___cuentas___ ovejas°. 99

ovejas *sheep*

3 **Teaching Tip** To simplify, provide the first word for each sentence.

3 **Expansion** Give students these sentences as items 8–11: **8. la / ? / ustedes / cerrar / ventana / ¿ / poder** (¿Pueden ustedes cerrar la ventana?) **9. cine / del / tú / las / salir / once / a** (Tú sales del cine a las once.) **10. el / conmigo / a / en / ellos / tenis / el / jugar / parque** (Ellos juegan al tenis conmigo en el parque.) **11. que / partido / mañana / un / decir / hay / Javier** (Javier dice que hay un partido mañana.)

4 **Teaching Tips**
- To simplify, ask students to make a three-column chart with the headings **Por la mañana, Por la tarde,** and **Por la noche.** Have them brainstorm at least three verbs or verb phrases for each column and circle any stem-changing or irregular **yo** verbs.
- →■← Have students exchange paragraphs with a classmate for peer editing. Ask them to underline grammatical and spelling errors.

5 **Teaching Tip** Point out the inverted word order in line 2 of the rhyme and ask students what the phrase would be in everyday Spanish (**y deseas el sueño**).

5 **Expansion** Come up with similar rhymes and have students complete them. Ex: **Si no ____ descansar y diversión deseas, lo vas a encontrar si ____ con ellas.** (quieres, juegas)

TEACHING OPTIONS

Game ■↔■ Make a *Bingo* card of places at school or around town, such as dorm names, libraries, cafeterias, movie theaters, and cafés. Give each student a card and model possible questions (Ex: for a cafeteria, **¿Almuerzas en ____?/¿Dónde almuerzas?**). Encourage them to circulate around the room, asking only one question per person; if they get an affirmative answer, they should write that person's name in the square. The first student to complete a horizontal, vertical, or diagonal row and yell ¡Bingo! is the winner.

Heritage Speakers ←■→ Ask heritage speakers if counting sheep is common advice for sleeplessness in their families. Have them describe other insomnia remedies they have heard of or practiced.

Section Goals

In **Lectura**, students will:
- learn the strategy of predicting content by surveying the graphic elements in reading matter
- read a magazine article containing graphs and charts

Instructional Resource
Supersite

Estrategia Tell students that they can infer a great deal of information about the content of an article by surveying the graphic elements included in it. When students survey an article for its graphic elements, they should look for such things as:
- headlines or headings
- bylines
- photos
- photo captions
- graphs and tables

Examinar el texto Give students two minutes to take a look at the visual clues in the article and write down all the ideas the clues suggest.

Contestar After going over students' responses, ask them how accurate their predictions were from **Examinar el texto**.

Evaluación y predicción Write two headings on the board: **Entre los jóvenes del mundo hispano** and **Entre los jóvenes de nuestra universidad**. Ask for a show of hands to respond to your questions about the ranking of each sporting event. Tally the responses as you proceed. Ask: **¿Quiénes creen que entre los jóvenes hispanos la Copa Mundial de Fútbol es el evento más popular? ¿Quiénes creen que los Juegos Olímpicos son el evento más popular?** Then ask: **Entre los jóvenes de nuestra universidad, ¿quiénes de ustedes creen que la Copa Mundial de Fútbol es el evento más popular?** Briefly discuss the differences indicated by student responses.

Lectura

 NATIONAL STANDARDS communication cultures

Antes de leer

Estrategia
Predicting content from visuals

When you are reading in Spanish, be sure to look for visual clues that will orient you as to the content and purpose of what you are reading. Photos and illustrations, for example, will often give you a good idea of the main points that the reading covers. You may also encounter very helpful visuals that are used to summarize large amounts of data in a way that is easy to comprehend; these include bar graphs, pie charts, flow charts, lists of percentages, and other sorts of diagrams.

Examinar el texto

Take a quick look at the visual elements of the magazine article in order to generate a list of ideas about its content. Then compare your list with a classmate's. Are they the same or are they different? Discuss your lists and make any changes needed to produce a final list of ideas.

Contestar

Read the list of ideas you wrote in **Examinar el texto**, and look again at the visual elements of the magazine article. Then answer the questions.

1. Who is the woman in the photo, and what is her role? *María Úrsula Echevarría is the author of this article.*
2. What is the article about? *The article is about sports in the Spanish-speaking world.*
3. What is the subject of the pie chart? *The most popular sports among college students.*
4. What is the subject of the bar graph? *Spanish-speaking countries in world soccer championships.*

More activities

vhlcentral   Online activities

por María Úrsula Echevarría

El fútbol es el deporte más popular en el mundo° hispano, según° una encuesta° reciente realizada entre jóvenes universitarios. Mucha gente practica este deporte y tiene un equipo de fútbol favorito. Cada cuatro años se realiza la Copa Mundial°. Argentina y Uruguay han ganado° este campeonato° más de una vez°. Los aficionados siguen los partidos de fútbol en casa por tele y en muchos otros lugares como bares, restaurantes, estadios y clubes deportivos. Los jóvenes juegan al fútbol con sus amigos en parques y gimnasios.

Países hispanos en campeonatos mundiales de fútbol (1930–2018)

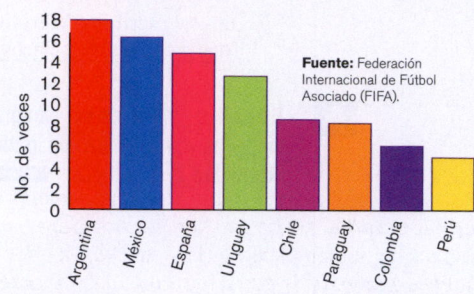

Fuente: Federación Internacional de Fútbol Asociado (FIFA).

Pero, por supuesto°, en los países de habla hispana también hay otros deportes populares. ¿Qué deporte sigue al fútbol en estos países? Bueno, ¡depende del país y de otros factores!

Después de leer

Evaluación y predicción

Which of the following sporting events would be most popular among the college students surveyed? Rate them from one (most popular) to five (least popular). Which would be the most popular at your college or university? *Answers will vary.*

_____ 1. la Copa Mundial de Fútbol

_____ 2. los Juegos Olímpicos

_____ 3. el Campeonato de Wimbledon

_____ 4. la Serie Mundial de Béisbol

_____ 5. el Tour de Francia

TEACHING OPTIONS

Variación léxica Remind students that the term **fútbol** in the Spanish-speaking world refers to soccer, and that in the English-speaking world outside of the United States and Canada, soccer is called *football*. The game that English speakers in the U.S. and Canada call *football* is **fútbol americano** in the Spanish-speaking world.

Extra Practice Ask questions that require students to refer to the article. Model the use of the definite article with percentages. **¿Qué porcentaje prefiere el fútbol?** (el 69 por ciento) **¿Qué porcentaje prefiere el vóleibol?** (el 2 por ciento)

No sólo el fútbol

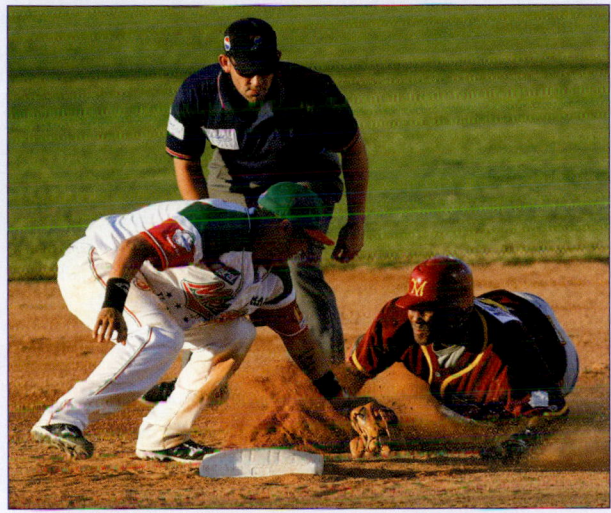

En Colombia, el béisbol también es muy popular después del fútbol, aunque° esto varía según la región del país. En la costa del norte de Colombia, el béisbol es una pasión. Y el ciclismo también es un deporte que los colombianos siguen con mucho interés.

Donde el béisbol es más popular

En los países del Caribe, el béisbol es el deporte predominante. Éste es el caso en Puerto Rico, Cuba y la República Dominicana. Los niños empiezan a jugar cuando son muy pequeños. En Puerto Rico y la República Dominicana, la gente también quiere participar en otros deportes, como el baloncesto, o ver los partidos en la tele. Y para los espectadores aficionados del Caribe, el boxeo es número dos.

Donde el fútbol es más popular

En México, el béisbol es el segundo° deporte más popular después° del fútbol. Pero en Argentina, después del fútbol, el rugby tiene mucha importancia. En Perú a la gente le gusta mucho ver partidos de vóleibol. ¿Y en España? Muchas personas prefieren el baloncesto, el tenis y el ciclismo.

Deportes más populares

- Fútbol (69%)
- Béisbol (10%)
- Baloncesto (8%)
- Ciclismo (4%)
- Tenis (4%)
- Boxeo (3%)
- Vóleibol (2%)

mundo *world* **según** *according to* **encuesta** *survey* **se realiza la Copa Mundial** *the World Cup is held* **han ganado** *have won* **campeonato** *championship* **más de una vez** *more than once* **por supuesto** *of course* **segundo** *second* **después** *after* **aunque** *although*

¿Cierto o falso?

Indicate whether each sentence is **cierto** or **falso**, then correct the false statements.

	Cierto	Falso
1. El vóleibol es el segundo deporte más popular en México. *Es el béisbol.*	○	●
2. En España a la gente le gustan varios deportes como el baloncesto y el ciclismo.	●	○
3. En la costa del norte de Colombia, el tenis es una pasión. *El béisbol es una pasión.*	○	●
4. En el Caribe, el deporte más popular es el béisbol.	●	○

Preguntas

Answer these questions. *Answers will vary.*

1. ¿Dónde ven el fútbol los aficionados? Y tú, ¿cómo ves tus deportes favoritos?
2. ¿Te gusta el fútbol? ¿Por qué?
3. ¿Miras la Copa Mundial en la televisión?
4. ¿Qué deportes miras en la televisión?
5. En tu opinión, ¿cuáles son los tres deportes más populares en tu universidad? ¿En tu comunidad? ¿En tu país?
6. ¿Practicas deportes en tus ratos libres?

¿Cierto o falso? After completing the activity, ask students to write an additional sentence about sports in each country or region mentioned. Ex: **El fútbol es el deporte más popular en México.**

Preguntas Give students these questions as items 7–10: **7. ¿Cuál es el deporte más popular en el mundo hispano? (el fútbol) 8. ¿En qué países es el béisbol el deporte más popular? (en los países del Caribe) 9. ¿Pueden nombrar algunos jugadores de béisbol hispanos en los Estados Unidos? (Answers will vary.) 10. ¿Participan muchos países hispanos en campeonatos mundiales de fútbol? (sí)**

Escritura

Estrategia
Using a dictionary

A common mistake made by beginning language learners is to embrace the dictionary as the ultimate resource for reading, writing, and speaking. While it is true that the dictionary is a useful tool that can provide valuable information about vocabulary, using the dictionary correctly requires that you understand the elements of each entry.

If you glance at a Spanish-English dictionary, you will notice that its format is similar to that of an English dictionary. The word is listed first, usually followed by its pronunciation. Then come the definitions, organized by parts of speech. Sometimes the most frequently used definitions are listed first.

To find the best word for your needs, you should refer to the abbreviations and the explanatory notes that appear next to the entries. For example, imagine that you are writing about your pastimes. You want to write, "I want to buy a new racket for my match tomorrow," but you don't know the Spanish word for "racket." In the dictionary, you may find an entry like this:

> **racket** *s* **1.** alboroto; **2.** raqueta (*dep.*)

The abbreviation key at the front of the dictionary says that *s* corresponds to **sustantivo** (*noun*). Then, the first word you see is **alboroto**. The definition of **alboroto** is *noise* or *racket*, so **alboroto** is probably not the word you're looking for. The second word is **raqueta**, followed by the abbreviation *dep.*, which stands for **deportes**. This indicates that the word **raqueta** is the best choice for your needs.

Tema

Escribir un folleto

Choose one topic to write a brochure. Answers will vary.

1. You are the head of the Homecoming Committee at your school this year. Create a pamphlet that lists events for Friday night, Saturday, and Sunday. Include a brief description of each event and its time and location. Include activities for different age groups, since some alumni will bring their families.

2. You are on the Freshman Student Orientation Committee and are in charge of creating a pamphlet for new students that describes the sports offered at your school. Write the flyer and include activities for both men and women.

3. You work for the Chamber of Commerce in your community. It is your job to market your community to potential residents. Write a brief pamphlet that describes the recreational opportunities your community provides, the areas where the activities take place, and the costs, if any. Be sure to include activities that will appeal to singles as well as couples and families; you should include activities for all age groups and for both men and women.

EVALUATION: Folleto

Criteria	Scale
Appropriate details	1 2 3 4
Organization	1 2 3 4
Use of vocabulary	1 2 3 4
Grammatical accuracy	1 2 3 4
Mechanics	1 2 3 4

Scoring	
Excellent	18–20 points
Good	14–17 points
Satisfactory	10–13 points
Unsatisfactory	< 10 points

Escuchar

Antes de escuchar

Estrategia

Listening for the gist

Listening for the general idea, or gist, can help you follow what someone is saying even if you can't hear or understand some of the words. When you listen for the gist, you simply try to capture the essence of what you hear without focusing on individual words.

 To help you practice this strategy, you will listen to a paragraph made up of three sentences. Jot down a brief summary of what you hear.

Preparación

Based on the photo, what do you think Anabela is like? Do you and Anabela have similar interests? *Answers will vary.*

Ahora escucha

Pasatiempos favoritos

You will hear first José talking, then Anabela. As you listen, check off each person's favorite activities.

Pasatiempos favoritos de José

1. ✔ leer el correo electrónico
2. _____ jugar al béisbol
3. ✔ ver películas de acción
4. ✔ ir al café
5. ✔ ir a partidos de béisbol
6. _____ ver películas románticas
7. ✔ dormir la siesta
8. ✔ escribir mensajes electrónicos

Pasatiempos favoritos de Anabela

9. ✔ esquiar
10. ✔ nadar
11. ✔ practicar el ciclismo
12. ✔ jugar al golf
13. _____ jugar al baloncesto
14. _____ ir a ver partidos de tenis
15. ✔ escalar montañas
16. _____ ver televisión

Comprensión

Preguntas

Answer these questions about José's and Anabela's pastimes.

1. ¿Quién practica más deportes?
   Anabela
2. ¿Quién piensa que es importante descansar?
   José
3. ¿A qué deporte es aficionado José?
   Le gusta el béisbol.
4. ¿Por qué Anabela no practica el baloncesto?
   Ella no es alta.
5. ¿Qué películas le gustan a la novia de José?
   Le gustan las películas románticas.
6. ¿Cuál es el deporte favorito de Anabela?
   el ciclismo

Seleccionar

Which person do these statements best describe?

1. Le gusta practicar deportes.   Anabela
2. Prefiere las películas de acción.   José
3. Le gustan las computadoras.   José
4. Le gusta nadar.   Anabela
5. Siempre (*Always*) duerme una siesta por la tarde.   José
6. Quiere ir de vacaciones a las montañas.   Anabela

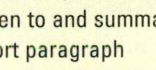

realidad todos los deportes. No, eso no es cierto; no juego al baloncesto porque no soy alta. Para mis vacaciones, quiero esquiar o escalar la montaña, depende si nieva. Suena divertido, ¿no?

Section Goals

In **Escuchar**, students will:
- listen to and summarize a short paragraph
- learn the strategy of listening for the gist
- answer questions based on the content of a recorded conversation

Instructional Resources
Supersite: Audio (Textbook MP3s); Resources (Scripts)

Estrategia

Script Buenas tardes y bienvenidos a la clase de español. En esta clase van a escuchar, escribir y conversar en cada clase, y ustedes también deben estudiar y practicar todos los días. Ahora encuentran el español difícil, pero cuando termine el curso van a comprender y comunicarse bien en español.

Teaching Tip

⬅️🧍➡️ Have students look at the photo and write a short paragraph describing what they see. Guide them in saying what **Anabela** is like and guessing what her favorite pastimes might be.

Ahora escucha

Script JOSÉ: No me gusta practicar deportes, pero sí tengo muchos pasatiempos. Me gusta mucho escribir y recibir correo electrónico. Me gusta también ir con mis amigos a mi café favorito. Siempre duermo una siesta por la tarde. A veces voy a ver un partido de béisbol. Me gusta mucho ver películas de acción pero mi novia prefiere las de romance… y por lo tanto veo muchas películas de romance. ANABELA: Todos mis parientes dicen que soy demasiado activa. Soy aficionada a los deportes, pero también estudio mucho y necesito diversión. Aunque prefiero practicar el ciclismo, me gustan mucho la natación, el tenis, el golf… bueno, en

(Script continues at far left in the bottom panels.)

En pantalla Video

BMX, skateboarding, surfing, and other extreme sports are passions for many young men and women who, in search of speed and adrenaline, make their bikes and boards the center of their lives. Communities around the world are responding to the demand for extreme sports by constructing bike and skate parks, and Spanish-speaking countries are no exception. The UCI BMX World Championship was held in Medellín in 2016. Colombian Olympic Gold Medalist Mariana Pajón has won gold at the games three times (2011, 2014, 2016).

Vocabulario útil

andar	*to go*
bici	*bike*
callejón	*alley*
campeonato	*championship*
conocer	*to be acquainted with*
molar	*to be cool*
rampas	*ramps*

Preparación

What role do sports play in your life? Which sports do you enjoy? Why? Answers will vary.

Comprensión

Indicate whether each statement is **cierto** or **falso**.

	Cierto	Falso
1. A Diego le gusta la bici.	○	●
2. Sarini cree que patinar es un arte.	●	○
3. Pequesaurio prefiere la patineta.	○	●
4. A Pequesaurio le gusta la rampa.	●	○

Conversación

With a partner, discuss these questions in Spanish. Answers will vary.

1. ¿Qué deportes se pueden practicar fácilmente en tu comunidad? ¿Qué deportes son fomentados (*encouraged*) en tu comunidad?

2. ¿Cuál es la diferencia entre un deporte y un juego? ¿Cuál es la diferencia entre un deporte y un deporte extremo?

Me quedo con la bici *I'll stick with the bike*

Ejes

Patino por pasión más que por otra cosa.

Es un deporte también, pero creo que es un arte.

A mí me gusta la bici y me quedo con la bici°.

More activities

vhlcentral / Online activities

TEACHING OPTIONS

Language Notes In its normal usage, **andar** means *to walk*. However, in many cases, **andar** can mean *to travel* or *to go*: **Ando en bicicleta para ir a la escuela.** In some cases, **andar** can be followed by a gerund to form a continuous tense: **Mi hermano anda estudiando mucho.** Sometimes it is a synonym of **estar**: **Mi madre siempre anda muy ocupada.** Note that **andar** is irregular in the indicative preterite and the past subjunctive tenses. The verb **molar** is used to express that something is cool: **La bici mola.** It can also be conjugated like the verb **gustar**: **¿Te mola el rap?** It is mainly used in Spain. **¡Cómo mola! Patinar, el patín,** and **el *skate*** are used by the Spanish teenagers in the video to talk about skateboarding.

Video

The rivalry between the teams **Real Madrid** and **FC Barcelona** is perhaps the fiercest in all of soccer—just imagine if they occupied the same city! Well, each team also has competing clubs within its respective city: Spain's capital has the **Club Atlético de Madrid**, and Barcelona is home to **Espanyol**. In fact, across the Spanish-speaking world, it is common for a city to have more than one professional team, often with strikingly dissimilar origins, identity, and fan base. For example, in Bogotá, the **Millonarios** were so named for the large sums spent on players, while the **Santa Fe** team is one of the most traditional in Colombian soccer. **River Plate** and **Boca Juniors**, who enjoy a famous rivalry, are just two of twenty-four clubs in Buenos Aires—the city with the most professional soccer teams in the world.

Vocabulario útil

afición	*fans*
celebran	*they celebrate*
preferido/a	*favorite*
rivalidad	*rivalry*
se junta con	*it's tied up with*

Preparación

What is the most popular sport at your school? What teams are your rivals? How do students celebrate a win?
Answers will vary.

Escoger

Select the correct answer.

1. Un partido entre el Barça y el Real Madrid es un ___evento___ (deporte/evento) importante en toda España.

2. Los aficionados ___celebran___ (miran/celebran) las victorias de sus equipos en las calles (*streets*).

3. La rivalidad entre el Real Madrid y el Barça está relacionada con la ___política___ (religión/política).

¡Fútbol en España!

(Hay mucha afición al fútbol en España.)

¿Y cuál es vuestro jugador favorito?

—**¿Y quién va a ganar?**
—**El Real Madrid.**

More activities
vhlcentral · VM pp. 43–44 · Online activities

Section Goals

In **Flash cultura**, students will:
- read about soccer rivalries in the Spanish-speaking world
- watch a video about soccer in Spain

Instructional Resources
Supersite: Video (*Flash cultura*); Resources (Scripts, Translations, Answer Keys)
WebSAM
Video Manual

Introduction To check comprehension, ask these questions. 1. What are the two main soccer clubs in Madrid? 2. What are the two main soccer teams in Barcelona? 3. How did the team **Millonarios** get its name? 4. How many professional soccer teams are there in Buenos Aires?

Antes de ver
- Have students look at the video stills, read the captions, and predict the content of the video.
- Read through **Vocabulario útil** with students. Model the pronunciation.
- Explain that students do not need to understand every word they hear. Tell them to rely on visual cues, cognates, and words from **Vocabulario útil**.

Preparación Survey the class to find out what sport is the most popular and who the main rivals are. Discuss how long these rivalries have existed, and ask students how they feel about the rival schools/students due to the competitive atmosphere.

Escoger To challenge students, makes copies of this activity with the words in parentheses removed. Pass out the copies and have students close their books. Write all the possible answers for the activity in one list on the board and tell students to fill in the blanks using these words.

TEACHING OPTIONS

Small Groups In small groups, have students research one of the teams on this page. Have them focus on the team's key players, colors, team song (**himno**), any historical or political points of interest, and its fan base. Have groups present their findings to the class.

Heritage Speakers Ask heritage speakers to share their experiences with soccer as they were growing up. Ask them to discuss whether they played/watched formal or informal matches, whether girls were allowed or expected to play, and if they would watch soccer in their household and celebrate wins.

Section Goals

Section Goals

In **Panorama**, students will read about:
- the geography, history, economy, and culture of Mexico
- Mexico's relationship with the United States

Instructional Resources
Supersite: Video (*Panorama cultural*); Resources (Scripts, Translations, Digital Image Bank, Answer Keys)
WebSAM
Workbook

Teaching Tips
- Use the **Lección 4 Panorama** digital images to assist with this presentation.
- Have students look at the map of Mexico. Ask them questions about the locations of cities and natural features of Mexico. Ex: **¿Dónde está la capital?** (**en el centro del país**)

El país en cifras Ask questions related to section content. Ex: After looking at the map, ask: **¿Qué ciudad mexicana está en la frontera con El Paso, Texas? (Ciudad Juárez)** Ask students if they can name other sister cities (**ciudades hermanas**) on the Mexico-U.S. border. (Tijuana/ San Diego, Calexico/Mexicali, Laredo/Nuevo Laredo, etc.)

México

(sello: NATIONAL STANDARDS — connections cultures)

El país en cifras

▶ **Área:** 1.972.550 km² (761.603 millas²), casi° tres veces° el área de Texas

La situación geográfica de México, al sur° de los Estados Unidos, ha influido en° la economía y la sociedad de los dos países. Una de las consecuencias es la emigración de la población mexicana al país vecino°. Hoy día, más de 34 millones de personas de ascendencia mexicana viven en los Estados Unidos.

▶ **Población:** 124.574.000
▶ **Capital:** Ciudad de México (y su área metropolitana)—20.999.000
▶ **Ciudades principales:** Guadalajara —4.843.000, Monterrey—4.513.000, Puebla—2.984.000, Ciudad Juárez—1.391.000
▶ **Moneda:** peso mexicano
▶ **Idiomas:** español (oficial), náhuatl, otras lenguas indígenas

Bandera de México

Mexicanos célebres

▶ **Benito Juárez,** héroe nacional (1806–1872)
▶ **Octavio Paz,** poeta (1914–1998)
▶ **Elena Poniatowska,** periodista y escritora (1932–)
▶ **Mario Molina,** Premio Nobel de Química, 1995; químico (1943–)
▶ **Paulina Rubio,** cantante (1971–)

casi *almost* veces *times* sur *south* ha influido en *has influenced* vecino *neighboring*

(Mapa de México con etiquetas:) Cabo San Lucas, ESTADOS UNIDOS, Ciudad Juárez, Río Grande, Golfo de California, Baja California, Sierra Madre Oriental, Río Bravo del Norte, Sierra Madre Occidental, Monterrey, Océano Pacífico, Ciudad de México, Puerto Vallarta, Guadalajara, Puebla, Acapulco

(Mapa pequeño:) ESTADOS UNIDOS, MÉXICO, OCÉANO ATLÁNTICO, OCÉANO PACÍFICO, AMÉRICA DEL SUR

Autorretrato con collar de espinas, 1940, Frida Kahlo

Artesanías en Taxco, Guerrero

Pirámide de Kukulcán en Chichén Itzá

More activities
vhlcentral | WB pp. 47–48 | Online activities

ACTIVIDADES

1 **¿Cierto o falso?** Indica si lo que dice cada oración es **cierto** o **falso**.

1. México está en América del Sur. falso
2. La moneda de México es el dólar estadounidense. falso
3. Mario Molina tiene un Premio Nobel de Química. cierto
4. Cabo San Lucas es una iglesia mexicana. falso
5. Encuentras artesanías en Taxco. cierto
6. Muchos inmigrantes y turistas van a la Ciudad de México. cierto
7. Uno puede ver obras de Frida Kahlo en el Museo de Arte Moderno de la Ciudad de México. cierto
8. Tenochtitlán, la capital azteca, es la Ciudad de México hoy día. cierto
9. Zacatecas es una ciudad principal de México. falso
10. Cada año, el dos de noviembre, los mexicanos ponen flores en los cementerios. cierto

TEACHING OPTIONS

Extra Practice Mexico is a large and diverse nation, with many regions and regional cultures. Have students select a region that interests them, research it, and present a short oral report to the class. Encourage them to include information about the cities, art, history, geography, customs, and cuisine of the region.

Small Groups Many of the dishes that distinguish Mexican cuisine have pre-Hispanic origins. To these native dishes have been added elements of Spanish and French cuisines, making Mexican food, like Mexican civilization, a dynamic mix of ingredients. Have groups of students research recipes that exemplify this fusion of cultures. Have each group describe one recipe's origins to the class.

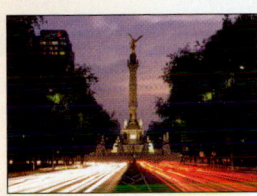

Ciudades • Ciudad de México

La Ciudad de México, fundada° en 1525, también es conocida como el D.F. o el Distrito Federal. Muchos turistas e inmigrantes vienen a la ciudad porque es el centro cultural y económico del país. El crecimiento° de la población es de los más altos° del mundo. La población de la Ciudad de México es mayor que la de ciudades como Nueva York, Madrid o París.

⊳ Artes • Diego Rivera y Frida Kahlo

Frida Kahlo y Diego Rivera eran° artistas mexicanos muy famosos. Se casaron° en 1929. Los dos se interesaron° en las condiciones sociales de la gente indígena de su país. Puedes ver algunas° de sus obras° en el Museo de Arte Moderno de la Ciudad de México.

⊳ Historia • Los aztecas

Los aztecas dominaron° en México del siglo° XIV al siglo XVI. Sus canales, puentes° y pirámides con templos religiosos eran muy importantes. El fin del imperio azteca comenzó° con la llegada° de los españoles en 1519, pero la presencia azteca sigue hoy. La Ciudad de México está situada en la capital azteca de Tenochtitlán, y muchos turistas van a visitar sus ruinas.

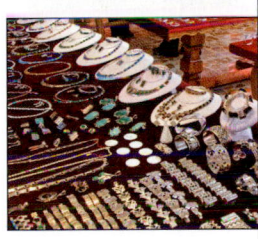

Economía • La plata

México es el mayor productor de plata° del mundo°. Estados como Zacatecas y Durango tienen ciudades fundadas cerca de los más grandes yacimientos° de plata del país. Estas ciudades fueron° en la época colonial unas de las más ricas e importantes. Hoy en día, aún° conservan mucho de su encanto° y esplendor.

Golfo de México

Península de Yucatán

Bahía de Campeche

Mérida

Cancún

...acruz

Istmo de Tehuantepec

BELICE

GUATEMALA

fundada *founded* crecimiento *growth* más altos *highest* eran *were* Se casaron *They got married* se interesaron *were interested* algunas *some* obras *works* dominaron *dominated* siglo *century* puentes *bridges* comenzó *started* llegada *arrival* plata *silver* mundo *world* yacimientos *deposits* fueron *were* aún *still* encanto *charm*

¡Increíble pero cierto!

Cada dos de noviembre los cementerios de México se llenan de luz°, música y flores°. El Día de Muertos° no es un evento triste; es una fiesta en honor a las personas muertas. En ese día, los mexicanos se ríen° de la muerte°, lo cual se refleja° en detalles como las calaveras de azúcar° y el pan° de muerto (pan en forma de huesos°).

se llenan de luz *get filled with light* flores *flowers* Muertos *Dead* se ríen *laugh* muerte *death* lo cual se refleja *which is reflected* calaveras de azúcar *sugar skulls* pan *bread* huesos *bones*

---

2 ¿Qué aprendiste? Contesta las preguntas.

1. ¿Qué lenguas hablan los mexicanos?
   español y lenguas indígenas
2. ¿En qué se interesaron Frida Kahlo y Diego Rivera?
   las condiciones sociales de la gente indígena de su país
3. Nombra algunas de las estructuras de la arquitectura azteca.
   canales, puentes y pirámides con templos religiosos
4. ¿Qué estados de México tienen los mayores yacimientos de plata? Zacatecas y Durango

3 Turistas En parejas, imaginen que viajan a México. Hablen de las cosas que quieren ver y hacer allí.

modelo
Estudiante 1: *Quiero ir a Chichén Itzá.*
Estudiante 2: *Sí. Quiero ver la pirámide de Kukulcán.*

TEACHING OPTIONS

Variación léxica Over 52 languages are spoken by indigenous communities in Mexico today; of these, Mayan languages are the most prevalent. Also, **náhuatl,** the language of the Aztecs, is spoken by a significant part of the population. Some **náhuatl** words have entered Mexican Spanish, such as **aguacate** (*avocado*), **guajolote** (*turkey*), **cacahuate** (*peanut*), **ejote**

(*green bean*), **chile** (*chili pepper*), and **elote** (*corn*). Two food names of **náhuatl** origin that are now used in world languages are *tomato* and *chocolate*, as these foods are native to Mexico and were brought to Europe in the sixteenth century.

Ciudad de México Mexicans usually refer to their capital as **México** or **el D.F.** The monument pictured here is **El Ángel de la Independencia**, located on the **Paseo de la Reforma**.

Diego Rivera y Frida Kahlo Show students paintings by **Rivera** and **Kahlo**, and discuss the indigenous Mexican themes that dominate their works: **Rivera's** murals have largely proletarian and political messages, while **Kahlo** incorporated indigenous motifs in her portrayals of suffering. You may want to play the **Panorama cultural** video for this paragraph.

Los aztecas Explain that the coat of arms on the Mexican flag represents an Aztec prophecy. Legend states that nomadic Aztecs wandered present-day Mexico in search of a place to establish a city. According to their gods, the precise location would be indicated by an eagle devouring a snake while perched atop a nopal cactus. The Aztecs saw this sign on an island in Lake Texcoco, where they founded Tenochtitlán. You may want to play the **Panorama cultural** video for this paragraph.

La plata Taxco, in the state of Guerrero, is the home to the annual **Feria Nacional de la Plata**.

¡Increíble pero cierto! Mexico's **Día de Muertos**, like many holidays in Latin America, blends indigenous and Catholic practices. The date coincides with the Catholic All Saints' Day; however, the holiday's indigenous origins are evident in the gravesite offerings, **el pan de muertos**, and the belief that on this day the deceased can communicate with the living. Students will see a **Día de Muertos** celebration in the **Lección 9 Fotonovela**.

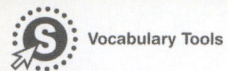
Teaching Tip You may want to assign the **Prueba de práctica**, with its diagnostics and review activities, in the online-only **Repaso** section on the Supersite. There is also a **Repaso oral** in this section. For the Sixth Edition, a new summative vocabulary activity with speech recognition has been added to the **Repaso** section.

Pasatiempos

andar en patineta	to skateboard
bucear	to scuba dive
escalar montañas (f., pl.)	to climb mountains
escribir una carta	to write a letter
escribir un mensaje electrónico	to write an e-mail
esquiar	to ski
ganar	to win
ir de excursión	to go on a hike
leer el correo electrónico	to read e-mail
leer un periódico	to read a newspaper
leer una revista	to read a magazine
nadar	to swim
pasear	to take a walk
pasear en bicicleta	to ride a bicycle
patinar	to skate
practicar deportes (m., pl.)	to play sports
tomar el sol	to sunbathe
ver películas (f., pl.)	to watch movies
visitar monumentos (m., pl.)	to visit monuments
la diversión	fun activity; entertainment; recreation
el fin de semana	weekend
el pasatiempo	pastime; hobby
los ratos libres	spare (free) time
el videojuego	video game

Deportes

el baloncesto	basketball
el béisbol	baseball
el ciclismo	cycling
el equipo	team
el esquí (acuático)	(water) skiing
el fútbol	soccer
el fútbol americano	football
el golf	golf
el hockey	hockey
el/la jugador(a)	player
la natación	swimming
el partido	game; match
la pelota	ball
el tenis	tennis
el vóleibol	volleyball

Adjetivos

deportivo/a	sports-related
favorito/a	favorite

Lugares

el café	café
el centro	downtown
el cine	movie theater
el gimnasio	gymnasium
la iglesia	church
el lugar	place
el museo	museum
el parque	park
la piscina	swimming pool
la plaza	city or town square
el restaurante	restaurant

Verbos

almorzar (o:ue)	to have lunch
cerrar (e:ie)	to close
comenzar (e:ie)	to begin
conseguir (e:i)	to get; to obtain
contar (o:ue)	to count; to tell
decir (e:i)	to say; to tell
dormir (o:ue)	to sleep
empezar (e:ie)	to begin
encontrar (o:ue)	to find
entender (e:ie)	to understand
hacer	to do; to make
ir	to go
jugar (u:ue)	to play (a sport or a game)
mostrar (o:ue)	to show
oír	to hear
pedir (e:i)	to ask for; to request
pensar (e:ie)	to think
pensar (+ inf.)	to intend
pensar en	to think about
perder (e:ie)	to lose; to miss
poder (o:ue)	to be able to; can
poner	to put; to place
preferir (e:ie)	to prefer
querer (e:ie)	to want; to love
recordar (o:ue)	to remember
repetir (e:i)	to repeat
salir	to leave
seguir (e:i)	to follow; to continue
suponer	to suppose
traer	to bring
ver	to see
volver (o:ue)	to return

***Decir* expressions**	*See page 136.*
Expresiones útiles	*See page 121.*

More activities

vhlcentral   LM p. 24

Las vacaciones

Communicative Goals

You will learn how to:
- Discuss and plan a vacation
- Describe a hotel
- Talk about how you feel
- Talk about the seasons and the weather

A PRIMERA VISTA
- ¿La persona es vieja o joven?
- ¿Lleva una pelota o una mochila?
- ¿Pasea o ve una película? ¿Anda en patineta o va de excursión?
- ¿Es posible nadar en este lugar?

Lesson Goals

In **Lección 5**, students will be introduced to the following:
- terms for traveling and vacations
- seasons and months
- weather expressions
- ordinal numbers (1st–10th)
- **El Viejo San Juan**
- **Punta del Este**, Uruguay
- **estar** with conditions and emotions
- adjectives for conditions and emotions
- present progressive of regular and irregular verbs
- comparison of the uses of **ser** and **estar**
- direct object nouns and pronouns
- personal **a**
- scanning to find specific information
- making an outline
- writing a brochure for a hotel
- listening for key words
- a Panamanian tourism ad
- a video about **Machu Picchu**
- cultural, geographic, and historical information about Puerto Rico

A primera vista Here are some additional questions you can ask to personalize the photo: **¿Dónde te gusta pasar tus ratos libres? ¿Qué haces en tus ratos libres? ¿Te gusta explorar otras culturas? ¿Te gusta viajar a otros países? ¿Adónde quieres ir en las próximas vacaciones?**

Teaching Tip Look for these icons for additional communicative practice:

→■←	Interpretive communication
←■→	Presentational communication
■↔■	Interpersonal communication

INSTRUCTIONAL RESOURCES

Supersite (vhlcentral.com)
Video: *Fotonovela, Flash cultura, En pantalla, Panorama cultural*
Audio: Textbook and Lab MP3 Files

Activity Pack: Information Gap Activities, games, additional activity handouts
Resources: SAM Answer Key, Scripts, Translations, **Vocabulario adicional**, sample lesson plan, Grammar Presentation Slides, Digital Image Bank

Testing Program: Quizzes, Tests, Exams, MP3s
Student Activities Manual: Workbook/Video Manual/Lab Manual
WebSAM (online Student Activities Manual)

Section Goals

In **Contextos**, students will learn and practice:
- travel- and vacation-related vocabulary
- seasons and months of the year
- weather expressions
- ordinal numbers

Instructional Resources

Supersite: Audio (Textbook and Lab MP3 Files); Resources (Digital Image Bank, **Vocabulario adicional**, Activity Pack, Scripts, Answer Keys); Testing Program (Quizzes)
WebSAM
Workbook
Lab Manual

Teaching Tips

- Ask: **¿A quién le gusta mucho viajar? ¿Cómo prefieres viajar?** Introduce cognates as suggestions: **¿Te gusta viajar en auto?** Write each term on the board as you say it. Ask: **¿Adónde te gusta viajar? ¿A México?** Ask students about their classmates' statements: **¿Adónde le gusta viajar a _____? ¿Cómo puede viajar?**
- Ask questions about transportation in your community. Ex: **Si quiero ir de la universidad al aeropuerto, ¿cómo puedo ir?** Ask what type of transportation students use to go home on school break.
- Use the **Lección 5 Contextos** digital images to assist with this presentation.

Note: At this point you may want to present *Vocabulario adicional: Más vocabulario para las vacaciones* from the Supersite.

Las vacaciones

Más vocabulario

la cama	bed
la habitación individual, doble	single, double room
la llave	key
el piso	floor (of a building)
la planta baja	ground floor
el campo	countryside
el paisaje	landscape
la estación de autobuses, del metro, de tren	bus, subway, train station
el/la inspector(a) de aduanas	customs inspector
la llegada	arrival
el pasaje (de ida y vuelta)	(round-trip) ticket
el pasaporte	passport
la salida	departure; exit
la tabla de (wind)surf	surfboard/sailboard
acampar	to camp
confirmar una reservación	to confirm a reservation
estar de vacaciones	to be on vacation
hacer las maletas	to pack (one's suitcases)
hacer un viaje	to take a trip
hacer (wind)surf	to (wind)surf
ir de compras	to go shopping
ir de vacaciones	to go on vacation
ir en autobús (m.), auto(móvil) (m.), motocicleta (f.)	to go by bus, car, motorcycle
jugar a las cartas	to play cards

Variación léxica

automóvil	⟷	coche (*Esp.*), carro (*Amér. L.*)
autobús	⟷	camión (*Méx.*), guagua (*Caribe*)
motocicleta	⟷	moto (*coloquial*)

More activities

vhlcentral	LM p. 25	WB pp. 49–50	Online activities

el aeropuerto
el avión
el autobús
el viajero
Monta a caballo. (montar)
Saca/Toma fotos. (sacar, tomar)
la playa
Hace surf. (hacer)
la tabla de surf
Va en barco. (ir)
el mar

TEACHING OPTIONS

Extra Practice 👥↔👥 Ask questions about the people, places, and activities in **Contextos**. Ex: **¿Qué actividades pueden hacer los turistas en una playa? ¿Pueden nadar? ¿Tomar el sol? ¿Sacar fotos?** Then expand questions to ask students what they specifically do at these places. **_____, ¿qué haces tú cuando vas a la playa?** Students should respond in complete sentences.

Variación léxica Point out that these are just some of the different Spanish names for vehicles. Ask heritage speakers if they are familiar with other terms. While some of these terms are mutually understood in different regions (**el coche, el carro, el auto, el automóvil**), others are specific to a region and may not be understood by others (**la guagua, el camión**). Stress that the feminine article **la** is used with the abbreviation **moto**.

Práctica

HOTEL BUENA VISTA

el hotel

el ascensor

el empleado

el huésped

la huésped

el equipaje

el taxi

Pesca. (pescar)

1 **Escuchar** Check **aeropuerto**, **hotel**, or **playa** to indicate where you would find each thing you hear.

	Aeropuerto	Hotel	Playa
1.	○	●	○
2.	●	○	○
3.	○	●	○
4.	○	○	●
5.	○	●	○
6.	○	○	●
7.	●	○	○
8.	○	○	●

2 **¿Cierto o falso?** Indicate whether each statement about the drawing is **cierto** or **falso**.

1. _falso_   5. _cierto_
2. _cierto_   6. _cierto_
3. _falso_   7. _cierto_
4. _falso_   8. _falso_

3 **Escoger** Choose the best answer for each sentence.

1. Abrimos la puerta con __a__.
   a. una llave   b. un caballo   c. una llegada
2. Un huésped es una persona que __b__.
   a. toma fotos   b. está en un hotel   c. pesca en el mar
3. Enrique tiene __a__ porque va a viajar a otro (*another*) país.
   a. un pasaporte   b. una foto   c. una llegada
4. Antes de (*Before*) ir de vacaciones, hay que __c__.
   a. pescar   b. ir en tren   c. hacer las maletas
5. Nosotros vamos en __a__ al aeropuerto.
   a. autobús   b. pasaje   c. viajero
6. Me gusta mucho ir al campo. El __a__ es increíble.
   a. paisaje   b. pasaje   c. equipaje

4 **Preguntas** Answer the questions.

el ascensor	la cama	el pasaje	la salida
el auto	el equipaje	la playa	el viajero

1. ¿Dónde duermes cada (*each*) noche? _la cama_
2. ¿Qué necesitas para ir en tren? _el pasaje_
3. ¿Quién va en avión? _el viajero_
4. ¿Qué tomas para llegar al piso de tu habitación en un hotel grande? _el ascensor_
5. ¿Qué necesitas para hacer las maletas? _el equipaje_
6. ¿Adónde vas para tomar el sol, nadar y hacer surf? _la playa_

Las estaciones y los meses del año

el invierno: diciembre, enero, febrero

la primavera: marzo, abril, mayo

el verano: junio, julio, agosto

el otoño: septiembre, octubre, noviembre

—**¿Cuál es la fecha de hoy?**
—**Es el primero de octubre.**
—**Es el dos de marzo.**
—**Es el diez de noviembre.**

What is today's date?
It's the first of October.
It's March 2nd.
It's November 10th.

Más vocabulario	
Está (muy) nublado.	*It's (very) cloudy.*
Hace fresco.	*It's cool.*
Hace (mucho) sol.	*It's (very) sunny.*
Hace (mucho) viento.	*It's (very) windy.*

El tiempo

—**¿Qué tiempo hace?**
—**Hace buen/mal tiempo.**

How's the weather?
The weather is good/bad.

Hace (mucho) calor.
It's (very) hot.

Hace (mucho) frío.
It's (very) cold.

Llueve. (llover o:ue)
It's raining.
Está lloviendo.
It's raining.

Nieva. (nevar e:ie)
It's snowing.
Está nevando.
It's snowing.

5 **El Hotel Regis** Label the floors of the hotel.

Números ordinales	
primer (before a masculine singular noun), **primero/a**	first
segundo/a	second
tercer (before a masculine singular noun), **tercero/a**	third
cuarto/a	fourth
quinto/a	fifth
sexto/a	sixth
séptimo/a	seventh
octavo/a	eighth
noveno/a	ninth
décimo/a	tenth

a. <u>séptimo</u> piso
b. <u>sexto</u> piso
c. <u>quinto</u> piso
d. <u>cuarto</u> piso
e. <u>tercer</u> piso
f. <u>segundo</u> piso
g. <u>primer</u> piso
h. <u>planta</u> baja

---

6 **Contestar** In pairs, take turns asking each other these questions. Use the illustrations on the previous page to answer the questions about the seasons.

> **modelo**
> **Estudiante 1:** ¿Cuál es el primer mes de la primavera?
> **Estudiante 2:** marzo

1. ¿Cuál es el primer mes del invierno?   diciembre
2. ¿Cuál es el tercer mes del otoño?   noviembre
3. ¿Cuál es el segundo mes de la primavera?   abril
4. ¿Cuál es el primer mes del año?   enero
5. ¿Cuál es el octavo mes del año?   agosto
6. ¿Cuál es el quinto mes del año?   mayo
7. ¿Cuál es el décimo mes del año?   octubre
8. ¿Cuál es el segundo mes del verano?   julio
9. ¿Cuál es el tercer mes del invierno?   febrero
10. ¿Cuál es el sexto mes del año?   junio

---

7 **Las estaciones** Name the season that applies to the description.   Some answers may vary.

1. Las clases terminan.   la primavera
2. Vamos a la playa.   el verano
3. Nieva mucho.   el invierno
4. Acampamos.   el verano
5. Las clases empiezan.   el otoño
6. Llueve mucho.   la primavera
7. Hace mucho calor.   el verano
8. Esquiamos.   el invierno
9. el entrenamiento (*training*) de béisbol   la primavera
10. el Día de Acción de Gracias (*Thanksgiving*)   el otoño

---

8 **¿Cuál es la fecha?** Give the dates for these holidays.

> **modelo**
> el día de San Valentín   **14 de febrero**

1. el día de Halloween   31 de octubre
2. el día de San Patricio   17 de marzo
3. el primer día de verano   20–23 de junio
4. el Año Nuevo   primero de enero
5. mi cumpleaños (*birthday*)   Answers will vary.
6. mi día de fiesta favorito   Answers will vary.

TEACHING OPTIONS

TPR Ask ten volunteers to line up facing the class. Make sure students know the starting point and what number in line they are. At random, call out ordinal numbers. The student to which each ordinal number corresponds has three seconds to step forward. If the student does not, he or she sits down and the order changes for the rest of the students further down the line. Who will be the last student(s) standing?

Game Ask four or five volunteers to come to the front of the room and hold races. (Make it difficult to reach the finish line; for example, have students hop on one foot or recite the ordinal numbers backward.) Teach the words **llegó** and **fue** and, after each race, ask the class to summarize the results. Ex: _____ **llegó en quinto lugar.** _____ **fue la tercera persona (en llegar).**

---

5 Teaching Tips
• Point out that for numbers greater than ten, Spanish speakers tend to use cardinal numbers instead: **Está en el piso veintiuno.**
• Add a visual aspect to this vocabulary presentation. Write out each ordinal number on a separate sheet of paper and distribute them at random among ten students. Ask them to go to the front of the class, hold up their signs, and stand in the correct order.
• Explain that **la planta baja** is used for the ground floor of a building. In Spanish-speaking countries, **el primer piso** is the floor above **la planta baja**.

5 Expansion Ask students questions about their lives, using ordinal numbers. Ex: **¿En qué piso vives? ¿En qué piso está mi oficina?**

6 Teaching Tip Before beginning this activity, have students close their books. Review seasons and months of the year by asking questions. Ex: **¿Qué estación tiene los meses de junio, julio y agosto?**

7 Expansion
↔ Ask volunteers to describe events, situations, or holidays that are important to them or their families. Have the class guess the event and name the season that applies.

8 Teaching Tip Bring in a Spanish-language calendar. Ask students to name the important events and their scheduled dates.

8 Expansion
• Give these holidays to students as items 7–10:
7. Independencia de los EE.UU. (4 de julio) 8. Navidad (25 de diciembre) 9. Día de Acción de Gracias (cuarto jueves de noviembre) 10. Día de los Inocentes (primero de abril)
• Ask heritage speakers to provide other important holidays, such as saints' days.

9 Teaching Tip Review weather expressions by asking students about current weather conditions around the world. Ex: **¿Hace calor en Alaska hoy? ¿Nieva en Puerto Rico?**

9 Expansion Use the alternate choices in the exercise to ask students weather-related questions. Ex: **No nieva en Yucatán. ¿Dónde nieva?**

10 Teaching Tip Point out the words **soleado, lluvia**, and **nieve** in the key. Have students guess the meaning of these words based on the context. Finally, explain that **soleado** is an adjective and **lluvia** and **nieve** are nouns related to **llover** and **nevar**.

10 Expansion
• Ask students questions that compare and contrast the weather conditions presented in the activity or on the weather page of a Spanish-language newspaper. Ex: **Cuando la temperatura está a 85 grados en Buenos Aires, ¿a cuánto está en Tokio?**
• To challenge students, ask them to predict tomorrow's weather for these cities, based on the same cues. Have them use **ir a + [infinitive]**. Ex: **En Montreal, mañana va a nevar y va a hacer mucho frío.**

11 Teaching Tip Model the activity by completing the first two sentences about yourself.

11 Expansion
Tell students to imagine that they are six years old again. Then have them write a short paragraph repeating the activity.

9 Seleccionar Choose the word or phrase that best completes each sentence.

1. A mis padres les gusta ir a Yucatán porque (hace sol, nieva). *hace sol*
2. Mis amigos van a esquiar si (nieva, está nublado). *nieva*
3. Mi primo de Kansas dice que durante (*during*) un tornado, hace mucho (sol, viento). *viento*
4. Tomo el sol cuando (hace calor, llueve). *hace calor*
5. Nosotros vamos a ver una película si hace (buen, mal) tiempo. *mal*
6. Mi hermana prefiere correr cuando (hace mucho calor, hace fresco). *hace fresco*
7. Mi padre no quiere jugar al golf si (hace fresco, llueve). *llueve*
8. Mis tíos van de excursión si hace (buen, mal) tiempo. *buen*
9. Cuando hace mucho (sol, frío), tomo chocolate caliente (*hot*). *frío*
10. Hoy mi sobrino va al parque porque (está lloviendo, hace buen tiempo). *hace buen tiempo*

10 El clima With a partner, take turns asking and answering questions about the weather and temperatures in these cities. *Answers will vary.*

modelo

Estudiante 1: ¿Qué tiempo hace hoy en Nueva York?
Estudiante 2: Hace frío y hace viento.
Estudiante 1: ¿Cuál es la temperatura máxima?
Estudiante 2: Treinta y un grados (*degrees*).
Estudiante 1: ¿Y la temperatura mínima?
Estudiante 2: Diez grados.

soleado   lluvia   nieve   nublado   viento

Nueva York	Miami	Chicago	París	Madrid	Tokio
Máx. 31°	Máx. 84°	Máx. 23°	Máx. 38°	Máx. 42°	Máx. 49°
Mín. 10°	Mín. 62°	Mín. 5°	Mín. 26°	Mín. 27°	Mín. 34°

Montreal	México D.F.	Cozumel	Caracas	Quito	Buenos Aires
Máx. 18°	Máx. 76°	Máx. 91°	Máx. 80°	Máx. 60°	Máx. 85°
Mín. 2°	Mín. 41°	Mín. 73°	Mín. 72°	Mín. 51°	Mín. 59°

11 Completar Complete these sentences with your own ideas. *Answers will vary.*

1. Cuando hace sol, yo…
2. Cuando llueve, mis amigos y yo…
3. Cuando hace calor, mi familia…
4. Cuando hace viento, la gente…
5. Cuando hace frío, yo…
6. Cuando hace mal tiempo, mis amigos…
7. Cuando nieva, muchas personas…
8. Cuando está nublado, mis amigos y yo…
9. Cuando hace fresco, mis padres…
10. Cuando hace buen tiempo, mis amigos…

NOTA CULTURAL

In most Spanish-speaking countries, temperatures are given in degrees Celsius. Use these formulas to convert between **grados centígrados** and **grados Fahrenheit**.

degrees C × 9 ÷ 5 + 32 = degrees F

degrees F - 32 × 5 ÷ 9 = degrees C

CONSULTA

Calor and **frío** can apply to both weather and people. Use **hacer** to describe weather conditions or climate.

Hace frío en Santiago. *It's cold in Santiago.*

Use **tener** to refer to people.

El viajero tiene frío. *The traveler is cold.*

See **Estructura 3.4**, p. 101.

TEACHING OPTIONS

TPR Have volunteers mime situations that elicit weather-related vocabulary from the class. Ex: A shiver might elicit **hace frío**.
Heritage Speakers Ask heritage speakers to talk about typical weather-dependent activities in their families' countries of origin. Refer them to **Actividad 11** as a model. Ex: **En México, cuando hace frío, la gente bebe ponche de frutas (una bebida caliente).**

Small Groups Have students form groups of two to four. Hand out cards that contain the name of a holiday or other annual event. The group must come up with at least three sentences to describe the holiday or occasion without mentioning its name. They can, however, mention the season of the year. After discussing, other groups must first guess the month and day on which the event takes place, then name the holiday or event itself.

Comunicación

12 **Preguntas personales** In pairs, ask each other these questions. *Answers will vary.*

1. ¿Cuál es la fecha de hoy? ¿Qué estación es?
2. ¿Te gusta esta estación? ¿Por qué?
3. ¿Qué estación prefieres? ¿Por qué?
4. ¿Prefieres el mar o las montañas? ¿La playa o el campo? ¿Por qué?
5. Cuando haces un viaje, ¿qué te gusta hacer y ver?
6. ¿Piensas ir de vacaciones este verano? ¿Adónde quieres ir? ¿Por qué?
7. ¿Qué deseas ver y qué lugares quieres visitar?
8. ¿Cómo te gusta viajar? ¿En avión? ¿En motocicleta...?

13 **Encuesta** Your instructor will give you a worksheet. How does the weather affect what you do? Walk around the class and ask your classmates what they prefer or like to do in the weather conditions given. Note their responses on your worksheet. Make sure to personalize your survey by adding a few original questions. *Answers will vary.*

14 **La reservación** In pairs, prepare a conversation between a hotel receptionist and a tourist calling to make a reservation. Read only the information that pertains to you. Then role-play the situation.

Turista

Vas a viajar a Yucatán con un amigo. Llegan a Cancún el 23 de febrero y necesitan una habitación con baño privado para cuatro noches. Ustedes quieren descansar y prefieren una habitación con vista (*view*) al mar. Averigua (*Find out*) toda la información que necesitas (el costo, cuántas camas, etc.) y decide si quieres hacer la reservación o no.

Empleado/a

Trabajas en la recepción del Hotel Oceanía en Cancún. Para el mes de febrero, sólo quedan (*remain*) dos habitaciones: una individual ($168/noche) en el primer piso y una doble ($134/noche) en el quinto piso que tiene descuento porque no hay ascensor. Todas las habitaciones tienen baño privado y vista (*view*) a la piscina.

15 **Minidrama** With two or three classmates, prepare a skit about people who are on vacation or are planning a vacation. The skit should take place in one of these locations. *Answers will vary.*

- la playa
- una casa
- un aeropuerto, una estación de tren/autobuses
- un hotel
- el campo

Síntesis

16 **Un viaje** You are planning a trip to Mexico and have many questions about your itinerary on which your partner, a travel agent, will advise you. Your instructor will give you and your partner each a sheet with different instructions for acting out the roles. *Answers will vary.*

---

12 **Expansion** Have pairs imagine that one of them is a journalist and the other is a celebrity. Then have them conduct the interview using questions 3–8.

13 **Teaching Tip** Model the activity by asking volunteers what they enjoy doing in hot weather. Ex: **Cuando hace calor, ¿qué haces? (Nado.)** Then distribute the *Hojas de actividades* (Activity Pack/Supersite). Have students report their findings to the class.

14 **Teaching Tips**
- Have students sit back-to-back to better simulate a phone conversation.
- Survey the class to see which room was the most popular. Have volunteers explain why.

15 **Teaching Tip** To simplify, ask the class to brainstorm a list of people and things that may be encountered in each situation. Write the lists on the board.

15 **Expansion** Have students rate the skits as most original, funniest, most realistic, etc.

16 **Teaching Tip** Divide the class into pairs and distribute the handouts from the Activity Pack (Activity Pack/Supersite) that correspond to this Information Gap Activity. Give students ten minutes to complete the activity.

16 **Expansion** Have pairs put together an ideal itinerary for someone else traveling to Mexico, like a classmate, a relative, someone famous, or **el/la profesor(a)**.

¡Vamos a la playa!

Los seis amigos hacen un viaje a la playa.

PERSONAJES **FELIPE** **JUAN CARLOS**

 Video

TÍA ANA MARÍA ¿Están listos para su viaje a la playa?
TODOS Sí.
TÍA ANA MARÍA Excelente... ¡A la estación de autobuses!
MARU ¿Dónde está Miguel?
FELIPE Yo lo traigo.

(*se escucha un grito de Miguel*)
FELIPE Ya está listo. Y tal vez enojado. Ahorita vamos.

EMPLEADO Bienvenidas. ¿En qué puedo servirles?
MARU Hola. Tenemos una reservación para seis personas para esta noche.
EMPLEADO ¿A nombre de quién?
JIMENA ¿Díaz? ¿López? No estoy segura.

EMPLEADO No encuentro su nombre. Ah, no, ahora sí lo veo, aquí está. Díaz. Dos habitaciones en el primer piso para seis huéspedes.

FELIPE No está nada mal el hotel, ¿verdad? Limpio, cómodo... ¡Oye, Miguel! ¿Todavía estás enojado conmigo? (*a Juan Carlos*) Miguel está de mal humor. No me habla.
JUAN CARLOS ¿Todavía?

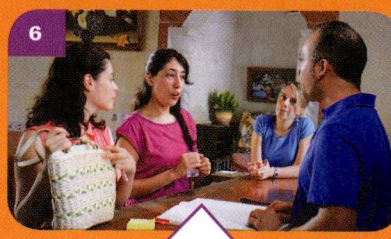

EMPLEADO Aquí están las llaves de sus habitaciones.
MARU Gracias. Una cosa más. Mi novio y yo queremos hacer windsurf, pero no tenemos tablas.
EMPLEADO El botones las puede conseguir para ustedes.

MARISSA
 JIMENA
 MARU
 MIGUEL
 MAITE FUENTES
ANA MARÍA
EMPLEADO

JUAN CARLOS ¿Qué hace este libro aquí? ¿Estás estudiando en la playa?

JIMENA Sí, es que tengo un examen la próxima semana.

JUAN CARLOS Ay, Jimena. ¡No! ¿Vamos a nadar?

JIMENA Bueno, como estudiar es tan aburrido y el tiempo está tan bonito...

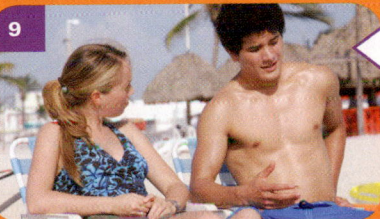

MARISSA Yo estoy un poco cansada. ¿Y tú? ¿Por qué no estás nadando?

FELIPE Es por causa de Miguel.

MARISSA Hmm, estoy confundida.

FELIPE Esta mañana. ¡Sigue enojado conmigo!

MARISSA No puede seguir enojado tanto tiempo.

More activities

vhlcentral | VM pp. 9–10 | Online activities

Expresiones útiles

Talking with hotel personnel

¿En qué puedo servirles?
How can I help you?
Tenemos una reservación.
We have a reservation.
¿A nombre de quién?
In whose name?
¿Quizás López? ¿Tal vez Díaz?
Maybe López? Maybe Díaz?
Ahora lo veo, aquí está. Díaz.
Now I see it. Here it is. Díaz.
Dos habitaciones en el primer piso para seis huéspedes.
Two rooms on the first floor for six guests.
Aquí están las llaves.
Here are the keys.

Describing a hotel

No está nada mal el hotel.
The hotel isn't bad at all.
Todo está tan limpio y cómodo.
Everything is so clean and comfortable.
Es excelente/estupendo/fabuloso/ fenomenal/increíble/magnífico/ maravilloso/perfecto.
It's excellent/stupendous/fabulous/ phenomenal/incredible/magnificent/ marvelous/perfect.

Talking about how you feel

Yo estoy un poco cansado/a.
I am a little tired.
Estoy confundido/a. *I'm confused.*
Todavía estoy/Sigo enojado/a contigo.
I'm still angry with you.

Additional vocabulary

afuera *outside*
amable *nice; friendly*
el balde *bucket*
el/la botones *bellhop*
la crema de afeitar *shaving cream*
el frente (frío) *(cold) front*
el grito *scream*
la temporada *period of time*
entonces *so, then*
es igual *it's the same*

Expresiones útiles Remind students that **está, están,** and **estoy** are present-tense forms of the verb **estar,** which is often used with adjectives that describe conditions and emotions. Remind students that **Es** is a present-tense form of the verb **ser,** which is often used to describe characteristics of people and things and to make generalizations. Draw students' attention to video stills 7 and 9. Point out that **Estás estudiando** and **estás nadando** are examples of the present progressive, which is used to emphasize an action in progress. Finally, point out the captions for video stills 1, 4, and 6 and explain that **lo** and **las** are examples of direct object pronouns. Explain that these are words that replace direct object nouns in order to avoid repetition. Tell students that they will learn more about these concepts in **Estructura.**

Teaching Tip
Have students work in groups of six to read the **Fotonovela** captions aloud (have one student read the role of both **tía Ana María** and the **empleado**). Then have one group come to the front of the class and role-play the scenes. Encourage them to use props and gestures.

Nota cultural The **Yucatán** peninsula is warm year-round, but there are rainy and dry seasons. Generally, the dry season lasts from November to April and the wet season runs from May through October. Hurricanes occur in the late summer and fall. The **Yucatán's** average temperature is 25°C to 27°C (77°F to 81°F), rarely dropping below 16°C (61°F) or rising above 49°C (120°F).

¿Qué pasó?

1 Completar Complete these sentences.

aburrido	botones	la llave
el aeropuerto	la estación de autobuses	montar a caballo
amable	habitaciones	reservación

1. Los amigos van a **la estación de autobuses** para ir a la playa.
2. La **reservación** del hotel está a nombre de los Díaz.
3. Los amigos tienen dos **habitaciones** para seis personas.
4. El **botones** puede conseguir tablas de windsurf para Maru.
5. Jimena dice que estudiar en vacaciones es muy **aburrido**.

CONSULTA
The meaning of some adjectives, such as **aburrido**, changes depending on whether they are used with **ser** or **estar**. See **Estructura 5.3**, pp. 170–171.

2 Identificar Identify the person who made each statement.

1. Aquí están las llaves de sus habitaciones. El botones puede llevar su equipaje al primer piso. **empleado**
2. ¿Qué hace este libro aquí? ¿Estás estudiando en la playa? **Juan Carlos**
3. Tenemos una reservación para seis personas para esta noche. **Maru**
4. Miguel está de mal humor. No me habla. **Felipe**
5. ¿Están listos para su viaje a la playa? **Ana María**

 EMPLEADO **MARU**
 FELIPE
 JUAN CARLOS **TÍA ANA MARÍA**

3 Ordenar Place these events in the correct order.

- **3** a. El empleado busca la reservación.
- **5** b. Marissa dice que está confundida.
- **1** c. Los amigos están listos para ir a la playa.
- **4** d. El empleado da (*gives*) las llaves de las habitaciones a las chicas.
- **2** e. Miguel grita (*screams*).

4 Conversar With a partner, create a conversation between a hotel employee and a guest in Mexico. *Answers will vary.*

 Huésped   **Empleado/a**

Say hi to the employee and ask for your reservation. → Tell the guest that you can't find his/her reservation.

Tell the employee that the reservation is in your name. → Tell him/her that you found the reservation and that it's for a double room.

Tell the employee that the hotel is very clean and comfortable. → Say that you agree with the guest, welcome him/her, and give him/her the keys.

 NATIONAL communication STANDARDS

Pronunciación
Spanish b and v

 Tutorial

---

bueno **vóleibol** **biblioteca** **vivir**

There is no difference in pronunciation between the Spanish letters **b** and **v**. However, each letter can be pronounced two different ways, depending on which letters appear next to them.

bonito **viajar** **también** **investigar**

B and v are pronounced like the English hard *b* when they appear either as the first letter of a word, at the beginning of a phrase, or after **m** or **n**.

deber **novio** **abril** **cerveza**

In all other positions, **b** and **v** have a softer pronunciation, which has no equivalent in English. Unlike the hard **b**, which is produced by tightly closing the lips and stopping the flow of air, the soft **b** is produced by keeping the lips slightly open.

bola **vela** **Caribe** **declive**

In both pronunciations, there is no difference in sound between **b** and **v**. The English *v* sound, produced by friction between the upper teeth and lower lip, does not exist in Spanish. Instead, the soft **b** comes from friction between the two lips.

Verónica y su esposo cantan boleros.

When **b** or **v** begins a word, its pronunciation depends on the previous word. At the beginning of a phrase or after a word that ends in **m** or **n**, it is pronounced as a hard **b**.

Benito es de Boquerón pero vive en Victoria.

Words that begin with **b** or **v** are pronounced with a soft **b** if they appear immediately after a word that ends in a vowel or any consonant other than **m** or **n**.

Práctica Read these words aloud to practice the **b** and the **v**.

1. hablamos
2. trabajar
3. botones
4. van
5. contabilidad
6. bien
7. doble
8. novia
9. béisbol
10. nublado
11. llave
12. invierno

Hombre prevenido vale por dos.[2]

Oraciones Read these sentences aloud to practice the **b** and the **v**.

1. Vamos a Guaynabo en autobús.
2. Voy de vacaciones a la Isla Culebra.
3. Tengo una habitación individual en el octavo piso.
4. Víctor y Eva van en avión al Caribe.
5. La planta baja es bonita también.
6. ¿Qué vamos a ver en Bayamón?
7. Beatriz, la novia de Víctor, es de Arecibo, Puerto Rico.

No hay mal que por bien no venga.[1]

Refranes Read these sayings aloud to practice the **b** and the **v**.

More activities

vhlcentral

LM p. 26

1 *Every cloud has a silver lining.*
2 *An ounce of prevention equals a pound of cure.*

Section Goal

In **Pronunciación**, students will be introduced to the pronunciation of **b** and **v**.

Instructional Resources
Supersite: Audio (Textbook and Lab MP3 Files); Resources (Scripts, Answer Keys)
WebSAM
Lab Manual

Teaching Tips
- Emphasize that **b** (alta/grande) and **v** (baja/chica) are pronounced identically in Spanish, but depending on the letter's position in a word, each can be pronounced two ways. Pronounce **vóleibol** and **vivir** and have students listen for the difference between the initial and medial sounds represented by **b** and **v**.
- Explain the cases in which **b** and **v** are pronounced like English *b* in *boy* and model the pronunciation of **bonito, viajar, también,** and **investigar**.
- Point out that before **b** or **v**, **n** is usually pronounced **m**.
- Explain that in all other positions, **b** and **v** are fricatives. Pronounce **deber, novio, abril,** and **cerveza** and stress that the friction is between the two lips.
- Remind the class that Spanish has no sound like the English **v**. Pronounce **vida, vacaciones, avión,** and **automóvil**.
- Explain that the same rules apply in connected speech. Practice with phrases like **de vacaciones** and **de ida y vuelta**.

Práctica/Oraciones/Refranes
These exercises are recorded on the *Textbook MP3s*. You may want to play the audio so that students practice listening to Spanish spoken by speakers other than yourself.

EN DETALLE

El Viejo San Juan

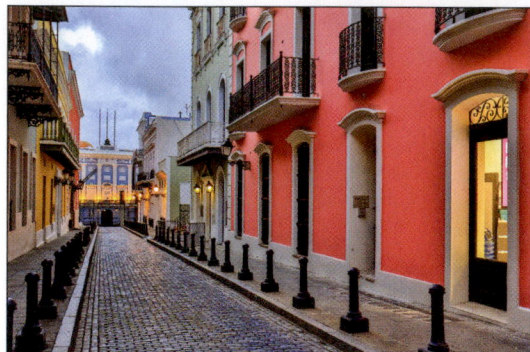

San Juan, the capital of Puerto Rico, was founded by Juan Ponce de León in 1508. The original settlement was called **Caparra**. In 1521 the name was formally changed to **San Juan Bautista°** de Puerto Rico. The city has served as the island's capital ever since. The oldest part of the capital, known as **el Viejo San Juan**, is an international tourist destination. Many Caribbean cruise ships make stops there.

El Viejo San Juan is most famous for its Spanish colonial architecture, which according to strict regulations can neither be altered nor demolished. Furthermore, all new construction must maintain the integrity of the Spanish colonial style.

Visitors flock to this historic site to stroll the colonial **callejones°**, tour monuments such as the **Casa Blanca** and the fortress known as **El Morro**, and enjoy the climate of **la Isla del Encanto°**.

El Viejo San Juan was added to the U.S. National Register of Historic Places in 1966, and in 1983 it was designated a World Heritage Site by UNESCO.

In 2017, Hurricane María severely damaged parts of the old city, causing a disruption to tourism. In time, the people of the city cleaned up and repaired. As one reporter put it, "Old San Juan has already survived 500 hurricane seasons. It will survive this one, too!"

Plaza de Armas

San Juan Bautista *Saint John the Baptist* callejones *narrow lanes, alleyways* la Isla del Encanto *the Isle of Enchantment (nickname for Puerto Rico)*

Sitios históricos del Viejo San Juan

- **Plaza de Armas:** the main public square in el Viejo San Juan
- **Catedral Metropolitana Basílica de San Juan Bautista:** the second oldest cathedral in the Western Hemisphere
- **El Morro** and **Castillo de San Cristóbal:** forts built to protect the city and San Juan Bay
- **Casa Blanca:** historic house and museum, residence of Ponce de León's family from 1521 to the mid-18th century

ACTIVIDADES

1 **¿Cierto o falso?** Indicate whether these statements are **cierto** or **falso**. Correct the false statements.

1. **Caparra** was the name of the original settlement. **Cierto.**
2. Puerto Rico's capital is named after a saint. **Cierto.**
3. To protect its historic sites, most of **el Viejo San Juan** is off-limits to the public. **Falso.** It is a popular tourist destination.
4. The buildings in **el Viejo San Juan** maintain a Spanish colonial architectural style. **Cierto.**
5. The city is culturally important in the United States but not internationally. **Falso.** The city is a UNESCO World Heritage Site.
6. Hurricane María completely spared **el Viejo San Juan**. **Falso.** It caused severe damage to parts of the old city.
7. **El Viejo San Juan** does not have a main public square. **Falso.** La Plaza de Armas is its main public square.
8. The second oldest cathedral in the Americas is in San Juan. **Cierto.**
9. **El Castillo de San Cristóbal** was principally a colonial trading post. **Falso.** It is a fort that protected the city and San Juan Bay.
10. You can visit Ponce de León's family home in **el Viejo San Juan**. **Cierto.**

ASÍ SE DICE
Viajes y turismo

el asiento del medio, del pasillo, de la ventanilla	center, aisle, window seat
el itinerario	itinerary
media pensión	breakfast and one meal included
el ómnibus (Perú)	el autobús
pensión completa	all meals included
el puente	long weekend (lit., bridge)

EL MUNDO HISPANO
Destinos populares

- **Las playas del Parque Nacional Manuel Antonio** (Costa Rica) ofrecen° la oportunidad de nadar y luego caminar por el bosque tropical°.
- **Teotihuacán** (México) Desde antes de la época° de los aztecas, aquí se celebra el equinoccio de primavera en la Pirámide del Sol.
- **Puerto Chicama** (Perú), con sus olas° de cuatro kilómetros de largo°, es un destino para surfistas expertos.
- **Tikal** (Guatemala) Aquí puedes ver las maravillas de la selva° y ruinas de la civilización maya.
- **Las playas de Rincón** (Puerto Rico) Son ideales para descansar y observar ballenas°.

ofrecen *offer* bosque tropical *rain forest*
Desde antes de la época *Since before the time* olas *waves*
de largo *in length* selva *jungle* ballenas *whales*

PERFIL
Punta del Este

One of South America's largest and most fashionable beach resort towns is Uruguay's **Punta del Este**, a narrow strip of land containing twenty miles of pristine beaches. Its peninsular shape gives it two very different seascapes. **La Playa Mansa**, facing the bay and therefore the more protected side, has calm waters. Here, people practice water sports like swimming, water skiing, windsurfing, and diving. **La Playa Brava**, facing the east, receives the Atlantic Ocean's powerful, wave-producing winds, making it popular for surfing, body boarding, and kite surfing. Besides the beaches, posh shopping, and world-famous nightlife, **Punta** offers its 620,000 yearly visitors yacht and fishing clubs, golf courses, and excursions to observe sea lions at the **Isla de Lobos** nature reserve.

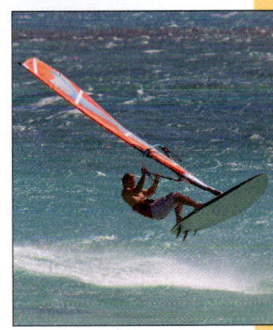

CON RITMO HISPANO
Luis Fonsi (1978–)
Birthplace: San Juan, Puerto Rico

He has released ten albums and worked with artists such as Christina Aguilera, David Bisbal, Laura Pausini, and Juan Luis Guerra. His song "Despacito," featuring Daddy Yankee, was an international hit.

Go to **vhlcentral.com** to find out more about **Luis Fonsi** and his music.

ACTIVIDADES

2 Comprensión Complete the sentences.
1. En las playas de Rincón puedes ver <u>ballenas</u>.
2. Cerca de 620.000 turistas visitan <u>Punta del Este</u> cada año.
3. En el avión pides un <u>asiento de la ventanilla</u> si te gusta ver el paisaje.
4. En Punta del Este, la gente prefiere nadar en la Playa <u>Mansa</u>.
5. El <u>ómnibus</u> es un medio de transporte en Perú.

3 De vacaciones Spring break is coming up, and you want to go on a short vacation with some friends. Working in a small group, decide which of the locations featured on these pages best suits the group's likes and interests. Come to an agreement about how you will get there, where you prefer to stay and for how long, and what each of you will do during free time. Answers will vary.

More activities
 vhlcentral Online activities

Section Goals

In **Estructura 5.1**, students will learn:
- to use **estar** to describe conditions and emotions
- adjectives that describe conditions and emotions

Instructional Resources

Supersite: Audio (Lab MP3 Files); Resources (Grammar Presentation Slides, Activity Pack, Scripts, Answer Keys); Testing Program (Quizzes)
WebSAM
Workbook
Lab Manual

Teaching Tips

- →👤← Ask students to find examples of **estar** used with adjectives in the **Fotonovela**. Have volunteers explain why **estar** instead of **ser** is used in each example.
- Remind students that adjectives agree in number and gender with the nouns they modify.
- Add a visual aspect to this grammar presentation. Bring in personal or magazine photos of people with varying facial expressions. Hold up each one and state the person's emotion. Ex: **Mi esposa y yo estamos contentos.**
- Point to objects and people and have volunteers supply the correct form of **estar** + [adjective]. Ex: Point to windows. (**Están abiertas.**)
- Use TPR to practice the adjectives. Have the class stand, and signal a student. Say: ____, **estás enojado/a.** (Student will make an angry face.) Vary by indicating more than one student.
- Point out the use of **de** with **enamorado/a** and **por** with **preocupado/a.** Write cloze sentences on the board and have students complete them. Ex: **Michelle Obama está ____ Barack Obama.** (**enamorada de**)

5.1 Estar with conditions and emotions

ANTE TODO As you learned in **Lecciones 1** and **2**, the verb **estar** is used to talk about how you feel and to say where people, places, and things are located. **Estar** is also used with adjectives to talk about certain emotional and physical conditions.

▶ Use **estar** with adjectives to describe the physical condition of places and things.

La habitación **está** sucia.
The room is dirty.

La puerta **está** cerrada.
The door is closed.

▶ Use **estar** with adjectives to describe how people feel, both mentally and physically.

Yo estoy cansada.

¿Están listos para su viaje?

▶ **¡Atención!** Two important expressions with **estar** that you can use to talk about conditions and emotions are **estar de buen humor** (*to be in a good mood*) and **estar de mal humor** (*to be in a bad mood*).

CONSULTA

To review the present tense of **estar**, see **Estructura 2.3**, p. 59.

•••

To review the present tense of **ser**, see **Estructura 1.3**, p. 20.

Adjectives that describe emotions and conditions

abierto/a	open	**contento/a**	content	**listo/a**	ready
aburrido/a	bored	**desordenado/a**	disorderly	**nervioso/a**	nervous
alegre	happy	**enamorado/a (de)**	in love (with)	**ocupado/a**	busy
avergonzado/a	embarrassed	**enojado/a**	angry	**ordenado/a**	orderly
cansado/a	tired	**equivocado/a**	wrong	**preocupado/a (por)**	worried (about)
cerrado/a	closed	**feliz**	happy	**seguro/a**	sure
cómodo/a	comfortable	**limpio/a**	clean	**sucio/a**	dirty
confundido/a	confused			**triste**	sad

👁 **¡INTÉNTALO!** Provide the present tense forms of **estar**, and choose which adjective best completes the sentence.

1. La biblioteca ___está___ (cerrada / nerviosa) los domingos por la noche. *cerrada*
2. Nosotros ___estamos___ muy (ocupados / equivocados) todos los lunes. *ocupados*
3. Ellas ___están___ (alegres / confundidas) porque tienen vacaciones. *alegres*
4. Javier ___está___ (enamorado / ordenado) de Maribel. *enamorado*
5. Yo ___estoy___ (nerviosa / abierta) por el viaje. *nerviosa*
6. Diana ___está___ (enojada / limpia) con su novio. *enojada*
7. La habitación siempre ___está___ (ordenada / segura) cuando vienen sus padres. *ordenada*
8. Ustedes no comprenden; ___están___ (equivocados / tristes). *equivocados*

More activities

vhlcentral

LM
p. 27

WB
pp. 51–52

Online activities

TEACHING OPTIONS

TPR Call out a sentence using an adjective and have students mime the emotion or show the condition. Ex: **Sus libros están abiertos.** (Students show their open books.) **Ustedes están alegres.** (Students act happy.) Next, call on volunteers to act out an emotion or condition, and have the class tell what is going on. Ex: A student pretends to cry. (**Carlos está triste.**)

Video →👤← Replay the **Fotonovela** episode and ask comprehension questions using **estar** and adjectives expressing emotions or conditions. Ex: **¿Cómo está el hotel?** (**Está limpio y cómodo.**) **¿Está de mal humor Miguel?** (**Sí, está de mal humor.**) **¿Quién está cansado?** (**Marissa está cansada.**)

Práctica y Comunicación

1 **¿Cómo están?** In the first blank of each statement made by Martín, fill in the correct form of **estar**. In the second blank, fill in the adjective that best fits the context. *Some answers may vary.*

1. Yo ___estoy___ un poco ___nervioso___ porque tengo un examen mañana.
2. Mis hermanos Juan y José salen de la casa a las cinco de la mañana. Por la noche, siempre ___están___ muy ___cansados___.
3. Mi hermana Patricia ___está___ muy ___contenta___ porque mañana va a hacer una excursión al campo.
4. Mi amigo Ramiro ___está___ ___enamorado___; su novia se llama Adela.
5. Mi papá y sus colegas ___están___ muy ___ocupados___ hoy. ¡Hay mucho trabajo!
6. Patricia y yo ___estamos___ un poco ___preocupados___ por ellos porque trabajan mucho.
7. Mi amiga Mónica ___está___ un poco ___triste/enojada___ porque su novio no puede salir esta noche.
8. Esta clase no es muy interesante. ¿Tú ___estás___ ___aburrido/a___ también?

2 **Describir** Describe these people and places. *Answers will vary. Sample answers:*

1. Anabela
Está cómoda/ocupada.

2. Juan y Luisa
Están enamorados/felices/contentos.

3. la habitación de Teresa
Está ordenada/limpia.

4. César
Está ocupado/cansado.

3 **Situaciones** With a partner, use **estar** to talk about how you feel in these situations. *Answers will vary.*

1. Cuando hace sol…
2. Cuando tomas un examen…
3. Cuando viajas en avión…
4. Cuando estás en la clase de español…
5. Cuando ves una película con tu actor/actriz favorito/a…

4 **En la tele** In small groups, imagine that you are a family that stars on a reality TV show. You are vacationing together, but the trip isn't going well for everyone. Write the script of a scene from the show and then act it out. Use at least six adjectives from the previous page and be creative!

modelo

Papá: ¿Por qué estás enojada, María Rosa? El hotel es muy bonito y las habitaciones están limpias.

Mamá: ¡Pero mira, Roberto! Las maletas de Elisa están abiertas y, como siempre, sus cosas están muy desordenadas.

---

1 Teaching Tip Have a volunteer model the first sentence by supplying the correct form of **estar** and an appropriate adjective. Ask the student to explain his or her choices.

1 Expansion Have students write five additional sentences missing **estar** and an adjective. Then have them exchange papers and complete the sentences.

2 Expansion
• Have students write a few sentences about the photos explaining why the people feel the way they do and why the room looks this way.
• Have students pretend they are **Anabela, Juan,** or **Luisa** and give a short oral description of who they are and how they feel today.

3 Teaching Tip Have partners alternate completing the sentences until each has answered all items.

3 Expansion Ask students to keep a record of their partners' responses. Take a classroom poll to see what percentage of students felt a particular way for each situation.

4 Teaching Tip As an alternative, have students imagine that they are a family that is currently appearing on a reality show.

5.2   The present progressive Tutorial

ANTE TODO   Both Spanish and English use the present progressive, which consists of the present tense of the verb *to be* and the present participle of another verb (the *-ing* form in English).

Las chicas están hablando con el empleado del hotel.

¿Estás estudiando en la playa?

▶ Form the present progressive with the present tense of **estar** and a present participle.

FORM OF ESTAR + PRESENT PARTICIPLE	FORM OF ESTAR + PRESENT PARTICIPLE
Estoy **pescando.**	**Estamos** **comiendo.**
I am *fishing.*	*We are* *eating.*

▶ The present participle of regular **-ar**, **-er**, and **-ir** verbs is formed as follows:

INFINITIVE	STEM	ENDING	PRESENT PARTICIPLE
hablar	habl-	**-ando**	habl**ando**
comer	com-	**-iendo**	com**iendo**
escribir	escrib-	**-iendo**	escrib**iendo**

▶ **¡Atención!** When the stem of an **-er** or **-ir** verb ends in a vowel, the present participle ends in **-yendo**.

INFINITIVE	STEM	ENDING	PRESENT PARTICIPLE
leer	le-	**-yendo**	le**yendo**
oír	o-	**-yendo**	o**yendo**
traer	tra-	**-yendo**	tra**yendo**

▶ **Ir**, **poder**, and **venir** have irregular present participles (**yendo**, **pudiendo**, **viniendo**). Several other verbs have irregular present participles that you will need to learn.

▶ **-Ir** stem-changing verbs have a stem change in the present participle.

-ir stem-changing verbs

e:ie in the present tense	**e → i** in the present participle
preferir	pref**i**riendo
e:i in the present tense	**e → i** in the present participle
conseguir	cons**i**guiendo
o:ue in the present tense	**o → u** in the present participle
dormir	d**u**rmiendo

COMPARE & CONTRAST

The use of the present progressive is much more restricted in Spanish than in English. In Spanish, the present progressive is mainly used to emphasize that an action is in progress at the time of speaking.

Maru **está escuchando** música latina **ahora mismo**.
Maru is listening to Latin music right now.

Felipe y su amigo **todavía están jugando** al fútbol.
Felipe and his friend are still playing soccer.

In English, the present progressive is often used to talk about situations and actions that occur over an extended period of time or in the future. In Spanish, the simple present tense is often used instead.

Xavier **estudia** computación este semestre.
Xavier is studying computer science this semester.

Marissa **sale** mañana para los Estados Unidos.
Marissa is leaving tomorrow for the United States.

¿Está pensando en su futuro?
Nosotros, sí.

🏛 BANCO
CONGRESO 🏛

Preparándolo para el mañana

¡INTÉNTALO!   Create complete sentences by putting the verbs in the present progressive.

1. mis amigos / descansar en la playa   *Mis amigos están descansando en la playa.*
2. nosotros / practicar deportes   *Estamos practicando deportes.*
3. Carmen / comer en casa   *Carmen está comiendo en casa.*
4. yo / leer el periódico   *Estoy leyendo el periódico.*
5. nuestro equipo / ganar el partido   *Nuestro equipo está ganando el partido.*
6. él / pensar comprar una bicicleta   *Está pensando comprar una bicicleta.*
7. ustedes / jugar a las cartas   *Ustedes están jugando a las cartas.*
8. Marcela / leer el correo electrónico   *Marcela está leyendo el correo electrónico.*
9. José y Francisco / dormir   *José y Francisco están durmiendo.*
10. yo / preparar sándwiches   *Estoy preparando sándwiches.*
11. Carlos / tomar fotos   *Carlos está tomando fotos.*
12. ¿dormir / tú?   *¿Estás durmiendo?*

Práctica

1 **Completar** Use the present progressive of the verb to complete Alfredo's description of what everyone in his class is doing to prepare for a trip to Puerto Rico.

1. Yo ___estoy investigando___ (investigar) la situación política de la isla (*island*).
2. Marta y José Luis ___están buscando___ (buscar) información sobre San Juan en Internet.
3. La esposa del profesor ___está haciendo___ (hacer) las maletas.
4. Enrique y yo ___estamos leyendo___ (leer) un correo electrónico de nuestro amigo puertorriqueño.
5. Javier ___está aprendiendo___ (aprender) mucho sobre la cultura puertorriqueña.
6. Y tú ___estás practicando___ (practicar) el español, ¿verdad?

2 **¿Qué están haciendo?** Complete María's description of what she and her friends are doing right now as they vacation in Puerto Rico.

1. Alejandro y Rebeca
están jugando a las cartas.

2. Javier
está buceando en el mar.

3. Yo
estoy dibujando.

4. Celia y yo
estamos nadando.

5. Samuel
está haciendo surf.

6. Lorenzo
está durmiendo.

3 **Personajes famosos** Say what these celebrities are doing right now. Answers will vary.

modelo
Shakira
Shakira está cantando una canción ahora mismo.

A		B	
Isabel Allende	Daymé Arocena	bailar	hacer
Rachael Ray	Kevin Durant	cantar	jugar
James Cameron	Las Rockettes de	correr	preparar
Venus y Serena	Nueva York	escribir	¿?
Williams	¿?	hablar	¿?
José Altuve	¿?		

TEACHING OPTIONS

Pairs Have students bring in photos from a vacation. Ask them to describe the photos to a partner. Students should explain what the weather is like, who is in the photo, and what they are doing. The partner should try to guess the location the student is describing. Students can ask additional questions until they guess correctly.

Game Have the class form a circle. Appoint one student to be the starter, who will mime an action (Ex: eating) and say what he or she is doing (Ex: **Estoy comiendo.**). The next student mimes the same action, says what that person is doing (_____ **está comiendo.**), and then mimes and states a different action (Ex: sleeping/**Estoy durmiendo.**). Have students continue until the chain breaks. Have students see how long the chain can get in three minutes.

Comunicación

4 **Preguntar** With a partner, take turns asking each other what you are doing at these times. Answers will vary.

> **modelo**
> 8:00 a.m.
> **Estudiante 1:** ¡Hola, Andrés! Son las ocho de la mañana. ¿Qué estás haciendo?
> **Estudiante 2:** Estoy desayunando.

1. 5:00 a.m.	3. 11:00 a.m.	5. 2:00 p.m.	7. 9:00 p.m.
2. 9:30 a.m.	4. 12:00 p.m.	6. 5:00 p.m.	8. 11:30 p.m.

5 **Describir** Work with a partner and use the present progressive to describe what is going on in this Spanish beach scene. Answers will vary.

NOTA CULTURAL

Nearly 70 million tourists travel to Spain every year, many of them drawn by the warm climate and beautiful coasts. Tourists wanting a beach vacation go mostly to the **Costa del Sol** or the Balearic Islands, in the Mediterranean.

Felipe · Enrique · Iván · Sr. Cantú · Sra. Morales · Dra. Núñez · Georgina · Sr. Morales

6 **Conversar** With a partner, prepare a phone conversation between two babysitters. Be creative and add further comments. Answers will vary.

Estudiante 1	**Estudiante 2**
Say hello and ask what the kids are doing.	Say hello and tell your partner that two of your kids are doing their homework. Then ask what the kids at his/her house are doing.
Tell your partner that two of your kids are running and dancing in the house.	Tell your partner that one of the kids is reading.
Tell your partner that you are tired and that two of your kids are watching TV and eating pizza.	Tell your partner that one of the kids is sleeping.
Tell your partner you have to go; the kids are playing soccer in the house.	Say goodbye and good luck (**¡Buena suerte!**).

Síntesis

7 **¿Qué están haciendo?** A group of classmates is traveling to San Juan, Puerto Rico, for a week-long Spanish immersion program. In order for the participants to be on time for their flight, you and your partner must locate them. Your instructor will give you each a handout to help you complete this task. Answers will vary.

TEACHING OPTIONS

Video Show the **Fotonovela** episode again, pausing after each exchange. Ask students to describe what each person in the shot is doing at that moment.
TPR Write sentences with the present progressive on strips of paper. Call on volunteers to draw papers out of a hat to act out. The class should guess what the sentences are. Ex: **Yo estoy durmiendo en la cama.**

Pairs Add an auditory aspect to this grammar practice. Ask students to write a short paragraph using the present progressive. Students should try to make their sentences as complex as possible. Have students dictate their sentences to a partner. After pairs have finished dictating their sentences, have them exchange papers to check for accuracy. Circulate around the room and look over students' work.

---

4 **Teaching Tip** To simplify, first have students outline their daily activities and at what time they do them. Remind students to use **a la(s)** when expressing time.

4 **Expansion** Reverse the activity by having students state what they are doing. Their partner should guess the time of day. Alternatively, students could say that they are doing season-specific activities (Ex: **Estoy tomando el sol.**) and their partner will guess the month.

5 **Teaching Tip** Use the **Lección 5 Estructura** digital images to assist with the presentation of this activity.

5 **Expansion** In pairs, have students write a conversation between two or more of the people in the drawing. Conversations should consist of at least three exchanges.

6 **Teaching Tip** To simplify, before beginning their conversation, have students prepare for their roles by brainstorming two lists: one with verbs that describe what the children are doing at home and the other with adjectives that describe how the babysitter feels.

6 **Expansion** Ask pairs to tell each other what the parents of the two sets of children are doing. Ex: **Los padres de los niños buenos están visitando el museo. Los padres de los niños malos están en una fiesta.**

7 **Teaching Tip** Divide the class into pairs and distribute the handouts from the Activity Pack (Activity Pack/Supersite) that correspond to this Information Gap Activity.

7 **Expansion** Have pairs discuss what each program participant is doing in flight. Ex: **Pedro está leyendo una novela.**

5.3 Ser and estar Tutorial

ANTE TODO You have already learned that **ser** and **estar** both mean *to be* but are used for different purposes. These charts summarize the key differences in usage between **ser** and **estar**.

Uses of ser

1. Nationality and place of origin .... Juan Carlos **es** argentino.
   Es de Buenos Aires.
2. Profession or occupation .... Adela **es** inspectora de aduanas.
   Francisco **es** médico.
3. Characteristics of people and things ... José y Clara **son** simpáticos.
   El clima de Puerto Rico **es** agradable.
4. Generalizations .... ¡**Es** fabuloso viajar!
   Es difícil estudiar a la una de la mañana.
5. Possession .... **Es** la pluma de Jimena.
   Son las llaves del señor Díaz.
6. What something is made of .... La bicicleta **es** de metal.
   Los pasajes **son** de papel.
7. Time and date .... Hoy **es** martes. **Son** las dos.
   Hoy **es** el primero de julio.
8. Where or when an event takes place. . El partido **es** en el estadio Santa Fe.
   La conferencia **es** a las siete.

Ellos son mis amigos.

Miguel está enojado conmigo.

Uses of estar

1. Location or spatial relationships ..... El aeropuerto **está** lejos de la ciudad.
   Tu habitación **está** en el tercer piso.
2. Health .... ¿Cómo **estás**?
   Estoy bien, gracias.
3. Physical states and conditions....... El profesor **está** ocupado.
   Las ventanas **están** abiertas.
4. Emotional states .... Marissa **está** feliz hoy.
   Estoy muy enojado con Maru.
5. Certain weather expressions .... **Está** lloviendo.
   Está nublado.
6. Ongoing actions (progressive tenses) .. **Estamos** estudiando para un examen.
   Ana **está** leyendo una novela.

Ser and estar with adjectives

▶ With many descriptive adjectives, **ser** and **estar** can both be used, but the meaning will change.

Juan **es** delgado.
Juan is thin.

Juan **está** más delgado hoy.
Juan looks thinner today.

Ana **es** nerviosa.
Ana is a nervous person.

Ana **está** nerviosa por el examen.
Ana is nervous because of the exam.

▶ In the examples above, the statements with **ser** are general observations about the inherent qualities of Juan and Ana. The statements with **estar** describe conditions that are variable.

▶ Here are some adjectives that change in meaning when used with **ser** and **estar**.

With ser	With estar
El chico **es listo**. *The boy is smart.*	El chico **está listo**. *The boy is ready.*
La profesora **es mala**. *The professor is bad.*	La profesora **está mala**. *The professor is sick.*
Jaime **es aburrido**. *Jaime is boring.*	Jaime **está aburrido**. *Jaime is bored.*
Las peras **son verdes**. *Pears are green.*	Las peras **están verdes**. *The pears are not ripe.*
El gato **es muy vivo**. *The cat is very clever.*	El gato **está vivo**. *The cat is alive.*
Iván **es un hombre seguro**. *Iván is a confident man.*	Iván no **está seguro**. *Iván is not sure.*

¡ATENCIÓN!

When referring to objects, **ser seguro/a** means *to be safe*.
El puente es seguro.
The bridge is safe.

More activities

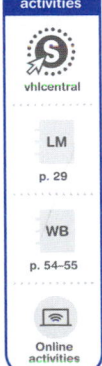

vhlcentral

LM
p. 29

WB
p. 54–55

Online activities

 ¡INTÉNTALO! Form complete sentences by using the correct form of **ser** or **estar** and making any other necessary changes.

1. Alejandra / cansado
   Alejandra está cansada.

2. ellos / pelirrojo
   Ellos son pelirrojos.

3. yo / la clase de español
   Estoy en la clase de español.

4. Carmen / alto
   Carmen es alta.

5. película / a las once
   La película es a las once.

6. hoy / viernes
   Hoy es viernes.

7. Romeo y Julieta / enamorado
   Romeo y Julieta están enamorados.

8. Antonio / médico
   Antonio es médico.

9. nosotras / enojado
   Nosotras estamos enojadas.

10. libros / de Ana
    Los libros son de Ana.

11. Mariana y Juan / estudiando
    Mariana y Juan están estudiando.

12. partido de baloncesto / gimnasio
    El partido de baloncesto es en el gimnasio.

Teaching Tips

- Ask students if they notice any context clues in the examples that would help them choose between **ser** and **estar**.
- Write sentences like these on the board: 1. Pilar is worried because she has a quiz tomorrow. (**Pilar está preocupada porque tiene una prueba mañana.**) 2. The male employee is very busy right now. (**El empleado está muy ocupado ahora.**) 3. The beach is pretty. (**La playa es bonita.**) 4. **Juan** is/looks very handsome today. (**Juan está muy guapo hoy.**) Have students translate the sentences into Spanish, and ask them why they chose either **ser** or **estar** for their translation.
- Ask students questions to practice the different meanings of adjectives, depending on whether they are used with **ser** or **estar**. Ex: 1. **Manuel es un muchacho muy inteligente. ¿Está listo o es listo?** 2. **No me gusta la clase de física. ¿Está aburrida o es aburrida?** 3. **No sé si Carlos tiene 50 o 51 años. ¿No estoy seguro/a o no soy seguro/a?** 4. **¿El color del taxi es verde o está verde?** 5. **El profesor no enseña muy bien. ¿Está malo o es malo?**

The Affective Dimension

If students feel anxious that Spanish has two verbs that mean *to be*, reassure them that they will soon feel more comfortable with this concept as they read more examples and have more practice. Point out that **ser** and **estar** express rich shades of meaning.

TEACHING OPTIONS

Extra Practice Ask students to write sentences illustrating the contrasting meanings of adjectives used with **ser** or **estar**. Have students exchange papers for peer editing before going over them with the class.
Video → Show the **Fotonovela** episode again. Have students jot down the forms of **ser** or **estar** that they hear. Discuss each use of **ser** and **estar**.

Pairs Tell students to imagine that they are going to interview a celebrity visiting their hometown. Ask them to write questions with at least ten different uses of **ser** and **estar**. Next, have them interview a partner and record the answers. Have students write a summary of their interviews.

Práctica

1 Teaching Tip Have students identify the use(s) of **ser** or **estar** for each item.

1 Expansion To challenge students, ask them to use each adjective in a sentence. If the adjective can take both verbs, have them provide two sentences.

2 Teaching Tip To simplify, ask students to point out context clues that will help them determine whether to use **ser** or **estar**. Ex: The word **hoy** in line 2 suggests that **guapo** is a variable physical state.

2 Expansion Have pairs write a continuation of the conversation and then present it to the class.

3 Teaching Tip Use the **Lección 5 Estructura** digital images to assist with the presentation of this activity.

3 Expansion Add another visual aspect to this grammar practice. Bring in photos or magazine pictures that show many different people performing a variety of activities. Have students use **ser** and **estar** to write short descriptions of the scenes.

---

1 **¿Ser o estar?** Indicate whether each adjective takes **ser** or **estar**. ¡Ojo! Three of them can take both verbs.

	ser	estar			ser	estar
1. canadiense	☑	○	5. enojada	○	☑
2. delgada	☑	☑	6. seguro	☑	☑
3. enamorado	○	☑	7. importante	☑	○
4. lista	☑	☑	8. avergonzada	○	☑

2 **Completar** Complete this conversation with the appropriate forms of **ser** and **estar**.

EDUARDO ¡Hola, Ceci! ¿Cómo (1)___estás___?

CECILIA Hola, Eduardo. Bien, gracias. ¡Qué guapo (2)___estás___ hoy!

EDUARDO Gracias. (3)___Eres___ muy amable. Oye, ¿qué (4)___estás___ haciendo? (5)¿___Estás___ ocupada?

CECILIA No, sólo le (6)___estoy___ escribiendo una carta a mi prima Pilar.

EDUARDO ¿De dónde (7)___es___ ella?

CECILIA Pilar (8)___es___ de Ecuador. Su papá (9)___es___ médico en Quito. Pero ahora Pilar y su familia (10)___están___ de vacaciones en Ponce, Puerto Rico.

EDUARDO Y… ¿cómo (11)___es___ Pilar?

CECILIA (12)___Es___ muy lista. Y también (13)___es___ alta, rubia y muy bonita.

3 **En el parque** With a partner, take turns describing the people in the drawing. Your descriptions should answer the questions. Answers will vary.

1. ¿Quiénes son?
2. ¿Dónde están?
3. ¿Cómo son?
4. ¿Cómo están?
5. ¿Qué están haciendo?
6. ¿Qué estación es?
7. ¿Qué tiempo hace?
8. ¿Quiénes están de vacaciones?

Comunicación

4 Describir With a classmate, take turns describing these people. Mention where they are from, what they are like, how they are feeling, and what they are doing right now. *Answers will vary.*

> **modelo**
>
> tu compañero/a de cuarto
>
> Mi compañera de cuarto es de San Juan, Puerto Rico. Es muy inteligente. Está cansada pero está estudiando porque tiene un examen.

1. tu mejor (*best*) amigo/a
2. tu actor/actriz favorito/a
3. tu profesor(a) favorito/a
4. tu novio/a o esposo/a
5. tus abuelos
6. tus padres

5 Adivinar Get together with a partner and take turns describing a celebrity. Don't mention the celebrity's name. Can your partner guess who you are describing? *Answers will vary.*

- descripción física
- cómo está ahora
- origen
- dónde está ahora
- qué está haciendo ahora
- profesión u ocupación

6 En el aeropuerto In groups of three, take turns assuming the identity of a character from this drawing. Your partners will ask you questions using **ser** and **estar** until they figure out who you are. *Answers will vary.*

> **modelo**
>
> Estudiante 3: ¿Dónde estás?
> Estudiante 1: Estoy cerca de la puerta.
> Estudiante 2: ¿Qué estás haciendo?
> Estudiante 1: Estoy escuchando a otra persona.
> Estudiante 3: ¿Eres uno de los pasajeros?
> Estudiante 1: No, soy empleado del aeropuerto.
> Estudiante 2: ¿Eres Camilo?

Síntesis

7 Conversación With a partner, role-play a conversation between two airline passengers seated next to each other. *Answers will vary.*

TEACHING OPTIONS

Small Groups Have students work in small groups to write a television commercial for a vacation resort in the Spanish-speaking world. Ask them to employ as many uses of **ser** and **estar** as they can. If possible, after they have written the commercial, have them tape it to show to the class.

TPR Call on a volunteer and whisper the name of a celebrity in his or her ear. The volunteer acts out verbs and characteristics and uses props to elicit descriptions from the class. Ex: The volunteer points to the U.S. on a map. (**Es de los Estados Unidos.**) He or she then indicates a tall, thin man. (**Es un hombre atlético y delgado.**) He or she acts out swimming. (**Está nadando. ¿Es Michael Phelps?**)

---

4 Expansion Have pairs select two descriptions to present to the class.

5 Teaching Tip Model the activity for the class. You may want to tell students to use **una persona** to create ambiguity in their descriptions. Ex: **Es una persona alta…**

6 Teaching Tip Use the **Lección 5 Estructura** digital images to assist with the presentation of this activity.

6 Expansion Have students pick one of the individuals pictured and write a one-paragraph description, employing as many different uses of **ser** and **estar** as possible.

7 Teaching Tips
- To simplify, first have students write a character description for the person they will be playing. Then, as a class, brainstorm topics of conversation.
- Make sure that students use **ser** and **estar**, the present progressive, and stem-changing verbs in their conversations, as well as vacation-, pastime-, and family-related vocabulary. Have pairs act out their conversation for the class.

The Affective Dimension
Encourage students to consider pair and group activities as a cooperative venture in which group members support and motivate each other.

5.4 Direct object nouns and pronouns Tutorial

SUBJECT	VERB	DIRECT OBJECT NOUN
Juan Carlos y Jimena	están tomando	fotos.
Juan Carlos and Jimena	*are taking*	*photos.*

▶ A direct object noun receives the action of the verb directly and generally follows the verb. In the example above, the direct object noun answers the question *What are Juan Carlos and Jimena taking?*

▶ When a direct object noun in Spanish is a person or a pet, it is preceded by the word **a**. This is called the personal **a**; there is no English equivalent for this construction.

Mariela mira **a** Carlos.
Mariela is watching Carlos.

Mariela mira televisión.
Mariela is watching TV.

▶ In the first sentence above, the personal **a** is required because the direct object is a person. In the second sentence, the personal **a** is not required because the direct object is a thing, not a person.

No tenemos tablas de windsurf.

Miguel no me perdona.

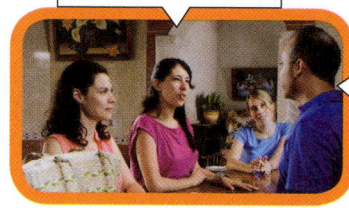

El botones las puede conseguir para ustedes.

▶ Direct object pronouns are words that replace direct object nouns. Like English, Spanish uses a direct object pronoun to avoid repeating a noun already mentioned.

	DIRECT OBJECT			DIRECT OBJECT PRONOUN	
Maribel hace	las maletas.	▶	Maribel	las	hace.
Felipe compra	el sombrero.		Felipe	lo	compra.
Vicky tiene	la llave.		Vicky	la	tiene.

Direct object pronouns

SINGULAR		PLURAL	
me	*me*	**nos**	*us*
te	*you* (fam.)	**os**	*you* (fam.)
lo	*you* (m., form.)	**los**	*you* (m.)
	him; it (m.)		*them* (m.)
la	*you* (f., form.)	**las**	*you* (f.)
	her; it (f.)		*them* (f.)

Section Goals

In **Estructura 5.4**, students will study:
• direct object nouns
• the personal **a**
• direct object pronouns

Instructional Resources
Supersite: Audio (Lab MP3 Files); Resources (Grammar Presentation Slides, Activity Pack, Scripts, Answer Keys); Testing Program (Quizzes)
WebSAM
Workbook
Lab Manual

Teaching Tips
• Write these sentences on the board: —**¿Quién tiene el pasaporte? —Juan lo tiene.** Underline **pasaporte** and explain that it is a direct object noun. Then underline **lo** and explain that it is the masculine singular direct object pronoun. Translate both sentences. Continue with: —**¿Quién saca fotos? —Simón las saca. —¿Quién tiene la llave? —Pilar la tiene.**
• Read this exchange aloud: —**¿Haces las maletas? —No, no hago las maletas. —¿Por qué no haces las maletas? —No hago las maletas porque las maletas no están aquí.** Ask students if the exchange sounds natural to them. Then write it on the board and ask students to use direct object pronouns to avoid repetition. If students try to say **no las están** in the last sentence, point out that direct object pronouns cannot replace the subject of a verb. The only option is to eliminate the subject: **no están.**
• Ask individuals questions to elicit the personal **a**: **¿Visitas a tu abuela los fines de semana? ¿Llamas a tu padre los sábados?**
• Ask questions to elicit third-person direct object pronouns. Ex: **¿Quién ve el lápiz de Marcos? ¿Quién quiere estos diccionarios?**

TEACHING OPTIONS

TPR Call out a series of sentences with direct object nouns, some of which require the personal **a** and some of which do not. Ex: **Visito muchos museos. Visito a mis tíos.** Have students raise their hands if the personal **a** is used.

Extra Practice Write six sentences on the board that have direct object nouns. Use two verbs in the simple present tense, two in the present progressive, and two using **ir a** + [*infinitive*]. Draw a line through the direct objects as students call them out. Have students state which pronouns to write to replace them. Then, draw an arrow from each pronoun to where it goes in the sentence, as indicated by students.

▶ In affirmative sentences, direct object pronouns generally appear before the conjugated verb. In negative sentences, the pronoun is placed between the word **no** and the verb.

Adela practica **el tenis.**	Gabriela no tiene **las llaves.**
Adela **lo** practica.	Gabriela **no las** tiene.
Carmen compra **los pasajes.**	Diego no hace **las maletas.**
Carmen **los** compra.	Diego **no las** hace.

▶ When the verb is an infinitive construction, such as **ir a** + [*infinitive*], the direct object pronoun can be placed before the conjugated form or attached to the infinitive.

Ellos van a escribir **unas postales.**
- Ellos **las** van a escribir.
- Ellos van a escribir**las.**

Lidia quiere ver **una película.**
- Lidia **la** quiere ver.
- Lidia quiere ver**la.**

▶ When the verb is in the present progressive, the direct object pronoun can be placed before the conjugated form or attached to the present participle. **¡Atención!** When a direct object pronoun is attached to the present participle, an accent mark is added to maintain the proper stress.

Gerardo está leyendo **la lección.**
- Gerardo **la** está leyendo.
- Gerardo está leyéndo**la.**

Toni está mirando **el partido.**
- Toni **lo** está mirando.
- Toni está mirándo**lo.**

CONSULTA

To learn more about accents, see **Lección 4, Pronunciación,** p. 123, **Lección 10, Ortografía,** p. 339, and **Lección 11, Ortografía,** p. 375.

 ¡INTÉNTALO! Choose the correct direct object pronoun for each sentence.

1. Tienes el libro de español. *c*
   a. La tienes.   b. Los tienes.   c. Lo tienes.
2. Marcos busca la llave. *b*
   a. Me busca.   b. La busca.   c. Las busca.
3. El artista quiere dibujar a Luisa y a su mamá. *c*
   a. Quiere dibujarme.   b. Quiere dibujarla.   c. Quiere dibujarlas.
4. Voy a ver el partido de baloncesto. *a*
   a. Voy a verlo.   b. Voy a verte.   c. Voy a vernos.
5. Puedo oír a Gerardo y a Miguel. *b*
   a. Puedo oírte.   b. Puedo oírlos.   c. Puedo oírlo.
6. Rita me lleva al aeropuerto y también lleva a Tomás. *a*
   a. Nos lleva.   b. Las lleva.   c. Te lleva.
7. Quieren estudiar la gramática. *c*
   a. Quieren estudiarnos.   b. Quieren estudiarlo.   c. Quieren estudiarla.
8. ¿Practicas los verbos irregulares? *a*
   a. ¿Los practicas?   b. ¿Las practicas?   c. ¿Lo practicas?
9. Ignacio ve la película. *a*
   a. La ve.   b. Lo ve.   c. Las ve.
10. Sandra va a invitar a Mario a la excursión. También me va a invitar a mí. *c*
    a. Los va a invitar.   b. Lo va a invitar.   c. Nos va a invitar.

More activities

vhlcentral

LM p. 30

WB p. 56

Online activities

Teaching Tips
- Play a memory game. In view of the class, quickly distribute various items in quantities of either one or two to many different students, then tell them to hide the objects in their bag or backpack. Ask the class who has what. Ex: **¿Quién tiene las plumas? (David las tiene.) ¿Quién tiene el marcador? (Jessica lo tiene.)**
- Elicit first- and second-person direct object pronouns by asking questions first of individual students and then groups of students. Ex: **¿Quién te invita a bailar con frecuencia? (Mi novio me invita a bailar con frecuencia.) ¿Quién te comprende? (Mi amigo me comprende.)**
- Ask questions directed at the class as a whole to elicit first-person plural direct object pronouns. Ex: **¿Quiénes los llaman los fines de semana? (Nuestros padres nos llaman.) ¿Quiénes los esperan después de la clase? (Los amigos nos esperan.)**
- Add a visual aspect to this grammar presentation. Use magazine pictures to practice the third-person direct object pronouns with infinitives and the present progressive. Ex: **¿Quién está practicando el tenis? (Rafael Nadal lo está practicando./Rafael Nadal está practicándolo.) ¿Quién va a mirar la televisión? (El hombre pelirrojo la va a mirar./El hombre pelirrojo va a mirarla.)**
- Point out that the direct object pronoun **los** refers to both masculine and mixed groups. **Las** refers only to feminine groups.

TEACHING OPTIONS

Large Group Make a list of 20 questions requiring direct object pronouns in the answer. Arrange students in two concentric circles. Students in the center circle ask questions from the list to those in the outer circle until you say stop (**¡Paren!**). The outer circle moves one person to the right and the questions begin again. Continue for five minutes, then have the students in the outer circle ask the questions.

Pairs Have students write ten sentences about a vacation they want to take using direct object nouns. Their sentences should also include a mixture of verbs in the present progressive, simple present, and **ir a** + [*infinitive*]. Ask students to exchange their sentences with a partner, who will rewrite them using direct object pronouns. Students should check their partner's work.

Práctica

1 **Teaching Tip** To simplify, ask individual students to identify the direct object in each sentence before beginning the activity.

1 **Simplificar** Describe preparations for a class trip to Costa Rica by changing the direct object nouns into direct object pronouns.

> **modelo**
> La profesora Vega tiene su pasaporte.
> *La profesora Vega lo tiene.*

1. Nosotros leemos los folletos (*brochures*). Nosotros los leemos.
2. Gustavo y Héctor confirman las reservaciones. Gustavo y Héctor las confirman.
3. Ana María estudia el mapa. Ana María lo estudia.
4. Yo aprendo los nombres de los monumentos de San José. Yo los aprendo.
5. Alicia escucha a la profesora. Alicia la escucha.
6. Miguel escribe las instrucciones para ir al hotel. Miguel las escribe.
7. Esteban busca el pasaje. Esteban lo busca.
8. Nosotros planeamos una excursión. Nosotros la planeamos.

¡LENGUA VIVA!
There are many Spanish words that correspond to *ticket*. **Billete** and **pasaje** usually refer to a ticket for travel, such as an airplane ticket. **Entrada** refers to a ticket to an event, such as a concert or a movie. **Boleto** can be used in either case.

2 **Expansion** Ask questions (using direct objects) about the people in the activity to elicit **Sí/No** answers. Ex: **¿Tiene Ramón reservaciones en el hotel? (Sí, las tiene.) ¿Tiene su mochila? (No, no la tiene.)**

2 **Vacaciones** Restate Ramón's thoughts about his trip to San Juan more succinctly using direct object pronouns.

> **modelo**
> Quiero hacer una excursión.
> *Quiero hacerla./La quiero hacer.*

1. Marcos está pidiendo el folleto turístico. Marcos está pidiéndolo./Marcos lo está pidiendo.
2. Necesitamos llevar los pasaportes. Necesitamos llevarlos./Los necesitamos llevar.
3. Voy a hacer mi maleta. Voy a hacerla./La voy a hacer.
4. Javier debe llamar a sus padres. Javier debe llamarlos./Javier los debe llamar.
5. Ellos desean visitar el Viejo San Juan. Ellos desean visitarlo./Ellos lo desean visitar.
6. Puedo llamar a Javier por la mañana. Puedo llamarlo./Lo puedo llamar.
7. Prefiero llevar mi cámara. Prefiero llevarla./La prefiero llevar.
8. No queremos perder nuestras reservaciones de hotel. No queremos perderlas./No las queremos perder.

NOTA CULTURAL
Puerto Rico is a U.S. territory, so people do not need travel documents when traveling to and from Puerto Rico from the U.S. mainland. However, everyone must meet all requirements for entering the U.S. when traveling directly to Puerto Rico from abroad.

3 **Expansion**
• Ask students questions about who does what in the activity. Ex: **¿La señora Garza busca la cámara? (No, María la busca.)**
• Ask additional questions about the family's preparations, allowing students to decide who does what. Ex: **¿Quién compra una revista para leer en el avión? ¿Quién llama al taxi? ¿Quién practica el español?**

3 **¿Quién?** Answer the questions about the Garza family's trip to Puerto Rico. Use direct object pronouns in your answers.

> **modelo**
> ¿Quién hace las reservaciones para el hotel? (el Sr. Garza)
> *El Sr. Garza las hace.*

1. ¿Quién compra los pasajes para el vuelo (*flight*)? (la Sra. Garza) La Sra. Garza los compra.
2. ¿Quién tiene que hacer las maletas de los niños? (María) María tiene que hacerlas./María las tiene que hacer.
3. ¿Quién compra un mapa de Puerto Rico? (Antonio) Antonio lo compra.
4. ¿Quién va a confirmar las reservaciones de hotel? (la Sra. Garza) La Sra. Garza va a confirmarlas./La Sra. Garza las va a confirmar.
5. ¿Quién busca la cámara? (María) María la busca.
6. ¿Quiénes buscan los pasaportes? (Antonio y María) Antonio y María los buscan.

TEACHING OPTIONS

Small Groups Split the class into small groups. Have students take turns asking the group who does these activities: **leer revistas, practicar el ciclismo, ganar todos los partidos, visitar a sus padres durante las vacaciones, escuchar a sus profesores, practicar la natación.** Ex: —¿Quién lee revistas? —Yo las leo.

Heritage Speakers Pair heritage speakers with other students. Ask the pairs to create a dialogue between a travel agent and client. Assign the role of traveler to the heritage speaker, who would like to visit his or her family's home country. Encourage both students to draw on their experiences from past vacations and trips to Spanish-speaking countries. Have students role-play their dialogues for the class.

Comunicación

4 **Entrevista** Take turns asking and answering these questions with a classmate. Be sure to use direct object pronouns in your responses.   *Answers will vary.*

1. ¿Ves mucho la televisión?
2. ¿Cuándo vas a ver tu programa favorito?
3. ¿Quién prepara la comida (*food*) en tu casa?
4. ¿Te visita mucho tu familia?
5. ¿Visitas mucho a tus abuelos?
6. ¿Nos entienden nuestros padres a nosotros?
7. ¿Cuándo ves a tus amigos/as?
8. ¿Cuándo te llaman tus amigos/as?

5 **Los pasajeros** Get together with a partner and take turns asking each other questions about the drawing. Use the verbs and direct object pronouns.   *Answers will vary.*

AYUDA
For travel-related vocabulary, see **Contextos**, pp. 152–153.

modelo
Estudiante 1: ¿Quién está leyendo el libro?
Estudiante 2: Susana lo está leyendo./Susana está leyéndolo.

buscar	escuchar	llevar	tener	¿?
encontrar	leer	mirar	traer	

Síntesis

6 **Adivinanzas** In pairs, take turns describing a person, place, or thing for your partner to guess. Each of you should give at least five descriptions.   *Answers will vary.*

modelo
Estudiante 1: Lo uso para (*I use it to*) escribir en mi cuaderno. No es muy grande y tiene borrador. ¿Qué es?
Estudiante 2: ¿Es un lápiz?
Estudiante 1: ¡Sí!

4 Teaching Tip Ask students to record their partner's answers. After the interviews, have students review answers in groups and report the most common responses to the class.

4 Expansion ⬥↔⬥ Have students write five additional questions, then continue their interviews. Encourage students to comment on their partner's answers.

5 Teaching Tip Before assigning the activity, ask individual students to identify different objects in the picture that might be used as direct objects in questions and answers.

5 Expansion
• Reverse the activity by having students say what the people are doing. Their partner will guess who it is. Ex: **Está escribiendo en su cuaderno. (Es Miguelito.)**
• ⬥↔⬥ Have students use **ser** and **estar** to write descriptions of the people in the drawing.

6 Teaching Tip To simplify this activity, have students first write out their descriptions.

6 Expansion ⬥↔⬥ Have pairs write out five additional riddles. Have volunteers read them aloud for the class to answer.

TEACHING OPTIONS

Game Play a game of **20 Preguntas**. Divide the class into two teams. Think of an object in the room and alternate calling on teams to ask questions. Once a team knows the answer, the team captain should raise his or her hand. If right, the team gets a point. If wrong, the team loses a point. Play until one team has earned five points.

Pairs Have students create five questions that include the direct object pronouns **me**, **te**, and **nos**. Then have them ask their partners the questions on their list. Ex: —¿Quién te llama mucho? —**Mi novia me llama mucho.** —¿Quién nos escucha cuando hacemos preguntas en español? —**El/La profesor(a) y los estudiantes nos escuchan.**

Section Goal

In **Recapitulación**, students will review the grammar concepts from this lesson.

Instructional Resource
Supersite

Teaching Tip You may want to assign this **Recapitulación** activity on the Supersite because it has diagnostics. There is an online-only review activity for each grammar point. The Supersite also has a **Repaso de vocabulario** activity with diagnostics.

1 Expansion Create a list of present participles and have students supply the infinitive. Ex: **durmiendo (dormir)**

2 Teaching Tip Ask students to explain why they chose **ser** or **estar** for each item.

2 Expansion
←📱→ Have students use **ser** and **estar** to write a brief paragraph describing **Julia's** first few days in Paris.

3 Teaching Tip To simplify, have students begin by underlining the direct object nouns and identifying the corresponding direct object pronouns.

Recapitulación

Review the grammar concepts you have learned in this lesson by completing these activities.

1 Completar Complete the chart with the correct present participle of these verbs. **16 pts.**

Infinitive	Present participle	Infinitive	Present participle
hacer	haciendo	estar	estando
acampar	acampando	ser	siendo
tener	teniendo	vivir	viviendo
venir	viniendo	estudiar	estudiando

2 Vacaciones en París Complete this paragraph with the correct form of **ser** or **estar**. **24 pts.**

Hoy (1) __es__ (es/está) el 3 de julio y voy a París por tres semanas. (Yo) (2) __Estoy__ (Soy/Estoy) muy feliz porque voy a ver a mi mejor amiga. Ella (3) __es__ (es/está) de Puerto Rico, pero ahora (4) __está__ (es/está) viviendo en París. También (yo) (5) __estoy__ (soy/estoy) un poco nerviosa porque (6) __es__ (es/está) mi primer viaje a Francia. El vuelo (*flight*) (7) __es__ (es/está) hoy por la tarde, pero ahora (8) __está__ (es/está) lloviendo. Por eso (9) __estamos__ (somos/estamos) preocupadas, porque probablemente el avión va a salir tarde. Mi equipaje ya (10) __está__ (es/está) listo. (11) __Es__ (Es/Está) tarde y me tengo que ir. ¡Va a (12) __ser__ (ser/estar) un viaje fenomenal!

3 ¿Qué hacen? Respond to these questions by indicating what people do with the items mentioned. Use direct object pronouns. **10 pts.**

> **modelo**
> ¿Qué hacen ellos con la película? (ver)
> La ven.

1. ¿Qué haces tú con el libro de viajes? (leer) __Lo leo.__
2. ¿Qué hacen los turistas en la ciudad? (explorar) __La exploran.__
3. ¿Qué hace el botones con el equipaje? (llevar) __Lo lleva (a la habitación).__
4. ¿Qué hace la agente con las reservaciones? (confirmar) __Las confirma.__
5. ¿Qué hacen ustedes con los pasaportes? (mostrar) __Los mostramos.__

RESUMEN GRAMATICAL

5.1 Estar with conditions and emotions *p. 164*

► Yo est**oy** aburrido/a, feliz, nervioso/a.
► El cuarto est**á** desordenado, limpio, ordenado.
► Estos libros est**án** abiertos, cerrados, sucios.

5.2 The present progressive *pp. 166–167*

► The present progressive is formed with the present tense of **estar** plus the present participle.

Forming the present participle

infinitive	stem	ending	present participle
hablar	habl-	-ando	habl**ando**
comer	com-	-iendo	com**iendo**
escribir	escrib-	-iendo	escrib**iendo**

-ir stem-changing verbs

	infinitive	present participle
e:ie	preferir	pref**i**riendo
e:i	conseguir	cons**i**guiendo
o:ue	dormir	d**u**rmiendo

► Irregular present participles: **yendo (ir), pudiendo (poder), viniendo (venir)**

5.3 Ser and estar *pp. 170–171*

► Uses of **ser**: nationality, origin, profession or occupation, characteristics, generalizations, possession, what something is made of, time and date, time and place of events

► Uses of **estar**: location, health, physical states and conditions, emotional states, weather expressions, ongoing actions

► Many adjectives can be used with both **ser** and **estar**, but the meaning of the adjectives will change.

Juan **es** delgado.   Juan **está** más delgado hoy.
Juan is thin.   *Juan looks thinner today.*

TEACHING OPTIONS

Extra Practice Add an auditory aspect to this grammar review. Go around the room and read a sentence with a direct object. Each student must repeat the sentence using a direct object pronoun. Ex: **María y Jennifer están comprando sus libros para la clase. (María y Jennifer los están comprando./María y Jennifer están comprándolos.)**
TPR Divide the board into two columns, with the heads **ser**

and **estar**. Ask a volunteer to stand in front of each verb. The rest of the class should take turns calling out a use of **ser** or **estar**. The volunteer standing in front of the correct verb should step forward and give an example sentence. Ex: nationality or origin (**Soy norteamericano/a.**) After each volunteer has given two sentences, call on different students to take their places. Continue this way until everyone has had a turn.

4 Opuestos Complete these sentences with the appropriate form of the verb **estar** and an antonym for the underlined adjective. **10 pts.**

modelo
Mis respuestas están <u>bien</u>, pero las de Susana **están mal**.

1. Las tiendas están <u>abiertas</u>, pero la estación del metro ___está___ ___cerrada___.
2. No me gustan las habitaciones <u>desordenadas</u>. Incluso (*Even*) mi habitación de hotel ___está___ ___ordenada___.
3. Nosotras estamos <u>tristes</u> cuando trabajamos. Hoy comienzan las vacaciones y ___estamos___ ___contentas/alegres/felices___.
4. En esta ciudad los autobuses están <u>sucios</u>, pero los taxis ___están___ ___limpios___.
5. —El avión sale a las 5:30, ¿verdad? —No, estás <u>confundida</u>. Yo ___estoy___ ___seguro/a___ de que el avión sale a las 5:00.

5 En la playa Describe what these people are doing. Complete the sentences using the present progressive tense. **8 pts.**

1. El Sr. Camacho ___está sacando/tomando fotos___.
2. Felicia ___está haciendo surf___.
3. Ana ___está montando a caballo___.
4. Nosotros ___estamos nadando___.

6 Antes del viaje Write a paragraph of at least six sentences describing the time right before you go on a trip. Say how you feel and what you are doing. You can use **Actividad 2** as a model. **32 pts.** *Answers will vary.*

modelo
Hoy es viernes, 27 de octubre. Estoy en mi habitación...

7 Refrán Complete this Spanish saying by filling in the missing present participles. Refer to the translation and the drawing. **4 EXTRA points!**

¡LA CIUDAD ESTÁ MUY SUCIA!

"Se consigue más ___haciendo___ que ___diciendo___."

(You can accomplish more by doing than by saying.)

5.4 Direct object nouns and pronouns *pp. 174–175*

Direct object pronouns

Singular		Plural	
me	lo	nos	los
te	la	os	las

In affirmative sentences:
Adela practica **el tenis**. → Adela **lo** practica.

In negative sentences: Adela no **lo** practica.

With an infinitive:
Adela **lo** va a practicar./Adela va a practicar**lo**.

With the present progressive:
Adela **lo** está practicando./Adela está practicándo**lo**.

4 Expansion Have students create three sentences about their own lives, using antonyms. Ex: **Mi hermano es desordenado, pero yo soy muy ordenado.** Tell them to make one of the sentences false. Then, in pairs, have students read their sentences aloud. Their partner should try to guess which statement is false.

5 Expansion To challenge students, have them imagine that the people in the illustration are now in a hotel. Ask students to say what they are doing. Ex: **Ana está mirando un programa sobre caballos.**

6 Teaching Tips
• Have students exchange papers with a partner for peer editing.
• To make this activity more challenging, require students to include at least two examples each of **ser**, **estar**, and direct object pronouns.

7 Teaching Tip Explain the use of the impersonal **se** and explain that **Se consigue** means *You can accomplish* (as in the translation) or *One can accomplish*. Students will learn the impersonal **se** in **Estructura 10.3**.

7 Expansion To challenge students, have them work in pairs to create a short dialogue that ends with this saying. Encourage them to be creative.

Section Goals

In **Lectura**, students will:
• learn the strategy of scanning to find specific information in reading matter
• read a brochure about ecotourism in Puerto Rico

Instructional Resource
Supersite

Estrategia Explain to students that a good way to get an idea of what an article or other text is about is to scan it before reading. Scanning means running one's eyes over a text in search of specific information that can be used to infer the content of the text. Explain that scanning a text before reading it is a good way to improve Spanish reading comprehension.

The Affective Dimension
Point out to students that becoming familiar with cognates will help them feel less overwhelmed when they encounter new Spanish texts.

Examinar el texto Do the activity orally as a class. Some cognates that give a clue to the content of the text are: **turismo ecológico, teléfono, TV por cable, Internet, hotel, aire acondicionado, perfecto, Parque Nacional Foresta, Museo de Arte Nativo, Reserva, Biosfera, Santuario**. These clues should tell a reader scanning the text that it is about a hotel promoting ecotourism.

Preguntas Ask the questions orally of the class. Possible responses: 1. travel brochure 2. Puerto Rico 3. photos of beautiful tropical beaches, bays, and forests; The document is trying to attract the reader. 4. **Hotel Vistahermosa** in Lajas, Puerto Rico; attract guests

---

Lectura

 communication cultures NATIONAL STANDARDS

Antes de leer

Estrategia

Scanning

Scanning involves glancing over a document in search of specific information. For example, you can scan a document to identify its format, to find cognates, to locate visual cues about the document's content, or to find specific facts. Scanning allows you to learn a great deal about a text without having to read it word for word.

Examinar el texto

Scan the reading selection for cognates and write down a few of them. Answers will vary.

1. _____   4. _____
2. _____   5. _____
3. _____   6. _____

Based on the cognates you found, what do you think this document is about?

_____

Preguntas

Read these questions. Then scan the document again to look for answers. Answers will vary.

1. What is the format of the reading selection?

_____

2. Which place is the document about?

_____

3. What are some of the visual cues this document provides? What do they tell you about the content of the document?

_____

4. Who produced the document, and what do you think it is for?

_____

More activities

vhlcentral   Online activities

Turismo ecológico en Puerto Rico

Hotel Vistahermosa
~ Lajas, Puerto Rico ~

• 40 habitaciones individuales
• 15 habitaciones dobles
• Teléfono / TV por cable / Internet
• Aire acondicionado
• Restaurante (Bar)
• Piscina
• Área de juegos
• Cajero automático°

El hotel está situado en Playa Grande, un pequeño pueblo de pescadores del mar Caribe. Es el lugar perfecto para el viajero que viene de vacaciones. Las playas son seguras y limpias, ideales para tomar el sol, descansar, tomar fotografías y nadar. Está abierto los 365 días del año. Hay una rebaja° especial para estudiantes universitarios.

DIRECCIÓN: Playa Grande 406, Lajas, PR 00667, cerca del Parque Nacional Foresta.

Cajero automático *ATM* rebaja *discount*

TEACHING OPTIONS

Heritage Speakers Ask heritage speakers of Puerto Rican descent who have lived on or visited the island to talk briefly about any experiences they have had with the beaches, nature preserves, or wildlife of Puerto Rico.
Small Groups Have students work in small groups to research and prepare a short presentation about the climate, geography, or people of Puerto Rico. If possible, ask them to

illustrate their presentations with photos or illustrations.
Small Groups Lead a discussion about vacations. Have students work in groups to brainstorm what are important aspects of an "ideal" vacation. Each student should contribute at least one idea. When each group has its list, ask for volunteers to share the information with the rest of the class. How do the groups differ? How are they similar?

Atracciones cercanas

Playa Grande ¿Busca la playa perfecta? Playa Grande es la playa que está buscando. Usted puede pescar, sacar fotos, nadar y pasear en bicicleta. Playa Grande es un paraíso para el turista que quiere practicar deportes acuáticos. El lugar es bonito e interesante y usted va a tener muchas oportunidades para descansar y disfrutar en familia.

Valle Niebla Ir de excursión, tomar café, montar a caballo, caminar, hacer picnics. Más de cien lugares para acampar.

Bahía Fosforescente Sacar fotos, salidas de noche, excursión en barco. Una maravillosa experiencia llena de luz°.

Arrecifes de Coral Sacar fotos, bucear, explorar. Es un lugar único en el Caribe.

Playa Vieja Tomar el sol, pasear en bicicleta, jugar a las cartas, escuchar música. Ideal para la familia.

Parque Nacional Foresta Sacar fotos, visitar el Museo de Arte Nativo. Reserva Mundial de la Biosfera.

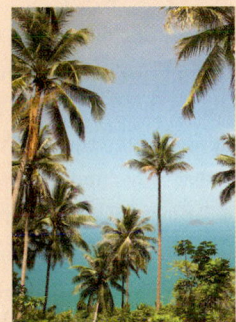

Santuario de las Aves Sacar fotos, observar aves°, seguir rutas de excursión.

llena de luz *full of light*   aves *birds*

Después de leer

Listas

Which amenities of Hotel Vistahermosa would most interest these potential guests? Explain your choices. Answers will vary.

1. dos padres con un hijo de seis años y una hija de ocho años

   _____

2. un hombre y una mujer en su luna de miel (*honeymoon*)

   _____

3. una persona en un viaje de negocios (*business trip*)

   _____

Conversaciones

With a partner, take turns asking each other these questions. Answers will vary.

1. ¿Quieres visitar el Hotel Vistahermosa? ¿Por qué?

2. Tienes tiempo de visitar sólo tres de las atracciones turísticas que están cerca del hotel. ¿Cuáles vas a visitar? ¿Por qué?

3. ¿Qué prefieres hacer en Valle Niebla? ¿En Playa Vieja? ¿En el Parque Nacional Foresta?

Situaciones

You have just arrived at Hotel Vistahermosa. Your partner is the concierge. Use the phrases to express your interests and ask for suggestions about where to go. Answers will vary.

1. montar a caballo
2. bucear
3. pasear en bicicleta
4. pescar
5. observar aves

Contestar

Answer these questions. Answers will vary.

1. ¿Quieres visitar Puerto Rico? Explica tu respuesta.

   _____

2. ¿Adónde quieres ir de vacaciones el verano que viene? Explica tu respuesta.

   _____

Listas
- Ask these comprehension questions. 1. ¿El Hotel Vistahermosa está situado cerca de qué mar? (el mar Caribe) 2. ¿Qué playa es un paraíso para el turista? (la Playa Grande) 3. ¿Dónde puedes montar a caballo? (en el Valle Niebla)
- Encourage discussion of each of the items by asking questions such as: En tu opinión, ¿qué tipo de atracciones buscan los padres con hijos de seis y ocho años? ¿Qué esperan de un hotel? Y una pareja en su luna de miel, ¿qué tipo de atracciones espera encontrar en un hotel? En tu opinión, ¿qué busca una persona en un viaje de negocios?

Conversaciones Ask individuals about what their partners said. Ex: ¿Por qué (no) quiere _____ visitar el Hotel Vistahermosa? ¿Qué atracciones quiere ver? Ask other students: Y tú, ¿quieres visitar el Parque Nacional Foresta o prefieres visitar otro lugar?

Situaciones
- Give students a couple of minutes to review **Más vocabulario** on page 152 and **Expresiones útiles** on page 159.
- To challenge students, add to the list activities such as **sacar fotos, correr, nadar,** and **ir de excursión**.

Contestar Have volunteers explain how the reading selection might influence their choice of a vacation destination for next summer.

TEACHING OPTIONS

Pairs Have pairs of students work together to read the brochure aloud and write three questions about it. After they have finished, ask pairs to exchange papers with another pair, who will work together to answer them. Alternatively, you might pick pairs to read their questions to the class. Ask volunteers to answer them.

Small Groups To practice scanning written material to infer its content, bring in short, simple Spanish-language magazine or newspaper articles you have read. Have small groups scan the articles to determine what they are about. Have them write down all the clues that help them. When each group has come to a decision, ask it to present its findings to the class. Confirm the accuracy of the inferences.

Escritura

Estrategia
Making an outline

When we write to share information, an outline can serve to separate topics and subtopics, providing a framework for the presentation of data. Consider the following excerpt from an outline of the tourist brochure on pages 180–181.

IV. Descripción del sitio (con foto)
  A. Playa Grande
    1. Playas seguras y limpias
    2. Ideal para tomar el sol, descansar, tomar fotografías, nadar
  B. El hotel
    1. Abierto los 365 días del año
    2. Rebaja para estudiantes universitarios

Mapa de ideas

Idea maps can be used to create outlines. The major sections of an idea map correspond to the Roman numerals in an outline. The minor idea map sections correspond to the outline's capital letters, and so on. Examine the idea map that led to the outline above.

Tema

Escribir un folleto

Write a tourist brochure for a hotel or resort you have visited. If you wish, you may write about an imaginary location. You may want to include some of this information in your brochure:

- the name of the hotel or resort
- phone and fax numbers that tourists can use to make contact
- the hotel website that tourists can consult
- an e-mail address that tourists can use to request information
- a description of the exterior of the hotel or resort
- a description of the interior of the hotel or resort, including facilities and amenities
- a description of the surrounding area, including its climate
- a listing of nearby scenic natural attractions
- a listing of nearby cultural attractions
- a listing of recreational activities that tourists can pursue in the vicinity of the hotel or resort

EVALUATION: Folleto

Criteria	Scale
Appropriate details	1 2 3 4 5
Organization	1 2 3 4 5
Use of vocabulary	1 2 3 4 5
Grammatical accuracy	1 2 3 4 5

Scoring	
Excellent	18–20 points
Good	14–17 points
Satisfactory	10–13 points
Unsatisfactory	< 10 points

Escuchar

Antes de escuchar

Estrategia
Listening for key words

By listening for key words or phrases, you can identify the subject and main ideas of what you hear, as well as some of the details.

  To practice this strategy, you will now listen to a short paragraph. As you listen, jot down the key words that help you identify the subject of the paragraph and its main ideas.

Preparación

Based on the illustration, who do you think Hernán Jiménez is, and what is he doing? What key words might you listen for to help you understand what he is saying?

Ahora escucha

El pronóstico del tiempo

Now you are going to listen to a weather report by Hernán Jiménez. Note which phrases are correct according to the key words and phrases you hear.

Santo Domingo
1. hace sol ✔
2. va a hacer frío
3. una mañana de mal tiempo
4. va a estar nublado ✔
5. buena tarde para tomar el sol
6. buena mañana para la playa ✔

San Francisco de Macorís
1. hace frío ✔
2. hace sol
3. va a nevar
4. va a llover ✔
5. hace calor
6. mal día para excursiones ✔

Comprensión

¿Cierto o falso?

Indicate whether each statement is **cierto** or **falso**, based on the weather report. Correct the false statements.

1. Según el meteorólogo, la temperatura en Santo Domingo es de 26 grados.
   Cierto.

2. La temperatura máxima en Santo Domingo hoy va a ser de 30 grados.
   Cierto.

3. Está lloviendo ahora en Santo Domingo.
   Falso. Hace sol.

4. En San Francisco de Macorís la temperatura mínima de hoy va a ser de 20 grados.
   Falso. La temperatura mínima va a ser de 18 grados.

5. Va a llover mucho hoy en San Francisco de Macorís.
   Cierto.

Preguntas

Answer these questions about the weather report.

1. ¿Hace viento en Santo Domingo ahora?
   Sí, hace viento en Santo Domingo.
2. ¿Está nublado en Santo Domingo ahora?
   No, no está nublado ahora en Santo Domingo.
3. ¿Está nevando ahora en San Francisco de Macorís?
   No, no está nevando ahora en San Francisco de Macorís.
4. ¿Qué tiempo hace en San Francisco de Macorís?
   Hace frío.

de estas 24 horas va a ser de 18 grados. Va a llover casi todo el día. ¡No es buen día para excursiones a las montañas!

Hasta el noticiero del mediodía, me despido de ustedes. ¡Que les vaya bien!

Section Goals

In **Escuchar**, students will:
- learn the strategy of listening for key words
- listen to a short paragraph and note the key words
- answer questions based on the content of a recorded conversation

Instructional Resources
Supersite: Audio (Textbook MP3s); Resources (Scripts)

Estrategia
Script Aquí está la foto de mis vacaciones en la playa. Ya lo sé; no debo pasar el tiempo tomando el sol. Es que vivo en una ciudad donde llueve casi todo el año y mis actividades favoritas son bucear, pescar en el mar y nadar.

Teaching Tip
Have students look at the drawing and describe what they see. Guide them in saying what **Hernán Jiménez** is like and what he is doing.

Ahora escucha
Script Buenos días, queridos televidentes, les saluda el meteorólogo Hernán Jiménez, con el pronóstico del tiempo para nuestra bella isla.

Hoy, 17 de octubre, a las diez de la mañana, la temperatura en Santo Domingo es de 26 grados. Hace sol con viento del este a 10 kilómetros por hora.

En la tarde, va a estar un poco nublado con la posibilidad de lluvia. La temperatura máxima del día va a ser de 30 grados. Es una buena mañana para ir a la playa.

En las montañas hace bastante frío ahora, especialmente en el área de San Francisco de Macorís. La temperatura mínima

(Script continues at far left in the bottom panels.)

Section Goals

In **En pantalla**, students will:
• read about the geography and attractions of Panama
• watch an ad promoting tourism in Panama

Instructional Resources
Supersite: Video (*En pantalla*); Resources (Scripts, Translations)

Introduction To check comprehension, ask these questions. 1. What countries does Panama border? (Colombia, Costa Rica) 2. Which bodies of water are connected by the Panama Canal? (the Atlantic and Pacific Oceans) 3. How many bird species are there in Panama? (over 900)

Antes de ver Ask students what they see in the three photos. Have them predict the content and the nature of the ad. What activities does Panama offer to visitors?

Preparación Conduct a class survey to see what students like to do and where they like to go on vacation.

¿Qué hacen?
• Before you show the video, ask students to make a list of the activities they think will be shown in the ad. Have them check off activities as they watch.
• Have students create sentences using the present progressive to say what people in the ad are and aren't doing. Ex: **Están acampando. No están buceando**.

Conversación Have students report their partner's answers to the class.

En pantalla Video

Known as the "Crossroads of the Americas," Panama is a Central American country that borders Colombia in the southeast and Costa Rica in the northwest. The Panama Canal bridges the Atlantic and Pacific Oceans. Panama boasts an amazing variety of flora and fauna with over 900 different bird species, as well as rivers, mountains, rain forests, and hiking trails both near and far from urban areas. Visitors can enjoy an array of water sports as well as culturally diverse activities in fairly moderate temperatures, ranging from 75° to 90°F, year-round.

Vocabulario útil	
a nadie le viene mal	doesn't hurt anyone
aventura	adventure
estrellas	stars
redes	(social) networks

Preparación

Where do you like to go on vacation? What do you like to do there? Answers will vary.

¿Qué hacen?

Check **sí** if the activity is shown in the ad or **no** if it's not.

		Sí	No
1.	bucear	○	☑
2.	acampar	☑	○
3.	pescar	○	☑
4.	hacer surf	○	☑
5.	escalar montañas	☑	○
6.	nadar en una piscina	○	☑
7.	ir de excursión	☑	○
8.	montar a caballo	○	☑

Conversación

With a partner, take turns asking each other these questions. Answers will vary.

1. ¿Quieres ir de vacaciones a Panamá? Explica tu respuesta.

2. ¿Qué prefieres: la montaña o la playa?

3. ¿Qué deportes o actividades del anuncio te gusta practicar?

cortada *cut through* ríos *rivers* trochas *narrow paths* senderos *trails* Deja atrás *Leave behind*

Autoridad de Turismo de Panamá

Tu Panamá está cortada° por ríos°, trochas° y senderos°...

Deja atrás° la ciudad.

Nos vemos en el camino.

 communication cultures STANDARDS

More activities

 vhlcentral / Online activities

TEACHING OPTIONS

Worth Noting The man featured in the ad is Robin Durán, a Panamanian actor and producer. He is the son of the famous boxer Roberto Durán.
Pairs Have partners research Panama's weather and climate. Have them identify the rainy season and the dry season, as well as the hottest and coldest months.

Extra Practice Ask students to create sentences about the ad using **ser** and **estar**. Ex: **El hombre es panameño. Está lejos de la ciudad.**
Language Note While **trocha** can be a *path*, it can also mean *shortcut*. And, in a railway context, it can indicate *gauge*.

Video

¡Vacaciones en Perú!

Between 1438 and 1533, when the vast and powerful Incan Empire was at its height, the Incas built an elaborate network of **caminos** (*trails*) that traversed the Andes Mountains and converged on the empire's capital, Cuzco. Today, hundreds of thousands of tourists come to Peru annually to walk the surviving trails and enjoy the spectacular scenery. The most popular trail, **el Camino Inca**, leads from Cuzco to **Intipunku** (*Sun Gate*), the entrance to the ancient mountain city of Machu Picchu.

Vocabulario útil

ciudadela	*citadel*
de cultivo	*farming*
el/la guía	*guide*
maravilla	*wonder*
quechua	*Quechua (indigenous Peruvian)*
sector (urbano)	*(urban) sector*

Preparación

Have you ever visited an archeological or historic site? Where? Why did you go there? Answers will vary.

Completar

Complete these sentences. Make the necessary changes.

1. Las ruinas de Machu Picchu son una antigua _ciudadela_ inca.

2. La ciudadela estaba (*was*) dividida en tres sectores: _urbano_, religioso y de cultivo.

3. Cada año los _guías_ reciben a cientos de turistas de diferentes países.

4. Hoy en día, la cultura _quechua_ está presente en las comunidades andinas (*Andean*) de Perú.

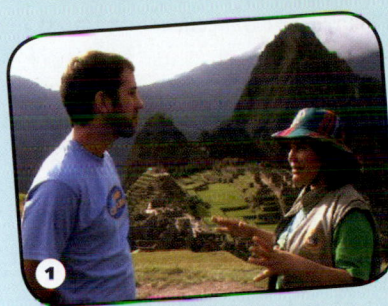

Machu Picchu [...] se encuentra aislada sobre° esta montaña...

... siempre he querido° venir [...] Me encantan° las civilizaciones antiguas°.

Somos una familia francesa [...] Perú es un país muy, muy bonito de verdad.

More activities

vhlcentral | VM pp. 45–46 | Online activities

se encuentra aislada sobre *it is isolated on* siempre he querido *I have always wanted* Me encantan *I love* antiguas *ancient*

Section Goals

In **Flash cultura**, students will:
- read about Incan trails
- watch a video about **Machu Picchu**

Instructional Resources

Supersite: Video (*Flash cultura*); Resources (Scripts, Translations, Answer Keys)
WebSAM
Video Manual

Introduction To check comprehension, ask these questions. 1. During what years was the Incan empire at its most powerful? (between 1438 and 1533) 2. How many tourists walk the Incan trails each year? (hundreds of thousands) 3. What is the most famous Incan trail called and to where does it lead? (**el Camino Inca**; to **Machu Picchu**)

Antes de ver
- Have students look at the video stills, read the captions, and predict the content of the video.
- Read through **Vocabulario útil** with students. Model the pronunciation.
- Explain that students do not need to understand every word they hear. Tell them to rely on visual cues, cognates, and words from **Vocabulario útil**.

Preparación Ask students how they felt while visiting the site, and what they learned about the people who created it.

Completar Have students write three additional cloze sentences for a partner to complete based on the content of the video.

TEACHING OPTIONS

Pairs Tell students to imagine that they are archeologists that belong to a future civilization and they are examining the remains of your university. In pairs, have students write a list of what they found. Then, based on this list, tell them to write and act out a dialogue where they discuss the kind of people that inhabited the university. Encourage them to use props. (Ex: **Son teleadictos. Hay restos de televisores por todas partes.**)

You may wish to introduce key vocabulary or cognates, such as **restos, habitantes,** and **intacto/a**.
Extra Practice For homework, have students research and write a report about the different ways tourists can reach **Machu Picchu**. Have them state which method they prefer and why, and create a trip itinerary.

Puerto Rico

NATIONAL connections cultures STANDARDS

El país en cifras

▸ **Área:** 8.959 km² (3.459 millas²) menor° que el área de Connecticut
▸ **Población:** 3.351.000

Puerto Rico es una de las islas más densamente pobladas° del mundo. Más de la mitad de la población vive en San Juan, la capital.

▸ **Capital:** San Juan—2.463.000
▸ **Ciudades principales:** Arecibo, Bayamón, Fajardo, Mayagüez, Ponce
▸ **Moneda:** dólar estadounidense
▸ **Idiomas:** español (oficial); inglés (oficial)

Aproximadamente la cuarta parte de la población puertorriqueña habla inglés, pero en las zonas turísticas este porcentaje es mucho más alto. El uso del inglés es obligatorio para documentos federales.

Bandera de Puerto Rico

Puertorriqueños célebres

▸ **Raúl Juliá,** actor (1940–1994)
▸ **Roberto Clemente,** beisbolista (1934–1972)
▸ **Julia de Burgos,** escritora (1914–1953)
▸ **Benicio del Toro,** actor y productor (1967–)
▸ **Rosie Pérez,** actriz y bailarina (1964–)
▸ **José Rivera,** dramaturgo y guionista (1955–)

menor *less* pobladas *populated*

Playa en San Juan
Faro en Arecibo

Océano Atlántico

Arecibo
San Juan ⭐
Bayamón
Río Grande de Añasco
Mayagüez
Cordillera Central
Sierra de Caye
Ponce
Mar Caribe

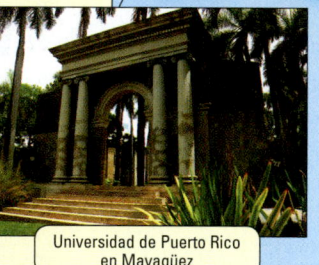
Universidad de Puerto Rico en Mayagüez

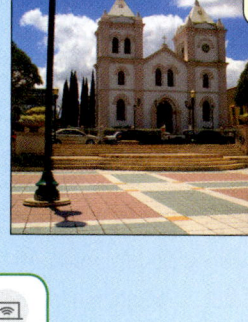
Iglesia en Ponce

OCÉANO ATLÁNTICO
PUERTO RIC
OCÉANO PACÍFICO

More activities

vhlcentral | WB pp. 57–58 | Online activities

ACTIVIDADES

1 **¿Cierto o falso?** Indica si lo que dice cada oración es **cierto** o **falso**.

1. Benicio del Toro es un beisbolista puertorriqueño. falso
2. María es un famoso río de Puerto Rico. falso
3. La salsa es un estilo musical que nace en el barrio latino de Nueva York. cierto
4. En el Observatorio de Arecibo es posible estudiar el arte y la arquitectura de Puerto Rico. falso
5. El Morro, hoy en día, es un museo que recibe muchos turistas. cierto
6. Los puertorriqueños son ciudadanos estadounidenses desde 1898. falso
7. Felipe Rodríguez es un músico famoso de Nueva York. falso
8. Más de la mitad (*half*) de la población de Puerto Rico vive en la capital. cierto

Lugares • El Morro

El Morro es una fortaleza que se construyó para proteger° la bahía° de San Juan desde principios del siglo° XVI hasta principios del siglo XX. Hoy día muchos turistas visitan este lugar, convertido en un museo. Es el sitio más fotografiado de Puerto Rico. La arquitectura de la fortaleza es impresionante. Tiene misteriosos túneles, oscuras mazmorras° y vistas fabulosas de la bahía.

ⓘ Artes • Salsa

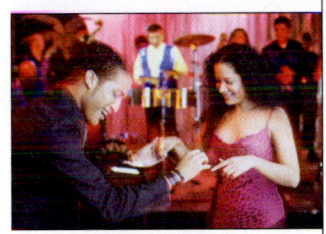

La salsa, un estilo musical de origen puertorriqueño y cubano, nació° en el barrio latino de la ciudad de Nueva York. Dos de los músicos de salsa más famosos son Tito Puente y Willie Colón, los dos de Nueva York. Las estrellas° de la salsa en Puerto Rico son Felipe Rodríguez y Héctor Lavoe. Hoy en día, Puerto Rico es el centro internacional de este estilo musical. El Gran Combo de Puerto Rico es una de las orquestas de salsa más famosas del mundo°.

Isla de Culebra

Fajardo

Isla de Vieques

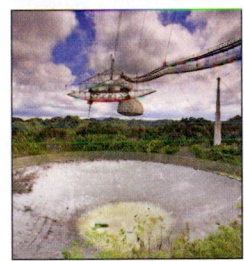

ⓘ Ciencias • El Observatorio de Arecibo

El Observatorio de Arecibo tiene uno de los radiotelescopios más grandes del mundo. Gracias a este telescopio, los científicos° pueden estudiar las propiedades de la Tierra°, la Luna° y otros cuerpos celestes. También pueden analizar fenómenos celestiales como los quasares y pulsares, y detectar emisiones de radio de otras galaxias, en busca de inteligencia extraterrestre.

Historia • Relación con los Estados Unidos

Puerto Rico pasó a ser° parte de los Estados Unidos después de° la guerra° de 1898 y se hizo° un estado libre asociado en 1952. Los puertorriqueños, ciudadanos° estadounidenses desde° 1917, tienen representación política en el Congreso, pero sólo pueden participar en las elecciones presidenciales si viven en los Estados Unidos continentales. En el referendo de 2017, los puertorriqueños votaron° "sí" a favor de convertirse° en el estado 51 de los Estados Unidos. Sin embargo, la decisión final depende del Congreso estadounidense.

proteger *protect* bahía *bay* siglo *century* mazmorras *dungeons* nació *was born* estrellas *stars* mundo *world* científicos *scientists* Tierra *Earth* Luna *Moon* pasó a ser *became* después de *after* guerra *war* se hizo *became* ciudadanos *citizens* desde *since* votaron *voted* convertirse *to become*

¡Increíble pero cierto!

El 20 de septiembre de 2017, el huracán María atravesó° Puerto Rico. Pasó a sólo 25 millas de San Juan, a una velocidad° de 155 millas por hora. María afectó° a toda la población. Miles de personas perdieron° sus casas y, además, quedaron incomunicadas° por la falta de energía eléctrica°.

atravesó *crossed* Pasó *It passed* velocidad *speed* afectó *affected* perdieron *lost* quedaron incomunicadas *were cut off* falta de energía eléctrica *lack of electrical power*

---

2 **¿Qué aprendiste?** Responde a cada pregunta.

1. ¿Cuál es la moneda de Puerto Rico?
   el dólar estadounidense
2. ¿Qué idiomas se hablan (*are spoken*) en Puerto Rico?
   español e inglés
3. ¿Cuál es el sitio más fotografiado de Puerto Rico?
   El Morro
4. ¿Qué es el Gran Combo?
   una orquesta de salsa

3 **Adivinanzas** Describe dos lugares o personas de Puerto Rico a un(a) compañero/a. Cada uno/a debe adivinar (*guess*) qué está describiendo el/la otro/a.

modelo

Estudiante 1: *Es un cantante de salsa.*
Estudiante 2: *¿Es Héctor Lavoe?*
Estudiante 1: *Sí.*

TEACHING OPTIONS

Variación léxica When the first Spanish colonists arrived on the island they were to name Puerto Rico, they found it inhabited by the Taínos, who called the island **Boriquen**. Puerto Ricans still use **Borinquen** to refer to the island, and they frequently call themselves **boricuas**. The Puerto Rican national anthem is ***La borinqueña***. Some other Taíno words that have entered Spanish (and English) are **huracán**, **hamaca**, **canoa**, and **iguana**. **Juracán** was the name of the

Taíno god of the winds whose anger stirred up the great storms that periodically devastated the island. The hammock, of course, was the device the Taínos slept in, and canoes were the boats made of great hollowed-out logs with which they paddled between islands. The Taíno language also survives in many Puerto Rican place names: **Arecibo, Bayamón, Guayama, Sierra de Cayey, Yauco,** and **Coamo**.

El Morro Remind students that at the time **El Morro** was built, piracy was a major concern for Spain and its Caribbean colonies.

Salsa With students, listen to **salsa** or **merengue** from the Dominican Republic, and **rumba** or **mambo** from Cuba. Encourage them to identify common elements in the music (strong percussion patterns rooted in African traditions, alternating structure of soloist and ensemble, incorporation of Western instruments and musical vocabulary). Then, have them point out contrasts. You may want to play the **Panorama cultural** video for this paragraph.

El Observatorio de Arecibo The Arecibo Ionospheric Observatory has the world's most sensitive radio telescope. It can detect objects up to 13 billion light years away. The telescope dish is 1,000 feet in diameter and covers 20 acres. The dish is made of about 40,000 aluminum mesh panels. The Arecibo Observatory celebrated its 50th anniversary in 2013. Hurricane María destroyed some of the dish's reflective panels and most of an antenna in 2017. You may want to play the **Panorama cultural** video for this paragraph.

Relación con los Estados Unidos Point out that only Puerto Ricans living on the island vote in plebiscites (or referenda) on the question of the island's political relationship with the United States.

¡Increíble pero cierto! Hurricane María also affected telecommunication networks in Puerto Rico. That is why AT&T used COW (Cell on Wings) drones for the first time to provide service to the people affected and to facilitate rescue efforts in remote areas.

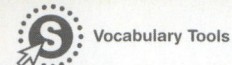
Instructional Resources
Supersite: Audio (Textbook & Lab MP3s); Testing Program (Tests, MP3s)
WebSAM
Lab Manual

Teaching Tip You may want to assign the **Prueba de práctica**, with its diagnostics and review activities, in the online-only **Repaso** section on the Supersite. There is also a **Repaso oral** in this section. For the Sixth Edition, a new summative vocabulary activity with speech recognition has been added to the **Repaso** section.

Los viajes y las vacaciones

acampar	to camp
confirmar una reservación	to confirm a reservation
estar de vacaciones (*f. pl.*)	to be on vacation
hacer las maletas	to pack (one's suitcases)
hacer un viaje	to take a trip
hacer (wind)surf	to (wind)surf
ir de compras (*f. pl.*)	to go shopping
ir de vacaciones	to go on vacation
ir en autobús (*m.*), auto(móvil) (*m.*), avión (*m.*), barco (*m.*), moto(cicleta) (*f.*), taxi (*m.*)	to go by bus, car, plane, boat, motorcycle, taxi
jugar a las cartas	to play cards
montar a caballo (*m.*)	to ride a horse
pescar	to fish
sacar/tomar fotos (*f. pl.*)	to take photos
el/la inspector(a) de aduanas	customs inspector
el/la viajero/a	traveler
el aeropuerto	airport
el campo	countryside
el equipaje	luggage
la estación de autobuses, del metro, de tren	bus, subway, train station
la llegada	arrival
el mar	sea
el paisaje	landscape
el pasaje (de ida y vuelta)	(round-trip) ticket
el pasaporte	passport
la playa	beach
la salida	departure; exit
la tabla de (wind)surf	surfboard/sailboard

El hotel

el ascensor	elevator
la cama	bed
el/la empleado/a	employee
la habitación individual, doble	single, double room
el hotel	hotel
el/la huésped	guest
la llave	key
el piso	floor (of a building)
la planta baja	ground floor

Adjetivos

abierto/a	open
aburrido/a	bored; boring
alegre	happy
amable	nice; friendly
avergonzado/a	embarrassed
cansado/a	tired
cerrado/a	closed
cómodo/a	comfortable
confundido/a	confused
contento/a	content
desordenado/a	disorderly
enamorado/a (de)	in love (with)
enojado/a	angry
equivocado/a	wrong
feliz	happy
limpio/a	clean
listo/a	ready; smart
nervioso/a	nervous
ocupado/a	busy
ordenado/a	orderly
preocupado/a (por)	worried (about)
seguro/a	sure; safe; confident
sucio/a	dirty
triste	sad

Los números ordinales

primer, primero/a	first
segundo/a	second
tercer, tercero/a	third
cuarto/a	fourth
quinto/a	fifth
sexto/a	sixth
séptimo/a	seventh
octavo/a	eighth
noveno/a	ninth
décimo/a	tenth

Palabras adicionales

ahora mismo	right now
el año	year
¿Cuál es la fecha (de hoy)?	What is the date (today)?
de buen/mal humor	in a good/bad mood
la estación	season
el mes	month
todavía	yet; still

Seasons, months, and dates	See page 154.
Weather expressions	See page 154.
Direct object pronouns	See page 174.
Expresiones útiles	See page 159.

More activities

 vhlcentral LM p. 30

¡De compras!

6

Lesson Goals

In **Lección 6**, students will be introduced to the following:
- terms for clothing and shopping
- colors
- open-air markets
- Venezuelan clothing designer **Carolina Herrera**
- the verbs **saber** and **conocer**
- indirect object pronouns
- preterite tense of regular verbs
- demonstrative adjectives and pronouns
- skimming a document
- how to report an interview
- writing a report
- listening for linguistic cues
- A television commercial for the Spanish toy store **Juguettos**
- a video about open-air markets
- cultural, geographic, economic, and historical information about Cuba

A primera vista Here are some additional questions you can ask to personalize the photo: *¿Te gusta ir de compras? ¿Por qué? ¿Estás de buen humor cuando vas de compras? ¿Piensas ir de compras este fin de semana? ¿Adónde? ¿Qué compras cuando estás de vacaciones?*

Teaching Tip Look for these icons for additional communicative practice:

→👤👤	Interpretive communication
←👤👤	Presentational communication
👤↔👤	Interpersonal communication

🔍 A PRIMERA VISTA
- ¿Está buscando algo la chica?
- ¿Hace las maletas o va de compras?
- ¿Está de buen o mal humor?
- ¿Es rubia o morena?

INSTRUCTIONAL RESOURCES

Supersite (vhlcentral.com)
Video: *Fotonovela, Flash cultura, En pantalla, Panorama cultural*
Audio: Textbook and Lab MP3 Files

Activity Pack: Information Gap Activities, games, additional activity handouts
Resources: SAM Answer Key, Scripts, Translations, **Vocabulario adicional**, sample lesson plan, Grammar Presentation Slides, Digital Image Bank

Testing Program: Quizzes, Tests, Exams, MP3s, Oral Testing Suggestions
Student Activities Manual: Workbook/Video Manual/Lab Manual
WebSAM (online Student Activities Manual)

¡De compras!

Más vocabulario

el abrigo	*coat*
los calcetines (el calcetín)	*sock(s)*
el cinturón	*belt*
las gafas (de sol)	*(sun)glasses*
los guantes	*gloves*
el impermeable	*raincoat*
las medias	*pantyhose; stockings*
la ropa	*clothes*
la ropa interior	*underwear*
el traje	*suit*
los zapatos de tenis	*sneakers*
el regalo	*gift*
el almacén	*department store*
el centro comercial	*shopping mall*
el mercado (al aire libre)	*(open-air) market*
el precio (fijo)	*(fixed; set) price*
la rebaja	*sale*
la tarjeta de débito	*debit card*
la tienda	*store*
comprar en línea	*to buy online*
costar (o:ue)	*to cost*
gastar	*to spend (money)*
pagar	*to pay*
regatear	*to bargain*
vender	*to sell*
hacer juego (con)	*to match (with)*
llevar	*to wear; to take*
usar	*to wear; to use*

Variación léxica

calcetines	⟷	medias (*Amér. L.*)
cinturón	⟷	correa (*Col., Venez.*)
gafas/lentes	⟷	espejuelos (*Cuba, P.R.*), anteojos (*Arg., Chile*)
zapatos de tenis	⟷	zapatillas de deporte (*Esp.*), zapatillas (*Arg., Perú*)

More activities

vhlcentral | LM p. 31 | WB pp. 59–60 | Online activities

Image labels: el traje de baño, el vestido, la dependienta/la vendedora, el dependiente/el vendedor, el dinero en efectivo, la tarjeta de crédito, la cartera, la bolsa, la caja, el suéter, los (blue)jeans, los pantalones cortos, los zapatos, la clienta, las sandalias, el cliente

Práctica

1 Indicar Check **invierno** or **verano** to indicate when someone would be most likely to wear each item you hear.

	Invierno	Verano		Invierno	Verano
1.	●	○	5.	○	●
2.	●	○	6.	○	●
3.	○	●	7.	●	○
4.	●	○	8.	○	●

2 ¿Lógico o ilógico? Indicate whether each statement you hear is **lógico** or **ilógico**.

1. _ilógico_   3. _ilógico_   5. _lógico_   7. _ilógico_
2. _lógico_   4. _ilógico_   6. _lógico_   8. _lógico_

3 Escoger Choose the item in each group that does not belong.

1. almacén • centro comercial • mercado • (sombrero)
2. jeans • (bolsa) • falda • pantalones
3. camisa • camiseta • blusa • (botas)
4. abrigo • suéter • (corbata) • chaqueta
5. (pagar) • llevar • hacer juego (con) • usar
6. mercado • tienda • almacén • (cartera)
7. botas • sandalias • zapatos de tenis • (traje)
8. vender • regatear • (ropa interior) • gastar

4 Completar Complete each sentence with the correct word(s), adding definite or indefinite articles when necessary.

caja	medias	tarjeta de crédito
centro comercial	par	traje de baño
dependientas	ropa	vendedores

1. Hoy voy a ir de compras al __centro comercial__.
2. Voy a ir a la tienda de ropa para mujeres. Siempre hay muchas rebajas y las __dependientas__ son muy simpáticas.
3. Necesito comprar __un par__ de zapatos.
4. También voy a comprar unas __medias__ para mi mamá.
5. Y tengo que comprar __un traje de baño__ porque el sábado voy a la playa con mis amigos.
6. Voy a pagar todo (*everything*) en __la caja__.
7. Pero hoy no tengo dinero. Voy a tener que usar mi __tarjeta de crédito__.
8. Mañana voy al mercado al aire libre. Me gusta regatear con los __vendedores__.

Labels (illustration):
- el sombrero
- la camisa
- la blusa
- la chaqueta
- la falda
- la bota
- la corbata
- los pantalones
- la camiseta
- un par de zapatos

Los colores

amarillo/a • azul • gris • anaranjado/a • blanco/a • marrón, café • morado/a • negro/a • rojo/a • rosado/a • verde

---

5 Contrastes Complete each phrase with the opposite of the underlined word.

1. un vestido <u>corto</u> • una falda… **larga**
2. unas vendedoras <u>malas</u> • unos dependientes… **buenos**
3. una corbata <u>barata</u> • unas camisas… **caras**
4. un hombre muy <u>pobre</u> • una mujer muy… **rica**
5. una cartera <u>nueva</u> • un cinturón… **viejo**
6. unos trajes <u>hermosos</u> • unos jeans… **feos**
7. unos calcetines <u>blancos</u> • unas medias… **negras**
8. un impermeable <u>caro</u> • unos suéteres… **baratos**

Adjetivos

barato/a	cheap
bueno/a	good
cada	each
caro/a	expensive
corto/a	short (in length)
elegante	elegant
hermoso/a	beautiful
largo/a	long
loco/a	crazy
nuevo/a	new
otro/a	other; another
pobre	poor
rico/a	rich

6 Preguntas Answer these questions with a classmate.

modelo
¿De qué color es el flamenco (flamingo)?
Es rosado.

1. ¿De qué color es la nieve? **Es blanca.**
2. ¿De qué color es el océano Atlántico? **Es azul.**
3. ¿De qué color es la casa donde vive el presidente de los EE.UU.? **Es blanca.**
4. ¿De qué color es la bandera (*flag*) de Canadá? **Es roja y blanca.**
5. ¿De qué color es el sol? **Es amarillo.**
6. ¿De qué color es la pelota de baloncesto? **Es marrón./Es café./Es anaranjada.**
7. ¿De qué color es el dólar de los EE.UU.? **Es verde y blanco.**
8. ¿De qué color es la cebra (*zebra*)? **Es negra y blanca.**

Comunicación

7 **Las maletas** With a classmate, answer these questions about the drawings.

1. ¿Qué hay al lado de la maleta de Carmela?
   Hay unas gafas de sol, una camiseta, unos pantalones cortos y un traje de baño.
2. ¿Qué hay en la maleta?
   Hay un sombrero y un par de sandalias.
3. ¿De qué color son las sandalias? ¿Y la camiseta?
   Las sandalias son rojas. La camiseta es rosada.
4. ¿Adónde va Carmela?
   Va a la playa.

▶ 5. ¿Qué tiempo va a hacer?
   Va a hacer sol./ Va a hacer calor.

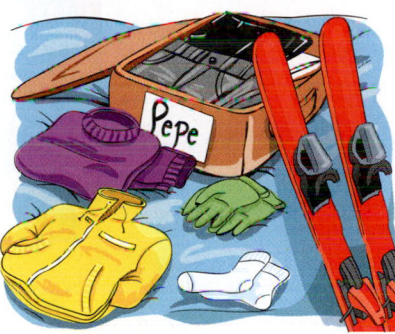

6. ¿Qué hay al lado de la maleta de Pepe?
   Hay un par de calcetines, un par de guantes, un suéter y un abrigo.
7. ¿Qué hay en la maleta?
   Hay dos pantalones.
8. ¿De qué color es el suéter? ¿Y los pantalones?
   El suéter es morado. Los pantalones son negros y grises.

▶ 9. ¿Qué va a hacer Pepe en Bariloche?
   Va a esquiar.

10. ¿Qué tiempo va a hacer?
   Va a hacer frío./ Va a nevar.

CONSULTA

To review weather, see **Lección 5, Contextos**, p. 154.

NOTA CULTURAL

Bariloche is a popular resort for skiing in South America. Located in Argentina's Patagonia region, the town is also known for its chocolate factories and its beautiful lakes, mountains, and forests.

8 **El viaje** You are going on vacation with two classmates. Pick a destination and then draw three suitcases. Write in each one what clothing each person is taking. Present your drawings to the rest of the class, answering these questions. Answers will vary.

- ¿Adónde van?
- ¿Qué tiempo va a hacer allí?
- ¿Qué van a hacer allí?
- ¿Qué hay en sus maletas?
- ¿De qué color es la ropa que llevan?

9 **Preferencias** Take turns asking and answering these questions with a classmate. Answers will vary.

1. ¿Adónde vas a comprar ropa? ¿Por qué?
2. ¿Qué tipo de ropa prefieres? ¿Por qué?
3. ¿Cuáles son tus colores favoritos?
4. En tu opinión, ¿es importante comprar ropa nueva frecuentemente? ¿Por qué?
5. ¿Gastas mucho dinero en ropa cada mes? ¿Buscas rebajas?
6. ¿Regateas cuando compras ropa? ¿Usas tarjetas de crédito?
7. ¿Cómo prefieres pagar? ¿Con dinero en efectivo? ¿Con tarjeta de crédito o débito?
8. ¿Prefieres ir de compras o comprar en línea? ¿Por qué?

---

7 **Teaching Tip** Tell students to include the color for each piece of clothing and accessory.

7 **Expansion**
- In pairs, have students discuss what essential items might be missing from the suitcases. Students may agree or disagree with their partner's suggestions. Ex:
  —**Pepe debe llevar unas botas y unas gafas de sol.**
  —**Sí, Pepe necesita unas botas para esquiar.**
- Ask volunteers what kind of clothing they would take with them to these destinations: **Seattle en la primavera, la Florida en el verano, Toronto en el invierno, San Francisco en el otoño.**

8 **Teaching Tip** One class period before doing this activity, assign groups and have them discuss where they are going.

8 **Expansion** Have students guess where the groups are going, based on the content of the suitcases. Facilitate guessing by asking items 2–5 from the list.

9 **Expansion**
- Ask students to report the findings of their interviews to the class. Ex: _____ **va a H&M para comprar ropa porque allí la ropa no es cara. Prefiere ropa informal...**
- Have students work with different partners. Tell students to assume the identity of a famous person and explain their clothing preferences, using questions similar to those in **Actividad 9**.

TEACHING OPTIONS

Pairs Have students form pairs, and tell them they are going on a shopping spree. On paper strips, write varying dollar amounts, from ten dollars to three thousand, and distribute them. Have pairs discuss what they will buy. Encourage creativity. Ex: **Tenemos quince dólares y vamos a _Old Navy_. Ella va a comprar medias amarillas. Yo voy a comprar un sombrero en rebaja.**

Extra Practice Add an auditory aspect to this vocabulary practice. Ask students to write an anonymous description of the article of clothing or outfit that best defines them. Collect the papers, shuffle them, and read the descriptions aloud for the class to guess.

Pairs Have pairs take turns describing classmates' clothing and guessing the person. Ex: **Esta persona lleva jeans y una blusa marrón. Lleva sandalias blancas. (Es _____.)**

En el mercado

Los chicos van de compras al mercado. ¿Quién hizo la mejor compra?

PERSONAJES

 FELIPE JUAN CARLOS

 Video

1

MARISSA Oigan, vamos al mercado.

JUAN CARLOS ¡Sí! Los chicos en un equipo y las chicas en otro.

FELIPE Tenemos dos horas para ir de compras.

MARU Y don Guillermo decide quién gana.

2

JIMENA Esta falda azul es muy elegante.

MARISSA ¡Sí! Además, este color está de moda.

MARU Éste rojo es de algodón.

(*Las chicas encuentran unas bolsas.*)

VENDEDOR Ésta de rayas cuesta 190 pesos, ésta 120 pesos y ésta 220 pesos.

3

MARISSA ¿Me das aquella blusa rosada? Me parece que hace juego con esta falda, ¿no? ¿No tienen otras tallas?

JIMENA Sí, aquí. ¿Qué talla usas?

MARISSA Uso talla 4.

JIMENA La encontré. ¡Qué ropa más bonita!

5

6

(*En otra parte del mercado*)

FELIPE Juan Carlos compró una camisa de muy buena calidad.

MIGUEL (*a la vendedora*) ¿Puedo ver ésos, por favor?

VENDEDORA Sí, señor. Le doy un muy buen precio.

4

VENDEDOR Son 530 por las tres bolsas. Pero como ustedes son tan bonitas, son 500 pesos.

MARU Señor, no somos turistas ricas. Somos estudiantes pobres.

VENDEDOR Bueno, son 480 pesos.

MARISSA **JIMENA** **MARU** **MIGUEL** **DON GUILLERMO** **VENDEDORA** **VENDEDOR**

7

JUAN CARLOS Miren, mi nueva camisa. Elegante, ¿verdad?

FELIPE A ver, Juan Carlos... te queda bien.

8

MARU ¿Qué compraste?

MIGUEL Sólo esto.

MARU ¡Qué bonitos aretes! Gracias, mi amor.

9

JUAN CARLOS Y ustedes, ¿qué compraron?

JIMENA Bolsas.

MARU Acabamos de comprar tres bolsas por sólo 480 pesos. ¡Una ganga!

10

FELIPE Don Guillermo, usted tiene que decidir quién gana. ¿Los chicos o las chicas?

DON GUILLERMO El ganador es... Miguel. ¡Porque no compró nada para él, sino para su novia!

More activities

S vhlcentral | VM pp. 11–12 | Online activities

Expresiones útiles

Talking about clothing

¡Qué ropa más bonita!
What nice clothing!
Esta falda azul es muy elegante.
This blue skirt is very elegant.
Está de moda.
It's in style.
Éste rojo es de algodón/lana.
This red one is cotton/wool.
Ésta de rayas/lunares/cuadros es de seda.
This striped / polka-dotted / plaid one is silk.
Es de muy buena calidad.
It's very good quality.
¿Qué talla usas/llevas?
What size do you wear?
Uso/Llevo talla 4.
I wear a size 4.
¿Qué número calza?
What size shoe do you wear?
Yo calzo siete.
I wear a size seven.

Negotiating a price

¿Cuánto cuesta?
How much does it cost?
Demasiado caro/a.
Too expensive.
Es una ganga.
It's a bargain.

Saying what you bought

¿Qué compraste?/¿Qué compró usted?
What did you buy?
Sólo compré esto.
I only bought this.
¡Qué bonitos aretes!
What beautiful earrings!
Y ustedes, ¿qué compraron?
And you guys, what did you buy?

Additional vocabulary

híjole *wow*

¿Qué pasó?

1 ¿Cierto o falso? Indicate whether each sentence is **cierto** or **falso**. Correct the false statements.

	Cierto	Falso	
1. Jimena dice que la falda azul no es elegante.	○	✓	Jimena dice que la falda azul es muy elegante.
2. Juan Carlos compra una camisa.	✓	○	
3. Marissa dice que el azul es un color que está de moda.	✓	○	
4. Miguel compra unas sandalias para Maru.	○	✓	Miguel compra unos aretes para Maru.

2 Identificar Provide the first initial of the person who says the equivalent of each statement.

MARU

FELIPE

JIMENA

M 1. Gracias por los aretes.
F 2. Te queda muy bien esa camisa, Juan Carlos.
M 3. No podemos pagar 500, señor, eso es muy caro.
J 4. ¿Qué talla necesitas, Marissa?
J 5. Esta falda me gusta mucho, el color azul es muy elegante.
F 6. ¿Ganan los chicos o las chicas?

3 Completar Answer the questions.

1. ¿Qué talla usa Marissa? Marissa usa talla 4.
2. ¿Cuánto les pide el vendedor por las tres bolsas? Las bolsas cuestan 500 pesos.
3. ¿Cuál es el precio que pagan las tres amigas por las bolsas? El precio que pagan es 480 pesos.
4. ¿Qué dice Juan Carlos sobre su nueva camisa? Juan Carlos dice que su nueva camisa es elegante.
5. ¿Quién ganó al hacer las compras? ¿Por qué? Ganó Miguel porque le compró unos aretes a su novia.

4 Conversar With a partner, role-play a conversation between a customer and a salesperson in an open-air market. Use these expressions and also look at **Expresiones útiles** on the previous page. Answers will vary.

¿Qué desea?	Estoy buscando...	Prefiero el/la rojo/a.
What would you like?	*I'm looking for...*	*I prefer the red one.*

Cliente/a — **Vendedor(a)**

Say good afternoon. → Greet the customer and ask what he/she would like.

Explain that you are looking for a particular item of clothing. → Show him/her some items and ask what he/she prefers.

Discuss colors and sizes. → Discuss colors and sizes.

Ask for the price and begin bargaining. → Tell him/her a price. Negotiate a price.

Settle on a price and purchase the item. → Accept a price and say thank you.

---

## Side column (left margin)

1 Expansion Once statements have been corrected, ask pairs to find the places in the episode that support their answers. Have pairs role-play the scenes for the class. Ask comprehension questions as a follow-up.

2 Expansion Give students these statements as items 7–9:
7. Somos estudiantes y por eso no tenemos mucho dinero. (M)
8. Compramos unas camisetas. (F)
9. Don Guillermo debe decidir el ganador en dos horas. (M)

3 Expansion Ask pairs to write two additional questions. Then have pairs exchange papers and answer each other's questions.

Nota cultural Shoe sizes in Mexico are different from the U.S. and Canada. Men's sizes in Mexico are 2 numbers smaller, and women's, 3 sizes smaller. For example, a man's size 11 shoe in the U.S. and Canada would be a size 9 in Mexico, and a woman's size 7.5 would be a 4.5.

4 Possible Conversation
E1: Buenas tardes.
E2: Buenas tardes. ¿Qué desea?
E1: Estoy buscando una camisa.
E2: Pues, tengo estas camisas de algodón y estas camisas de seda. ¿Cuál prefiere usted?
E1: Busco una camisa blanca o azul de algodón. Uso talla mediana.
E2: Las camisas de algodón son de talla mediana. Tengo esta camisa azul de algodón.
E1: Quiero comprarla, pero no soy rico/a. ¿Cuánto cuesta?
E2: Veinte dólares. Pero para usted... sólo diecisiete dólares.
E1: Muy bien. La compro, pero sólo tengo quince dólares.
E2: Está bien. Muchas gracias.

TEACHING OPTIONS

Extra Practice Have the class answer questions about the **Fotonovela**. Ex: **1.** ¿Quién piensa que el color azul está de moda? (Marissa) **2.** ¿Quiénes regatean por tres bolsas? (Maru, Jimena y Marissa) **3.** ¿Qué acaba de comprar Miguel? (Acaba de comprar unos aretes para Maru.)

Pairs Divide the class into pairs. Tell them to imagine that they are awards show commentators on the red carpet (**la alfombra roja**). Ask each pair to choose six celebrities and write a description of their outfits. Encourage creativity, and provide additional vocabulary if needed. Then have pairs read their descriptions for the class. Ex: **Aquí estamos en la alfombra roja de los *Video Music Awards*. Ahora viene Beyoncé con Jay-Z. Ella lleva un vestido azul de seda y sandalias grises. ¡Qué ropa tan bonita! Jay-Z usa jeans y...**

Pronunciación
The consonants **d** and **t**

Tutorial

¿Dónde?	**ven**d**er**	**na**d**ar**	**ver**d**ad**

Like **b** and **v**, the Spanish **d** can have a hard sound or a soft sound, depending on which letters appear next to it.

Don	**d**inero	**tien**d**a**	**fal**d**a**

At the beginning of a phrase and after **n** or **l**, the letter **d** is pronounced with a hard sound. This sound is similar to the English *d* in *dog*, but a little softer and duller. The tongue should touch the back of the upper teeth, not the roof of the mouth.

med**ias**	**ver**d**e**	**vesti**d**o**	**huéspe**d

In all other positions, **d** has a soft sound. It is similar to the English *th* in *there*, but a little softer.

Don Diego no tiene el diccionario

When **d** begins a word, its pronunciation depends on the previous word. At the beginning of a phrase or after a word that ends in **n** or **l**, it is pronounced as a hard **d**.

Doña Dolores es de la capital

Words that begin with **d** are pronounced with a soft **d** if they appear immediately after a word that ends in a vowel or any consonant other than **n** or **l**.

traje	**pan**t**alones**	**tarje**t**a**	**t**ienda

When pronouncing the Spanish **t**, the tongue should touch the back of the upper teeth, not the roof of the mouth. Unlike the English *t*, no air is expelled from the mouth.

Práctica Read these phrases aloud to practice the **d** and the **t**.

1. Hasta pronto.
2. De nada.
3. Mucho gusto.
4. Lo siento.
5. No hay de qué.
6. ¿De dónde es usted?
7. ¡Todos a bordo!
8. No puedo.
9. Es estupendo.
10. No tengo computadora.
11. ¿Cuándo vienen?
12. Son las tres y media.

Oraciones Read these sentences aloud to practice the **d** and the **t**.

1. Don Teodoro tiene una tienda en un almacén en La Habana.
2. Don Teodoro vende muchos trajes, vestidos y zapatos todos los días.
3. Un día un turista, Federico Machado, entra en la tienda para comprar un par de botas.
4. Federico regatea con don Teodoro y compra las botas y también un par de sandalias.

Refranes Read these sayings aloud to practice the **d** and the **t**.

En la variedad está el gusto.[1]

Aunque la mona se vista de seda, mona se queda.[2]

More activities

vhlcentral   LM p. 32

[1] Variety is the spice of life. [2] You can't make a silk purse out of a sow's ear.

Section Goal

In **Pronunciación**, students will be introduced to the pronunciation of the letters **d** and **t**.

Instructional Resources
Supersite: Audio (Textbook and Lab MP3 Files); Resources (Scripts, Answer Keys)
WebSAM
Lab Manual

Teaching Tips

- Explain that **d** has a hard sound at the beginning of a phrase or after **n** or **l**. Write **don, dinero, tienda,** and **falda** on the board and have the class pronounce them.
- Explain that **d** has a soft sound in all other positions. Pronounce **medias, verde, vestido,** and **huésped** and have the class repeat.
- Point out that within phrases, **d** at the beginning of a word has a hard or soft sound depending on the last sound of the preceding word. Read the examples aloud and have the class repeat.
- Explain that **t** is pronounced with the tongue at the back of the upper teeth and that, unlike English, no air is expelled from the mouth. Pronounce **traje, pantalones, tarjeta,** and **tienda** and have the class repeat. Then pronounce pairs of similar-sounding Spanish and English words, having students focus on the difference between the **t** sounds: **ti**/*tea*; **tal**/*tall*; **todo**/*toad*; **tema**/*tame*; **tela**/*tell*.

Práctica/Oraciones/Refranes These exercises are recorded on the *Textbook MP3s*. You may want to play the audio so that students practice listening to Spanish spoken by speakers other than yourself.

Section Goals

In **Cultura**, students will:
- read about open-air markets
- learn clothing-related terms
- read about Venezuelan clothing designer **Carolina Herrera**
- read about the fashions of Hispanic designers

Instructional Resource
Supersite

En detalle
Antes de leer
👥↔👤 Lead a discussion about open-air markets, such as a flea market. Have students share their experiences, including the market's location, goods sold there, and prices. Ask them to predict what might be sold at a market in a Spanish-speaking country.

Lectura
- Explain that open-air markets that specialize in second-hand or low-priced goods are often referred to as **mercados de pulgas** (*flea markets*).
- Point out that many local artists take advantage of open-air markets to sell their pieces or display new works.
- Explain that **la ñapa** can be considered similar to the Anglo tradition of a baker's dozen.

Después de leer Ask students what facts are new or surprising to them.

1 **Expansion** Give students these statements as items 9–11: 9. The **Tianguis Cultural del Chopo** is not a good place to go if you are interested in Mexican crafts and art. (**Falso.** The **Tianguis Cultural del Chopo** has crafts and art.) 10. Market stands are referred to as **puestos.** (**Cierto.**) 11. Bargaining often raises the price of an item significantly. (**Falso.** It usually lowers the price significantly.)

Los mercados al aire libre

Mercados al aire libre are an integral part of commerce and culture in the Spanish-speaking world. Whether they take place daily or weekly, these markets are an important forum where tourists, locals, and vendors interact. People come to the marketplace to shop, socialize, taste local foods, and watch street performers. Wandering from one **puesto** (*stand*) to the next, one can browse for fresh fruits and vegetables, clothing, CDs and DVDs, and **artesanías** (*crafts*). Some markets offer a mix of products, while others specialize in food, fashion, or used merchandise, such as antiques and books.

When shoppers see an item they like, they can bargain with the vendor. Friendly bargaining is an expected ritual and may result in a significantly lower price. When selling food, vendors may give the customer a little extra of what they purchase; this free addition is known as **la ñapa**.

Many open-air markets are also tourist attractions. The market in Otavalo, Ecuador, is world-famous and has taken place every Saturday since pre-Incan times. This market is well-known for the colorful textiles woven by the **otavaleños**, the indigenous people of the area. One can also find leather goods and wood carvings from nearby towns. Another popular market is **El Rastro**, held every Sunday in Madrid, Spain. Sellers set up **puestos** along the streets to display their wares, which range from local artwork and antiques to inexpensive clothing and electronics.

Mercado de Otavalo

Otros mercados famosos

Mercado	Lugar	Productos
Feria Artesanal de Recoleta	Buenos Aires, Argentina	artesanías
Mercado Central	Santiago, Chile	mariscos°, pescado°, frutas, verduras°
Tianguis Cultural del Chopo	Ciudad de México, México	ropa, música, revistas, libros, arte, artesanías
El mercado de Chichicastenango	Chichicastenango, Guatemala	frutas y verduras, flores°, cerámica, textiles

mariscos *seafood* pescado *fish* verduras *vegetables* flores *flowers*

---

1 **¿Cierto o falso?** Indicate whether these statements are **cierto** or **falso**. Correct the false statements.

1. Generally, open-air markets specialize in one type of goods. **Falso.** They sell a variety of goods.
2. Bargaining is commonplace at outdoor markets. **Cierto.**
3. Only new goods can be found at open-air markets. **Falso.** They sell both new and used goods.
4. A Spaniard in search of antiques could search at **El Rastro. Cierto.**
5. If you are in Guatemala and want to buy ceramics, you can go to Chichicastenango. **Cierto.**
6. A **ñapa** is a tax on open-air market goods. **Falso.** A **ñapa** is a free addition sometimes given to customers.
7. The **otavaleños** weave colorful textiles to sell on Saturdays. **Cierto.**
8. Santiago's **Mercado Central** is known for books and music. **Falso.** It's known for seafood, fish, fruits, and vegetables.

TEACHING OPTIONS

TPR Create a series of true/false statements about goods one can purchase at the open-air markets mentioned in **En detalle.** Tell students to raise their right hand if a statement is true or their left hand if it is false. Ex: **Compro mariscos en El Rastro.** (left hand) **Compro flores en el mercado de Chichicastenango.** (right hand)

Small Groups ←👥→ Have students work in groups of three. For homework, have them research another famous open-air market in the Spanish-speaking world. Ex: **Pisac** (Peru), **La Romana** (Dominican Republic), **La Cancha** (Bolivia). In class, have each group present the location of the market, how often it takes place, what is sold, and any other significant information. Encourage students to bring in photos.

ASÍ SE DICE

La ropa

la chamarra (Méx.)	la chaqueta
de manga corta/larga	*short/long-sleeved*
los mahones (P. Rico); el pantalón de mezclilla (Méx.); los tejanos (Esp.); los vaqueros (Arg., Cuba, Esp., Uru.)	los bluejeans
la marca	*brand*
la playera (Méx.); la remera (Arg.)	la camiseta

EL MUNDO HISPANO

Diseñadores de moda

- **Adolfo Domínguez** (España) Su ropa tiene un estilo minimalista y práctico. Usa telas° naturales y cómodas en sus diseños.

- **Silvia Tcherassi** (Colombia) Los colores vivos y las líneas asimétricas de sus vestidos y trajes muestran influencias tropicales.

- **Óscar de la Renta** (República Dominicana) Diseñó ropa opulenta para la mujer clásica.

- **Narciso Rodríguez** (EE.UU.) En sus diseños delicados y finos predominan los colores blanco y negro. Hizo° el vestido de boda° de Carolyn Bessette Kennedy. También diseñó varios vestidos para Michelle Obama.

telas *fabrics* Hizo *He made* de boda *wedding*

PERFIL

Carolina Herrera

In 1980, at the urging of some friends, **Carolina Herrera** created a fashion collection as a "test." The Venezuelan designer received such a favorable response that within one year she moved her family from Caracas to New York City and created her own label, Carolina Herrera, Ltd.

"I love elegance and intricacy, but whether it is in a piece of clothing or a fragrance, the intricacy must appear as simplicity," Herrera once stated. She quickly found that many sophisticated women agreed; from the start, her sleek and glamorous designs have been in constant demand. Over the years, Herrera has grown her brand into a veritable fashion empire that encompasses her fashion and bridal collections, cosmetics, perfume, and accessories that are sold around the globe.

CON RITMO HISPANO

Gente de Zona (2000–)
Place of origin: Havana, Cuba

This duo, consisting of Alexander Delgado and Randy Malcolm Martínez, gained worldwide recognition thanks to the song "Bailando," in collaboration with Enrique Iglesias.

Go to **vhlcentral.com** to find out more about **Gente de Zona** and their music.

ACTIVIDADES

2 **Comprensión** Complete these sentences.

1. Adolfo Domínguez usa telas ___naturales___ y ___cómodas___ en su ropa.
2. Si hace fresco en el D.F., puedes llevar una ___chamarra___.
3. La diseñadora ___Carolina Herrera___ hace ropa, perfumes y más.
4. La ropa de ___Silvia Tcherassi___ muestra influencias tropicales.
5. Los ___mahones___ son una ropa casual en Puerto Rico.

3 **Mi ropa favorita** Write a brief description of your favorite article of clothing. Mention what store it is from, the brand, colors, fabric, style, and any other information. Then get together with a small group, collect the descriptions, and take turns reading them aloud at random. Can the rest of the group guess whose favorite piece of clothing is being described? Answers will vary.

More activities
 vhlcentral
 Online activities

Section Goals

In **Estructura 6.1**, students will learn:
• the uses of **saber** and **conocer**
• more uses of the personal **a**
• other verbs conjugated like **conocer**

Instructional Resources

Supersite: Audio (Lab MP3 Files); Resources (Grammar Presentation Slides, Activity Pack, Scripts, Answer Keys); Testing Program (Quizzes)
WebSAM
Workbook
Lab Manual

Teaching Tips

• Use the **Lección 6** Grammar Presentation Slides to assist with this presentation.
• Point out the irregular **yo** forms of **saber** and **conocer**.
• Divide the board into two columns with the headings **saber** and **conocer**. In the first column, write the uses of **saber** and model them by asking individuals what they know how to do and what factual information they know. Ex: ____, **¿sabes bailar salsa? ¿Sabes mi número de teléfono?** In the second column, write the uses of **conocer** and model them by asking individuals about people and places they know. Ex: ____, **¿conoces Cuba? ¿Conoces a Yasiel Puig?**
• Further distinguish the uses of **saber** and **conocer** by making statements such as: **Sé quién es el presidente de este país, pero no lo conozco.**
• Point out the first **¡Atención!** bullet. Ask volunteers to write the full conjugation of these verbs on the board.
• Point out the similar **yo** form for **conocer, parecer, ofrecer, conducir,** and **traducir**.
• Ask questions using the new verbs. Ex: **¿Quiénes conducen? ¿Qué carro conduces?**

6.1 Saber and conocer Tutorial

ANTE TODO Spanish has two verbs that mean *to know*: **saber** and **conocer**. They cannot be used interchangeably. Note the irregular **yo** forms.

The verbs saber and conocer

		saber *(to know)*	conocer *(to know)*
SINGULAR FORMS	yo	**sé**	**conozco**
	tú	**sabes**	**conoces**
	Ud./él/ella	**sabe**	**conoce**
PLURAL FORMS	nosotros/as	**sabemos**	**conocemos**
	vosotros/as	**sabéis**	**conocéis**
	Uds./ellos/ellas	**saben**	**conocen**

▶ **Saber** means *to know a fact or piece(s) of information* or *to know how to do something.*

No **sé** tu número de teléfono.
I don't know your phone number.

Mi hermana **sabe** hablar francés.
My sister knows how to speak French.

▶ **Conocer** means *to know* or *be familiar/acquainted* with a person, place, or thing.

¿Conoces la ciudad de Nueva York?
Do you know New York City?

No **conozco** a tu amigo Esteban.
I don't know your friend Esteban.

▶ When the direct object of **conocer** is a person or pet, the personal **a** is used.

¿Conoces La Habana? *but* ¿Conoces **a** Celia Cruz?
Do you know Havana? *Do you know Celia Cruz?*

▶ **¡Atención!** **Parecer** (*to seem*) and **ofrecer** (*to offer*) are conjugated like **conocer**.

▶ **¡Atención!** **Conducir** (*to drive*) and **traducir** (*to translate*) also have an irregular **yo** form, but since they are **-ir** verbs, they are conjugated differently from **conocer**.

conducir	**conduzco**, conduces, conduce, condu**cimos**, condu**cís**, conducen
traducir	**traduzco**, traduces, traduce, tradu**cimos**, tradu**cís**, traducen

 ¡INTÉNTALO! Provide the appropriate forms of these verbs.

saber
1. José no __sabe__ la hora.
2. Sara y yo __sabemos__ jugar al tenis.
3. ¿Por qué no __sabes__ tú estos verbos?
4. Mis padres __saben__ hablar japonés.
5. Yo __sé__ a qué hora es la clase.
6. Nosotros __sabemos__ muchas cosas.
7. Mi hermano no __sabe__ nadar.
8. Usted no __sabe__ dónde vivo.

conocer
1. Usted y yo __conocemos__ bien Miami.
2. ¿Tú __conoces__ a mi amigo Manuel?
3. Sergio y Taydé __conocen__ mi pueblo.
4. Yo __conozco__ muy bien el centro.
5. Emiliano __conoce__ a mis padres.
6. ¿Ustedes __conocen__ la tienda Gigante?
7. Nosotras __conocemos__ una playa hermosa.
8. ¿Usted __conoce__ a mi profesora?

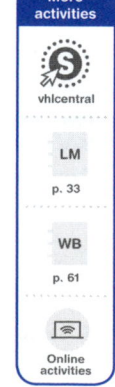

TEACHING OPTIONS

TPR Divide the class into two teams, **saber** and **conocer**, and have them line up. Indicate the first member of each team and call out a sentence in English that uses *to know.* (Ex: We know the answer.) The team member whose verb corresponds to the English sentence has to step forward and provide the Spanish translation.

Extra Practice Ask students to jot down three things they know how to do well (**saber** + [*infinitive*] + **bien**). Collect the papers, shuffle them, and read the sentences aloud. Have the rest of the class guess who wrote the sentences.

Práctica y Comunicación

1

Completar Indicate the correct verb for each sentence.

1. —¿(Conocen/**Saben**) ustedes dónde está el estadio? —No, no lo (conocemos/**sabemos**).
2. Mis hermanos (conocen/**saben**) conducir, pero yo no (**sé**/conozco).
3. —¿(**Conoces**/Sabes) a Lady Gaga? —Bueno, (**sé**/conozco) quién es, pero no la (**conozco**/sé).
4. Mi profesora (sabe/**conoce**) Cuba y también (conoce/**sabe**) bailar salsa.

2

Combinar Combine elements from each column to create sentences. *Answers will vary.*

A	B	C
Shakira	(no) conocer	Jimmy Kimmel
los Yankees	(no) saber	cantar y bailar
el primer ministro		La Habana Vieja
de Canadá		muchas personas importantes
mis amigos y yo		hablar dos lenguas extranjeras
tú		jugar al béisbol

3

Preguntas In pairs, ask each other these questions. Answer with complete sentences.
Answers will vary.

1. ¿Conoces a un(a) cantante famoso/a? ¿Te gusta cómo canta?
2. En tu familia, ¿quién sabe cantar bien? ¿Tu opinión es objetiva?
3. Y tú, ¿conduces bien o mal? ¿Y tus amigos?
4. Si un(a) amigo/a no conduce muy bien, ¿le ofreces crítica constructiva?
5. ¿Cómo parece estar el/la profesor(a) hoy? ¿Y tus compañeros de clase?

4

Entrevista Jot down three things you know how to do, three people you know, and three places
you are familiar with. Then, in a small group, find out what you have in common. *Answers will vary.*

> **modelo**
> **Estudiante 1:** ¿Conocen ustedes a David Lomas?
> **Estudiante 2:** Sí, conozco a David. Vivimos en la misma residencia estudiantil.
> **Estudiante 3:** No, no lo conozco. ¿Cómo es?

5

Anuncio In groups, answer these questions about
the ad. *Answers will vary.*

1. Busquen ejemplos de los verbos
   saber y **conocer**.
2. ¿Qué saben del Centro Comercial Málaga?
3. ¿Qué pueden hacer en el Centro
   Comercial Málaga?
4. ¿Conocen otros centros comerciales
   similares? ¿Cómo se llaman? ¿Dónde están?
5. ¿Conocen un centro comercial
   en otro país? ¿Cómo es?

Él sabe dónde **comer** lo que más le gusta.

Él sabe cómo **jugar** cuatro horas seguidas.

Él sabe dónde está su **regalo** de cumpleaños.

Él sabe dónde **divertirse...**

... y usted sabe dónde puede encontrar un poco de todo.
¿Conoce algún otro lugar como éste?

CENTRO COMERCIAL
MÁLAGA
SABE LO QUE TE GUSTA.

---

1 Teaching Tip To challenge
students, write this activity on
the board as cloze sentences.

1 Expansion Give students
these sentences as items 5–8:
**5. No (sé/conozco) a qué hora es
el examen. (sé) 6. (Conoces/
Sabes) el Viejo San Juan,
¿verdad? (Conoces) 7. ¿Quieren
(saber/conocer) dónde va a ser
la fiesta? (saber) 8. Esta noche
voy a salir con mi novia, pero mis
padres no lo (conocen/saben).
Todavía no la (conocen/saben)…
¡no (conocen/saben) quién es
ella! (saben, conocen, saben)**

2 Teaching Tip To simplify,
before beginning the activity,
read through column C and
have students determine
whether each item takes the
verb **saber** or **conocer**.

2 Expansion
• Add more elements to
  column A (Ex: **yo, mis padres,
  mi profesor(a) de español**)
  and continue the activity.
• Ask students questions
  about what certain celebrities know how to do or
  whom they know. Ex: **Javier
  Bardem, ¿conoce a Penélope
  Cruz? (Sí, la conoce.) Miguel
  Cabrera, ¿sabe jugar al
  béisbol? (Sí, sabe jugarlo.)**

3 Expansion
In pairs, have students
create three additional
questions using the verbs
conducir, ofrecer, and
traducir. Then have pairs
join other pairs to ask and
answer their questions.

4 Teaching Tip To simplify,
have students divide a sheet
of paper into three columns
with the headings **Sé, Conozco
a,** and **Conozco.** Then have
them complete their lists.

5 Expansion
Ask each group to
create an advertisement
using two examples each
of **saber** and **conocer.**

TEACHING OPTIONS

Extra Practice Use the Internet to research advertising slogans
that use verbs from **Estructura 6.1.** In groups, have students
guess the company or product for each slogan. Ex: **Sabemos por
qué vuelas. (American Airlines)**
Small Groups Ask students to write down four
sentences (two true, two false) using **saber** and **conocer.** In
groups of three, have them read their sentences aloud. The

group should ask questions to guess if the person is lying or
telling the truth.
Large Group Ask students to write down six things they
know how to do. Have them circulate around the room to find
out who else knows how to do those things, jotting down the
names of those that answer **sí.** Have students report back to
the class. Ex: **Keisha y yo sabemos tocar el piano.**

Section Goals

In **Estructura 6.2**, students will learn:

- to identify an indirect object noun
- how to use indirect object pronouns

Instructional Resources

Supersite: Audio (Lab MP3 Files); Resources (Grammar Presentation Slides, Activity Pack, Scripts, Answer Keys); Testing Program (Quizzes)
WebSAM
Workbook
Lab Manual

Teaching Tips

- Write on the board: **Mi novio me escribe un mensaje de texto.** Ask students what the direct object of the verb is. Then tell them that an indirect object answers the questions *to whom* or *for whom.*

- Write the indirect object pronouns on the board. Ask how their forms differ from those of direct object pronouns.

- Ask volunteers to read aloud the video-still captions, and have the class identify the indirect object pronoun in each.

- Point out that the redundant use of both an indirect object pronoun and an indirect object noun is common in Spanish and that, unlike in English, it is the indirect object noun that is optional, not the pronoun.

6.2 # Indirect object pronouns Tutorial

ANTE TODO   In **Lección 5**, you learned that a direct object receives the action of the verb directly. In contrast, an indirect object receives the action of the verb indirectly.

SUBJECT	I.O. PRONOUN	VERB	DIRECT OBJECT	INDIRECT OBJECT
Roberto	**le**	presta	cien pesos	**a Luisa.**
Roberto	*lends*		*100 pesos*	*to Luisa.*

An indirect object is a noun or pronoun that answers the question *to whom* or *for whom* an action is done. In the preceding example, the indirect object answers this question: **¿A quién le presta Roberto cien pesos?** *To whom does Roberto lend 100 pesos?*

Indirect object pronouns

Singular forms		**Plural forms**	
me	(to, for) *me*	**nos**	(to, for) *us*
te	(to, for) *you* (fam.)	**os**	(to, for) *you* (fam.)
le	(to, for) *you* (form.) (to, for) *him; her*	**les**	(to, for) *you* (to, for) *them*

▶ **¡Atención!** The forms of indirect object pronouns for the first and second persons (**me, te, nos, os**) are the same as the direct object pronouns. Indirect object pronouns agree in number with the corresponding nouns, but not in gender.

Bueno, le doy un descuento.

Acabo de mostrarles que sí sabemos regatear.

Using indirect object pronouns

▶ Spanish speakers commonly use both an indirect object pronoun and the noun to which it refers in the same sentence. This is done to emphasize and clarify to whom the pronoun refers.

I.O. PRONOUN		INDIRECT OBJECT	I.O. PRONOUN		INDIRECT OBJECT

Ella **le** vende la ropa **a Elena.**   **Les** prestamos el dinero **a Inés y a Álex.**

▶ Indirect object pronouns are also used without the indirect object noun when the person for whom the action is being done is known.

Ana **le** presta la falda **a Elena.**   También **le** presta unos jeans.
Ana lends her skirt to Elena.   *She also lends her a pair of jeans.*

TEACHING OPTIONS

Extra Practice Write sentences like these on the board: **1. Ana te prepara unos tacos. 2. Le presto dinero a Luisa. 3. Les compramos unos regalos a los niños.** Ask students to come to the board and underline the direct objects and circle the indirect objects.

Small Groups Have students work in groups of three. Have Student A "lend" an object to Student B and say: **Te presto mi...** Student B responds: **Me prestas tu...** Student C says: _____ **le presta a _____ su...** Have groups practice until each member has begun the chain twice. Practice plural pronouns by having two groups join together and two students "lend" something to two other students.

▶ Indirect object pronouns are usually placed before the conjugated form of the verb. In negative sentences the pronoun is placed between **no** and the conjugated verb.

Martín **me** compra un regalo.
Martín is buying me a gift.

Eva **no me** escribe cartas.
Eva doesn't write me letters.

CONSULTA

For more information on accents, see **Lección 4, Pronunciación**, p. 123, **Lección 10, Ortografía**, p. 339, and **Lección 11, Ortografía**, p. 375.

▶ When a conjugated verb is followed by an infinitive or the present progressive, the indirect object pronoun may be placed before the conjugated verb or attached to the infinitive or present participle. **¡Atención!** When an indirect object pronoun is attached to a present participle, an accent mark is added to maintain the proper stress.

Él no quiere **pagarte**./
Él no **te** quiere pagar.
He does not want to pay you.

Él está **escribiéndole** una postal a ella./
Él **le** está escribiendo una postal a ella.
He is writing a postcard to her.

▶ Because the indirect object pronouns **le** and **les** have multiple meanings, Spanish speakers often clarify to whom the pronouns refer with the preposition **a** + [*pronoun*] or **a** + [*noun*].

UNCLARIFIED STATEMENTS
Yo **le** compro un abrigo.

Ella **le** describe un libro.

CLARIFIED STATEMENTS
Yo **le** compro un abrigo **a usted/él/ella**.

Ella **le** describe un libro **a Juan**.

UNCLARIFIED STATEMENTS
Él **les** vende unos sombreros.

Ellos **les** hablan muy claro.

CLARIFIED STATEMENTS
Él **les** vende unos sombreros **a ustedes/ellos/ellas**.

Ellos **les** hablan muy claro **a los clientes**.

▶ The irregular verbs **dar** (*to give*) and **decir** (*to say; to tell*) are often used with indirect object pronouns.

The verbs dar and decir

	Singular forms			Plural forms	
	dar	decir		dar	decir
yo	**doy**	**digo**	nosotros/as	**damos**	**decimos**
tú	**das**	**dices**	vosotros/as	**dais**	**decís**
Ud./él/ella	**da**	**dice**	Uds./ellos/ellas	**dan**	**dicen**

Me dan una fiesta cada año.
They give (throw) me a party every year.

Voy a **darle** consejos.
I'm going to give her advice.

Te digo la verdad.
I'm telling you the truth.

No **les digo** mentiras a mis padres.
I don't tell lies to my parents.

¡INTÉNTALO! Provide the correct indirect object pronoun for each sentence.

1. Juan _____le_____ quiere dar un regalo. (*to Elena*)
2. María _____nos_____ prepara un café. (*for us*)
3. Beatriz y Felipe _____me_____ escriben desde (*from*) Cuba. (*to me*)
4. Los vendedores _____te_____ venden ropa. (*to you, fam. sing.*)
5. Marta y yo _____les_____ compramos unos guantes. (*for them*)
6. La dependienta _____nos_____ muestra los guantes. (*to us*)

Teaching Tips
- Point out that the position of indirect object pronouns in a sentence is the same as that of direct object pronouns.
- Ask individuals questions using indirect object pronouns. Ex: ¿A quién le ofreces ayuda? ¿Les das consejos a tus amigos? ¿Qué te dicen tus padres que no debes hacer? ¿Les dices mentiras a tus padres? ¿Cuándo vas a escribirles a tus abuelos? Have students respond with complete sentences, and ask follow-up questions if necessary.
- After going over the ¡Inténtalo! orally with the class, ask students which items might require clarification (items 1 and 4). Ask them what they would add to each sentence in order to clarify le or les.
- As a comprehension check, have students write answers to these questions: 1. Es el cumpleaños de tu mejor amigo. ¿Qué vas a comprarle? 2. ¿A quiénes les hablas todos los días? 3. ¿Quién te presta dinero cuando lo necesitas? 4. ¿Quién les está enseñando español a ustedes?
- In pairs, have students write the dialogue of an argument between two roommates, using dar and decir. Have volunteers role-play their conversations for the class. Encourage them to be creative and act out the argument with props, if possible.

TEACHING OPTIONS

Video Replay the **Fotonovela**. Ask students to note each time an indirect object pronoun is used. Then, have students find each use of **le** and state to whom it refers.
Game Give each student an envelope and a sheet of paper. Ask them to write a sentence using an indirect object pronoun, cut the paper into strips (one word per strip), shuffle them, and place them in the envelope. Then have students pass their envelopes to the person sitting behind them. Allow thirty seconds for them to unscramble the sentence and write it down, before placing the shuffled strips back into the envelope and passing it on. After three minutes, the row with the most correctly deciphered sentences wins.

Práctica

1 Completar Fill in the blanks with the correct pronouns to complete Mónica's description of her family's holiday shopping.

1. Juan y yo ___le___ damos una blusa a nuestra hermana Gisela.
2. Mi tía ___nos___ da a nosotros una mesa para la casa.
3. Mis padres ___me___ dan un traje nuevo a mí.
4. A mi mamá yo ___le___ doy un par de guantes negros.
5. A mi profesora ___le___ doy dos libros de José Martí.
6. Juan ___les___ da un regalo a mis padres.
7. Gisela ___le___ da dos corbatas a su novio.
8. Y a ti, yo ___te___ doy un regalo también. ¿Quieres verlo?

2 En La Habana Describe what happens on Pascual's trip to Cuba.

1. yo / preparar el almuerzo (*lunch*) / (ti)
Yo te preparo el almuerzo (a ti).

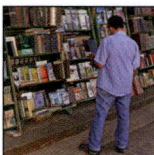

2. él / comprar / libros / (sus hijos) / Plaza de Armas
Él les compra libros (a sus hijos) en la Plaza de Armas.

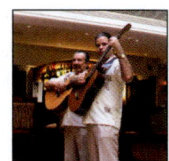

3. ellos / cantar / canción / (mí)
Ellos me cantan una canción (a mí).

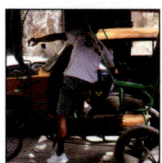

4. él / explicar cómo llegar / (conductor)
Él le explica cómo llegar (al conductor).

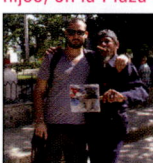

5. mi novia / sacar / foto / (nosotros)
Mi novia nos saca una foto (a nosotros).

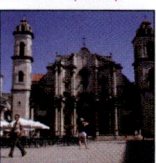

6. el guía (*guide*) / mostrar / catedral de San Cristóbal / (ustedes)
El guía les muestra la catedral de San Cristóbal (a ustedes).

3 Combinar Use an item from each column and an indirect object pronoun to create logical sentences. Answers will vary.

> **modelo**
> Mis padres les dan regalos a mis primos.

A	B	C	D
yo	comprar	mensajes electrónicos	mí
el dependiente	dar	corbata	ustedes
el profesor Arce	decir	dinero en efectivo	clienta
la vendedora	escribir	tarea	novia
mis padres	explicar	problemas	primos
tú	pagar	regalos	ti
nosotros/as	prestar	ropa	nosotros
¿?	vender	¿?	¿?

Comunicación

4 **Preguntas** In pairs, take turns asking and answering to/for whom you do these activities. Answers will vary.

cantar canciones de amor (*love songs*)	escribir mensajes electrónicos
comprar ropa	mostrar fotos de un viaje
dar una fiesta	pedir dinero
decir mentiras	preparar comida (*food*) mexicana

modelo

escribir mensajes electrónicos
Estudiante 1: ¿A quién le escribes mensajes electrónicos?
Estudiante 2: Le escribo mensajes electrónicos a mi hermano.

5 **¡Somos ricos!** You and your classmates chipped in on a lottery ticket and you won! Now you want to spend money on your loved ones. In groups of three, discuss what each person is buying for family and friends. Answers will vary.

modelo

Estudiante 1: Quiero comprarle un vestido de Carolina Herrera a mi madre.
Estudiante 2: Y yo voy a darles un automóvil nuevo a mis padres.
Estudiante 3: Voy a comprarles una casa a mis padres, pero a mis amigos no les voy a dar nada.

6 **Entrevista** Use these questions to interview a classmate. Answers will vary.

1. ¿Qué tiendas, almacenes o centros comerciales prefieres?
2. ¿A quién le compras regalos cuando hay rebajas?
3. ¿A quién le prestas dinero cuando lo necesita?
4. Quiero ir de compras. ¿Cuánto dinero me puedes prestar?
5. ¿Te dan tus padres su tarjeta de crédito cuando vas de compras?

Síntesis

7 **Minidrama** In groups of three, take turns playing the roles of two shoppers and a clerk in a clothing store. The shoppers should talk about the articles of clothing they are looking for and for whom they are buying the clothes. The clerk should recommend several items based on the shoppers' descriptions. Use these expressions and also look at **Expresiones útiles** on page 195. Answers will vary.

Me queda grande/pequeño.	¿Está en rebaja?
It's big/small on me.	*Is it on sale?*
¿Tiene otro color?	También estoy buscando...
Do you have another color?	*I'm also looking for...*

4 Teaching Tips
- Have two volunteers read the model aloud. Then go through the phrases in the word bank and model question formation.
- 👤↔👤 To challenge students, have them ask follow-up questions for each item. Ex: **¿A quién le compras ropa? ¿Qué ropa le compras? ¿Dónde la compras?**

4 Expansion
👤↔👤 In pairs, give students five minutes to brainstorm as many questions as they can using different forms of the verbs in the word bank. Invite two pairs to come to the front of the class. Each pair takes a turn asking the other its questions. Encourage students to ask follow-up questions.

5 Teaching Tip Give each group a different lottery payout. Remind students they have to split it equally among the group members.

5 Expansion
←👤→ Have students research one of the different lotteries in Spain, such as **el Gordo** or **ONCE**. Have them write a brief description of how the lottery works, what it costs, and how much recent winners received.

6 Teaching Tip Take a class survey of the answers and write the results on the board.

6 Expansion
👤↔👤 Have students work in pairs and write a conversation between a parent and a child, using item 4 as a starting point. Ask students to role-play their dialogues for the class.

7 Teaching Tip To simplify, have students begin by brainstorming phrases for their role. Remind them that, except for the dialogue *between* the two shoppers, they should use **usted** in their conversations.

6.3 Preterite tense of regular verbs Tutorial

ANTE TODO In order to talk about events in the past, Spanish uses two simple tenses: the preterite and the imperfect. In this lesson, you will learn how to form the preterite tense, which is used to express actions or states completed in the past.

Preterite of regular -ar, -er, and -ir verbs

		-ar verbs comprar	-er verbs vender	-ir verbs escribir
SINGULAR FORMS	yo	compr**é** *I bought*	vend**í** *I sold*	escrib**í** *I wrote*
	tú	compr**aste**	vend**iste**	escrib**iste**
	Ud./él/ella	compr**ó**	vend**ió**	escrib**ió**
PLURAL FORMS	nosotros/as	compr**amos**	vend**imos**	escrib**imos**
	vosotros/as	compr**asteis**	vend**isteis**	escrib**isteis**
	Uds./ellos/ellas	compr**aron**	vend**ieron**	escrib**ieron**

▶ **¡Atención!** The **yo** and **Ud./él/ella** forms of all three conjugations have written accents on the last syllable to show that it is stressed.

▶ As the chart shows, the endings for regular **-er** and **-ir** verbs are identical in the preterite.

¿Qué compraste?

Compré estos aretes.

▶ Note that the **nosotros/as** forms of regular **-ar** and **-ir** verbs in the preterite are identical to the present tense forms. Context will help you determine which tense is being used.

En invierno **compramos** ropa.
In the winter, we buy clothes.

Anoche **compramos** unos zapatos.
Last night we bought some shoes.

▶ **-Ar** and **-er** verbs that have a stem change in the present tense are regular in the preterite. They do *not* have a stem change.

		PRESENT	**PRETERITE**
cerrar (e:ie)		La tienda **cierra** a las seis.	La tienda **cerró** a las seis.
volver (o:ue)		Carlitos **vuelve** tarde.	Carlitos **volvió** tarde.
jugar (u:ue)		Él **juega** al fútbol.	Él **jugó** al fútbol.

▶ **¡Atención!** **-Ir** verbs that have a stem change in the present tense also have a stem change in the preterite.

CONSULTA
There are a few high-frequency irregular verbs in the preterite. You will learn more about them in **Estructura 9.1**, p. 310.

CONSULTA
You will learn about the preterite of **-ir** stem-changing verbs in **Estructura 8.1**, p. 274.

▶ Verbs that end in **-car**, **-gar**, and **-zar** have a spelling change in the first person singular (**yo** form) in the preterite.

bus**car**		busc-		qu-		yo bus**qué**
lle**gar**	▶	lleg-	▶	gu-	▶	yo lle**gué**
empe**zar**		empez-		c-		yo empe**cé**

▶ Except for the **yo** form, all other forms of **-car**, **-gar**, and **-zar** verbs are regular in the preterite.

▶ Three other verbs—**creer**, **leer**, and **oír**—have spelling changes in the preterite. The **i** of the verb endings of **creer**, **leer**, and **oír** carries an accent in the **yo**, **tú**, **nosotros/as**, and **vosotros/as** forms, and changes to **y** in the **Ud./él/ella** and **Uds./ellos/ellas** forms.

creer		cre-		cre**í**, cre**í**ste, cre**yó**, cre**í**mos, cre**í**steis, cre**yeron**
leer	▶	le-	▶	le**í**, le**í**ste, le**yó**, le**í**mos, le**í**steis, le**yeron**
oír		o-		o**í**, o**í**ste, o**yó**, o**í**mos, o**í**steis, o**yeron**

▶ **Ver** is regular in the preterite, but none of its forms has an accent.

ver ⟶ vi, viste, vio, vimos, visteis, vieron

Words commonly used with the preterite

anoche	*last night*	**pasado/a (*adj.*)**	*last; past*
anteayer	*the day before yesterday*	**el año pasado**	*last year*
		la semana pasada	*last week*
ayer	*yesterday*	**una vez**	*once*
de repente	*suddenly*	**dos veces**	*twice*
desde... hasta...	*from... until...*	**ya**	*already*

Ayer llegué a Santiago de Cuba.   **Anoche** oí un ruido extraño.
Yesterday I arrived in Santiago de Cuba.   *Last night I heard a strange noise.*

▶ **Acabar de** + [*infinitive*] is used to say that something has just occurred. Note that **acabar** is in the present tense in this construction.

Acabo de comprar una falda.   **Acabas de ir** de compras.
I just bought a skirt.   *You just went shopping.*

More activities

vhlcentral

LM p. 35

WB pp. 64–65

Online activities

 ¡INTÉNTALO!   Provide the appropriate preterite forms of the verbs.

	comer	**salir**	**comenzar**	**leer**
1. ellas	comieron	salieron	comenzaron	leyeron
2. tú	comiste	saliste	comenzaste	leíste
3. yo	comí	salí	comencé	leí
4. nosotros	comimos	salimos	comenzamos	leímos
5. usted	comió	salió	comenzó	leyó

Teaching Tips

• Point out that verbs ending in **-car** and **-gar** are regular and have logical spelling changes in the **yo** form in order to preserve the hard **c** and **g** sounds.

• Students will learn the preterite of **dar** in **Estructura 9.1**. If you wish to present it for recognition only at this point, you can tell them that the endings are identical to **ver** in the preterite.

• Provide sentence starters using the present indicative and have students complete them in a logical manner. Ex: **Todos los días los estudiantes llegan temprano, pero anteayer… (llegaron tarde.)**

• Practice verbs with spelling changes in the preterite by asking students about things they read, heard, and saw yesterday. Ex: **¿Leíste las noticias ayer? ¿Quiénes vieron el pronóstico del tiempo? Yo oí que va a llover hoy. ¿Qué oyeron ustedes?**

• Add a visual aspect to this grammar presentation. Use magazine pictures to demonstrate **acabar de**. Ex: **¿Quién acaba de ganar? (Serena Williams acaba de ganar.) ¿Qué acaban de ver ellos? (Acaban de ver una película.)**

TEACHING OPTIONS

Game Divide the class into teams of six and have them sit in rows. Call out the infinitive of a verb. The first person writes the preterite **yo** form on a sheet of paper and passes it to the second person, who writes the **tú** form, and so on. The sixth checks spelling. If all forms are correct, the team gets a point. Continue play, having team members rotate positions for each round. The team with the most points after six rounds wins.

Extra Practice Have students write down five things they did yesterday. Ask students questions about what they did to elicit as many different conjugations as possible. Ex: _____, ¿leíste las noticias ayer? ¿Quién más leyó las noticias ayer?... _____ y _____, ustedes dos leyeron las noticias ayer, ¿verdad? ¿Quiénes leyeron las noticias ayer?

Práctica

1 Completar   Complete each sentence by choosing the correct verb and putting it in the preterite.

1. El viernes a las cuatro de la tarde, la profesora Mora ___asistió___ (asistir, costar, usar) a una reunión (*meeting*) de profesores.
2. A la una, yo ___llegué___ (llegar, bucear, llevar) a la tienda con mis amigos.
3. Mis amigos y yo ___compramos___ (comprar, regatear, gastar) dos o tres cosas.
4. Yo ___compré___ (costar, comprar, escribir) unos pantalones negros y mi amigo Mateo ___compró___ (gastar, pasear, comprar) una camisa azul.
5. Después, nosotros ___comimos___ (llevar, vivir, comer) cerca de un mercado.
6. A las tres, Pepe ___habló___ (hablar, pasear, nadar) con su novia por teléfono.
7. El sábado por la tarde, mi mamá ___escribió___ (escribir, beber, vivir) una carta.
8. El domingo mi tía ___decidió___ (decidir, salir, escribir) comprarme un traje.
9. A las cuatro de la tarde, mi tía ___encontró___ (beber, salir, encontrar) el traje y después nosotras ___vimos___ (acabar, ver, salir) una película.

2 Preguntas   Ask a partner if he/she did these activities. Your partner will respond that he/she already did or has just done them. Take turns asking and answering.

> **modelo**
>
> leer la lección
> **Estudiante 1:** *¿Leíste la lección?*
> **Estudiante 2:** *Sí, ya la leí./Sí, acabo de leerla.*

1. lavar (*to wash*) la ropa
2. escribir el mensaje electrónico
3. oír las noticias (*news*)
4. comprar pantalones cortos
5. practicar los verbos
6. pagar la cuenta (*bill*)
7. empezar la composición
8. ver la película *Diarios de motocicleta*

1. E1: ¿Lavaste la ropa?
   E2: Sí, ya la lavé./Acabo de lavarla.
2. E1: ¿Escribiste el mensaje electrónico?
   E2: Sí, ya lo escribí./Acabo de escribirlo.
3. E1: ¿Oíste las noticias?
   E2: Sí, ya las oí./Acabo de oírlas.
4. E1: ¿Compraste pantalones cortos?
   E2: Sí, ya los compré./Acabo de comprarlos.
5. E1: ¿Practicaste los verbos?
   E2: Sí, ya los practiqué./Acabo de practicarlos.
6. E1: ¿Pagaste la cuenta?
   E2: Sí, ya la pagué./Acabo de pagarla.
7. E1: ¿Empezaste la composición?
   E2: Sí, ya la empecé./Acabo de empezarla.
8. E1: ¿Viste la película *Diarios de motocicleta*?
   E2: Sí, ya la vi./Acabo de verla.

NOTA CULTURAL

Based on Ernesto "Che" Guevara's diaries, *Diarios de motocicleta* (2004) traces the road trip of Che (played by Gael García Bernal) with his friend Alberto Granado (played by Rodrigo de la Serna) through Argentina, Chile, Peru, Colombia, and Venezuela.

3 ¿Cuándo?   Use the time expressions to talk about when you and others did the activities.   Answers will vary.

| anoche | anteayer | el mes pasado | una vez |
| ayer | la semana pasada | el año pasado | dos veces |

1. mi compañero/a de cuarto: llegar tarde (*late*) a clase
2. mi mejor (*best*) amigo/a: salir con un(a) chico/a guapo/a
3. mis padres: ver una película
4. yo: llevar un traje/vestido
5. el presidente/primer ministro de mi país: asistir a una conferencia internacional
6. mis amigos y yo: comer en un restaurante
7. ¿?: comprar algo (*something*) bueno, bonito y barato

1 Teaching Tip To simplify, tell students to read through the items once and circle the correct infinitive for each sentence. Then ask them to read the sentences a second time and underline the subject for each verb. Finally, have them conjugate the infinitives.

1 Expansion
Ask questions about the speaker's weekend. Have students answer with complete sentences. Ex: **¿Quién asistió a una reunión? ¿Qué compraron los amigos?**

2 Expansion Have students repeat the activity, using **ustedes** as the subject of the questions and **nosotros** in the answers.

3 Teaching Tips
- To simplify, have students work with a partner to quickly review the preterite forms of the verbs in the activity.
- After students have completed item 7, discuss **las tres bes.** Ask students which one is most important to them when they go shopping.

3 Expansion
Have students share their responses with a partner, who will ask follow-up questions. Ex: **—Mis padres vieron una película la semana pasada. —¿Qué película vieron? —Vieron *The Post*. —¿Qué les pareció? —Les pareció muy buena.**

TEACHING OPTIONS

TPR Have students stand in a circle. Begin by tossing a ball to a student and naming an infinitive and subject pronoun (Ex: **cerrar/tú**). The student who catches the ball has four seconds to provide the correct preterite form, toss the ball to another student, and name another infinitive and pronoun.
Extra Practice Ask students to imagine they have just visited an open-air market for the first time. Have them write a letter to a friend describing what they saw and did there. Then, ask students to exchange their letters with a classmate, who will respond.
Small Groups In groups of three, have students write down three sentences using verbs in the preterite. Then ask each group to act out its sentences for the class. When someone guesses the action, the group writes the sentence on the board.

Comunicación

4 **Ayer** Jot down at what time you did these activities yesterday. Then get together with a classmate and find out at what time he or she did these activities. Answers will vary.

1. desayunar
2. empezar la primera clase
3. almorzar
4. ver a un(a) amigo/a
5. salir de clase
6. volver a la residencia/casa

5 **Las vacaciones** Get together with a partner and use the pictures to tell him or her about your vacation with friends. Answers will vary.

6 **El fin de semana** Your instructor will give you and your partner different incomplete charts about what four employees at **Almacén Gigante** did last weekend. After you fill out the chart based on each other's information, you will fill out the final column about your partner. Answers will vary.

Síntesis

7 **Conversación** Get together with a partner and have a conversation about what you did last week using the verbs. Don't forget to include school activities, shopping, and pastimes. Answers will vary.

acampar	comer	gastar	tomar
asistir	comprar	hablar	trabajar
bailar	correr	jugar	vender
beber	escribir	leer	ver
buscar	estudiar	oír	viajar

TEACHING OPTIONS

Large Group Have students stand up. Tell them to create a story chain about a student who had a very bad day. Begin the story by saying: **Ayer, Rigoberto pasó un día desastroso.** In order to sit down, students must contribute to the story. Call on a student to tell how **Rigoberto** began his day. The second person tells what happened next, and so on, until only one student remains. That person must conclude the story.

Extra Practice For homework, have students make a "to do" list at the beginning of their day. Then, ask students to return to their lists at the end of the day and write sentences stating which activities they completed. Ex: **estudiar; No, no estudié.**

---

4 **Teaching Tips**
- After forming pairs, model question formation and possible responses for the first two items.
- 👥 Encourage students to ask follow-up questions. Ex: **1. ¿Dónde desayunaste, en casa o en la cafetería? ¿Qué comiste?**

5 **Teaching Tips**
- You may wish to provide extra vocabulary. Ex: **la discoteca**
- 👥 Have students first state where they traveled and when. Then have them identify the people in the photos, stating their names and their relationship to them and describing their personalities. Finally, students should tell what everyone did on the trip. Encourage students to ask each other follow-up questions to learn more about their partner's trip.

5 **Expansion**
👥 After completing the activity orally, have students write a paragraph about their vacation, basing their account on the photos.

6 **Teaching Tip** Divide the class into pairs and distribute the handouts from the Activity Pack (Activity Pack/Supersite) that correspond to this Information Gap Activity. Give students ten minutes to complete the activity.

6 **Expansion** Have students tell the class about any activities that both their partner and one of the **Almacén Gigante** employees did. Ex: **La señora Zapata leyó un libro y _____ también. Los dos leyeron un libro.**

7 **Teaching Tips**
- 👥 Have volunteers rehearse their conversation, then present it to the class.
- Have volunteers report to the class what their partners did last week.

Estructura **209**

6.4 Demonstrative adjectives and pronouns

Demonstrative adjectives   Tutorial

ANTE TODO   In Spanish, as in English, demonstrative adjectives are words that "demonstrate" or "point out" nouns. Demonstrative adjectives precede the nouns they modify and, like other Spanish adjectives you have studied, agree with them in gender and number. Observe these examples and then study the chart.

esta camisa	**ese** vendedor	**aquellos** zapatos
this shirt	*that salesman*	*those shoes (over there)*

Demonstrative adjectives

	Singular		Plural		
	MASCULINE	FEMININE	MASCULINE	FEMININE	
	este	**esta**	**estos**	**estas**	*this; these*
	ese	**esa**	**esos**	**esas**	*that; those*
	aquel	**aquella**	**aquellos**	**aquellas**	*that; those (over there)*

▶ There are three sets of demonstrative adjectives. To determine which one to use, you must establish the relationship between the speaker and the noun(s) being pointed out.

▶ The demonstrative adjectives **este**, **esta**, **estos**, and **estas** are used to point out things that are close to the speaker and the listener.

Me gustan estos zapatos.

▶ The demonstrative adjectives **ese**, **esa**, **esos**, and **esas** are used to point out things that are not close in space and time to the speaker. They may, however, be close to the listener.

Prefiero esos zapatos.

▶ The demonstrative adjectives **aquel**, **aquella**, **aquellos**, and **aquellas** are used to point out things that are far away from the speaker and the listener.

> *Aquel auto es de mi hermana.*

Demonstrative pronouns

▶ Demonstrative pronouns are identical to their corresponding demonstrative adjectives, with the exception that they traditionally carry an accent mark on the stressed vowel. The **Real Academia** no longer requires this accent, but it is still used.

Demonstrative pronouns

Singular		Plural	
MASCULINE	FEMININE	MASCULINE	FEMININE
éste	ésta	éstos	éstas
ése	ésa	ésos	ésas
aquél	aquélla	aquéllos	aquéllas

—¿Quieres comprar **este suéter**?
Do you want to buy this sweater?

—No, no quiero **éste**. Quiero **ése**.
No, I don't want this one. I want that one.

—¿Vas a leer **estas revistas**?
Are you going to read these magazines?

—Sí, voy a leer **éstas**. También voy a leer **aquéllas**.
Yes, I'm going to read these. I'll also read those (over there).

▶ **¡Atención!** Like demonstrative adjectives, demonstrative pronouns agree in gender and number with the corresponding noun.

Este libro es de Pablito.   **Éstos** son de Juana.

▶ There are three neuter demonstrative pronouns: **esto**, **eso**, and **aquello**. These forms refer to unidentified or unspecified things, situations, ideas, and concepts. They do not change in gender or number and never carry an accent mark.

—¿Qué es **esto**?
What's this?

—**Eso** es interesante.
That's interesting.

—**Aquello** es bonito.
That's pretty.

 ¡INTÉNTALO! Provide the correct form of the demonstrative adjective for these nouns.

1. la falda / este   esta falda
2. los países / aquel   aquellos países
3. los estudiantes / este   estos estudiantes
4. la ventana / ese   esa ventana
5. el chico / aquel   aquel chico
6. los periodistas / ese   esos periodistas
7. las sandalias / este   estas sandalias
8. las chicas / aquel   aquellas chicas

More activities

vhlcentral

LM p. 36

WB pp. 66–68

Online activities

Práctica

1 **Expansion** To challenge students, ask them to expand each sentence with a phrase that includes a demonstrative pronoun. Ex: **Aquellos sombreros son muy elegantes, pero éstos son más baratos.**

1 Cambiar Make the singular sentences plural and the plural sentences singular.

> **modelo**
> Estas camisas son blancas.
> *Esta camisa es blanca.*

1. Aquellos sombreros son muy elegantes. *Aquel sombrero es muy elegante.*
2. Ese abrigo es muy caro. *Esos abrigos son muy caros.*
3. Estos cinturones son hermosos. *Este cinturón es hermoso.*
4. ¿Quieres ir a aquel almacén? *¿Quieres ir a aquellos almacenes?*
5. Estas faldas son muy cortas. *Esta falda es muy corta.*
6. Esos precios son muy buenos. *Ese precio es muy bueno.*
7. Esas blusas son baratas. *Esa blusa es barata.*
8. Esta corbata hace juego con mi traje. *Estas corbatas hacen juego con mis trajes.*

2 **Teaching Tips**
• To simplify, have students underline the nouns that will be replaced by demonstrative pronouns.
• As you go over the activity, write each demonstrative pronoun on the board so that students may verify that they have placed the accent marks correctly. You may choose to have your students leave out the accents.

2 Completar Complete the sentences with the correct demonstrative pronouns.

1. Esta guayabera es bonita, pero prefiero ____ésa____. (*that one*)
2. Estas corbatas rojas son muy bonitas, pero ____ésas____ son fabulosas. (*those*)
3. No me gustan esos zapatos. Voy a comprar ____éstos____. (*these*)
4. ¿Vas a comprar ese traje o ____éste____? (*this one*)
5. Estos cinturones cuestan demasiado. Prefiero ____aquéllos____. (*those over there*)
6. ¿Te gustan esas botas o ____éstas____? (*these*)
7. Esa bolsa roja es bonita, pero prefiero ____aquélla____. (*that one over there*)
8. ¿Prefieres estos pantalones o ____ésos____? (*those*)
9. No voy a comprar estas botas; voy a comprar ____aquéllas____. (*those over there*)
10. Me gusta este vestido, pero voy a comprar ____ése____. (*that one*)
11. Me gusta ese almacén, pero ____aquél____ es mejor (*better*). (*that one over there*)
12. Esa blusa es bonita, pero cuesta demasiado. Voy a comprar ____ésta____. (*this one*)

3 **Expansion**
Ask students to find a photo featuring different articles of clothing or to draw several articles of clothing. Have them write five statements like that of the **Estudiante 1** model in part one of this activity. Then have students exchange their statements and photo/drawing with a partner to write responses like that of the **Estudiante 2** model.

3 Describir With your partner, look for two items in the classroom that are one of these colors: **amarillo, azul, blanco, marrón, negro, verde, rojo.** Take turns pointing them out to each other, first using demonstrative adjectives, and then demonstrative pronouns. *Answers will vary.*

> **modelo**
> azul
> **Estudiante 1:** *Esta silla es azul. Aquella mochila es azul.*
> **Estudiante 2:** *Ésta es azul. Aquélla es azul.*

Now use demonstrative adjectives and pronouns to discuss the colors of your classmates' clothing. One of you can ask a question about an article of clothing, using the wrong color. Your partner will correct you and point out that color somewhere else in the room.

> **modelo**
> **Estudiante 1:** *¿Esa camisa es negra?*
> **Estudiante 2:** *No, ésa es azul. Aquélla es negra.*

TEACHING OPTIONS

Pairs Have pairs role-play a dialogue between friends shopping for clothes. Student A tries to convince the friend that the clothes he or she wants to buy are not attractive. Student A suggests other items of clothing, but the friend does not agree. Students should use as many demonstrative adjectives and pronouns as possible.
Game Divide the class into two teams. Post pictures of different versions of the same object (Ex: sedan, sports car, all-terrain vehicle) on the board. Assign each a dollar figure, but do not share the prices with the class. Team A guesses the price of each object, using demonstrative adjectives and pronouns. Team B either agrees or guesses a higher or lower price. The team that guesses the closest price, wins. Ex: **Este carro cuesta $20.000, ése cuesta $35.000 y aquél cuesta $18.000.**

Comunicación

4 **Conversación** With a classmate, use demonstrative adjectives and pronouns to ask each other questions about the people around you. *Answers will vary.*

> ¿A qué hora…?   ¿Cuántos años tiene(n)…?
> ¿Cómo es/son…?   ¿De dónde es/son…?
> ¿Cómo se llama…?   ¿De quién es/son…?
> ¿Cuándo…?   ¿Qué clases toma(n)…?

modelo

Estudiante 1: ¿Cómo se llama esa chica?
Estudiante 2: Se llama Rebeca.
Estudiante 1: ¿A qué hora llegó aquel chico a la clase?
Estudiante 2: A las nueve.

4 Teaching Tip
👥↔👤 To challenge students, have both partners ask a question for each item in the word bank and at least one other question using an interrogative expression that is not included. Encourage students to ask follow-up questions.

5 **En una tienda** You and a classmate are in Madrid shopping at Zara. Study the floor plan, then have a conversation about your surroundings. Use demonstrative adjectives and pronouns. *Answers will vary.*

modelo

Estudiante 1: Me gusta este suéter gris.
Estudiante 2: Yo prefiero aquella chaqueta azul.

NOTA CULTURAL

Zara is an international clothing company based in Spain. Its innovative processes take a product from the design room to the manufacturing shelves in less than a month. This means that the merchandise is constantly changing to keep up with the most current trends.

Hombres — chaquetas — suéteres — camisas — camisetas — botas — pantalones cortos — pantalones — Estudiante 1

blusas — chaquetas — **Mujeres** — vestidos — pantalones cortos — zapatos — faldas — Estudiante 2

5 Expansion
👥↔👥 Divide the class into small groups and have students role-play a situation between a salesperson and two customers. The customers should ask about the different items of clothing pictured and the salesperson will answer. They talk about how the items fit and their cost. The customers then express their preferences and decide which items to buy.

Síntesis

6 **Diferencias** Your instructor will give you and a partner each a drawing of a store. They are almost identical, but not quite. Use demonstrative adjectives and pronouns to find seven differences. *Answers will vary.*

modelo

Estudiante 1: Aquellas gafas de sol son feas, ¿verdad?
Estudiante 2: No. Aquellas gafas de sol son hermosas.

6 Teaching Tip Divide the class into pairs and distribute the handouts from the Activity Pack (Activity Pack/Supersite) that correspond with this Information Gap Activity. Give students ten minutes to complete the activity.

6 Expansion Have pairs work together with another pair to compare the seven responses that confirmed the seven differences. Ex: **No. Aquellas gafas de sol no son feas. Aquéllas son hermosas.** Ask a few groups to share some of the sentences with the class.

TEACHING OPTIONS

Pairs ↔👤→ Ask students to write a conversation between two people sitting at a busy sidewalk café in the city. They are watching the people who walk by, asking each other questions about what the passersby are doing, and making comments on their clothing. Students should use as many demonstrative adjectives and pronouns as possible in their conversations. Invite several pairs to present their conversations to the class.

Small Groups 👥↔👤 Ask students to bring in pictures of their families, a sports team, a group of friends, etc. Have them take turns asking about and identifying the people in the pictures. Ex: —¿Quién es aquella mujer? —¿Cuál? —Aquélla con la camiseta roja. —Es mi…

Recapitulación

RESUMEN GRAMATICAL

Review the grammar concepts you have learned in this lesson by completing these activities.

1 Completar Complete the chart with the correct preterite or infinitive form of the verbs. **30 pts.**

Infinitive	yo	ella	ellos
tomar	tomé	tomó	tomaron
abrir	abrí	abrió	abrieron
comprender	comprendí	comprendió	comprendieron
leer	leí	leyó	leyeron
pagar	pagué	pagó	pagaron

2 En la tienda Complete the conversation with demonstrative adjectives and pronouns. **14 pts.**

CLIENTE Buenos días, señorita. Deseo comprar (1) ____esta____ corbata.

VENDEDORA Muy bien, señor. ¿No le interesa mirar (2) ____aquellos____ trajes que están allá? Hay unos que hacen juego con la corbata.

CLIENTE (3) ____Aquéllos____ de allá son de lana, ¿no? Prefiero ver (4) ____ese____ traje marrón que está detrás de usted.

VENDEDORA Estupendo. Como puede ver, es de seda. Cuesta seiscientos cincuenta dólares.

CLIENTE Ah… eh… no, creo que sólo voy a comprar la corbata, gracias.

VENDEDORA Bueno… si busca algo más económico, hay rebaja en (5) ____aquellos____ sombreros de allá. Cuestan sólo treinta dólares.

CLIENTE ¡Magnífico! Me gusta (6) ____aquél____, el blanco que está hasta arriba (*at the top*). Y quiero pagar todo con (7) ____esta____ tarjeta.

VENDEDORA Sí, señor. Ahora mismo le traigo el sombrero.

6.1 Saber and conocer *p. 200*

saber	conocer
sé	conozco
sabes	conoces
sabe	conoce
sabemos	conocemos
sabéis	conocéis
saben	conocen

► **saber** = to know facts/how to do something
► **conocer** = to know a person, place, or thing

6.2 Indirect object pronouns *pp. 202–203*

Indirect object pronouns

Singular	Plural
me	nos
te	os
le	les

► **dar** = **doy**, das, da, damos, dais, dan
► **decir (e:i)** = **digo**, dices, dice, decimos, decís, dicen

6.3 Preterite tense of regular verbs *pp. 206–207*

comprar	vender	escribir
compré	vendí	escribí
compraste	vendiste	escribiste
compró	vendió	escribió
compramos	vendimos	escribimos
comprasteis	vendisteis	escribisteis
compraron	vendieron	escribieron

Verbs with spelling changes in the preterite

► -car: buscar → yo busqué
► -gar: llegar → yo llegué
► -zar: empezar → yo empecé
► creer: creí, creíste, creyó, creímos, creísteis, creyeron
► leer: leí, leíste, leyó, leímos, leísteis, leyeron
► oír: oí, oíste, oyó, oímos, oísteis, oyeron
► ver: vi, viste, vio, vimos, visteis, vieron

3 **¿Saber o conocer?** Complete each dialogue with the correct form of **saber** or **conocer**. **20 pts.**

1. —¿Qué ____sabes____ hacer tú?
   —(Yo) ____Sé____ jugar al fútbol.
2. —¿____Conoces____ tú esta tienda de ropa?
   —No, (yo) no la ____conozco____. ¿Es buena?
3. —¿Tus padres no ____conocen____ a tu novio?
   —No, ¡ellos no ____saben____ que tengo novio!
4. —Mi compañero de cuarto todavía no me ____conoce____ bien.
   —Y tú, ¿lo quieres ____conocer____ a él?
5. —¿____Saben____ ustedes dónde está el mercado?
   —No, nosotros no ____conocemos____ bien esta ciudad.

4 **Oraciones** Form complete sentences using the information provided. Use indirect object pronouns and the present tense of the verbs. **10 pts.**

1. Javier / prestar / el abrigo / a Maripili
   Javier le presta el abrigo a Maripili.
2. nosotros / vender / ropa / a los clientes
   Nosotros les vendemos ropa a los clientes.
3. el vendedor / traer / las camisetas / a mis amigos y a mí
   El vendedor nos trae las camisetas (a mis amigos y a mí).
4. yo / querer dar / consejos / a ti
   Yo quiero darte consejos (a ti)./Yo te quiero dar consejos (a ti).
5. ¿tú / ir a comprar / un regalo / a mí?
   ¿Tú vas a comprarme un regalo (a mí)?/¿Tú me vas a comprar un regalo (a mí)?

5 **Mi última compra** Write a short paragraph describing the last time you went shopping. Use at least four verbs in the preterite tense. **26 pts.** *Answers will vary.*

> **modelo**
> El viernes pasado, busqué unos zapatos en el centro comercial...

6 **Poema** Write the missing words to complete the excerpt from the poem *Romance sonámbulo* by Federico García Lorca. **4 EXTRA points!**

> 66 Verde que ___te___ quiero verde.
> Verde viento. Verdes ramas°.
> El barco sobre la mar
> y el caballo en la montaña, [...]
> Verde que te quiero ___verde___ (*green*). 99

ramas *branches*

6.4 Demonstrative adjectives and pronouns · pp. 210–211

Demonstrative adjectives

Singular		Plural	
Masc.	Fem.	Masc.	Fem.
este	esta	estos	estas
ese	esa	esos	esas
aquel	aquella	aquellos	aquellas

Demonstrative pronouns

Singular		Plural	
Masc.	Fem.	Masc.	Fem.
éste	ésta	éstos	éstas
ése	ésa	ésos	ésas
aquél	aquélla	aquéllos	aquéllas

3 Teaching Tip Ask students to explain why they chose **saber** or **conocer** in each case.

3 Expansion
Have students choose one dialogue from this activity and write a continuation. Encourage them to use at least one more example each of **saber** and **conocer**.

4 Teaching Tips
- Ask a volunteer to model the first sentence for the class.
- Before forming sentences, have students identify the indirect object in each item.
- Remind students of the possible positions for indirect object pronouns when using an infinitive.

4 Expansion
- Ask students to create three dehydrated sentences similar to those in **Actividad 4**. Have them exchange papers with a classmate and form complete sentences.
- For items 1–4, have students write questions that would elicit these statements. Ex: **1. ¿A quién le presta el abrigo Javier?/¿Qué le presta Javier a Maripili?** For item 5, have them write a response.

5 Teaching Tip To add a visual aspect to this activity, have students create a time line of what they did when they went shopping.

6 Teaching Tips
- Tell students to read through the whole excerpt before filling in the blanks.
- Have a volunteer read the excerpt aloud.

TEACHING OPTIONS

Extra Practice Add an auditory aspect to this grammar review. Read each of these sentences twice, pausing after the second time for students to write: **1. Ayer empecé a leer sobre los diseñadores hispanos. 2. Ellas buscaron unas bolsas en el mercado al aire libre. 3. El dependiente vendió cinco camisetas. 4. Nosotras oímos una explosión. 5. El joven le leyó el libro a su hermanito. 6. Raúl vio una película anoche.**

Game Divide the class into two teams. Indicate a member of each team and call out a color. The first student to find an object or article of clothing in the room, point to it, and use the correct form of a demonstrative adjective earns a point for their team. Ex: **¡Aquella camiseta es morada!** The team with the most points at the end wins.

Lectura

communication cultures
NATIONAL STANDARDS

Antes de leer

Estrategia

Skimming

Skimming involves quickly reading through a document to absorb its general meaning. This allows you to understand the main ideas without having to read word for word. When you skim a text, you might want to look at its title and subtitles. You might also want to read the first sentence of each paragraph.

 Examinar el texto

Look at the format of the reading selection. How is it organized? What does the organization of the document tell you about its content?

Buscar cognados

Scan the reading selection to locate at least five cognates. Based on the cognates, what do you think the reading selection is about? *Answers will vary. Suggested answers for 1–5: elegancia, blusas, accesorios, pantalones, precio.*

1. _____   4. _____
2. _____   5. _____
3. _____

The reading selection is about <u>a sale in a store</u>.

Impresiones generales

Now skim the reading selection to understand its general meaning. Jot down your impressions. What new information did you learn about the document by skimming it? Based on all the information you now have, answer these questions in Spanish.

1. Who created this document? *un almacén/una tienda*
2. What is its purpose? *vender ropa*
3. Who is its intended audience? *gente que quiere comprar ropa*

More activities

vhlcentral | Online activities

 Corona

http://corona.cl

Corona

¡Corona tiene las ofertas más locas del verano!

La tienda más elegante de la ciudad con precios increíbles

niños | **mujeres** | casa | baño | equipaje

Faldas largas
ROPA BONITA
Algodón. De distintos colores
Talla mediana
Precio especial: 8.000 pesos

Blusas de seda
BAMBÚ
De cuadros y de lunares
Ahora: 21.000 pesos
40% de rebaja

Vestido de algodón
PANAMÁ
Colores blanco, azul y verde
Ahora: 18.000 pesos
30% de rebaja

Accesorios
BELLEZA
Cinturones, gafas de sol, sombreros, medias
Diversos estilos
Todos con un 40% de rebaja

Carteras
ELEGANCIA
Colores anaranjado, blanco, rosado y amarillo
Ahora: 15.000 pesos
50% de rebaja

Sandalias de playa
GINO
Números del 35 al 38
A sólo 12.000 pesos
50% de descuento

Lunes a sábado de 9 a 21 horas.
Domingo de 10 a 14 horas.

Después de leer

Real° Liquidación° ¡Grandes rebajas!

¡La rebaja está de moda en Corona!

y con la tarjeta de crédito más conveniente del mercado.

| bebé | hombres | jardín | joyas | electrónica |

Chaquetas
CASINO
Microfibra. Colores negro, café y gris.
Tallas: P, M, G, XG
Ahora: 22.500 pesos

Traje inglés
GALES
Modelos originales
Ahora: 105.000 pesos
30% de rebaja

Pantalones
OCÉANO
Colores negro, gris y café
Ahora: 11.500 pesos
30% de rebaja

Accesorios
GUAPO
Gafas de sol, corbatas, cinturones, calcetines
Diversos estilos
Todos con un 40% de rebaja

Zapatos
COLOR
Italianos y franceses
Números del 40 al 45
A sólo 20.000 pesos

Ropa interior
ATLÁNTICO
Tallas: P, M, G
Colores blanco, negro y gris
40% de rebaja

Real *Royal* Liquidación *Clearance sale*

Por la compra de 40.000 pesos, puede llevar un regalo gratis.
- Un hermoso cinturón de mujer
- Un par de calcetines
- Una corbata de seda
- Una bolsa para la playa
- Una mochila
- Unas medias

Completar

Complete this paragraph with the correct forms of the words.

almacén	hacer juego	tarjeta de crédito
caro	increíble	tienda
dinero	pantalones	verano
falda	rebaja	zapato

En este anuncio, el ___almacén___ Corona anuncia la liquidación de ___verano___ con grandes ___rebajas___. Con muy poco ___dinero___ usted puede conseguir ropa fina y elegante. Si no tiene dinero en efectivo, puede utilizar su ___tarjeta de crédito___ y pagar luego. Para el hombre con gustos refinados, hay ___zapatos___ importados de París y Roma. La señora elegante puede encontrar blusas de seda que ___hacen juego___ con todo tipo de ___pantalones/faldas___ o ___faldas/pantalones___. Los precios de esta liquidación son realmente ___increíbles___.

¿Cierto o falso?

Indicate whether each statement is **cierto** or **falso**. Correct the false statements.

1. Hay sandalias de playa. Cierto.
2. Las corbatas tienen una rebaja del 30%. Falso. Tienen una rebaja del 40%.
3. El almacén Corona tiene un departamento de zapatos. Cierto.
4. Normalmente las sandalias cuestan 22.000 pesos. Falso. Normalmente cuestan 24.000 pesos.
5. Cuando gastas 30.000 pesos en la tienda, llevas un regalo gratis. Falso. Cuando gastas 40.000 pesos en la tienda, llevas un regalo gratis.
6. Tienen carteras amarillas. Cierto.

Preguntas

In pairs, take turns asking and answering these questions. Answers will vary.

1. Imagina que vas a ir a la tienda Corona. ¿Qué departamentos vas a visitar? ¿El departamento de ropa para mujeres, el departamento de ropa para hombres...?
2. ¿Qué vas a buscar en Corona?
3. ¿Hay tiendas similares a la tienda Corona en tu pueblo o ciudad? ¿Cómo se llaman? ¿Tienen muchas gangas?

Completar Have students quickly review the lesson vocabulary on pages 190–192 and 195 before they do this activity. Make sure that they understand the meaning of **el hombre con gustos refinados.**

¿Cierto o falso? Give students these sentences as items 7–10: **7. Las sandalias de playa no tienen una rebaja grande.** (Falso. Tienen una rebaja del 50%.) **8. El almacén Corona está cerrado los domingos.** (Falso. El almacén Corona está abierto de 10:00 a 14:00 los domingos.) **9. Se pueden conseguir carteras rosadas y blancas en rebaja.** (Cierto.) **10. Un señor puede comprar una chaqueta gris de talla pequeña.** (Cierto.)

Preguntas
Have small groups put together an ad for a store where they shop. Have them use the **Almacén Corona** ad as a model. If two or more groups chose the same store, compare their ads in a follow-up discussion with the class.

TEACHING OPTIONS

TPR Write items of clothing on slips of paper. Have a volunteer choose a slip and mime putting on the item of clothing that he or she draws. The first student to correctly identify the item receives a point. The student with the most points at the end wins.
Heritage Speakers Ask heritage speakers to share phrases they know to ask the price of items. Ex: **¿Cuánto vale?** or **¿A cómo está(n)...?**

Game In pairs, have students play a modified version of **20 Preguntas**. Student A thinks of an item of clothing. Student B asks questions and guesses the name of the item. Student A keeps track of the number of questions and guesses. Allow partners to ask a total of ten questions and attempt to guess three times before moving on to the next item. The pair with the fewest questions overall wins.

Section Goals

In **Escritura**, students will:
- conduct an interview
- integrate vocabulary and structures taught in **Lección 6** into a written report
- report on an interview

Instructional Resource
Supersite

Estrategia Model an interview for students by asking a volunteer a few of the questions on this page. Then model how to report on an interview by transcribing verbatim a section of the dialogue on the board. Then give an example each of summarizing and summarizing but quoting occasionally.

Tema Tell students that they may interview a classmate or another Spanish-speaking student they know. Encourage them to take notes as they conduct the interview or record it. They might want to brainstorm additional questions with a classmate that they are not planning to interview. Introduce terms such as **entrevista, entrevistar, diálogo,** and **citas** as you present the activity.

Escritura

Estrategia

How to report an interview

There are several ways to prepare a written report about an interview. For example, you can transcribe the interview verbatim, you can simply summarize it, or you can summarize it but quote the speakers occasionally. In any event, the report should begin with an interesting title and a brief introduction, which may include the five Ws (*what, where, when, who, why*) and the H (*how*) of the interview. The report should end with an interesting conclusion. Note that when you transcribe dialogue in Spanish, you should pay careful attention to format and punctuation.

Writing dialogue in Spanish

- If you need to transcribe an interview verbatim, you can use speakers' names to indicate a change of speaker.

  CARMELA ¿Qué compraste? ¿Encontraste muchas gangas?

  ROBERTO Sí, muchas. Compré un suéter, una camisa y dos corbatas. Y tú, ¿qué compraste?

  CARMELA Una blusa y una falda muy bonitas. ¿Cuánto costó tu camisa?

  ROBERTO Sólo diez dólares. ¿Cuánto costó tu blusa?

  CARMELA Veinte dólares.

- You can also use a dash (*raya*) to mark the beginning of each speaker's words.

  —¿Qué compraste?

  —Un suéter y una camisa muy bonitos. Y tú, ¿encontraste muchas gangas?

  —Sí... compré dos blusas, tres camisetas y un par de zapatos.

  —¡A ver!

Tema

Escribe un informe

Write a report for the school newspaper about an interview you conducted with a student about his or her shopping habits and clothing preferences. First, brainstorm a list of interview questions. Then conduct the interview using the questions as a guide, but feel free to ask other questions as they occur to you.

Examples of questions:

- ► ¿Cuándo vas de compras?
- ► ¿Adónde vas de compras?
- ► ¿Con quién vas de compras?
- ► ¿Qué tiendas, almacenes o centros comerciales prefieres?
- ► ¿Compras ropa de catálogos o en línea?
- ► ¿Prefieres comprar ropa cara o barata? ¿Por qué? ¿Te gusta buscar gangas?
- ► ¿Qué ropa llevas cuando vas a clase?
- ► ¿Qué ropa llevas cuando sales a bailar?
- ► ¿Qué ropa llevas cuando practicas un deporte?
- ► ¿Cuáles son tus colores favoritos? ¿Compras mucha ropa de esos colores?
- ► ¿Les das ropa a tu familia o a tus amigos/as?

EVALUATION: Informe

Criteria	Scale
Content	1 2 3 4 5
Organization	1 2 3 4 5
Accuracy	1 2 3 4 5
Creativity	1 2 3 4 5

Scoring	
Excellent	18–20 points
Good	14–17 points
Satisfactory	10–13 points
Unsatisfactory	< 10 points

Escuchar

Antes de escuchar

> ### Estrategia
> #### Listening for linguistic cues
>
> You can enhance your listening comprehension by listening for specific linguistic cues. For example, if you listen for the endings of conjugated verbs, or for familiar constructions, such as **acabar de** + [*infinitive*] or **ir a** + [*infinitive*], you can find out whether an event already took place, is taking place now, or will take place in the future. Verb endings also give clues about who is participating in the action.
>
> To practice listening for linguistic cues, you will now listen to four sentences. As you listen, note whether each sentence refers to a past, present, or future action. Also jot down the subject of each sentence.

Preparación

Based on the photograph, what do you think Marisol has recently done? What do you think Marisol and Alicia are talking about? What else can you guess about their conversation from the visual clues in the photograph?

Ahora escucha

 La ropa

Now you are going to hear Marisol and Alicia's conversation. Make a list of the clothing items that each person mentions. Then put a check mark after the item if the person actually purchased it.

Marisol		Alicia	
1.	pantalones ✔	1.	falda
2.	blusa ✔	2.	blusa
3.	_____	3.	zapatos
4.	_____	4.	cinturón

Marisol   Alicia

Comprensión

¿Cierto o falso?

Indicate whether each statement is **cierto** or **falso.** Then correct the false statements.

1. Marisol y Alicia acaban de ir de compras juntas (*together*).   Falso. Marisol acaba de ir de compras.
2. Marisol va a comprar unos pantalones y una blusa mañana.   Falso. Marisol ya los compró.
3. Marisol compró una blusa de cuadros.   Cierto.
4. Alicia compró unos zapatos nuevos hoy.   Falso. Alicia va a comprar unos zapatos nuevos.
5. Alicia y Marisol van a ir al café.   Cierto.
6. Marisol gastó todo el dinero de la semana en ropa nueva.   Cierto.

Preguntas

Discuss the following questions with a classmate.   Answers will vary.
1. ¿Crees que Alicia y Marisol son buenas amigas? ¿Por qué?
2. ¿Cuál de las dos estudiantes es más ahorradora (*frugal*)? ¿Por qué?
3. ¿Crees que a Alicia le gusta la ropa que Marisol compró?
4. ¿Crees que la moda es importante para Alicia? ¿Para Marisol? ¿Por qué?
5. ¿Es importante para ti estar a la moda? ¿Por qué?

NATIONAL communication STANDARDS

---

no aguanta más. Y trabajé poco la semana pasada. ¡Acabo de gastar todo el dinero para la semana!

A: ¡Ay, chica! Fui al centro comercial el mes pasado y encontré unos zapatos muy, pero muy de moda. Muy caros… pero buenos. No me los compré porque no los tenían en mi número. Voy a comprarlos cuando lleguen más… el vendedor me va a llamar.

M: Ajá… ¿Y va a invitarte a salir con él?

A: ¡Ay! ¡No seas así! Ven, vamos al café. Te ves muy bien y no hay que gastar eso aquí.

M: De acuerdo. Vamos.

Section Goals

In **Escuchar**, students will:
- listen for specific linguistic cues in oral sentences
- answer questions based on a recorded conversation

> **Instructional Resources**
> **Supersite:** Audio (Textbook MP3s); Resources (Scripts)

Estrategia
Script 1. Acabamos de pasear por la ciudad y encontramos unos monumentos fenomenales. 2. Estoy haciendo las maletas. 3. Carmen y Alejandro decidieron ir a un restaurante. 4. Mi familia y yo vamos a ir a la playa.

Teaching Tip Ask students to look at the photo of **Marisol** and **Alicia** and predict what they are talking about.

Ahora escucha
Script MARISOL: Oye, Alicia, ¿qué estás haciendo?
ALICIA: Estudiando no más. ¿Qué hay de nuevo?
M: Acabo de comprarme esos pantalones que andaba buscando.
A: ¿Los encontraste en el centro comercial? ¿Y cuánto te costaron?
M: Míralos. ¿Te gustan? En el almacén Melo tienen tremenda rebaja. Como estaban baratos me compré una blusa también. Es de cuadros, pero creo que hace juego con los pantalones por el color rojo. ¿Qué piensas?
A: Es de los mismos colores que la falda y la blusa que llevaste cuando fuimos al cine anoche. La verdad es que te quedan muy bien esos colores. ¿No encontraste unos zapatos y un cinturón para completar el juego?
M: No lo digas ni de chiste. Mi tarjeta de crédito está que

(Script continues at far left in the bottom panels.)

En pantalla Video

Juguettos, first established in Villena (Comunidad de Valencia), Spain, in the 1980s, now has chain stores all over the country. Juguettos offers both brand-name toys you would recognize (and maybe own) and those that specifically cater to a child's life and cultural experiences in Spain. But children's toys, like their imaginations, are very similar throughout the world. Indeed, the company declares it has founded its own "country," el País de Siempre Jugar.

Vocabulario útil	
copionas	copycats
despistado/a	distracted
sean	they may be
pidan	they may ask for

Preparación

¿Cómo eres? Escribe tres adjetivos que te describan. ¿Qué actividades ilustran (*illustrate*) tu personalidad? *Answers will vary.*

Emparejar

Match the personality trait with its visual representation in the ad.

_e_ 1. valiente
_c_ 2. galáctico/a
_d_ 3. artista
_b_ 4. generoso/a
_a_ 5. intrépido/a

   a. Tienen una batalla (*battle*) imaginaria.
   b. Le compra juguetes a su mascota (*pet*).
   c. Está en un cartón con forma de nave espacial (*spaceship*).
   d. Hacen música con parte de una basurera (*trashcan*).
   e. Imagina que puede volar (*fly*).

Conversación

Answer these questions with a classmate. *Answers will vary.*

1. ¿Por qué es importante la imaginación en la vida de los niños?
2. ¿Qué importancia tiene la imaginación en la vida de los adultos?

Anuncio de Juguettos

Me lo pido.

Me pido éste, éste.

¿Te lo pido?

More activities
vhlcentral / Online activities

Video

In the Spanish-speaking world, most city dwellers shop at large supermarkets and little stores that specialize in just one item, such as a butcher shop (**carnicería**), vegetable market (**verdulería**), perfume shop (**perfumería**), or hat shop (**sombrerería**). In small towns where supermarkets are less common, many people rely exclusively on specialty shops. This requires shopping more frequently—often every day or every other day for perishable items—but also means that the foods they consume are fresher and the goods are usually locally produced. Each neighborhood generally has its own shops, so people don't have to walk far to find fresh bread (at a **panadería**) for the midday meal.

Vocabulario útil

colones (pl.)	*currency from Costa Rica*
¿Cuánto vale?	*¿Cuánto cuesta?*
descuento	*discount*
disculpe	*excuse me*
¿Dónde queda...?	*Where is... located?*
los helados	*ice cream*
el regateo	*bargaining*

Preparación

Have you ever been to an open-air market? What did you buy? Have you ever negotiated a price? What did you say? Answers will vary.

¿Cierto o falso?

Indicate whether each statement is **cierto** or **falso**.

	Cierto	Falso
1. Randy lleva una camiseta verde.	⊘	○
2. El Mercado de Guadalupe está abierto cada domingo.	○	⊘
3. Randy regatea cuando compra papayas.	⊘	○
4. El Mercado Central es un mercado al aire libre.	○	⊘
5. Venden zapatos en el Mercado Central.	⊘	○

Comprar en los mercados

Trescientos colones.

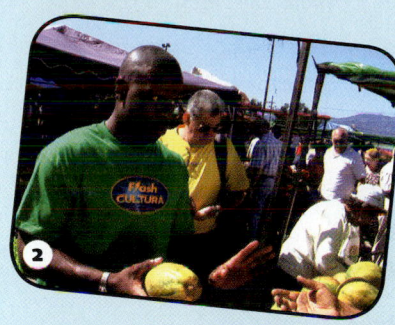

... pero me hace un buen descuento.

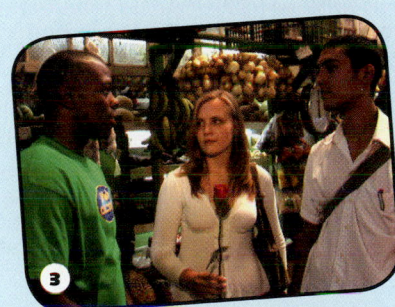

¿Qué compran en el Mercado Central?

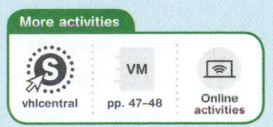

More activities

vhlcentral — VM pp. 47–48 — Online activities

Section Goals

In **Flash cultura**, students will:
• read about specialty shops in Spanish-speaking countries
• watch a video about open-air markets

Instructional Resources

Supersite: Video (*Flash cultura*); Resources (Scripts, Translations, Answer Keys)
WebSAM
Video Manual

Introduction To check comprehension, have students indicate whether these statements are true or false. 1. Supermarkets do not exist in Spanish-speaking countries. (False.) 2. In general, people that live in small towns only shop at specialty shops. (True.) 3. Specialty shops usually sell just one type of food or merchandise. (True.)

Antes de ver
• Read through the **Vocabulario útil** and model pronunciation. Present mini-conversations with these words, using contexts that are familiar to students. Ex: —**Disculpe, ¿me puede decir dónde queda la residencia estudiantil Evans? —Sí, claro. Está al lado de la cafetería.**
• Assure students that they do not need to understand every Spanish word they hear in the video. Tell them to rely on visual cues and to listen for words from **Vocabulario útil**.

Preparación Ask students if they have ever held a yard sale or garage sale. Did the buyers try to bargain?

¿Cierto o falso?
• Have students correct the false statements.
• Ask students to write three additional true/false statements about this episode for a partner to complete.

TEACHING OPTIONS

Extra Practice Have students write a summary of this episode in their own words.

Extra Practice 👥↔👤 Tell students to imagine that they are at one of the markets featured in the video. Ask them to jot down what they would like to buy there. Then have them write a dialogue of the conversation they would have in order to bargain for the goods they want to buy. Ask volunteers to role-play their dialogues for the class.

Cuba

connections cultures
NATIONAL STANDARDS

El país en cifras

▸ **Área:** 110.860 km² (42.803 millas²), *aproximadamente el área de Pensilvania*
▸ **Población:** 11.147.400
▸ **Capital:** La Habana—2.137.000

La Habana Vieja fue declarada° Patrimonio° Cultural de la Humanidad por la UNESCO en 1982. Este distrito es uno de los lugares más fascinantes de Cuba. En la Plaza de Armas, se puede visitar el majestuoso Palacio de Capitanes Generales, que ahora es un museo. En la calle° Obispo, frecuentada por el autor Ernest Hemingway, hay hermosos cafés, clubes nocturnos y tiendas elegantes.

▸ **Ciudades principales:** Santiago de Cuba, Camagüey, Holguín, Guantánamo
▸ **Moneda:** peso cubano
▸ **Idiomas:** español (oficial)

Bandera de Cuba

Cubanos célebres
▸ **Carlos Finlay,** doctor y científico (1833–1915)
▸ **José Martí,** político y poeta (1853–1895)
▸ **Fidel Castro,** ex primer ministro, ex comandante en jefe° de las fuerzas armadas (1926–2016)
▸ **Zoé Valdés,** escritora (1959–)
▸ **Ibrahim Ferrer,** músico (1927–2005)
▸ **Carlos Acosta,** bailarín (1973–)

fue declarada *was declared* Patrimonio *Heritage* calle *street*
comandante en jefe *commander in chief*

Gran Teatro de La Habana

Golfo de México

ESTADOS UNIDOS

Plaza del Capitolio

Océano Atlántico

Los coco taxis son un medio de transporte cubano muy popular.

⭐ **La Habana**

Cordillera de Guaniguanico

ESTADOS UNIDOS
CUBA
OCÉANO PACÍFICO
OCÉANO ATLÁNTICO
AMÉRICA DEL SUR

Isla de la Juventud

Mar Caribe

Camagüe

La música es parte esencial de la vida en Cuba.

More activities

vhlcentral | WB pp. 69–70 | Online activities

ACTIVIDADES

1 **Completar** Completa las oraciones con la información correcta.

1. La moneda oficial de Cuba es el __peso cubano__.
2. __Zoé Valdés__ es una escritora cubana.
3. __La Habana Vieja__ es Patrimonio Cultural de la Humanidad desde 1982.
4. El ave más pequeña del mundo es __el colibrí abeja__ y está en Cuba.
5. El Palacio de Capitanes Generales es actualmente un __museo__.
6. En la calle __Obispo__ encontramos cafés y tiendas elegantes.
7. Los __coco taxis__ son un medio de transporte muy popular en Cuba.
8. Alicia Alonso es una __bailarina__ cubana muy famosa.

▶ **Baile** • **Ballet Nacional de Cuba**

La bailarina Alicia Alonso fundó el Ballet Nacional de Cuba en 1948, después de° convertirse en una estrella° internacional en el Ballet de Nueva York y en Broadway. El Ballet Nacional de Cuba es famoso en todo el mundo por su creatividad y perfección técnica.

▶ **Economía** • **La caña de azúcar y el tabaco**

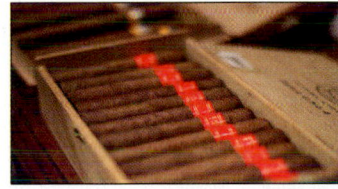

La caña de azúcar° es el producto agrícola° que más se cultiva en la isla y su exportación es muy importante para la economía del país. El tabaco, que se usa para fabricar los famosos puros° cubanos, es otro cultivo° de mucha importancia.

Gente • **Población**

La población cubana tiene raíces° muy heterogéneas. La inmigración a la isla fue determinante° desde la colonia hasta mediados° del siglo° XX. Los cubanos de hoy son descendientes de africanos, europeos, chinos y antillanos, entre otros.

Música • **Buena Vista Social Club**

En 1997 nace° el fenómeno musical conocido como *Buena Vista Social Club*. Este proyecto reúne° a un grupo de importantes músicos de Cuba, la mayoría ya mayores, con una larga trayectoria interpretando canciones clásicas del son° cubano. Ese mismo año ganaron un *Grammy*. Hoy en día estos músicos son conocidos en todo el mundo, y personas de todas las edades bailan al ritmo° de su música.

Holguín
Santiago de Cuba
Guantánamo
Sierra Maestra

después de *after* estrella *star* caña de azúcar *sugar cane* agrícola *farming* puros *cigars* cultivo *crop* raíces *roots* determinante *deciding* mediados *halfway through* siglo *century* nace *is born* reúne *gets together* son *Cuban musical genre* ritmo *rhythm*

¡Increíble pero cierto!

Pequeño y liviano°, el colibrí abeja° de Cuba es una de las más de 320 especies de colibrí y es también el ave° más pequeña del mundo°. Menores que muchos insectos, estas aves minúsculas miden° 5 centímetros y pesan° sólo 1,95 gramos.

liviano *light* colibrí abeja *bee hummingbird* ave *bird* mundo *world* miden *measure* pesan *weigh*

---

2 **¿Qué aprendiste?** Responde a las preguntas.

1. ¿Qué autor está asociado con La Habana Vieja?
   Ernest Hemingway
2. ¿Por qué es famoso el Ballet Nacional de Cuba?
   por su creatividad y perfección técnica
3. ¿Cuáles son los dos cultivos más importantes para la economía cubana? la caña de azúcar y el tabaco
4. ¿En qué año ganó un *Grammy* el disco *Buena Vista Social Club*?
   1997

3 **Conversar** En parejas, háganse preguntas sobre lo que saben y conocen sobre Cuba.

modelo

Estudiante 1: *¿Sabes cuál es la capital de Cuba?*

Estudiante 2: *Sí, es La Habana.*

Language Notes Some Cuban songs mention beings with names that do not sound Spanish, such as **Obatalá**, **Elegguá**, and **Babaluayé**. These are divinities (**orichas**) of the Afro-Cuban religion, which has its origins in Yoruba-speaking West Africa. Forcibly converted to Catholicism upon their arrival in Cuba, Africans developed a syncretized religion in which they worshiped the gods they had brought from Africa in the form of Catholic saints. **Babaluayé**, for instance, is worshiped as **San Lázaro**. **Obatalá** is **Nuestra Señora de las Mercedes**. Cuban popular music is deeply rooted in the songs and dances with which Afro-Cubans expressed their devotion to the **orichas**.

Ballet Nacional de Cuba

Although the **Ballet Nacional de Cuba** specializes in classical dance, Cuban popular dances (**habanera, mambo, rumba**) have gained worldwide popularity. Students can interview grandparents or other adults to see what they remember about Cuban dances. You may want to play the **Panorama cultural** video for this paragraph.

La caña de azúcar y el tabaco

With the collapse of the Soviet bloc and the end of subsidies, Cuba's economy suffered. In 1990, Cuba entered **el período especial en tiempo de paz**. Government planners have developed tourism, which formerly was seen as bourgeois and corrupting, as a means of gaining badly needed foreign currency. You may want to play the **Panorama cultural** video for this paragraph.

Población

◄▪► Have students pick an immigrant group and research its history in Cuba. Have them note general dates of arrival, what their community contributed to Cuban culture, and current demographics.

Buena Vista Social Club

If students are not familiar with the film or the music of *Buena Vista Social Club*, play some songs from the soundtrack for students to hear. Read some song titles and have students make predictions about the music before they listen.

¡Increíble pero cierto! Due to the patterns of evolution and adaptation common to islands, Cuba has many examples of unique flora and fauna. Have students research other examples.

Teaching Tip You may want to assign the **Prueba de práctica**, with its diagnostics and review activities, in the online-only **Repaso** section on the Supersite. There is also a **Repaso oral** in this section. For the Sixth Edition, a new summative vocabulary activity with speech recognition has been added to the **Repaso** section.

La ropa

el abrigo	coat
los (blue)jeans	jeans
la blusa	blouse
la bolsa	purse; bag
la bota	boot
los calcetines (el calcetín)	sock(s)
la camisa	shirt
la camiseta	t-shirt
la cartera	wallet
la chaqueta	jacket
el cinturón	belt
la corbata	tie
la falda	skirt
las gafas (de sol)	(sun)glasses
los guantes	gloves
el impermeable	raincoat
las medias	pantyhose; stockings
los pantalones	pants
los pantalones cortos	shorts
la ropa	clothes
la ropa interior	underwear
las sandalias	sandals
el sombrero	hat
el suéter	sweater
el traje	suit
el traje de baño	bathing suit
el vestido	dress
los zapatos de tenis	sneakers

Verbos

conducir	to drive
conocer	to know; to be acquainted with
dar	to give
ofrecer	to offer
parecer	to seem
saber	to know; to know how
traducir	to translate

Ir de compras

el almacén	department store
la caja	cash register
el centro comercial	shopping mall
el/la cliente/a	customer
el/la dependiente/a	clerk
el dinero	money
(en) efectivo	cash
el mercado (al aire libre)	(open-air) market
un par (de zapatos)	a pair (of shoes)
el precio (fijo)	(fixed; set) price
la rebaja	sale
el regalo	gift
la tarjeta de crédito	credit card
la tarjeta de débito	debit card
la tienda	store
el/la vendedor(a)	salesperson
comprar en línea	to buy online
costar (o:ue)	to cost
gastar	to spend (money)
hacer juego (con)	to match (with)
llevar	to wear; to take
pagar	to pay
regatear	to bargain
usar	to wear; to use
vender	to sell

Adjetivos

barato/a	cheap
bueno/a	good
cada	each
caro/a	expensive
corto/a	short (in length)
elegante	elegant
hermoso/a	beautiful
largo/a	long
loco/a	crazy
nuevo/a	new
otro/a	other; another
pobre	poor
rico/a	rich

Los colores

el color	color
amarillo/a	yellow
anaranjado/a	orange
azul	blue
blanco/a	white
gris	gray
marrón, café	brown
morado/a	purple
negro/a	black
rojo/a	red
rosado/a	pink
verde	green

Palabras adicionales

acabar de (+ *inf.*)	to have just done something
anoche	last night
anteayer	the day before yesterday
ayer	yesterday
de repente	suddenly
desde	from
dos veces	twice
hasta	until
pasado/a (*adj.*)	last; past
el año pasado	last year
la semana pasada	last week
prestar	to lend; to loan
una vez	once
ya	already

Indirect object pronouns	See page 202.
Demonstrative adjectives and pronouns	See page 210.
Expresiones útiles	See page 195.

More activities

vhlcentral LM p. 36

La rutina diaria

7

Communicative Goals

You will learn how to:
- Describe your daily routine
- Talk about personal hygiene
- Reassure someone

A PRIMERA VISTA
- ¿Está él en casa o en una tienda?
- ¿Está contento o enojado?
- ¿Lleva camisa?
- ¿De qué color es la crema de afeitar?

Lesson Goals

In **Lección 7**, students will be introduced to the following:
- terms for daily routines
- reflexive verbs
- adverbs of time
- the custom of **la siesta**
- drinking **mate** as part of a daily routine
- indefinite and negative words
- preterite of **ser** and **ir**
- verbs like **gustar**
- predicting content from the title
- sequencing events
- writing a description of a place
- listening for background information
- a television commercial for **Asepxia** makeup
- a video about **tapas**
- cultural, geographic, and historical information about Peru

A primera vista Here are some additional questions you can ask to personalize the photo: **¿Con quién vives? ¿Qué le dices antes de salir de casa? ¿Qué tipo de ropa llevas para ir a tus clases? ¿Les prestas esta ropa a tus amigos/as? ¿Qué ropa usaste en el verano? ¿Y en el invierno?**

Teaching Tip Look for these icons for additional communicative practice:

→🧍	Interpretive communication
←🧍	Presentational communication
🧍↔	Interpersonal communication

INSTRUCTIONAL RESOURCES

Supersite (vhlcentral.com)
Video: *Fotonovela, Flash cultura, En pantalla, Panorama cultural*
Audio: Textbook and Lab MP3 Files

Activity Pack: Information Gap Activities, games, additional activity handouts
Resources: SAM Answer Key, Scripts, Translations, **Vocabulario adicional**, sample lesson plan, Grammar Presentation Slides, Digital Image Bank

Testing Program: Quizzes, Tests, Exams, MP3s
Student Activities Manual: Workbook/Video Manual/Lab Manual
WebSAM (online Student Activities Manual)

La rutina diaria

En la habitación por la mañana

Más vocabulario

el baño, el cuarto de baño	bathroom
el inodoro	toilet
el jabón	soap
el maquillaje	makeup
la rutina diaria	daily routine
bañarse	to take a bath
cepillarse el pelo	to brush one's hair
dormirse (o:ue)	to go to sleep; to fall asleep
lavarse la cara	to wash one's face
levantarse	to get up
maquillarse	to put on makeup
antes (de)	before
después	afterward; then
después (de)	after
durante	during
entonces	then
luego	then
más tarde	later (on)
por la mañana	in the morning
por la noche	at night
por la tarde	in the afternoon; in the evening
por último	finally

Variación léxica

afeitarse	⟷	rasurarse (*Méx., Amér. C.*)
ducha	⟷	regadera (*Col., Méx., Venez.*)
ducharse	⟷	bañarse (*Amér. L.*)
pantuflas	⟷	chancletas (*Méx., Col.*); zapatillas (*Esp.*)

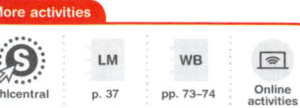

More activities

vhlcentral	LM p. 37	WB pp. 73–74	Online activities

Se viste. (vestirse)

el despertador

Se despierta. (despertarse)

En el baño por la mañana

el espejo

Se afeita. (afeitarse)

Se pone crema de afeitar. (ponerse)

Se ducha. (ducharse)

la crema de afeitar

el champú

el lavabo

la ducha

En la habitación por la noche

Se acuesta. (acostarse)

Se peina. (peinarse)

En el baño por la noche

Se cepilla los dientes. (cepillarse los dientes)

la toalla

Se lava las manos. (lavarse las manos)

las pantuflas

la pasta de dientes

Práctica

1 **Escuchar** Indica si, en general, las personas hacen las acciones que vas a escuchar por la mañana o por la noche.

	Por la mañana	Por la noche
1.	○	◉
2.	◉	○
3.	◉	○
4.	○	◉
5.	◉	○
6.	◉	○
7.	◉	○
8.	◉	○

2 **¿Lógico o ilógico?** Indica si lo que dice cada oración es **lógico** o **ilógico**.

1. lógico
2. ilógico
3. ilógico
4. ilógico
5. lógico
6. lógico
7. ilógico
8. lógico

3 **Seleccionar** Selecciona la palabra que no está relacionada con cada grupo.

1. manos • antes de • después de • por último _____ manos
2. lavabo • toalla • despertador • jabón _____ despertador
3. acostarse • jabón • despertarse • dormirse _____ jabón
4. espejo • lavabo • despertador • entonces _____ entonces
5. dormirse • toalla • vestirse • levantarse _____ toalla
6. espejo • champú • jabón • pasta de dientes _____ espejo
7. pelo • cara • manos • inodoro _____ inodoro
8. maquillarse • vestirse • peinarse • dientes _____ dientes
9. baño • dormirse • despertador • acostarse _____ baño
10. ducharse • luego • bañarse • lavarse _____ luego

4 **La rutina de Andrés** Ordena esta rutina de una manera lógica.

a. Se afeita después de cepillarse los dientes. __4__
b. Se acuesta a las once y media de la noche. __9__
c. Después de afeitarse, sale para las clases. __5__
d. Por último, se duerme. __10__
e. Asiste a todas sus clases y vuelve a su casa. __6__
f. Andrés se despierta a las seis y media de la mañana. __1__
g. Después de volver a casa, come un poco. Luego estudia en su habitación. __7__
h. Se viste y entonces se cepilla los dientes. __3__
i. Se cepilla los dientes antes de acostarse. __8__
j. Se ducha antes de vestirse. __2__

---

1 **Teaching Tip** You may want to do this activity as a TPR exercise. Have students raise their left hand for **por la mañana** and their right hand for **por la noche**.

1 **Script** 1. acostarse
2. vestirse 3. levantarse
4. dormirse 5. afeitarse
6. despertarse 7. maquillarse
8. peinarse
Textbook MP3s

2 **Expansion** Have students correct the illogical statements to make them logical.

2 **Script** 1. Sofía se lava las manos antes de comer. 2. Claudia se maquilla antes de dormirse. 3. Sebastián se cepilla los dientes con champú. 4. Joaquín se baña antes de despertarse. 5. Daniel se viste después de ducharse. 6. Carlos se afeita con crema de afeitar. 7. María Teresa se baña después de maquillarse. 8. Isabel se levanta después de despertarse.
Textbook MP3s

3 **Expansion** Go over the answers and explain why a particular item does not belong. Ex: **El lavabo, la toalla y el jabón son para lavarse. El despertador es para despertarse.**

4 **Teaching Tip** To simplify, first ask students to identify the adverbs of time in the sentences. Then have them read through all the items before attempting to put them in order.

4 **Expansion** Ask students if **Andrés's** schedule represents that of a "typical" student. Ask: **Un estudiante típico, ¿se despierta normalmente a las seis y media de la mañana? ¿A qué hora se despiertan ustedes?**

5 **La rutina diaria** Identifica las actividades de las personas.

> **modelo**
> dormirse

1.

bañarse

2.

ducharse

3.

maquillarse

4.

lavarse las manos

5.

afeitarse

6.

cepillarse el pelo

7.

cepillarse los dientes

6 **Identificar** Con un(a) compañero/a, identifica las cosas que cada persona necesita. Sigue el modelo.
Some answers will vary.

> **modelo**
> Jorge / lavarse la cara
> **Estudiante 1:** ¿Qué necesita Jorge para lavarse la cara?
> **Estudiante 2:** Necesita jabón y una toalla.

1. Gerardo / despertarse   un despertador
2. Mariana / maquillarse   maquillaje y un espejo
3. Gabriel / ducharse   una ducha, una toalla y jabón
4. Roberto / afeitarse   un espejo y crema de afeitar
5. Sonia / lavarse el pelo   champú y una toalla
6. Vanesa / lavarse las manos   un lavabo, jabón y una toalla
7. Manuel / vestirse   su ropa/una camiseta/unos pantalones/etc.
8. Simón / acostarse   una cama

TEACHING OPTIONS

Extra Practice Name daily routine activities and have students list all the words that they associate with each activity, such as things, places, and parts of the body. Ex: **lavarse las manos: el jabón, el cuarto de baño, el agua, la toalla.**

Small Groups In groups of three or four, have students think of a famous person or character and describe his or her daily routine. In their descriptions, students may use names of friends or family of the famous person or character. Have groups read their descriptions aloud for the rest of the class to guess.

Comunicación

7 **La farmacia** Lee el anuncio y responde a las preguntas con un(a) compañero/a.

Answers will vary.

---

www.lafarmacianuevosol.com

LA FARMACIA NUEVO SOL tiene todo lo que necesitas para la vida diaria.

| Esta semana tenemos grandes rebajas. | Con poco dinero puedes comprar lo que necesitas para el cuarto de baño ideal. |

Para los hombres ofrecemos…
Excelentes cremas de afeitar de Guapo y Máximo

Para las mujeres ofrecemos…
Nuevo maquillaje de Marisol y jabones de baño
Ilusiones y Belleza

Y para todos tenemos los mejores jabones, pastas de dientes
y cepillos de dientes.

¡Visita LA FARMACIA NUEVO SOL!

Tenemos los mejores precios. Visita nuestra tienda muy cerca de tu casa.

---

1. ¿Qué tipo de tienda es? Es una farmacia.
2. ¿Qué productos ofrecen para las mujeres? maquillaje, jabones de baño
3. ¿Qué productos ofrecen para los hombres? cremas de afeitar
4. Haz (*Make*) una lista de los verbos que asocias con los productos del anuncio.
5. ¿Dónde compras tus productos de higiene? Answers will vary. Suggested answers: afeitarse, maquillarse, cepillarse los dientes, ducharse/bañarse
6. ¿Tienes una tienda favorita? ¿Cuál es? Answers will vary.

8 **Preguntas** En parejas, túrnense para hacerse estas preguntas. Answers will vary.

> **modelo**
> **Estudiante 1:** ¿Qué hay en tu cuarto de baño?
> **Estudiante 2:** Hay un lavabo, un espejo, un inodoro y una ducha.

1. ¿Cómo es tu cuarto de baño?
2. ¿Cuántas personas comparten tu cuarto de baño?
3. ¿Qué pasta de dientes usas?
4. ¿De qué color es tu toalla?
5. ¿Cuánto cuesta tu jabón?
6. ¿Qué champú usas?
7. ¿A qué hora oyes tu despertador?
8. ¿Cuándo estudias? ¿Por la mañana, por la tarde, por la noche?

7 Expansion
• ⬅🔲➡ Ask small groups to write a competing ad for another pharmacy. Have each group present its ad to the class, who will vote for the most persuasive one.
• 🔲↔🔲 In pairs, have students write a conversation between a customer and an employee at **La Farmacia Nuevo Sol**. Encourage creativity. Have a few volunteers role-play their conversations for the class.

8 Teaching Tip Take a class survey of the answers and write the results on the board.

TEACHING OPTIONS

Small Groups 🔲↔🔲 In small groups, have students write and act out a brief skit. Tell them to imagine that they are roommates who are trying to get ready for their morning classes at the same time, but there is only one bathroom in the house or apartment. Have the class vote for the most original or funniest skit.

Heritage Speakers ⬅🔲➡ Ask heritage speakers to write paragraphs in which they describe their daily routine when at home with their family. If they are not talking about their current situation, be sure that they keep their narration in the historical present. Have students present their paragraphs orally to the class. Verify comprehension by asking other students to paraphrase portions of each speaker's description.

¡Necesito arreglarme!

Es viernes por la tarde y Marissa, Jimena y Felipe se preparan para salir.

PERSONAJES MARISSA JIMENA

MARISSA ¿Hola? ¿Está ocupado?
JIMENA Sí. Me estoy lavando la cara.
MARISSA Necesito usar el baño.

MARISSA Tengo que terminar de arreglarme. Voy al cine esta noche.
JIMENA Yo también tengo que salir. ¿Te importa si me maquillo primero? Me voy a encontrar con mi amiga Elena en una hora.

JIMENA No te preocupes, Marissa. Llegaste primero. Entonces, te arreglas el pelo y después me maquillo.
FELIPE ¿Y yo? Tengo crema de afeitar en la cara. No me voy a ir. Estoy aquí y aquí me quedo.

JIMENA ¡Felipe! ¿Qué estás haciendo?
FELIPE Me estoy afeitando. ¿Hay algún problema?
JIMENA ¡Siempre haces lo mismo!
FELIPE Pues, yo no vi a nadie aquí.

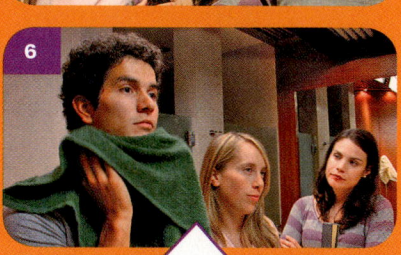

JIMENA ¿Por qué no te afeitaste por la mañana?
FELIPE Porque cada vez que quiero usar el baño, una de ustedes está aquí. O bañándose o maquillándose.

MARISSA Tú ganas. ¿Adónde vas a ir esta noche, Felipe?
FELIPE Juan Carlos y yo vamos a ir a un café en el centro. Siempre hay música en vivo. (Sale.) Me siento guapísimo. Todavía me falta cambiarme la camisa.

FELIPE

7

MARISSA ¿Adónde vas esta noche?

JIMENA A la biblioteca.

MARISSA ¡Es viernes! ¡Nadie debe estudiar los viernes! Voy a ver una película de Pedro Almodóvar con unas amigas.

8

MARISSA ¿Por qué no vienen tú y Elena al cine con nosotras? Después, podemos ir a ese café y molestar a Felipe.

9

JIMENA No sé.

MARISSA ¿Cuándo fue la última vez que viste a Juan Carlos?

JIMENA Cuando fuimos a Mérida.

10

MARISSA A ti te gusta ese chico.

JIMENA No tengo idea de qué estás hablando. Si no te importa, nos vemos en el cine.

More activities

vhlcentral

VM
pp. 13–14

Online activities

Expresiones útiles

Talking about getting ready

Necesito arreglarme.
I need to get ready.
Me estoy lavando la cara.
I'm washing my face.
¿Te importa si me maquillo primero?
Is it OK with you if I put on my makeup first?
Tú te arreglas el pelo y después yo me maquillo.
You fix your hair and then I'll put on my makeup.
Todavía me falta cambiarme la camisa.
I still have to change my shirt.

Reassuring someone

Tranquilo/a.
Relax.
No te preocupes.
Don't worry.

Talking about past actions

¿Cuándo fue la última vez que viste a Juan Carlos?
When was the last time you saw Juan Carlos?
Cuando fuimos a Mérida.
When we went to Mérida.

Talking about likes and dislikes

Me fascinan las películas de Almodóvar.
I love Almodóvar's movies.
Me encanta la música en vivo.
I love live music.
Me molesta compartir el baño.
It bothers me to share the bathroom.

Additional vocabulary

encontrarse con *to meet up with*
molestar *to bother*
nadie *no one*

Expresiones útiles Draw attention to the verb forms **fue** and **fuimos** in the caption of video still 9. Tell students that these are preterite forms of the verbs **ser** and **ir**, respectively. Then explain that the context clarifies which verb is used. Point out the phrases **Me estoy lavando, me maquillo, te arreglas,** and **No te preocupes.** Tell the class that these are forms of the reflexive verbs **lavarse, maquillarse, arreglarse,** and **preocuparse.** Then, point out the phrases **Me fascinan, Me encanta,** and **Me molesta.** Explain that these are examples of verbs that have constructions similar to that of **gustar.** Finally, draw attention to the caption for video still 3 and point out the words **algún, Siempre,** and **nadie.** Explain that **algún** and **Siempre** are indefinite words and **nadie** is a negative word. Tell students that they will learn more about these concepts in **Estructura.**

Teaching Tip
👤↔👤 Have students get together in groups of three to role-play the episode. Encourage students to ad-lib when possible. Then, ask one or two groups to present the episode to the class.

Nota cultural In the Spanish-speaking world, young people tend to dress more formally than their U.S. counterparts, not only for parties, but also to go see a movie or attend class. This concept is known as **lucir bien** (*to look good*). In some countries, for people of all ages, dressing in an overly casual manner may result in poorer service at certain establishments.

TEACHING OPTIONS

TPR Ask students to write **Marissa, Jimena,** and **Felipe** on separate pieces of paper. Read aloud statements from the perspective of the characters and have students hold up the corresponding name. Ex: **Me quiero arreglar el pelo. (Marissa) Mi hermano se está afeitando. (Jimena)**
Small Groups ↔👤→ Ask students to select one of the characters and write a short description about what they think his or her daily routine is like. Then have students who picked the same character get together to find similarities and differences in their descriptions.
Pairs Ask pairs of students to work together to create six true/false sentences about the **Fotonovela.** Have pairs exchange papers and complete the activity.

¿Qué pasó?

1 **¿Cierto o falso?** Indica si lo que dicen estas oraciones es cierto o falso. Corrige las oraciones falsas.

1. Marissa va a ver una película de Pedro Almodóvar con unas amigas.
   Cierto.
2. Jimena se va a encontrar con Elena en dos horas.
   Falso. Jimena se va a encontrar con Elena en una hora.
3. Felipe se siente muy feo después de afeitarse.
   Falso. Felipe se siente guapísimo después de afeitarse.
4. Jimena quiere maquillarse.
   Cierto.
5. Marissa quiere ir al café para molestar a Juan Carlos.
   Falso. Marissa quiere ir al café para molestar a Felipe.

2 **Identificar** Identifica quién dice estas oraciones.

1. No me voy a ir. Estoy aquí y aquí me quedo. _____Felipe_____
2. Tengo que terminar de arreglarme. Voy al cine esta noche.
   _____Marissa_____
3. Me voy a encontrar con mi amiga Elena en una hora.
   _____Jimena_____
4. Juan Carlos y yo vamos a ir a un café en el centro.
   _____Felipe_____
5. ¿Cuándo fue la última vez que viste a Juan Carlos?
   _____Marissa_____
6. ¿Por qué no te afeitaste por la mañana? _____Jimena_____

MARISSA

FELIPE

JIMENA

3 **Ordenar** Ordena correctamente los planes que tiene Marissa.

- __5__ a. Voy al café.
- __2__ b. Me arreglo el pelo.
- __6__ c. Molesto a Felipe.
- __3__ d. Me encuentro con unas amigas.
- __1__ e. Entro al baño.
- __4__ f. Voy al cine.

4 **En el baño** Trabajen en parejas para representar los papeles de dos compañeros/as de cuarto que deben usar el baño al mismo tiempo para hacer su rutina diaria. *Answers will vary.*

Estudiante 1	**Estudiante 2**
Di (*Say*) que quieres arreglarte porque vas a ir al cine.	→ Di (*Say*) que necesitas arreglarte porque te vas a encontrar con tus amigos/as.
Pregunta si puedes secarte (*dry*) el pelo.	→ Responde que no porque necesitas lavarte la cara.
Di que puede lavarse la cara, pero que después necesitas secarte el pelo.	→ Di que puede secarse el pelo, pero que después necesitas peinarte.

---

1 **Expansion** Give students these true/false statements as items 6–7: **6. Felipe va a encontrarse con Juan Carlos en una discoteca. (Falso. Ellos van a encontrarse en un café.) 7. La última vez que Jimena vio a Juan Carlos fue ayer. (Falso. Fue en Mérida.)**

Nota cultural Internationally renowned, Spanish filmmaker **Pedro Almodóvar's** films are generally characterized by complex narratives and themes of family, identity, and desire. His movie *Todo sobre mi madre* (1999) won the Best Foreign Language Film Oscar. The 1988 film *Mujeres al borde de un ataque de nervios*, his first movie to have major international success, was adapted as a musical.

2 **Expansion** Give students these sentences as items 7–8: **7. Todavía me falta cambiarme la camisa. (Felipe) 8. ¿Por qué no vienen tú y Elena al cine con nosotras? (Marissa)**

3 **Expansion** Ask pairs to imagine another character's plans and list them using the **yo** form of the verbs, as in the activity. Then have pairs share their lists with the class.

4 **Possible Conversation**
E1: Quiero arreglarme porque voy a ir al cine.
E2: Pues, necesito arreglarme porque voy a encontrarme con mis amigos.
E1: ¿Puedo secarme el pelo?
E2: No, porque necesito lavarme la cara.
E1: Está bien. Puedes lavarte la cara, pero después necesito secarme el pelo.
E2: De acuerdo. Puedes secarte el pelo, pero después necesito peinarme.

TEACHING OPTIONS

Extra Practice →👤← Add an auditory aspect to this vocabulary practice. Ask students to close their books. Then read aloud the sentences from **Actividad 3**, in the correct order. Read each sentence twice slowly to give students an opportunity to write them down. Then read them again at normal speed, without pausing, to allow students to check for accuracy or fill in any gaps. Ask comprehension questions as a follow-up.

Small Groups 👤↔👤 Have students get together in small groups to discuss and compare their daily routines. Have them use as many of the words and expressions from this lesson as they can. Then ask for a few volunteers to describe the daily routine of one of their group members.

Pronunciación
 Tutorial

The consonant r

ropa	**rutina**	**rico**	**Ramón**

In Spanish, **r** has a strong trilled sound at the beginning of a word. No English words have a trill, but English speakers often produce a trill when they imitate the sound of a motor.

gustar	**durante**	**primero**	**crema**

In any other position, **r** has a weak sound similar to the English *tt* in *better* or the English *dd* in *ladder*. In contrast to English, the tongue touches the roof of the mouth behind the teeth.

pizarra	**corro**	**marrón**	**aburrido**

The letter combination **rr**, which only appears between vowels, always has a strong trilled sound.

caro	**carro**	**pero**	**perro**

Between vowels, the difference between the strong trilled **rr** and the weak **r** is very important, as a mispronunciation could lead to confusion between two different words.

Práctica Lee las palabras en voz alta, prestando (*paying*) atención a la pronunciación de la **r** y la **rr**.

1. Perú
2. Rosa
3. borrador
4. madre
5. comprar
6. favor
7. rubio
8. reloj
9. Arequipa
10. tarde
11. cerrar
12. despertador

Oraciones Lee las oraciones en voz alta, prestando atención a la pronunciación de la **r** y la **rr**.

1. Ramón Robles Ruiz es programador. Su esposa Rosaura es artista.
2. A Rosaura Robles le encanta regatear en el mercado.
3. Ramón nunca regatea… le aburre regatear.
4. Rosaura siempre compra cosas baratas.
5. Ramón no es rico, pero prefiere comprar cosas muy caras.
6. ¡El martes Ramón compró un carro nuevo!

Refranes Lee en voz alta los refranes, prestando atención a la **r** y a la **rr**.

Perro que ladra no muerde.[1]

No se ganó Zamora en una hora.[2]

More activities

vhlcentral   LM p. 38

1 *A dog's bark is worse than its bite.*   2 *Rome wasn't built in a day.*

Section Goal

In **Pronunciación**, students will be introduced to the pronunciation of the consonant **r** and the letter combination **rr**.

Instructional Resources
Supersite: Audio (Textbook and Lab MP3 Files); Resources (Scripts, Answer Keys)
WebSAM
Lab Manual

Teaching Tips
- Explain that **r** is trilled at the beginning of a word, and that there are no words that have a trill in American English. Model the pronunciation of **ropa, rutina, rico,** and **Ramón** and have the class repeat.
- Point out that in any other position, **r** is pronounced like the *tt* in American English *better*. Write the words **gustar, durante, primero,** and **crema** on the board and ask a volunteer to pronounce each word.
- Point out that **rr** always has a strong trilled sound and that it only appears between vowels. Pronounce the words **pizarra, corro, marrón,** and **aburrido** and have the class repeat.
- To help students discriminate between **r** and **rr**, write on the board the pairs **caro/carro** and **pero/perro**. Then pronounce each pair several times in random order, pausing after each for students to repeat. Ex: **caro, carro, caro, carro, carro, caro**
- If students struggle with the trill of **rr**, have them repeat the phrases *better butter* or *I edited it* in rapid succession.

Práctica/Oraciones/Refranes
These exercises are recorded on the *Textbook MP3s*. You may want to play the audio so that students practice listening to Spanish spoken by speakers other than yourself.

TEACHING OPTIONS

Extra Practice Write the names of a few Peruvian cities on the board and ask for a volunteer to pronounce each name. Ex: **Huaraz, Cajamarca, Trujillo, Puerto Maldonado, Cerro de Pasco, Piura.** Then write the names of a few Peruvian literary figures on the board and repeat the process. Ex: **Ricardo Palma, Ciro Alegría, Mario Vargas Llosa, César Vallejo.**

Small Groups Have students work in small groups and take turns reading aloud sentences from the **Fotonovela** episode in this lesson and in previous lessons, focusing on the correct pronunciation of **r** and **rr**.
Extra Practice Write this rhyme on the board and have students practice trilling: **Erre con erre, cigarro, erre con erre, barril, rápido corren los carros, sobre los rieles del ferrocarril.**

EN DETALLE

La siesta

¿Sientes cansancio° después de comer?
¿Te cuesta° volver al trabajo° o a clase después del almuerzo? Estas sensaciones son normales. A muchas personas les gusta relajarse° después de almorzar. Este momento de descanso es **la siesta**. La siesta es popular en los países hispanos y viene de una antigua costumbre° del área del Mediterráneo. La palabra *siesta* viene del latín y significa "sexta hora". La sexta hora del día es después del mediodía, el momento de más calor. Debido al° calor y al cansancio, los habitantes de España, Italia, Grecia y Portugal tienen la costumbre de dormir la siesta desde hace° más de° dos mil años. Los españoles y los portugueses llevaron la costumbre a los países americanos.

Aunque° hoy día esta costumbre está desapareciendo° en las grandes ciudades, la siesta todavía es importante en la cultura hispana. En pueblos pequeños, por ejemplo, muchas oficinas° y tiendas tienen la costumbre de cerrar por dos o tres horas después del mediodía. Los empleados van a su casa, almuerzan con sus familias, duermen la siesta o hacen actividades, como ir al gimnasio, y luego regresan al trabajo entre las 2:30 y las 4:30 de la tarde.

Los estudios científicos explican que una siesta corta después de almorzar ayuda° a trabajar más y mejor° durante la tarde. Pero, ¡cuidado! Esta siesta sólo debe durar° entre veinte y cuarenta minutos. Si dormimos más, entramos en la fase de sueño profundo y es difícil despertarse.

Hoy, algunas empresas° de los EE.UU., Canadá, Japón, Inglaterra y Alemania tienen salas° especiales donde los empleados pueden dormir la siesta.

¿Dónde duermen la siesta?

■ Costumbre antigua
■ Costumbre nueva

En los lugares donde la siesta es una costumbre antigua, las personas la duermen en su casa. En los países donde la siesta es una costumbre nueva, la gente duerme en sus lugares de trabajo o en centros de siesta.

Sientes cansancio *Do you feel tired* Te cuesta *Is it hard for you* trabajo *work* relajarse *to relax* antigua costumbre *old custom* Debido al *Because (of)* desde hace *for* más de *more than* Aunque *Although* está desapareciendo *is disappearing* oficinas *offices* ayuda *helps* mejor *better* durar *last* algunas empresas *some businesses* salas *rooms*

ACTIVIDADES

1 ¿Cierto o falso? Indica si lo que dicen las oraciones es cierto o falso. Corrige la información falsa.

1. La costumbre de la siesta empezó en Asia. **Falso.** La costumbre de la siesta empezó en el área del Mediterráneo.
2. La palabra *siesta* está relacionada con la sexta hora del día. **Cierto.**
3. Los españoles y los portugueses llevaron la costumbre de la siesta a Latinoamérica. **Cierto.**
4. La siesta ayuda a trabajar más y mejor durante la tarde. **Cierto.**
5. Los horarios de trabajo de las grandes ciudades hispanas son los mismos que los de pueblos pequeños. **Falso.** En las grandes ciudades hispanas la costumbre de la siesta está desapareciendo.
6. Una siesta larga siempre es mejor que una siesta corta. **Falso.** La siesta debe durar entre veinte y cuarenta minutos.
7. En los Estados Unidos, los empleados de algunas empresas pueden dormir la siesta en el trabajo. **Cierto.**
8. Es fácil despertar de un sueño profundo. **Falso.** Es difícil despertar de un sueño profundo.

ASÍ SE DICE

El cuidado personal

el aseo; el excusado; el servicio; el váter (Esp.)	el baño
el cortaúñas	*nail clippers*
el desodorante	*deodorant*
el enjuague bucal	*mouthwash*
el hilo dental/ la seda dental	*dental floss*
la máquina de afeitar/ de rasurar (Méx.)	*electric razor*

EL MUNDO HISPANO

Costumbres especiales

- **México y El Salvador** Los vendedores pasan por las calles anunciando a gritos° su mercancía°: tanques de gas y flores° en México; pan y tortillas en El Salvador.

- **Costa Rica** Para encontrar las direcciones°, los costarricenses usan referencias de anécdotas, lugares o características geográficas. Por ejemplo: *200 metros norte de la iglesia, frente al° supermercado Mi Mega.*

- **Argentina** En Tigre, una ciudad junto al Río° de la Plata, la gente usa barcos particulares°, barcos colectivos y barcos-taxi para ir de una isla a otra. Todas las mañanas, un barco colectivo recoge° a los niños y los lleva a la escuela.

gritos *shouts* mercancía *merchandise* flores *flowers* direcciones *addresses* frente al *opposite* Río *River* particulares *private* recoge *picks up*

PERFIL

El mate

El mate es una parte muy importante de la rutina diaria en muchos países. Es una bebida° muy similar al té que se consume en Argentina, Uruguay y Paraguay. Tradicionalmente se bebe caliente° con una *bombilla*° y en un recipiente° que también se llama *mate*. Por ser amarga°, algunos le agregan° azúcar para suavizar su sabor°. El mate se puede tomar a cualquier°

hora y en cualquier lugar, aunque en Argentina las personas prefieren sentarse en círculo e ir pasando el mate de mano en mano mientras° conversan. Los uruguayos, por otra parte, acostumbran llevar el agua° caliente para el mate en

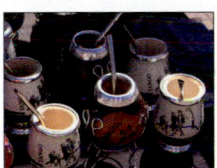

un termo° bajo el brazo° y lo beben mientras caminan. Si ves a una persona con un termo bajo el brazo y un mate en la mano, ¡es casi seguro que es de Uruguay!

bebida *drink* caliente *hot* bombilla *straw (in Argentina)* recipiente *container* amarga *bitter* agregan *add* suavizar su sabor *soften its flavor* cualquier *any* mientras *while* agua *water* termo *thermos* bajo el brazo *under their arm*

CON RITMO HISPANO

Susana Baca (1944–)

Lugar de nacimiento: Lima, Perú

Susana Baca es representante destacada de la música afroperuana. Fue ministra de Cultura de Perú y presidenta de la Comisión Interamericana de Cultura.

Go to **vhlcentral.com** to find out more about **Susana Baca** and her music.

ACTIVIDADES

2 **Comprensión** Completa las oraciones.

1. Uso <u>el hilo dental/la seda dental</u> para limpiar (*to clean*) entre los dientes.

2. En <u>El Salvador</u> las personas compran pan y tortillas a los vendedores que pasan por la calle.

3. El <u>mate</u> es una bebida similar al té.

4. Los uruguayos beben mate mientras <u>caminan</u>.

3 **¿Qué costumbres tienes?** Escribe cuatro oraciones sobre una costumbre que compartes con tus amigos o con tu familia (por ejemplo: ir al cine, ir a eventos deportivos, leer, comer juntos, etc.). Explica qué haces, cuándo lo haces y con quién. Answers will vary.

More activities

 vhlcentral

 Online activities

Section Goals

In **Estructura 7.1**, students will learn:
- the conjugation of reflexive verbs
- common reflexive verbs

Instructional Resources

Supersite: Audio (Lab MP3 Files); Resources (Grammar Presentation Slides, Activity Pack, Scripts, Answer Keys); Testing Program (Quizzes)
WebSAM
Workbook
Lab Manual

Teaching Tips

- Model the first-person reflexive by talking about yourself. Ex: **Me levanto muy temprano. Me levanto a las cinco de la mañana.** Then model the second person by asking questions with a verb you have already used in the first person. Ex: **Y tú, _____, ¿a qué hora te levantas? (Me levanto a las ocho.)**
- Introduce the third person by making statements and asking questions about what a student has told you. Ex: _____ **se levanta muy tarde, ¿no? (Sí, se levanta muy tarde.)**
- Add a visual aspect to this grammar presentation. Use magazine pictures to clarify meanings between third-person singular and third-person plural forms. Ex: **Se lava las manos** and **Se lavan las manos.**
- On the board summarize the three possible positions for reflexive pronouns. You may want to demonstrate this visually by using an **X** to represent the reflexive pronoun: **X verbo conjugado, infinitivoX, gerundioX.** Remind students that they have already learned these positions for direct and indirect object pronouns.

7.1 Reflexive verbs Tutorial

ANTE TODO A reflexive verb is used to indicate that the subject does something to or for himself or herself. In other words, it "reflects" the action of the verb back to the subject. Reflexive verbs always use reflexive pronouns.

SUBJECT   REFLEXIVE VERB

Joaquín   **se ducha** por la mañana.

The verb **lavarse** (*to wash oneself*)

SINGULAR FORMS			
yo	**me lavo**	*I wash (myself)*
tú	**te lavas**	*you wash (yourself)*
Ud.	**se lava**	*you wash (yourself)*
él/ella	**se lava**	*he/she washes (himself/herself)*

PLURAL FORMS			
nosotros/as	**nos lavamos**	*we wash (ourselves)*
vosotros/as	**os laváis**	*you wash (yourselves)*
Uds.	**se lavan**	*you wash (yourselves)*
ellos/ellas	**se lavan**	*they wash (themselves)*

▶ The pronoun **se** attached to an infinitive identifies the verb as reflexive: **lavarse**.

▶ When a reflexive verb is conjugated, the reflexive pronoun agrees with the subject.

Me afeito.   **Te despiertas** a las siete.

¿Te importa si me maquillo primero?

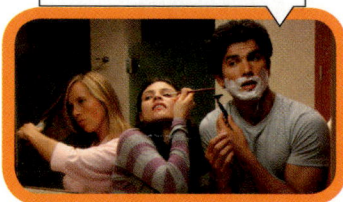

A las chicas les encanta maquillarse durante horas y horas.

▶ Like object pronouns, reflexive pronouns generally appear before a conjugated verb. With infinitives and present participles, they may be placed before the conjugated verb or attached to the infinitive or present participle.

Ellos **se** van a vestir.
Ellos van a vestir**se**.
They are going to get dressed.

Nos estamos lavando las manos.
Estamos lavándo**nos** las manos.
We are washing our hands.

▶ **¡Atención!** When a reflexive pronoun is attached to a present participle, an accent mark is added to maintain the original stress.

bañando ⟶ bañ**á**ndo**se**   durmiendo ⟶ durmi**é**ndo**se**

Except for **se**, reflexive pronouns have the same forms as direct and indirect object pronouns.

• • •

Se is used for both singular and plural subjects—there is no individual plural form:
Pablo **se** lava.
Ellos **se** lavan.

TEACHING OPTIONS

Extra Practice To provide oral practice with reflexive verbs, create sentences that follow the pattern of the sentences in the examples. Say the sentence, have students repeat it, then say a different subject, varying the gender and number. Have students then say the sentence with the new subject, changing pronouns and verb forms as necessary.

Extra Practice ←👤→ Have students describe daily routines in their families. Encourage heritage speakers to use their own linguistic variation of words presented in this lesson. Ex: **regarse** (e:ie), **pintarse**. Have students work together to compare and contrast activities as well as lexical variations.

Common reflexive verbs

acordarse (de) (o:ue)	to remember		llamarse	to be called; to be named
acostarse (o:ue)	to go to bed			
afeitarse	to shave		maquillarse	to put on makeup
bañarse	to take a bath		peinarse	to comb one's hair
cepillarse	to brush		ponerse	to put on
despertarse (e:ie)	to wake up		ponerse (+ adj.)	to become (+ adj.)
dormirse (o:ue)	to go to sleep; to fall asleep		preocuparse (por)	to worry (about)
			probarse (o:ue)	to try on
ducharse	to take a shower		quedarse	to stay
enojarse (con)	to get angry (with)		quitarse	to take off
irse	to go away; to leave		secarse	to dry (oneself)
lavarse	to wash (oneself)		sentarse (e:ie)	to sit down
levantarse	to get up		sentirse (e:ie)	to feel
			vestirse (e:i)	to get dressed

COMPARE & CONTRAST

Unlike English, a number of verbs in Spanish can be reflexive or non-reflexive. If the verb acts upon the subject, the reflexive form is used. If the verb acts upon something other than the subject, the non-reflexive form is used. Compare these sentences.

Lola **lava** los platos.

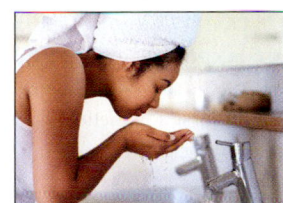

Lucía **se lava** la cara.

As the preceding sentences show, reflexive verbs sometimes have different meanings than their non-reflexive counterparts. For example, **lavar** means *to wash*, while **lavarse** means *to wash oneself, to wash up*.

▶ **¡Atención!** Parts of the body or clothing are generally not referred to with possessives, but with articles.

La niña se quitó **un** zapato.   Necesito cepillarme **los** dientes.

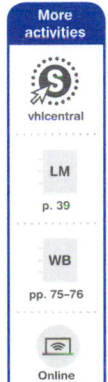

More activities

vhlcentral

LM p. 39

WB pp. 75–76

Online activities

¡INTÉNTALO! Indica el presente de estos verbos reflexivos.

despertarse
1. Mis hermanos _se despiertan_ tarde.
2. Tú _te despiertas_ tarde.
3. Nosotros _nos despertamos_ tarde.
4. Yo _me despierto_ tarde.
5. Benito _se despierta_ tarde.

ponerse
1. Él _se pone_ una chaqueta.
2. Yo _me pongo_ una chaqueta.
3. Las niñas _se ponen_ una chaqueta.
4. Nosotras _nos ponemos_ una chaqueta.
5. Usted _se pone_ una chaqueta.

TEACHING OPTIONS

TPR Model gestures for a few of the reflexive verbs. Ex: **acordarse** (tap side of head), **acostarse** (lay head on folded hands). Have students stand. Begin by practicing as a class using only the **nosotros** form, saying expressions at random. (Ex: **Nos lavamos la cara.**) Then vary the verb forms and point to the student who should perform the appropriate gesture. Keep a brisk pace. Vary by pointing to more than one student. (Ex: **Ustedes se peinan.**)

Pairs Have students write a short account of their daily routine. Then have pairs compare and contrast their routines using a Venn diagram (see **Lección 9, Escritura**). Have the pair label the circles with their names and write **Los/Las dos** where they overlap. Then have them list their activities in the appropriate section. Remind them to use the **nosotros/as** form for verbs under **Los/Las dos.**

Práctica

1 **La fiesta elegante** Selecciona el verbo apropiado y completa las oraciones con la forma correcta.

1. Nosotros ___nos bañamos___ (bañar / bañarse) antes de ir a la fiesta.
2. Tú ___lavas___ (lavar / lavarse) el auto antes de ir a la fiesta.
3. Para llegar a tiempo, Raúl y Marta ___acuestan___ (acostar / acostarse) a los niños antes de salir.
4. Cecilia ___se maquilla___ (maquillar / maquillarse) antes de salir.
5. Mis amigos siempre ___se visten___ (vestir / vestirse) con ropa muy elegante.
6. Julia y Ana ___se ponen___ (poner / ponerse) los vestidos nuevos.
7. Usted ___va___ (ir / irse) a llegar antes que (*before*) los demás invitados, ¿no?
8. En general, ___me afeito___ (afeitar / afeitarse) yo mismo, pero hoy es un día especial y el barbero (*barber*) me ___afeita___ (afeitar / afeitarse). ¡Será una fiesta inolvidable!

2 **Nuestra rutina** Escribe oraciones sobre la rutina diaria de la familia de Blanca.

> **modelo**
> mamá / despertarse a las 5:00
> **Mamá se despierta a las cinco.**

1. Roberto y yo / levantarse a las 7:00 Roberto y yo nos levantamos a las siete.
2. papá / ducharse primero y / luego afeitarse Papá se ducha primero y luego se afeita.
3. mamá / peinarse y / luego maquillarse Mamá se peina y luego se maquilla.
4. yo / lavarse la cara y / vestirse antes de tomar café Yo me lavo la cara y me visto antes de tomar café.
5. todos (nosotros) / sentarse a la mesa para comer Todos nos sentamos a la mesa para comer.
6. Roberto / cepillarse los dientes después de comer Roberto se cepilla los dientes después de comer.
7. yo / ponerse el abrigo antes de salir Yo me pongo el abrigo antes de salir.
8. nosotros / irse Nosotros nos vamos.

3 **Describir** Describe lo que estas personas hacen. Some answers may vary.

> **modelo**
> Toni **Toni se enoja.**

1. el joven
El joven se quita los calcetines.

2. Carmen
Carmen se duerme.

3. Juan
Juan se prueba la camiseta.

4. los pasajeros
Los pasajeros se van.

5. Estrella
Estrella se seca el pelo.

Comunicación

4 **Preguntas personales** En parejas, túrnense para hacerse estas preguntas. *Answers will vary.*

1. ¿A qué hora te levantas durante la semana?
2. ¿A qué hora te levantas los fines de semana?
3. ¿Prefieres levantarte tarde o temprano? ¿Por qué?
4. ¿Te enojas frecuentemente con tus amigos?
5. ¿Te preocupas fácilmente? ¿Qué te preocupa?
6. ¿Qué haces cuando te sientes triste? ¿Y cuando te sientes alegre?
7. ¿Te acuestas tarde o temprano durante la semana?
8. ¿A qué hora te acuestas los fines de semana?

5 **Charadas** En grupos, jueguen a las charadas. Cada persona debe pensar en dos oraciones con verbos reflexivos. La primera persona que adivina la charada dramatiza la siguiente. *Answers will vary.*

6 **Debate** En grupos, discutan este tema: ¿Quiénes necesitan más tiempo para arreglarse (*to get ready*) antes de salir, los hombres o las mujeres? Hagan una lista de las razones (*reasons*) que tienen para defender sus ideas e informen a la clase. *Answers will vary.*

7 **Mi rutina diaria** Escribe un párrafo para describir cómo fue tu rutina diaria ayer. Usa los verbos. *Answers will vary.*

acostarse	despertarse
afeitarse/maquillarse	dormirse
bañarse/ducharse	levantarse
cepillarse	vestirse

Síntesis

8 **La familia ocupada** Tú y tu compañero/a asisten a un programa de verano en Lima, Perú. Viven con la familia Ramos. Tu profesor(a) te va a dar la rutina incompleta que la familia sigue en las mañanas. Trabaja con tu compañero/a para completarla. *Answers will vary.*

> **modelo**
> **Estudiante 1:** ¿Qué hace el señor Ramos a las seis y cuarto?
> **Estudiante 2:** El señor Ramos se levanta.

Expansion
Ask volunteers to call out some of their answers. The class should add information by speculating on the reason behind each answer. Ex: **Hablas por teléfono con tus amigos cuando te sientes triste porque ellos te comprenden muy bien.** Have the volunteer confirm or refute the speculation.

5 Teaching Tip Ask each group to present their best **charada** to the class.

6 Teaching Tip Before assigning groups, go over some of the things men and women do to get ready to go out. Ex: **Las mujeres se maquillan. Los hombres se afeitan.** Then ask students to indicate their opinion on the question, and divide the class into groups accordingly.

7 Expansion Have groups of three compare their routines of yesterday.

8 Teaching Tip Divide the class into pairs and distribute the handouts from the Activity Pack (Activity Pack/Supersite) that correspond to this Information Gap Activity. Give students ten minutes to complete this activity.

8 Expansion Ask small groups to imagine that they all live in the same house, and have them put together a message board to reflect their different schedules.

7.2 Indefinite and negative words Tutorial

ANTE TODO Indefinite words refer to people and things that are not specific, for example, *someone* or *something*. Negative words deny the existence of people and things or contradict statements, for instance, *no one* or *nothing*. Spanish indefinite words have corresponding negative words, which are opposite in meaning.

Indefinite and negative words

Indefinite words		Negative words	
algo	*something; anything*	**nada**	*nothing; not anything*
alguien	*someone; somebody; anyone*	**nadie**	*no one; nobody; not anyone*
alguno/a(s), algún	*some; any*	**ninguno/a, ningún**	*no; none; not any*
o... o	*either... or*	**ni... ni**	*neither... nor*
siempre	*always*	**nunca, jamás**	*never, not ever*
también	*also; too*	**tampoco**	*neither; not either*

▶ There are two ways to form negative sentences in Spanish. You can place the negative word before the verb, or you can place **no** before the verb and the negative word after.

Nadie se levanta temprano.
No one gets up early.

No se levanta nadie temprano.
No one gets up early.

Ellos **nunca gritan**.
They never shout.

Ellos **no gritan nunca**.
They never shout.

¿Hay algún problema?

Siempre haces esto.

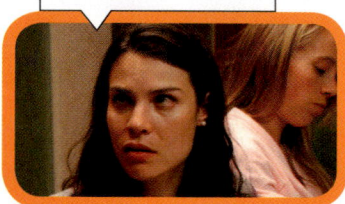

▶ Because they refer to people, **alguien** and **nadie** are often used with the personal **a**. The personal **a** is also used before **alguno/a, algunos/as,** and **ninguno/a** when these words refer to people and they are the direct object of the verb.

—Perdón, señor, ¿busca usted **a alguien**?
—No, gracias, señorita, no busco **a nadie**.

—Tomás, ¿buscas **a alguno** de tus hermanos?
—No, mamá, no busco **a ninguno**.

▶ **¡Atención!** Before a masculine singular noun, **alguno** and **ninguno** are shortened to **algún** and **ningún**.

—¿Tienen ustedes **algún** amigo peruano?

—No, no tenemos **ningún** amigo peruano.

COMPARE & CONTRAST

In English, it is incorrect to use more than one negative word in a sentence. In Spanish, however, sentences frequently contain two or more negative words. Compare these Spanish and English sentences.

Nunca le escribo a **nadie**.
I never write to anyone.

No me preocupo **nunca** por **nada**.
I do not ever worry about anything.

As the preceding sentences show, once an English sentence contains one negative word (for example, *not* or *never*), no other negative word may be used. Instead, indefinite (or affirmative) words are used. In Spanish, however, once a sentence is negative, no other affirmative (that is, indefinite) word may be used. Instead, all indefinite ideas must be expressed in the negative.

▶ **Pero** is used to mean *but*. The meaning of **sino** is *but rather* or *on the contrary*. It is used when the first part of the sentence is negative and the second part contradicts it.

Los estudiantes no se acuestan temprano **sino** tarde.
The students don't go to bed early, but rather late.

Esas gafas son caras, **pero** bonitas.
Those glasses are expensive, but pretty.

María no habla francés **sino** español.
María doesn't speak French, but rather Spanish.

José es inteligente, **pero** no saca buenas notas.
José is intelligent but doesn't get good grades.

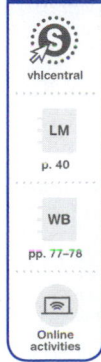

More activities

vhlcentral

LM
p. 40

WB
pp. 77–78

Online activities

¡INTÉNTALO!   Cambia las oraciones para que sean negativas.

1. Siempre se viste bien.
   _____Nunca_____ se viste bien.
   _____No_____ se viste bien _____nunca_____.

2. Alguien se ducha.
   _____Nadie_____ se ducha.
   _____No_____ se ducha _____nadie_____.

3. Ellas van también.
   Ellas _____tampoco_____ van.
   Ellas _____no_____ van _____tampoco_____.

4. Voy a traer algo.
   _____No_____ voy a traer _____nada_____.

5. Tú siempre te lavas las manos.
   Tú _____nunca / jamás_____ te lavas las manos.
   Tú _no_ te lavas las manos _____nunca / jamás_____.

6. Alguien se pone nervioso.
   _____Nadie_____ se pone nervioso.
   _____No_____ se pone nervioso _____nadie_____.

7. Juan se afeita también.
   Juan _____tampoco_____ se afeita.
   Juan _____no_____ se afeita _____tampoco_____.

8. Mis amigos viven en una residencia o en casa.
   Mis amigos _____no_____ viven _____ni_____ en una residencia _____ni_____ en casa.

9. La profesora hace algo en su escritorio.
   La profesora _____no_____ hace _____nada_____ en su escritorio.

10. Tienen un espejo en su casa.
    _____No_____ tienen _____ningún_____ espejo en su casa.

11. Tú y yo vamos al mercado.
    _____Ni_____ tú _____ni_____ yo vamos al mercado.

12. Algunos niños se ponen los abrigos.
    _____Ningún_____ niño se pone el abrigo.

TEACHING OPTIONS

Video →👤← Show the **Fotonovela** again to give students more input containing indefinite and negative words. Stop the video where appropriate to discuss how these words are used.
Pairs ←👤→ Have pairs create sentences about your community using indefinite and negative words. Ex: **En nuestra ciudad no hay ningún mercado al aire libre. Hay algunos restaurantes de tapas.**

Small Groups ←👤→ Give small groups five minutes to write a description of **un señor muy, pero muy antipático**. Tell them to use as many indefinite and negative words as possible to describe what makes this person so unpleasant. Encourage exaggeration and creativity.

Teaching Tips
- Emphasize that there is no limit to the number of negative words that can be strung together in a sentence in Spanish. Ex: **No hablo con nadie nunca de ningún problema, ni con mi familia ni con mis amigos.**
- Ask volunteers questions about their activities since the last class, reiterating the answers. Ex: **¿Quién compró algo nuevo? Sólo dos personas. Nadie más compró algo nuevo. Yo no compré nada nuevo tampoco.**
- Elicit negative responses by asking questions whose answers will clearly be negative. Ex: **¿Alguien lleva zapatos de lunares? (No, nadie lleva zapatos de lunares.) ¿Piensas comprar un barco mañana? (No, no pienso comprar ninguno/ningún barco.) ¿Tienes nietos? (No, no tengo ninguno/ningún nieto.)**
- Give examples of **pero** and **sino** using the seating of the students. Ex: _____ se sienta al lado de _____, pero no al lado de _____. No se sienta a la izquierda de _____, sino a la derecha. _____ no se sienta al lado de la ventana, pero está cerca de la puerta.

Práctica

1 Teaching Tips

- To challenge students, ask them to change each sentence so that the opposite choice (**pero** or **sino**) would be correct. Ex: **Muchos estudiantes no viven en la residencia estudiantil, sino en apartamentos.**
- Display a magazine picture that shows a group of people involved in a specific activity. Then talk about the picture, modeling the types of constructions required in **Actividad 1**. Ex: **Todos trabajan en la oficina, pero ninguno tiene computadora.**

1 Expansion
Have pairs create four sentences, two with **sino** and two with **pero**. Have them "dehydrate" their sentences and exchange papers with another pair, who will write the complete sentences.

2 Teaching Tip
Review indefinite and negative words by using them in short sentences and asking volunteers to contradict your statements. Ex: **Veo a alguien en la puerta. (No, usted no ve a nadie en la puerta.) Nunca vengo a clase con el libro. (No, usted siempre viene a clase con el libro.)**

2 Expansion
↤🔆↦ After students have role-played the conversation, ask them to summarize it. **Ana María no encontró ningún regalo para Eliana. Tampoco vio a ninguna amiga en el centro comercial....**

1 **¿Pero o sino?** Forma oraciones sobre estas personas usando **pero** o **sino**.

> **modelo**
>
> muchos estudiantes viven en residencias estudiantiles / muchos de ellos quieren vivir fuera del (*off*) campus
>
> *Muchos estudiantes viven en residencias estudiantiles, pero muchos de ellos quieren vivir fuera del campus.*

1. Lisa y Katarina no se acuestan temprano / muy tarde
   Lisa y Katarina no se acuestan temprano sino muy tarde.
2. Marcos nunca se despierta temprano / siempre llega puntual a clase
   Marcos nunca se despierta temprano, pero siempre llega puntual a clase.
3. Alfonso es inteligente / algunas veces es antipático
   Alfonso es inteligente, pero algunas veces es antipático.
4. los directores de la residencia no son ecuatorianos / peruanos
   Los directores de la residencia no son ecuatorianos sino peruanos.
5. no nos acordamos de comprar champú / compramos jabón
   No nos acordamos de comprar champú, pero compramos jabón.
6. no quiero levantarme / tengo que ir a clase
   No quiero levantarme, pero tengo que ir a clase.
7. Emilia no es estudiante / profesora
   Emilia no es estudiante sino profesora.
8. Miguel no se afeita por la mañana / por la noche
   Miguel no se afeita por la mañana sino por la noche.

2 **Completar** Completa esta conversación. Usa expresiones negativas en tus respuestas. Luego, dramatiza la conversación con un(a) compañero/a. *Answers will vary.*

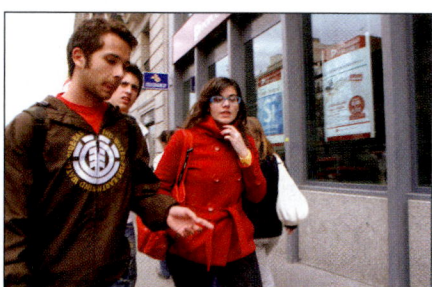

AURELIO Ana María, ¿encontraste algún regalo para Eliana?
ANA MARÍA (1) *No, no encontré ningún regalo/nada para Eliana.*

AURELIO ¿Viste a alguna amiga en el centro comercial?
ANA MARÍA (2) *No, no vi a ninguna amiga/ninguna/nadie en el centro comercial.*

AURELIO ¿Me llamó alguien?
ANA MARÍA (3) *No, nadie te llamó./No, no te llamó nadie.*

AURELIO ¿Quieres ir al teatro o al cine esta noche?
ANA MARÍA (4) *No, no quiero ir ni al teatro ni al cine.*

AURELIO ¿No quieres salir a comer?
ANA MARÍA (5) *No, no quiero salir a comer (tampoco).*

AURELIO ¿Hay algo interesante en la televisión esta noche?
ANA MARÍA (6) *No, no hay nada interesante en la televisión.*

AURELIO ¿Tienes algún problema?
ANA MARÍA (7) *No, no tengo ningún problema/ninguno.*

TEACHING OPTIONS

Small Groups ↤🔆↦ Add a visual aspect to this grammar practice. Have students bring in pairs of photos or magazine pictures, such as two photos of different family members, to compare and contrast. Divide the class into groups of three and have each student present his or her pictures to the group. Ex: **Éste es mi tío Ignacio. Siempre viene a casa los domingos. Ésta es mi tía Yolanda. Vive en Lima y por eso nunca viene a casa.**

Extra Practice To provide oral practice with indefinite and negative words, create prompts that follow the pattern of the sentences in **Actividad 1** and **Actividad 2**. Say the first part of the sentence, then have students repeat it and finish the sentence. Ex: **1. _____ no se viste de azul hoy, sino _____ . (de verde) 2. _____ no llegó temprano a clase hoy, sino _____ . (tarde)**

Comunicación

3 Opiniones Completa estas oraciones de una manera lógica. Luego, compara tus respuestas con las de un(a) compañero/a. *Answers will vary.*

1. Mi habitación es _____, pero _____.
2. Por la noche me gusta _____, pero _____.
3. Un(a) profesor(a) ideal no es _____, sino _____.
4. Mis amigos son _____, pero _____.

4 En el campus En parejas, háganse preguntas sobre qué hay en su universidad: residencias bonitas, departamento de ingeniería, cines, librerías baratas, estudiantes guapos/as, equipo de fútbol, playa, clases fáciles, museo, profesores/as estrictos/as. Sigan el modelo. *Answers will vary.*

> **modelo**
> **Estudiante 1:** ¿Hay algunas residencias bonitas?
> **Estudiante 2:** Sí, hay una/algunas. Está(n) detrás del estadio.
> **Estudiante 1:** ¿Hay algún museo?
> **Estudiante 2:** No, no hay ninguno.

5 Quejas En parejas, hagan una lista de cinco quejas (*complaints*) comunes que tienen los estudiantes. Usen expresiones negativas. *Answers will vary.*

> **modelo**
> Nadie me entiende.

6 Anuncios En parejas, lean el anuncio y contesten las preguntas.
Some answers will vary.

1. ¿Es el anuncio positivo o negativo? ¿Por qué? *Answers will vary.*
2. ¿Qué palabras indefinidas hay? *algún, siempre, algo*
3. Escriban el texto del anuncio cambiando todo por expresiones negativas. *¿No buscas ningún producto especial? ¡Nunca hay nada para nadie en las tiendas García!*

Ahora preparen su propio (*own*) anuncio usando expresiones indefinidas y negativas.

¿Buscas algún producto especial?

¡Siempre hay algo para todos en las tiendas García!

Síntesis

7 Encuesta Tu profesor(a) te va a dar una hoja de actividades para hacer una encuesta. Circula por la clase y pídeles a tus compañeros que comparen las actividades que hacen durante la semana con las que hacen durante los fines de semana. Escribe las respuestas. *Answers will vary.*

TEACHING OPTIONS

Large Groups Write the names of four vacation spots on four slips of paper and post them in different corners of the room. Ask students to pick their vacation preference by going to one of the corners. Then, have each group produce a short paragraph describing the five reasons for their choice as well as one complaint about each of the other places.

Extra Practice Have students complete this cloze activity using **pero, sino,** and **tampoco:** Yo me levanto temprano y hago mi tarea, _____ mi compañera de apartamento prefiere hacerla por la noche y acostarse muy tarde. (pero) Ella no tiene exámenes este semestre _____ proyectos. (sino) Yo no tengo exámenes _____. (tampoco) Sólo tengo mucha, mucha tarea.

7.3 # Preterite of **ser** and **ir** Tutorial

ANTE TODO In **Lección 6**, you learned how to form the preterite tense of regular **-ar**, **-er**, and **-ir** verbs. The following chart contains the preterite forms of **ser** (*to be*) and **ir** (*to go*). Since these forms are irregular, you will need to memorize them.

Preterite of ser and ir

		ser (to be)	**ir** (to go)
SINGULAR FORMS	yo	**fui**	**fui**
	tú	**fuiste**	**fuiste**
	Ud./él/ella	**fue**	**fue**
PLURAL FORMS	nosotros/as	**fuimos**	**fuimos**
	vosotros/as	**fuisteis**	**fuisteis**
	Uds./ellos/ellas	**fueron**	**fueron**

AYUDA
Note that, whereas regular **-er** and **-ir** verbs have accent marks in the **yo** and **Ud./él/ella** forms of the preterite, **ser** and **ir** do not.

▶ Since the preterite forms of **ser** and **ir** are identical, context clarifies which of the two verbs is being used.

Él **fue** a comprar champú y jabón.
He went to buy shampoo and soap.

¿Cómo **fue** la película anoche?
How was the movie last night?

¿Cuándo fue la última vez que viste a Juan Carlos?

Cuando fuimos a Mérida.

¡INTÉNTALO! Completa las oraciones usando el pretérito de **ser** e **ir**.

ir

1. Los viajeros _____fueron_____ a Perú.
2. Patricia _____fue_____ a Cuzco.
3. Gregorio y yo _____fuimos_____ a Lima.
4. Tú _____fuiste_____ a Iquitos.
5. Yo _____fui_____ a Trujillo.
6. Ustedes _____fueron_____ a Arequipa.
7. Mi padre _____fue_____ a Lima.
8. Él _____fue_____ a Machu Picchu.
9. Nosotras _____fuimos_____ a Cuzco.
10. Usted _____fue_____ a Nazca.

ser

1. Usted _____fue_____ muy amable.
2. Yo _____fui_____ muy cordial.
3. Ellos _____fueron_____ simpáticos.
4. Nosotros _____fuimos_____ muy tontos.
5. Tú _____fuiste_____ muy generoso.
6. Ella _____fue_____ antipática.
7. Ustedes _____fueron_____ cordiales.
8. Tomás y yo _____fuimos_____ muy felices.
9. La gente _____fue_____ amable.
10. Los profesores _____fueron_____ buenos.

More activities

vhlcentral

LM
p. 41

WB
p. 79

Online activities

Práctica y Comunicación

1   **Completar**   Completa estas conversaciones con la forma correcta del pretérito de **ser** o **ir**. Indica el infinitivo de cada forma verbal.

Conversación 1

		ser	ir
RAÚL	¿Adónde (1) ___fueron___ ustedes de vacaciones?	○	⊘
PILAR	(2) ___Fuimos___ a Perú.	○	⊘
RAÚL	¿Cómo (3) ___fue___ el viaje?	⊘	○
▶ **PILAR**	¡(4) ___Fue___ estupendo! Machu Picchu y El Callao son increíbles.	⊘	○
RAÚL	¿(5) ___Fue___ caro el viaje?	⊘	○
PILAR	No, el precio (6) ___fue___ muy bajo. Sólo costó tres mil dólares.	⊘	○

Conversación 2

		ser	ir
ISABEL	Tina y Vicente (7) ___fueron___ novios, ¿no?	⊘	○
LUCÍA	Sí, pero ahora no. Anoche Tina (8) ___fue___ a comer con Gregorio y la semana pasada ellos (9) ___fueron___ al partido de fútbol.	○	⊘
ISABEL	¿Ah sí? Javier y yo (10) ___fuimos___ al partido y no los vimos.	○	⊘

2   **Descripciones**   Forma oraciones con estos elementos. Usa el pretérito.   Answers will vary.

A	B	C	D
yo	(no) ir	a un restaurante	ayer
tú	(no) ser	en autobús	anoche
mi compañero/a		estudiante	anteayer
nosotros		muy simpático/a	la semana pasada
mis amigos		a la playa	año pasado
ustedes		dependiente/a en una tienda	

3   **Preguntas**   En parejas, túrnense para hacerse estas preguntas.   Answers will vary.

1. ¿Cuándo fuiste al cine por última vez? ¿Con quién fuiste?
2. ¿Fuiste en auto, en autobús o en metro? ¿Cómo fue el viaje?
3. ¿Cómo fue la película?
4. ¿Fue una película de terror, de acción o un drama?
5. ¿Fue una de las mejores películas que viste? ¿Por qué?
6. ¿Fueron buenos los actores o no? ¿Cuál fue el mejor?
7. ¿Adónde fuiste/fueron después?
8. ¿Fue una buena idea ir al cine?

4   **El viaje**   En parejas, preparen un diálogo de un(a) viajero/a hablando con un(a) amigo/a sobre un viaje que hizo recientemente. Usen el pretérito de **ser** e **ir**.   Answers will vary.

> **modelo**
> **Amigo:** *¿Cómo fue el viaje?*
> **Viajero:** *El viaje fue maravilloso/horrible…*

1   **Teaching Tip**   Before assigning the activity, write cloze sentences on the board and ask volunteers to fill in the blanks. Ex: ¿**Cómo _____ los guías turísticos durante tu viaje?** (fueron) ¿**Quién _____ con Marcela al baile?** (fue)

1   **Expansion**   Ask small groups to write four questions based on the conversations. Have groups exchange papers to discuss and answer the questions they receive. Then have them confirm their answers with the group who wrote the questions.

2   **Expansion**   Ask a volunteer to say one of his or her sentences aloud. Point to another student, and call out an interrogative word in order to cue a question. Ex: **E1: No fui a un restaurante anoche.** Say: **¿Adónde? E2: ¿Adónde fuiste? E1: Fui al cine.**

3   **Expansion**   Have students form new pairs and describe the movie that their first partner saw, based on the information they learned from items 3–6. The other student should guess what movie it was, asking for more information as needed.

4   **Expansion**   Ask pairs to write a similar conversation within a different context (Ex: **un día horrible**).

TEACHING OPTIONS

Small Groups   Have small groups of students role-play a TV interview with astronauts who have just returned from a long stay on Mars. Have students review previous lesson vocabulary lists as necessary in preparation. Give groups sufficient time to plan and practice their skits. When all groups have completed the activity, ask a few of them to perform their role-play for the class.

TPR   Read aloud a series of sentences using **ser** and **ir** in the preterite. Have students raise their right hand if the verb is **ser**, and their left hand for **ir**. Ex: **Yo fui camarero a los dieciocho años.** (right hand)

Section Goal

In **Estructura 7.4**, students will learn verbs that follow the pattern of **gustar**.

Instructional Resources

Supersite: Audio (Lab MP3 Files); Resources (Grammar Presentation Slides, Activity Pack, Scripts, Answer Keys); Testing Program (Quizzes)
WebSAM
Workbook
Lab Manual

Teaching Tips

• Review the verb **gustar**. Write the headings **Les gusta(n)** and **No les gusta(n)** on the board. Have the class brainstorm a list of likes and dislikes among the college population including music, artists, movies, clothes, or hobbies. Use the lists to form statements and questions illustrating the use of the verb **gustar**. Use different indirect object pronouns. Ex: **A los estudiantes universitarios no les gusta el jazz. A mis amigos y a mí, sí nos gusta el jazz.**

• Use the previously generated lists of likes and dislikes to present verbs like **gustar**. Ex: **A los estudiantes les aburren los documentales. A mí tampoco me interesan esas películas.**

7.4 **Verbs like gustar** Tutorial

 ANTE TODO In **Lección 2**, you learned how to express preferences with **gustar**. You will now learn more about the verb **gustar** and other similar verbs. Observe these examples.

Me gusta ese champú.

> **ENGLISH EQUIVALENT**
> *I like that shampoo.*
> **LITERAL MEANING**
> *That shampoo is pleasing to me.*

¿Te gustaron las clases?

> **ENGLISH EQUIVALENT**
> *Did you like the classes?*
> **LITERAL MEANING**
> *Were the classes pleasing to you?*

 As the examples show, constructions with **gustar** do not have a direct equivalent in English. The literal meaning of this construction is *to be pleasing to* (*someone*), and it requires the use of an indirect object pronoun.

INDIRECT OBJECT PRONOUN	VERB	SUBJECT		SUBJECT	VERB	DIRECT OBJECT
Me	**gusta**	ese champú.		*I*	*like*	*that shampoo.*

▶ In the diagram above, observe how in the Spanish sentence the object being liked (**ese champú**) is really the subject of the sentence. The person who likes the object, in turn, is an indirect object because it answers the question: *To whom is the shampoo pleasing?*

¿Te gusta Juan Carlos?

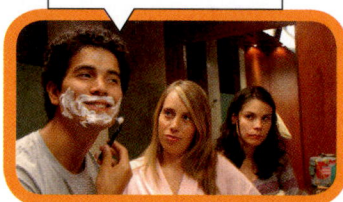

Me gustan los cafés que tienen música en vivo.

▶ Other verbs in Spanish are used in the same way as **gustar**. Here is a list of the most common ones.

Verbs like gustar

aburrir	to bore	**importar**	to be important to; to matter
encantar	to like very much; to love (inanimate objects)	**interesar**	to be interesting to; to interest
faltar	to lack; to need	**molestar**	to bother; to annoy
fascinar	to fascinate; to like very much	**quedar**	to be left over; to fit (clothing)

¡ATENCIÓN!

Faltar expresses what is lacking or missing. **Me falta una página.** *I'm missing one page.*

Quedar expresses how much of something is left. **Nos quedan tres pesos.** *We have three pesos left.*

•••

Quedar also means *to fit.* It can be used to tell how something looks (on someone).

Estos zapatos me quedan bien. *These shoes fit me well.*

Esa camisa te queda muy bien. *That shirt looks good on you.*

TEACHING OPTIONS

Pairs Have students work in pairs to compare and contrast activities they like to do with activities their parents/grandparents like to do. Encourage them to use the verb **gustar** and others that follow the same pattern.

Game Divide the class into small teams. Give a prompt including subject and object (Ex: **ella/películas de horror**). Allow teams one minute to construct a sentence using one of the verbs that follow the pattern of **gustar**. Then one member from each team will write the sentence on the board. Award one point to each team for each correct response.

▶ The most commonly used verb forms of **gustar** and similar verbs are the third person (singular and plural). When the object or person being liked is singular, the singular form (**gusta**) is used. When two or more objects or persons are being liked, the plural form (**gustan**) is used. Observe the following diagram:

	SINGULAR	
me, te, le, nos, os, les	encanta / interesó	la película / el concierto
	PLURAL	
	importan / fascinaron	las vacaciones / los museos de Lima

▶ To express what someone likes or does not like to do, use an appropriate verb followed by an infinitive. The singular form is used even if there is more than one infinitive.

Nos molesta comer a las nueve.   **Les encanta bailar** y **cantar** en las fiestas.
It bothers us to eat at nine o'clock.   *They love to dance and sing at parties.*

▶ As you learned in **Lección 2**, the construction a + [*pronoun*] (**a mí, a ti, a usted, a él,** etc.) is used to clarify or to emphasize who is pleased, bored, etc. The construction **a** + [*noun*] can also be used before the indirect object pronoun to clarify or to emphasize who is pleased.

A los turistas les gustó mucho   **A ti** te gusta cenar en casa, pero
Machu Picchu.   **a mí** me aburre.
The tourists liked Machu Picchu a lot.   *You like eating dinner at home, but I get bored.*

▶ **¡Atención! Mí** (*me*) has an accent mark to distinguish it from the possessive adjective **mi** (*my*).

AYUDA

Note that the **a** must be repeated if there is more than one person.
A Armando y a **Carmen** les molesta levantarse temprano.

¡INTÉNTALO!   Indica el pronombre de objeto indirecto y la forma del tiempo presente adecuados en cada oración.

fascinar

1. A él _le fascina_ viajar.
2. A nosotras _nos fascina_ cantar.
3. A mí _me fascina_ bailar.
4. A ustedes _les fascina_ leer.
5. A ti _te fascina_ correr y patinar.
6. A ellos _les fascinan_ los aviones.
7. A usted _le fascina_ jugar al tenis.
8. A mis padres _les fascina_ caminar.
9. A mi esposo y a mí _nos fascina_ dormir.
10. A Alberto _le fascina_ dibujar y pintar.
11. A todos _nos/les fascina_ opinar.
12. A Pili _le fascinan_ los sombreros.

aburrir

1. A ellos _les aburren_ los deportes.
2. A ti _te aburren_ las películas.
3. A usted _le aburren_ los viajes.
4. A Jorge y a Luis _les aburren_ los perros.
5. A mí _me aburren_ las revistas.
6. A nosotros _nos aburren_ las vacaciones.
7. A ustedes _les aburre_ el béisbol.
8. A Marcela _le aburren_ los libros.
9. A mis amigos _les aburren_ los museos.
10. A ella _le aburre_ el ciclismo.
11. A ti y a mí _nos aburre_ el baile.
12. A Omar _le aburre_ ir de compras.

More activities

vhlcentral

LM
p. 42

WB
pp. 80–82

Online activities

Teaching Tips
• Write a model sentence on the board such as those found in the examples. Ex: **A Carlos le encanta la pasta de dientes** *Crest*. Then change the noun and ask volunteers to say the new sentence. Ex: **A nosotros** (**A nosotros nos encanta la pasta de dientes** *Crest*.)
• Ask students about their preferences, using verbs that follow the pattern of **gustar**. Ex: **A mí me encantan las lenguas, pero me aburren las matemáticas. ¿Qué les interesa a ustedes? ¿Qué les aburre?**
• Point out the third bullet on this page. Give students some sample phrases to complete. Ex: **A _____ me encantan las películas. A _____ les aburre ir de compras. A _____ le gusta viajar.** Explain that some phrases have many possible answers.

TEACHING OPTIONS

Large Group Have the class sit in a circle. Student A begins by saying **Me encanta** and an activity he or she enjoys. Ex: **Me encanta correr.** Student B reports what student A said and adds his or her own favorite activity. **A Frank le encanta correr. A mí me fascina bailar.** Student C reports the preferences of the first two students and adds his or her own, and so forth. This activity may be used with any verb that follows the pattern of **gustar**.

Extra Practice →📖← To add an auditory aspect to this grammar presentation, read a series of sentences aloud, pausing for students to write. Ex: **1. A todos en mi familia nos encanta viajar. 2. Nos gusta viajar en avión, pero nos molestan los aviones pequeños. 3. A mi hijo le interesan las culturas latinoamericanas, a mi esposo le encantan los países de Asia y a mí me fascina Europa.** Ask comprehension questions as a follow-up.

Práctica

1

Completar Completa las oraciones con todos los elementos necesarios.

1. ____A____ Adela __le encanta__ (encantar) la música de Tito "El Bambino".
2. A ____mí____ me ____interesa____ (interesar) la música de otros países.
3. A Juan y ____a____ Rafael no les ____molesta____ (molestar) la música alta (*loud*).
4. A mis amigos ____les encantan____ (encantar) las canciones (*songs*) de Calle 13.
5. ____A____ nosotros ____nos fascinan____ (fascinar) los grupos de pop latino.
6. ____Al____ señor Ruiz ____le interesa____ (interesar) más la música clásica.
7. A ____mí____ me ____aburre____ (aburrir) la música clásica.
8. ¿A ____ti____ te ____falta____ (faltar) dinero para el concierto de Carlos Santana?
9. No. Ya compré el boleto y ____me quedan____ (quedar) cinco dólares.
10. ¿Cuánto dinero te ____queda____ (quedar) a ____ti____?

NOTA CULTURAL

Hoy día, la música latina es popular en los EE.UU. gracias a artistas como **Shakira**, de nacionalidad colombiana, y **Tito "El Bambino"**, puertorriqueño. Otros artistas, como **Carlos Santana** y **Gloria Estefan**, difundieron (*spread*) la música latina en los años 60, 70, 80 y 90.

2

Describir Usa los verbos para describir lo que está pasando. *Answers will vary. Suggested answers:*

aburrir	faltar	molestar
encantar	interesar	quedar

1. a Ramón *A Ramón le molesta despertarse temprano.*

2. a nosotros *A nosotros nos encanta esquiar.*

3. a Sara *A Sara le interesan los libros de arte moderno.*

4. a ti *A ti no te queda bien este vestido. A ti te queda mal/grande este vestido.*

3

Gustos Forma oraciones con los elementos de las columnas. *Answers will vary.*

modelo

Tú interesar las ruinas

A ti te interesan las ruinas de Machu Picchu.

A	B	C
yo	aburrir	despertarse temprano
tú	encantar	mirarse en el espejo
mi mejor amigo/a	faltar	la música rock
mis amigos y yo	fascinar	las pantuflas rosadas
Bart y Homero Simpson	interesar	la pasta de dientes con menta (*mint*)
Shakira	molestar	las ruinas de Machu Picchu
Gael García Bernal		los zapatos caros

Comunicación

4

Preguntas En parejas, túrnense para hacer y contestar estas preguntas. Answers will vary.

1. ¿Te gusta levantarte temprano o tarde? ¿Por qué? ¿Y a tu compañero/a de cuarto?
2. ¿Te gusta acostarte temprano o tarde? ¿Y a tu compañero/a de cuarto?
3. ¿Te gusta dormir la siesta?
4. ¿Te encanta acampar o prefieres quedarte en un hotel cuando estás de vacaciones?
5. ¿Qué te gusta hacer en el verano?
6. ¿Qué te fascina de esta universidad? ¿Qué te molesta?
7. ¿Te interesan más las ciencias o las humanidades? ¿Por qué?
8. ¿Qué cosas te aburren?

5

Completar Trabajen en parejas. Túrnense para completar estas frases de una manera lógica. Answers will vary.

1. A mi novio/a le fascina(n)…
2. A mi mejor (*best*) amigo/a no le interesa(n)…
3. A mis padres les importa(n)…
4. A nosotros nos molesta(n)…
5. A mis hermanos les aburre(n)…
6. A mi compañero/a de cuarto le aburre(n)…
7. A los turistas les interesa(n)…
8. A los jugadores profesionales les encanta(n)…
9. A nuestro/a profesor(a) le molesta(n)…
10. A mí me importa(n)…

Warm-up Two.

6

La residencia Tú y tu compañero/a de clase son los directores de una residencia estudiantil en Perú. Su profesor(a) les va a dar a cada uno de ustedes las descripciones de cinco estudiantes. Con la información tienen que escoger quiénes van a ser compañeros de cuarto. Después, completen la lista. Answers will vary.

Síntesis

7

Situación Trabajen en parejas para representar los papeles de un(a) cliente/a y un(a) dependiente/a en una tienda de ropa. Answers will vary.

Dependiente/a	**Cliente/a**
Saluda al/a la cliente/a y pregúntale en qué le puedes servir.	Saluda al/a la dependiente/a y dile (*tell him/her*) qué quieres comprar y qué colores prefieres.
Pregúntale si le interesan los estilos modernos y empieza a mostrarle la ropa.	Explícale que los estilos modernos te interesan. Escoge las cosas que te interesan.
Habla de los gustos del/de la cliente/a.	Habla de la ropa (me queda(n) bien/mal, me encanta(n)…).
Da opiniones favorables al/a la cliente/a (las botas te quedan fantásticas…).	Decide cuáles son las cosas que te gustan y qué vas a comprar.

TEACHING OPTIONS

Pairs ▰↔▰ Have pairs prepare short TV commercials in which they use the target verbs presented in **Estructura 7.4** to sell a particular product. Group three pairs together to present their skits.
Extra Practice Add a visual aspect to this grammar practice. Bring in magazine pictures of people enjoying or not enjoying what they are doing. Have students create sentences with verbs like **gustar**. Ex: **A los chicos no les interesa estudiar.**

Game ↔▰ Give groups of students five minutes to write a description of social life during a specific historical period, such as the French Revolution or prehistoric times, using as many of the target verbs presented in **Estructura 7.4** as possible. When finished, ask groups how many of these verbs they used in their descriptions. Have the top three read their descriptions for the class, who vote for their favorite description.

---

4 Teaching Tip Take a class survey of the answers and write the results on the board. Ask volunteers to use verbs like **gustar** to summarize them.

5 Teaching Tip For items that start with **A mi(s)…** , have pairs compare their answers and then report to the class: first, the answers they had in common; then, the answers that differed. Ex: **A mis padres les importan los estudios, pero a los padres de _____ les importa más el dinero.**

6 Teaching Tip Divide the class into pairs and distribute the handouts from the Activity Pack (Activity Pack/Supersite) that correspond to this Information Gap Activity. Give students ten minutes to complete this activity.

6 Expansion
• Have pairs circulate around the classroom and compare their matches.
• ▰↔▰ Have pairs choose one of the students and write his or her want ad looking for a suitable roommate.

7 Teaching Tip To simplify, have students prepare for their roles by brainstorming a list of words and phrases. Remind students to use the formal register in this conversation.

7 Expansion
▰↔▰ Ask pairs to role-play their conversation for the class, or have them record it.

Recapitulación

Completa estas actividades para repasar los conceptos de gramática que aprendiste en esta lección.

1 Completar Completa la tabla con la forma correcta de los verbos. **24 pts.**

yo	tú	nosotros	ellas
me levanto	te levantas	nos levantamos	se levantan
me afeito	**te afeitas**	nos afeitamos	se afeitan
me visto	te vistes	**nos vestimos**	se visten
me seco	te secas	nos secamos	**se secan**

2 Hoy y ayer Cambia los verbos del presente al pretérito. **10 pts.**

1. Vamos de compras hoy. _Fuimos_ de compras hoy.
2. Por último, voy a poner el despertador. Por último, _fui_ a poner el despertador.
3. Lalo es el primero en levantarse. Lalo _fue_ el primero en levantarse.
4. ¿Vas a tu habitación? ¿_Fuiste_ a tu habitación?
5. Ustedes son profesores. Ustedes _fueron_ profesores.

3 Reflexivos Completa cada conversación con la forma correcta de los verbos reflexivos. **22 pts.**

TOMÁS Yo siempre (1) _me baño_ (bañarse) antes de (2) _acostarme_ (acostarse). Esto me relaja porque no (3) _me duermo_ (dormirse) fácilmente. Y así puedo (4) _levantarme_ (levantarse) más tarde. Y tú, ¿cuándo (5) _te duchas_ (ducharse)?

LETI Pues por la mañana, para poder (6) _despertarme_ (despertarse).

DAVID ¿Cómo (7) _se siente_ (sentirse) Pepa hoy?

MARÍA Todavía está enojada.

DAVID ¿De verdad? Ella nunca (8) _se enoja_ (enojarse) con nadie.

BETO ¿(Nosotros) (9) _Nos vamos_ (irse) de esta tienda? Estoy cansado.

SARA Pero antes vamos a (10) _probarnos_ (probarse) estos sombreros. Si quieres, después (nosotros) (11) _nos sentamos_ (sentarse) un rato.

RESUMEN GRAMATICAL

7.1 Reflexive verbs *pp. 236–237*

lavarse	
me lavo	nos lavamos
te lavas	os laváis
se lava	se lavan

7.2 Indefinite and negative words *pp. 240–241*

Indefinite words	Negative words
algo	nada
alguien	nadie
alguno/a(s), algún	ninguno/a, ningún
o... o	ni... ni
siempre	nunca, jamás
también	tampoco

7.3 Preterite of ser and ir *p. 244*

► The preterite of **ser** and **ir** are identical. Context will determine the meaning.

ser and ir	
fui	fuimos
fuiste	fuisteis
fue	fueron

7.4 Verbs like gustar *pp. 246–247*

aburrir	importar
encantar	interesar
faltar	molestar
fascinar	quedar

SINGULAR
me, te, le, nos, os, les ⟩ encanta / interesó ⟩ la película / el concierto

PLURAL
importan / fascinaron ⟩ las vacaciones / los museos

► Use the construction a + [*noun/pronoun*] to clarify the person in question.

A mí me encanta ver películas, ¿y a ti?

---

4 **Conversaciones** Completa cada conversación de manera lógica con palabras de la lista. `18 pts.`

algo	nada	ningún	siempre
alguien	nadie	nunca	también
algún	ni... ni	o... o	tampoco

1. —¿Tienes __algún__ plan para esta noche?

   —No, prefiero quedarme en casa. Hoy no quiero ver a __nadie__.

   —Yo __también__ me quedo. Estoy muy cansado.

2. —¿Puedo entrar? ¿Hay __alguien__ en el cuarto de baño?

   —Sí. ¡Un momento! Ahora mismo salgo.

3. —¿Puedes prestarme __algo__ para peinarme? No encuentro __ni__ mi cepillo __ni__ mi peine.

   —Lo siento, yo __tampoco__ encuentro los míos (*mine*).

4. —¿Me prestas tu maquillaje?

   —Lo siento, no tengo. __Nunca__ me maquillo.

5 **Oraciones** Forma oraciones completas con los elementos dados (*given*). Usa el presente de los verbos. `8 pts.`

1. David y Juan / molestar / levantarse temprano
   A David y a Juan les molesta levantarse temprano.
2. Lucía / encantar / las películas de terror   *A Lucía le encantan las películas de terror.*
3. todos (nosotros) / importar / la educación   *A todos nos importa la educación.*
4. tú / aburrir / ver / la televisión   *A ti te aburre ver la televisión.*

6 **Rutinas** Escribe seis oraciones que describan las rutinas de dos personas que conoces. `18 pts.`
Answers will vary.

> **modelo**
> Mi tía se despierta temprano, pero mi primo...

7 **Adivinanza** Completa la adivinanza con las palabras que faltan y adivina la respuesta. `¡4 puntos EXTRA!`

"Cuanto más° __te seca__ (*it dries you*), más se moja°."
¿Qué es? __La toalla__

Cuanto más *The more* se moja *it gets wet*

---

4 Expansion
Have students write additional mini-conversations using the remaining indefinite and negative words from the word bank.

5 Expansion Give students these sentences as items 5–8: **5.** yo / faltar / dinero (A mí me falta dinero.) **6.** Pedro y yo / fascinar / cantar y bailar (A Pedro y a mí nos fascina cantar y bailar.) **7.** usted / quedar / muy bien / esas gafas de sol (A usted le quedan muy bien esas gafas de sol.) **8.** ¿ / ustedes / interesar / conocer / otros países / ? (¿A ustedes les interesa conocer otros países?)

6 Expansion
Have volunteers share their sentences with the class. Encourage classmates to ask them follow-up questions. Ex: **¿Por qué se despierta temprano tu tía?**

7 Expansion
To challenge students, have them work in small groups to create a riddle using grammar and/or vocabulary from this lesson. Have groups share their riddles with the class.

Lectura

communication cultures
NATIONAL STANDARDS

Antes de leer

Estrategia
Predicting content from the title

Prediction is an invaluable strategy in reading for comprehension. For example, we can usually predict the content of a newspaper article from its headline. We often decide whether to read the article based on its headline. Predicting content from the title will help you increase your reading comprehension in Spanish.

Examinar el texto
Lee el título de la lectura y haz tres predicciones sobre el contenido. Escribe tus predicciones en una hoja de papel. Answers will vary.

Compartir
Comparte tus ideas con un(a) compañero/a de clase.

Cognados
Haz una lista de seis cognados que encuentres en la lectura. Answers will vary.

1. _____
2. _____
3. _____
4. _____
5. _____
6. _____

¿Qué te dicen los cognados sobre el tema de la lectura?

More activities
vhlcentral | Online activities

✉ Mensaje

⬆ Anterior ⬇ Siguiente ✉ Responder ✉ Reenviar

De	Guillermo Zamora
Para	Lupe; Marcos; Sandra; Jorge
Asunto	¡Qué día!

Hola, chicos:

La semana pasada me di cuenta° de que necesito organizar mejor° mi rutina... pero especialmente debo prepararme mejor para los exámenes. Me falta disciplina, me molesta no tener control de mi tiempo y nunca deseo repetir los eventos de la semana pasada. ☹️

El miércoles pasé todo el día y 😴 toda la noche estudiando para el examen de biología del jueves por la mañana. Me aburre la biología y no empecé a estudiar hasta el día antes del examen. El jueves a las 8, después de no dormir en toda la noche, fui exhausto al examen. Fue difícil, pero afortunadamente° me acordé de todo el material. Esa noche me acosté temprano y dormí mucho. 😴

Me desperté a las 7, y fue extraño° ver a mi compañero de cuarto, Andrés, preparándose para ir a dormir. Como° siempre se enferma°, tiene problemas para dormir y no hablamos mucho, no le comenté nada. Fui al baño a cepillarme los dientes para ir a clase. ¿Y Andrés? Él se acostó. "Debe estar enfermo°, ¡otra vez!", pensé. 😮

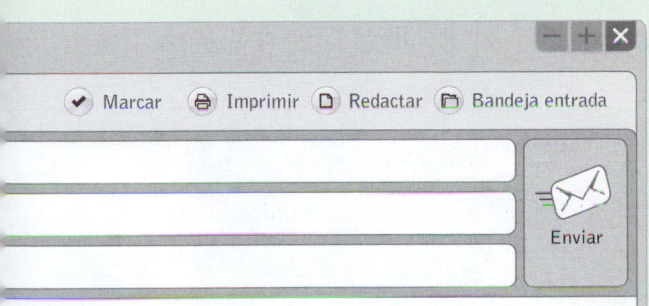

Mi clase es a las 8, y fue necesario hacer las cosas rápido. Todo empezó a ir mal... eso pasa siempre cuando uno tiene prisa. Cuando busqué mis cosas para el baño, no las encontré. Entonces me duché sin jabón, me cepillé los dientes sin cepillo de dientes y me peiné con las manos. Tampoco encontré ropa limpia y usé la sucia. Rápido, tomé mis libros. ¿Y Andrés? Roncando°... ¡a las 7:50!

Cuando salí corriendo para la clase, la prisa no me permitió ver el campus desierto. Cuando llegué a la clase, no vi a nadie. No vi al profesor ni a los estudiantes. Por último miré mi reloj, y vi la hora. Las 8 en punto... ¡de la noche!

¡Dormí 24 horas!

Guillermo

me di cuenta *I realized* mejor *better* afortunadamente *fortunately*
extraño *strange* Como *Since* se enferma *he gets sick* enfermo *sick*
Roncando *Snoring*

Después de leer

Seleccionar
Selecciona la respuesta correcta.
1. ¿Quién es el/la narrador(a)? c
   a. Andrés
   b. una profesora
   c. Guillermo
2. ¿Qué le molesta al narrador? b
   a. Le molestan los exámenes de biología.
   b. Le molesta no tener control de su tiempo.
   c. Le molesta mucho organizar su rutina.
3. ¿Por qué está exhausto? c
   a. Porque fue a una fiesta la noche anterior.
   b. Porque no le gusta la biología.
   c. Porque pasó la noche anterior estudiando.
4. ¿Por qué no hay nadie en clase? a
   a. Porque es de noche.
   b. Porque todos están de vacaciones.
   c. Porque el profesor canceló la clase.
5. ¿Cómo es la relación de Guillermo y Andrés? b
   a. Son buenos amigos.
   b. No hablan mucho.
   c. Tienen una buena relación.

Ordenar
Ordena los sucesos de la narración. Utiliza los números del 1 al 9.
   a. Toma el examen de biología. _2_
   b. No encuentra sus cosas para el baño. _5_
   c. Andrés se duerme. _7_
   d. Pasa todo el día y toda la noche estudiando para un examen. _1_
   e. Se ducha sin jabón. _6_
   f. Se acuesta temprano. _3_
   g. Vuelve a su cuarto después de las 8 de la noche. _9_
   h. Se despierta a las 7 y su compañero de cuarto se prepara para dormir. _4_
   i. Va a clase y no hay nadie. _8_

Contestar
Contesta estas preguntas. Answers will vary.
1. ¿Cómo es tu rutina diaria? ¿Muy organizada?
2. ¿Cuándo empiezas a estudiar para los exámenes?
3. ¿Tienes compañero/a de cuarto? ¿Es tu amigo/a?
4. Para comunicarte con tus amigos/as, ¿prefieres el teléfono o el correo electrónico? ¿Por qué?

Seleccionar Before beginning the activity, have students summarize the reading selection by listing all the verbs in the preterite. Then, have them use these verbs to talk about **Guillermo's** day.

Ordenar
- Before beginning, ask a volunteer to summarize in Spanish, using the third-person present tense, the first two sentences of the reading selection.
- As writing practice, have students use the sentence in each item as the topic sentence of a short paragraph about **Guillermo** or **Andrés**.

Contestar Have students work in small groups to tell each other about a day when everything turned out wrong due to a miscalculation. Have groups vote for the most unusual story to share with the class.

TEACHING OPTIONS

Pairs Add a visual aspect to this reading. Have pairs reconstruct **Guillermo's** confusing day graphically by means of one or more time lines (or other graphic representation). They should compare what **Guillermo** assumed was going on with what was actually occurring.

Pairs Have pairs of students work together to read the selection and write two questions about each paragraph. When they have finished, have them exchange papers with another pair, who can work together to answer the questions.

Escritura

Estrategia
Sequencing events

Paying strict attention to sequencing in a narrative will ensure that your writing flows logically from one part to the next.

Every composition should have an introduction, a body, and a conclusion. The introduction presents the subject, the setting, the situation, and the people involved. The main part, or the body, describes the events and people's reactions to these events. The conclusion brings the narrative to a close.

Adverbs and adverbial phrases are sometimes used as transitions between the introduction, the body, and the conclusion. Here is a list of commonly used adverbs in Spanish:

Adverbios	
además; también	*in addition; also*
al principio; en un principio	*at first*
antes (de)	*before*
después	*then*
después (de)	*after*
entonces; luego	*then*
más tarde	*later (on)*
primero	*first*
pronto	*soon*
por fin; finalmente	*finally*
al final	*finally*

Tema

 Escribe tu rutina

Imagina tu rutina diaria en uno de estos lugares:

▶ una isla desierta
▶ el Polo Norte
▶ un crucero° transatlántico
▶ un desierto

Escribe una composición en la que describes tu rutina diaria en uno de estos lugares o en algún otro lugar interesante que imagines°. Mientras planeas tu composición, considera cómo cambian algunos de los elementos más básicos de tu rutina diaria en el lugar que escogiste°. Por ejemplo, ¿dónde te acuestas en el Polo Norte? ¿Cómo te duchas en el desierto?

Usa el presente de los verbos reflexivos que conoces e incluye algunos de los adverbios de esta página para organizar la secuencia de tus actividades. Piensa también en la información que debes incluir en cada sección de la narración. Por ejemplo, en la introducción puedes hacer una descripción del lugar y de las personas que están allí, y en la conclusión puedes dar tus opiniones acerca del° lugar y de tu vida diaria allí.

crucero *cruise ship* que imagines *that you dream up* escogiste *you chose* acerca del *about the*

EVALUATION: Descripción

Criteria	Scale
Content	1 2 3 4 5
Organization	1 2 3 4 5
Use of vocabulary	1 2 3 4 5
Grammatical accuracy	1 2 3 4 5

Scoring	
Excellent	18–20 points
Good	14–17 points
Satisfactory	10–13 points
Unsatisfactory	< 10 points

Escuchar
Antes de escuchar

Estrategia
Using background information

Once you discern the topic of a conversation, pause to think about what you already know about the subject. Using this background information will help you guess the meaning of unknown words or structures.

  To help you practice this strategy, you will now listen to a short paragraph. Jot down the subject of the paragraph, and then use your knowledge of the subject to listen for and write down the paragraph's main points.

Preparación

Según la foto, ¿dónde están Carolina y Julián? Piensa en lo que sabes de este tipo de situación. ¿De qué van a hablar? **Answers will vary.**

Ahora escucha

La entrevista

Ahora escucha la entrevista y piensa en lo que sabes sobre este tipo de situación. Elige la información que completa correctamente cada oración.

1. Julián es ___c___.
   a. político
   b. deportista profesional
   c. artista de cine
2. El público de Julián quiere saber de ___b___.
   a. sus películas
   b. su vida
   c. su novia
3. Julián habla de ___a___.
   a. sus viajes y sus rutinas
   b. sus parientes y amigos
   c. sus comidas favoritas
4. Julián ___b___.
   a. se levanta y se acuesta a diferentes horas todos los días
   b. tiene una rutina diaria
   c. no quiere hablar de su vida

Comprensión

¿Cierto o falso?

Indica si las oraciones son **ciertas** o **falsas** según la información que Julián da en la entrevista.

1. Es difícil despertarme; generalmente duermo hasta las diez. **Falsa**
2. Pienso que mi vida no es más interesante que las vidas de ustedes. **Cierta**
3. Me gusta tener tiempo para pensar y meditar. **Cierta**
4. Nunca hago mucho ejercicio; no soy una persona activa. **Falsa**
5. Me fascinan las actividades tranquilas, como escribir y escuchar música clásica. **Cierta**
6. Los viajes me parecen aburridos. **Falsa**

Preguntas **Answers will vary.**

1. ¿Qué tiene Julián en común con otras personas de su misma profesión?
2. ¿Te parece que Julián siempre fue rico? ¿Por qué?
3. ¿Qué piensas de Julián como persona?

C: Cuando no estás filmando, ¿te quedas en casa durante el día?
J: Pues, en esos momentos, uso el tiempo libre para sentarme en casa a escribir. Pero sí tengo una rutina diaria de ejercicio. Corro unas cinco millas diarias y si hace mal tiempo voy al gimnasio.
C: Veo que eres una persona activa. Te mantienes en muy buena forma. ¿Qué más nos puedes decir de tu vida?
J: Bueno, no puedo negar que me encanta viajar. ¡Y la elegancia de algunos hoteles es increíble! Estuve en un hotel en Londres que tiene una ducha del tamaño de un cuarto normal.
C: Ya vemos que tu vida no es nada aburrida. Qué gusto hablar contigo hoy, Julián.
J: El placer es mío. Gracias por la invitación, Carolina.

En pantalla Video

La fiesta de quince años se celebra en algunos países de Latinoamérica cuando las chicas cumplen° quince años. Los quince años representan la transición de niña a mujer. Los orígenes de esta ceremonia son mayas y aztecas, pero también tiene influencias del catolicismo. La celebración varía según el país, pero es común en todas la importancia del vestido de la quinceañera°, el baile de la quinceañera con su padre y con otros familiares° y el banquete para los invitados°.

Vocabulario útil

cubren	*cover*
granos	*zits, pimples*
hice	*I did*
peor	*worse*
tapar	*to cover*
tenía	*I had*

Preparación

¿Qué fechas especiales son importantes para ti? ¿Por qué? Answers will vary.

Escoger

Escoge la opción correcta para cada oración.
1. La chica se levantó **a** el día de las fotos.
   a. con granos   b. muy tarde
2. Después de levantarse, la chica **b**.
   a. se bañó   b. se maquilló
3. Para las fotos, la chica tapó los granos con **a**.
   a. la flora y la fauna   b. maquillaje Asepxia
4. Ahora la chica **b**.
   a. tiene muchos granos   b. usa maquillaje Asepxia

Una fiesta

Habla con un(a) compañero/a sobre la última fiesta a la que fuiste. Puedes usar estas preguntas como guía. Luego, presenta la experiencia de tu compañero/a a la clase. Answers will vary.

▶ ¿Qué te gustó más? ¿Te aburrió algo?

▶ ¿Cuántas personas fueron?

▶ ¿Cómo te preparaste para la fiesta? ¿Te duchaste antes de ir a la fiesta? ¿Te maquillaste? ¿Te afeitaste?

cumplen *turn* **quinceañera** *young woman celebrating her fifteenth birthday* **familiares** *family members* **invitados** *guests* **Tuve que** *I had to* **lo que pude** *what I could*

Anuncio de Asepxia

Me levanté con una invasión de granos.

Tuve que° taparlos con lo que pude°...

Ahora Florencia usa maquillajes Asepxia.

COMMUNICATION CULTURES STANDARDS

More activities

vhlcentral   Online activities

Video

En este episodio de *Flash cultura* vas a conocer unos entremeses° españoles llamados **tapas**. Hay varias teorías sobre el origen de su nombre. Una dice que viene de la costumbre antigua° de **tapar**° los vasos de vino para evitar° que insectos o polvo entren en° ellos. Otra teoría cuenta que el rey Alfonso X debía° beber un poco de vino por indicación médica y decidió acompañarlo° con algunos bocados° para tapar los efectos del alcohol. Cuando el rey estuvo° mejor, ordenó que siempre en Castilla se sirviera° algo de comer con las bebidas° alcohólicas.

Vocabulario útil

económicas	inexpensive
montaditos	bread slices with assorted toppings
pagar propinas	to tip
tapar el hambre	to take the edge off (lit. putting the lid on one's hunger)

Preparación

En el área donde vives, ¿qué hacen las personas normalmente después del trabajo (*work*)? ¿Van a sus casas? ¿Salen con amigos? ¿Comen? Answers will vary.

Ordenar

Ordena estos sucesos.

__5__ a. El empleado cuenta los palillos (*counts the toothpicks*) de los montaditos que Mari Carmen comió.

__2__ b. Mari Carmen va al barrio de la Ribera.

__1__ c. Un hombre en un bar explica cuándo sale a tomar tapas.

__3__ d. Un hombre explica la tradición de los montaditos o pinchos.

__4__ e. Carmen le pregunta a la chica si los montaditos son buenos para la salud.

entremeses *appetizers* antigua *ancient* tapar *cover* evitar *avoid* entren en *would get in* debía *should* acompañarlo *accompany it* bocados *snacks* estuvo *was* se sirviera *they should serve* bebidas *drinks* sueles *do you tend*

Tapas para todos los días

Estamos en la Plaza Cataluña, el puro centro de Barcelona.

—¿Cuándo sueles° venir a tomar tapas?
—Generalmente, después del trabajo.

Éstos son los montaditos, o también llamados pinchos. ¿Te gustan?

More activities
vhlcentral / VM pp. 49–50 / Online activities

Section Goals

In **Flash cultura**, students will:
- read about the origins of **tapas**
- watch a video about **tapas**

Instructional Resources
Supersite: Video (*Flash cultura*); Resources (Scripts, Translations, Answer Keys)
WebSAM
Video Manual

Introduction To check comprehension, ask students these questions: 1. ¿En qué país se comen las tapas? (en España) 2. ¿Se sabe con exactitud de dónde viene el nombre *tapa*? (No, hay varias teorías.) 3. ¿Cuál fue la solución para mantener limpios los vasos de vino? (taparlos) 4. ¿Qué ordenó Alfonso X? (que se sirviera algo de comer con las bebidas alcohólicas)

Antes de ver
- Read through the **Vocabulario útil** and model pronunciation.
- Assure students that they do not need to understand every Spanish word they hear in the video. Tell them to rely on visual cues and to listen for cognates and words from **Vocabulario útil**.

Preparación Ask students to compare the custom of **tapas** to typical North American customs, like brunch or "happy hour."

Ordenar To simplify, have students read through the items before watching the video.

TEACHING OPTIONS

Extra Practice Have students research and prepare an oral report about a **tapas** bar in Madrid. Have them include information about the location, ambience, menu, and hours of operation. They should present images from the Internet, if possible. Also have students say what they would order there.

Cultural Note Explain that the Spanish tendency to socialize outside of the home is due in part to the nature of the country's cities and apartments. Since city apartments tend to be small, people generally meet with friends outside of the home. Also, the walkable nature of Spanish cities makes it easy to get together spontaneously with others and go **tapas**-hopping.

Video

Perú

El país en cifras

▶ **Área:** 1.285.220 km² (496.224 millas²), *un poco menos que el área de Alaska*

▶ **Población:** 31.036.000

▶ **Capital:** Lima—9.897.000

▶ **Ciudades principales:** Arequipa—850.000, Trujillo, Chiclayo, Callao, Iquitos

Iquitos es un puerto muy importante en el río Amazonas. Desde Iquitos se envían° muchos productos a otros lugares, incluyendo goma°, nueces°, madera°, arroz°, café y tabaco. Iquitos es también un destino popular para los ecoturistas que visitan la selva°.

▶ **Moneda:** nuevo sol

▶ **Idiomas:** español (oficial); quechua, aimara y otras lenguas indígenas (oficiales en los territorios donde se usan)

Bandera de Perú

Peruanos célebres

▶ **Clorinda Matto de Turner,** escritora (1852–1909)

▶ **César Vallejo,** poeta (1892–1938)

▶ **Javier Pérez de Cuéllar,** diplomático (1920–)

▶ **Juan Diego Flórez,** cantante de ópera (1973–)

▶ **Mario Vargas Llosa,** escritor (1936–)

Mario Vargas Llosa, Premio Nobel de Literatura 2010

se envían *are shipped* goma *rubber* nueces *nuts* madera *timber* arroz *rice* selva *jungle*

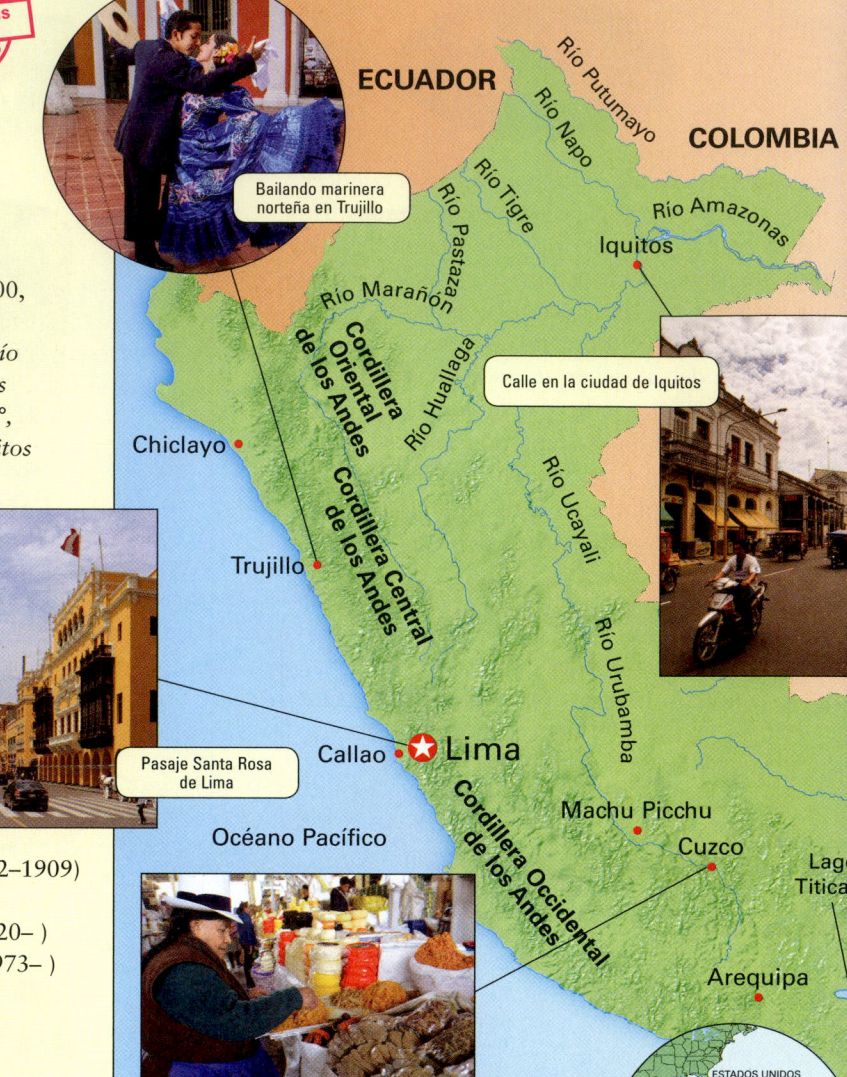

Bailando marinera norteña en Trujillo

ECUADOR

COLOMBIA

Río Putumayo
Río Napo
Río Tigre
Río Pastaza
Río Amazonas
Iquitos
Río Marañón
Cordillera Oriental de los Andes
Río Huallaga
Río Ucayali
Calle en la ciudad de Iquitos
Chiclayo
Cordillera Central de los Andes
Trujillo
Río Urubamba
Pasaje Santa Rosa de Lima
Callao • ★ Lima
Cordillera Occidental de los Andes
Machu Picchu
Océano Pacífico
Cuzco
Lago Titicaca
Arequipa

Mercado indígena en Cuzco

ESTADOS UNIDOS
OCÉANO ATLÁNTICO
OCÉANO PACÍFICO
AMÉRICA DEL SUR
PERÚ

More activities
 vhlcentral
WB pp. 83–84
Online activities

ACTIVIDADES

1 **¿Cierto o falso?** Indica si lo que dice cada oración es **cierto** o **falso.**

1. Ni Arequipa ni Callao son ciudades principales de Perú. falso
2. El nuevo sol es la moneda de Perú. cierto
3. Juan Diego Flórez nunca canta en público. falso
4. El escritor peruano Mario Vargas Llosa ganó el Premio Nobel de Literatura en el año 2010. cierto
5. Hay algunas lenguas indígenas en Perú. cierto
6. Hiram Bingham descubrió las Líneas de Nazca en 1911. falso
7. En el Museo Oro del Perú y en el Museo Nacional de Antropología y Arqueología podemos ver exhibiciones sobre los aztecas. falso
8. Los españoles nunca encontraron Machu Picchu durante la Conquista. cierto
9. La música andina tiene influencias francesas e italianas. falso
10. Los peruanos usan las llamas para la carga y el transporte. cierto

---

TEACHING OPTIONS

Heritage Speakers Ask heritage speakers of Peruvian origin or students who have visited Peru to make a short presentation to the class about their impressions. Encourage them to speak of the region they are from or have visited and how it differs from other regions in this vast country. If they have photographs, ask them to bring them to class to illustrate their talk.

TPR Invite students to take turns guiding the class on tours of Peru's waterways: one student gives directions, and the others follow by tracing the route on their map of Peru. For example: **Comenzamos en el río Amazonas, pasando por Iquitos hasta llegar al río Ucayali....**

Lugares • Lima

Lima es una ciudad moderna y antigua° a la vez°. La Iglesia de San Francisco es notable por su arquitectura barroca colonial. También son fascinantes las exhibiciones sobre los incas en el Museo Oro del Perú y en el Museo Nacional de Antropología y Arqueología. Barranco, el barrio° bohemio de la ciudad, es famoso por su ambiente cultural y sus bares y restaurantes.

⊙ Historia • Machu Picchu

A 80 kilómetros al noroeste de Cuzco está Machu Picchu, una antigua ciudad del Imperio inca. Está a una altitud de 2.430 metros (7.972 pies), entre dos cimas° de los Andes. Cuando los españoles llegaron a Perú y recorrieron la región, nunca encontraron Machu Picchu. En 1911, el arqueólogo estadounidense Hiram Bingham la redescubrió. Todavía no se sabe ni cómo se construyó° una ciudad a esa altura, ni por qué los incas la abandonaron. Sin embargo°, esta ciudad situada en desniveles° naturales es el ejemplo más conocido de la arquitectura inca.

⊙ Artes • La música andina

Machu Picchu aún no existía° cuando se originó la música cautivadora° de las culturas indígenas de los Andes. Los ritmos actuales de la música andina tienen influencias españolas y africanas. Varios tipos de flauta°, entre ellos la quena y la zampoña, caracterizan esta música. En las décadas de los sesenta y los setenta se popularizó un movimiento para preservar la música andina, y hasta° Simon y Garfunkel incorporaron a su repertorio la canción *El cóndor pasa*.

Economía • Llamas y alpacas

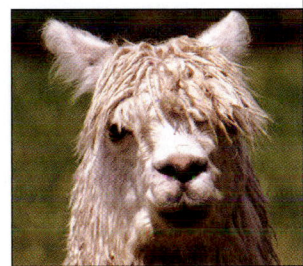

Perú se conoce por sus llamas, alpacas, guanacos y vicuñas, todos ellos animales mamíferos° parientes del camello. Estos animales todavía tienen una enorme importancia en la economía del país. Dan lana para exportar a otros países y para hacer ropa, mantas°, bolsas y otros artículos artesanales. La llama se usa también para la carga y el transporte.

antigua *old* a la vez *at the same time* barrio *neighborhood* cimas *summits* se construyó *was built* Sin embargo *However* desniveles *uneven pieces of land* aún no existía *didn't exist yet* cautivadora *captivating* flauta *flute* hasta *even* mamíferos *mammalian* mantas *blankets*

¡Increíble pero cierto!

Hace más de° dos mil años la civilización nazca de Perú grabó° más de dos mil kilómetros de líneas en el desierto. Los dibujos sólo son descifrables desde el aire. Uno de ellos es un cóndor del tamaño° de un estadio. Las Líneas de Nazca son uno de los grandes misterios de la humanidad.

Hace más de *More than... ago* grabó *engraved* tamaño *size*

---

2 **¿Qué aprendiste?** Contesta las preguntas.

1. ¿Cuáles son las lenguas oficiales de Perú?
   el español, el quechua, el aimara y otras lenguas indígenas
2. ¿Por qué es notable la Iglesia de San Francisco en Lima?
   por su arquitectura barroca colonial
3. ¿Qué información sobre Machu Picchu no se sabe todavía?
   ni cómo se construyó ni por qué la abandonaron
4. ¿Qué son la quena y la zampoña?
   tipos de flauta
5. ¿Qué hacen los peruanos con la lana de sus llamas y alpacas?
   ropa, mantas, bolsas y otros artículos artesanales

3 **Descripción** Viajaste a Perú y conociste los lugares turísticos más importantes de este país. Describe a un(a) compañero/a el lugar que más te gustó.

modelo
Cuando fui a Perú, conocí Machu Picchu.
Fue un viaje muy interesante porque...

Lima Lima, rich in colonial architecture, is also home to the **Universidad Nacional Mayor de San Marcos,** which was established in 1551 and is the oldest university in South America.

Machu Picchu Another invention of the Incas was the **quipus,** clusters of knotted strings that were a means of keeping records and sending messages. A **quipu** consisted of a series of small, knotted cords attached to a larger cord. Each cord's color, place, size, and the knots it contained all had significance. You may want to play the **Panorama cultural** video for this paragraph.

La música andina Ancient tombs belonging to pre-Columbian cultures like the **Nazca** and **Moche** have yielded instruments and other artifacts indicating that the precursors of Andean music go back at least two millennia. You may want to play the **Panorama cultural** video for this paragraph.

Llamas y alpacas Of the camel-like animals of the Andes, only the sturdy **llama** has been domesticated as a pack animal. Its long, thick coat also provides fiber that is woven into a coarser grade of cloth. The more delicate **alpaca** and **vicuña** are raised only for their beautiful coats, which are used to create extremely high-quality cloth. The **guanaco** has never been domesticated.

¡Increíble pero cierto! In recent years, the **El Niño** weather phenomenon has caused flooding in the deserts of southern Peru. The Peruvian government is working to preserve the **Líneas de Nazca** from further deterioration in the hope that someday scientists will discover more about their origins and meaning.

Instructional Resources
Supersite: Audio (Textbook & Lab MP3s); Testing Program (Tests, MP3s)
WebSAM
Lab Manual

Teaching Tip You may want to assign the **Prueba de práctica**, with its diagnostics and review activities, in the online-only **Repaso** section on the Supersite. There is also a **Repaso oral** in this section. For the Sixth Edition, a new summative vocabulary activity with speech recognition has been added to the **Repaso** section.

Los verbos reflexivos

acordarse (de) (o:ue)	to remember
acostarse (o:ue)	to go to bed
afeitarse	to shave
bañarse	to take a bath
cepillarse el pelo	to brush one's hair
cepillarse los dientes	to brush one's teeth
despertarse (e:ie)	to wake up
dormirse (o:ue)	to go to sleep; to fall asleep
ducharse	to take a shower
enojarse (con)	to get angry (with)
irse	to go away; to leave
lavarse la cara	to wash one's face
lavarse las manos	to wash one's hands
levantarse	to get up
llamarse	to be called; to be named
maquillarse	to put on makeup
peinarse	to comb one's hair
ponerse	to put on
ponerse (+ *adj.*)	to become (+ *adj.*)
preocuparse (por)	to worry (about)
probarse (o:ue)	to try on
quedarse	to stay
quitarse	to take off
secarse	to dry (oneself)
sentarse (e:ie)	to sit down
sentirse (e:ie)	to feel
vestirse (e:i)	to get dressed

Palabras de secuencia

antes (de)	before
después	afterward; then
después (de)	after
durante	during
entonces	then
luego	then
más tarde	later (on)
por último	finally

Palabras indefinidas y negativas

algo	something; anything
alguien	someone; somebody; anyone
alguno/a(s), algún	some; any
jamás	never; not ever
nada	nothing; not anything
nadie	no one; nobody; not anyone
ni… ni	neither… nor
ninguno/a, ningún	no; none; not any
nunca	never; not ever
o… o	either… or
siempre	always
también	also; too
tampoco	neither; not either

En el baño

el baño, el cuarto de baño	bathroom
el champú	shampoo
la crema de afeitar	shaving cream
la ducha	shower
el espejo	mirror
el inodoro	toilet
el jabón	soap
el lavabo	sink
el maquillaje	makeup
la pasta de dientes	toothpaste
la toalla	towel

Verbos similares a *gustar*

aburrir	to bore
encantar	to like very much; to love (inanimate objects)
faltar	to lack; to need
fascinar	to fascinate; to like very much
importar	to be important to; to matter
interesar	to be interesting to; to interest
molestar	to bother; to annoy
quedar	to be left over; to fit (clothing)

Palabras adicionales

el despertador	alarm clock
las pantuflas	slippers
la rutina diaria	daily routine
por la mañana	in the morning
por la noche	at night
por la tarde	in the afternoon; in the evening

Expresiones útiles	*See page 231.*

More activities

vhlcentral   LM   p. 42

La comida

Communicative Goals

You will learn how to:
- Order food in a restaurant
- Talk about and describe food

Lesson Goals

In **Lección 8**, students will be introduced to the following:
- food terms
- meal-related words
- fruits and vegetables native to the Americas
- Spanish chef **Ferran Adrià**
- preterite of stem-changing verbs
- double object pronouns
- converting **le** and **les** to **se** with double object pronouns
- comparisons
- superlatives
- reading for the main idea
- expressing and supporting opinions
- writing a restaurant review
- taking notes while listening
- a television commercial for **Sopas Roa**, a Colombian brand of packaged soups
- a video about Latin food in the U.S.
- cultural, geographic, and historical information about Guatemala

A primera vista Here are some additional questions you can ask to personalize the photo: **¿Dónde te encanta comer? ¿Por qué? ¿Fuiste a algún lugar especial para comer la semana pasada? ¿Compras comida? ¿Dónde? ¿Prefieres cocinar o comer en un restaurante?**

Teaching Tip Look for these icons for additional communicative practice:

→👤←	Interpretive communication
←👤→	Presentational communication
👤←→👤	Interpersonal communication

INSTRUCTIONAL RESOURCES

Supersite (vhlcentral.com)
Video: ***Fotonovela, Flash cultura, En pantalla, Panorama cultural***
Audio: Textbook and Lab MP3 Files

Activity Pack: Information Gap Activities, games, additional activity handouts
Resources: SAM Answer Key, Scripts, Translations, **Vocabulario adicional**, sample lesson plan, Grammar Presentation Slides, Digital Image Bank

Testing Program: Quizzes, Tests, Exams, MP3s
Student Activities Manual: Workbook/Video Manual/Lab Manual
WebSAM (online Student Activities Manual)

La comida

Más vocabulario

el/la camarero/a	waiter/waitress
la comida	food; meal
la cuenta	bill
el/la dueño/a	owner
los entremeses	appetizers
el menú	menu
el plato (principal)	(main) dish
la propina	tip
la sección de (no) fumar	(non) smoking section
el agua (f.) (mineral)	(mineral) water
la bebida	drink
la cerveza	beer
la leche	milk
el refresco	soft drink
el ajo	garlic
las arvejas	peas
los cereales	cereal; grains
los frijoles	beans
el melocotón	peach
el pollo (asado)	(roast) chicken
el queso	cheese
el sándwich	sandwich
el yogur	yogurt
el aceite	oil
la margarina	margarine
la mayonesa	mayonnaise
el vinagre	vinegar
delicioso/a	delicious
sabroso/a	tasty; delicious
saber (a)	to taste (like)

Variación léxica

arvejas	⟷	chícharos (*Méx.*), guisantes (*Esp.*)
camarones	⟷	gambas (*Esp.*)
camarero	⟷	mesero (*Amér. L.*), mesonero (*Ven.*), mozo (*Arg., Chile, Urug., Perú*)
refresco	⟷	gaseosa (*Amér. C., Amér. S.*)

Frutas y verduras

el jamón
las uvas
el limón
la pera
el tomate
la zanahoria
la banana
el maíz
la lechuga
la cebolla
el champiñón
la naranja

More activities

vhlcentral | LM p. 43 | WB pp. 85–86 | Online activities

TEACHING OPTIONS

Extra Practice To review vocabulary for colors, ask students what colors these food items are: **las bananas (amarillas), las uvas (verdes o moradas), las zanahorias (anaranjadas), los tomates (rojos, verdes o amarillos), los frijoles (blancos, marrones, verdes, rojos o negros), la lechuga (verde), las cebollas (blancas o moradas).**

Heritage Speakers Point out that food vocabulary varies according to region in the Spanish-speaking world. Ask heritage speakers to share food-related terms with which they are familiar and where the terms are used. Possible responses: **el banano (Col.), el cambur (Ven.), el choclo (Chile, Perú), el elote (Méx.), la patata (Esp.)**

Las carnes

el pollo

el pavo

la chuleta (de cerdo)

la carne de res

Pescados y mariscos

la langosta

el salmón

el atún

los camarones (el camarón)

¡LENGUA VIVA!

You learned the verb **saber** in **Lección 6.** This verb is also used to describe food.

Use **saber** + [adjective] to explain how something *tastes*.

Ex: **Este plato sabe dulce/rico/amargo.**
(*This dish tastes sweet/delicious/bitter.*)

Use **saber** + a to say what something *tastes like.*

Ex: **Sabe a ajo.**
(*It tastes like garlic.*)

Estas langostas no saben a nada.
(*These lobsters don't taste like anything./ These lobsters don't have any flavor.*)

Práctica

1 **Escuchar** Indica si un vegano puede comer las comidas que vas a escuchar.

	Sí	No		Sí	No
1.	○	◉	5.	○	◉
2.	○	◉	6.	◉	○
3.	◉	○	7.	○	◉
4.	○	◉	8.	◉	○

2 **Escoger** Indica en qué casos se habla de bebidas y en qué casos se habla de comidas.

1. _____comida_____
2. _____bebida_____
3. _____comida_____
4. _____comida_____
5. _____bebida_____
6. _____bebida_____
7. _____comida_____
8. _____comida_____

3 **Identificar** Identifica la palabra que no está relacionada con cada grupo.

1. champiñón • cebolla • propina • zanahoria   propina
2. camarones • ajo • atún • salmón   ajo
3. pollo • naranja • limón • melocotón   pollo
4. jamón • chuleta de cerdo • vinagre • carne de res   vinagre
5. cerveza • lechuga • arvejas • frijoles   cerveza
6. carne • pescado • mariscos • camarero   camarero
7. aceite • leche • refresco • agua mineral   aceite
8. maíz • queso • tomate • champiñón   queso
9. cuenta • menú • camarera • mayonesa   mayonesa
10. uva • pera • langosta • banana   langosta

4 **Completar** Completa las oraciones con las palabras más lógicas.

1. Camarero, ¿puedo ver el __c__, por favor?
   a. aceite   b. maíz   c. menú
2. ¡Me gusta mucho este plato! Sabe __b__.
   a. mal   b. delicioso   c. antipático
3. Carlos y yo bebemos siempre agua __b__.
   a. cómoda   b. mineral   c. principal
4. El plato del día es __a__.
   a. pollo asado   b. mayonesa   c. ajo
5. Margarita es vegetariana. Ella come __a__.
   a. frijoles   b. chuletas   c. jamón
6. Mi hermana le da __c__ a su niña.
   a. ajo   b. vinagre   c. yogur

Teaching Tips

- 🙋↔🙋 Involve the class in a conversation about meals. Say: **Por lo general, desayuno sólo café con leche y pan tostado, pero cuando tengo mucha hambre desayuno dos huevos y una salchicha también. ____, ¿qué desayunas tú?** Ask follow-up questions to continue the discussion.

- Use the **Lección 8 Contextos** digital images to assist with this vocabulary presentation.

- Have students look at the illustrations on this page and say: **Mira el desayuno aquí. ¿Qué desayuna esta persona?** Then continue to **el almuerzo** and **la cena.** Have students identify the food items and talk about their eating habits, including what, when, and where they eat. Say: **Yo siempre desayuno en casa, pero casi nunca almuerzo en casa. ¿A qué hora almuerzan ustedes por lo general?**

- Ask students to tell you their favorite foods to eat for each of the three meals. Ex: ____, **¿qué te gusta desayunar?** Introduce additional items such as **los espaguetis, la pasta, la pizza.**

Nota cultural Point out that in Spanish-speaking countries, **el almuerzo,** also called **la comida,** usually is the main meal of the day, consists of several courses, and is enjoyed at a leisurely pace. **La cena** is typically much lighter than **el almuerzo.**

Note: At this point you may want to present *Vocabulario adicional: Más vocabulario relacionado con la comida* from the Supersite.

el desayuno

el pan (tostado) · el azúcar · el café · el jugo (de fruta) · el huevo · la mantequilla · la salchicha

el almuerzo

la hamburguesa · el pan · el té helado · la manzana · las papas/patatas fritas

la cena

la sopa · la ensalada · el vino tinto · la sal · el bistec · el arroz · la pimienta · los espárragos

NOTA CULTURAL

En Guatemala, un desayuno típico incluye huevos, frijoles, fruta, tortillas, jugo y café.
Otros desayunos populares son:
madalenas (*muffins*) España
pan dulce (*assorted breads/pastries*) México
champurradas (*sugar cookies*) Guatemala
gallo pinto (*fried rice and beans*) Costa Rica
perico (*scrambled eggs with peppers and onions*) Venezuela

Más vocabulario

escoger	*to choose*
merendar (e:ie)	*to snack*
probar (o:ue)	*to taste; to try*
recomendar (e:ie)	*to recommend*
servir (e:i)	*to serve*
el té	*tea*
el vino blanco	*white wine*

TEACHING OPTIONS

Small Groups ←🙋→ In small groups, have students create a menu for a special occasion. Ask them to describe what they are going to serve for **el entremés, el plato principal,** and **bebidas.** Write **el postre** on the board and explain that it means *dessert.* Explain that in Spanish-speaking countries fresh fruit and cheese are common as dessert, but you may also want to introduce the words **el pastel** (*pie, cake*) and **el helado** (*ice*

cream). Have groups present their menus to the class.
Extra Practice →🙋← Add an auditory aspect to this vocabulary presentation. Prepare descriptions of five to seven different meals, with a mix of breakfasts, lunches, and dinners. As you read each description aloud, have students write down what you say as a dictation and then guess the meal it describes.

5 **En el supermercado** Completa la conversación.

aceite	carne	escojo	meriendo	tinto
arroz	cena	espárragos	recomiendo	vino

LAURA ¿Sabes qué necesitamos comprar para la (1)___cena___ de hoy?

EDUARDO No lo sé, quiero probar ese (2)___arroz___ especial que tú haces.

LAURA Bueno, para ese plato necesitamos también (3)___espárragos___.

EDUARDO ¿Verdes o blancos?

LAURA Verdes, por supuesto. Y también (4)___aceite___ de oliva.

EDUARDO ¿Y compramos (5)___carne___?

LAURA No, ahora soy vegetariana.

EDUARDO Ah. Y para beber, ¿compramos (6)___vino___?

LAURA Sí, te (7)___recomiendo___ uno blanco, porque el vino (8)___tinto___ no va bien con este plato.

EDUARDO Mira, ¿(9)___escojo___ éste? Está a buen precio.

LAURA Sí. Bueno, vamos rápido a casa, ¡ya tengo mucha hambre!

6 **Adivinanzas** En parejas, completen las adivinanzas (*riddles*).

bistec	manzana	pimienta	sopa
ensalada	pan	refresco	té
langosta	papas fritas	sal	yogur

1. Es un condimento blanco. sal
2. Es una fruta que puede ser de color rojo, verde o amarillo. manzana
3. Puede tener lechuga, tomates y zanahoria. ensalada
4. Es una bebida que puede saber a naranja. refresco
5. Es una carne roja. bistec
6. Puedes beberlo frío o caliente. té
7. Lo necesitas para hacer un sándwich. pan
8. Es un marisco muy caro. langosta
9. Puedes comerlo en el desayuno con cereales. yogur
10. Es un condimento negro. pimienta

5 **Expansion**
• Ask questions about the conversation: **¿Quién quiere comer arroz?** (Eduardo) **¿Qué verdura van a comprar?** (espárragos verdes) **¿Quién no come carne?** (Laura) **¿Qué vino recomienda Laura?** (el vino blanco)
• Have pairs of students write a conversation between **Laura** and **Eduardo** as they are preparing and eating dinner. Have volunteers act out their conversations for the class.

6 **Expansion** Have students write their own food riddles for a partner to solve.

TEACHING OPTIONS

Heritage Speakers Ask heritage speakers to talk about food items or dishes unique to their families' countries of origin that are not typically found in this country. Have them describe what the item looks and tastes like. If the item is a dish, they should briefly describe how to prepare it if they know how to do so. Have the class ask follow-up questions to find out more information, such as when and where these items are eaten.

Extra Practice Have students describe to the class what they typically eat for breakfast, lunch, and dinner.

Margin notes (left column)

7 Expansion Have students write four more illogical statements for a partner to correct.

8 Expansion To simplify, ask individual students what people in the activity logically do. Point out that there are many possible answers to your questions. Ex: **¿Qué hace la camarera en el restaurante? ¿Qué hace el dueño?**

Nota cultural Ask students what they consider to be the staples of the North American diet. Ask them if there are any essential items in their personal diets they cannot live without.

9 Expansion Have pairs present their menus to the class. Ask students why they chose their food items—because they are personal preferences, for their health benefits, or because they go well with other foods. Ex: **¿Por qué escogieron espárragos? ¿Les gustan mucho? ¿Son saludables? Van bien con el pescado, ¿verdad?**

7

Cambiar En parejas, corrijan las oraciones para que sean lógicas.   Answers will vary. Sample answers:

> **modelo**
> El cereal favorito de mi hermana es la banana.
> *La fruta favorita de mi hermana es la banana.*

1. El pollo y el bistec son entremeses.
   El pollo y el bistec son platos principales.
2. El camarero va a darnos una propina.
   El camarero va a darnos la cuenta.
3. Los niños de Susana beben café todas las mañanas.
   Los niños de Susana beben jugo/leche todas las mañanas.
4. Marcos siempre come su yogur con camarones.
   Marcos siempre come su yogur con frutas/cereal.
5. Me encantan los pescados, en especial el pavo.
   Me encantan los pescados, en especial el salmón/atún.
6. Las arvejas y los espárragos son anaranjados.
   Las arvejas y los espárragos son verdes.
7. Sirven té helado con frijoles.
   Sirven té helado con limón/azúcar.
8. Muchas personas desayunan langosta.
   Muchas personas desayunan yogur/pan tostado/huevos/cereal.
9. Para beber, quiero un jugo de pimienta, por favor.
   Para beber, quiero un jugo de naranja/manzana/uva, por favor.
10. Para hacer pizza, necesitas arroz.
    Para hacer pizza, necesitas queso/aceite/tomates/ajo.

8

Combinar Combina palabras de cada columna, en cualquier (*any*) orden, para formar diez oraciones lógicas.   Answers will vary.

> **modelo**
> **La camarera nos sirve la ensalada.**

A	B	C
el/la camarero/a	almorzar	la sección de no fumar
el/la dueño/a	escoger	el desayuno
mi familia	gustar	la ensalada
mi novio/a	merendar	las uvas
mis amigos y yo	pedir	el restaurante
mis padres	preferir	el jugo de naranja
mi hermano/a	probar	el refresco
el/la médico/a	recomendar	el plato
yo	servir	el arroz

NOTA CULTURAL

El arroz es un alimento básico en el Caribe, Centroamérica y México, entre otros países. Aparece frecuentemente como acompañamiento del plato principal y muchas veces se sirve con frijoles. Un plato muy popular en varios países es **el arroz con pollo** *(chicken and rice casserole).*

9

Un menú En parejas, van a crear un menú para una cena especial. Incluyan los entremeses, los platos principales y las bebidas.   Answers will vary.

> **modelo**
> *La cena especial que vamos a preparar es deliciosa. Primero, hay dos entremeses: ensalada César y sopa de langosta. El plato principal es salmón con salsa de ajo y espárragos. También vamos a servir arroz…*

TEACHING OPTIONS

Extra Practice To review and practice the preterite along with food vocabulary, have students write a paragraph in which they describe what they ate yesterday. Students should also indicate whether this collection of meals represents a typical day for them. If not, they should explain why.

Small Groups In small groups, have students role-play a situation in a restaurant. Two students play the customers and the other plays the **camarero/a**. Write these sentences on the board as suggested phrases: **¿Están listos/as para pedir?, ¿Qué nos recomienda usted?, ¿Me trae _____, por favor?, ¿Y para empezar?, A sus órdenes, La especialidad de la casa.**

Comunicación

10 **Conversación** En parejas, túrnense para hacerse estas preguntas. *Answers will vary.*

1. ¿Qué te gusta cenar?
2. ¿A qué hora, dónde y con quién almuerzas?
3. ¿Cuáles son las comidas más (*most*) típicas de tu almuerzo?
4. ¿Desayunas? ¿Qué comes y bebes por la mañana?
5. ¿Qué comida te gusta más? ¿Qué comida no conoces y quieres probar?
6. ¿Cuáles son las comidas y bebidas más frecuentes en tu dieta?
7. ¿Qué comida recomiendas a tus amigos? ¿Por qué?
8. ¿Te gusta preparar la comida? ¿Qué comidas preparas para tus amigos? ¿Para tu familia?

11 **Describir** Con dos compañeros/as de clase, describe las dos fotos, contestando estas preguntas. *Answers will vary.*

▶ ¿Quiénes están en las fotos?

▶ ¿Dónde están?

▶ ¿Qué hora es?

▶ ¿Qué comen y qué beben?

12 **Crucigrama** Tu profesor(a) les va a dar a ti y a tu compañero/a un crucigrama (*crossword puzzle*) incompleto. Tú tienes las palabras que necesita tu compañero/a y él/ella tiene las palabras que tú necesitas. Tienen que darse pistas (*clues*) para completarlo. No pueden decir la palabra; deben utilizar definiciones, ejemplos y frases. *Answers will vary.*

 modelo

6 vertical: Es un condimento que normalmente viene con la sal.
12 horizontal: Es una fruta amarilla.

10 Teaching Tip Ask the same questions of individual students. Ask other students to restate what their partners answered.

10 Expansion
Have pairs join other pairs and share their answers to items 6 and 7. Then have them decide which student is the most adventurous eater of the group and report back to the class. You may wish to teach the phrase **el/la más aventurero/a del grupo,** thus previewing superlatives, which are presented in **Estructura 8.4.**

11 Expansion
Add an additional visual aspect to this vocabulary practice. Using magazine pictures that show dining situations, have students describe what is going on: who the people are, what they are eating and drinking, and so forth.

12 Teaching Tip Divide the class into pairs and distribute the handouts from the Activity Pack (Activity Pack/ Supersite) that correspond to this Information Gap Activity. Give students ten minutes to complete this activity.

12 Expansion Have groups create another type of word puzzle, such as a word-find, to share with the class. It should contain additional food- and meal-related vocabulary.

TEACHING OPTIONS

Small Groups In small groups, ask students to prepare brief skits related to food. The skits may involve being in a market, in a restaurant, in a café, inviting people over for dinner, and so forth. Allow groups time to rehearse before performing their skits for the class, who will vote for the most creative one.

Game Play a game of continuous narration. One student begins with: **Voy a preparar** (*name of dish*) **y voy al mercado. Necesito comprar…** and names one food item. The next student then repeats the entire narration, adding another food item. Continue on with various students. When the possibilities for that particular dish are used up, have another student begin with another dish.

Una cena... romántica

Maru y Miguel quieren tener una cena romántica, pero les espera una sorpresa.

PERSONAJES   MARU   MIGUEL

 Video

1

MARU No sé qué pedir. ¿Qué me recomiendas?

MIGUEL No estoy seguro. Las chuletas de cerdo se ven muy buenas.

MARU ¿Vas a pedirlas?

MIGUEL No sé.

2

MIGUEL ¡Qué bonitos! ¿Quién te los dio?

MARU Me los compró un chico muy guapo e inteligente.

MIGUEL ¿Es tan guapo como yo?

MARU Sí, como tú, guapísimo.

MIGUEL Por nosotros.

MARU Dos años.

3

(El camarero llega a la mesa.)

CAMARERO ¿Les gustaría saber nuestras especialidades del día?

MARU Sí, por favor.

CAMARERO Para el entremés, tenemos ceviche de camarón. De plato principal ofrecemos bistec con verduras a la plancha.

5

6

4

MARU Voy a probar el jamón.

CAMARERO Perfecto. ¿Y para usted, caballero?

MIGUEL Pollo asado con champiñones y papas, por favor.

CAMARERO Excelente.

(en otra parte del restaurante)

JUAN CARLOS Disculpe. ¿Qué me puede contar del pollo? ¿Dónde lo consiguió el chef?

CAMARERO ¡Oiga! ¿Qué está haciendo?

Section Goals

In **Fotonovela**, students will:
- receive comprehensible input from free-flowing discourse
- learn functional phrases that preview lesson grammatical structures

Instructional Resources
Supersite: Video (**Fotonovela**); Resources (Scripts, Translations, Answer Keys)
WebSAM
Video Manual

Video Recap: Lección 7
Before doing this **Fotonovela** section, review the previous episode with these questions:
1. ¿Adónde va a ir Marissa? (Va al cine.) 2. ¿Qué necesita hacer antes de salir? (Necesita arreglarse el pelo.) 3. ¿Qué está haciendo Felipe en el baño? (Está afeitándose.) 4. ¿Qué planes tiene Jimena? ¿Adónde decide ir al final? (Tiene que estudiar en la biblioteca. Decide ir al cine con Marissa.)

Video Synopsis
Miguel and **Maru** are at one of Mexico City's best restaurants enjoying a romantic dinner to celebrate their second anniversary. **Felipe** and **Juan Carlos** show up and, while **Juan Carlos** distracts the waiter, **Felipe** serves the couple their food, making a mess of the table. To set things right with the manager, they must pay for dinner and wash the dishes.

Teaching Tips
- Have the class predict the content of this episode based on its title and the video stills.
- Quickly review the predictions and ask the class a few questions to help them summarize this episode.

TEACHING OPTIONS

Video Tips General suggestions for using video clips in the classroom can be found in the front matter of this Instructor's Annotated Edition.
Una cena... romántica ➔ Play the first half of the **Una cena... romántica** segment and have the class give you a description of what they see. Write their observations on the board, pointing out any inaccuracies. Repeat this process to allow the class to pick up more details of the plot. Then ask students to use the information they have accumulated to guess what happens in the rest of the segment. Write their predictions on the board. Then play the entire segment and, through discussion, help the class summarize the plot.

CAMARERO **JUAN CARLOS** **FELIPE** **GERENTE**

FELIPE Los espárragos están sabrosísimos esta noche. Usted pidió el pollo, señor. Estos champiñones saben a mantequilla.

GERENTE ¿Qué pasa aquí, Esteban?

CAMARERO Lo siento, señor. Me quitaron la comida.

GERENTE (*a Felipe*) Señor, ¿quién es usted? ¿Qué cree que está haciendo?

JUAN CARLOS Felipe y yo les servimos la comida a nuestros amigos. Pero desafortunadamente, salió todo mal.

FELIPE Soy el peor camarero del mundo. ¡Lo siento! Nosotros vamos a pagar la comida.

JUAN CARLOS ¿Nosotros?

FELIPE Todo esto fue idea tuya, Juan Carlos.

JUAN CARLOS ¿Mi idea? ¡Felipe! (*al gerente*) Señor, él es más responsable que yo.

GERENTE Tú y tú, vamos.

More activities

vhlcentral | VM pp. 15–16 | Online activities

Expresiones útiles

Ordering food

¿Qué me recomiendas?
What do you recommend?
Las chuletas de cerdo se ven muy buenas.
The pork chops look good.
¿Les gustaría saber nuestras especialidades del día?
Would you like to hear our specials?
Para el entremés, tenemos ceviche de camarón.
For an appetizer, we have shrimp ceviche.
De plato principal ofrecemos bistec con verduras a la plancha.
For a main course, we have beef with grilled vegetables.
Voy a probar el jamón.
I am going to try the ham.

Describing people and things

¡Qué bonitos! ¿Quién te los dio?
How pretty! Who gave them to you?
Me los compró un chico muy guapo e inteligente.
A really handsome, intelligent guy bought them for me.
¿Es tan guapo como yo?
Is he as handsome as I am?
Sí, como tú, guapísimo.
Yes, like you, gorgeous.
Soy el peor camarero del mundo.
I am the worst waiter in the world.
Él es más responsable que yo.
He is more responsible than I am.

Additional vocabulary

el/la gerente *manager*
caballero *gentleman, sir*

Expresiones útiles Point out some of the unfamiliar structures, which will be taught in detail in **Estructura**. Have the class read the caption for video still 2, and draw attention to the double object pronouns **te los** and **Me los**. Explain that these are examples of indirect object pronouns and direct object pronouns used together. Then point out that **tan guapo como** is an example of a comparison of two things that are equal. Have the class read the caption for video still 10, and tell them that **más responsable que** is an example of a comparison of two unequal things. Then, for video still 9, point out **el peor camarero del mundo** and explain that this is an example of a superlative. Finally, draw attention to **guapísimo** in video still 2, and **sabrosísimos** in video still 7, and explain that these are absolute superlatives. Tell students that they will learn more about these concepts in **Estructura**.

Teaching Tips
- Have the class read through the entire **Fotonovela**, with volunteers playing the parts of **Miguel, Maru, Felipe, Juan Carlos,** the waiter, and the manager. Have students take turns playing the roles so that more students participate.
- For video still 2, point out the question **¿Quién te los dio?** and explain that **dio** is the third-person preterite form of the verb **dar**. You may want to tell them that **dar** has the same preterite endings as **ver**. Students will learn the remaining preterite forms of **dar** in **Lección 9**.

Nota cultural The precise origins of **ceviche** are unknown, but each former Spanish colony has its own version of this dish, which consists of seafood marinated in citrus juices, usually lemon or lime, which "cook" the protein.

¿Qué pasó?

1

Escoger Escoge la respuesta que completa mejor cada oración.

1. Miguel lleva a Maru a un restaurante para ___c___.
   a. almorzar   b. desayunar   c. cenar
2. El camarero les ofrece ___b___ como plato principal.
   a. ceviche de camarón   b. bistec con verduras a la plancha
   c. pescado, arroz y ensalada
3. Miguel va a pedir ___a___.
   a. pollo asado con champiñones y papas
   b. langosta al horno   c. pescado con verduras a la mantequilla
4. Felipe les lleva la comida a sus amigos y prueba ___c___.
   a. el jamón y los vinos   b. el atún y la lechuga
   c. los espárragos y los champiñones

NOTA CULTURAL

El **ceviche** es un plato típico de varios países hispanos como México, Perú y Costa Rica. En México, se prepara con pescado o mariscos frescos, jugo de limón, jitomate, cebolla, chile y cilantro. Se puede comer como plato fuerte, pero también como entremés o botana (*snack*). Casi siempre se sirve con tostadas (*fried tortillas*) o galletas saladas (*crackers*).

2

Identificar Indica quién dice las oraciones equivalentes.

1. ¡Qué desastre! Soy un camarero muy malo. Felipe
2. Tenemos bistec con verduras a la plancha. camarero
3. Recomiendo las chuletas de cerdo, creo que son muy sabrosas. Miguel
4. Vamos a la cocina. gerente
5. Quiero el jamón con los espárragos, por favor. Maru
6. No fue mi idea. Felipe es más responsable que yo. Juan Carlos

FELIPE   MARU   JUAN CARLOS

CAMARERO   MIGUEL   GERENTE

3

Preguntas Contesta estas preguntas. Some answers may vary. Sample answers:

1. ¿Por qué fueron Maru y Miguel a un restaurante?
   Maru y Miguel fueron a un restaurante para tener una cena romántica.
2. ¿Qué entremés es una de las especialidades del día?
   El ceviche de camarón es el entremés del día.
3. ¿Qué pidió Maru?
   Maru pidió vino, sopa de frijoles y jamón con espárragos.
4. ¿Quiénes van a pagar la cuenta?
   Juan Carlos y Felipe van a pagar la cuenta.

4

En el restaurante Answers will vary.

1. Prepara con un(a) compañero/a una conversación en la que le preguntas si conoce algún buen restaurante en tu comunidad. Tu compañero/a responde que él/ella sí conoce un restaurante que sirve una comida deliciosa. Lo/La invitas a cenar y tu compañero/a acepta. Determinan la hora para verse en el restaurante.

2. Trabaja con un(a) compañero/a para representar los papeles de un(a) cliente/a y un(a) camarero/a en un restaurante. El/La camarero/a te pregunta qué te puede servir y tú preguntas cuál es la especialidad de la casa. El/La camarero/a te dice cuál es la especialidad y te recomienda algunos platos del menú. Tú pides entremeses, un plato principal y escoges una bebida. El/La camarero/a te sirve la comida y tú le das las gracias.

CONSULTA

To review indefinite words like **algún**, see **Estructura 7.2**, p. 240.

Instructor's side notes (left column)

1 Teaching Tip To challenge students, give them these items as cloze sentences.

2 Teaching Tip Add an auditory aspect to this exercise. Have students close their books. Then read each item aloud and have the class identify the character.

2 Expansion Give the class these sentences as items 7–9:
7. Voy a probar la ensalada de pera con queso. (Miguel)
8. De entremés ofrecemos ceviche de camarón. (camarero)
9. Quiero saber dónde consigue el pollo el chef. ¿Me lo puede explicar? (Juan Carlos)

3 Expansion In pairs, have students write a follow-up question for each item, and exchange papers with another pair. Ex: **1. ¿Cuánto tiempo llevan juntos? 2. ¿Cuál es la otra especialidad del día?**

4 Possible Conversations
Conversation 1:
E1: Oye, María, ¿conoces un buen restaurante en esta ciudad?
E2: Sí… el restaurante El Pescador sirve comida riquísima.
E1: ¿Por qué no vamos a El Pescador esta noche?
E2: ¿A qué hora?
E1: ¿A las ocho?
E2: Perfecto.
E1: Está bien. Nos vemos a las ocho.
E2: Adiós.
Conversation 2:
E1: ¿Qué le puedo traer?
E2: Bueno, ¿cuáles son las especialidades de la casa?
E1: Hay ceviche de atún. También le recomiendo la langosta con arroz y verduras.
E2: Mmm… voy a pedir el ceviche y el bistec con verduras. De tomar, voy a pedir el jugo de piña.
E1: Gracias, señor.

Pronunciación
 Tutorial

ll, ñ, c, and z

pollo	llave	ella	cebolla

Most Spanish speakers pronounce **ll** like the *y* in *yes*.

mañana	señor	baño	niña

The letter **ñ** is pronounced much like the *ny* in *canyon*.

café	colombiano	cuando	rico

Before **a**, **o**, or **u**, the Spanish **c** is pronounced like the *c* in *car*.

cereales	delicioso	conducir	conocer

Before **e** or **i**, the Spanish **c** is pronounced like the *s* in *sit*. (In parts of Spain, **c** before **e** or **i** is pronounced like the *th* in *think*.)

zeta	zanahoria	almuerzo	cerveza

The Spanish **z** is pronounced like the *s* in *sit*. (In parts of Spain, **z** is pronounced like the *th* in *think*.)

Práctica   Lee las palabras en voz alta.

1. mantequilla
2. cuñado
3. aceite
4. manzana
5. español
6. cepillo
7. zapato
8. azúcar
9. quince
10. compañera
11. almorzar
12. calle

Oraciones   Lee las oraciones en voz alta.

1. Mi compañero de cuarto se llama Toño Núñez. Su familia es de la Ciudad de Guatemala y de Quetzaltenango.
2. Dice que la comida de su mamá es deliciosa, especialmente su pollo al champiñón y sus tortillas de maíz.
3. Creo que Toño tiene razón porque hoy cené en su casa y quiero volver mañana para cenar allí otra vez.

Refranes   Lee los refranes en voz alta.

Panza llena, corazón contento.[2]

Las apariencias engañan.[1]

More activities

vhlcentral   LM   p. 44

1 Looks can be deceiving.   2 A full belly makes a happy heart.

Section Goals

In **Cultura**, students will:
- read about fruits and vegetables native to the Americas
- learn food-related terms
- read about Spanish chef **Ferran Adrià**
- read about typical dishes from Peru, Spain, and Colombia

Instructional Resource
Supersite

En detalle

Antes de leer Ask students if they can name any fruits and vegetables that are native to the Americas.

Lectura
- The Aztec and Maya's beverage made of cacao, chile, and other spices was far thicker and more bitter than the hot chocolate most North Americans consume today.
- Point out that many words, such as **tomate, chocolate, aguacate, tamale,** and **mole,** come from Nahuatl, the language of the Aztecs. **Papa** comes from the Quechua word for *potato.* Explain that **salsa** is a general term for *sauce.*
- Explain that **tamales** are corn dough (usually filled with meat or cheese), which is wrapped in plant leaves or corn husks and steamed. **Arepas** are a type of thin corn cake, and **mole** is a Mexican sauce made of chile peppers, spices, and unsweetened chocolate.

Después de leer Ask students if they were surprised to learn that these foods were unknown to Europe and the rest of the world until about 500 years ago. Ask them to name dishes they would miss without these fruits and vegetables.

1 Expansion Ask students to write three additional true/false statements for a classmate to answer.

Frutas y verduras de América

Imagínate una pizza sin salsa° de tomate o una hamburguesa sin papas fritas. Ahora piensa que quieres ver una película, pero las palomitas de maíz° y el chocolate no existen. ¡Qué mundo° tan insípido°! Muchas de las comidas más populares del mundo tienen ingredientes esenciales que son originarios del continente americano. Después de la conquista de América, estas frutas y verduras fueron introducidas en Europa.

El tomate, por ejemplo, cuando llegó por primera vez a Europa, fue usado como planta ornamental porque pensaron que era° venenoso°. El maíz, por su parte, era ya la base de la comida de muchos países latinoamericanos muchos siglos° antes de la llegada de los españoles.

La papa fue un alimento° básico para los incas. Incluso consiguieron deshidratarla para almacenarla° por largos períodos de tiempo. El cacao (planta con la que se hace el chocolate) fue muy importante para los aztecas y los mayas. Ellos usaban sus semillas° como moneda° y como ingrediente de diversas salsas. También las molían° para preparar una bebida: las mezclaban° con agua ¡y con chile!

El aguacate°, la guayaba°, la papaya, la piña y el maracuyá (o fruta de la pasión) son otros ejemplos de frutas originarias de América que son hoy día conocidas en todo el mundo.

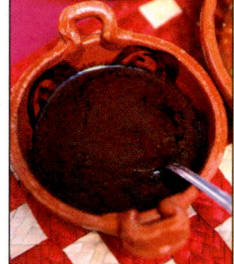

Mole

¿En qué alimentos encontramos estas frutas y verduras?

Tomate: pizza, ketchup, salsa de tomate, sopa de tomate

Maíz: palomitas de maíz, tamales, tortillas, arepas (Colombia y Venezuela), pan

Papa: papas fritas, frituras de papa°, puré de papas°, sopa de papas, tortilla de patatas (España)

Cacao: mole (México), chocolatinas°, cereales, helados°, tartas°

Aguacate: guacamole (México), coctel de camarones, sopa de aguacate, nachos, enchiladas hondureñas

---

salsa *sauce* palomitas de maíz *popcorn* mundo *world* insípido *flavorless* era *was* venenoso *poisonous* siglos *centuries* alimento *food* almacenarla *to store it* semillas *seeds* moneda *currency* las molían *they used to grind them* mezclaban *they used to mix* aguacate *avocado* guayaba *guava* frituras de papa *chips* puré de papas *mashed potatoes* chocolatinas *chocolate bars* helados *ice cream* tartas *cakes*

ACTIVIDADES

1 ¿Cierto o falso? Indica si lo que dicen las oraciones es cierto o falso. Corrige la información falsa.

1. El tomate se introdujo a Europa como planta ornamental.
   Cierto.
2. Los incas sólo consiguieron almacenar las papas por poco tiempo.
   Falso. Los incas pudieron almacenar las papas por largo tiempo.
3. Los aztecas y los mayas usaron las papas como moneda. **Falso.** Los aztecas y los mayas usaron las semillas de cacao como moneda.
4. El maíz era una comida poco popular en Latinoamérica.
   Falso. El maíz era muy popular en Latinoamérica.
5. El aguacate era el alimento básico de los incas.
   Falso. La papa era el alimento básico de los incas.
6. En México se hace una salsa con chocolate.
   Cierto.
7. El aguacate, la guayaba, la papaya, la piña y el maracuyá son originarios de América.
   Cierto.
8. Las arepas se hacen con cacao.
   Falso. Las arepas se hacen con maíz.
9. El aguacate es un ingrediente del cóctel de camarones.
   Cierto.
10. En España hacen una tortilla con papas.
    Cierto.

TEACHING OPTIONS

Game Have students make a *Bingo* card of fruits and vegetables mentioned in **Contextos** and on page 272, with one "free" square in the middle. Draw cards with different dishes and call them out. Have students cover the square on their card of the fruit or vegetable that is used in that dish. Ex: **tortilla de patatas** (Student covers **la papa**). The winner is the first student to fill a row (horizontally, vertically, or diagonally) and yell ¡*Bingo*!

Extra Practice Tell students to imagine they are Europeans who traveled to the Americas 500 years ago and are tasting a fruit or vegetable for the first time. Have them write a letter to a friend or family member describing the look and taste of the fruit or vegetable. Encourage them to use verbs like **gustar** in the letter. You may want to brainstorm a list of possible adjectives on the board for students to use in their descriptions.

ASÍ SE DICE
La comida

el banano (Col.), el cambur (Ven.), el guineo (Nic.), el plátano (Amér. L., Esp.)	la banana
el choclo (Amér. S.), el elote (Méx.), el jojoto (Ven.), la mazorca (Esp.)	*corncob*
las caraotas (Ven.), los porotos (Amér. S.), las habichuelas (P. R.)	los frijoles
el durazno (Méx.)	el melocotón
el jitomate (Méx.)	el tomate

EL MUNDO HISPANO
Algunos platos típicos

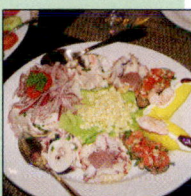

- **Ceviche peruano:** Es un plato de pescado crudo° que se marina° en jugo de limón, con sal, pimienta, cebolla y ají°. Se sirve con lechuga, maíz, camote° y papa amarilla.
- **Gazpacho andaluz:** Es una sopa fría típica del sur de España. Se hace con verduras crudas y molidas°: tomate, ají, pepino° y ajo. También lleva pan, sal, aceite y vinagre.
- **Sancocho colombiano:** Es una sopa de pollo, pescado o carne con plátano, maíz, zanahoria, yuca, papa, cebolla, cilantro y ajo. Se sirve con arroz blanco.

crudo *raw* se marina *gets marinated* ají *pepper* camote *sweet potato* molidas *mashed* pepino *cucumber*

PERFIL
Ferran Adrià: arte en la cocina°

¿Qué haces si un amigo te invita a comer croquetas líquidas o paella de *Kellogg's*? ¿Piensas que es una broma°? ¡Cuidado! Puedes estar perdiendo la oportunidad de probar los platos de uno de los chefs más innovadores del mundo°: **Ferran Adrià.**

Este artista de la cocina basa su éxito° en la creatividad y en la química. Adrià modifica combinaciones de ingredientes y juega con contrastes de gustos y sensaciones: frío-caliente, crudo-cocido°, dulce°-salado°... A partir de nuevas técnicas, altera la textura de los alimentos sin alterar su sabor°. Sus platos sorprendentes° y divertidos atraen a muchos nuevos chefs a su academia de cocina experimental. Quizás un día compraremos° en el supermercado té esférico°, carne líquida y espuma° de tomate.

Aire de zanahorias

cocina *kitchen* broma *joke* mundo *world* éxito *success* cocido *cooked* dulce *sweet* salado *savory* sabor *taste* sorprendentes *surprising* compraremos *we will buy* esférico *spheric* espuma *foam*

CON RITMO HISPANO
Ricardo Arjona (1964–)
Lugar de nacimiento: Jocotenango, Guatemala

Las canciones de Ricardo Arjona abordan (*tackle*) temas como el amor, el racismo y la política. Antes de ser cantante, fue jugador de baloncesto y profesor de escuela primaria.

Go to **vhlcentral.com** to find out more about **Ricardo Arjona** and his music.

ACTIVIDADES

2 Comprensión Empareja cada palabra con su definición.

1. fruta amarilla d
2. sopa típica de Colombia c
3. ingrediente del ceviche e
4. chef español d

a. gazpacho
b. Ferran Adrià
c. sancocho
d. guineo
e. pescado

3 ¿Qué plato especial hay en tu región? Escribe cuatro oraciones sobre un plato típico de tu región. Explica los ingredientes que contiene y cómo se sirve. Answers will vary.

More activities
vhlcentral / Online activities

8.1 Preterite of stem-changing verbs

 Tutorial

ANTE TODO As you learned in **Lección 6**, **–ar** and **–er** stem-changing verbs have no stem change in the preterite. **–Ir** stem-changing verbs, however, do have a stem change. Study the following chart and observe where the stem changes occur.

CONSULTA

There are a few high-frequency irregular verbs in the preterite. You will learn more about them in **Estructura 9.1**, p. 310.

Preterite of –ir stem-changing verbs		
	servir *(to serve)*	**dormir** *(to sleep)*
SINGULAR FORMS yo	serví	dormí
tú	serviste	dormiste
Ud./él/ella	s**i**rvió	d**u**rmió
PLURAL FORMS nosotros/as	servimos	dormimos
vosotros/as	servisteis	dormisteis
Uds./ellos/ellas	s**i**rvieron	d**u**rmieron

▶ Stem-changing **–ir** verbs, in the preterite only, have a stem change in the third-person singular and plural forms. The stem change consists of either **e** to **i** or **o** to **u**.

(e → i) pedir: p**i**dió, p**i**dieron   (o → u) morir *(to die)*: m**u**rió, m**u**rieron

¿Quién pidió el jamón?

Yo lo pedí.

✓ 🔊 **¡INTÉNTALO!** Cambia cada infinitivo al pretérito.

1. Yo _____serví, dormí, pedí..._____. (servir, dormir, pedir, preferir, repetir, seguir)
preferí, repetí, seguí

2. Usted _____. (morir, conseguir, pedir, sentirse, servir, vestirse)
murió, consiguió, pidió, se sintió, sirvió, se vistió

3. Ellas _____. (repetir, dormir, seguir, preferir, morir, servir)
repitieron, durmieron, siguieron, prefirieron, murieron, sirvieron

4. Tú _____. (conseguir, servir, morir, pedir, dormir, repetir)
conseguiste, serviste, moriste, pediste, dormiste, repetiste

5. Nosotros _____. (seguir, preferir, servir, vestirse, pedir, dormirse)
seguimos, preferimos, servimos, nos vestimos, pedimos, nos dormimos

6. Ustedes _____. (sentirse, vestirse, conseguir, pedir, repetir, dormirse)
se sintieron, se vistieron, consiguieron, pidieron, repitieron, se durmieron

7. Él _____. (dormir, morir, preferir, repetir, seguir, pedir)
durmió, murió, prefirió, repitió, siguió, pidió

More activities

🔊 vhlcentral

LM p. 45

WB pp. 87–88

Online activities

Práctica

1

Completar Completa estas oraciones.

▶ 1. Paula y Humberto Suárez llegaron al restaurante El Famoso a las ocho y ___siguieron___ (seguir) al camarero a una mesa en la sección de no fumar.
2. El señor Suárez ___pidió___ (pedir) una chuleta de cerdo.
3. La señora Suárez ___prefirió___ (preferir) probar los camarones.
4. De tomar, los dos ___pidieron___ (pedir) vino tinto.
5. El camarero ___repitió___ (repetir) el pedido (*the order*) para confirmarlo.
6. La comida tardó mucho (*took a long time*) en llegar y los señores Suárez ___se durmieron___ (dormirse) esperando la comida.
7. A las nueve y media el camarero les ___sirvió___ (servir) la comida.
8. Después de comer la chuleta, el señor Suárez ___se sintió___ (sentirse) muy mal.
9. Pobre señor Suárez… ¿por qué no ___pidió___ (pedir) los camarones?

2

El camarero loco Indica lo que los clientes pidieron y lo que el camarero les sirvió por error.

> **modelo**
> Armando / papas fritas
> Armando pidió papas fritas, pero el camarero le sirvió pan.

1. nosotros / jugo de naranja Nosotros pedimos jugo de naranja, pero el camarero nos sirvió ensalada.

2. Beatriz / queso Beatriz pidió queso, pero el camarero le sirvió bistec/ carne (de res).

3. tú / arroz Tú pediste arroz, pero el camarero te sirvió sopa.

4. Elena y Alejandro / atún Elena y Alejandro pidieron atún, pero el camarero les sirvió camarones/mariscos.

5. usted / agua mineral Usted pidió agua mineral, pero el camarero le sirvió té helado.

6. yo / hamburguesa Yo pedí una hamburguesa, pero el camarero me sirvió pollo asado.

Comunicación

3

El almuerzo Trabajen en parejas. Túrnense para completar las oraciones de una manera lógica. *Answers will vary.*

> **modelo**
>
> Mi compañero de cuarto se despertó temprano, pero yo…
>
> *Mi compañero de cuarto se despertó temprano, pero yo me desperté tarde.*

1. Yo llegué al restaurante a tiempo, pero mis amigos…
2. Beatriz pidió la ensalada de frutas, pero yo…
3. Yolanda les recomendó el bistec, pero Eva y Paco…
4. Nosotros preferimos las papas fritas, pero Yolanda…
5. El camarero sirvió la carne, pero yo…
6. Beatriz y yo pedimos café, pero Yolanda y Paco…
7. Eva se sintió enferma, pero Paco y yo…
8. Nosotros repetimos postre (*dessert*), pero Eva…
9. Ellos salieron tarde, pero yo…
10. Yo me dormí temprano, pero mi compañero de cuarto…

¡LENGUA VIVA!

In Spanish, the verb **repetir** is used to express *to have a second helping (of something).*

Cuando mi mamá prepara sopa de champiñones, yo siempre repito.

When my mom makes mushroom soup, I always have a second helping.

◀

4

Entrevista Trabajen en parejas y túrnense para entrevistar a su compañero/a. *Answers will vary.*

1. ¿Te acostaste tarde o temprano anoche? ¿A qué hora te dormiste? ¿Dormiste bien?
2. ¿A qué hora te despertaste esta mañana? Y, ¿a qué hora te levantaste?
3. ¿A qué hora vas a acostarte esta noche?
4. ¿Qué almorzaste ayer? ¿Quién te sirvió el almuerzo?
5. ¿Qué cenaste ayer?
6. ¿Cenaste en un restaurante recientemente? ¿Con quién(es)?
7. ¿Qué pediste en el restaurante? ¿Qué pidieron los demás?
8. ¿Se durmió alguien en alguna de tus clases la semana pasada? ¿En qué clase?

Síntesis

5

Describir En grupos, describan la primera (¿y la última?) cita de César y Libertad. *Answers will vary.* ◀

▶ ¿Adónde salieron a cenar?

▶ ¿Qué pidieron?

▶ ¿Les gustó la comida?

▶ ¿Quién prefirió una cena vegetariana? ¿Por qué?

▶ ¿Cómo se vistieron?

▶ ¿De qué hablaron? ¿Les gustó la conversación?

▶ ¿Van a volver a verse? ¿Por qué?

CONSULTA

To review words commonly associated with the preterite, such as **anoche**, see **Estructura 6.3**, p. 207.

TEACHING OPTIONS

Pairs ← In pairs, have students take turns telling each other about a memorable experience in a restaurant (a date, dinner with family or friends, etc.). Encourage students to take notes as their partners narrate. Then have students reveal to the class what their partners told them.

Extra Practice ← Add a visual aspect to this grammar practice. As you hold up magazine pictures that show restaurant scenes, have students describe them in the past tense, using the preterite. You may want to write on the board some stem-changing **–ir** verbs that might apply to the situations pictured in the photographs.

8.2 Double object pronouns

  Tutorial

ANTE TODO   In **Lecciones 5** and **6**, you learned that direct and indirect object pronouns replace nouns and that they often refer to nouns that have already been referenced. You will now learn how to use direct and indirect object pronouns together. Observe the following diagram.

Indirect Object Pronouns			Direct Object Pronouns	
me	nos	**+**	lo	los
te	os		la	las
le (se)	les (se)			

▶ When direct and indirect object pronouns are used together, the indirect object pronoun always precedes the direct object pronoun.

		DOUBLE OBJECT PRONOUNS
I.O. D.O.		
La camarera **me** muestra **el menú**.	→	La camarera **me lo** muestra.
The waitress shows me the menu.		*The waitress shows it to me.*
I.O. D.O.		**DOUBLE OBJECT PRONOUNS**
Nos sirven **los platos**.	→	**Nos los** sirven.
They serve us the dishes.		*They serve them to us.*
I.O. D.O.		**DOUBLE OBJECT PRONOUNS**
Maribel **te** pidió **una hamburguesa**.	→	Maribel **te la** pidió.
Maribel ordered a hamburger for you.		*Maribel ordered it for you.*

¿Quién te los dio?

Me los compró un chico muy guapo.

▶ In Spanish, two pronouns that begin with the letter **l** cannot be used together. Therefore, the indirect object pronouns **le** and **les** always change to **se** when they are used with **lo, los, la,** and **las**.

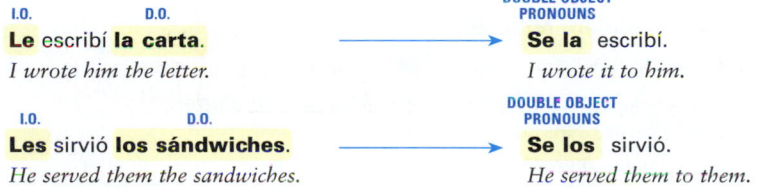

I.O. D.O.		**DOUBLE OBJECT PRONOUNS**
Le escribí **la carta**.	→	**Se la** escribí.
I wrote him the letter.		*I wrote it to him.*
I.O. D.O.		**DOUBLE OBJECT PRONOUNS**
Les sirvió **los sándwiches**.	→	**Se los** sirvió.
He served them the sandwiches.		*He served them to them.*

▶ Because **se** has multiple meanings, Spanish speakers often clarify to whom the pronoun refers by adding **a usted, a él, a ella, a ustedes, a ellos,** or **a ellas.**

¿El sombrero? Carlos **se** lo
    vendió **a ella.**
The hat? Carlos sold it to her.

¿Las verduras? Ellos **se** las
    compran **a usted.**
The vegetables? They are buying them for you.

▶ Double object pronouns are placed before a conjugated verb. With infinitives and present participles, they may be placed before the conjugated verb or attached to the end of the infinitive or present participle.

DOUBLE OBJECT PRONOUNS
Te lo voy a mostrar.

DOUBLE OBJECT PRONOUNS
Voy a mostrár**telo.**

DOUBLE OBJECT PRONOUNS
Nos las están comprando.

DOUBLE OBJECT PRONOUNS
Están comprándo**noslas.**

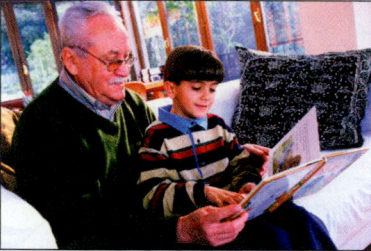

Mi abuelo **me lo** está leyendo.
Mi abuelo está leyéndo**melo.**

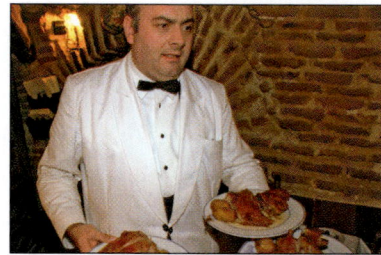

El camarero **se los** va a servir.
El camarero va a servír**selos.**

▶ As you can see above, when double object pronouns are attached to an infinitive or a present participle, an accent mark is added to maintain the original stress.

¡INTÉNTALO! Escribe el pronombre de objeto directo o indirecto que falta en cada oración.

Objeto directo

1. ¿La ensalada? El camarero nos ___la___ sirvió.
2. ¿El salmón? La dueña me ___lo___ recomienda.
3. ¿La comida? Voy a preparárte___la___.
4. ¿Los refrescos? Te ___los___ puedo traer ahora.
5. ¿Las bebidas? Estamos pidiéndose___las___.
6. ¿Los platos de arroz? Van a servírnos___los___ después.

Objeto indirecto

1. ¿Puedes traerme tu plato? No, no ___te___ lo puedo traer.
2. ¿Quieres mostrarle la carta? Sí, voy a mostrár___se___la ahora.
3. ¿Les serviste la carne? No, no ___se___ la serví.
4. ¿Me recomiendas la langosta? Sí, ___te___ la recomiendo.
5. ¿Vas a leerle el menú? No, no ___se___ lo voy a leer.
6. ¿Cuándo vas a prepararnos la cena? ___Se___ la voy a preparar en una hora.

More activities

vhlcentral

LM
p. 46

WB
pp. 89–90

Online activities

Práctica

1   **Responder**   Trabajas de camarero/a en un restaurante. Responde a los pedidos (*requests*) de estos clientes usando pronombres.

> **modelo**
>
> Sra. Gómez: Una ensalada, por favor.
> Sí, señora. Enseguida (*Right away*) se la traigo.

1. Sra. Lugones: El pollo asado, por favor.   Sí, señora. Enseguida se lo traigo.
2. Srta. Rivas: Los camarones, por favor.   Sí, señorita. Enseguida se los traigo.
3. Sres. López: La mantequilla, por favor.   Sí, señores. Enseguida se la traigo.
4. Tus compañeros/as de cuarto: Café, por favor.   Sí, chicos/as. Enseguida se lo traigo.
5. Tu profesor(a) de español: Papas fritas, por favor.   Sí, profesor(a). Enseguida se las traigo.
6. Dra. González: La chuleta de cerdo, por favor.   Sí, doctora. Enseguida se la traigo.
7. Tu padre: Los champiñones, por favor.   Sí, papá. Enseguida te los traigo.
8. Dr. Torres: La cuenta, por favor.   Sí, doctor. Enseguida se la traigo.

AYUDA

Here are some other useful expressions:

ahora mismo
right now

inmediatamente
immediately

¡A la orden!
At your service!

¡Ya voy!
I'm on my way!

2   **¿Quién?**   La señora Cevallos está planeando una cena. En parejas, túrnense para decir lo que ella está pensando. Cambien los sustantivos subrayados por pronombres de objeto directo y hagan los otros cambios necesarios.

> **modelo**
>
> ¡No tengo carne! ¿Quién va a traerme la carne del supermercado? (mi esposo)
> Mi *esposo va a traérmela./Mi esposo me la va a traer.*

1. ¡Las invitaciones! ¿Quién les manda las invitaciones a los invitados (*guests*)? (mi hija)   Mi hija se las manda.
2. No tengo tiempo de ir a la bodega. ¿Quién me puede comprar el vino? (mi hijo)   Mi hijo puede comprármelo./Mi hijo me lo puede comprar.
3. Nos falta mantequilla. ¿Quién nos trae la mantequilla? (mi cuñada)   Mi cuñada nos la trae.
4. ¡Ay! No tengo suficientes platos (*plates*). ¿Quién puede prestarme los platos que necesito? (mi mamá)   Mi mamá puede prestármelos./Mi mamá me los puede prestar.
5. ¡Los entremeses! ¿Quién está preparándonos los entremeses? (Silvia y Renata)   Silvia y Renata están preparándonoslos./Silvia y Renata nos los están preparando.
6. No tengo tiempo de pedirle el aceite a Mónica. ¿Quién puede pedirle el aceite? (mi hijo)   Mi hijo puede pedírselo./Mi hijo se lo puede pedir.
7. No hay suficientes sillas. ¿Quién nos trae las sillas que faltan? (Héctor y Lorena)   Héctor y Lorena nos las traen.
8. ¿Quién va a servirles la cena a los invitados? (mis hijos)   Mis hijos van a servírsela./Mis hijos se la van a servir.
9. Quiero poner buena música de fondo (*background*). ¿Quién me va a recomendar la música? (mi esposo)   Mi esposo va a recomendármela./Mi esposo me la va a recomendar.
10. ¡Los postres! ¿Quién va a preparar los postres para los invitados? (Sra. Villalba)   La señora Villalba va a preparárselos./La señora Villalba se los va a preparar.

NOTA CULTURAL

Los vinos de Chile son conocidos internacionalmente. **Concha y Toro** es el productor y exportador más grande de vinos de Chile. Las zonas más productivas de vino están al norte de Santiago, en el Valle Central.

1 **Teaching Tip** Do the activity with the whole class, selecting a student to play the role of customer and another to play the role of server for each item.

Ayuda Model the helpful phrases in sentences. Point out that **Ahora mismo, Inmediatamente,** and **Ya** can replace **Enseguida** in the **modelo** for **Actividad 1.**

2 **Expansion**
- For each item, change the subject in parentheses so that students practice different forms of the verbs.
- Add a visual aspect to this activity. Hold up magazine pictures and ask students to state who is doing what to or for whom. Ex: **La señora les muestra la casa a los jóvenes. Se la muestra a los jóvenes.**

TEACHING OPTIONS

Heritage Speakers Ask heritage speakers to talk about a favorite gift they received. Write **regalar** on the board and explain that it means *to give (a gift)*. Have students talk about what they received, who gave it to them (**regalar**), and why. Ask the rest of the class comprehension questions.
Game Play **Concentración**. Write sentences that use double object pronouns on each of eight cards. Ex: **Óscar se las**

muestra. On another eight cards, draw or paste a picture that matches each sentence. Ex: A photo of a boy showing photos to his grandparents. Place the cards face-down in four rows of four. In pairs, students select two cards. If the two cards match, the pair keeps them. If they do not match, students replace them in their original position. The pair with the most cards at the end wins.

Comunicación

3 **Contestar** Trabajen en parejas. Túrnense para hacer preguntas, usando las palabras interrogativas **¿Quién?** o **¿Cuándo?**, y para responderlas. Answers will vary.

> **modelo**
> nos enseña español
> **Estudiante 1:** ¿Quién nos enseña español?
> **Estudiante 2:** La profesora Camacho nos lo enseña.

1. te puede explicar la tarea cuando no la entiendes
2. les vende el almuerzo a los estudiantes
3. vas a comprarme boletos (*tickets*) para un concierto
4. te escribe mensajes de texto
5. nos prepara los entremeses
6. me vas a prestar tu computadora
7. te compró esa bebida
8. nos va a recomendar el menú de la cafetería
9. le enseñó español al/a la profesor(a)
10. me vas a mostrar tu casa o apartamento

4 **Preguntas** En parejas, túrnense para hacerse estas preguntas. Answers will vary.

> **modelo**
> **Estudiante 1:** ¿Les prestas tu casa a tus amigos? ¿Por qué?
> **Estudiante 2:** No, no se la presto a mis amigos porque no son muy responsables.

1. ¿Me prestas tu auto? ¿Ya le prestaste tu auto a otro/a amigo/a?
2. ¿Quién te presta dinero cuando lo necesitas?
3. ¿Les prestas dinero a tus amigos? ¿Por qué?
4. ¿Nos compras el almuerzo a mí y a los otros compañeros de clase?
5. ¿Les escribes mensajes electrónicos a tus amigos? ¿Y a tu familia?
6. ¿Les das regalos a tus amigos? ¿Cuándo?
7. ¿Quién te va a preparar la cena esta noche?
8. ¿Quién te va a preparar el desayuno mañana?

Síntesis

5 **Regalos de Navidad** Tu profesor(a) te va a dar a ti y a un(a) compañero/a una parte de la lista de los regalos de Navidad (*Christmas*) que Berta pidió y los regalos que sus parientes le compraron. Conversen para completar sus listas. Answers will vary.

> **modelo**
> **Estudiante 1:** ¿Qué le pidió Berta a su mamá?
> **Estudiante 2:** Le pidió una computadora. ¿Se la compró?
> **Estudiante 1:** Sí, se la compró.

NOTA CULTURAL

Las fiestas navideñas (*Christmas season*) en los países hispanos duran hasta enero. En muchos lugares celebran **la Navidad** (*Christmas*), pero no se dan los regalos hasta el seis de enero, **el Día de los Reyes Magos** (*Three Kings' Day/The Feast of the Epiphany*).

TEACHING OPTIONS

Heritage Speakers Ask heritage speakers if they or their families celebrate **el Día de los Reyes Magos** (The Feast of the Epiphany, January 6). Ask them to expand on the information given in the **Nota cultural** box and to tell whether **el Día de los Reyes** is more important for them than **la Navidad**.

Large Groups Divide the class into two groups. Give each member of the first group a strip of paper with a question on it. Ex: **¿Te compró ese suéter tu novia?** Give each member of the second group a piece of paper with an answer to one of the questions. Ex: **Sí, ella me lo compró.** Students must find their partners. Take care not to create sentences that can have more than one match.

8.3 Comparisons Tutorial

ANTE TODO   Both Spanish and English use comparisons to indicate which of two people or things has a lesser, equal, or greater degree of a quality.

menos interesante	más grande	tan sabroso como
less interesting	*bigger*	*as delicious as*

Comparisons of inequality

▶ Comparisons of inequality are formed by placing **más** (*more*) or **menos** (*less*) before adjectives, adverbs, and nouns and **que** (*than*) after them.

$$\text{más/menos} + \begin{bmatrix} \textit{adjective} \\ \textit{adverb} \\ \textit{noun} \end{bmatrix} + \text{que}$$

▶ **¡Atención!** Note that while English has a comparative form for short adjectives (*tall**er***), such forms do not exist in Spanish (**más** alto).

adjectives

Los bistecs son **más caros que** el pollo.   Estas uvas son **menos ricas que** esa pera.
Steaks are more expensive than chicken.   *These grapes are less tasty than that pear.*

adverbs

Me acuesto **más tarde que** tú.   Luis se despierta **menos temprano que** yo.
I go to bed later than you (do).   *Luis wakes up less early than I (do).*

nouns

Juan prepara **más platos que** José.   Susana come **menos carne que** Enrique.
Juan prepares more dishes than José (does).   *Susana eats less meat than Enrique (does).*

La ensalada es menos cara que la sopa.

¿El pollo es más rico que el jamón?

▶ When the comparison involves a numerical expression, **de** is used before the number instead of **que**.

Hay más **de** cincuenta naranjas.   Llego en menos **de** diez minutos.
There are more than fifty oranges.   *I'll be there in less than ten minutes.*

▶ With verbs, this construction is used to make comparisons of inequality.

$$[\textit{verb}] + \text{más/menos que}$$

Mis hermanos **comen más que** yo.   Arturo **duerme menos que** su padre.
My brothers eat more than I (do).   *Arturo sleeps less than his father (does).*

Comparisons of equality

▶ This construction is used to make comparisons of equality.

tan + [*adjective adverb*] + **como**   **tanto/a(s)** + [*singular noun plural noun*] + **como**

¿Es tan guapo como yo?

¿Aquí vienen tantos mexicanos como extranjeros?

▶ **¡Atención!** Note that unlike **tan**, **tanto** acts as an adjective and therefore agrees in number and gender with the noun it modifies.

Estas uvas son **tan ricas como** aquéllas.   Yo probé **tantos platos como** él.
These grapes are as tasty as those ones (are).   *I tried as many dishes as he did.*

▶ **Tan** and **tanto** can also be used for emphasis, rather than to compare, with these meanings: **tan** *so,* **tanto** *so much,* **tantos/as** *so many.*

¡Tu almuerzo es **tan** grande!   ¡Comes **tantas** manzanas!
Your lunch is so big!   *You eat so many apples!*

¡Comes **tanto**!   ¡Preparan **tantos** platos!
You eat so much!   *They prepare so many dishes!*

▶ Comparisons of equality with verbs are formed by placing **tanto como** after the verb. Note that in this construction **tanto** does not change in number or gender.

[*verb*] + **tanto como**

Tú viajas **tanto como** mi tía.   Ellos hablan **tanto como** mis hermanas.
You travel as much as my aunt (does).   *They talk as much as my sisters.*

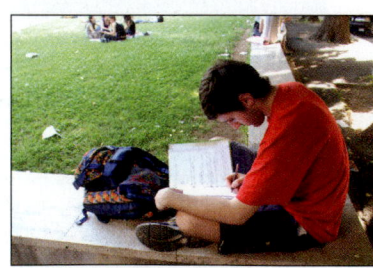

Sabemos **tanto como** ustedes.   No estudio **tanto como** Felipe.
We know as much as you (do).   *I don't study as much as Felipe (does).*

Irregular comparisons

▶ Some adjectives have irregular comparative forms.

Irregular comparative forms

Adjective		Comparative form	
bueno/a	*good*	**mejor**	*better*
malo/a	*bad*	**peor**	*worse*
grande	*grown, adult*	**mayor**	*older*
pequeño/a	*young*	**menor**	*younger*
joven	*young*	**menor**	*younger*
viejo/a	*old*	**mayor**	*older*

CONSULTA

To review how descriptive adjectives like **bueno**, **malo**, and **grande** are shortened before nouns, see **Estructura 3.1**, p. 90.

▶ When **grande** and **pequeño/a** refer to age, the irregular comparative forms, **mayor** and **menor**, are used. However, when these adjectives refer to size, the regular forms, **más grande** and **más pequeño/a**, are used.

Yo soy **menor** que tú.
I'm younger than you.

Pedí un plato **más pequeño**.
I ordered a smaller dish.

Nuestro hijo es **mayor** que el hijo de los Andrade.
Our son is older than the Andrades' son.

La ensalada de Isabel es **más grande** que ésa.
Isabel's salad is bigger than that one.

▶ The adverbs **bien** and **mal** have the same irregular comparative forms as the adjectives **bueno/a** and **malo/a**.

Julio nada **mejor** que los otros chicos.
Julio swims better than the other boys.

Ellas cantan **peor** que las otras chicas.
They sing worse than the other girls.

More activities

vhlcentral

LM
p. 47

WB
pp. 91–92

Online activities

¡INTÉNTALO!   Escribe el equivalente de las palabras en inglés.

1. Ernesto mira más televisión ___que___ (*than*) Alberto.
2. La camarera sirve ___tanta___ (*as much*) carne como pescado.
3. Tú eres ___menos___ (*less*) simpático que Federico.
4. No estudio ___tanto como___ (*as much as*) tú.
5. Recibo ___más___ (*more*) propinas que tú.
6. ¿Sabes jugar al tenis tan bien ___como___ (*as*) tu hermana?
7. ¿Puedes beber ___tantos___ (*as many*) refrescos como yo?
8. Mis amigos parecen ___tan___ (*as*) simpáticos como ustedes.

TEACHING OPTIONS

Large Groups Divide the class into groups of six. Give cards with adjectives listed on page 283 to one group. Give cards with the corresponding irregular comparative form to another group. Students must find their partners. To avoid confusion, make duplicate cards of **mayor** and **menor**.
Pairs Write on the board the heading **Nuestra universidad vs.** [*another nearby university*]. Underneath, write a list of categories.

Ex: **la ciudad universitaria, los estudiantes, las residencias estudiantiles, el equipo de fútbol americano** Have pairs take turns making comparisons about the universities. Encourage them to be creative and to use a variety of comparative forms. Ex: **Los estudiantes de nuestra universidad estudian tanto como los estudiantes de** [*other university*].

Teaching Tips
• Practice the differences between **grande—mayor** and **pequeño/a—menor** when referring to age by having two students stand. Ask **E1: ____ , ¿cuántos años tienes?** (E1: Tengo dieciocho años.) Then ask **E2: Y tú, ____ , ¿cuántos años tienes?** (E2: Tengo diecinueve años.) Now ask the class: **¿Quién es mayor? ¿Y quién es más grande?**
• Ask questions and give examples to practice irregular comparative forms. Ex: (pointing to two students) **Lisa tiene diecinueve años y Shawn tiene veintiún años. ¿Lisa es mayor que Shawn?** (No, Lisa es menor que Shawn.) Then ask questions about celebrities. Ex: **¿Quién canta mejor, Adele o Rihanna?** Have students state their opinions in complete sentences. Ex: **Adele canta mejor que Rihanna.**

Práctica

1 **Escoger** Escoge la palabra correcta para comparar a dos hermanas muy diferentes. Haz los cambios necesarios.

1. Lucila es más alta y más bonita ___que___ Tita. (de, más, menos, que)
2. Tita es vegetariana y por eso come ___más___ verduras que su hermana. (de, más, menos, que)
3. Lucila es más ___simpática___ que Tita porque es alegre. (listo, simpático, bajo)
4. A Tita le gusta comer en casa. Va a ___menos___ restaurantes que su hermana. (más, menos, que) Es tímida, pero activa. Hace ___más___ ejercicio (*exercise*) que su hermana. (más, tanto, menos) Todos los días toma más ___de___ cinco vasos (*glasses*) de agua mineral. (que, tan, de)
5. Lucila come muchas papas fritas y se preocupa ___menos___ que Tita por comer frutas. (de, más, menos) ¡Son ___tan___ diferentes! Pero se llevan (*they get along*) muy bien. (como, tan, tanto)

2 **Emparejar** Compara a Mario y a Luis, los novios de Lucila y Tita, completando las oraciones con las palabras o frases apropiadas.

A	B
1. Mario es ___tan interesante___ como Luis.	tantas
2. Luis toma ___tantas___ clases de cocina (*cooking*) como Mario.	diferencia
3. Mario viaja tanto ___como___ Luis.	tan interesante
4. Luis habla ___francés___ tan bien como Mario.	amigos extranjeros
5. Mario tiene tantos ___amigos extranjeros___ como Luis.	como
6. ¡Qué casualidad (*coincidence*)! Mario y Luis también son hermanos, pero no hay tanta ___diferencia___ entre ellos como entre Lucila y Tita.	francés

3 **Oraciones** Combina elementos de las columnas para hacer comparaciones. Escribe oraciones completas. Answers will vary.

> **modelo**
> Chris Hemsworth tiene tantos autos como Emma Stone.
> Emma Stone es menos musculosa que Chris Hemsworth.

A	B	C
la comida japonesa	costar	la gente de Montreal
el fútbol	saber	la música *country*
Chris Hemsworth	ser	el brócoli
el pollo	tener	el presidente de los EE.UU.
la gente de Vancouver	¿?	la comida italiana
la primera dama (*lady*) de los EE.UU.		el hockey
las universidades privadas		Emma Stone
las espinacas		las universidades públicas
la música rap		la carne de res

Comunicación

4   **Intercambiar** En parejas, hagan comparaciones sobre diferentes cosas. Pueden usar las sugerencias de la lista u otras ideas. Answers will vary.

AYUDA

You can use these adjectives in your comparisons:

bonito/a
caro/a
elegante
interesante
inteligente

> **modelo**
>
> **Estudiante 1:** *Los pollos de Pollitos del Corral son muy ricos.*
> **Estudiante 2:** *Pues yo creo que los pollos de Rostipollos son tan buenos como los pollos de Pollitos del Corral.*
> **Estudiante 1:** *Ummm... no tienen tanta mantequilla como los pollos de Pollitos del Corral. Tienes razón. Son muy sabrosos.*

> podcasts favoritos
> revistas favoritas
> libros favoritos

> comidas favoritas
> los profesores
> los cursos que toman

> restaurantes en tu ciudad/pueblo
> cafés en tu comunidad
> tiendas en tu ciudad/pueblo

5   **Conversar** En grupos, túrnense para hacer comparaciones entre ustedes mismos (*yourselves*) y una persona de cada categoría de la lista. Answers will vary.

▶ una persona de tu familia
▶ un(a) amigo/a especial
▶ una persona famosa

Síntesis

6   **La familia López** En grupos, túrnense para hablar de Sara, Sabrina, Cristina, Ricardo y David y hacer comparaciones entre ellos. Answers will vary.

> **modelo**
>
> **Estudiante 1:** *Sara es tan alta como Sabrina.*
> **Estudiante 2:** *Sí, pero David es más alto que ellas.*
> **Estudiante 3:** *En mi opinión, él es guapo también.*

Section Goals

In **Estructura 8.4**, students will be introduced to:
- superlatives
- irregular superlative forms

Instructional Resources
Supersite: Audio (Lab MP3 Files); Resources (Grammar Presentation Slides, Activity Pack, Scripts, Answer Keys); Testing Program (Quizzes)
WebSAM
Workbook
Lab Manual

Teaching Tips
- Give names of famous people or places and have students make superlative statements about their most obvious quality. Ex: **Bill Gates (Es uno de los hombres más ricos del mundo.); el monte Denali (Es la montaña más alta de Norteamérica.)**
- Ask questions and give examples to practice irregular superlative forms. Ex: **¿Quién es el menor de tu familia? ¿Ah, sí? ¿Cuántos hermanos mayores tienes?**
- Practice superlative questions by asking for students' opinions. Ex: **¿Cuál es la clase más difícil de esta universidad? ¿Y la más fácil?**
- Use magazine pictures to compare and contrast absolute superlatives. Ex: **Este edificio parece modernísimo, pero éste no. Parece viejísimo.**
- →👤← Ask volunteers to identify people you describe using absolute superlatives. Ex: **Tiene un canal y varios programas de televisión. Se le conoce por ser una filántropa muy generosa. Es riquísima. (Oprah Winfrey)**

8.4 Superlatives Tutorial

ANTE TODO   Both English and Spanish use superlatives to express the highest or lowest degree of a quality.

el/la mejor	**el/la peor**	**el/la más alto/a**
the best	*the worst*	*the tallest*

▶ This construction is used to form superlatives. Note that the noun is always preceded by a definite article and that **de** is equivalent to the English *in* or *of*.

$$\boxed{\text{el/la/los/las} + \fbox{noun} + \text{más/menos} + \fbox{adjective} + \text{de}}$$

▶ The noun can be omitted if the person, place, or thing referred to is clear.

¿El restaurante Las Delicias?
Es **el más elegante** de la ciudad.
The restaurant Las Delicias?
It's the most elegant (one) in the city.

Recomiendo el pollo asado.
Es **el más sabroso** del menú.
I recommend the roast chicken.
It's the most delicious on the menu.

▶ Here are some irregular superlative forms.

Irregular superlatives

Adjective		Superlative form	
bueno/a	*good*	**el/la mejor**	*(the) best*
malo/a	*bad*	**el/la peor**	*(the) worst*
grande	*grown, adult*	**el/la mayor**	*(the) oldest*
pequeño/a	*young*	**el/la menor**	*(the) youngest*
joven	*young*	**el/la menor**	*(the) youngest*
viejo/a	*old*	**el/la mayor**	*(the) oldest*

▶ The absolute superlative is equivalent to *extremely*, *super*, or *very*. To form the absolute superlative of most adjectives and adverbs, drop the final vowel, if there is one, and add **-ísimo/a(s)**.

malo → mal- → malísimo   **mucho → much- → muchísimo**

¡El bistec está **malísimo**!   Comes **muchísimo**.

▶ Note these spelling changes.

rico → riquísimo   **largo → larguísimo**   **feliz → felicísimo**

fácil → facilísimo   **joven → jovencísimo**   **trabajador → trabajadorcísimo**

∞ **¡INTÉNTALO!**   Escribe el equivalente de las palabras en inglés.

1. Mónica es <u>la más inteligente</u> (*the most intelligent*) de todas.
2. Ricardo y Tomás son <u>los menos aburridos</u> (*the least boring*) de la fiesta.
3. Mi profesor de biología es <u>el mayor</u> (*the oldest*) de la universidad.
4. Miguel y Antonio son <u>los peores</u> (*the worst*) estudiantes de la clase.

¡ATENCIÓN!

While **más** alone means *more*, after **el**, **la**, **los**, or **las**, it means *most*. Likewise, **menos** can mean *less* or *least*.

Es **el café más rico del** país.
It's the most delicious coffee in the country.

Es **el menú menos caro de** todos éstos.
It is the least expensive menu of all of these.

CONSULTA

The rule you learned in **Estructura 8.3** (p. 283) regarding the use of **mayor/menor** with age, but not with size, is also true with superlative forms.

More activities

vhlcentral

LM
p. 48

WB
pp. 93–94

Online activities

TEACHING OPTIONS

Heritage Speakers ←👤→ Ask heritage speakers to discuss whether absolute superlatives are common in their culture (some regions and countries use them less frequently than others). Also have them discuss under what circumstances absolute superlatives are most frequently used, such as when talking about food, people, events, and so forth. Then have the class work in pairs to create mini-conversations

based on the superlatives mentioned.
Extra Practice Ask students questions with superlatives about things and places at your university, in your community, in the class, and so forth. Include a mix of regular and irregular superlative forms. Ex: **¿Cuál es el edificio más grande del campus? ¿Cuál es la peor clase de la universidad?**

Práctica y Comunicación

1 El más...
Responde a las preguntas afirmativamente. Usa las palabras entre paréntesis.

> **modelo**
> El cuarto está sucísimo, ¿no? (residencia)
> Sí, es el más sucio de la residencia.

1. La silla de tu madre es comodísima, ¿no? (casa) *Sí, es la más cómoda de la casa.*
2. El almacén Velasco es buenísimo, ¿no? (centro comercial) *Sí, es el mejor del centro comercial.*
3. Ángela y Julia están nerviosísimas por el examen, ¿no? (clase) *Sí, son las más nerviosas de la clase.*
4. Jorge es jovencísimo, ¿no? (mis amigos) *Sí, es el menor de mis amigos.*

2 Completar
Tu profesor(a) te va a dar una hoja de actividades con descripciones de José Valenzuela Carranza y Ana Orozco Hoffman. Completa las oraciones con las palabras de la lista.

Some answers may vary. Suggested answers:

altísima	del	mayor	peor
atlética	guapísimo	mejor	periodista
bajo	la	menor	trabajadorcísimo
de	más	Orozco	Valenzuela

1. José tiene 22 años; es el ___menor___ y el más ___bajo___ de su familia. Es ___guapísimo___ y ___trabajadorcísimo___. Es el mejor ___periodista___ de la ciudad y el ___peor___ jugador de baloncesto.
2. Ana es la más ___atlética___ y ___la___ mejor jugadora de baloncesto del estado. Es la ___mayor___ de sus hermanos (tiene 28 años) y es ___altísima___. Estudió la profesión ___más___ difícil ___de___ todas: medicina.
3. Jorge es el ___mejor___ jugador de videojuegos de su familia.
4. Mauricio es el menor de la familia ___Orozco___.
5. El abuelo es el ___mayor___ de todos los miembros de la familia Valenzuela.
6. Fifí es la perra más antipática ___del___ mundo.

3 Superlativos
Trabajen en parejas para hacer comparaciones. Usen los superlativos.

Answers will vary.

> **modelo**
> Emma Watson, Bill Gates, Warren Buffett
> **Estudiante 1:** Bill Gates es el más rico de los tres.
> **Estudiante 2:** Sí, ¡es riquísimo! Y Warren Buffett es el mayor de los tres.

1. Guatemala, Argentina, España
2. Jaguar, Prius, Smart
3. la comida mexicana, la comida francesa, la comida árabe
4. Amy Adams, Cate Blanchett, Jennifer Lawrence
5. Ciudad de México, Buenos Aires, Nueva York
6. *Don Quijote de la Mancha, Cien años de soledad, Como agua para chocolate*
7. el fútbol americano, el golf, el béisbol
8. las películas románticas, las películas de acción, las películas cómicas

(NATIONAL communication STANDARDS)

TEACHING OPTIONS

Extra Practice Add an auditory aspect to this grammar practice. Prepare ten superlative sentences and read them aloud slowly, pausing after each sentence to allow students to write the direct opposite. Ex: **Ernesto es el menor de la familia. (Ernesto es el mayor de la familia.)**

Pairs Bring in clothing catalogs and have students work in pairs to create superlative statements about the prices of different items. Ask volunteers to share some of their statements with the class. You may want to have students review clothing-related vocabulary from **Lección 6.**

---

1 Expansion
- Give these sentences to students as items 5–7:
  5. Esas películas son malísimas, ¿no? (Hollywood) (Sí, son las peores de Hollywood.) 6. El centro comercial Galerías es grandísimo, ¿no? (ciudad) (Sí, es el más grande de la ciudad.) 7. Tus bisabuelos son viejísimos, ¿no? (familia) (Sí, son los mayores de mi familia.)
- To challenge students, after they have completed the activity, have them repeat it by answering in the negative. Ex: **1. No, es el peor del centro comercial.**

2 Teaching Tip Distribute the *Hojas de actividades* (Activity Pack/Supersite) that correspond to this activity.

2 Expansion
In pairs, have students select a family member or a close friend and describe him or her using comparatives and superlatives. Ask volunteers to share their descriptions with the class.

3 Teaching Tips
- To simplify, read through the items with students and, in English, brainstorm points of comparison between the three people or things. For item 6, briefly describe these novels for students who are not familiar with them.
- Encourage students to create as many superlatives as they can for each item. Have volunteers share their most creative statements with the class.

Recapitulación

Completa estas actividades para repasar los conceptos de gramática que aprendiste en esta lección.

1 **Completar** Completa la tabla con la forma correcta del pretérito. `18 pts.`

Infinitive	yo	usted	ellos
dormir	dormí	durmió	durmieron
servir	serví	sirvió	sirvieron
vestirse	me vestí	se vistió	se vistieron

2 **La cena** Completa la conversación con el pretérito de los verbos. `14 pts.`

PAULA ¡Hola, Daniel! ¿Qué tal el fin de semana?

DANIEL Muy bien. Marta y yo (1) ___conseguimos___ (conseguir) hacer muchas cosas, pero lo mejor fue la cena del sábado.

PAULA Ah, ¿sí? ¿Adónde fueron?

DANIEL Al restaurante Vistahermosa. Es elegante, así que (nosotros) (2) ___nos vestimos___ (vestirse) bien.

PAULA Y, ¿qué platos (3) ___pidieron___ (pedir, ustedes)?

DANIEL Yo (4) ___pedí___ (pedir) camarones y Marta (5) ___prefirió___ (preferir) el pollo. Y al final, el camarero nos (6) ___sirvió___ (servir) flan.

PAULA ¡Qué rico!

DANIEL Sí. Pero después de la cena Marta no (7) ___se sintió___ (sentirse) bien.

3 **Camareros** Completa la conversación usando pronombres. `8 pts.`

JEFE Úrsula, ¿le ofreciste agua fría al cliente de la mesa 22?

ÚRSULA Sí, (1) ___se la ofrecí___ de inmediato.

JEFE Genaro, ¿los clientes de la mesa 5 te pidieron ensaladas?

GENARO Sí, (2) ___me las pidieron___.

ÚRSULA Genaro, ¿recuerdas si ya me mostraste los vinos nuevos?

GENARO Sí, ya (3) ___te los mostré___.

JEFE Genaro, ¿van a pagarte la cuenta los clientes de la mesa 5?

GENARO Sí, (4) ___me la van a pagar/van a pagármela___ ahora mismo.

RESUMEN GRAMATICAL

8.1 **Preterite of stem-changing verbs** *p. 274*

servir	dormir
serví	dormí
serviste	dormiste
sirvió	durmió
servimos	dormimos
servisteis	dormisteis
sirvieron	durmieron

8.2 **Double object pronouns** *pp. 277–278*

Indirect Object Pronouns: me, te, le (se), nos, os, les (se)

Direct Object Pronouns: lo, la, los, las

Le escribí la carta. → Se la escribí.
Nos van a servir los platos. → Nos los van a servir./ Van a servírnoslos.

8.3 **Comparisons** *pp. 281–283*

Comparisons of inequality		
más/menos +	*adj., adv., n.*	**+ que**
verb + **más/menos + que**		

Comparisons of equality		
tan +	*adj., adv.*	**+ como**
tanto/a(s) +	*noun*	**+ como**
verb + **tanto como**		

Irregular comparative forms	
bueno/a	mejor
malo/a	peor
grande	mayor
pequeño/a	menor
joven	menor
viejo/a	mayor

8.4 **Superlatives** *p. 286*

el/la/ los/las +	noun	+ más/ menos +	adjective	+ de

▶ Irregular superlatives follow the same pattern as irregular comparatives.

4 **El menú** Completa las oraciones basándote en los elementos dados. Usa comparativos y superlativos. **14 pts.**

Ensaladas	*Precio*	*Calorías*
Ensalada de tomates	$9.00	170
Ensalada de mariscos	$12.99	325
Ensalada de zanahorias	$9.00	200
Platos principales		
Pollo con champiñones	$13.00	495
Cerdo con papas	$10.50	725
Atún con espárragos	$18.95	495

1. ensalada de mariscos / otras ensaladas / costar
   La ensalada de mariscos ___cuesta más que___ las otras ensaladas.
2. pollo con champiñones / cerdo con papas / calorías
   El pollo con champiñones tiene ___menos calorías que___ el cerdo con papas.
3. atún con espárragos / pollo con champiñones / calorías
   El atún con espárragos tiene ___tantas calorías como___ el pollo con champiñones.
4. ensalada de tomates / ensalada de zanahorias / caro
   La ensalada de tomates es ___tan cara como___ la ensalada de zanahorias.
5. cerdo con papas / platos principales / caro
   El cerdo con papas es ___el menos caro de___ los platos principales.
6. ensalada de zanahorias / ensalada de tomates / costar
   La ensalada de zanahorias ___cuesta tanto como___ la ensalada de tomates.
7. ensalada de mariscos / ensaladas / caro
   La ensalada de mariscos es ___la más cara de___ las ensaladas.

5 **Dos restaurantes** ¿Cuál es el mejor restaurante que conoces? ¿Y el peor? Escribe un párrafo de por lo menos (*at least*) seis oraciones donde expliques por qué piensas así. Puedes hablar de la calidad de la comida, el ambiente, los precios, el servicio, etc. **46 pts.** Answers will vary.

6 **Adivinanza** Completa la adivinanza y adivina la respuesta. **¡4 puntos EXTRA!**

"En el campo yo nací°,
mis hermanos son
los ___ajos___ (*garlic, pl.*),
y aquél que llora° por mí
me está partiendo°
en pedazos°. "
¿Quién soy? ___La cebolla___

nací *was born*   llora *cries*   partiendo *cutting*   pedazos *pieces*

Audio: Reading

Section Goals

In **Lectura**, students will:
- learn to identify the main idea in a text
- read a content-rich menu and restaurant review

Instructional Resource
Supersite

Estrategia Tell students that recognizing the main idea of a text will help them unlock the meaning of unfamiliar words and phrases they come across while reading. Tell them to first check the title, where the main idea is often expressed. Then have them read the topic sentence of each paragraph before they read the full text to get a sense of the main idea.

Examinar el texto First, have students scan the menu. Ask how the title and subheadings help predict the content. Ask volunteers to state the meaning of each category of food served. Then have students scan the newspaper article. Ask them how the title and the format (the box with ratings) of the text give clues to the content.

Identificar la idea principal Ask students to read the column heading and the title of the article and predict the subject of the article and the author's purpose. Then have students read the topic sentence of the first paragraph and state the main idea. Finally, have them read the entire paragraph.

Lectura

 communication cultures NATIONAL STANDARDS

Antes de leer

Estrategia
Reading for the main idea

As you know, you can learn a great deal about a reading selection by looking at the format and looking for cognates, titles, and subtitles. You can skim to get the gist of the reading selection and scan it for specific information. Reading for the main idea is another useful strategy; it involves locating the topic sentences of each paragraph to determine the author's purpose for writing a particular piece. Topic sentences can provide clues about the content of each paragraph, as well as the general organization of the reading. Your choice of which reading strategies to use will depend on the style and format of each reading selection.

Examinar el texto

En esta sección tenemos dos textos diferentes. ¿Qué estrategias puedes usar para leer la crítica culinaria°? ¿Cuáles son las apropiadas para familiarizarte con el menú? Utiliza las estrategias más eficaces° para cada texto. ¿Qué tienen en común? ¿Qué tipo de comida sirven en el restaurante?

Identificar la idea principal

Lee la primera oración de cada párrafo de la crítica culinaria del restaurante **La feria del maíz**. Apunta° el tema principal de cada párrafo. Luego lee todo el primer párrafo. ¿Crees que el restaurante le gustó al autor de la crítica culinaria? ¿Por qué? Ahora lee la crítica entera. En tu opinión, ¿cuál es la idea principal de la crítica? ¿Por qué la escribió el autor? Compara tus opiniones con las de un(a) compañero/a.

More activities

vhlcentral | Online activities

crítica culinaria *restaurant review* eficaces *effective*
Apunta *Jot down*

MENÚ

Entremeses
Tortilla servida con
- Ajiaceite (chile, aceite)
- Ajicomino (chile, comino)

Pan tostado servido con
- Queso frito a la pimienta
- Salsa de ajo y mayonesa

Sopas
- Tomate
- Cebolla
- Verduras
- Pollo y huevo
- Carne de res
- Mariscos

Entradas
Tomaticán
(tomate, papas, maíz, chile, arvejas y zanahorias)

Tamales
(maíz, azúcar, ajo, cebolla)

Frijoles enchilados
(frijoles negros, carne de cerdo o de res, arroz, chile)

Chilaquil
(tortilla de maíz, queso, hierbas y chile)

Tacos
(tortillas, pollo, verduras y salsa)

Cóctel de mariscos
(camarones, langosta, vinagre, sal, pimienta, aceite)

Postres°
- Plátanos caribeños
- Cóctel de frutas al ron°
- Uvate (uvas, azúcar de caña y ron)
- Flan napolitano
- Helado° de piña y naranja
- Pastel° de yogur

Después de leer

Preguntas

En parejas, contesten estas preguntas sobre la crítica culinaria de **La feria del maíz.**

1. ¿Quién es el dueño y chef de **La feria del maíz**? Ernesto Sandoval
2. ¿Qué tipo de comida se sirve en el restaurante? tradicional
3. ¿Cuál es el problema con el servicio? Se necesitan más camareros.
4. ¿Cómo es el ambiente del restaurante? agradable
5. ¿Qué comidas probó el autor? las tortillas, el ajiaceite, la sopa de mariscos, los tamales, los tacos de pollo y los plátanos caribeños
6. ¿Quieren ir ustedes al restaurante **La feria del maíz**? ¿Por qué? Answers will vary.

TEACHING OPTIONS

Small Groups Ask groups to create a dinner menu featuring their favorite dishes, including lists of ingredients similar to those in the menu above. Have groups present their menus to the class.

Heritage Speakers Ask a heritage speaker of Guatemalan origin or a student who has visited Guatemala and dined in restaurants or cafés to prepare a short presentation about his or her experiences there. Of particular interest would be a comparison and contrast of city vs. small-town restaurants. If possible, the presentation should be illustrated with menus from the restaurants, advertisements, or photos of and articles about the country.

Escuchar

Antes de escuchar

Estrategia

Jotting down notes as you listen

Jotting down notes while you listen to a conversation in Spanish can help you keep track of the important points or details. It will help you to focus actively on comprehension rather than on remembering what you have heard.

To practice this strategy, you will now listen to a paragraph. Jot down the main points you hear.

Preparación Mira la foto. ¿Dónde están estas personas y qué hacen? ¿Sobre qué crees que están hablando?

Ahora escucha

En el restaurante

Rosa y Roberto están en un restaurante. Escucha la conversación y toma nota de cuáles son los especiales del día, qué pidieron y qué bebidas se mencionan.

Especiales del día

Entremeses
salmón y langosta

Plato principal
arroz con pollo
cerdo con salsa de champiñones y papas
bistec a la criolla

¿Qué pidieron?

Roberto
cerdo con salsa de champiñones y papas

Rosa
especial de arroz con pollo

Bebidas

Inca Kola
jugo de naranja

Comprensión

Seleccionar

Usa tus notas para seleccionar la opción correcta para completar cada oración.

1. Dos de los mejores platos del restaurante son ___c___.
   a. los entremeses del día y el cerdo
   b. el salmón y el arroz con pollo
   c. la carne y el arroz con pollo

2. La camarera ___b___.
   a. los lleva a su mesa, les muestra el menú y les sirve el postre
   b. les habla de los especiales del día, les recomienda unos platos y ellos deciden qué van a comer
   c. les lleva unas bebidas, les recomienda unos platos y les sirve pan

3. Roberto va a comer ___a___ Rosa.
   a. tantos platos como
   b. más platos que
   c. menos platos que

Preguntas

En grupos de tres o cuatro, respondan a las preguntas: ¿Conocen los platos que Rosa y Roberto pidieron? ¿Conocen platos con los mismos ingredientes? ¿En qué son diferentes o similares? ¿Cuál les gusta más? ¿Por qué? Answers will vary.

ROSA: Bueno, yo voy a pedir el especial de arroz con pollo. Y tú, Roberto, ¿sabes lo que vas a pedir?
ROBERTO: Voy a pedir el cerdo con salsa de champiñones y papas.
CAMARERA: Muy bien. ¿Y para tomar?
ROBERTO: Yo quiero una Inca Kola.

ROSA: Y yo quiero jugo de naranja.
CAMARERA: Muy bien. Ya les traigo el pedido.
ROSA: Ah, por favor, ¿nos puede traer un poco de pan con mantequilla?
CAMARERA: Sí, claro, enseguida.

Section Goals

In **Escuchar**, students will:
- use the strategy of jotting down notes
- listen to a short paragraph and write down its main points
- answer questions based on a recorded conversation

Instructional Resources
Supersite: Audio (Textbook MP3s); Resources (Scripts)

Estrategia
Script Sandra está avergonzada. Ayer fue a sus clases sin peinarse ni maquillarse. ¡Y la ropa que llevaba! ¡Una camiseta vieja con unos pantalones morados y unas sandalias rosadas! Hablé con ella y me contó que tiene muchos problemas. Salió muy mal en el examen, su abuela está enferma y también su novio se enojó con ella anteayer.

Teaching Tip Invite students to look at the photo and predict where **Roberto** and **Rosa** are and what they are doing.

Ahora escucha
Script CAMARERA: Buenas noches y bienvenidos a El Chaltén. Aquí les traigo el menú y también les cuento cuáles son los especiales del día.
Para empezar, hay entremeses de salmón y langosta. Los especiales para plato principal son: arroz con pollo, cerdo con salsa de champiñones acompañado de papas y, finalmente, bistec a la criolla, que es carne con una salsa de tomates y cebollas.
ROSA: Hmm… ¡Qué delicia!
ROBERTO: Sí, muy rico. ¿Qué nos recomiendas tú?
CAMARERA: Definitivamente, recomiendo los entremeses de salmón y langosta. ¡Son deliciosos! Como plato principal, el especial de arroz con pollo es muy bueno. El especial de carne es también uno de los mejores platos de este restaurante.

(Script continues at far left in the bottom panels.)

En pantalla Video

La sopa es un plato muy importante en las cocinas° del mundo hispano. Se pueden tomar° frías, como el famoso gazpacho español, a base de tomate y otras verduras y servida totalmente líquida. La mayoría se sirven calientes, como el pozole de México, un plato precolombino preparado con nixtamal°, cerdo, chiles y otras especias°. Otra sopa de origen indígena es la changua, de la región andina central de Colombia. Aunque° las sopas normalmente forman parte del almuerzo, la changua siempre se toma en el desayuno: se hace con agua, leche, huevo y cilantro.

Vocabulario útil	
bajar	*to descend*
la escalera	*staircase*
lo que yo quiera	*whatever I want*
sabor marinero	*seafood flavor*

Preparación
¿Qué comidas son irresistibles para ti? ¿Te gusta la sopa?
Answers will vary.

Ordenar
Ordena cronológicamente estas oraciones.
- __2__ a. El niño abre la puerta.
- __4__ b. El niño decide almorzar.
- __1__ c. El niño baja la escalera con una maleta.
- __5__ d. El niño se va a lavar las manos.
- __3__ e. La madre dice que la sopa está servida.

Sopas
En parejas, túrnense para describir su sopa favorita. ¿Cuál es tu sopa favorita? ¿Quién la prepara o dónde la compras? ¿Qué ingredientes tiene? ¿Con qué se sirve? ¿Cómo la prefieres, caliente o fría? ¿La tomas en el almuerzo o en la cena? ¿En invierno o en verano?
Answers will vary.

cocinas *cuisines* tomar *to eat (soup)* nixtamal *hominy* especias *spices*
Aunque *Although* está servida *it is served*

Anuncio de Sopas Roa

Me voy de esta casa.

Ya está servida° la sopa...

... y lavarme las manos.

More activities
vhlcentral   Online activities

Video

España y la mayoría de los países de Latinoamérica tienen una abundante producción de frutas y verduras. Es por esto que en los hogares° hispanos se acostumbra° cocinar° con productos frescos° más que con alimentos° que vienen en latas° o en frascos°. Las salsas mexicanas, el gazpacho español y el sancocho colombiano, por ejemplo, deben prepararse con ingredientes frescos para que mantengan° su sabor° auténtico. Actualmente, en los Estados Unidos está creciendo el interés en cocinar con productos frescos y orgánicos. Cada vez hay más mercados donde los agricultores° pueden vender sus frutas y verduras directamente° al público. Además, las personas prefieren consumir productos locales de temporada°. En este episodio de *Flash cultura* vas a ver algunas de las frutas y verduras típicas de la comida hispana.

Vocabulario útil

blanda	*soft*
cocinar	*to cook*
dura	*hard*
¿Está lista para ordenar?	*Are you ready to order?*
pruébala	*try it, taste it*
las ventas	*sales*

Preparación

¿Probaste alguna vez comida latina? ¿La compraste en un supermercado o fuiste a un restaurante? ¿Qué plato(s) probaste? ¿Te gustó? Answers will vary.

¿Cierto o falso?

Indica si cada oración es **cierta** o **falsa**.

1. En Los Ángeles hay comida de países latinoamericanos y de España. Cierto.
2. Leticia explica que la tortilla del taco americano es blanda y la del taco mexicano es dura. Falso.
3. Las ventas de salsa son bajas en los Estados Unidos. Falso.
4. Leticia fue a un restaurante ecuatoriano. Falso.
5. Leticia probó Inca Kola en un supermercado. Cierto.

hogares *homes* se acostumbra *they are used* cocinar *to cook* frescos *fresh* alimentos *foods* latas *cans* frascos *jars* para que mantengan *so that they keep* sabor *flavor* agricultores *farmers* directamente *directly* de temporada *seasonal* mostrará *will show*

La comida latina

La mejor comida latina no sólo se encuentra en los grandes restaurantes.

Marta nos mostrará° algunos de los platos de la comida mexicana.

... hay más lugares donde podemos comprar productos hispanos.

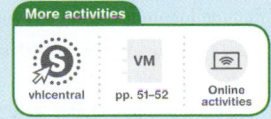

More activities

| vhlcentral | VM pp. 51–52 | Online activities |

Section Goals

In **Flash cultura**, students will:
- read about the importance of fresh produce in the Spanish-speaking world
- watch a video about Latin food in the U.S.

Instructional Resources
Supersite: Video (*Flash cultura*); Resources (Scripts, Translations, Answer Keys)
WebSAM
Video Manual

Introduction To check comprehension, give students these true/false statements: **1. No hay buena producción de frutas y verduras en Suramérica.** (Falso.) **2. En los países hispanos no es común cocinar con productos de lata.** (Cierto.) **3. En los Estados Unidos hay lugares donde la gente puede conseguir frutas y verduras directamente con los agricultores.** (Cierto.)

Antes de ver
- Have students look at the video stills, read the captions, and predict the content of the video.
- Read through **Vocabulario útil** with students. Model the pronunciation. Point out that **blanda, dura,** and **lista** are adjectives; have students name the masculine forms as well.
- Explain that students do not need to understand every word they hear. Tell them to rely on visual cues, cognates, and words from **Vocabulario útil.**

Preparación Ask students if their families purchase any food items that are imported from Spanish-speaking countries.

¿Cierto o falso? Have students work in pairs and correct the false statements.

TEACHING OPTIONS

Extra Practice ←👥→ Ask students to imagine that they are immigrants from a Spanish-speaking country who have recently arrived in your community. Have them draft a letter to a friend or family member in their home country, describing their first culinary experiences in comparison with those back home. Encourage them to describe the food available here and to use as many comparatives and superlatives as they can.

Extra Practice →👥← Have students search the Internet for a typical recipe from a Spanish-speaking country. Have them make a list of the ingredients that can be found in their regular local supermarket. Then have them find out where in the community they can purchase the remaining items.

Section Goal

In **Panorama**, students will read about the geography, history, and culture of Guatemala.

Instructional Resources

Supersite: Video (*Panorama cultural*); Resources (Scripts, Translations, Digital Image Bank, Answer Keys)
WebSAM
Workbook

Teaching Tips

• Use the **Lección 8 Panorama** digital images to assist with this presentation.

• As students examine the map in their books, point out that Guatemala has three main climatic regions: the tropical Pacific and Caribbean coasts, the highlands (southwest), and jungle lowlands (north). Ask volunteers to read aloud the names of the cities, mountains, and rivers of Guatemala. Point out that indigenous languages are the source of many place names.

El país en cifras As you read about the languages of Guatemala, you might point out that while some Guatemalans are monolingual in either Spanish or a Mayan language, many are bilingual, speaking an indigenous language and Spanish.

Guatemala

El país en cifras

▸ **Área:** 108.890 km² (42.042 millas²), *un poco más pequeño que Tennessee*

▸ **Población:** 15.460.732

▸ **Capital:** Ciudad de Guatemala—2.918.000

▸ **Ciudades principales:** Quetzaltenango, Escuintla, Mazatenango, Puerto Barrios

▸ **Moneda:** quetzal

▸ **Idiomas:** español (oficial), lenguas mayas, xinca, garífuna
El español es la lengua de 69 por ciento° de la población; el otro 31 por ciento tiene como lengua materna el xinca, el garífuna o, en su mayoría°, una de las lenguas mayas (cakchiquel, quiché y kekchícomo, entre otras). Una palabra que las lenguas mayas tienen en común es ixim, que significa 'maíz', un cultivo° de mucha importancia en estas culturas.

Bandera de Guatemala

Guatemaltecos célebres

▸ **Carlos Mérida,** pintor (1891–1984)

▸ **Miguel Ángel Asturias,** escritor (1899–1974)

▸ **Margarita Carrera,** poeta y ensayista (1929–)

▸ **Rigoberta Menchú Tum,** activista (1959–), Premio Nobel de la Paz° en 1992

▸ **Jaime Viñals Massanet,** montañista (1966–)

por ciento *percent* en su mayoría *most of them* cultivo *crop*
Paz *Peace*

Lago de Atitlán

Palacio Nacional de la Cultura en la Ciudad de Guatemala

Iglesia de la Merced en Antigua Guatemala

More activities

vhlcentral | WB pp. 95–96 | Online activities

ACTIVIDADES

1 **¿Cierto o falso?** Indica si lo que dice cada oración es **cierto** o **falso.**

1. Huipil es una de las ciudades más importantes de Guatemala. **falso**
2. Carlos Mérida murió en 1974. **falso**
3. Miguel Ángel Asturias fue un importante pintor guatemalteco. **falso**
4. La lengua materna del noventa por ciento de los guatemaltecos es el español. **falso**
5. Tennessee es más grande que Guatemala. **cierto**
6. La famosa Iglesia de la Merced se encuentra en Antigua Guatemala. **cierto**
7. Un terremoto destruyó Antigua Guatemala en 1773. **cierto**
8. El quetzal está en peligro de extinción. **cierto**
9. Los mayas inventaron un calendario preciso. **cierto**
10. Los guatemaltecos muestran en su ropa el amor a la arquitectura. **falso**

TEACHING OPTIONS

Worth Noting Although the indigenous population of Guatemala is Mayan, many place names in southwestern Guatemala are in Nahuatl, the language of the Aztecs of central Mexico. In the sixteenth century, Guatemala was conquered by Spaniards who came from the Valley of Mexico after having overthrown the Aztec rulers there. The Spanish were accompanied by large numbers of Nahuatl-speaking allies, who renamed the captured Mayan strongholds with Nahuatl names. The suffix **–tenango**, which appears in many of these names, means *place with a wall*, that is, a fortified place. **Quetzaltenango**, then, means *fortified place of the quetzal bird;* **Mazatenango** means *fortified place of the deer.*

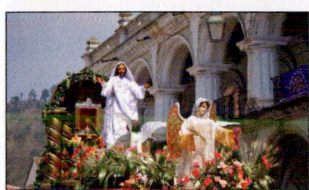

⊳ Ciudades • Antigua Guatemala

Antigua Guatemala fue fundada en 1543. Fue una capital de gran importancia hasta 1773, cuando un terremoto° la destruyó. Sin embargo, conserva el carácter original de su arquitectura y hoy es uno de los centros turísticos del país. Su celebración de la Semana Santa° es, para muchas personas, la más importante del hemisferio.

⊳ Naturaleza • El quetzal

El quetzal simbolizó la libertad para los antiguos° mayas porque creían° que este pájaro° no podía° vivir en cautiverio°. Hoy el quetzal es el símbolo nacional. El pájaro da su nombre a la moneda nacional y aparece también en los billetes° del país. Desafortunadamente, está en peligro° de extinción. Para su protección, el gobierno mantiene una reserva ecológica especial.

Historia • Los mayas

Desde 1500 a.C. hasta 900 d.C., los mayas habitaron gran parte de lo que ahora es Guatemala. Su civilización fue muy avanzada. Los mayas fueron arquitectos y constructores de pirámides, templos y observatorios. También descubrieron° el cero y lo usaron antes que los europeos, e inventaron un calendario complejo° y preciso.

Artesanía • La ropa tradicional

La ropa tradicional de los guatemaltecos es el *huipil* y muestra el amor° de la cultura maya por la naturaleza. Ellos se inspiran en las flores°, las plantas y los animales para crear sus diseños° de colores vivos° y formas geométricas. El diseño y los colores de cada *huipil* indican el pueblo de origen y a veces también el sexo y la edad° de la persona que lo lleva.

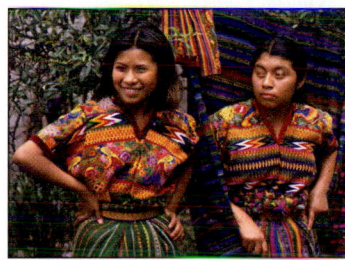

terremoto *earthquake* Semana Santa *Holy Week* antiguos *ancient* creían *they believed* pájaro *bird* no podía *couldn't* cautiverio *captivity* los billetes *bills* peligro *danger* descubrieron *they discovered* complejo *complex* amor *love* flores *flowers* diseños *designs* vivos *bright* edad *age*

¡Increíble pero cierto!

¿Qué "ingrediente" secreto se encuentra en las telas° tradicionales de Guatemala? ¡El mosquito! El excepcional tinte° de estas telas es producto de una combinación de flores y de mosquitos aplastados°. El insecto hace que los colores no se destiñan°. Quizás es por esto que los artesanos representan la figura del mosquito en muchas de sus telas.

telas *fabrics* tinte *dye* aplastados *crushed* hace... destiñan *keeps the colors from running*

2 ¿Qué aprendiste? Contesta las preguntas.

1. ¿Qué significa la palabra *ixim*?
   "maíz"
2. ¿Quién es Rigoberta Menchú?
   una activista de Guatemala
3. ¿Qué simbolizó el quetzal para los mayas?
   la libertad
4. ¿De qué fueron arquitectos los mayas?
   pirámides, templos y observatorios
5. ¿Qué descubrieron los mayas antes que los europeos?
   el cero

3 Comparaciones Escribe seis comparaciones entre Guatemala y otros lugares de América Latina. Después, comparte tu lista con un(a) compañero/a y discutan si están de acuerdo con lo que escribieron de estos lugares.

> **modelo**
> *Guatemala es más pequeño que México...*

TEACHING OPTIONS

Worth Noting Spanish is a second language for more than 30% of Guatemalans. Students may be interested to learn that Guatemala has many bilingual education programs, where native languages are used in addition to Spanish for instructional purposes. There are also many government-sponsored Spanish as a Second Language (SSL) programs, offered through schools and radio or television. Speakers of Guatemala's indigenous languages often encounter problems similar to those found by other learners of Spanish: difficulty with agreement of number and gender.

Antigua Guatemala
→⟡← Have students use tour books and the Internet to read more about **Semana Santa** celebrations in this Guatemalan city, usually referred to simply as Antigua. You may want to play the **Panorama cultural** video for this paragraph.

El quetzal Recent conservation efforts in Guatemala, Costa Rica, and other Central American nations have focused on preserving the cloud forests (**bosques nubosos**) that are home to the **quetzal**. You may want to play the **Panorama cultural** video for this paragraph.

Los mayas Today ethnobotanists work with Mayan traditional healers to learn about medicinal uses of plants of the region.

La ropa tradicional Many indigenous Guatemalans still wear traditional clothing richly decorated with embroidery. The **huipil** is a long, sleeveless tunic worn by women. A distinctively woven **faja**, or waist sash, identifies the town or village each woman comes from.

¡Increíble pero cierto! Guatemala is internationally renowned for the wealth and diversity of its textile arts. Each village has a traditional, "signature" weaving style that allows others to quickly identify where each beautiful piece comes from.

Mar Caribe

Golfo de Honduras

erto ríos

NDURAS

Teaching Tip You may want to assign the **Prueba de práctica**, with its diagnostics and review activities, in the online-only **Repaso** section on the Supersite. There is also a **Repaso oral** in this section. For the Sixth Edition, a new summative vocabulary activity with speech recognition has been added to the **Repaso** section.

Las comidas

el/la camarero/a	waiter/waitress
la comida	food; meal
la cuenta	bill
el/la dueño/a	owner
el menú	menu
la propina	tip
la sección de (no) fumar	(non) smoking section
el almuerzo	lunch
la cena	dinner
el desayuno	breakfast
los entremeses	appetizers
el plato (principal)	(main) dish
delicioso/a	delicious
rico/a	tasty; delicious
sabroso/a	tasty; delicious

Las frutas

la banana	banana
las frutas	fruits
el limón	lemon
la manzana	apple
el melocotón	peach
la naranja	orange
la pera	pear
la uva	grape

Las verduras

las arvejas	peas
la cebolla	onion
el champiñón	mushroom
la ensalada	salad
los espárragos	asparagus
los frijoles	beans
la lechuga	lettuce
el maíz	corn
las papas/patatas (fritas)	(fried) potatoes; French fries
el tomate	tomato
las verduras	vegetables
la zanahoria	carrot

La carne y el pescado

el atún	tuna
el bistec	steak
los camarones	shrimp
la carne	meat
la carne de res	beef
la chuleta (de cerdo)	(pork) chop
la hamburguesa	hamburger
el jamón	ham
la langosta	lobster
los mariscos	shellfish
el pavo	turkey
el pescado	fish
el pollo (asado)	(roast) chicken
la salchicha	sausage
el salmón	salmon

Otras comidas

el aceite	oil
el ajo	garlic
el arroz	rice
el azúcar	sugar
los cereales	cereal; grains
el huevo	egg
la mantequilla	butter
la margarina	margarine
la mayonesa	mayonnaise
el pan (tostado)	(toasted) bread
la pimienta	black pepper
el queso	cheese
la sal	salt
el sándwich	sandwich
la sopa	soup
el vinagre	vinegar
el yogur	yogurt

Las bebidas

el agua (f.) (mineral)	(mineral) water
la bebida	drink
el café	coffee
la cerveza	beer
el jugo (de fruta)	(fruit) juice
la leche	milk
el refresco	soft drink
el té (helado)	(iced) tea
el vino (blanco/ tinto)	(white/red) wine

Verbos

escoger	to choose
merendar (e:ie)	to snack
morir (o:ue)	to die
pedir (e:i)	to order (food)
probar (o:ue)	to taste; to try
recomendar (e:ie)	to recommend
saber (a)	to taste (like)
servir (e:i)	to serve

Las comparaciones

como	like; as
más de (+ number)	more than
más... que	more... than
menos de (+ number)	fewer than
menos... que	less... than
tan... como	as... as
tantos/as... como	as many... as
tanto... como	as much... as
el/la mayor	the oldest
el/la mejor	the best
el/la menor	the youngest
el/la peor	the worst
mejor	better
peor	worse

Expresiones útiles	See page 269.

More activities

vhlcentral   LM
              p. 48

Las fiestas

9

Communicative Goals

You will learn how to:
- Express congratulations
- Express gratitude
- Ask for and pay the bill at a restaurant

A PRIMERA VISTA
- ¿Se visten ellos con ropa elegante?
- ¿Cómo se sienten, alegres o tristes?
- ¿Quién es el menor?
- ¿Qué lleva la chica?

Lesson Goals

In **Lección 9**, students will be introduced to the following:
- terms for parties and celebrations
- words for stages of life and personal relationships
- **Semana Santa** celebrations
- **Noche Valdiviana** in Chile
- irregular preterites
- verbs that change meaning in the preterite
- uses of ¿qué? and ¿cuál?
- pronouns after prepositions
- recognizing word families
- using a Venn diagram to organize information
- writing a comparative analysis
- using context to infer the meaning of unfamiliar words
- a television commercial about **Las Fiestas Patrias** and other celebrations in Chile
- a video about **las fiestas de la calle San Sebastián** in San Juan, Puerto Rico
- cultural, geographic, and economic information about Chile

A primera vista You may want to tell students that the girl is wearing **una diadema** (*tiara*). Here are some additional questions you can ask to personalize the photo: **¿Fuiste a una fiesta importante el año pasado? ¿Cuál fue la ocasión? ¿Sirvieron comida en la fiesta? ¿Qué sirvieron?**

Teaching Tip Look for these icons for additional communicative practice:

→👥←	Interpretive communication
←👥←	Presentational communication
👤↔👤	Interpersonal communication

INSTRUCTIONAL RESOURCES

Supersite (vhlcentral.com)
Video: *Fotonovela, Flash cultura, En pantalla, Panorama cultural*
Audio: Textbook and Lab MP3 Files

Activity Pack: Information Gap Activities, games, additional activity handouts
Resources: SAM Answer Key, Scripts, Translations, **Vocabulario adicional**, sample lesson plan, Grammar Presentation Slides, Digital Image Bank

Testing Program: Quizzes, Tests, Exams, MP3s, Oral Testing Suggestions
Student Activities Manual: Workbook/Video Manual/Lab Manual
WebSAM (online Student Activities Manual)

Section Goals

In **Contextos**, students will learn and practice:

• vocabulary related to parties and celebrations
• vocabulary used to talk about stages of life and personal relationships

Instructional Resources

Supersite: Audio (Textbook and Lab MP3 Files); Resources (Digital Image Bank, **Vocabulario adicional,** Activity Pack, Scripts, Answer Keys); Testing Program (Quizzes)
WebSAM
Workbook
Lab Manual

Teaching Tips

• Ask about parties. Ex: **¿Fuiste a una fiesta el fin de semana pasado? ¿Qué tomaste allí? ¿Comiste algo? ¿Bailaste? ¿Escuchaste música?** Write **divertirse** on the board and explain what it means. Ask: **¿Te divertiste?** Also write **pasarlo bien** on the board. Say: **Ah, te divertiste mucho allí. Entonces, lo pasaste bien, ¿no? No lo pasaste mal.**

• Use the **Lección 9 Contextos** digital images to assist with this presentation.

• Have students respond to true/false statements about the illustrations in **Contextos.** Ex: **1. Es una boda. (Cierto.) 2. Muchas personas lo pasan mal en la fiesta. (Falso.)** Next, ask students about parties. Ex: **¿Qué tipo de fiesta te gusta más? ¿Te gusta recibir regalos?**

Note: At this point you may want to present **Vocabulario adicional: Más vocabulario para las celebraciones** from the Supersite.

Las fiestas

Felicitaciones

Más vocabulario

la alegría	*happiness*
la amistad	*friendship*
el amor	*love*
la sorpresa	*surprise*
el aniversario (de bodas)	*(wedding) anniversary*
la boda	*wedding*
el cumpleaños	*birthday*
el día de fiesta	*holiday*
el divorcio	*divorce*
el matrimonio	*marriage*
la Navidad	*Christmas*
la pareja	*(married) couple; partner*
la quinceañera	*young woman celebrating her fifteenth birthday*
cambiar (de)	*to change*
celebrar	*to celebrate*
divertirse (e:ie)	*to have fun*
graduarse (de/en)	*to graduate (from/in)*
invitar	*to invite*
jubilarse	*to retire (from work)*
nacer	*to be born*
odiar	*to hate*
pasarlo bien/mal	*to have a good/bad time*
reírse (e:i)	*to laugh*
relajarse	*to relax*
sonreír (e:i)	*to smile*
sorprender	*to surprise*
juntos/as	*together*
¡Felicidades!/ ¡Felicitaciones!	*Congratulations!*

Variación léxica

pastel ⟷ torta (*Arg., Col., Venez.*)
comprometerse ⟷ prometerse (*Esp.*)

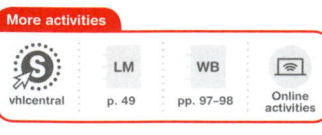

More activities

| vhlcentral | LM p. 49 | WB pp. 97–98 | Online activities |

los recién casados

el beso

regalar

la botella de vino

el champán

los dulces

los postres

el helado

las galletas

TEACHING OPTIONS

Extra Practice Ask students questions about birthdays and other celebrations and what days and months they fall on. Ask: _____, **¿cuándo es tu cumpleaños? (¿Qué día naciste?) ¿Estás casado/a? ¿Cuándo es tu aniversario de bodas?** Verify comprehension by asking other students to repeat. Then ask more general questions: **¿Cuándo es la Navidad?**

Worth Noting Point out that in addition to or instead of celebrating their birthday, many Hispanics celebrate their **día del santo,** or Saint's Day. This is the day that celebrates the saint for whom a person was named. In many Hispanic countries, the **día del santo** is just as important and significant in an individual's life as his or her birthday.

Relaciones personales

casarse (con)	to get married (to)
comprometerse (con)	to get engaged (to)
divorciarse (de)	to get divorced (from)
enamorarse (de)	to fall in love (with)
llevarse bien/mal (con)	to get along well/ badly (with)
romper (con)	to break up (with)
salir (con)	to go out (with); to date
separarse (de)	to separate (from)
tener una cita	to have a date; to have an appointment

la invitada

brindar

el flan de caramelo

el pastel (de chocolate)

Práctica

1 Connotaciones Indica si las palabras que vas a escuchar tienen connotaciones **positivas** o **negativas**.

	Positivo	Negativo		Positivo	Negativo
1.	○	◉	5.	○	◉
2.	◉	○	6.	◉	○
3.	◉	○	7.	◉	○
4.	◉	○	8.	○	◉

2 ¿Lógico o ilógico? Indica si cada afirmación es **lógica** o **ilógica**.

1. lógico
2. ilógico
3. ilógico
4. lógico
5. ilógico
6. ilógico
7. lógico
8. ilógico

3 Emparejar Indica la frase que mejor completa cada oración.

cambió de	nos divertimos	se llevan bien
lo pasaron mal	se casaron	sonrió
nació	se jubiló	tenemos una cita

1. Manuel y Felipe __lo pasaron mal__ en el cinc. La película fue muy mala.
2. Pablo y yo __nos divertimos__ en la fiesta. Bailamos y comimos.
3. Jaime y Laura __se casaron__ el septiembre pasado. La boda fue maravillosa.
4. ¡Tengo una nueva sobrina! Ella __nació__ ayer.
5. Mi madre __cambió de__ profesión. Ahora es artista.
6. Mi padre __se jubiló__ el año pasado. Ahora no trabaja.
7. Jorge y yo __tenemos una cita__ esta noche. Vamos a ir a un restaurante muy elegante.
8. María y sus compañeras de cuarto __se llevan bien__. Son buenas amigas.

4 Acciones Escoge la acción apropiada y escribe una oración. *Answers may vary. Suggested answers:*

> **modelo**
> Camila terminó sus estudios. (enamorarse/nacer/graduarse)
> *Se graduó.*

1. Liliana ya no trabaja más. (jubilarse/salir/graduarse) *Se jubiló.*
2. Francisco sale con Elena. (separarse/tener una cita/jubilarse) *Tienen una cita.*
3. Carlos terminó su relación sentimental. (separarse/casarse/llevarse bien) *Se separó.*
4. Marcela quiere estar siempre con Javier. (pasarlo mal/relajarse/casarse) *Van a casarse.*
5. Gabriel y Mauricio siempre se divierten juntos. (odiar/romper/llevarse bien) *Se llevan bien.*

Las etapas de la vida de Sergio

el nacimiento

la niñez

la adolescencia

la juventud

la madurez

la vejez

Más vocabulario	
la edad	age
el estado civil	marital status
las etapas de la vida	the stages of life
la muerte	death
casado/a	married
divorciado/a	divorced
separado/a	separated
soltero/a	single
viudo/a	widower/widow

5 **Las etapas de la vida** Identifica las etapas de la vida que se describen.

> **modelo**
> Mi hermano acaba de graduarse de la universidad.
> la juventud

1. Mi abuela se jubiló y se mudó (*moved*) a Viña del Mar. la vejez
2. Mi padre trabaja para una compañía grande en Santiago. la madurez
3. ¿Viste a mi nuevo sobrino en el hospital? Es precioso y ¡tan pequeño! el nacimiento
4. Mi hermana celebró su fiesta de quince años. la adolescencia
5. Mi abuelo murió este año. la vejez/la muerte
6. Mi hermana pequeña juega con muñecas (*dolls*). la niñez

6 **Cambiar** En parejas, túrnense para decir que las afirmaciones son falsas y corregirlas cambiando las expresiones subrayadas (*underlined*).

> **modelo**
> **Estudiante 1:** La <u>niñez</u> es cuando trabajamos mucho.
> **Estudiante 2:** No, te equivocas. La madurez es cuando trabajamos mucho.

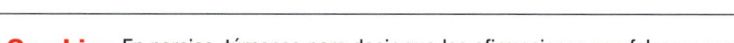

1. <u>La juventud</u> es la etapa cuando nos jubilamos. La vejez
2. <u>El nacimiento</u> es el fin de la vida. La muerte
3. A los sesenta y cinco años, muchas personas <u>comienzan a trabajar.</u> se jubilan
4. Julián y nuestra prima <u>se divorcian</u> mañana. se casan
5. Mamá <u>odia</u> a su hermana. quiere/se lleva bien con
6. El abuelo murió, por eso la abuela es <u>separada</u>. viuda
7. Mi tío nunca se casó; es <u>viudo</u>. soltero
8. Cuando te gradúas de la universidad, estás en la etapa de <u>la adolescencia</u>. la juventud

Comunicación

7 **Una fiesta** Trabaja con un(a) compañero/a para planear una fiesta. Recuerda incluir la siguiente información. *Answers will vary.*

1. ¿Qué tipo de fiesta es? ¿Dónde va a ser? ¿Cuándo va a ser?
2. ¿A quiénes van a invitar?
3. ¿Qué van a comer? ¿Quiénes van a llevar o a preparar la comida?
4. ¿Qué van a beber? ¿Quiénes van a traer las bebidas?
5. ¿Cómo planean entretener a los invitados? ¿Van a bailar o a jugar algún juego?
6. Después de la fiesta, ¿quiénes van a limpiar (*to clean*)?

8 **Encuesta** Tu profesor(a) va a darte una hoja de actividades. Haz las preguntas de la hoja a dos o tres compañeros/as de clase para saber qué actitudes tienen en sus relaciones personales. *Answers will vary.*

Preguntas	Nombres	Actitudes
1. ¿Te importa la amistad? ¿Por qué?		
2. ¿Es mejor tener un(a) buen(a) amigo/a o muchos/as amigos/as?		
3. ¿Cuáles son las características que buscas en tus amigos/as?		
4. ¿Tienes novio/a? ¿A qué edad es posible enamorarse?		
5. ¿Deben las parejas hacer todo juntos? ¿Deben tener las mismas opiniones? ¿Por qué?		

¡LENGUA VIVA!

While a **buen(a) amigo/a** is a *good friend*, the term **amigo/a íntimo/a** refers to a *close friend*, or a very good friend, without any romantic overtones.

9 **Minidrama** En parejas, consulten la ilustración de la página 302 y luego, usando las palabras de la lista, preparen un minidrama para representar las etapas de la vida de Sergio. Pueden inventar más información sobre su vida. *Answers will vary.*

amor	celebrar	enamorarse	romper
boda	comprometerse	graduarse	salir
cambiar	cumpleaños	jubilarse	separarse
casarse	divorciarse	nacer	tener una cita

---

7 Teaching Tip To simplify, create a seven-column chart on the board with the headings **Lugar, Fecha y hora, Invitados, Comida, Bebidas, Actividades,** and **Limpieza.** Have groups brainstorm a few items for each category.

7 Expansion
- Ask volunteer groups to describe the party they have just planned.
- Have students make invitations for their party. Ask the class to judge which invitation is the cleverest, funniest, most elegant, etc.

8 Teaching Tip Distribute the *Hojas de actividades* (Activity Pack/Supersite). Give students ten minutes to ask other group members the questions. Have groups share their results and conclusions with the class.

8 Expansion Take a survey of the attitudes found in the entire class. Ex: **¿Quiénes creen que es más importante tener un buen amigo que muchos amigos? ¿Quiénes creen que es más importante tener muchos amigos que un buen amigo?**

9 Teaching Tip To simplify, read through the word list as a class and have students name the stage or stages of life that correspond to each word.

9 Expansion After all skits have been presented, have the class vote on the most original, funniest, truest to life, etc.

TEACHING OPTIONS

Extra Practice Add a visual aspect to this vocabulary practice. Using magazine pictures, display images that pertain to parties or celebrations, stages of life, or interpersonal relations. Have students describe the pictures and make guesses about who the people are, how they are feeling, and so forth.

Extra Practice Add an auditory aspect to this vocabulary practice. As a listening comprehension activity, prepare short descriptions of five easily recognizable people. Use as much active lesson vocabulary as possible. Write their names on the board in random order. Then read the descriptions aloud and have students match each one to the appropriate name. Ex: **Me divorcié tres veces, la última vez de otro cantante latino. Yo canto, pero también soy actriz y tengo mi propia marca de perfumes. (Jennifer López)**

El Día de Muertos

La familia Díaz conmemora el Día de Muertos.

PERSONAJES

 MARISSA   JIMENA FELIPE JUAN CARLOS

 Video

1

MAITE FUENTES El Día de Muertos se celebra en México el primero y el segundo de noviembre. Como pueden ver, hay calaveras de azúcar, flores, música y comida por todas partes. Ésta es una fiesta única que todos deben ver por lo menos una vez en la vida.

MARISSA *Holy moley!* ¡Está delicioso!

TÍA ANA MARÍA Mi mamá me enseñó a prepararlo. El mole siempre fue el plato favorito de mi papá. Mi hijo Eduardo nació el día de su cumpleaños. Por eso le pusimos su nombre.

2

MARISSA ¿Cómo se conocieron?

TÍA ANA MARÍA En la fiesta de un amigo. Fue amor a primera vista.

MARISSA (*Señala la foto.*) La voy a llevar al altar.

TÍO RAMÓN ¿Dónde están mis hermanos?

JIMENA Mi papá y Felipe están en el otro cuarto. Esos dos antipáticos no quieren decirnos qué están haciendo. Y la tía Ana María...

TÍO RAMÓN ... está en la cocina.

3

5

TÍA ANA MARÍA Marissa, ¿le puedes llevar esa foto que está ahí a Carolina? La necesita para el altar.

MARISSA Sí. ¿Son sus padres?

TÍA ANA MARÍA Sí, el día de su boda.

4

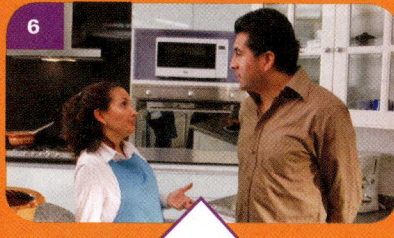

6

TÍA ANA MARÍA Ramón, ¿cómo estás?

TÍO RAMÓN Bien, gracias. ¿Y Mateo? ¿No vino contigo?

TÍA ANA MARÍA No. Ya sabes que me casé con un doctor y, pues, trabaja muchísimo.

yo

SRA. DÍAZ

SR. DÍAZ

TÍA ANA MARÍA

TÍO RAMÓN

TÍA NAYELI

DON DIEGO

MARTA

VALENTINA

MAITE FUENTES

7

SR. DÍAZ Familia Díaz, deben prepararse...

FELIPE ... ¡para la sorpresa de sus vidas!

8

JUAN CARLOS Gracias por invitarme.

SR. DÍAZ Juan Carlos, como eres nuestro amigo, ya eres parte de la familia.

9

(En el cementerio)

JIMENA Yo hice las galletas y el pastel. ¿Dónde los puse?

MARTA Postres... ¿Cuál prefiero? ¿Galletas? ¿Pastel? ¡Dulces!

VALENTINA Me gustan las galletas.

10

SR. DÍAZ Brindamos por ustedes, mamá y papá.

TÍO RAMÓN Todas las otras noches estamos separados. Pero esta noche estamos juntos.

TÍA ANA MARÍA Con gratitud y amor.

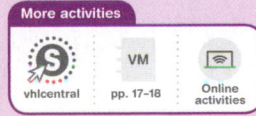
More activities

vhlcentral | VM pp. 17–18 | Online activities

Expresiones útiles

Discussing family history

El mole siempre fue el plato favorito de mi papá.
Mole was always my dad's favorite dish.
Mi hijo Eduardo nació el día de su cumpleaños.
My son Eduardo was born on his birthday.
Por eso le pusimos su nombre.
That's why we named him after him (after my father).
¿Cómo se conocieron sus padres?
How did your parents meet?
En la fiesta de un amigo. Fue amor a primera vista.
At a friend's party. It was love at first sight.

Talking about a party/celebration

Ésta es una fiesta única que todos deben ver por lo menos una vez.
This is a unique celebration that everyone should see at least once.
Gracias por invitarme.
Thanks for inviting me.
Brindamos por ustedes.
A toast to you.

Additional vocabulary

alma *soul*
altar *altar*
ángel *angel*
calavera de azúcar
skull made out of sugar
cementerio *cemetery*
cocina *kitchen*
disfraz *costume*

Expresiones útiles Draw attention to **pusimos** and explain that it is an irregular preterite form of the verb **poner**. Then point out the forms **vino** (video still 6) and **hice** and **puse** (video still 9) and tell students that these are irregular preterite forms of the verbs **venir**, **hacer**, and **poner**. Finally, draw attention to the phrase **Cómo se conocieron** and explain that **conocer** in the preterite means *to meet*. Tell students that they will learn more about these concepts in **Estructura**.

Teaching Tip Go through the **Fotonovela**, asking volunteers to read the various parts.

Nota cultural El Día de Muertos is an example of a holiday that blends indigenous and Catholic customs and beliefs. In pre-Columbian times, this celebration of deceased ancestors was a month-long festival that fell in the ninth month of the Aztec calendar, in August. The Spaniards moved it to coincide with the Catholic holidays of All Saints' Day and All Souls' Day.

TEACHING OPTIONS

Extra Practice Photocopy the **Fotonovela** Videoscript (Supersite) and white out words related to celebrations and personal relationships, in order to make a master for a cloze activity. Have students fill in the missing words as they watch the episode.
Extra Practice Have students research a **Día de Muertos** celebration in another Spanish-speaking country, such as Bolivia, Ecuador, or Guatemala, and prepare a brief report in which they

compare it to Mexico's celebration of **Día de Muertos**.
Game Divide the class into two teams, A and B. Give a member from team A a card with the name of an item from the **Fotonovela** or **Expresiones útiles** (Ex: **flores, cocina, foto**). He or she has thirty seconds to draw the item, while team A has to guess what it is. Award one point per correct answer. If team A cannot guess the item within the time limit, team B may try to "steal" the point.

¿Qué pasó?

1 **Completar** Completa las oraciones.

1. El Día de Muertos es una _____fiesta_____ única que todos deben ver.
2. La tía Ana María preparó _____mole_____ para celebrar.
3. Marissa lleva la _____foto_____ al altar.
4. Jimena hizo las _____galletas_____ y el _____pastel_____.
5. Marta no sabe qué _____postre_____ prefiere.

2 **Identificar** Identifica quién dice estas oraciones.

SR. DÍAZ   **MAITE FUENTES**

JUAN CARLOS   **VALENTINA**

TÍA ANA MARÍA

1. Es difícil hacer las cosas bien la primera vez, Jimena. tía Ana María
2. Como pueden ver, hay calaveras de azúcar, flores, música y comida por todas partes. Maite Fuentes
3. Gracias por invitarme. Juan Carlos
4. Ya sabes que me casé con un doctor y, pues, trabaja muchísimo. tía Ana María
5. Me gustan mucho las galletas. Valentina
6. Juan Carlos, como eres nuestro amigo, ya eres parte de la familia. Sr. Díaz

3 **Seleccionar** Selecciona algunas de las opciones para completar las oraciones.

amor	días de fiesta	pasarlo bien	salieron
el champán	divorciarse	postres	se enamoraron
cumpleaños	flan	la quinceañera	una sorpresa

1. El Sr. Díaz y Felipe prepararon ____una sorpresa____ para la familia.
2. Los ____días de fiesta____, como el Día de Muertos, se celebran con la familia.
3. Eduardo, el hijo de Ana María, nació el día del ____cumpleaños____ de su abuelo.
4. La tía Ana María siente gratitud y ____amor____ hacia (*toward*) sus padres.
5. Los días de fiesta también son para ____pasarlo bien____ con los amigos.
6. El Día de Muertos se hacen muchos ____postres____.
7. Los padres de la tía Ana María ____se enamoraron____ a primera vista.

4 **Una cena** Trabajen en grupos para representar una conversación en una cena de Año Nuevo. Answers will vary.

- Una persona brinda por el año que está por comenzar y por estar con su familia y amigos.
- Cada persona del grupo habla de cuál es su comida favorita en año nuevo.
- Después de la cena, una persona del grupo dice que es hora de (*it's time to*) comer las uvas.
- Cada persona del grupo dice qué desea para el año que empieza.
- Después, cada persona del grupo debe desear Feliz Año Nuevo a las demás.

NOTA CULTURAL

Comer doce uvas a las doce de la noche del 31 de diciembre de cada año es una costumbre que nació en España y que también se observa en varios países de Latinoamérica. Se debe comer una uva por cada una de las 12 campanadas (*strokes*) del reloj y se cree que (*it's believed that*) quien lo hace va a tener un año próspero.

TEACHING OPTIONS

Large Groups In groups, have students ad-lib the **Fotonovela** episode. Assure them that it is not necessary to memorize the episode or stick strictly to its content. They should try to get the general meaning across with the vocabulary and expressions they know, and they should also feel free to be creative. Then have volunteers act out the episode for the class.

Pairs Have students work in pairs to tell each other about celebrations they have with their own families. Remind them to use as many expressions as possible from the **Expresiones útiles** on page 305, as well as the vocabulary on pages 300–301. Follow up by asking a few students to describe celebrations in their partners' families.

Pronunciación

 Tutorial

The letters h, j, and g

helado	hombre	hola	hermosa

The Spanish **h** is always silent.

José	jubilarse	dejar	pareja

The letter **j** is pronounced much like the English *h* in *his*.

agencia	general	Gil	Gisela

The letter **g** can be pronounced three different ways. Before **e** or **i**, the letter **g** is pronounced much like the English *h*.

Gustavo, gracias por llamar el domingo.

At the beginning of a phrase or after the letter **n**, the Spanish **g** is pronounced like the English *g* in *girl*.

Me gradué en agosto.

In any other position, the Spanish **g** has a somewhat softer sound.

guerra	conseguir	guantes	agua

In the combinations **gue** and **gui**, the **g** has a hard sound and the **u** is silent. In the combination **gua**, the **g** has a hard sound and the **u** is pronounced like the English *w*.

Práctica Lee las palabras en voz alta, prestando atención a la **h**, la **j** y la **g**.

1. hamburguesa
2. jugar
3. oreja
4. guapa
5. geografía
6. magnífico
7. espejo
8. hago
9. seguir
10. gracias
11. hijo
12. galleta
13. Jorge
14. tengo
15. ahora
16. guantes

Oraciones Lee las oraciones en voz alta, prestando atención a la **h**, la **j** y la **g**.

1. Hola. Me llamo Gustavo Hinojosa Lugones y vivo en Santiago de Chile.
2. Tengo una familia grande; somos tres hermanos y tres hermanas.
3. Voy a graduarme en mayo.
4. Para celebrar mi graduación, mis padres van a regalarme un viaje a Egipto.
5. ¡Qué generosos son!

Refranes Lee los refranes en voz alta, prestando atención a la **h**, la **j** y la **g**.

A la larga, lo más dulce amarga.[1]

El hábito no hace al monje.[2]

1 Too much of a good thing.
2 The clothes don't make the man.

More activities

vhlcentral | LM p. 50

Section Goal

In **Pronunciación**, students will be introduced to the pronunciation of **h**, **j**, and **g**.

Instructional Resources
Supersite: Audio (Textbook and Lab MP3 Files); Resources (Scripts, Answer Keys)
WebSAM
Lab Manual

Teaching Tips
• Ask the class how the Spanish **h** is pronounced. Ask volunteers to pronounce the example words. Contrast the pronunciations of the English *hotel* and the Spanish **hotel**.
• Explain that **j** is pronounced much like the English *h*.
• Draw attention to the fact that the letter **g** is pronounced like the English *h* before **e** or **i**. Write the example words on the board and ask volunteers to pronounce them.
• Point out that the letter **g** is pronounced like the English *g* in *good* at the beginning of a phrase or after the letter **n**.
• Explain that in any other position, particularly between vowels, **g** has a softer sound.
• Tell the class that in the combinations **gue** and **gui**, **g** has a hard sound and **u** is not pronounced. Explain that in the combination **gua**, the **u** sounds like the English *w*.

Práctica/Oraciones/Refranes
These exercises are recorded on the *Textbook MP3s*. You may want to play the audio so that students practice listening to Spanish spoken by speakers other than yourself.

TEACHING OPTIONS

Extra Practice Write the names of these Chilean cities on the board and ask for a volunteer to pronounce each one: **Santiago, Antofagasta, Rancagua, Coihaique.** Repeat the process with the names of these Chilean writers: **Alberto Blest Gana, Vicente Huidobro, Gabriela Mistral, Juan Modesto Castro.**

Pairs Have students work in pairs to read aloud the sentences in **Actividad 6, Cambiar,** page 302. Remind them to pay attention to the pronunciation of the letters **h**, **j**, and **g**. Encourage students to help their partners if they have trouble pronouncing a particular word.

EN DETALLE

Semana Santa: más que una celebración

De todas las celebraciones hispanas, la **Semana Santa°** es una de las más importantes. Esta fiesta religiosa se celebra la semana antes de Pascua° y conmemora la muerte y resurrección de Jesucristo, figura central del cristianismo.

Procesión en Sevilla, España

Pero, ¿por qué es tan importante esta celebración? Para los cristianos, durante la Semana Santa se recuerdan los principales hechos° que forman la base de su religión. Cada día tiene su significado. Por ejemplo, el Viernes Santo, con la representación del Vía Crucis°, se recuerdan el juicio° y la muerte de Jesucristo. Por esta razón, cada año tienen lugar diferentes celebraciones populares, famosas alrededor del mundo gracias a su originalidad y despliegue°. Así, aunque algunas personas aprovechan° estos días para viajar, muchas prefieren participar en estas celebraciones religiosas

en las calles°. Por ejemplo, en **Sevilla**, España, los fieles° sacan a las calles imágenes religiosas sobre plataformas decoradas con abundantes flores° y velas°. En **Antigua**, Guatemala, los fieles hacen alfombras° de flores y altares, además de organizar Vía Crucis y danzas. Estos son sólo algunos ejemplos del tipo de celebraciones que se presentan en casi todos los países hispanos durante la Semana Santa.

Alfombra de flores en Antigua, Guatemala

Esta fiesta religiosa es una muestra innegable de la cultura y de las creencias religiosas de muchos hispanos.

Otras celebraciones famosas

Ayacucho, Perú: Además de alfombras de flores y procesiones, aquí hay una antigua tradición llamada "quema de la chamiza"°.

Iztapalapa, Ciudad de México: Es famoso el Vía Crucis del cerro° de la Estrella. Es una representación del recorrido° de Jesucristo con la cruz°.

Popayán, Colombia: En las procesiones "chiquitas" los niños llevan imágenes que son copias pequeñas de las que llevan los adultos.

Semana Santa *Holy Week* Pascua *Easter Sunday* hechos *events* Vía Crucis *Stations of the Cross* juicio *trial* despliegue *display* aprovechan *take advantage of* fieles *faithful* velas *candles* alfombras *carpets* quema de la chamiza *burning of brushwood* cerro *hill* recorrido *route* cruz *cross*

ACTIVIDADES

1 ¿Cierto o falso? Indica si lo que dicen las oraciones es cierto o falso. Corrige las oraciones falsas.

1. La Semana Santa se celebra después de Pascua.
   Falso. La Semana Santa se celebra la semana antes de Pascua.
2. La Semana Santa conmemora el nacimiento de la Virgen María.
   Falso. Conmemora la muerte y resurrección de Jesucristo.
3. La celebración es importante porque recuerda los eventos más importantes que forman la base del cristianismo. **Cierto.**
4. Todos los días de la Semana Santa tienen el mismo significado.
   Falso. Cada día de la Semana Santa tiene un significado diferente.

5. El Viernes Santo se recuerda la resurrección de Jesucristo.
   Falso. Se recuerdan el juicio y la muerte de Jesucristo.
6. Las personas tienen días libres durante la Semana Santa.
   Cierto.
7. Todas las personas asisten a las celebraciones religiosas.
   Falso. Algunas personas aprovechan estos días para viajar.
8. En los países hispanos, las celebraciones se hacen en las calles.
   Cierto.
9. España es el único país donde se celebra la Semana Santa con procesiones. **Falso. La Semana Santa se celebra de esta manera en muchos países hispanos.**
10. Las procesiones "chiquitas" son famosas en Sevilla, España.
    Falso. Son famosas en Popayán, Colombia.

ASÍ SE DICE

Fiestas y celebraciones

la despedida de soltero/a	*bachelor(ette) party*
el día feriado/festivo	el día de fiesta
disfrutar	*to enjoy*
festejar	celebrar
los fuegos artificiales	*fireworks*
pasarlo en grande	divertirse mucho
la vela	*candle*

EL MUNDO HISPANO

Celebraciones latinoamericanas

- **Oruro, Bolivia** Durante el carnaval de Oruro se realiza la famosa Diablada, una antigua danza° que muestra la lucha° entre el Bien y el Mal: ángeles contra° demonios.

- **Panchimalco, El Salvador** La primera semana de mayo, Panchimalco se cubre de flores y de color. También hacen el Desfile de las palmas° y bailan danzas antiguas.

- **Quito, Ecuador** El mes de agosto es el Mes de las Artes. Danza, teatro, música, cine, artesanías° y otros eventos culturales inundan la ciudad.

- **San Pedro Sula, Honduras** En junio se celebra la Feria Juniana. Hay comida típica, bailes, desfiles, conciertos, rodeos, exposiciones ganaderas° y eventos deportivos y culturales.

danza *dance* lucha *fight* contra *versus* palmas *palm leaves* artesanías *handcrafts* exposiciones ganaderas *cattle shows*

PERFIL

Noche Valdiviana

El fin de las vacaciones de verano llega a Chile en febrero, y se celebra en la ciudad de Valdivia durante una semana entera con conciertos y puestos° de artesanías.

La última noche, llamada **Noche Valdiviana**, el río Calle-Calle se llena de luces°. A las nueve, la gente va a la costanera° para observar los botes cargados de° velas que

forman un desfile° en el agua. La Reina de los Ríos° inicia el desfile y la siguen más de cuarenta embarcaciones°, decoradas con diferentes motivos, que compiten por varios

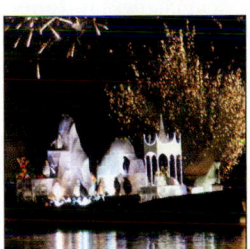

premios. Al final, una lluvia de fuegos artificiales despide° el verano y a los turistas hasta el próximo año.

puestos *stands* se llena de luces *is filled with lights* costanera *promenade* cargados de *loaded with* desfile *parade* Reina de los Ríos *Queen of the Rivers* embarcaciones *vessels* despide *bids farewell*

CON RITMO HISPANO

Ana Tijoux (1977–)
Lugar de nacimiento: Lille, Francia

Ana Tijoux, hija de la socióloga chilena María Emilia Tijoux, es una de las raperas más importantes de América Latina. Desde 1997 hasta 2006 formó parte de la banda de rap Makiza.

Go to **vhlcentral.com** to find out more about **Ana Tijoux** and her music.

ACTIVIDADES

2 Comprensión Responde a las preguntas.

1. ¿Cuántas embarcaciones participan en el desfile de Valdivia? *más de cuarenta*
2. ¿Qué es la Diablada? *Es una antigua danza que muestra la lucha entre el bien y el mal.*
3. ¿Qué celebran en Quito en agosto? *Celebran el Mes de las Artes.*
4. Nombra dos atracciones en la Feria Juniana de San Pedro Sula. *Answers will vary.*
5. ¿Cuándo se celebra la Noche Valdiviana? *Se celebra en febrero.*

3 ¿Cuál es tu celebración favorita? Escribe un pequeño párrafo sobre la celebración que más te gusta de tu comunidad. Explica cómo se llama, cuándo ocurre y cómo es. *Answers will vary.*

More activities

 vhlcentral Online activities

TEACHING OPTIONS

Pairs Have students work in pairs to research and plan a trip to a festival mentioned in the reading. Students should explain why they want to visit that particular festival, how they will get there, and present an itinerary to the class.

TPR Divide the class into five groups: **Valdivia**, **Oruro**, **Panchimalco**, **Quito**, and **San Pedro Sula**. Call out a series of statements about the festivals without mentioning the city in which they take place. Have groups stand up when the festival refers to their city. Ex: **Su festival tiene lugar la primera semana de mayo.** (Group **Panchimalco** stands.)

Section Goal

In **Estructura 9.1**, students will be introduced to the irregular preterites of several common verbs.

Instructional Resources

Supersite: Audio (Lab MP3 Files); Resources (Grammar Presentation Slides, Activity Pack, Scripts, Answer Keys); Testing Program (Quizzes)
WebSAM
Workbook
Lab Manual

Teaching Tips

- Quickly review the present tense of a stem-changing verb such as **pedir**. Write the paradigm on the board and ask volunteers to point out the stem-changing forms.
- Work through the preterite paradigms of **tener**, **venir**, and **decir**, modeling the pronunciation.
- 👥 Add a visual aspect to this grammar presentation. Use magazine pictures to ask about social events in the past. Ex: **¿Con quién vino este chico a la fiesta? (Vino con esa chica rubia.) ¿Qué se puso esta señora para ir a la boda? (Se puso un sombrero.) ¿Qué trajo esta chica a clase? (Trajo una mochila.) ¿Y qué hizo? (Se durmió.)**
- Write the preterite paradigm for **estar** on the board. Then erase the initial **es-** for each form and point out that the preterite of **estar** and **tener** are identical except for the initial **es-**.

9.1 Irregular preterites Tutorial

ANTE TODO You already know that the verbs **ir** and **ser** are irregular in the preterite. You will now learn other verbs whose preterite forms are also irregular.

Preterite of **tener, venir,** and **decir**

		tener (**u**-stem)	venir (**i**-stem)	decir (**j**-stem)
SINGULAR FORMS	yo	tuve	vine	dije
	tú	tuv**iste**	vin**iste**	dij**iste**
	Ud./él/ella	tuv**o**	vin**o**	dij**o**
PLURAL FORMS	nosotros/as	tuv**imos**	vin**imos**	dij**imos**
	vosotros/as	tuv**isteis**	vin**isteis**	dij**isteis**
	Uds./ellos/ellas	tuv**ieron**	vin**ieron**	dij**eron**

▶ **¡Atención!** The endings of these verbs are the regular preterite endings of **-er/-ir** verbs, except for the **yo** and **usted/él/ella** forms. Note that these two endings are unaccented.

▶ These verbs observe similar stem changes to **tener, venir,** and **decir**.

INFINITIVE	U-STEM	PRETERITE FORMS
poder	pud-	pude, pudiste, pudo, pudimos, pudisteis, pudieron
poner	pus-	puse, pusiste, puso, pusimos, pusisteis, pusieron
saber	sup-	supe, supiste, supo, supimos, supisteis, supieron
estar	estuv-	estuve, estuviste, estuvo, estuvimos, estuvisteis, estuvieron

INFINITIVE	I-STEM	PRETERITE FORMS
querer	quis-	quise, quisiste, quiso, quisimos, quisisteis, quisieron
hacer	hic-	hice, hiciste, hizo, hicimos, hicisteis, hicieron

¡ATENCIÓN!
Note the **c → z** spelling change in the third-person singular form of **hacer**: **hizo**.

INFINITIVE	J-STEM	PRETERITE FORMS
traer	traj-	traje, trajiste, trajo, trajimos, trajisteis, trajeron
conducir	conduj-	conduje, condujiste, condujo, condujimos, condujisteis, condujeron
traducir	traduj-	traduje, tradujiste, tradujo, tradujimos, tradujisteis, tradujeron

▶ **¡Atención!** Most verbs that end in **-cir** are **j**-stem verbs in the preterite. For example, **producir → produje, produjiste,** etc.

> **Produjimos** un documental sobre los accidentes en la casa.
> *We produced a documentary about accidents in the home.*

▶ Notice that the preterites with **j**-stems omit the letter **i** in the **ustedes/ellos/ellas** form.

> Mis amigos **trajeron** comida a la fiesta.
> *My friends brought food to the party.*

> Ellos **dijeron** la verdad.
> *They told the truth.*

TEACHING OPTIONS

Extra Practice Do a pattern practice drill. Name an infinitive and ask individuals to provide conjugations for the different subject pronouns and/or names you provide. Reverse the activity by saying a conjugated form and asking students to give an appropriate subject pronoun.

Game Divide the class into two teams. Indicate one team member at a time, alternating between teams. Give a verb in its infinitive form and a subject pronoun (Ex: **querer/tú**). The team member should give the correct preterite form (Ex: **quisiste**). Give one point per correct answer. Deduct one point for each wrong answer. The team with the most points at the end wins.

The preterite of **dar**

SINGULAR FORMS		PLURAL FORMS	
yo	d**i**	nosotros/as	d**imos**
tú	d**iste**	vosotros/as	d**isteis**
Ud./él/ella	d**io**	Uds./ellos/ellas	d**ieron**

▶ The endings for **dar** are the same as the regular preterite endings for **-er** and **-ir** verbs, except that there are no accent marks.

La camarera me **dio** el menú.
The waitress gave me the menu.

Los invitados le **dieron** un regalo.
The guests gave him/her a gift.

Le **di** a Juan algunos consejos.
I gave Juan some advice.

Nosotros **dimos** una gran fiesta.
We gave a great party.

▶ The preterite of **hay** (*inf.* **haber**) is **hubo** (*there was; there were*).

CONSULTA

Note that there are other ways to say *there was* or *there were* in Spanish. See **Estructura** 10.1, p. 342.

Marissa le dio la foto a la Sra. Díaz.

Hubo una celebración en casa de los Díaz.

¡INTÉNTALO!   Escribe la forma correcta del pretérito de cada verbo.

1. (querer) tú _quisiste_
2. (hacer) nosotras _hicimos_
3. (decir) usted _dijo_
4. (traer) yo _traje_
5. (conducir) ellas _condujeron_
6. (estar) ella _estuvo_
7. (tener) tú _tuviste_
8. (dar) ella y yo _dimos_
9. (haber) ayer _hubo_
10. (traducir) yo _traduje_
11. (saber) usted _supo_
12. (poner) ellos _pusieron_
13. (venir) yo _vine_
14. (poder) tú _pudiste_
15. (querer) ustedes _quisieron_
16. (estar) nosotros _estuvimos_
17. (decir) tú _dijiste_
18. (hacer) él _hizo_
19. (saber) ellos _supieron_
20. (poner) yo _puse_
21. (traer) nosotras _trajimos_
22. (dar) tú _diste_
23. (tener) yo _tuve_
24. (poder) ustedes _pudieron_

More activities

vhlcentral

LM p. 51

WB pp. 99–100

Online activities

Teaching Tips

• →🔲← Use the preterite forms of these verbs by talking about what you did in the recent past and then asking students questions that involve them in a conversation about what they did in the recent past. You may want to avoid the preterite of **poder, saber,** and **querer** for the moment. Ex: **El sábado pasado tuve que ir a la fiesta de cumpleaños de mi sobrina. Cumplió siete años. Le di un bonito regalo. ____, ¿tuviste que ir a una fiesta el sábado? ¿No? Pues, ¿qué hiciste el sábado?**

• Point out that **dar** has the same preterite endings as **ver.**

• Drill the preterite of **dar** by asking students about what they gave their family members for their last birthdays or other special occasion. Ex: **¿Qué le diste a tu hermano para su cumpleaños?** Then ask what other family members gave them. Ex: **¿Qué te dio tu padre? ¿Y tu madre?**

• ←🔲→ In a dramatically offended tone, say: **Di una fiesta el sábado. Los invité a todos ustedes y ¡no vino nadie!** Complain about all the work you did to prepare for the party. Ex: **Limpié toda la casa, preparé tortilla española, fui al supermercado y compré refrescos, puse la mesa con platos bonitos, puse música salsa…** Then write **¿Por qué no viniste a mi fiesta?** and **Lo siento, profesor(a), no pude venir a su fiesta porque tuve que…** on the board and give students one minute to write a creative or humorous excuse. Have volunteers read their excuses aloud. Ex: **Lo siento, profesor, no pude venir a su fiesta porque tuve que lavarme el pelo….**

TEACHING OPTIONS

Video →🔲← Show the **Fotonovela** again to give students more input containing irregular preterite forms. Stop the video where appropriate to discuss how certain verbs were used and to ask comprehension questions.

Extra Practice 🔲↔🔲 Have students write down six things they brought to class today. Then have them circulate around the room, asking other students if they also brought those items (**¿Trajiste tus llaves a clase hoy?**). When they find a student that answers **sí,** they ask that student to sign his or her name next to that item (**Firma aquí, por favor.**). Can students get signatures for all the items they brought to class?

Práctica

1 Teaching Tip
To simplify, have students begin by identifying the subject in each sentence. Help them see that, for item 1, the subject is implied.

1 Expansion
• 👤↔👤 Ask individual students about the last time they threw a party. Ex: **La última vez que diste una fiesta, ¿quiénes estuvieron allí? ¿Fue alguien que no invitaste? ¿Qué llevaron los invitados?**

• 👤↔👤 Assign students to groups of three. Tell them they are going to write a narrative about a wedding. You will begin the story, then each student will add a sentence using an irregular verb in the preterite. Each group member should have at least two turns. Ex: **El domingo se casaron Carlos y Susana. (E1: Tuvieron una boda muy grande. E2: Vinieron muchos invitados. E3: Hubo un pastel enorme y elegante.)**

2 Teaching Tip
↔👤→ To challenge students, have them see how many sentences they can come up with to describe each drawing using the target verbs.

2 Expansion
↔👤→ Using magazine pictures, show images similar to those in the activity. Have students narrate what happened in the images using irregular preterite verb forms.

1 **Completar** Completa estas oraciones con el pretérito de los verbos.

1. El sábado _____hubo_____ (haber) una fiesta sorpresa para Elsa en mi casa.
2. Sofía _____hizo_____ (hacer) un pastel para la fiesta y Miguel _____trajo_____ (traer) un flan.
3. Los amigos y parientes de Elsa _____vinieron_____ (venir) y _____trajeron_____ (traer) regalos.
4. El hermano de Elsa no _____vino_____ (venir) porque _____tuvo_____ (tener) que trabajar.
5. Su tía María Dolores tampoco _____pudo_____ (poder) venir.
6. Cuando Elsa abrió la puerta, todos gritaron: "¡Feliz cumpleaños!" y su esposo le _____dio_____ (dar) un beso.
7. Elsa no _____supo_____ (saber) cómo reaccionar (*react*). _____Estuvo_____ (estar) un poco nerviosa al principio, pero pronto sus amigos _____pusieron_____ (poner) música y ella _____pudo_____ (poder) relajarse bailando con su esposo.
8. Al final de la noche, todos _____dijeron_____ (decir) que se divirtieron mucho.

NOTA CULTURAL
El **flan** es un postre muy popular en los países de habla hispana. Se prepara con huevos, leche y azúcar y se sirve con salsa de caramelo. Existen variedades deliciosas como el flan de chocolate o el flan de coco.

2 **Describir** En parejas, usen los verbos para describir lo que estas personas hicieron.

Some answers may vary. Suggested answers:

conducir	estar	poner	traducir
dar	hacer	tener	traer

1. Gabriel y Natalia
Gabriel y Natalia tuvieron una cita.

2. Sergio
Sergio hizo el pastel de cumpleaños.

3. anoche nosotros
Anoche nosotros tuvimos/hicimos/dimos una fiesta de Navidad./Anoche nosotros estuvimos en una fiesta de Navidad.

4. la señora Rojas
La señora Rojas condujo el auto.

TEACHING OPTIONS

Extra Practice ↔👤→ Ask students to write a description of a party they once attended. They should include information on what kind of party it was, who was there, what people brought, what the guests did, and so forth. Have students exchange papers with a classmate for peer editing.

Small Groups In small groups, have each student write three sentences using irregular preterites. Two of the sentences should be true and the third should be false. As students read their sentences aloud to the group, the other members have to guess which of the sentences is the false one, discussing their reasoning with the group.

Comunicación

3 **Preguntas** En parejas, túrnense para hacerse y responder a estas preguntas. Answers will vary.

1. ¿Fuiste a una fiesta de cumpleaños el año pasado? ¿De quién?
2. ¿Quiénes fueron a la fiesta?
3. ¿Quién condujo el auto?
4. ¿Cómo estuvo el ambiente de la fiesta?
5. ¿Quién llevó regalos, bebidas o comida? ¿Llevaste algo especial?
6. ¿Hubo comida? ¿Quién la hizo? ¿Hubo champán?
7. ¿Qué regalo hiciste tú? ¿Qué otros regalos trajeron los invitados?
8. ¿Cuántos invitados hubo en la fiesta?

4 **Encuesta** Tu profesor(a) va a darte una hoja de actividades. Para cada una de las actividades de la lista, encuentra a alguien que hizo esa actividad. Answers will vary.

> **modelo**
> traer dulces a clase
> **Estudiante 1:** ¿Trajiste dulces a clase?
> **Estudiante 2:** Sí, traje galletas y helado a la fiesta del fin del semestre.

Actividades   **Nombres**
1. ponerse un disfraz (*costume*) de Halloween
2. traer dulces a clase
3. conducir su auto a clase
4. estar en la biblioteca ayer
5. dar un regalo a alguien ayer
6. poder levantarse temprano esta mañana
7. hacer un viaje a un país hispano en el verano
8. tener una cita anoche
9. ir a una fiesta el fin de semana pasado
10. tener que trabajar el sábado pasado

Síntesis

5 **Conversación** En parejas, preparen una conversación en la que uno/a de ustedes va a visitar a su hermano/a para explicarle por qué no fue a su fiesta de graduación y para saber cómo estuvo la fiesta. Incluyan esta información en la conversación: Answers will vary.

- cuál fue el menú
- quiénes vinieron a la fiesta y quiénes no pudieron venir
- quiénes prepararon la comida o trajeron algo
- si él/ella tuvo que preparar algo
- lo que la gente hizo antes y después de comer
- cómo lo pasaron, bien o mal

Section Goal

In **Estructura 9.2**, students will be introduced to verbs that change meaning in the preterite tense.

Instructional Resources
Supersite: Audio (Lab MP3 Files); Resources (Grammar Presentation Slides, Activity Pack, Scripts, Answer Keys); Testing Program (Quizzes)
WebSAM
Workbook
Lab Manual

Teaching Tips

- Introduce the preterite of **conocer**. Say: **Ahora conozco a ustedes muy bien. Pero me acuerdo del día en que los conocí. ¿Ustedes se acuerdan del día en que nos conocimos? ¿Cuándo fue?** Ask volunteers to compare and contrast the meanings of **conocer** in your example.

- Stress the meaning of **poder** in the preterite by giving both affirmative (*to manage; to succeed*) and negative (*to try and fail*) examples. Ex: **Pude leer todas sus composiciones anoche, pero no pude leer las composiciones de la otra clase.**

- Stress the meaning of **querer** in the preterite by giving both affirmative (*to try*) and negative (*to refuse*) examples. Ex: **Quisimos ver una película el sábado, pero no quise ver ninguna película violenta.**

9.2 Verbs that change meaning in the preterite

 Tutorial

ANTE TODO The verbs **conocer, saber, poder,** and **querer** change meanings when used in the preterite. Because of this, each of them corresponds to more than one verb in English, depending on its tense.

Verbs that change meaning in the preterite

Present	**Preterite**
conocer	
to know; to be acquainted with	*to meet*
Conozco a esa pareja.	**Conocí** a esa pareja ayer.
I know that couple.	*I met that couple yesterday.*
saber	
to know information; to know how to do something	*to find out; to learn*
	Supimos la verdad anoche.
Sabemos la verdad.	*We found out (learned) the truth*
We know the truth.	*last night.*
poder	
to be able; can	*to manage; to succeed (could and did)*
Podemos hacerlo.	**Pudimos** hacerlo ayer.
We can do it.	*We managed to do it yesterday.*
querer	
to want; to love	*to try*
Quiero ir, pero tengo que trabajar.	**Quise** evitarlo, pero fue imposible.
I want to go, but I have to work.	*I tried to avoid it, but it was impossible.*

> **¡ATENCIÓN!**
>
> In the preterite, the verbs **poder** and **querer** have different meanings, depending on whether they are used in affirmative or negative sentences.
> **pude** *I succeeded*
> **no pude** *I failed (to)*
> **quise** *I tried (to)*
> **no quise** *I refused (to)*

¡INTÉNTALO! Elige la respuesta más lógica.

1. Hablamos por primera vez con Nuria y Ana en la boda. **a**
   a. Las conocimos en la boda.   b. Les dijimos en la boda.

2. Yo no hice lo que me pidieron mis padres. ¡Tengo mis principios! **a**
   a. No quise hacerlo.   b. No supe hacerlo.

3. Por fin hablé con mi hermano después de llamarlo siete veces. **b**
   a. No quise hablar con él.   b. Pude hablar con él.

4. Josefina se acostó para relajarse. Se durmió inmediatamente. **a**
   a. Pudo relajarse.   b. No pudo relajarse.

5. Después de mucho buscar, encontraste la definición en el diccionario. **b**
   a. No supiste la respuesta.   b. Supiste la respuesta.

6. Las chicas fueron a la fiesta. Cantaron y bailaron mucho. **a**
   a. Ellas pudieron divertirse.   b. Ellas no supieron divertirse.

More activities

vhlcentral

LM
p. 52

WB
p. 101

Online activities

TEACHING OPTIONS

Extra Practice Prepare sentences using **conocer, saber, poder,** and **querer** in the present tense that will be logical when converted into the preterite. Have students convert them and explain how the meanings of the sentences change. Ex: **Sé la fecha de la fiesta. (Supe la fecha de la fiesta.)**

Heritage Speakers Ask heritage speakers to talk about one of these situations in the past: (1) when they found out there was no Santa Claus (**saber**), (2) when they met their best friend (**conocer**), or (3) something they tried to do but could not (**querer/ no poder**). Verify student comprehension by asking other students to relate what was said.

Práctica y Comunicación

1 **Carlos y Eva** Forma oraciones con los siguientes elementos. Usa el pretérito y haz todos los cambios necesarios. Al final, inventa la razón del divorcio de Carlos y Eva.

1. anoche / mi esposa y yo / saber / qué / Carlos y Eva / divorciarse
   Anoche mi esposa y yo supimos que Carlos y Eva se divorciaron.

2. los / conocer / viaje / isla de Pascua
   Los conocimos en un viaje a la isla de Pascua.

3. no / poder / hablar / mucho / con / ellos / ese día
   No pudimos hablar mucho con ellos ese día.

4. pero / ellos / ser / simpático / y / nosotros / hacer planes / vernos / con más / frecuencia
   Pero ellos fueron simpáticos y nosotros hicimos planes para vernos con más frecuencia.

5. yo / poder / encontrar / su / número / teléfono / páginas / amarillo
   Yo pude encontrar su número de teléfono en las páginas amarillas.

6. (yo) querer / llamar / los / ese día / pero / no / tener / tiempo
   Quise llamarlos ese día, pero no tuve tiempo.

7. cuando / los / llamar / nosotros / poder / hablar / Eva
   Cuando los llamé, nosotros pudimos hablar con Eva.

8. nosotros / saber / razón / divorcio / después / hablar / ella
   Nosotros supimos la razón del divorcio después de hablar con ella.

9. _____
   Answers will vary.

NOTA CULTURAL

La isla de Pascua es un remoto territorio chileno situado en el océano Pacífico Sur. Sus inmensas estatuas son uno de los mayores misterios del mundo: nadie sabe cómo o por qué se crearon. Para más información, véase **Panorama**, p. 329.

---

2 **Completar** Completa estas frases de una manera lógica. *Answers will vary.*

1. Ayer mi compañero/a de cuarto supo…
2. Esta mañana no pude…
3. Conocí a mi mejor amigo/a en…
4. Mis padres no quisieron…
5. Mi mejor amigo/a no pudo…
6. Mi novio/a y yo nos conocimos en…
7. La semana pasada supe…
8. Ayer mis amigos quisieron…

---

3 **Telenovela** En parejas, escriban el diálogo para una escena de una telenovela (*soap opera*). La escena trata de una situación amorosa entre tres personas: Mirta, Daniel y Raúl. Usen el pretérito de **conocer, poder, querer** y **saber** en su diálogo. *Answers will vary.*

modelo

Mirta: ¿Cómo supiste?
Daniel: Vi un mensaje electrónico de Raúl…

La mujer doble

⚬ Pasión   ⚬ Aventura   ⚬ Suspenso   ⚬ Venganza

Síntesis

4 **Conversación** En una hoja de papel, escribe dos listas: las cosas que hiciste durante el fin de semana y las cosas que quisiste hacer, pero no pudiste. Luego, compara tu lista con la de un(a) compañero/a, y expliquen ambos por qué no pudieron hacer esas cosas. *Answers will vary.*

---

1 Expansion
- In pairs, students create five additional dehydrated sentences for their partners to complete, using the verbs **conocer, saber, poder,** and **querer.** After pairs have finished, ask volunteers to share some of their dehydrated sentences. Write them on the board and have the rest of the class "hydrate" them.
- 🏃↔🏃 To challenge students, have pairs use preterite forms of **conocer, saber, poder,** and **querer** to role-play **Carlos** and **Eva** explaining their separate versions of the divorce to their friends.

2 Teaching Tip Before assigning the activity, share with the class some recent things you found out, tried to do but could not, or the names of people you met, inviting students to respond.

3 Teaching Tips
- Explain that **telenovelas** are soap operas aired in a miniseries format. They typically run for a limited duration (averaging 120 episodes) and have a conclusion. In Mexico, historical romances are very popular, usually set in the colonial or revolutionary periods.
- Before students begin writing, brainstorm as a class some of the characteristics of soap operas, including how they create suspense and melodrama. You may wish to provide some extra vocabulary or key expressions.

4 Expansion
⬅🏃 Have pairs repeat the activity, this time describing another person. Ask students to share their descriptions with the class, who will guess the person being described.

9.3 ¿Qué? and ¿cuál? Tutorial

ANTE TODO You've already learned how to use interrogative words and phrases. As you know, *¿qué?* and *¿cuál?* or *¿cuáles?* mean *what?* or *which?* However, they are not interchangeable.

▶ **¿Qué?** is used to ask for a definition or an explanation.

¿**Qué** es el flan?	¿**Qué** estudias?
What is flan?	*What do you study?*

▶ **¿Cuál(es)?** is used when there is more than one possibility to choose from.

¿**Cuál** de los dos prefieres, el vino o el champán?	¿**Cuáles** son tus medias, las negras o las blancas?
Which of these (two) do you prefer, wine or champagne?	*Which ones are your socks, the black ones or the white ones?*

▶ **¿Cuál?** should not be used before a noun; in this case, **¿qué?** is used.

¿**Qué** sorpresa te dieron tus amigos?	¿**Qué** colores te gustan?
What surprise did your friends give you?	*What colors do you like?*

▶ **¿Qué?** used before a noun has the same meaning as **¿cuál?**

¿**Qué regalo** te gusta?	¿**Qué dulces** quieren ustedes?
What (Which) gift do you like?	*What (Which) sweets do you want?*

Review of interrogative words and phrases

¿a qué hora?	at what time?	¿cuántos/as?	how many?
¿adónde?	(to) where?	¿de dónde?	from where?
¿cómo?	how?	¿dónde?	where?
¿cuál(es)?	what?; which?	¿por qué?	why?
¿cuándo?	when?	¿qué?	what?; which?
¿cuánto/a?	how much?	¿quién(es)?	who?

¡INTÉNTALO! Completa las preguntas con **¿qué?** o **¿cuál(es)?**, según el contexto.

1. ¿ **Cuál** de los dos te gusta más?
2. ¿ **Qué** tipo de pastel pediste?
3. ¿ **Cuál** es tu teléfono?
4. ¿ **Qué** es una galleta?
5. ¿ **Qué** haces ahora?
6. ¿ **Cuáles** son tus platos favoritos?
7. ¿ **Qué** bebidas te gustan más?
8. ¿ **Cuál** es el mejor?
9. ¿ **Qué** es esto?
10. ¿ **Cuál** es tu opinión?
11. ¿ **Qué** fiestas celebras tú?
12. ¿ **Qué** botella de vino prefieres?
13. ¿ **Qué** pones en la mesa?
14. ¿ **Cuál** es tu helado favorito?
15. ¿ **Qué** restaurante prefieres?
16. ¿ **Qué** estudiantes estudian más?
17. ¿ **Cuál** es la sorpresa mañana?
18. ¿ **Qué** quieres comer esta noche?
19. ¿ **Qué** postre prefieres?
20. ¿ **Qué** opinas?

More activities

vhlcentral

LM
p. 53

WB
p. 102

Online activities

Práctica y Comunicación

1 **Completar** Completa estas preguntas con alguna(s) palabra(s) interrogativa(s). Luego, con un(a) compañero/a, hagan y contesten las preguntas.

1. ¿___Cuál___ es la fecha de tu cumpleaños?
2. ¿___Dónde/Cuándo/A qué hora___ naciste?
3. ¿___Cuál___ es tu estado civil?
4. ¿___Quién/Cómo___ es tu mejor amigo/a?
5. ¿___Qué___ cosas te hacen reír?
6. ¿___Cómo/Cuándo/Dónde___ te relajas?
7. ¿___Qué___ postres te gustan? ¿___Cuál___ te gusta más?
8. ¿___Qué___ problemas tuviste en la primera cita con alguien?

2 **Una invitación** En parejas, túrnense para hacer y contestar preguntas con **qué** y **cuál** basadas en la información de la invitación. *Answers will vary.*

modelo
> **Estudiante 1:** ¿Cuál es el nombre del padre de la novia?
> **Estudiante 2:** Su nombre es Fernando Sandoval Valera.

> *Fernando Sandoval Valera*   *Lorenzo Vásquez Amaral*
> *Isabel Arzipe de Sandoval*   *Elena Soto de Vásquez*
>
> tienen el agrado de invitarlos a la boda de sus hijos
>
> **María Luisa y José Antonio**
>
> La ceremonia religiosa tendrá lugar
> el sábado 10 de junio a las dos de la tarde
> en el Templo de Santo Domingo
> (Calle Santo Domingo, 961).
>
> Después de la ceremonia, sírvanse pasar a la recepción en
> el salón de baile del Hotel Metrópoli (Sotero del Río, 465).

3 **Quinceañera** Trabaja con un(a) compañero/a. Uno/a de ustedes es el/la director(a) del salón de fiestas "Renacimiento". La otra persona es el padre/la madre de Sandra, quien quiere hacer la fiesta de quince años de su hija gastando menos de $25 por invitado. Su profesor(a) va a darles la información necesaria para confirmar la reservación. *Answers will vary.*

modelo
> **Estudiante 1:** ¿Cuánto cuestan los entremeses?
> **Estudiante 2:** Depende. Puede escoger champiñones por 50 centavos o
>   camarones por dos dólares.
> **Estudiante 1:** ¡Uf! A mi hija le gustan los camarones, pero son muy caros.
> **Estudiante 2:** Bueno, también puede escoger quesos por un dólar por invitado.

9.4 Pronouns after prepositions

 Tutorial

 NATIONAL comparisons STANDARDS

ANTE TODO

In Spanish, as in English, the object of a preposition is the noun or pronoun that follows a preposition. Observe the following diagram.

PREPOSITION	NOUN	PREPOSITION	PRONOUN
La sopa es para	Alicia	y para	él.

Prepositional pronouns

	Singular			Plural	
	mí	me		**nosotros/as**	us
	ti	you (fam.)		**vosotros/as**	you (fam.)
preposition +	**Ud.**	you (form.)		**Uds.**	you
	él	him		**ellos**	them (m.)
	ella	her		**ellas**	them (f.)

▶ Note that, except for **mí** and **ti,** these pronouns are the same as the subject pronouns. **¡Atención! Mí** (*me*) has an accent mark to distinguish it from the possessive adjective **mi** (*my*).

▶ The preposition **con** combines with **mí** and **ti** to form **conmigo** and **contigo**, respectively.

—¿Quieres venir **conmigo** a Concepción?
Do you want to come with me to Concepción?

—Sí, gracias, me gustaría ir **contigo**.
Yes, thanks, I would like to go with you.

▶ The preposition **entre** is followed by **tú** and **yo** instead of **ti** and **mí**.

Papá va a sentarse **entre tú y yo**.
Dad is going to sit between you and me.

CONSULTA

For more prepositions, refer to **Estructura 2.3,** p. 60.

¡INTÉNTALO! Completa estas oraciones con las preposiciones y los pronombres apropiados.

1. (*with him*) No quiero ir _con él_.
2. (*for her*) Las galletas son _para ella_.
3. (*for me*) Los mariscos son _para mí_.
4. (*with you*, pl.) Preferimos estar _con ustedes_.
5. (*with me*) ¿Por qué no quieres tener una cita _conmigo_? *without me; sin mí*
6. (*with you*, sing. fam.) Me gusta salir _contigo_. *without you: sin ti*
7. (*for her*) La cuenta es _para ella_.
8. (*for them*, m.) La habitación es muy pequeña _para ellos_.
9. (*for you*, sing. fam.) Este beso es _para ti_.
10. (*with them*, f.) Anoche celebré la Navidad _con ellas_ / *without them: sin ellas*
11. (*with you*, sing. fam.) Nunca me aburro _contigo_.
12. (*with you*, pl.) ¡Qué bien que vamos _con ustedes_!
13. (*for them*, f.) _Para ellas_ no hay sorpresas.
14. (*for you*, sing. fam.) _Para ti_ la vida es muy fácil.

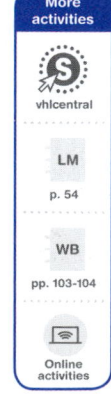

More activities

vhlcentral

LM
p. 54

WB
pp. 103-104

Online activities

TEACHING OPTIONS

Extra Practice →👤← Describe someone in the classroom using prepositions of location, without saying the student's name. Ex: **Esta persona está entre la ventana y ____. No está al lado de____.** The rest of the class has to guess the person being described. Once students have this model, ask individuals to create similar descriptions so that their classmates may guess.

Game 👤↔👤 Divide the class into two teams. One student from the first team chooses an item in the classroom and writes it down. Call on five students from the other team to ask questions about the item's location. Ex: **¿Está cerca de mí?** The first student can respond with **sí, no, caliente,** or **frío**. If a team guesses the item within five tries, give it a point. If not, give the other team a point. The team with the most points wins.

Práctica y Comunicación

1 Completar Escoge los pronombres adecuados para completar el mensaje electrónico.

www.micorreo.com

✉ Mi Correo

Para: Antonio   Asunto: Cena romántica con Claudia

Hola, Antonio:
¿Recuerdas a Claudia? Hoy voy a cenar con (1) _____ella_____ (usted/ ella). Vamos a ir al restaurante italiano que conocí (2) _____contigo_____ (conmigo/contigo) el mes pasado. Aunque a (3) _____ti_____ (él/ ti) no te gustó la pasta, a (4) _____mí_____ (ellos/mí) me encantó la pizza.

Claudia me dijo que después de la cena quiere ir a bailar (5) _____conmigo_____ (contigo/conmigo). Creo que va a ser una noche muy especial para (6) _____nosotros_____ (nosotros/él) y te lo quería contar a (7) _____ti_____ (ti/usted) porque eres mi mejor amigo.

Hasta pronto,
Diego

2 Preguntas En parejas, túrnense para hacerse estas preguntas. Usa los pronombres apropiados en tus respuestas. *Answers will vary.*

1. ¿Quieres practicar el español conmigo?
2. ¿Te gusta viajar con tus padres?
3. ¿Tus padres se preocupan mucho por ti?
4. ¿Tu familia vive contigo?
5. ¿Aprendes mucho con tus profesores?
6. ¿Siempre lo pasas bien con tu mejor amigo/a?
7. ¿Te llevas bien con tus compañeros de clase?
8. ¿Compras regalos para tus amigos?

NATIONAL **communication** STANDARDS

3 Compartir Tu profesor(a) va a darte una hoja de actividades en la que hay un dibujo. En parejas, hagan preguntas para saber dónde está cada una de las personas en el dibujo. Ustedes tienen dos versiones diferentes de la ilustración. Al final deben saber dónde está cada persona. *Answers will vary.*

AYUDA

Here are some useful prepositions: **al lado de, debajo de, a la derecha de, a la izquierda de, cerca de, lejos de, delante de, detrás de, entre.**

modelo
Estudiante 1: ¿Quién está al lado de Óscar?
Estudiante 2: Alfredo está al lado de él.

Alfredo	Dolores	Graciela	Raúl
Sra. Blanco	Enrique	Leonor	Rubén
Carlos	Sra. Gómez	Óscar	Yolanda

Recapitulación

Section Goal

In **Recapitulación**, students will review the grammar concepts from this lesson.

Instructional Resource
Supersite

Teaching Tip You may want to assign this **Recapitulación** activity on the Supersite because it has diagnostics. There is an online-only review activity for each grammar point. The Supersite also has a **Repaso de vocabulario** activity with diagnostics.

1 Teaching Tip Ask students to identify which verb changes meaning in the preterite.

1 Expansion
• To challenge students, ask them to provide the **tú** and **ustedes** forms of the verbs.
• Have students provide the conjugations of **conocer, dar,** and **venir**.

2 Teaching Tip To simplify, have students circle the subject of each verb before filling in the blanks.

2 Expansion
Have students work in pairs to write a response e-mail from **Omar**. Tell them to use the preterite tense to ask for more details about the party. Ex: **¿Qué más tuviste que hacer para preparar la fiesta? ¿Qué regalos te dieron tus amigos?**

Completa estas actividades para repasar los conceptos de gramática que aprendiste en esta lección.

1 Completar Completa la tabla con el pretérito de los verbos. **18 pts.**

Infinitive	yo	ella	nosotros
conducir	conduje	condujo	condujimos
hacer	hice	hizo	hicimos
saber	supe	supo	supimos

2 Mi fiesta Completa este mensaje electrónico con el pretérito de los verbos. Vas a usar cada verbo sólo una vez. **20 pts.**

dar	haber	tener
decir	hacer	traer
estar	poder	venir
	poner	

Hola, Omar:

Como tú no (1) ___pudiste___ venir a mi fiesta de cumpleaños, quiero contarte cómo fue. El día de mi cumpleaños, muy temprano por la mañana, mis hermanos me (2) ___dieron___ una gran sorpresa: ellos (3) ___pusieron___ un regalo delante de la puerta de mi habitación: ¡una bicicleta roja preciosa! Mi madre nos preparó un desayuno riquísimo. Después de desayunar, mis hermanos y yo (4) ___tuvimos___ que limpiar toda la casa, así que (*therefore*) no (5) ___hubo___ más celebración hasta la tarde. A las seis y media (nosotros) (6) ___hicimos___ una barbacoa en el patio de la casa. Todos los invitados (7) ___trajeron___ bebidas y regalos. (8) ___Vinieron___ todos mis amigos, excepto tú, ¡qué pena! :-(La fiesta (9) ___estuvo___ muy animada hasta las diez de la noche, cuando mis padres (10) ___dijeron___ que los vecinos (*neighbors*) iban a (*were going to*) protestar y entonces todos se fueron a sus casas.

RESUMEN GRAMATICAL

9.1 Irregular preterites *pp. 310–311*

u-stem	estar poder poner saber tener	estuv- pud- pus- sup- tuv-	
i-stem	hacer querer venir	hic- quis- vin-	-e, -iste, -o, -imos, -isteis, -(i)eron
j-stem	conducir decir traducir traer	conduj- dij- traduj- traj-	

▶ Preterite of **dar**: di, diste, dio, dimos, disteis, dieron
▶ Preterite of **hay** (*inf.* **haber**): hubo

9.2 Verbs that change meaning in the preterite *p. 31*

Present	Preterite
conocer	
to know; to be acquainted with	to meet
saber	
to know info.; to know how to do something	to find out; to learn
poder	
to be able; can	to manage; to succeed
querer	
to want; to love	to try

9.3 ¿Qué? and ¿cuál? *p. 316*

▶ Use **¿qué?** to ask for a definition or an explanation.
▶ Use **¿cuál(es)?** when there is more than one possibility to choose from.
▶ **¿Cuál?** should not be used before a noun; use **¿qué?** instead.
▶ **¿Qué?** used before a noun has the same meaning as **¿cuál?**

TEACHING OPTIONS

TPR Have students stand and form a circle. Call out an infinitive from **Resumen gramatical** and a subject pronoun (Ex: **poder/nosotros**) and toss a ball to a student, who will give the correct preterite form (Ex: **pudimos**). He or she then tosses the ball to another student, who must use the verb correctly in a sentence before throwing the ball back to you. Ex: **No pudimos comprar los regalos**.

Small Groups Tell small groups to imagine that one of them has received an anonymous birthday gift from a secret admirer. Have them create a dialogue in which friends ask questions about the gift and the potential admirer. Students must use at least two irregular preterites, two examples of **¿qué?** or **¿cuál?**, and three pronouns after prepositions.

3 ¿Presente o pretérito? Escoge la forma correcta de los verbos.   `12 pts.`

1. Después de muchos intentos (*tries*), (podemos/**pudimos**) hacer una piñata.
2. —¿Conoces a Pepe?
   —Sí, lo (conozco/**conocí**) en tu fiesta.
3. Como no es de aquí, Cristina no (**sabe**/supo) mucho de las celebraciones locales.
4. Yo no (**quiero**/quise) ir a un restaurante grande, pero tú decides.
5. Ellos (quieren/**quisieron**) darme una sorpresa, pero Nina me lo dijo todo.
6. Mañana se terminan las vacaciones; por fin (**podemos**/pudimos) volver a la escuela.

> **9.4 Pronouns after prepositions**   *p. 318*
>
> **Prepositional pronouns**
>
> | | Singular | Plural |
> |---|---|---|
> | | mí | nosotros/as |
> | | ti | vosotros/as |
> | Preposition + | Ud. | Uds. |
> | | él | ellos |
> | | ella | ellas |
>
> ► Exceptions: conmigo, contigo, entre tú y yo

4 Preguntas Escribe una pregunta para cada respuesta con los elementos dados. Empieza con **qué, cuál** o **cuáles** de acuerdo con el contexto y haz los cambios necesarios.   `8 pts.`

1. —¿? / pastel / querer —Quiero el pastel de chocolate.   *1. ¿Qué pastel quieres?*
2. —¿? / ser / sangría —La sangría es una bebida típica española.   *2. ¿Qué es la sangría?*
3. —¿? / ser / restaurante favorito —Mis restaurantes favoritos son Dalí y Jaleo.   *3. ¿Cuáles son tus restaurantes favoritos?*
4. —¿? / ser / dirección electrónica —Mi dirección electrónica es paco@email.com.   *4. ¿Cuál es tu dirección electrónica?*

5 ¿Dónde me siento? Completa la conversación con los pronombres apropiados.   `14 pts.`

JUAN A ver, te voy a decir dónde te vas a sentar. Manuel, ¿ves esa silla? Es para _____*ti*_____. Y esa otra silla es para tu novia, que todavía no está aquí.

MANUEL Muy bien, yo la reservo para _____*ella*_____.

HUGO ¿Y esta silla es para _____*mí*_____ (*me*)?

JUAN No, Hugo. No es para _____*ti*_____. Es para Carmina, que viene con Julio.

HUGO No, Carmina y Julio no pueden venir. Hablé con _____*ellos*_____ y me avisaron.

JUAN Pues ellos se lo pierden (*it's their loss*). ¡Más comida para _____*nosotros*_____ (*us*)!

CAMARERO Aquí tienen el menú. Les doy un minuto y enseguida estoy con _____*ustedes*_____.

6 Cumpleaños feliz Escribe cinco oraciones que describan cómo celebraste tu último cumpleaños. Usa el pretérito y los pronombres que aprendiste en esta lección.   `28 pts.`   *Answers will vary.*

7 Poema Completa este fragmento del poema *Elegía nocturna* de Carlos Pellicer con el pretérito de los verbos.   `¡4 puntos EXTRA!`

   **"Ay de mi corazón° que nadie _____*quiso*_____ (querer)
tomar de entre mis manos desoladas.
Tú _____*viniste*_____ (venir) a mirar sus llamaradas°
y le miraste arder° claro° y sereno. "**

corazón *heart*   llamaradas *flames*   arder *to burn*   claro *clear*

---

3 Teaching Tip To challenge students, ask them to explain why they chose the preterite or present tense in each case.

4 Expansion Give students these answers as items 5–8:
5. —¿? / libro / comprar —Voy a comprar el libro de viajes. (¿Qué libro vas a comprar?) 6. —¿? / ser / última película / ver —Vi la película *Los abrazos rotos.* (¿Cuál fue la última película que viste?) 7. —¿? / ser / número de la suerte —Mi número de la suerte es el ocho. (¿Cuál es tu número de la suerte?) 8. —¿? / ser / nacimiento —El nacimiento es la primera etapa de la vida. (¿Qué es el nacimiento?)

5 Expansion Have four volunteers role-play the dialogue for the class. Encourage them to ad-lib as they present.

6 Teaching Tip To simplify, have students begin by making an idea map. In the center circle, have them write **Mi último cumpleaños**. Help them brainstorm labels for the surrounding circles, such as **lugar, invitados, comida, regalos**. You also may want to provide a list of infinitives that students may use in their descriptions.

7 Teaching Tip You may want to point out the example of leísmo in line 4 (**le miraste**). Explain that some Spanish speakers tend to use **le** or **les** as direct object pronouns. In this case, **le** replaces the direct object pronoun **lo**, which refers to **mi corazón**.

Nota cultural Mexican poet **Carlos Pellicer** mixes in his works the splendor of nature with the most intimate emotions. Some of his most important works are *Práctica de vuelo*, *Hora de junio*, and *Camino.* Also a museologist, he helped create the **Museo Casa de Frida Kahlo** and the **Anahuacalli**, which exhibits pre-Hispanic art donated by **Diego Rivera**.

Lectura

Antes de leer

Estrategia
Recognizing word families

Recognizing root words can help you guess the meaning of words in context, ensuring better comprehension of a reading selection. Using this strategy will enrich your Spanish vocabulary as you will see below.

Examinar el texto

Familiarízate con el texto usando las estrategias de lectura más efectivas para ti. ¿Qué tipo de documento es? ¿De qué tratan° las cuatro secciones del documento? Explica tus respuestas.

Raíces°

Completa el cuadro° para ampliar tu vocabulario. Usa palabras de la lectura de esta lección y vocabulario de las lecciones anteriores. ¿Qué significan las palabras que escribiste?
Some answers may vary. Suggested answers:

Verbos	Sustantivos	Otras formas
1. agradecer *to thank, to be grateful for*	agradecimiento/ gracias *gratitude/thanks*	agradecido *grateful, thankful*
2. estudiar	estudiante *student*	estudiado *studied*
3. celebrar *to celebrate*	celebración *celebration*	celebrado
4. bailar *to dance*	baile	bailable *danceable*
5. bautizar	bautismo *baptism*	bautizado *baptized*

¿De qué tratan...? *What are... about?* **Raíces** *Roots* **cuadro** *chart*

More activities

vhlcentral — Online activities

Matrimonio

Espinoza Álvarez- Reyes Salazar

El día sábado 17 de junio a las 19 horas, se celebró el matrimonio de Silvia Reyes y Carlos Espinoza en la catedral de Santiago. La ceremonia fue oficiada por el pastor Federico Salas y participaron los padres de los novios, el señor Jorge Espinoza y señora y el señor José Alfredo Reyes y señora. Después de la ceremonia, los padres de los recién casados ofrecieron una fiesta bailable en el restaurante La Misión.

Bautismo

José María recibió el bautismo el 26 de junio.

Sus padres, don Roberto Lagos Moreno y doña María Angélica Sánchez, compartieron la alegría de la fiesta con todos sus parientes y amigos. La ceremonia religiosa tuvo lugar° en la catedral de Aguas Blancas. Después de la ceremonia, padres, parientes y amigos celebraron una fiesta en la residencia de la familia Lagos.

Entretenimiento   Deportes   Economía

Fiesta de quince años

El doctor don Amador Larenas Fernández y la señora Felisa Vera de Larenas celebraron los quince años de su hija Ana Ester junto a sus parientes y amigos. La quinceañera reside en la ciudad de Valparaíso y es estudiante del Colegio Francés. La fiesta de presentación en sociedad de la señorita Ana Ester fue el día viernes 2 de mayo a las 19 horas en el Club Español. Entre los invitados especiales asistieron el alcalde° de la ciudad, don Pedro Castedo, y su esposa. La música estuvo a cargo de la Orquesta Americana. ¡Feliz cumpleaños, le deseamos a la señorita Ana Ester en su fiesta bailable!

. . . .

Expresión de gracias
Carmen Godoy Tapia

Agradecemos° sinceramente a todas las personas que nos acompañaron en el último adiós a nuestra apreciada esposa, madre, abuela y tía, la señora Carmen Godoy Tapia. El funeral tuvo lugar el día 28 de junio en la ciudad de Viña del Mar. La vida de Carmen Godoy fue un ejemplo de trabajo, amistad, alegría y amor para todos nosotros. Su esposo, hijos y familia agradecen de todo corazón° su asistencia° al funeral a todos los parientes y amigos.

tuvo lugar *took place* **alcalde** *mayor* **Agradecemos** *We thank* **de todo corazón** *sincerely* **asistencia** *attendance*

Después de leer

Corregir

Escribe estos comentarios otra vez para corregir la información errónea.

1. El alcalde y su esposa asistieron a la boda de Silvia y Carlos. *El alcalde y su esposa asistieron a la fiesta de quince años de Ana Ester.*

2. Todos los anuncios (*announcements*) describen eventos felices. *Tres de los anuncios tratan de eventos felices. Uno trata de una muerte.*

3. Felisa Vera de Larenas cumple quince años. *Ana Ester Larenas cumple quince años.*

4. Roberto Lagos y María Angélica Sánchez son hermanos. *Roberto Lagos y María Angélica Sánchez están casados/son esposos.*

5. Carmen Godoy Tapia les dio las gracias a las personas que asistieron al funeral. *La familia de Carmen Godoy Tapia les dio las gracias a las personas que asistieron al funeral.*

Identificar

Escribe el nombre de la(s) persona(s) descrita(s) (*described*).

1. Dejó viudo a su esposo el 28 de junio. *Carmen Godoy Tapia*

2. Sus padres y todos los invitados brindaron por él, pero él no entendió por qué. *José María*

3. El Club Español les presentó una cuenta considerable. *don Amador Larenas Fernández y doña Felisa Vera de Larenas*

4. Unió a los novios en matrimonio. *el pastor Federico Salas*

5. Su fiesta de cumpleaños se celebró en Valparaíso. *Ana Ester*

Un anuncio

Trabajen en grupos pequeños para inventar un anuncio breve sobre una celebración importante. Puede ser una graduación, un matrimonio o una gran fiesta en la que ustedes participan. Incluyan la siguiente información. *Answers will vary.*

1. nombres de los participantes

2. la fecha, la hora y el lugar

3. qué se celebra

4. otros detalles de interés

Section Goals

In **Escritura**, students will:
- create a Venn diagram to organize information
- learn words and phrases that signal similarity and difference
- write a comparative analysis

Instructional Resource
Supersite

Estrategia Explain that a graphic organizer, such as a Venn diagram, is a useful way to record information and visually organize details to be compared and contrasted in a comparative analysis. On the board, draw a Venn diagram with the headings **La boda de mi hermano, El bautismo de mi sobrina,** and the subheadings **Diferencias** and **Similitudes**. Tell students they are going to complete a Venn diagram to compare two celebrations. Discuss with the class how these events are alike and how they are different, using some of the terms to signal similarities and differences.

Tema Explain to students that to write a comparative analysis, they will need to use words or phrases that signal similarities (**similitudes**) and differences (**diferencias**). Model the pronunciation of the words and expressions under **Escribir una composición**. Then have volunteers use them in sentences to express the similarities and differences listed in the Venn diagram.

Escritura

Estrategia

Planning and writing a comparative analysis

Writing any kind of comparative analysis requires careful planning. Venn diagrams are useful for organizing your ideas visually before comparing and contrasting people, places, objects, events, or issues. To create a Venn diagram, draw two circles that overlap one another and label the top of each circle. List the differences between the two elements in the outer rings of the two circles, then list their similarities where the two circles overlap. Review the following example.

Diferencias y similitudes

Boda de Silvia Reyes y Carlos Espinoza

Diferencias:
1. Primero hay una celebración religiosa.
2. Se celebra en un restaurante.

Similitudes:
1. Las dos fiestas se celebran por la noche.
2. Las dos fiestas son bailables.

Fiesta de quince años de Ana Ester Larenas Vera

Diferencias:
1. Se celebra en un club.
2. Vienen invitados especiales.

La lista de palabras y expresiones a la derecha puede ayudarte a escribir este tipo de ensayo (*essay*).

Tema

Escribir una composición

Compara una celebración familiar (como una boda, una fiesta de cumpleaños o una graduación) a la que tú asististe recientemente con otro tipo de celebración. Utiliza palabras y expresiones de esta lista.

NATIONAL communication STANDARDS

Para expresar similitudes	
además; también	*in addition; also*
al igual que	*the same as*
como	*as; like*
de la misma manera	*in the same manner (way)*
del mismo modo	*in the same manner (way)*
tan + [*adjetivo*] + como	*as + [adjective] + as*
tanto/a(s) + [*sustantivo*] + como	*as many/much + [noun] + as*

Para expresar diferencias	
a diferencia de	*unlike*
a pesar de	*in spite of*
aunque	*although*
en cambio	*on the other hand*
más/menos… que	*more/less … than*
no obstante	*nevertheless; however*
por el contrario	*on the contrary*
por otro lado	*on the other hand*
sin embargo	*nevertheless; however*

EVALUATION: Composición

Criteria	Scale
Content	1 2 3 4
Organization	1 2 3 4
Use of comparisons/contrasts	1 2 3 4
Use of vocabulary	1 2 3 4
Accuracy	1 2 3 4

Scoring	
Excellent	18–20 points
Good	14–17 points
Satisfactory	10–13 points
Unsatisfactory	< 10 points

Escuchar
Antes de escuchar

Estrategia
Guessing the meaning of words through context

When you hear an unfamiliar word, you can often guess its meaning by listening to the words and phrases around it.

 To practice this strategy, you will now listen to a paragraph. Jot down the unfamiliar words that you hear. Then listen to the paragraph again and jot down the word or words that give the most useful clues to the meaning of each unfamiliar word.

Preparación
Lee la invitación. ¿De qué crees que van a hablar Rosa y Josefina?

Ahora escucha

Josefina y Rosa
Ahora escucha la conversación entre Josefina y Rosa. Cuando oigas una de las palabras de la columna A, usa el contexto para identificar el sinónimo o la definición en la columna B.

A	B
_d_ 1. festejar	a. conmemoración religiosa de una muerte
_c_ 2. dicha	b. tolera
_h_ 3. bien parecido	c. suerte
_g_ 4. finge (fingir)	d. celebrar
_b_ 5. soporta (soportar)	e. me divertí
_e_ 6. yo lo disfruté (disfrutar)	f. horror
	g. crea una ficción
	h. guapo

Margarita Robles de García
y Roberto García Olmos

Piden su presencia en la celebración
del décimo aniversario de bodas
el día 13 de marzo
con una misa en la Iglesia Virgen del Coromoto
a las 6:30

seguida por cena y baile
en el restaurante El Campanero,
Calle Principal, Las Mercedes
a las 8:30

Comprensión

¿Cierto o falso?
Lee cada oración e indica si lo que dice es **cierto** o **falso**. Corrige las oraciones falsas.

1. No invitaron a mucha gente a la fiesta de Margarita y Roberto porque ellos no conocen a muchas personas.
   Falso. Fueron muchos invitados.

2. Algunos fueron a la fiesta con pareja y otros fueron sin compañero/a. Cierto.

3. Margarita y Roberto decidieron celebrar el décimo aniversario porque no hicieron una fiesta el día de su boda. Falso. Celebraron el décimo aniversario porque les gustan las fiestas.

4. Rafael les parece interesante a Rosa y a Josefina. Cierto.

5. Josefina se divirtió mucho en la fiesta porque bailó toda la noche con Rafael. Falso. Josefina se divirtió mucho, pero bailó con otros, no con Rafael.

Preguntas
Responde a estas preguntas con oraciones completas.
Answers will vary.

1. ¿Son solteras Rosa y Josefina? ¿Cómo lo sabes?

2. ¿Tienen las chicas una amistad de mucho tiempo con la pareja que celebra su aniversario? ¿Cómo lo sabes?

Section Goals
In **Escuchar**, students will:
• use context to infer meaning of unfamiliar words
• answer questions based on a recorded conversation

Instructional Resources
Supersite: Audio (Textbook MP3s); Resources (Scripts)

Estrategia
Script Hoy mi sobrino Gabriel cumplió seis años. Antes de la fiesta, ayudé a mi hermana a decorar la sala con globos de todos los colores, pero ¡qué bulla después!, cuando los niños se pusieron a estallarlos todos. El pastel de cumpleaños estaba riquísimo, y cuando Gabriel sopló las velas, apagó las seis. Los otros niños le regalaron un montón de juguetes, y nos divertimos mucho.

Teaching Tip
Have students read the invitation and guess what **Rosa** and **Josefina** will be talking about in the audio.

Ahora escucha
Script JOSEFINA: Rosa, ¿te divertiste anoche en la fiesta?
ROSA: Sí, me divertí más en el aniversario que en la boda. ¡La fiesta estuvo fenomenal! Fue buena idea festejar el aniversario en un restaurante. Así todos pudieron relajarse.
J: En parte, yo lo disfruté porque son una pareja tan linda; qué dicha que estén tan enamorados después de diez años de matrimonio. Me gustaría tener una relación como la de ellos. Y también saberlo celebrar con tanta alegría. ¡Pero qué cantidad de comida y bebida!
R: Es verdad que Margarita y Roberto exageran un poco con sus fiestas, pero son de la clase de gente que le gusta celebrar los eventos de la vida. Y como tienen tantas amistades y dos familias tan grandes...
J: Oye, Rosa, hablando de

(Script continues at far left in the bottom panels.)

---

familia, ¿llegaste a conocer al cuñado de Magali? Es soltero, ¿no? Quise bailar con él, pero no me sacó a bailar. R: Hablas de Rafael. Es muy bien parecido; ¡ese pelo...! Estuve hablando con él después del brindis. Me dijo que no le gusta ni el champán ni el vino; él finge tomar cuando

brindan porque no lo soporta. No te sacó a bailar porque él y Susana estaban juntos en la fiesta.
J: De todos modos, aun sin Rafael, bailé toda la noche.
Lo pasé muy, pero muy bien.

Section Goals

In **En pantalla**, students will:
- read about **las Fiestas Patrias** in Chile
- watch a television commercial about **las Fiestas Patrias** and other celebrations in Chile

Instructional Resources
Supersite: Video (**En pantalla**); Resources (Scripts, Translations)

Introduction To check comprehension, have students indicate whether these statements are **cierto** or **falso** and correct the false statements. **1. Durante las Fiestas Patrias todos los niños tienen que ir a la escuela. (Falso. Durante las Fiestas Patrias se cierran casi todas las escuelas.) 2. La cueca es un plato tradicional de Chile. (Falso. Es el baile nacional de Chile.) 3. Los chilenos vuelan volantines durante las Fiestas Patrias. (Cierto.)**

Antes de ver
- Have students look at the video stills, read the captions, and predict what is being celebrated in each visual.
- Read through the **Vocabulario útil** with students and model the pronunciation.

Preparación Have students tell the class about their favorite holiday.

Seleccionar
- For items 1–3, have students name a holiday that they associate with the three related words.
- Have students write a sentence using each of the words that doesn't belong.

Fiesta
←👤→ Have students imagine that one of their friends is timid and reluctant to come to the party. Ask them to write a dialogue in which they try to convince their friend to come.

En pantalla Video

Desfiles°, música, asados°, fuegos artificiales° y baile son los elementos de una buena fiesta. ¿Celebrar durante toda una semana? ¡Eso sí que es una fiesta espectacular! El 18 de septiembre Chile conmemora su independencia de España y los chilenos demuestran su orgullo° nacional durante una semana llena de celebraciones. Durante las Fiestas Patrias° casi todas las oficinas° y escuelas se cierran para que la gente se reúna° a festejar. Desfiles y rodeos representan la tradición de los vaqueros° del país, y la gente baila cueca, el baile nacional. Otra de las tradiciones de estas fiestas es hacer volar cometas°, llamadas volantines.

Vocabulario útil

conejo	bunny
disfraces	costumes
mariscal	traditional Chilean soup with raw seafood
sustos	frights
vieja (Chi.)	mother

Preparación

¿Cuál es tu día de fiesta favorito?
¿Cómo lo celebras?

🔁 Seleccionar

Selecciona la palabra que no está relacionada con cada grupo.
1. disfraces • noviembre • arbolito • sustos   arbolito
2. volantines • arbolito • regalos • diciembre   volantines
3. conejo • enero • huevitos • chocolates   enero
4. septiembre • volantines • disfraces • asado   disfraces

👥 Fiesta

Trabajen en grupos de tres. Imaginen que van a organizar una fiesta para celebrar el 4 de julio. Escriban una invitación electrónica para invitar a sus parientes y amigos a la fiesta. Describan los planes que tienen para la fiesta y díganles a sus amigos qué tiene que traer cada uno.   Answers will vary.

Desfiles/Paradas *Parades* asados *barbecues* fuegos artificiales *fireworks* orgullo *pride* Fiestas Patrias *Independence Day celebrations* oficinas *offices* se reúna *would get together* vaqueros *cowboys* cometas/volantines *kites*

Fiestas patrias: Chilevisión

Noviembre: disfraces, dulces...

Mayo: besito, tarjeta, tecito con la mamá...

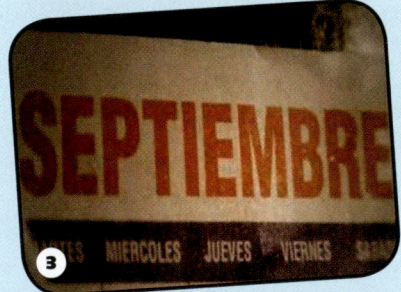

Septiembre... Septiembre: familia, parada militar...

 communication cultures NATIONAL STANDARDS

More activities

vhlcentral   Online activities

TEACHING OPTIONS

Small Groups ←👤→ Have small groups create a commercial similar to the one for **Chilevisión**, but that includes other important holidays. Allow groups to choose any Spanish-speaking country they want, including the U.S. and Canada. Have groups bring in visuals to represent each celebration and hold up the visuals as they read the script aloud for the class. Each group member should read a portion of the script.

Heritage Speakers 👤↔👤 If heritage speakers have attended parties for young people in a Spanish-speaking country (such as a **miniteca** in Colombia), have them describe certain aspects of the party. Is it common to bring food or drink to a friend's party? Are parties more or less formal than in the U.S.? Do people dance or just listen to music? Have the rest of the class compare and contrast these customs with their own.

Video

El Día de los Reyes Magos* es una celebración muy popular en muchos países hispanos. No sólo es el día en que los reyes les traen regalos a los niños, también es una fiesta llena° de tradiciones. La tarde del 5 de enero, en muchas ciudades como Barcelona, España, se hace un desfile° en que los reyes regalan dulces a los niños y reciben sus cartas con peticiones. Esa noche, antes de irse a dormir, los niños deben dejar un zapato junto a la ventana y un bocado° para los reyes. En Puerto Rico, por ejemplo, los niños ponen una caja con hierba° bajo su cama para alimentar a los camellos° de los reyes.

Vocabulario útil

los cabezudos	*carnival figures with large heads*
los carteles	*posters*
fiesta de pueblo	*popular celebration*
santos de palo	*wooden saints*

Preparación

¿Se celebra la Navidad en tu país? ¿Qué otras fiestas importantes se celebran? ¿Cuánto tiempo duran? ¿Cuáles son las tradiciones y actividades típicas?

Answers will vary.

¿Cierto o falso?

Indica si cada oración es **cierta** o **falsa**.

1. En Puerto Rico se celebra la Navidad hasta febrero. Falso.
2. San Sebastián fue un soldado romano que ayudó a los cristianos. Cierto.
3. Los cabezudos son unas máscaras que vienen de las fiestas españolas. Cierto.
4. Diego Palacio compra un helado de chocolate. Falso.
5. El güiro y el pandero son comidas puertorriqueñas. Falso.

* *According to the Christian tradition, the Three Wise Men were the three kings that traveled to Bethlehem after the birth of Baby Jesus, carrying with them gifts of gold, frankincense, and myrrh to pay him homage.*

llena *full* desfile *parade* bocado *snack* hierba *grass* alimentar los camellos *feed the camels*

Las fiestas

Los cabezudos son una tradición [...] de España.

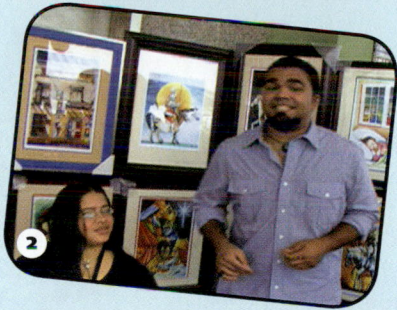
Hay mucha gente y mucho arte.

Es una fiesta de pueblo... una tradición. Vengo todos los años.

More activities
vhlcentral   VM pp. 53–54   Online activities

Chile

NATIONAL connections cultures STANDARDS

El país en cifras

▶ **Área:** 756.950 km² (292.259 millas²), *dos veces el área de Montana*
▶ **Población:** 17.789.000 *Aproximadamente el 85 por ciento de la población del país es urbana.*
▶ **Capital:** Santiago de Chile—6.507.000
▶ **Ciudades principales:** Valparaíso—907.000, Concepción, Viña del Mar, Temuco
▶ **Moneda:** peso chileno
▶ **Idiomas:** español (oficial), mapuche

Bandera de Chile

Chilenos célebres
▶ **Bernardo O'Higgins,** militar° y héroe nacional (1778–1842)
▶ **Gabriela Mistral,** Premio Nobel de Literatura, 1945; poeta y diplomática (1889–1957)
▶ **Pablo Neruda,** Premio Nobel de Literatura, 1971; poeta (1904–1973)
▶ **Isabel Allende,** novelista (1942–)
▶ **Javiera Mena,** cantante (1983–)

Pablo Neruda

militar *soldier*

PERÚ

Pampa del Tamarugal

El puerto de Valparaíso

La costa de Viña del Mar

BOLIVIA

Edificio antiguo en Santiago

Cordillera de los Andes

Océano Pacífico

Viña del Mar
Valparaíso

Santiago de Chile

ARGENTINA

Concepción

Temuco

Torres del Paine

Una celebración en Temuco

Lago Buenos Aires

Océano Atlántico

Punta Arenas

Estrecho de Magallanes

Isla Grande de Tierra del Fuego

More activities
vhlcentral | WB pp. 105–106 | Online activities

ACTIVIDADES

1 ¿Cierto o falso? Indica si lo que dicen las oraciones es **cierto** o **falso.**

1. Valparaíso es la capital de Chile. Falso
2. Isabel Allende nació en el año 1942. Cierto
3. Javiera Mena canta. Cierto
4. Le dieron el Premio Nobel de Literatura a Pablo Neruda en 1945. Falso
5. Viña del Mar es un día de fiesta en Chile. Falso
6. Los exploradores holandeses llegaron a la isla de Pascua por primera vez el día de Pascua de 1722. Cierto
7. No puedes esquiar en el Parque Nacional Villarrica. Falso
8. Todos los observatorios de Chile son viejos. Falso
9. Los vinos de Aconcagua y del valle del Maipo son los más conocidos. Cierto
10. Atacama, en el norte de Chile, es el desierto más seco del mundo. Cierto

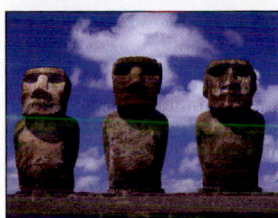

▶ Lugares • La isla de Pascua

La isla de Pascua° recibió ese nombre porque los exploradores holandeses° llegaron a la isla por primera vez el día de Pascua de 1722. Ahora es parte del territorio de Chile. La isla de Pascua es famosa por los *moái*, estatuas enormes que representan personas con rasgos° muy exagerados. Los *rapa nui*, antiguos habitantes de la zona, construyeron estas estatuas. Todavía no se sabe mucho sobre los *rapa nui*, ni tampoco se sabe por qué decidieron abandonar la isla.

▶ Deportes • Los deportes de invierno

Hay muchos lugares para practicar deportes de invierno en Chile porque las montañas nevadas de los Andes ocupan gran parte del país. El Parque Nacional Villarrica, por ejemplo, situado al pie de un volcán y junto a° un lago, es un sitio popular para el esquí y el *snowboard*. Para los que prefieren deportes más extremos, el centro de esquí Valle Nevado organiza excursiones para practicar heliesquí.

Ciencias • Astronomía

Los observatorios chilenos, situados en los Andes, son lugares excelentes para las observaciones astronómicas. Científicos° de todo el mundo van a Chile para estudiar las estrellas° y otros cuerpos celestes. Hoy día, Chile está construyendo nuevos observatorios y telescopios para mejorar las imágenes del universo.

Economía • El vino

La producción de vino comenzó en Chile en el siglo° XVI. Ahora la industria del vino constituye una parte importante de la actividad agrícola del país y la exportación de sus productos está aumentando° cada vez más. Los vinos chilenos son muy apreciados internacionalmente por su gran variedad, sus ricos y complejos sabores° y su precio moderado. Los más conocidos son los vinos de Aconcagua y del valle del Maipo.

isla de Pascua *Easter Island*   holandeses *Dutch*   rasgos *features*   junto a *beside*   Científicos *Scientists*   estrellas *stars*   siglo *century*   aumentando *increasing*   complejos sabores *complex flavors*

¡Increíble pero cierto!

El desierto° de Atacama, en el norte de Chile, es el más seco° del mundo°. Con más de cien mil km² de superficie, algunas zonas de este desierto nunca han tenido° lluvia. Atacama ha sido usado° como escenario para representar a Marte° en películas y series de televisión.

desierto *desert*   el más seco *the driest*   mundo *world*   han tenido *have had*   ha sido usado *has been used*   Marte *Mars*

---

 2 ¿Qué aprendiste? Contesta las preguntas.

1. ¿Qué porcentaje de la población chilena es urbana?
   el 85 por ciento
2. ¿Qué son los *moái*? ¿Dónde están?
   estatuas enormes en la isla de Pascua
3. ¿Qué deporte extremo ofrece el centro de esquí Valle Nevado?
   heliesquí
4. ¿Por qué van a Chile científicos de todo el mundo? los observatorios son excelentes para las observaciones astronómicas
5. ¿Por qué son apreciados los vinos chilenos? por su variedad, sus ricos y complejos sabores y su precio moderado

3 Preguntas En parejas, túrnense para hacer preguntas sobre Chile con las palabras interrogativas qué y cuál.

 modelo

Estudiante 1: ¿Cuál es la capital de Chile?
Estudiante 2: La capital de Chile es Santiago.

TEACHING OPTIONS

Worth Noting The native Mapuche people of southern Chile are a small minority of the Chilean population today, but have maintained a strong cultural identity since the time of their first contact with Europeans. In fact, they resisted conquest so well that it was only in the late nineteenth century that the government of Chile could assert sovereignty over the region south of the Bío-Bío River. However, the majority of Chileans are of European descent. Chilean Spanish is much less infused with indigenous lexical items than the Spanish of countries such as Guatemala and Mexico, where the larger indigenous population has made a greater impact on the language.

La isla de Pascua With its vibrant Polynesian culture, Easter Island is unlike anywhere else in Chile. Located 2,000 miles from the nearest island and 4,000 from the Chilean coast, it is one of the most isolated places on Earth. Until the 1960s, it was visited once a year by a Chilean warship bringing supplies. Now there are regular air connections to Santiago. You may want to play the **Panorama cultural** video for this paragraph.

Los deportes de invierno Remind students that some of the highest mountains in South America lie along the border Chile shares with Argentina. In the south is the **Parque Nacional Torres del Paine**, a national park featuring ice caverns, deep glacial trenches, and other spectacular features. You may want to play the **Panorama cultural** video for this paragraph.

Astronomía In 1962, the Cerro Tololo Inter-American Observatory was founded as a joint project between Chilean and U.S. astronomers. Since that time, so many other major telescopes have been installed for research purposes that Chile is home to the highest concentration of telescopes in the world.

El vino ←🚶→ Invite students to research the wine-growing regions of Chile and to compare them to those of California, Spain, or other wine-producing areas. Encourage students to share their findings with the class.

¡Increíble pero cierto! The Atacama Desert covers the northern third of the country. It is considered one of the best places in the world for astronomical observations, due to its high altitude, absence of cloud cover, dry air, and lack of light pollution and radio interference.

Teaching Tip You may want to assign the **Prueba de práctica**, with its diagnostics and review activities, in the online-only **Repaso** section on the Supersite. There is also a **Repaso oral** in this section. For the Sixth Edition, a new summative vocabulary activity with speech recognition has been added to the **Repaso** section.

Las celebraciones

el aniversario (de bodas)	(wedding) anniversary
la boda	wedding
el cumpleaños	birthday
el día de fiesta	holiday
la fiesta	party
el/la invitado/a	guest
la Navidad	Christmas
la quinceañera	young woman celebrating her fifteenth birthday
la sorpresa	surprise
brindar	to toast (drink)
celebrar	to celebrate
divertirse (e:ie)	to have fun
invitar	to invite
pasarlo bien/mal	to have a good/bad time
regalar	to give (a gift)
reírse (e:i)	to laugh
relajarse	to relax
sonreír (e:i)	to smile
sorprender	to surprise

Los postres y otras comidas

la botella (de vino)	bottle (of wine)
el champán	champagne
los dulces	sweets; candy
el flan (de caramelo)	baked (caramel) custard
la galleta	cookie
el helado	ice cream
el pastel (de chocolate)	(chocolate) cake; pie
el postre	dessert

Las relaciones personales

la amistad	friendship
el amor	love
el divorcio	divorce
el estado civil	marital status
el matrimonio	marriage
la pareja	(married) couple; partner
el/la recién casado/a	newlywed
casarse (con)	to get married (to)
comprometerse (con)	to get engaged (to)
divorciarse (de)	to get divorced (from)
enamorarse (de)	to fall in love (with)
llevarse bien/mal (con)	to get along well/ badly (with)
odiar	to hate
romper (con)	to break up (with)
salir (con)	to go out (with); to date
separarse (de)	to separate (from)
tener una cita	to have a date; to have an appointment
casado/a	married
divorciado/a	divorced
juntos/as	together
separado/a	separated
soltero/a	single
viudo/a	widower/widow

Las etapas de la vida

la adolescencia	adolescence
la edad	age
las etapas de la vida	the stages of life
la juventud	youth
la madurez	maturity; middle age
la muerte	death
el nacimiento	birth
la niñez	childhood
la vejez	old age
cambiar (de)	to change
graduarse (de/en)	to graduate (from/in)
jubilarse	to retire (from work)
nacer	to be born

Palabras adicionales

la alegría	happiness
el beso	kiss
conmigo	with me
contigo	with you
¡Felicidades!/ ¡Felicitaciones!	Congratulations!
¡Feliz cumpleaños!	Happy birthday!

Expresiones útiles	See page 305.

More activities

vhlcentral   LM p. 54

En el consultorio 10

Lesson Goals

In **Lección 10**, students will be introduced to the following:

- names of parts of the body
- health-related terms
- medical-related vocabulary
- health services in Spanish-speaking countries
- healers and shamans
- the imperfect tense
- uses of the preterite and imperfect tenses
- impersonal **se** constructions
- using **se** for unplanned events
- forming adverbs using [*adjective*] + –**mente**
- common adverbs and adverbial expressions
- activating background knowledge
- mastering the simple past tenses
- writing about an illness or accident
- listening for specific information
- a public service ad for the **Asociación Parkinson Alicante**
- a video about hospitals in Argentina
- cultural, geographic, and economic information about Costa Rica

A primera vista Ask these additional questions: ¿Cuándo fue la última vez que viste a tu médico/a? ¿Estuviste en su consultorio la semana pasada? ¿Cuáles son las mejores comidas para sentirte bien?

Teaching Tip Look for these icons for additional communicative practice:

→👤👤	Interpretive communication
👤👤→	Presentational communication
👤↔👤	Interpersonal communication

🔊 A PRIMERA VISTA

- ¿Están en una farmacia o en un hospital?
- ¿La mujer es médica o dentista?
- ¿Qué hace ella, una operación o un examen médico?
- ¿En qué etapa de la vida está la paciente?

INSTRUCTIONAL RESOURCES

Supersite (vhlcentral.com)
Video: *Fotonovela, Flash cultura, En pantalla, Panorama cultural*
Audio: Textbook and Lab MP3 Files

Activity Pack: Information Gap Activities, games, additional activity handouts
Resources: SAM Answer Key, Scripts, Translations, **Vocabulario adicional**, sample lesson plan, Grammar Presentation Slides, Digital Image Bank

Testing Program: Quizzes, Tests, Exams, MP3s
Student Activities Manual: Workbook/Video Manual/Lab Manual
WebSAM (online Student Activities Manual)

Section Goals

In **Contextos**, students will learn and practice:
• names of parts of the body
• vocabulary for talking about illnesses and accidents
• vocabulary associated with medical visits

Instructional Resources
Supersite: Audio (Textbook and Lab MP3 Files); Resources (Digital Image Bank, **Vocabulario adicional**, Activity Pack, Scripts, Answer Keys); Testing Program (Quizzes)
WebSAM
Workbook
Lab Manual

Teaching Tips

• →👤← Pretend to have had an accident-filled day. Ex: **Ayer pasé un día horrible. Fui a pasear en bicicleta y me caí. Me lastimé las rodillas y los brazos. Luego, cuando llegué a casa, me di con la puerta y me lastimé el ojo. Esta mañana cerré la puerta del auto y me lastimé el dedo.** Then ask comprehension questions about what hurts. Ex: **¿Me duele la garganta? (No.)** Finally, ask students about likely treatment options.

• Use the **Lección 10 Contextos** digital images to assist with this presentation.

• 👥 Have students refer to the scene and the vocabulary boxes as you give yes/no statements about the new vocabulary. Ex: **¿Sí o no? La enfermera le toma la temperatura a la paciente. (Sí.) La doctora le pone una inyección al hombre. (No.)** Then ask volunteers to describe what is going on in the scene, using as much of the new vocabulary as possible.

En el consultorio

Más vocabulario

la clínica	clinic
el consultorio	doctor's office
el/la dentista	dentist
el examen médico	physical exam
la farmacia	pharmacy
el hospital	hospital
la operación	operation
la sala de emergencia(s)	emergency room
el cuerpo	body
el oído	(sense of) hearing; inner ear
el accidente	accident
la salud	health
el síntoma	symptom
caerse	to fall (down)
darse con	to bump into; to run into
doler (o:ue)	to hurt
enfermarse	to get sick
estar enfermo/a	to be sick
lastimarse (el pie)	to injure (one's foot)
poner una inyección	to give an injection
recetar	to prescribe
romperse (la pierna)	to break (one's leg)
sacar(se) un diente	to have a tooth removed
sufrir una enfermedad	to suffer an illness
torcerse (o:ue) (el tobillo)	to sprain (one's ankle)
toser	to cough

Variación léxica

gripe	←→	gripa (*Col., Gua., Méx.*)
resfriado	←→	catarro (*Cuba, Esp., Gua.*)
sala de emergencia(s)	←→	sala de urgencias (*Arg., Col., Esp., Méx.*)
romperse	←→	quebrarse (*Arg., Gua.*)

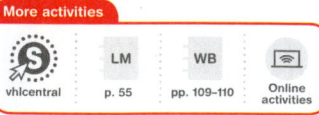

More activities

| S vhlcentral | LM p. 55 | WB pp. 109–110 | Online activities |

Labels on illustration: la doctora, el paciente, la cabeza, el ojo, la nariz, la oreja, el cuello, la boca, la garganta, el estómago, la rodilla, el corazón, el dedo, el dedo del pie

La medicina

el antibiótico	antibiotic
la aspirina	aspirin
el medicamento	medication
la pastilla	pill
la receta	prescription

TEACHING OPTIONS

TPR Play a game of **Simón dice**. Write **toquen** on the board and explain that it means *touch*. Start by saying: **Simón dice… que toquen la nariz.** Students are to touch their noses and keep their hands there until instructed to do otherwise. Work through various parts of the body. Be sure to give instructions occasionally without saying **Simón dice…**

Variación léxica Point out differences in health-related vocabulary, as well as some false cognates. **Embarazada** means *pregnant*, not *embarrassed*. You may also want to present **constipado/a** and explain that it does not mean *constipated*, but rather *congested* or *stuffed up*. Point out that, whereas in English people have ten fingers and ten toes, in Spanish people have twenty **dedos: diez dedos de las manos y diez de los pies**.

Práctica

la radiografía

el hueso

la enfermera

Toma la temperatura.

la paciente

el brazo

Estornuda.

la pierna

el tobillo

Síntomas y condiciones médicas

el dolor (de cabeza)	(head)ache; pain
la gripe	flu
la infección	infection
el resfriado	cold
la tos	cough
congestionado/a	congested
embarazada	pregnant
grave	grave; serious
mareado/a	dizzy; nauseated
médico/a	medical
saludable	healthy
sano/a	healthy
ser alérgico/a (a)	to be allergic (to)
tener dolor (m.)	to have pain
tener fiebre (f.)	to have a fever

---

1 **Escuchar** Escucha las preguntas y selecciona la respuesta más adecuada.

- a. Debes ir a la farmacia.
- b. No fui a la clase porque estaba (*I was*) enfermo.
- c. Me caí la semana pasada jugando al tenis.
- d. Tengo dolor de cabeza y fiebre.
- e. Porque tengo gripe.
- f. Sí, tengo mucha tos por las noches.
- g. Lo llevaron directamente a la sala de emergencia.
- h. No sé. Todavía tienen que tomarme la temperatura.

1. __c__   3. __g__   5. __f__   7. __d__
2. __e__   4. __a__   6. __h__   8. __b__

---

2 **¿Cierto o falso?** Indica si las oraciones sobre la conversación que vas a escuchar son **ciertas** o **falsas**.

	Cierto	Falso
1. El doctor habla con su paciente por teléfono.	○	⊘
2. El doctor le receta pastillas a la paciente.	⊘	○
3. La paciente estornuda mucho.	○	⊘
4. El doctor piensa que la paciente tiene un resfriado.	⊘	○
5. La paciente tiene dolor de cabeza.	⊘	○
6. La enfermera le pone una inyección a la paciente.	○	⊘

---

3 **Completar** Completa las oraciones con una palabra de la misma familia de la palabra subrayada. Usa la forma correcta de cada palabra.

> **modelo**
> Si tienes buena <u>salud</u>, eres una persona __saludable__.

1. Cuando <u>oyes</u> algo, usas el __oído__.
2. ¿Vas al __consultorio__ para <u>consultar</u> al médico?
3. ¿Alguien __estornudó__? Creo que oí un <u>estornudo</u> (*sneeze*).
4. No puedo <u>arrodillarme</u> (*kneel down*) porque me lastimé la __rodilla__ en un accidente de coche.
5. Cuando te <u>enfermas</u>, te sientes __enfermo/a__ y necesitas ir al consultorio para ver a la __enfermera__.
6. Si te rompes un <u>diente</u>, vas al __dentista__.

---

4 **Contestar** Mira el dibujo y contesta las preguntas. *Answers will vary.*

1. ¿Qué hace la enfermera?
2. ¿Qué hay en la pared (*wall*)?
3. ¿Qué hace la doctora?
4. ¿Qué hace el paciente?
5. ¿A quién le duele la garganta?
6. ¿Qué tiene la paciente?

---

1 **Teaching Tip** Before playing the audio, have students read through the list of responses. Explain that not all the questions are directed at the same person.

1 **Script** 1. ¿Cuándo te caíste? 2. ¿Por qué vas al médico? 3. ¿Adónde llevaron a Juan después del accidente? 4. ¿Adónde debo ir para conseguir estas pastillas? 5. ¿Tienes mucha tos? 6. ¿Tienes fiebre? 7. ¿Cuáles son sus síntomas, señor? 8. Ayer no te vi en la clase de biología. ¿Por qué? *Textbook MP3s*

2 **Teaching Tip** Have students read the statements before listening to the conversation.

2 **Script** PACIENTE: Vengo porque me siento muy enferma. DOCTOR: ¿Cuáles son sus síntomas? PACIENTE: Me duele mucho la cabeza, estoy congestionada y toso mucho. DOCTOR: Parece un simple resfriado. Se va a poner bien con estas pastillas. PACIENTE: Muy bien, doctor. ¡Gracias por no ponerme una inyección! *Textbook MP3s*

3 **Teaching Tip** Have students identify the part of speech of each underlined word and each fill-in-the-blank answer.

3 **Expansion** Have students write two additional cloze sentences for a partner to complete.

4 **Teaching Tip** Have pairs play a memory game. Have them study the drawing for 30 seconds, then ask each other the questions.

5 Teaching Tip Point out that there are several parts of the body that may be associated with each activity. Encourage students to list as many as they can.

5 Expansion Do the activity in reverse. Name parts of the body and ask students to associate them with as many activities as they can.

6 Expansion

• Ask for a show of hands for those who fall into the different health levels based on point totals. Analyze the trends of the class—are your students healthy or unhealthy?

• ← Ask for volunteers from each of the three groups to explain whether they think the results of the survey are accurate or not. Ask them to give examples based on their own eating, exercise, and other health habits.

• You may want to have students brainstorm a few additional health-related questions and responses, and adjust the point totals accordingly. Ex: **¿Con qué frecuencia te lavas las manos? ¿Con qué frecuencia usas seda dental? ¿Tomas el sol sin bloqueador solar? ¿Comes comida rápida (McDonald's, etc.)? ¿Fumas cigarros? ¿Consumes mucha cafeína?**

Note: At this point you may want to present *Vocabulario adicional: Más vocabulario para el consultorio* from the Supersite.

---

5 Asociaciones Trabajen en parejas para identificar las partes del cuerpo que ustedes asocian con estas actividades. Answers will vary.

> **modelo**
> nadar
> **Estudiante 1:** Usamos los brazos para nadar.
> **Estudiante 2:** Usamos las piernas también.

1. hablar por teléfono
2. conducir
3. correr en el parque
4. escuchar música
5. ver una película
6. toser
7. llevar zapatos
8. comprar perfume
9. estudiar biología
10. comer pollo asado

> **AYUDA**
> Remember that in Spanish, parts of the body are usually referred to with an article and not a possessive adjective: **Me duelen los pies.** The indirect object pronoun **me** is used to express the concept of *my*.

6 Cuestionario Contesta el cuestionario seleccionando las respuestas que reflejen mejor tus experiencias. Suma (*Add*) los puntos de cada respuesta y anota el resultado. Después, con el resto de la clase, compara y analiza los resultados del cuestionario y comenta lo que dicen de la salud y de los hábitos de todo el grupo. Answers will vary.

¿Tienes buena salud?

27–30 puntos	Salud y hábitos excelentes
23–26 puntos	Salud y hábitos buenos
22 puntos o menos	Salud y hábitos problemáticos

1. ¿Con qué frecuencia te enfermas? (resfriados, gripe, etc.)
Cuatro veces por año o más. (1 punto)
Dos o tres veces por año. (2 puntos)
Casi nunca. (3 puntos)

2. ¿Con qué frecuencia tienes dolores de estómago o problemas digestivos?
Con mucha frecuencia. (1 punto)
A veces. (2 puntos)
Casi nunca. (3 puntos)

3. ¿Con qué frecuencia sufres de dolores de cabeza?
Frecuentemente. (1 punto)
A veces. (2 puntos)
Casi nunca. (3 puntos)

4. ¿Comes verduras y frutas?
No, casi nunca como verduras ni frutas. (1 punto)
Sí, a veces. (2 puntos)
Sí, todos los días. (3 puntos)

5. ¿Eres alérgico/a a algo?
Sí, a muchas cosas. (1 punto)
Sí, a algunas cosas. (2 puntos)
No. (3 puntos)

6. ¿Haces ejercicios aeróbicos?
No, casi nunca hago ejercicios aeróbicos. (1 punto)
Sí, a veces. (2 puntos)
Sí, con frecuencia. (3 puntos)

7. ¿Con qué frecuencia te haces un examen médico?
Nunca o casi nunca. (1 punto)
Cada dos años. (2 puntos)
Cada año y/o antes de empezar a practicar un deporte. (3 puntos)

8. ¿Con qué frecuencia vas al dentista?
Nunca voy al dentista. (1 punto)
Sólo cuando me duele un diente. (2 puntos)
Por lo menos una vez por año. (3 puntos)

9. ¿Qué comes normalmente por la mañana?
No como nada por la mañana. (1 punto)
Tomo una bebida dietética. (2 puntos)
Como cereal y fruta. (3 puntos)

10. ¿Con qué frecuencia te sientes mareado/a?
Frecuentemente. (1 punto)
A veces. (2 puntos)
Casi nunca. (3 puntos)

TEACHING OPTIONS

Small Groups On the board, write popular expressions related to parts of the body and guide students in guessing their meanings. Ex: **tomarle el pelo (a alguien), no tener pelos en la lengua, salvarse por un pelo, costar un ojo de la cara, no tener dos dedos de frente, ponerle los pelos de punta, hablar hasta por los codos**. In small groups, have students create a sentence about a famous person or classmate for each expression.

Ex: **El presidente no tiene pelos en la lengua.**
Game Play a modified version of **20 Preguntas**. Ask a volunteer to think of a part of the body. Other students get one chance each to ask a yes/no question until someone guesses the correct body part. Limit attempts to ten questions per item. Encourage students to guess by associating activities with various parts of the body.

Comunicación

7 ¿Qué les pasó? Trabajen en un grupo de dos o tres personas. Hablen de lo que les pasó y de cómo se sienten las personas. *Answers will vary.*

1. Pilar

2. Francisco

3. Adela

4. Félix

5. Cristina

6. Pedro

8 Un accidente Cuéntale a un(a) compañero/a de un accidente o una enfermedad que tuviste. Incluye información que conteste estas preguntas. *Answers will vary.*

✓ ¿Qué ocurrió?
✓ ¿Dónde ocurrió?
✓ ¿Cuándo ocurrió?
✓ ¿Cómo ocurrió?
✓ ¿Quién te ayudó y cómo?
✓ ¿Tuviste algún problema después del accidente o después de la enfermedad?
✓ ¿Cuánto tiempo tuviste el problema?

9 Crucigrama Tu profesor(a) les va a dar a ti y a un(a) compañero/a un crucigrama (*crossword*) incompleto. Tú tienes las palabras que necesita tu compañero/a y él/ella tiene las palabras que tú necesitas. Tienen que darse pistas para completarlo. No pueden decir la palabra necesaria; deben utilizar definiciones, ejemplos y frases. *Answers will vary.*

modelo
10 horizontal: La usamos para hablar.
14 vertical: Es el médico que examina los dientes.

Section Goals

In **Fotonovela**, students will:
• receive comprehensible input from free-flowing discourse
• learn functional phrases that preview lesson grammatical structures

Instructional Resources
Supersite: Video (*Fotonovela*); Resources (Scripts, Translations, Answer Keys)
WebSAM
Video Manual

Video Recap: Lección 9
Before doing this **Fotonovela** section, review the previous episode with these questions:
1. ¿Qué les enseñó a hacer la tía Ana María a Jimena y a Marissa? (Les enseñó a hacer mole.) 2. ¿Quiénes prepararon una sorpresa para llevar al cementerio? (El Sr. Díaz y Felipe la prepararon.) 3. ¿Qué postres hizo Jimena? (Ella hizo galletas y pastel.) 4. ¿Por quiénes brindaron Ana María, Roberto y Ramón? (Ellos brindaron por sus padres.)

Video Synopsis
While out with her friend **Elena**, Jimena's cold symptoms start bothering her. Despite taking **don Diego's** and **Elena's** home remedies, the cold symptoms persist. At her mother's insistence, **Jimena** goes to the doctor, who prescribes some medicine.

Teaching Tips
• Have students scan the **Fotonovela** for words and expressions related to illness, injury, and health care. Then have them predict what will happen in this episode.
• Review the predictions and ask a few questions to guide students in summarizing this episode.

¡Qué dolor!

Jimena no se siente bien y tiene que ir al doctor.

PERSONAJES ELENA JIMENA

 Video

ELENA ¿Cómo te sientes?

JIMENA Me duele un poco la garganta. Pero no tengo fiebre.

ELENA Creo que tienes un resfriado. Te voy a llevar a casa.

ELENA ¿Don Diego ya fue a la farmacia? ¿Cuánto tiempo hace que lo llamaste?

JIMENA Hace media hora. Ay, qué cosas, de niña apenas me enfermaba. No perdí ni un solo día de clases.

ELENA Yo tampoco.

ELENA Nunca tenía resfriados, pero me rompí el brazo dos veces. Mi hermana y yo estábamos paseando en bicicleta y casi me di con un señor que caminaba por la calle. Me caí y me rompí el brazo.

JIMENA ¿Qué es esto?

ELENA Es té de jengibre. Cuando me dolía el estómago, mi mamá siempre me hacía tomarlo. Se dice que es bueno para el dolor de estómago.

JIMENA Pero no me duele el estómago.

JIMENA Hola, don Diego. Gracias por venir.

DON DIEGO Fui a la farmacia. Aquí están las pastillas para el resfriado. Se debe tomar una cada seis horas con las comidas. Y no se deben tomar más de seis pastillas al día.

(*La Sra. Díaz llama a Jimena.*)

JIMENA Hola, mamá. Don Diego me trajo los medicamentos... ¿Al doctor? ¿Estás segura? Allá nos vemos. (*A Elena*) Mi mamá ya hizo una cita para mí con el Dr. Meléndez.

TEACHING OPTIONS

Video Tips General suggestions for using video clips in the classroom can be found in the front matter of this Instructor's Annotated Edition.
¡Qué dolor! ➜ Play the **¡Qué dolor!** episode and have students jot down key words that they hear. Then have them work in small groups to prepare a brief plot summary based on their lists of key words. Play the segment again and have students return to their groups to refine their summaries. Finally, discuss the plot of this episode with the entire class and correct any errors of fact or sequencing.
Extra Practice ➜ Photocopy the **Fotonovela** Videoscript (Supersite) and white out words related to injuries and illnesses in order to make a master for a cloze activity. Have students fill in the missing words as they watch the episode.

DON DIEGO
 SRA. DÍAZ
 DR. MELÉNDEZ

SRA. DÍAZ ¿Te pusiste un suéter anoche?

JIMENA No, mamá. Se me olvidó.

SRA. DÍAZ Doctor, esta jovencita salió anoche, se le olvidó ponerse un suéter y parece que le dio un resfriado.

DR. MELÉNDEZ Jimena, ¿cuáles son tus síntomas?

JIMENA Toso con frecuencia y me duele la garganta.

DR. MELÉNDEZ ¿Cuánto tiempo hace que tienes estos síntomas?

JIMENA Hace dos días que me duele la garganta.

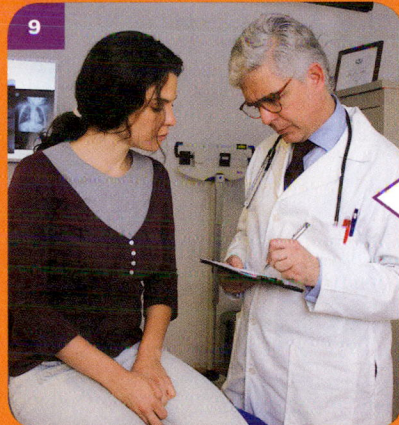

DR. MELÉNDEZ Muy bien. Aquí no tienes infección. No tienes fiebre. Te voy a mandar algo para la garganta. Puedes ir por los medicamentos inmediatamente a la farmacia.

SRA. DÍAZ Doctor, ¿cómo está? ¿Es grave?

DR. MELÉNDEZ No, no es nada grave. Jimena, la próxima vez, escucha a tu mamá. ¡Tienes que usar suéter!

More activities
vhlcentral | VM pp. 19–20 | Online activities

Expresiones útiles

Discussing medical conditions

¿Cómo te sientes?
How do you feel?
Me duele un poco la garganta.
My throat hurts a little.
No me duele el estómago.
My stomach doesn't hurt.
De niño/a apenas me enfermaba.
As a child, I rarely got sick.
¡Soy alérgico/a a chile!
I'm allergic to chili powder!

Discussing remedies

Se dice que el té de jengibre es bueno para el dolor de estómago.
They say ginger tea is good for stomachaches.
Aquí están las pastillas para el resfriado.
Here are the pills for your cold.
Se debe tomar una cada seis horas.
You should take one every six hours.

Expressions with hacer

Hace + [*period of time*] **que** + [*present/preterite*]
¿Cuánto tiempo hace que tienes estos síntomas?
How long have you had these symptoms?
Hace dos días que me duele la garganta.
My throat has been hurting for two days.
¿Cuánto tiempo hace que lo llamaste?
How long has it been since you called him?
Hace media hora.
It's been a half hour (since I called).

Additional vocabulary

canela *cinnamon*
miel *honey*
terco *stubborn*

Expresiones útiles Point out the phrase **apenas me enfermaba**. Explain that **apenas** is an adverb, and that **me enfermaba** is an imperfect tense form, used here to talk about habitual events in the past. Then draw attention to **Se dice que** and **Se debe tomar** and explain that these are examples of impersonal constructions with **se**. Finally, point out **Se me olvidó** and **se le olvidó** under video still 7 and tell students that **se** is also used to describe unplanned or accidental events. Tell students that they will learn more about these concepts in **Estructura**.

Teaching Tip
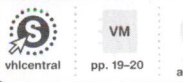 Ask students to read the **Fotonovela** captions in groups of five. Ask one or two groups to role-play the dialogue for the class.

Nota cultural In Celsius, normal body temperature is 37 degrees. If a temperature reading is above 37 but below 38, it is considered **febrícula**, or low-grade fever. Any temperature from 38 to 40 degrees Celsius is considered a fever (**fiebre**).

¿Qué pasó?

1 Expansion Give students these sentences as items 6–7:
6. Toma té de jengibre porque le duele el estómago. (Falso. No le duele el estómago.) 7. Tose con frecuencia. (Cierto.)

1 **¿Cierto o falso?** Decide si lo que dicen estas oraciones sobre Jimena es **cierto** o **falso**. Corrige las oraciones falsas.

		Cierto	Falso	
1.	Dice que de niña apenas se enfermaba.	◉	○	
2.	Tiene dolor de garganta y fiebre.	○	◉	Tiene dolor de garganta, pero no tiene fiebre.
3.	Olvidó ponerse un suéter anoche.	◉	○	
4.	Hace tres días que le duele la garganta.	○	◉	Hace dos días que le duele la garganta.
5.	El doctor le dice que tiene una infección.	○	◉	El doctor le dice que no tiene una infección.

2 Expansion Give students these sentences as items 7–8:
**7. Si quieres, ya puedes ir a la farmacia. (Dr. Meléndez)
8. Me duele la cabeza. (Elena)**

2 **Identificar** Identifica quién dice las oraciones equivalentes.

1. Como dice tu mamá, tienes que usar suéter. Dr. Meléndez
2. Por pasear en bicicleta me rompí el brazo dos veces. Elena
3. ¿Cuánto tiempo hace que toses y te duele la garganta? Dr. Meléndez
4. Tengo cita con el Dr. Meléndez. Jimena
5. Dicen que el té de jengibre es muy bueno para los dolores de estómago. Elena
6. Nunca perdí un día de clases porque apenas me enfermaba. Jimena

DR. MELÉNDEZ

ELENA

JIMENA

Nota cultural In the Dominican Republic, drinking **té de jengibre** is a Christmas tradition. It is made with fresh ginger root, cinnamon sticks, and sugar, and served hot.

3 **Ordenar** Pon estos sucesos en el orden correcto.

a. Jimena va a ver al doctor. __4__
b. El doctor le dice a la Sra. Díaz que no es nada serio. __6__
c. Elena le habla a Jimena de cuando se rompió el brazo. __2__
d. El doctor le receta medicamentos. __5__
e. Jimena le dice a Elena que le duele la garganta. __1__
f. Don Diego le trae a Jimena las pastillas para el resfriado. __3__

3 Teaching Tip ➔👤◄ Write each sentence from this activity on separate strips of paper and shuffle them. Divide the class into groups of three and distribute a set of sentences to each group; each student should receive two sentences. Have groups put the sentences in correct order and then return them to a group representative, who will read them aloud.

4 **En el consultorio** Trabajen en parejas para representar los papeles de un(a) médico/a y su paciente.

El/La médico/a	**El/La paciente**
Pregúntale al / a la paciente qué le pasó.	→ Dile que te caíste en casa. Describe tu dolor.
Pregúntale cuánto tiempo hace que se cayó.	→ Describe la situación. Piensas que te rompiste el dedo.
Mira el dedo. Debes recomendar un tratamiento (*treatment*) al / a la paciente.	→ Debes hacer preguntas al / a la médico/a sobre el tratamiento (*treatment*).

AYUDA
Here are some useful expressions:
¿Cómo se lastimó...?
¿Qué le pasó?
¿Cuánto tiempo hace que...?
Tengo...
Estoy...
¿Es usted alérgico/a a algún medicamento?
Usted debe...

4 Possible Conversation
E1: Buenos días. ¿Cómo se lastimó?
E2: Doctor, me caí en casa. Me duele mucho la mano.
E1: ¿Y cuánto tiempo hace que se cayó?
E2: Hace más de dos horas. Creo que me rompí el dedo.
E1: ¿Ah, sí? ¿Le duele mucho?
E2: Me duele muchísimo, doctor. Y estoy mareada.
E1: Bueno, le voy a sacar una radiografía primero.
E2: ¿Me rompí el dedo?
E1: No se preocupe. No se rompió el dedo. Como le duele mucho, le voy a recetar unas pastillas.
E2: Sí, doctor. Gracias.

TEACHING OPTIONS

Heritage Speakers ◄👤► Ask heritage speakers to prepare a poster about the health care system of their families' countries of origin or other Spanish-speaking countries they have visited. Have them present their posters to the class, and invite students to ask questions about the information.

Extra Practice Ask students questions about the **Fotonovela**. Ex: 1. ¿Quién fue a la farmacia para conseguirle unas pastillas a Jimena? (Don Diego fue a la farmacia.) 2. ¿Quién se rompió el mismo brazo dos veces? (Elena se lo rompió dos veces.) 3. ¿Por qué la mamá de Elena le daba té de jengibre? (Porque le dolía el estómago.) 4. ¿Cuáles son los síntomas de Jimena? (Tose mucho y le duele la garganta.)

Ortografía

S Tutorial

El acento y las sílabas fuertes

In Spanish, written accent marks are used on many words. Here is a review of some of the principles governing word stress and the use of written accents.

---

as-pi-ri-na   gri-pe   to-man   an-tes

In Spanish, when a word ends in a vowel, **-n**, or **-s**, the spoken stress usually falls on the next-to-last syllable. Words of this type are very common and do not need a written accent.

---

a-sí   in-glés   in-fec-ción   hé-ro-e

When a word ends in a vowel, **-n**, or **-s**, and the spoken stress does *not* fall on the next-to-last syllable, then a written accent is needed.

---

hos-pi-tal   na-riz   re-ce-tar   to-ser

When a word ends in any consonant *other* than **-n** or **-s**, the spoken stress usually falls on the last syllable. Words of this type are very common and do not need a written accent.

---

lá-piz   fút-bol   hués-ped   sué-ter

When a word ends in any consonant *other* than **-n** or **-s** and the spoken stress does *not* fall on the last syllable, then a written accent is needed.

---

far-ma-cia   bio-lo-gí-a   su-cio   frí-o

Diphthongs (two weak vowels or a strong and weak vowel together) are normally pronounced as a single syllable. A written accent is needed when a diphthong is broken into two syllables.

---

sol   pan   mar   tos

Spanish words of only one syllable do not usually carry a written accent (unless it is to distinguish meaning: **se** and **sé**).

CONSULTA

In Spanish, **a**, **e**, and **o** are considered strong vowels while **i** and **u** are weak vowels. To review this concept, see **Lección 3**, **Pronunciación**, p. 85.

Práctica Busca las palabras que necesitan acento escrito y escribe su forma correcta.

1. sal-mon   salmón
2. ins-pec-tor
3. nu-me-ro   número
4. fa-cil   fácil
5. ju-go
6. a-bri-go
7. ra-pi-do   rápido
8. sa-ba-do   sábado
9. vez
10. me-nu   menú
11. o-pe-ra-cion   operación
12. im-per-me-a-ble
13. a-de-mas   además
14. re-ga-te-ar
15. an-ti-pa-ti-co   antipático
16. far-ma-cia
17. es-qui   esquí
18. pen-sion   pensión
19. pa-is   país
20. per-don   perdón

El ahorcado Juega al ahorcado (*hangman*) para adivinar las palabras.

1. _ l _ _ _ _ _ a   Vas allí cuando estás enfermo.   clínica
2. _ _ _ _ e _ c _ _ _ n   Se usa para poner una vacuna (*vaccination*).   inyección
3. _ _ _ d _ o _ _ _ _ _ a   Permite ver los huesos.   radiografía
4. _ _ _ _ i _ o   Trabaja en un hospital.   médico
5. a _ _ _ b _ _ _ _ _ _ _   Es una medicina.   antibiótico

More activities

S vhlcentral   **LM** p. 56

Section Goals

In **Ortografía**, students will review:
- word stress
- the use of written accent marks

Instructional Resources
Supersite: Audio (Lab MP3 Files); Resources (Scripts, Answer Keys)
WebSAM
Lab Manual

Teaching Tips

- You may want to explain that all words in which the spoken stress falls on the antepenultimate or preantepenultimate syllable will carry a written accent, regardless of the word's final letter.
- As you go through each point in the explanation, write the example words on the board, pronounce them, and have students repeat. Then, ask students to provide words they learned in previous lessons that exemplify each point.
- Make a list of unfamiliar words on the board, leaving out any written accent marks. Pronounce them, and ask students if a written accent mark is needed, and if so, where it should be placed. Include words that carry a written accent mark as well as some that do not.
- Point out that **Ortografía** replaces **Pronunciación** in the Student Edition for **Lecciones 10–18**, but not in the Lab Manual. The box references the **Pronunciación** sections found in all lessons of the Lab Manual.

TEACHING OPTIONS

Extra Practice Add an auditory aspect to this **Ortografía** section. Have students close their books. Then read aloud the questions in **Actividad 6, Cuestionario,** page 334. Say each sentence twice slowly and once at normal speed to give students enough time to write. Then have them open their books and check their work.

Pairs Ask students to work in pairs and explain why each word in the **Práctica** activity does or does not have a written accent mark. The same process can be followed with the words in the **El ahorcado** activity.

Section Goals

In **Cultura**, students will:
- read about health services in Spanish-speaking countries
- learn health-related terms
- read about **curanderos** and **chamanes**
- read about home remedies and medicinal plants

Instructional Resource
Supersite

En detalle

Antes de leer Ask students about their experiences with health care while traveling. Ex: **¿Alguna vez te enfermaste durante un viaje? ¿Dónde? ¿Fuiste al hospital o al médico? ¿Quién lo pagó?**

Lectura
- Point out that many over-the-counter health care products in the U.S. are available by request at pharmacies in Spanish-speaking countries (e.g., facial cleansers, sunscreen, contact lens solution).
- Tell students that most pharmacies are closed on Sundays.
- While traditional pharmacies are privately owned and consist of a small counter and retail space, large chain pharmacies are entering the market, especially in Latin America.

Después de leer
- Ask students which three factors described in the article would be most important in devising an ideal health care system.

1 Expansion Give students these true/false statements as items 9–10: **9. El sistema de salud en Cuba no es muy desarrollado. (Falso. Es muy desarrollado.) 10. Las farmacias generalmente tienen un horario comercial. (Cierto.)**

EN DETALLE

Servicios de salud

¿Sabías que en los países hispanos no necesitas pagar por los servicios de salud? Ésta es una de las diferencias que hay entre países como los Estados Unidos y los países hispanos.

En la mayor parte de estos países, el gobierno ofrece servicios médicos muy baratos o gratuitos° a sus ciudadanos°. Los turistas y extranjeros también pueden tener acceso a los servicios médicos a bajo° costo. La Seguridad Social y organizaciones similares son las responsables de gestionar° estos servicios.

Naturalmente, esto no funciona igual° en todos los países. En Ecuador, México y Perú, la situación varía según las regiones. Los habitantes de las ciudades y pueblos grandes tienen acceso a más servicios médicos, mientras que quienes viven en pueblos remotos sólo cuentan con° pequeñas clínicas.

Por su parte, Costa Rica, Colombia, Cuba y España tienen sistemas de salud muy desarrollados°.

Cruz verde de farmacia en Madrid, España

En España, por ejemplo, la mayoría de la gente tiene acceso a ellos y en muchos casos son completamente gratuitos. Según un informe de la Organización Mundial de la Salud, el sistema de salud español ocupa uno de los primeros diez lugares del mundo. Esto se debe no sólo al buen funcionamiento° del sistema, sino también al nivel de salud general de la población. Impresionante, ¿no?

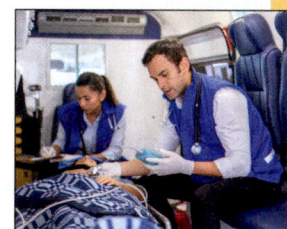

Paramédicos colombianos

Las farmacias

Farmacia de guardia: Las farmacias generalmente tienen un horario comercial. Sin embargo°, en cada barrio° hay una farmacia de guardia que abre las veinticuatro horas del día.

Productos farmacéuticos: Hay muchas farmacias tradicionales especializadas en medicinas y en productos farmacéuticos. No venden una gran variedad de productos.

Recetas: Muchos medicamentos se venden sin receta médica. Los farmacéuticos aconsejan° a las personas sobre problemas de salud y les dan las medicinas.

Cruz° verde: En muchos países, las farmacias tienen como símbolo una cruz verde. Cuando la cruz verde está encendida°, la farmacia está abierta.

gratuitos *free (of charge)* ciudadanos *citizens* bajo *low*
gestionar *to manage* igual *in the same way* cuentan con *have*
desarrollados *developed* funcionamiento *operation*
Sin embargo *However* barrio *neighborhood* aconsejan *advise*
Cruz *Cross* encendida *lit (up)*

ACTIVIDADES

1 ¿Cierto o falso? Indica si lo que dicen las oraciones es **cierto** o **falso**. Corrige la información falsa.

1. En los países hispanos los gobiernos ofrecen servicios de salud accesibles a sus ciudadanos. **Cierto.**

2. En los países hispanos los extranjeros tienen que pagar mucho dinero por los servicios médicos. **Falso.** Los extranjeros tienen acceso a los servicios médicos a bajo costo.

3. El sistema de salud español es uno de los mejores del mundo. **Cierto.**

4. Las farmacias de guardia abren sólo los sábados y domingos. **Falso.** Las farmacias de guardia abren las 24 horas del día.

5. En los países hispanos las farmacias venden una gran variedad de productos. **Falso.** En los países hispanos las farmacias están especializadas en medicinas y en productos farmacéuticos.

6. Los farmacéuticos de los países hispanos aconsejan a los enfermos y venden algunas medicinas sin necesidad de receta. **Cierto.**

7. En México y otros países, los pueblos remotos cuentan con grandes centros médicos. **Falso.** Cuentan con pequeñas clínicas.

8. Muchas farmacias usan una cruz verde como símbolo. **Cierto.**

TEACHING OPTIONS

Cultural Comparison ←👤→ Ask students to write a short paragraph in which they compare the health care systems in the U.S. or Canada with those of different Spanish-speaking countries. You may want to have students review comparisons (**Estructura 8.3**) before writing.

Pairs 👤↔👤 Ask pairs to write a dialogue in which a foreign tourist in Costa Rica goes to the emergency room due to an injury. Have them use vocabulary from **Contextos** and **Expresiones útiles**. Have students role-play their dialogues for the class.

ASÍ SE DICE

La salud

el chequeo (Esp., Méx.)	el examen médico
la droguería (Col.)	la farmacia
la herida	*injury; wound*
la píldora	la pastilla
los primeros auxilios	*first aid*
la sangre	*blood*

EL MUNDO HISPANO

Remedios caseros° y plantas medicinales

- **Achiote°** En Suramérica se usa para curar inflamaciones de garganta. Las hojas° de achiote se cuecen° en agua, se cuelan° y se hacen gárgaras° con esa agua.

- **Ají** En Perú se usan cataplasmas° de las semillas° de ají para aliviar los dolores reumáticos y la tortícolis°.

- **Azúcar** En Nicaragua y en otros países centroamericanos se usa el azúcar para detener° la sangre en pequeñas heridas.

- **Sábila (aloe vera)** En Latinoamérica, el jugo de las hojas de sábila se usa para reducir cicatrices°. Se recomienda aplicarlo sobre la cicatriz dos veces al día, durante varios meses.

Remedios caseros *Home remedies* Achiote *Annatto* hojas *leaves* se cuecen *are cooked* se cuelan *they are drained* gárgaras *gargles* cataplasmas *pastes* semillas *seeds* tortícolis *stiff neck* detener *to stop* cicatrices *scars*

PERFIL

Curanderos° y chamanes

¿Quieres ser doctor(a), juez(a)°, político/a o psicólogo/a? En algunas sociedades de las Américas **los curanderos** y **los chamanes** no tienen que escoger entre estas profesiones porque ellos son mediadores de conflictos y dan consejos a la comunidad. Su opinión es muy respetada.

Desde las culturas antiguas° de las Américas muchas personas piensan que la salud del cuerpo y de la mente sólo puede existir si hay un equilibrio entre el ser humano y la naturaleza. Los curanderos y los chamanes son quienes cuidan este equilibrio.

Códice Florentino, México, siglo XVI

Los curanderos se especializan más en enfermedades físicas, mientras que los chamanes están

Cuzco, Perú

más relacionados con los males° de la mente y el alma°. Ambos° usan plantas, masajes y rituales y sus conocimientos se basan en la tradición, la experiencia, la observación y la intuición.

Curanderos *Healers* juez(a) *judge* antiguas *ancient* males *illnesses* alma *soul* Ambos *Both*

CON RITMO HISPANO

Cocofunka (2008–)

Lugar de origen: San José, Costa Rica

Los miembros de Cocofunka son Javier Arce, Reynaldo Escobedo, Miguel Vega, Horacio París, Nacho Páez y Gustavo Gutiérrez. Sus canciones son una mezcla de rock, funk, reggae y diversos géneros latinos.

Go to **vhlcentral.com** to find out more about **Cocofunka**.

ACTIVIDADES

2 **Comprensión** Contesta las preguntas.

1. ¿Cómo se les llama a las farmacias en Colombia? droguerías
2. ¿Qué parte del achiote se usa para curar la garganta? las hojas
3. ¿Cómo se aplica la sábila para reducir cicatrices? Se aplica sobre la cicatriz dos veces al día.
4. En algunas partes de las Américas, ¿quiénes mantienen el equilibrio entre el ser humano y la naturaleza? los chamanes y curanderos
5. ¿Qué usan los curanderos y los chamanes para curar? Usan plantas, masajes y rituales.

3 **¿Qué haces cuando tienes gripe?** Escribe cuatro oraciones sobre las cosas que haces cuando tienes gripe. Explica si vas al médico, si tomas medicamentos o si sigues alguna dieta especial. Después, comparte tu texto con un(a) compañero/a. Answers will vary.

More activities
vhlcentral | Online activities

Así se dice
- You may want to point out that in Spain a **droguería** is not a pharmacy, but rather a shop selling cleaning and decorating materials, as well as cosmetics.
- To challenge students, add these health-related words to the list: **la espalda** (*back*); **la fractura** (*fracture*); **el hombro** (*shoulder*); **el jarabe** (*cough syrup*); **la lengua** (*tongue*); **la muñeca** (*wrist*); **sangrar** (*to bleed*); **tener escalofríos** (*to have chills*); **el vendaje** (*bandage*).

Perfil **Curanderos** sometimes experience discrimination in the medical field. However, recently, some medical doctors have grown to understand the beliefs of **los curanderos** and are working with them to help support their ceremonies and natural care while providing additional modern medical attention.

El mundo hispano
- Ask students: ¿**Conocen otros remedios caseros o naturales?**
- Ask heritage speakers to describe home remedies used in their families.

Con ritmo hispano Point out to students that they will find supporting activities and information at **vhlcentral.com**.

2 Expansion Give students these questions as items 6–8: 6. ¿**Para qué se usa el azúcar en Centroamérica?** (para detener la sangre) 7. ¿**Quiénes curan los males de la mente y el alma?** (los chamanes) 8. ¿**En qué se basan los conocimientos de los curanderos y de los chamanes?** (en la tradición, la experiencia, la observación y la intuición)

3 Teaching Tip As a variant, have students create a list of recommendations for a friend who has the flu. Ex: **Debes tomar sopa de pollo con verduras.**

TEACHING OPTIONS

TPR Divide the class into two teams, **remedios naturales** and **medicina moderna**, and have them stand at opposite sides of the room. Read a medical scenario aloud. The team whose name defines the situation most accurately has five seconds to step forward. Ex: **1. Juan sufre de dolores de cabeza. Hoy tiene una migraña. Decide comprar vitamina B2. (remedios naturales) 2. María tiene mucha ansiedad. Además siente estrés por su** trabajo. **Toma pastillas calmantes. (medicina moderna)**

Small Groups Have small groups create a television commercial for a new natural product. Encourage them to include a customer testimonial stating how long they have had these symptoms (**hace** + [*time period*] + **que** + [*present*]), when they started using the product (**hace** + [*time period*] + **que** + [*preterite*]), and how they feel now.

10.1 The imperfect tense Tutorial

ANTE TODO In **Lecciones 6–9,** you learned the preterite tense. You will now learn the imperfect, which describes past activities in a different way.

The imperfect of regular verbs

		cantar	**beber**	**escribir**
SINGULAR FORMS	yo	cant**aba**	beb**ía**	escrib**ía**
	tú	cant**abas**	beb**ías**	escrib**ías**
	Ud./él/ella	cant**aba**	beb**ía**	escrib**ía**
PLURAL FORMS	nosotros/as	cant**ábamos**	beb**íamos**	escrib**íamos**
	vosotros/as	cant**abais**	beb**íais**	escrib**íais**
	Uds./ellos/ellas	cant**aban**	beb**ían**	escrib**ían**

¡ATENCIÓN!

Note that the imperfect endings of **-er** and **-ir** verbs are the same. Also note that the **nosotros** form of **-ar** verbs always carries an accent mark on the first **a** of the ending. All forms of **-er** and **-ir** verbs in the imperfect carry an accent on the first **i** of the ending.

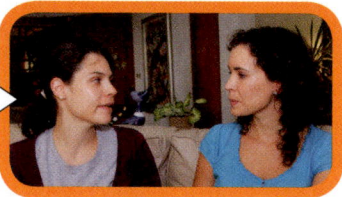

De niña apenas me enfermaba.

Cuando me dolía el estómago, mi mamá me daba té de jengibre.

▶ There are no stem changes in the imperfect.

entender (e:ie)	**Entendíamos** japonés.
	We used to understand Japanese.
servir (e:i)	El camarero les **servía** el café.
	The waiter was serving them coffee.
doler (o:ue)	A Javier le **dolía** el tobillo.
	Javier's ankle was hurting.

▶ The imperfect form of **hay** is **había** (*there was; there were; there used to be*).

▶ **¡Atención!** **Ir, ser,** and **ver** are the only verbs that are irregular in the imperfect.

AYUDA

Like **hay, había** can be followed by a singular or plural noun.
Había un solo médico en la sala.
Había dos pacientes allí.

The imperfect of irregular verbs

		ir	**ser**	**ver**
SINGULAR FORMS	yo	**iba**	**era**	**veía**
	tú	**ibas**	**eras**	**veías**
	Ud./él/ella	**iba**	**era**	**veía**
PLURAL FORMS	nosotros/as	**íbamos**	**éramos**	**veíamos**
	vosotros/as	**ibais**	**erais**	**veíais**
	Uds./ellos/ellas	**iban**	**eran**	**veían**

Section Goal

In **Estructura 10.1**, students will learn the imperfect tense.

Instructional Resources

Supersite: Audio (Lab MP3 Files); Resources (Grammar Presentation Slides, Activity Pack, Scripts, Answer Keys); Testing Program (Quizzes)
WebSAM
Workbook
Lab Manual

Teaching Tips

- Explain to students that they can already express the past with the preterite tense, and now they are learning the imperfect tense, which also expresses the past but in a different way.
- As you work through the discussion of the imperfect, test comprehension by asking volunteers to supply the correct form of verbs for the subjects you name. Ex: **romper/nosotros (rompíamos)**
- Point out that **había** is impersonal and can be followed by a singular or plural noun. Ex: **Había una enfermera. Había muchos pacientes.**

¡Atención! To demonstrate that the accents on **–er** and **–ir** verbs break diphthongs, write **farmacia** and **vendia** on the board. Ask volunteers to pronounce each word, and have the class identify which needs a written accent to break the diphthong (**vendía**).

TEACHING OPTIONS

Extra Practice To provide oral practice with the imperfect tense, change the subjects in **¡Inténtalo!** on page 343. Have students give the appropriate forms for each infinitive listed.
Large Groups Write a list of activities on the board.
Ex: **1. tenerle miedo a la oscuridad 2. ir a la escuela en autobús 3. llevar el almuerzo a la escuela 4. comer brócoli 5. ser atrevido/a en clase 6. creer en Santa Claus** Have students copy the list on a sheet of paper and check off the items that they used to do when they were in the second grade. Then have them circulate around the room and find other students that used to do the same activities. Ex: **¿Le tenías miedo a la oscuridad?** When they find a student who used to do the same activity, have them write that student's name next to the item. Then have students report back to the class. Ex: **Mark y yo creíamos en Santa Claus.**

CONSULTA

You will learn more about the contrast between the preterite and the imperfect in **Estructura 10.2**, pp. 346–347.

Uses of the imperfect

▶ As a general rule, the imperfect is used to describe actions that are seen by the speaker as incomplete or "continuing," while the preterite is used to describe actions that have been completed. The imperfect expresses what was happening at a certain time or how things used to be. The preterite, in contrast, expresses a completed action.

—¿Qué te **pasó**?
What happened to you?

—¿Dónde **vivías** de niño?
Where did you live as a child?

—Me **torcí** el tobillo.
I sprained my ankle.

—**Vivía** en San José.
I lived in San José.

▶ These expressions are often used with the imperfect because they express habitual or repeated actions: **de niño/a** (*as a child*), **todos los días** (*every day*), **mientras** (*while*).

Uses of the imperfect

1. Habitual or repeated actions . . . . **Íbamos** al parque los domingos.
We used to go to the park on Sundays.

2. Events or actions that were in progress — Yo **leía** mientras él **estudiaba**.
I was reading while he was studying.

3. Physical characteristics . . . . **Era** alto y guapo.
He was tall and handsome.

4. Mental or emotional states . . . . **Quería** mucho a su familia.
He loved his family very much.

5. Telling time . . . . **Eran** las tres y media.
It was 3:30.

6. Age . . . . Los niños **tenían** seis años.
The children were six years old.

More activities

vhlcentral

LM
p. 57

WB
pp. 111–112

Online activities

🔲 **¡INTÉNTALO!** Indica la forma correcta de cada verbo en el imperfecto.

1. Mis hermanos _____veían_____ (ver) televisión todas las tardes.
2. Yo _____viajaba_____ (viajar) en el tren de las 3:30.
3. ¿Dónde _____vivía_____ (vivir) Samuel de niño?
4. Leonardo y yo _____corríamos_____ (correr) por el parque.
5. Tú _____hablabas_____ (hablar) con Javier.
6. Ustedes _____iban_____ (ir) a la clínica.
7. Nadia _____bailaba_____ (bailar) merengue.
8. Yo _____era_____ (ser) muy feliz.
9. ¿Cuándo _____asistías_____ (asistir) tú a clase de español?
10. Nosotras _____comprendíamos_____ (comprender) las preguntas.

Teaching Tips

• Ask students to compare and contrast a home video with a snapshot in the family picture album. Then call their attention to the brief description of the uses of the imperfect. Which actions would be best captured by a home video? (Continuing actions; incomplete actions; what was happening; how things used to be.) Which actions are best captured in a snapshot? (A completed action.)

• Ask students to answer questions about themselves in the past. Ex: **Y tú, _____, ¿ibas al parque los domingos cuando eras niño/a? ¿Qué hacías mientras tu madre preparaba la comida? ¿Cómo eras de niño/a?**

• Ask questions about the **Fotonovela** characters using the imperfect. Ex: **De niña, ¿Jimena se enfermaba mucho o poco? (Se enfermaba poco.) ¿Elena tenía muchos resfriados? (No, no tenía muchos resfriados.) ¿Qué tomaban para los dolores de estómago en la casa de Elena? (Tomaban té de jengibre.) ¿Qué remedio para la garganta usaban en la casa de don Diego? (Usaban miel con canela.)**

Successful Language Learning Ask students to think about what they used to do when they were younger and imagine how to say it in Spanish. This is good practice for real-life conversations because people often talk about their childhood when making new friends.

TEACHING OPTIONS

Extra Practice Prepare a list of sentences in the present tense. Ex: **Todos los días jugamos al tenis.** Read each sentence twice, pausing to allow students to convert the present tense to the imperfect. Ex: **Todos los días jugábamos al tenis.**
Extra Practice ←🔲→ Ask students to write a description of their first-grade classroom and teacher, using the imperfect. Ex: **En la sala de clases había… La maestra se llamaba… Ella era…**

Have students share their descriptions with a classmate.
Large Groups Have the class stand and form a circle. Call out a name or subject pronoun and an infinitive (Ex: **ellas/ver**). Toss a ball to a student, who will say the correct imperfect form (Ex: **veían**). He or she should then name a new subject and infinitive and throw the ball to another student.

Práctica

1 Teaching Tips
• Before assigning the activity, review the forms of the imperfect by calling out an infinitive and a series of subject pronouns. Ask volunteers to give the corresponding forms. Ex: **querer: usted (quería); yo (quería); nosotras (queríamos).** Include irregular verbs.
• As a model, write these sentences on the board and have volunteers supply the verb forms and then reorder the sentences. **No ____ (dormir) bien. (dormía/1) ____ (ser) la una de la mañana cuando llamé al doctor. (Era/3) Me desperté a las once porque ____ (sentirse) mal. (me sentía/2)**

1 Expansion
←👤→ Have students write a conversation between **Miguelito** and his friends in which he relates what happened after the accident.

2 Expansion To challenge students, ask them to state the reason the imperfect is used in each sentence.

3 Expansion Write these sentences on the board, and have students work in pairs to complete them. **1. Fui al doctor porque ____. 2. Tuvo que ir al dentista porque ____. 3. El médico le dio unas pastillas porque ____. 4. La enfermera le tomó la temperatura porque ____.**

1 Completar Primero, completa las oraciones con el imperfecto de los verbos. Luego, pon las oraciones en orden lógico y compáralas con las de un(a) compañero/a.

a. Miguelito ___tenía___ (tener) la nariz hinchada (*swollen*). Fueron al hospital. __4__
b. El doctor ___quería___ (querer) ver la nariz del niño. __6__
c. Su mamá ___estaba___ (estar) dibujando cuando Miguelito entró llorando. __3__
d. Miguelito no ___iba___ (ir) a jugar más. Ahora quería ir a casa a descansar. __8__
e. El doctor dijo que no ___era___ (ser) nada grave. __7__
f. Miguelito y sus amigos ___jugaban___ (jugar) al béisbol en el patio. __2__
g. ___Eran___ (ser) las dos de la tarde. __1__
h. Miguelito le dijo a la enfermera que ___le dolía___ (dolerle) la nariz. __5__

2 Transformar Forma oraciones completas para describir lo que hacían Julieta y César. Usa las formas correctas del imperfecto y añade todas las palabras necesarias.

1. Julieta y César / ser / paramédicos
   Julieta y César eran paramédicos.
2. trabajar / juntos y / llevarse / muy bien
   Trabajaban juntos y se llevaban muy bien.
3. cuando / haber / accidente, / siempre / analizar / situación / con cuidado
   Cuando había un accidente, siempre analizaban la situación con cuidado.
4. preocuparse / mucho / por / pacientes
   Se preocupaban mucho por los pacientes.
5. si / paciente / tener / mucho / dolor, / ponerle / inyección
   Si el paciente tenía mucho dolor, le ponían una inyección.

3 En la escuela de medicina Usa los verbos para completar las oraciones con las formas correctas del imperfecto. Algunos verbos se usan más de una vez. Some answers may vary. Suggested answers:

caerse	enfermarse	ir	querer	tener
comprender	estornudar	pensar	sentirse	tomar
doler	hacer	poder	ser	toser

1. Cuando Javier y Victoria ___eran___ estudiantes de medicina, siempre ___tenían___ que ir al médico.
2. Cuando Victoria ___hacía___ ejercicios aeróbicos, siempre ___se sentía___ mareada.
3. Cada vez que él ___tomaba___ un examen, a Javier le ___dolía___ mucho la cabeza.
4. Victoria también ___se caía___ de su bicicleta camino a la escuela.
5. Todas las primaveras, Javier ___estornudaba/tosía___ mucho porque es alérgico al polen.
6. Después de comer en la cafetería, a Victoria siempre le ___dolía___ el estómago.
7. Javier ___quería/pensaba___ ser médico para ayudar a los demás.
8. Pero no ___comprendía___ por qué él ___se enfermaba___ con tanta frecuencia.
9. Cuando Victoria ___tenía___ fiebre, no ___podía___ ni leer el termómetro.
10. A Javier ___le dolían___ los dientes, pero nunca ___quería___ ir al dentista.
11. Victoria ___tosía/estornudaba___ mucho cuando ___se sentía___ congestionada.
12. Javier y Victoria ___pensaban___ que nunca ___iban___ a graduarse.

TEACHING OPTIONS

TPR Model gestures for physical or emotional states using the imperfect. Ex: **Me dolía la cabeza.** (Furrow your brow and rub your forehead.) **Tenía fiebre.** (Fan yourself.) Have students stand. Say an expression at random (Ex: **Estornudabas**) and signal a student to perform the appropriate gesture. Keep a brisk pace. Vary by pointing to multiple students. (Ex: **Ustedes se enfermaban.**)

Small Groups ←👤→ In small groups, have students talk about doctors or dentists that they used to visit. Tell each group to select the best and worst experience and write a description of each to share with the class.
Extra Practice ←👤→ If possible, have students bring in video clips from popular movies or *YouTube.* Choose three or four clips and have the students describe the events after viewing each one.

Comunicación

4 **Entrevista** Trabajen en parejas. Un(a) estudiante usa estas preguntas para entrevistar a su compañero/a. *Answers will vary.*

1. Cuando eras estudiante de primaria, ¿te gustaban tus profesores/as?
2. ¿Veías mucha televisión cuando eras niño/a?
3. Cuando tenías diez años, ¿cuál era tu programa de televisión favorito?
4. Cuando eras niño/a, ¿qué hacía tu familia durante las vacaciones?
5. ¿Cuántos años tenías en 2010?
6. Cuando estabas en el quinto año escolar, ¿qué hacías con tus amigos/as?
7. Cuando tenías once años, ¿cuál era tu grupo musical favorito?
8. Antes de tomar esta clase, ¿sabías hablar español?

5 **Describir** En parejas, túrnense para describir cómo eran sus vidas cuando eran niños. Pueden usar las sugerencias u otras ideas. *Answers will vary.*

> **modelo**
> De niña, mi familia y yo siempre íbamos a Tortuguero. Tomábamos un barco desde Limón, y por las noches mirábamos las tortugas en la playa. Algunas veces teníamos suerte, porque las tortugas venían a poner huevos. Otras veces, volvíamos al hotel sin ver ninguna tortuga.

- las vacaciones
- ocasiones especiales
- qué hacías durante el verano
- celebraciones con tus amigos/as
- celebraciones con tu familia
- cómo era tu escuela
- cómo eran tus amigos/as
- los viajes que hacías
- a qué jugabas
- qué hacías cuando te sentías enfermo/a

NOTA CULTURAL

El Parque Nacional Tortuguero está en la costa del Caribe, al norte de la ciudad de Limón, en Costa Rica. Varias especies de tortuga (*turtle*) van a las playas del parque para poner (*lay*) sus huevos. Esto ocurre de noche, y hay guías que llevan pequeños grupos de turistas a observar este fenómeno biológico.

Síntesis

6 **En el consultorio** Tu profesor(a) te va a dar una lista incompleta con los pacientes que fueron al consultorio del doctor Donoso ayer. En parejas, conversen para completar sus listas y saber a qué hora llegaron las personas al consultorio y cuáles eran sus problemas. *Answers will vary.*

Teaching Tip (4)
To simplify, have students record the results of their interviews in a Venn diagram, which they can use to present the information to the class.

Teaching Tips (5)
- After students have completed the activity in pairs, divide the class into small groups. Then, after each student reports to the class about his/her partner's life, have groups decide on a follow-up question to ask.
- You may want to assign this activity as a short written composition.

Teaching Tip (6)
Divide the class into pairs and distribute the handouts from the Activity Pack (Activity Pack/Supersite) that correspond to this Information Gap Activity. Give students ten minutes to complete this activity.

Expansion (6)
Have pairs write Dr. Donoso's advice for three of the patients. Then have them read the advice to the class and compare it with what other pairs wrote for the same patients.

TEACHING OPTIONS

Large Groups Label the four corners of the room **La Revolución Americana, Tiempos prehistóricos, El Imperio Romano,** and **El Japón de los samurai.** Have students go to the corner that best represents the historical period they would visit if they could. Each group should then discuss their reasons for choosing that period using the imperfect tense. A spokesperson will report the group's responses to the rest of the class.

Game Divide the class into teams of three. Each team should choose a fictional villain. When it is their turn, they will give the class one hint. The other teams are allowed three questions, which must be answered truthfully. At the end of the question/answer session, teams must guess the person's identity. Award one point for each correct guess and two to any team able to stump the class.

Section Goal

In **Estructura 10.2**, students will compare and contrast the uses and meanings of the preterite and imperfect tenses.

Instructional Resources

Supersite: Audio (Lab MP3 Files); Resources (Grammar Presentation Slides, Activity Pack, Scripts, Answer Keys); Testing Program (Quizzes)
WebSAM
Workbook
Lab Manual

Teaching Tips

- Draw a simple time line on the board. Mark the year you were born and the present year. Invite students to guess how old you were at key points in your life. Ex: **¿Qué creen ustedes? ¿Cuántos años tenía yo cuando aprendí a conducir?** Mark the appropriate spot on the time line and write the corresponding phrase (**Aprendí a conducir.**).
- Give personalized examples as you contrast the preterite and the imperfect. Ex: **La semana pasada tuve que ir al dentista. Me dolía mucho el diente.**
- 👥↔👤 Involve the class in a conversation about what they did in the past. Ask: ____, **¿paseabas en bicicleta cuando eras niño/a? ¿Te caíste alguna vez? ____, ¿cuando eras niño/a iba tu familia de vacaciones todos los años? ¿Adónde iban?**
- ←👤→ Add a visual aspect to this grammar presentation. Create or bring in a series of simple drawings. As you hold up each one, have students narrate the events in English and say whether they would use the preterite or imperfect in each case. Ex: 1. The man was sleeping (imperfect). It was midnight (imperfect). The door was open (imperfect). 2. It was 12:05 (imperfect). The man heard a noise (preterite)... Then have volunteers narrate the scenes in Spanish.

10.2 # The preterite and the imperfect   Tutorial

NATIONAL STANDARDS comparisons

ANTE TODO   Now that you have learned the forms of the preterite and the imperfect, you will learn more about how they are used. The preterite and the imperfect are not interchangeable. In Spanish, the choice between these two tenses depends on the context and on the point of view of the speaker.

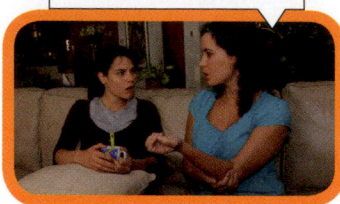

Me rompí el brazo cuando estaba paseando en bicicleta.

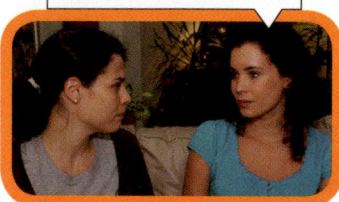

Tenía dolor de cabeza, pero me tomé una aspirina y se me fue.

COMPARE & CONTRAST

Use the preterite to...

1. Express actions that are viewed by the speaker as completed

   Sandra **se rompió** la pierna.
   Sandra broke her leg.

   Fueron a Buenos Aires ayer.
   They went to Buenos Aires yesterday.

2. Express the beginning or end of a past action

   La película **empezó** a las nueve.
   The movie began at nine o'clock.

   Ayer **terminé** el proyecto para la clase de química.
   Yesterday I finished the project for chemistry class.

3. Narrate a series of past actions or events

   La doctora me **miró** los oídos, me **hizo** unas preguntas y **escribió** la receta.
   The doctor looked in my ears, asked me some questions, and wrote the prescription.

   Me di con la mesa, **me caí** y me **lastimé** el pie.
   I bumped into the table, I fell, and I injured my foot.

Use the imperfect to...

1. Describe an ongoing past action with no reference to its beginning or end

   Sandra **esperaba** al doctor.
   Sandra was waiting for the doctor.

   El médico **se preocupaba** por sus pacientes.
   The doctor worried about his patients.

2. Express habitual past actions and events

   Cuando **era** joven, **jugaba** al tenis.
   When I was young, I used to play tennis.

   De niño, Eduardo **se enfermaba** con mucha frecuencia.
   As a child, Eduardo used to get sick very frequently.

3. Describe physical and emotional states or characteristics

   La chica **quería** descansar. **Se sentía** mal y **tenía** dolor de cabeza.
   The girl wanted to rest. She felt ill and had a headache.

   Ellos **eran** altos y **tenían** ojos verdes.
   They were tall and had green eyes.

   Estábamos felices de ver a la familia.
   We were happy to see our family.

AYUDA

These words and expressions, as well as similar ones, commonly occur with the preterite: **ayer, anteayer, una vez, dos veces, tres veces, el año pasado, de repente.** They usually imply that an action has happened at a specific point in time. For a review, see **Estructura 6.3**, p. 207.

AYUDA

These words and expressions, as well as similar ones, commonly occur with the imperfect: **de niño/a, todos los días, mientras, siempre, con frecuencia, todas las semanas.** They usually express habitual or repeated actions in the past.

TEACHING OPTIONS

Extra Practice Write in English a simple, humorous retelling of a well-known fairy tale. Read it to the class, pausing after each verb in the past to ask the class whether the imperfect or preterite would be used in Spanish. Ex: *Once upon a time there was a girl named Little Red Riding Hood. She wanted to take lunch to her ailing grandmother. She put a loaf of bread, a wedge of cheese, and a bottle of Beaujolais in a basket and set off through the* woods. *Meanwhile, farther down the path, a big, ugly, snaggle-toothed wolf was leaning against a tree, filing his nails…*

Pairs On separate slips of paper, have students write six personalized statements, one for each of the uses of the preterite and imperfect in **Compare & Contrast**. Have them shuffle the slips and exchange them with a partner, who will identify which preterite or imperfect use each of the sentences illustrates.

▶ The preterite and the imperfect often appear in the same sentence. In such cases, the imperfect describes what *was happening*, while the preterite describes the action that "interrupted" the ongoing activity.

Miraba la tele cuando **sonó** el teléfono.
I was watching TV when the phone rang.

Felicia **leía** el periódico cuando **llegó** Ramiro.
Felicia was reading the newspaper when Ramiro arrived.

▶ You will also see the preterite and the imperfect together in narratives such as fiction, news, and the retelling of events. The imperfect provides background information, such as time, weather, and location, while the preterite indicates the specific events that occurred.

Eran las dos de la mañana y el detective ya no **podía** mantenerse despierto. **Se bajó** lentamente del coche, **estiró** las piernas y **levantó** los brazos hacia el cielo oscuro.
It was two in the morning, and the detective could no longer stay awake. He slowly stepped out of the car, stretched his legs, and raised his arms toward the dark sky.

La luna **estaba** llena y no **había** en el cielo ni una sola nube. De repente, el detective **escuchó** un grito espeluznante proveniente del parque.
The moon was full and there wasn't a single cloud in the sky. Suddenly, the detective heard a piercing scream coming from the park.

Un médico colombiano desarrolló una vacuna contra la malaria

En 1986, el doctor colombiano Manuel Elkin Patarroyo creó la primera vacuna sintética para combatir la malaria. Esta enfermedad parecía haberse erradicado hacía décadas en muchas partes del mundo. Sin embargo, justo cuando Patarroyo terminó de elaborar la inmunización, los casos de malaria empezaban a aumentar de nuevo. En mayo de 1993, el doctor colombiano cedió la patente de la vacuna a la Organización Mundial de la Salud en nombre de Colombia. Los grandes laboratorios farmacéuticos presionaron a la OMS porque querían la vacuna. Las presiones no tuvieron éxito y, en 1995, el doctor Patarroyo y la OMS pactaron continuar con el acuerdo inicial: la vacuna seguía siendo propiedad de la OMS.

 ¡INTÉNTALO!   Elige el pretérito o el imperfecto para completar la historia. Explica por qué se usa ese tiempo verbal en cada ocasión. *Answers for the second part will vary.*

1. _____Eran_____ (Fueron/Eran) las doce.
2. Todos los días yo __almorzaba__ (almorcé/almorzaba) con Tomás al mediodía.
3. _____Había_____ (Hubo/Había) mucha gente en la calle.
4. A las doce y media, Tomás y yo __entramos__ (entramos/entrábamos) en el restaurante Tárcoles.
5. El camarero _____llegó_____ (llegó/llegaba) inmediatamente con el menú.
6. Nosotros __empezamos__ (empezamos/empezábamos) a leerlo.
7. Yo _____pedí_____ (pedí/pedía) el pescado.
8. De repente, el camarero __volvió__ (volvió/volvía) a nuestra mesa.
9. Y nos _____dio_____ (dio/daba) una mala noticia.
10. Desafortunadamente, no __tenían__ (tuvieron/tenían) más pescado.
11. Por eso Tomás y yo __decidimos__ (decidimos/decidíamos) comer en otro lugar.
12. __Llovía__ (Llovió/Llovía) mucho cuando __salimos__ (salimos/salíamos) del restaurante.
13. Así que __regresamos__ (regresamos/regresábamos) al restaurante Tárcoles.
14. Esta vez, __pedí__ (pedí/pedía) arroz con pollo.

More activities

vhlcentral

LM
p. 58

WB
pp. 113–116

Online activities

Teaching Tips

- →👤← Give further examples from your own experiences that contrast the imperfect and the preterite. Ex: **Quería ver la nueva película ____, pero anoche sólo pude ir a las diez de la noche. La película fue buena, pero terminó muy tarde. Era la una cuando llegué a casa. Me acosté muy tarde y esta mañana, cuando me levanté, estaba cansadísimo/a.**
- Have students find the example of an interrupted action in the realia.
- →👤← Create a *PowerPoint* presentation or *Word* document of a simple narration in Spanish, in such a way that the first screen shows only the sentences with imperfect verbs and the second screen has only the preterite. Show the first group of sentences and read it aloud. Ask students what tense is used (imperfect) and if they know what happened and why not (no, it only sets the scene). Then show the second set of sentences. After reading through the sentences, ask students the tense (preterite), if they know what happened (yes), and if this is an interesting story (no). Then show a final screen that combines the tenses and read through the complete narration. Explain that, now that students have learned both the imperfect and the preterite, they are able to communicate in a more complete, interesting way.
- After completing ¡Inténtalo!, have students explain why the preterite or imperfect was used in each case. Then call on different students to create new sentences illustrating the same uses.

Práctica

1 Expansion Ask comprehension questions about the article. Ex: **¿Qué pasó ayer?** (Hubo un accidente.) **¿Dónde hubo un accidente?** (en el centro de San José) **¿Qué tiempo hacía?** (Estaba muy nublado y llovía.) **¿Qué le pasó a la mujer que conducía?** (Murió al instante.) **¿Y a su pasajero?** (Sufrió varias fracturas.) **¿Qué hizo el conductor del autobús?** (Intentó dar un viraje brusco y perdió control del autobús.) **¿Qué les pasó a los pasajeros del autobús?** (Nada; no se lastimó ninguno.)

1 **En el periódico** Completa esta noticia con las formas correctas del pretérito o el imperfecto.

Un accidente trágico

Ayer temprano por la mañana (1) __hubo__ (haber) un trágico accidente en el centro de San José cuando el conductor de un autobús no (2) __vio__ (ver) venir un carro. La mujer que (3) __conducía__ (conducir) el carro (4) __murió__ (morir) al instante y los paramédicos (5) __tuvieron__ (tener) que llevar al pasajero al hospital porque (6) __sufrió__ (sufrir) varias fracturas. El conductor del autobús (7) __dijo__ (decir) que no (8) __vio__ (ver) el carro hasta el último momento porque (9) __estaba__ (estar) muy nublado y (10) __llovía__ (llover). Él (11) __intentó__ (intentar) (*to attempt*) dar un viraje brusco (*to swerve*), pero (12) __perdió__ (perder) el control del autobús y no (13) __pudo__ (poder) evitar (*to avoid*) el accidente. Según nos informaron, no (14) __se lastimó__ (lastimarse) ningún pasajero del autobús.

AYUDA

Reading Spanish-language newspapers is a good way to practice verb tenses. You will find that both the imperfect and the preterite occur with great regularity. Many newsstands carry international papers, and many Spanish-language newspapers (such as Spain's *El País*, Mexico's *Reforma*, and Argentina's *Clarín*) are on the Web.

2 Teaching Tip To simplify, begin by reading through the items as a class. Have students label each blank with an *I* for *imperfect* or *P* for *preterite*.

2 Expansion Have volunteers explain why they chose the preterite or imperfect in each case. Ask them to point out any words or expressions that triggered one tense or the other.

2 **Seleccionar** Utiliza el tiempo verbal adecuado, según el contexto. Answers will vary. Suggested answers:

1. La semana pasada, Manolo y Aurora __querían__ (querer) dar una fiesta. __Decidieron__ (decidir) invitar a seis amigos y servirles mucha comida.
2. Manolo y Aurora __estaban__ (estar) preparando la comida cuando Elena __llamó__ (llamar). Como siempre, __tenía__ (tener) que estudiar para un examen.
3. A las seis, __volvió__ (volver) a sonar el teléfono. Su amigo Francisco tampoco __podía__ (poder) ir a la fiesta, porque __tenía__ (tener) fiebre. Manolo y Aurora __se sentían__ (sentirse) muy tristes, pero __tenían__ (tener) que preparar la comida.
4. Después de otros quince minutos, __sonó__ (sonar) el teléfono. Sus amigos, los señores Vega, __estaban__ (estar) en camino (*en route*) al hospital: a su hijo le __dolía__ (doler) mucho el estómago. Sólo dos de los amigos __podían__ (poder) ir a la cena.
5. Por supuesto, __iban__ (ir) a tener demasiada comida. Finalmente, cinco minutos antes de las ocho, __llamaron__ (llamar) Ramón y Javier. Ellos __pensaban__ (pensar) que la fiesta __era__ (ser) la próxima semana.
6. Tristes, Manolo y Aurora __se sentaron__ (sentarse) a comer solos. Mientras __comían__ (comer), pronto __llegaron__ (llegar) a la conclusión de que __era__ (ser) mejor estar solos: ¡La comida __estaba__ (estar) malísima!

3 Expansion
• After students compare their sentences, ask them to report to the class the most interesting things their partners said.
• To challenge students, ask them to expand on one of their sentences, creating a paragraph about an imaginary or actual past experience.

3 **Completar** Completa las frases de una manera lógica. Usa el pretérito o el imperfecto. En parejas, comparen sus respuestas. Answers will vary.

in class (& collect)

1. De niño/a, yo...
2. Yo conducía el auto mientras...
3. Anoche mi novio/a...
4. Ayer el/la profesor(a)...
5. La semana pasada un(a) amigo/a...
6. Con frecuencia mis padres...
7. Esta mañana en la cafetería...
8. Hablábamos con el doctor cuando...

TEACHING OPTIONS

Small Groups In groups of four, have students write a short article about an imaginary trip they took last summer. Students should use the imperfect to set the scene and the preterite to narrate the events. Each student should contribute three sentences to the article. When finished, have students read their articles to the class.

Heritage Speakers Ask heritage speakers to write a brief narration of a well-known fairy tale, such as *Little Red Riding Hood* (*Caperucita Roja*). Allow them to change details as they see fit, modernizing the story or setting it in another country, for example, but tell them to pay special attention to the use of preterite and imperfect verbs. Have them share their retellings with the class.

Comunicación

4 **Entrevista** Usa estas preguntas para entrevistar a un(a) compañero/a acerca de su primer(a) novio/a. Si quieres, puedes añadir otras preguntas. *Answers will vary.*

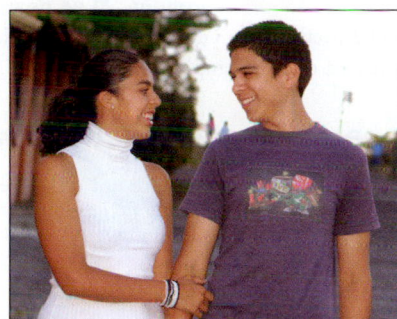

1. ¿Quién fue tu primer(a) novio/a?
2. ¿Cuántos años tenías cuando lo/la conociste?
3. ¿Cómo era él/ella?
4. ¿Qué le gustaba hacer? ¿Tenían ustedes los mismos pasatiempos?
5. ¿Por cuánto tiempo salieron ustedes?
6. ¿Adónde iban cuando salían?
7. ¿Pensaban casarse?
8. ¿Cuándo y por qué rompieron?

5 **La sala de emergencias** En parejas, inventen qué les pasó a estas personas que están en la sala de emergencias. *Answers will vary.*

> **modelo**
>
> Eran las tres de la tarde. Como todos los días, Pablo jugaba al fútbol con sus amigos. Estaba muy *contento*. De repente, se cayó y se rompió el brazo. Entonces fue a la sala de emergencias.

Paciente	Edad	Hora	Estado
1. Pablo Romero	9 años	15:20	hueso roto (el brazo)
2. Estela Rodríguez	45 años	15:25	tobillo torcido
3. Lupe Quintana	29 años	15:37	embarazada, dolores
4. Manuel López	52 años	15:45	infección de garganta
5. Marta Díaz	3 años	16:00	congestión, fiebre
6. Roberto Salazar	32 años	16:06	dolor de oído
7. Marco Brito	18 años	16:18	daño en el cuello, posible fractura
8. Ana María Ortiz	66 años	16:29	reacción alérgica a un medicamento

6 **Situación** Anoche alguien robó (*stole*) el examen de la **Lección 10** de la oficina de tu profesor(a) y tú tienes que averiguar quién lo hizo. Pregúntales a tres compañeros dónde estaban, con quién estaban y qué hicieron entre las ocho y las doce de la noche. *Answers will vary.*

Síntesis

7 **La primera vez** En grupos, cuéntense cómo fue la primera vez que les pusieron una inyección, se rompieron un hueso, pasaron la noche en un hospital, estuvieron mareados/as, etc. Incluyan estos datos en su conversación: una descripción del tiempo que hacía, sus edades, qué pasó y cómo se sentían. *Answers will vary.*

TEACHING OPTIONS

Small Groups Have small groups write a skit and perform it for the class. Three students walk into the campus clinic. Each explains to the nurse what happened and why he or she should be seen first. Students should use the preterite and imperfect.
Game Create a short narrative in the past based on a well-known story. Allow space between sentences so they may be easily cut into strips. Then make a copy of the narrative and edit it, changing all preterites to imperfects and vice versa. Make two copies of each version and cut the sentences apart. Place a complete set of both the versions into two separate bags, mix the strips up, and challenge two teams to reconstruct the correct version. The team that does so first wins.

10.3 Constructions with se Tutorial

ANTE TODO In **Lección 7,** you learned how to use **se** as the third person reflexive pronoun (**Él se despierta. Ellos se visten. Ella se baña.**). **Se** can also be used to form constructions in which the person performing the action is not expressed or is de-emphasized.

Impersonal constructions with se

▶ In Spanish, verbs that are not reflexive can be used with **se** to form impersonal constructions. These are statements in which the person performing the action is not defined.

Se habla español en Costa Rica.
Spanish is spoken in Costa Rica.

Se puede leer en la sala de espera.
You can read in the waiting room.

Se hacen operaciones aquí.
They perform operations here.

Se necesitan medicinas enseguida.
They need medicine right away.

> **AYUDA**
> In English, the passive voice or indefinite subjects (*you, they, one*) are used where Spanish uses impersonal constructions with **se**.

▶ **¡Atención!** Note that the third person singular verb form is used with singular nouns and the third person plural form is used with plural nouns.

Se vende ropa.   **Se venden** camisas.

▶ You often see the impersonal **se** in signs, advertisements, and directions.

Se prohíbe nadar

Se necesitan programadores
Grupo Tecno

← **ENTRADA**

Se entra por la izquierda

Se for unplanned events

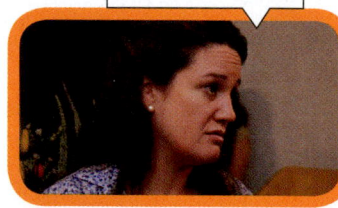

¿Te pusiste un suéter anoche?

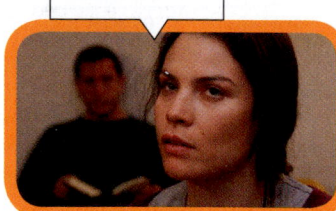

No, mamá. Se me olvidó.

▶ **Se** also describes accidental or unplanned events. In this construction, the person who performs the action is de-emphasized, implying that the accident or unplanned event is not his or her direct responsibility. Note this construction.

se	+	[**INDIRECT OBJECT PRONOUN**]	+	[**VERB**]	+	[**SUBJECT**]
Se		me		cayó		la pluma.

▶ In this type of construction, what would normally be the direct object of the sentence becomes the subject, and it agrees with the verb, not with the indirect object pronoun.

I.O. PRONOUN	VERB		SUBJECT
Se	me, te, le, nos, os, les	quedó / cayó / dañó **SINGULAR**	la receta. / la taza. / el radio.
		rompieron / olvidaron / perdieron **PLURAL**	las botellas. / las pastillas. / las llaves.

▶ These verbs are the ones most frequently used with **se** to describe unplanned events.

Verbs commonly used with se

caer	to fall; to drop	**perder (e:ie)**	to lose
dañar	to damage; to break down	**quedar**	to be left behind
olvidar	to forget	**romper**	to break

Se me perdió el teléfono de la farmacia.
I lost the pharmacy's phone number.

Se nos olvidaron los pasajes.
We forgot the tickets.

▶ **¡Atención!** While Spanish has a verb for *to fall* (**caer**), there is no direct translation for *to drop*. **Dejar caer** (*To let fall*) or a **se** construction is often used to mean *to drop*.

El médico **dejó caer** la aspirina.
The doctor dropped the aspirin.

A mí **se me cayeron** los cuadernos.
I dropped the notebooks.

CONSULTA

For an explanation of prepositional pronouns, refer to **Estructura 9.4**, p. 318.

▶ To clarify or emphasize who the person involved in the action is, this construction commonly begins with the preposition **a** + [*noun*] or **a** + [*prepositional pronoun*].

Al paciente se le perdió la receta.
The patient lost his prescription.

A ustedes se les quedaron los libros en casa.
You left the books at home.

 ¡INTÉNTALO! Completa las oraciones con **se** impersonal y los verbos en presente.

A

1. _Se enseñan_ (enseñar) cinco lenguas en esta universidad.
2. _Se come_ (comer) muy bien en Las Delicias.
3. _Se sirven_ (servir) platos exquisitos cada noche.
4. _Se venden_ (vender) muchas camisetas allí.

Completa las oraciones con **se** y los verbos en pretérito.

B

1. _Se me rompieron_ (*I broke*) las gafas.
2. _Se le quedó_ (*You* (form., sing.) *left*) aquí la radiografía.
3. _Se les perdió_ (*They lost*) la receta.
4. _Se te cayeron_ (*You* (fam., sing.) *dropped*) las pastillas.

More activities

vhlcentral

LM p. 59

WB pp. 117–118

Online activities

---

1 Expansion
- Change the date from 1901 to 2011 and go through the exercise again orally.
- ↤🔳↦ In pairs, have students use constructions with **se** to write a description of a period in history such as the French or American Revolution, the Sixties, and Prohibition. Then have pairs form groups of six and read their descriptions aloud to their group.
- Have pairs use **se** constructions to note cultural differences between Spanish-speaking countries and their own. Ex: **Aquí se habla inglés, pero en ____ se habla español.**

2 Teaching Tips
- Model the activity by asking volunteers to restate similar phrases. Ex: **Buscamos enfermero/a (Se busca enfermero/a); Compramos libros usados (Se compran libros usados)**
- 🔳↔🔳 Ask students to discuss with a partner where these signs could be found locally.

3 Teaching Tip To simplify, have students work in pairs to brainstorm verbs that could be used to complete this activity.

3 Expansion
↤🔳↦ Add another visual aspect to this activity. Use magazine pictures to have students continue describing past events using constructions with **se**.

Práctica

1 ¿Cierto o falso? Indica si lo que dice cada oración sobre la vida en 1901 es **cierto** o **falso**. Luego corrige las oraciones falsas.

1. Se viajaba mucho en tren. Cierto.
2. Se escribían muchos libros. Cierto.
3. Se veía mucha televisión. Falso. No se veía televisión. Se leía mucho.
4. Se montaba a caballo. Cierto.
5. Se mandaba correo electrónico. Falso. No se mandaba correo electrónico. Se mandaban cartas y postales.
6. Se preparaban comidas en casa. Cierto.
7. Se pasaba mucho tiempo con la familia. Cierto.
8. Se llevaban minifaldas. Falso. No se llevaban minifaldas. Se llevaban faldas largas.

2 Letreros y anuncios Reescribe los letreros (*signs*) y anuncios usando el **se** impersonal.

> **modelo**
> Buscamos vendedores con experiencia
> *Se buscan vendedores con experiencia*

1. Necesitamos profesores de matemáticas Se necesitan profesores de matemáticas
2. Hablamos español Se habla español
3. Aceptamos tarjetas de crédito Se aceptan tarjetas de crédito
4. Está prohibido hablar por teléfono Se prohíbe hablar por teléfono
5. Vendemos libros Se venden libros
6. Buscamos dentista con experiencia Se busca dentista con experiencia

3 ¿Qué pasó? Indica lo que pasó en cada dibujo. Some answers will vary. Suggested answers:

1. Sr. Álvarez / computadora
Al señor Álvarez se le dañó la computadora.

2. camarero / pastel
Al camarero se le cayó el pastel.

3. Arturo / huevos
A Arturo se le olvidaron los huevos.

4. Carla y Lupe / botellas
A Carla y a Lupe se les rompieron las botellas.

5. Sra. Domínguez / llaves
A la Sra. Domínguez se le perdieron las llaves.

6. Juana / bolsa
A Juana se le quedó la bolsa.

TEACHING OPTIONS

Extra Practice ↤🔳↦ Have students imagine that they have just seen a movie about the future. Have them work in groups to prepare a description of the way of life portrayed in the movie using the imperfect tense and constructions with **se**. Ex: **No se necesitaba trabajar. Se usaban robots para hacer todo. Se viajaba por telepatía. No se comía nada sino en los fines de semana.**

Game Divide the class into teams of four. Have each team think of a famous place or public building and compose four signs that could be found on the premises. Teams will take turns reading their signs aloud. Each team that correctly identifies the place or building receives one point. The team with the most points wins.

En el consultorio
trescientos cincuenta y tres
353

Comunicación

4

¿Distraído/a yo? Trabajen en parejas y usen estas preguntas para averiguar cuál de los/las dos es más distraído/a (*absentminded*). Answers will vary.

¿Alguna vez…
1. se te olvidó invitar a alguien a una fiesta o comida? ¿A quién?
2. se te quedó algo importante en la casa? ¿Qué?
3. se te perdió algo importante durante un viaje? ¿Qué?
4. se te rompió algo muy caro? ¿Qué?

¿Sabes…
5. si se permite el ingreso (*admission*) de perros al parque cercano a la universidad?
6. si en el supermercado se aceptan cheques?
7. dónde se arreglan zapatos y botas?
8. qué se sirve en la cafetería de la universidad los lunes?

5

Opiniones En parejas, terminen cada oración con ideas originales. Answers will vary.

1. No se tiene que dejar propina cuando…
2. Antes de viajar, se debe…
3. Si se come bien, …
4. Para tener una vida sana, se debe…
5. Se sirve la mejor comida en…
6. Se hablan muchas lenguas en…

Síntesis

6

Anuncios En grupos, preparen dos anuncios de televisión para presentar a la clase. Usen el imperfecto y por lo menos dos construcciones con **se** en cada uno. Answers will vary.

> **modelo**
>
> Se me cayeron unos libros en el pie y me dolía mucho. Pero ahora no, gracias a SuperAspirina 500. ¡Dos pastillas y se me fue el dolor! Se puede comprar SuperAspirina 500 en todas las farmacias Recetamax.

4 Teaching Tip Encourage students to give detailed responses. Model this by choosing from the first set of questions and providing as many details as possible. Ex: **Una vez cuando era adolescente se me rompió un plato muy caro de mi abuela. Pero ella no se enojó. Me dijo: No te preocupes por el plato. ¿Te lastimaste?**

4 Expansion
←🔁→ Have each pair decide on the most unusual answer to the questions. Ask the student who gave it to describe the event to the class.

5 Teaching Tip Have students compare their answers with the rest of the class to see which pair had the best ideas.

5 Expansion Ask pairs to write similar beginnings to three different statements using **se** constructions. Have pairs exchange papers and finish each other's sentences.

6 Expansion
←🔁→ After all the groups have presented their ads, have each group write a letter of complaint. Their letter should be directed to one of the other groups, claiming false advertising.

TEACHING OPTIONS

Extra Practice Write these sentence fragments on the board and ask students to supply at least two logical endings using a construction with **se**. **1. Una vez, cuando yo comía en un restaurante elegante, _____. (se me rompió un vaso; se me perdió la tarjeta de crédito) 2. Ayer cuando yo venía a clase, _____. (se me dañó la bicicleta; me caí y se me rompió el brazo)**

3. Cuando era niño/a, siempre _____. (se me olvidaban las cosas; se me perdían las cosas) 4. El otro día cuando yo lavaba los platos, _____. (se me rompieron tres vasos; se me acabó el detergente)

Section Goals

In **Estructura 10.4**, students will learn:

- the formation of adverbs using [*adjective*] + –**mente**
- common adverbs and adverbial expressions

Instructional Resources

Supersite: Audio (Lab MP3 Files); Resources (Grammar Presentation Slides, Activity Pack, Scripts, Answer Keys); Testing Program (Quizzes)
WebSAM
Workbook
Lab Manual

Teaching Tips

- Add a visual aspect to this grammar presentation. Use magazine pictures to review known adverbs. Ex: **Miren la foto que tengo** *aquí.* **Hoy esta chica se siente** *bien,* **pero** *ayer* **se sentía** *mal.* Write the adverbs on the board as you proceed.
- After presenting the formation of adverbs that end in –**mente**, ask volunteers to convert known adjectives into adverbs and then use them in a sentence. Ex: **cómodo/cómodamente: Alberto se sentó cómodamente en la silla.**
- Name celebrities and have students create sentences about them, using adverbs. Ex: **Shakira (Shakira baila maravillosamente.)**

10.4 Adverbs Tutorial

ANTE TODO Adverbs are words that describe how, when, and where actions take place. They can modify verbs, adjectives, and even other adverbs. In previous lessons, you have already learned many Spanish adverbs, such as the ones below.

aquí	hoy	nunca
ayer	mal	siempre
bien	muy	temprano

▶ The most common adverbs end in -**mente**, equivalent to the English ending *-ly*.

verdaderamente *truly, really*   **generalmente** *generally*   **simplemente** *simply*

▶ To form these adverbs, add -**mente** to the feminine form of the adjective. If the adjective does not have a special feminine form, just add -**mente** to the standard form. **¡Atención!** Adjectives do not lose their accents when adding -**mente**.

ADJECTIVE		FEMININE FORM		SUFFIX		ADVERB
seguro		segura		-mente		seguramente
fabuloso		fabulosa		-mente		fabulosamente
enorme				-mente		enormemente
fácil				-mente		fácilmente

▶ Adverbs that end in -**mente** generally follow the verb, while adverbs that modify an adjective or another adverb precede the word they modify.

Maira dibuja **maravillosamente**.
Maira draws wonderfully.

Sergio está **casi siempre** ocupado.
Sergio is almost always busy.

Common adverbs and adverbial expressions

a menudo	*often*	**así**	*like this; so*	**menos**	*less*
a tiempo	*on time*	**bastante**	*enough; rather*	**muchas veces**	*a lot; many times*
a veces	*sometimes*	**casi**	*almost*		
además (de)	*furthermore; besides*	**con frecuencia**	*frequently*	**poco**	*little*
				por lo menos	*at least*
apenas	*hardly; scarcely*	**de vez en cuando**	*from time to time*		
				pronto	*soon*
		despacio	*slowly*	**rápido**	*quickly*

More activities

vhlcentral

LM p. 60

WB pp. 119–120

Online activities

¡ATENCIÓN!

When a sentence contains two or more adverbs in sequence, the suffix -**mente** is dropped from all but the last adverb.
Ex: **El médico nos habló simple y abiertamente.** *The doctor spoke to us simply and openly.*

¡ATENCIÓN!

Rápido functions as an adjective (**Ella tiene una computadora rápida.**) as well as an adverb (**Ellas corren rápido.**). Note that as an adverb, **rápido** does not need to agree with any other word in the sentence. You can also use the adverb **rápidamente** (**Ella corre rápidamente.**).

 ¡INTÉNTALO! Transforma los adjetivos en adverbios.

1. alegre   *alegremente*
2. perfecto   *perfectamente*
3. gradual   *gradualmente*
4. constante   *constantemente*
5. regular   *regularmente*
6. frecuente   *frecuentemente*
7. tranquilo   *tranquilamente*
8. real   *realmente*
9. maravilloso   *maravillosamente*
10. básico   *básicamente*
11. normal   *normalmente*
12. afortunado   *afortunadamente*

TEACHING OPTIONS

Heritage Speakers ⟵🔹⟶ Have heritage speakers talk about daily life when they were children or adolescents. Tell them to use at least eight of the common adverbs and adverbial expressions listed. Then have the rest of the class write sentences comparing and contrasting their experiences with those of the heritage speakers.

Extra Practice Have pairs of students write sentences using adverbs such as **nunca, hoy**, and **despacio**. When they have finished, ask volunteers to dictate their sentences to you to write on the board. After you have written a sentence and checked it for accuracy, ask a volunteer to create a sentence that uses the antonym of the adverb.

Práctica

1 **Escoger** Completa la historia con los adverbios adecuados.

1. La cita era a las dos, pero llegamos _____tarde_____. (menos, nunca, tarde)
2. El problema fue que ___ayer___ se nos dañó el despertador. (aquí, ayer, despacio)
3. La recepcionista no se enojó porque sabe que normalmente llego ____a tiempo____. (a veces, a tiempo, poco)
4. ___Por lo menos___ el doctor estaba listo. (Por lo menos, Muchas veces, Casi)
5. ___Apenas___ tuvimos que esperar cinco minutos. (Así, Además, Apenas)
6. El doctor dijo que nuestra hija Irene necesitaba cambiar su rutina diaria ___inmediatamente___. (temprano, menos, inmediatamente)
▶ 7. El doctor nos explicó _____bien_____ las recomendaciones del Cirujano General (*Surgeon General*) sobre la salud de los jóvenes. (de vez en cuando, bien, apenas)
8. ___Afortunadamente___ nos dijo que Irene estaba bien, pero tenía que hacer más ejercicio y comer mejor. (Bastante, Afortunadamente, A menudo)

Comunicación

2 **Aspirina** Responde a las preguntas con un(a) compañero/a. *Answers will vary.*

No hay tiempo para el dolor de cabeza.

Si tienes prisa, o simplemente quieres que tu dolor de cabeza se vaya muy pronto, piensa en Capalivia. Se asimila mejor y actúa rápidamente. Ya no se puede perder tiempo por un dolor de cabeza.

ASPIRINA

1. ¿Cuáles son los adverbios que aparecen en el anuncio?
2. Según el anuncio, ¿cuáles son las ventajas (*advantages*) de este tipo de aspirina?
3. ¿Tienen ustedes dolores de cabeza? ¿Qué toman para curarlos?
4. ¿Qué productos ven con frecuencia en los anuncios de televisión? Escriban descripciones de varios de estos anuncios. Usen adverbios en sus descripciones.

Section Goal

In **Recapitulación**, students will review the grammar concepts from this lesson.

Instructional Resource
Supersite

Teaching Tip You may want to assign this **Recapitulación** activity on the Supersite because it has diagnostics. There is an online-only review activity for each grammar point. The Supersite also has a **Repaso de vocabulario** activity with diagnostics.

1 Teaching Tip Ask students to identify the infinitive for each row.

1 Expansion Ask students to provide the forms for **ir, ver**, and **doler**.

2 Expansion
• To challenge students, have them create sentences to express the opposite meaning for each item. Ex: **1. Pablito se cae muy poco.**
• ←🏃→ Ask students to write a paragraph in which they use at least five of the listed adverbs. Then have them exchange papers with a partner for peer editing.

Recapitulación

RESUMEN GRAMATICAL

Completa estas actividades para repasar los conceptos de gramática que aprendiste en esta lección.

1 **Completar** Completa el cuadro con la forma correcta del imperfecto. **24 pts.**

yo/Ud./él/ella	tú	nosotros	Uds./ellos/ellas
era	eras	éramos	eran
cantaba	**cantabas**	cantábamos	cantaban
venía	venías	**veníamos**	venían
quería	querías	queríamos	**querían**

2 **Adverbios** Escoge el adverbio correcto de la lista para completar estas oraciones. Lee con cuidado las oraciones; los adverbios sólo se usan una vez. **16 pts.**

a menudo	apenas	fácilmente
a tiempo	casi	maravillosamente
además	despacio	por lo menos

1. Pablito se cae ___a menudo___; un promedio (*average*) de cuatro veces por semana.

2. No me duele nada y no sufro de ninguna enfermedad; me siento ___maravillosamente___ bien.

3. —Doctor, ¿cómo supo que tuve una operación de garganta?
   —Muy ___fácilmente___, lo leí en su historial médico (*medical history*).

4. ¿Le duele mucho la espalda (*back*)? Entonces tiene que levantarse ___despacio___.

5. Ya te sientes mucho mejor, ¿verdad? Mañana puedes volver al trabajo; tu temperatura es ___casi___ normal.

6. Es importante hacer ejercicio con regularidad, ___por lo menos___ tres veces a la semana.

7. El examen médico no comenzó ni tarde ni temprano. Comenzó ___a tiempo___, a las tres de la tarde.

8. Parece que ya te estás curando del resfriado. ___Apenas___ estás congestionada.

RESUMEN GRAMATICAL

10.1 **The imperfect tense** *pp. 342–343*

The imperfect of regular verbs

cantar	beber	escribir
cantaba	bebía	escribía
cantabas	bebías	escribías
cantaba	bebía	escribía
cantábamos	bebíamos	escribíamos
cantabais	bebíais	escribíais
cantaban	bebían	escribían

▶ There are no stem changes in the imperfect: entender (e:ie) → entendía; servir (e:i) → servía; doler (o:ue) → dolía

▶ The imperfect of hay is había.

▶ Only three verbs are irregular in the imperfect.
ir: iba, ibas, iba, íbamos, ibais, iban
ser: era, eras, era, éramos, erais, eran
ver: veía, veías, veía, veíamos, veíais, veían

10.2 **The preterite and the imperfect** *pp. 346–347*

Preterite	Imperfect
1. Completed actions **Fueron** a Buenos Aires ayer.	1. Ongoing past action Usted **miraba** el fútbol.
2. Beginning or end of past action La película **empezó** a las nueve.	2. Habitual past actions Todos los domingos yo **visitaba** a mi abuela.
3. Series of past actions or events **Me caí** y **me lastimé** el pie.	3. Description of states or characteristics Ella **era** alta. **Quería** descansar.

10.3 **Constructions with se** *pp. 350–351*

Impersonal constructions with se

Se	prohíbe fumar.
	habla español.
	hablan varios idiomas.

TEACHING OPTIONS

TPR Divide the class into three groups: **-ar** verbs, **-er** verbs, and **-ir** verbs. Read a series of sentences that contain the imperfect tense. Have groups stand up when their verb form is used. Ex: **Mi escuela primaria tenía un patio grande. (-er** verb group stands)

Extra Practice ←🏃→ Ask students to use the preterite and imperfect to write a paragraph about an imaginary scenario in which a celebrity got injured and went to the emergency room. Have students describe the person's age, where he or she was, the weather, the time, what he or she was doing when the accident occurred, and what happened at the hospital. Ask volunteers to read their paragraphs aloud.

3 Un accidente Escoge el imperfecto o el pretérito según el contexto para completar esta conversación. **20 pts.**

NURIA Hola, Felipe. ¿Estás bien? ¿Qué es eso?
¿(1) (Te lastimaste/Te lastimabas) el pie?

FELIPE Ayer (2) (tuve/tenía) un pequeño accidente.

NURIA Cuéntame. ¿Cómo (3) (pasó/pasaba)?

FELIPE Bueno, (4) (fueron/eran) las cinco de la tarde y (5) (llovió/llovía) mucho cuando (6) (salí/salía) de la casa en mi bicicleta. No (7) (vi/veía) a una chica que (8) (caminó/caminaba) en mi dirección, y los dos (9) (nos caímos/nos caíamos) al suelo (*ground*).

NURIA Y la chica, ¿está bien ella?

FELIPE Sí. Cuando llegamos al hospital, ella sólo (10) (tuvo/tenía) dolor de cabeza.

4 Oraciones Escribe oraciones con **se** a partir de los elementos dados (*given*). Usa el tiempo especificado y añade pronombres cuando sea necesario. **10 pts.**

modelo
Carlos / quedar / la tarea en casa (pretérito)
A Carlos se le quedó la tarea en casa.

1. en la farmacia / vender / medicamentos (presente) En la farmacia se venden medicamentos.
2. ¿(tú) / olvidar / las llaves / otra vez? (pretérito) ¿Se te olvidaron las llaves otra vez?
3. (yo) / dañar / la computadora (pretérito) Se me dañó la computadora.
4. en esta clase / prohibir / hablar inglés (presente) En esta clase se prohíbe hablar inglés.
5. ellos / romper / las gafas / en el accidente (pretérito) A ellos se les rompieron las gafas en el accidente.

5 En la consulta Escribe al menos cinco oraciones sobre tu última visita al médico. Incluye cinco verbos en pretérito y cinco en imperfecto. Habla de qué te pasó, cómo te sentías, cómo era el/la doctor(a), qué te dijo, etc. Usa tu imaginación. **30 pts.** Answers will vary.

6 Refrán Completa el refrán con las palabras que faltan. **¡4 puntos EXTRA!**

❝Lo que ___bien___ (*well*) se aprende, nunca ___se___ pierde.❞

Lectura

Antes de leer

> **Estrategia**
> **Activating background knowledge**
>
> Using what you already know about a particular subject will often help you better understand a reading selection. For example, if you read an article about a recent medical discovery, you might think about what you already know about health in order to understand unfamiliar words or concepts.

Examinar el texto

Utiliza las estrategias de lectura que tú consideras más efectivas para hacer algunas observaciones preliminares acerca del texto. Después trabajen en parejas para comparar sus observaciones acerca del texto. Luego contesten estas preguntas:
- Analicen el formato del texto: ¿Qué tipo de texto es? ¿Dónde creen que se publicó este artículo?
- ¿Quiénes son Carla Baron y Tomás Monterrey?
- Miren la foto del libro. ¿Qué sugiere el título del libro sobre su contenido?

Conocimiento previo

Ahora piensen en su conocimiento previo° sobre el cuidado de la salud en los viajes. Consideren estas preguntas:
- ¿Viajaron alguna vez a otro estado o a otro país?
- ¿Tuvieron problemas durante sus viajes con el agua, la comida o el clima del lugar?
- ¿Olvidaron poner en su maleta algún medicamento que después necesitaron?
- Imaginen que su compañero/a se va de viaje. Díganle por lo menos cinco cosas que debe hacer para prevenir cualquier problema de salud.

conocimiento previo *background knowledge*

More activities

 vhlcentral Online activities

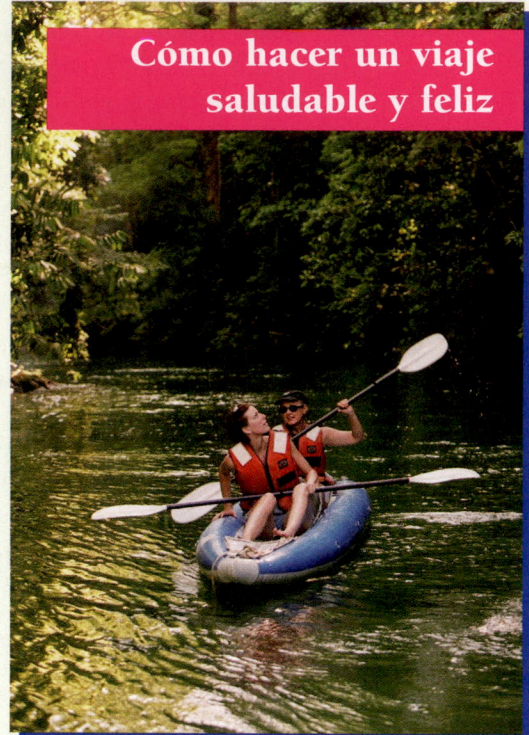

Libro de la semana

Cómo hacer un viaje saludable y feliz

Después de leer

Correspondencias

Busca las correspondencias entre los problemas y las recomendaciones.

Problemas

1. el agua ___b___   4. la identificación ___e___
2. el sol ___d___   5. el clima ___c___
3. la comida ___a___

Recomendaciones

a. Hay que adaptarse a los ingredientes desconocidos (*unknown*).
b. Toma sólo productos purificados (*purified*).
c. Es importante llevar ropa adecuada cuando viajas.
d. Lleva loción o crema con alta protección solar.
e. Lleva tu pasaporte.

Correspondencias Ask students to work together in pairs and use cognates or context clues to match **Problemas** with **Recomendaciones**.

Entrevista a Carla Baron
por Tomás Monterrey

Tomás: ¿Por qué escribió su libro *Cómo hacer un viaje saludable y feliz*?

Carla: Me encanta viajar, conocer otras culturas y escribir. Mi primer viaje lo hice cuando era estudiante universitaria. Todavía recuerdo el día en que llegamos a San Juan, Puerto Rico. Era el panorama ideal para unas vacaciones maravillosas, pero al llegar a la habitación del hotel, bebí mucha agua de la llave° y luego pedí un jugo de frutas con mucho hielo°. El clima en San Juan es tropical y yo tenía mucha sed y calor. Los síntomas llegaron en menos de media hora: pasé dos días con dolor de estómago y corriendo al cuarto de baño cada diez minutos. Desde entonces, siempre que viajo sólo bebo agua mineral y llevo un pequeño bolso con medicinas necesarias, como pastillas para el dolor y también bloqueador solar, una crema repelente de mosquitos y un desinfectante.

Tomás: ¿Son reales° las situaciones que se narran en su libro?

Carla: Sí, son reales y son mis propias° historias°. A menudo los autores crean caricaturas divertidas de un turista en dificultades. ¡En mi libro la turista en dificultades soy yo!

Tomás: ¿Qué recomendaciones puede encontrar el lector en su libro?

Carla: Bueno, mi libro es anecdótico y humorístico, pero el tema de la salud se trata° de manera seria. En general, se dan recomendaciones sobre ropa adecuada para cada sitio, consejos para protegerse del sol, y comidas y bebidas adecuadas para el turista que viaja al Caribe o Suramérica.

Tomás: ¿Tiene algún consejo para las personas que se enferman cuando viajan?

Carla: Muchas veces los turistas toman el avión sin saber nada acerca del país que van a visitar. Ponen toda su ropa en la maleta, toman el pasaporte, la cámara fotográfica y ¡a volar°! Es necesario tomar precauciones porque nuestro cuerpo necesita adaptarse al clima, al sol, a la humedad, al agua y a la comida. Se trata de° viajar, admirar las maravillas del mundo y regresar a casa con hermosos recuerdos. En resumen, el secreto es "prevenir en vez de° curar".

llave *faucet* hielo *ice* reales *true* propias *own* historias *stories*
se trata *is treated* ¡a volar! *Off they go!* Se trata de *It's a question of*
en vez de *instead of*

Seleccionar
- Have students check their work by locating the sections in the text where the information can be found.
- Ask the class the questions. Have volunteers answer orally or write their answers on the board.

Seleccionar

Selecciona la respuesta correcta.

1. El tema principal de este libro es ___d___.
   a. Puerto Rico   b. la salud y el agua   c. otras culturas
   d. el cuidado de la salud en los viajes

2. Las situaciones narradas en el libro son ___a___.
   a. autobiográficas   b. inventadas   c. ficticias
   d. imaginarias

3. ¿Qué recomendaciones no vas a encontrar en este libro? ___d___
   a. cómo vestirse adecuadamente
   b. cómo prevenir las quemaduras solares
   c. consejos sobre la comida y la bebida
   d. cómo dar propina en los países del Caribe o de Suramérica

4. En opinión de la señorita Baron, ___b___.
   a. es bueno tomar agua de la llave y beber jugo de frutas con mucho hielo
   b. es mejor tomar solamente agua embotellada (*bottled*)
   c. los minerales son buenos para el dolor abdominal
   d. es importante visitar el cuarto de baño cada diez minutos

5. ¿Cuál de estos productos no lleva la autora cuando viaja a otros países? ___c___
   a. desinfectante
   b. crema repelente
   c. detergente
   d. pastillas medicinales

TEACHING OPTIONS

Pairs Ask pairs to use the items in **Correspondencias** on page 358 as a model. Have them work together to write additional possibilities for **Problemas** and **Recomendaciones**. Ex: **Problema: el dinero; Recomendación: Lleva una tarjeta de crédito internacional.** When pairs have completed five more items, have them exchange their items with another pair, who will match them.

Heritage Speakers ←👤→ Ask heritage speakers to describe a few health tips for traveling in their families' countries of origin, such as any immunizations that may be required; appropriate clothing; spicy regional foods or dishes that may cause digestive problems; and so forth. Have the rest of the class ask follow-up questions.

Escritura

Estrategia
Mastering the simple past tenses

In Spanish, when you write about events that occurred in the past you will need to know when to use the preterite and when to use the imperfect tense. A good understanding of the uses of each tense will make it much easier to determine which one to use as you write.

Look at the summary of the uses of the preterite and the imperfect and write your own example sentence for each of the rules described.

Preterite vs. imperfect

Preterite
1. Completed actions
   _____
   _____
2. Beginning or end of past actions
   _____
   _____
3. Series of past actions
   _____
   _____

Imperfect
1. Ongoing past actions
   _____
   _____
2. Habitual past actions
   _____
   _____
3. Mental, physical, and emotional states and characteristics in the past
   _____
   _____

Get together with a few classmates to compare your example sentences. Then use these sentences and the chart as a guide to help you decide which tense to use as you are writing a story or other type of narration about the past.

Tema

Escribir una historia

Escribe una historia acerca de una experiencia tuya° (o de otra persona) con una enfermedad, accidente o problema médico. Tu historia puede ser real o imaginaria y puede tratarse de un incidente divertido, humorístico o desastroso. Incluye todos los detalles relevantes. Consulta la lista de sugerencias° con detalles que puedes incluir.

▶ Descripción del/de la paciente
  nombre y apellidos
  edad
  características físicas
  historial médico°

▶ Descripción de los síntomas
  enfermedades
  accidente
  problemas médicos

▶ Descripción del tratamiento°
  tratamientos
  recetas
  operaciones

NATIONAL communication STANDARDS

tuya *of yours* **sugerencias** *suggestions* **historial médico** *medical history* **tratamiento** *treatment*

EVALUATION: Historia

Criteria	Scale
Content	1 2 3 4
Organization	1 2 3 4
Use of preterite and imperfect	1 2 3 4
Use of vocabulary	1 2 3 4
Accuracy and mechanics	1 2 3 4

Scoring	
Excellent	18–20 points
Good	14–17 points
Satisfactory	10–13 points
Unsatisfactory	< 10 points

Escuchar

Antes de escuchar

Estrategia

Listening for specific information

You can listen for specific information effectively once you identify the subject of a conversation and use your background knowledge to predict what kinds of information you might hear.

To practice this strategy, you will listen to a paragraph from a letter Marta wrote to a friend about her fifteenth birthday celebration. Before you listen to the paragraph, use what you know about this type of party to predict the content of the letter. What kinds of details might Marta include in her description of the celebration? Now listen to the paragraph and jot down the specific information Marta relates. Then compare these details to the predictions you made about the letter.

Preparación

Mira la foto. ¿Con quién crees que está conversando Carlos Peña? ¿De qué están hablando? **Answers will vary.**

Ahora escucha

Síntomas

Ahora escucha la conversación de la señorita Méndez y Carlos Peña. Marca las oraciones donde se mencionan los síntomas de Carlos.

1. ____ Tiene infección en los ojos.
2. ____ Se lastimó el dedo.
3. ✔ No puede dormir.
4. ✔ Siente dolor en los huesos.
5. ____ Está mareado.
6. ✔ Está congestionado.
7. ____ Le duele el estómago.
8. ✔ Le duele la cabeza.
9. ____ Es alérgico a la aspirina.
10. ✔ Tiene tos.
11. ✔ Le duele la garganta.
12. ____ Se rompió la pierna.
13. ____ Tiene dolor de oído.
14. ✔ Tiene frío.

Comprensión

Preguntas

1. ¿Tiene fiebre Carlos? Carlos no sabe si tiene fiebre pero tiene mucho frío y le duelen los huesos.
2. ¿Cuánto tiempo hace que le duele la garganta a Carlos? Hace cinco días que le duele la garganta.
3. ¿Qué tiene que hacer el médico antes de recetarle algo a Carlos? Tiene que ver si tiene una infección.
4. ¿A qué hora es su cita con el médico? Es a las tres de la tarde.
5. Después de darle una cita con el médico, ¿qué otra información le pide a Carlos la señorita del consultorio? Le pide su nombre, su fecha de nacimiento y su número de teléfono.
6. En tu opinión, ¿qué tiene Carlos? ¿Gripe? ¿Un resfriado? ¿Alergias? Explica tu opinión. **Answers will vary.**

Diálogo

Con un(a) compañero/a, escribe el diálogo entre el Dr. Aguilar y Carlos Peña en el consultorio del médico. Usa la información del diálogo telefónico para pensar en lo que dice el médico mientras examina a Carlos. Imagina cómo responde Carlos y qué preguntas le hace al médico. ¿Cuál es el diagnóstico del médico?

Section Goals

In **Escuchar**, students will:
- listen to a short paragraph and jot down specific information
- answer questions based on the content of a recorded conversation

Instructional Resources
Supersite: Audio (Textbook MP3s); Resources (Scripts)

Estrategia
Script Ya sé que no pudiste venir a mi quinceañera. ¡Cuánto lo siento, Juanita! Vinieron muchos invitados, ¡creo que eran más de cien! Todos se divirtieron y yo lo pasé fenomenal. Llevé un traje largo y rosado con mucho encaje, y guantes y zapatos del mismo color. Mi tía Rosa, la madrina de la fiesta, me preparó el pastel. Me imagino que sabes que el pastel era de chocolate porque me fascina el chocolate. Me dieron muchos regalos. ¡Imagínate!, mis abuelos me regalaron un viaje para ir a visitarte.

Teaching Tip Have students look at the photo and guide them to see that **Carlos Peña** is talking to a health care provider about his illness.

Ahora escucha
Script SRTA. MÉNDEZ: Consultorio del Dr. Aguilar. Buenos días.
CARLOS PEÑA: Buenos días, señorita. Habla Carlos Peña. Mire, no me siento nada bien.
M: ¿Qué tiene?
C: Tengo mucha tos. Apenas me deja dormir. Estoy muy congestionado y tengo un tremendo dolor de cabeza.
M: ¿Cuánto tiempo hace que se siente así?
C: Bueno, hace cinco días que me empezó a doler la garganta. Fue de mal en peor.
M: ¿Tiene fiebre?
C: Pues, en realidad, no lo sé. No me tomé la temperatura,

(Script continues at far left in the bottom panels.)

---

pero creo que sí tengo fiebre porque tengo mucho frío y me duelen los huesos.
M: Pienso que usted tiene la gripe. Primero hay que verificar que no tiene una infección, pero creo que el doctor le va a recetar algo que va a ayudarle. Le puedo dar una cita con el médico hoy a las tres de la tarde.
C: Excelente.
M: ¿Cómo me dijo que se llama?

C: Carlos Peña, señorita.
M: ¿Y su fecha de nacimiento y su teléfono, por favor?
C: 4 de octubre de 1983, y mi teléfono... seis cuarenta y tres, veinticinco, cincuenta y dos.
M: Muy bien. Hasta las tres.
C: Sí. Muchas gracias, señorita, y hasta luego.

En pantalla Video

El objetivo de esta original y divertida campaña es informar y sensibilizar° a la sociedad sobre la enfermedad del Parkinson y el sufrimiento que ocasiona° a los que la padecen°. Además de darse a conocer° y enfrentarse a° la indiferencia, con esta campaña también se pretende° recaudar fondos°, ya que la Asociación Parkinson Alicante se ha visto afectada por la crisis económica española, disminuyendo así el número de ayudas recibidas.

Vocabulario útil

aullar	to howl
hombre lobo	werewolf
lucha	fight, battle
manada	pack (of wolves)
subvenciones	subsidies
tiembla	trembles, shakes

Preparación

¿Conoces alguna ONG (organización no gubernamental)? ¿Cuál? ¿Qué cosas se hacen en esa organización para ayudar a los demás? Utiliza construcciones con *se*. Answers will vary.

Escoger

Elige la opción correcta.

1. Las __a__ a la asociación estaban fallando.
   a. subvenciones   b. peticiones
2. La asociación decidió inventar una __b__ para el Parkinson.
   a. pastilla   b. causa
3. Michael J. Fox hizo el papel de un __a__ y tiene Parkinson.
   a. hombre lobo   b. hombre araña
4. La forma para llegar a todo el mundo es __b__ lo más fuerte (*loud*) posible.
   a. cantar   b. aullar

Una campaña

En parejas, creen una campaña para transformar una organización, real o ficticia. Utilicen el imperfecto y construcciones con *se*. Answers will vary.

sensibilizar *to raise awareness* ocasiona *causes* la padecen *suffer from it*
darse a conocer *spreading the word* enfrentarse a *to fight against*
se pretende *the hope is to* recaudar fondos *to raise money*

Asociación Parkinson Alicante

Hemos decidido inventarnos una causa para el Parkinson.

Tal vez la gente pueda creerse que ser hombre lobo provoque Parkinson.

Queremos que la gente conozca la asociación y nos ayude en esta lucha.

More activities

vhlcentral   Online activities

NATIONAL communication cultures STANDARDS

Video

Argentina tiene una gran tradición médica influenciada desde el siglo XIX por la medicina francesa. Tres de los cinco premios Nobel de esta nación están relacionados con investigaciones médicas que han hecho° grandes aportes° al avance de las ciencias de la salud. Además, existen otros adelantos° de médicos argentinos que han hecho historia. Entre ellos se cuentan el *bypass* coronario, desarrollado° por el cirujano° René Favaloro en 1967, y la técnica de cirugía cardiovascular sin circulación extracorpórea° desarrollada en 1978 por Federico Benetti, quien es considerado uno de los padres de la cirugía cardíaca moderna.

Vocabulario útil

la cita previa	previous appointment
la guardia	emergency room
Me di un golpe.	I got hit.
la práctica	rotation (hands-on medical experience)

Preparación

¿Qué haces si tienes un pequeño accidente o quieres hacer una consulta? ¿Visitas a tu médico general o vas al hospital? ¿Debes pedir un turno (*appointment*)?

Answers will vary.

¿Cierto o falso?

Indica si las oraciones son **ciertas** o **falsas**.

1. Silvina tuvo un accidente en su automóvil. Falso.
2. Silvina fue a la guardia del hospital. Cierto.
3. La guardia del hospital está abierta sólo durante el día y es necesario tener cita previa. Falso.
4. Los entrevistados (*interviewees*) tienen enfermedades graves. Falso.
5. En Argentina, los médicos reciben la certificación cuando terminan la práctica. Cierto.

han hecho *have made* aportes *contributions* adelantos *advances*
desarrollado *developed* cirujano *surgeon* extracorpórea *out-of-body*
podría *could*

La salud

1

¿Le podría° pedir que me explique qué es la guardia?

2

Nuestro hospital público es gratuito para todas las personas.

3

... la carrera de medicina comienza con el primer año de la universidad.

More activities
vhlcentral   VM pp. 55–56   Online activities

Video

Costa Rica

NATIONAL connections cultures STANDARDS

El país en cifras

▶ **Área:** 51.100 km² (19.730 millas²), *aproximadamente el área de Virginia Occidental°*

▶ **Población:** 4.930.000
Costa Rica es el país de Centroamérica con la población más homogénea. El 84% de sus habitantes es blanco y mestizo°. Más del 50% de la población es de ascendencia° española y un alto porcentaje tiene sus orígenes en otros países europeos.

▶ **Capital:** San José—1.170.000

▶ **Ciudades principales:** Alajuela, Cartago, Puntarenas, Heredia

▶ **Moneda:** colón costarricense

▶ **Idioma:** español (oficial)

Bandera de Costa Rica

Costarricenses célebres
▶ **Carmen Lyra,** escritora (1888–1949)
▶ **Chavela Vargas,** cantante (1919–2012)
▶ **Óscar Arias Sánchez,** expresidente de Costa Rica (1941–)
▶ **Laura Chinchilla Miranda,** expresidenta de Costa Rica (1959–)
▶ **Claudia Poll,** nadadora° olímpica (1972–)

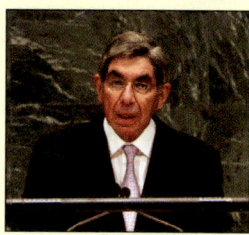

Óscar Arias recibió el Premio Nobel de la Paz en 1987.

Virginia Occidental *West Virginia* mestizo *of indigenous and white parentage* ascendencia *descent* nadadora *swimmer*

Mercado Central en San José

Vista del volcán Aren

NICARAGUA

Río San Juan

Río Tempisque

Cordillera de Guanacaste

Cordillera Central

Volcán Arenal

Cordillera de Tilarán

Alajuela

Puntarenas

Río Grande de Tárcoles

Heredia

Volcán Irazu

San José

Cartago

Cordille

Edificio Metálico en San José

Océano Pacífico

Basílica de Nuestra Señora de los Ángeles en Cartago

ESTADOS UNIDOS

OCÉANO ATLÁNTICO

COSTA RICA

OCÉANO PACÍFICO

AMÉRICA DEL SUR

More activities

vhlcentral | WB pp. 121–122 | Online activities

ACTIVIDADES

1 **¿Cierto o falso?** Indica si lo que dicen las oraciones es **cierto** o **falso**.

1. El colón costarricense es la moneda de Costa Rica. Cierto
2. Laura Chinchilla Miranda es la presidenta de Costa Rica. Falso
3. Óscar Arias Sánchez trabaja en un consultorio. Falso
4. Se pueden ver quetzales, monos y jaguares en algunos de los parques nacionales de Costa Rica. Cierto
5. En Centroamérica, Costa Rica fue el primer país que desarrolló la industria del café. Cierto
6. Pocas personas saben leer y escribir en Costa Rica. Falso
7. Costa Rica gasta mucho dinero en su ejército. Falso
8. La educación en Costa Rica es gratuita para todos sus ciudadanos. Cierto
9. En Costa Rica, las carretas de bueyes se utilizaban para transportar el maíz. Falso
10. El Museo Nacional de Costa Rica fue antes un cuartel del ejército. Cierto

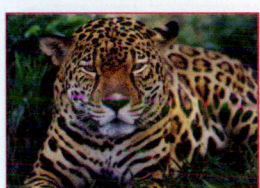

Lugares • Los parques nacionales

El sistema de parques nacionales de Costa Rica ocupa aproximadamente el 12% de su territorio y fue establecido° para la protección de su biodiversidad. En los parques, los ecoturistas pueden admirar montañas, cataratas° y una gran variedad de plantas exóticas. Algunos ofrecen también la oportunidad de ver quetzales°, monos°, jaguares, armadillos y mariposas° en su hábitat natural.

▷ Economía • Las plantaciones de café

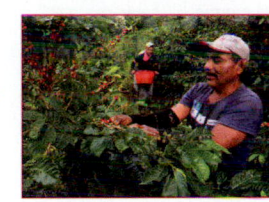

Costa Rica fue el primer país centroamericano en desarrollar° la industria del café. En el siglo° XIX, los costarricenses empezaron a exportar esta semilla a Inglaterra°, lo que significó una contribución importante a la economía de la nación. Actualmente, más de 50.000 costarricenses trabajan en el cultivo del café. Este producto representa cerca del 10% de sus exportaciones anuales.

Sociedad • Una nación progresista

Costa Rica es un país progresista. Tiene un nivel de alfabetización° del 96%, uno de los más altos de Latinoamérica. En 1871, esta nación centroamericana abolió la pena de muerte°, y en 1948 eliminó el ejército° e hizo obligatoria y gratuita° la educación para todos sus ciudadanos.

▷ Artesanía • La carreta

PANAMÁ

La carreta de bueyes es uno de los símbolos nacionales de Costa Rica. Entre 1850 y 1935, se utilizó principalmente para transportar el café desde las montañas del Valle Central hasta los puertos del océano Pacífico, y desde allí se exportaba a Europa. Su decorado de figuras geométricas de colores brillantes la convierte en la artesanía costarricense más famosa.

establecido *established* cataratas *waterfalls* quetzales *type of tropical bird* monos *monkeys* mariposas *butterflies* en desarrollar *to develop* siglo *century* Inglaterra *England* nivel de alfabetización *literacy rate* pena de muerte *death penalty* ejército *army* gratuita *free*

Parque Morazán en San José

¡Increíble pero cierto!

Costa Rica no tiene ejército. Sin gastos° militares, el gobierno puede invertir° más dinero en la educación y en las artes. En la foto aparece el Museo Nacional de Costa Rica, antiguo cuartel° del ejército.

gastos *expenditures* invertir *to invest* cuartel *barracks*

---

2 ¿Qué aprendiste? Contesta las preguntas.

1. ¿Cómo se llama la capital de Costa Rica? San José
2. ¿Quién es Claudia Poll? una nadadora olímpica
3. ¿Qué porcentaje del territorio de Costa Rica ocupan los parques nacionales? aproximadamente el 12%
4. ¿Cuántos costarricenses trabajan en las plantaciones de café hoy día? más de 50.000 costarricenses
5. ¿Cuándo eliminó Costa Rica la pena de muerte? en 1871

3 ¿Qué se hace? En parejas, túrnense para decir qué se hace en Costa Rica.

modelo

Estudiante 1: En Costa Rica se habla español.
Estudiante 2: En Costa Rica se exporta café.

Los parques nacionales
Costa Rica's system of national parks was begun in the 1960s. With the addition of buffer zones in which some logging and farming are allowed, the percentage of Costa Rica's territory protected by environmental legislation rose to 27%.

Las plantaciones de café
Invite students to prepare a coffee-tasting session, where they sample the coffees of Central America. You may wish to compare them to South American or African coffees as well. Teach vocabulary to describe the flavors: **rico, amargo, fuerte,** and so forth. You may want to play the **Panorama cultural** video for this paragraph.

Una nación progresista
Because of its mild climate (in terms of weather *and* politics), Costa Rica has become a major destination for retired and expatriate North Americans. Survey students to see how many have visited Costa Rica already, and how many know of friends or family who have visited or live there.

La carreta UNESCO declared the Costa Rican oxcart an Intangible Cultural Heritage of Humanity in 2005. You may want to play the **Panorama cultural** video for this paragraph.

¡Increíble pero cierto! Costa Rica has one of the most long-standing democratic traditions in the Americas. Although it has no army, it does have a national police force and a rural guard.

TEACHING OPTIONS

Worth Noting Costa Rica has three types of lands protected by ecological legislation: **parques nacionales, refugios silvestres,** and **reservas biológicas**. Costa Rica's most famous protected area is the **Reserva Biológica Bosque Nuboso Monteverde** (Monteverde Cloud Forest Biological Reserve), where over 400 different species of birds have been recorded. The town of Monteverde was founded in 1950 by Quakers from the United States, who began dairy farming and cheese-making there. In order to protect the watershed, the settlers decided to preserve about a third of their property as a biological reserve. In 1972 this area more than doubled, and then became the **Reserva Biológica**. Today Monteverde still has a cheese factory (**La Fábrica de Quesos Monteverde**) and its cheeses are sold throughout the country.

Teaching Tip You may want to assign the **Prueba de práctica**, with its diagnostics and review activities, in the online-only **Repaso** section on the Supersite. There is also a **Repaso oral** in this section. For the Sixth Edition, a new summative vocabulary activity with speech recognition has been added to the **Repaso** section.

El cuerpo

la boca	mouth
el brazo	arm
la cabeza	head
el corazón	heart
el cuello	neck
el cuerpo	body
el dedo	finger
el dedo del pie	toe
el estómago	stomach
la garganta	throat
el hueso	bone
la nariz	nose
el oído	(sense of) hearing; inner ear
el ojo	eye
la oreja	(outer) ear
el pie	foot
la pierna	leg
la rodilla	knee
el tobillo	ankle

La salud

el accidente	accident
el antibiótico	antibiotic
la aspirina	aspirin
la clínica	clinic
el consultorio	doctor's office
el/la dentista	dentist
el/la doctor(a)	doctor
el dolor (de cabeza)	(head)ache; pain
el/la enfermero/a	nurse
el examen médico	physical exam
la farmacia	pharmacy
la gripe	flu
el hospital	hospital
la infección	infection
el medicamento	medication
la medicina	medicine
la operación	operation
el/la paciente	patient
la pastilla	pill
la radiografía	X-ray
la receta	prescription
el resfriado	cold (illness)
la sala de emergencia(s)	emergency room
la salud	health
el síntoma	symptom
la tos	cough

Verbos

caerse	to fall (down)
dañar	to damage; to break down
darse con	to bump into; to run into
doler (o:ue)	to hurt
enfermarse	to get sick
estar enfermo/a	to be sick
estornudar	to sneeze
lastimarse (el pie)	to injure (one's foot)
olvidar	to forget
poner una inyección	to give an injection
prohibir	to prohibit
recetar	to prescribe
romper	to break
romperse (la pierna)	to break (one's leg)
sacar(se) un diente	to have a tooth removed
ser alérgico/a (a)	to be allergic (to)
sufrir una enfermedad	to suffer an illness
tener dolor (m.)	to have pain
tener fiebre (f.)	to have a fever
tomar la temperatura	to take someone's temperature
torcerse (o:ue) (el tobillo)	to sprain (one's ankle)
toser	to cough

Adjetivos

congestionado/a	congested
embarazada	pregnant
grave	grave; serious
mareado/a	dizzy; nauseated
médico/a	medical
saludable	healthy
sano/a	healthy

Adverbios

a menudo	often
a tiempo	on time
a veces	sometimes
además (de)	furthermore; besides
apenas	hardly; scarcely
así	like this; so
bastante	enough; rather
casi	almost
con frecuencia	frequently
de niño/a	as a child
de vez en cuando	from time to time
despacio	slowly
menos	less
muchas veces	a lot; many times
poco	little
por lo menos	at least
pronto	soon
rápido	quickly
todos los días	every day

Conjunción

mientras	while

Expresiones útiles	See page 337.

More activities

vhlcentral | LM p. 60

La tecnología

Communicative Goals

You will learn how to:

- Talk about using technology and electronics
- Use common expressions on the telephone
- Talk about car trouble

Lesson Goals

In **Lección 11**, students will be introduced to the following:

- terms related to technology, electronics, and the Internet
- terms related to cars and their accessories
- social networks in Spanish-speaking countries
- text messaging
- familiar (**tú**) commands
- uses of **por** and **para**
- reciprocal reflexive verbs
- stressed possessive adjectives and pronouns
- recognizing borrowed words
- listing key words before writing
- giving instructions in an e-mail
- recognizing the genre of spoken discourse
- a video from Spain promoting the use of physical books
- a video about technology in Peru
- cultural, geographic, and historical information about Argentina

A primera vista Here are some additional questions you can ask: ¿**Te gustan los teléfonos celulares? ¿Para qué usas tu teléfono celular? ¿Cómo te comunicas con tus amigos? ¿Por chat, por teléfono o se escriben mensajes electrónicos?**

Teaching Tip Look for these icons for additional communicative practice:

→👥←	Interpretive communication
←👤→	Presentational communication
👥↔	Interpersonal communication

🔊 A PRIMERA VISTA

- ¿Qué hacen las chicas?
- ¿Lo pasan bien o mal?
- ¿Son unas chicas saludables?
- ¿Qué partes del cuerpo se ven en la foto?

INSTRUCTIONAL RESOURCES

Supersite (vhlcentral.com)
Video: **Fotonovela, Flash cultura, En pantalla, Panorama cultural**
Audio: Textbook and Lab MP3 Files

Activity Pack: Information Gap Activities, games, additional activity handouts
Resources: SAM Answer Key, Scripts, Translations, **Vocabulario adicional**, sample lesson plan, Grammar Presentation Slides, Digital Image Bank

Testing Program: Quizzes, Tests, Exams, MP3s
Student Activities Manual: Workbook/Video Manual/Lab Manual
WebSAM (online Student Activities Manual)

La tecnología

Más vocabulario

la batería	battery
la cámara digital	digital camera
el canal	(TV) channel
el correo de voz	voice mail
el archivo	file
la arroba	@ symbol
el blog	blog
el buscador	browser
la conexión inalámbrica	wireless connection
la contraseña	password
la dirección electrónica	e-mail address
la impresora	printer
Internet	Internet
la página principal	home page
el perfil	profile
el programa de computación	software
la red	network; Web
el sitio web	website
apagar	to turn off
borrar	to erase
cargar	to charge; to upload
chatear	to chat
conectarse a Internet	to get connected to the Internet
descargar	to download
funcionar	to work
grabar	to record
guardar	to save
imprimir	to print
llamar	to call
poner, prender	to turn on
sonar (o:ue)	to ring
descompuesto/a	not working; out of order
lento/a	slow
lleno/a	full

Variación léxica

computadora ⟷ ordenador (*Esp.*), computador (*Col.*)
descargar ⟷ bajar (*Arg., Col., Esp., Ven.*)

el televisor

el (teléfono) celular

la tableta

la pantalla

la computadora (portátil)

el teclado

el ratón

el mensaje de texto

textear

Práctica

el control remoto

escanear

la aplicación

el cargador

1 **¿Lógico o ilógico?** Indica si las situaciones que vas a escuchar son **lógicas** o **ilógicas**.

1. ilógico
2. ilógico
3. lógico
4. lógico
5. ilógico
6. lógico
7. ilógico
8. lógico

2 **Nuevo celular** Escucha la conversación entre Liliana y un empleado de una tienda de artículos electrónicos e indica si cada afirmación es **cierta** o **falsa**.

	Cierto	Falso
1. Liliana quiere comprar un celular con acceso a Internet.	●	○
2. En la tienda no hay nuevos modelos de celulares.	○	●
3. El celular tiene acceso a Internet pero no tiene cámara.	○	●
4. En el celular se pueden usar muchas aplicaciones.	●	○
5. Liliana también quiere ver algunas cámaras digitales.	○	●
6. En la tienda no hay tabletas.	○	●

3 **Emparejar** Empareja las palabras de forma lógica.

_e_ 1. conexión inalámbrica	a. archivo
_a_ 2. imprimir	b. arroba
_f_ 3. textear	c. batería
_d_ 4. control remoto	d. canal
_h_ 5. perfil	e. lenta
_c_ 6. cargador	f. mensaje de texto
_g_ 7. página principal	g. sitio web
_b_ 8. dirección electrónica	h. red social

4 **Oraciones** Escribe oraciones usando estos elementos. Usa el pretérito y añade las palabras necesarias.

1. Jaime / decidir / comprar / tableta
   Jaime decidió comprar una tableta.
2. tú / apagar / televisor / diez / noche
   Tú apagaste el televisor a las diez de la noche.
3. Daniel y su esposa / comprar / computadora portátil / ayer
   Daniel y su esposa compraron una computadora portátil ayer.
4. Sara y yo / ir / tienda / para / buscar / impresora
   Sara y yo fuimos a la tienda para buscar una impresora.
5. yo / descargar / fotos
   Yo descargué las fotos.
6. teléfono celular / sonar / pero / yo / no contestar
   El teléfono celular sonó, pero yo no contesté.

TEACHING OPTIONS

Pairs 👤↔👤 Have pairs of students role-play one of these situations. 1. An irate customer claims that his/her new laptop computer doesn't work and wants to exchange it. The store employee says there's nothing wrong with it. 2. A customer can't decide which smartphone to get. The store employee explains the different features.

Heritage Speakers ↔👤→ Ask heritage speakers to describe their experiences with Spanish-language Web applications, such as e-mail, instant messenger, or websites. Do they or their families regularly visit Spanish-language websites? Which ones?

En la gasolinera

el capó, el cofre
el parabrisas
el volante
el navegador GPS
el radio
el baúl
la gasolina
la llanta
Revisa el aceite. (revisar)
Llena el tanque. (llenar)
el carro, el coche

5774 ZGZ

Más vocabulario

la autopista	highway
la calle	street
la carretera	highway; (main) road
la circulación, el tráfico	traffic
el garaje, el taller (mecánico)	garage; (mechanic's) repair shop
la licencia de conducir	driver's license
el/la mecánico/a	mechanic
la policía	police (force)
la velocidad máxima	speed limit
arrancar	to start
arreglar	to fix; to arrange
bajar(se) de	to get off of/out of (a vehicle)
conducir, manejar	to drive
estacionar	to park
parar	to stop
subir(se) a	to get on/into (a vehicle)

5 **Conversación** Completa la conversación.

el aceite	la gasolina	llenar	el parabrisas	el taller
el baúl	las llantas	manejar	revisar	el volante

EMPLEADO Bienvenido al (1) ___taller___ mecánico *Óscar*. ¿En qué le puedo servir?

JUAN Buenos días. Quiero (2) ___llenar___ el tanque y revisar (3) ___el aceite___, por favor.

EMPLEADO Con mucho gusto. Si quiere, también le limpio (4) ___el parabrisas___.

JUAN Sí, gracias. Está un poquito sucio. La próxima semana tengo que (5) ___manejar___ hasta Buenos Aires. ¿Puede cambiar (6) ___las llantas___? Están gastadas (*worn*).

EMPLEADO Claro que sí, pero voy a tardar (*it will take me*) un par de horas.

JUAN Mejor regreso mañana. Ahora no tengo tiempo. ¿Cuánto le debo por (7) ___la gasolina___?

EMPLEADO Sesenta pesos. Y veinticinco por (8) ___revisar___ y cambiar el aceite.

◄ **CONSULTA**

For more information about **Buenos Aires**, see **Panorama**, p. 400.

6 **Completar** Completa estas oraciones.

1. Otra palabra para coche es… carro.
2. Para poder conducir legalmente, necesitas… una licencia de conducir.
3. Si tu carro no funciona, debes llevarlo a… un mecánico/taller/garaje.
4. Para llenar el tanque de tu coche, necesitas ir a… la gasolinera.
5. Antes de un viaje largo, es importante revisar… el aceite.
6. Otra palabra para autopista es… carretera.
7. Mientras hablas por teléfono celular, no es buena idea… manejar/conducir.
8. Puedes poner las maletas en… el baúl.

◄ **¡LENGUA VIVA!**

Aunque **carro** es el término que se usa en la mayoría de países hispanos, no es el único. En España, por ejemplo, se dice **coche**, y en Argentina, Chile y Uruguay se dice **auto**.

Comunicación

7 **Preguntas** Trabajen en parejas y túrnense para contestar estas preguntas. Answers will vary.

1. a. ¿Tienes un teléfono celular? ¿Para qué lo usas?
   b. ¿Qué utilizas más: el teléfono o el correo electrónico? ¿Por qué?
   c. En tu opinión, ¿cuáles son las ventajas (*advantages*) y desventajas de los diferentes modos de comunicación?
2. a. ¿Con qué frecuencia usas la computadora?
   b. ¿Para qué usas Internet?
   c. ¿Tienes tu propio blog? ¿Cómo es?
3. a. ¿Miras la televisión con frecuencia? ¿Qué programas ves?
   b. ¿Dónde miras tus programas favoritos, en la tele o en la computadora?
   c. ¿Ves películas en la computadora? ¿Cuál es tu película favorita de todos los tiempos (*of all time*)?
   d. ¿A través de (*By*) qué medio escuchas música? ¿Radio, teléfono celular o computadora?
4. a. ¿Tienes licencia de conducir?
   b. ¿Tienes carro? Descríbelo.

NOTA CULTURAL

Algunos sitios web utilizan códigos para identificar su país de origen. Éstos son los códigos para algunos países hispanohablantes:

Argentina	.ar
Colombia	.co
España	.es
México	.mx
Venezuela	.ve

8 **Postal** En parejas, lean la tarjeta postal. Después contesten las preguntas. Answers will vary.

19 julio de 1979

Hola, Paco:

¡Saludos! Estamos de viaje por unas semanas. La Costa del Sol es muy bonita. No hemos encontrado (*we haven't found*) a tus amigos porque nunca están en casa cuando llamamos. El teléfono suena y suena y nadie contesta. Vamos a seguir llamando.

Sacamos muchas fotos muy divertidas. Cuando regresemos y las revelemos (*get them developed*), te las voy a enseñar. Las playas son preciosas. Hasta ahora el único problema fue que la oficina en la cual reservamos un carro perdió nuestros papeles y tuvimos que esperar mucho tiempo.

También tuvimos un pequeño problema con el hotel. La agencia de viajes nos reservó una habitación en un hotel que está muy lejos de todo. No podemos cambiarla, pero no me importa mucho. A pesar de eso, estamos contentos.

Tu hermana, Gabriela

Francisco Jiménez
San Lorenzo 3250
Rosario, Argentina 2000

1. ¿Cuáles son los problemas que ocurren en el viaje de Gabriela?
2. Con la tecnología de hoy, ¿existen los mismos problemas cuando se viaja? ¿Por qué?
3. Hagan una comparación entre la tecnología de los años 70 y 80 y la de hoy.
4. Imaginen que la hija de Gabriela escribe un mensaje electrónico sobre el mismo tema con fecha de hoy. Escriban ese mensaje, incorporando la tecnología actual (teléfonos celulares, Internet, cámaras digitales, etc.). Inventen nuevos problemas.

7 **Teaching Tip** For item 2, if few or no students have their own blogs, ask them if they follow any and what they are about. Encourage them to seek out some blogs related to learning Spanish as a foreign language.

7 **Expansion** Write names of different communication devices on the board (Ex: **teléfono celular, computadora**). Then survey the class to find out how many people own or use these items. Analyze the trends of the class.

8 **Teaching Tip** Possible answers: **1.** Gabriela no encuentra a los amigos de Paco porque nunca están en casa, tuvo que esperar mucho por el carro y su hotel estaba muy lejos de todo. **2.** No existen los mismos problemas porque existen el correo de voz y los teléfonos celulares, se puede reservar un carro en Internet y se puede buscar información sobre un hotel en la red antes del viaje.

8 **Expansion** Ask groups to write a postcard similar to the one in the activity, except that in theirs the problems encountered during the trip are a direct result of the existence of technology, not its absence.

Note: At this point you may want to present *Vocabulario adicional: Más vocabulario para el carro y la tecnología* from the Supersite.

TEACHING OPTIONS

Extra Practice For homework, have students do an Internet research project on technology and technology terminology in the Spanish-speaking world. Suggest possible topics and websites where students may look for information. Have students write out their reports and present them to the class.

Large Groups Stage a debate about the role of technology in today's world. Divide the class into two groups and assign each side a position. Propose this debate topic: **La tecnología: ¿beneficio o no?** Allow groups time to plan their arguments before staging the debate.

Section Goals

In **Fotonovela**, students will:
- receive comprehensible input from free-flowing discourse
- learn functional phrases that preview lesson grammatical structures

Instructional Resources

Supersite: Video (*Fotonovela*); Resources (Scripts, Translations, Answer Keys)
WebSAM
Video Manual

Video Recap: Lección 10

Before doing this **Fotonovela** section, review the previous episode with these questions:
1. ¿Qué estaba haciendo Jimena cuando empezó a sentirse mal? (Estaba estudiando con Elena.) 2. ¿Quién llevó a Jimena al médico? (Elena la llevó.) 3. ¿Cuáles eran los síntomas de Jimena? (Tosía, le dolía la garganta y estaba congestionada.) 4. ¿Qué le recetó el médico? (Algo / Una medicina para la garganta.)

Video Synopsis

Miguel's car has broken down again, and he has to take it to his friend **Jorge's** repair shop. In the meantime, **Maru** has bad luck with her computer. Their friends do their best to help them with their technological problems. **Miguel's** car is saved one last time, but **Maru** may not be so lucky with her computer.

Teaching Tips

- Have students predict the content of this episode based on the video stills only.
- Quickly review students' predictions and ask a few questions to guide them in summarizing this episode.

En el taller

El coche de Miguel está descompuesto y Maru tiene problemas con su computadora.

 Video

PERSONAJES

 MIGUEL   JORGE

1

MIGUEL ¿Cómo lo ves?

JORGE Creo que puedo arreglarlo. ¿Me pasas la llave?

2

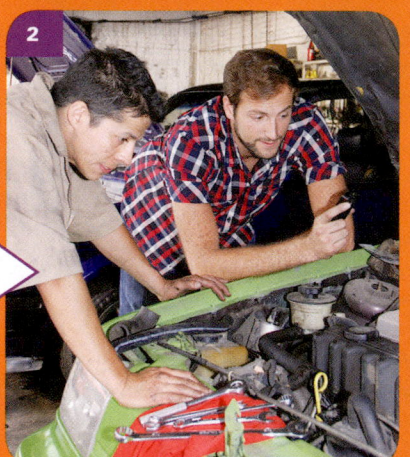

JORGE ¿Y dónde está Maru?

MIGUEL Acaba de enviarme un mensaje de texto: "Última noticia sobre la computadora portátil: todavía está descompuesta. Moni intenta arreglarla. Voy para allá".

JORGE ¿Está descompuesta tu computadora?

MIGUEL No, la mía no, la suya. Una amiga la está ayudando.

JORGE Un mal día para la tecnología, ¿no?

3

MIGUEL Ella está preparando un proyecto para ver si puede hacer sus prácticas profesionales en el Museo de Antropología.

JORGE ¿Y todo está en la computadora?

MIGUEL Y claro.

4

MARU Buenos días, Jorge.

JORGE ¡Qué gusto verte, Maru! ¿Cómo está la computadora?

MARU Mi amiga Mónica recuperó muchos archivos, pero muchos otros se borraron.

5

6

MARU Estamos en una triste situación. Yo necesito una computadora nueva, y Miguel necesita otro coche.

JORGE Y un televisor nuevo para mí, por favor.

TEACHING OPTIONS

Video Tips General suggestions for using video clips in the classroom can be found in the front matter of this Instructor's Annotated Edition.

En el taller →👤← Show the **En el taller** episode once without sound and have the class create a plot summary based on the visual cues. Then show the episode with sound and have the class make corrections and fill in any gaps in the plot summary.

MARU

MARU ¿Qué vamos a hacer, Miguel?

MIGUEL Tranquila, cariño. Por eso tenemos amigos como Jorge y Mónica. Nos ayudamos los unos a los otros.

JORGE ¿No te sientes afortunada, Maru? No te preocupes. Sube.

MIGUEL ¡Por fin!

MARU Gracias, Jorge. Eres el mejor mecánico de la ciudad.

MIGUEL ¿Cuánto te debo por el trabajo?

JORGE Hombre, no es nada. Guárdalo para el coche nuevo. Eso sí, recomiéndame con tus amigos.

MIGUEL Gracias, Jorge.

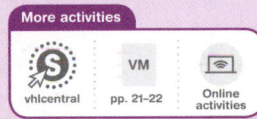

JORGE No manejes en carretera. Revisa el aceite cada 1.500 kilómetros y asegúrate de llenarle el tanque... No manejes con el cofre abierto. Nos vemos.

Expresiones útiles

Giving instructions to a friend
¿Me pasas la llave?
Can you pass me the wrench?
No lo manejes en carretera.
Don't drive it on the highway.
Revisa el aceite cada 1.500 kilómetros.
Check the oil every 1,500 kilometers.
Asegúrate de llenar el tanque.
Make sure to fill up the tank.
No manejes con el cofre abierto.
Don't drive with the hood open.
Recomiéndame con tus amigos.
Recommend me to your friends.

Taking a phone call
Aló./Bueno./Diga.
Hello.
¿Quién habla?/¿De parte de quién?
Who is speaking/calling?
Con él/ella habla.
Speaking.
¿Puedo dejar un recado?
May I leave a message?

Reassuring someone
Tranquilo/a, cariño.
Relax, sweetie.
Nos ayudamos los unos a los otros.
We help each other out.
No te preocupes.
Don't worry.

Additional vocabulary
entregar *to hand in*
el intento *attempt*
la noticia *news*
el proyecto *project*
recuperar *to recover*

More activities — vhlcentral | VM pp. 21–22 | Online activities

Expresiones útiles Point out the phrases **No lo manejes, Revisa, Asegúrate, No manejes, Recomiéndame,** and **No te preocupes.** Explain that these are **tú** commands, a direct way of telling someone to do or not to do something. Then draw attention to the words **Nos ayudamos** and tell students that this is a reciprocal reflexive construction that expresses a shared action. Point out the words **la mía** and **la suya** in the caption of video still 3 and tell the class that these are examples of possessive pronouns. Tell students that they will learn more about these concepts in **Estructura.**

Teaching Tip Ask students to read the **Fotonovela** captions aloud in groups of three. Then have one or two groups role-play the dialogue for the class. Encourage them to ad-lib whenever possible.

Nota cultural **Prácticas profesionales** are similar to unpaid internships in the U.S. Normally, they are carried out as a requirement for a study program, in the form of a professional practicum or fieldwork.

¿Qué pasó?

1 **Seleccionar** Selecciona las respuestas que completan correctamente estas oraciones.

1. Jorge intenta arreglar ___b___.
   a. la computadora de Maru   b. el coche de Miguel   c. el teléfono celular de Felipe
2. Maru dice que se borraron muchos ___a___ de su computadora.
   a. archivos   b. sitios web   c. mensajes de texto
3. Jorge dice que necesita un ___c___.
   a. navegador GPS   b. radio   c. televisor
4. Maru dice que Jorge es el mejor ___a___.
   a. mecánico de la ciudad   b. amigo del mundo   c. compañero de la clase
5. Jorge le dice a Miguel que no maneje su coche en ___c___.
   a. el tráfico   b. el centro de la ciudad   c. la carretera

2 **Identificar** Identifica quién dice estas oraciones.

1. Hombre, no es nada. Guárdalo para el coche nuevo.   Jorge
2. ¿Y qué pasó con tu proyecto?   Miguel
3. Si no puedo usar mi computadora, ¿me prestas la tuya?   Maru
4. Revisa el aceite cada 1.500 kilómetros y asegúrate de llenarle el tanque.   Jorge
5. La copia que tengo más actualizada es de la semana pasada. El problema es que hice muchos cambios desde entonces.   Maru

MARU

MIGUEL

JORGE

3 **Problema mecánico** Trabajen en parejas para representar los papeles de un(a) mecánico/a y un(a) cliente/a que está llamando al taller porque su carro está descompuesto.   Answers will vary.

Mecánico/a	**Cliente/a**
Contesta el teléfono con un saludo y el nombre del taller.	→ Saluda y explica que tu carro está descompuesto.
Pregunta qué tipo de problema tiene exactamente.	→ Explica que tu carro no arranca cuando hace frío.
Di que debe traer el carro al taller.	→ Pregunta cuándo puedes llevarlo.
Ofrece una hora para revisar el carro.	→ Acepta la hora que ofrece el/la mecánico/a.

Ahora cambien los papeles y representen otra conversación. Ustedes son un(a) técnico/a y un(a) cliente/a. Usen estas ideas:

- el celular no guarda mensajes
- la computadora no descarga fotos
- la impresora imprime muy lentamente
- el televisor está descompuesto

NATIONAL communication STANDARDS

---

1 **Teaching Tip** Read the activity items to the class as true/false statements. Ask students to correct the false statements. Ex: **Jorge intenta arreglar el coche de Miguel.** **(Cierto.)**

2 **Expansion** Give students these sentences as items 6–8:
6. Creo que puedo arreglarlo. (Jorge) 7. Moni es mi única salvación. (Maru) 8. Nos ayudamos los unos a los otros. (Miguel)

3 **Possible Conversation**
E1: ¿Bueno? Taller Mendoza.
E2: Buenos días. Tengo un problema con mi carro.
E1: ¿Qué pasó? ¿Cuál es el problema exactamente?
E2: El carro no arranca cuando hace frío.
E1: Tengo que revisarlo. ¿Puede venir al taller?
E2: Creo que sí. ¿A qué hora debo pasar?
E1: Tengo tiempo esta tarde a las tres.
E2: Muy bien. Es una buena hora para mí también.
E1: Nos vemos a las tres. Gracias, y hasta esta tarde.
E2: Hasta luego.

3 **Teaching Tip** For the second conversation, have students brainstorm a list of phrases for their roles. Encourage them to follow a similar outline to that of the first conversation.

The Affective Dimension
Talking on the phone can be more stressful than talking with someone in person because one does not see the other person's facial expressions or gestures. Remind students that they do not need to understand every word, and that they should ask the other person to repeat if necessary.

TEACHING OPTIONS

Extra Practice ←🚶→ Have each student choose one of the **Fotonovela** characters and prepare a five-sentence summary of the day's events from that person's point of view. As volunteers read their summaries to the class, have the class guess which character would have given each summary.

Small Groups Have the class work in small groups to write questions about the **Fotonovela**. Have each group hand its questions to another group to write the answers. Ex: **G1: ¿A quién le mandó un mensaje de texto Maru? G2: Maru le mandó un mensaje de texto a Miguel.**

Ortografía

 Tutorial

La acentuación de palabras similares

Although accent marks usually indicate which syllable in a word is stressed, they are also used to distinguish between words that have the same or similar spellings.

Él maneja **el** coche. | **Sí**, voy **si** quieres.

Although one-syllable words do not usually carry written accents, some *do* have accent marks to distinguish them from words that have the same spelling but different meanings.

Sé cocinar. | **Se** baña. | ¿Tomas **té**? | **Te** duermes.

Sé (*I know*) and **té** (*tea*) have accent marks to distinguish them from the pronouns **se** and **te**.

para **mí** | **mi** cámara | **Tú** lees. | **tu** estéreo

Mí (*Me*) and **tú** (*you*) have accent marks to distinguish them from the possessive adjectives **mi** and **tu**.

¿**Por qué** vas? | Voy **porque** quiero.

Several words of more than one syllable also have accent marks to distinguish them from words that have the same or similar spellings.

Éste es rápido. | **Este** tren es rápido.

Demonstrative pronouns may have accent marks to distinguish them from demonstrative adjectives.

¿**Cuándo** fuiste? | Fui **cuando** me llamó.
¿**Dónde** trabajas? | Voy al taller **donde** trabajo.

Adverbs have accent marks when they are used to convey a question.

 Práctica Marca los acentos en las palabras que los necesitan.

ANA Alo, soy Ana. ¿Que tal? *Aló/¿Qué?*
JUAN Hola, pero... ¿por que me llamas tan tarde? *¿por qué?*
ANA Porque mañana tienes que llevarme a la universidad. Mi auto esta dañado. *está*
JUAN ¿Como se daño? *¿Cómo?/dañó*
ANA Se daño el sabado. Un vecino (*neighbor*) choco con (*crashed into*) el. *dañó/sábado/chocó/él*

 Crucigrama Utiliza las siguientes pistas (*clues*) para completar el crucigrama. ¡Ojo con los acentos!

Horizontales
1. Él _____ levanta.
4. No voy _____ no puedo.
7. Tú _____ acuestas.
9. ¿ _____ es el examen?
10. Quiero este video y _____.

Verticales
2. ¿Cómo _____ usted?
3. Eres _____ mi hermano.
5. ¿ _____ tal?
6. Me gusta _____ suéter.
8. Pongo las maletas _____ el baúl.

Crossword answers:
S E / C
S / P O R Q U E
T E / M U S
C U Á N D O / É S E

 More activities vhlcentral / LM p. 62

Section Goals

In **Cultura**, students will:
- read about social networks in Spanish-speaking countries
- learn technology-related terms
- read about different types of **bicimotos**
- read about text messaging

Instructional Resource
Supersite

En detalle

Antes de leer

👥↔👥 Survey the class about social networks. Ask: **¿Usan las redes sociales? ¿Cuáles? ¿Con qué frecuencia usan las redes sociales?**

Lectura

- Point out the boxed feature on page 376. Ask students what they think are the two languages used most on social networks. (English, Chinese)

- Explain that **tuitear** and **wasapear** are new Spanish verbs that refer to using Twitter and WhatsApp.

Después de leer

↔👤→ Ask students: **En tu opinión, ¿nos comunicábamos mejor antes o después del invento de las redes sociales? ¿Por qué?** Have students write their answers in a short paragraph, and encourage volunteers to share their responses with the class.

1 Expansion Ask students to write three additional true/false statements. Then have them exchange papers with a classmate and complete the activity.

EN DETALLE

Las redes sociales

¿Cómo te comunicas con tu familia y con tus amigos? Al igual que° en los Estados Unidos, en los países hispanohablantes las redes sociales han tenido° un gran impacto en los últimos años. Los usos básicos de los teléfonos celulares ya no son las llamadas° y los mensajes de texto, sino el contacto entre amigos y familiares por medio de° redes sociales y de aplicaciones como Facebook, Twitter, WhatsApp o Instagram.

La mayoría de los hispanos tiene un perfil en Facebook o en Twitter, pero el método de comunicación más popular en los países hispanohablantes es WhatsApp. Por medio de esta aplicación de mensajería los usuarios° pueden crear grupos y enviarse° un número ilimitado de imágenes, videos y mensajes de texto y de audio. Su popularidad se debe a que es una forma rápida y prácticamente gratuita° de comunicarse.

Hoy en día, los teléfonos inteligentes y los contratos telefónicos son más asequibles°, por lo que la mayoría de los hispanos disfruta de estos celulares y de sus ventajas tecnológicas. Gracias a las redes sociales y a las aplicaciones, las personas pueden estar en constante comunicación con sus seres queridos° más lejanos°. La inevitable pregunta es: ¿qué ocurre con los seres queridos que están cerca? La influencia que tienen las redes sociales en las relaciones humanas es cada vez un tema más polémico.

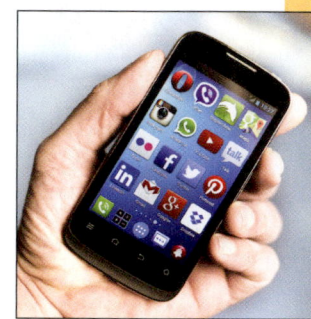

El español en las redes sociales

- El español es la tercera lengua más utilizada en las redes sociales.

- El español es la segunda lengua más usada en Twitter, con un crecimiento° de más de 1.100% en los últimos diez años.

- Facebook tiene más de 80 millones de usuarios hispanohablantes.

- Sólo en España, WhatsApp tiene 15 millones de usuarios que usan la aplicación un promedio° de 45 minutos al día.

Al igual que *Like* **han tenido** *have had* **llamadas** *calls* **por medio de** *through* **usuarios** *users* **enviarse** *send each other* **gratuita** *free* **asequibles** *affordable* **seres queridos** *loved ones* **lejanos** *distant* **crecimiento** *growth* **promedio** *average*

ACTIVIDADES

1 ¿Cierto o falso? Indica si lo que dicen estas oraciones es **cierto** o **falso**. Corrige la información falsa.

1. Los hispanos prefieren las llamadas para comunicarse con sus familias y con sus amigos. Falso. Los hispanos prefieren comunicarse por medio de redes sociales y de aplicaciones.
2. Twitter no se usa en Latinoamérica. Falso. La mayoría de los hispanos tiene un perfil en Facebook o en Twitter.
3. WhatsApp es un método de comunicación muy común en los países hispanos. Cierto.

4. WhatsApp permite enviar fotos a los contactos del celular. Cierto.
5. Pocos hispanos pueden comprar un teléfono inteligente. Falso. Hoy en día los teléfonos inteligentes son más asequibles.
6. Una ventaja de las redes sociales es el contacto con las personas que están lejos. Cierto.
7. El español es la segunda lengua más utilizada en las redes sociales. Falso. El español es la tercera lengua más utilizada en las redes sociales.
8. Los españoles usan mucho la aplicación WhatsApp. Cierto.

TEACHING OPTIONS

Extra Practice ↔👤→ Tell students to imagine that they are writing to a friend who refuses to use social networks. Have students persuade their friend by describing how it has changed their own lives. If necessary, review comparatives and superlatives, **hace** + [*time period*] + **que** + [*present*] and **hace** + [*time period*] + **que** + [*preterite*].

Heritage Speakers ↔👤→ Ask heritage speakers to describe social network use in their families.
Pairs In pairs, have students list, in order of importance, the top five reasons to use social networks. Have pairs share their lists with the class to see if a consensus can be reached. Make sure students write their lists in Spanish.

ASÍ SE DICE

La tecnología

los audífonos (Méx., Col.), los auriculares (Arg.), los cascos (Esp.)	headset; earphones
el móvil (Esp.)	el celular
el manos libres (Amér. S.)	hands-free system
la memoria	memory
mensajear (Méx.)	textear

EL MUNDO HISPANO

Las bicimotos

- **Argentina** El *ciclomotor* se usa mayormente° para repartir a domicilio° comidas y medicinas.

- **Perú** La *motito* se usa mucho para el reparto a domicilio de pan fresco todos los días.

- **México** La *Vespa* se usa para evitar° el tráfico en grandes ciudades.

- **España** La población usa el *Vespino* para ir y volver al trabajo cada día.

- **Puerto Rico** Una *scooter* es el medio de transporte favorito en las zonas rurales.

- **República Dominicana** Las *moto-taxis* son el medio de transporte más económico, ¡pero no olvides el casco°!

mayormente *mainly* repartir a domicilio *home delivery of* evitar *to avoid* casco *helmet*

PERFIL

Los mensajes de texto

¿Qué tienen en común un **mensaje de texto** y un telegrama?: la necesidad de decir lo máximo en el menor espacio posible —y rápidamente—.
Así como los abuelos se las arreglaron° para hacer más baratos sus telegramas, que se cobraban° por número de palabras, ahora los jóvenes buscan ahorrar° espacio, tiempo y dinero, en sus mensajes de texto. Esta economía del lenguaje dio origen al **lenguaje chat**, una forma de escritura muy creativa y compacta. Olvídate de la gramática, la puntuación y la ortografía: es tan flexible que evoluciona° todos los días con el uso que cada quien° le da, aunque° hay muchas palabras y expresiones ya establecidas°. Fácilmente encontrarás° abreviaturas (**xq?**, "¿Por qué?"; **tkm**, "Te quiero mucho."), sustitución de sonidos por números (**a2**, "Adiós."; **5mntrios**, "Sin comentarios."), símbolos (**ad+**, "además") y omisión de vocales y acentos (**tb**, "también"; **k tl?**, "¿Qué tal?"). Ahora que lo sabes, si un amigo te envía: **cont xfa, m dbs \$!°**, puedes responderle: **ntp, ns vms + trd°**.

se las arreglaron *they managed to* se cobraban *were charged* ahorrar *to save* evoluciona *evolves* cada quien *each person* aunque *although* establecidas *fixed* encontrarás *you will find* cont xfa, m dbs \$! Contesta, por favor, ¡me debes dinero! ntp, ns vms +trd No te preocupes, nos vemos más tarde.

CON RITMO HISPANO

Andrés Calamaro (1961–)
Lugar de nacimiento: Buenos Aires, Argentina

Andrés Calamaro es uno de los rockeros más influyentes de Latinoamérica. Formó parte de Los Abuelos de la Nada y de Los Rodríguez.

Go to **vhlcentral.com** to find out more about **Andrés Calamaro** and his music.

ACTIVIDADES

2 Comprensión Responde a las preguntas.

1. ¿Cuáles son tres formas de decir *headset*? los audífonos, los auriculares, los cascos
2. ¿Para qué se usan las bicimotos en Argentina? para repartir a domicilio comidas y medicinas
3. ¿Qué dio origen al "lenguaje chat"? la necesidad de ahorrar espacio, tiempo y dinero
4. ¿Es importante escribir los acentos en los mensajes de texto? No. La gramática, la ortografía y la puntuación no importan en un mensaje de texto.

3 ¿Cómo te comunicas? Escribe un párrafo breve en donde expliques qué utilizas para comunicarte con tus amigos/as (correo electrónico, redes sociales, teléfono, etc.) y de qué hablan cuando se llaman por teléfono. Answers will vary.

More activities

vhlcentral

Online activities

Section Goals

In **Estructura 11.1**, students will learn:
- affirmative **tú** commands
- negative **tú** commands

Instructional Resources
Supersite: Audio (Lab MP3 Files); Resources (Grammar Presentation Slides, Activity Pack, Scripts, Answer Keys); Testing Program (Quizzes)
WebSAM
Workbook
Lab Manual

Teaching Tips
- Model the use of informal commands with simple examples using TPR and gestures. Ex: Point to a student and say: _____ , **levántate. Gracias, ahora siéntate.** Give other commands using **camina, vuelve, toca,** and **corre.**
- Help students recognize that the affirmative **tú** command forms of regular verbs are the same as the third-person singular forms.
- Emphasize that **tú** commands are spoken to people one addresses as **tú.**

11.1 Familiar commands Tutorial

ANTE TODO In Spanish, the command forms are used to give orders or advice. You use **tú** commands (**mandatos familiares**) when you want to give an order or advice to someone you normally address with the familiar **tú.**

Affirmative tú commands

Infinitive	Present tense él/ella form	Affirmative tú command
hablar	habla	**habla** (tú)
guardar	guarda	**guarda** (tú)
prender	prende	**prende** (tú)
volver	vuelve	**vuelve** (tú)
pedir	pide	**pide** (tú)
imprimir	imprime	**imprime** (tú)

▶ Affirmative **tú** commands usually have the same form as the **él/ella** form of the present indicative.

Guarda el documento antes de cerrarlo.
Save the document before closing it.

Imprime tu tarea para la clase de inglés.
Print your homework for English class.

▶ The following verbs have irregular affirmative **tú** commands.

Irregular affirmative tú commands

decir	**di**	salir	**sal**
hacer	**haz**	ser	**sé**
ir	**ve**	tener	**ten**
poner	**pon**	venir	**ven**

¡**Sal** ahora mismo!
Leave at once!

Haz los ejercicios.
Do the exercises.

▶ Since **ir** and **ver** have the same **tú** command (**ve**), context will determine the meaning.

Ve al taller con Yolanda.
Go to the repair shop with Yolanda.

Ve ese programa... es muy interesante.
See that program... it's very interesting.

Súbete al coche y préndelo.

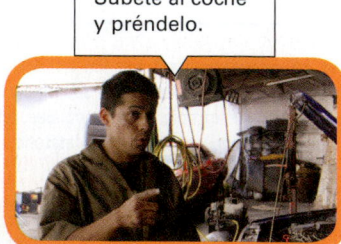

No lo manejes en la carretera.

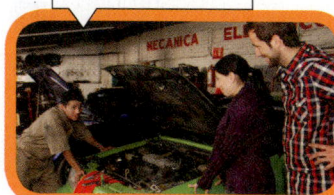

TEACHING OPTIONS

TPR Ask individual students to comply with a series of commands requiring them to perform actions or move around the room. While the student follows the command, the class writes it down as a volunteer writes it on the board. Be sure to use both affirmative and negative commands. Ex: **Recoge ese papel. Ponlo en la basura. Regresa a tu escritorio. No te sientes. Siéntate ahora.**

Pairs Ask students to imagine they are starting a computer club. Have them make a list of five things to do in order to get ready for the first meeting and five things not to do to make sure everything runs smoothly, using infinitives. Then have students take turns telling partners what to do or not do.

The negative **tú** commands are formed by dropping the final **-o** of the **yo** form of the present tense. For **-ar** verbs, add **-es**. For **-er** and **-ir** verbs, add **-as**.

Negative tú commands

Infinitive	Present tense yo form	Negative tú command
hablar	hablo	**no hables** (tú)
guardar	guardo	**no guardes** (tú)
prender	prendo	**no prendas** (tú)
volver	vuelvo	**no vuelvas** (tú)
pedir	pido	**no pidas** (tú)

Héctor, **no pares** el carro aquí.
Héctor, don't stop the car here.

No prendas la computadora todavía.
Don't turn on the computer yet.

Verbs with irregular **yo** forms maintain the same irregularity in their negative **tú** commands. These verbs include **conducir, conocer, decir, hacer, ofrecer, oír, poner, salir, tener, traducir, traer, venir,** and **ver**.

No pongas el disco en la computadora.
Don't put the disk in the computer.

No conduzcas tan rápido.
Don't drive so fast.

Note also that stem-changing verbs keep their stem changes in negative **tú** commands.

No p**ie**rdas tu celular.
Don't lose your cell phone.

No v**ue**lvas a esa gasolinera.
Don't go back to that gas station.

No rep**i**tas las instrucciones.
Don't repeat the instructions.

Verbs ending in **-car**, **-gar**, and **-zar** have a spelling change in the negative **tú** commands.

sa**car**	c → **qu**	no sa**qu**es
apa**gar**	g → **gu**	no apa**gu**es
almor**zar**	z → **c**	no almuer**c**es

The following verbs have irregular negative **tú** commands.

Irregular negative tú commands

dar	**no des**
estar	**no estés**
ir	**no vayas**
saber	**no sepas**
ser	**no seas**

¡INTÉNTALO! Indica los mandatos familiares afirmativos y negativos de estos verbos.

1. correr — _Corre_ más rápido. / No _corras_ más rápido.
2. llenar — _Llena_ el tanque. / No _llenes_ el tanque.
3. salir — _Sal_ ahora. / No _salgas_ ahora.
4. descargar — _Descarga_ ese documento. / No _descargues_ ese documento.
5. hacerlo — _Hazlo_ ya. / No _lo hagas_ ahora.
6. levantarse — _Levántate_ temprano. / No _te levantes_ temprano.

¡ATENCIÓN!

In affirmative commands, reflexive, indirect, and direct object pronouns are always attached to the end of the verb. In negative commands, these pronouns always precede the verb.

Bórralos./No los borres.
Escríbeles un mensaje electrónico./**No les escribas** un mensaje electrónico.

• • •

When a pronoun is attached to an affirmative command that has two or more syllables, an accent mark is added to maintain the original stress:

borra → bórralos
prende → préndela
imprime → imprímelo

Práctica

1 Expansion Continue this activity orally with the class, using regular verbs. Call out a negative command and designate individuals to make corresponding affirmative commands. Ex: **No sirvas la comida ahora.** (**Sirve la comida ahora./Sírvela ahora.**)

2 Expansion
Ask volunteers to role-play the exchanges between **Pedro** and **Marina**. Encourage them to ad-lib and add more to the exchanges as they go along.

3 Teaching Tip To simplify, review the vocabulary in the word bank by asking students to make associations with each word. Ex: **imprimir (documento), descargar (programa)**

1 Completar Completa los comentarios con el mandato de cada verbo.

1. ____Apaga____ tu teléfono celular, pero no ____apagues____ la computadora. (apagar)
2. ____Haz____ tu tarea después. No la ____hagas____ ahora. (hacer)
3. No ____vayas____ a la tienda a comprar papel para la impresora. ____Ve____ a la cafetería a comprarme algo de comer. (ir)
4. No ____me digas____ que no puedes abrir un archivo. ____Dime____ que el programa de computación funciona sin problemas. (decirme)
5. ____Sé____ generoso con tu tiempo y no ____seas____ antipático si no entiendo fácilmente. (ser)
6. ____Ten____ mucha paciencia y no ____tengas____ prisa. (tener)
7. No ____vengas____ en una hora. ____Ven____ ahora mismo. (venir)

in class

2 Cambiar Cuando Pedro dice que algo es necesario, Marina expresa una opinión diferente. Usa la información entre paréntesis para formar las órdenes que Marina le da a Pedro.

> **modelo**
> **Pedro:** Necesito revisar el aceite del carro. (seguir hasta el próximo pueblo)
> **Marina:** *No revises el aceite del carro. Sigue hasta el próximo pueblo.*

1. Necesito poner el radio. (hablarme) *No pongas el radio. Háblame.*
2. Necesito conducir más rápido. (parar el carro) *No conduzcas más rápido. Para el carro.*
3. Necesito almorzar ahora. (comer más tarde) *No almuerces ahora. Come más tarde.*
4. Necesito sacar una foto. (manejar con cuidado) *No saques… Maneja…*
5. Necesito estacionar el carro en esta calle. (pensar en otra opción) *No estaciones… Piensa…*
6. Necesito volver a esa gasolinera. (arreglar el carro en un taller) *No vuelvas… Arregla…*
7. Necesito leer el mapa. (pedirle ayuda a aquella señora) *No leas… Pídele…*
8. Necesito dormir en el carro. (acostarse en una cama) *No duermas… Acuéstate…*

in class

3 Problemas Tú y tu compañero/a trabajan en el centro de computadoras de la universidad. Muchos estudiantes están llamando con problemas. Denles órdenes para ayudarlos a resolverlos.

Answers will vary. Suggested answers:

> **modelo**
> **Problema:** *No veo nada en la pantalla.*
> **Tu respuesta:** *Prende la pantalla de tu computadora.*

| apagar… | conectarse… | funcionar… | guardar… | prender… |
| borrar… | descargar… | grabar… | imprimir… | volver… |

1. No me gusta este programa de computación. *Descarga otro.*
2. Tengo miedo de perder mi documento. *Guárdalo.*
3. Prefiero leer este sitio web en papel. *Imprímelo.*
4. Mi correo electrónico funciona muy lentamente. *Borra los mensajes más viejos.*
5. Busco información sobre los gauchos de Argentina. *Conéctate a Internet.*
6. Tengo demasiados archivos en mi computadora. *Borra algunos archivos.*
7. Mi computadora se congeló (*froze*). *Apaga la computadora y luego préndela.*
8. Quiero ver las fotos del cumpleaños de mi hermana. *Descárgalas.*

NOTA CULTURAL

Los gauchos (*nomadic cowboys*), conocidos por su habilidad (*skill*) para montar a caballo y utilizar el lazo, viven en la Región Pampeana, una llanura muy extensa ubicada en el centro de Argentina y dedicada a la agricultura (*agriculture*).

TEACHING OPTIONS

TPR Have pairs of students brainstorm a list of actions that can be mimed. Then have them give each other **tú** commands based on the actions. Call on several pairs to demonstrate their actions for the class. When a repertoire of mimable actions is established, do TPR with the class using these commands/actions.
Pairs Tell students to imagine that they belong to their grandparents' generation and are not very familiar with new

technology. Have them write three questions about electronic devices to ask a partner, who will answer using affirmative and negative commands. If the response uses a negative command, it should be followed by an affirmative command. Ex: **¿Debo apagar la computadora cada vez que salgo de la casa? (No, no la apagues. Pero guarda todos tus documentos.)** Students should ask follow-up questions when necessary.

Comunicación

4 **Órdenes** Intercambia mandatos negativos y afirmativos con tu compañero/a. Debes seguir las órdenes que él o ella te da o reaccionar apropiadamente. Answers will vary.

> **modelo**
> **Estudiante 1:** Dame todo tu dinero.
> **Estudiante 2:** No, no quiero dártelo. Muéstrame tu cuaderno.
> **Estudiante 1:** Aquí está.
> **Estudiante 2:** Ve a la pizarra y escribe tu nombre.
> **Estudiante 1:** No quiero. Hazlo tú.

5 **Consejos** En parejas, imaginen que un(a) amigo/a de ustedes tiene muy poca experiencia en el uso de nuevas tecnologías. Denle consejos a su amigo/a.

> **modelo**
> Apaga tu teléfono celular antes de clase.

6 **Anuncios** En grupos pequeños, preparen tres anuncios adicionales para tres escuelas que compiten (*compete*) con ésta. Answers will vary.

INFORMÁTICA ARGENTINA

Toma nuestros cursos y aprende a usar la computadora

abre y lee tus archivos

imprime tus documentos

entra al campo de la tecnología

¡Ponte en contacto con nosotros llamando al **11-4-129-1508** HOY!

Síntesis

7 **¡Tanto que hacer!** Tu profesor(a) te va a dar una lista de diligencias (*errands*). Algunas las hiciste tú y algunas las hizo tu compañero/a. Las diligencias que ya hicieron tienen esta marca ✔. Pero quedan cuatro diligencias por hacer. Dale órdenes a tu compañero/a y él/ella responde para confirmar si hay que hacerla o si ya la hizo. Answers will vary.

> **modelo**
> **Estudiante 1:** Llena el tanque.
> **Estudiante 2:** Ya llené el tanque. / ¡Ay, no! Tenemos que llenar el tanque.

4 **Teaching Tip** To simplify, ask students to brainstorm a list of what they might ask their classmates to do.

4 **Expansion** ←👥→ Have volunteers report to the class what they were asked to do, what they did, and what they did not do.

5 **Teaching Tip** Before assigning the activity, have students make a list of verbs that could be used for technology-related commands. You may want to refer them to the word bank on page 380 for ideas.

6 **Teaching Tip** Ask comprehension questions about the ad. **¿Qué se anuncia?** (cursos de informática) **¿Cómo puedes informarte?** (llamar por teléfono) **¿Dónde se encuentra este tipo de anuncio?** (en periódicos y revistas)

6 **Expansion** Post the finished ads in different places around the classroom. Have groups circulate and write one question for each poster. Then have group members ask their questions. Group answers should include a **tú** command.

7 **Teaching Tips**
• Divide the class into pairs and distribute the handouts from the Activity Pack (Activity Pack/Supersite) that correspond to this Information Gap Activity. Give students ten minutes to complete this activity.
• Ask volunteers to give examples of **tú** commands that college students usually give to their roommates. Ex: **Apaga la tele. No te acuestes en el sofá.**

11.2 Por and para Tutorial

ANTE TODO Unlike English, Spanish has two words that mean *for*: **por** and **para**. These two prepositions are not interchangeable. Study the following charts to see how they are used.

▶ **Por** and **para** are most commonly used to describe aspects of movement, time, and action, but in different circumstances.

Por	Para
Movement	
Through or by a place	**Toward a destination**
La excursión nos llevó **por** el centro.	Mis amigos van **para** el estadio.
The tour took us through downtown.	*My friends are going to the stadium.*
Time	
Duration of an event	**Action deadline**
Ana chateó **por** dos horas.	Tengo que escribir un ensayo **para** mañana.
Ana chatted for two hours.	*I have to write an essay by tomorrow.*
Action	
Reason or motive for an action or circumstance	**Indication of for whom something is intended or done**
Llegué a casa tarde **por** el tráfico.	Estoy preparando una sorpresa **para** Eduardo.
I got home late because of the traffic.	*I'm preparing a surprise for Eduardo.*

▶ Here is a list of the uses of **por** and **para**.

Por is used to indicate…

1. **Movement:** Motion or a general location.. (around, through, along, by)

   Pasamos **por** el parque y **por** el río.
   We passed by the park and along the river.

2. **Time:** Duration of an action . . . . (for, during, in)

   Estuve en la Patagonia **por** un mes.
   I was in Patagonia for a month.

3. **Action:** Reason or motive for an action . . (because of, on account of, on behalf of)

   Lo hizo **por** su familia.
   She did it on behalf of her family.

4. **Object of a search** . . . . (for, in search of)

   Vengo **por** ti a las ocho.
   I'm coming for you at eight.
   Manuel fue **por** su cámara digital.
   Manuel went in search of his digital camera.

5. **Means by which something is done** . . . (by, by way of, by means of)

   Ellos viajan **por** la autopista.
   They travel by (by way of) the highway.

6. **Exchange or substitution** . . . . (for, in exchange for)

   Le di dinero **por** el cargador.
   I gave him money for the charger.

7. **Unit of measure** . . . . (per, by)

   José manejaba a 120 kilómetros **por** hora.
   José was driving 120 kilometers per hour.

¡ATENCIÓN!

Por is also used in several idiomatic expressions, including:

por aquí *around here*
por ejemplo *for example*
por eso *that's why; therefore*
por fin *finally*

AYUDA

Remember that when giving an exact time, **de** is used instead of **por** before **la mañana, la tarde,** or **la noche.**
La clase empieza a las nueve **de** la mañana.

• • •

In addition to **por, durante** is also commonly used to mean *for* when referring to time.
Esperé al mecánico **durante** cincuenta minutos.

Para is used to indicate…

1. **Movement: Destination** . . . . (*toward, in the direction of*)	Salimos **para** Córdoba el sábado. *We are leaving for Córdoba on Saturday.*
2. **Time: Deadline or a specific time** **in the future** . . . . (*by, for*)	Él va a arreglar el carro **para** el viernes. *He will fix the car by Friday.*
3. **Action: Purpose or goal** + [*infinitive*] . . . . (*in order to*)	Juan estudia **para** (ser) mecánico. *Juan is studying to be a mechanic.*
4. **Purpose** + [*noun*] . . . . (*for, used for*)	Es una llanta **para** el carro. *It's a tire for the car.*
5. **The recipient of something** . . . . (*for*)	Compré una impresora **para** mi hijo. *I bought a printer for my son.*
6. **Comparison with others or an opinion** . . (*for, considering*)	**Para** un joven, es demasiado serio. *For a young person, he is too serious.* **Para** mí, esta lección no es difícil. *For me, this lesson isn't difficult.*
7. **In the employment of** . . . . (*for*)	Sara trabaja **para** Telecom Argentina. *Sara works for Telecom Argentina.*

▶ In many cases it is grammatically correct to use either **por** or **para** in a sentence. The meaning of the sentence is different, however, depending on which preposition is used.

Caminé **por** el parque.
I walked through the park.

Caminé **para** el parque.
I walked to (toward) the park.

Trabajó **por** su padre.
He worked for (in place of) his father.

Trabajó **para** su padre.
He worked for his father('s company).

More activities

vhlcentral

LM
p. 64

WB
pp. 127–128

Online activities

¡INTÉNTALO!   Completa estas oraciones con las preposiciones **por** o **para**.

1. Fuimos al café __por__ la tarde.
2. Necesitas un navegador GPS __para__ encontrar la casa de Luis.
3. Entraron __por__ la puerta.
4. Quiero un pasaje __para__ Buenos Aires.
5. __Para__ arrancar el carro, necesito la llave.
6. Estuvieron nerviosos __por__ el examen.
7. Arreglé el televisor __para__ mi amigo.
8. ¿No hay una gasolinera __por__ aquí?
9. El radio es __para__ usted.

10. __Para__ mí, el español es fácil.
11. Estuvimos en Canadá __por__ dos meses.
12. Juan está enfermo. Tengo que trabajar __por__ él.
13. Tengo que estudiar la lección __para__ el lunes.
14. Compré dulces __para__ mi novia.
15. Voy a ir __por__ la carretera.
16. Compramos el auto __por__ un buen precio.

Teaching Tips

- Create a matching activity for the uses of **para**. Write sentences exemplifying each use of **para** listed, but not in the order they are given in the text. Ex: **1. Maru escribió un mensaje para Miguel. 2. Este autobús va para Mérida. 3. Para Jimena, los estudios son importantes. 4. Jorge trabaja para un taller. 5. Estudia para llegar a ser doctora. 6. El baúl es para las maletas. 7. Tengo que entregar el proyecto para la semana que viene.** Call on individual students to match each sentence with its usage.
- Have students make two flashcards. On one they write **por** and on the other **para**. Call out one of the uses for either word. Students hold up the appropriate card. Then call on a volunteer to write a sentence illustrating that use on the board. The class verifies the accuracy of the sentence.
- Add a visual aspect to this grammar presentation. Use magazine pictures to practice sentences demonstrating the uses of **por** and **para**. Ex: **Este señor hace la cena para su esposa. Los novios montan a caballo por el campo.**

TEACHING OPTIONS

Large Group 👤↔👤 Give each student in the class a strip of paper on which you have written one of the uses of **por** or **para**, or a sentence that exemplifies one of the uses. Have students circulate around the room until they find the person who has the match for their use or sentence. After everyone has found a partner, the pairs read their sentences and uses to the class.

Game Play **Concentración**. Create one card for each use of **por** and **para**, and one card with a sentence illustrating each use, for a total of 28 cards. Shuffle the cards and lay them face down. Then, taking turns, students uncover two cards at a time, trying to match a use to a sentence. The student with the most matches wins.

Práctica

1 **Completar** Completa este párrafo con las preposiciones **por** o **para**.

El mes pasado mi esposo y yo hicimos un viaje a Buenos Aires y sólo pagamos dos mil dólares (1)__por__ los pasajes. Estuvimos en Buenos Aires (2)__por__ una semana y paseamos por toda la ciudad. Durante el día caminamos (3)__por__ la plaza San Martín, el microcentro y el barrio de La Boca, donde viven muchos artistas. (4)__Por__ la noche fuimos a una tanguería, que es una especie de teatro, (5)__para__ mirar a la gente bailar tango. Dos días después decidimos hacer una excursión (6)__por__ las pampas (7)__para__ ver el paisaje y un rodeo con gauchos. Alquilamos (*We rented*) un carro y manejamos (8)__por__ todas partes y pasamos unos días muy agradables. El último día que estuvimos en Buenos Aires fuimos a Galerías Pacífico (9)__para__ comprar recuerdos (*souvenirs*) (10)__para__ nuestros hijos y nietos. Compramos tantos regalos que tuvimos que pagar impuestos (*duties*) en la aduana al regresar.

2 **Oraciones** Crea oraciones originales con los elementos de las columnas. Une los elementos usando **por** o **para**. Answers will vary.

> **modelo**
> Fuimos a Mar del Plata por razones de salud para visitar a un especialista.

(no) fue al mercado	por/para	comprar frutas	por/para	¿?
(no) fuimos a las montañas	por/para	tres días	por/para	¿?
(no) fuiste a Mar del Plata	por/para	razones de salud	por/para	¿?
(no) fueron a Buenos Aires	por/para	tomar el sol	por/para	¿?

3 **Describir** Usa **por** o **para** y el tiempo presente para describir estos dibujos. Answers will vary. Suggested answers:

1. Salen para Mendoza.

2. Habla por celular.

3. Trabaja para el Taller Juárez.

4. El regalo es para ella.

5. Camina por el parque.

6. Maneja a 100 kilómetros por hora.

Comunicación

4 **Descripciones** Usa **por** o **para** y completa estas frases de manera lógica. Luego, compara tus respuestas con las de un(a) compañero/a. *Answers will vary.*

1. En casa, hablo con mis amigos…
2. Mi padre/madre trabaja…
3. Ayer fui al taller…
4. Los miércoles tengo clases…
5. A veces voy a la biblioteca…
6. Esta noche tengo que estudiar…
7. Necesito… dólares…
8. Compré un regalo…
9. Mi mejor amigo/a estudia…
10. Necesito hacer la tarea…

5 **Situación** En parejas, dramaticen esta situación. Utilicen muchos ejemplos de **por** y **para**. *Answers will vary.*

Hijo/a	**Padre/Madre**
Pídele dinero a tu padre/madre.	→ Pregúntale para qué lo necesita.
Dile que quieres comprar un carro.	→ Pregúntale por qué necesita un carro.
Explica tres razones por las que necesitas un carro.	→ Explica por qué sus razones son buenas o malas.
Dile que por no tener un carro tu vida es muy difícil.	→ Decide si vas a darle el dinero y explica por qué.

Síntesis

6 **Una subasta** (*auction*) Cada estudiante debe traer a la clase un objeto o una foto del objeto para vender. En grupos, túrnense para ser el/la vendedor(a) y los postores (*bidders*). Para empezar, el/la vendedor(a) describe el objeto y explica para qué se usa y por qué alguien debe comprarlo.
Answers will vary.

modelo

Vendedora: Aquí tengo una tableta fantástica. Pueden usarla para conectarse a Internet, chatear con sus amigos y tomar notas en la universidad. La batería funciona perfectamente. ¿Quién ofrece $500 para empezar?

Postor(a) 1: Pero una computadora portátil nueva cuesta eso. Te doy $25.

Vendedora: Ah, pero ésta es muy especial porque viene con un teclado y un ratón, los dos inalámbricos.

Postor(a) 2: Ah, ¡entonces te doy $50!

---

4 Teaching Tip Model the activity by completing item 1 in two different ways.

4 Expansion Have students create new sentences, employing additional uses of **por** and **para**.

5 Teaching Tip
←👤→ Ask students questions about the car in the picture. Ex: **¿Te gusta este carro? ¿Cuánto se paga por un carro así? ¿A cuántas millas por hora corre este carro?** Have students write their answers using complete sentences.

5 Expansion
• 👤↔👤 Ask volunteers to role-play their conversation for the class.
• ←👤→ Show a picture of an old used car and ask students to create a new conversation. The parents are offering to buy their son/daughter this car instead of the one shown in the activity.

6 Teaching Tips
• 👤↔👤 Before the bidding begins, display the items to be auctioned off and name them. Invite students to walk around with their group members and discuss what the items are, their purposes, and how much they will pay for them.
• ←👤→ Have groups prepare the opening statements for the items their members brought. Students then take turns opening up the bidding for the entire class. Non-group members may bid on each item. Group members should place bids to keep the bidding alive.

TEACHING OPTIONS

Small Groups ←👤→ Have students create a television advertisement for a car or piece of technological equipment. Students should describe the item; explain why the customer should buy it; tell how much it costs; explain that the item is on sale only until a certain date; and detail any possible trade-ins. Students should use **por** and **para** as much as possible in their ad.

Extra Practice For students still having trouble distinguishing between **por** and **para**, have them create a mnemonic device, like a story or chant, for remembering the different uses. Ex: **Vine por la tarde y busqué por el parque, por el río y por el centro. Busqué por horas. Viajé por carro, por tren y por avión.** Do the same for **para**.

Section Goal

In **Estructura 11.3**, students will learn the use of reciprocal reflexives.

Instructional Resources
Supersite: Audio (Lab MP3 Files); Resources (Grammar Presentation Slides, Activity Pack, Scripts, Answer Keys); Testing Program (Quizzes)
WebSAM
Workbook
Lab Manual

Teaching Tips
• Ask a volunteer to explain what reflexive verbs are. Ask other students to provide examples. Review reflexive verbs and pronouns by asking students questions about their personal routine. Ex: **Yo me desperté a las seis de la mañana. Y tú, _____, ¿a qué hora te despertaste?**

• After going over the example sentences, ask students questions that contain or require reciprocal constructions. Ex: **¿Los estudiantes y los profesores siempre se saludan? ¿Se ven ustedes con frecuencia durante la semana? En las elecciones, ¿los candidatos siempre se respetan?**

• ←🚶→ Add a visual aspect to this grammar presentation. Hold up images of pairs of celebrities and have students write descriptions about them, using reciprocal reflexives. Remind students they can use the present, preterite, or imperfect tense.

11.3 Reciprocal reflexives Tutorial

ANTE TODO In **Lección 7**, you learned that reflexive verbs indicate that the subject of a sentence does the action to itself. Reciprocal reflexives, on the other hand, express a shared or reciprocal action between two or more people or things. In this context, the pronoun means *(to) each other* or *(to) one another*.

Luis y Marta **se** miran en el espejo.
Luis and Marta look at themselves in the mirror.

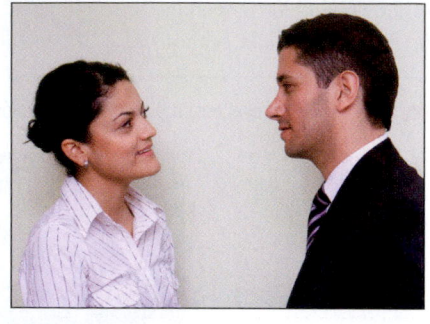

Luis y Marta **se** miran.
Luis and Marta look at each other.

▶ Only the plural forms of the reflexive pronouns (**nos, os, se**) are used to express reciprocal actions because the action must involve more than one person or thing.

Cuando **nos vimos** en la calle, **nos abrazamos**.
When we saw each other on the street, we hugged (one another).

Ustedes **se** van a **encontrar** en el café, ¿no?
You are meeting (each other) at the café, right?

Nos ayudamos cuando usamos la computadora.
We help each other when we use the computer.

Las amigas **se saludaron** y **se besaron**.
The friends greeted each other and kissed (one another).

> **¡ATENCIÓN!**
> Here is a list of common verbs that can express reciprocal actions:
> **abrazar(se)** *to hug; to embrace (each other)*
> **ayudar(se)** *to help (each other)*
> **besar(se)** *to kiss (each other)*
> **encontrar(se)** *to meet (each other); to run into (each other)*
> **saludar(se)** *to greet (each other)*

🔗 ¡INTÉNTALO! Indica el reflexivo recíproco adecuado de estos verbos en el presente o el pretérito.

presente

1. (escribir) Los novios _se escriben_.
   Nosotros _nos escribimos_.
   Ana y Ernesto _se escriben_.
2. (llamar) Ellas _se llaman_.
   Mis hermanos _se llaman_.
   Pepa y yo _nos llamamos_.
3. (ver) Nosotros _nos vemos_.
   Fernando y Tomás _se ven_.
   Ustedes _se ven_.
4. (escuchar) Mis tíos _se escuchan_.
   Nosotros _nos escuchamos_.
   Ellos _se escuchan_.

pretérito

1. (saludar) Nicolás y tú _se saludaron_.
   Nuestros vecinos _se saludaron_.
   Nosotros _nos saludamos_.
2. (conocer) Alberto y yo _nos conocimos_.
   Ustedes _se conocieron_.
   Ellos _se conocieron_.
3. (hablar) Los amigos _se hablaron_.
   Elena y yo _nos hablamos_.
   Ustedes _se hablaron_.
4. (encontrar) Ana y Javier _se encontraron_.
   Los primos _se encontraron_.
   Mi hermana y yo _nos encontramos_.

More activities

S vhlcentral
LM p. 65
WB pp. 129–130
Online activities

TEACHING OPTIONS

Extra Practice ←🚶→ Have students describe what they and their significant other or best friend do together, or what their friends do together. Have them use these verbs: **llamarse por teléfono, verse, decirse, ayudarse, encontrarse, reunirse.** Ex: **Mi amigo y yo siempre nos ayudamos con las tareas. Nos reunimos en la biblioteca o en mi casa y estudiamos por horas. Cuando hay examen de español, nos hacemos preguntas sobre** el vocabulario y la gramática.

Pairs 🚶↔🚶 Have students write a conversation in which they discuss two friends who are romantically involved, but have had a misunderstanding. Ask them to incorporate these verbs: **conocerse, encontrarse, quererse, hablarse, enojarse, besarse, mirarse,** and **entenderse.** Have pairs role-play their conversations for the class.

Práctica y Comunicación

1 Un amor recíproco Describe a Laura y a Elián usando los verbos recíprocos.   *use imperfect*

> **modelo**
>
> Laura veía a Elián todos los días. Elián veía a Laura todos los días.
> Laura y Elián se veían todos los días.

1. Laura conocía bien a Elián. Elián conocía bien a Laura.
   Laura y Elián se conocían bien.
2. Laura miraba a Elián con amor. Elián la miraba con amor también.
   Laura y Elián se miraban con amor.
3. Laura entendía bien a Elián. Elián entendía bien a Laura.
   Laura y Elián se entendían bien.
4. Laura ayudaba a Elián con sus problemas. Elián la ayudaba también
   con sus problemas. *Laura y Elián se ayudaban con sus problemas.*
5. Laura hablaba con Elián todas las noches por teléfono. Elián hablaba
   con Laura todas las noches por teléfono.
   Laura y Elián se hablaban todas las noches por teléfono.

2 Describir Describe lo que estas personas hicieron.   Answers will vary.
Suggested answers:

1. Ellos _____se besaron_____.

2. Las amigas _____se abrazaron_____.

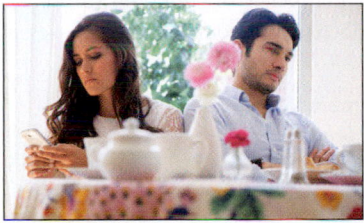

3. Gilberto y Mercedes _____no se miraron_____ /
   _____no se hablaron_____ / _____se enojaron_____.

4. Tú y yo _____nos saludamos_____ /
   _____nos encontramos_____.

NATIONAL communication STANDARDS

3 Preguntas En parejas, túrnense para hacerse estas preguntas.   Answers will vary.

1. ¿Se vieron tú y tu mejor amigo/a ayer? ¿Cuándo se ven ustedes normalmente?
2. ¿Dónde se encuentran tú y tus amigos?
3. ¿Se ayudan tú y tu mejor amigo/a con sus problemas?
4. ¿Se entienden bien tus compañeros de clase?
5. ¿Dónde se conocieron tú y tu mejor amigo/a? ¿Cuánto tiempo hace que se
   conocen ustedes?
6. ¿Cuándo se dan regalos tú y tu novio/a?
7. ¿Se escriben tú y tus amigos mensajes de texto o prefieren llamarse por teléfono?
8. ¿Siempre se llevan bien tú y tu compañero/a de cuarto? Explica.

11.4 Stressed possessive adjectives and pronouns

 Tutorial

 NATIONAL STANDARDS comparisons

ANTE TODO Spanish has two types of possessive adjectives: the unstressed (or short) forms you learned in **Lección 3** and the stressed (or long) forms. The stressed forms are used for emphasis or to express *of mine*, *of yours*, and so on.

Stressed possessive adjectives

Masculine singular	Feminine singular	Masculine plural	Feminine plural	
mío	mía	míos	mías	my; (of) mine
tuyo	tuya	tuyos	tuyas	your; (of) yours (fam.)
suyo	suya	suyos	suyas	your; (of) yours (form.); his; (of) his; her; (of) hers; its
nuestro	nuestra	nuestros	nuestras	our; (of) ours
vuestro	vuestra	vuestros	vuestras	your; (of) yours (fam.)
suyo	suya	suyos	suyas	your; (of) yours; their; (of) theirs

▶ **¡Atención!** Used with **un/una**, these possessives are similar in meaning to the English expression *of mine/yours*/etc.

Juancho es **un** amigo **mío**.
Juancho is a friend of mine.

Ella es **una** compañera **nuestra**.
She is a classmate of ours.

▶ Stressed possessive adjectives agree in gender and number with the nouns they modify. While unstressed possessive adjectives are placed before the noun, stressed possessive adjectives are placed after the noun they modify.

su impresora
her printer

la impresora **suya**
her printer

nuestros televisores
our television sets

los televisores **nuestros**
our television sets

▶ A definite article, an indefinite article, or a demonstrative adjective usually precedes a noun modified by a stressed possessive adjective.

Me encantan { **unos** blogs **tuyos**. *I love some of your blogs.*
{ **los** blogs **tuyos**. *I love your blogs.*
{ **estos** blogs **tuyos**. *I love these blogs of yours.*

▶ Since **suyo, suya, suyos,** and **suyas** have more than one meaning, you can avoid confusion by using the construction: [*article*] + [*noun*] + **de** + [*subject pronoun*].

el teclado **suyo**

el teclado **de él/ella/usted**
el teclado **de ustedes/ellos/ellas**

CONSULTA

This is the same construction you learned in **Lección 3** for clarifying **su** and **sus**. To review unstressed possessive adjectives, see **Estructura 3.2**, p. 93.

Possessive pronouns

▶ Possessive pronouns are used to replace a noun + [*possessive adjective*]. In Spanish, the possessive pronouns have the same forms as the stressed possessive adjectives, but they are preceded by a definite article.

la cámara **nuestra**   **la nuestra**
el navegador GPS **tuyo**   **el tuyo**
los archivos **suyos**   **los suyos**

▶ A possessive pronoun agrees in number and gender with the noun it replaces.

—Aquí está **mi coche**. ¿Dónde está **el tuyo**?
Here's my car. Where is yours?

—¿Tienes **las revistas** de Carlos?
Do you have Carlos' magazines?

—**El mío** está en el taller de mi hermano.
Mine is at my brother's garage.

—No, pero tengo **las nuestras**.
No, but I have ours.

¿También está descompuesta tu computadora?

No, la mía no, la suya.

More activities

vhlcentral

LM
p. 66

WB
pp. 131–132

Online activities

¡INTÉNTALO!   Indica las formas tónicas (*stressed*) de estos adjetivos posesivos y los pronombres posesivos correspondientes.

	adjetivos	pronombres
1. su cámara digital	la cámara digital suya	la suya
2. mi televisor	el televisor mío	el mío
3. tus aplicaciones	las aplicaciones tuyas	las tuyas
4. nuestros radios	los radios nuestros	los nuestros
5. su ratón	el ratón suyo	el suyo
6. mis videos	los videos míos	los míos
7. nuestra impresora	la impresora nuestra	la nuestra
8. nuestro blog	el blog nuestro	el nuestro
9. tu perfil	el perfil tuyo	el tuyo
10. mi computadora	la computadora mía	la mía

Teaching Tips
• Ask students questions using unstressed possessive adjectives or the [*article*] + [*noun*] + **de** construction before a name, having them answer with a possessive pronoun. Ex: **¿Tienes tu cuaderno? Sí, tengo el mío.**
• Point out that the function of the stressed possessives is to give emphasis. They are often used to point out contrasts. Ex: **¿Tu carro es azul? Pues, el carro mío es rojo. ¿Tu cámara digital no es buena? La mía es excelente.**

TEACHING OPTIONS

Video →👤← Replay the **Fotonovela**, having students listen for each use of an unstressed possessive adjective and write down the sentence in which it occurs. Next, have students rewrite those sentences using a stressed possessive adjective. Then, discuss how the use of stressed possessive adjectives affected the meaning or fluidity of the sentences.

Pairs 👤↔👤 Tell students that their laundry has gotten mixed up with their roommate's and since they are the same size and have the same tastes in clothing, they cannot tell what belongs to whom. Have them ask each other questions about different articles of clothing. Ex: —**¿Son tuyos estos pantalones de rayas?** —**Sí, son míos.** —**Y, ¿estos calcetines rojos son tuyos?** —**Sí, son míos, pero esta camisa grandísima no es mía.**

Práctica

1 **Oraciones** Forma oraciones con estas palabras. Usa el presente y haz los cambios necesarios.

1. un / amiga / suyo / vivir / Mendoza *Una amiga suya vive en Mendoza.*
2. ¿me / prestar / calculadora / tuyo? *¿Me prestas la calculadora tuya?*
3. el / coche / suyo / nunca / funcionar / bien *El coche suyo nunca funciona bien.*
4. yo / querer / cámara digital / mío / ahora mismo *Yo quiero la cámara digital mía ahora mismo.*
5. no / nos / interesar / problemas / suyo *No nos interesan los problemas suyos.*
6. un / amigos / nuestro / manejar / como / loco *Unos amigos nuestros manejan como locos.*

2 **¿Es suyo?** Un policía ha capturado (*has captured*) al hombre que robó (*robbed*) en tu casa. Ahora quiere saber qué cosas son tuyas. Túrnate con un(a) compañero/a para hacer el papel del policía y usa las pistas (*clues*) para contestar las preguntas.

> **modelo**
> no/viejo
> **Policía:** Esta impresora, ¿es suya?
> **Estudiante:** No, no es mía. La mía era más vieja.

1. sí E1: Este radio, ¿es suyo?
E2: Sí, es mío.

2. no/grande E1: Esta cámara digital, ¿es suya?
E2: No, no es mía. La mía era más grande.

3. sí E1: Estos teléfonos celulares, ¿son suyos?
E2: Sí, son míos.

4. sí E1: Esta computadora portátil, ¿es suya?
E2: Sí, es mía.

5. no/pequeño E1: Este televisor, ¿es suyo?
E2: No, no es mío. El mío era más pequeño.

6. no/caro E1: Estas tabletas, ¿son suyas?
E2: No, no son mías. Las mías eran más caras.

3 **Conversaciones** Completa estas conversaciones con las formas adecuadas de los pronombres posesivos.

1. —A Carmen le encanta su televisor nuevo.
   —¿Sí? A José no le gusta ___el suyo___.
2. —La casa de ellos estaba en la Avenida Alvear. ¿Dónde estaba la casa de ustedes?
   —___La nuestra___ estaba en la calle Bolívar.
3. —Puse mis libros aquí. ¿Dónde pusiste ___los tuyos___, Alfonso?
   —Puse ___los míos___ en el escritorio.
4. —Se me olvidó traer mis llaves. ¿Trajeron ustedes ___las suyas___?
   —No, dejamos ___las nuestras___ en casa.
5. —Yo compré mi computadora en una tienda y Marta compró ___la suya___ en Internet. Y ___la tuya___, ¿dónde la compraste?
   —___La mía___ es de Cíbermax.

Comunicación

4 **Vendedores competitivos** Trabajen en grupos de tres. Uno/a de ustedes va a una tienda a comprar un aparato tecnológico (tableta, computadora portátil, impresora, etc.). Los/Las otros/as dos son empleados/as de dos marcas rivales y compiten para convencer al/a la cliente/a de que compre su producto. Usen los adjetivos posesivos y túrnense para comprar y vender. *Answers will vary.*

> **modelo**
>
> **Estudiante 1:** *Buenos días, quiero comprar una impresora.*
> **Estudiante 2:** *Tengo lo que necesita. La mía imprime con excelente calidad.*
> **Estudiante 3:** *La tuya es vieja: necesita cable y es muy lenta. La mía puede imprimir hasta desde el teléfono celular, ¡sin usar ningún cable!*

5 **Comparar** Trabajen en parejas. Intenta (*Try to*) convencer a tu compañero/a de que algo que tú tienes es mejor que lo que él/ella tiene. Pueden hablar de sus carros, computadoras, teléfonos celulares, clases, horarios o trabajos. *Answers will vary.*

> **modelo**
>
> **Estudiante 1:** *Mi computadora tiene una pantalla de quince pulgadas (inches). ¿Y la tuya?*
> **Estudiante 2:** *La mía es mejor porque tiene una pantalla de diecisiete pulgadas.*
> **Estudiante 1:** *Pues la mía…*

Síntesis

6 **Inventos locos** En grupos pequeños, imaginen que construyeron un aparato tecnológico revolucionario. Dibujen su invento y descríbanlo contestando estas preguntas. Utilicen los posesivos, **por** y **para** y el vocabulario de **Contextos**. *Answers will vary.*

> **modelo**
>
> *Nuestro aparato se usa para cocinar huevos y funciona de una manera muy fácil...*

- ¿Para qué se usa?
- ¿Cómo es?
- ¿Cuánto cuesta?

- ¿Qué personas van a comprar este aparato?

Section Goal

In **Recapitulación**, students will review the grammar concepts from this lesson.

Instructional Resource
Supersite

Teaching Tip You may want to assign this **Recapitulación** activity on the Supersite because it has diagnostics. There is an online-only review activity for each grammar point. The Supersite also has a **Repaso de vocabulario** activity with diagnostics.

1 Teaching Tip Remind students that the –s ending is only present in negative familiar commands.

1 Expansion
←🔲→ To challenge students, have them write mini-dialogues that include these command forms.

2 Teaching Tip Ask students to identify the rule associated with each use of **por** or **para** in the sentences.

2 Expansion Ask questions using **por** and **para**. Ex: **¿Hablan mucho por** *Skype*? **¿Para qué clase estudian más, la clase de español o la clase de matemáticas?**

3 Expansion Make plural nouns singular and singular nouns plural in each question and have students repeat the activity. Ex: **1. ¿Éstos son mis videos? (Sí, son los tuyos.)**

Recapitulación

Completa estas actividades para repasar los conceptos de gramática que aprendiste en esta lección.

1 Completar Completa la tabla con las formas de los mandatos familiares. **16 pts.**

Infinitivo	Mandato	
	Afirmativo	**Negativo**
comer	come	no comas
hacer	haz	no hagas
sacar	saca	no saques
venir	ven	no vengas
ir	ve	no vayas

2 Por y para Completa el diálogo con **por** o **para**. **20 pts.**

MARIO Hola, yo trabajo (1) ___para___ el periódico de la universidad. ¿Puedo hacerte unas preguntas?

INÉS Sí, claro.

MARIO ¿Navegas mucho (2) ___por___ la red?

INÉS Sí, todos los días me conecto a Internet (3) ___para___ leer mi correo y navego (4) ___por___ una hora. También me gusta hablar (5) ___por___ *Skype* con mis amigos. Es muy bueno y, (6) ___para___ mí, es divertido.

MARIO ¿Y qué piensas sobre hacer la tarea en la computadora?

INÉS En general, me parece bien, pero (7) ___por___ ejemplo, anoche hice unos ejercicios (8) ___para___ la clase de álgebra y al final me dolieron los ojos. (9) ___Por___ eso a veces prefiero hacer la tarea a mano.

MARIO Muy bien. Muchas gracias (10) ___por___ tu tiempo.

3 Posesivos Completa las oraciones y confirma de quién son las cosas. **12 pts.**

1. —¿Éste es mi video? —Sí, es el ___tuyo___ (*fam.*).
2. —¿Ésta es la cámara de tu papá? —Sí, es la ___suya___.
3. —¿Ese teléfono es de Pilar? —Sí, es el ___suyo___.
4. —¿Éstos son los cargadores de ustedes? —No, no son ___nuestros___.
5. —¿Ésta es tu computadora portátil? —No, no es ___mía___.
6. —¿Ésas son mis fotos? —Sí, son las ___suyas___ (*form.*).

RESUMEN GRAMATICAL

11.1 Familiar commands *pp. 378–379*

tú commands		
Infinitive	**Affirmative**	**Negative**
guardar	guarda	no guardes
volver	vuelve	no vuelvas
imprimir	imprime	no imprimas

► Irregular **tú** command forms

dar → no des	saber → no sepas
decir → di	salir → sal
estar → no estés	ser → sé, no seas
hacer → haz	tener → ten
ir → ve, no vayas	venir → ven
poner → pon	

► Verbs ending in -car, -gar, -zar have a spelling change in the negative **tú** commands:

sacar → no saques
apagar → no apagues
almorzar → no almuerces

11.2 Por and para *pp. 382–383*

► Uses of **por**:

motion or general location; duration; reason or motive; object of a search; means by which something is done; exchange or substitution; unit of measure

► Uses of **para**:

destination; deadline; purpose or goal; recipient of something; comparison or opinion; in the employment of

11.3 Reciprocal reflexives *p. 386*

► Reciprocal reflexives express a shared or reciprocal action between two or more people or things. Only the plural forms (**nos, os, se**) are used.

Cuando **nos vimos** en la calle, **nos abrazamos.**

► Common verbs that can express reciprocal actions:

abrazar(se), ayudar(se), besar(se), conocer(se), encontrar(se), escribir(se), escuchar(se), hablar(se), llamar(se), mirar(se), saludar(se), ver(se)

TEACHING OPTIONS

Pairs ←🔲→ Have pairs create a short survey about technology use. Encourage them to use **por** and **para**, as well as adverbs like **a menudo, normalmente**, etc. Then have them exchange their surveys with another pair and complete them. Ask volunteers to share their survey results with the class.

Extra Practice 🔲↔🔲 Tell students that you are a new student in class who likes to take people's things. Go around the room and gather students' belongings (books, pens, bags, etc.). In each case, insist that the item is yours. Ex: **Esta mochila es mía.** Have students protest and take their item back. Ex: **Esta mochila no es tuya, es mía.** Have other students contribute by asking, **¿Esta mochila es suya o es mía?**

4 **Ángel y diablito** A Juan le gusta pedir consejos a su ángel y a su diablito imaginarios. Completa las respuestas con mandatos familiares desde las dos perspectivas. **16 pts.**

1. Estoy manejando. ¿Voy más rápido?
   Á No, no _____vayas_____ más rápido.
   D Sí, _____ve_____ más rápido.
2. Es el cargador de mi hermana. ¿Lo pongo en mi mochila?
   Á No, no _____lo pongas_____ en tu mochila.
   D Sí, _____ponlo_____ en tu mochila.
3. Necesito estirar (*to stretch*) las piernas. ¿Doy un paseo?
   Á Sí, _____da_____ un paseo.
   D No, no _____des_____ un paseo.
4. Mi amigo necesita imprimir algo. ¿Apago la impresora?
   Á No, no _____apagues_____ la impresora.
   D Sí, _____apaga_____ la impresora.

11.4 **Stressed possessive adjectives and pronouns**
pp. 388–389

Stressed possessive adjectives	
Masculine	**Feminine**
mío(s)	mía(s)
tuyo(s)	tuya(s)
suyo(s)	suya(s)
nuestro(s)	nuestra(s)
vuestro(s)	vuestra(s)
suyo(s)	suya(s)

la impresora **suya** → la **suya**

las llaves **mías** → las **mías**

5 **Oraciones** Forma oraciones para expresar acciones recíprocas con el tiempo indicado. **12 pts.**

> **modelo**
> tú y yo / conocer / bien (presente) *Tú y yo nos conocemos bien.*

1. José y Paco / llamar / una vez por semana (imperfecto)
   José y Paco se llamaban una vez por semana.
2. mi novia y yo / ver / todos los días (presente)
   Mi novia y yo nos vemos todos los días.
3. los compañeros de clase / ayudar / con la tarea (pretérito)
   Los compañeros de clase se ayudaron con la tarea.
4. tú y tu mamá / escribir / por correo electrónico / cada semana (imperfecto)
   Tú y tu mamá se escribían por correo electrónico cada semana.
5. mis hermanas y yo / entender / perfectamente (presente)
   Mis hermanas y yo nos entendemos perfectamente.
6. los profesores / saludar / con mucho respeto (pretérito)
   Los profesores se saludaron con mucho respeto.

6 **La tecnología** Escribe al menos seis oraciones diciéndole a un(a) amigo/a qué hacer para tener "una buena relación" con la tecnología. Usa mandatos familiares afirmativos y negativos. **24 pts.**

Answers will vary.

7 **Saber compartir** Completa la expresión con los dos pronombres posesivos que faltan.

¡4 puntos EXTRA!

❝Lo que° es _____mío_____ es _____tuyo/suyo_____.❞

Lo que *What*

4 **Teaching Tip**
👥↔👥 Have volunteers role-play each exchange for the class. Encourage them to ad-lib as they go.

4 **Expansion** Give students these situations as items 5–8:
5. Mi amigo tiene las respuestas del examen final de historia. ¿Se las pido? (No, no se las pidas.; Sí, pídeselas.) 6. Es el cumpleaños de mi compañero de cuarto. ¿Le compro algo? (Sí, cómprale algo.; No, no le compres nada.) 7. Rompí la computadora portátil de mi padre. ¿Se lo digo? (Sí, díselo; No, no se lo digas.) 8. No tengo nada de dinero. ¿Busco trabajo? (Sí, búscalo.; No, no lo busques.)

5 **Expansion** Have students create two additional dehydrated sentences. Then have them exchange papers with a classmate and complete the exercise.

6 **Teaching Tip**
←👤→ To challenge students, have them first write a letter from the point of view of the friend who needs help with technology. Then have students write their suggestions according to the problems outlined in the letter.

7 **Teaching Tip** Explain that this expression takes the masculine possessive form because it does not refer to anything specific, as denoted by **lo que**.

TEACHING OPTIONS

Game Divide the class into two teams, **por** and **para**, and have them line up. Choose a volunteer to go first from each team, and say an English sentence using an equivalent of **por** or **para**. Ex: Yesterday I got sick and my brother worked *for* me. The student whose team corresponds to the correct Spanish equivalent of *for* has five seconds to step forward and give the Spanish translation. Ex: **Ayer me enfermé y mi hermano trabajó *por* mí.** Award one point for every

correct answer. The team with the most points at the end wins.
Small Groups 👥↔👥 As a class, brainstorm a list of infinitives that can be made reciprocal (**llamar, abrazar, conocer**, etc.) and write them on the board. In small groups, have students create a dialogue using at least six of these infinitives. Then have students act out their dialogues for the class. Encourage students to use lesson vocabulary.

Section Goals

In **Lectura**, students will:
- learn to recognize borrowed words
- increase their reading comprehension in Spanish by using borrowed words to predict content
- read a content-rich text with borrowed words

Instructional Resource
Supersite

Estrategia Tell students that recognizing words borrowed from English will help them understand unfamiliar texts.

Examinar el texto If students struggle answering these questions, have them focus on the character in red shorts and what he is holding and saying.

Buscar Invite students to speculate as to why so many words related to technology are loan words from English.

Sobre el autor **Juan Matías Loiseau** has also made two award-winning short films, *El Ángel de Dorotea* (2005) and *Abismos* (2006).

Lectura

Antes de leer

Estrategia
Recognizing borrowed words

One way languages grow is by borrowing words from each other. English words that relate to technology often are borrowed by Spanish and other languages throughout the world. Sometimes the words are modified slightly to fit the sounds of the languages that borrow them. When reading in Spanish, you can often increase your understanding by looking for words borrowed from English or other languages you know.

Examinar el texto
Observa la tira cómica°. ¿De qué trata°? ¿Cómo lo sabes? Answers will vary.

Buscar
Esta lectura contiene una palabra tomada° del inglés. Trabaja con un(a) compañero/a para encontrarla.

    el celular

Repasa° las palabras nuevas relacionadas con la tecnología que aprendiste en **Contextos** y expande la lista de palabras tomadas del inglés. Answers will vary.

_____   _____

_____   _____

_____   _____

Sobre el autor
Juan Matías Loiseau (1974–). Más conocido como Tute, este artista nació en Buenos Aires, Argentina. Estudió diseño gráfico, humorismo y cine. Sus tiras cómicas se publican en Estados Unidos, Francia y toda Latinoamérica.

tira cómica *comic strip* **¿De qué trata?** *What is it about?* **tomada** *taken* **Repasa** *Review*

More activities

 vhlcentral   Online activities

Después de leer

Comprensión

Indica si las oraciones son **ciertas** o **falsas**. Corrige las falsas.

Cierto	Falso	
✓	___	1. Hay tres personajes en la tira cómica: un usuario de teléfono, un amigo y un empleado de la empresa (*company*) telefónica.
___	✓	2. El nuevo servicio de teléfono incluye las llamadas telefónicas únicamente. También viene con un tipo que te sigue a todos lados.
___	✓	3. El empleado duerme en su casa. Duerme al lado de la cama del usuario.
✓	___	4. El contrato de teléfono dura (*lasts*) un año.
___	✓	5. El usuario y el amigo están trabajando (*working*). Están de vacaciones.

Preguntas

Responde a estas preguntas con oraciones completas. Usa el pretérito y el imperfecto.

1. ¿Al usuario le gustaba usar el teléfono celular todo el tiempo?
   No, al usuario le molestaba usar el celular todo el tiempo.

2. ¿Por qué el usuario decidió tirar el teléfono al mar?
   Porque el celular y el tipo lo tenían harto.

3. Según el amigo, ¿para qué tenía el usuario que tirar el teléfono celular al mar?
   El usuario tenía que tirar el teléfono al mar para recuperar su libertad.

4. ¿Qué ocurrió cuando el usuario tiró el teléfono?
   El empleado fue a buscar el teléfono.

5. ¿Qué le dijo el empleado al usuario cuando salió del mar?
   El empleado le dijo que tenía una llamada perdida.

Conversar

En grupos pequeños, hablen de estos temas. Answers will vary.

1. ¿Se sienten identificados/as con el usuario de teléfono de la tira cómica? ¿Por qué?

2. ¿Cuáles son los aspectos positivos y los negativos de tener teléfono celular?

3. ¿Cuál es para ustedes el límite que debe tener la tecnología en nuestras vidas?

---

te viene *comes with* tipo *guy, dude* te avisa *alerts you* escuchás *listen (Arg.)*
distraídos *careless* piso *floor* bolsa de dormir *sleeping bag* darle de baja *to suspend*
harto *fed up* revolear *throw it away with energy (S. America)* bien hecho *well done*
llamada perdida *missed call*

Comprensión Have students write three additional true/false statements for a classmate to complete.

Preguntas
- Have students work in pairs to answer these questions.
- Assign a number to each panel in the comic. Then have students identify the panel(s) where they found the information needed for their answers.

Conversar For item 2, survey the class and write their answers on the board in a two-column chart with the headings **Lo positivo** and **Lo negativo**. Then ask the class to determine which column wins out overall.

TEACHING OPTIONS

Large Groups ←👤→ Ask students to work in groups of six. Tell them to improvise and create a humorous story as a group. Ask one person in the group to start it off by giving an introductory sentence, such as: **Ayer estuvimos en el coche y ocurrió algo muy raro.** Have the others add sentences with additional details to complete the story. Encourage students to be creative and make the story as long as they wish.

Pairs ←👤→ In pairs, have students create a comic strip about cars or car accessories. Tell them that they may use the same main character as the comic on these pages, or they may develop new character(s). Have students present their comics to the class.

Escritura

Estrategia

Listing key words

Once you have determined the purpose for a piece of writing and identified your audience, it is helpful to make a list of key words you can use while writing. If you were to write a description of your campus, for example, you would probably need a list of prepositions that describe location, such as **al lado de** and **detrás de**. Likewise, a list of descriptive adjectives would be useful to you if you were writing about the people and places of your childhood.

By preparing a list of potential words ahead of time, you will find it easier to avoid using the dictionary while writing your first draft. You will probably also learn a few new words in Spanish while preparing your list of key words.

Listing useful vocabulary is also a valuable organizational strategy, since the act of brainstorming key words will help you to form ideas about your topic. In addition, a list of key words can help you avoid redundancy when you write.

If you were going to help someone write a personal ad, what words would be most helpful to you? Jot a few of them down and compare your list with a partner's. Did you choose the same words? Would you choose any different or additional words, based on what your partner wrote?

1. _____
2. _____
3. _____
4. _____
5. _____
6. _____

Tema

Escribir instrucciones

Un(a) amigo/a tuyo/a quiere escribir un anuncio personal en un sitio web para citas románticas. Tú tienes experiencia con esto y vas a decirle qué debe y no debe decir en su perfil.

Escríbele un mensaje electrónico en el que le explicas claramente° cómo hacerlo.

Cuando escribas tu mensaje, considera esta información:

- ▶ el nombre del sitio web
- ▶ mandatos afirmativos que describen en detalle lo que tu amigo/a debe escribir
- ▶ una descripción física, sus pasatiempos, sus actividades favoritas y otras cosas originales como el tipo de carro que tiene o su signo del zodiaco
- ▶ su dirección electrónica, su número de teléfono celular, etc.
- ▶ mandatos negativos sobre cosas que tu amigo/a no debe escribir en el anuncio

claramente *clearly*

EVALUATION: Instrucciones

Criteria	Scale
Content	1 2 3 4 5
Organization	1 2 3 4 5
Use of vocabulary	1 2 3 4 5
Grammatical accuracy	1 2 3 4 5

Scoring	
Excellent	18–20 points
Good	14–17 points
Satisfactory	10–13 points
Unsatisfactory	< 10 points

Escuchar
Antes de escuchar

Estrategia

Recognizing the genre of spoken discourse

You will encounter many different genres of spoken discourse in Spanish. For example, you may hear a political speech, a radio interview, a commercial, a voicemail message, or a news broadcast. Try to identify the genre of what you hear so that you can activate your background knowledge about that type of discourse and identify the speakers' motives and intentions.

 To practice this strategy, you will now listen to two short selections. Identify the genre of each one.

Preparación

Mira la foto de Ricardo Moreno. ¿Puedes imaginarte qué tipo de discurso vas a oír?

Ahora escucha

 En la radio

Mientras escuchas a Ricardo Moreno, responde a las preguntas.

1. ¿Qué tipo de discurso es?
   a. las noticias (*news*) por radio o televisión
   b. una conversación entre amigos
   c. un anuncio comercial
   d. una reseña (*review*) de una película

2. ¿De qué habla?
   a. del tiempo   c. de un producto o servicio
   b. de su vida   d. de algo que oyó o vio

3. ¿Cuál es el propósito (*purpose*)?
   a. informar   c. relacionarse con alguien
   b. vender   d. dar opiniones

Comprensión

Identificar

Indica si esta información está incluida en el discurso; si está incluida, escribe los detalles que escuchaste.

	Sí	No
1. El anuncio describe un servicio.	⊙	○
Venden computadoras y productos para computadoras.		
2. Explica cómo está de salud.	○	⊙
3. Informa sobre la variedad de productos.	⊙	○
programas de computación, impresoras, computadoras portátiles		
4. Pide tu opinión.	○	⊙
5. Explica por qué es la mejor tienda.	⊙	○
Tiene buenos precios y los dependientes conocen los últimos avances.		
6. Informa sobre el tiempo para mañana.	⊙	○
7. Informa dónde se puede conseguir el servicio.	⊙	○
en Mundo de Computación o en el sitio web		
8. Informa sobre las noticias del mundo.	○	⊙

Haz un anuncio

Con tres o cuatro compañeros, hagan un anuncio comercial de algún producto. No se olviden de dar toda la información necesaria. Después presenten su anuncio a la clase. Entre todos, decidan cuál es el mejor anuncio.

Section Goals

In **Escuchar**, students will:
- practice recognizing the genre of two short examples of spoken discourse
- answer questions based on a broadcast advertisement for a computer store

Instructional Resources
Supersite: Audio (Textbook MP3s); Resources (Scripts)

Estrategia
Script 1. Buenos días. Hoy tenemos la gran oportunidad de conversar con el futbolista Carlos Roa del equipo argentino. Carlos, ¿qué opinas del partido que ganaron contra Chile? 2. Buenos días. Ésta es la residencia del arquitecto Rivera. No hay nadie en casa en estos momentos. Por favor, deje un mensaje y lo llamaré lo más pronto posible.

Teaching Tip Make sure students correctly identified the two genres in the **Estrategia** recording as **entrevista** and **mensaje de correo de voz**. Then, have them look at the photo and describe what they see. Guide them to see that **Ricardo Moreno** is broadcasting from a radio studio.

Ahora escucha
Script Necesita, ¿navegar en Internet o imprimir documentos? ¿Descargar fotos? Si usted está buscando una computadora y no está seguro del tipo de computadora que necesita, hable con nosotros. Le ayudamos a escoger la computadora más adecuada para usted. ¡Es facilísimo! Los dependientes de nuestra tienda de computación conocen los últimos avances en programas de computación, conexiones a Internet, computadoras portátiles, impresoras y más. También tenemos los mejores precios. Venga inmediatamente a Mundo de Computación en Paseo Las Américas para ver qué fácil es comprar la computadora perfecta. O visite nuestro sitio web en la dirección www.mundodecom.ar.

En pantalla Video

¿Para qué sirven la tecnología y los aparatos digitales? La tecnología cambia las actividades diarias y los deseos de las personas. Las compañías que venden objetos tradicionales necesitan imaginación para vender sus productos en el mundo digital. La compañía **Popular libros**, un distribuidor español de libros en Internet, hizo este video como un proyecto cultural para promover los libros impresos y la lectura, de una manera creativa y divertida.

Vocabulario útil	
atril	*stand*
búsqueda	*search*
colgarse	*to crash*
disfrutar (de)	*to enjoy*
reiniciar	*to restart, reboot*
toma de corriente	*(electric) outlet*
ventajas	*advantages*

Preparación

¿Te gusta más leer libros y revistas en papel o en formato electrónico? ¿Por qué? ¿Qué ventajas tiene cada uno de estos formatos? Answers will vary.

Emparejar

¿Para qué sirve? Empareja los elementos según el contenido del video.

1. atril d
2. índice e
3. lapicero a
4. marcapáginas c
5. papel opaco b

a. tomar notas personales
b. duplicar la información
c. abrir el libro en un punto exacto
d. leer sin usar las manos
e. señalar la localización exacta de información

Anuncios

Este anuncio habla de cómo leer de manera tradicional, pero de una manera cómica y usando el vocabulario del mundo digital. Trabaja con un grupo pequeño para hacer lo mismo con las actividades siguientes: escribir cartas a los amigos, encontrar un lugar en una ciudad, comprar música u otro tema que consideren interesante. Answers will vary.

BOOK

Compacto y portátil, BOOK puede ser utilizado en cualquier lugar.

Una simple sacudida de dedo nos lleva a la siguiente página.

...sin necesidad de usar las manos.

 NATIONAL communication cultures STANDARDS

 More activities / vhlcentral / Online activities

TEACHING OPTIONS

Heritage Speakers Have heritage speakers share ways in which their culture of origin approaches everyday tasks with regard to the use of digital and traditional tools. How does the attitude toward digital tools (and having the latest digital device) compare to that which they have observed in the United States? Can they identify any trends in attitude toward digital devices used in everyday tasks or for connecting people with each other?

Expansion Have students do a survey among various student groups in their school to determine the use of and the attitudes toward digital devices. Begin with the class defining activities (such as reading, writing, listening to music, or doing research). Then establish columns for information such as preferred devices, advantages, disadvantages, or changes in use over time. Have students share and pool their findings and graph the results.

Video

Maravillas de la tecnología

Hoy día, en cualquier ciudad grande latinoamericana puedes encontrar **un cibercafé**. Allí uno puede disfrutar de° un refresco o de un café mientras escribe mensajes electrónicos o chatea. De hecho°, el negocio° del cibercafé está mucho más desarrollado° en Latinoamérica que en los Estados Unidos. En una ciudad hispana, es común ver varios en una misma cuadra°. Los cibercafés ofrecen servicios especializados que permiten su coexistencia. Por ejemplo, mientras que el cibercafé Videomax atrae° a los niños con videojuegos, el Conécta-T ofrece servicio de chat con cámara para jóvenes, y el Mundo° Ejecutivo atrae a profesionales, todos en la misma calle.

Vocabulario útil

comunidad indígena	indigenous community
localizados	located
usuarios	users

Preparación

¿Con qué frecuencia te conectas a Internet? ¿Dónde lo haces, en tu casa o en un lugar público? Answers will vary.

¿Cierto o falso?

Indica si cada oración es **cierta** o **falsa**.

	Cierto	Falso
1. A Omar lo llama su tía.		⊘
2. Omar entrevista a varios habitantes de Cuzco.	⊘	
3. En Perú sólo hay cibercafés en la ciudad de Cuzco.		⊘
4. Sólo los turistas van a los cibercafés.		⊘
5. Algunos peruanos utilizan Internet para vender sus productos.	⊘	

disfrutar de *enjoy* De hecho *In fact* negocio *business* desarrollado *developed* cuadra *(city) block* atrae *attracts* Mundo *World*

... los cibercafés se conocen comúnmente como "cabinas de Internet" y están localizados por todo el país.

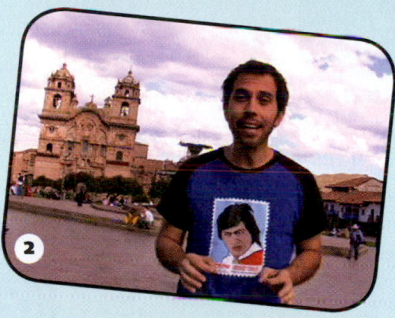

... el primer *hotspot* de Cuzco [...] permite a los usuarios navegar de manera inalámbrica...

Puedo usar Internet en medio de la plaza y nadie me molesta.

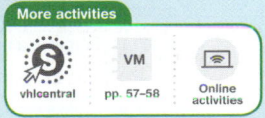

More activities — vhlcentral — VM pp. 57–58 — Online activities

Section Goals
In **Flash cultura**, students will:
- read about cybercafés in Latin America
- watch a video about technology in Peru

Instructional Resources
Supersite: Video (*Flash cultura*); Resources (Scripts, Translations, Answer Keys)
WebSAM
Video Manual

Introduction To check comprehension, give students these true/false statements: 1. Normalmente no se bebe en los cibercafés. (Falso.) 2. Hay más cibercafés en Latinoamérica que en los Estados Unidos. (Cierto.) 3. Normalmente hay varios cibercafés en la misma cuadra. (Cierto.) 4. Generalmente todos los cibercafés ofrecen los mismos servicios. (Falso.)

Antes de ver
- Have students look at the video stills, read the captions, and predict the content of the video.
- Have students look at the captions for cognates and loan words related to technology.

Preparación
- Have students name what they use to get connected to the Internet.
- ⬤↔⬤ Survey the class to find the students that spend the most time on the Internet per day. Have volunteers ask them questions and comment on their Internet use. Ex: —¿Siete horas cada día? ¿Qué haces? —Miro películas y hablo con mis amigos en *Skype*. —Yo hablo con mis amigos también, pero por sólo una hora.

¿Cierto o falso?
- Have students correct the false statements.
- Ask students to write three additional true/false statements about this episode for a partner to complete.

TEACHING OPTIONS

Extra Practice ←⬤→ Have students conduct online research to find out what kinds of products indigenous groups in Peru sell on the Internet. Have students find a few websites through which they could purchase products, and prepare a short oral report on the items' cultural significance, cost, and shipping.
Small Groups ←⬤→ Have small groups discuss how they would design and run their own cybercafé. Encourage them to be

creative and include specific details. Have groups present their businesses to the class.
Small Groups ←⬤→ Have small groups research one of the indigenous groups of Peru. Each group member should write a paragraph about one topic, such as history, language, music, or cultural customs in modern-day Peru. Have groups combine their paragraphs into a report.

Section Goal

In **Panorama**, students will read about the geography, history, and culture of Argentina.

Instructional Resources
Supersite: Video (*Panorama cultural*); Resources (Scripts, Translations, Digital Image Bank, Answer Keys)
WebSAM
Workbook

Teaching Tips
- Use the **Lección 11 Panorama** digital images to assist with this presentation.
- Have students look at the map of Argentina and guide them to recognize Argentina's great size and the variety of topographical features, such as mountains (**los Andes**), vast plains (**las pampas**), and large rivers.
- Point out that Argentina is one of the largest beef producers in the world and that **gauchos** have played an important role in the culture of the country. Bariloche is an important winter recreation area. Remind students that June–August is winter in the southern hemisphere.

El país en cifras Patagonia is very sparsely populated, but Buenos Aires is a metropolis about the size of New York City. Invite students to mention anything they know about Argentina.

Argentina

NATIONAL STANDARDS — connections cultures

El país en cifras

- ▶ **Área:** 2.780.400 km² (1.074.000 millas²)
  Argentina es el país de habla española más grande del mundo. Su territorio es dos veces el tamaño° de Alaska.
- ▶ **Población:** 44.293.000
- ▶ **Capital:** Buenos Aires (y su área metropolitana)—15.180.000
  En el gran Buenos Aires vive más del treinta por ciento de la población total del país. La ciudad es conocida° como el "París de Suramérica" por su estilo parisino°.

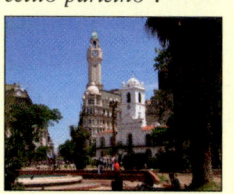
Buenos Aires

- ▶ **Ciudades principales:**
  Córdoba—1.511.000, Rosario—1.381.000, Mendoza—1.009.000
- ▶ **Moneda:** peso argentino
- ▶ **Idiomas:** español (oficial), lenguas indígenas

Bandera de Argentina

Argentinos célebres
- ▶ **Jorge Luis Borges,** escritor (1899–1986)
- ▶ **María Eva Duarte de Perón ("Evita"),** primera dama° (1919–1952)
- ▶ **Mercedes Sosa,** cantante (1935–2009)
- ▶ **Leandro "Gato" Barbieri,** saxofonista (1932–2016)
- ▶ **Adolfo Pérez Esquivel,** activista (1931–), Premio Nobel de la Paz en 1980

tamaño *size* conocida *known* parisino *Parisian* primera dama *First Lady*

Gaucho de las pampas

ESTADOS UNIDOS
OCÉANO ATLÁNTICO
OCÉANO PACÍFICO
AMÉRICA DEL SUR
ARGENTINA

BOLIVIA
PARAGUAY
Las cata del Igu

San Miguel de Tucumán
Córdoba
URUGU
La Cordillera de los Andes
Aconcagua
Mendoza
Rosario
Río Paraná
CHILE
La Pampa
Buenos Aires
Mar del Plata
San Carlos de Bariloche
Patagonia
Monte Fitz Roy (Chaltén)
Artesano en Buenos Aires
Océano Atlántico
Vista de San Carlos de Bariloche
Tierra del Fuego

More activities
vhlcentral | WB pp. 133–134 | Online activities

ACTIVIDADES

1 ¿Cierto o falso? Indica si lo que dicen las oraciones es **cierto** o **falso**.

1. La ciudad de Buenos Aires es conocida como el "Madrid de Suramérica". falso
2. La moneda oficial de Argentina es el peso argentino. cierto
3. Jorge Luis Borges era un cantante de tango argentino. falso
4. Para Adolfo Pérez Esquivel, el activismo es importante. cierto
5. El río Paraná pasa por Argentina. cierto

6. Argentina es el país más "europeo" por los inmigrantes italianos, alemanes, españoles e ingleses. cierto
7. El tango se originó en el siglo XX. falso
8. Las cataratas del Iguazú se encuentran en la frontera con Chile. falso
9. Los productos de exportación más importantes de Argentina son el mate y el café. falso
10. La Avenida 9 de Julio es una de las calles más anchas del mundo. cierto

TEACHING OPTIONS

Worth Noting The Argentinian cowboy, the **gaucho**, has played as significant a role in the folklore of Argentina as the cowboy of the Old West has played in that of the United States. Two classic works of Argentinian literature focus on the **gaucho**. *El gaucho Martín Fierro*, an epic poem by **José Hernández** (1834–1886), celebrates the **gaucho's** fiercely independent way of life, whereas **Domingo Faustino Sarmiento's** (1811–1888)

biography, *Facundo: Civilización y barbarie*, describes the nomadic, uneducated **gauchos** as hindrances in Argentina's pursuit of economic, social, and political progress.

Extra Practice Have students listen to a song on one of the many recordings by singer **Mercedes Sosa**. Then, have pairs work together to transcribe the lyrics. Invite volunteers to share their work with the class.

BRASIL

Historia • Inmigración europea

Se dice que Argentina es el país más "europeo" de toda Latinoamérica. Después del año 1880, inmigrantes italianos, alemanes, españoles e ingleses llegaron para establecerse en esta nación. Esta diversidad cultural ha dejado° una profunda huella° en la música, en el cine y en la arquitectura argentinos.

⊳ Artes • El tango

El tango es uno de los símbolos culturales más importantes de Argentina. Este género° musical es una mezcla de ritmos de origen africano, italiano y español, y se originó a finales del siglo XIX entre los porteños°. Poco después se hizo popular entre el resto de los argentinos y su fama llegó hasta París. Como baile, el tango en un principio° era provocativo y violento, pero se hizo más romántico durante los años 30. Hoy día, este estilo musical tiene adeptos° en muchas partes del mundo°.

⊳ Lugares • Las cataratas del Iguazú

Las famosas cataratas° del Iguazú se encuentran entre las fronteras de Argentina, Paraguay y Brasil, al norte de Buenos Aires. Cerca de ellas confluyen° los ríos Iguazú y Paraná. Estas extensas caídas de agua tienen hasta 80 metros (262 pies) de altura°, y en época° de lluvias llegan a medir 4 kilómetros (2,5 millas) de ancho. Situadas en el Parque Nacional Iguazú, las cataratas son un destino° turístico muy visitado.

Economía • La soja, el maíz y los camiones

La economía de Argentina es la tercera más importante de América Latina, después de las de Brasil y México. Sus productos más emblemáticos son la carne, el vino y el mate, cuyas industrias se asociaron en 2017 para consolidarse internacionalmente. Los principales productos de exportación de Argentina son los derivados de la soja°, el maíz, el trigo° y los camiones de reparto°.

ha dejado *has left* **huella** *mark* **género** *genre* **porteños** *people of Buenos Aires* **en un principio** *at first* **adeptos** *followers* **mundo** *world* **cataratas** *waterfalls* **confluyen** *converge* **altura** *height* **época** *season* **destino** *destination* **soja** *soybean* **trigo** *wheat* **camiones de reparto** *delivery trucks*

¡Increíble pero cierto!

La Avenida 9 de Julio en Buenos Aires es una de las calles más anchas° del mundo. De lado a lado mide° cerca de 140 metros, lo que es equivalente a un campo° y medio de fútbol. Su nombre conmemora el Día de la Independencia de Argentina.

anchas *wide* **mide** *it measures* **campo** *field*

---

2 **¿Qué aprendiste?** Contesta las preguntas.

1. ¿Qué porcentaje de la población de Argentina vive en el gran Buenos Aires? *más del treinta por ciento*
2. ¿Quién era Mercedes Sosa? *una cantante argentina*
3. ¿Qué tipo de baile es uno de los símbolos culturales más importantes de Argentina? *el tango*
4. ¿Cómo era el baile del tango originalmente? *provocativo y violento*
5. ¿En qué parque nacional están las cataratas del Iguazú? *el Parque Nacional Iguazú*

3 **Describir** En parejas, imaginen que visitaron Argentina y túrnense para describir cómo fue su experiencia. Utilicen las preposiciones **por** y **para**.

modelo

Estudiante 1: Yo compré boletos para un show de tango.

TEACHING OPTIONS

Variación léxica Argentinians frequently use the word **¡che!** to get the attention of someone they are talking to. **Che** also serves as a kind of spoken exclamation point with which Argentinians pepper their speech. This is so noticeable to outsiders that Argentinians are often given the nickname **Che** in other parts of the Spanish-speaking world. Another notable feature of Argentine Spanish is the existence, alongside **tú**, of **vos** as the second-person singular familiar pronoun. **Vos** is also heard in other parts of Latin America, and it is accompanied by corresponding verb forms in the present tense. Here are some equivalents: **vos contás / tú cuentas, vos pensás / tú piensas, vos sos / tú eres, vos ponés / tú pones, vos venís / tú vienes.**

Inmigración europea Among the waves of immigrants were thousands of European Jews. An interesting chapter in the history of the **pampas** features Jewish **gauchos**. A generous, pre-Zionist philanthropist purchased land for Jews who settled on the Argentine grasslands. At one time, the number of Yiddish-language newspapers in Argentina was second only to that in New York City.

El tango **Carlos Gardel** (1890–1935) is considered the great classic interpreter of **tango**. If possible, bring in a recording of his version of a **tango** such as *Cuesta abajo* or *Volver*. **Astor Piazzola** (1921–1992) was a modern exponent of **tango**. His **tango nuevo** has found interpreters such as cellist Yo-Yo Ma and the Kronos Quartet. You may want to play the **Panorama cultural** video for this paragraph.

Las cataratas del Iguazú At just over ten miles away, **Puerto Iguazú** is the closest city to the falls. Other nearby attractions include the **Itaipú** dam, which is the world's biggest hydroelectric facility, and the **Parque de las Aves**, where one can observe many near-extinct and exotic species of birds. You may want to play the **Panorama cultural** video for this paragraph.

La soja, el maíz y los camiones Argentina also exports citrus fruits, honey, sorghum, sunflower seeds, and fish.

¡Increíble pero cierto! **Avenida 9 de Julio** is so wide that pedestrians need a few minutes and several green lights to cross it (there are stoplights to control pedestrian traffic). To help alleviate this, some urban planners have advocated making the central part of the avenue subterranean.

Instructional Resources

Supersite: Audio (Textbook & Lab MP3s); Testing Program (Tests, MP3s)

WebSAM

Lab Manual

Teaching Tip You may want to assign the **Prueba de práctica**, with its diagnostics and review activities, in the online-only **Repaso** section on the Supersite. There is also a **Repaso oral** in this section. For the Sixth Edition, a new summative vocabulary activity with speech recognition has been added to the **Repaso** section.

La tecnología

la aplicación	app
la batería	battery
la cámara digital	digital camera
el canal	(TV) channel
el cargador	charger
el control remoto	remote control
el correo de voz	voice mail
el radio	radio (set)
el (teléfono) celular	(cell) phone
el televisor	television set
apagar	to turn off
funcionar	to work
llamar	to call
poner, prender	to turn on
sonar (o:ue)	to ring
textear	to text
descompuesto/a	not working; out of order
lento/a	slow
lleno/a	full

Verbos

abrazar(se)	to hug; to embrace (each other)
ayudar(se)	to help (each other)
besar(se)	to kiss (each other)
encontrar(se) (o:ue)	to meet (each other); to run into (each other)
saludar(se)	to greet (each other)

La computadora

el archivo	file
la arroba	@ symbol
el blog	blog
el buscador	browser
la computadora (portátil)	(portable) computer; (laptop)
la conexión inalámbrica	wireless connection
la contraseña	password
la dirección electrónica	e-mail address
la impresora	printer
Internet	Internet
el mensaje de texto	text message
la página principal	home page
la pantalla	screen
el perfil	profile
el programa de computación	software
el ratón	mouse
la red	network; Web
el sitio web	website
la tableta	tablet (computer)
el teclado	keyboard
borrar	to erase
cargar	to charge; to upload
chatear	to chat
conectarse a Internet	to get connected to the Internet
descargar	to download
escanear	to scan
grabar	to record
guardar	to save
imprimir	to print

El carro

la autopista	highway
el baúl	trunk
la calle	street
la carretera	highway; (main) road
el capó, el cofre	hood
el carro, el coche	car
la circulación, el tráfico	traffic
el garaje, el taller (mecánico)	garage; (mechanic's) repair shop
la gasolina	gasoline
la gasolinera	gas station
la licencia de conducir	driver's license
la llanta	tire
el/la mecánico/a	mechanic
el navegador GPS	GPS
el parabrisas	windshield
la policía	police (force)
la velocidad máxima	speed limit
el volante	steering wheel
arrancar	to start
arreglar	to fix; to arrange
bajar(se) de	to get off of/out of (a vehicle)
conducir, manejar	to drive
estacionar	to park
llenar (el tanque)	to fill (the tank)
parar	to stop
revisar (el aceite)	to check (the oil)
subir(se) a	to get on/into (a vehicle)

Otras palabras y expresiones

por aquí	around here
por ejemplo	for example
por eso	that's why; therefore
por fin	finally

Por and **para**	See pages 382–383.
Stressed possessive adjectives and pronouns	See pages 388–389.
Expresiones útiles	See page 373.

More activities

vhlcentral | LM p. 66

La vivienda

12

Communicative Goals

You will learn how to:

- Welcome people to your home
- Describe your house or apartment
- Talk about household chores
- Give instructions

A PRIMERA VISTA

- ¿Está el chico en casa?
- ¿Vive en una casa o en un apartamento?
- ¿De qué color es la camiseta suya?
- ¿Está limpia o sucia la ventana?

Lesson Goals

In **Lección 12**, students will be introduced to the following:

- terms for parts of a house
- names of common household objects
- terms for household chores
- central patios
- floating islands in Lake Titicaca
- relative pronouns
- formal (**usted/ustedes**) commands
- object pronouns with formal commands
- present subjunctive
- subjunctive with verbs and expressions of will and influence
- locating the main parts of a sentence
- using linking words
- writing a lease agreement
- using visual cues while listening
- a commercial for **Conforama** home stores
- a video about the **Museo Casa de Frida Kahlo**
- cultural and geographic information about Panama

A primera vista Here are some additional questions you can ask to personalize the photo: **¿Dónde vives? ¿Con quién vives? ¿Cómo es tu casa? ¿Qué haces en casa por la noche? ¿Qué haces los fines de semana? ¿Tienes computadora en casa? ¿Qué otros aparatos tecnológicos tienes?**

Teaching Tip Look for these icons for additional communicative practice:

→■←	Interpretive communication
←■→	Presentational communication
■↔■	Interpersonal communication

INSTRUCTIONAL RESOURCES

Supersite (vhlcentral.com)
Video: *Fotonovela, Flash cultura, En pantalla, Panorama cultural*
Audio: Textbook and Lab MP3 Files

Activity Pack: Information Gap Activities, games, additional activity handouts
Resources: SAM Answer Key, Scripts, Translations, **Vocabulario adicional**, sample lesson plan, Grammar Presentation Slides, Digital Image Bank

Testing Program: Quizzes, Tests, Exams, MP3s, Oral Testing Suggestions
Student Activities Manual: Workbook/Video Manual/Lab Manual
WebSAM (online Student Activities Manual)

La vivienda

Section Goals

In **Contextos**, students will learn and practice:
• names of rooms in a house
• names of common household objects
• terms for household chores

Instructional Resources

Supersite: Audio (Textbook and Lab MP3 Files); Resources (Digital Image Bank, **Vocabulario adicional**, Activity Pack, Scripts, Answer Keys); Testing Program (Quizzes)
WebSAM
Workbook
Lab Manual

Teaching Tips

• Use the **Lección 12 Contextos** digital images to assist with this presentation.
• As students look at the illustration in their books, describe the house, naming the kinds of rooms and introducing those that are not shown. Ex: **Ésta es la casa de los Hernández. Hay una sala grande, un dormitorio, una oficina, una cocina y un altillo. También hay un cuarto de baño, un sótano y un garaje, pero no vemos estos cuartos en la ilustración.**
• Ask open-ended questions about the house and housework pictured in the illustration. Ex: **¿Dónde se pone la comida después de regresar del supermercado?** Ask personalized questions. Ex: **____, ¿vives en una residencia o en un apartamento? ¿Cuántos cuartos hay?**

Note: At this point you may want to present **Vocabulario adicional: Más vocabulario para el hogar** from the Supersite.

Más vocabulario

las afueras	suburbs; outskirts
el alquiler	rent (payment)
el amo/a (m., f.) de casa	homemaker
el barrio	neighborhood
el edificio de apartamentos	apartment building
el/la vecino/a	neighbor
la vivienda	housing
el balcón	balcony
la entrada	entrance
la escalera	stairs
el garaje	garage
el jardín	garden; yard
el patio	patio; yard
el pasillo	hallway
el sótano	basement
la cafetera	coffee maker
el electrodoméstico	electrical appliance
el horno (de microondas)	(microwave) oven
la lavadora	washing machine
la luz	light; electricity
la secadora	clothes dryer
la tostadora	toaster
el cartel	poster
la mesita de noche	night stand
los muebles	furniture
alquilar	to rent
mudarse	to move (from one house to another)

Variación léxica

dormitorio	⟷	alcoba (Arg.); aposento (Rep. Dom.); recámara (Méx.)
apartamento	⟷	departamento (Arg., Chile, Méx.); piso (Esp.)
lavar los platos	⟷	lavar/fregar los trastes (Amér. C., Rep. Dom.)

More activities

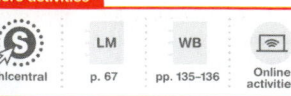

S vhlcentral | LM p. 67 | WB pp. 135–136 | Online activities

Los quehaceres domésticos

arreglar	to straighten up
barrer el suelo	to sweep the floor
ensuciar	to get (something) dirty
hacer quehaceres domésticos	to do household chores
lavar (el suelo, los platos)	to wash (the floor, the dishes)
limpiar la casa	to clean the house
planchar la ropa	to iron the clothes
quitar la mesa	to clear the table
quitar el polvo	to dust
sacar la basura	to take out the trash

el dormitorio

el cuadro/la pintura
Hace la cama. (hacer)
el armario
la almohada
la manta
la cómoda

la sala

la lámpara
las cortinas
Pasa la aspiradora. (pasar)
el sofá
la mesita
la alfombra

TEACHING OPTIONS

Extra Practice Ask students to complete these analogies.
1. aspiradora : ____ :: lavadora : ropa (alfombra)
   (Aspiradora es a ____ como lavadora es a ropa.)
2. frío : calor :: congelador : ____ (horno)
3. cama : dormitorio :: ____ : oficina (escritorio)
4. platos : cocina :: carro : ____ (garaje)

Heritage Speakers Ask heritage speakers to tell the class any other terms their families use to refer to rooms in a home or household appliances. Ex: **el lavaplatos = el lavavajillas; el altillo = el ático, el desván.**

el altillo

la oficina

la pared

el estante

Sacude los muebles. (sacudir)

el sillón

la cocina

el congelador

el refrigerador

Cocina. (cocinar)

la cocina, la estufa

el horno

el lavaplatos

Práctica

1 **¿Dónde?** Indica el lugar de la casa donde se presentan las situaciones.

1. el dormitorio
2. la cocina
3. el sótano
4. el garaje
5. la sala
6. la oficina
7. la cocina
8. el dormitorio

2 **¿Cierto o falso?** Indica si las oraciones son **ciertas** o **falsas**.

	Cierto	Falso
1. El nombre de los apartamentos es Buena Vida.	○	⦿
2. Los apartamentos son ideales para personas solteras.	○	⦿
3. Cada apartamento tiene tres dormitorios.	⦿	○
4. Hay una oficina en cada apartamento.	⦿	○
5. Es posible encontrar un parque cerca de los apartamentos.	⦿	○
6. Cada apartamento tiene sólo un baño.	○	⦿
7. Cerca de los apartamentos hay un museo.	○	⦿
8. Cada apartamento tiene una bonita cocina.	⦿	○

3 **Escoger** Escoge la letra de la respuesta correcta.

1. Ponemos cuadros y pinturas en _____ a _____.
   a. las paredes   b. los quehaceres   c. los jardines
2. Si no quieres vivir en el centro, puedes mudarte _____ b _____.
   a. al alquiler   b. a las afueras   c. a la vivienda
3. Guardamos (*We keep*) los pantalones, las camisas y los zapatos en _____ b _____.
   a. la secadora   b. el armario   c. el patio
4. Para subir de la planta baja al primer piso, usas _____ c _____.
   a. la entrada   b. el cartel   c. la escalera
5. Cuando quieres tener una lámpara y un despertador cerca de tu cama, puedes ponerlos en _____ c _____.
   a. el barrio   b. el cuadro   c. la mesita de noche

4 **Definiciones** En parejas, identifiquen cada cosa que se describe. Luego inventen sus propias descripciones de algunas palabras y expresiones de **Contextos**.

modelo

Estudiante 1: *Es donde pones los libros.*
Estudiante 2: *el estante*

1. Son las personas que viven en tu barrio. los vecinos
2. Es el quehacer doméstico que haces después de comer. lavar los platos/ quitar la mesa
3. Algunos de ellos son las cómodas y los sillones. los muebles
4. Es donde pones la cabeza cuando duermes. la/una almohada

1 **Expansion** Ask students to write two more situations for a partner to indicate the corresponding part(s) of the house.

1 **Script** 1. Tienes que hacer la cama. 2. Voy a poner el pollo en el horno. 3. Ella bajó del primer piso para planchar la ropa. 4. Nos subimos al coche. 5. Quieren sentarse en el sofá y ver un programa de televisión. 6. Necesito silencio para trabajar en mi proyecto. 7. Él debe lavar los platos. 8. Me acosté anoche a las once. *Textbook MP3s*

2 **Teaching Tip** You may want to do this activity as a TPR exercise. Have students give a thumbs-up for **cierto** and a thumbs-down for **falso**.

2 **Expansion** Have pairs of students write their own radio ad for a new housing development.

2 **Script** Los apartamentos Buen Vivir tienen todo lo que usted y su familia necesitan: tres dormitorios grandes, una oficina, dos baños y una hermosa cocina. Estos apartamentos son ideales para la familia: el barrio es tranquilo y seguro y, además, hay un parque y una escuela cerca. Para más información sobre los apartamentos, pueden llamar al número 05347881. ¡Los esperamos! *Textbook MP3s*

3 **Expansion** To challenge students, write these items on the board as a cloze activity.

4 **Expansion** Have pairs give each other words from **Contextos** for their partners to define. Ex: **el pasillo (Pasas por este lugar cuando vas de un cuarto al otro.)**

Teaching Tips
• Use the **Lección 12 Contextos** digital images to assist with this vocabulary presentation.
• Ask volunteers to name the items on the table. Then talk about the uses of the silverware (**cubiertos**), glassware (**cristalería**), and china (**vajilla**) pictured. Ex: **La copa sirve para tomar vino.** Also ask questions, such as: **Tomamos café en un vaso, ¿verdad? (No, tomamos café en una taza.)**
• 🔵↔🔵 Add a visual aspect to this vocabulary presentation. Bring in silverware, plates, and glasses. As you hold up each item, engage students in a conversation. Have them name each item and guide you in setting the table. Ex: **¿Dónde pongo el tenedor, a la derecha o a la izquierda del plato?** Then model table manners common to many Spanish-speaking countries and contrast them to dining in the U.S. Ex: resting wrists (never elbows!) on the table, rather than placing one hand in your lap

5 Expansion
• Ask students additional questions modeled on the sentence starters in **Actividad 5**. Ex: **¿Qué se necesita para comer la carne?**
• Add a visual aspect to this activity. Using pictures of different foods or dishes, ask students what utensils are needed. Ex: **¿Qué se necesita para comer este plato de espaguetis? (un tenedor y una cuchara)**

6 Teaching Tip
→🔵← Before forming groups, model the activity with your own information. Ex: **En casa, mi esposa siempre pasa la aspiradora, pero yo sacudo los muebles. Mi hijo…**

el comedor

5 **Completar** Completa estas frases con las palabras más adecuadas.

1. Para tomar café necesitas… una taza
2. Para comer una ensalada necesitas… un tenedor/un plato
3. Para tomar vino necesitas… una copa
4. Para poner la comida en la mesa necesitas… un plato/poner la mesa
5. Para limpiarte la boca después de comer necesitas… una servilleta
6. Para cortar (*to cut*) un bistec necesitas… un cuchillo (y un tenedor)
7. Para tomar agua necesitas… un vaso/una copa
8. Para tomar sopa necesitas… una cuchara/un plato

6 **Los quehaceres** Trabajen en grupos para indicar quién hace estos quehaceres domésticos en sus casas. Luego contesten las preguntas. Answers will vary.

barrer el suelo	lavar los platos	planchar la ropa
cocinar	lavar la ropa	sacar la basura
hacer las camas	pasar la aspiradora	sacudir los muebles

modelo
Estudiante 1: ¿Quién pasa la aspiradora en tu casa?
Estudiante 2: Mi hermano y yo pasamos la aspiradora.

1. ¿Quién hace más quehaceres, tú o tus compañeros/as?
2. ¿Quiénes hacen la mayoría de los quehaceres, los hombres o las mujeres?
3. ¿Piensas que debes hacer más quehaceres? ¿Por qué?

TEACHING OPTIONS

Heritage Speakers ←🔵→ Ask heritage speakers to talk about special features, details, or areas of their homes that are particular to their family's culture. Ex: In Colombian homes, decorating the dining room with a **bodegón** (still-life painting of fruit). Also, if their families have told them about houses and apartments in their countries of origin, have them share these details with the class.

Extra Practice Write these sentence starters on the board, and have the students complete them with appropriate chores.
1. Antes de pasar la aspiradora, tienes que… (sacudir los muebles.) **2. Después de lavar y secar la ropa, normalmente…** (tienes que plancharla.) **3. Después de comer, tienes que…** (lavar los platos.) **4. Tienes que levantarte antes de…** (hacer la cama.) **5. Antes de sentarte a comer, tienes que…** (poner la mesa.)

Comunicación

7 **La vida doméstica** En parejas, describan las habitaciones que ven en estas fotos. Identifiquen y describan cinco muebles o adornos (*accessories*) de cada foto y digan dos quehaceres que se pueden hacer en cada habitación. Answers will vary.

8 **Mi apartamento** Dibuja el plano (*floor plan*) de un apartamento amueblado (*furnished*) imaginario y escribe los nombres de las habitaciones y de los muebles. En parejas, siéntense espalda contra espalda (*sit back to back*). Uno/a de ustedes describe su apartamento mientras su compañero/a lo dibuja según la descripción. Cuando terminen, miren el segundo dibujo. ¿Es similar al dibujo original? Answers will vary.

CONSULTA

To review bathroom-related vocabulary, see **Lección 7, Contextos,** p. 226.

9 **¡Corre, corre!** Tu profesor(a) va a darte una serie incompleta de dibujos que forman una historia. Tú y tu compañero/a tienen dos series diferentes. Descríbanse los dibujos para completar la historia.
Answers will vary.

> **modelo**
> **Estudiante 1:** Marta quita la mesa.
> **Estudiante 2:** Francisco...

10 **¡A arreglar!** Tu compañero/a de apartamento y tú dieron ayer una gran fiesta en casa, y ahora tienen que arreglarla. En parejas, pónganse de acuerdo sobre qué va a hacer cada uno/a de ustedes.
Answers will vary.

> **modelo**
> **Estudiante 1:** La alfombra de la sala está muy sucia. Yo paso la aspiradora allí. Y tú, ¿qué haces?
> **Estudiante 2:** Si quieres, yo puedo sacar la basura. Y luego, ¿qué hacemos?

Extra Practice Have students complete this cloze activity.
La vida doméstica de un estudiante universitario puede ser un desastre, ¿no? Nunca hay tiempo para hacer los _____ (quehaceres) domésticos. Sólo _____ (pasa) la aspiradora una vez al semestre y nunca _____ (sacude) los muebles. Los _____ (platos) sucios se acumulan en la _____ (cocina). Saca la ropa de la _____ (secadora) y se la pone sin _____ (planchar). Y,
¿por qué hacer la _____ (cama)? Se va a acostar en ella de nuevo este mismo día, ¿no?
Game Have students bring in real estate ads. Ask teams of three to write a description of a property. Teams then take turns reading their descriptions aloud. Other teams guess the price. The team that guesses the amount closest to the real price without going over scores one point.

7 **Teaching Tip**
→🔁← Model the activity using magazine pictures. Have students guess which photo you are describing. Ex: **¡Qué comedor más desordenado! ¡Es un desastre! Alguien debe quitar los platos sucios de la mesa. También es necesario sacudir los muebles y pasar la aspiradora.**

8 **Teaching Tips**
• ←🔁→ Draw a floor plan of a four-room apartment on the board. Ask volunteers to describe it.
• Have students draw their floor plans before you assign pairs. Make sure they understand the activity so that their floor plans do not become too complicated.

8 **Expansion**
• Have students talk about the changes needed to improve the drawing and then make the suggested changes to their floor plans.
• Have pairs repeat the activity, drawing floor plans of their actual homes or apartments.
• 🔁↔🔁 In pairs, tell students to imagine that they are interior decorators. Give each pair the same catalogue from IKEA or Pottery Barn, but set different budgets. Tell them they must design the apartment of their dreams without going over the spending limit. Have students describe their dream houses to the class while volunteers draw them on the board.

9 **Teaching Tip** Divide the class into pairs and distribute the handouts from the Activity Pack (Activity Pack/Supersite) that correspond to this Information Gap Activity.

10 **Expansion**
🔁↔🔁 Have pairs tell each other about an occasion when they have had to clean up their home for a particular reason. Encourage pairs to ask each other questions to find out additional information. Then ask volunteers to share their partners' stories with the class.

Los quehaceres

Jimena y Felipe deben limpiar el apartamento para poder ir de viaje con Marissa.

PERSONAJES JIMENA FELIPE

 Video

Section Goals

In **Fotonovela**, students will:
- receive comprehensible input from free-flowing discourse
- learn functional phrases that preview lesson grammatical structures

Instructional Resources

Supersite: Video (*Fotonovela*); Resources (Scripts, Translations, Answer Keys)
WebSAM
Video Manual

Video Recap: Lección 11

Before doing this **Fotonovela** section, review the previous episode with these questions:
**1. ¿Qué se borró de la computadora de Maru? (Se borraron muchos archivos.)
2. ¿Quién intenta arreglar la computadora de Maru? (Mónica intenta arreglarla.) 3. ¿Dónde está Miguel? (Él está en el taller de Jorge.) 4. ¿Cuánto le pagó Miguel a Jorge para arreglar su coche? (No le pagó nada.)**

Video Synopsis

Felipe and **Jimena** have promised to clean the apartment in exchange for permission to take a trip to the **Yucatán** Peninsula. **Marissa, Juan Carlos,** and **don Diego** help them finish on time.

Teaching Tips

- Have students predict the content of this episode, based on the title and video stills.
- Ask the class if this episode was what they expected, based on the predictions they made.

1

SR. DÍAZ Quieren ir a Yucatán con Marissa, ¿verdad?

SRA. DÍAZ Entonces, les sugiero que arreglen este apartamento. Regresamos más tarde.

SR. DÍAZ Les aconsejo que preparen la cena para las 8:30.

2

MARISSA ¿Qué pasa?

JIMENA Nuestros papás quieren que Felipe y yo arreglemos toda la casa.

FELIPE Y que, además, preparemos la cena.

MARISSA ¡Pues, yo les ayudo!

(*Don Diego llega a ayudar a los chicos.*)

FELIPE Tenemos que limpiar la casa hoy.

JIMENA ¿Nos ayuda, don Diego?

DON DIEGO Claro. Recomiendo que se organicen en equipos para limpiar.

3

MARISSA Mis padres siempre quieren que mis hermanos y yo ayudemos con los quehaceres. No me molesta ayudar. Pero odio limpiar el baño.

JIMENA Lo que más odio yo es sacar la basura.

5

6

JUAN CARLOS Hola, Jimena. ¿Está Felipe? (*a Felipe*) Te olvidaste del partido de fútbol.

FELIPE Juan Carlos, ¿verdad que mi papá te considera como de la familia?

JUAN CARLOS Sí.

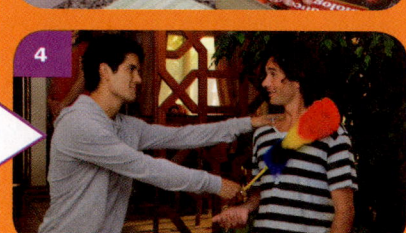

4

MARISSA Yo lleno el lavaplatos... después de vaciarlo.

DON DIEGO Juan Carlos, ¿por qué no terminas de pasar la aspiradora? Y Felipe, tú limpia el polvo. ¡Ya casi acaban!

TEACHING OPTIONS

Video Tips General suggestions for using video clips in the classroom can be found in the front matter of this Instructor's Annotated Edition.

Los quehaceres →👤← Play the last half of the **Los quehaceres** episode and have students summarize what they see and hear. Then, have the class predict what happens in the first half of the

episode, based on their observations. Write their predictions on the board. Then play the entire episode and through discussion, guide the class to a correct summary of the plot.

SRA. DÍAZ   **SR. DÍAZ**   **MARISSA**   **JUAN CARLOS**   **DON DIEGO**

7

(Los chicos preparan la cena y ponen la mesa.)

JUAN CARLOS ¿Dónde están los tenedores?

JIMENA Allá.

JUAN CARLOS ¿Y las servilletas?

MARISSA Aquí están.

8

FELIPE La sala está tan limpia. Le pasamos la aspiradora al sillón y a las cortinas. ¡Y también a las almohadas!

JIMENA Yucatán, ¡ya casi llegamos!

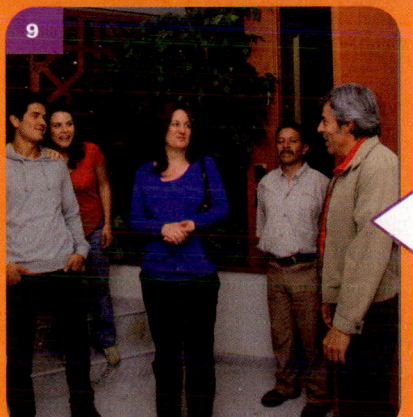

9

(Papá y mamá regresan a casa.)

SRA. DÍAZ ¡Qué bonita está la casa!

SR. DÍAZ Buen trabajo, muchachos. ¿Qué hay para cenar?

JIMENA Quesadillas. Vengan.

10

SRA. DÍAZ Don Diego, quédese a cenar con nosotros. Venga.

SR. DÍAZ Sí, don Diego. Pase.

DON DIEGO Gracias.

More activities

vhlcentral | VM pp. 23–24 | Online activities

Expresiones útiles

Making recommendations

Le(s) sugiero que arregle(n) este apartamento.
I suggest you tidy up this apartment.
Le(s) aconsejo que prepare(n) la cena para las ocho y media.
I recommend that you have dinner ready for eight thirty.

Organizing work

Recomiendo que se organicen en equipos para limpiar.
I recommend that you divide yourselves into teams to clean.
Yo lleno el lavaplatos... después de vaciarlo.
I'll fill the dishwasher... after I empty it.
¿Por qué no terminas de pasar la aspiradora?
Why don't you finish vacuuming?
¡Ya casi acaban!
You're almost finished!
Felipe, tú quita el polvo.
Felipe, you dust.

Making polite requests

Don Diego, quédese a cenar con nosotros.
Don Diego, stay and have dinner with us.
Venga.
Come on.
Don Diego, pase.
Don Diego, come in.

Additional vocabulary

el plumero *duster*

¿Qué pasó?

1

¿Cierto o falso? Indica si lo que dicen estas oraciones es **cierto** o **falso**. Corrige las oraciones falsas.

	Cierto	Falso
1. Felipe y Jimena tienen que preparar el desayuno.	○	⊘
Felipe y Jimena tienen que preparar la cena.		
2. Don Diego ayuda a los chicos organizando los quehaceres domésticos.	⊘	○
3. Jimena le dice a Juan Carlos dónde están los tenedores.	⊘	○
4. A Marissa no le molesta limpiar el baño.	○	⊘
Marissa odia limpiar el baño.		
5. Juan Carlos termina de lavar los platos.	○	⊘
Juan Carlos termina de pasar la aspiradora.		

2

Identificar Identifica quién dice las oraciones equivalentes.

1. Yo les ayudo, no me molesta hacer quehaceres domésticos. Marissa
2. No me gusta sacar la basura. Jimena
3. Es importante que termines de pasar la aspiradora, Juan Carlos. don Diego
4. Pasamos la aspiradora en toda la sala. Felipe
5. ¡Buen trabajo, chicos! ¿Qué vamos a cenar? Sr. Díaz

 JIMENA
 DON DIEGO
 FELIPE
 SR. DÍAZ
 MARISSA

3

Completar Los chicos y don Diego están haciendo los quehaceres. Adivina en qué cuarto está cada uno de ellos.

1. Jimena limpia el congelador. Jimena está en ____la cocina____.
2. Don Diego limpia el escritorio. Don Diego está en ____la oficina____.
3. Felipe pasa la aspiradora debajo de la mesa y las sillas. Felipe está en ____el comedor____.
4. Juan Carlos sacude el sillón. Juan Carlos está en ____la sala____.
5. Marissa hace la cama. Marissa está en ____el dormitorio____.

4

Mi casa Dibuja el plano de una casa o de un apartamento. Puede ser el plano de la casa o del apartamento donde vives o de donde te gustaría (*you would like*) vivir. Después, trabajen en parejas y describan lo que se hace en cuatro de las habitaciones. Para terminar, pídanse (*ask for*) ayuda para hacer dos quehaceres domésticos. Answers will vary.

Quiero mostrarte…	Al fondo hay...
Ésta es (la cocina).	Quiero que me ayudes a (sacar la basura).
Allí yo (preparo la comida).	Por favor, ayúdame con…

 NATIONAL communication STANDARDS

TEACHING OPTIONS

Small Groups Have the class label various parts of the classroom with the names of rooms one would typically find in a house. If possible, rearrange the classroom desks and chairs to represent the different rooms and their furniture. Then have students work in small groups to write a skit about a family that is cleaning up the house in preparation for a dinner party. Have groups perform their skits for the class. Be sure to give them time to rehearse.

Game Have students write a few sentences that one of the characters in this **Fotonovela** episode would say. They can look at the captions on pages 408–409 for ideas, but they should not copy sentences word for word. Then have students read their sentences to the class. The class will guess which character would say those sentences.

Ortografía
Mayúsculas y minúsculas

Tutorial

Here are some of the rules that govern the use of capital letters (**mayúsculas**) and lowercase letters (**minúsculas**) in Spanish.

Los estudiantes llegaron al aeropuerto a las dos.
Luego fueron al hotel.

In both Spanish and English, the first letter of every sentence is capitalized.

Rubén Blades   **Panamá**   **Colón**   **los Andes**

The first letter of all proper nouns (names of people, countries, cities, geographical features, etc.) is capitalized.

Cien años de soledad   **Don Quijote de la Mancha**
El País   **Muy Interesante**

The first letter of the first word in titles of books, films, and works of art is generally capitalized, as well as the first letter of any proper names. In newspaper and magazine titles, as well as other short titles, the initial letter of each word is often capitalized.

---

la señora Ramos   **don Francisco**
el presidente   **Sra. Vives**

Titles associated with people are *not* capitalized unless they appear as the first word in a sentence. Note, however, that the first letter of an abbreviated title is capitalized.

Último   **Álex**   **MENÚ**   **PERDÓN**

Accent marks should be retained on capital letters. In practice, however, this rule is often ignored.

---

lunes   **viernes**   **marzo**   **primavera**

The first letter of days, months, and seasons is <u>not</u> capitalized.

---

español   **estadounidense**   **japonés**   **panameños**

The first letter of nationalities and languages is <u>not</u> capitalized.

Profesor Herrera, ¿es cierto que somos venenosas°?

Sí, Pepito. ¿Por qué lloras?

Práctica Corrige las mayúsculas y minúsculas incorrectas.

1. soy lourdes romero. Soy Colombiana.
   Soy Lourdes Romero. Soy colombiana.
2. éste Es mi Hermano álex.
   Éste es mi hermano Álex.
3. somos De panamá. *Somos de Panamá.*
4. ¿es ud. La sra. benavides?
   ¿Es Ud. la Sra. Benavides?
5. ud. Llegó el Lunes, ¿no?
   Ud. llegó el lunes, ¿no?

Palabras desordenadas Lee el diálogo de las serpientes. Ordena las letras para saber de qué palabras se trata. Después escribe las letras indicadas para descubrir por qué llora Pepito.

m n a a P á   ⭕☐☐☐☐☐
s t e m r a   ⭕☐☐☐☐☐
i g s l é n   ☐☐☐⭕☐☐
y a U r u g u   ☐☐☐⭕☐☐☐
r o ñ e s a   ☐☐☐☐☐⭕

¡ ☐orque ☐e acabo de morder° la ☐en ☐u ☐!

Respuestas: Panamá, martes, inglés, Uruguay, señora.
¡Porque me acabo de morder la lengua!

More activities
vhlcentral   LM p. 68

venenosas *venomous* morder *to bite*

Section Goal

In **Ortografía**, students will learn about the rules for capitalization in Spanish.

Instructional Resources
Supersite: Audio (Lab MP3 Files); Resources (Scripts, Answer Keys)
WebSAM
Lab Manual

Teaching Tips
- Explain that in a few Spanish city and country names the definite article is considered part of the name, and is thus capitalized. Ex: **La Habana, La Coruña, La Haya, El Salvador**.
- As in English, Spanish titles of books, films, and works of art are italicized in print; however, capitalization rules differ. In Spanish, only the first word and any proper noun gets an initial capital. Spanish treatment of the names of newspapers and magazines is the same as in English; they are italicized in print and each word is capitalized. Tell students that *El País* is a Spanish newspaper and *Muy Interesante* is a popular science magazine.
- After going through the explanation, write example titles, names, sentences, etc., all in lowercase on the board. Then, ask pairs to decide which letters should be capitalized.
- Point out that **Ortografía** replaces **Pronunciación** in the Student Edition for **Lecciones 10–18**, but not in the Lab Manual. The box references the **Pronunciación** sections found in all lessons of the Lab Manual.

TEACHING OPTIONS

Extra Practice Have students scan the reading on the next page. Have them circle all the capital letters and explain why each is capitalized. Then point out the words **árabe, españoles,** and **islámica** and have volunteers explain why they are not capitalized.
Extra Practice Add an auditory aspect to this **Ortografía** section. Read this sentence aloud for students to write down: **El doctor Guzmán, el amigo panameño de la señorita Rivera, llegó a Quito el lunes, doce de mayo.** To allow students time to write, read the sentence twice slowly and once at full speed. Tell the class to abbreviate all titles. Have volunteers write their version of the sentence on the board, and as a class correct any mistakes they may have made.

EN DETALLE

El patio central

En las tardes cálidas° de Oaxaca, México, Córdoba, España, o Popayán, Colombia, es un placer sentarse en **el patio central** de una casa y tomar un refresco disfrutando de° una buena conversación. Esta característica arquitectónica°, de influencia árabe, fue traída° a las Américas por los españoles. En la época° colonial, se construyeron casas, palacios, monasterios, hospitales y escuelas con patio central. Éste es un espacio privado e íntimo en donde se disfruta del sol y de la brisa, y, al mismo tiempo, se puede estar aislado° de la calle.

El centro del patio es un espacio abierto. Alrededor de° él, separado por columnas, hay un pasillo cubierto°. Así, en el patio hay zonas de sol y de sombra°. El patio es una parte importante de la vivienda familiar y su decoración se cuida° mucho. En el centro del patio muchas veces hay una fuente°, plantas e incluso árboles°. El agua es un elemento muy importante en la cultura islámica porque simboliza la purificación del cuerpo y del alma°. Por esta razón y también para disminuir° la temperatura, el agua es muy importante en estas construcciones. Así, mientras el agua y la vegetación ayudan a mantener la temperatura fresca, el patio proporciona° luz y ventilación a todas las habitaciones.

La distribución

Las casas con patio central eran usualmente las viviendas de familias adineradas°. Son casas de dos o tres pisos. Los cuartos de la planta baja son las áreas comunes: cocina, comedor, sala, etc., y tienen puertas al patio. En los pisos superiores están las habitaciones privadas de la familia.

cálidas *hot* **disfrutando de** *enjoying* **arquitectónica** *architectural* **traída** *brought* **época** *era* **brisa** *breeze* **aislado** *isolated* **Alrededor de** *Surrounding* **cubierto** *covered* **sombra** *shade* **se cuida** *is looked after* **fuente** *fountain* **árboles** *trees* **alma** *soul* **disminuir** *lower* **proporciona** *provides* **adineradas** *wealthy*

ACTIVIDADES

1 ¿Cierto o falso? Indica si lo que dicen las oraciones es **cierto** o **falso**. Corrige las falsas.

1. Los patios centrales de Latinoamérica tienen su origen en la tradición indígena. **Falso. Los patios centrales tienen su origen en la arquitectura árabe.**
2. Los españoles llevaron a América el concepto de patio. **Cierto.**
3. En la época colonial las casas eran las únicas construcciones con patio central. **Falso. Se construyeron casas, palacios, monasterios, hospitales y escuelas.**
4. El patio es una parte importante en estas construcciones, y es por eso que se le presta atención a su decoración. **Cierto.**
5. El patio central es un lugar de descanso que da luz y ventilación a las habitaciones. **Cierto.**
6. Las fuentes en los patios tienen importancia por razones culturales y porque bajan la temperatura. **Cierto.**
7. En la cultura española el agua simboliza la salud y el bienestar del cuerpo y del alma. **Falso. En la cultura islámica el agua simboliza la salud y el bienestar del cuerpo y del alma.**
8. Las casas con patio central eran para personas adineradas. **Cierto.**
9. Los cuartos de la planta baja son privados. **Falso. Los cuartos de la planta baja son las áreas comunes.**
10. Los dormitorios están en los pisos superiores. **Cierto.**

ASÍ SE DICE

La vivienda

el ático, el desván	el altillo
la cobija (Col., Méx.), la frazada (Arg., Cuba, Ven.)	la manta
el escaparate (Cuba, Ven.), el ropero (Méx.)	el armario
el fregadero	*kitchen sink*
el frigidaire (Perú); el frigorífico (Esp.), la nevera	el refrigerador
el lavavajillas (Arg., Esp., Méx.)	el lavaplatos

EL MUNDO HISPANO

Los muebles

- **Mecedora°** La mecedora es un mueble típico de Latinoamérica, especialmente de la zona del Caribe. A las personas les gusta relajarse mientras se mecen° en el patio.

- **Mesa camilla** Era un mueble popular en España hasta hace algunos años. Es una mesa con un bastidor° en la parte inferior° para poner un brasero°. En invierno, las personas se sentaban alrededor de la mesa camilla para conversar, jugar a las cartas o tomar café.

- **Hamaca** Se cree que los taínos hicieron las primeras hamacas con fibras vegetales. Su uso es muy popular en toda Latinoamérica para dormir y descansar.

Mecedora *Rocking chair* **se mecen** *they rock themselves* **bastidor** *frame* **inferior** *bottom* **brasero** *container for hot coals*

PERFIL

Las islas flotantes del lago Titicaca

Bolivia y Perú comparten el **lago Titicaca**, donde viven **los uros**, uno de los pueblos indígenas más antiguos de América. Hace muchos años, los uros fueron a vivir al lago escapando de **los incas.** Hoy en día, siguen viviendo allí en **islas flotantes** que ellos mismos hacen con unos juncos° llamados **totora**. Primero, tejen° grandes plataformas. Luego, con el mismo material, construyen sus casas sobre las plataformas. La totora es resistente, pero con el tiempo el agua la pudre°. Los habitantes de las islas

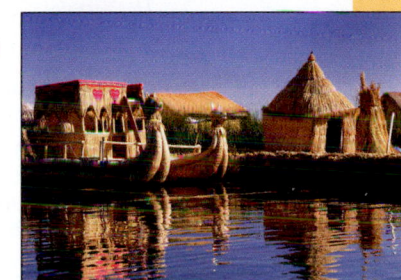

necesitan renovar continuamente las plataformas y las casas. Sus muebles y sus barcos también están hechos° de juncos. Los uros viven de la pesca y del turismo; en las islas hay unas tiendas donde venden artesanías° hechas con totora.

PERÚ

Lago Titicaca →

BOLIVIA

juncos *reeds* **tejen** *they weave* **la pudre** *rots it* **hechos** *made* **artesanías** *handcrafts*

CON RITMO HISPANO

Erika Ender (1974–)
Lugar de nacimiento: Ciudad de Panamá, Panamá

Erica Ender es hija de padre estadounidense y madre brasileña. Compuso con Luis Fonsi el éxito internacional "Despacito".

Go to **vhlcentral.com** to find out more about **Erika Ender** and her music.

ACTIVIDADES

2 **Comprensión** Responde a las preguntas.

1. Tu amigo mexicano te dice: "La **cobija** azul está en el **ropero**". ¿Qué quiere decir? La manta azul está en en el armario

2. ¿Quiénes hicieron las primeras hamacas? ¿Qué material usaron? los taínos; fibras vegetales

3. ¿Qué grupo indígena vive en el lago Titicaca? Los uros viven en el lago Titicaca.

4. ¿Qué pueden comprar los turistas en las islas flotantes del lago Titicaca? Pueden comprar artesanías hechas con totora.

3 **Viviendas tradicionales** Escribe cuatro oraciones sobre una vivienda tradicional que conoces. Explica en qué lugar se encuentra, de qué materiales está hecha y cómo es. Answers will vary.

More activities

vhlcentral Online activities

TEACHING OPTIONS

Small Groups ←👤→ In small groups, have students research the floating islands of Lake Titicaca and make a poster or collage. Tell them to include information about the **uro** way of life, tourism, and any other significant details about the islands. Have groups present their posters to the class.

Extra Practice ←👤→ Ask students to write a short description of their favorite room in their family's house or apartment. Encourage them to give details about the furniture and decorations. Have them share their paragraphs with a partner, who will ask clarifying questions about the room.

Section Goal

In **Estructura 12.1**, students will learn the relative pronouns **que, quien(es), lo que** and their uses.

Instructional Resources

Supersite: Audio (Lab MP3 Files); Resources (Grammar Presentation Slides, Activity Pack, Scripts, Answer Keys); Testing Program (Quizzes)
WebSAM
Workbook
Lab Manual

Teaching Tips

• Have students look at the **Fotonovela** on pages 408–409. Ask questions about the episode. Restate each student response as a sentence using a relative pronoun. Write the sentences on the board and underline the relative pronouns. Ex:

1. ¿Quiénes van a arreglar la casa? (Felipe y Jimena) Sí, ellos son las personas que van a limpiar la casa. 2. ¿Qué cuarto tiene lavaplatos? (la cocina) Sí, la cocina es el cuarto que tiene lavaplatos.

• Compare and contrast the use of **que** and **quien** by writing some examples on the board. Ex: **Es la chica que vino con Carlos a mi fiesta. Es la chica a quien conocí en mi fiesta.** Have students deduce the rule.

12.1 Relative pronouns Tutorial

ANTE TODO In both English and Spanish, relative pronouns are used to combine two sentences or clauses that share a common element, such as a noun or pronoun. Study this diagram.

Mis padres me regalaron **la aspiradora**.
My parents gave me the vacuum cleaner.

La aspiradora funciona muy bien.
The vacuum cleaner works really well.

La aspiradora **que** mis padres me regalaron funciona muy bien.
The vacuum cleaner that my parents gave me works really well.

Lourdes es muy inteligente.
Lourdes is very intelligent.

Lourdes estudia español.
Lourdes is studying Spanish.

Lourdes, **quien** estudia español, es muy inteligente.
Lourdes, who studies Spanish, is very intelligent.

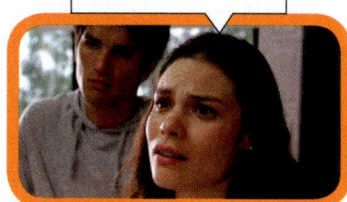

Eso fue todo lo que dijimos.

Mi papá se lleva bien con Juan Carlos, quien es como mi hermano.

▶ Spanish has three frequently used relative pronouns. **¡Atención!** Even though interrogative words (**qué**, **quién**, etc.) always carry an accent, relative pronouns never carry a written accent.

que	*that; which; who*
quien(es)	*who; whom; that*
lo que	*that which; what*

▶ **Que** is the most frequently used relative pronoun. It can refer to things or to people. Unlike its English counterpart, *that*, **que** is never omitted.

¿Dónde está la cafetera **que** compré?
Where is the coffee maker (that) I bought?

El hombre **que** limpia es Pedro.
The man who is cleaning is Pedro.

▶ The relative pronoun **quien** refers only to people, and is often used after a preposition or the personal **a**. **Quien** has only two forms: **quien** (singular) and **quienes** (plural).

¿Son las chicas **de quienes** me hablaste la semana pasada?
Are they the girls (that) you told me about last week?

Eva, **a quien** conocí anoche, es mi nueva vecina.
Eva, whom I met last night, is my new neighbor.

TEACHING OPTIONS

Extra Practice Write these sentences on the board, and have students supply the correct relative pronoun.
1. Hay una escalera _____ sube al primer piso. (que)
2. Elena es la muchacha a _____ le presté la aspiradora. (quien)
3. ¿Dónde pusiste la ropa _____ acabas de quitarte? (que)
4. ¿Cuáles son los estudiantes a _____ les alquilas tu casa? (quienes)

5. La cómoda _____ compramos la semana pasada está en el dormitorio de mi hermana. (que)
Heritage Speakers Using complex sentences with relative pronouns, have heritage speakers describe a location in their families' communities where people can get together. Ex: town square, park, café, etc.

▶ **Quien(es)** is occasionally used instead of **que** in clauses set off by commas.

Lola, **quien** es cubana, es médica.
Lola, who is Cuban, is a doctor.

Su tía, **que** es alemana, ya llegó.
His aunt, who is German, already arrived.

▶ Unlike **que** and **quien(es)**, **lo que** doesn't refer to a specific noun. It refers to an idea, a situation, or a past event and means *what, that which*, or *the thing that*.

Lo que me molesta es el calor.
What bothers me is the heat.

Lo que quiero es una casa.
What I want is a house.

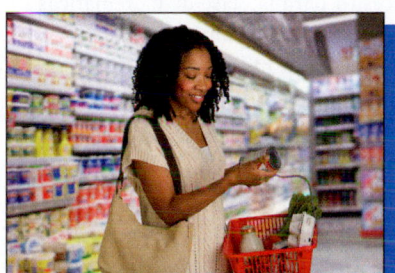

Este supermercado tiene todo **lo que** necesito.

A Samuel no le gustó **lo que** le dijo Violeta.

¡INTÉNTALO! Completa estas oraciones con pronombres relativos.

1. Voy a utilizar los platos ___que___ me regaló mi abuela.
2. Ana comparte un apartamento con la chica a ___quien___ conocimos en la fiesta de Jorge.
3. Puedes estudiar en el dormitorio ___que___ está a la derecha de la cocina.
4. Esta oficina tiene todo ___lo que___ necesitamos.
5. Los señores ___que___ viven en esa casa acaban de llegar de Centroamérica.
6. Los niños a ___quienes___ viste en nuestro jardín son mis sobrinos.
7. La piscina ___que___ ves desde la ventana es la piscina de mis vecinos.
8. Úrsula, ___que/quien___ ayudó a mamá a limpiar el refrigerador, es muy simpática.
9. ___Lo que___ te dijo Pablo no es cierto.
10. El hombre de ___quien___ hablo es mi padre.
11. Tengo que sacudir los muebles ___que___ están en el altillo una vez al mes.
12. No entiendo por qué no lavaste los vasos ___que___ te dije.
13. La mujer a ___quien___ saludaste vive en las afueras.
14. ¿Sabes ___lo que___ necesita este dormitorio? ¡Unas cortinas!
15. No me gusta vivir con personas a ___quienes___ no conozco.
16. No quiero volver a hacer ___lo que___ hice ayer.

Práctica

1 Expansion Ask students to write alternate endings for each of the sentences. Then ask several volunteers to read their sentences aloud.

2 Expansion Ask questions about the content of the activity. Ex: **1. ¿Quiénes quieren comprar una casa? (Jaime y Tina) 2. ¿Qué casa quieren comprar? (una casa que está en las afueras de la ciudad) 3. ¿De quién era la casa? (de una artista famosa) 4. ¿Cómo venden la casa? (con todos los muebles que tenía) 5. ¿Qué tipo de alfombra tiene la sala? (una alfombra que la artista trajo de Kuwait)**

3 Teaching Tip Ask a volunteer to read the **modelo** aloud. Ask another volunteer to explain what word is replaced by the relative pronoun **que**.

3 Expansion
←🔁→ Have pairs write three more sentences that contain relative pronouns and refer to the newlyweds' new home.

1
Combinar Combina elementos de las dos columnas para formar oraciones lógicas.

A	B
1. ¿Cómo se llama el programa __g__ ?	a. con quien bailaba es mi vecina
2. Rubén Blades, __c__ .	b. que te compró Cecilia
3. No traje __e__ .	c. quien es de Panamá, es un cantante muy bueno
4. ¿Te gusta la manta __b__ ?	d. que arregló mi lavadora
5. Ése es el hombre __d__ .	e. lo que necesito para la clase de matemáticas
6. La mujer __a__ .	f. que comiste en el restaurante
	g. que escuchaste en la radio anoche

NOTA CULTURAL

Rubén Blades es un cantante, compositor y actor panameño muy famoso. Este versátil abogado fue también Ministro de Turismo en su país (2004–2009) y fue nombrado Embajador contra el racismo por las Naciones Unidas en el 2000.

2
Completar Completa la historia con los pronombres relativos **que, quien, quienes** o **lo que**.

1. Jaime y Tina son los chicos a ___quienes___ conocí la semana pasada.
2. Quieren comprar una casa ___que___ está en las afueras de la ciudad.
3. Es una casa ___que___ era de una artista famosa.
4. La artista, a ___quien___ yo conocía, murió el año pasado y no tenía hijos.
5. Ahora se vende la casa con todos los muebles ___que___ ella tenía.
6. La casa tiene muchos estantes, ___lo que___ a Tina le encanta.
7. La sala tiene una alfombra ___que___ ella trajo de Kuwait.

3
Oraciones Combina las declaraciones de dos recién casados para formar una sola oración con los pronombres relativos **que, quien(es)** y **lo que**.

modelo
Vamos a usar los vasos nuevos mañana. Los pusimos en el comedor.
Mañana vamos a usar los vasos nuevos que pusimos en el comedor.

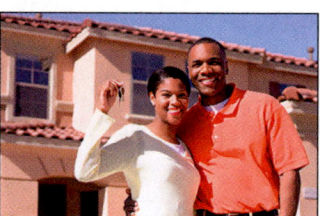

1. Esos platos no nos costaron mucho. Están encima del horno.
   Esos platos que están encima del horno no nos costaron mucho.
2. Tenemos una cómoda nueva. Es bueno porque no hay espacio en el armario.
   Tenemos una cómoda nueva, lo que es bueno porque no hay espacio en el armario.
3. Tenemos una cafetera nueva. Mi prima nos la regaló.
   Tenemos una cafetera nueva que mi prima nos regaló.
4. Esas copas me las regaló mi amiga Amalia. Ella viene a visitarme mañana.
   Esas copas me las regaló mi amiga Amalia, quien/que viene a visitarme mañana.
5. La lavadora está casi nueva. Nos la regalaron mis suegros.
   La lavadora que nos regalaron mis suegros está casi nueva.
6. La vecina nos dio una manta de lana. Ella la compró en México.
   La vecina nos dio una manta de lana que compró en México.

TEACHING OPTIONS

Extra Practice Have students use relative pronouns to complete this series. **1.** _____ tenemos que hacer es buscar otro apartamento. (Lo que) **2.** El apartamento _____ tenemos sólo tiene dos dormitorios. (que) **3.** Ayer hablamos con un compañero _____ alquila una casa cerca de aquí. (que) **4.** Buscamos algo similar a _____ él tiene: tres dormitorios, dos cuartos de baño, una cocina,

una sala, un comedor… ¡y un alquiler bajo! (lo que) **5.** Nos dio el nombre de unos agentes a _____ podemos contactar. (quienes)
Pairs ←🔁→ Ask pairs of students to write a description of a new household gadget, using relative pronouns. Their descriptions should include the purpose of the gadget and how it is used.

Comunicación

4 **Entrevista** En parejas, túrnense para hacerse estas preguntas. *Answers will vary.*

1. ¿Qué es lo que más te gusta de vivir en las afueras o en la ciudad?
2. ¿Quién es la persona que hace los quehaceres domésticos en tu casa?
3. ¿Hay vecinos que te caen bien? ¿Quiénes?
4. ¿De qué vecino es el coche que más te gusta?
5. ¿Cuál es el barrio de tu ciudad que más te gusta y por qué?
6. ¿Cuál es el lugar de la casa donde te sientes más cómodo/a? ¿Por qué?
7. ¿Qué es lo que más te gusta de tu barrio?
8. ¿Qué es lo que menos te gusta de tu barrio?

5 **Adivinanza** En grupos, túrnense para describir distintas partes de una vivienda usando pronombres relativos. Los demás compañeros tienen que hacer preguntas hasta que adivinen (*they guess*) la palabra. *Answers will vary.*

> **modelo**
>
> **Estudiante 1:** Es lo que tenemos en el dormitorio.
> **Estudiante 2:** ¿Es el mueble que usamos para dormir?
> **Estudiante 1:** No. Es lo que usamos para guardar la ropa.
> **Estudiante 3:** Lo sé. Es la cómoda.

6 **Describir** En parejas, imaginen que el semestre pasado participaron en un programa de intercambio estudiantil (*student exchange program*) en una ciudad de Latinoamérica. Túrnense para describir cómo era el lugar y contar cómo fue la experiencia. Usa los pronombres **que**, **quien(es)** y **lo que**. *Answers will vary.*

> **modelo**
>
> Yo estuve en Bogotá, Colombia, y compartí un apartamento
> con dos chicas colombianas, quienes eran muy amables.
> El apartamento, que estaba en el décimo piso, tenía vistas
> increíbles de la ciudad…

Síntesis

7 **Definir** En parejas, definan las palabras. Usen los pronombres relativos **que**, **quien(es)** y **lo que**. Luego compartan sus definiciones con la clase. *Answers will vary.*

alquiler	flan	patio	tenedor
amigos	guantes	postre	termómetro
aspiradora	jabón	sillón	vaso
enfermera	manta	sótano	vecino

> **modelo**
>
> lavadora   Es lo que se usa para lavar la ropa.
> pastel   Es un postre que comes en tu cumpleaños.

AYUDA

Remember that **de**, followed by the name of a material, means *made of*.

Es de algodón.
It's made of cotton.

•••

Es un tipo de means *It's a kind/sort of…*

Es un tipo de flor.
It's a kind of flower.

---

4 Teaching Tip Have students take notes on the answers provided by their partners to use in expansion activities.

4 Expansion
- Have pairs team up to form groups of four. Each student will report on his or her partner, using the information obtained in the interview.
- Have pairs of students write four additional questions. Ask pairs to exchange their questions with another pair, and then interview each other using the new set of questions. Students should ask their partner follow-up questions as needed.

5 Expansion Have groups choose their three best **adivinanzas** and present them to the class.

6 Teaching Tip Ask students to imagine details about the location, the rooms, the furniture, the appliances, and the decor of their fictional Latin American residence for their description.

7 Expansion Have pairs choose one of the items listed in the activity and develop a magazine ad. Their ad should include at least three sentences with relative pronouns.

TEACHING OPTIONS

Small Groups Have students bring in pictures of houses (exterior only). Have them work in groups of three to write a description of what they imagine the interiors to be like. Remind them to use relative pronouns in their descriptions.

Extra Practice Add an auditory aspect to this grammar practice. Prepare short descriptions of easily recognizable residences, such as the White House, Hearst Castle, Alcatraz prison, Graceland, and Buckingham Palace. Write their names on the board in random order. Then read your descriptions aloud and have students match each one to the appropriate name. Ex: **Es un castillo que está situado en una pequeña montaña cerca del océano Pacífico de California. Lo construyó un norteamericano considerado bastante excéntrico. Es un sitio que visitan muchos turistas cada año. (Hearst Castle)**

Section Goals

In **Estructura 12.2**, students will learn:

- formal (**usted/ustedes**) commands
- use of object pronouns with formal commands

Instructional Resources

Supersite: Audio (Lab MP3 Files); Resources (Grammar Presentation Slides, Activity Pack, Scripts, Answer Keys); Testing Program (Quizzes)
WebSAM
Workbook
Lab Manual

Teaching Tips

- Model the use of formal commands with simple examples using TPR and gestures. Ex: **Levántense. Siéntense.** Then point to individual students and give commands in an exaggerated formal tone. Ex: **Señor(ita) _____, levántese.** Give other commands using **salga/salgan, vuelva/vuelvan,** and **venga/vengan.**
- Write these sentences on the board, contrasting their meaning with the examples in the text: **Habla con ellos. Come frutas y verduras. Lavan los platos ahora mismo. Beben menos té y café.**
- Have volunteers give the command forms for other verbs, such as **alquilar, correr,** or **imprimir.**

12.2 Formal (usted/ustedes) commands

 Tutorial

ANTE TODO As you learned in **Lección 11**, the command forms are used to give orders or advice. Formal commands are used with people you address as **usted** or **ustedes**. Observe these examples, then study the chart.

Hable con ellos, don Francisco.
Talk with them, Don Francisco.

Laven los platos ahora mismo.
Wash the dishes right now.

Coma frutas y verduras.
Eat fruits and vegetables.

Beban menos té y café.
Drink less tea and coffee.

AYUDA

By learning formal commands, it will be easier for you to learn the subjunctive forms that are presented in **Estructura 12.3**, p. 422.

Formal commands (Ud. and Uds.)

Infinitive	Present tense yo form	Ud. command	Uds. command
limpiar	limpi**o**	limpi**e**	limpi**en**
barrer	barr**o**	barr**a**	barr**an**
sacudir	sacud**o**	sacud**a**	sacud**an**
decir (e:i)	dig**o**	dig**a**	dig**an**
pensar (e:ie)	piens**o**	piens**e**	piens**en**
volver (o:ue)	vuelv**o**	vuelv**a**	vuelv**an**
servir (e:i)	sirv**o**	sirv**a**	sirv**an**

▶ The **usted** and **ustedes** commands, like the negative **tú** commands, are formed by dropping the final **-o** of the **yo** form of the present tense. For **-ar** verbs, add **-e** or **-en**. For **-er** and **-ir** verbs, add **-a** or **-an**.

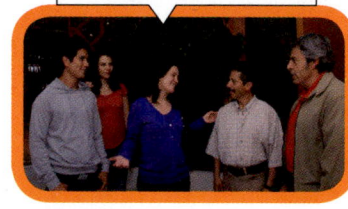

Don Diego, quédese a cenar con nosotros.

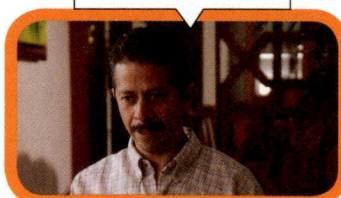

No se preocupen, yo los ayudo.

▶ Verbs with irregular **yo** forms maintain the same irregularity in their formal commands. These verbs include **conducir, conocer, decir, hacer, ofrecer, oír, poner, salir, tener, traducir, traer, venir,** and **ver.**

Oiga, don Manolo...
Listen, Don Manolo...

Ponga la mesa, por favor.
Set the table, please.

¡Salga inmediatamente!
Leave immediately!

Hagan la cama antes de salir.
Make the bed before leaving.

▶ Note also that verbs maintain their stem changes in **usted** and **ustedes** commands.

e:ie	o:ue	e:i
No **pierda** la llave.	**Vuelva** temprano, joven.	**Sirva** la sopa, por favor.
Cierren la puerta.	**Duerman** bien, chicos.	**Repitan** las frases.

TEACHING OPTIONS

Video ➡ Replay the **Fotonovela**, having students focus on formal commands. Ask them to write down each formal command that they hear. Then form groups of three and have students compare their lists.
Extra Practice Describe situations and have students call out **ustedes** commands that would be used. Ex: A mother sending her kids off to overnight camp. (**Cepíllense los**

dientes antes de dormir.**)
TPR Have students stand. Using the verbs presented in the discussion of formal commands, give commands at random (Ex: **Barra el suelo.**) and point to a student who should perform the appropriate gesture. Keep a brisk pace. Vary by pointing to more than one student. Ex: **Pongan la mesa.**

AYUDA

These spelling changes are necessary to ensure that the words are pronounced correctly. See **Lección 8, Pronunciación,** p. 271, and **Lección 9, Pronunciación,** p. 307.

•••

It may help you to study the following series of syllables. Note that, within each series, the consonant sound doesn't change.

ca que qui co cu
za ce ci zo zu
ga gue gui go gu
ja ge gi jo ju

▶ Verbs ending in **-car**, **-gar**, and **-zar** have a spelling change in the command forms.

sa**car**	c → qu	sa**que**, sa**quen**
ju**gar**	g → gu	jue**gue**, jue**guen**
almor**zar**	z → c	almuer**ce**, almuer**cen**

▶ These verbs have irregular formal commands.

Infinitive	Ud. command	Uds. command
dar	**dé**	**den**
estar	**esté**	**estén**
ir	**vaya**	**vayan**
saber	**sepa**	**sepan**
ser	**sea**	**sean**

▶ To make a formal command negative, simply place **no** before the verb.

No ponga las maletas en la cama.   **No ensucien** los sillones.
Don't put the suitcases on the bed.   *Don't dirty the armchairs.*

▶ In affirmative commands, reflexive, indirect, and direct object pronouns are always attached to the end of the verb.

Siénten**se**, por favor.   Acuésten**se** ahora.
Sígue**me**, Laura.   Pónganl**as** en el suelo, por favor.

▶ **¡Atención!** When a pronoun is attached to an affirmative command that has two or more syllables, an accent mark is added to maintain the original stress.

limpie → **límpielo**   **lean** → **léanlo**
diga → **dígamelo**   **sacudan** → **sacúdanlos**

▶ In negative commands, these pronouns always precede the verb.

No **se** preocupe.   No **los** ensucien.
No **me lo** dé.   No **nos las** traigan.

▶ **Usted** and **ustedes** can be used with the command forms to strike a more formal tone. In such instances, they follow the command form.

Muéstrele usted la foto a su amigo.   **Tomen ustedes** esta mesa.
Show the photo to your friend.   *Take this table.*

More activities

vhlcentral

LM
p. 70

WB
pp. 139–140

Online activities

 ¡INTÉNTALO!   Indica los mandatos (*commands*) afirmativos y negativos correspondientes.

1. escucharlo (Ud.) ___Escúchelo___ . ___No lo escuche___ .
2. salir (Ud.) ___Salga___ . ___No salga___ .
3. decírmelo (Uds.) ___Díganmelo___ . ___No me lo digan___ .
4. servírnoslo (Uds.) ___Sírvannoslo___ . ___No nos lo sirvan___ .
5. barrerla (Ud.) ___Bárrala___ . ___No la barra___ .
6. hacerlo (Ud.) ___Hágalo___ . ___No lo haga___ .

Teaching Tips
• Ask volunteers to write formal command forms of other verbs with spelling changes on the board. Ex: **empezar (empiece); comenzar (comience); buscar (busque); pagar (pague); llegar (llegue).**
• Test comprehension as you proceed by asking volunteers to supply the correct form of other infinitives you name.
• Point out that the written accent mark on **dé** serves to distinguish the verb form from the preposition **de**.
• Point out that the affirmative answer for item 4 of **¡Inténtalo!** is spelled with a double n: **Sírvannoslo.**

TEACHING OPTIONS

Extra Practice Write a list of situations on the board using singular and plural forms. Ex: **La cocina está sucia. Mis amigos y yo tenemos hambre. Tenemos miedo.** Then have students write responses in the form of commands. Ex: **Límpiela. Hagan la cena. No tengan miedo.**

Heritage Speakers Ask heritage speakers to make a list of ten commands they would hear in their homes that may not be heard elsewhere. Ex: **Sírvale el café al niño. Acuéstese después de almorzar.**

Práctica

1 **Completar** Indica el mandato formal de cada verbo para ayudar a la señora González, que quiere mudarse.

1. ___Lea___ los anuncios del periódico y ___guárdelos___ . (leer, guardarlos)
2. ___Vaya___ personalmente y ___vea___ las casas usted misma. (ir, ver)
3. Decida qué casa quiere y ___llame___ al agente. ___Pídale___ un contrato de alquiler. (llamar, pedirle)
4. ___Contrate___ un camión (*truck*) para ese día y ___pregúnteles___ la hora exacta de llegada. (contratar, preguntarles)
5. El día de la mudanza (*On moving day*) ___esté___ tranquila. ___Vuelva___ a revisar su lista para completar todo lo que tiene que hacer. (estar, volver)
6. Primero, ___dígales___ a todos en casa que usted va a estar ocupada. No ___les diga___ que usted va a hacerlo todo. (decirles, decirles)
7. ___Saque___ tiempo para hacer las maletas tranquilamente. No ___les haga___ las maletas a los niños más grandes. (sacar, hacerles)
8. No ___se preocupe___ . ___Sepa___ que todo va a salir bien. (preocuparse, saber)

2 **¿Qué dicen?** Mira los dibujos y escribe un mandato lógico para cada uno.

Answers will vary. Suggested answers:

1. El ascensor no funciona. Usen la escalera, por favor.

2. Apague las luces, por favor.

3. Ponga los libros en el estante, por favor.

4. Arreglen el cuarto, por favor. Está desordenado.

5. Cierre las cortinas, por favor.

6. La cocina está sucia. Bárranla, por favor.

---

1 Expansion
- Ask volunteers to give additional organizational tips for **señora González**.
- To challenge students, have them work in pairs to formulate a list of instructions for the movers. Ex: **Tengan cuidado con los platos. No pongan los cuadros en una caja.** Then, with the class, compare and contrast the commands the pairs have formulated.

2 Teaching Tip
To simplify, before starting the activity, have volunteers describe the situation in each of the drawings and identify who is speaking to whom.

2 Expansion Continue the exercise by using magazine pictures. Ex: **Tengan paciencia con los niños.**

Extra Practice
To add an auditory aspect to this grammar practice, prepare several different series of formal commands that would be expressed in particular circumstances. After you read each set of commands aloud, students should guess the situation. Ex: **Por favor, siéntense todos. Abróchense los cinturones de seguridad y apaguen todos los aparatos electrónicos. Ahora coloquen el respaldo de su asiento en posición vertical y aseguren la mesa de servicio. (un avión)**

TEACHING OPTIONS

Small Groups Form small groups of students who have similar living arrangements, such as dormitories, at home, or in an apartment. Then have the groups write suggestions for a newly arrived resident, using formal commands. Ex: **No ponga usted la tele después de las diez. Saque la basura temprano. No estacione el carro en la calle. No invite a sus amigos a la casa después de las once.**

Extra Practice Add an auditory aspect to this grammar practice. Prepare a series of sentences that contain formal commands. Read each twice, pausing after the second time for students to write. Then ask volunteers to write their sentences on the board and correct them as a class. Ex: **1. Saquen la basura a la calle. 2. Almuerce usted conmigo hoy. 3. Niños, jueguen en el patio. 4. Váyase inmediatamente. 5. Esté usted aquí a las diez.**

Comunicación

3 **Solucionar** Trabajen en parejas. Un(a) estudiante presenta los problemas de la columna A y el/la otro/a los de la columna B. Usen mandatos formales y túrnense para ofrecer soluciones. *Answers will vary.*

modelo

Estudiante 1: Vilma se torció un tobillo jugando al tenis. Es la tercera vez.
Estudiante 2: *No juegue más al tenis. / Vaya a ver a un especialista.*

A

1. Se me perdió el libro de español con todas mis notas.
2. A Vicente se le cayó la botella de vino para la cena.
3. ¿Cómo? ¿Se le olvidó traer el traje de baño a la playa?
4. Se nos quedaron los pasaportes en la casa. El avión sale en una hora.

B

1. Mis hijas no se levantan temprano. Siempre llegan tarde a la escuela.
2. A mi abuela le robaron (*stole*) las maletas. Era su primer día de vacaciones.
3. Nuestra casa es demasiado pequeña para nuestra familia.
4. Me preocupo constantemente por Roberto. Trabaja demasiado.

4 **Conversaciones** En parejas, escojan dos situaciones y preparen conversaciones para presentar a la clase. Usen mandatos formales. *Answers will vary.*

modelo

Lupita: Señor Ramírez, siento mucho llegar tan tarde. Mi niño se enfermó. ¿Qué debo hacer?
Sr. Ramírez: *No se preocupe. Siéntese y descanse un poco.*

SITUACIÓN 1 Profesor Rosado, no vine la semana pasada porque el equipo jugaba en Boquete. ¿Qué debo hacer para ponerme al día (*catch up*)?
SITUACIÓN 2 Los invitados de la boda llegan a las cuatro de la tarde, las mesas están sin poner y el champán sin servir. Son las tres de la tarde y los camareros apenas están llegando. ¿Qué deben hacer los camareros?
SITUACIÓN 3 Mi novio es un poco aburrido. No le gustan ni el cine, ni los deportes, ni salir a comer. Tampoco habla mucho. ¿Qué puedo hacer?
▶ **SITUACIÓN 4** Tengo que preparar una presentación para mañana sobre el Canal de Panamá. ¿Por dónde comienzo?

Síntesis

5 **Presentar** En grupos, preparen un anuncio de televisión para presentar a la clase. El anuncio debe tratar de un detergente, un electrodoméstico o una agencia inmobiliaria (*real estate agency*). Usen mandatos, los pronombres relativos y el **se** impersonal. *Answers will vary.*

modelo

Compre el lavaplatos Destellos. Tiene todo lo que usted desea. Es el lavaplatos que mejor funciona. Venga a verlo ahora mismo... No pierda ni un minuto más. Se aceptan tarjetas de crédito.

Section Goals

In **Estructura 12.3**, students will learn:

- the present subjunctive of regular verbs
- the present subjunctive of stem-changing verbs
- irregular verbs in the present subjunctive

Instructional Resources

Supersite: Audio (Lab MP3 Files); Resources (Grammar Presentation Slides, Activity Pack, Scripts, Answer Keys); Testing Program (Quizzes)
WebSAM
Workbook
Lab Manual

Teaching Tips

- On the board, make two columns labeled **Indicativo** and **Subjuntivo,** and write sentences like these under each column: Column 1: **Mi esposo lava los platos. Mi esposo barre el suelo. Mi esposo cocina.** Column 2: **Es importante que mi esposo lave los platos. Es urgente que mi esposo barra el suelo. Es bueno que mi esposo cocine.** Underline **mi esposo lave,** guiding students to notice the difference between the indicative and subjunctive forms. Do the same for the other sentences.
- Check for understanding by asking volunteers to give subjunctive forms of other regular verbs from this lesson such as **planchar, barrer,** and **sacudir.**
- Emphasize that the formation of the subjunctive is very similar to formal commands and negative **tú** commands.

12.3 The present subjunctive Tutorial

ANTE TODO With the exception of commands, all the verb forms you have been using have been in the indicative mood. The indicative is used to state facts and to express actions or states that the speaker considers to be real and definite. In contrast, the subjunctive mood expresses the speaker's attitudes toward events, as well as actions or states the speaker views as uncertain or hypothetical.

> Por favor, quiten los platos de la mesa.

> Les aconsejo que preparen la cena.

▶ The present subjunctive is formed very much like **usted**, **ustedes**, and *negative* **tú** commands. From the **yo** form of the present indicative, drop the **-o** ending, and replace it with the subjunctive endings.

INFINITIVE	PRESENT INDICATIVE	VERB STEM	PRESENT SUBJUNCTIVE
hablar comer escribir	hablo como escribo	habl- com- escrib-	hable coma escriba

▶ The present subjunctive endings are:

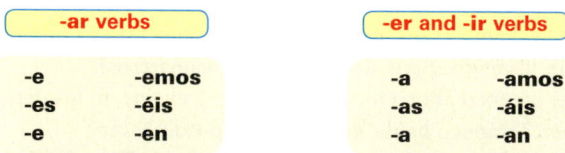

-ar verbs		-er and -ir verbs	
-e	-emos	-a	-amos
-es	-éis	-as	-áis
-e	-en	-a	-an

Present subjunctive of regular verbs

		hablar	comer	escribir
SINGULAR FORMS	yo	hable	coma	escriba
	tú	hables	comas	escribas
	Ud./él/ella	hable	coma	escriba
PLURAL FORMS	nosotros/as	hablemos	comamos	escribamos
	vosotros/as	habléis	comáis	escribáis
	Uds./ellos/ellas	hablen	coman	escriban

AYUDA

Note that, in the present subjunctive, **-ar** verbs use endings normally associated with present tense **-er** and **-ir** verbs. Likewise, **-er** and **-ir** verbs in the present subjunctive use endings normally associated with **-ar** verbs in the present tense. Note also that, in the present subjunctive, the **yo** form is the same as the **Ud./él/ella** form.

¡LENGUA VIVA!

You may think that English has no subjunctive, but it does! While once common, it now survives mostly in set expressions such as *If I were you...* and *Be that as it may...*

TEACHING OPTIONS

Large Group Have the class stand in a circle. Name an infinitive of a regular verb and subject pronoun (Ex: **alquilar/yo**), and toss a ball to a student. He or she must provide the correct subjunctive form (Ex: **alquile**) and toss the ball back. You may want to have students give an entire phrase (Ex: **que yo alquile**) so that they become accustomed to this structure.

Extra Practice Read aloud sentences that use the subjunctive, and have students repeat. Then call out a different subject for the subordinate clause, and have students say the new sentence, making all the necessary changes. Ex: **Es malo que ustedes trabajen mucho. Javier. (Es malo que Javier trabaje mucho.) Es necesario que lleguen temprano. Nosotras. (Es necesario que lleguemos temprano.)**

▶ Verbs with irregular **yo** forms show the same irregularity in all forms of the present subjunctive.

Infinitive	Present indicative	Verb stem	Present subjunctive
conducir	conduzco	conduzc-	conduzca
conocer	conozco	conozc-	conozca
decir	digo	dig-	diga
hacer	hago	hag-	haga
ofrecer	ofrezco	ofrezc-	ofrezca
oír	oigo	oig-	oiga
parecer	parezco	parezc-	parezca
poner	pongo	pong-	ponga
tener	tengo	teng-	tenga
traducir	traduzco	traduzc-	traduzca
traer	traigo	traig-	traiga
venir	vengo	veng-	venga
ver	veo	ve-	vea

▶ To maintain the **c, g,** and **z** sounds, verbs ending in **-car, -gar,** and **-zar** have a spelling change in all forms of the present subjunctive.

sacar:	saque, saques, saque, saquemos, saquéis, saquen
jugar:	juegue, juegues, juegue, juguemos, juguéis, jueguen
almorzar:	almuerce, almuerces, almuerce, almorcemos, almorcéis, almuercen

Present subjunctive of stem-changing verbs

AYUDA

Note that stem-changing verbs and verbs that have a spelling change have the same ending as regular verbs in the present subjunctive.

▶ **-Ar** and **-er** stem-changing verbs have the same stem changes in the subjunctive as they do in the present indicative.

pensar (e:ie):	piense, pienses, piense, pensemos, penséis, piensen
mostrar (o:ue):	muestre, muestres, muestre, mostremos, mostréis, muestren
entender (e:ie):	entienda, entiendas, entienda, entendamos, entendáis, entiendan
volver (o:ue):	vuelva, vuelvas, vuelva, volvamos, volváis, vuelvan

▶ **-Ir** stem-changing verbs have the same stem changes in the subjunctive as they do in the present indicative, but in addition, the **nosotros/as** and **vosotros/as** forms undergo a stem change. The unstressed **e** changes to **i**, while the unstressed **o** changes to **u**.

pedir (e:i):	pida, pidas, pida, pidamos, pidáis, pidan
sentir (e:ie):	sienta, sientas, sienta, sintamos, sintáis, sientan
dormir (o:ue):	duerma, duermas, duerma, durmamos, durmáis, duerman

Teaching Tips
• It may be helpful for students to be aware how English uses the subjunctive mood. Ex: *I wish she were here. I insist that he take notes. I suggest you be there tomorrow. If it were me, I would be happy.*
• Point out the stem changes that occur in the **nosotros/as** and **vosotros/as** forms of **–ir** stem-changing verbs.
• Write a few simple cloze sentences on the board and have students complete them in a logical manner. Ex: **Es bueno que mis padres ____. Es importante que yo ____. Es urgente que la profesora ____.** Then have students write three original sentences using the same impersonal expressions.

TEACHING OPTIONS

Pairs Have pairs of students role-play a conversation between a landlord and his/her new tenant. Give pairs sufficient time to plan and practice. When all pairs have completed the activity, ask a few of them to introduce their characters and perform the conversation for the class.

Extra Practice Ask students to compare family members' attitudes toward domestic life using the subjunctive. Ex: **Según los padres, es necesario que los hijos... Según los hijos, es malo que...** You may wish to repeat this activity several times, varying the age group of the children (**niños pequeños, adolescentes, adultos**). Make a three-column chart on the board and write students' sentences under the appropriate age group.

Irregular verbs in the present subjunctive

▶ These five verbs are irregular in the present subjunctive.

		dar	estar	ir	saber	ser
SINGULAR FORMS	yo	dé	esté	vaya	sepa	sea
	tú	des	estés	vayas	sepas	seas
	Ud./él/ella	dé	esté	vaya	sepa	sea
PLURAL FORMS	nosotros/as	demos	estemos	vayamos	sepamos	seamos
	vosotros/as	deis	estéis	vayáis	sepáis	seáis
	Uds./ellos/ellas	den	estén	vayan	sepan	sean

▶ **¡Atención!** The subjunctive form of **hay** (_there is, there are_) is also irregular: **haya.**

General uses of the subjunctive

▶ The subjunctive is mainly used to express: 1) will and influence, 2) emotion, 3) doubt, disbelief, and denial, and 4) indefiniteness and nonexistence.

▶ The subjunctive is most often used in sentences that consist of a main clause and a subordinate clause. The main clause contains a verb or expression that triggers the use of the subjunctive. The conjunction **que** connects the subordinate clause to the main clause.

Main clause   **Connector**   **Subordinate clause**

Es muy importante   que   **vayas** al hotel ahora mismo.

▶ These impersonal expressions are always followed by clauses in the subjunctive:

Es bueno que… _It's good that…_	**Es mejor que…** _It's better that…_	**Es malo que…** _It's bad that…_
Es importante que… _It's important that…_	**Es necesario que…** _It's necessary that…_	**Es urgente que…** _It's urgent that…_

More activities

vhlcentral

LM
p. 71

WB
pp. 141–142

Online activities

🔊 **¡INTÉNTALO!**   Indica el presente de subjuntivo de estos verbos.

1. (alquilar, beber, vivir)   que yo <u>alquile, beba, viva</u>
2. (estudiar, aprender, asistir)   que tú <u>estudies, aprendas, asistas</u>
3. (encontrar, poder, tener)   que él <u>encuentre, pueda, tenga</u>
4. (hacer, pedir, dormir)   que nosotras <u>hagamos, pidamos, durmamos</u>
5. (dar, hablar, escribir)   que ellos <u>den, hablen, escriban</u>
6. (ser, ir, saber)   que yo <u>sea, vaya, sepa</u>
7. (pagar, empezar, buscar)   que ustedes <u>paguen, empiecen, busquen</u>
8. (estar, dar, oír)   que tú <u>estés, des, oigas</u>

Práctica y Comunicación

1

Completar Completa las oraciones con el presente de subjuntivo de los verbos. Luego empareja las oraciones del primer grupo con las del segundo grupo.

A

▶ 1. Es importante que ____visites____ las casas colgadas de Cuenca. (tú, visitar) __c__
2. Es mejor que ____cenemos____ en casa. (nosotros, cenar) __b__
3. Señora, es urgente que le ____saque____ el diente. Tiene una infección. (yo, sacar) __e__
4. Es malo que Ana les ____dé____ tantos dulces a los niños. (dar) __a__
5. Es necesario que ____lleguen____ a la una de la tarde. (ustedes, llegar) __f__
6. Es importante que __nos acostemos__ temprano. (nosotros, acostarse) __d__

B

a. Es importante que ____coman____ más verduras. (ellos, comer)
b. No, es mejor que ____salgamos____ a comer. (nosotros, salir)
c. Y yo creo que es bueno que ____vaya____ a Madrid después. (yo, ir)
d. En mi opinión, no es necesario que ____durmamos____ tanto. (nosotros, dormir)
e. ¿Ah, sí? ¿Es necesario que me ____tome____ un antibiótico también? (yo, tomar)
f. Para llegar a tiempo, es necesario que __almorcemos__ temprano. (nosotros, almorzar)

2

Minidiálogos En parejas, completen los minidiálogos con expresiones impersonales de una manera lógica. Answers will vary.

modelo

Miguelito: Mamá, no quiero arreglar mi cuarto.
Sra. Casas: *Es necesario que lo arregles. Y es importante que sacudas los muebles también.*

1. **MIGUELITO** Mamá, no quiero estudiar. Quiero salir a jugar con mis amigos.
   SRA. CASAS _____

2. **MIGUELITO** Mamá, es que no me gustan las verduras. Prefiero comer pasteles.
   SRA. CASAS _____

3. **MIGUELITO** ¿Tengo que poner la mesa, mamá?
   SRA. CASAS _____

4. **MIGUELITO** No me siento bien, mamá. Me duele todo el cuerpo y tengo fiebre.
   SRA. CASAS _____

3

Entrevista Trabajen en parejas. Entrevístense usando estas preguntas. Expliquen sus respuestas.
Answers will vary.
1. ¿Es importante que las personas sepan una segunda lengua? ¿Por qué?
2. ¿Es urgente que los norteamericanos aprendan otras lenguas?
3. Si un(a) norteamericano/a quiere aprender francés, ¿es mejor que lo aprenda en Francia?
4. ¿Es necesario que una persona sepa decir "te amo" en la lengua nativa de su pareja?
5. ¿Es importante que un cantante de ópera entienda italiano?
6. ¿Es bueno que los turistas extranjeros digan unas frases en la lengua del país que visitan?

---

1 Expansion
After students have paired the sentences from each group, have them continue a couple of the short conversations with three more sentences using the subjunctive. Ex: **No es posible que encontremos un restaurante con mesas disponibles a las siete. Es mejor que salgamos ahora mismo para no tener ese problema. Sin embargo, es importante que no manejemos muy rápido; no quiero causar un accidente.**

2 Teaching Tip To simplify, before assigning the activity, have students brainstorm impersonal expressions that a mother would say to her young son.

2 Expansion
• Ask volunteers to share their mi_____ rest of t_____ them to _____
• Ask que_____ Migueli_____
Ex: **Para la señora Casas, ¿es necesario que Miguelito coma pasteles? (No. Es necesario que Miguelito coma las verduras.) ¿Qué quiere Miguelito? (Quiere salir a jugar con sus amigos.)** Have a volunteer explain why the second response does not take the subjunctive. (There isn't a change of subject and **que** is absent.)

3 Expansion
Ask students to report on their partner's answers using complete sentences and explanations.
Ex: **¿Qué opina _____ sobre los cantantes de ópera? ¿Cree que es importante que entiendan italiano?** Ask follow-up questions as necessary.

12.4 Subjunctive with verbs of will and influence Tutorial

ANTE TODO   You will now learn how to use the subjunctive with verbs and expressions of will and influence.

▶ Verbs of will and influence are often used when someone wants to affect the actions or behavior of other people.

Enrique **quiere** que salgamos a cenar.
Enrique wants us to go out to dinner.

Paola **prefiere** que cenemos en casa.
Paola prefers that we have dinner at home.

▶ Here is a list of widely used verbs of will and influence.

Verbs of will and influence

aconsejar	to advise	**pedir** (e:i)	to ask (for)
desear	to wish; to desire	**preferir** (e:ie)	to prefer
importar	to be important; to matter	**prohibir**	to prohibit
		querer (e:ie)	to want
insistir (en)	to insist (on)	**recomendar** (e:ie)	to recommend
mandar	to order	**rogar** (o:ue)	to beg
necesitar	to need	**sugerir** (e:ie)	to suggest

▶ Some impersonal expressions, such as **es necesario que, es importante que, es mejor que,** and **es urgente que,** are considered expressions of will or influence.

▶ When the main clause contains an expression of will or influence, the subjunctive is required in the subordinate clause, provided that the two clauses have different subjects.

Mi mamá **prefiere**   que   yo **saque** la basura.

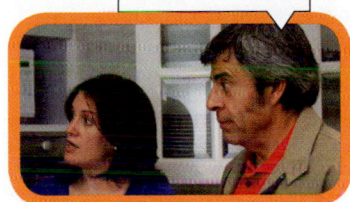

Les sugiero que arreglen este apartamento.

Recomiendo que se organicen en equipos.

▶ Indirect object pronouns are often used with the verbs **aconsejar, importar, mandar, pedir, prohibir, recomendar, rogar,** and **sugerir.**

Te aconsejo que estudies.
I advise you to study.

Le sugiero que vaya a casa.
I suggest that he go home.

Les recomiendo que barran el suelo.
I recommend that you sweep the floor.

Le ruego que no venga.
I'm begging you not to come.

▶ Note that all the forms of **prohibir** in the present tense carry a written accent, except for the **nosotros/as** form: **prohíbo, prohíbes, prohíbe, prohibimos, prohibís, prohíben.**

Ella les **prohíbe** que miren la televisión.
She prohibits them from watching TV.

Nos **prohíben** que nademos en la piscina.
They prohibit us from swimming in the swimming pool.

▶ The infinitive is used with words or expressions of will and influence if there is no change of subject in the sentence.

No quiero **sacudir** los muebles.
I don't want to dust the furniture.

Paco prefiere **descansar.**
Paco prefers to rest.

Es importante **sacar** la basura.
It's important to take out the trash.

No es necesario **quitar** la mesa.
It's not necessary to clear the table.

More activities

vhlcentral

LM
p. 72

WB
pp. 143–144

Online activities

¡INTÉNTALO!   Completa cada oración con la forma correcta del verbo.

1. Te sugiero que _____vayas_____ (ir) con ella al supermercado.
2. Mis papás quieren que yo _____limpie_____ (limpiar) mi cuarto.
3. No queremos que tú _____hagas_____ (hacer) nada especial para nosotros.
4. Él necesita que yo le _____preste_____ (prestar) dinero.
5. Nos piden que la _____ayudemos_____ (ayudar) a preparar la comida.
6. Quieren que tú _____saques_____ (sacar) la basura todos los días.
7. Es importante que ustedes _____limpien_____ (limpiar) los estantes.
8. Quiero _____descansar_____ (descansar) esta noche.
9. Su tía les manda que _____pongan_____ (poner) la mesa.
10. Te aconsejo que no _____salgas_____ (salir) con él.
11. Prefiero _____ir_____ (ir) al cine.
12. Mi tío insiste en que mi prima _____haga_____ (hacer) la cama.
13. Es necesario _____estudiar_____ (estudiar).
14. Recomiendo que ustedes _____pasen_____ (pasar) la aspiradora.

Práctica

1 Teaching Tip Before beginning the activity, ask a volunteer to read the first line of the dialogue aloud. Guide students to see that the subject of the verb in the blank is **yo**, which is implied by **me** in the main clause.

1 Completar Completa el diálogo.

cocina	haga	quiere	sea
comas	ponga	saber	ser
diga	prohíbe	sé	vaya

IRENE   Tengo problemas con Vilma. Sé que debo hablar con ella. ¿Qué me recomiendas que le (1)___diga___?

JULIA   Pues, necesito (2)___saber___ más antes de darte consejos.

IRENE   Bueno, para empezar me (3)___prohíbe___ que traiga dulces a la casa.

JULIA   Pero chica, tiene razón. Es mejor que tú no (4)___comas___ cosas dulces.

IRENE   Sí, ya lo sé. Pero quiero que (5)___sea___ más flexible. Además, insiste en que yo (6)___haga___ todo en la casa.

JULIA   Yo (7)___sé___ que Vilma (8)___cocina___ y hace los quehaceres todos los días.

IRENE   Sí, pero siempre que hay fiesta me pide que (9)___ponga___ los cubiertos (*silverware*) y las copas en la mesa y que (10)___vaya___ al sótano por las servilletas y los platos. ¡Es lo que más odio: ir al sótano!

JULIA   Mujer, ¡Vilma sólo (11)___quiere___ que ayudes en la casa!

1 Expansion
↤🚶↦ Have pairs write a summary of the dialogue in the third person. Ask one or two volunteers to read their summaries to the class.

2 Aconsejar En parejas, den consejos lógicos usando verbos como **aconsejar, recomendar** y **prohibir.** Sus consejos deben ser diferentes de lo que la persona quiere hacer. Answers will vary.

> **modelo**
>
> **Isabel:**   Quiero conseguir un comedor con los muebles más caros del mundo.
>
> **Consejo:** *Te aconsejamos que consigas unos muebles menos caros.*

1. **DAVID**   Pienso poner el cuadro del lago de Maracaibo en la cocina.
2. **SARA**   Voy en bicicleta a comprar unas copas de cristal.
3. **SR. ALARCÓN**   Insisto en comenzar a arreglar el jardín en marzo.
4. **SRA. VILLA**   Quiero ver las tazas y los platos de la tienda El Ama de Casa Feliz.
5. **DOLORES**   Voy a poner servilletas de tela (*cloth*) para los cuarenta invitados.
6. **SR. PARDO**   Pienso poner todos mis muebles nuevos en el altillo.
7. **SRA. GONZÁLEZ**   Hay una fiesta en casa esta noche, pero no quiero limpiarla.
8. **CARLITOS**   Hoy no tengo ganas de hacer las camas ni de quitar la mesa.

2 Teaching Tip Ask two volunteers to read the **modelo.** Then ask other volunteers to offer additional suggestions for **Isabel.**

2 Expansion Have students create two suggestions for each person. In the second they should use one of the impersonal expressions listed on page 424.

NOTA CULTURAL

En el **lago de Maracaibo,** en Venezuela, hay casas suspendidas sobre el agua que se llaman **palafitos.** Este tipo de construcciones les recordó a los conquistadores la ciudad de Venecia, Italia, de donde viene el nombre "Venezuela", que significa "pequeña Venecia".

3 Preguntas En parejas, túrnense para contestar las preguntas. Usen el subjuntivo. Answers will vary.

1. ¿Te dan consejos tus amigos/as? ¿Qué te aconsejan? ¿Aceptas sus consejos? ¿Por qué?
2. ¿Qué te sugieren tus profesores que hagas antes de terminar los cursos que tomas?
3. ¿Insisten tus amigos/as en que salgas mucho con ellos?
4. ¿Qué quieres que te regalen tu familia y tus amigos/as en tu cumpleaños?
5. ¿Qué le recomiendas tú a un(a) amigo/a que no quiere salir los sábados con su novio/a?
6. ¿Qué les aconsejas a los nuevos estudiantes de tu universidad?

3 Expansion
🚶↔🚶 Have a conversation with the class about the information they learned in their interviews. Ask: **¿A quiénes siempre les dan consejos sus amigos? ¿Quiénes siempre les dan consejos a los amigos suyos? ¿Qué tipo de consejos ofrecen?**

TEACHING OPTIONS

Small Groups 🚶↔🚶 Have small groups prepare skits in which a group of roommates is discussing how to divide the household chores equitably. Give groups time to prepare and practice their skits before presenting them to the class.

Pairs ↤🚶↦ Give pairs of students five minutes to write a conversation in which they logically use as many of the verbs of will and influence with the subjunctive as they can. After the time is up, ask pairs to count the number of subjunctive constructions they used in their conversations. Have the top three or four perform their conversations for the class.

Comunicación

4 **Inventar** En parejas, preparen una lista de seis personas famosas. Un(a) estudiante da el nombre de una persona famosa y el/la otro/a le da un consejo. *Answers will vary.*

> **modelo**
>
> **Estudiante 1:** Judge Judy.
> **Estudiante 2:** Le recomiendo que sea más simpática con la gente.
> **Estudiante 2:** Chris Pine.
> **Estudiante 1:** Le aconsejo que haga más películas.

5 **Hablar** En parejas, imaginen que Gerardo es su hermano y necesita ayuda para arreglar su casa y resolver sus problemas románticos y económicos. Usen expresiones impersonales y verbos como **aconsejar**, **sugerir** y **recomendar**. *Answers will vary.*

> **modelo**
>
> Es mejor que arregles el apartamento más a menudo.
> Te aconsejo que no dejes para mañana lo que puedes hacer hoy.

Síntesis

6 **La doctora Salvamórez** Hernán tiene problemas con su novia y le escribe a la doctora Salvamórez, columnista del periódico *Panamá y su gente*. Ella responde a las cartas de personas con problemas románticos. En parejas, usen el subjuntivo para escribir los consejos de la doctora. *Answers will vary.*

> Estimada doctora Salvamórez:
>
> Mi novia nunca quiere que yo salga de casa. No le molesta que vengan mis amigos a visitarme. Pero insiste en que nosotros sólo miremos los programas de televisión que ella quiere. Necesita saber dónde estoy en cada momento, y yo necesito que ella me dé un poco de independencia. ¿Qué hago?
>
> Hernán

Sidebar (right column)

4 Teaching Tip Ask volunteers to read the **modelo** aloud and provide other suggestions for Judge Judy and Chris Pine.

4 Expansion Ask each pair to pick its favorite response and share it with the class, who will vote for the most clever, shocking, or humorous suggestion.

5 Teaching Tips
• Use the **Lección 12 Estructura** digital images to assist with the presentation of this activity.
• ↤👥↦ Ask volunteers to describe the drawing, naming everything they see and all the chores that need to be done.

5 Expansion
👤↔👤 Have students change partners and take turns playing the roles of **Gerardo** and his sibling giving him advice. Ex: **Te sugiero que pongas la pizza en la basura....**

6 Expansion
• 👤↔👤 Have pairs compare their responses in groups of four. Ask groups to choose which among all of the suggestions are the most likely to work for **Hernán**, and have them share these with the class.
• ↤👤↦ Have pairs choose a famous couple in history or fiction. Ex: Elizabeth Bennet and Mr. Darcy or Napoleon and Josephine. Then have them write a letter from one of the couples to **doctora Salvamórez**. Finally, have them exchange their letters with another pair and write the corresponding responses from the doctor.

TEACHING OPTIONS

Heritage Speakers 👤↔👤 Have heritage speakers write a list of five suggestions for other class members participating in an exchange program in their cultural communities. Their suggestions should focus on participating in the daily life of their host family's home. Ask students to share their suggestions with the class. Facilitate conversation by having students respond to the suggestions or ask additional questions.

Small Groups 👤↔👤 Divide the class into small groups. Write the names of famous historical figures on slips of paper and place them in small paper bags; give each group a bag. Have students take turns drawing names and giving three pieces of "advice" about what the person should do. The other students will try to guess who it is. They are allowed to ask additional questions, if necessary, to figure out the person's identity.

Section Goal

In **Recapitulación**, students will review the grammar concepts from this lesson.

Instructional Resource
Supersite

Teaching Tip You may want to assign this **Recapitulación** activity on the Supersite because it has diagnostics. There is an online-only review activity for each grammar point. The Supersite also has a **Repaso de vocabulario** activity with diagnostics.

1 **Expansion** Give students additional verbs to conjugate in the subjunctive. Ex: **comer, dar, estar, saber, traer**.

2 **Expansion**
• Have volunteers take turns reading aloud portions of the brochure.
• ↤▲↦ To challenge students, ask them to work in pairs to write four pieces of advice for a real estate agent, using impersonal expressions. Ex: **Es importante que sea honesto....** Have a few pairs read their sentences for the class.

Extra Practice

▲↔▲ On note cards or sticky notes, write names of well-known characters from literature, film, or television. Making sure that students do not see the name assigned to them, stick a note on the back of each student's shirt. Have students circulate around the room, giving each other hints about the identity of their characters, using the subjunctive. Tell students to be sure to use only the present tense in the main clause. Ex: **Tu madre dice que es importante que te cases con el conde París. / Tu novio te pide que te cases con él en secreto. / Deseas que toda tu familia crea que estás muerta. (Julieta Capuleto)**

Recapitulación

RESUMEN GRAMATICAL

Completa estas actividades para repasar los conceptos de gramática que aprendiste en esta lección.

1 **Completar** Completa el cuadro con la forma correspondiente del presente de subjuntivo. **24 pts.**

yo/él/ella	tú	nosotros/as	Uds./ellos/ellas
limpie	limpies	limpiemos	limpien
venga	**vengas**	vengamos	vengan
quiera	quieras	**queramos**	quieran
ofrezca	ofrezcas	ofrezcamos	**ofrezcan**

2 **El apartamento ideal** Completa este folleto (*brochure*) informativo con la forma correcta del presente de subjuntivo. **16 pts.**

> ### ¿Eres joven y buscas tu primera vivienda? Te ofrezco estos consejos:
>
> ■ Te sugiero que primero (tú) (1) __escribas__ (escribir) una lista de las cosas que quieres en un apartamento.
>
> ■ Quiero que después (2) __pienses__ (pensar) muy bien cuáles son tus prioridades. Es necesario que cada persona (3) __tenga__ (tener) sus prioridades claras, porque el hogar (*home*) perfecto no existe.
>
> ■ Antes de decidir en qué área quieren vivir, les aconsejo a ti y a tu futuro/a compañero/a de apartamento que (4) __salgan__ (salir) a ver la ciudad y que (5) __conozcan__ (conocer) los distintos barrios y las afueras.
>
> ■ Pidan que el agente les (6) __muestre__ (mostrar) todas las partes de cada casa.
>
> ■ Finalmente, como consumidores, es importante que nosotros (7) __sepamos__ (saber) bien nuestros derechos (*rights*); por eso, deben insistir en que todos los puntos del contrato (8) __estén__ (estar) muy claros antes de firmarlo (*signing it*).
>
> ### ¡Buena suerte!

12.1 **Relative pronouns** *pp. 414–415*

Relative pronouns

que	*that; which; who*
quien(es)	*who; whom; that*
lo que	*that which; what*

12.2 **Formal commands** *pp. 418–419*

Formal commands (Ud. and Uds.)

Infinitive	Present tense yo form	Ud(s). command
limpiar	limpi**o**	limpi**e(n)**
barrer	barr**o**	barr**a(n)**
sacudir	sacud**o**	sacud**a(n)**

► Verbs with stem changes or irregular **yo** forms maintain the same irregularity in the formal commands:

hacer: yo ha**go** → **Ha**gan la cama.

Irregular formal commands

dar	dé (Ud.); den (Uds.)
estar	esté(n)
ir	vaya(n)
saber	sepa(n)
ser	sea(n)

12.3 **The present subjunctive** *pp. 422–424*

Present subjunctive of regular verbs

hablar	comer	escribir
habl**e**	com**a**	escrib**a**
habl**es**	com**as**	escrib**as**
habl**e**	com**a**	escrib**a**
habl**emos**	com**amos**	escrib**amos**
habl**éis**	com**áis**	escrib**áis**
habl**en**	com**an**	escrib**an**

TEACHING OPTIONS

TPR Add an auditory aspect to this grammar review. Have students imagine they are landlords with students as tenants. Prepare statements about the tenants, using impersonal expressions. As you read each statement, have students give a thumbs-up if they like what they hear or a thumbs-down if they do not. Ex: **Es importante que los estudiantes mantengan el apartamento limpio.** (thumbs-up) **Es urgente que den fiestas todos los sábados.** (thumbs-down)

Extra Practice Write items like these on the board and have students give the subjunctive forms: **1. barrer: yo/ella/ustedes (que yo barra, que ella barra, que ustedes barran) 2. mudarse: ellos/usted/tú (que ellos se muden, que usted se mude, que tú te mudes) 3. dormir: nosotros/tú/ella (que nosotros durmamos, que tú duermas, que ella duerma)**

3 **Relativos** Completa las oraciones con **lo que**, **que** o **quien(es)**. `16 pts.`

1. Me encanta la alfombra ___que___ está en el comedor.
2. Mi amiga Tere, con ___quien___ trabajo, me regaló ese cuadro.
3. Todas las cosas ___que___ tenemos vienen de la casa de mis abuelos.
4. Hija, no compres más cosas. ___Lo que___ debes hacer ahora es organizarlo todo.
5. La agencia de decoración de ___que___ le hablé se llama Casabella.
6. Esas flores las dejaron en la puerta mis nuevos vecinos, a ___quienes___ aún (*yet*) no conozco.
7. Leonor no compró nada, porque ___lo que___ le gustaba era muy caro.
8. Mi amigo Aldo, a ___quien___ visité ayer, es un cocinero excelente.

Irregular verbs in the present subjunctive

dar		dé, des, dé, demos, deis, den
estar	est- +	-é, -és, -é, -emos, -éis, -én
ir	vay- +	
saber	sep- +	-a, -as, -a, -amos, -áis, -an
ser	se- +	

12.4 **Subjunctive with verbs of will and influence**
pp. 426–427

▶ Verbs of will and influence: **aconsejar, desear, importar, insistir (en), mandar, necesitar, pedir (e:i), preferir (e:ie), prohibir, querer (e:ie), recomendar (e:ie), rogar (o:ue), sugerir (e:ie)**

4 **Preparando la casa** Completa las instrucciones con mandatos formales. Usa cada verbo una sola vez y agrega pronombres de objeto directo o indirecto si es necesario. `20 pts.`

arreglar	dejar	hacer	pedir	sacudir
barrer	ensuciar	limpiar	poner	tener

Primero, (1) ___hagan___ ustedes las maletas. Las cosas que no se llevan a Costa Rica, (2) ___pónganlas___ en el altillo. Ángela, (3) ___arregle/limpie___ las habitaciones y Martín, (4) ___limpie/arregle___ usted la cocina y el baño. Después, los dos (5) ___barran___ el suelo y (6) ___sacudan___ los muebles de toda la casa. Ángela, no (7) ___deje___ sus joyas (*jewelry*) en el apartamento. (8) ___Tengan___ cuidado ¡y no (9) ___ensucien___ nada antes de irse! Por último, (10) ___pídanle___ a alguien que recoja (*pick up*) su correo.

5 **Los quehaceres** A tu compañero/a de cuarto no le gusta ayudar con los quehaceres. Escribe al menos seis oraciones dándole consejos para hacer más divertidos los quehaceres. `24 pts.`

Answers will vary.

> **modelo**
> Te sugiero que pongas música mientras lavas los platos...

6 **El circo** Completa esta famosa frase que tiene su origen en el circo (*circus*). `¡4 puntos EXTRA!`

"¡ ___Pasen___ (pasar) ustedes y ___vean___ (ver)! El espectáculo va a comenzar."

3 **Teaching Tip** Have students circle the noun or idea to which each relative pronoun refers.

3 **Expansion**
- Ask volunteers to give the corresponding questions for each item. Ex: **1. ¿Qué alfombra te encanta?**
- Have students work in pairs to create four additional sentences using relative pronouns.

4 **Teaching Tips**
- To simplify, have students begin by scanning the paragraph and identifying which blanks call for **usted** commands and which call for **ustedes** commands.
- Tell students that some answers will contain object pronouns (items 2 and 10).

5 **Teaching Tip**
👥↔👥 Before beginning this activity, have pairs discuss their own habits regarding chores.

5 **Expansion** Have students imagine they have two roommates, and ask them to rewrite their sentences using **ustedes** commands.

6 **Expansion** To challenge students, ask them to write two **ustedes** commands for people attending a circus and one **usted** command for the master of ceremonies.

TEACHING OPTIONS

Extra Practice Call out formal commands. Ex: **Sacudan los muebles.** Have students respond by naming the infinitive and subject. Ex: **sacudir, ustedes.** Reverse the drill by calling out verb phrases and either **usted** or **ustedes.** Have students give the command form.
Large Groups Review present subjunctive and vocabulary from previous lessons. Divide the class into two teams and have

them line up. Name a person or group of people. Ex: **estudiantes de computación, Taylor Swift, un niño en su primer día de la escuela primaria.** Then point to the first member of team A, who has three seconds to create a piece of advice. Ex: **Quiero que apaguen las computadoras.** Then the first member of team B has to give another sentence. Continue until the chain is broken, then name a new person.

Section Goals

In **Lectura**, students will:
- learn to locate the main parts of a sentence
- read a content-rich text with long sentences

Instructional Resource
Supersite

Estrategia Tell students that if they have trouble reading long sentences in Spanish, they should pause to identify the main verb of the sentence and its subject. They should then reread the entire sentence.

Lectura

 NATIONAL STANDARDS communication cultures

Antes de leer

Estrategia
Locating the main parts of a sentence

Did you know that a text written in Spanish is an average of 15% longer than the same text written in English? Since the Spanish language tends to use more words to express ideas, you will often encounter long sentences when reading in Spanish. Of course, the length of sentences varies with genre and with authors' individual styles. To help you understand long sentences, identify the main parts of the sentence before trying to read it in its entirety. First locate the main verb of the sentence, along with its subject, ignoring any words or phrases set off by commas. Then reread the sentence, adding details like direct and indirect objects, transitional words, and prepositional phrases.

Examinar el texto Students should see from the layout (cover page with title, photo, and phone number; interior pages with an introduction and several headings followed by short paragraphs) that this is a brochure. Revealing cognates are: **información** (cover) and **residencia oficial del Presidente de Panamá** (introduction).

Examinar el texto
Mira el formato de la lectura. ¿Qué tipo de documento es? ¿Qué cognados encuentras en la lectura? ¿Qué te dicen sobre el tema de la selección?

¿Probable o improbable? Ask volunteers to read aloud each item and give the answer. Have a volunteer rephrase the improbable statement so that it is probable.

¿Probable o improbable?
Mira brevemente el texto e indica si estas oraciones son probables o improbables.

1. Este folleto° es de interés turístico. probable
2. Describe un edificio moderno cubano. improbable
3. Incluye algunas explicaciones de arquitectura. probable
4. Espera atraer° a visitantes al lugar. probable

Oraciones largas
Mira el texto y busca algunas oraciones largas. Con un(a) compañero/a, identifiquen las partes principales de la oración y después examinen las descripciones adicionales. ¿Qué significan las oraciones?

More activities
 vhlcentral | Online activities

folleto *brochure* atraer *to attract* épocas *time periods*

Oraciones largas Ask pairs to create a couple of long sentences. Have them point out the main verb and subject.

Bienvenidos al Palacio de las Garzas

El palacio está abierto de martes a domingo. Para más información, llame al teléfono 507-226-7000. También puede solicitar° un folleto a la casilla° 3467, Ciudad de Panamá, Panamá.

Después de leer

Ordenar
Pon estos eventos en el orden cronológico adecuado.

<u> 3 </u> El palacio se convirtió en residencia presidencial.

<u> 2 </u> Durante diferentes épocas°, maestros, médicos y banqueros ejercieron su profesión en el palacio.

<u> 4 </u> El Dr. Belisario Porras ocupó el palacio por primera vez.

<u> 1 </u> Los españoles construyeron el palacio.

<u> 5 </u> Se renovó el palacio.

<u> 6 </u> Los turistas pueden visitar el palacio de martes a domingo.

TEACHING OPTIONS

Heritage Speakers ←👤→ Ask heritage speakers to give a brief presentation about a famous government building in their family's home country. Tell them to include recommendations about what rooms and objects are particularly noteworthy and should not be missed. If possible, they should illustrate their presentation with photographs or brochures.

Extra Practice ←👤→ Ask students to write ten statements using the subjunctive to describe their dream house (**la casa de mis sueños**). Ex: **Para mí es importante que haya una piscina de tamaño olímpico en la casa de mis sueños. Recomiendo que la cocina sea grande porque me gusta cocinar. Es necesario que tenga varios dormitorios porque siempre tengo huéspedes.** Have students share their sentences with a partner.

El Palacio de las Garzas° es la residencia oficial del Presidente de Panamá desde 1903. Fue construido en 1673 para ser la casa de un gobernador español. Con el paso de los años fue almacén, escuela, hospital, aduana, banco y por último, palacio presidencial.

En la actualidad el edificio tiene tres pisos, pero los planos originales muestran una construcción de un piso con un gran patio en el centro. La restauración del palacio comenzó en el año 1922 y los trabajos fueron realizados por el arquitecto Villanueva-Meyer y el pintor Roberto Lewis. El palacio, un monumento al estilo colonial, todavía conserva su elegancia y buen gusto, y es una de las principales atracciones turísticas del barrio Casco Viejo°.

Planta baja

EL PATIO DE LAS GARZAS

Una antigua puerta de hierro° recibe a los visitantes. El patio interior todavía conserva los elementos originales de la construcción: piso de mármol°, columnas cubiertas° de nácar° y una magnífica fuente° de agua en el centro. Aquí están las nueve garzas que le dan el nombre al palacio y que representan las nueve provincias de Panamá.

Primer piso

EL SALÓN AMARILLO

Aquí el turista puede visitar una galería de cuarenta y un retratos° de gobernadores y personajes ilustres de Panamá. La principal atracción de este salón es el sillón presidencial, que se usa especialmente cuando hay cambio de presidente. Otros atractivos de esta área son el comedor Los Tamarindos, que se destaca° por la elegancia de sus muebles y sus lámparas de cristal, y el Patio Andaluz, con sus coloridos mosaicos que representan la unión de la cultura indígena y la española.

EL SALÓN DR. BELISARIO PORRAS

Este elegante y majestuoso salón es uno de los lugares más importantes del Palacio de las Garzas. Lleva su nombre en honor al Dr. Belisario Porras, quien fue tres veces presidente de Panamá (1912–1916, 1918–1920 y 1920–1924).

Segundo piso

Es el área residencial del palacio y el visitante no tiene acceso a ella. Los armarios, las cómodas y los espejos de la alcoba fueron comprados en Italia y Francia por el presidente Porras, mientras que las alfombras, cortinas y frazadas° son originarias de España.

solicitar *request* **casilla** *post office box* **Garzas** *Herons* **Casco Viejo** *Old Quarter*
hierro *iron* **mármol** *marble* **cubiertas** *covered* **nácar** *mother-of-pearl*
fuente *fountain* **retratos** *portraits* **se destaca** *stands out* **frazadas** *blankets*

Preguntas

Contesta las preguntas.

1. ¿Qué sala es notable por sus muebles elegantes y sus lámparas de cristal? el comedor Los Tamarindos

2. ¿En qué parte del palacio se encuentra la residencia del presidente? en el segundo piso

3. ¿Dónde empiezan los turistas su visita al palacio? en el Patio de las Garzas

4. ¿En qué lugar se representa artísticamente la rica herencia cultural de Panamá? en el Patio Andaluz

5. ¿Qué salón honra la memoria de un gran panameño? el Salón Dr. Belisario Porras

6. ¿Qué partes del palacio te gustaría (*would you like*) visitar? ¿Por qué? Explica tu respuesta.
Answers will vary.

Conversación

En grupos de tres o cuatro, hablen sobre lo siguiente:
Answers will vary.

1. ¿Qué tiene en común el Palacio de las Garzas con otras residencias presidenciales u otras casas muy grandes?

2. ¿Te gustaría vivir en el Palacio de las Garzas? ¿Por qué?

3. Imagina que puedes diseñar tu palacio ideal. Describe los planos para cada piso del palacio.

Ordenar Quickly go over the correct order by asking a volunteer to read the sentence he or she believes should be first, another volunteer to read the sentence that should be second, and so forth.

Preguntas
- Go over the answers as a class.
- To add a visual aspect to this reading, have students work in pairs to create a detailed floor plan of the **Palacio de las Garzas**. Then have volunteers use **usted** commands to tell you how to draw the floor plan on the board. Ex: **Dibuje la planta baja. Ponga una fuente de agua en el centro.**

Conversación
After groups have finished their conversations, encourage the class to discuss the three questions. Ask additional questions, such as: **¿En qué se diferencia el Palacio de las Garzas con otras casas? ¿A quién no le gustaría vivir en el Palacio de las Garzas? ¿Por qué? ¿Quién está de acuerdo?**

Escritura

Estrategia

Using linking words

You can make your writing sound more sophisticated by using linking words to connect simple sentences or ideas and create more complex sentences. Consider these passages, which illustrate this effect:

Without linking words

En la actualidad el edificio tiene tres pisos. Los planos originales muestran una construcción de un piso con un gran patio en el centro. La restauración del palacio comenzó en el año 1922. Los trabajos fueron realizados por el arquitecto Villanueva-Meyer y el pintor Roberto Lewis.

With linking words

En la actualidad el edificio tiene tres pisos, pero los planos originales muestran una construcción de un piso con un gran patio en el centro. La restauración del palacio comenzó en el año 1922 y los trabajos fueron realizados por el arquitecto Villanueva-Meyer y el pintor Roberto Lewis.

Linking words

cuando	when
mientras	while
o	or
pero	but
porque	because
pues	since
que	that; who; which
quien(es)	who
sino	but (rather)
y	and

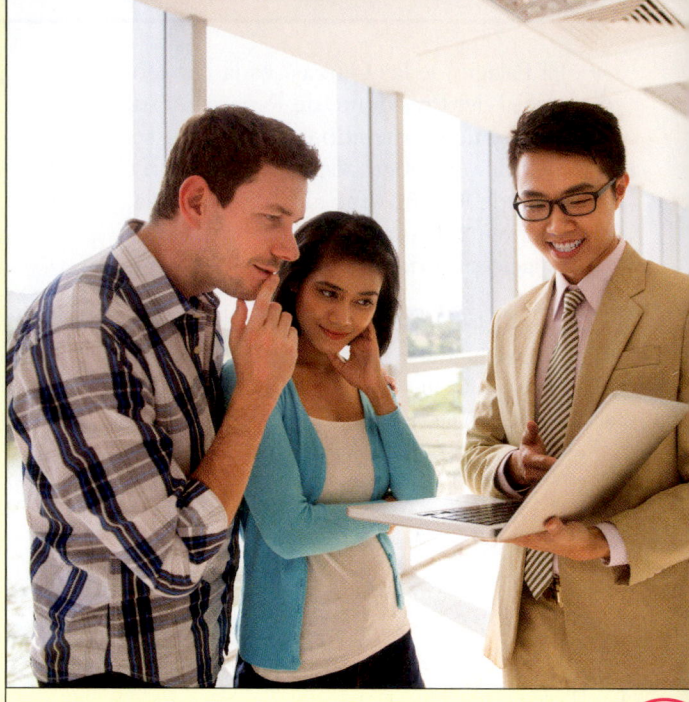

Tema

Escribir un contrato de arrendamiento°

Eres el/la administrador(a)° de un edificio de apartamentos. Prepara un contrato de arrendamiento para los nuevos inquilinos°. El contrato debe incluir estos detalles:

▶ la dirección° del apartamento y del/de la administrador(a)

▶ las fechas del contrato

▶ el precio del alquiler y el día que se debe pagar

▶ el precio del depósito

▶ información y reglas° acerca de:
  la basura
  el correo
  los animales domésticos
  el ruido°
  los servicios de electricidad y agua
  el uso de electrodomésticos

▶ otros aspectos importantes de la vida comunitaria

contrato de arrendamiento *lease* administrador(a) *manager* inquilinos *tenants* dirección *address* reglas *rules* ruido *noise*

Escuchar

Antes de escuchar

Estrategia

Using visual cues

Visual cues like illustrations and headings provide useful clues about what you will hear.

To practice this strategy, you will listen to a passage related to the following photo. Jot down the clues the photo gives you as you listen.

Preparación

Mira el dibujo. ¿Qué pistas te da para comprender lo que vas a escuchar? ¿Qué significa *bienes raíces*?

Ahora escucha

La vivienda

Mira los anuncios de esta página y escucha la conversación. Luego indica si cada descripción se refiere a la casa ideal de Adriana y Felipe, a la casa del anuncio o al apartamento del anuncio.

Oraciones	La casa ideal	La casa del anuncio	El apartamento del anuncio
Es barato.	___	___	✔
Tiene 4 dormitorios.	___	✔	___
Tiene una oficina.	✔	___	___
Tiene un balcón.	___	___	✔
Tiene una cocina moderna.	___	✔	___
Tiene un jardín muy grande.	___	✔	___
Tiene un patio.	✔	___	___

18G

Bienes raíces

Se vende.
4 dormitorios,
3 baños, cocina
moderna, jardín
con árboles frutales.
B/. 225.000

Se alquila.
2 dormitorios,
1 baño.
Balcón.
Urbanización
Las Brisas. B/. 525

Comprensión

Preguntas

1. ¿Cuál es la relación entre el señor Núñez, Adriana y Felipe? ¿Cómo lo sabes? El Sr. Núñez es el padre de Adriana y Felipe es su esposo.
2. ¿Qué diferencia de opinión hay entre Adriana y Felipe sobre dónde quieren vivir? Felipe prefiere vivir en la ciudad, pero Adriana quiere vivir en las afueras.
3. Usa la información de los dibujos y la conversación para entender lo que dice Adriana al final. ¿Qué significa "todo a su debido tiempo"? Answers will vary.

Conversación

En parejas, túrnense para hacer y contestar las preguntas. Answers will vary.

1. ¿Qué tienen en común el apartamento y la casa del anuncio con el lugar donde tú vives?
2. ¿Qué piensas de la recomendación del señor Núñez?
3. ¿Qué tipo de sugerencias te da tu familia sobre dónde vivir?
4. ¿Dónde prefieres vivir tú, en un apartamento o en una casa? Explica por qué.

NATIONAL communication STANDARDS

---

una oficina para mí y un patio para las plantas.
S: Como no tienen mucho dinero ahorrado, es mejor que alquilen un apartamento pequeño por un tiempo. Así pueden ahorrar su dinero para comprar la casa ideal. Miren este apartamento. Tiene un balcón precioso y está en un barrio muy seguro y

bonito. Y el alquiler es muy razonable.
F: Adriana, me parece que tu padre tiene razón. Con un alquiler tan barato, podemos comprar muebles y también ahorrar dinero cada mes.
A: ¡Ay!, quiero mi casa. Pero, bueno, ¡todo a su debido tiempo!

Section Goals

In **Escuchar**, students will:
- use visual cues to help them understand an oral passage
- answer questions based on the content of a recorded conversation

Instructional Resources
Supersite: Audio (Textbook MP3s); Resources (Scripts)

Estrategia

Script En mi niñez lo pasé muy bien. Vivíamos en una pequeña casa en la isla Colón con vistas al mar. Pasaba las horas buceando alrededor de los arrecifes de coral. A veces me iba a pasear por las plantaciones de bananos o a visitar el pueblo de los indios guaymí. Otros días iba con mi hermano al mar en una pequeña lancha para pescar. Era una vida feliz y tranquila. Ahora vivo en la Ciudad de Panamá. ¡Qué diferencia!

Ahora escucha

Script ADRIANA: Mira, papá, tienen una sección especial de bienes raíces en el periódico. Felipe, mira esta casa... tiene un jardín enorme.
FELIPE: ¡Qué linda! ¡Uy, qué cara! ¿Qué piensa usted? ¿Debemos buscar una casa o un apartamento?
SR. NÚÑEZ: Bueno, hijos, hay muchas cosas que deben considerar. Primero, ¿les gustaría vivir en las afueras o en el centro de la ciudad?
F: Pues, señor Núñez, yo prefiero vivir en la ciudad. Así tenemos el teatro, los parques, los centros comerciales... todo cerca de casa. Sé que Adriana quiere vivir en las afueras porque es más tranquilo.
S: De todos modos van a necesitar un mínimo de dos dormitorios, un baño, una sala grande... ¿Qué más?
A: Es importante que tengamos

(Script continues at far left in the bottom panels.)

En pantalla Video

La compañía francesa Conforama abrió sus puertas en España en el año 1992. Actualmente°, tiene 28 tiendas en total y planea abrir otras 22 a pesar de la crisis económica que afectó el mercado español entre los años 2008 y 2014. La cadena° ofrece una amplia gama° de muebles y electrodomésticos a precios asequibles°. El propósito° de este anuncio es promover° la presencia de Conforama en España y sugerir que en sus tiendas hay muebles y electrodomésticos para todos los gustos.

Vocabulario útil	
caber	*to fit*
colchón	*mattress*
duro	*hard*
madera	*wood*
me da igual	*it's all the same to me*

Preparación
¿Qué muebles tienes en tu casa? ¿Qué muebles te faltan o te gustaría comprar para decorar más tu casa? **Answers will vary.**

✇ ¿Qué buscan?
Indica lo que buscan estas personas en la tienda.

1. chico **d**
2. familia de cinco **a**
3. niña **b**
4. Juan y su esposa **e**
5. hombre **c**

a. un sofá
b. una cama
c. una cocina de madera
d. un televisor
e. un colchón

👥 De compras
En parejas, escriban un diálogo entre dos compañeros de cuarto o dos esposos que van a Conforama para comprar algo. Utilicen el subjuntivo. **Answers will vary.**

> **modelo**
>
> **Esposo:** *Es importante que compremos un sofá cómodo.*
> **Esposa:** *Quiero que el sofá sea grande...*

Actualmente *Currently* **cadena** *chain* **gama** *range* **asequibles** *affordable* **propósito** *purpose* **promover** *to promote* **colcha** *bedspread* **piedra** *stone*

Anuncio de Conforama

Aquí cabemos todos, ¿no?

Tenemos la cama de rayas, la colcha° de rayas, el sofá de rayas, las cortinas de rayas.

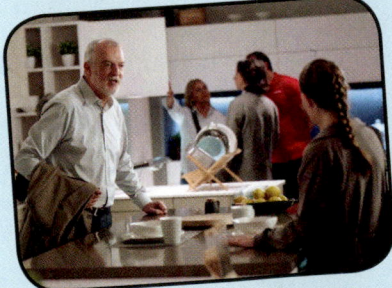

Piedra°. Una cocina tiene que ser de piedra.

More activities
vhlcentral | Online activities

Video

En el sur de la Ciudad de México hay una construcción que fusiona° el funcionalismo con elementos de la cultura mexicana. Es la casa y estudio° donde el muralista Diego Rivera y su esposa, Frida Kahlo, vivieron desde 1934. El creador fue el destacado° arquitecto y pintor mexicano Juan O'Gorman, amigo de la pareja. Como Frida y Diego necesitaban cada uno un lugar tranquilo para trabajar, O'Gorman hizo dos casas, cada una con un taller°, conectadas por un puente° en la parte superior°. En 1981, años después de la muerte de los artistas, se creó ahí el Museo Casa Estudio Diego Rivera y Frida Kahlo. Este museo busca conservar, investigar y difundir° la obra° de estos dos mexicanos, como lo hace el Museo Casa de Frida Kahlo, que vas a ver a continuación.

Vocabulario útil

jardinero	gardener
muros	walls
la silla de ruedas	wheelchair
las valiosas obras	valuable works

Preparación

Imagina que eres un(a) artista, ¿cómo sería (would be) tu casa? ¿Sería muy diferente de la casa en donde vives ahora? Answers will vary.

¿Cierto o falso?

Indica si lo que dicen estas oraciones es **cierto** o **falso**.

1. La casa de Frida Kahlo está en el centro de la Ciudad de México. Falso.
2. La casa de Frida se transformó en un museo en los años 50. Cierto.
3. Frida Kahlo vivió sola en su casa. Falso.
4. Entre las obras que se exhiben está el cuadro (painting) *Las dos Fridas.* Cierto.
5. El jardinero actual (current) jamás conoció ni a Frida ni a Diego. Falso.
6. En el museo se exhiben la silla de ruedas y los aparatos ortopédicos de Frida. Cierto.

fusiona *fuses* estudio *studio* destacado *prominent* taller *art studio*
puente *bridge* parte superior *top* difundir *to spread* obra *work*

La casa de Frida

El hogar en que nació la pintora Frida Kahlo en 1907 se caracteriza por su arquitectura típicamente mexicana...

Esta casa tiene varios detalles que revelan el amor de esta mexicana por la cultura de su país, por ejemplo, la cocina.

Uno de los espacios más atractivos de esta casa es este estudio que Diego instaló...

More activities

vhlcentral | VM pp. 59–60 | Online activities

Panamá

connections cultures NATIONAL STANDARDS

El país en cifras

- ▸ **Área:** 75.420 km² (29.119 millas²), *aproximadamente el área de Carolina del Sur*
- ▸ **Población:** 3.753.000
- ▸ **Capital:** Ciudad de Panamá—1.673.000
- ▸ **Ciudades principales:** Colón, David
- ▸ **Moneda:** balboa; es equivalente al dólar estadounidense.

En Panamá circulan los billetes de dólar estadounidense. El país centroamericano, sin embargo, acuña° su propia moneda. "El peso" es una moneda grande equivalente a cincuenta centavos°. La moneda de cinco centavos es llamada frecuentemente "real".

- ▸ **Idiomas:** español (oficial), lenguas indígenas, inglés
Muchos panameños son bilingües. La lengua materna del 14% de los panameños es el inglés.

Mujer kuna vendiendo molas

Bandera de Panamá

Panameños célebres
- ▸ **Mariano Rivera,** beisbolista (1969–)
- ▸ **Mireya Moscoso,** política (1946–)
- ▸ **Rubén Blades,** músico y político (1948–)
- ▸ **Danilo Pérez,** pianista (1965–)
- ▸ **Jorge Cham,** caricaturista (1976–)

acuña *mints* centavos *cents*

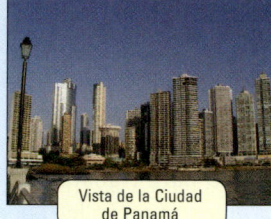
Una turista disfruta del bosque tropical colgado de un cable.

Vista de la Ciudad de Panamá

COSTA RICA
Lago Gatún
Canal de Panamá
Islas San Blas
Cordillera de San
Río Chep
Bocas del Toro
Mar Caribe
Colón
Serranía de Tabasará
Ciudad de Panamá
David
Isla del Rey
Río Cobre
Océano Pacífico
Golfo de Panamá
Isla de Coiba

ESTADOS UNIDOS
OCÉANO ATLÁNTICO
PANAMÁ
AMÉRICA DEL SUR

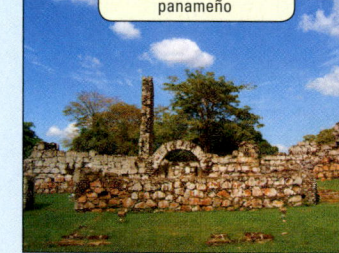
Ruinas de un fuerte panameño

More activities
vhlcentral | WB pp. 145–146 | Online activities

ACTIVIDADES

1 **¿Cierto o falso?** Indica si lo que dicen las oraciones es **cierto** o **falso**.

1. El balboa es la única (*only*) moneda aceptada en Panamá. falso
2. Rubén Blades es el beisbolista más famoso de Panamá. falso
3. Jorge Cham, quien nació en 1976, es un caricaturista panameño. cierto
4. El canal de Panamá se terminó de construir en 1903. falso
5. Un promedio de 40 barcos usa el Canal de Panamá en un solo día. cierto
6. Las molas que hacen los kunas tienen colores vivos. cierto
7. Antiguamente, las molas se usaban como mantas y servilletas. falso
8. Panamá es frecuentado gracias a sus extensas montañas. falso
9. En el Parque Nacional Marino Isla Bastimentos hay gran diversidad de fauna marina. cierto
10. La diversidad étnica y cultural de Panamá se presenta también en su arte y en su gastronomía. cierto

⊙ Lugares • El Canal de Panamá

El Canal de Panamá conecta el océano Pacífico con el océano Atlántico. La construcción de este cauce° artificial empezó en 1903 y concluyó diez años después. Es una de las principales fuentes° de ingresos° del país, gracias al dinero que aportan los más de 14.000 buques° que transitan anualmente por esta ruta y a las actividades comerciales que se han desarrollado° en torno a° ella.

⊙ Artes • La mola

La mola es una forma de arte textil de los kunas, una tribu indígena que vive principalmente en las islas San Blas. Esta pieza artesanal se confecciona con fragmentos de tela° de colores vivos. Algunos de sus diseños son abstractos, inspirados en las formas del coral, y otros son geométricos, como en las molas más tradicionales. Antiguamente, estos tejidos se usaban sólo como ropa, pero hoy día también sirven para decorar las casas.

Naturaleza • El mar

Panamá, cuyo° nombre significa "lugar de muchos peces°", es un país muy frecuentado por los aficionados al buceo y a la pesca. El territorio panameño cuenta con una gran variedad de playas en los dos lados del istmo°, con el mar Caribe a un lado y el océano Pacífico al otro. Algunas zonas costeras están destinadas al turismo. Otras están protegidas por la diversidad de su fauna marina, en la que abundan los arrecifes° de coral, como el Parque Nacional Marino Isla Bastimentos.

Gente • Diversidad étnica y cultural

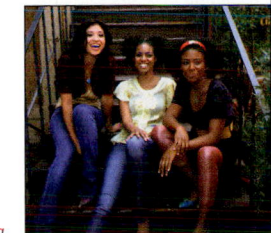

La población de Panamá está conformada por indígenas, blancos, mestizos°, afrodescendientes y asiáticos, provenientes de países como los Estados Unidos, Colombia, España, Argentina, China, India, República Dominicana y Turquía, entre otros. Este mestizaje°, que también se percibe en la gastronomía, la música, el arte y la moda, convierte a Panamá en uno de los países más multiétnicos y multiculturales del mundo.

cauce *channel* fuentes *sources* ingresos *income* buques *ships* han desarrollado *have developed* en torno a *around* tela *fabric*
cuyo *whose* peces *fish* istmo *isthmus* arrecifes *reefs* mestizos *people of indigenous and white parentage* mestizaje *cultural mixing*

COLOMBIA

¡Increíble pero cierto!

¿Conocías estos datos sobre el Canal de Panamá?
- Gracias al Canal de Panamá, el viaje en barco de Nueva York a Tokio es 3.000 millas más corto.
- Su construcción costó 639 millones de dólares.
- Hoy lo usan en promedio° 40 barcos al día.
- El peaje° promedio cuesta 54.000 dólares.

promedio *average* peaje *toll*

---

2 **¿Qué aprendiste?** Contesta las preguntas.

1. ¿Cuál es la lengua materna del catorce por ciento de los panameños? el inglés
2. ¿A qué unidad monetaria es equivalente el balboa? al dólar estadounidense
3. ¿Qué océanos une el Canal de Panamá? los océanos Atlántico y Pacífico
4. ¿Quién es Mariano Rivera? un beisbolista panameño
5. ¿Qué significa "Panamá"? "lugar de muchos peces"

3 **Consejos** Aconseja a tu compañero/a sobre lo que debe hacer en su viaje a Panamá. Utilicen el subjuntivo.

modelo
Estudiante 1: Te aconsejo que visites el canal.
Estudiante 2: Te sugiero que vayas a la playa.

El Canal de Panamá The Panama Canal is a lake-and-lock type of canal, connecting the Atlantic and Pacific oceans at one of the lowest points on the Continental Divide. It is about 40 miles long and is one of the two most strategic man-made waterways on earth (the Suez Canal is the other). You may want to play the **Panorama cultural** video for this paragraph.

La mola The Kuna originally lived on mainland Panama, but the majority chose to move to the San Blas Islands, where they could maintain their way of life. Elaborate traditions accompany every life-cycle event in Kuna culture, and many of these ceremonies are depicted on the elaborate appliqué **molas**. You may want to play the **Panorama cultural** video for this paragraph.

El mar The **Parque Nacional Bastimentos** is located in the **Archipiélago de Bocas del Toro**. In this nature reserve, turtles nest on some of the beaches. Its coral reefs are home to more than 200 species of tropical fish, in addition to lobsters, manatees, and other marine life. The park is also known for its mangroves, which offer snorkelers another aquatic experience.

Diversidad étnica y cultural A popular nickname for Panama is **puente del mundo, corazón del universo**.

¡Increíble pero cierto! The opening of the Panama Canal not only dramatically reduced the distance ships had to travel to get from the Atlantic Ocean to the Pacific, it also provided a much safer route than the stormy, perilous route around Cape Horn and through the Straits of Magellan.

Instructional Resources
Supersite: Audio (Textbook & Lab MP3s); Testing Program (Tests, MP3s, Oral Testing Suggestions)
WebSAM
Lab Manual

Teaching Tip You may want to assign the **Prueba de práctica**, with its diagnostics and review activities, in the online-only **Repaso** section on the Supersite. There is also a **Repaso oral** in this section. For the Sixth Edition, a new summative vocabulary activity with speech recognition has been added to the **Repaso** section.

Las viviendas

las afueras	suburbs; outskirts
el alquiler	rent (payment)
el amo/a (m., f.) de casa	homemaker
el barrio	neighborhood
el edificio de apartamentos	apartment building
el/la vecino/a	neighbor
la vivienda	housing
alquilar	to rent
mudarse	to move (from one house to another)

Los cuartos y otros lugares

el altillo	attic
el balcón	balcony
la cocina	kitchen
el comedor	dining room
el dormitorio	bedroom
la entrada	entrance
la escalera	stairs
el garaje	garage
el jardín	garden; yard
la oficina	office
el pasillo	hallway
el patio	patio; yard
la sala	living room
el sótano	basement

Los muebles y otras cosas

la alfombra	carpet; rug
la almohada	pillow
el armario	closet
el cartel	poster
la cómoda	chest of drawers
las cortinas	curtains
el cuadro	picture
el estante	bookcase; bookshelves
la lámpara	lamp
la luz	light; electricity
la manta	blanket
la mesita	end table
la mesita de noche	night stand
los muebles	furniture
la pared	wall
la pintura	painting; picture
el sillón	armchair
el sofá	sofa

Los electrodomésticos

la cafetera	coffee maker
la cocina, la estufa	stove
el congelador	freezer
el electrodoméstico	electric appliance
el horno (de microondas)	(microwave) oven
la lavadora	washing machine
el lavaplatos	dishwasher
el refrigerador	refrigerator
la secadora	clothes dryer
la tostadora	toaster

La mesa

la copa	wineglass
la cuchara	(table or large) spoon
el cuchillo	knife
el plato	plate
la servilleta	napkin
la taza	cup
el tenedor	fork
el vaso	glass

Los quehaceres domésticos

arreglar	to straighten up
barrer el suelo	to sweep the floor
cocinar	to cook
ensuciar	to get (something) dirty
hacer la cama	to make the bed
hacer quehaceres domésticos	to do household chores
lavar (el suelo, los platos)	to wash (the floor, the dishes)
limpiar la casa	to clean the house
pasar la aspiradora	to vacuum
planchar la ropa	to iron the clothes
poner la mesa	to set the table
quitar la mesa	to clear the table
quitar el polvo	to dust
sacar la basura	to take out the trash
sacudir los muebles	to dust the furniture

Verbos y expresiones verbales

aconsejar	to advise
insistir (en)	to insist (on)
mandar	to order
recomendar (e:ie)	to recommend
rogar (o:ue)	to beg
sugerir (e:ie)	to suggest
Es bueno que…	It's good that…
Es importante que…	It's important that…
Es malo que…	It's bad that…
Es mejor que…	It's better that…
Es necesario que…	It's necessary that…
Es urgente que…	It's urgent that…

Relative pronouns	See page 414.
Expresiones útiles	See page 409.

More activities

vhlcentral   LM p. 72

La naturaleza

13

Lesson Goals

In **Lección 13**, students will be introduced to the following:

- terms to describe nature, the environment, conservation, and recycling
- the Andes mountain range
- Colombia's Santa Marta mountain range
- subjunctive with verbs and expressions of emotion
- subjunctive with verbs and expressions of doubt, disbelief, and denial
- expressions of certainty
- subjunctive with conjunctions
- when to use the infinitive instead of the subjunctive
- identifying a text's purpose
- considering audience and purpose when writing
- writing a persuasive text
- using background knowledge and context to guess meaning
- a Spanish government TV ad about geothermal energy
- a video about nature in Costa Rica
- cultural, geographic, and historical information about Colombia

A PRIMERA VISTA

- ¿Está mareada esta mujer?
- ¿Es importante que use ropa cómoda?
- ¿Es necesario que tenga cuidado?
- ¿Le interesa la naturaleza?

A primera vista Ask these additional questions: **¿Te interesa la ecología? ¿Te gusta entrar en contacto con la naturaleza? ¿Cómo te sientes cuando estás fuera de la ciudad? ¿Te preocupa la ecología de la región donde vives?**

Teaching Tip Look for these icons for additional communicative practice:

→👥←	Interpretive communication
←👥→	Presentational communication
👥↔👥	Interpersonal communication

INSTRUCTIONAL RESOURCES

Supersite (vhlcentral.com)
Video: **Fotonovela, Flash cultura, En pantalla, Panorama cultural**
Audio: Textbook and Lab MP3 Files

Activity Pack: Information Gap Activities, games, additional activity handouts
Resources: SAM Answer Key, Scripts, Translations, **Vocabulario adicional**, sample lesson plan, Grammar Presentation Slides, Digital Image Bank

Testing Program: Quizzes, Tests, Exams, MP3s
Student Activities Manual: Workbook/Video Manual/Lab Manual
WebSAM (online Student Activities Manual)

La naturaleza

Más vocabulario

el desierto	*desert*
la naturaleza	*nature*
la selva, la jungla	*jungle*
el sendero	*trail; path*
la tierra	*land; soil*
el valle	*valley*
el animal	*animal*
la ballena	*whale*
la tortuga (marina)	*(sea) turtle*
la vaca	*cow*
el cielo	*sky*
la estrella	*star*
la luna	*moon*
el calentamiento global	*global warming*
el cambio climático	*climate change*
la conservación	*conservation*
la ecología	*ecology*
el/la ecologista	*ecologist*
el ecoturismo	*ecotourism*
la energía (nuclear; solar)	*(nuclear; solar) energy*
la extinción	*extinction*
el medio ambiente	*environment*
el peligro	*danger*
el recurso natural	*natural resource*
la solución	*solution*
el gobierno	*government*
la ley	*law*
la (sobre)población	*(over)population*
ecológico/a	*ecological*
puro/a	*pure*
renovable	*renewable*

Variación léxica

hierba ⟷ pasto (*Perú*); grama (*Venez., Col.*); zacate (*Méx.*)

el mono
el árbol
el bosque (tropical)
el río
la flor
la hierba
la contaminación del aire
la deforestación
la fábrica
el perro
el gato

---

el sol
el ave, el pájaro
la nube
la planta
el pez (sing.), los peces (pl.)
la piedra
el lago
el cráter
el volcán
la contaminación del agua

Práctica

1 Escuchar Mientras escuchas estas oraciones, anota los sustantivos (*nouns*) que se refieren a las plantas, los animales, la tierra y el cielo.

Plantas	Animales	Tierra	Cielo
flores	tortugas marinas	bosques tropicales	nubes
hierba	peces	volcán	estrellas

2 Una invitación Completa las oraciones sobre la invitación de Claudia.

1. Hay muchos tipos de ____aves____ y de árboles en el parque.
2. Claudia quiere almorzar sobre la ____hierba____.
3. Hay un ____lago____ muy grande en el parque.
4. Claudia quiere estar en contacto con la ____naturaleza____.

3 Seleccionar Selecciona la palabra que no está relacionada.

1. estrella • gobierno • luna • sol   gobierno
2. flor • hierba • renovable • árbol   renovable
3. vaca • ballena • pájaro • población   población
4. cielo • cráter • aire • nube   cráter
5. desierto • solución • selva • bosque   solución
6. lago • río • mar • peligro   peligro

4 Definiciones Indica la palabra adecuada para cada definición.

> **modelo**
> lugar que está lleno de árboles
> *el bosque*

1. animal que produce la leche que tomamos ____la vaca____
2. estrella más grande de nuestro sistema planetario ____el sol____
3. lugar donde llueve poco ____el desierto____
4. cuando la temperatura del planeta sube ____el calentamiento global____
5. cuando una especie animal ya no existe más ____la extinción____
6. parte de un volcán ____el cráter____

5 Describir Trabajen en parejas para describir estas fotos. Answers will vary.

not assigned

1 Teaching Tip To simplify, have students brainstorm a few words for each category before listening.

1 Script 1. Mi novio siempre me compra flores para nuestro aniversario. 2. Llueve mucho en los bosques tropicales. 3. Hoy día, en Latinoamérica hay seis especies de tortugas marinas en peligro de extinción. 4. Anoche, las nubes grises cubrían toda la ciudad. 5. En el mar Caribe hay muchos peces exóticos. 6. Me gusta ver las estrellas. 7. Se prohíbe caminar sobre la hierba. 8. El Puracé es un volcán activo en los Andes colombianos. *Textbook MP3s*

2 Teaching Tip Have students read the sentences before listening to the audio.

2 Script Hola, Nicolás. ¿Quieres ir mañana al Parque Natural Los Senderos? Dicen que tiene muchos tipos de aves y de árboles. Además, hay un lago muy grande donde podemos pescar; tiene muchos tipos de peces. En la tarde, podemos almorzar sobre la hierba. Quiero tener aire puro y estar en contacto con la naturaleza. Llámame, chau. *Textbook MP3s*

3 Expansion Have students state a category for the related words. Ex: **1. cosas que están en el cielo**

4 Expansion Ask students to create three additional definitions and give them to a partner, who will provide the answers.

5 Teaching Tip To simplify, give students these guidelines to help them prepare their descriptions: objects in the photos, colors, what the weather is like, the time of day, the location where the photo was taken.

El reciclaje

Recicla la lata de aluminio. (reciclar)

Recoge la botella de vidrio. (recoger)

el envase de plástico

Más vocabulario

cazar	to hunt
conservar	to conserve
contaminar	to pollute
controlar	to control
cuidar	to take care of
dejar de (+ *inf.*)	to stop (doing something)
desarrollar	to develop
descubrir	to discover
destruir	to destroy
estar afectado/a (por)	to be affected (by)
estar contaminado/a	to be polluted
evitar	to avoid
mejorar	to improve
proteger	to protect
reducir	to reduce
resolver (o:ue)	to resolve; to solve
respirar	to breathe

6 Completar Selecciona la palabra o la expresión adecuada para completar cada oración.

contaminar	destruyen	reciclamos
controlan	están afectadas	recoger
cuidan	mejoramos	resolver
descubrir	proteger	se desarrollaron

1. Si vemos basura en las calles, la debemos ___recoger___.
2. Los científicos trabajan para ___descubrir___ nuevas soluciones.
3. Todas las personas ___están afectadas___ por la contaminación.
4. Debemos ___proteger___ el medio ambiente porque hoy día está en peligro.
5. Es necesario que todos trabajemos juntos para ___resolver___ los problemas del medio ambiente.
6. Las primeras civilizaciones ___se desarrollaron___ cerca de los ríos y los mares.
7. Muchas leyes nuevas ___controlan___ el nivel de emisiones que producen las fábricas.
8. Los turistas deben tener cuidado de no ___contaminar___ los lugares que visitan.
9. Podemos conservar los recursos si ___reciclamos___ el aluminio, el vidrio y el plástico.
10. La contaminación y la deforestación ___destruyen___ el medio ambiente.

Comunicación

7 **Preguntas** En parejas, túrnense para hacerse estas preguntas. Answers will vary.

1. ¿Te preocupas por el medio ambiente? ¿Por qué?
2. ¿Qué forma de energía prefieres? ¿Por qué?
3. ¿Cómo podemos reducir la cantidad de basura?
4. ¿Crees que es importante reciclar? ¿Lo haces? ¿Por qué?
5. ¿Cómo podemos proteger los animales en peligro de extinción?
6. ¿Qué lugares están contaminados en tu estado o región?
7. ¿Qué podemos hacer para mejorar la calidad del aire?
8. ¿Quiénes deben resolver los problemas del medio ambiente? ¿Los gobiernos, los ecologistas…?

8 **Alternativas** En parejas, hablen sobre las alternativas y el efecto que tienen en el medio ambiente. Answers will vary.

- manejar un coche o pasear en bicicleta
- ser vegetariano/a o comer carne
- ducharse o bañarse
- lavar los platos a mano o usar el lavaplatos
- leer libros en papel o electrónicos
- hacer ecoturismo o turismo tradicional

9 **Situaciones** Trabajen en grupos pequeños para representar estas situaciones. Answers will vary.

1. Unos/as representantes de una agencia ambiental (*environmental*) hablan con el/la presidente/a de una fábrica que está contaminando el aire o el río de la zona.
2. Un(a) guía de ecoturismo habla con un grupo sobre cómo disfrutar (*enjoy*) de la naturaleza y conservar el medio ambiente.
3. Un(a) representante de la universidad habla con un grupo de nuevos estudiantes sobre la campaña (*campaign*) ambiental de la universidad y trata de reclutar (*tries to recruit*) miembros para un club que trabaja para la protección del medio ambiente.

10 **Escribir una carta** Trabajen en parejas para escribir una carta a una fábrica real o imaginaria que esté contaminando el medio ambiente. Expliquen las consecuencias que sus acciones van a tener para el medio ambiente. Sugiéranle algunas ideas para que solucione el problema. Answers will vary.

11 **A debatir** Trabajen en grupos y discutan cuáles creen que son los problemas ambientales más graves que afectan nuestro planeta. Cada uno/a debe escoger dos o tres opciones y decir por qué son problemas serios. Después, ofrezcan posibles soluciones para cada problema. Answers will vary.

- contaminación del aire
- contaminación del agua
- pérdida (*loss*) de biodiversidad
- cambio climático/calentamiento global
- disminución de la capa de ozono
- agotamiento (*depletion*) de recursos naturales
- residuos (*waste*) industriales
- actividades mineras
- deforestación
- sobrepoblación
- lluvia ácida
- exceso de basura

7 Expansion Ask students to report on their partner's answers.

8 Expansion Have a class discussion about the effects of these activities on the environment.

9 Teaching Tip Divide the class into small groups. Have each group choose a situation, but make sure that each situation is selected by at least one group. Have students take turns playing each role. After groups have had time to prepare their situations, ask volunteers to present them to the class.

10 Teaching Tips
- Remind students that a business letter in Spanish begins with a salutation, such as **Estimado(s) señor(es)**, and ends with a closing such as **Atentamente**.
- With the class, brainstorm a list of agencies or companies that are known not to be environmentally conscious. Ask the class to categorize the companies by how they harm the environment. Then divide the class into pairs and have them choose a company for the activity. Alternately, you can vary the activity to have it focus on green companies.

11 Teaching Tip Poll the class to see what students think are the top three environmental problems.

TEACHING OPTIONS

Heritage Speakers Ask heritage speakers to interview family members or people in their community about the environmental challenges in their families' countries of origin. Encourage them to find out how the problems affect the land and the people. Have students report their findings to the class.
Large Groups Prepare two sets of index cards, one with environmental problems and the other with possible solutions.

Ex: **la destrucción de los bosques – reducir las áreas de deforestación; la contaminación de los ríos – controlar el tipo de sustancias que hay en el agua.** Shuffle the two sets of cards and distribute them. Have students with problem cards circulate around the room, asking their classmates questions until they find a viable solution.

Aventuras en la naturaleza

Las chicas visitan un santuario de tortugas, mientras los chicos pasean por la selva.

PERSONAJES — **MARISSA** — **JIMENA**

 Video

1

MARISSA Querida tía Ana María, lo estoy pasando muy bien. Es maravilloso que México tenga tantos programas estupendos para proteger a las tortugas. Hoy estamos en Tulum, y ¡el paisaje es espectacular! Con cariño, Marissa.

2

MARISSA Estoy tan feliz de que estés aquí conmigo.

JIMENA Es mucho más divertido cuando se viaja con amigos.

(*Llegan Felipe y Juan Carlos*)

JIMENA ¿Qué pasó?

JUAN CARLOS No lo van a creer.

FELIPE Juan Carlos encontró al grupo. ¡Yo esperaba encontrarlos también! ¡Pero nunca vinieron por mí! Yo estaba asustado. Regresé al lugar de donde salimos y esperé. Me perdí todo el recorrido.

3

GUÍA A menos que protejamos a los animales de la contaminación y la deforestación, muchos van a estar en peligro de extinción. Por favor, síganme y eviten pisar las plantas.

5

4

FELIPE Nos retrasamos sólo cinco minutos... Qué extraño. Estaban aquí hace unos minutos.

JUAN CARLOS ¿Adónde se fueron?

FELIPE No creo que puedan ir muy lejos.

(*Se separan para buscar al grupo.*)

6

FELIPE Decidí seguir un río y...

MARISSA No es posible que un guía continúe el recorrido cuando hay dos personas perdidas.

JIMENA Vamos a ver, chicos, ¿qué pasó? Díganos la verdad.

JUAN CARLOS

FELIPE

GUÍA

7

JUAN CARLOS Felipe se cayó. Él no quería contarles.

JIMENA ¡Lo sabía!

FELIPE Y ustedes, ¿qué hicieron hoy?

JIMENA Marissa y yo fuimos al santuario de las tortugas.

8

9

MARISSA Aprendimos sobre las normas que existen para proteger a las tortugas marinas.

JIMENA Pero no cabe duda de que necesitamos aprobar más leyes para protegerlas.

MARISSA Fue muy divertido verlas tan cerca.

10

JUAN CARLOS Entonces se divirtieron. ¡Qué bien!

JIMENA Gracias, y tú, pobrecito, pasaste todo el día con mi hermano. Siempre te mete en problemas.

Expresiones útiles

Talking about the environment

Aprendimos sobre las normas que existen para proteger a las tortugas marinas.
We learned about the regulations that exist to protect sea turtles.

Afortunadamente, ahora la población está aumentando.
Fortunately, the population is now growing.

No cabe duda de que necesitamos aprobar más leyes para protegerlas.
There is no doubt that we need to pass more laws to protect them.

Es maravilloso que México tenga tantos programas estupendos para proteger a las tortugas.
It's marvelous that Mexico has so many wonderful programs to protect the turtles.

A menos que protejamos a los animales de la contaminación y la deforestación, muchos van a estar en peligro de extinción.
Unless we protect animals from pollution and habitat loss, many of them will become endangered.

Additional vocabulary

aumentar
to grow; to get bigger
meterse en problemas
to get into trouble
perdido/a
lost
el recorrido
tour
sobre todo
above all

More activities

vhlcentral | VM pp. 25–26 | Online activities

Expresiones útiles

- Point out the sentence that begins with **A menos que protejamos...** and explain that **a menos que** is a conjunction that is always followed by the subjunctive. Then draw attention to the captions for video stills 1 and 2. Tell students that **Es maravilloso que México tenga...** and **Estoy tan feliz de que estés aquí conmigo** are examples of the subjunctive used with verbs and expressions of emotion. Finally, draw attention to the sentence **No creo que puedan ir muy lejos** under video still 4. Explain that this is an example of the subjunctive used with an expression of doubt.

- Point out the phrase **meterse en problemas** and have students read through the caption for video still 10.

Teaching Tips

- 👤↔👤 Continue the conversation that you began in **Contextos** about the state of the environment in your area. Integrate **Expresiones útiles** into the conversation.

- Have the class work in groups to read through the entire **Fotonovela** aloud, with volunteers playing the various parts.

Nota cultural Mexico is believed to be the home of roughly ten percent of all known species. These include 500 species of mammals, 300 species of birds, and 25,000 species of plants. Human interference with natural habitats and climate changes have, however, placed many of these species in danger. Among those under threat of extinction are the jaguar, the golden eagle, and the **vaquita** (the world's smallest porpoise).

TEACHING OPTIONS

TPR →👤← As you play the episode, have students raise their hands each time they hear the subjunctive.

Extra Practice →👤← Photocopy the **Fotonovela** Videoscript (Supersite) and white out target vocabulary and expressions in order to create a master for a cloze activity. Have students fill in the blanks as they watch the episode.

Large Groups ←👤→ Divide the class into four groups and assign each one a nature reserve (**reserva natural**) in a Spanish-speaking country. (Ex: **La Pedregoza** in Colombia, **Reserva Marina de Galápagos** in Ecuador, Costa Rica's **Reserva Ecológica Manuel Antonio**, and Mexico's **Reserva Natural Cuatro Ciénagas**.) For homework, have each group prepare a presentation, including size, flora and fauna, environmental issues the reserve faces, and any other significant information.

¿Qué pasó?

1 **Teaching Tip** To challenge students, write these sentences on the board without the multiple choice items and have students complete them.

2 **Expansion** Have pairs of students write questions or statements that could have elicited these comments.

Nota cultural **Tulum** is the third most visited archeological site in Mexico, after **Teotihuacán** and **Chichén Itzá**.

3 **Expansion** Ask students to write three additional questions for a classmate to answer.

4 **Possible Conversation**
E1: **¿Hay problemas de contaminación donde vives?**
E2: **Sí, tenemos un problema muy grave de contaminación en los ríos. Hay muchos papeles, botellas y latas en ellos. En las montañas, los ríos no están tan afectados por la contaminación pero en las ciudades, sí. ¿En tu región hay problemas de contaminación?**
E1: **Sí, tenemos un problema gravísimo de contaminación del aire. Esto causa enfermedades para los habitantes.**
E2: **Qué terrible. ¿Cómo podemos resolver los problemas de la contaminación?**
E1: **Bueno, nosotros ahora tenemos un programa de reciclaje. También algunas personas tratan de no usar el auto. Usan el metro o caminan.**

The Affective Dimension
Many students feel nervous when called on to give an answer or to read aloud. You can minimize anxiety by asking for volunteers and by having students work in pairs or groups.

1 **Seleccionar** Selecciona la respuesta más lógica para completar cada oración.

1. México tiene muchos programas para __c__ a las tortugas.
   a. destruir   b. reciclar   c. proteger
2. Según la guía, muchos animales van a estar en peligro de __b__ si no los protegemos.
   a. reciclaje   b. extinción   c. deforestación
3. La guía les pide a los visitantes que eviten pisar __a__.
   a. las plantas   b. las piedras   c. la tierra
4. Felipe no quería contarles a las chicas que se __c__.
   a. divirtió   b. alegró   c. cayó
5. Jimena dice que debe haber más __b__ para proteger a las tortugas.
   a. playas   b. leyes   c. gobiernos

2 **Identificar** Identifica quién dice estas oraciones.

1. Aprendimos sobre las normas que existen para proteger a las tortugas marinas. *Marissa*
2. A menos que protejamos a los animales de la contaminación y la deforestación, muchos van a estar en peligro de extinción. *guía*
3. Hoy estamos en Tulum, y ¡el paisaje es espectacular! *Marissa*
4. Me perdí todo el recorrido. *Felipe*
5. Creo que éste es nuestro último viaje del año. *Jimena*
6. Entonces se divirtieron. ¡Qué bien! *Juan Carlos*
7. Ése es el árbol de la especie de chaká. *guía*
8. Dígannos la verdad. *Jimena*

 FELIPE **MARISSA**
 JIMENA
 GUÍA **JUAN CARLOS**

NOTA CULTURAL

Tulum es una importante zona arqueológica que se localiza en la costa del estado de Quintana Roo, México. La ciudad amurallada (*walled*), construida (*built*) por los mayas, es famosa por su ubicación (*location*) dramática en un acantilado (*cliff*) frente al mar.

3 **Preguntas** Contesta estas preguntas.

1. ¿Qué lugar visitan Marissa y Jimena?
   Marissa y Jimena visitan un santuario de tortugas.
2. ¿Adónde fueron Juan Carlos y Felipe?
   Juan Carlos y Felipe fueron a la selva.
3. Según la guía, ¿por qué muchos animales están en peligro de extinción?
   Muchos animales están en peligro de extinción por la contaminación y la deforestación.
4. ¿Por qué Jimena y Marissa no creen la historia de Felipe?
   Porque no es posible que un guía continúe el recorrido cuando hay dos personas perdidas.
5. ¿Qué esperaba Felipe cuando se perdió?
   Felipe esperaba encontrar al grupo.

4 **El medio ambiente** En parejas, discutan algunos problemas ambientales y sus posibles soluciones. Usen estas preguntas y frases en su conversación. *Answers will vary.*

- ¿Hay problemas de contaminación donde vives?
- Tenemos un problema muy grave de contaminación de...
- ¿Cómo podemos resolver los problemas de la contaminación?

TEACHING OPTIONS

Extra Practice Add an auditory aspect to this vocabulary practice. Use the sentences in **Actividad 1** or **Actividad 2** for a dictation activity. Have students close their books; then read each sentence twice slowly and once at regular speed. Then have students open their books and check their work for accuracy. Ask comprehension questions as a follow-up.

Small Groups Have students work in groups of three to write a short article about their environmental concerns for a local newsletter (**boletín informativo**). Their articles should include a description of a few environmental problems and some suggestions for solving them. Have groups share their articles with the class.

Ortografía

 Tutorial

Los signos de puntuación

In Spanish, as in English, punctuation marks are important because they help you express your ideas in a clear, organized way.

> No podía ver las llaves**.** Las buscó por los estantes**,** las mesas**,** las sillas**,** el suelo**;** minutos después**,** decidió mirar por la ventana**.** Allí estaban**…**

The **punto y coma (;),** the **tres puntos (…),** and the **punto (.)** are used in very similar ways in Spanish and English.

> Argentina**,** Brasil**,** Paraguay **y** Uruguay son miembros de Mercosur.

In Spanish, the **coma (,)** is not used before **y** or **o** in a series.

| 13**,**5% | 29**,**2° | 3**.**000**.**000 | $2**.**999**,**99 |

In numbers, Spanish uses a **coma** where English uses a decimal point and a **punto** where English uses a comma.

 ¿**Cómo te llamas**?   ¿**Dónde está**?   ¡**Ven aquí**!   **Hola**

Questions in Spanish are preceded and followed by **signos de interrogación (¿ ?),** and exclamations are preceded and followed by **signos de exclamación (¡ !).**

Práctica Lee el párrafo e indica los signos de puntuación necesarios. *Answers will vary.*

Ayer recibí la invitación de boda de Marta mi amiga colombiana inmediatamente empecé a pensar en un posible regalo fui al almacén donde Marta y su novio tenían una lista de regalos había de todo copas cafeteras tostadoras finalmente decidí regalarles un perro ya sé que es un regalo extraño pero espero que les guste a los dos

¿Palabras de amor? El siguiente diálogo tiene diferentes significados (*meanings*) dependiendo de los signos de puntuación que utilices y el lugar donde los pongas. Intenta encontrar los diferentes significados. *Answers will vary.*

JULIÁN	me quieres
MARISOL	no puedo vivir sin ti
JULIÁN	me quieres dejar
MARISOL	no me parece mala idea
JULIÁN	no eres feliz conmigo
MARISOL	no soy feliz

 More activities

vhlcentral   LM p. 74

Section Goals

In **Cultura**, students will:
- read about the Andes mountain range
- learn nature-related terms
- read about Colombia's **Sierra Nevada de Santa Marta**
- read about important bodies of water in Latin America

Instructional Resource
Supersite

En detalle

Antes de leer Preview the reading by asking these questions: **¿Qué montañas conocen? ¿Qué les parece más interesante, pasar tiempo en la playa o en las montañas? ¿Por qué?**

Lectura
- Point out that the Andes pass through seven different countries.
- Tell students that the highest area of the Andes is known as the **altiplano**, where farmers raise sheep, llamas, alpacas, and vicuñas. They use these animals' wool to make clothing and blankets.
- Add a visual aspect to this reading. Bring in topographic maps of Spain, Central America, and South America and indicate other important mountain ranges in Spanish-speaking countries, such as **los Pirineos** (Spain), or **la Sierra Madre Occidental** and **Oriental** (Mexico).

Después de leer
👥↔👥 Ask students to discuss with a partner what facts from this reading are new or surprising to them.

1 Teaching Tip To challenge students, rephrase the items as comprehension questions. Ex: **2. ¿Qué es "la espina dorsal de Suramérica"?**

EN DETALLE

¡Los Andes se mueven!

Los Andes, la cadena° de montañas más extensa de América, son conocidos como "la espina dorsal° de Suramérica". Sus 7.240 kilómetros (4.500 millas) van desde el norte° de la región entre Venezuela y Colombia, hasta el extremo sur°, entre Argentina y Chile, y pasan por casi todos los países suramericanos. La cordillera° de los Andes, formada hace 27 millones de años, es la segunda más alta del mundo, después de la del Himalaya (aunque° esta última es mucho más "joven", ya que se formó hace apenas cinco millones de años).

Para poder atravesar° de un lado a otro de los Andes, existen varios pasos o puertos° de montaña. Situados a grandes alturas°, son generalmente estrechos° y peligrosos. En algunos de ellos hay, también, vías ferroviarias°.

De acuerdo con° varias instituciones científicas, la cordillera de los Andes se eleva° y se hace más angosta° cada año. La capital de Chile se acerca° a la capital de Argentina a un ritmo° de 19,4 milímetros por año. Si ese ritmo se mantiene°, Santiago y Buenos Aires podrían unirse° en unos... 63 millones de años, ¡casi el mismo tiempo que ha transcurrido° desde la extinción de los dinosaurios!

Arequipa, Perú

Los Andes en números

3 Cordilleras que forman los Andes: Las cordilleras Central, Occidental y Oriental

900 (A.C.°) Año aproximado en que empezó el desarrollo° de la cultura chavín, en los Andes peruanos

600 Número aproximado de volcanes que hay en los Andes

6.962 Metros (22.841 pies) de altura del Aconcagua (Argentina), el pico° más alto de los Andes

cadena *range* espina dorsal *spine* norte *north* sur *south* cordillera *mountain range* aunque *although* atravesar *to cross* puertos *passes* alturas *heights* estrechos *narrow* vías ferroviarias *railroad tracks* De acuerdo con *According to* se eleva *rises* angosta *narrow* se acerca *gets closer* ritmo *rate* se mantiene *keeps going* podrían unirse *could join together* ha transcurrido *has gone by* A.C. *Before Christ* desarrollo *development* pico *peak*

ACTIVIDADES

1 **Escoger** Escoge la opción que completa mejor cada oración.

1. Los Andes son la cadena montañosa más extensa del...
   a. mundo.   **b. continente americano.**   c. hemisferio norte.
2. "La espina dorsal de Suramérica" es...
   a. los Andes.   b. el Himalaya.   c. el Aconcagua.
3. La cordillera de los Andes se extiende...
   a. de este a oeste.   b. de sur a oeste.   **c. de norte a sur.**
4. El Himalaya y los Andes tienen...
   a. diferente altura.   b. la misma altura.   c. el mismo color.
5. Es posible atravesar los Andes por medio de...
   a. montañas   **b. puertos**   c. metro
6. En algunos de los puertos de montaña de los Andes hay...
   a. puertas.   **b. vías ferroviarias.**   c. cordilleras.
7. En 63 millones de años, Buenos Aires y Santiago podrían...
   a. separarse.   b. desarrollarse.   **c. unirse.**
8. El Aconcagua es...
   a. una montaña.   b. un grupo indígena.   c. un volcán.

TEACHING OPTIONS

Extra Practice List on the board: **3; 900; 600; 6.962; 27 millones; 63 millones; 7.240; 19,4; 4.500.** Have students form sentences about the reading using each number. Ex: **Hay tres cordilleras que forman los Andes.**

Cultural Comparison ←👥→ For homework, ask students to research a North American mountain range and compare and contrast it with one of the ranges mentioned on these pages. To simplify, brainstorm a list of research categories, such as climate, local industries, tourism, flora and fauna, and inhabitants.

Pairs Have pairs create questions and corresponding answers about the reading. One student should create the answers. The other student then develops the questions. After five minutes, have partners switch roles.

ASÍ SE DICE

La naturaleza

el arco iris	*rainbow*
la cascada; la catarata	*waterfall*
el cerro; la colina; la loma	*hill, hillock*
la cima; la cumbre; el tope (Col.)	*summit; mountaintop*
la maleza; los rastrojos (Col.); la yerba mala (Cuba); los hierbajos (Méx.); los yuyos (Arg.)	*weeds*
la niebla	*fog*

EL MUNDO HISPANO

Cuerpos de agua

- **Lago de Maracaibo** es el lago natural más grande de Suramérica y tiene una conexión directa y natural con el mar.

- **Lago Titicaca** es el lago navegable más alto del mundo. Se encuentra a más de 3.800 metros de altitud.

- **Bahía Mosquito** es una bahía bioluminiscente. En sus aguas viven unos microorganismos que emiten luz° cuando sienten que algo las agita°.

emiten luz *emit light* agita *shakes*

PERFIL

La Sierra Nevada de Santa Marta

La Sierra Nevada de Santa Marta es una cadena de montañas en la costa norte de Colombia. Se eleva abruptamente desde las costas del mar Caribe y en apenas 42 kilómetros llega a una altura de 5.775 metros

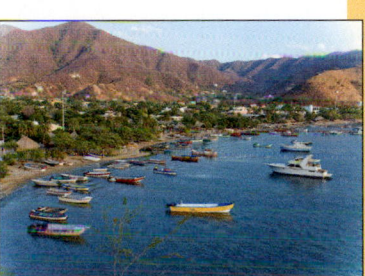

(18.947 pies) en sus picos nevados°. Tiene las montañas más altas de Colombia y es la formación montañosa costera° más alta del mundo.

Los pueblos indígenas que habitan allí lograron° mantener los frágiles ecosistemas de estas montañas a través de° un sofisticado sistema de terrazas° y senderos empedrados° que permitieron° el control de las aguas en una región de

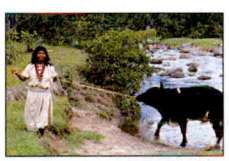

muchas lluvias, evitando así la erosión de la tierra. La Sierra fue nombrada Reserva de la Biosfera por la UNESCO en 1979.

nevados *snowcapped* costera *coastal* lograron *managed* a través de *by means of* terrazas *terraces* empedrados *cobblestone* permitieron *allowed*

CON RITMO HISPANO

ChocQuibTown (2000–)
Lugar de nacimiento: Quibdó y Condoto, Colombia

El nombre de este trío de hip hop y música alternativa significa Chocó Quibdó nuestro pueblo, y es un homenaje a esta región del Pacífico colombiano.

Go to **vhlcentral.com** to find out more about **ChocQuibTown** and their music.

ACTIVIDADES

2 Comprensión Indica si lo que dice cada oración es **cierto** o **falso**. Corrige la información falsa.

1. En Colombia, *weeds* se dice **hierbajos**. Falso. Se dice rastrojos.
2. El lago Titicaca es el más grande del mundo. Falso. Es el lago navegable más alto del mundo.
3. La Sierra Nevada de Santa Marta es la formación montañosa costera más alta del mundo. Cierto.
4. Los indígenas destruyeron el ecosistema de Santa Marta. Falso. Lograron mantener los ecosistemas de las montañas.

3 Maravillas de la naturaleza Escribe un párrafo breve donde describas alguna maravilla de la naturaleza que has (*you have*) visitado y que te impresionó. Puede ser cualquier (*any*) sitio natural: un río, una montaña, una selva, etc. Answers will vary.

More activities

vhlcentral | Online activities

Así se dice
- To challenge students, add these nature-related words to the list: **el acantilado** (*cliff*); **la marisma, el pantano** (*swamp; wetlands*).
- Ask questions using the terms. Ex: **¿Es fácil manejar cuando hay niebla?**

Perfil
- Point out the **Sierra Nevada de Santa Marta** on the map on page 472.
- As students read, have them think about the similarities and differences between the **Sierra Nevada de Santa Marta** and the Andes.

El mundo hispano Use a map to point out the locations (Venezuela; between Peru and Bolivia; and Vieques, Puerto Rico, respectively) of these bodies of water.

Con ritmo hispano Point out to students that they will find supporting activities and information at **vhlcentral.com**.

2 Expansion Give students these statements as items 5–7: **5. La Sierra Nevada de Santa Marta es más extensa que la cordillera de los Andes.** (Falso. La cordillera de los Andes es más extensa.) **6. El lago Titicaca está a más de 3.000 metros de altitud.** (Cierto.) **7. Un arco iris se ve cuando hay precipitación y sol a la vez.** (Cierto.)

3 Teaching Tips
- To add a visual aspect to this activity, have students make a simple drawing or collage.
- If students have not visited any place in nature that impressed them, give them the option of researching a place that they would like to visit.

TEACHING OPTIONS

TPR Add an auditory aspect to this **Cultura** presentation. Prepare descriptions of the bodies of water and mountain ranges mentioned on these pages. Ex: **Es la formación montañosa más alta del mundo. Cada año se eleva un poco más. Está formada por tres cordilleras.** Give each student a set of cards with the names of geographical features, and have them hold up the corresponding name for each sentence you read.

Large Groups Give five volunteers each a slip of paper with a different body of water or mountain range: **el lago Titicaca, el lago de Maracaibo, la Bahía Mosquito, los Andes,** and **la Sierra Nevada de Santa Marta**. Then have the class circulate around the room and ask questions to find out what body of water or mountain range each volunteer represents. Ex: **¿Eres un cuerpo de agua o una montaña? ¿En qué país(es) estás?**

Section Goals

In **Estructura 13.1**, students will learn:
- to use the subjunctive with verbs and expressions of emotion
- common verbs and expressions of emotion

Instructional Resources

Supersite: Audio (Lab MP3 Files); Resources (Grammar Presentation Slides, Activity Pack, Scripts, Answer Keys); Testing Program (Quizzes)
WebSAM
Workbook
Lab Manual

Teaching Tips

- Ask students to call out some of the verbs that, when placed in the main clause, trigger the subjunctive in the subordinate clause (see **Estructura 12.4**). List the verbs on the board and ask students to use them in sentences as a review of the conjugation of regular **–ar**, **–er**, and **–ir** verbs.
- Model the use of some common verbs and expressions of emotion. Ex: **Me molesta mucho que recojan la basura sólo una vez a la semana. Me sorprende que algunas personas no se preocupen por el medio ambiente.** Then ask volunteers to use other verbs and expressions in sentences.

13.1 The subjunctive with verbs of emotion

Tutorial

ANTE TODO In the previous lesson, you learned how to use the subjunctive with expressions of will and influence. You will now learn how to use the subjunctive with verbs and expressions of emotion.

Main clause ——— **Subordinate clause**

Marta **espera** (que) yo **vaya** al lago este fin de semana.

▶ When the verb in the main clause of a sentence expresses an emotion or feeling, such as hope, fear, joy, pity, or surprise, the subjunctive is required in the subordinate clause.

Nos alegramos de que te **gusten** las flores.
We are happy that you like the flowers.

Siento que tú no **puedas** venir mañana.
I'm sorry that you can't come tomorrow.

Temo que Ana no **pueda** ir mañana con nosotros.
I'm afraid that Ana won't be able to go with us tomorrow.

Le **sorprende** que Juan **sea** tan joven.
It surprises him that Juan is so young.

Es una lástima que ellos no estén aquí con nosotros.

Me alegro de que te diviertas.

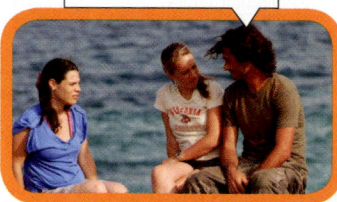

Common verbs and expressions of emotion

alegrarse (de)	*to be happy*	**tener miedo (de)**	*to be afraid (of)*
esperar	*to hope; to wish*	**es extraño**	*it's strange*
gustar	*to like*	**es una lástima**	*it's a shame*
molestar	*to bother*	**es ridículo**	*it's ridiculous*
sentir (e:ie)	*to be sorry; to regret*	**es terrible**	*it's terrible*
sorprender	*to surprise*	**es triste**	*it's sad*
temer	*to be afraid*	**ojalá (que)**	*I hope (that); I wish (that)*

CONSULTA

Certain verbs of emotion, like **gustar, molestar,** and **sorprender,** require indirect object pronouns. For more examples, see **Estructura 7.4,** pp. 246–247.

Me molesta que la gente no **recicle** el plástico.
It bothers me that people don't recycle plastic.

Es triste que **tengamos** problemas como el cambio climático.
It's sad that we have problems like climate change.

TEACHING OPTIONS

Large Groups Have students circulate around the room, interviewing each other about their hopes and fears for the future of the environment. Ex: **¿Qué deseas para el futuro del medio ambiente? (Deseo que encontremos una solución al problema de la contaminación.) ¿Qué es lo que más temes? (Temo que destruyamos los bosques tropicales.)** Encourage students to use the common verbs and expressions of emotion.

Extra Practice Ask students to imagine that they have just finished watching a documentary about the effects of pollution. Have them write five responses to what they saw and heard, using different verbs or expressions of emotion in each sentence. Ex: **Me sorprende que el río esté contaminado....**

▶ As with expressions of will and influence, the infinitive, not the subjunctive, is used after an expression of emotion when there is no change of subject. Compare these sentences.

Temo **llegar** tarde.
I'm afraid I'll arrive late.

Temo que mi novio **llegue** tarde.
I'm afraid my boyfriend will arrive late.

▶ The expression **ojalá (que)** means *I hope* or *I wish*, and it is always followed by the subjunctive. Note that the use of **que** with this expression is optional.

Ojalá (que) se conserven nuestros recursos naturales.
I hope (that) our natural resources will be conserved.

Ojalá (que) recojan la basura hoy.
I hope (that) they collect the garbage today.

Ojalá que

su aseguradora escuche sus necesidades con la misma atención.

Por fin usted se puede poner en manos de **una compañía confiable.**

COLMENA
salud - medicina
Con su familia, por su futuro.

¡INTÉNTALO! Completa las oraciones con las formas correctas de los verbos.

1. Ojalá que ellos <u>descubran</u> (descubrir) nuevas formas de energía.
2. Espero que Ana nos <u>ayude</u> (ayudar) a recoger la basura en la carretera.
3. Me alegro de que mis amigos <u>quieran</u> (querer) conservar la naturaleza.
4. Esperamos <u>proteger</u> (proteger) a las tortugas marinas que llegan a esta playa.
5. Es una lástima que la gente no <u>recicle</u> (reciclar) más.
6. A mis padres les gusta que nosotros <u>participemos</u> (participar) en la reunión.
7. Es malo <u>contaminar</u> (contaminar) el medio ambiente.
8. Espero que tú <u>vengas</u> (venir) a la reunión (*meeting*) del Club de Ecología.
9. Es terrible que nuestras ciudades <u>estén</u> (estar) afectadas por la contaminación.
10. Ojalá que yo <u>pueda</u> (poder) hacer algo para reducir el calentamiento global.

Práctica

1 Teaching Tips
• To simplify, start by having students read the items listed in the word bank. Ask volunteers to point out which verbs are in the subjunctive and which words trigger it.
• Ask individuals to explain why they chose the verbs or expressions they did.

1 Expansion
👥↔👥 Ask pairs to write a new conversation based on the one in the activity. Students should use the subjunctive at least six times. Call on pairs to perform their conversations for the class. Have the class vote for the funniest or most original one.

2 Teaching Tip Have volunteers look at the dehydrated sentences and name elements that could trigger the subjunctive in a following clause.
Ex: **esperar, ojalá, molestarme**

1 **Completar** Completa el diálogo con palabras de la lista. Compara tus respuestas con las de un(a) compañero/a.

Bogotá, Colombia

alegro	molesta	salga
encuentren	ojalá	tengo miedo de
estén	puedan	vayan
lleguen	reduzcan	visitar

OLGA Me alegro de que Adriana y Raquel (1)___vayan___ a Colombia. ¿Van a estudiar?

SARA Sí. Es una lástima que (2)___lleguen___ una semana tarde. Ojalá que la universidad las ayude a buscar casa. (3)___Tengo miedo de___ que no consigan dónde vivir.

OLGA Me (4)___molesta___ que seas tan pesimista, pero sí, yo también espero que (5)___encuentren___ gente simpática y que hablen mucho español.

SARA Sí, ojalá. Van a hacer un estudio sobre la deforestación en las costas. Es triste que en tantos países los recursos naturales (6)___estén___ en peligro.

OLGA Pues, me (7)___alegro___ de que no se queden mucho en la capital por la contaminación. (8)___Ojalá___ tengan tiempo de viajar por el país.

SARA Sí, espero que (9)___puedan___ ir a Medellín.
Sé que también quieren (10)___visitar___ la Catedral de Sal de Zipaquirá.

NOTA CULTURAL

Los principales factores que determinan la temperatura de **Bogotá, Colombia,** son su proximidad al ecuador y su altitud, 2.640 metros (8.660 pies) sobre el nivel (*level*) del mar. Con un promedio (*average*) de 13° C (56° F), Bogotá disfruta de un clima templado (*mild*) durante la mayor parte del año. Hay, sin embargo, variaciones considerables entre el día (18° C) y la noche (7° C).

2 **Transformar** Transforma estos elementos en oraciones completas para formar un diálogo entre Juan y la madre de Raquel. Añade palabras si es necesario. Luego, con un(a) compañero/a, presenta el diálogo a la clase.

1. Juan, / esperar / (tú) escribirle / Raquel. / Ser / tu / novia. / Ojalá / no / sentirse / sola. *Juan, espero que (tú) le escribas a Raquel. Es tu novia. Ojalá (que) no se sienta sola.*

2. molestarme / (usted) decirme / lo que / tener / hacer. / Ahora / mismo / le / estar / escribiendo *Me molesta que (Ud.) me diga lo que tengo que hacer. Ahora mismo le estoy escribiendo.*

3. alegrarme / oírte / decir / eso. / Ser / terrible / estar / lejos / cuando / nadie / recordarte *Me alegro de oírte decir eso. Es terrible estar lejos cuando nadie te recuerda.*

4. señora, / ¡yo / tener / miedo de / (ella) no recordarme / mí! / Ser / triste / estar / sin / novia *Señora, ¡yo tengo miedo de que (ella) no me recuerde a mí! Es triste estar sin novia.*

5. ser / ridículo / (tú) sentirte / así. / Tú / saber / ella / querer / casarse / contigo *Es ridículo que te sientas así. Tú sabes que ella quiere casarse contigo.*

6. ridículo / o / no, / sorprenderme / (todos) preocuparse / ella / y / (nadie) acordarse de / mí *Ridículo o no, me sorprende que todos se preocupen por ella y nadie se acuerde de mí.*

TEACHING OPTIONS

Game Write each of the common verbs and expressions of emotion on slips of paper and put them in a large bag. On separate strips, write an equal number of infinitives and subject pronouns. Place these in a separate bag and divide the class into two teams. One member of each team draws a slip of paper from each bag and writes a sentence on the board using the elements on both slips. If the sentence makes sense and the grammar is correct, that team gets one point. The team with the most points at the end wins.

Pairs 👥↔👥 Have students write five sentences describing nature or the environment. Students then read their sentences to a partner who will respond to each one, expressing a feeling or hope. Ex: **Hay muchos animales que están en peligro de extinción. (Es terrible que haya muchos animales en peligro de extinción.)**

Comunicación

3 **Comentar** En parejas, túrnense para formar oraciones sobre su comunidad, sus clases, su gobierno o algún otro tema, usando expresiones como **me alegro de que**, **temo que** y **es extraño que**. Luego, reaccionen a los comentarios de su compañero/a. Answers will vary.

> **modelo**
>
> **Estudiante 1:** Me alegro de que vayan a limpiar el río.
> **Estudiante 2:** Yo también. Me preocupa que el agua del río esté tan sucia.

4 **Contestar** Lee el mensaje electrónico. Luego, en parejas, contesten el mensaje usando expresiones como **me sorprende que**, **me molesta que** y **es una lástima que**. Answers will vary.

De:	Raquel
Para:	Juan
Asunto:	¡Hola!

Hola, Juan:

Mi amor, siento no escribirte más frecuentemente. La verdad es que estoy muy ocupada todo el tiempo. No sabes cuánto me estoy divirtiendo en Colombia. Me sorprende haber podido adaptarme tan bien. Es bueno tener tanto trabajo. Aprendo mucho más aquí que en el laboratorio de la universidad. Me encanta que me den responsabilidades y que compartan sus muchos conocimientos conmigo. Ay, pero pienso mucho en ti. Qué triste es que no podamos estar juntos por tanto tiempo. Ojalá que los días pasen rápido. Bueno, querido, es todo por ahora. Escríbeme pronto.

Te quiero y te extraño mucho,

Raquel

AYUDA
Echar de menos (a alguien) and **extrañar (a alguien)** are two ways of saying *to miss (someone)*.

Síntesis

5 **No te preocupes** Estás muy preocupado/a por los problemas del medio ambiente y le comentas a tu compañero/a todas tus preocupaciones. Él/Ella va a darte la solución adecuada para tus preocupaciones. Su profesor(a) les va a dar una hoja distinta a cada uno/a con la información necesaria para completar la actividad. Answers will vary.

> **modelo**
>
> **Estudiante 1:** Me molesta que las personas tiren basura en las calles.
> **Estudiante 2:** Por eso es muy importante que los políticos hagan leyes para conservar las ciudades limpias.

---

3 Teaching Tips
- To simplify, have students divide a sheet of paper into four columns, with these headings: **Nuestra ciudad**, **Las clases**, **El gobierno**, and another subject of their choosing. Ask them to brainstorm topics or issues for each column.
- 🖿↔🖿 Have groups write statements about these issues and exchange them with another group, who will write down their reactions.

4 Expansion
↔🖿 In pairs, have students tell each other about a memorable event in their lives, such as a recent trip, birthday celebration, or exciting purchase they made. Using verbs and expressions of emotion, partners should draft an e-mail to express their reactions.

5 Teaching Tip Divide the class into pairs and distribute the handouts from the Activity Pack (Activity Pack/Supersite) that correspond to this Information Gap Activity. Give students ten minutes to complete the activity.

5 Expansion
↔🖿 Have students work in groups of three to create a public service announcement. Groups should choose one of the ecological problems they mentioned in the activity, and include the proposed solutions for that problem in their announcement.

TEACHING OPTIONS

Small Groups 🖿↔🖿 Divide the class into groups of three. Have students write three predictions about the future on separate pieces of paper and put them in a bag. Students take turns drawing predictions and reading them to the group. Each group member should respond with an appropriate expression of emotion. Ex: **Voy a ganar millones de dólares algún día. (—Me alegro de que vayas a ganar millones de dólares. —Yo también.**

¡Ojalá que a mí me pase lo mismo!
Extra Practice ↔🖿 Ask students to imagine that they are world leaders speaking at an environmental summit. Have students deliver a short speech to the class addressing one or two of the world's environmental problems and how they hope to solve them. Students should use as many verbs and expressions of emotion as possible.

Section Goals

In **Estructura 13.2**, students will learn:

- to use the subjunctive with verbs and expressions of doubt, disbelief, and denial
- common verbs and expressions of doubt, disbelief, and denial
- expressions of certainty

Instructional Resources

Supersite: Audio (Lab MP3 Files); Resources (Grammar Presentation Slides, Activity Pack, Scripts, Answer Keys); Testing Program (Quizzes)
WebSAM
Workbook
Lab Manual

Teaching Tips

- Introduce a few of the expressions of doubt, disbelief, or denial by talking about a topic familiar to the class. Ex: **Dudo que el equipo de baloncesto vaya a ganar el partido este fin de semana. Es probable que el otro equipo gane.** As you introduce each expression of doubt, disbelief, or denial, write it on the board, making sure that students understand its meaning and recognize the subjunctive verb in the subordinate clause.
- Ask volunteers to read the captions to the video stills, having them identify the phrase that triggers the subjunctive and the verb in the subjunctive.
- Add a visual aspect to this grammar presentation. Bring in articles and photos from Spanish-language tabloids. As you hold up each one, have students react, using expressions of doubt, disbelief, and denial. Ex: **Es improbable que una señora hable con extraterrestres.**

13.2 # The subjunctive with doubt, disbelief, and denial Tutorial

ANTE TODO Just as the subjunctive is required with expressions of emotion, influence, and will, it is also used with expressions of doubt, disbelief, and denial.

Main clause **Subordinate clause**

Dudan (que) su hijo les **diga** la verdad.

▶ The subjunctive is always used in a subordinate clause when there is a change of subject and the expression in the main clause implies negation or uncertainty.

No creo que puedan ir muy lejos.

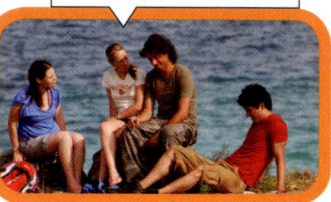

No es posible que el guía continúe el recorrido sin ustedes.

▶ Here is a list of some common expressions of doubt, disbelief, or denial.

Expressions of doubt, disbelief, or denial

dudar	*to doubt*	**no es seguro**	*it's not certain*
negar (e:ie)	*to deny*	**no es verdad**	*it's not true*
no creer	*not to believe*	**es imposible**	*it's impossible*
no estar seguro/a (de)	*not to be sure*	**es improbable**	*it's improbable*
no es cierto	*it's not true; it's not certain*	**(no) es posible**	*it's (not) possible*
		(no) es probable	*it's (not) probable*

El gobierno **niega** que el agua **esté** contaminada.
The government denies that the water is contaminated.

Dudo que el gobierno **resuelva** el problema.
I doubt that the government will solve the problem.

Es probable que **haya** menos bosques y selvas en el futuro.
It's probable that there will be fewer forests and jungles in the future.

No es verdad que mi hermano **estudie** ecología.
It's not true that my brother studies ecology.

¡LENGUA VIVA!

In English, the expression *it is probable* indicates a fairly high degree of certainty. In Spanish, however, **es probable** implies uncertainty and therefore triggers the subjunctive in the subordinate clause: **Es probable que venga Elena (pero quizás no puede).**

TEACHING OPTIONS

Extra Practice Write these statements on the board. Ask students to write their reactions using a different expression of doubt, disbelief, or denial for each. **1. Muchos tipos de peces viven en el desierto. 2. El cielo se está cayendo. 3. Los carros pequeños no contaminan. 4. No hay ningún animal en peligro de extinción.** Then have students discuss their answers with a partner.

Pairs Ask students to write five absurd statements and read them aloud to a partner, who will react with an expression of doubt, disbelief, or denial. Ex: **Unos hombres verdes me visitan todos los días. (No creo que unos hombres verdes te visiten todos los días.)** Students should respond to their partner's reactions.

▶ The indicative is used in a subordinate clause when there is no doubt or uncertainty in the main clause. Here is a list of some expressions of certainty.

Expressions of certainty

no dudar	*not to doubt*	**estar seguro/a (de)**	*to be sure*
no cabe duda de	*there is no doubt*	**es cierto**	*it's true; it's certain*
no hay duda de	*there is no doubt*	**es seguro**	*it's certain*
no negar (e:ie)	*not to deny*	**es verdad**	*it's true*
creer	*to believe*	**es obvio**	*it's obvious*

No negamos que **hay** demasiados carros en las carreteras.
We don't deny that there are too many cars on the highways.

No hay duda de que el Amazonas **es** uno de los ríos más largos.
There is no doubt that the Amazon is one of the longest rivers.

Es verdad que Colombia **es** un país bonito.
It's true that Colombia is a beautiful country.

Es obvio que las ballenas **están** en peligro de extinción.
It's obvious that whales are in danger of extinction.

▶ In affirmative sentences, the verb **creer** expresses belief or certainty, so it is followed by the indicative. In negative sentences, however, when doubt is implied, **creer** is followed by the subjunctive.

Creo que **debemos** usar exclusivamente la energía solar.
I believe we should use solar energy exclusively.

No creo que **haya** vida en el planeta Marte.
I don't believe that there is life on the planet Mars.

▶ The expressions **quizás** and **tal vez** are usually followed by the subjunctive because they imply doubt about something.

Quizás haga sol mañana.
Perhaps it will be sunny tomorrow.

Tal vez veamos la luna esta noche.
Perhaps we will see the moon tonight.

¡INTÉNTALO!   Completa estas oraciones con la forma correcta del verbo.

1. Dudo que ellos <u>trabajen</u> (trabajar).
2. Es cierto que él <u>come</u> (comer) mucho.
3. Es imposible que ellos <u>salgan</u> (salir).
4. No creo que ella <u>vuelva</u> (volver).
5. No niego que ustedes <u>estudian</u> (estudiar).
6. Es posible que nosotros <u>vayamos</u> (ir).
7. Dudamos que tú <u>recicles</u> (reciclar).
8. Creo que ellos <u>juegan</u> (jugar) al fútbol.
9. Es probable que ustedes <u>ganen</u> (ganar).
10. Es posible que ella no <u>venga</u> (venir) a casa.
11. Es probable que Lucio y Carmen <u>duerman</u> (dormir).
12. Es posible que mi prima Marta <u>llame</u> (llamar).
13. No es cierto que Paco y Daniel nos <u>ayuden</u> (ayudar).
14. Tal vez Juan no nos <u>oiga</u> (oír).

More activities

vhlcentral

LM
p. 76

WB
pp. 153–154

Online activities

Teaching Tips
- Have students respond to statements that elicit expressions of doubt, disbelief, or denial and expressions of certainty. Ex: **Terminan la nueva residencia antes del próximo año. (Es seguro que la terminan antes del próximo año.) La universidad va a tener un nuevo presidente pronto. (No es verdad que la universidad vaya a tener un nuevo presidente pronto.)**
- Have students change the items in **¡Inténtalo!**, making the affirmative expressions in the main clauses negative, and the negative ones affirmative, and making all corresponding changes. Ex: **1. No dudo que ellos trabajan.**

TEACHING OPTIONS

TPR Call out a series of sentences, using either an expression of certainty or an expression of doubt, disbelief, or denial. Have students stand if they hear an expression of certainty or remain seated if they hear an expression of doubt. Ex: **Es cierto que algunos pájaros hablan.** (Students stand.)
Heritage Speakers Ask heritage speakers to jot down a few statements about things unique to their cultural communities.

Ex: **Como chiles en el desayuno.** Have the class react using expressions of doubt, disbelief, denial, or certainty. Ex: **Dudo que comas chiles en el desayuno.**
Extra Practice Ask students to write sentences about three things of which they are certain and three things they doubt or cannot believe. Have students share some of their sentences with the class.

Práctica

1 Expansion

↔ Have pairs prepare another conversation between **Raúl** and his father using expressions of doubt, disbelief, and denial, as well as expressions of certainty. This time, **Raúl** is explaining the advantages of the Internet to his reluctant father and trying to persuade him to use it. Have pairs role-play their conversations for the class.

1 Escoger Escoge las respuestas correctas para completar el diálogo. Luego dramatiza el diálogo con un(a) compañero/a.

RAÚL Ustedes dudan que yo realmente (1)_**estudie**_ (estudio/estudie). No niego que a veces me (2)_**divierto**_ (divierto/divierta) demasiado, pero no cabe duda de que (3)_**tomo**_ (tomo/tome) mis estudios en serio. Estoy seguro de que cuando me vean graduarme van a pensar de manera diferente. Creo que no (4)_**tienen**_ (tienen/tengan) razón con sus críticas.

PAPÁ Es posible que tu mamá y yo no (5)_**tengamos**_ (tenemos/tengamos) razón. Es cierto que a veces (6)_**dudamos**_ (dudamos/dudemos) de ti. Pero no hay duda de que te (7)_**pasas**_ (pasas/pases) toda la noche en Internet y oyendo música. No es nada seguro que (8)_**estés**_ (estás/estés) estudiando.

RAÚL Es verdad que (9)_**uso**_ (uso/use) mucho la computadora pero, ¡piensen! ¿No es posible que (10)_**sea**_ (es/sea) para buscar información para mis clases? ¡No hay duda de que Internet (11)_**es**_ (es/sea) el mejor recurso del mundo! Es obvio que ustedes (12)_**piensan**_ (piensan/piensen) que no hago nada, pero no es cierto.

PAPÁ No dudo que esta conversación nos (13)_**va**_ (va/vaya) a ayudar. Pero tal vez esta noche (14)_**puedas**_ (puedes/puedas) trabajar sin música. ¿Está bien?

2 Dudas Usa las expresiones entre paréntesis para expresar tus dudas sobre lo que una amiga te dice.

> **modelo**
>
> El próximo año Marta y yo vamos de vacaciones por diez meses. (dudar)
>
> *¡Ja! Dudo que vayan de vacaciones por ese tiempo. ¡Ustedes no son ricas!*

1. Estoy escribiendo una novela en español. (no creer)
   No creo que estés escribiendo una novela en español.
2. Mi tía es la directora de PETA. (no ser verdad)
   No es verdad que tu tía sea la directora de PETA.
3. Dos profesores míos juegan para los Osos (*Bears*) de Chicago. (ser imposible)
   Es imposible que dos profesores tuyos jueguen para los Osos de Chicago.
4. Yo ya tengo un doctorado (*doctorate*) en lenguas. (ser improbable)
   Es improbable que ya tengas un doctorado en lenguas.
5. Mi padre es dueño del Centro Rockefeller. (no ser posible)
   No es posible que tu padre sea dueño del Centro Rockefeller.
6. Mi mejor amiga conoce al chef Bobby Flay. (no ser cierto)
   No es cierto que tu mejor amiga conozca al chef Bobby Flay.

3 Combinar Combina elementos de las columnas para formar oraciones lógicas. **Answers will vary.**

> **modelo**
>
> *Dudo que el gobierno nacional limpie todos los ríos.*

dudo que	los ecologistas	cazar animales
es verdad que	el gobierno local	respirar aire puro
es improbable que	el gobierno nacional	proteger el medio ambiente
es posible que	los estadounidenses	desarrollar una solución
no es cierto que	todo el mundo	limpiar todos los ríos

Comunicación

4 **Entrevista** En parejas, imaginen que tienen que hacerle una entrevista a la ecologista Mary Axtmann, quien colaboró en la fundación de la organización Ciudadanos Pro Bosque San Patricio, en Puerto Rico. Escriban seis preguntas para la entrevista después de leer las declaraciones de Axtmann. Al final, inventen las respuestas de Axtmann. Answers will vary.

NOTA CULTURAL

La asociación de **Mary Axtmann** trabaja para la conservación del Bosque San Patricio. También ofrece conferencias sobre temas ambientales, hace un censo anual de pájaros y tiene un grupo de guías voluntarios. La comunidad hace todo el trabajo; la asociación no recibe ninguna ayuda del gobierno.

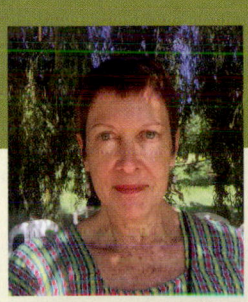

Declaraciones de Mary Axtmann:

"... que el bosque es un recurso ecológico educativo para la comunidad."

"El Bosque San Patricio es un pulmón (*lung*) que produce oxígeno para la ciudad."

"El Bosque San Patricio está en medio de la ciudad de San Juan. Por eso digo que este bosque es una esmeralda (*emerald*) en un mar de concreto."

"El bosque pertenece (*belongs*) a la comunidad."

"Nosotros salvamos este bosque mediante la propuesta (*proposal*) y no la protesta."

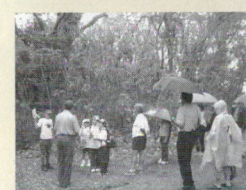

5 **Adivinar** Escribe cinco oraciones sobre tu vida presente y futura. Cuatro deben ser falsas y sólo una debe ser cierta. Presenta tus oraciones al grupo. El grupo adivina cuál es la oración cierta y expresa sus dudas sobre las oraciones falsas. Answers will vary.

AYUDA

Here are some useful verbs for talking about plans.
esperar → to hope
querer → to want
pretender → to intend
pensar → to plan
Note that **pretender** and *pretend* are false cognates. To express *to pretend*, use the verb **fingir**.

modelo
Estudiante 1: Quiero irme un año a la selva a trabajar.
Estudiante 2: Dudo que te guste vivir en la selva.
Estudiante 3: En cinco años voy a ser presidente de los Estados Unidos.
Estudiante 2: No creo que seas presidente de los Estados Unidos en cinco años. ¡Tal vez en treinta!

Síntesis

6 **Intercambiar** En grupos, escriban un párrafo sobre los problemas del medio ambiente en su estado o en su comunidad. Compartan su párrafo con otro grupo, que va a ofrecer opiniones y soluciones. Luego presenten su párrafo, con las opiniones y soluciones del otro grupo, a la clase. Answers will vary.

TEACHING OPTIONS

Small Groups In groups of three, have students pretend they are filming a live newscast on a local news station. Give each group a breaking news story and have one student play the reporter that interviews the other two about what is happening. The interviewees should use the expressions from the lesson when responding to the reporter's questions. Possible news stories: protest in favor of animal rights, a volcano about to erupt, a local ecological problem.
Game Divide the class into two teams. Team A writes sentences with expressions of certainty, while team B writes sentences with expressions of doubt, disbelief, or denial. Put all the sentences in a hat. Each team takes turns drawing sentences and stating the opposite of what the sentence says. The team with the most correct sentences at the end wins.

4 Teaching Tip Before starting, have the class brainstorm different topics that might be discussed with Mary Axtmann.

4 Expansion Ask pairs to role-play their interviews for the class.

5 Teaching Tip Tell groups to choose a secretary, who will write down the group members' true statements and present them to the class.

6 Teaching Tip Assign students to groups of four. Ask group members to appoint a mediator to lead the discussion, a secretary to write the paragraph, a proofreader to check what was written, and a stenographer to take notes on the opinions and solutions of the other group.

6 Expansion Have students create a poster illustrating the environmental problems in their community and proposing possible solutions.

13.3 The subjunctive with conjunctions Tutorial

ANTE TODO Conjunctions are words or phrases that connect other words and clauses in sentences. Certain conjunctions commonly introduce adverbial clauses, which describe *how, why, when,* and *where* an action takes place.

Main clause	Conjunction	Adverbial clause
Vamos a visitar a Carlos	**antes de que**	**regrese** a California.

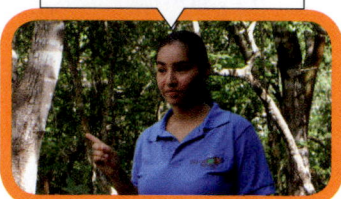

Muchos animales van a estar en peligro de extinción, a menos que los protejamos.

Marissa habla con Jimena antes de que lleguen los chicos.

▶ With certain conjunctions, the subjunctive is used to express a hypothetical situation, uncertainty as to whether an action or event will take place, or a condition that may or may not be fulfilled.

Voy a dejar un recado **en caso de que Gustavo me llame.**
I'm going to leave a message in case Gustavo calls me.

Voy al supermercado **para que tengas** algo de comer.
I'm going to the store so that you'll have something to eat.

▶ Here is a list of the conjunctions that always require the subjunctive.

Conjunctions that require the subjunctive

a menos que	*unless*	**en caso (de) que**	*in case (that)*
antes (de) que	*before*	**para que**	*so that*
con tal (de) que	*provided that*	**sin que**	*without*

Algunos animales van a morir **a menos que** haya leyes para protegerlos.
Some animals are going to die unless there are laws to protect them.

Ellos nos llevan a la selva **para que** veamos las plantas tropicales.
They are taking us to the jungle so that we may see the tropical plants.

▶ The infinitive, not **que** + [*subjunctive*], is used after the prepositions **antes de, para,** and **sin** when there is no change of subject. **¡Atención!** While you may use a present participle with the English equivalent of these phrases, in Spanish you cannot.

Te llamamos **antes de salir** de la casa.
We will call you before leaving the house.

Te llamamos mañana **antes de que salgas.**
We will call you tomorrow before you leave.

Conjunctions with subjunctive or indicative

Voy a formar un club de ecología tan pronto como vuelva al D.F.

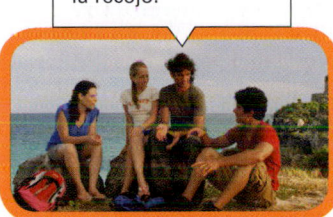

Cuando veo basura, la recojo.

Conjunctions used with subjunctive or indicative

cuando	*when*	**hasta que**	*until*
después de que	*after*	**tan pronto como**	*as soon as*
en cuanto	*as soon as*		

▶ With the conjunctions above, use the subjunctive in the subordinate clause if the main clause expresses a future action or command.

Vamos a resolver el problema **cuando desarrollemos** nuevas tecnologías.
We are going to solve the problem when we develop new technologies.

Después de que ustedes **tomen** sus refrescos, reciclen las botellas.
After you drink your soft drinks, recycle the bottles.

▶ With these conjunctions, the indicative is used in the subordinate clause if the verb in the main clause expresses an action that habitually happens, or that happened in the past.

Contaminan los ríos **cuando construyen** nuevos edificios.
They pollute the rivers when they build new buildings.

Contaminaron el río **cuando construyeron** ese edificio.
They polluted the river when they built that building.

 ¡INTÉNTALO!   Completa las oraciones con las formas correctas de los verbos.

1. Voy a estudiar ecología cuando ___vuelva___ (volver) a la universidad.
2. No podemos evitar el cambio climático, a menos que todos ___trabajemos___ (trabajar) juntos.
3. No podemos conducir sin ___contaminar___ (contaminar) el aire.
4. La gente recicla con tal de que no ___sea___ (ser) difícil.
5. Elisa habló con el presidente del Club de Ecología después de que ___terminó___ (terminar) la reunión.
6. Siempre recogemos mucha basura cuando ___vamos___ (ir) al parque.
7. La contaminación va a ser un problema muy serio hasta que nosotros ___cambiemos___ (cambiar) nuestros sistemas de producción y transporte.
8. El gobierno debe crear más parques nacionales antes de que los bosques y ríos ___estén___ (estar) completamente contaminados.
9. Vamos de excursión para ___observar___ (observar) los animales y las plantas.

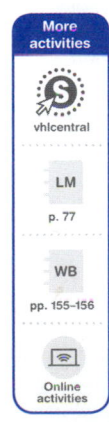

More activities

vhlcentral

LM
p. 77

WB
pp. 155–156

Online activities

Teaching Tips
• Write sentences that use **antes de** and **para** and ask volunteers to rewrite them so that they end with subordinate clauses instead of a preposition and an infinitive. Ex: **Voy a hablar con Paula antes de ir a clase.** (… **antes de que ella vaya a clase;** … **antes de que Sergio le hable;** … **antes de que ella compre esas botas.**)
• As students complete the **¡Inténtalo!** activity, have them circle the conjunctions that always require the subjunctive.

TEACHING OPTIONS

TPR Have students write **I** for **infinitivo** on one piece of paper and **S** for **subjuntivo** on another. Make several statements, some with prepositions followed by the infinitive and some with conjunctions followed by the subjunctive. Students should hold up the paper that represents what they heard. Ex: **Juan habla despacio para que todos lo entiendan. (S) No necesitan un carro para ir a la universidad. (I)**

Extra Practice Have students use these prepositions and conjunctions to make statements about the environment: **para, para que, sin, sin que, antes de,** and **antes de que.** Ex: **Es importante empezar un programa de reciclaje antes de que tengamos demasiada basura. No es posible conservar los bosques sin que se deje de cortar tantos árboles....**

Práctica

1 **Completar** Completa las oraciones con la forma correcta de cada verbo.

1. Voy a llevar a mis hijos al parque para que ___aprendan___ (aprender) sobre la naturaleza.
2. Voy a pasar todo el día allí a menos que ___haga___ (hacer) mucho frío.
3. Podemos explorar el parque en bicicleta sin ___caminar___ (caminar) demasiado.
4. Siempre llevamos al perro cuando ___vamos___ (ir) al parque.
5. No pensamos ir muy lejos en caso de que ___llueva___ (llover).
6. Vamos a bajar al cráter con tal de que no se ___prohíba___ (prohibir).
7. Vamos a almorzar a la orilla (*shore*) del río cuando nosotros ___terminemos___ (terminar) de preparar la comida.
8. Mis hijos van a dejar todo limpio antes de ___salir___ (salir) del parque.

2 **Frases** Completa estas frases de una manera lógica. *Answers will vary.*

1. No podemos controlar la contaminación del aire a menos que…
2. Voy a reciclar los productos de papel y de vidrio en cuanto…
3. Debemos comprar coches eléctricos tan pronto como…
4. Protegemos los animales en peligro de extinción para que…
5. Mis amigos y yo vamos a recoger la basura de la universidad después de que…
6. No podemos desarrollar nuevas fuentes (*sources*) de energía sin…
7. Hay que eliminar la contaminación del agua para…
8. No podemos proteger la naturaleza sin que…

3 **Organizaciones colombianas** En parejas, lean las descripciones de las organizaciones de conservación. Luego expresen en sus propias (*own*) palabras las opiniones de cada organización. *Answers will vary.*

Organización:
Fundación Río Orinoco

Problema:
La destrucción de los ríos

Solución:
Programa para limpiar las orillas de los ríos y reducir la erosión y así proteger los ríos

Organización:
Oficina de Turismo Internacional

Problema:
Necesidad de mejorar la imagen del país en el mercado turístico internacional

Solución:
Plan para promover el ecoturismo en los 54 parques nacionales, usando agencias de publicidad e implementando un plan agresivo de conservación

Organización:
Asociación Nabusimake-Pico Colón

Problema:
Un lugar turístico popular en la Sierra Nevada de Santa Marta necesita mejor mantenimiento

Solución:
Programa de voluntarios para limpiar y mejorar los senderos

AYUDA

Here are some expressions you can use as you complete **Actividad 3**.

Se puede evitar… con tal de que…

Es necesario… para que…

Debemos prohibir… antes de que…

No es posible… sin que…

Vamos a… tan pronto como…

A menos que… no vamos a…

Handwritten margin notes: Online / In class / In class

TEACHING OPTIONS

Pairs ←👤→ Ask students to imagine that, unless some dramatic environmental actions are taken, the world as we know it will end in five days. It is their responsibility as community leaders to give a speech warning people what will happen unless everyone takes action. Have students work with a partner to prepare a three-minute presentation for the class, using as many different conjunctions that require the subjunctive as possible.

Small Groups Divide the class into groups of four. The first student begins a sentence, the second picks a conjunction, and the third student finishes the sentence. The fourth student writes the sentence down. Students should take turns playing the different roles until they have created eight sentences.

Comunicación

4 **Preguntas** En parejas, túrnense para hacerse estas preguntas. *Answers will vary.*

1. ¿Qué haces cada noche antes de acostarte?
2. ¿Qué haces después de salir de la universidad?
3. ¿Qué hace tu familia para que puedas asistir a la universidad?
4. ¿Qué piensas hacer tan pronto como te gradúes?
5. ¿Qué quieres hacer mañana, a menos que haga mal tiempo?
6. ¿Qué haces en tus clases sin que los profesores lo sepan?

5 **Comparar** En parejas, comparen una actividad rutinaria que ustedes hacen con algo que van a hacer en el futuro. *Answers will vary.*

antes de	después de que	hasta que	sin (que)
antes de que	en caso de que	para (que)	tan pronto como

modelo

Estudiante 1: El sábado vamos al lago. Tan pronto como volvamos, vamos a estudiar para el examen.

Estudiante 2: Todos los sábados llevo a mi primo al parque para que juegue. Pero el sábado que viene, con tal de que no llueva, lo voy a llevar a las montañas.

Síntesis

6 **Tres en raya (Tic-Tac-Toe)** Formen dos equipos. Con el vocabulario de esta lección, una persona comienza una frase y otra persona de su equipo la termina usando palabras de la gráfica. El primer equipo que forme tres oraciones seguidas (*in a row*) gana el tres en raya. Hay que usar la conjunción o la preposición y el verbo correctamente. Si no, ¡no cuenta! *Answers will vary.*

¡LENGUA VIVA!

Tic-Tac-Toe has various names in the Spanish-speaking world, including **tres en raya, tres en línea, ta-te-ti, gato, la vieja,** and **triqui-triqui.**

modelo

Equipo 1
Estudiante 1: Dudo que podamos eliminar la deforestación…
Estudiante 2: sin que nos ayude el gobierno.
Equipo 2
Estudiante 1: Creo que podemos conservar nuestros recursos naturales…
Estudiante 2: con tal de que todos hagamos algo para ayudar.

cuando	con tal de que	para que
antes de que	para	sin que
hasta que	en caso de que	antes de

4 Expansion When pairs have finished asking and answering the questions, work with the whole class, asking several individuals each of the questions and asking other students to react to their responses. Ex: ____ hace ejercicios aeróbicos antes de acostarse. ¿Quién más hace ejercicio? ¡Uf! Hacer ejercicio a esa hora me parece excesivo. ¿Quiénes ven la tele? ¿Nadie lee un libro antes de acostarse?

5 Teaching Tip Have partners compare the routines of other people they know and what they are going to do in the future. Have them do the same with celebrities, making guesses about their routines.

6 Teaching Tips
• Have groups prepare *Tic-Tac-Toe* cards like the one shown in the activity.
• Regroup the students to do a second round of *Tic-Tac-Toe*.

TEACHING OPTIONS

Heritage Speakers Ask heritage speakers if they played *Tic-Tac-Toe* when growing up. What did they call it? Have them look at the names listed in **¡Lengua viva!** to see if any are familiar. Ask them the names of other childhood games they played and to describe them. Are the games similar to those played by other students in the class?

Pairs Ask partners to interview each other about what they must do today for their future goals to become a reality. Students should state what their goals are, the necessary conditions to achieve them, and talk about obstacles they may encounter. Students should use as many conjunctions as possible in their interviews. Have pairs present their interviews to the class.

Recapitulación

Completa estas actividades para repasar los conceptos de gramática que aprendiste en esta lección.

1 **Subjuntivo con conjunciones** Escoge la forma correcta del verbo para completar las oraciones. `16 pts.`

1. En cuanto (empiecen/empiezan) las vacaciones, vamos a viajar.
2. Por favor, llámeme a las siete y media en caso de que no (me despierto/me despierte).
3. Toni va a usar su bicicleta hasta que los coches híbridos (cuesten/cuestan) menos dinero.
4. Tan pronto como supe la noticia (*news*) (te llamé/te llame).
5. Debemos conservar el agua antes de que no (queda/quede) nada para beber.
6. ¿Siempre recoges la basura después de que (terminas/termines) de comer en un picnic?
7. Siempre quiero vender mi camioneta (*SUV*) cuando (*yo*) (piense/pienso) en la contaminación.
8. Estudiantes, pueden entrar al parque natural con tal de que no (tocan/toquen) las plantas.

2 **Creer o no creer** Completa estos diálogos con la forma correcta del presente de indicativo o de subjuntivo, según el contexto. `16 pts.`

CAROLA Creo que (1) _debemos_ (nosotras, deber) escribir nuestra presentación sobre el reciclaje.

MÓNICA Hmm, no estoy segura de que el reciclaje (2) _sea_ (ser) un buen tema. No hay duda de que la gente ya (3) _sabe_ (saber) reciclar.

CAROLA Sí, pero dudo que todos lo (4) _practiquen_ (practicar).

• • •

PACO ¿Sabes, Néstor? El sábado voy a ir a limpiar el río con un grupo de voluntarios. ¿Quieres venir?

NÉSTOR No es seguro que (5) _pueda_ (yo, poder) ir. El lunes hay un examen y tengo que estudiar.

PACO ¿Estás seguro de que no (6) _tienes_ (tener) tiempo? Es imposible que (7) _vayas_ (ir) a estudiar todo el fin de semana.

NÉSTOR Pues sí, pero es muy probable que (8) _llueva_ (llover).

RESUMEN GRAMATICAL

13.1 The subjunctive with verbs of emotion
pp. 452–453

Verbs and expressions of emotion	
alegrarse (de)	tener miedo (de)
esperar	es extraño
gustar	es una lástima
molestar	es ridículo
sentir (e:ie)	es terrible
sorprender	es triste
temer	ojalá (que)

Main clause		Subordinate clause
Marta **espera** Ojalá	**que**	yo **vaya** al lago mañana. **comamos** en casa.

13.2 The subjunctive with doubt, disbelief, and denial
pp. 456–457

Expressions of doubt, disbelief, or denial (used with subjunctive)	
dudar	no es verdad
negar (e:ie)	es imposible
no creer	es improbable
no estar seguro/a (de)	(no) es posible
no es cierto	(no) es probable
no es seguro	

Expressions of certainty (used with indicative)	
no dudar	estar seguro/a (de)
no cabe duda de	es cierto
no hay duda de	es seguro
no negar (e:ie)	es verdad
creer	es obvio

► The infinitive is used after these expressions when there is no change of subject.

13.3 The subjunctive with conjunctions
pp. 460–461

Conjunctions that require the subjunctive	
a menos que	en caso (de) que
antes (de) que	para que
con tal (de) que	sin que

> ► The infinitive is used after the prepositions **antes de**, **para**, and **sin** when there is no change of subject.
>
> Te llamamos **antes de salir** de casa.
>
> Te llamamos mañana **antes de que salgas**.

Conjunctions used with subjunctive or indicative	
cuando	hasta que
después de que	tan pronto como
en cuanto	

3 **Reacciones** Reacciona a estas oraciones según las pistas (*clues*). Sigue el modelo. **20 pts.**

modelo

Tú casi nunca reciclas nada.

(yo, molestar)

A mí me molesta que tú casi nunca recicles nada.

1. La Ciudad de México tiene un problema grave de contaminación. (ser una lástima)
   Es una lástima que la Ciudad de México tenga un problema grave de contaminación.
2. En ese safari permiten tocar a los animales. (ser extraño)
   Es extraño que en ese safari permitan tocar a los animales.
3. Julia y Víctor no pueden ir a las montañas. (yo, sentir)
   Yo siento que Julia y Víctor no puedan ir a las montañas.
4. El nuevo programa de reciclaje es un éxito. (nosotros, esperar)
   Nosotros esperamos que el nuevo programa de reciclaje sea un éxito.
5. A María no le gustan los perros. (ser una lástima)
   Es una lástima que a María no le gusten los perros.
6. Existen leyes ecológicas en este país. (Juan, alegrarse de)
   Juan se alegra de que existan leyes ecológicas en este país.
7. El gobierno no busca soluciones. (ellos, temer)
   Ellos temen que el gobierno no busque soluciones.
8. La mayoría de la población no cuida el medio ambiente. (ser triste)
   Es triste que la mayoría de la población no cuide el medio ambiente.
9. Muchas personas cazan animales en esta región. (yo, sorprender)
   A mí me sorprende que muchas personas cacen animales en esta región.
10. La situación mejora día a día. (ojalá que) Ojalá que la situación mejore día a día.

4 **Oraciones** Forma oraciones con estos elementos. Usa el subjuntivo cuando sea necesario. **10 pts.**

1. ser ridículo / los coches / contaminar tanto Es ridículo que los coches contaminen tanto.
2. no caber duda de / tú y yo / poder / hacer mucho más No cabe duda de que tú y yo podemos hacer mucho más.
3. los ecologistas / temer / no conservarse / los recursos naturales Los ecologistas temen que no se conserven los recursos naturales.
4. yo / alegrarse de / en mi ciudad / reciclarse / el plástico, el vidrio y el aluminio Yo me alegro de que en mi ciudad se reciclen el plástico, el vidrio y el aluminio.
5. todos (nosotros) / ir a respirar / mejor / cuando / (nosotros) llegar / a la montaña Todos vamos a respirar mejor cuando lleguemos a la montaña.

5 **Escribir** Escribe un diálogo de al menos siete oraciones en el que un(a) amigo/a hace comentarios pesimistas sobre la situación del medio ambiente en tu región y tú respondes con comentarios optimistas. Usa verbos y expresiones de esta lección. **38 pts.** Answers will vary.

6 **Canción** Completa estos versos de una canción de Juan Luis Guerra. **¡4 puntos EXTRA!**

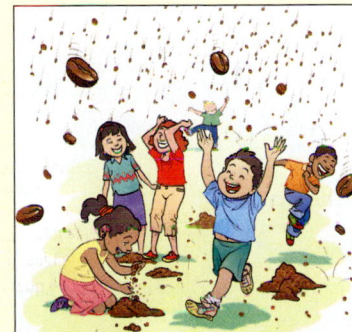

" Ojalá que ___llueva___ (llover) café en el campo.

Pa'° que todos los niños ___canten___ (cantar) en el campo. "

Pa' *short for* Para

3 **Teaching Tip** Have a volunteer read the model aloud. Remind students that an indirect object pronoun is used with verbs like **molestar**.

3 **Expansion**
- To challenge students, have them rewrite each item, using other verbs or expressions of emotion.
- Give students these sentences as items 11–12:
  11. No hay un programa de reciclaje en la universidad. (ser ridículo) (Es ridículo que no haya un programa de reciclaje en la universidad.)
  12. Los voluntarios trabajan para limpiar el río. (yo, gustar) (A mí me gusta que los voluntarios trabajen para limpiar el río.)

4 **Expansion** Ask students to create three additional dehydrated sentences. Then have them exchange papers with a partner and hydrate each other's sentences.

5 **Teaching Tip** Remind students that, with the exception of **ojalá**, the word **que** must be present and there must be a change of subject in order to use the subjunctive.

6 **Expansion** Have students create their own song verse by replacing **llueva café** and **canten** with other verbs in the subjunctive. Ex: **nieve helado** and **bailen**

TEACHING OPTIONS

Game Have students make *Bingo* cards of different verbs, expressions, and conjunctions that require the subjunctive. Read aloud sentences using the subjunctive. If students have the verb, expression, or phrase on their card, they should cover the space. The first student to complete a horizontal, vertical, or diagonal row is the winner.

Pairs Ask students to write down two true sentences and two false ones. Encourage them to write sentences that are all very likely. In pairs, have students take turns reading their sentences. Their partner should react, using expressions of doubt, disbelief, denial, or certainty. The student who stumps his or her partner with all four statements wins. Have pairs share their most challenging sentences with the class.

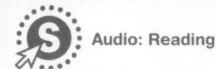

Section Goals

In **Lectura**, students will:
- learn that recognizing the purpose of a text can help them understand it
- read two fables

Instructional Resource
Supersite

Estrategia Tell students that recognizing the writer's purpose will help them comprehend an unfamiliar text.

Examinar los textos Have students scan the texts, using the reading strategies they have learned to determine the authors' purposes. Then have them work with a partner to answer the questions. Students should recognize that the texts are fables because the characters are animals.

Predicciones
- Tell pairs that where their predictions differ they should refer back to the texts for resolution.
- Give students these additional predictions: **5. Los textos son infantiles. 6. Se trata de una historia romántica.**

Determinar el propósito
- Tell students to take notes about the characters as they read. Remind students that they should be able to retell the stories in their own words.
- ← ♦ → Ask students who generally reads fables. Ex: **Por lo general, ¿las fábulas se escriben para niños, adultos o ambos?** Then have them write a few sentences explaining their answer.

Lectura

Antes de leer

 NATIONAL STANDARDS / communication cultures

Estrategia
Recognizing the purpose of a text

When you are faced with an unfamiliar text, it is important to determine the writer's purpose. If you are reading an editorial in a newspaper, for example, you know that the journalist's objective is to persuade you of his or her point of view. Identifying the purpose of a text will help you better comprehend its meaning.

Examinar los textos
Primero, utiliza la estrategia de lectura para familiarizarte con los textos. Después, contesta estas preguntas y compara tus respuestas con las de un(a) compañero/a. Answers will vary.

- ¿De qué tratan los textos?°
- ¿Son fábulas°, poemas, artículos de periódico…?
- ¿Cómo lo sabes?

Predicciones
Lee estas predicciones sobre la lectura e indica si estás de acuerdo° con ellas. Después, compara tus opiniones con las de un(a) compañero/a. Answers will vary.

1. Los textos son del género° de ficción.
2. Los personajes son animales.
3. La acción de los textos tiene lugar en un zoológico.
4. Hay alguna moraleja°.

Determinar el propósito
Con un(a) compañero/a, hablen de los posibles propósitos° de los textos. Consideren estas preguntas: Answers will vary.

- ¿Qué te dice el género de los textos sobre los posibles propósitos de ellos?
- ¿Piensas que los textos pueden tener más de un propósito? ¿Por qué?

More activities

 vhlcentral / Online activities

¿De qué tratan los textos? What are the texts about? **fábulas** *fables* **estás de acuerdo** *you agree* **género** *genre* **moraleja** *moral* **propósitos** *purposes*

Sobre el autor

Félix María Samaniego (1745–1801) nació en España y escribió las *Fábulas morales* que ilustran de manera humorística el carácter humano. Los protagonistas de muchas de sus fábulas son animales que hablan.

El **perro** y el **cocodrilo**

Bebiendo un perro en el Nilo°,
al mismo tiempo corría.
"Bebe quieto°", le decía
un taimado° cocodrilo.

Díjole° el perro prudente:
"Dañoso° es beber y andar°;
pero ¿es sano el aguardar
a que me claves el diente°? "

¡Oh qué docto° perro viejo!
Yo venero° su sentir°
en esto de no seguir
del enemigo el consejo.

Nilo *Nile* **quieto** *in peace* **taimado** *sly* **Díjole** *Said to him* **Dañoso** *Harmful* **andar** *to walk* **¿es sano… diente?** *Is it good for me to wait for you to sink your teeth into me?* **docto** *wise* **venero** *revere* **sentir** *wisdom*

Sobre el autor

Tomás de Iriarte (1750–1791) nació en las islas Canarias y tuvo gran éxito° con su libro *Fábulas literarias*. Su tendencia a representar la lógica a través de° símbolos de la naturaleza fue de gran influencia para muchos autores de su época°.

El **pato**° y la **serpiente**

A orillas° de un estanque°,
diciendo estaba un pato:
"¿A qué animal dio el cielo°
los dones que me ha dado°?

"Soy de agua, tierra y aire:
cuando de andar me canso°,
si se me antoja, vuelo°;
si se me antoja, nado".

Una serpiente astuta
que le estaba escuchando,
le llamó con un silbo°,
y le dijo "¡Seo° guapo!

"No hay que echar tantas plantas°;
pues ni anda como el gamo°,
ni vuela como el sacre°,
ni nada como el barbo°;

"y así tenga sabido
que lo importante y raro°
no es entender de todo,
sino ser diestro° en algo".

éxito *success* a través de *through* época *time* pato *duck* orillas *banks* estanque *pond* cielo *heaven* los dones... dado *the gifts that it has given me* me canso *I get tired* si se... vuelo *if I feel like it, I fly* silbo *hiss* Seo *Señor* No hay... plantas *There's no reason to boast* gamo *deer* sacre *falcon* barbo *barbel (a type of fish)* raro *rare* diestro *skillful*

Después de leer

Comprensión

Escoge la mejor opción para completar cada oración.

1. El cocodrilo _____ perro.
   a. está preocupado por el   b. quiere comerse al
   c. tiene miedo del

2. El perro _____ cocodrilo.
   a. tiene miedo del   b. es amigo del
   c. quiere quedarse con el

3. El pato cree que es un animal _____.
   a. muy famoso   b. muy hermoso
   c. de muchos talentos

4. La serpiente cree que el pato es _____.
   a. muy inteligente   b. muy tonto   c. muy feo

Preguntas

Contesta las preguntas.   Answers will vary.

1. ¿Qué representa el cocodrilo?
   _____

2. ¿Qué representa el pato?
   _____

3. ¿Cuál es la moraleja (*moral*) de "El perro y el cocodrilo"?
   _____

4. ¿Cuál es la moraleja de "El pato y la serpiente"?
   _____

Coméntalo

En parejas, túrnense para hacerse estas preguntas. ¿Estás de acuerdo con las moralejas de estas fábulas? ¿Por qué? ¿Cuál de estas fábulas te gusta más? ¿Por qué? ¿Conoces otras fábulas? ¿Cuál es su propósito?   Answers will vary.

Escribir

Escribe una fábula para compartir con la clase. Puedes escoger algunos animales de la lista o escoger otros. ¿Qué características deben tener estos animales?   Answers will vary.

- una abeja (*bee*)
- un gato
- un mono
- un burro
- un perro
- una tortuga
- un águila (*eagle*)
- un pavo real (*peacock*)

Comprensión

- To simplify, before beginning the activity, call on volunteers to explain the fables in their own words using Spanish.
- Encourage students to justify their answers by citing the text.

Preguntas
For items 1 and 2, have the class brainstorm a list of adjectives to describe each animal.

Coméntalo
For additional class discussion, have students imagine they must rewrite fables with the same morals, but using other animals as the protagonists. Ask students: **¿Qué animales escogen para sustituir a estos animales? ¿Cómo cambia la historia?**

Escribir
- Before writing, encourage students to outline their fables. Have them include the characters, the setting, the basic plot, and the moral in their outlines.
- If needed, supply additional vocabulary for students to describe the animals' characteristics. Ex: **sabio, perezoso, terco, fiel, lento, inquieto, orgulloso, egoísta, (im)paciente**

TEACHING OPTIONS

Extra Practice To challenge students, have them write a story from the viewpoint of the dog, the crocodile, the duck, or the snake, in which they explain their encounter with another animal and what they learned from the experience. You may want to review the imperfect and preterite tenses before assigning this activity.

Small Groups If time and resources permit, bring in other fables in Spanish, such as **Samaniego's** *El herrero y el perro* or *La abeja haragana* by **Horacio Quiroga**. Have students work in small groups to read and analyze one fable in terms of its characters and moral. Then have volunteers summarize their analyses for the class.

Escritura

Estrategia
Considering audience and purpose

Writing always has a specific purpose. During the planning stages, a writer must determine to whom he or she is addressing the piece, and what he or she wants to express to the reader. Once you have defined both your audience and your purpose, you will be able to decide which genre, vocabulary, and grammatical structures will best serve your literary composition.

Let's say you want to share your thoughts on local traffic problems. Your audience can be either the local government or the community. You could choose to write a news article, a letter to the editor, or a letter to the city's governing board. But first you should ask yourself these questions:

1. Are you going to comment on traffic problems in general, or are you going to point out several specific problems?

2. Are you simply intending to register a complaint?

3. Are you simply intending to inform others and increase public awareness of the problems?

4. Are you hoping to persuade others to adopt your point of view?

5. Are you hoping to inspire others to take concrete actions?

The answers to these questions will help you establish the purpose of your writing and determine your audience. Of course, your writing can have more than one purpose. For example, you may intend for your writing to both inform others of a problem and inspire them to take action.

Tema
Escribir una carta o un artículo

Escoge uno de estos temas. Luego decide si vas a escribir una carta a un(a) amigo/a, una carta a un periódico, un artículo de periódico o de revista, etc.

1. Escribe sobre los programas que existen para proteger la naturaleza en tu comunidad. ¿Funcionan bien? ¿Participan todos los vecinos de tu comunidad en los programas? ¿Tienes dudas sobre la eficacia° de estos programas?

2. Describe uno de los atractivos naturales de tu región. ¿Te sientes optimista sobre el futuro del medio ambiente en tu región? ¿Qué están haciendo el gobierno y los ciudadanos° de tu región para proteger la naturaleza? ¿Es necesario hacer más?

3. Escribe sobre algún programa para la protección del medio ambiente a nivel° nacional. ¿Es un programa del gobierno o de una empresa° privada°? ¿Cómo funciona? ¿Quiénes participan? ¿Tienes dudas sobre el programa? ¿Crees que debe cambiarse o mejorarse? ¿Cómo?

eficacia *effectiveness* ciudadanos *citizens* nivel *level* empresa *company* privada *private*

EVALUATION: Una carta o un artículo

Criteria	Scale
Content	1 2 3 4
Organization	1 2 3 4
Use of vocabulary	1 2 3 4
Accuracy and mechanics	1 2 3 4
Creativity	1 2 3 4

Scoring	
Excellent	18–20 points
Good	14–17 points
Satisfactory	10–13 points
Unsatisfactory	< 10 points

Escuchar
Antes de escuchar

Estrategia
**Using background knowledge/
Guessing meaning from context**

Listening for the general idea, or gist, can help you follow what someone is saying even if you can't hear or understand some of the words. When you listen for the gist, you simply try to capture the essence of what you hear without focusing on individual words.

To practice these strategies, you will listen to a paragraph written by Jaime Urbinas, an urban planner. Before listening to the paragraph, write down what you think it will be about, based on Jaime Urbinas' profession. As you listen to the paragraph, jot down any words or expressions you don't know and use context clues to guess their meanings.

Preparación

Mira el dibujo. ¿Qué pistas (*clues*) te da sobre el tema del discurso (*speech*) de Soledad Morales? **Answers will vary.**

Ahora escucha

Discurso

Vas a escuchar un discurso de Soledad Morales, una activista preocupada por el medio ambiente. Antes de escuchar, indica las palabras y frases que tú crees que ella va a usar en su discurso. Después, indica las palabras y frases que escuchaste.

Palabras	Antes de escuchar	Después de escuchar
el futuro	_____	✔
el cine	_____	_____
los recursos naturales	_____	✔
el aire	_____	✔
los ríos	_____	✔
la contaminación	_____	✔
el reciclaje	_____	_____
las diversiones	_____	_____

¡PROTEJAMOS LA TIERRA!

Nuestro patrimonio

Comprensión

Escoger

Indica el equivalente correcto de cada palabra.
1. patrimonio (fatherland, heritage, acrimony)   heritage
2. ancianos (elderly, ancient, antiques)   elderly
3. entrelazadas (destined, interrupted, intertwined)   intertwined
4. aguantar (to hold back, to destroy, to pollute)   to hold back
5. apreciar (to value, to imitate, to consider)   to value
6. tala (planting, cutting, watering)   cutting

Ahora ustedes

Trabaja con un(a) compañero/a. Escriban seis recomendaciones que creen que la señora Morales va a darle al gobierno colombiano para mejorar los problemas del medio ambiente.   **Answers will vary.**

1. _____
2. _____
3. _____
4. _____
5. _____
6. _____

problema grave… hoy día, cuando llueve, el río Cauca se llena de tierra porque no hay árboles que aguanten la tierra. La contaminación del río está afectando gravemente la ecología de las playas de Barranquilla, una de nuestras joyas.

Ojalá que me oigan y piensen bien en el futuro de nuestra comunidad. Espero que aprendamos a conservar la naturaleza y que podamos cuidar el patrimonio de nuestros hijos.

Section Goals
In **Escuchar**, students will:
• use background knowledge and context to guess the meaning of unknown words
• listen to a short speech

Instructional Resources
Supersite: Audio (Textbook MP3s); Resources (Scripts)

Estrategia
Script Es necesario que las casas del futuro sean construidas en barrios que tengan todos los recursos esenciales para la vida cotidiana: tiendas, centros comerciales, cines, restaurantes y parques, por ejemplo. El medio ambiente ya no soporta tantas autopistas llenas de coches y, por lo tanto, es importante que la gente pueda caminar para ir de compras o para ir a divertirse. Recomiendo que vivamos en casas con jardines compartidos para usar menos espacio y, más importante, para que los vecinos se conozcan.

Teaching Tip Have students look at the drawing and guess what it depicts.

Ahora escucha
Script Les vengo a hablar hoy porque aunque espero que el futuro sea color de rosa, temo que no sea así. Vivimos en esta tierra de preciosos recursos naturales —nuestros ríos de los cuales dependemos para el agua que nos da vida, el aire que respiramos, los árboles que nos protegen, los animales cuyas vidas están entrelazadas con nuestras vidas. Es una lástima que no apreciemos lo mucho que tenemos.
Es terrible que haya días con tanta contaminación del aire que nuestros ancianos se enferman y nuestros hijos no pueden respirar. La tala de árboles es un

(Script continues at far left in the bottom panels.)

En pantalla Video

¿Viste alguna vez de cerca un pozo termal° como los que hay en Costa Rica, Perú o España? ¿Y los géiseres? ¿Sabes de dónde provienen y por qué las aguas termales se consideran beneficiosas para la salud y el bienestar? Imagina poder climatizar tu hogar y obtener agua caliente sanitaria ecológicamente usando la misma fuente° de energía: el calor natural del subsuelo°. Hay quienes creen que el uso de la energía geotérmica no sólo contribuye a solucionar los problemas del medio ambiente, sino que resulta en ahorros significativos para llevar una vida moderna.

Vocabulario útil

calefacción	*heating*
dañino	*harmful*
geotérmica	*geothermal*
madalena	*cupcake*

Preparación

¿Qué tipos de energía conoces? ¿Cuáles son más limpios? ¿Cuáles son renovables? Answers will vary.

Elegir

Selecciona las expresiones que se relacionan con la energía geotérmica.

- (a.) recurso natural
- b. contaminante
- c. peligrosa
- (d.) en el interior de la tierra
- e. dulce
- (f.) ecológica
- g. afuera de la tierra
- (h.) limpia

Anuncio

¿De qué otras formas creativas se puede explicar el mismo concepto? En parejas, escriban su propio anuncio que promueva la energía geotérmica. Utilicen el subjuntivo. Answers will vary.

pozo termal *hot springs* **fuente** *source* **subsuelo** *subsoil* **te gustaría que tuviera** *you would like it if it had*

Anuncio de IDAE

¿Qué es la energía geotérmica?

Pero te gustaría que tuviera° chocolate, ¿no?

Hay reservas de energía en el interior de la madalena.

vhlcentral / Online activities

communication cultures NATIONAL STANDARDS

Video

Centroamérica es una región con un gran crecimiento° en el turismo, especialmente ecológico, y no por pocas razones°. Con solamente el uno por ciento° de la superficie terrestre°, esta zona tiene el ocho por ciento de las reservas naturales del planeta. Algunas de estas maravillas son la isla Coiba en Panamá, la Reserva de la Biosfera Maya en Guatemala, el volcán Mombacho en Nicaragua, el parque El Imposible en El Salvador y Pico Bonito en Honduras. En este episodio de *Flash cultura* vas a conocer más tesoros° naturales en un país ecológico por tradición: Costa Rica.

Vocabulario útil

aguas termales	hot springs
hace erupción	erupts
los poderes curativos	healing powers
rocas incandescentes	incandescent rocks

Preparación

¿Qué sabes de los volcanes de Costa Rica? ¿Y de sus aguas termales? Si no sabes nada, escribe tres predicciones sobre cada tema. Answers will vary.

¿Cierto o falso?

Indica si estas oraciones son **ciertas** o **falsas**.

1. Centroamérica es una zona de pocos volcanes.
   Falso.
2. El volcán Arenal está en un parque nacional.
   Cierto.
3. El volcán Arenal hace erupción pocas veces.
   Falso.
4. Las aguas termales cerca del volcán vienen del mar.
   Falso.
5. Cuando Alberto sale del agua, tiene calor.
   Falso.
6. Se pueden ver las rocas incandescentes desde algunos hoteles.
   Cierto.

crecimiento *growth* razones *reasons* por ciento *percent*
superficie terrestre *earth's surface* tesoros *treasures* rugido *roar*

Naturaleza en Costa Rica

Aquí existen más de cien volcanes. Hoy visitaremos el Parque Nacional Volcán Arenal.

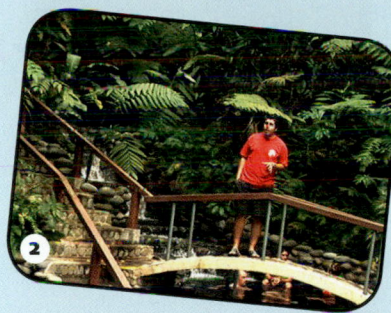

En los alrededores del volcán [...] nacen aguas termales de origen volcánico...

Puedes escuchar cada rugido° del volcán Arenal...

More activities
vhlcentral   VM pp. 61–62   Online activities

Section Goal

In **Panorama**, students will read about the geography, history, and culture of Colombia.

Instructional Resources
Supersite: Video (*Panorama cultural*); Resources (Scripts, Translations, Digital Image Bank, Answer Keys)
WebSAM
Workbook

Teaching Tips
• Use the **Lección 13 Panorama** digital images to assist with this presentation.
• Have students look at the map of Colombia and talk about the physical features of the country. Point out the three parallel ranges of the Andes in the west. After students look at the call-out photos and read the captions, point out that there are no major cities in the eastern half of the country. Ask students to suggest reasons for the lack of population in that area.

El país en cifras After reading the **Población** section, ask students what the impact might be of having 55% of the nation's territory unpopulated, and the sort of problems this might create for a national government. Point out that, although Spanish is the official language, some indigenous peoples speak **chibcha** and **araucano**.

Colombia

connections cultures NATIONAL STANDARDS

El país en cifras

▶ **Área:** 1.138.910 km² (439.734 millas²), *tres veces el área de Montana*

▶ **Población:** 47.698.000

De todos los países de habla hispana, sólo México tiene más habitantes que Colombia. Casi toda la población colombiana vive en las áreas montañosas y la costa occidental° del país. Aproximadamente el 55% de la superficie° del país está sin poblar°.

▶ **Capital:** Bogotá—9.765.000

▶ **Ciudades principales:** Medellín—3.911.000, Cali—2.646.000, Barranquilla—1.991.000, Cartagena—1.092.000

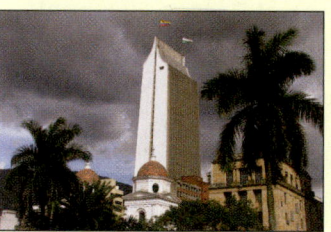
Medellín

▶ **Moneda:** peso colombiano

▶ **Idiomas:** español (oficial); lenguas indígenas, criollas y gitanas

Bandera de Colombia

Colombianos célebres

▶ **Edgar Negret,** escultor°, pintor (1920–2012)
▶ **Juan Pablo Montoya,** automovilista (1975–)
▶ **Fernando Botero,** pintor, escultor (1932–)
▶ **Shakira,** cantante (1977–)
▶ **Sofía Vergara,** actriz (1972–)

occidental *western* superficie *surface* sin poblar *unpopulated*
escultor *sculptor*

Palacio de San Francisco, Bogotá

Desfile en Cartagena

Barranquilla
Cartagena
Mar Caribe
PANAMÁ
Sierra Nevada de Santa Marta
VENEZUELA

ESTADOS UNIDOS
OCÉANO ATLÁNTICO
COLOMBIA
OCÉANO PACÍFICO
AMÉRICA DEL SUR

Cordillera Occidental de los Andes
Cordillera Central de los Andes
Río Magdalena
Medellín
Río Meta
Cali
Volcán Nevado del Huila
Bogotá
Cordillera Oriental de los Andes
Océano Pacífico

Feria de Cali

ECUADOR

PERÚ

More activities
vhlcentral | WB pp. 157–158 | Online activities

ACTIVIDADES

1 ¿Cierto o falso? Indica si lo que dicen las oraciones es **cierto** o **falso.**

1. Colombia tiene la población más grande de todos los países de habla hispana. falso

2. En Colombia sólo se habla español. falso

3. Fernando Botero es un famoso pintor colombiano. cierto

4. Juan Pablo Montoya es ecologista. falso

5. El río Magdalena pasa por Colombia. cierto

6. El Museo del Oro fue fundado en el año 1533. falso

7. El libro más conocido de Gabriel García Márquez es *Cien años de soledad.* cierto

8. Se conservan muchos edificios de la época colonial en Cartagena de Indias. cie[rto]

9. El evento más importante del Carnaval de Barranquilla es la Batalla de Flores. cie[rto]

10. La leyenda de El Dorado nació en la laguna de Guatavita. cierto

---

TEACHING OPTIONS

La música One of Colombia's contributions to Latin popular music is the dance called the **cumbia**. The **cumbia** was born out of the fusion of musical elements contributed by each of Colombia's three main ethnic groups: indigenous Andeans, Africans, and Europeans. According to ethnomusicologists, the flutes and wind instruments characteristically used in the **cumbia** derive from indigenous Andean music, the rhythms have their origin in African music, and the melodies are shaped by popular Spanish melodies. **Cumbias** are popular outside of Colombia, particularly in Mexico. Another Colombian dance, native to the Caribbean coast, is the **vallenato**, a fusion of African and European elements. If possible, bring in examples of **cumbias** and **vallenatos** for the class to listen to and compare and contrast.

▷ Lugares • El Museo del Oro

El famoso Museo del Oro del Banco de la República fue fundado° en Bogotá en 1939 para preservar las piezas de orfebrería° de la época precolombina. Tiene más de 30.000 piezas de oro y otros materiales; en él se pueden ver joyas°, ornamentos religiosos y figuras que representaban ídolos. El cuidado con el que se hicieron los objetos de oro refleja la creencia° de las tribus indígenas de que el oro era la expresión física de la energía creadora° de los dioses°.

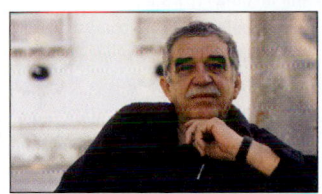

Literatura • Gabriel García Márquez (1927–2014)

Gabriel García Márquez, ganador del Premio Nobel de Literatura en 1982, es considerado uno de los escritores más importantes de la literatura universal. García Márquez publicó su primer cuento° en 1947, cuando era estudiante universitario. Su libro más conocido, *Cien años de soledad*, está escrito en el estilo° literario llamado "realismo mágico", un estilo que mezcla° la realidad con lo irreal y lo mítico°.

Historia • Cartagena de Indias

Los españoles fundaron la ciudad de Cartagena de Indias en 1533 y construyeron a su lado la fortaleza° más grande de las Américas: el Castillo de San Felipe de Barajas. En la ciudad de Cartagena se conservan muchos edificios de la época colonial, como iglesias, monasterios, palacios y mansiones. Cartagena es conocida también por el Festival Internacional de Música y por su prestigioso Festival Internacional de Cine.

▷ Costumbres • El Carnaval

Durante el Carnaval de Barranquilla, la ciudad vive casi exclusivamente para esta fiesta. Este festival es una fusión de las culturas que han llegado° a las costas caribeñas de Colombia y de sus grupos autóctonos°. El evento más importante es la Batalla° de Flores, un desfile° de carrozas° decoradas con flores. En 2003, la UNESCO declaró este carnaval como Patrimonio de la Humanidad°.

fundado *founded* orfebrería *goldsmithing* joyas *jewelry* creencia *belief* creadora *creative* dioses *gods* cuento *story* estilo *style* mezcla *mixes* mítico *mythical* fortaleza *fortress* han llegado *have arrived* autóctonos *indigenous* Batalla *Battle* desfile *parade* carrozas *floats* Patrimonio de la Humanidad *World Heritage*

BRASIL

¡Increíble pero cierto!
En el siglo XVI los exploradores españoles oyeron la leyenda de El Dorado. Esta leyenda cuenta que los indios, como parte de un ritual en honor a los dioses, arrojaban° oro° a la laguna de Guatavita y el cacique° se sumergía en sus aguas cubierto de oro. Aunque esto era cierto, muy pronto la exageración llevó° al mito de una ciudad de oro.

arrojaban *threw* oro *gold* cacique *chief* llevó *led*

2 ¿Qué aprendiste? Contesta las preguntas.
1. ¿Cuáles son las principales ciudades de Colombia? Bogotá, Medellín, Cali, Barranquilla y Cartagena
2. ¿Quién era Edgar Negret? un escultor y pintor colombiano
3. ¿Para qué fue fundado el Museo del Oro? para preservar las piezas de orfebrería de la época precolombina
4. ¿Quién ganó el Premio Nobel de Literatura en 1982? Gabriel García Márquez
5. ¿Qué construyeron los españoles al lado de la ciudad de Cartagena de Indias? el Castillo de San Felipe de Barajas

3 Impresiones En parejas, túrnense para formar oraciones sobre Colombia. Utilicen expresiones como es extraño que, me alegro de que, me sorprende que y ojalá que.

modelo
Es obvio que Gabriel García Márquez es el escritor más importante de Colombia.

Instructional Resources
Supersite: Audio (Textbook & Lab MP3s); Testing Program (Tests, MP3s)
WebSAM
Lab Manual

Teaching Tip You may want to assign the **Prueba de práctica**, with its diagnostics and review activities, in the online-only **Repaso** section on the Supersite. There is also a **Repaso oral** in this section. For the Sixth Edition, a new summative vocabulary activity with speech recognition has been added to the **Repaso** section.

La naturaleza

el árbol	tree
el bosque (tropical)	(tropical; rain) forest
el cielo	sky
el cráter	crater
el desierto	desert
la estrella	star
la flor	flower
la hierba	grass
el lago	lake
la luna	moon
la naturaleza	nature
la nube	cloud
la piedra	stone
la planta	plant
el río	river
la selva, la jungla	jungle
el sendero	trail; path
el sol	sun
la tierra	land; soil
el valle	valley
el volcán	volcano

Los animales

el animal	animal
el ave, el pájaro	bird
la ballena	whale
el gato	cat
el mono	monkey
el perro	dog
el pez (sing.), los peces (pl.)	fish
la tortuga (marina)	(sea) turtle
la vaca	cow

El medio ambiente

el calentamiento global	global warming
el cambio climático	climate change
la conservación	conservation
la contaminación (del aire; del agua)	(air; water) pollution
la deforestación	deforestation
la ecología	ecology
el/la ecologista	ecologist
el ecoturismo	ecotourism
la energía (nuclear, solar)	(nuclear, solar) energy
el envase	container
la extinción	extinction
la fábrica	factory
el gobierno	government
la lata	(tin) can
la ley	law
el medio ambiente	environment
el peligro	danger
la (sobre)población	(over)population
el reciclaje	recycling
el recurso natural	natural resource
la solución	solution
cazar	to hunt
conservar	to conserve
contaminar	to pollute
controlar	to control
cuidar	to take care of
dejar de (+ *inf.*)	to stop (doing something)
desarrollar	to develop
descubrir	to discover
destruir	to destroy
estar afectado/a (por)	to be affected (by)
estar contaminado/a	to be polluted
evitar	to avoid
mejorar	to improve
proteger	to protect
reciclar	to recycle
recoger	to pick up
reducir	to reduce
resolver (o:ue)	to resolve; to solve
respirar	to breathe
de aluminio	(made) of aluminum
de plástico	(made) of plastic
de vidrio	(made) of glass
ecológico/a	ecological
puro/a	pure
renovable	renewable

Las emociones

alegrarse (de)	to be happy
esperar	to hope; to wish
sentir (e:ie)	to be sorry; to regret
temer	to be afraid
es extraño	it's strange
es una lástima	it's a shame
es ridículo	it's ridiculous
es terrible	it's terrible
es triste	it's sad
ojalá (que)	I hope (that); I wish (that)

Las dudas y certezas

(no) creer	(not) to believe
(no) dudar	(not) to doubt
(no) negar (e:ie)	(not) to deny
es imposible	it's impossible
es improbable	it's improbable
es obvio	it's obvious
no cabe duda de	there is no doubt that
no hay duda de	there is no doubt that
(no) es cierto	it's (not) certain
(no) es posible	it's (not) possible
(no) es probable	it's (not) probable
(no) es seguro	it's (not) certain
(no) es verdad	it's (not) true

Conjunciones

a menos que	unless
antes (de) que	before
con tal (de) que	provided (that)
cuando	when
después de que	after
en caso (de) que	in case (that)
en cuanto	as soon as
hasta que	until
para que	so that
sin que	without
tan pronto como	as soon as

Expresiones útiles	See page 447.

More activities

vhlcentral | LM p. 77

En la ciudad

14

Communicative Goals

You will learn how to:
- Give advice to others
- Give and receive directions
- Discuss daily errands and city life

Lesson Goals

In **Lección 14**, students will be introduced to the following:
- names of commercial establishments
- banking terminology
- citing locations
- city transportation
- Mexican architect **Luis Barragán**
- subjunctive in adjective clauses
- **nosotros/as** commands
- forming regular past participles
- irregular past participles
- past participles used as adjectives
- visualizing
- avoiding redundancy
- writing an e-mail
- listening for specific information and linguistic cues
- a TV commercial for a bank in Honduras
- a video about Mexico City's subway system
- geographic, economic, and historical information about Venezuela

A primera vista Here are some additional questions you can ask based on the photo: ¿Cómo es la vida en la ciudad? ¿Y en el campo? ¿Dónde prefieres vivir? ¿Por qué? ¿Es posible que una ciudad esté completamente libre de contaminación? ¿Cómo? ¿Qué responsabilidades tienen las personas que viven en una ciudad para proteger el medio ambiente?

Teaching Tip Look for these icons for additional communicative practice:

→👤←	Interpretive communication
←👤→	Presentational communication
👤↔👤	Interpersonal communication

🔊 A PRIMERA VISTA
- ¿Está la mujer en una ciudad o en un bosque?
- ¿Tiene una lata o un mapa en la mano?
- ¿Hay árboles?
- ¿Tiene balcones el edificio?

INSTRUCTIONAL RESOURCES

Supersite (vhlcentral.com)
Video: *Fotonovela, Flash cultura, En pantalla, Panorama cultural*
Audio: Textbook and Lab MP3 Files

Activity Pack: Information Gap Activities, games, additional activity handouts
Resources: SAM Answer Key, Scripts, Translations, **Vocabulario adicional**, sample lesson plan, Grammar Presentation Slides, Digital Image Bank

Testing Program: Quizzes, Tests, Exams, MP3s
Student Activities Manual: Workbook/Video Manual/Lab Manual
WebSAM (online Student Activities Manual)

En la ciudad

Más vocabulario

la carnicería	*butcher shop*
la heladería	*ice cream shop*
la panadería	*bakery*
el supermercado	*supermarket*
la cuadra	*(city) block*
la dirección	*address*
la esquina	*corner*
el estacionamiento	*parking lot*
derecho	*straight (ahead)*
enfrente de	*opposite; facing*
hacia	*toward*
cruzar	*to cross*
doblar	*to turn*
hacer diligencias	*to run errands*
quedar	*to be located*
el cheque	*check*
la cuenta corriente	*checking account*
la cuenta de ahorros	*savings account*
ahorrar	*to save (money)*
cobrar	*to cash (a check)*
depositar	*to deposit*
firmar	*to sign*
llenar (un formulario)	*to fill out (a form)*
pagar a plazos	*to pay in installments*
pagar al contado/ en efectivo	*to pay in cash*
pedir prestado/a	*to borrow*
pedir un préstamo	*to apply for a loan*
ser gratis	*to be free of charge*

Variación léxica

cuadra	⟷	manzana (*Esp.*)
estacionamiento	⟷	aparcamiento (*Esp.*)
doblar	⟷	girar; virar; dar vuelta
hacer diligencias	⟷	hacer mandados

More activities

vhlcentral	LM p. 79	WB pp. 159–160	Online activities

la joyería — Todo Brillo — BANCAJA — **el banco** — **la peluquería, el salón de belleza** — Corto y Cambio — ABIERTO — LA VUELTA DEL CALCETÍN — **la lavandería** — DON MELÓN — **el letrero** — **la pastelería** — Indica cómo llegar. (indicar) — ¡68! — Diente Dulce — Está perdida. (estar) — **la frutería**

Práctica

el cajero automático

Pie de Rey

la zapatería

Bajo el Mar

la pescadería

1 **Emparejar** Empareja las oraciones con las tiendas apropiadas.

1. __d__
2. __b__
3. __c__
4. __e__
5. __a__
6. __f__
7. __h__
8. __g__

a. la joyería
b. la pastelería
c. la carnicería
d. la frutería
e. la zapatería
f. la pescadería
g. la panadería
h. el banco

2 **Cita** Indica si cada afirmación es **cierta** o **falsa**.

1. Sandra fue a la peluquería. _cierto_
2. Jorge fue a la zapatería. _cierto_
3. Sandra fue a la lavandería. _falso_
4. Jorge va a encontrarse con Sandra en la pastelería. _falso_
5. Sandra también quiere ir a una heladería. _cierto_
6. La panadería queda en la esquina. _cierto_

3 **Seleccionar** Indica dónde haces estas diligencias.

banco	joyería	pescadería
carnicería	lavandería	salón de belleza
frutería	pastelería	zapatería

modelo
pedir un préstamo _banco_

1. comprar galletas _pastelería_
2. comprar manzanas _frutería_
3. lavar la ropa _lavandería_
4. comprar pollo _carnicería_
5. comprar mariscos _pescadería_
6. comprar sandalias _zapatería_

4 **Completar** Completa las oraciones con las palabras más adecuadas.

1. El banco me regaló un reloj. Fue ___gratis___.
2. La cajera me dijo que tenía que ___firmar___ el cheque en el dorso (_on the back_) para cobrarlo.
3. Me gusta ___ahorrar___ dinero, pero no me molesta gastarlo.
4. Para pagar con un cheque, necesito tener dinero en mi ___cuenta corriente___.
5. Mi madre va a un ___cajero automático___ para obtener dinero en efectivo cuando el banco está cerrado.
6. Julio debe pedir un ___préstamo___ para pagar sus estudios.
7. Ana ___deposita___ su cheque en su cuenta de ahorros.
8. Siempre pago mis compras en efectivo o con tarjeta de crédito; no me gusta pagar ___a plazos___.

1 **Expansion** Have students create sentences for three other businesses: **la heladería, la lavandería, el supermercado.**

1 **Script** 1. Quiero seis naranjas y dos melocotones. 2. Prefiero el flan de caramelo. 3. Necesito cuatro chuletas de cerdo. 4. Deseo probarme estas botas, en el número siete. 5. ¿Puedo ver estos aretes? 6. ¿Hay langostas hoy? 7. ¿Qué debo hacer para abrir una cuenta de ahorros? 8. Me gusta el pan de queso. *Textbook MP3s*

2 **Teaching Tip** Have students read the statements before listening to the audio.

2 **Expansion** Ask students to correct the false statements.

2 **Script** S: Jorge, lo siento. Tuve un día muy ocupado y no pude llamarte antes. Primero fui al banco, luego a la peluquería que está al lado y después al supermercado.
J: No te preocupes. Yo también hice algunas diligencias hoy: fui a la lavandería y luego a la zapatería. ¿Nos vemos esta tarde en la panadería de la esquina? Quiero hablar contigo.
S: Claro, pero nos tomamos un café. Además, también quiero llevarte a una heladería que te va a encantar.
J: Qué bueno, nos vemos más tarde. *Textbook MP3s*

3 **Expansion** After students finish, ask them what else can be bought or done in each establishment. Ex: **¿Qué más podemos comprar en la pastelería?**

4 **Expansion** Ask students to compare and contrast aspects of banking. Ex: ATM vs. traditional tellers; paying bills online vs. by check; savings account vs. checking account. Have them work in groups of three to make a list of **Ventajas** and **Desventajas.**

TEACHING OPTIONS

Game Add a visual aspect to this vocabulary presentation by playing **Concentración**. On eight cards, write names of types of commercial establishments. On another eight cards, draw or paste a picture that matches each commercial establishment. Place the cards facedown in four rows of four. In pairs, students select two cards. If the cards match, the pair keeps them. If the cards do not match, students replace them in their original position. The pair with the most cards at the end wins.
Pairs Have each student write a shopping list with ten items. Have students include items found in different stores. Then have them exchange their shopping list with a partner. Each student tells his or her partner where to go to get each item. Ex: **unas botas (Para comprar unas botas, tienes que ir a la zapatería que queda en la calle ____.)**

Teaching Tips
- Use the **Lección 14 Contextos** digital images to assist with this vocabulary presentation.
- 👥↔👥 Ask students questions about the scene to elicit active vocabulary. Ex: **¿Qué hace el señor en la ventanilla? Y las personas que esperan detrás de él, ¿qué hacen?** Then, involve students in a conversation about sending mail and the post office. Ex: **Necesito estampillas. ¿Dónde está el correo que está más cerca de aquí? A mí me parece que la carta es una forma de escritura en vías de extinción. Desde que uso el correo electrónico y los mensajes de texto, casi nunca escribo cartas. ¿Quiénes todavía escriben cartas?**

5 Expansion
- 👥↔👥 After you have gone over the activity, have pairs role-play the conversation. Encourage them to ad-lib as they go.
- ←👥→ Have pairs create short conversations similar to the one presented in the activity, but set in a different place of business. Ex: **el salón de belleza, la pescadería**

6 Teaching Tips
- To simplify, create a word bank of useful phrases on the board. Ask volunteers to suggest expressions.
- Go over the new vocabulary by asking questions. Ex: **¿Cuándo pedimos un préstamo? ¿Los cheques son para una cuenta corriente o una cuenta de ahorros?**

En el correo

Manda/Envía un paquete. (mandar, enviar)

el cartero

la estampilla, el sello

el correo

Hacen cola. (hacer)

Echa una carta al buzón. (echar)

el sobre

¡LENGUA VIVA!
Note that **correo** can mean either *mail* or *post office*. Other ways to say *post office* are **la oficina de correos** and **correos**.

5 **Conversación** Completa la conversación con las palabras más adecuadas.

CARTERO Buenas tardes, ¿es usted la señorita Ramírez? Le traigo un (1) ___paquete___.

JUANITA Sí, soy yo. ¿Quién lo envía?

CARTERO La señora Brito. Y también tiene dos (2) ___cartas___.

JUANITA Ay, pero ¡ninguna es de mi novio! ¿No llegó nada de Manuel Fuentes?

CARTERO Sí, pero él echó la carta al (3) ___buzón___ sin poner un (4) ___sello___ en el sobre.

JUANITA Entonces, ¿qué recomienda usted que haga?

CARTERO Sugiero que vaya al (5) ___correo___. Con tal de que pague el costo del sello, se le puede dar la carta sin ningún problema.

JUANITA Uy, otra diligencia, y no tengo mucho tiempo esta tarde para (6) ___hacer___ cola en el correo, pero voy enseguida. ¡Ojalá que sea una carta de amor!

¡LENGUA VIVA!
In Spanish, **Soy yo** means *That's me* or *It's me*. **¿Eres tú?/ ¿Es usted?** means *Is that you?*

6 **Situaciones** En parejas, hagan una lista de las palabras que pueden necesitar para representar estas situaciones. Answers will vary.

- Dos compañeros/as de cuarto van a la lavandería.
- Un(a) cliente/a habla con un(a) empleado/a de banco sobre abrir una cuenta corriente.
- Una pareja de recién casados quiere pedir un préstamo para comprar una casa.
- Dos amigos no recuerdan dónde estacionaron el carro.
- Una persona habla con un(a) empleado/a de correo sobre mandar un paquete.

Ahora, escojan una de las cinco situaciones y represéntenla para la clase.

TEACHING OPTIONS

Extra Practice ←👥→ Ask students to research specific information about a bank in a Spanish-speaking country. Have them write a summary of branches, services, rates, and hours.
Pairs ←👥→ Have pairs list the five best places for local students. Ex: **la mejor pizza, el mejor corte de pelo**. Then have them write directions to each place from campus. Expand by having students debate their choices.

Game Divide the class into two teams and have them sit in two rows facing one another, so that a person from team A is directly across from a person from team B. Begin with the first two students and work your way down the rows. Say a word, and the first student to say an associated word wins a point for his or her team. Ex: You say: **correo**. The first person from team B answers: **sello**. Team B wins one point.

Comunicación

7

Diligencias En parejas, decidan quién va a hacer cada diligencia y cuál es la manera más rápida de llegar a los diferentes lugares desde el campus. *Answers will vary.*

modelo

comprar una pizza

Estudiante 1: Yo voy a comprar una pizza. ¿Cómo llego al restaurante italiano?

Estudiante 2: Conduce hacia el norte hasta cruzar la calle Oak.
El restaurante queda en la esquina a la izquierda.

1. enviar un paquete
2. comprar botas nuevas
3. comprar un pastel de cumpleaños
4. lavar unas camisas
5. comprar helado
6. cortarse (*to cut*) el pelo

8

El Hatillo Trabajen en parejas para representar los papeles de un(a) turista que está perdido/a en El Hatillo y de un(a) residente de la ciudad que quiere ayudarlo/la. *Answers will vary.*

Plaza Bolívar
Plaza Sucre
banco
Casa de la Cultura
farmacia
iglesia
terminal
escuela
estacionamiento
joyería
zapatería
café Primavera

modelo

Plaza Sucre, café Primavera

Estudiante 1: Perdón, ¿por dónde queda la Plaza Sucre?

Estudiante 2: Del café Primavera, camine derecho por la calle Sucre
hasta cruzar la calle Comercio...

1. Plaza Bolívar, farmacia
2. Casa de la Cultura, Plaza Sucre
3. banco, terminal
4. estacionamiento (este), escuela
5. Plaza Sucre, estacionamiento (oeste)
6. joyería, banco
7. farmacia, joyería
8. zapatería, iglesia

9

Cómo llegar En grupos, escriban un minidrama en el que unos/as turistas están preguntando cómo llegar a diferentes sitios de la comunidad en la que ustedes viven. *Answers will vary.*

Section Goals

In **Fotonovela**, students will:
- receive comprehensible input from free-flowing discourse
- learn functional phrases that preview lesson grammatical structures

Instructional Resources

Supersite: Video (*Fotonovela*); Resources (Scripts, Translations, Answer Keys)
WebSAM
Video Manual

Video Recap: Lección 13

Before doing this **Fotonovela** section, review the previous one with these questions:
1. ¿Adónde fueron Marissa y Jimena? (Fueron al santuario de tortugas.) 2. ¿Qué aprendieron allí? (Aprendieron sobre las normas para proteger a las tortugas.) 3. ¿Qué le pasó a Felipe durante el recorrido por la selva? (Se cayó.) 4. ¿Qué mentira les dijo Felipe a las chicas? (Les dijo que se perdió todo el recorrido.)

Video Synopsis
Maru is racing against the clock to deliver her application for an internship at the **Museo de Antropología**. However, with **Miguel's** car broken down again, long lines at the bank, and heavy traffic, **Maru** needs her friend **Mónica's** help to meet the deadline.

Teaching Tip
Ask students to predict what they would see and hear in an episode in which one of the characters runs into trouble when trying to get somewhere on time in a big city. Then, ask them a few questions to help them summarize this episode.

Corriendo por la ciudad

Maru necesita entregar unos documentos en el Museo de Antropología.   PERSONAJES

 MARU   **MIGUEL**

 Video

1

MARU Miguel, ¿estás seguro de que tu coche está estacionado en la calle de Independencia? Estoy en la esquina de Zaragoza y Francisco Sosa. OK. Estoy enfrente del salón de belleza.

2

MIGUEL Dobla a la avenida Hidalgo. Luego cruza la calle Independencia y dobla a la derecha. El coche está enfrente de la pastelería.

MARU ¡Ahí está! Gracias, cariño. Hablamos luego.

3

MARU Vamos, arranca. Pensé que podías aguantar unos kilómetros más. Necesito un coche que funcione bien. (*en el teléfono*) Miguel, tu coche está descompuesto. Voy a pasar al banco porque necesito dinero, y luego me voy en taxi al museo.

4

MARU Hola, Moni. Lo siento, tengo que ir a entregar un paquete y todavía tengo que ir a un cajero.

MÓNICA ¡Uf! Y la cola está súper larga.

MARU ¿Me puedes prestar algo de dinero?

MÓNICA Déjame ver cuánto tengo. Estoy haciendo diligencias, y me gasté casi todo el efectivo en la carnicería y en la panadería y en la frutería.

5

6

MÓNICA ¿Estás bien? Te ves pálida. Sentémonos un minuto.

MARU ¡No tengo tiempo! Tengo que llegar al Museo de Antropología. Necesito entregar...

MÓNICA ¡Ah, sí, tu proyecto!

TEACHING OPTIONS

Video Tips General suggestions for using video clips in the classroom can be found in the front matter of this Instructor's Annotated Edition.

Corriendo por la ciudad Play the **Corriendo por la ciudad** episode without sound and ask the class to summarize what they see. Then, ask them to predict the content of the episode, and write their predictions on the board. Then play the entire episode with sound. Finally, through questions and discussion, lead the class to an accurate summary of the plot.

MÓNICA

MÓNICA ¿Puedes mandarlo por correo? El correo está muy cerca de aquí.

MARU El plazo para mandarlo por correo se venció la semana pasada. Tengo que entregarlo personalmente.

MARU ¿Me podrías prestar tu coche?

MÓNICA Estás muy nerviosa para manejar con este tráfico. Te acompaño. ¡No!, mejor, yo te llevo. Mi coche está en el estacionamiento de la calle Constitución.

MARU En esta esquina dobla a la derecha. En el semáforo, a la izquierda y sigue derecho.

MÓNICA Hay demasiado tráfico. No sé si podemos...

MARU Hola, Miguel. No, no hubo más problemas. Lo entregué justo a tiempo. Nos vemos más tarde. (*a Mónica*) ¡Vamos a celebrar!

More activities

vhlcentral | VM pp. 27–28 | Online activities

Expresiones útiles

Getting/giving directions

Estoy en la esquina de Zaragoza y Francisco Sosa.
I'm at the corner of Zaragoza and Francisco Sosa.
Dobla a la avenida Hidalgo.
Turn on Hidalgo Avenue.
Luego cruza la calle Independencia y dobla a la derecha.
Then cross Independencia Street and turn right.
El coche está enfrente de la pastelería.
The car is in front of the bakery.
En el semáforo, a la izquierda y sigue derecho.
Left at the light, then straight ahead.

Talking about errands

Voy a pasar al banco porque necesito dinero.
I'm going to the bank because I need money.
No tengo tiempo.
I don't have time.
Estoy haciendo diligencias, y me gasté casi todo el efectivo.
I'm running errands, and I spent most of my cash.

Asking for a favor

¿Me puedes prestar algo de dinero?
Could you lend me some money?
¿Me podrías prestar tu coche?
Could I borrow your car?

Talking about deadlines

Tengo que entregar mi proyecto.
I have to turn in my project.
El plazo para mandarlo por correo se venció la semana pasada.
The deadline to mail it in passed last week.

Additional vocabulary

acompañar *to accompany*
aguantar *to endure, to hold up*
ándale *come on*
pálido/a *pale*
¿Qué onda? *What's up?*

Expresiones útiles Draw attention to the word **estacionado** in the caption for video still 1 and **descompuesto** next to video still 3. Tell students that these are examples of past participles used as adjectives, and when used with **estar**, they describe a condition or state that results from an action. Then, in the caption for video still 3, point out the statement **Necesito un coche que funcione bien.** Explain that the subordinate clause functions as an adjective, and in this case requires the subjunctive because the existence of the car is unknown or indefinite. Finally, draw attention to the verb **Sentémonos** under video still 6 and explain that this is an example of a **nosotros/as** command. Tell students that they will learn more about these concepts in **Estructura**.

Teaching Tip
👥↔👤 Have students work in pairs to read the **Fotonovela** captions aloud. (Have the same student read both **Miguel** and **Mónica's** roles.) Then have volunteers ad-lib this episode for the class.

Nota cultural Taxis are cheap, quick, and easy to find in Mexico City. In fact, there are more than 250,000 taxis regulated by the government. Riders should be wary of the approximately 45,000 illegal taxis, or **taxis pirata**.

TEACHING OPTIONS

Extra Practice →👤← Photocopy the **Fotonovela** Videoscript (Supersite) and white out key vocabulary in order to make a master for a cloze activity. Distribute the copies and, as you play the **Corriendo por la ciudad** episode, have students fill in the blanks.

Pairs 👤↔👤 Ask pairs to create a skit in which a tourist asks for directions in a Spanish-speaking country. Tell them to use phrases from **Expresiones útiles**. Give the class sufficient time to prepare and rehearse the skits; then ask a few volunteers to role-play their skits for the class.

¿Qué pasó?

1 Expansion Give students these true/false statements as items 5–6: **5. Maru va al museo en taxi.** (Falso. Mónica la lleva en su coche.) **6. Hay mucha gente en el cajero.** (Cierto.)

Nota cultural For timely delivery of correspondence in Mexico City, courier services are often used within the city limits, rather than the postal service. Some companies even have their own in-house messengers for such purposes.

2 Teaching Tip Write these sentences on separate slips of paper so that students can arrange them in the correct sequence.

3 Expansion Have pairs come up with an additional situation and then make a list of the errands that **Maru, Mónica,** and **Miguel** need to do in order to complete the task. Then have them read the list of errands aloud so that the class can guess what the situation might be.

4 Possible Conversation
E1: Voy al supermercado y a la heladería. ¿Quieres ir conmigo?
E2: Sí, en cuanto termine mi almuerzo, te acompaño.
E1: Tengo que pasar por el banco porque necesito dinero.
E2: Yo también necesito ir al banco. ¿Hay un banco por aquí con cajero automático?
E1: Hay un cajero automático a tres cuadras de aquí. Queda en la calle Libertad.
E2: También necesito ir a la lavandería y al correo.
E1: No hay problema… el correo y la lavandería están cerca del banco.
E2: Oye, ¿qué vas a hacer esta noche?
E1: Voy a ir a la fiesta que celebran para un amigo. ¿Quieres ir?
E2: ¡Sí, gracias!

1
¿Cierto o falso? Decide si lo que dicen estas oraciones es **cierto** o **falso**. Corrige las oraciones falsas.

	Cierto	Falso	
1. Miguel dice que su coche está estacionado enfrente de la carnicería.	○	◉	Miguel dice que su coche está estacionado enfrente de la pastelería.
2. Maru necesita pasar al banco porque necesita dinero.	◉	○	
3. Mónica gastó el efectivo en la joyería y el supermercado.	○	◉	Mónica gastó el efectivo en la carnicería, la panadería y la frutería.
4. Maru puede mandar el paquete por correo.	○	◉	Maru no puede mandar el paquete por correo.

2
Ordenar Pon los sucesos en el orden correcto.

a. Maru le pide dinero prestado a Mónica. __3__
b. Maru entregó el paquete justo a tiempo (*just in time*). __6__
c. Mónica dice que hay una cola súper larga en el banco. __2__
d. Mónica lleva a Maru en su coche. __4__
e. Maru dice que se va a ir en taxi al museo. __1__
f. Maru le dice a Mónica que doble a la derecha en la esquina. __5__

3
Otras diligencias En parejas, hagan una lista de las diligencias que Miguel, Maru y Mónica necesitan hacer para completar estas actividades. Answers will vary.

1. enviar un paquete por correo
2. pedir una beca (*scholarship*)
3. visitar una nueva ciudad
4. abrir una cuenta corriente
5. celebrar el cumpleaños de Mónica
6. comprar una nueva computadora portátil

MARU

MIGUEL

MÓNICA

4
Conversación Un(a) compañero/a y tú son vecinos/as. Uno/a de ustedes acaba de mudarse y necesita ayuda porque no conoce la ciudad. Los/Las dos tienen que hacer algunas diligencias y deciden hacerlas juntos/as. Preparen una conversación breve incluyendo planes para ir a estos lugares. Answers will vary.

modelo

Estudiante 1: Necesito lavar mi ropa. ¿Sabes dónde queda una lavandería?
Estudiante 2: Sí. Aquí a dos cuadras hay una. También tengo que lavar mi ropa. ¿Qué te parece si vamos juntos?

▶ un cajero automático

▶ una lavandería

▶ un supermercado

▶ una heladería

▶ una panadería

AYUDA

primero *first*
luego *then*
¿Sabes dónde queda…? *Do you know where…is?*
¿Qué te parece? *What do you think?*
¡Cómo no! *But of course!*

NATIONAL communication STANDARDS

TEACHING OPTIONS

Extra Practice Add an auditory aspect to this vocabulary practice. Prepare several sets of directions that explain how to get to well-known places on campus or in your community, without mentioning the destinations by name. Read each set of directions aloud and ask the class to tell you where they would end up if they followed your directions.

Pairs Tell pairs of students to imagine that one of them is a new student who is having trouble navigating the campus while doing some errands (Ex: mailing letters, getting cash from the ATM, and going to the bookstore). Ask them to write a dialogue between the new student and a passerby who helps him or her. Have a few pairs perform their dialogues for the class.

Ortografía

 Tutorial

Las abreviaturas

In Spanish, as in English, abbreviations are often used in order to save space and time while writing. Here are some of the most commonly used abbreviations in Spanish.

usted ⟶ **Ud.**   ustedes ⟶ **Uds.**

As you have already learned, the subject pronouns **usted** and **ustedes** are often abbreviated

don ⟶ **D.**   doña ⟶ **Dña.**   doctor(a) ⟶ **Dr(a).**
señor ⟶ **Sr.**   señora ⟶ **Sra.**   señorita ⟶ **Srta.**

These titles are frequently abbreviated.

centímetro ⟶ **cm**   metro ⟶ **m**   kilómetro ⟶ **km**
litro ⟶ **l**   gramo ⟶ **g**   kilogramo ⟶ **kg**

The abbreviations for these units of measurement are often used, but without periods.

por ejemplo ⟶ **p. ej.**   página(s) ⟶ **pág(s).**

These abbreviations are often seen in books.

derecha ⟶ **dcha.**   izquierda ⟶ **izq., izqda.**
código postal ⟶ **C.P.**   número ⟶ **n.º**

These abbreviations are often used in mailing addresses.

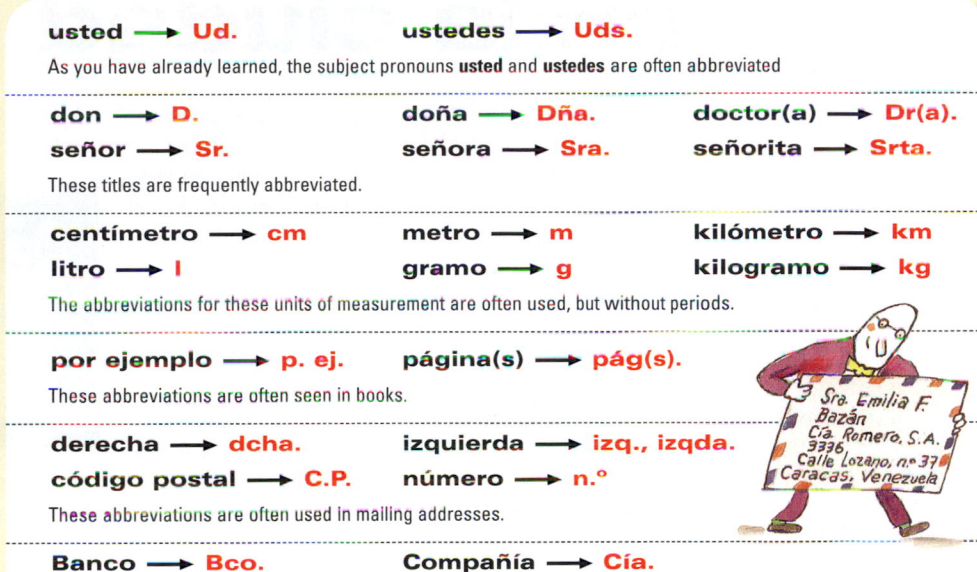

Sra. Emilia F. Bazán
Cía. Romero, S.A.
3336
Calle Lozano, n.º 37
Caracas, Venezuela

Banco ⟶ **Bco.**   Compañía ⟶ **Cía.**
cuenta corriente ⟶ **c/c.**   Sociedad Anónima (*Inc.*) ⟶ **S.A.**

These abbreviations are frequently used in the business world.

Práctica Escribe otra vez esta información usando las abreviaturas adecuadas.

1. doña María   Dña. María
2. señora Pérez   Sra. Pérez
3. Compañía Mexicana de Inversiones   Cía. Mexicana de Inversiones
4. usted   Ud.
5. Banco de Santander   Bco. de Santander
6. doctor Medina   Dr. Medina
7. Código Postal 03697   C.P. 03697
8. cuenta corriente número 20-453   c/c., n.º 20-453

Emparejar En la tabla hay nueve abreviaturas. Empareja los cuadros necesarios para formarlas.   S.A., Bco., cm, Dña., c/c., dcha., Srta., C.P., Ud.

S.	c.	C.	c	co.	U
B	c/	Sr	A.	D	dc
ta.	P.	ña.	ha.	m	d.

More activities

vhlcentral   LM p. 80

Section Goals

In **Cultura**, students will:
- read about bicycles in Latin American cities
- learn transportation-related terms
- read about Mexican architect **Luis Barragán**
- read about nicknames for Latin American and Spanish cities

Instructional Resource
Supersite

En detalle

Antes de leer

←👤→ Ask students to predict the content of this reading based on the title and photos. Have them share with the class their experiences with bicycling in cities.

Lectura
- Explain that safety is one of the main concerns in planning solutions for traffic and promoting a more humane city, where pedestrians and cyclists no longer feel like "second-class citizens." The biggest threat to cyclists comes from buses, taxis, cars, and official vehicles.
- Since half of the population in Latin America uses the public transportation system, the goal is to achieve transport integration: this means that whatever types of transportation exist in a city (rail, road, air, or water), they all operate as a single system for the benefit of users.

Después de leer Ask students about measures to promote bicycle use in their community.

1 Expansion Ask students to write three additional true/false statements for a partner to complete.

EN DETALLE

Las bicicletas en la ciudad

La bicicleta es un medio de transporte que tiene múltiples beneficios. Es ideal a la hora de recorrer la ciudad si se quieren evitar los atascos° y, además, su uso no sólo evita la contaminación ambiental, también es una forma de cuidar la salud.

En este sentido°, las ciudades de Latinoamérica están desarrollando políticas para la promoción del uso de las bicicletas en la vida urbana. El objetivo es lograr° que las calles se conviertan en un espacio seguro y respetuoso° para todos.

Desde hace años, Bogotá está a la cabeza de la iniciativa que propone el uso de la bicicleta como medio de transporte alternativo y amigable° con el medio ambiente. De esta manera, todos los domingos y días festivos, desde las siete de la mañana hasta las dos de la tarde, se prohíbe la circulación de carros por las principales calles de esta ciudad de nueve millones de habitantes: sólo pueden pasear por estas calles los peatones° y las bicicletas. Se calcula que cerca de un millón y medio de bicicletas llenan la ciudad en esos días. Hay también ciclovías° nocturnas, es decir, vías vehiculares que, por unas horas en las noches, permiten el uso exclusivo de bicicletas, y ciclopaseos, que son visitas programadas a lugares históricos de la ciudad.

Además, desde el año 2000, el primer jueves de febrero se celebra en la ciudad el Día sin carro.

En otras ciudades la gran novedad es el sistema de bicicletas compartidas. En Buenos Aires, el programa Ecobici nació en 2010 y funciona todos los días del año durante las 24 horas. Cualquier persona (incluso los turistas) puede buscar una bicicleta en una estación automática cercana, pasear en ella por la ciudad y devolverla° en otra estación. ¡Y es totalmente gratis! La ciudad tiene 190 kilómetros de ciclovías y 200 estaciones con 2.450 bicicletas públicas. Y el programa sigue aumentando.

Otros sistemas de bicicletas compartidas

Caracas, Venezuela: Caracas Rueda Libre (2015)
Ciudad de México, México: ECOBICI (2010)
Medellín, Colombia: EnCicla (2011)
Montevideo, Uruguay: Movete (2014)
Quito, Ecuador: BiciQuito (2012)
Santiago, Chile: Bikesantiago (2013)

atascos *traffic jams* **sentido** *regard* **lograr** *to achieve* **respetuoso** *respectful* **amigable** *friendly* **peatones** *pedestrians* **ciclovías** *bikeways* **devolverla** *return it*

ACTIVIDADES

1 **¿Cierto o falso?** Indica si lo que dice cada oración es **cierto** o **falso**. Corrige la información falsa.

1. Todos los domingos y días festivos, sólo los peatones y las bicicletas pueden pasear por las principales calles de Bogotá. **Cierto.**
2. En Bogotá se prohíbe la circulación de los carros desde las siete de la mañana hasta las seis de la tarde. **Falso.** Se prohíbe desde las siete de la mañana hasta las dos de la tarde.
3. Los ciclopaseos son calles sólo para bicicletas. **Falso.** Los ciclopaseos son visitas a lugares históricos de Bogotá.
4. En Bogotá está prohibido usar carros durante todo el mes de febrero. **Falso.** En Bogotá hay un día sin carro el primer jueves de febrero.
5. Ecobici es un sistema de bicicletas compartidas en Buenos Aires. **Cierto.**
6. Puedes usar bicicletas de Ecobici sólo de lunes a viernes. **Falso.** Puedes usar las bicicletas todos los días.
7. Los ciclistas pagan para usar Ecobici. **Falso.** Es gratis.
8. El sistema de bicicletas compartidas de Medellín se llama EnCicla. **Cierto.**

TEACHING OPTIONS

Small Groups ←👤→ Have students work in small groups, research one of the bike-sharing programs in Latin America or Spain, and create an informational poster. Tell them to include a map, the pricing scheme, a brief history, and any other significant information. Have groups present their posters to the class.

Pairs 👤↔👤 "The bicycle symbolizes individuality, civil rights, women's rights, urban mobility, simplicity, the new urbanism, and, of course, environmental consciousness." These are the words of Jaime Ortiz Mariño, one of the three friends who started the bike revolution in Bogotá in the 1970s. Have students discuss with a partner whether they agree with his interpretation of the bicycle.

ASÍ SE DICE

En la ciudad

el parqueadero (Col., Pan.)	el estacionamiento
el parqueo (Bol., Cuba, Amér. C.)	
dar un aventón (Méx.); dar botella (Cuba)	to give (someone) a ride
el subterráneo, el subte (Arg.)	el metro

EL MUNDO HISPANO

Apodos de ciudades

Así como Nueva York es la Gran Manzana, muchas ciudades hispanas tienen un apodo°.

- **La tacita de plata°** A Cádiz, España, se le llama así por sus edificios blancos de estilo árabe.

- **Ciudad de la eterna primavera** Arica, Chile; Cuernavaca, México, y Medellín, Colombia, llevan este sobrenombre por su clima templado° durante todo el año.

- **La docta°** Así se conoce a la ciudad argentina de Córdoba por su gran tradición universitaria.

- **La ciudad de los reyes** Así se conoce Lima, Perú, porque fue la capital del Virreinato° del Perú y allí vivían los virreyes°.

- **La arenosa** A Barranquilla, Colombia, se le llama así porque sus calles y espacios públicos siempre están cubiertos° de arena debido a los vientos constantes.

apodo *nickname* plata *silver* templado *mild* docta *erudite*
Virreinato *Viceroyalty* virreyes *viceroys* cubiertos *covered*

PERFIL

Luis Barragán: arquitectura y emoción

Para el arquitecto mexicano **Luis Barragán** (1902–1988) los sentimientos° y emociones que despiertan sus diseños eran muy importantes. Afirmaba° que la arquitectura tiene una dimensión espiritual. Para él, era belleza, inspiración, magia°, serenidad, misterio, silencio, privacidad, asombro°...

Casa Barragán, Ciudad de México, 1947-1948

Las obras de Barragán muestran un suave° equilibrio entre la naturaleza y la creación humana. Su estilo también combina la arquitectura tradicional

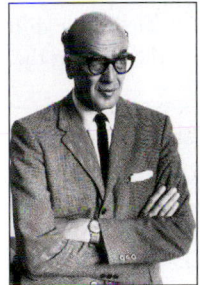

mexicana con conceptos modernos. Una característica de sus casas son las paredes envolventes° de diferentes colores con muy pocas ventanas.

En 1980, Barragán obtuvo° el Premio Pritzker, algo así como el Premio Nobel de Arquitectura. Está claro que este artista logró° que sus casas transmitieran sentimientos especiales.

sentimientos *feelings* Afirmaba *He stated* magia *magic* asombro *amazement*
suave *smooth* envolventes *enveloping* obtuvo *received* logró *managed*

CON RITMO HISPANO

Oscar D'León (1943–)
Lugar de nacimiento: Caracas, Venezuela

Oscar D'León es uno de los grandes cantantes de salsa de América Latina. Fue mecánico y taxista antes de ser músico.

Go to **vhlcentral.com** to find out more about **Oscar D'León** and his music.

ACTIVIDADES

2 Comprensión Contesta las preguntas.

1. ¿En qué país estás si te dicen "Dame botella al parqueo"? *en Cuba*
2. ¿Qué ciudades tienen clima templado todo el año? *Arica, Chile; Cuernavaca, México, y Medellín, Colombia*
3. ¿Qué es más importante en los diseños de Barragán: la naturaleza o la creación humana? *Son igual de importantes.*
4. ¿Qué premio obtuvo Barragán y cuándo? *Barragán obtuvo el Premio Pritzker en 1980.*

3 ¿Qué ciudad te gusta? Escribe un párrafo breve sobre el sentimiento que despiertan las construcciones que hay en una ciudad o un pueblo que te guste mucho. Explica cómo es y cómo te sientes cuando estás allí. Inventa un apodo para este lugar. *Answers will vary.*

More activities

vhlcentral — Online activities

Section Goal

In **Estructura 14.1**, students will learn the use of the subjunctive in adjective clauses.

Instructional Resources
Supersite: Audio (Lab MP3 Files); Resources (Grammar Presentation Slides, Activity Pack, Scripts, Answer Keys); Testing Program (Quizzes)
WebSAM
Workbook
Lab Manual

Teaching Tips

• Add a visual aspect to this grammar presentation. Use magazine pictures to compare and contrast the uses of the indicative and subjunctive in adjective clauses. Ex: **Esta casa tiene una fuente en el jardín. Yo busco una casa que tenga piscina. Este señor come insectos vivos. ¿Conocen a alguien que coma insectos vivos?**

• Ask volunteers to answer questions that describe their wishes. Ex: **¿Qué buscas en una casa? ¿Qué buscas en un(a) compañero/a de cuarto?**

• Ask volunteers to read the captions to the video stills and point out the subordinate adjective clause and its antecedent, then indicate whether the indicative or subjunctive is used in the clause, and why.

• Make sure to point out the role of the indefinite article vs. the definite article in determining the use of the subjunctive in adjective clauses. Show students the two sentences in **¡Atención!** and have them explain why the subjunctive is used in one, but not the other.

14.1 # The subjunctive in adjective clauses Tutorial

ANTE TODO In **Lección 13**, you learned that the subjunctive is used in adverbial clauses after certain conjunctions. You will now learn how the subjunctive can be used in adjective clauses to express that the existence of someone or something is uncertain or indefinite.

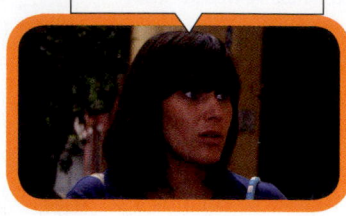

¿Conoces una joyería que esté cerca?

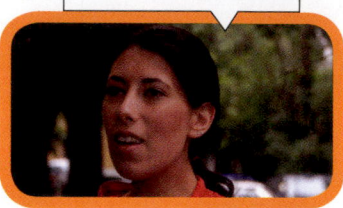

No, no conozco ninguna joyería que esté cerca de aquí.

▶ The subjunctive is used in an adjective (or subordinate) clause that refers to a person, place, thing, or idea that either does not exist or whose existence is uncertain or indefinite. In the examples below, compare the differences in meaning between the statements using the indicative and those using the subjunctive.

Indicative	Subjunctive
Necesito **el libro** que **tiene** información sobre Venezuela. *I need **the book** that has information about Venezuela.*	Necesito **un libro** que **tenga** información sobre Venezuela. *I need **a book** that has information about Venezuela.*
Quiero vivir en **esta casa** que **tiene** jardín. *I want to live in **this house** that has a garden.*	Quiero vivir en **una casa** que **tenga** jardín. *I want to live in **a house** that has a garden.*
En mi barrio, hay **una heladería** que **vende** helado de mango. *In my neighborhood, **there's an ice cream shop** that sells mango ice cream.*	En mi barrio no hay **ninguna heladería** que **venda** helado de mango. *In my neighborhood, **there is no ice cream shop** that sells mango ice cream.*

▶ When the adjective clause refers to a person, place, thing, or idea that is clearly known, certain, or definite, the indicative is used.

Quiero ir **al supermercado** que **vende** productos venezolanos.
I want to go to the supermarket that sells Venezuelan products.

Busco **al profesor** que **enseña** japonés.
I'm looking for the professor who teaches Japanese.

Conozco **a alguien** que **va** a esa peluquería.
I know someone who goes to that beauty salon.

Tengo **un amigo** que **vive** cerca de mi casa.
I have a friend who lives near my house.

¡ATENCIÓN!

Adjective clauses are subordinate clauses that modify a noun or pronoun in the main clause of a sentence. That noun or pronoun is called the *antecedent*.

¡ATENCIÓN!

Observe the important role that the indefinite article vs. the definite article plays in determining the use of the subjunctive in adjective clauses. Read the following sentences and notice why they are different:

¿Conoces *un* restaurante italiano que *esté* cerca de mi casa?

¿Conoces *el* restaurante italiano que *está* cerca de mi casa?

TEACHING OPTIONS

Extra Practice To provide oral practice with adjective clauses in the subjunctive and indicative, create sentences that follow the pattern of the sentences in the examples. Say a sentence, have students repeat it, then change the main clause. Have students then say the sentence with the new clause, changing the subordinate clause as necessary. **Conozco una tienda donde venden helados riquísimos. (Busco una tienda donde…)**

Heritage Speakers Ask heritage speakers to describe business establishments in their cultural communities. They should use both the indicative and the subjunctive, varying the verbs in the main clause as much as possible. Have the rest of the class compare and contrast these establishments with those around your university.

▶ The personal **a** is not used with direct objects that are hypothetical people. However, as you learned in **Lección 7**, **alguien** and **nadie** are always preceded by the personal **a** when they function as direct objects.

Necesitamos **un empleado** que
sepa usar computadoras.
*We need an employee who knows
how to use computers.*

Necesitamos **al empleado** que
sabe usar computadoras.
*We need the employee who knows how
to use computers.*

Buscamos **a alguien** que
pueda cocinar.
We're looking for someone who can cook.

No conocemos **a nadie** que
pueda cocinar.
We don't know anyone who can cook.

▶ The subjunctive is commonly used in questions with adjective clauses when the speaker is trying to find out information about which he or she is uncertain. However, if the person who responds to the question knows the information, the indicative is used.

—¿Hay un parque que **esté** cerca de
nuestro hotel?
Is there a park that's near our hotel?

—Sí, hay un parque que **está** muy
cerca del hotel.
Yes, there's a park that's very near the hotel.

▶ **¡Atención!** Here are some verbs that are commonly followed by adjective clauses in the subjunctive:

Verbs commonly used with subjunctive	
buscar	haber
conocer	necesitar
encontrar	querer

http://paginasamarillas.com   03:54

**paginas
amarillas.com**

Busque cualquier información que necesite.

More
activities

vhlcentral

LM
p. 81

WB
pp. 161–162

Online
activities

¡INTÉNTALO!   Escoge entre el subjuntivo y el indicativo para completar cada oración.

1. Necesito una persona que ___pueda___ (puede/pueda) cantar bien.
2. Buscamos a alguien que ___tenga___ (tiene/tenga) paciencia.
3. ¿Hay restaurantes aquí que ___sirvan___ (sirven/sirvan) comida japonesa?
4. Tengo una amiga que ___saca___ (saca/saque) fotografías muy bonitas.
5. No vemos ningún apartamento que nos ___interese___ (interesa/interese).
6. Hay una carnicería que ___está___ (está/esté) cerca de aquí.
7. Conozco a un estudiante que ___come___ (come/coma) hamburguesas todos los días.
8. ¿Hay alguien que ___diga___ (dice/diga) la verdad?

Práctica

1

Completar Completa estas oraciones con la forma correcta del indicativo o del subjuntivo de los verbos.

1. Buscamos un hotel que ____tenga____ (tener) piscina.
2. ¿Sabe usted dónde ____queda____ (quedar) el Correo Central?
3. ¿Hay algún buzón por aquí donde yo ____pueda____ (poder) echar una carta?
4. Ana quiere ir a la carnicería que ____está____ (estar) en la avenida Lecuna.
5. No hay nada en este mundo que ____sea____ (ser) gratis.
6. ¿Conoces a alguien que ____sepa____ (saber) mandar un *fax* por computadora?
7. Llamas al empleado que ____entiende____ (entender) este nuevo programa de computación.
8. Encontramos un restaurante que ____sirve____ (servir) comida típica venezolana.

2

Oraciones Forma oraciones con estos elementos, usando el presente de indicativo o de subjuntivo. Haz los cambios que sean necesarios.

1. yo / conocer / un / panadería / que / vender / pan / cubano
   Yo conozco una panadería que vende pan cubano.
2. ¿hay / alguien / que / saber / dirección / de / un / buen / carnicería?
   ¿Hay alguien que sepa la dirección de una buena carnicería?
3. yo / querer / comprarle / mi / hija / un / zapatos / que / gustar
   Yo quiero comprarle a mi hija unos zapatos que le gusten.
4. ella / no / encontrar / nada / que / gustar / en / ese / zapatería
   Ella no encuentra nada que le guste en esa zapatería.
5. ¿tener / dependientas / algo / que / ser / más / barato?
   ¿Tienen las dependientas algo que sea más barato?
6. nosotras / no / conocer / nadie / que / hacer / tanto / diligencias / como / nosotras
   Nosotras no conocemos a nadie que haga tantas diligencias como nosotras.
7. ¿conocer / tú / alguno / banco / que / ofrecer / cuentas / corrientes / gratis?
   ¿Conoces tú algún banco que ofrezca cuentas corrientes gratis?
8. nosotras / necesitar / un / línea / de / metro / que / nos / llevar / a / casa
   Nosotras necesitamos una línea de metro que nos lleve a casa.

3

Anuncios clasificados En parejas, describan el tipo de persona u objeto que se busca en cada anuncio. Answers will vary.

CLASIFICADOS

CLASES DE INGLÉS Profesor de Inglaterra con diez años de experiencia ofrece clases para grupos o instrucción privada para individuos. Llamar al 933-4110 de 16:30 a 18:30.

SE BUSCA CONDOMINIO Se busca condominio en Sabana Grande con 3 dormitorios, 2 baños, sala, comedor y aire acondicionado. Tel: 977-2018.

EJECUTIVO DE CUENTAS Se requiere joven profesional con al menos dos años de experiencia en el sector financiero. Se ofrecen beneficios excelentes. Enviar currículum vitae al Banco Unión, Avda. Urdaneta 263, Caracas.

VENDEDOR(A) Se necesita persona dinámica y responsable con buena presencia. Experiencia mínima de un año. Horario de trabajo flexible. Llamar a Joyería Aurora de 10 a 13h y de 16 a 18h. Tel: 263-7553

PELUQUERÍA UNISEX Se busca persona con experiencia en peluquería y maquillaje para trabajar tiempo completo. Llamar de 9 a 13: 30h. Tel: 261-3548

COMPARTIR APARTAMENTO Se necesita compañera para compartir apartamento de 2 dormitorios en el Chaco. Alquiler $500 por mes. No fumar. Llamar al 951-3642 entre 19 y 22h.

Teaching notes (margin)

1 **Teaching Tip** Briefly review the use of the indicative and subjunctive in adjective clauses. Write two contrasting sentences on the board. Ex: **Conozco una pastelería donde sirven café. No hay ninguna pastelería en este barrio donde sirvan café.** Then ask volunteers to explain why the indicative or subjunctive was used in each sentence.

2 **Teaching Tip** Have volunteers write each "rehydrated" sentence on the board. Ask other volunteers to point out why the subjunctive or indicative was used in each sentence.

2 **Expansion** Ask pairs to invent an ending to a day of running errands by writing a few sentences using the subjunctive in adjective clauses. Ex: **No encuentro una estación de metro que quede cerca....**

3 **Teaching Tips**
- Ask volunteers to discuss the types of information found in classified ads. Write them on the board.
- Have students do the activity by studying the ads for a few minutes and then discussing them with a partner with their books closed.

3 **Expansion** Have pairs compose their own classified ad for one of the topics listed on the board but not covered in the activity.

Comunicación

4

Subjuntivo Completa estas frases de una manera lógica. Luego, con un(a) compañero/a, túrnense para comparar sus respuestas. Answers will vary.

> **modelo**
>
> **Estudiante 1:** Tengo una novia que sabe bailar tango. ¿Y tú?
> **Estudiante 2:** Yo tengo un novio que habla alemán.

1. Deseo un trabajo (*job*) que…
2. Algún día espero tener un apartamento/una casa que…
3. Mis padres buscan un carro que…, pero yo quiero un carro que…
4. Tengo un(a) novio/a que…
5. Un(a) consejero/a (*advisor*) debe ser una persona que…
6. Me gustaría (*I would like*) conocer a alguien que…
7. En esta clase no hay nadie que…
8. No tengo ningún profesor que…

5

Encuesta Tu profesor(a) va a darte una hoja de actividades. Circula por la clase y pregúntales a tus compañeros/as si conocen a alguien que haga cada actividad de la lista. Si responden que sí, pregúntales quién es y anota sus respuestas. Luego informa a la clase de los resultados de tu encuesta. Answers will vary.

6

¿Compatibles? Vas a mudarte a un apartamento con dos dormitorios. Como no quieres pagar el alquiler tú solo/a, estás buscando a un(a) compañero/a para que viva contigo. Escribe un anuncio buscando a alguien con cuatro características que consideres importantes y pégalo en la pared de la clase. Puedes usar algunas de estas opciones u otras en tu anuncio y no olvides usar el subjuntivo. Answers will vary.

- cocinar
- escuchar hip-hop
- estar informado/a
- gustarle la política/el arte/los deportes
- llevarse bien con los animales
- ser vegetariano/a / limpio/a / optimista
- tener paciencia

> **modelo**
>
> Busco a alguien a quien no le guste el fútbol, que sea vegetariano,
> juegue videojuegos y le fascine la ciencia ficción.

Luego lee los anuncios de tus compañeros/as. ¿Con quién(es) podrías compartir tu apartamento? Busca tres candidatos/as y entrevístalos/las en dos minutos. Túrnate para entrevistar y ser entrevistado. ¿Encontraste a la persona ideal para que viva contigo? Answers will vary.

Síntesis

7

Busca los cuatro Tu profesor(a) te va a dar una hoja con ocho anuncios clasificados y a tu compañero/a otra hoja con ocho anuncios distintos a los tuyos. Háganse preguntas para encontrar los cuatro anuncios de cada hoja que tienen su respuesta en la otra. Answers will vary.

---

4 Teaching Tip Model the activity by giving a personal example. Write a sentence starter on the board and then complete it. Ex: **No conozco ningún restaurante cercano que… (No conozco ningún restaurante cercano que tenga un patio grande.)**

4 Expansion Assign students to groups of six and ask them to pick two responses and make a visual representation of them. Designate a student from each group to show the visual for the class to guess what the response was. Guesses should include an adjective clause.

5 Teaching Tip Distribute the *Hojas de actividades* (Activity Pack/Supersite) that correspond to this activity.

5 Expansion Have pairs write six original sentences with adjective clauses based on the answers of the **encuesta**. Three sentences should have subordinate clauses in the subjunctive.

6 Teaching Tip During the interview phase of the activity, encourage students to ask follow-up questions to gather more information that will aid them in determining compatibility. For example, if the interviewee generally likes animals and the interviewer has a cat, they should make sure that the potential roommate doesn't have any issues with cats.

7 Teaching Tip Divide the class into pairs and distribute the handouts from the Activity Pack (Activity Pack/Supersite) that correspond to this Information Gap Activity.

7 Expansion Have pairs write counterparts for two of the ads that do not have them. One ad should be for someone seeking to buy something and the other should be a "for sale" ad.

14.2 Nosotros/as commands Tutorial

ANTE TODO You have already learned familiar (**tú**) commands and formal (**usted/ustedes**) commands. You will now learn **nosotros/as** commands, which are used to give orders or suggestions that include yourself and other people.

▶ **Nosotros/as** commands correspond to the English *Let's*.

▶ Both affirmative and negative **nosotros/as** commands are generally formed by using the first-person plural form of the present subjunctive.

Crucemos la calle.
Let's cross the street.

No crucemos la calle.
Let's not cross the street.

▶ The affirmative *Let's* + [*verb*] command may also be expressed with **vamos a** + [*infinitive*]. However, remember that **vamos a** + [*infinitive*] can also mean *we are going to (do something)*. Context and tone of voice determine which meaning is being expressed.

Vamos a cruzar la calle.
Let's cross the street.

Vamos a trabajar mucho.
We're going to work a lot.

▶ To express *Let's go*, the present indicative form of **ir** (**vamos**) is used, not the subjunctive. For the negative command, however, the subjunctive is used.

Vamos a la pescadería.

No **vayamos** a la pescadería.

Pensemos, ¿adónde fuiste hoy?

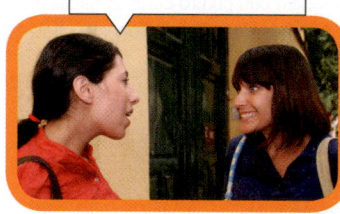

¡Eso es! ¡El carro de Miguel! Vamos.

▶ Object pronouns are always attached to affirmative **nosotros/as** commands. A written accent is added to maintain the original stress.

Firmemos el cheque.
Firmémoslo.

Escribamos a Ana y Raúl.
Escribámosles.

▶ Object pronouns are placed in front of negative **nosotros/as** commands.

No **les paguemos** el préstamo.

No **se lo digamos** a ellos.

🔗 **¡INTÉNTALO!** Indica los mandatos afirmativos y negativos de **nosotros/as** de estos verbos.

1. estudiar ___estudiemos, no estudiemos___
2. decidir ___decidamos, no decidamos___
3. leer ___leamos, no leamos___
4. cenar ___cenemos, no cenemos___
5. decir ___digamos, no digamos___
6. cerrar ___cerremos, no cerremos___
7. levantarse ___levantémonos, no nos levantemos___
8. irse ___vámonos, no nos vayamos___

Práctica

1

Completar Completa esta conversación con mandatos de **nosotros/as**. Luego, representa la conversación con un(a) compañero/a.

MARÍA Sergio, ¿quieres hacer diligencias ahora o por la tarde?

SERGIO No (1)_las dejemos_ (dejarlas) para más tarde. (2)_Hagámoslas_ (hacerlas) ahora. ¿Qué tenemos que hacer?

MARÍA Necesito sacar dinero de mi cuenta corriente.

SERGIO Bueno, (3)_busquemos_ (buscar) un cajero automático.

MARÍA ¿Tienes hambre?

SERGIO Sí. (4)_Crucemos_ (cruzar) la calle y (5)_entremos_ (entrar) en ese café.

MARÍA Buena idea.

SERGIO ¿Nos sentamos aquí?

MARÍA No, no (6)_nos sentemos_ (sentarse) aquí; (7)_sentémonos_ (sentarse) enfrente de la ventana.

SERGIO ¿Qué pedimos?

MARÍA (8)_Pidamos_ (pedir) café y pan dulce.

2

Responder Responde a cada mandato de **nosotros/as** según las indicaciones. Sustituye los sustantivos por los objetos directos e indirectos.

> **modelo**
> Vamos a vender el carro.
> *Sí, vendámoslo./No, no lo vendamos.*

1. Vamos a levantarnos a las seis. (sí)
   Sí, levantémonos a las seis.
2. Vamos a enviar los paquetes. (no)
   No, no los enviemos.
3. Vamos a depositar el cheque. (sí)
   Sí, depositémoslo.
4. Vamos al supermercado. (no)
   No, no vayamos al supermercado.
5. Vamos a bailar. (sí)
   Sí, bailemos.
6. Vamos a pintar la sala. (no)
   No, no la pintemos.
7. Vamos a limpiar la habitación. (sí)
   Sí, limpiémosla.
8. Vamos a mirar la televisión. (no)
   No, no la miremos.

3

Mandatos Forma mandatos de **nosotros/as** con estos elementos. Answers may vary. Suggested answers:

> **modelo**
> sacar / dinero / este cajero automático
> *Saquemos dinero de este cajero automático.*

1. no / beber / café / esta pastelería
   No bebamos café en esta pastelería.
2. pagar / el sofá / plazos
   Paguemos el sofá a plazos.
3. no / poner / la radio / el estacionamiento
   No pongamos la radio en el estacionamiento.
4. ir / la pescadería / comprar salmón
   Vamos a la pescadería a comprar salmón.
5. llevar / este paquete / correo
   Llevemos este paquete al correo.

1 Teaching Tip
Encourage pairs performing in front of the class to ad-lib additional material as they see fit.

1 Expansion
In pairs, have students write three cloze mini-conversations between two friends in which they use **nosotros/as** commands. Each dialogue should take place in a different commercial establishment, but students should leave out details that explicitly give away the friends' location. Then, have pairs exchange papers with another pair, who will fill in the blanks and try to identify the setting of each mini-conversation. They should end by acting it out for the class.

2 Expansion To challenge students, have pairs create another logical **nosotros/as** command for each item. Ex: **1. Vamos a levantarnos a las seis. (Sí, levantémonos a las seis. Y acostémonos temprano por la noche.)**

2 Expansion Have students rewrite the affirmative **nosotros/as** commands as negative ones and vice versa.

TEACHING OPTIONS

Small Groups Divide the class into groups of three. Student A writes a sentence that contains a **nosotros/as** command with direct or indirect objects. Ex: **Firmemos el cheque.** Student B must rewrite the sentence using pronouns. Ex: **Firmémoslo.** Then, student C must express the statement negatively. Ex: **No lo firmemos.** Have them switch roles and continue writing sentences until each has played student A twice.

Game Divide the class into teams of three. Teams will take turns responding to your cues with a **nosotros/as** command. Ex: **Necesitamos pan. (Vamos a la panadería.)** Give the cue. Allow the team members to confer and come up with a team answer, and then call on a team. Each correct answer earns one point. The team with the most points at the end wins.

Comunicación

4 **Expansion** To challenge students, ask them to expand their answers with a reason for their choice. Ex: **Paguemos en efectivo porque tenemos suficiente dinero.**

4

Preguntar Tú y tu compañero/a están de vacaciones en Caracas y se hacen sugerencias para resolver las situaciones que se presentan. Inventen mandatos afirmativos o negativos de **nosotros/as**.

Answers will vary.

> **modelo**
> Se nos olvidaron las tarjetas de crédito.
> *Paguemos en efectivo./No compremos más regalos.*

A

1. El museo está a sólo una cuadra de aquí.
2. Tenemos hambre.
3. Hay una cola larga en el cine.

B

1. Perdimos una maleta en el aeropuerto.
2. Tenemos prisa para llegar al cine.
3. Estamos cansados y queremos dormir.

5 **Expansion**
 Have groups bring in tourist information for another city in the Spanish-speaking world and repeat the activity. Encourage them to make copies of this information for the class. They should then present to the class their suggestions for what to do, using **nosotros/as** commands.

5

Decisiones Trabajen en grupos pequeños. Ustedes están en Caracas por dos días. Decidan qué van a hacer hoy por la mañana, por la tarde y por la noche. Hagan oraciones con mandatos afirmativos o negativos de **nosotros/as**. Answers will vary.

> **modelo**
> *Visitemos el Museo de Arte Contemporáneo de Caracas
> esta tarde. Quiero ver las esculturas de Jesús Rafael Soto.*

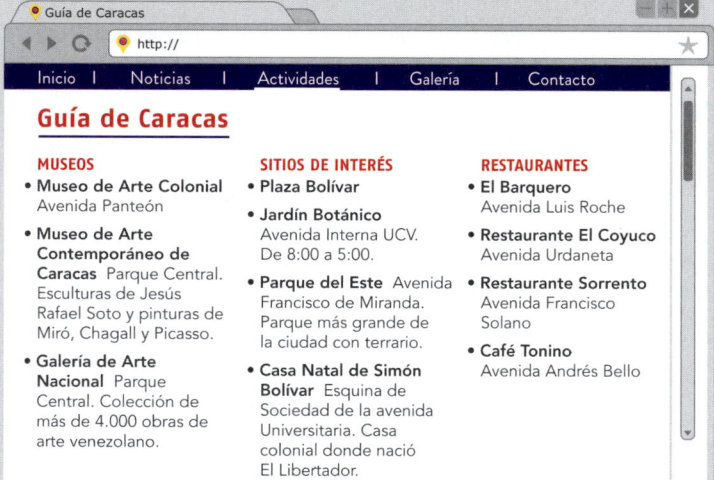

NOTA CULTURAL

Jesús Rafael Soto (1923–2005) fue un escultor y pintor venezolano. Sus obras cinéticas (*kinetic works*) frecuentemente incluyen formas que brillan (*shimmer*) y vibran. En muchas de ellas el espectador se puede integrar a la obra.

Síntesis

6 **Teaching Tip** To simplify, have students brainstorm different financial problems and solutions encountered by roommates sharing an apartment. Write their responses on the board.

6

Situación Tú y un(a) compañero/a viven juntos/as en un apartamento y tienen problemas económicos. Describan los problemas y sugieran algunas soluciones. Hagan oraciones con mandatos afirmativos o negativos de **nosotros/as**. Answers will vary.

> **modelo**
> *Hagamos un presupuesto (budget).*
> *No gastemos tanto dinero.*

6 **Expansion**
Call on pairs to perform their **Situación** for the class. Encourage them to ad-lib as they go.

TEACHING OPTIONS

Heritage Speakers Ask heritage speakers to write a conversation using **nosotros/as** commands. The topic of the conversation should be typical errands they run in their communities. Have them read their conversations to the class, making sure to note any new vocabulary on the board.
Pairs Have pairs create a guide for their favorite city, based on the **Guía de Caracas** in **Actividad 5**. Have them exchange their guides with another pair. That pair should decide which places they will visit and which they will avoid. Have them express their preferences using **nosotros/as** commands.
Pairs Have students create a dialogue in which two friends are deciding which local restaurant to go to for dinner. Students should use **nosotros/as** commands as much as possible. Have pairs perform their role-plays for the class.

14.3 Past participles used as adjectives Tutorial

comparisons

ANTE TODO   In **Lección 5**, you learned about present participles (**estudiando**). Both Spanish and English have past participles. The past participles of English verbs often end in **-ed** (*to turn* → *turned*), but many are also irregular (*to buy* → *bought*; *to drive* → *driven*).

▶ In Spanish, regular **-ar** verbs form the past participle with **-ado**. Regular **-er** and **-ir** verbs form the past participle with **-ido**.

INFINITIVE	STEM	PAST PARTICIPLE
bailar	bail-	**bailado**
comer	com-	**comido**
vivir	viv-	**vivido**

▶ **¡Atención!** The past participles of **-er** and **-ir** verbs whose stems end in **-a**, **-e**, or **-o** carry a written accent mark on the **i** of the **-ido** ending.

caer	**caído**	reír	**reído**
creer	**creído**	sonreír	**sonreído**
leer	**leído**	traer	**traído**
oír	**oído**		

Irregular past participles

abrir	**abierto**	morir	**muerto**
decir	**dicho**	poner	**puesto**
describir	**descrito**	resolver	**resuelto**
descubrir	**descubierto**	romper	**roto**
escribir	**escrito**	ver	**visto**
hacer	**hecho**	volver	**vuelto**

▶ In Spanish, as in English, past participles can be used as adjectives. They are often used with the verb **estar** to describe a condition or state that results from an action. Like other Spanish adjectives, they must agree in gender and number with the nouns they modify.

En la entrada hay algunos letreros **escritos** en español.
In the entrance, there are some signs written in Spanish.

Tenemos la mesa **puesta** y la cena **hecha**.
We have the table set and dinner made.

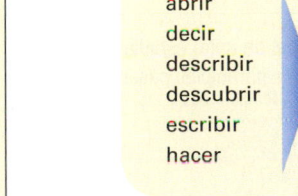
¡INTÉNTALO!   Indica la forma correcta del participio pasado de estos verbos.

1. hablar ___hablado___
2. beber ___bebido___
3. decidir ___decidido___
4. romper ___roto___
5. escribir ___escrito___
6. cantar ___cantado___
7. traer ___traído___
8. oír ___oído___
9. correr ___corrido___
10. ver ___visto___
11. leer ___leído___
12. hacer ___hecho___

Práctica

1 **Completar** Completa las oraciones con la forma adecuada del participio pasado del verbo.

1. Hoy mi peluquería favorita está __cerrada__ (cerrar).
2. Por eso, voy a otro salón de belleza que está __abierto__ (abrir) todos los días.
3. Queda en la Plaza Bolívar, una plaza muy __conocida__ (conocer).
4. El nombre del salón está __escrito__ (escribir) en el letrero y en la acera (*sidewalk*).
5. Todos los productos y servicios de esta tienda están __descritos__ (describir) en un catálogo.
6. Cuando la tarea esté __hecha__ (hacer), necesito pasar por el banco.

NOTA CULTURAL

Simón Bolívar (1783–1830) es considerado el "libertador" de cinco países de Suramérica: Venezuela, Perú, Bolivia, Colombia y Ecuador. Su apellido se ve en nombres como Bolivia, Ciudad Bolívar, la Universidad Simón Bolívar, el bolívar (la moneda venezolana) y en los nombres de muchas plazas y calles.

2 **Preparativos** Tú y tu compañero/a van a hacer un viaje. Túrnense para hacerse estas preguntas sobre los preparativos (*preparations*). Respondan afirmativamente y usen el participio pasado en sus respuestas.

modelo

Estudiante 1: ¿Enviaste el mensaje electrónico?
Estudiante 2: Sí, el mensaje electrónico ya está enviado.

1. ¿Compraste los pasajes para el avión? Sí, los pasajes ya están comprados.
2. ¿Confirmaste las reservaciones para el hotel? Sí, las reservaciones ya están confirmadas.
3. ¿Hiciste todas las diligencias? Sí, todas las diligencias ya están hechas.
4. ¿Lavaste la ropa? Sí, la ropa ya está lavada.
5. ¿Resolviste el problema con el banco? Sí, el problema con el banco ya está resuelto.
6. ¿Pagaste todas las cuentas? Sí, las cuentas ya están pagadas.
7. ¿Firmaste tu pasaporte? Sí, mi pasaporte ya está firmado.
8. ¿Hiciste las maletas? Sí, las maletas ya están hechas.

3 **El estudiante competitivo** En parejas, túrnense para hacer el papel de un(a) estudiante que es muy competitivo/a y siempre quiere ser mejor que los demás. Usen los participios pasados de los verbos subrayados. Answers will vary. Sample answers:

modelo

Estudiante 1: A veces se me daña la computadora.
Estudiante 2: Yo sé mucho de computadoras. Mi computadora nunca está dañada.

1. Yo no hago la cama todos los días.
   Soy muy ordenado/a. Mi cama siempre está hecha.
2. Casi nunca resuelvo mis problemas.
   Soy muy eficiente. Mis problemas siempre están resueltos.
3. Nunca guardo mis documentos importantes.
   Soy muy organizado/a. Mis documentos importantes siempre están guardados.
4. Es difícil para mí terminar mis tareas.
   Soy muy responsable. Mis tareas siempre están terminadas.
5. No quiero escribir la composición para mañana.
   Soy muy buen(a) estudiante. Mi composición ya está escrita.
6. Nunca pongo la mesa cuando ceno.
   Soy muy organizado/a. Mi mesa siempre está puesta.
7. Siempre se me olvida firmar mis tarjetas de crédito.
   Soy muy responsable. Todas mis tarjetas de crédito están firmadas.
8. Casi nunca lavo mi carro.
   Yo soy muy limpio/a. Mi carro siempre está lavado.

1 **Expansion** Have pairs make a list of new nouns of different gender and/or number, one for each item in the activity, to replace the original nouns being modified by past participles. They should double-check that the new sentences will make sense. Have them exchange their list with another pair, who should rewrite the sentences, then return them to the first pair for correction.

2 **Expansion** Have students redo the activity using a negative response and a different past participle used as an adjective to provide a reason. Ex: **No, no están confirmadas porque el teléfono del hotel está ocupado.**

3 **Expansion** Ask pairs to write 2–4 additional situations. Have them exchange papers with another pair and complete the activity.

TEACHING OPTIONS

Pairs In pairs, have students take turns miming actions for places or situations that you name. Their partners should describe the result of the action, using past participles. Ex: You say: **el banco** and a student mimes signing a check. (**El cheque está firmado.**)
Extra Practice Write these cloze sentences on the board. Have students copy them, provide the correct past participle, and draw a happy or sad face next to each to show the situations and/or feelings expressed. **1. Con el dinero ____(ahorrar) en las compras, podemos ir al cine. (ahorrado/☺) 2. Todo el dinero está ____(perder). (perdido/☹) 3. Con el préstamo del banco está ____(resolver) nuestro problema. (resuelto/☺) 4. Vamos a la pastelería ____(abrir) recientemente. (abierta/☺)**

Comunicación

4 **Preguntas** En parejas, túrnense para hacerse estas preguntas. *Answers will vary.*

1. ¿Dejas alguna luz prendida en tu casa por la noche?
2. ¿Está ordenado tu cuarto?
3. ¿Prefieres comprar libros usados o nuevos? ¿Por qué?
4. ¿Tienes mucho dinero ahorrado?
5. ¿Necesitas pedirles dinero prestado a tus padres?
6. ¿Estás preocupado/a por el medio ambiente?
7. ¿Qué haces cuando no estás preparado/a para una clase?
8. ¿Qué haces cuando estás perdido/a en una ciudad?

5 **Describir** Tú y un(a) compañero/a son agentes de policía y tienen que investigar un crimen. Describan lo que encontraron en la habitación del señor Villalonga. Usen el participio pasado en la descripción. Luego, comparen su descripción con la de otra pareja. *Answers will vary.*

> **modelo**
> La puerta del baño no estaba cerrada.

Síntesis

6 **Entre líneas** En parejas, representen una conversación entre un empleado de banco y una clienta. Usen las primeras dos líneas del diálogo para empezar y la última para terminar, pero inventen las líneas del medio (*middle*). Usen participios pasados. *Answers will vary.*

EMPLEADO Buenos días, señora Ibáñez. ¿En qué la puedo ayudar?
CLIENTA Tengo un problema con este banco. ¡Todavía no está resuelto!
...
CLIENTA ¡No vuelvo nunca a este banco!

---

4 **Teaching Tip** Tell students to use complex sentences whenever possible. Ex: **Nunca dejo la luz prendida en mi cuarto porque quiero ahorrar energía.**

4 **Expansion** Have one member of each pair write down the answers, choosing only one per question and mixing up his or her own with his or her partner's. Then have pairs exchange papers with another pair, who will read the list of answers and guess who from the first pair gave each answer. Have pairs work in groups of four to correct each other's guesses.

5 **Teaching Tips**
- To simplify, before assigning the activity to pairs, allow students a couple of minutes to make notes about the crime scene.
- Have students give their answers in round-robin format. Remind them that each contribution has to contain new information not previously supplied.

6 **Teaching Tip** Have the class brainstorm a list of banking problems an individual might have. Write the list on the board.

6 **Expansion** Invite volunteers to role-play their conversations for the class.

TEACHING OPTIONS

Pairs Have pairs make a promotional flyer for a new business in town. Their flyers should include at least three sentences with past participles used as adjectives. When they have finished, circulate the flyers in the class. Have students say which businesses they would most like to visit and why.

Game Divide the class into teams of three. Each team should think of a famous place or a historical monument. The other teams will take turns asking questions about the monument. Questions can only be answered with **sí/no** and each one should have a past participle used as an adjective. Ex: **¿Está abierto al público? ¿Es conocido solamente en este país?** The first team to guess the identity of the site wins a point.

Section Goal

In **Recapitulación**, students will review the grammar concepts from this lesson.

Instructional Resource
Supersite

Teaching Tip You may want to assign this **Recapitulación** activity on the Supersite because it has diagnostics. There is an online-only review activity for each grammar point. The Supersite also has a **Repaso de vocabulario** activity with diagnostics.

1 Teaching Tips
- Before beginning the activity, ask students to identify any verbs that have irregular past participles.
- Make sure that students understand to fill in the first column of blanks with the feminine form of the past participle, and the second column of blanks with the masculine form.
- Have students check their answers by going over **Actividad 1** as a class.

1 Expansion Ask students to create sentences using the past participles from the chart. Remind them that they must agree with the noun they modify. Ex: **Los exámenes ya están corregidos.**

2 Teaching Tip Have students begin by identifying which commands are negative. Call on a volunteer to explain the difference in the formation of affirmative and negative **nosotros/as** commands.

2 Expansion
↩ Have students work in pairs to create an original dialogue using **nosotros/as** commands.

Recapitulación

Completa estas actividades para repasar los conceptos de gramática que aprendiste en esta lección.

1 Completar Completa la tabla con la forma correcta de los verbos. **16 pts.**

Infinitivo	Participio	Infinitivo	Participio
completar	completada	hacer	hecho
corregir	corregida	pagar	pagado
creer	creída	pedir	pedido
decir	dicha	perder	perdido
escribir	escrita	poner	puesto

2 Los novios Completa este diálogo entre dos novios con mandatos en la forma de **nosotros/as**. **20 pts.**

SIMÓN ¿Quieres ir al cine mañana?

CARLA Sí, ¡qué buena idea! (1) _Compremos_ (comprar) los boletos (*tickets*) por Internet.

SIMÓN No, mejor (2) _pidámoselos_ (pedírselos) a mi prima, quien trabaja en el cine y los consigue gratis.

CARLA ¡Fantástico!

SIMÓN Y también quiero visitar la nueva galería de arte el fin de semana que viene.

CARLA ¿Por qué esperar? (3) _Visitémosla_ (visitarla) esta tarde.

SIMÓN Bueno, pero primero tengo que limpiar mi apartamento.

CARLA No hay problema. (4) _Limpiémoslo_ (limpiarlo) juntos.

SIMÓN Muy bien. ¿Y tú no tienes que hacer diligencias hoy? (5) _Hagámoslas_ (hacerlas) también.

CARLA Sí, tengo que ir al correo y al banco. (6) _Vamos_ (ir) al banco hoy, pero no (7) _vayamos_ (ir) al correo todavía. Antes tengo que escribir una carta.

SIMÓN ¿Una carta misteriosa? (8) _Escribámosla_ (escribirla) ahora.

CARLA No, mejor no (9) _la escribamos_ (escribirla) hasta que regresemos de la galería donde venden un papel reciclado muy lindo (*cute*).

SIMÓN ¿Papel lindo? Pues, ¿para quién es la carta?

CARLA No importa. (10) _Empecemos_ (empezar) a limpiar.

RESUMEN GRAMATICAL

14.1 The subjunctive in adjective clauses
pp. 486–487

▶ When adjective clauses refer to something that is known, certain, or definite, the indicative is used.

Necesito el **libro** que **tiene** fotos.

▶ When adjective clauses refer to something that is uncertain or indefinite, the subjunctive is used.

Necesito un **libro** que **tenga** fotos.

14.2 Nosotros/as commands *p. 490*

▶ Same as **nosotros/as** form of present subjunctive.

Affirmative	Negative
Démosle un libro a Lola.	No le demos un libro a Lola.
Démoselo.	No se lo demos.

▶ While the subjunctive form of the verb **ir** is used for the negative **nosotros/as** command, the indicative is used for the affirmative command.

No **vayamos** a la plaza. **Vamos** a la plaza.

14.3 Past participles used as adjectives *p. 493*

Past participles		
Infinitive	Stem	Past participle
bailar	bail-	bail**ado**
comer	com-	com**ido**
vivir	viv-	viv**ido**

Irregular past participles			
abrir	**abierto**	morir	**muerto**
decir	**dicho**	poner	**puesto**
describir	**descrito**	resolver	**resuelto**
descubrir	**descubierto**	romper	**roto**
escribir	**escrito**	ver	**visto**
hacer	**hecho**	volver	**vuelto**

▶ Like common adjectives, past participles must agree with the noun they modify.

Hay unos letreros **escritos** en español.

TEACHING OPTIONS

Large Groups Have students stand and form a circle. Have one student step inside the circle and describe a situation. Ex: **Tenemos un examen de español mañana.** The student to the right should step forward and propose a solution, using a **nosotros/as** command form. Ex: **Estudiemos el subjuntivo.** Continue around the circle until each student has had a turn forming commands. Then have another student start the activity again with a new situation.

Game Divide the class into two teams. Alternating between teams, select one student from each group to take a turn. Call out an infinitive and have the team member give the correct past participle. Award one point for each correct answer. The team with the most points wins.

3 **Verbos** Escribe los verbos en el presente de indicativo o de subjuntivo. **20 pts.**

1. —¿Sabes dónde hay un restaurante donde nosotros (1) _podamos_ (poder) comer paella valenciana? —No, no conozco ninguno que (2) _sirva_ (servir) paella, pero conozco uno que (3) _se especializa_ (especializarse) en tapas españolas.

2. Busco vendedores que (4) _sean_ (ser) bilingües. No estoy seguro de conocer a alguien que (5) _tenga_ (tener) esa característica. Pero ahora que lo pienso, ¡sí! Tengo dos amigos que (6) _trabajan_ (trabajar) en el almacén Excelencia. Los voy a llamar. Debo decirles que necesitamos que (ellos) (7) _sepan_ (saber) hablar inglés.

3. Se busca apartamento que (8) _esté_ (estar) bien situado, que (9) _cueste_ (costar) menos de $800 al mes y que (10) _permita_ (permitir) tener perros.

4 **La mamá de Pedro** Completa las respuestas de Pedro a las preguntas de su mamá. **10 pts.**

> **modelo**
> **MAMÁ:** ¿Te ayudo a guardar la ropa?
> **PEDRO:** La ropa ya *está guardada*.

1. **MAMÁ** ¿Cuándo se van a vestir tú y tu hermano para la fiesta?
   PEDRO Nosotros ya _estamos_ _vestidos_.

2. **MAMÁ** Hijo, ¿puedes ordenar tu habitación?
   PEDRO La habitación ya _está_ _ordenada_.

3. **MAMÁ** ¿Ya se murieron tus peces?
   PEDRO No, todavía no _están_ _muertos_.

4. **MAMÁ** ¿Te ayudo a hacer tus diligencias?
   PEDRO Gracias, mamá, pero las diligencias ya _están_ _hechas_.

5. **MAMÁ** ¿Cuándo terminas tu proyecto?
   PEDRO El proyecto ya _está_ _terminado_.

5 **La ciudad ideal** Escribe un párrafo de al menos seis oraciones describiendo cómo es la comunidad ideal donde te gustaría (*you would like*) vivir en el futuro y compárala con la comunidad donde vives ahora. Usa cláusulas adjetivas y el vocabulario de esta lección. **34 pts.** Answers will vary.

6 **Adivinanza** Completa la adivinanza y adivina la respuesta. **¡4 puntos EXTRA!**

" Me llegan las cartas
y no sé _leer_ (*to read*)
y, aunque° me las como,
no mancho° el papel. "
¿Quién soy? _el buzón_

aunque *although* no mancho *I don't stain*

Section Goals

In **Lectura**, students will:
- learn to visualize while reading
- read an authentic narrative in Spanish

Instructional Resource
Supersite

Estrategia Use stories that students are familiar with, such as fairy tales, as examples to talk about visualizing.

¿Qué va a pasar? Ask students to make their own predictions about what is going to happen in the story.

Visualizar Have students close their eyes and visualize the story as you read it aloud or play the audio.

Lectura

Antes de leer

Estrategia
Visualizing

Visualizing a text as you read can help you comprehend it. Before you begin, read the title and create a picture in your mind. Then skim each paragraph and visualize what you read. As you create these mental pictures, think about not only the sights, but also the sounds, smells, tastes, and feelings that are conveyed in the text. These visualizations will help you create an image of what the story will be about.

¿Qué va a pasar?

Responde a estas preguntas para hacer predicciones sobre el cuento.   Answers will vary.

1. ¿Quién es Olegario?
   _____

2. ¿Cuál es la emergencia?
   _____

3. ¿Tiene un final feliz el cuento?
   _____

Visualizar

Lee el título y echa una ojeada (*skim*) a los párrafos del cuento. ¿Qué visualizas?   Answers will vary.
_____
_____

Sobre el autor

Mario Benedetti (1920-2009) fue un escritor uruguayo. Aunque es conocido principalmente por sus poemas, escribió también ensayos, novelas y cuentos. Gran parte de la obra de Benedetti se centra en la temática urbana y se caracteriza por su compromiso político y social.

More activities

vhlcentral | Online activities

Los bomberos

Mario Benedetti

Olegario no sólo fue un as del presentimiento°, sino que además siempre estuvo muy orgulloso° de su poder. A veces se quedaba absorto° por un instante, y luego decía: "Mañana va a llover". Y llovía. Otras veces se rascaba la nuca° y anunciaba: "El martes saldrá° el 57 a la cabeza". Y el martes salía el 57 a la cabeza. Entre sus amigos gozaba de° una admiración sin límites.

Algunos de ellos recuerdan el más famoso de sus aciertos°. Caminaban con él frente a la Universidad, cuando de pronto el aire matutino° fue atravesado° por el sonido y la furia de los bomberos°. Olegario sonrió de modo casi imperceptible, y dijo: "Es posible que mi casa se esté quemando".

Llamaron un taxi y encargaron° al chofer que siguiera de cerca a los bomberos. Éstos tomaron por Rivera, y Olegario dijo: "Es casi seguro que mi casa se esté quemando". Los amigos guardaron un respetuoso y afable silencio; tanto lo admiraban.

Los bomberos siguieron por Pereyra y la nerviosidad llegó a su colmo°. Cuando doblaron por la calle en que vivía Olegario, los amigos se pusieron tiesos° de expectativa. Por fin, frente mismo a la llameante° casa de Olegario, el carro de bomberos se detuvo° y los hombres comenzaron rápida y serenamente los preparativos de rigor. De vez en cuando, desde las ventanas de la planta alta, alguna astilla° volaba por los aires.

Con toda parsimonia°, Olegario bajó del taxi. Se acomodó el nudo° de la corbata, y luego, con un aire de humilde vencedor°, se aprestó° a recibir las felicitaciones y los abrazos de sus buenos amigos.

as del presentimiento *master of premonition* **orgulloso** *proud* **absorto** *absorbed* **se rascaba la nuca** *he scratched the back of his neck* **saldrá** *will leave* **gozaba de** *he enjoyed* **aciertos** *correct predictions* **matutino** *morning* **atravesado** *pierced* **bomberos** *firefighters* **encargaron** *asked* **colmo** *peak* **tiesos** *tense, stiff* **llameante** *flaming* **se detuvo** *stopped* **astilla** *splinter* **parsimonia** *lack of urgency* **nudo** *knot* **vencedor** *victor* **se aprestó** *he prepared*

Después de leer

Comprensión

Indica si las oraciones son **ciertas** o **falsas**. Corrige las oraciones falsas.

1. Las predicciones de Olegario a veces son correctas.
   Falso. Las predicciones de Olegario siempre son correctas.
2. Los amigos de Olegario dudan de sus predicciones. **Falso.** Lo admiran porque sus predicciones se convierten en realidad.
3. Un día, Olegario y sus amigos caminaban por la calle cuando oyeron el carro de los bomberos. **Cierto.**
4. Olegario y sus amigos siguieron a los bomberos en un taxi. **Cierto.**
5. Los amigos de Olegario tuvieron miedo al ver que su casa se quemaba. **Falso.** Los amigos de Olegario se alegraron cuando vieron que su predicción fue correcta y lo felicitaron.

Interpretación

Responde a las preguntas con oraciones completas.
Answers will vary.

1. Busca las dos predicciones de Olegario en el primer párrafo del cuento. ¿Expresan un grado de certeza (*certainty*) alto o bajo?

2. Ahora, busca las dos predicciones que hace sobre la casa. ¿Expresan certeza o dejan lugar a dudas?

3. Al final, ¿crees que a Olegario le importa que se queme su casa? Explica tu respuesta.

4. ¿Tiene Olegario una actitud arrogante con respecto a su talento? ¿Por qué?

Comentar

En parejas, comenten el cuento. Usen como guía estas preguntas. Answers will vary.

- ¿Cómo creen que ocurrió el incendio (*fire*)?
- ¿Creen que el final del cuento es lógico? ¿Por qué?
- ¿Les gustaría predecir el futuro? ¿Por qué?
- ¿Cómo usarían el poder de predecir el futuro?

Comprensión Have students write three additional true/false statements about the story for a partner to answer.

Interpretación Have students discuss their answers with a partner.

Comentar Use the questions to conduct a class discussion. Ask students what they think about the ending.

Escritura

Estrategia

Avoiding redundancies

Redundancy is the needless repetition of words or ideas. To avoid redundancy with verbs and nouns, consult a Spanish language thesaurus (**Diccionario de sinónimos**). You can also avoid redundancy by using object pronouns, possessive adjectives, demonstrative adjectives and pronouns, and relative pronouns. Remember that, in Spanish, subject pronouns are generally used only for clarification, emphasis, or contrast. Study the example.

> **Redundant:**
>
> Susana quería visitar a su amiga. Susana estaba en la ciudad. Susana tomó el tren y perdió el mapa de la ciudad. Susana estaba perdida en la ciudad. Susana estaba nerviosa. Por fin, la amiga de Susana la llamó a Susana y le indicó cómo llegar.
>
> **Improved:**
>
> Susana, quien estaba en la ciudad, quería visitar a su amiga. Tomó el tren y perdió el mapa. Estaba perdida y nerviosa. Por fin, su amiga la llamó y le indicó cómo llegar.

Tema

Escribir un mensaje electrónico

Vas a visitar a un(a) amigo/a que vive en una ciudad que no conoces. Vas a pasar allí una semana y tienes que hacer también un trabajo para tu clase de literatura. Tienes planes de alquilar un carro, pero no sabes cómo llegar del aeropuerto a la casa de tu amigo/a.

Escríbele a tu amigo/a un mensaje electrónico describiendo lo que te interesa hacer allí y dale sugerencias de actividades que pueden hacer juntos/as. Menciona lo que necesitas para hacer tu trabajo. Puedes basarte en una visita real o imaginaria.

Considera esta lista de datos que puedes incluir:

▸ El nombre de la ciudad que vas a visitar
▸ Los lugares que más te interesa visitar
▸ Lo que necesitas para hacer tu trabajo:
    acceso a Internet
    saber cómo llegar a la biblioteca pública
    tiempo para estar solo/a
    libros para consultar
▸ Mandatos para las actividades que van a compartir

EVALUATION: Mensaje electrónico

Criteria	Scale
Content	1 2 3 4 5
Organization	1 2 3 4 5
Use of vocabulary	1 2 3 4 5
Grammatical accuracy	1 2 3 4 5

Scoring	
Excellent	18–20 points
Good	14–17 points
Satisfactory	10–13 points
Unsatisfactory	< 10 points

Escuchar

Antes de escuchar

Estrategia

Listening for specific information/ Listening for linguistic cues

As you already know, you don't have to hear or understand every word when listening to Spanish. You can often get the facts you need by listening for specific pieces of information. You should also be aware of the linguistic structures you hear. For example, by listening for verb endings, you can ascertain whether the verbs describe past, present, or future actions, and they can also indicate who is performing the action.

To practice these strategies, you will listen to a short paragraph about an environmental issue. What environmental problem is being discussed? What is the cause of the problem? Has the problem been solved, or is the solution under development?

Preparación

Describe la foto. Según la foto, ¿qué información específica piensas que vas a oír en el diálogo?
Answers will vary.

Ahora escucha

Los tiempos verbales

Lee estas frases y luego escucha la conversación entre Alberto y Eduardo. Indica si cada verbo se refiere a algo en el pasado, en el presente o en el futuro.

Acciones

1. Demetrio / comprar en Macro ___pasado___
2. Alberto / comprar en Macro ___futuro___
3. Alberto / estudiar psicología ___pasado___
4. carro / tener frenos malos ___presente___
5. Eduardo / comprar un anillo para Rebeca ___pasado___
6. Eduardo / estudiar ___futuro___

Comprensión

Descripciones

Indica las oraciones que describen correctamente a Alberto.

1. ___✔___ Es organizado en sus estudios.
2. _____ Compró unas flores para su novia.
3. _____ No le gusta tomar el metro.
4. ___✔___ No conoce bien la zona de Sabana Grande y Chacaíto.
5. ___✔___ No tiene buen sentido de la orientación (*sense of direction*).
6. ___✔___ Le gusta ir a los lugares que están de moda.

Preguntas

1. ¿Por qué Alberto prefiere ir en metro a Macro?
   Porque es muy difícil estacionar el carro en Sabana Grande.
2. ¿Crees que Alberto y Eduardo viven en una ciudad grande o en un pueblo? ¿Cómo lo sabes?
   Viven en una ciudad grande porque tiene metro.
3. ¿Va Eduardo a acompañar a Alberto? ¿Por qué?
   No puede porque tiene que estudiar y tiene una cita con Rebeca.

Conversación

En grupos pequeños, hablen de sus tiendas favoritas y de cómo llegar a ellas desde la universidad. ¿En qué lugares tienen la última moda? ¿Los mejores precios? ¿Hay buenas tiendas cerca de la universidad? *Answers will vary.*

manejarlo tampoco porque los frenos están malos.
E: Bueno, súbete al metro en la línea amarilla hasta Plaza Venezuela. Cuando salgas de la estación de metro dobla a la izquierda hacia Chacaíto. Sigue derecho por dos cuadras.
A: Ah, sí, enfrente de la joyería donde le compraste el anillo a Rebeca.
E: No, la joyería queda una cuadra hacia el sur. Pasa el Banco

Mercantil y dobla a la derecha. Tan pronto como pases la pizzería Papagallo, vas a ver un letrero rojo grandísimo a mano izquierda que dice Macro.
A: Gracias, Eduardo. ¿No quieres ir? Así no me pierdo.
E: No, hoy no puedo. Tengo que estudiar y a las cuatro tengo una cita con Rebeca. Pero estoy seguro que vas a llegar lo más bien.

En pantalla Video

En algunas partes de Centroamérica, Bolivia, Chile, Colombia, Ecuador y Perú y en la mayor parte de Argentina, Uruguay y Paraguay, las personas tienen la costumbre° de usar **vos** en lugar de **tú** al hablar o escribir. Este uso es conocido como **voseo** y se refleja también en la manera de conjugar los verbos. Por ejemplo, el presente del indicativo de los verbos regulares se conjuga con las terminaciones **-ás** (**vos hablás**), **-és** (**vos comés**) e **-ís** (**vos vivís**).

Vocabulario útil	
cargar	*to carry*
parecerse a	*to look like*
peluquero	*hairdresser*
ponerle	*name him*
segundo nombre	*middle name*
trato	*treatment*

Preparación
¿Te gusta ahorrar? ¿Dónde guardas tu dinero?
Answers will vary.

Escoger
Elige la opción correcta.

1. El peluquero de la mamá del bebé se llama ___a___.
   a. José   b. Tomás

2. Al papá del bebé le gustan las películas de ___b___.
   a. Harry Potter   b. Sylvester Stallone

3. Tomás es el nombre del ___a___ de la mamá del bebé.
   a. abuelo   b. hermano

4. El regalo para el bebé está ___b___.
   a. en el banco   b. personalizado

En el banco
En parejas, describan cinco pasos para abrir una cuenta de ahorros conjunta (*joint*). Usen mandatos de **nosotros/as.**
Answers will vary.

costumbre *custom*

Anuncio de Banco Ficensa

¡Felicitaciones! ¿Cómo se va a llamar?

Bueno, yo le puse José.

¿Y si le ponen Tomás?

More activities

 vhlcentral   Online activities

Video

En una ciudad tan grande como la Ciudad de México la vida es más fácil gracias al Sistema de Transporte Colectivo Metro y los viajes muchas veces pueden ser interesantes: en el metro se promueve° la cultura. Allí se construyó el primer museo del mundo en un transporte colectivo. También hay programas de préstamo de libros para motivar a los usuarios a leer en el tiempo muerto° que pasan dentro° del sistema. ¿Quieres saber más? Descubre qué hace tan especial al Metro de la Ciudad de México en este episodio de *Flash cultura*.

Vocabulario útil

concurrido	*busy, crowded*
se esconde	*is hidden*
transbordo	*transfer, change*
tranvía	*streetcar*

Preparación

Imagina que estás en la Ciudad de México, una de las ciudades más grandes del mundo. ¿Qué transporte usas para ir de un lugar a otro? ¿Por qué? Answers will vary.

Seleccionar

Selecciona la respuesta correcta.

1. El Bosque de Chapultepec es uno de los lugares más (solitarios/concurridos) de la ciudad.

2. En las estaciones (de transbordo/subterráneas) los pasajeros pueden cambiar de trenes para llegar fácilmente a su destino.

3. Algunas líneas del Metro no son subterráneas, sino superficiales, es decir, (paran/circulan) al nivel de la calle.

4. Dentro de algunas estaciones hay (danzas indígenas/exposiciones de arte).

se promueve *is promoted* tiempo muerto *down time* dentro *inside*

El Metro del D.F.

Viajando en el Metro... puedes conocer más acerca de la cultura de este país.

Para la gente... mayor de 60 años, es el transporte totalmente gratuito.

... el Metro [...] está conectado con los demás sistemas de transporte...

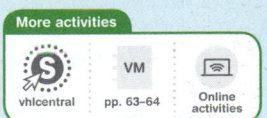
More activities
vhlcentral | VM pp. 63–64 | Online activities

Section Goals

In **Flash cultura**, students will:
- read about Mexico City's subway system and how it promotes culture
- watch a video about Mexico City's subway system

Instructional Resources

Supersite: Video (*Flash cultura*); Resources (Scripts, Translations, Answer Keys)
WebSAM
Video Manual

Introduction To check comprehension, give students these true/false statements.
1. En la Ciudad de México, el metro se llama Sistema Colectivo de Transporte. (Falso. Se llama Sistema de Transporte Colectivo Metro.) 2. Hay un museo dentro del Metro. (Cierto.) 3. En el Metro de la Ciudad de México regalan libros a los pasajeros. (Falso. Hay programas de préstamo.) 4. Se promueve la cultura mexicana en el Metro de la Ciudad de México (Cierto.)

Antes de ver
- Read through the **Vocabulario útil** and model pronunciation.
- Assure students that they do not need to understand every Spanish word they hear in the video. Tell them to rely on visual cues and to listen for cognates and words from **Vocabulario útil**.

Preparación Encourage students to brainstorm a list of all possible modes of city transportation (subway, bus, bicycle, etc.) and then express their preferred means.

Seleccionar To challenge students, eliminate the choices in parentheses.

TEACHING OPTIONS

Cultural Comparison 👤↔👤 In pairs, have students compare and contrast Mexico City's subway system with one in the U.S. or Canada.
Small Groups →👤 Have students watch a short film or TV clip that has to do with public transportation, such as the short films **Momentos de estación** (2001, Argentina) or **Panchito** (2010, Spain). Then, in small groups, have students analyze the role that transportation played in developing the story, such as symbolic value.
Extra Practice ↔👤→ Have students research public transportation systems in other Spanish-speaking countries. Have them choose one and write a brief paragraph comparing it to Mexico City's **metro** in terms of cost, cultural features, ease of use, and so on.

Section Goal

In **Panorama**, students will read about the history, geography, and economy of Venezuela.

Instructional Resources

Supersite: Video (*Panorama cultural*); Resources (Scripts, Translations, Digital Image Bank, Answer Keys)
WebSAM
Workbook

Teaching Tips

• Use the **Lección 14 Panorama** digital images to assist with this presentation.
• Have students look at the map of Venezuela and talk about the physical features of the country. Have students trace the Orinoco River and notice the types of terrain it runs through. Note that the principal cities are all located along the Caribbean coast.

El país en cifras Point out that the national currency is named for **Simón Bolívar,** the Latin American hero who played a central role in the struggle for independence from Spain. Point out that **Bolívar's** birthplace was Caracas. After reading about the **yanomami,** point out the vastness of Venezuela's jungle area, and remind students that various indigenous groups inhabit this largely undeveloped area.

Venezuela

El país en cifras

▸ **Área:** 912.050 km² (352.144 millas²), *aproximadamente dos veces el área de California*
▸ **Población:** 31.304.000
▸ **Capital:** Caracas—2.916.000
▸ **Ciudades principales:** Maracaibo—2.196.000, Valencia—1.734.000, Barquisimeto—1.039.000, Maracay—1.166.000
▸ **Moneda:** bolívar
▸ **Idiomas:** español (oficial), lenguas indígenas (oficiales)

El yanomami es uno de los idiomas indígenas que se habla en Venezuela. La cultura de los yanomami tiene su centro en el sur de Venezuela, en el bosque tropical. Son cazadores° y agricultores y viven en comunidades de hasta 400 miembros.

Bandera de Venezuela

Venezolanos célebres

▸ **Teresa Carreño,** compositora y pianista (1853–1917)
▸ **Rómulo Gallegos,** escritor y político (1884–1969)
▸ **Andrés Eloy Blanco,** poeta (1896–1955)
▸ **Gustavo Dudamel,** director de orquesta (1981–)
▸ **Baruj Benacerraf,** científico (1920–2011)

En 1980, Baruj Benacerraf, junto con dos de sus colegas, recibió el Premio Nobel por sus investigaciones en el campo° de la inmunología y las enfermedades autoinmunes. Nacido en Caracas, Benacerraf también vivió en París y los Estados Unidos.

cazadores *hunters* campo *field*

Isla Margarita

Maracaibo • Valencia • ★ Caracas

Lago de Maracaibo

Cordillera Central de la Costa

Río Orinoco

Macizo de las Guayanas

GUYA

Río Orinoco

BRASIL

Vista de Caracas

Una piragua

ESTADOS UNIDOS
OCÉANO ATLÁNTICO
VENEZUELA
OCÉANO PACÍFICO

More activities
vhlcentral | WB pp. 167–168 | Online activities

ACTIVIDADES

1 **¿Cierto o falso?** Indica si lo que dicen las oraciones es **cierto** o **falso**.

1. El yanomami es una lengua indígena que se habla en Venezuela. **cierto**
2. Gustavo Dudamel es un científico venezolano ganador de un Premio Nobel. **falso**
3. Nacido en Caracas, Baruj Benacerraf también vivió en París. **cierto**
4. La mayor concentración de petróleo de Venezuela se encuentra en la Isla Margarita. **falso**
5. Maracaibo queda al norte de Venezuela. **cierto**
6. El arpa, las maracas y las guitarras son los instrumentos más comunes del joropo venezolano. **cierto**
7. Simón Bolívar es conocido como "El Libertador". **cierto**
8. El Salto Ángel es la tercera catarata más alta del mundo. **falso**
9. La arepa está hecha de maíz cocido y molido. **cierto**

TEACHING OPTIONS

Variación léxica Venezuelan Spanish has a rich repertoire of regionalisms and colloquialisms. If students go to Caracas, they are certainly going to hear the word **pana**, which means both **amigo** and **amiga**. Ex: ¡Eso es chévere, pana! The Venezuelan equivalent of *guy* or *girl* is **chamo/a**. An inhabitant of the city of Caracas is a **caraqueño/a**. Some other words that are specific to Venezuela are **cambur** for **banana** and **caraota** for **frijol**.

Worth Noting **Rómulo Gallegos's** great novel, *Doña Bárbara*, is set in the **Llanos** of Venezuela, a region known for its cattle raising culture. The theme of the novel is one that has been explored by many Latin American writers—the struggle between **civilización y barbarie**.

⊳ Economía • El petróleo

La industria petrolera° es muy importante para la economía venezolana. La mayor concentración de petróleo del país se encuentra debajo del lago Maracaibo. En 1976 se nacionalizaron las empresas° petroleras y pasaron a ser propiedad° del Estado con el nombre de *Petróleos de Venezuela*. Este producto representa más del 90% de las exportaciones del país.

Música y danza • El joropo

El joropo venezolano es un género musical y también una danza popular de origen europeo, árabe, africano e indígena. Sus instrumentos más comunes son el arpa, las maracas y distintos tipos de guitarras. Las personas bailan joropo zapateando°, tomadas de la mano o separadas, y realizando diferentes figuras. Fue declarado patrimonio cultural de Venezuela en 2014.

Historia • Simón Bolívar (1783–1830)

A principios del siglo° XIX, el territorio de la actual Venezuela, al igual que gran parte de América, todavía estaba bajo el dominio de la Corona° española. El general Simón Bolívar, nacido en Caracas, es llamado "El Libertador" porque fue el líder del movimiento independentista suramericano en el área que hoy es Venezuela, Colombia, Ecuador, Perú y Bolivia.

⊳ Comida • La arepa

La arepa es una de las comidas más representativas de Venezuela. Es de origen indígena y está hecha de maíz cocido° y molido°. Se prepara frita o a la plancha°, y se come con queso, verduras y carnes como el jamón, el pollo o el solomillo°. La palabra **arepa** viene de **aripo**, que era una base de arcilla° donde se cocinaban las arepas.

industria petrolera *oil industry* empresas *companies* propiedad *property* zapateando *stomping* siglo *century* Corona *Crown* cocido *cooked* molido *ground*
a la plancha *grilled* solomillo *sirloin* arcilla *clay*

¡Increíble pero cierto!

Con una caída° de 979 metros (3.212 pies) desde la meseta de Auyan Tepuy, Salto Ángel°, en Venezuela, es la catarata° más alta del mundo, ¡diecisiete veces más alta que las cataratas del Niágara! James C. Angel la dio a conocer° en 1935. Los indígenas de la zona la denominan "Kerepakupai Merú".

caída *drop* Salto Ángel *Angel Falls* catarata *waterfall* la dio a conocer *made it known*

---

2 **¿Qué aprendiste?** Contesta cada pregunta con una oración completa.

1. ¿Cuál es la moneda de Venezuela?
   La moneda de Venezuela es el bolívar.
2. ¿Quién fue Rómulo Gallegos?
   Rómulo Gallegos fue un escritor y político venezolano.
3. ¿Cuándo se dio a conocer el Salto Ángel?
   El Salto Ángel se dio a conocer en 1935.
4. ¿Cuál es el producto más exportado de Venezuela?
   El producto más exportado de Venezuela es el petróleo.
5. ¿Cómo se llama la capital de Venezuela?
   La capital de Venezuela se llama Caracas.

3 **Impresiones** En parejas, imaginen que hacen un viaje a Venezuela. Describan lo que quieren hacer y lo que buscan en este país. Utilicen cláusulas adjetivas.

> **modelo**
> Yo busco un hotel que tenga la mejor vista de Caracas.

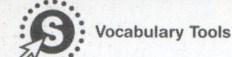 **Vocabulary Tools**

Teaching Tip You may want to assign the **Prueba de práctica**, with its diagnostics and review activities, in the online-only **Repaso** section on the Supersite. There is also a **Repaso oral** in this section. For the Sixth Edition, a new summative vocabulary activity with speech recognition has been added to the **Repaso** section.

En la ciudad

el banco	bank
la carnicería	butcher shop
el correo	post office
el estacionamiento	parking lot
la frutería	fruit store
la heladería	ice cream shop
la joyería	jewelry store
la lavandería	laundromat
la panadería	bakery
la pastelería	pastry shop
la peluquería, el salón de belleza	beauty salon
la pescadería	fish market
el supermercado	supermarket
la zapatería	shoe store
hacer cola	to stand in line
hacer diligencias	to run errands

En el banco

el cajero automático	ATM
el cheque	check
la cuenta corriente	checking account
la cuenta de ahorros	savings account
ahorrar	to save (money)
cobrar	to cash (a check)
depositar	to deposit
firmar	to sign
llenar (un formulario)	to fill out (a form)
pagar a plazos	to pay in installments
pagar al contado/ en efectivo	to pay in cash
pedir prestado/a	to borrow
pedir un préstamo	to apply for a loan
ser gratis	to be free of charge

Cómo llegar

la cuadra	(city) block
la dirección	address
la esquina	corner
el letrero	sign
cruzar	to cross
doblar	to turn
estar perdido/a	to be lost
indicar cómo llegar	to give directions
quedar	to be located
(al) este	(to the) east
(al) norte	(to the) north
(al) oeste	(to the) west
(al) sur	(to the) south
derecho	straight (ahead)
enfrente de	opposite; facing
hacia	toward

En el correo

el cartero	mail carrier
el correo	mail; post office
la estampilla, el sello	stamp
el paquete	package
el sobre	envelope
echar (una carta) al buzón	to put (a letter) in the mailbox; to mail
enviar, mandar	to send; to mail

Past participles used as adjectives	See page 493.
Expresiones útiles	See page 481.

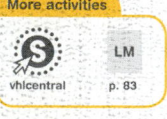
More activities

vhlcentral   LM p. 83

El bienestar

15

Communicative Goals

You will learn how to:
- **Talk about health, well-being, and nutrition**
- **Talk about physical activities**

A PRIMERA VISTA
- ¿Está la chica en un gimnasio o en un lugar al aire libre?
- ¿Practica ella deportes frecuentemente?
- ¿Es activa o sedentaria?
- ¿Tiene los ojos abiertos o cerrados?

Lesson Goals

In **Lección 15**, students will be introduced to the following:
- terms for health and exercise
- nutrition terms
- natural spas
- the health benefits of quinoa
- present perfect
- past perfect
- present perfect subjunctive
- analyzing story structure
- organizing information logically when writing
- writing a personal wellness plan
- listening for the gist and for cognates
- the short film ***Iker pelos tiesos***
- a video about places to relax and ways to deal with stress in Madrid, Spain
- cultural, geographic, and historical information about Bolivia

A primera vista Here are some additional questions you can ask: **¿Crees que tienes buena salud? ¿Vas al gimnasio regularmente? ¿Usas tu carro para hacer diligencias, o caminas? ¿Qué haces cuando te sientes nervioso/a o cansado/a? ¿Es importante que desayunes todas las mañanas? ¿Cuántas horas duermes cada noche?**

Teaching Tip Look for these icons for additional communicative practice:

Icon	Type
→👤←🢢	Interpretive communication
←👤→	Presentational communication
👤↔👤	Interpersonal communication

INSTRUCTIONAL RESOURCES

Supersite (vhlcentral.com)
Video: ***Fotonovela, Flash cultura, En pantalla, Panorama cultural***
Audio: Textbook and Lab MP3 Files

Activity Pack: Information Gap Activities, games, additional activity handouts
Resources: SAM Answer Key, Scripts, Translations, **Vocabulario adicional**, sample lesson plan, Grammar Presentation Slides, Digital Image Bank

Testing Program: Quizzes, Tests, Exams, MP3s, Oral Testing Suggestions
Student Activities Manual: Workbook/Video Manual/Lab Manual
WebSAM (online Student Activities Manual)

El bienestar

la cinta caminadora

Más vocabulario

adelgazar	to lose weight; to slim down
aliviar el estrés	to reduce stress
aliviar la tensión	to reduce tension
apurarse, darse prisa	to hurry; to rush
aumentar de peso, engordar	to gain weight
calentarse (e:ie)	to warm up
disfrutar (de)	to enjoy; to reap the benefits (of)
entrenarse	to train
estar a dieta	to be on a diet
estar en buena forma	to be in good shape
hacer gimnasia	to work out
llevar una vida sana	to lead a healthy lifestyle
mantenerse en forma	to stay in shape
sufrir muchas presiones	to be under a lot of pressure
tratar de (+ *inf.*)	to try (to do something)
la droga	drug
el/la drogadicto/a	drug addict
activo/a	active
débil	weak
en exceso	in excess; too much
flexible	flexible
fuerte	strong
sedentario/a	sedentary
tranquilo/a	calm; quiet
el bienestar	well-being

No fumar.

el masaje

Hace ejercicio. (hacer)

Hace ejercicios de estiramiento. (hacer)

el teleadicto

la entrenadora

Variación léxica

hacer ejercicios aeróbicos	⟷	hacer aeróbic *(Esp.)*
el/la entrenador(a)	⟷	el/la monitor(a)

Práctica

1 Emparejar Empareja las oraciones que vas a escuchar con las palabras más apropiadas.

a. débil	1.	b
b. fuerte	2.	d
c. activo	3.	f
d. masaje	4.	c
e. flexible	5.	e
f. sedentario	6.	h
g. engordar	7.	a
h. apurarse	8.	g

2 ¿Cierto o falso? Indica si lo que dice cada oración sobre el anuncio es **cierto** o **falso**.

1. El gimnasio sólo ofrece un servicio para las personas que quieren estar en buena forma.   falso
2. El gimnasio tiene un equipo de entrenadores.   cierto
3. El gimnasio tiene entrenadores personales.   cierto
4. Hay programas privados de pesas y masajes.   cierto
5. El gimnasio no abre los domingos.   falso
6. Puedes ir al gimnasio desde las siete de la mañana hasta las nueve de la noche.   falso

3 Identificar Identifica el antónimo (*antonym*) de cada palabra.

apurarse	fuerte
disfrutar	mantenerse en forma
engordar	sedentario
estar enfermo	sufrir muchas presiones
flexible	tranquilo

1. débil   fuerte
2. adelgazar   engordar
3. aliviar el estrés   sufrir muchas presiones
4. activo   sedentario
5. estar sano   estar enfermo
6. ir despacio   apurarse
7. nervioso   tranquilo
8. ser teleadicto   mantenerse en forma

4 Combinar Combina elementos de cada columna para formar oraciones lógicas.

1. David levanta pesas   h
2. Estás en buena forma   d
3. Felipe se lastimó   f
4. José y Rafael   e
5. Sara hace ejercicios de   b
6. Mi hermano   a
7. Mis primas se entrenan   c
8. Para llevar una vida sana,   g

a. aumentó de peso.
b. estiramiento.
c. para correr un maratón.
d. porque haces ejercicio.
e. sudan mucho en el gimnasio.
f. un músculo de la pierna.
g. no se debe fumar.
h. y corre mucho.

Levanta pesas. (levantar)

el entrenador

el músculo

Suda. (sudar)

Hacen ejercicios aeróbicos. (hacer)

la clase de ejercicios aeróbicos

1 Expansion Have students create sentences for three other vocabulary words.

1 Script 1. Levanto pesas todos los días. 2. Necesito aliviar la tensión. 3. Soy un teleadicto. 4. Me gusta correr y pasear en bicicleta. 5. Hago ejercicios de estiramiento. 6. Me doy prisa. 7. Estoy enfermo y no puedo levantarme. 8. Sólo como dulces; no me gustan ni las frutas ni las verduras. *Textbook MP3s*

2 Teaching Tip Have students read the statements before listening to the audio.

2 Expansion Ask students to correct the false statements.

2 Script Si quieres estar en buena forma, aliviar el estrés o adelgazar, nuestro gimnasio te ofrece una serie de programas que te van a encantar. Tenemos un equipo de entrenadores que te pueden ayudar a mantenerte en forma con las clases de ejercicios aeróbicos, yoga y gimnasia. Si sufres muchas presiones y lo que necesitas es un servicio más especial, puedes trabajar con un entrenador personal en nuestros programas privados de pesas y masajes. Abrimos de lunes a domingo, de las seis de la mañana a las diez de la noche. *Textbook MP3s*

3 Expansion Have students use each pair of opposite terms in sentences. Ex: **José está muy nervioso porque no estudió para el examen. Roberto estudió por dos horas; por eso está tranquilo.**

4 Expansion Have students create original endings for the sentence starters in the left column.

Note: At this point you may want to present *Vocabulario adicional: Más vocabulario para el bienestar* from the Supersite.

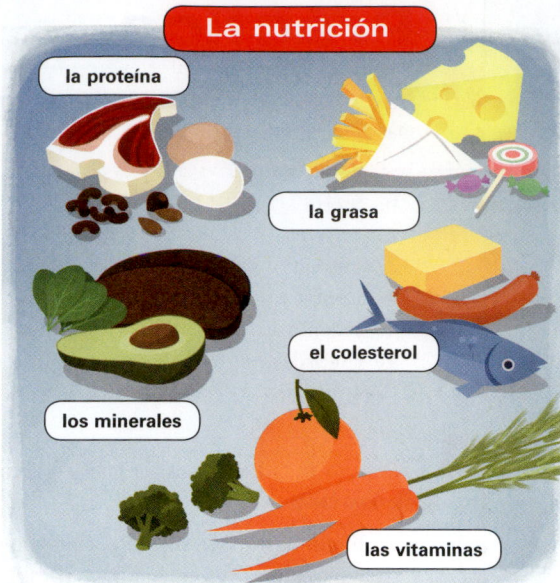

La nutrición

- la proteína
- la grasa
- el colesterol
- los minerales
- las vitaminas

Más vocabulario

la bebida alcohólica	*alcoholic beverage*
la cafeína	*caffeine*
la caloría	*calorie*
la merienda	*afternoon snack*
la nutrición	*nutrition*
el/la nutricionista	*nutritionist*
comer una dieta equilibrada	*to eat a balanced diet*
consumir alcohol	*to consume alcohol*
descafeinado/a	*decaffeinated*

5 **Completar** Completa cada oración con la palabra adecuada.

1. Mi entrenador no come queso ni papas fritas porque contienen ___c___.
   a. dietas   b. vitaminas   c. mucha grasa
2. Para ___c___, es necesario consumir comidas de todos los grupos alimenticios (*nutrition groups*).
   a. aliviar el estrés   b. correr   c. comer una dieta equilibrada
3. Mis primas ___a___ una buena comida.
   a. disfrutan de   b. tratan de   c. sudan
4. Después de hacer ejercicio, como pollo o bistec porque contienen ___b___.
   a. drogas   b. proteínas   c. grasa
5. Mi padre no come mantequilla porque él necesita reducir ___b___.
   a. la nutrición   b. el colesterol   c. el bienestar
6. Mi novio cuenta ___c___ porque está a dieta.
   a. las pesas   b. los músculos   c. las calorías

CONSULTA

To review what you have learned about nutrition and food, see **Contextos, Lección 8,** pp. 262–264.

6 **Frecuencia** Di con qué frecuencia haces estas actividades. *Answers will vary.*

siempre	una vez a la semana	una vez al año
todos los días	una vez al mes	nunca

modelo
fumar
Nunca fumo.

1. beber café descafeinado
2. hacer ejercicio
3. comer papas fritas
4. usar la cinta caminadora
5. levantar pesas
6. trabajar con un(a) entrenador(a)
7. salir a correr
8. tomar vitaminas

Comunicación

7

La nutrición En parejas, hablen de los tipos de comida que comen y las consecuencias que tienen para su salud. *Answers will vary.*

> **AYUDA**
>
> Some useful words:
> **sano = saludable**
> **en general = por lo general**
> **estricto**
> **normalmente**
> **muchas veces**
> **a veces**
> **de vez en cuando**

1. ¿Cuántas comidas con mucha grasa comes regularmente? ¿Piensas que debes comer menos comidas de este tipo? ¿Por qué?
2. ¿Compras comidas con muchos minerales y vitaminas? ¿Necesitas consumir más comidas que los contienen? ¿Por qué?
3. ¿Algún miembro de tu familia tiene problemas con el colesterol? ¿Qué haces para evitar problemas con el colesterol?
4. ¿Eres vegetariano/a? ¿Conoces a alguien que sea vegetariano/a? ¿Qué piensas de la idea de no comer carne u otros productos animales? ¿Es posible comer una dieta equilibrada sin comer carne? Explica.
5. ¿Tomas cafeína en exceso? ¿Qué ventajas (*advantages*) y desventajas tiene la cafeína? Da ejemplos de productos que contienen cafeína y de productos descafeinados.
6. ¿Llevas una vida sana? ¿Y tus amigos? ¿Crees que, en general, los estudiantes llevan una vida sana? ¿Por qué?

8

Un anuncio En grupos de cuatro, imaginen que son dueños/as de un gimnasio con un equipo (*equipment*) moderno, entrenadores cualificados y un(a) nutricionista. Preparen y presenten un anuncio para la televisión que hable del gimnasio y atraiga (*attracts*) a una gran variedad de nuevos clientes. No se olviden de presentar esta información: *Answers will vary.*

- ▶ las ventajas de estar en buena forma
- ▶ el equipo que tienen
- ▶ los servicios y clases que ofrecen
- ▶ las características únicas
- ▶ la dirección y el teléfono
- ▶ el precio para los socios (*members*)

9

Recomendaciones para la salud En parejas, imaginen que están preocupados/as por los malos hábitos de un(a) amigo/a que no está bien últimamente (*lately*). Escriban y representen una conversación en la cual hablen de lo que está pasando en la vida de su amigo/a y los cambios que necesita hacer para llevar una vida sana. *Answers will vary.*

10

El teleadicto Con un(a) compañero/a, representen los papeles de un(a) nutricionista y un(a) teleadicto/a. La persona sedentaria habla de sus malos hábitos para la comida y de que no hace ejercicio. También dice que toma demasiado café y que siente mucho estrés. El/La nutricionista le sugiere una dieta equilibrada con bebidas descafeinadas y una rutina para mantenerse en forma.
Answers will vary.

11

El gimnasio perfecto Tú y tu compañero/a quieren encontrar el gimnasio perfecto. Su profesor(a) les va a dar a cada uno/a de ustedes el anuncio de un gimnasio. Túrnense para hacerse preguntas sobre las actividades que se ofrecen en cada uno. Al final, decidan cuál es el mejor gimnasio y compartan su decisión con la clase. *Answers will vary.*

Chichén Itzá

Los chicos exploran Chichén Itzá y se relajan en un spa.

PERSONAJES MARISSA FELIPE

 Video

1

MARISSA ¡Chichén Itzá es impresionante! Qué lástima que Maru y Miguel no hayan podido venir. Sobre todo Maru.

FELIPE Ha estado bajo mucha presión.

2

MARISSA ¿Ustedes ya habían venido antes?

FELIPE Sí. Nuestros papás nos trajeron cuando éramos niños.

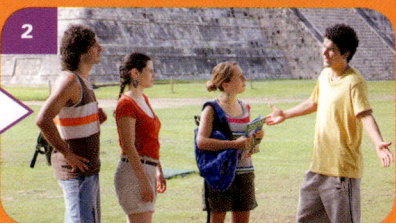

FELIPE El otro día le gané a Juan Carlos en el parque.

JUAN CARLOS Estaba mirando hacia otro lado, cuando me di cuenta, Felipe ya había empezado a correr.

3

(en otro lugar de las ruinas)

JUAN CARLOS ¡Hace calor!

JIMENA ¡Sí! Hay que estar en buena forma para recorrer las ruinas.

5

4

JUAN CARLOS Siempre había llevado una vida sana antes de entrar a la universidad.

JIMENA Tienes razón. La universidad hace que seamos muy sedentarios.

JUAN CARLOS ¡Busquemos a Felipe y a Marissa!

6

FELIPE ¡Gané!

JIMENA Qué calor. Tengo una idea. Vamos.

JUAN CARLOS **JIMENA** **EMPLEADA**

EMPLEADA Ofrecemos varios servicios para aliviar el estrés: masajes, saunas...

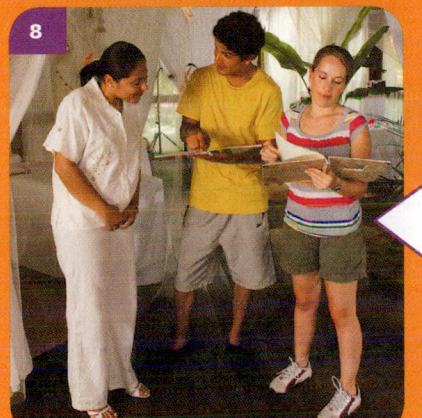

FELIPE Me gustaría un masaje.
MARISSA Yo prefiero un baño mineral.

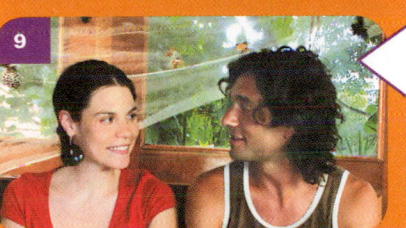

JUAN CARLOS ¿Crees que tienes un poco de tiempo libre la semana que viene? Me gustaría invitarte a salir.
JIMENA ¿Sin Felipe?
JUAN CARLOS Sin Felipe.

EMPLEADA ¿Ya tomaron una decisión?
JIMENA Sí.

More activities
vhlcentral | VM pp. 29–30 | Online activities

Expresiones útiles

Wishing a friend were with you

Qué lástima que no hayan podido venir.
What a shame that they were not able to come.
Sobre todo Maru.
Especially Maru.
Él/Ella ha estado bajo mucha presión.
He/She has been under a lot of pressure.
Creo que ellos ya habían venido antes.
I think they had already come (here) before.

Talking about trips

¿Ustedes ya habían venido antes?
Had you been (here) before?
Sí. He querido regresar desde que leí el Chilam Balam.
Yes. I have wanted to come back ever since I read the Chilam Balam.
¿Recuerdas cuando nos trajo papá?
Remember when Dad brought us?
Al llegar a la cima, comenzaste a llorar.
When we got to the top, you started to cry.

Talking about well-being

Siempre había llevado una vida sana antes de entrar a la universidad.
I had always maintained a healthy lifestyle before starting college.
Ofrecemos varios servicios para aliviar el estrés.
We offer many services to relieve stress.
Me gustaría un masaje.
I would like a massage.

Additional vocabulary

la cima *top, peak*
el escalón *step*
el muro *wall*
tomar una decisión *to make a decision*

¿Qué pasó?

1 Seleccionar Selecciona la respuesta que completa mejor cada oración.

1. Felipe y Marissa piensan que Maru ___c___.
   a. debe hacer ejercicio   b. aumentó de peso   c. ha estado bajo mucha presión
2. Felipe y Jimena visitaron Chichén Itzá ___b___.
   a. para aliviar el estrés   b. cuando eran niños   c. para llevar una vida sana
3. Jimena dice que la universidad hace a los estudiantes ___b___.
   a. comer una dieta equilibrada   b. ser sedentarios   c. levantar pesas
4. En el spa ofrecen servicios para ___b___.
   a. sudar   b. aliviar el estrés   c. ser flexibles
5. Felipe elige que le den un ___c___.
   a. baño mineral   b. almuerzo   c. masaje

2 Identificar Identifica quién dice estas oraciones.

MARISSA   FELIPE

JIMENA

JUAN CARLOS   EMPLEADA

1. Estaba mirando hacia otro lado, cuando me di cuenta, Felipe ya había empezado a correr. *Juan Carlos*
2. Chichén Itzá es impresionante. Qué lástima que Maru y Miguel no hayan podido venir. *Marissa*
3. Hay que estar en buena forma para recorrer las ruinas. *Jimena*
4. Ofrecemos varios servicios para aliviar el estrés: masajes, saunas, tratamientos con vitaminas y minerales para la piel... *empleada*
5. Estudié mucho antes de salir del D.F. *Jimena*
6. Creo que ésa fue la última vez que papá hizo ejercicio. *Felipe*

3 Inventar En parejas, hagan descripciones de los personajes de la **Fotonovela**. *Answers will vary.*

aliviar el estrés	hacer ejercicios de estiramiento	masaje
bienestar	llevar una vida sana	teleadicto/a
grasa	mantenerse en forma	vitamina

modelo
Estudiante 1: Felipe es activo, flexible y fuerte.
Estudiante 2: Marissa siempre hace ejercicios de estiramiento. Está en buena forma y lleva una vida muy sana...

1. A Juan Carlos le duelen los músculos después de hacer gimnasia.
2. Maru a veces sufre presiones y estrés en la universidad.
3. A Jimena le encanta salir con amigos o leer un buen libro.
4. Felipe trata de comer una dieta equilibrada.
5. Juan Carlos no es muy flexible.

NATIONAL communication STANDARDS

TEACHING OPTIONS

Extra Practice Ask the class a few additional questions about the **Fotonovela**. Ex: **¿Por qué Jimena lloraba mientras subía los escalones de El Castillo?** (Quería regresar al hotel y jugar en la playa.) **¿Qué servicios ofrece el spa para aliviar el estrés?** (Ofrece masajes, saunas y tratamientos con vitaminas y minerales para la piel.)
Pairs Have pairs prepare a television program in which

travelers are interviewed about their recent trip to the Mayan ruins of **Chichén Itzá**. Allow students to research more about the archeological site online before writing their scripts. Make sure to give them enough time to prepare and rehearse; then ask volunteers to present their programs to the class. Alternately, you may want students to make a video of their programs and play them for the class.

Ortografía

Tutorial

Las letras **b** y **v**

Since there is no difference in pronunciation between the Spanish letters **b** and **v**, spelling words that contain these letters can be tricky. Here are some tips.

| nombre | blusa | absoluto | descubrir |

The letter **b** is always used before consonants.

| bonita | botella | buscar | bienestar |

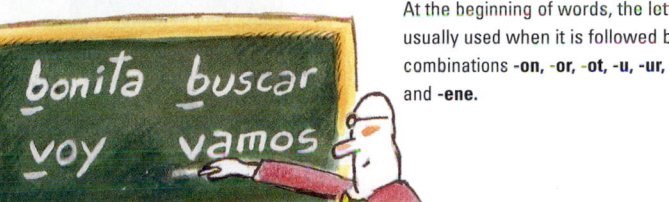

At the beginning of words, the letter **b** is usually used when it is followed by the letter combinations -**on**, -**or**, -**ot**, -**u**, -**ur**, -**us**, -**ien**, and -**ene**.

| adelgazaba | disfrutaban | ibas | íbamos |

The letter **b** is used in the verb endings of the imperfect tense for -**ar** verbs and the verb **ir**.

| voy | vamos | estuvo | tuvieron |

The letter **v** is used in the present tense forms of **ir** and in the preterite forms of **estar** and **tener**.

| octavo | huevo | activa | grave |

The letter **v** is used in these noun and adjective endings: -**avo/a**, -**evo/a**, -**ivo/a**, -**ave**, -**eve**.

Práctica Completa las palabras con las letras **b** o **v**.

1. Una _v_ez me lastimé el _b_razo cuando esta_b_a _b_uceando.
2. Manuela ol_v_idó sus li_b_ros en el auto_b_ús.
3. Ernesto tomó el _b_orrador y se puso todo _b_lanco de tiza.
4. Para tener una _v_ida sana y saluda_b_le, necesitas tomar _v_itaminas.
5. En mi pue_b_lo hay un _b_ule_v_ar que tiene muchos ár_b_oles.

El ahorcado (*Hangman*) Juega al ahorcado para adivinar las palabras.

1. n u b e s — Están en el cielo. nubes
2. b u z ó n — Relacionado con el correo buzón
3. b o t e l l a — Está llena de líquido. botella
4. n i e v e — Fenómeno meteorológico nieve
5. v e n t a n a s — Los "ojos" de la casa ventanas

More activities

vhlcentral

LM
p. 86

Section Goal

In **Ortografía**, students will learn about the spelling of words that contain **b** and **v**.

Instructional Resources
Supersite: Audio (Lab MP3 Files); Resources (Scripts, Answer Keys)
WebSAM
Lab Manual

Teaching Tips

- Ask the class if **b** or **v** is used before a consonant. Then say the words **nombre, blusa, absoluto,** and **descubrir** and have volunteers write them on the board.
- Write the words **bonita, botella, buscar,** and **bienestar** on the board. Ask the class to explain why these words start with a **b**.
- Ask the class if **b** or **v** is used in the endings of -**ar** verbs and the verb **ir** in the imperfect tense. Then say the words **adelgazaba, disfrutaban, ibas,** and **íbamos** and ask volunteers to write them on the board.
- Ask why the words **voy, vamos, estuvo,** and **tuvieron** are spelled with **v** and have volunteers write them on the board.
- Write the words **octavo, huevo, activa,** and **grave** on the board and ask the class to explain why these words are spelled with **v**.
- Point out that **Ortografía** replaces **Pronunciación** in the Student Edition for **Lecciones 10–18**, but not in the Lab Manual. The box references the **Pronunciación** sections found in all lessons of the Lab Manual.

EN DETALLE

Spas naturales

Muchas veces no hay nada mejor que un buen baño° para descansar y aliviar la tensión. Y si el baño se toma en una terma°, el beneficio° es mayor. Los tratamientos con agua y lodo° para mejorar la salud y el bienestar son populares en las Américas desde hace muchos siglos°. Las termas son manantiales° naturales de agua caliente. La temperatura de estos manantiales facilita la absorción de minerales y otros elementos que contiene el agua y que son buenos para la salud. El agua de las termas se usa en piscinas, baños y duchas o en el sitio natural en el que surge°: pozas°, estanques° o cuevas°.

En Baños de San Vicente, en Ecuador, son muy populares los tratamientos° con lodo volcánico.

El lodo caliente se extiende por el cuerpo; así la piel°

Volcán de lodo El Totumo, Colombia

Ecotermales en Arenal, Costa Rica

absorbe los minerales beneficiosos para la salud; también se usa para dar masajes. La lodoterapia es útil para tratar varias enfermedades, además hace que la piel se vea radiante.

En Costa Rica, la actividad volcánica también ha dado° origen a fuentes° y pozas termales. Si te gusta cuidarte y amas la naturaleza, recuerda estos nombres: Las Hornillas y Las Pailas. Son pozas naturales de aguas termales que están cerca del volcán Rincón de la Vieja. Un baño termal en medio de un paisaje tan hermoso es una experiencia única.

Otros balnearios°

Todos ofrecen piscinas, baños, pozas y duchas de aguas termales y además...

Lugar	Servicios
El Edén y Yanasara, Curgos (Perú)	cascadas° de aguas termales
Montbrió del Camp, Tarragona (España)	baños de algas°
Puyuhuapi (Chile)	duchas de agua de mar; baños de algas
Termas de Río Hondo, Santiago del Estero (Argentina)	baños de lodo
Tepoztlán, Morelos (México)	temazcales° aztecas
Uyuni, Potosí (Bolivia)	baños de sal

baño *bath* terma *hot spring* beneficio *benefit* lodo *mud* siglos *centuries* manantiales *springs* surge *springs forth* pozas *small pools* estanques *ponds* cuevas *caves* tratamientos *treatments* piel *skin* ha dado *has given* fuentes *springs* balnearios *spas* cascadas *waterfalls* algas *seaweed* temazcales *steam and medicinal herb baths*

ACTIVIDADES

1 ¿Cierto o falso? Indica si lo que dicen las oraciones es **cierto** o **falso**. Corrige la información falsa.

1. Las aguas termales son beneficiosas para algunas enfermedades, incluido el estrés. **Cierto.**
2. Los tratamientos con agua y lodo se conocen sólo desde hace pocos años. **Falso.** Son populares desde hace muchos siglos.
3. Las termas son manantiales naturales de agua caliente. **Cierto.**
4. La lodoterapia es un tratamiento con barro (*mud*). **Cierto.**
5. La temperatura de las aguas termales no afecta la absorción de los minerales. **Falso.** Facilita la absorción de minerales y otros elementos.
6. Mucha gente va a Baños de San Vicente, Ecuador, por sus playas. **Falso.** Mucha gente va por los tratamientos con lodo.
7. Las Hornillas son pozas de aguas termales en Costa Rica. **Cierto.**
8. Montbrió del Camp ofrece baños de sal. **Falso.** Montbrió del Camp ofrece baños de algas.
9. Es posible ver aguas termales en forma de cascadas. **Cierto.**
10. Tepoztlán ofrece temazcales aztecas. **Cierto.**

ASÍ SE DICE

El ejercicio

los abdominales	*sit-ups*
la bicicleta estática	*stationary bicycle*
el calambre muscular	*(muscular) cramp*
el (fisi)culturismo; la musculación (Esp.)	*bodybuilding*
las flexiones de pecho; las lagartijas (Méx.; Col.); **las planchas** (Esp.)	*push-ups*
la cinta (trotadora) (Arg.; Chile)	**la cinta caminadora**

EL MUNDO HISPANO

Creencias° sobre la salud

- **Colombia** Como algunos suelos son de baldosas°, se cree que si se camina descalzo° se enfrían° los pies y esto puede causar un resfriado o artritis.

- **Cuba** Por la mañana, muchas madres sacan a sus bebés a los patios y a las puertas de las casas. La creencia es que unos cinco minutos de sol ayudan a fijar° el calcio en los huesos y aumentan la inmunidad contra las enfermedades.

- **México** Muchas personas tienen la costumbre de tomar a diario un vaso de jugo del cactus conocido como "nopal". Se dice que es bueno para reducir el colesterol y el azúcar en la sangre y que ayuda a adelgazar.

Creencias *Beliefs* **baldosas** *tiles* **descalzo** *barefoot* **se enfrían** *get cold* **fijar** *to set*

PERFIL

La quinua

La quinua es una semilla° de gran valor° nutricional. Se produce en los Andes de Bolivia, Perú, Argentina, Colombia, Chile y Ecuador, y también en los Estados Unidos. Forma parte de la dieta básica de esos países andinos desde hace más de 5.000 años.

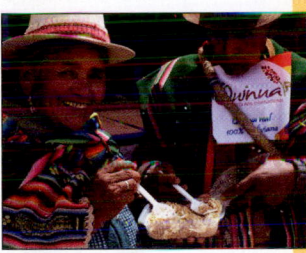

La quinua es rica en proteínas, hierro° y magnesio. Contiene los ocho aminoácidos básicos para el ser humano; por esto es un alimento muy completo, ideal para vegetarianos y veganos. Otra de las ventajas de la quinua es que no contiene gluten, por lo que la pueden consumir personas con alergias e intolerancia a esta proteína.

Aunque es técnicamente una semilla, la quinua es considerada un cereal por su composición y por su uso. Los granos° de la quinua pueden ser tostados para hacer harina° o se pueden cocinar de múltiples maneras. Se utiliza como

reemplazo° del arroz o de la pasta, con verduras, carnes, etc., en ensaladas, o como reemplazo de la avena° en el desayuno.

semilla *seed* **valor** *value* **hierro** *iron* **granos** *grains* **harina** *flour* **reemplazo** *replacement* **avena** *oats*

CON RITMO HISPANO

Chila Jatun (2008–)
Lugar de origen: Cochabamba, Bolivia

Este grupo de música andina está conformado por los hijos y los sobrinos de Los Kjarkas, una de las bandas de música folclórica más importantes de Bolivia. Su nombre, de origen quechua, significa "de pequeño a grande".

Go to **vhlcentral.com** to find out more about **Chila Jatun** and its music.

ACTIVIDADES

2 Comprensión Responde a las preguntas.

1. Una argentina te dice: "Voy a usar la cinta." ¿Qué va a hacer?
   Va a usar la cinta caminadora.
2. Según los colombianos, ¿qué efectos negativos tiene el no usar zapatos en casa? Puede causar un resfriado o artritis.
3. ¿Qué es la quinua? Es una semilla de gran valor nutricional.
4. ¿Qué proteína no contiene la quinua? No contiene gluten.

3 Para sentirte mejor Entrevista a un(a) compañero/a sobre las cosas que hace todos los días y las cosas que hace al menos una o dos veces a la semana para sentirse mejor. Hablen sobre actividades deportivas, la alimentación y lo que hacen en sus ratos libres.
Answers will vary.

More activities
vhlcentral / Online activities

Section Goal

In **Estructura 15.1**, students will learn the use of the present perfect.

Instructional Resources
Supersite: Audio (Lab MP3 Files); Resources (Grammar Presentation Slides, Activity Pack, Scripts, Answer Keys); Testing Program (Quizzes)
WebSAM
Workbook
Lab Manual

Teaching Tips
• Have students turn to pages 512–513. Ask them to read the **Fotonovela** captions again and write down the past participles they find. Ask students if they are used as adjectives or as parts of verbs.

• Model the present perfect by making statements about what you and others in the class have done, or by asking students questions. Ex: **Yo he preparado una lección. Ustedes han leído la sección de Estructura, ¿verdad? ¿Quién no la ha leído?**

Consulta Tell students that while the present perfect is generally used in Spanish just as it is in English, the expression *to have just done something* is expressed in Spanish by **acabar de** + [*infinitive*]. Write these sentences on the board and contrast them: **Acabo de venir del gimnasio. He venido del gimnasio.**

Nota cultural
The *Chilam Balam* texts are considered a challenge for translators because of the archaic, idiomatic, and metaphorical nature of the Yucatec Maya language. Have students research more about the language online and see if they can find any similarities to Spanish. Then have students share their findings with the class.

15.1 # The present perfect Tutorial

ANTE TODO In **Lección 14**, you learned how to form past participles. You will now learn how to form the present perfect indicative (**el pretérito perfecto de indicativo**), a compound tense that uses the past participle. The present perfect is used to talk about what someone *has done*. In Spanish, it is formed with the present tense of the auxiliary verb **haber** and a past participle.

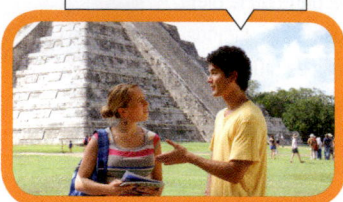

Maru ha estado bajo mucha presión.

He querido regresar desde que leí el *Chilam Balam*.

Present indicative of haber

Singular forms		Plural forms	
yo	**he**	nosotros/as	**hemos**
tú	**has**	vosotros/as	**habéis**
Ud./él/ella	**ha**	Uds./ellos/ellas	**han**

Tú no **has aumentado** de peso.
You haven't gained weight.

Yo ya **he leído** esos libros.
I've already read those books.

¿**Ha asistido** Juan a la clase de yoga?
Has Juan attended the yoga class?

Hemos conocido al entrenador.
We have met the trainer.

▶ The past participle does not change in form when it is part of the present perfect tense; it only changes in form when it is used as an adjective.

Clara **ha abierto** las ventanas.
Clara has opened the windows.

Yo **he cerrado** la puerta del gimnasio.
I've closed the door to the gym.

Las ventanas están **abiertas**.
The windows are open.

La puerta del gimnasio está **cerrada**.
The door to the gym is closed.

▶ In Spanish, the present perfect indicative generally is used just as in English: to talk about what someone has done or what has occurred. It usually refers to the recent past.

He trabajado cuarenta horas esta semana.
I have worked forty hours this week.

¿Cuál es el último libro que **has leído**?
What is the last book that you have read?

TEACHING OPTIONS

Extra Practice Ask students what they have done over the past week to lead a healthy lifestyle. Ask follow-up questions to elicit a variety of different conjugations of the present perfect. Ex: **¿Qué han hecho esta semana para llevar una vida sana? Y tú, ____, ¿qué has hecho? ¿Qué ha hecho ____ esta semana?**
Pairs Ask students to tell their partners five things they have done in the past to stay in shape. Partners repeat back what the

person has said, using the **tú** form of the present perfect.
Ex: **He levantado pesas. (Muy bien. Has levantado pesas.)**
Large Groups Have the class stand in a circle. Call out a subject pronoun and an infinitive. Ex: **yo/sufrir**. Toss a ball to a student, who will say the correct present perfect form (Ex: **yo he sufrido**) and toss the ball to another student, who will use the verb in a sentence.

▶ In English, the auxiliary verb and the past participle are often separated. In Spanish, however, these two elements—**haber** and the past participle—cannot be separated by any word.

> Siempre **hemos vivido** en Bolivia.
> *We have always lived in Bolivia.*

> Usted nunca **ha venido** a mi oficina.
> *You have never come to my office.*

¿Y Juan Carlos todavía no te ha invitado a salir?

Últimamente hemos sufrido muchas presiones en la universidad.

▶ The word **no** and any object or reflexive pronouns are placed immediately before **haber**.

> Yo **no he comido** la merienda.
> *I haven't eaten the snack.*

> ¿Por qué **no la has comido**?
> *Why haven't you eaten it?*

> Susana ya **se ha entrenado**.
> *Susana has already practiced.*

> Ellos **no lo han terminado**.
> *They haven't finished it.*

▶ Note that *to have* can be either a main verb or an auxiliary verb in English. As a main verb, it corresponds to **tener,** while as an auxiliary, it corresponds to **haber**.

> **Tengo** muchos amigos.
> *I have a lot of friends.*

> **He tenido** mucho éxito.
> *I have had a lot of success.*

▶ To form the present perfect of **hay,** use the third-person singular of **haber (ha) + habido**.

> **Ha habido** muchos problemas
> con el nuevo profesor.
> *There have been a lot of problems*
> *with the new professor.*

> **Ha habido** un accidente en
> la calle Central.
> *There has been an accident*
> *on Central Street.*

👁 **¡INTÉNTALO!** Indica el pretérito perfecto de indicativo de estos verbos.

1. (disfrutar, comer, vivir) yo _he disfrutado, he comido, he vivido_
2. (leer, resolver, poner) ella _ha leído, ha resuelto, ha puesto_
3. (venir, estar, correr) usted _ha venido, ha estado, ha corrido_
4. (traer, adelgazar, compartir) tú _has traído, has adelgazado, has compartido_
5. (decir, romper, hacer) ellos _han dicho, han roto, han hecho_
6. (mantenerse, dormirse) nosotros _nos hemos mantenido, nos hemos dormido_
7. (estar, escribir, ver) yo _he estado, he escrito, he visto_
8. (vivir, correr, morir) él _ha vivido, ha corrido, ha muerto_

Práctica

1 **Completar** Completa las oraciones con el pretérito perfecto de indicativo de los verbos.

adelgazar	aumentar	comer	hacer	llevar	sufrir

1. Juan y Raúl __han aumentado__ de peso porque no hacen ejercicio.
2. Luisa __ha sufrido__ muchas presiones este año.
3. Pero María y yo __hemos adelgazado__ porque trabajamos en exceso y nos olvidamos de comer.
4. Desde siempre, yo __he llevado__ una vida muy sana.
5. Pero tú y yo no __hemos hecho__ gimnasia este semestre.

2 **Oraciones** Combina los elementos para formar oraciones completas con el pretérito perfecto.

Answers may vary. Suggested answers:

> **modelo**
> tú / nunca / estar / a dieta   Tú nunca has estado a dieta.

1. ustedes / usar / muchas veces / la cinta caminadora
   Ustedes han usado muchas veces la cinta caminadora.
2. Patricia / asistir / una vez / a la clase de karate
   Patricia ha asistido una vez a la clase de karate.
3. yo / nunca / correr / más de cinco millas
   Yo nunca he corrido más de cinco millas.
4. los niños / nunca / comer / espárragos
   Los niños nunca han comido espárragos.
5. Antonio y yo / jamás / levantar / pesas
   Antonio y yo jamás hemos levantado pesas.
6. mis compañeros de clase / nunca / hacer ejercicios de estiramiento
   Mis compañeros de clase nunca han hecho ejercicios de estiramiento.

3 **¿Qué has hecho?** Indica si has hecho lo siguiente. Answers will vary.

> **modelo**
> escalar una montaña
> Sí, he escalado varias montañas./No, no he escalado nunca una montaña.

1. jugar al baloncesto
2. viajar a Bolivia
3. conocer a una persona famosa
4. recibir un masaje
5. bailar salsa
6. ver una película en español
7. estar despierto/a 24 horas
8. bucear

AYUDA

You may use some of these expressions in your answers:
una vez *once*
un par de veces *a couple of times*
algunas veces *a few times*
varias veces *several times*
muchas veces *many times, often*

4 **La vida sana** En parejas, túrnense para hacer preguntas sobre el tema de la vida sana.
Answers will vary.

> **modelo**
> encontrar un gimnasio
> **Estudiante 1:** ¿Has encontrado un buen gimnasio cerca de tu casa?
> **Estudiante 2:** Yo no he encontrado un gimnasio, pero sé que debo buscar uno.

1. tratar de estar en forma
2. dejar de tomar refrescos
3. hacerse una prueba del colesterol
4. entrenarse cinco días a la semana
5. cambiar de una vida sedentaria a una vida activa
6. hacer ejercicio para aliviar la tensión

TEACHING OPTIONS

Small Groups 🡒↔🡒 Divide the class into groups of four to write and perform skits in which one student plays a personal trainer, another plays a nutritionist, and the other two play clients. The personal trainer and nutritionist ask the clients whether they have done the things they have recommended. The clients explain what they have done and make excuses for what they have not done.

Pairs 🡒↔🡒 Have students discuss with a classmate five things they have already done today. Ex: **He estudiado la lección para esta clase. He ido al gimnasio. He ido a una clase de ejercicios aeróbicos. He almorzado con unos amigos. He escrito un mensaje electrónico a mis abuelos. ¿Qué has hecho tú?**

Comunicación

5

Descripción En parejas, describan lo que han hecho y no han hecho estas personas. Usen la imaginación. Answers will vary.

1. Jorge y Raúl

2. Luisa

3. Jacobo

4. Natalia y Diego

5. Ricardo

6. Carmen

6

Describir En parejas, identifiquen a una persona que lleva una vida muy sana. Puede ser una persona que conocen o un personaje que aparece en una película o programa de televisión. Entre los dos, escriban una descripción de lo que esta persona ha hecho para llevar una vida sana.
Answers will vary.

modelo
> Mario López siempre ha hecho todo lo posible para mantenerse en forma. Él…

Síntesis

7

Situación Trabajen en parejas para representar una conversación entre un(a) enfermero/a de la clínica de la universidad y un(a) estudiante. Answers will vary.

- El/La estudiante no se siente nada bien.
- El/La enfermero/a debe averiguar de dónde viene el problema e investigar los hábitos del/de la estudiante.
- El/La estudiante le explica lo que ha hecho en los últimos meses y cómo se ha sentido.
- Luego el/la enfermero/a le da recomendaciones de cómo llevar una vida más sana.

---

5 Teaching Tip
To simplify, before beginning the activity, ask volunteers to describe the people in the drawings and how they think they feel.

5 Expansion
In small groups, have students choose one of the drawings to elaborate on, using the preterite, present perfect, and present indicative. To begin, each student should take a turn telling a part of the story using the preterite, then as the story moves into the recent past, each group member should add to the story using the present perfect. To finish, the group should decide together what the people have just done and what they are going to do next. You may wish to assign one group member as the secretary to record the stories so that they can be shared with the class. Ex: **Carmen fue de vacaciones a Chile… En Portillo ella ha esquiado en una montaña… Carmen acaba de quitarse las botas de esquí y ahora va a almorzar en un restaurante.**

6 Teaching Tip
Have pairs describe eight things their chosen person has done that exemplify a healthy lifestyle. Remind them to include introductory and concluding statements in their descriptions.

6 Expansion
Have students choose someone who is the exact opposite of the healthy person they chose earlier and write a description of what that person has done that exemplifies an unhealthy lifestyle.

7 Expansion
While pairs are performing their role-plays for the class, stop the action after the patient has described his or her symptoms and what he or she has done in the last few months. Ask the class to make a diagnosis. Then have the pair finish their presentation.

TEACHING OPTIONS

Game Have students write three important things they have done over the past year on a slip of paper and put it in a box. Ex: **Este año he creado un blog.** Have students draw a paper from the box, then circulate around the room, asking classmates if they have done the activities listed, until they find the person who wrote the slip of paper. The first person to find a match wins.

Heritage Speakers Have heritage speakers interview a Spanish-speaking immigrant to find out how that person's life has changed since moving to this country. Tell them to find out if the interviewee's physical activity and diet have changed and report this information to the class. Have the rest of the class react and state to what degree the interviewee's lifestyle is typical of this country.

15.2 The past perfect Tutorial

ANTE TODO   The past perfect indicative (**el pretérito pluscuamperfecto de indicativo**) is used to talk about what someone *had done* or what *had occurred* before another past action, event, or state. Like the present perfect, the past perfect uses a form of **haber**—in this case, the imperfect—plus the past participle.

Past perfect indicative

		cerrar	perder	asistir
SINGULAR FORMS	yo	**había** cerrado	**había** perdido	**había** asistido
	tú	**habías** cerrado	**habías** perdido	**habías** asistido
	Ud./él/ella	**había** cerrado	**había** perdido	**había** asistido
PLURAL FORMS	nosotros/as	**habíamos** cerrado	**habíamos** perdido	**habíamos** asistido
	vosotros/as	**habíais** cerrado	**habíais** perdido	**habíais** asistido
	Uds./ellos/ellas	**habían** cerrado	**habían** perdido	**habían** asistido

Antes de 2014, **había vivido** en La Paz.
Before 2014, I had lived in La Paz.

Cuando llegamos, Luis ya **había salido**.
When we arrived, Luis had already left.

▶ The past perfect is often used with the word **ya** (*already*) to indicate that an action, event, or state had already occurred before another. Remember that, unlike its English equivalent, **ya** cannot be placed between **haber** and the past participle.

Ella **ya había salido** cuando llamaron.
She had already left when they called.

Cuando llegué, Raúl **ya se había acostado**.
When I arrived, Raúl had already gone to bed.

▶ **¡Atención!** The past perfect is often used in conjunction with **antes de** + [*noun*] or **antes de** + [*infinitive*] to describe when the action(s) occurred.

Antes de este año, nunca **había estudiado español**.
Before this year, I had never studied Spanish.

Luis **me había llamado antes de venir**.
Luis had called me before he came.

¡INTÉNTALO!   Indica el pretérito pluscuamperfecto de indicativo de cada verbo.

1. Nosotros ya ___habíamos cenado___ (cenar) cuando nos llamaron.
2. Eduardo nunca ___se había entrenado___ (entrenarse) tanto en invierno.
3. Antes de ir a México, ellos nunca ___habían ido___ (ir) a otro país.
4. Antes de tomar esta clase, yo no ___había estudiado___ (estudiar) nunca el español.
5. Tú siempre ___habías llevado___ (llevar) una vida sana antes del año pasado.
6. Antes de conocerte, yo ya te ___había visto___ (ver) muchas veces.

More activities
vhlcentral
LM p. 88
WB pp. 173–174
Online activities

Práctica

1 Completar Completa los minidiálogos con las formas correctas del pretérito pluscuamperfecto de indicativo.

1. **ANTONIO** Antes de este año, ¿ _había corrido_ (correr) usted en un maratón?
   SRA. VERA No, nunca lo _había hecho_ (hacer).

▶ 2. **DOLORES** Antes de ir a Argentina, ¿ _habían probado_ (probar) tú y tu familia el mate?
   TOMÁS Sí, ya _habíamos tomado_ (tomar) mate muchas veces.

3. **SARA** Antes de cumplir los 15 años, ¿ _habías estudiado_ (estudiar) tú otra lengua?
   JOSÉ Sí, _había tomado_ (tomar) clases de inglés y de italiano.

4. **SOFÍA** Antes de su enfermedad, ¿ _había sufrido_ (sufrir) muchas presiones tu tío?
   IRENE Sí... y él nunca _se había mantenido_ (mantenerse) en forma.

2 Quehaceres Indica lo que ya había hecho cada miembro de la familia antes de la llegada de la madre, la señora Ferrer. Answers will vary.

Cuando llegó la señora Ferrer,
ya _____ Tomás,

ya había   todavía no había

3 Tu vida Indica si ya habías hecho estas cosas antes de cumplir los dieciséis años. Answers will vary.

1. hacer un viaje en avión
2. escalar una montaña
3. escribir un poema
4. filmar un video
5. enamorarte
6. tomar clases de ejercicios aeróbicos
7. montar a caballo
8. acampar
9. manejar un carro
10. cantar frente a 50 o más personas

Comunicación

4

Lo dudo Tu profesor(a) va a darte una hoja de actividades. Escribe cinco oraciones, algunas ciertas y algunas falsas, sobre cosas que habías hecho antes de venir a la universidad. Luego, en grupos, túrnense para leer sus oraciones. Cada miembro del grupo debe decir "es cierto" o "lo dudo" después de cada una. Escribe la reacción de cada compañero/a en la columna apropiada. ¿Quién obtuvo más respuestas ciertas? Answers will vary.

Oraciones	Miguel	Ana	Beatriz
1. Cuando tenía 10 años, ya había manejado el carro de mi papá.	Lo dudo.	Es cierto.	Lo dudo.
2.			
3.			
4.			
5.			

Síntesis

5

Gimnasio Olímpico En parejas, contesten las preguntas sobre el anuncio.

¡ACABO DE DESCUBRIR UNA NUEVA VIDA!

Hasta el año pasado, siempre había mirado la tele sentado en el sofá durante mis ratos libres. ¡Era sedentario y teleadicto! Jamás había practicado ningún deporte y había aumentado mucho de peso.

Este año, he empezado a comer una dieta equilibrada y voy al gimnasio todos los días. He comenzado a ser una persona muy activa y he adelgazado. Disfruto de una vida sana. ¡Me siento muy feliz!

¡Venga al Gimnasio Olímpico hoy mismo!

MANTÉNGASE EN FORMA.

1. Identifiquen los elementos del pretérito pluscuamperfecto de indicativo en el anuncio. había mirado; había practicado; había aumentado
2. ¿Cómo era la vida del hombre cuando llevaba una vida sedentaria? ¿Cómo es ahora? Answers will vary.
3. ¿Se identifican ustedes con algunos de los hábitos, presentes o pasados, de este hombre? ¿Con cuáles? Answers will vary.
4. ¿Qué les recomienda el hombre del anuncio a los lectores? ¿Creen que les da buenos consejos? Answers will vary.

TEACHING OPTIONS

Small Groups Divide the class into groups of three. Student A begins a sentence with **antes de** + [*infinitive*]. Student B finishes the sentence with a verb in the past perfect. Student C writes the sentence down. Have students alternate their roles until they have created nine sentences. Then, have all group members check the sentences before sharing them with the class.

Large Groups Divide the class into large groups for a game of "one-upmanship." The first student states something he or she had done before a certain age. The second student tells what the first one had done, then counters with something even more outrageous that he or she had done, and so on, until everyone has participated. Ex: _____ **había viajado en avión antes de cumplir los cinco años, pero yo había viajado en barco antes de tener tres años.**

15.3 # The present perfect subjunctive Tutorial

ANTE TODO The present perfect subjunctive (**el pretérito perfecto de subjuntivo**), like the present perfect indicative, is used to talk about what *has happened*. The present perfect subjunctive is formed using the present subjunctive of the auxiliary verb **haber** and a past participle.

Present perfect indicative		Present perfect subjunctive	
PRESENT INDICATIVE OF **HABER**	PAST PARTICIPLE	PRESENT SUBJUNCTIVE OF **HABER**	PAST PARTICIPLE
yo he	hablado	yo haya	hablado

Present perfect subjunctive

		cerrar	**perder**	**asistir**
SINGULAR FORMS	yo	**haya** cerrado	**haya** perdido	**haya** asistido
	tú	**hayas** cerrado	**hayas** perdido	**hayas** asistido
	Ud./él/ella	**haya** cerrado	**haya** perdido	**haya** asistido
PLURAL FORMS	nosotros/as	**hayamos** cerrado	**hayamos** perdido	**hayamos** asistido
	vosotros/as	**hayáis** cerrado	**hayáis** perdido	**hayáis** asistido
	Uds./ellos/ellas	**hayan** cerrado	**hayan** perdido	**hayan** asistido

▶ The same conditions that trigger the use of the present subjunctive apply to the present perfect subjunctive.

Present subjunctive	Present perfect subjunctive
Espero que **duermas** bien. *I hope that you sleep well.*	Espero que **hayas dormido** bien. *I hope that you have slept well.*
No creo que **aumente** de peso. *I don't think he will gain weight.*	No creo que **haya aumentado** de peso. *I don't think he has gained weight.*

▶ The action expressed by the present perfect subjunctive is seen as occurring before the action expressed in the main clause.

Me alegro de que ustedes **se hayan reído** tanto esta tarde.
I'm glad that you have laughed so much this afternoon.

Dudo que tú **te hayas divertido** mucho con tu suegra.
I doubt that you have enjoyed yourself much with your mother-in-law.

¡ATENCIÓN!

In Spanish the present perfect subjunctive is used to express a recent action.

No creo que lo **hayas dicho** bien.
I don't think that you have said it right.

Espero que él **haya llegado.**
I hope that he has arrived.

More activities

vhlcentral

LM p. 89

WB pp. 175–176

Online activities

¡INTÉNTALO! Indica el pretérito perfecto de subjuntivo de los verbos.

1. Me gusta que ustedes __hayan dicho__ (decir) la verdad.
2. No creo que tú __hayas comido__ (comer) tanto.
3. Es posible que yo __haya adelgazado__ (adelgazar) un poco esta semana.
4. Me alegro de que tú y yo __hayamos merendado__ (merendar) juntas.
5. Es imposible que usted __haya podido__ (poder) hacer tal (*such a*) cosa.
6. Espero que ellas __se hayan sentido__ (sentirse) mejor después de la clase.

Section Goal

In **Estructura 15.3**, students will learn the use of the present perfect subjunctive.

Instructional Resources
Supersite: Audio (Lab MP3 Files); Resources (Grammar Presentation Slides, Activity Pack, Scripts, Answer Keys); Testing Program (Quizzes)
WebSAM
Workbook
Lab Manual

Teaching Tips
• Ask a volunteer to tell you something he or she has done this week. Respond with a comment using the present perfect subjunctive. Ex: **Me alegro de que hayas levantado pesas. ¡Ay, no exageres, chico/a! ¡Dudo que hayas trabajado tanto!** Write present perfect subjunctive forms on the board as you say them.
• Ask volunteers to tell you what they have done during the past week. Again, comment on their statements in ways that trigger the present perfect subjunctive, but this time elicit peer comments that use the present perfect subjunctive.

TEACHING OPTIONS

Extra Practice Ask students to write their reactions to these statements: 1. Ángela ha dejado de fumar. 2. Roberto ha estudiado ocho horas hoy. 3. Todos los teleadictos han comido una dieta equilibrada. 4. No he preparado la prueba para mañana. 5. Mi esposo y yo hemos estado enfermos. Ex: **Es bueno que Ángela haya dejado de fumar.**

Small Groups ←🔲→ Divide the class into small groups. Have students take turns telling the group three wishes they hope to have fulfilled by the end of the day. Ex: **Espero que mi compañero haya limpiado el apartamento. Ojalá que mi novia me haya escrito un mensaje electrónico. Espero que haya llegado el estante que compré por Internet.**

Práctica

1 Completar Completa las oraciones con la forma correcta del pretérito perfecto de subjuntivo de los verbos.

1. Es triste que Nuria y yo __hayamos perdido__ (perder) el partido. Esperamos que los entrenadores del gimnasio nos __hayan preparado__ (preparar) un buen programa para ponernos en forma.
2. No creo que Lourdes y su amiga __se hayan ido__ (irse) de ese trabajo donde siempre tienen tantos problemas. Espero que Lourdes __haya aprendido__ (aprender) a aliviar el estrés.
3. ¡Qué lástima que Julio __se haya sentido__ (sentirse) tan mal en la competencia! Dudo que __se haya entrenado__ (entrenarse) lo suficiente.
4. No estoy segura de que Samuel __haya llevado__ (llevar) una vida sana. Es bueno que él __haya decidido__ (decidir) mejorar su dieta.
5. Me preocupa mucho que Ana y Rosa __hayan fumado__ (fumar) tanto de jóvenes. Es increíble que ellas no __se hayan enfermado__ (enfermarse).
6. Me alegro de que mi abuela __haya disfrutado__ (disfrutar) de buena salud toda su vida. Es maravilloso que ella __haya cumplido__ (cumplir) noventa años.

2 Describir Usa el pretérito perfecto de subjuntivo para hacer dos comentarios sobre cada dibujo. Usa expresiones como **no creo que, dudo que, es probable que, me alegro de que, espero que** y **siento que**. Answers will vary.

CONSULTA
To review verbs of emotion, see **Estructura 13.1**, p. 452.
To review expressions of doubt, disbelief, and denial, see **Estructura 13.2**, p. 456.

modelo
Es probable que Javier haya levantado pesas durante muchos años.

Me alegro de que Javier se haya mantenido en forma.

Javier

1. Rosa y Carlos

2. Roberto

3. Mariela

4. Lorena y su amigo

5. la señora Matos

6. Sonia y René

in class

Comunicación

3 **¿Sí o no?** En parejas, comenten estas afirmaciones (*statements*) usando las expresiones de la lista. *Answers will vary.*

Dudo que…	Es imposible que…	Me alegro de que (no)…
Es bueno que (no)…	Espero que (no)…	No creo que…

modelo

Estudiante 1: Ya llegó el fin del año escolar.
Estudiante 2: Es imposible que haya llegado el fin del año escolar.

1. Recibí una A en la clase de español.
2. Tu mejor amigo/a aumentó de peso recientemente.
3. Beyoncé dio un concierto ayer con Jay-Z.
4. Mis padres ganaron un millón de dólares.
5. He aprendido a hablar japonés.
6. Nuestro/a profesor(a) nació en Bolivia.
7. Salí anoche con…
8. El año pasado mi familia y yo fuimos de excursión a…

4 **Quejas** Tu compañero/a y tú han ido a un gimnasio nuevo y no quedaron satisfechos/as ni con el lugar ni con el personal. En parejas, escriban seis quejas (*complaints*). Utilicen el pretérito perfecto de subjuntivo. Luego, representen la conversación. *Answers will vary.*

dudo que	es posible que	me molesta que
es improbable que	es terrible que	no creo que

modelo

Estudiante 1: ¿Has visto los baños? ¡Es posible que no los hayan limpiado en años!
Estudiante 2: Sí, ¡es bueno que no nos hayamos duchado allí!

5 **Propósitos** Una amiga hizo una lista con sus buenos propósitos (*resolutions*) de Año Nuevo. Sin embargo, sólo cumplió algunos de ellos. En parejas, den su opinión al respecto. Utilicen expresiones como **dudo que**, **espero que**, **no creo que**, **me alegro de que** y **es imposible que**. *Answers will vary.*

adelgazar	correr un maratón
beber menos café	ahorrar dinero
comer más frutas y verduras	ver menos televisión
ir al gimnasio todos los días	aprender chino

modelo

Dudo que haya visto menos televisión. ¡Ella es teleadicta!

Section Goal

In **Recapitulación**, students will review the grammar concepts from this lesson.

Instructional Resource
Supersite

Teaching Tip You may want to assign this **Recapitulación** activity on the Supersite because it has diagnostics. There is an online-only review activity for each grammar point. The Supersite also has a **Repaso de vocabulario** activity with diagnostics.

1 Teaching Tips
• Before beginning the activity, call on a volunteer to name the reflexive verbs in the exercise. Remind students that the reflexive pronoun should appear before the conjugated verb.
• Complete this activity orally as a class.

1 Expansion
• To challenge students, have them provide the remaining verb forms.
• Have volunteers create logical sentences using these verb forms.

2 Teaching Tips
• Call on volunteers to read the model aloud.
• To simplify, have students begin by identifying the subject and infinitive for each blank.

2 Expansion Have students change the response for each item to the present perfect. Ex: **1. No, he hecho ejercicio en el parque.**

Recapitulación

Completa estas actividades para repasar los conceptos de gramática que aprendiste en esta lección.

1 **Completar** Completa cada tabla con el pretérito pluscuamperfecto de indicativo y el pretérito perfecto de subjuntivo de los verbos. **24 pts.**

PRETÉRITO PLUSCUAMPERFECTO

Infinitivo	tú	nosotros	ustedes
disfrutar	habías disfrutado	habíamos disfrutado	habían disfrutado
apurarse	te habías apurado	nos habíamos apurado	se habían apurado

PRETÉRITO PERFECTO DE SUBJUNTIVO

Infinitivo	yo	él	ellas
tratar	haya tratado	haya tratado	hayan tratado
entrenarse	me haya entrenado	se haya entrenado	se hayan entrenado

2 **Preguntas** Completa las preguntas para estas respuestas usando el pretérito perfecto de indicativo. **16 pts.**

> **modelo**
> —¿Has llamado a tus padres? —Sí, los llamé ayer.

1. —¿Tú __has hecho__ ejercicio esta mañana en el gimnasio?
   —No, hice ejercicio en el parque.

2. —Y ustedes, ¿__han desayunado__ ya? —Sí, desayunamos en el hotel.

3. —Y Juan y Felipe, ¿adónde __han ido__? —Fueron al cine.

4. —Paco, ¿(nosotros) __hemos recibido__ la cuenta del gimnasio?
   —Sí, la recibimos la semana pasada.

5. —Señor Martín, ¿__ha pescado__ algo ya? —Sí, pesqué uno grande. Ya me puedo ir a casa contento.

6. —Inés, ¿__has visto__ mi pelota de fútbol? —Sí, la vi esta mañana en el coche.

7. —Yo no __he tomado__ café todavía. ¿Alguien quiere acompañarme? —No, gracias. Yo ya tomé mi café en casa.

8. —¿Ya te __ha dicho__ el doctor que puedes comer chocolate?
   —Sí, me lo dijo ayer.

RESUMEN GRAMATICAL

15.1 **The present perfect** *pp. 518–519*

Present indicative of haber	
he	hemos
has	habéis
ha	han

Present perfect: present tense of **haber** + past participle

Present perfect indicative	
he empezado	hemos empezado
has empezado	habéis empezado
ha empezado	han empezado

He empezado a ir al gimnasio con regularidad.
I have begun to go to the gym regularly.

15.2 **The past perfect** *p. 522*

Past perfect: imperfect tense of **haber** + past participle

Past perfect indicative	
había vivido	habíamos vivido
habías vivido	habíais vivido
había vivido	habían vivido

Antes de 2013, yo ya **había vivido** en tres países diferentes.
Before 2013, I had already lived in three different countries.

15.3 **The present perfect subjunctive** *p. 525*

Present perfect subjunctive: present subjunctive of **haber** + past participle

Present perfect subjunctive	
haya comido	hayamos comido
hayas comido	hayáis comido
haya comido	hayan comido

Espero que **hayas comido** bien.
I hope that you have eaten well.

TEACHING OPTIONS

Pairs Divide the class into pairs. Have students write and perform a conversation in which a student talks about the hard week he or she has had, using the present perfect. The other student should ask questions and offer advice, using the present perfect subjunctive.

Large Groups Have students form a circle. Throw a ball to a student and call out a time expression. Ex: **Antes de este semestre…** The student must complete the sentence using the past perfect (Ex: **Antes de este semestre, había estudiado japonés.**) and throw the ball to another student, who should do the same. Continue through a few more students, then provide a new sentence starter. Ex: **Antes de estudiar en esta universidad…**

3 Oraciones Forma oraciones completas con los elementos dados. Usa el pretérito pluscuamperfecto de indicativo y haz todos los cambios necesarios. Sigue el modelo. **8 pts.**

> **modelo**
> yo / ya / conocer / muchos amigos *Yo ya había conocido a muchos amigos.*

1. tú / todavía no / aprender / mantenerse en forma *Tú todavía no habías aprendido a mantenerte en forma.*
2. los hermanos Falcón / todavía no / perder / partido de vóleibol *Los hermanos Falcón todavía no habían perdido un partido de vóleibol.*
3. Elías / ya / entrenarse / para / maratón *Elías ya se había entrenado para el maratón.*
4. nosotros / siempre / sufrir / muchas presiones *Nosotros siempre habíamos sufrido muchas presiones.*

4 Una carta Completa esta carta con el pretérito perfecto de indicativo o de subjuntivo. **24 pts.**

Queridos papá y mamá:

¿Cómo (1) _han estado_ (estar)? Mamá, espero que no (2) _te hayas_ (tú, enfermarse) _enfermado_ otra vez. Yo sé que (3) _has seguido_ (tú, seguir) los consejos del doctor, pero estoy preocupada.

Y en mi vida, ¿qué (4) _ha pasado_ (pasar) últimamente (lately)? Pues, nada nuevo, sólo trabajo. Los problemas en la compañía, yo los (5) _he resuelto_ (resolver) casi todos. Pero estoy bien. Es verdad que (6) _he adelgazado_ (yo, adelgazar) un poco, pero no creo que (7) _haya sido_ (ser) a causa del estrés. Espero que no (8) _hayan sentido_ (ustedes, sentirse) mal porque no pude visitarlos. Es extraño que no (9) _hayan recibido_ (recibir) mis cartas. Tengo miedo de que (10) _se hayan perdido_ (las cartas, perderse).

Me alegro de que papá (11) _haya tomado_ (tomar) vacaciones para venir a visitarme. ¡Es increíble que nosotros no (12) _nos hayamos visto_ (verse) en casi un año!

Un abrazo y hasta muy pronto,
Belén

5 Manteniéndote en forma Escribe al menos cinco oraciones para describir cómo te has mantenido en forma este semestre. Di qué cosas han cambiado este semestre en relación con el año pasado. Usa las formas verbales que aprendiste en esta lección. **28 pts.** Answers will vary.

6 Poema Completa este fragmento de un poema de Nezahualcóyotl con el pretérito perfecto de indicativo de los verbos. **¡4 puntos EXTRA!**

" _He llegado_ (llegar) aquí,
soy Yoyontzin.
Sólo busco las flores
sobre la tierra, _he venido_ (venir)
a cortarlas. "

Section Goals

In **Lectura**, students will:
- learn to analyze story structure
- read an authentic narrative in Spanish

Instructional Resources
Supersite

Estrategia Have students identify the characters, setting, and plot of a well-known story.

Examinar el texto Ask students to predict what kind of consultation the story might have. Have them speculate about how the photos might illustrate some aspect of the story.

Estructura del cuento Have students take notes as they read the story and then answer the questions. Ask students to explain their answers.

Sobre el autor Explain that the author's real last name, **Leal**, means *loyal* and that his pseudonym, **Desleal**, means the opposite. His most famous work is *Luz negra* (1965), an example of theater of the absurd.

Lectura

Antes de leer

Estrategia

Analyzing story structure

You can understand a narrative more completely by analyzing story structure. Stories have characters, settings, and plots. A character is the fictional person in a story. The setting refers to the place and time of the action. The plot indicates what happens. Description, dialogue, and actions reveal information about characters, setting, and plot.

✎ Examinar el texto

Mira las fotos y lee el título. Haz predicciones sobre el cuento.

✎ Estructura del cuento

Mientras lees el cuento, contesta estas preguntas.
Answers may vary. Suggested answers:
1. ¿Quiénes son los personajes (*characters*) del cuento? el paciente, el psiquiatra y la secretaria

2. ¿Cuál es el ambiente (*setting*)? el consultorio del psiquiatra, en el presente
3. ¿Cuál es la trama (*plot*)? Un hombre va al psiquiatra porque piensa que tiene una personalidad dividida.
4. ¿Qué te dice algo sobre los personajes, el ambiente y la trama: la descripción, el diálogo y/o las acciones? la descripción, el diálogo y las acciones

Sobre el autor

Álvaro Menén Desleal es su pseudónimo. Su nombre real es Álvaro Menéndez Leal (1931–2000). Este salvadoreño fue un polifacético personaje con una vida muy intensa. Fue periodista de prensa y televisión, escritor de cuentos, poesía, ensayo y obras de teatro. Fue profesor, boxeador y diplomático. A lo largo de su vida obtuvo varios premios por su labor creativa: el Premio Nacional de Cultura, dos premios de teatro, dos de cuentos y uno de ensayo.

More activities

vhlcentral   Online activities

Después de leer

✎ Comprensión

Indica si las oraciones son **ciertas** o **falsas**. Corrige las oraciones falsas.

1. El paciente lleva un traje sucio.
   Falso. El hombre lleva un traje impoluto.
2. El paciente está sentado en una silla.
   Falso. El paciente está recostado en el diván.
3. El médico cree que el hombre tiene esquizofrenia.
   Falso. El médico no cree que el hombre tenga esquizofrenia.
4. La consulta dura casi dos horas. Cierto.

5. El paciente da respuestas cortas.
   Falso. El paciente da respuestas largas.
6. El paciente se despide del psiquiatra y le paga la consulta a la secretaria. Cierto.

TEACHING OPTIONS

Pairs ←👤→ Have students work in pairs to write a continuation of the story. Ask for volunteers to share their work with the class.

Large Group Have students generate a list of other short stories that contain fantastical elements.

Teaching Tip Explain that this story is from the author's collection *Una cuerda de nylon y oro y otros cuentos maravillosos* (1969).

LA CONSULTA

ÁLVARO MENÉN DESLEAL

—Tengo razones fundadas°, Doctor —dijo el hombre de impoluto° traje blanco, pacientemente recostado° en el diván del psiquiatra—, para suponer que padezco° de una personalidad dividida.

El psiquiatra anotó en su libretita° que, tentativamente, desechaba° la presencia de una esquizofrenia: en general, una persona afectada de tal dolencia° evita la consulta con el médico.

La consulta duró casi dos horas. Hubo preguntas cortas y respuestas largas. Aparentemente más tranquilo, el hombre se despidió del° psiquiatra, pagó a una secretaria el valor de la consulta, y ganó° la puerta.

En la calle, vestido de negro riguroso, le esperaba otro hombre.

—¿Lo confirmaste? —preguntó el hombre de negro.

—No sé —fue la respuesta del hombre de blanco.

Luego se fundieron° en un solo individuo, enfundado° en un traje gris. ◼

fundadas *well-founded* impoluto *spotless* recostado *lying down* padezco *I suffer* libretita *little notebook* desechaba *rejected* tal dolencia *such an illness* se despidió de *said goodbye to* ganó *reached* se fundieron *they merged* enfundado *wrapped*

Interpretación

Responde a las preguntas con oraciones completas. Answers will vary.

1. ¿El paciente está seguro de que tiene una personalidad dividida? ¿Por qué?

2. ¿El psiquiatra está seguro del diagnóstico? ¿Por qué?

3. ¿En qué se basa el médico para dar su diagnóstico?

4. Al final del cuento, ¿el hombre está seguro de que no padece de una personalidad dividida? ¿Por qué?

¿Qué piensas?

En parejas, respondan a estas preguntas. Answers will vary.

1. ¿Por qué creen que el hombre decide visitar al psiquiatra?

2. ¿Piensan que el hombre tiene o no tiene esquizofrenia?

3. ¿Creen que el hombre vestido de negro es real? ¿Por qué?

4. ¿Qué piensan que ocurre al final del cuento?

Comprensión Have students write two additional true/false statements about the story for a partner to answer.

Interpretación Have students discuss their answers with a partner.

¿Qué piensas? Use the questions to conduct a class discussion. Ask students what they think the ending means.

TEACHING OPTIONS

Pairs Bring in another short story with a surprising or unusual ending, such as *El eclipse* by **Augusto Monterroso**. Have pairs compare and contrast the endings.

Extra Practice Invite students to remember and write about a personal experience, or that of a friend or relative, with a surprising or unusual ending. If they don't have a real one to tell, ask them to imagine one. Ask volunteers to share their stories with the class.

Escritura

Estrategia
Organizing information logically

Many times a written piece may require you to include a great deal of information. You might want to organize your information in one of three different ways:

- ▶ chronologically (e.g., events in the history of a country)
- ▶ sequentially (e.g., steps in a recipe)
- ▶ in order of importance

Organizing your information beforehand will make both your writing and your message clearer to your readers. If you were writing a piece on weight reduction, for example, you would need to organize your ideas about two general areas: eating right and exercise. You would need to decide which of the two is more important according to your purpose in writing the piece. If your main idea is that eating right is the key to losing weight, you might want to start your piece with a discussion of good eating habits. You might want to discuss the following aspects of eating right in order of their importance:

- ▶ quantities of food
- ▶ selecting appropriate foods
- ▶ healthy recipes
- ▶ percentage of fat in each meal
- ▶ calorie count
- ▶ percentage of carbohydrates in each meal
- ▶ frequency of meals

You would then complete the piece by following the same process to discuss the various aspects of the importance of getting exercise.

Tema

 Escribir un plan personal de bienestar

Desarrolla un plan personal para mejorar tu bienestar, tanto físico como emocional. Tu plan debe describir:

1. lo que has hecho para mejorar tu bienestar y llevar una vida sana
2. lo que no has podido hacer todavía
3. las actividades que debes hacer en los próximos meses

Considera también estas preguntas:

La nutrición
- ▶ ¿Comes una dieta equilibrada?
- ▶ ¿Consumes suficientes vitaminas y minerales?
- ▶ ¿Consumes demasiada grasa?
- ▶ ¿Quieres aumentar de peso o adelgazar?
- ▶ ¿Qué puedes hacer para mejorar tu dieta?

El ejercicio
- ▶ ¿Haces ejercicio? ¿Con qué frecuencia?
- ▶ ¿Vas al gimnasio? ¿Qué tipo de ejercicios haces allí?
- ▶ ¿Practicas algún deporte?
- ▶ ¿Qué puedes hacer para mejorar tu bienestar físico?

El estrés
- ▶ ¿Sufres muchas presiones?
- ▶ ¿Qué actividades o problemas te causan estrés?
- ▶ ¿Qué haces (o debes hacer) para aliviar el estrés y sentirte más tranquilo/a?
- ▶ ¿Qué puedes hacer para mejorar tu bienestar emocional?

EVALUATION: Plan personal de bienestar

Criteria	Scale
Content	1 2 3 4
Organization	1 2 3 4
Use of vocabulary	1 2 3 4
Accuracy and mechanics	1 2 3 4
Creativity	1 2 3 4

Scoring	
Excellent	18–20 points
Good	14–17 points
Satisfactory	10–13 points
Unsatisfactory	< 10 points

Escuchar

Antes de escuchar

Estrategia

Listening for the gist/
Listening for cognates

Combining these two strategies is an easy way to get a good sense of what you hear. When you listen for the gist, you get the general idea of what you're hearing, which allows you to interpret cognates and other words in a meaningful context. Similarly, the cognates give you information about the details of the story that you might not have understood when listening for the gist.

To practice these strategies, you will listen to a short paragraph. Write down the gist of what you hear and jot down a few cognates. Based on the gist and the cognates, what conclusions can you draw about what you heard?

Preparación

Mira la foto. ¿Qué pistas (*clues*) te da de lo que vas a oír? Answers will vary.

Ahora escucha

Programa de radio

Escucha lo que dice Ofelia Cortez de Bauer. Anota algunos de los cognados que escuchas y también la idea general del discurso (*speech*). Answers will vary.

Idea general: _____

Ahora contesta las siguientes preguntas.

1. ¿Cuál es el género (*genre*) del discurso?
2. ¿Cuál es el tema?
3. ¿Cuál es el propósito (*purpose*)?

Comprensión

¿Cierto o falso?

Indica si lo que dicen estas oraciones es **cierto** o **falso**. Corrige las oraciones falsas.

	Cierto	Falso
1. La señora Bauer habla de la importancia de estar en buena forma y de hacer ejercicio.	◉	○
2. Según ella, lo más importante es que lleves el programa sugerido por los expertos.	○	◉
3. La señora Bauer participa en actividades individuales y de grupo.	◉	○
4. El único objetivo del tipo de programa que ella sugiere es adelgazar.	○	◉

2. Lo más importante es que lleves un programa variado que te guste.

4. Los objetivos de su programa son: condicionar el sistema cardiopulmonar, aumentar la fuerza muscular y mejorar la flexibilidad.

Preguntas

Responde a las preguntas. Answers will vary.

1. Imagina que el programa de radio sigue. Según las pistas que ella dio, ¿qué vas a oír en la segunda parte?
2. ¿A qué tipo de público (*audience*) le interesa el tema del que habla la señora Bauer?
3. ¿Sigues los consejos de la señora Bauer? Explica tu respuesta.
4. ¿Qué piensas de los consejos que ella da? ¿Hay otra información que ella debía haber incluido (*should have included*)?

con un buen calentamiento al comienzo. Tres días por semana corro en el parque, o si hace mal tiempo, uso una caminadora en el gimnasio. Luego levanto pesas y termino haciendo estiramientos de los músculos. Los fines de semana me mantengo activa pero hago una variedad de cosas de acuerdo a lo que quiere hacer la familia. A veces practico la natación; otras, vamos de excursión al campo, por ejemplo. Como les había

dicho la semana pasada, como unas 1.600 calorías al día, mayormente alimentos con poca grasa y sin sal. Disfruto mucho del bienestar que estos hábitos me producen. Ahora iremos a unos anuncios de nuestros patrocinadores. Cuando regresemos, voy a contestar sus preguntas acerca del ejercicio, la dieta o el bienestar en general. El teléfono es el 43.89.76. No se vayan. Ya regresamos con mucha más información.

En pantalla  Video

Para Iker, cada persona se parece a un animal. Por ejemplo, su papá es un oso°. A Iker le habría gustado° ser un oso también, pero él es otro animal. Y eso es algo que nadie sabe en la escuela. Iker ha conseguido mantenerlo así gracias a algunos trucos°, pero tiene miedo de que los demás lo sepan. ¿Qué podría° pasar si° sus compañeros descubren el secreto de Iker?

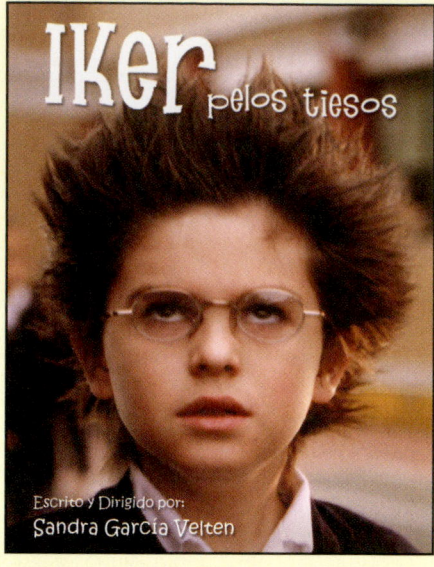

Escrito y Dirigido por:
Sandra García Velten

Preparación

 ¿Cierto o falso?

Lee la lista de **Expresiones útiles** e indica si lo que dice cada oración es **cierto** o **falso**. Corrige las oraciones falsas.

<u>cierto</u> 1. Me prestaste tu balón (*ball*) y yo te lo tengo que devolver.

<u>falso</u> 2. Si (*If*) quiero disimular algo, se lo digo a todos.
Si quiero disimular algo, no se lo digo a nadie.

<u>cierto</u> 3. Es común que una hija salga igual a su madre.

<u>cierto</u> 4. Para hacerme un peinado especial, voy al salón de belleza.

<u>falso</u> 5. Para cocinar el pan, lo meto en el congelador.
Para cocinar el pan, lo meto en la tostadora/el horno.

<u>cierto</u> 6. Si no hago ejercicios de estiramiento, me siento tieso.

 Rasgos de familia

En parejas, túrnense para hacerse estas preguntas.
Answers will vary.

1. ¿Tienes rasgos particulares? ¿Cuáles son de tu apariencia física (*physical appearance*)? ¿Cuáles son de tu personalidad?

2. ¿Cuáles de tus rasgos son buenos? ¿Cuáles son malos? ¿Cómo determinas que son buenos o malos?

3. ¿Cuáles de tus rasgos particulares, buenos y malos, te hacen una persona única?

4. ¿Alguno de esos rasgos es común en tu familia? ¿Ha pasado de generación en generación?

5. ¿Tienes compañeros que comparten tus mismos rasgos? ¿Qué tienen en común ustedes?

6. ¿Qué animal crees que serías (*you would be*) según (*according to*) tus rasgos? Explica tu respuesta.

oso *bear* le habría gustado *he would have liked*
trucos *tricks* podría *could* si *if*

Expresiones útiles

devolver	*to return, to give back*
disimular	*to hide, to disguise*
me hubiera gustado	*I would have liked*
meter	*to put (something) in, to introduce*
el peinado	*hairstyle*
salir (igual) a	*to take after*
si supieran	*if they knew*
tieso/a	*stiff*

Para hablar del corto

burlarse (de)	*to make fun (of)*
esconder(se)	*to hide (onself)*
la fuerza	*strength*
orgulloso/a	*proud*
pelear(se)	*to fight (with one another)*
el rasgo	*feature, characteristic*
sentirse cohibido/a	*to feel self-conscious*

NATIONAL
communication
cultures
STANDARDS

More activities
 vhlcentral
 Online activities

Escenas: Iker pelos tiesos

IKER: Tito es un mosquito; de esos que nunca dejan de molestar... ni en las noches.

IKER: Mi mamá es un perico (*parrot*), como todas las mamás.

NIÑO 3: Ey, no hay paso. (*Hey, there's no way through.*)

IKER: Pero, ¿por qué?

IKER: ... [yo] salí igual a mi abuelo... soy un puercoespín (*porcupine*).

IKER: ¿Qué me dirían si supieran mi secreto?

IKER: ¿Y por qué ese niño está pasando?

NIÑO 5: Porque éste es nuestro territorio.

I: ¿Qué me dirían si supieran mi secreto?
AMIGO: ¡Ah sí, te gané! Sí, mira, ¿ves?
I: ¿Cómo decías que se llamaba Miguel Hidalgo?
A: Michel... Michel Higalgo [*sic*].
NIÑO 3: Ey, no hay paso.
I: Pero, ¿por qué?
NIÑO 4: Porque nosotros decidimos quién pasa y quién no.
I: ¿Y por qué ese niño está pasando?

NIÑO 5: Porque éste es nuestro territorio.
I: ¡Déjenlo!
A: Mejor ya vámonos.
I: Sí.
N4: Y cuidadito y vayan de chismosas.
N5: Ey, ey, ey, ey, ésta sí pasa.
I: ¡Oye, dame mi balón!
N3: ¿Lo quieres?

(*Script continues on page 536.*)

Iker pelos tiesos
Script

HERMANA: Iker, ¡que ya te pares!
IKER: A veces pienso que todas las personas se parecen a un animal.
H: Iker, que ya te despiertes.
I: Mi hermana es un caballo.
H: ¡Yo contesto! (*A Iker*) ¡Que ya te pares!
I: Tito es un mosquito, de esos que nunca dejan de molestar... ni en las noches.
MAMÁ: No, amiga, esas oportunidades no las debes dejar ir tan fácilmente... no, se te van a escapar, ¡agárralas! No, si no, te va a pasar lo mismo que me paso a mí el otro día, acuérdate, con las galletas.
I: Mi mamá es un perico, como todas las mamás.
M: ¿Te conté lo de las galletas? No, no te lo conté. Ay, estaba yo en el supermercado comprando galletas, ya ves que soy una amante de las galletas, me encantan. Llego a la caja y no me quieren hacer el descuento, entonces les digo, "Óiganme, discúlpenme, pero tráiganme al gerente, a mí cómo que no me van a hacer ningún descuento, qué les pasa".
I: A mí me hubiera gustado ser oso, como mi papá.
I: Pero salí igual a mi abuelo... soy un puercoespín.
I: Casi siempre lo puedo disimular...
I: Bueno, casi siempre.
NIÑA 1: ¡¡¡Aaaaah!!!
MAESTRA: ¿Quién me dice qué otros animales habitan en el desierto? ¿Quién? Allá atrás.
NIÑO 1: Ratas.
MAE: Ratas, muy bien. ¿Qué más? Escorpiones, águilas, ¿qué más?
MAE: Tarántulas.
NIÑA 2: Tortugas.
MAE: Ese es un halcón. También hay tortugas, muy bien. Serpientes. También hay felinos.
NIÑO 2: Maestra, ¿y dónde habitan los hipopótamos?
MAE: Los hipopótamos habitan en la selva, junto a los ríos, Bruno.
N2: Oye, Francisco, ¿por qué no te vas a vivir para allá? Estarías más a gusto.

(*Script continues at far left in the bottom panels.*)

Escoger As a variant, provide these items as cloze sentences. Rather than the multiple-choice options, give students a word bank.

Preguntas
🔴↔🔴 Once pairs have completed the activity, have students debate the notion that we all, to some extent, conform to society with regard to our physical appearance.

Superhéroes If students have difficulty thinking of a superpower they would like to possess, have them begin by considering the fifth and sixth bullets; first, have them think about how they would like to improve the world and whom they would like to help.

Comprensión

Escoger

Escoge la opción que completa mejor cada oración.

1. Iker siempre __c__ su pelo tieso.
   - a. muestra
   - b. corta
   - c. disimula

2. En la familia de Iker, __b__ el mismo rasgo.
   - a. no hay dos personas con
   - b. él y su abuelo comparten
   - c. el abuelo y Tito tienen

3. Para Iker, su __b__ es un perico.
   - a. hermana
   - b. mamá
   - c. maestra (*teacher*)

4. Para Iker, es probable que sus compañeros __b__ si saben su secreto.
   - a. lo acepten
   - b. se burlen de él
   - c. se escondan

5. Iker se sintió __a__ cuando su compañero le dijo que le gustaba su peinado.
   - a. aliviado (*relieved*)
   - b. cohibido
   - c. enojado

6. Al final, Iker estaba __c__ de mostrar su peinado natural.
   - a. avergonzado
   - b. nervioso
   - c. orgulloso

Preguntas

En parejas, respondan a estas preguntas con oraciones completas. *Answers will vary. Sample answers:*

1. ¿En qué situaciones se le pone el pelo tieso a Iker? *Se le pone el pelo tieso cuando está enamorado y cuando está enojado.*

2. ¿Por qué esconde Iker su peinado natural? *Iker esconde su peinado natural porque se siente cohibido/inseguro.*

3. ¿Cómo se sintió Iker después de pelearse con los niños en el patio? *Se sintió contento y orgulloso de su peinado natural.*

4. ¿Se han sentido ustedes cohibidos/as alguna vez?

5. ¿Cuáles son las consecuencias positivas de presentarse ante el mundo tal y como son?

6. ¿Creen que la percepción que tienen de ustedes mismos/as influye en (*influences*) la manera en que ven a los demás? Expliquen su respuesta.

Superhéroes *Answers will vary.*

A. Imagina que un día descubres que tienes un superpoder (*superpower*). Escribe un párrafo donde describas tu experiencia. No te olvides de presentar esta información:

- ► cuál es tu superpoder
- ► cómo y cuándo lo descubriste
- ► quién, además de ti, sabe que tienes ese superpoder
- ► qué características positivas y negativas implica (*involves*) tener ese superpoder
- ► cómo has usado tu superpoder para ayudar a otros
- ► si has decidido usar tu superpoder para mejorar el mundo
- ► cuál es tu nombre de superhéroe/superheroína

> **modelo**
>
> Puedo saltar (*leap*) muros de hasta cinco metros de alto. Lo supe un día que mi gato quedó atrapado en el techo de un edificio…

B. En grupos pequeños, compartan sus párrafos. Conversen para decidir quiénes tienen los mejores superpoderes, los más divertidos, los más útiles (*useful*), etc., y quién escogió el mejor nombre de superhéroe/superheroína.

TEACHING OPTIONS

Large Groups 🔴↔🔴 Divide the class into two groups and tell them to imagine that they are administrators at **Iker's** school. Some parents have complained recently about the school uniform policy, and now the issue is up for debate. Have one group argue for the abolishment of school uniforms and one group argue that the dress code should remain in effect. As part of their arguments, students should consider the increase in bullying incidents at the school over the past year.

Pairs 🔴↔🔴 In pairs, have students write a conversation between **Iker** and his grandfather in which the boy tells about what happened at school and the grandfather shares a story from his youth. Encourage creativity. Have a few volunteers role-play their conversations for the class.

Video

¿Cómo sobrevivir° en la selva de concreto de una gran ciudad hispana? Sin duda, los parques públicos son la respuesta cuando se busca un oasis. Los Bosques de Palermo en Buenos Aires, el Bosque de Chapultepec en la Ciudad de México, el Parque Quinta Vergara en Viña del Mar o la Casa de Campo en Madrid son vitales para la salud física y mental de sus habitantes. Unos tienen museos, lagos y zoológicos, otros hasta parques de diversiones° y jardines. En ellos siempre vas a ver gente haciendo ejercicio, relajándose o reunida con familiares y amigos. A continuación conocerás uno de los muchos parques de Madrid, El Retiro, y vas a ver cómo se relajan los madrileños.

Vocabulario útil

árabe	Moorish, Arab
el bullicio	hustle and bustle
combatir el estrés	to fight stress
el ruido	noise

Preparación

¿Sufres de estrés? ¿Qué situaciones te producen estrés? ¿Qué haces para combatirlo? Answers will vary.

¿Cierto o falso?

Indica si las oraciones son **ciertas** o **falsas**.

1. Madrid es la segunda ciudad más grande de España, después de Barcelona.
   Falso. Es la ciudad más grande.
2. Madrid es una ciudad muy poco congestionada gracias a los policías de tráfico.
   Falso. Es una ciudad muy congestionada.
3. Un turista estadounidense intenta saltearse la cola (*cut the line*) para conseguir unos boletos para un espectáculo.
   Cierto.
4. En el Parque del Retiro, puedes descansar, hacer gimnasia, etc.
   Cierto.
5. Los baños termales Medina Mayrit son de influencia cristiana.
   Falso. Son de influencia árabe.
6. En Medina Mayrit es posible bañarse en aguas termales, tomar el té y hasta comer.
   Cierto.

sobrevivir *to survive* parques de diversiones *amusement parks*

¿Estrés? ¿Qué estrés?

El tráfico, el ruido de las calles... Todos quieren llegar al trabajo a tiempo.

... es un lugar donde la gente viene a "retirarse", a escapar del estrés y el bullicio de la ciudad.

... en pleno centro de Madrid, encontramos los Baños Árabes [...]

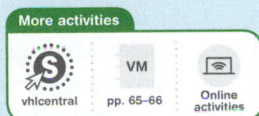

More activities

vhlcentral | VM pp. 65–66 | Online activities

Section Goals

In **Flash cultura**, students will:
• read about famous parks in Spanish-speaking cities
• watch a video about places to relax and ways to deal with stress in Madrid, Spain

Instructional Resources

Supersite: Video (*Flash cultura*); Resources (Scripts, Translations, Answer Keys)
WebSAM
Video Manual

Introduction To check comprehension, give students these true/false statements: **1. La Casa de Campo y el Retiro son dos parques públicos de Madrid. (Cierto.) 2. Ir a un parque en medio de la ciudad puede ayudar a una persona a eliminar el estrés mental. (Cierto.) 3. En el mundo hispano, la gente normalmente no hace ejercicio en los parques públicos. (Falso. Siempre vas a ver gente haciendo ejercicio.)**

Antes de ver

• Have students look at the video stills, read the captions, and predict the content of the video. Have students say how they would feel in each scene.
• Read through **Vocabulario útil** with students. Model the pronunciation. You may wish to add the term **la hora pico/punta** (*rush hour*) to the list.

Preparación

←👤→ Ask students if they deal with stress differently if they are at school or at home. Have pairs discuss and record their answers in a short paragraph. Have volunteers share their conversations with the class.

¿Cierto o falso?

←👤→ After completing the activity, ask students whether they would prefer to de-stress at **El Retiro** or **Medina Mayrit**, and write a short paragraph explaining why.

TEACHING OPTIONS

Extra Practice ←👤→ Have students research another Arab-influenced place in Madrid or another Spanish city, such as Granada, and prepare a written report about its history, uniquely Arabic characteristics, and current uses.
Pairs ←👤→ Have students work in pairs to research one of the city parks mentioned on this page. Have them create a tourist brochure that highlights the park's features and shows the activities one can

enjoy there. Have volunteers present their brochures to the class.
Heritage Speakers ←👤→ Ask heritage speakers if they are familiar with famous parks and places of leisure in their family's country of origin. Have them describe these places to the class.

Bolivia

 NATIONAL connections cultures STANDARDS

El país en cifras

▶ **Área:** 1.098.580 km² (424.162 millas²), *equivalente al área total de Francia y España*

▶ **Población:** 11.138.000

Los indígenas quechua y aimara constituyen más de la mitad° de la población de Bolivia. Estos grupos indígenas han mantenido sus culturas y lenguas tradicionales. Las personas de ascendencia° indígena y europea representan la tercera parte de la población. Los demás son de ascendencia europea nacida en Latinoamérica. Una gran mayoría de los bolivianos, más o menos el 70%, vive en el altiplano°.

▶ **Capital:** La Paz, sede° del gobierno, capital administrativa—1.816.000; Sucre, sede del Tribunal Supremo, capital constitucional y judicial

▶ **Ciudades principales:** Santa Cruz de la Sierra—2.107.000; Cochabamba, Oruro, Potosí

▶ **Moneda:** peso boliviano

▶ **Idiomas:** español (oficial), aimara (oficial), quechua (oficial)

Bandera de Bolivia

Carnaval de Oruro

Bolivianos célebres

▶ **Jesús Lara,** escritor (1898–1980)
▶ **Víctor Paz Estenssoro,** político y presidente (1907–2001)
▶ **María Luisa Pacheco,** pintora (1919–1982)
▶ **Matilde Casazola,** poeta (1943–)
▶ **Edmundo Paz Soldán,** escritor (1967–)

mitad *half* ascendencia *descent* altiplano *high plateau* sede *seat*

Plaza Murillo

Vista de la ciudad de Sucre

PERÚ
BRASIL
Río Beni
Río Mamoré
Illampu
Lago Titicaca
La Paz
Tiahuanaco
Cordillera Oriental de los Andes
Río Grande
Oruro
Cordillera Central de los Andes
Santa Cruz de la Sierra
Lago Poopó
Sucre
Cochabamba
Potosí
Río Pilcomayo
PARAGUAY
CHILE
ARGENTINA

ESTADOS UNIDOS
OCÉANO ATLÁNTICO
OCÉANO PACÍFICO
BOLIVIA

More activities
vhlcentral | WB pp. 177–178 | Online activities

ACTIVIDADES

1 **¿Cierto o falso?** Indica si lo que dicen las oraciones es **cierto** o **falso.**

1. Más de la mitad de la población de Bolivia corresponde a indígenas quechua y aimara. cierto
2. La población indígena de Bolivia ha cambiado su lengua y su cultura. falso
3. La moneda de Bolivia es el peso boliviano. cierto
4. Cochabamba es una merienda boliviana. falso
5. Edmundo Paz Soldán es un escritor boliviano. cierto

6. El lago Titicaca es el lago más grande de Suramérica. falso
7. La música andina tiene origen indígena. cierto
8. Tiahuanaco es un lugar muy activo. falso
9. La vestimenta de la chola paceña es blanca y negra. falso
10. Sucre es la capital más alta del mundo. falso

⊙ **Lugares** • **El lago Titicaca**

Titicaca, situado en los Andes de Bolivia y Perú, es el lago navegable más alto del mundo, a una altitud de 3.812 metros (12.506 pies). Con un área de más de 8.300 kilómetros² (3.200 millas²), también es el segundo lago más grande de Suramérica, después del lago de Maracaibo (Venezuela). La mitología inca cuenta que los hijos del dios° Sol emergieron de las profundas aguas del lago Titicaca para fundar su imperio°.

Artes • **La música andina**

La música andina, compartida por Bolivia, Perú, Ecuador, Chile y Argentina, es el aspecto más conocido de su folclore. Hay muchos conjuntos° profesionales que dan a conocer° esta música popular, de origen indígena, alrededor° del mundo. Algunos de los grupos más importantes y que llevan más de treinta años actuando en escenarios internacionales son Los Kjarkas (Bolivia), Inti Illimani (Chile), Los Chaskis (Argentina) e Illapu (Chile).

Historia • **Tiahuanaco**

Tiahuanaco, que significa "Ciudad de los dioses", es un sitio arqueológico de ruinas preincaicas situado cerca de La Paz y del lago Titicaca. Se piensa que los antepasados° de los indígenas aimara fundaron este centro ceremonial hace unos 15.000 años. En el año 1100, la ciudad tenía unos 60.000 habitantes. En este sitio se pueden ver el Templo de Kalasasaya, el Monolito Ponce, el Templete Subterráneo, la Puerta del Sol y la Puerta de la Luna. La Puerta del Sol es un impresionante monumento que tiene tres metros de alto y cuatro de ancho°, y pesa unas diez toneladas.

⊙ **Gente** • **La chola paceña**

La palabra **cholo** significa mestizo de sangre indígena y europea, y hace referencia al campesino que ha emigrado a la ciudad. Con el paso del tiempo, la chola paceña° se ha convertido en un símbolo de la identidad boliviana y en un ícono de la moda. Su vestimenta llena de color se compone de sombrero, mantón°, chaquetilla, falda, enagua°, botas y joyas, prendas que la chola lleva con elegancia y orgullo°.

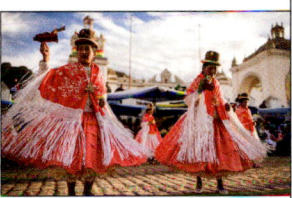

dios *god* imperio *empire* conjuntos *groups* dan a conocer *make known* alrededor *around* antepasados *ancestors* ancho *wide* paceña *from La Paz* mantón *shawl* enagua *petticoat* orgullo *pride*

¡Increíble pero cierto!

La Paz es la capital más alta del mundo. Su aeropuerto está situado a una altitud de 4.061 metros (13.325 pies). Ah, y si viajas en carro hasta La Paz, ¡no te olvides del paraguas°! En la carretera, que cruza 9.000 metros de densa selva, te encontrarás con una cascada°.

paraguas *umbrella* cascada *waterfall*

---

2 **¿Qué aprendiste?** Responde a las preguntas con una oración completa.

1. ¿Qué idiomas se hablan en Bolivia?
   En Bolivia se hablan español, quechua y aimara.
2. ¿Dónde vive la mayoría de los bolivianos?
   La mayoría de los bolivianos vive en el altiplano.
3. ¿Cuál es la capital administrativa de Bolivia?
   La capital administrativa de Bolivia es La Paz.
4. ¿De qué países es la música andina?
   La música andina es de Bolivia, Perú, Ecuador, Chile y Argentina.

3 **Preguntas** En parejas, imaginen que están en Bolivia y túrnense para preguntarse qué han hecho o qué lugares han conocido en este país. Utilicen el pretérito perfecto de indicativo.

> **modelo**
> **Estudiante 1:** ¿Has visitado el lago Titicaca?
> **Estudiante 2:** No, todavía no lo he visitado.

El lago Titicaca Sitting more than two miles above sea level, Lake Titicaca is larger than the area of Delaware and Rhode Island combined. Five major river systems feed into the lake, which has forty-one islands. Lake Titicaca is also the largest lake in South America as measured by water volume. You may want to play the **Panorama cultural** video for this paragraph.

La música andina Andean music is characterized by its plaintive, haunting melodies, often based in a minor or pentatonic scale.

Tiahuanaco The pre-Incan civilization that flourished at **Tiahuanaco** was probably a theocracy, governed by priest-kings. The primary deity was **Viracocha**, a sky and thunder god worshipped throughout much of the Andean world. The Tiahuanacan head of state was viewed as **Viracocha's** embodiment on earth.

La chola paceña The layered skirt that a **chola paceña** wears is called a **pollera**; it is wrapped around the waist and covers several petticoats. You may want to play the **Panorama cultural** video for this paragraph.

¡Increíble pero cierto! Visitors to La Paz and other Andean cities often experience **soroche**, or altitude sickness. Andean natives typically develop increased lung capacity and a greater capacity for diffusing oxygen to the body, helping to compensate for decreased oxygen levels at these heights.

TEACHING OPTIONS

Worth Noting Teams of scientists have extracted sediment samples from Titicaca's lakebed to study the history of climatological change in the region. Such research helps scientists build models to analyze contemporary trends in global climate change.

Worth Noting Students might enjoy learning this indigenous riddle about the **armadillo**, the animal whose outer shell is used to make the **charango**, a small guitar used in Andean music.
Vive en el cerro, lejos del mar.
De concha el saco sin abrochar.
Cuando se muere… ¡pues a cantar!

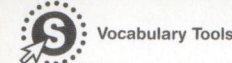
Teaching Tip You may want to assign the **Prueba de práctica**, with its diagnostics and review activities, in the online-only **Repaso** section on the Supersite. There is also a **Repaso oral** in this section. For the Sixth Edition, a new summative vocabulary activity with speech recognition has been added to the **Repaso** section.

El bienestar

el bienestar	well-being
la droga	drug
el/la drogadicto/a	drug addict
el masaje	massage
el/la teleadicto/a	couch potato
adelgazar	to lose weight; to slim down
aliviar el estrés	to reduce stress
aliviar la tensión	to reduce tension
apurarse, darse prisa	to hurry; to rush
aumentar de peso, engordar	to gain weight
disfrutar (de)	to enjoy; to reap the benefits (of)
estar a dieta	to be on a diet
(no) fumar	(not) to smoke
llevar una vida sana	to lead a healthy lifestyle
sufrir muchas presiones	to be under a lot of pressure
tratar de (+ *inf.*)	to try (to do something)
activo/a	active
débil	weak
en exceso	in excess; too much
flexible	flexible
fuerte	strong
sedentario/a	sedentary
tranquilo/a	calm; quiet

En el gimnasio

la cinta caminadora	treadmill
la clase de ejercicios aeróbicos	aerobics class
el/la entrenador(a)	trainer
el músculo	muscle
calentarse (e:ie)	to warm up
entrenarse	to train
estar en buena forma	to be in good shape
hacer ejercicio	to exercise
hacer ejercicios aeróbicos	to do aerobics
hacer ejercicios de estiramiento	to do stretching exercises
hacer gimnasia	to work out
levantar pesas	to lift weights
mantenerse en forma	to stay in shape
sudar	to sweat

La nutrición

la bebida alcohólica	alcoholic beverage
la cafeína	caffeine
la caloría	calorie
el colesterol	cholesterol
la grasa	fat
la merienda	afternoon snack
el mineral	mineral
la nutrición	nutrition
el/la nutricionista	nutritionist
la proteína	protein
la vitamina	vitamin
comer una dieta equilibrada	to eat a balanced diet
consumir alcohol	to consume alcohol
descafeinado/a	decaffeinated

Expresiones útiles	See page 513.

More activities
vhlcentral   LM   p. 89

El mundo del trabajo 16

Communicative Goals

You will learn how to:
- Talk about your future plans
- Talk about and discuss work
- Interview for a job
- Express agreement and disagreement

Lesson Goals

In **Lección 16**, students will be introduced to the following:
- terms for professions and occupations
- work-related vocabulary
- work benefits in the Spanish-speaking world
- **César Chávez**
- future tense
- irregular future tense verbs
- future perfect tense
- past subjunctive
- recognizing similes and metaphors
- using note cards in preparation for writing
- writing a composition on personal and professional goals
- using background knowledge when listening
- listening for specific information
- the short film *La leyenda del espantapájaros*
- a video about different work environments in Ecuador
- cultural and geographic information about Nicaragua
- cultural and geographic information about the Dominican Republic

A primera vista Here are some additional questions you can ask: ¿Has tenido un trabajo? ¿Dónde? ¿Qué hacías? ¿Te gusta trabajar? ¿Por qué? ¿Has sufrido presiones? ¿Qué haces para aliviar el estrés?

Teaching Tip Look for these icons for additional communicative practice:

→👥←	Interpretive communication
←👤→	Presentational communication
👤↔👤	Interpersonal communication

contextos
pages 542–545
- Professions and occupations
- The workplace
- Job interviews

fotonovela
pages 546–549
As Marissa prepares to go back to the States, the friends reflect on their plans for the future. In the meantime, Sra. Díaz helps Miguel with a mock job interview, and Maru gets some good news.

cultura
pages 550–551
- Work benefits
- César Chávez

estructura
pages 552–563
- The future
- The future perfect
- The past subjunctive
- **Recapitulación**

adelante
pages 564–575
Lectura: A poem
Escritura: An essay about your plans for the future
Escuchar: A job interview
En pantalla: A short film
Flash cultura: A video about the world of work in Ecuador
Panorama: Nicaragua y la República Dominicana

🐌 A PRIMERA VISTA
- ¿Están trabajando las personas en la foto?
- ¿Están en buena forma?
- ¿Son periodistas?
- ¿Están descansando o están ocupados?

INSTRUCTIONAL RESOURCES

Supersite (vistas.vhlcentral.com)
Video: *Fotonovela, Flash cultura, En pantalla, Panorama cultural*
Audio: Textbook and Lab MP3 Files

Activity Pack: Information Gap Activities, games, additional activity handouts
Resources: SAM Answer Key, Scripts, Translations, **Vocabulario adicional**, sample lesson plan, Grammar Presentation Slides, Digital Image Bank

Testing Program: Quizzes, Tests, Exams, MP3s
Student Activities Manual: Workbook/Video Manual/Lab Manual
WebSAM (online Student Activities Manual)

El mundo del trabajo

el bombero

la científica

el arquitecto

la pintora

el cocinero

el actor

la actriz

Más vocabulario

el/la abogado/a	lawyer
el/la consejero/a	counselor; advisor
el/la contador(a)	accountant
el/la corredor(a) de bolsa	stockbroker
el/la diseñador(a)	designer
el/la electricista	electrician
el/la gerente	manager
el hombre/la mujer de negocios	businessperson
el/la jefe/a	boss
el/la maestro/a	teacher
el/la político/a	politician
el/la psicólogo/a	psychologist
el/la secretario/a	secretary
el/la técnico/a	technician
el ascenso	promotion
el aumento de sueldo	raise
la carrera	career
la compañía, la empresa	company; firm
el empleo	job; employment
los negocios	business; commerce
la ocupación	occupation
el oficio	trade
la profesión	profession
la reunión	meeting
el teletrabajo	telecommuting
el trabajo	job; work
la videoconferencia	videoconference
dejar	to quit; to leave behind
despedir (e:i)	to fire
invertir (e:ie)	to invest
renunciar (a)	to resign (from)
tener éxito	to be successful
comercial	commercial; business-related

Variación léxica

abogado/a ←→ licenciado/a (*Amér. C.*)
contador(a) ←→ contable (*Esp.*)

More activities

🟡 vhlcentral   LM p. 91   WB pp. 181–182   📶 Online activities

Práctica

la peluquera

el carpintero

el pintor

la reportera

el arqueólogo

1 **Emparejar** Empareja las oraciones que vas a escuchar con las profesiones apropiadas.

1. __d__
2. __a__
3. __g__
4. __c__
5. __f__
6. __b__
7. __h__
8. __e__

a. la científica
b. el psicólogo
c. el reportero
d. la actriz
e. el carpintero
f. la contadora
g. el cocinero
h. la maestra

2 **¿Cierto o falso?** Indica si lo que dice cada oración sobre Diana Vargas es **cierto** o **falso**.

1. Su madre es actriz. falso
2. Su padre es pintor. cierto
3. Quería ser artista, pero no tenía talento. falso
4. Estudió negocios internacionales. cierto
5. Viaja mucho por su trabajo. cierto
6. Es gerente de una compañía multinacional. cierto
7. Prefiere utilizar las videoconferencias. falso
8. Hace negocios con empresas extranjeras. cierto

3 **Escoger** Escoge la ocupación que corresponda a cada descripción.

la arquitecta	el científico	la electricista
el bombero	el corredor de bolsa	el maestro
la carpintera	el diseñador	la técnica

1. Ayuda a la gente a invertir su dinero. el corredor de bolsa
2. Desarrolla teorías de biología, química, física, etc. el científico
3. Combate los incendios (*fires*) que destruyen edificios. el bombero
4. Nos ayuda a iluminar nuestras casas. la electricista
5. Enseña a los niños. el maestro
6. Diseña ropa. el diseñador
7. Arregla las computadoras. la técnica
8. Diseña edificios. la arquitecta

4 **Asociaciones** ¿Qué profesiones asocias con estas palabras? Answers may vary. Suggested answers:

modelo
emociones *psicólogo/a*

1. elecciones político/a
2. consejos consejero/a
3. pinturas pintor(a)
4. comida cocinero/a
5. leyes abogado/a
6. teatro actor/actriz
7. periódico reportero/a
8. pirámide arqueólogo/a
9. pelo peluquero/a

TEACHING OPTIONS

Pairs Have pairs arrange the professions into two lists based on distinct sets of criteria. Ex: **trabajos al aire libre/trabajos en lugares cerrados; profesiones/oficios; trabajos que requieren mucha fuerza/trabajos que no requieren mucha fuerza.** Have each pair read their lists aloud to the class.

Game Play a modified version of **20 Preguntas**. Ask a volunteer to think of a profession or occupation from the drawing or vocabulary list. Other students get one chance each to ask a yes/no question until someone guesses the profession or occupation correctly. Limit attempts to ten questions per item. Ex: **¿Es un oficio o una profesión? ¿Hay que hablar con mucha gente?**

Teaching Tip
👥↔👤 Introduce the vocabulary presented on this page by having a discussion with students about their experiences with interviews. Ex: **Algunas personas se ponen muy nerviosas antes de una entrevista. ¿Eso les pasa a ustedes? ¿Cómo se preparan para una entrevista?**

5 Teaching Tip
👤↔👤 Have pairs play the roles of **entrevistador** and **aspirante**. Each student should look at the entire conversation but should only complete the lines that correspond to his or her role. Have pairs rehearse by reading their sentences to each other for peer correction. Then have pairs role-play the conversation for the class. Encourage students to ad-lib as they go.

6 Expansion To challenge students, have them write logical sentences with the unused choices. Ex: **1. Me llamaron de una empresa porque me quieren entrevistar.**

7 Teaching Tip This activity may be done in pairs or in groups of three or four in round-robin fashion. Allow approximately ten minutes for completion of the activity. Then call on students to report on their group's responses.

5 Conversación Completa la entrevista con el nuevo vocabulario.

ENTREVISTADOR   Recibí la (1) _solicitud (de trabajo)_ que usted llenó y vi que tiene mucha experiencia.

ASPIRANTE   Por eso decidí mandar una copia de mi (2) _currículum_ cuando vi su (3) _anuncio_ en Internet.

ENTREVISTADOR   Me alegro de que lo haya hecho. Pero dígame, ¿por qué dejó usted su (4) _puesto_ anterior?

ASPIRANTE   Lo dejé porque quiero un mejor (5) _salario/sueldo_.

ENTREVISTADOR   ¿Y cuánto quiere (6) _ganar_ usted?

ASPIRANTE   Pues, eso depende de los (7) _beneficios_ que me puedan ofrecer.

ENTREVISTADOR   Muy bien. Pues, creo que usted tiene la experiencia necesaria, pero tengo que (8) _entrevistar_ a dos aspirantes más. Le vamos a llamar la semana que viene.

ASPIRANTE   Hasta pronto, y gracias por la (9) _entrevista_.

Más vocabulario

el anuncio	advertisement
el/la aspirante	candidate; applicant
los beneficios	benefits
el currículum	résumé
la entrevista	interview
el/la entrevistador(a)	interviewer
el puesto	position; job
el salario, el sueldo	salary
la solicitud (de trabajo)	(job) application
contratar	to hire
entrevistar	to interview
ganar	to earn
obtener	to obtain; to get
solicitar	to apply (for a job)

6 Completar Escoge la respuesta que completa cada oración.

1. Voy a ___b___ mi empleo.
   a. tener éxito   b. renunciar a   c. despedir
2. Quiero dejar mi ___c___ porque no me llevo bien con mi jefe.
   a. anuncio   b. gerente   c. puesto
3. Por eso, fui a una ___b___ con una consejera de carreras.
   a. profesión   b. reunión   c. ocupación
4. Ella me dijo que necesito revisar mi ___a___.
   a. currículum   b. compañía   c. aspirante
5. ¿Cuándo obtuviste ___c___ más reciente?, me preguntó.
   a. la reunión   b. la videoconferencia   c. el aumento de sueldo
6. Le dije que deseo trabajar en una empresa con excelentes ___a___.
   a. beneficios   b. entrevistas   c. solicitudes de trabajo
7. Y quiero tener la oportunidad de ___a___ en la nueva empresa.
   a. invertir   b. obtener   c. perder

◀ **¡LENGUA VIVA!**

Trabajo, empleo, and **puesto** can all be translated as *job*, but each has additional meanings: **trabajo** means *work*, **empleo** means *employment*, and **puesto** means *position*.

7 Preguntas Responde a cada pregunta con una respuesta breve. *Answers will vary.*

1. ¿Te gusta tu especialización?
2. ¿Lees los anuncios de empleo con regularidad?
3. ¿Piensas que una carrera que beneficia a otros es más importante que un empleo con un salario muy bueno? Explica tu respuesta.
4. ¿Obtienes siempre los puestos que quieres?
5. ¿Te preparas bien para las entrevistas?
6. ¿Crees que una persona debe renunciar a un puesto si no le ofrecen ascensos?
7. ¿Te gustaría (*Would you like*) más un teletrabajo o un trabajo tradicional en una oficina?
8. ¿Piensas que los jefes siempre tienen razón?
9. ¿Quieres crear tu propia empresa? ¿Por qué?
10. ¿Cuál es tu carrera ideal?

TEACHING OPTIONS

Heritage Speakers ←👤→ Ask heritage speakers to write a description of a job that is unique to their cultural community. Ex: **gestor(a), aparejador(a), curandero/a, puestero/a.** Have them read their descriptions to the class. Write unfamiliar vocabulary on the board.

Game Have students make a *Bingo* card with the names of professions, and then ask them to exchange their cards with a classmate. Read aloud simple descriptions, such as **Trabaja en una oficina.** If a student has a corresponding profession on his or her board, he or she makes a check mark in the corner of the box. To win, a student must mark five professions in a row, read them back to you, and supply appropriate descriptions.

Comunicación

8

Una entrevista Trabaja con un(a) compañero/a para representar los papeles de un(a) aspirante a un puesto y un(a) entrevistador(a). *Answers will vary.*

El/La entrevistador(a) debe describir...
▶ el puesto,
▶ las responsabilidades,
▶ el salario y
▶ los beneficios.

El/La aspirante debe...
▶ presentar su experiencia y
▶ obtener más información sobre el puesto.

Entonces...
▶ el/la entrevistador(a) debe decidir si va a contratar al/a la aspirante y
▶ el/la aspirante debe decidir si va a aceptar el puesto.

9

Un(a) consejero/a de carreras En parejas, representen los papeles de un(a) consejero/a de carreras y una persona que quiere saber cuál es la mejor ocupación para él/ella. El/La consejero/a debe hacerle preguntas sobre su educación, su experiencia y sus intereses y debe sugerir dos o tres profesiones posibles. Después, intercambien los papeles. *Answers will vary.*

10

Una feria de trabajo La clase va a celebrar una feria (*fair*) de trabajo. Unos estudiantes van a ser representantes de compañías que buscan empleados y otros van a estar buscando empleo.

• Los representantes deben preparar carteles con el nombre de su compañía y los puestos que ofrecen.
• Los que buscan empleo deben circular por la clase y hablar con tres representantes sobre sus experiencias de trabajo y el tipo de trabajo que están buscando.
• Los entrevistadores deben describir los puestos y conseguir los nombres y las referencias de los solicitantes. *Answers will vary.*

---

8 Teaching Tips
• 👥↔👥 To simplify, give students time to look at the photo and brainstorm. Then have a conversation with the class about the interview process. Ex: **En una entrevista, ¿quién explica las reponsabilidades del trabajo? ¿Quién pregunta sobre la experiencia de la otra persona?**
• Before beginning the activity, have students generate a list of different positions for which the **aspirante** could interview.

8 Expansion
👥↔👥 Ask volunteers to role-play their **entrevista** for the class.

9 Teaching Tips
• Have the class brainstorm questions an employment counselor might ask. Write the questions on the board.
• →👥← Model the activity by providing information for an imaginary client. Ex: **Una joven busca trabajo. Le gustan mucho los niños, pero no tiene carrera universitaria. Tiene muchos hermanos y gana dinero cuidando a los niños de sus vecinos.** Then, ask comprehension questions: **¿Qué trabajo le recomienda la consejera? (ayudante de maestra; trabajadora de guardería)**

10 Expansion
←👥→ After the **feria**, ask the **representantes de compañías** to say which candidate seemed like the best match for their company. Then ask the **solicitantes** to say which company seemed like the best match for them. Ask students to explain their choices.

TEACHING OPTIONS

Small Groups →👥← Have small groups write a résumé for a famous person. Write a suggested format on the board for the class. Ex: **Objetivos profesionales, Formación académica, Experiencia laboral.** Have groups peer edit and critique another group's completed résumé. Later, have groups review their classmates' comments.

Game ←👥→ Divide the class into teams and give them five minutes to write a job announcement. Explain that they should not specify the title of the position. Then have them take turns reading their announcements. The other teams must guess what job is being announced. Award one point for each correct guess.

La entrevista de trabajo

Los chicos hablan de sus planes para el futuro. Y la Sra. Díaz prepara a Miguel para unas entrevistas de trabajo.

PERSONAJES

 MARISSA

 FELIPE

Video

1

MARISSA En menos de dos meses, ya habré regresado a mi casa en Wisconsin.

FELIPE No pensé que el año terminara tan pronto.

JIMENA ¡Todavía no se ha acabado! Tengo que escribir tres ensayos.

2

MARISSA ¿Qué piensas hacer después de graduarte, Felipe?

JUAN CARLOS Vamos a crear una compañía de asesores de negocios.

FELIPE Les enseñaremos a las empresas a disminuir la cantidad de contaminación que producen.

(*Mientras tanto, en la oficina de la Sra. Díaz*)

MIGUEL Gracias por recibirme hoy.

SRA. DÍAZ De nada, Miguel. Estoy muy feliz de poder ayudarte con las entrevistas de trabajo.

3

MARISSA Estoy segura de que tendrán mucho éxito.

FELIPE También me gustaría viajar. Me muero por ir a visitarte a los Estados Unidos.

JIMENA Pues date prisa. Pronto estará lejos trabajando como arqueóloga.

5

4

MARISSA No sé cómo vaya a ser mi vida a los 30 años. Probablemente me habré ido de Wisconsin y seré arqueóloga en un país exótico.

JUAN CARLOS (*a Jimena*) Para entonces ya serás doctora.

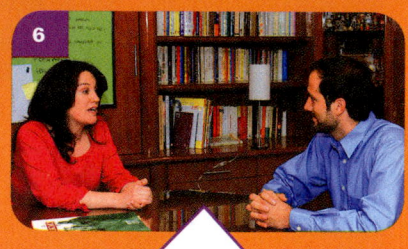

6

SRA. DÍAZ Durante la entrevista, tienes que convencer al entrevistador de que tú eres el mejor candidato. ¿Estás listo para comenzar?

MIGUEL Sí.

JIMENA **JUAN CARLOS** **MIGUEL** **SRA. DÍAZ**

7

MIGUEL Mucho gusto. Soy Miguel Ángel Lagasca Martínez.

SRA. DÍAZ Encantada, Miguel. Veamos. Hábleme sobre su trabajo en el Museo Guggenheim de Bilbao.

MIGUEL Estuve allí seis meses en una práctica.

8

SRA. DÍAZ ¿Cuáles son sus planes para el futuro?

MIGUEL Seguir estudiando historia del arte, especialmente la española y la latinoamericana. Me encanta el arte moderno. En el futuro, quiero trabajar en un museo y ser un pintor famoso.

9

SRA. DÍAZ ¿Qué te hace especial, Miguel?

MIGUEL ¿Especial?

SRA. DÍAZ Bueno. Paremos un momento. Necesitas relajarte. Vamos a caminar.

10

MIGUEL Estamos esperando noticias del museo. (*al teléfono*) Hola. ¿Maru? ¡Genial! (*a la Sra. Díaz*) ¡La aceptaron!

SRA. DÍAZ Felicidades. Ahora quiero que tomes ese mismo entusiasmo y lo lleves a la entrevista.

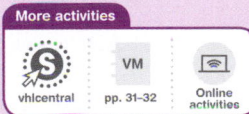

More activities

vhlcentral | VM pp. 31–32 | Online activities

Expresiones útiles

Talking about future plans

En menos de dos meses, ya habré regresado a mi casa en Wisconsin.
In less than two months, I'll have gone back home to Wisconsin.

¿Qué piensas hacer después de graduarte?
What do you think you'll be doing after graduation?

Vamos a crear una compañía de asesores de negocios.
We're going to open a consulting firm.

Les enseñaremos a las empresas a disminuir la cantidad de contaminación que producen.
We'll teach companies how to reduce the amount of pollution they produce.

No sé cómo vaya a ser mi vida a los treinta años.
I don't know what my life will be like when I am thirty.

Probablemente me habré ido de Wisconsin.
I'll probably have left Wisconsin.

Seré arqueóloga de un país exótico.
I'll be an archeologist in some exotic country.

Reactions

Estoy seguro/a de que tendrán mucho éxito.
I'm sure you'll be very successful.

¡Genial!
Great!

Additional Vocabulary

ejercer *to practice/exercise (a degree/profession)*
enterarse *to find out*
establecer *to establish*
extrañar *to miss*
por el porvenir *for/to the future*
el título *title*

¿Qué pasó?

1 **Expansion** Give the class these sentences as items 5–8:
5. Jimena va a ser profesora. (Falso. Va a ser doctora/médica.)
6. Marissa piensa buscar trabajo en Wisconsin. (Falso. Probablemente va a ser arqueóloga en un país exótico.)
7. A Miguel le interesa el arte moderno. (Cierto.) 8. Miguel contesta el teléfono cuando están en la oficina de la Sra. Díaz. (Falso. Contesta el teléfono mientras caminan enfrente del Palacio de Bellas Artes/afuera.)

2 **Teaching Tip** Have students close their books. Read each item aloud and have students identify the character who made the statement.

3 **Expansion** Ask pairs to read their definitions aloud. Have the class guess the corresponding professions.

4 **Possible Conversation**
E1: ¿Qué piensas hacer después de graduarte?
E2: Bueno, voy a trabajar en una escuela porque voy a ser maestro. Voy a dar clases de inglés. Voy a trabajar en una escuela en Ecuador.
E1: ¡Qué bien! ¿Quieres saber cuáles son mis planes para el futuro?
E2: Claro que sí. ¿Cuáles son tus planes?
E1: Pues, voy a ser mujer de negocios. El próximo verano voy a trabajar en la oficina de mi tío pero pienso crear mi propia compañía en cinco años.

1 **¿Cierto o falso?** Indica si lo que dicen estas oraciones es **cierto** o **falso**. Corrige las oraciones falsas.

	Cierto	Falso
1. Juan Carlos y Felipe quieren crear su propia empresa.	●	○
2. En el futuro, Marissa va a viajar porque va a ser psicóloga.	○	●
En el futuro, Marissa va a viajar porque va a ser arqueóloga.		
3. La Sra. Díaz ayuda a Miguel con su currículum.	○	●
La Sra. Díaz ayuda a Miguel con sus entrevistas de trabajo.		
4. Miguel quiere seguir estudiando historia del arte.	●	○

2 **Identificar** Identifica quién dice estas oraciones.

1. Les enseñaremos a las empresas a disminuir la cantidad de contaminación que producen. Felipe
2. Tengo que escribir tres ensayos, presentar dos exámenes finales y terminar un proyecto. Jimena
3. No sé cómo vaya a ser mi vida a los 30 años. Marissa
4. En el futuro, quiero trabajar en un museo y ser un pintor famoso. Miguel
5. Ahora, quiero que tomes ese mismo entusiasmo y lo lleves a la entrevista de la próxima semana. Sra. Díaz

 SRA. DÍAZ
 MIGUEL
JIMENA
MARISSA
FELIPE

3 **Profesiones** Los protagonistas mencionan estas profesiones. En parejas, túrnense para definir cada profesión. Answers will vary.

1. arqueólogo/a
2. doctor(a)
3. administrador(a) de empresas
4. artista
5. hombre/mujer de negocios
6. abogado/a
7. pintor(a)
8. profesor(a)

4 **Mis planes** En grupos, hablen de sus planes para el futuro. Utilicen estas preguntas y frases. Answers will vary.

- ¿Qué piensas hacer después de graduarte?
- ¿Quieres saber cuáles son mis planes para el futuro?
- ¿Cuáles son tus planes?
- ¿Dónde vas a trabajar?
- El próximo año/verano, voy a...
- Voy a ser...
- Voy a trabajar en...

AYUDA

Remember that the indefinite article is not used with professions, unless they are modified by an adjective.
José es **pintor**.
José es **un buen pintor**.

TEACHING OPTIONS

Pairs In pairs, have students write and act out the dialogue of **Miguel's** first real interview. Tell half of the class to create a scenario in which **Miguel** flubs the interview; the others should imagine a situation in which he was successful. Have a few volunteers role-play their interviews for the class.

Small Groups In small groups, have students discuss where they want to be and what they want to be doing in five years, in ten years, in thirty years, and so forth. Then ask a few volunteers to report on their classmates' plans.

Ortografía
y, ll y h

 Tutorial

The digraph **ll** and the letter **y** were not pronounced alike in Old Spanish. Nowadays, however, **ll** and **y** have the same or similar pronunciations in many parts of the Spanish-speaking world. This results in frequent misspellings. The letter **h**, as you already know, is silent in Spanish, and it is often difficult to know whether words should be written with or without it. Here are some of the word groups that are spelled with each letter.

talla	**sello**	**botella**	**amarillo**

The digraph **ll** is used in these endings: **-allo/a, -ello/a, -illo/a.**

llave	**llega**	**llorar**	**lluvia**

The digraph **ll** is used at the beginning of words in these combinations: **lla-, lle-, llo-, llu-.**

cayendo	**leyeron**	**oye**	**incluye**

The letter **y** is used in some forms of the verbs **caer, leer,** and **oír** and in verbs ending in **-uir.**

hiperactivo	**hospital**	**hipopótamo**	**humor**

The letter **h** is used at the beginning of words in these combinations: **hiper-, hosp-, hidr-, hipo-, hum-.**

hiato	**hierba**	**hueso**	**huir**

The letter **h** is also used in words that begin with these combinations: **hia-, hie-, hue-, hui-.**

Práctica Llena los espacios con **h, ll** o **y**. Después escribe una oración con cada una de las palabras.

1. cuchi<u>ll</u>o
2. <u>h</u>ielo
3. cue<u>ll</u>o
4. estampi<u>ll</u>a
5. estre<u>ll</u>a
6. <u>h</u>uésped
7. destru<u>y</u>ó
8. pla<u>y</u>a

Adivinanza Aquí tienes una adivinanza (*riddle*). Intenta descubrir de qué se trata.

Una cajita chiquita, blanca como la nieve: todos la saben abrir, nadie la sabe cerrar.[1]

Pista: Es una comida.

[1] El huevo

More activities

vhlcentral   LM   p. 92

Section Goal

In **Ortografía**, students will learn about the spelling of words that contain **y, ll**, and **h**.

Instructional Resources
Supersite: Audio (Lab MP3 Files); Resources (Scripts, Answer Keys)
WebSAM
Lab Manual

Teaching Tips
- Write the words **talla, sello, botella**, and **amarillo** on the board. Ask the class why these words are spelled with **ll**.
- Say the words **llave, llega, llorar**, and **lluvia** and ask volunteers to spell them aloud in Spanish.
- Say the words **cayendo, leyeron, oye**, and **incluye** and ask volunteers to write them on the board.
- Write the words **hiperactivo, hospital, hipopótamo**, and **humor** on the board and ask the class why these words are spelled with **h**.
- Say the words **hiato, hierba, hueso**, and **huir** and ask volunteers to spell them aloud.
- Point out that **Ortografía** replaces **Pronunciación** in the Student Edition for **Lecciones 10–18**, but not in the Lab Manual. The box references the **Pronunciación** sections found in all lessons of the Lab Manual.

TEACHING OPTIONS

Small Groups Have the class work in small groups and make a list of six words that are spelled with **y, ll,** or **h** (two words for each). They should not use the words that appear on this page. Have them write a creative, humorous sentence that includes all six of these words. Have a few groups share their sentences with the class.

Extra Practice Add an auditory aspect to this **Ortografía** presentation. Read aloud a list of words that contain **y, ll,** or **h**. Ex: **ayer, llegaban, oyó, llamamos, humano, huésped, millonario, cayeron, leyó.** For each word, have students say **i griega, elle,** or **hache** to indicate which is used.

Section Goals

In **Cultura**, students will:
- read about work benefits in the Spanish-speaking world
- learn employment-related terms
- read about Mexican American labor leader **César Chávez**
- read about labor equality

Instructional Resource
Supersite

En detalle

Antes de leer Ask volunteers to mention some common benefits for full-time employees (insurance, vacation days, retirement).

Lectura
- Explain that, since Spaniards tend to take their thirty vacation days in August, many small shops and family businesses close for the entire month.
- Point out the **currículum vitae** box. Ask students if they include or would include the same information in their own résumés.
- As students read, have them compare the information with what they know about their friends' and family members' jobs.

Después de leer
👥↔👥 Ask pairs of students to discuss what facts in this reading are new or surprising to them.

---

1 **Expansion** Give students these true/false statements as items 9–10: **9. Si una persona es soltera, es mal visto incluir esa información en el currículum vitae. (Falso. Es normal incluir información sobre el estado civil.) 10. En Chile, no hay una licencia pagada por maternidad. (Falso. Se ofrecen dieciocho semanas pagadas.)**

EN DETALLE

Beneficios en los empleos

de jubilación público. Es decir, las personas no tenían que pagar directamente por su jubilación, sino que el Estado la administraba. Sin embargo, en los últimos años las cosas han cambiado en Hispanoamérica: desde hace más de una década, casi todos los países han incorporado el sistema privado° de jubilación, y en muchos países podemos encontrar los dos sistemas (público y privado) funcionando al mismo tiempo, como en Colombia, Perú o Costa Rica.

¿Qué piensas si te ofrecen un trabajo que te da treinta días de vacaciones pagadas? Los beneficios laborales° en los Estados Unidos, España e Hispanoamérica son diferentes en varios sentidos°. En España, por ejemplo, todos los empleados, por ley, tienen treinta días de vacaciones pagadas al año. Otro ejemplo lo hallamos en las licencias por maternidad°. En los Estados Unidos se otorgan° doce semanas, dependiendo de la empresa si esos días son pagados o no. En muchos países hispanoamericanos, sin embargo, las leyes dictan que esta licencia sea pagada. Países como Chile y Venezuela ofrecen a las madres trabajadoras° dieciocho semanas de licencia pagada.

Otra diferencia está en los sistemas de jubilación° de los países hispanoamericanos. Hasta la década de 1990, la mayoría de los países de Centroamérica y Suramérica tenía un sistema

El currículum vitae

- El currículum vitae contiene información personal y es fundamental que sea muy detallado°. En ocasiones, mientras más páginas tenga, mejor.
- Normalmente incluye° la educación completa del aspirante, todos los trabajos que ha tenido e incluso sus gustos personales y pasatiempos.
- Puede también incluir detalles que no se suelen incluir en los Estados Unidos: una foto del aspirante, su estado civil e incluso si tiene auto y de qué tipo.

beneficios laborales *job benefits* **varios sentidos** *many ways*
licencias por maternidad *maternity leave* **se otorgan** *are given*
madres trabajadoras *working mothers* **jubilación** *retirement*
privado *private* **detallado** *detailed* **incluye** *includes*

ACTIVIDADES

1 **¿Cierto o falso?** Indica si lo que dicen estas oraciones es **cierto** o **falso**. Corrige la información falsa.

1. Los trabajadores de los Estados Unidos y los de España tienen beneficios laborales diferentes. **Cierto.**

2. La licencia por maternidad es igual en Hispanoamérica y en los Estados Unidos. **Falso. Son diferentes.**

3. En Venezuela, la licencia por maternidad es de cuatro meses y medio. **Cierto.**

4. En España, los empleados tienen treinta días de vacaciones al año. **Cierto.**

5. Hasta 1990, muchos países hispanoamericanos tenían un sistema de jubilación privado. **Falso.** La mayoría de los países hispanoamericanos tenía un sistema de jubilación público.

6. En Perú sólo tienen sistema de jubilación privado. **Falso.** En Perú tienen sistema de jubilación público y privado.

7. En general, el currículum vitae hispano y el estadounidense tienen contenido distinto. **Cierto.**

8. En Hispanoamérica, es importante que el currículum vitae tenga pocas páginas. **Falso.** Mientras más páginas tenga, mejor.

TEACHING OPTIONS

Extra Practice →👤← Have students imagine they are applying for a job in a Spanish-speaking country. Ask them to create a rough draft of their résumé, tailoring it according to the information in the reading. Encourage students to also look at sample résumés in Spanish on the Internet to get ideas. Have them exchange their papers for peer editing.

Pairs 👤↔👤 Have pairs pick a country or region mentioned in **En detalle** and create a conversation between an employer and a job applicant. If possible, have them use their résumés from the Extra Practice activity. The applicant should try to negotiate something with the employer, such as extra vacation time. Have pairs role-play their conversations for the class.

ASÍ SE DICE

El trabajo

la chamba (Méx.); el curro (Esp.); el laburo (Arg.); la pega (Chi.);	el trabajo
el/la cirujano/a	surgeon
la huelga	strike
el/la niñero/a	babysitter
el impuesto	tax

EL MUNDO HISPANO

Igualdad° laboral

- **United Fruit Company** fue, por casi cien años, la mayor corporación estadounidense. Monopolizó las exportaciones de frutas de Hispanoamérica, e influenció enormemente la economía y la política de la región hasta 1970.

- **Fair Trade Coffee** trabaja para proteger a los agricultores° de café de los abusos de las grandes compañías multinacionales. Ahora, en lugares como Centroamérica, los agricultores pueden obtener mayores ganancias° a través del comercio directo y los precios justos°.

- **FINCA International** trabaja en países como Guatemala, Honduras, Nicaragua y Ecuador para ofrecer pequeños préstamos y otros servicios financieros, como cuentas de ahorro, a las personas sin recursos económicos. El objetivo es desarrollar empresas que generen trabajos y mejoren la calidad de vida.

Igualdad Equality **agricultores** *farmers* **ganancias** *profits* **justos** *fair*

PERFIL

César Chávez

César Estrada Chávez (1927–1993) nació cerca de Yuma, Arizona. De padres mexicanos, empezó a trabajar en el campo a los diez años de edad. Comenzó a luchar contra la discriminación en los años 40, mientras estaba en la Marina°. Fue en esos tiempos cuando se sentó en la sección para blancos en un cine segregacionista y se negó° a moverse.

Junto a su esposa, Helen Fabela, fundó° en 1962 la Asociación Nacional de Trabajadores del Campo° que después se convertiría en la coalición Trabajadores del Campo Unidos. Participó y organizó muchas huelgas en grandes compañías para lograr mejores condiciones laborales° y salarios más altos y justos para los trabajadores. Es considerado un héroe del movimiento laboral estadounidense. Desde el año 2000, la

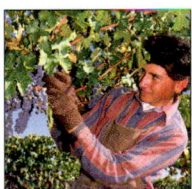

fecha de su cumpleaños es un día festivo pagado° en California y otros estados.

Marina Navy **se negó** *he refused* **fundó** *he established* **Trabajadores del Campo** *Farm Workers* **condiciones laborales** *working conditions* **día festivo pagado** *paid holiday*

CON RITMO HISPANO

La Cuneta Son Machín (2009–)

Lugar de origen: Managua, Nicaragua

Esta banda mezcla la cumbia, el rap, la marimba tradicional, el rock y la música "chinamera", o música popular nicaragüense. Además de tres álbumes de estudio, el grupo ha lanzado una línea de ropa llamada Jincho.

Go to **vhlcentral.com** to find out more about **La Cuneta Son Machín** and its music.

ACTIVIDADES

2 Comprensión Responde a las preguntas.

1. ¿Cómo dice un argentino "perdí mi trabajo"? Un argentino dice "perdí mi laburo".
2. ¿Cuál es el principio fundamental del Fair Trade Coffee? proteger a los agricultores de café
3. ¿Para qué César Chávez organizó huelgas contra grandes compañías? para lograr mejores condiciones laborales y salarios más altos y justos para los trabajadores
4. ¿Qué día es un día festivo pagado en California? el cumpleaños de César Chávez

3 Sus ambiciones laborales En parejas, hagan una lista con al menos tres ideas sobre las expectativas que tienen sobre su futuro como trabajadores/as. Pueden describir las ideas y ambiciones sobre el trabajo que quieren tener. ¿Conocen bien las reglas que deben seguir para conseguir un trabajo? ¿Les gustan? ¿Les disgustan? Luego van a exponer sus ideas ante la clase para un debate. Answers will vary.

More activities · vhlcentral · Online activities

TEACHING OPTIONS

Pairs Tell students to imagine they are organizing a student protest in order to convince the school cafeteria to serve Fair Trade Coffee. Have pairs write a letter in which they outline the advantages for the cafeteria and its clientele. Have students research online for more information about Fair Trade Coffee.
Heritage Speakers Ask heritage speakers to share other work-related terms they are familiar with, such as **la palanca, la**

conexión, or **el enchufe** to refer to preferential treatment.
Small Groups Have students look at job postings on Spanish-language websites and choose two job descriptions that interest them. In small groups, have students take turns describing the jobs and why they are appealing. Students should ask each other follow-up questions to learn more about the different jobs.

Section Goals

In **Estructura 16.1**, students will learn:
- the future tense
- irregular verbs in the future
- the future as a means of expressing conjecture or probability

Instructional Resources

Supersite: Audio (Lab MP3 Files); Resources (Grammar Presentation Slides, Activity Pack, Scripts, Answer Keys); Testing Program (Quizzes)
WebSAM
Workbook
Lab Manual

Teaching Tips

- Review the **ir a** + [*infinitive*] construction to express the future in Spanish. Then, work through the paradigm for the formation of the future. Go over regular and irregular verbs in the future point by point, calling students' attention to the information in **¡Atención!**
- Ask students about their future activities using **ir a** + [*infinitive*]. After they answer, repeat the information using the future. Ex: **¿A qué hora van a almorzar ustedes?** (**Vamos a almorzar a la una.**) **Ustedes almorzarán a la una.**
- Check for understanding by asking volunteers to give different forms of verbs that are not listed. Ex: **renunciar, ofrecer, invertir**

16.1 The future Tutorial

ANTE TODO   You have already learned ways of expressing the near future in Spanish. You will now learn how to form and use the future tense. Compare the different ways of expressing the future in Spanish and English.

Present indicative	Present subjunctive
Voy al cine mañana.	Ojalá **vaya al cine** mañana.
I'm going to the movies tomorrow.	*I hope I will go to the movies tomorrow.*

ir a + [*infinitive*]	Future
Voy a ir al cine.	**Iré** al cine.
I'm going to go to the movies.	*I will go to the movies.*

> ▶ In Spanish, the future is a simple tense that consists of one word, whereas in English it is made up of the auxiliary verb *will* or *shall*, and the main verb.

CONSULTA
To review **ir a** + [*infinitive*], see **Estructura 4.1**, p. 126.

Future tense

		estudiar	aprender	recibir
SINGULAR FORMS	yo	estudiar**é**	aprender**é**	recibir**é**
	tú	estudiar**ás**	aprender**ás**	recibir**ás**
	Ud./él/ella	estudiar**á**	aprender**á**	recibir**á**
PLURAL FORMS	nosotros/as	estudiar**emos**	aprender**emos**	recibir**emos**
	vosotros/as	estudiar**éis**	aprender**éis**	recibir**éis**
	Uds./ellos/ellas	estudiar**án**	aprender**án**	recibir**án**

¡ATENCIÓN!
Note that **-ar**, **-er**, and **-ir** verbs all have the same endings in the future tense.

> ▶ **¡Atención!** Note that all of the future endings have a written accent except the **nosotros/as** form.

¿Cuándo **recibirás** el ascenso?	Mañana **aprenderemos** más.
*When **will you receive** the promotion?*	*Tomorrow **we will learn** more.*

> ▶ The future endings are the same for regular and irregular verbs. For regular verbs, simply add the endings to the infinitive. For irregular verbs, add the endings to the irregular stem.

Irregular verbs in the future

INFINITIVE	STEM	FUTURE FORMS
decir	dir-	dir**é**
hacer	har-	har**é**
poder	podr-	podr**é**
poner	pondr-	pondr**é**
querer	querr-	querr**é**
saber	sabr-	sabr**é**
salir	saldr-	saldr**é**
tener	tendr-	tendr**é**
venir	vendr-	vendr**é**

TEACHING OPTIONS

Extra Practice To provide oral practice, create sentences using the future. Say a sentence, have students repeat it, then name a different subject. Have students then say the sentence with the new subject, conjugating as necessary.
Heritage Speakers Ask heritage speakers to share any song lyrics they know that use the future, such as *No seré* by **Julieta Venegas**, *El día de mi suerte* by **Héctor Lavoe**, or *Viviré* by

Juan Luis Guerra. Have the class analyze the use of the future.
Game Divide the class into teams of five. Each team should have a piece of paper. Give an infinitive in Spanish. The first team member will write the **yo** form of the verb and pass the paper to the second member, who will write the **tú** form, and so forth. The first team to finish the entire paradigm correctly wins a point. The team with the most points at the end wins.

▶ The future of **hay** (*inf.* **haber**) is **habrá** (*there will be*).

La próxima semana **habrá** dos reuniones.
Next week there will be two meetings.

Habrá muchos gerentes en la videoconferencia.
There will be many managers at the videoconference.

▶ Although the English word *will* can refer to future time, it also refers to someone's willingness to do something. In this case, Spanish uses **querer** + [*infinitive*], not the future tense.

¿Quieres llamarme, por favor?
Will you please call me?

¿Quieren ustedes escucharnos, por favor?
Will you please listen to us?

COMPARE & CONTRAST

In Spanish, the future tense has an additional use: expressing conjecture or probability. English sentences involving expressions such as *I wonder, I bet, must be, may, might*, and *probably* are often translated into Spanish using the *future of probability*.

—¿Dónde **estarán** mis llaves?
I wonder where my keys are.

—¿Qué hora **será**?
What time can it be? (I wonder what time it is.)

—**Estarán** en la cocina.
They're probably in the kitchen.

—**Serán** las once o las doce.
It must be (It's probably) eleven or twelve.

Note that although the future tense is used, these verbs express conjecture about *present* conditions, events, or actions.

CONSULTA

To review these conjunctions of time, see **Estructura 13.3**, p. 461.

▶ The future may also be used in the main clause of sentences in which the present subjunctive follows a conjunction of time such as **cuando, después (de) que, en cuanto, hasta que,** and **tan pronto como.**

Cuando llegues a la oficina, **hablaremos**.
When you arrive at the office, we will talk.

Saldremos tan pronto como termine su trabajo.
We will leave as soon as you finish your work.

¡INTÉNTALO! Conjuga en futuro los verbos.

1. (dejar, correr, invertir) yo dejaré, correré, invertiré
2. (hacer, poner, venir) Lola hará, pondrá, vendrá
3. (ir, ser, estar) ustedes irán, serán, estarán
4. (tener, decir, querer) nosotros tendremos, diremos, querremos
5. (renunciar, beber, vivir) tú renunciarás, beberás, vivirás
6. (solicitar, comer, repetir) usted solicitará, comerá, repetirá
7. (saber, salir, poder) yo sabré, saldré, podré
8. (encontrar, jugar, servir) tú encontrarás, jugarás, servirás

TEACHING OPTIONS

Pairs Ask students to write ten academic resolutions for the upcoming semester, using the future. Ex: **Haré dos o tres borradores de cada composición. Practicaré el español con los estudiantes hispanos.** Have students share their resolutions with a partner, who will then report back to the class. Ex: _____ **hará dos o tres borradores de cada composición.**

Extra Practice Ask students to finish these sentences logically: 1. **En cuanto encuentre trabajo,…** 2. **Tan pronto como termine mis estudios,…** 3. **El día que gane la lotería,…** 4. **Cuando lleguen las vacaciones,…** 5. **Hasta que tenga un puesto profesional,…** Encourage them to expand on their answers with additional information where appropriate.

Práctica

1 Planes Repite lo que Celia dice, usando el tiempo futuro.

> **modelo**
>
> Voy a consultar el índice de Empresas 500 en la biblioteca.
> *Consultaré el índice de Empresas 500 en la biblioteca.*

1. Álvaro y yo nos vamos a casar pronto. Nos casaremos…
2. Julián me va a decir dónde puedo buscar trabajo. Me dirá…
3. Voy a leer los anuncios clasificados todos los días. Leeré…
4. Voy a buscar un puesto con un buen sueldo. Buscaré…
5. Voy a obtener un puesto en mi especialización. Obtendré…
6. Mis amigos van a estar contentos por mí. Estarán…

2 La predicción inolvidable Completa el párrafo con el futuro de los verbos.
Some answers may vary. Sample answers:

acordarse	conseguir	estar	olvidar	tener
casarse	escribir	hacerse	ser	terminar

Nunca (1) ___olvidaré___ lo que me dijo la vidente (*clairvoyant*) antes de que se quedara sin batería mi teléfono celular: "En cinco años (2) ___se harán___ realidad todos tus deseos. (3) ___Terminarás___ tus estudios, (4) ___conseguirás___ un empleo rápidamente y tu éxito (5) ___será___ asombroso. (6) ___Te casarás___ con un hombre bueno y hermoso, del que (7) ___estarás___ enamorada. Pero en realidad (8) ___tendrás___ una vida muy triste porque un día, cuando menos lo esperes…"

3 Preguntas Imaginen que han aceptado uno de los puestos de los anuncios. En parejas, túrnense para hablar sobre los detalles (*details*) del puesto. Usen las preguntas como guía y hagan también sus propias preguntas. Answers will vary.

www.clasificados.com

LABORATORIOS LUNA

Se busca científico con mucha imaginación para crear nuevos productos. Mínimo 3 años de experiencia. Puesto con buen sueldo y buenos beneficios. Tel: 492-38-67

SE BUSCA CONTADOR(A)

Mínimo 5 años de experiencia. Debe hablar inglés, francés y alemán. Salario: 120.000 dólares al año. Envíen currículum por fax al: 924-90-34.

SE BUSCAN

Actores y actrices con experiencia para telenovela. Trabajarán por las noches. Salario: 40 dólares la hora. Soliciten puesto en persona. Calle El Lago n. 24, Managua.

SE NECESITAN

Jóvenes periodistas para el sitio web de un periódico nacional. Horario: 4:30 a 20:30. Comenzarán inmediatamente. Salario 20.000 dólares al año. Tel. contacto: 245-94-30.

1. ¿Cuál será el trabajo?
2. ¿Qué harás?
3. ¿Cuánto te pagarán?
4. ¿Sabes si te ofrecerán beneficios?
5. ¿Sabes el horario que tendrás? ¿Es importante saberlo?
6. ¿Crees que te gustará? ¿Por qué?
7. ¿Cuándo comenzarás a trabajar?
8. ¿Qué crees que aprenderás?

Comunicación

4 **Conversar** Tú y tu compañero/a viajarán a la República Dominicana por siete días. Indiquen lo que harán y no harán. Digan dónde, cómo, con quién o en qué fechas lo harán, usando el anuncio como guía. Pueden usar sus propias ideas también. Answers will vary.

> **modelo**
>
> **Estudiante 1:** ¿Qué haremos el martes?
> **Estudiante 2:** Visitaremos el Jardín Botánico.
> **Estudiante 1:** Pues, tú visitarás el Jardín Botánico y yo caminaré por el Mercado Modelo.

www.republicadominicana.com

¡BIENVENIDO a la República Dominicana!

Se divertirá desde el momento en que llegue al **Aeropuerto Internacional de las Américas.**

- Visite la ciudad colonial de **Santo Domingo** con su interesante arquitectura.
- Vaya al **Jardín Botánico** y disfrute de nuestra abundante naturaleza.
- En el **Mercado Modelo** no va a poder resistir la tentación de comprar artesanías.
- No deje de escalar el **Pico Duarte** (se recomiendan 3 días).
- ¿Le gusta bucear? **Cabarete** tiene todo el equipo que usted necesita.
- ¿Desea nadar? **Punta Cana** le ofrece hermosas playas.

5 **Planear** En parejas, hagan planes para formar una empresa privada. Usen las preguntas como guía. Answers will vary.

1. ¿Cómo se llamará y qué tipo de empresa será?
2. ¿Cuántos empleados tendrá y cuáles serán sus oficios o profesiones?
3. ¿Qué tipo de beneficios se ofrecerán?
4. ¿Quién será el/la gerente y quién será el jefe/la jefa? ¿Por qué?
5. ¿Permitirá su empresa el teletrabajo? ¿Por qué?
6. ¿Dónde pondrán anuncios para conseguir empleados?

Síntesis

6 **El futuro de Cristina** Tu profesor(a) va a darte una serie incompleta de dibujos sobre el futuro de Cristina. Tú y tu compañero/a tienen dos series diferentes. Háganse preguntas y respondan de acuerdo a los dibujos para completar la historia. Answers will vary.

> **modelo**
>
> **Estudiante 1:** ¿Qué hará Cristina en el año 2030?
> **Estudiante 2:** Ella se graduará en el año 2030.

16.2 The future perfect Tutorial

ANTE TODO Like other compound tenses you have learned, the future perfect (**el futuro perfecto**) is formed with a form of **haber** and the past participle. It is used to talk about what will have happened by some future point in time.

Future perfect

		hablar	comer	vivir
SINGULAR FORMS	yo	**habré** hablado	**habré** comido	**habré** vivido
	tú	**habrás** hablado	**habrás** comido	**habrás** vivido
	Ud./él/ella	**habrá** hablado	**habrá** comido	**habrá** vivido
PLURAL FORMS	nosotros/as	**habremos** hablado	**habremos** comido	**habremos** vivido
	vosotros/as	**habréis** hablado	**habréis** comido	**habréis** vivido
	Uds./ellos/ellas	**habrán** hablado	**habrán** comido	**habrán** vivido

¡ATENCIÓN!

As with other compound tenses, the past participle never varies in the future perfect; it always ends in **-o**.

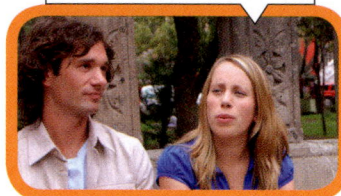

En dos meses, ya habré regresado a Wisconsin.

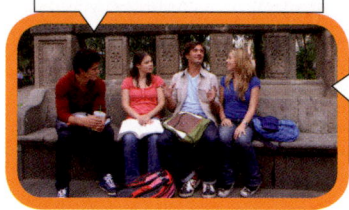

Tendremos una compañía muy exitosa.

Sí, porque muchas empresas habrán solicitado nuestros servicios.

▶ The phrases **para** + [*time expression*] and **dentro de** + [*time expression*] are used with the future perfect to talk about what will have happened by some future point in time.

Para el lunes, habré hecho todas las preparaciones.
By Monday, I will have made all the preparations.

Dentro de un año, habré renunciado a mi trabajo.
Within a year, I will have resigned from my job.

¡INTÉNTALO! Indica la forma apropiada del futuro perfecto.

1. Para el sábado, nosotros __habremos obtenido__ (obtener) el dinero.
2. Yo __habré terminado__ (terminar) el trabajo para cuando lleguen mis amigos.
3. Silvia __habrá hecho__ (hacer) todos los planes para el próximo fin de semana.
4. Para el cinco de junio, ustedes __habrán llegado__ (llegar) a Quito.
5. Para entonces, yo __habré vuelto__ (volver) de la República Dominicana.
6. Para el ocho de octubre, nosotros ya __habremos llegado__ (llegar) a Colombia.
7. Para esa fecha, Ernesto y tú __habrán recibido__ (recibir) muchas ofertas.
8. Para cuando yo te llame, ¿tú __habrás decidido__ (decidir) lo que vamos a hacer?
9. Para las ocho, tú y yo __habremos limpiado__ (limpiar) el piso.
10. Para las nueve, mi hermana __habrá salido__ (salir).

More activities

vhlcentral

LM
p. 94

WB
p. 185

Online activities

Práctica y Comunicación

1 **¿Qué habrá pasado?** Forma oraciones lógicas combinando ambas (*both*) columnas.

A

1. Para el año 2050, la población del mundo c
2. Antes de cumplir los 40 años, yo f
3. Para la semana que viene, el profesor b
4. Dentro de una semana, ellos e
5. Para cuando se dé cuenta, el científico g
6. Para fin de año, las termitas d

B

a. me habré jubilado.
b. habrá corregido los exámenes.
c. habrá aumentado un 47%.
d. habrán destruido su casa.
e. habrán atravesado el océano Pacífico.
f. habré escrito un libro, plantado un árbol y tenido tres hijos.
g. habrá hecho un gran daño a la humanidad.

2 **Escoger** Escoge los verbos que mejor completen cada oración y ponlos en el futuro perfecto.

casarse	leer	solicitar
comprar	romperse	tomar
graduarse	ser	viajar

1. Para mañana por la tarde, yo ya ___habré tomado___ mi examen de economía.
2. Para la semana que viene, el profesor ___habrá leído___ nuestros exámenes.
3. Dentro de tres meses, Juan y Marisa ___se habrán casado___ en Las Vegas.
4. Dentro de cinco meses, tú y yo ___nos habremos graduado___ de la universidad.
5. Para finales (*end*) de mayo, yo ___habré solicitado___ un trabajo en un banco.
6. Dentro de un año, tú ___habrás comprado___ una casa nueva.
7. Dentro de 25 años, Emilia ya ___habrá sido___ presidenta de los EE.UU.
8. Antes de cumplir los 50 años, usted ___habrá viajado___ a Europa.

3 **Encuesta** Tu profesor(a) te va a dar una hoja de actividades. Pregúntales a tres compañeros/as para cuándo habrán hecho las cosas relacionadas con sus futuras carreras que se mencionan en la lista. Toma nota de las respuestas y luego comparte con la clase la información que obtuviste.
Answers will vary.

Síntesis

4 **Competir** En parejas, preparen una conversación hipotética (8 líneas o más) que ocurra en una fiesta. Una persona dice lo que habrá hecho para algún momento del futuro; la otra responde, diciendo cada vez algo más exagerado. Prepárense para representar la conversación delante de la clase.
Answers will vary.

modelo
Estudiante 1: Cuando tenga 30 años, habré ganado un millón de dólares.
Estudiante 2: Y yo habré llegado a ser multimillonaria.
Estudiante 1: Para el 2030, me habrán escogido como la mejor escritora (*writer*) del país.
Estudiante 2: Pues, yo habré ganado el Premio Nobel de Literatura.

16.3 The past subjunctive Tutorial

ANTE TODO You will now learn how to form and use the past subjunctive (**el pretérito imperfecto de subjuntivo**), also called the imperfect subjunctive. Like the present subjunctive, the past subjunctive is used mainly in multiple-clause sentences that express states and conditions such as will, influence, emotion, commands, indefiniteness, and non-existence.

The past subjunctive

		estudiar	aprender	recibir
SINGULAR FORMS	yo	estudia**ra**	aprendie**ra**	recibie**ra**
	tú	estudia**ras**	aprendie**ras**	recibie**ras**
	Ud./él/ella	estudia**ra**	aprendie**ra**	recibie**ra**
PLURAL FORMS	nosotros/as	estudiá**ramos**	aprendié**ramos**	recibié**ramos**
	vosotros/as	estudia**rais**	aprendie**rais**	recibie**rais**
	Uds./ellos/ellas	estudia**ran**	aprendie**ran**	recibie**ran**

▶ The past subjunctive endings are the same for all verbs.

-ra	**-ramos**
-ras	**-rais**
-ra	**-ran**

▶ The past subjunctive is formed using the **Uds./ellos/ellas** form of the preterite. By dropping the **-ron** ending from this preterite form, you establish the stem of all the past subjunctive forms. To this stem you then add the past subjunctive endings.

INFINITIVE	PRETERITE FORM	PAST SUBJUNCTIVE
hablar	ellos **habla**ron	habla**ra**, habla**ras**, hablá**ramos**
beber	ellos **bebie**ron	bebie**ra**, bebie**ras**, bebié**ramos**
escribir	ellos **escribie**ron	escribie**ra**, escribie**ras**, escribié**ramos**

▶ For verbs with irregular preterites, add the past subjunctive endings to the irregular stem.

INFINITIVE	PRETERITE FORM	PAST SUBJUNCTIVE
dar	**die**ron	die**ra**, die**ras**, dié**ramos**
decir	**dije**ron	dije**ra**, dije**ras**, dijé**ramos**
estar	**estuvie**ron	estuvie**ra**, estuvie**ras**, estuvié**ramos**
hacer	**hicie**ron	hicie**ra**, hicie**ras**, hicié**ramos**
ir/ser	**fue**ron	fue**ra**, fue**ras**, fué**ramos**
poder	**pudie**ron	pudie**ra**, pudie**ras**, pudié**ramos**
poner	**pusie**ron	pusie**ra**, pusie**ras**, pusié**ramos**
querer	**quisie**ron	quisie**ra**, quisie**ras**, quisié**ramos**
saber	**supie**ron	supie**ra**, supie**ras**, supié**ramos**
tener	**tuvie**ron	tuvie**ra**, tuvie**ras**, tuvié**ramos**
venir	**vinie**ron	vinie**ra**, vinie**ras**, vinié**ramos**

¡ATENCIÓN!
Note that the **nosotros/as** form of the past subjunctive always has a written accent.

¡LENGUA VIVA!
The past subjunctive has another set of endings:

-se	-semos
-ses	-seis
-se	-sen

It's a good idea to learn to recognize these endings because they are sometimes used in literary and formal contexts.
Deseaba que mi esposo recibiese un ascenso.

¡LENGUA VIVA!
Quisiera, the past subjunctive form of **querer**, is often used to make polite requests.
Quisiera hablar con Marco, por favor.
I would like to speak to Marco, please.
¿Quisieran ustedes algo más?
Would you like anything else?

▶ **-Ir** stem-changing verbs and other verbs with spelling changes follow a similar process to form the past subjunctive.

INFINITIVE	PRETERITE FORM	PAST SUBJUNCTIVE
preferir	prefirie**ron**	prefirie**ra**, prefirie**ras**, prefirié**ramos**
repetir	repitie**ron**	repitie**ra**, repitie**ras**, repitié**ramos**
dormir	durmie**ron**	durmie**ra**, durmie**ras**, durmié**ramos**
conducir	conduje**ron**	conduje**ra**, conduje**ras**, condujé**ramos**
creer	creye**ron**	creye**ra**, creye**ras**, creyé**ramos**
destruir	destruye**ron**	destruye**ra**, destruye**ras**, destruyé**ramos**
oír	oye**ron**	oye**ra**, oye**ras**, oyé**ramos**

▶ The past subjunctive is used in the same contexts and situations as the present subjunctive and the present perfect subjunctive, except that it generally describes actions, events, or conditions that have already happened.

Me pidieron que no **llegara** tarde.
They asked me not to arrive late.

Me sorprendió que ustedes no **vinieran** a la cena.
It surprised me that you didn't come to the dinner.

Salió antes de que yo **pudiera** hablar contigo.
He left before I could talk to you.

Ellos querían que yo **escribiera** una novela romántica.
They wanted me to write a romantic novel.

Cuando llegaste, no creí que tuviéramos muchas cosas en común.

No pensé que el año terminara tan pronto.

¡INTÉNTALO! Indica la forma apropiada del pretérito imperfecto de subjuntivo de los verbos.

1. Quería que tú ___vinieras___ (venir) más temprano.
2. No creían que yo ___pudiera___ (poder) hacerlo.
3. Esperábamos que ustedes ___hablaran___ (hablar) mucho más en la reunión.
4. No deseaba que nosotros ___invirtiéramos___ (invertir) el dinero.
5. No había nadie que ___creyera___ (creer) tu historia.
6. No era necesario que ellas ___hicieran___ (hacer) todo.
7. Me pareció increíble que tú ___supieras___ (saber) dónde encontrarlo.
8. Sentí mucho que ustedes no ___estuvieran___ (estar) con nosotros anoche.
9. Mis padres insistieron en que yo ___fuera___ (ir) a la universidad.
10. Queríamos salir antes de que ustedes ___llegaran___ (llegar).

TEACHING OPTIONS

Extra Practice Review key moments of the **Fotonovela** up to this point and have students react by making statements using the past subjunctive. Ex: **Me pareció horrible que Felipe y Juan Carlos le dañaran la cena romántica de Maru y Miguel.**

Extra Practice Write this cloze paragraph on the board, asking students to complete it using the correct forms of these verbs: **querer, poder, estudiar, tener.**
Mis padres siempre querían que yo ____ una carrera universitaria. (estudiara/tuviera) **Nunca dudaron de que yo ____ llegar a ser lo que ____ .** (podía; quisiera) **Cuando ____ hijos, espero tener la misma confianza en ellos.** (tenga)

Práctica

1 Diálogos Completa los diálogos con el pretérito imperfecto de subjuntivo de los verbos. Después representa los diálogos con un(a) compañero/a.

1. —Cuánto me alegré de que tus hijas __vinieran__ (venir) ayer a visitarte. ¿Cuándo se van?
   —Bueno, yo esperaba que se __quedaran__ (quedar) dos semanas, pero no pueden. Ojalá __pudieran__ (poder). Hace mucho que no las veo.

2. —Qué lástima que ellos no te __ofrecieran__ (ofrecer) el puesto de gerente.
   —Querían a alguien que __tuviera__ (tener) experiencia en el sector público.
   —Pero, ¿cómo? ¿Y tu maestría? ¿No te molestó que te __dijeran__ (decir) eso?
   —No, no tengo experiencia en esa área, pero les gustó mucho mi currículum. Me pidieron que __volviera__ (volver) en un año y __solicitara__ (solicitar) el puesto otra vez. Para entonces habré obtenido la experiencia que necesito y podré conseguir el puesto que quiera.

3. —¿Qué le dijo el consejero a Andrés? Quisiera saberlo.
   —Le aconsejó que __dejara__ (dejar) los estudios de arte y que __estudiara__ (estudiar) una carrera que __pagara__ (pagar) mejor.
   —Siempre el dinero. ¿No se enojó Andrés de que le __aconsejara__ (aconsejar) eso?
   —Sí, y le dijo que no creía que ninguna otra carrera le __fuera__ (ir) a gustar más.

2 Año nuevo, vida nueva El año pasado, Marta y Alberto querían cambiar de vida. Aquí tienen las listas con sus propósitos para el Año Nuevo (*New Year's resolutions*). Ellos no consiguieron hacer realidad ninguno. En parejas, lean las listas y escriban por qué creen que no los consiguieron. Usen el pretérito imperfecto de subjuntivo. Answers will vary.

modelo

obtener un mejor puesto de trabajo
Era difícil que Alberto consiguiera un mejor puesto porque su novia le pidió que no cambiara de empleo.

AYUDA

Puedes usar estas expresiones:
No era verdad que…
Era difícil que…
Era imposible que…
No era cierto que…
Su novio/a no quería que…

Alberto
pedir un aumento de sueldo
tener una vida más sana
visitar más a su familia
dejar de fumar

Marta
querer mejorar su relación de pareja
terminar los estudios con buenas notas
cambiar de casa
ahorrar más

Comunicación

3

Reaccionar Tu amigo acaba de llegar de Nicaragua. Reacciona a lo que te dice usando el pretérito imperfecto de subjuntivo. Escribe las oraciones y luego compáralas con las de un(a) compañero/a. Answers will vary.

> **modelo**
> El día que llegué, me esperaban mi abuela y tres primos.
> ¡Qué bien! Me alegré de que vieras a tu familia después de tantos años.

1. Fuimos al volcán Masaya. ¡Y vimos la lava del volcán!
2. Visitamos la Catedral de Managua, que fue dañada por el terremoto (*earthquake*) de 1972.
3. No tuvimos tiempo de ir a la playa, pero pasamos unos días en el Hotel Dariense en Granada.
4. Fui a conocer el nuevo museo de arte y también fui al Teatro Rubén Darío.
5. Nos divertimos haciendo compras en Metrocentro.
6. Eché monedas (*I threw coins*) en la fuente (*fountain*) de la Plaza de la República y pedí un deseo.

Catedral de Managua, Nicaragua

NOTA CULTURAL

El nicaragüense **Rubén Darío** (1867–1916) es uno de los poetas más famosos de Latinoamérica. *Cantos de vida y esperanza* es una de sus obras.

4

Oraciones Escribe cinco oraciones sobre lo que otros esperaban de ti en el pasado y cinco más sobre lo que tú esperabas de ellos. Luego, en grupos, túrnense para compartir sus propias oraciones y para transformar las oraciones de sus compañeros/as. Sigan el modelo. Answers will vary.

> **modelo**
> **Estudiante 1:** Mi profesora quería que yo fuera a Granada para estudiar español.
> **Estudiante 2:** Su profesora quería que Mark fuera a Granada para estudiar español.
> **Estudiante 3:** Yo deseaba que mis padres me enviaran a España.
> **Estudiante 4:** Cecilia deseaba que sus padres la enviaran a España.

Síntesis

5

El despido Dos amigos/as trabajaban juntos/as en una compañía, pero uno/a de ellos/as fue despedido/a porque su jefe no estaba contento con él/ella. En parejas, inventen una conversación en la que intenten explicar las razones del despido. Usen el pretérito imperfecto de subjuntivo y después representen la conversación delante de la clase. Answers will vary.

> **modelo**
> **Estudiante 1:** ¡Yo no pensaba que fuera importante llegar a tiempo!
> **Estudiante 2:** ¡Claro que sí! Tu jefe te dijo muchas veces que no llegaras tarde.

Section Goal

In **Recapitulación**, students will review the grammar concepts from this lesson.

Instructional Resource
Supersite

1 Teaching Tip Complete this activity orally as a class.

1 Expansion
- To challenge students, add the verbs **poder, saber, tener, hacer,** and **venir** to the chart.
- Ask students how the conjugations of the verbs **poner, salir, tener,** and **venir** are similar in future tense. (The vowel of the verb ending is replaced by **d.**) Then ask how **poder** and **saber** are similar. (The vowel of the verb ending is eliminated.)

2 Teaching Tips
- Remind students that the **nosotros/as** form of the past subjunctive carries a written accent mark.
- After students complete the chart, read aloud the forms of **ir** and ask them what other verb has identical forms in the past subjunctive (**ser**).

2 Expansion
- Have students provide the remaining forms of the verbs.
- Have students create sentences that call for the past subjunctive, using the verb forms in the chart. Ex: **Me sorprendió que fueras a trabajar ayer.**

3 Teaching Tips
- To simplify, have students begin by identifying the past participle for each verb in parentheses. Call on a volunteer to conjugate **haber** in the future tense.
- Remind students that direct object pronouns and reflexive pronouns should appear directly before the conjugated verb.

Recapitulación

Completa estas actividades para repasar los conceptos de gramática que aprendiste en esta lección.

1 Completar Completa el cuadro con el futuro. **12 pts.**

Infinitivo	yo	ella	nosotros
decir	diré	dirá	diremos
poner	pondré	pondrá	pondremos
salir	saldré	saldrá	saldremos

2 Verbos Completa el cuadro con el pretérito imperfecto de subjuntivo. **12 pts.**

Infinitivo	tú	nosotros	ustedes
dar	dieras	diéramos	dieran
saber	supieras	supiéramos	supieran
ir	fueras	fuéramos	fueran

3 La oficina de empleo La nueva oficina de empleo está un poco desorganizada. Completa los diálogos con expresiones de probabilidad, utilizando el futuro perfecto de los verbos. **10 pts.**

SR. PÉREZ No encuentro el currículum de Mario Gómez.

SRA. MARÍN (1) ___Lo habrá tomado___ (tomarlo) la secretaria.

LAURA ¿De dónde vienen estas ofertas de trabajo?

ROMÁN No estoy seguro. (2) ___Habrán salido___ (salir) en el periódico de hoy.

ROMÁN ¿Has visto la lista nueva de aspirantes?

LAURA No, (3) ___la habrás puesto___ (tú, ponerla) en el archivo.

SR. PÉREZ José Osorio todavía no ha recibido el informe.

LAURA (4) ___Nos habremos olvidado___ (nosotros, olvidarse) de enviarlo por correo.

SRA. MARÍN ¿Sabes dónde están las solicitudes de los aspirantes?

ROMÁN (5) ___Las habré dejado___ (yo, dejarlas) en mi carro.

RESUMEN GRAMATICAL

16.1 The future *pp. 552–553*

Future tense of **estudiar***	
estudiaré	estudiaremos
estudiarás	estudiaréis
estudiará	estudiarán

*Same endings for **-ar, -er,** and **-ir** verbs.

Irregular verbs in the future		
Infinitive	Stem	Future forms
decir	dir-	diré
hacer	har-	haré
poder	podr-	podré
poner	pondr-	pondré
querer	querr-	querré
saber	sabr-	sabré
salir	saldr-	saldré
tener	tendr-	tendré
venir	vendr-	vendré

▶ The future of **hay** is **habrá** (*there will be*).
▶ The future can also express conjecture or probability.

16.2 The future perfect *p. 556*

Future perfect of **vivir**	
habré vivido	habremos vivido
habrás vivido	habréis vivido
habrá vivido	habrán vivido

▶ The future perfect can also express probability.

16.3 The past subjunctive *pp. 558–559*

Past subjunctive of **aprender***	
aprendiera	aprendiéramos
aprendieras	aprendierais
aprendiera	aprendieran

*Same endings for **-ar, -er,** and **-ir** verbs.

TEACHING OPTIONS

Large Groups Divide the class into two groups, **el futuro** and **el futuro perfecto**. Call out a statement in the present tense and select a member of each group. Students should step forward and change the sentence according to their assigned tense.
Extra Practice Tell students to imagine they were fired from a job. Now they must write a letter convincing their boss that they deserve a second chance. Give students fifteen minutes to complete this activity. Encourage use of lesson vocabulary and the future tense. Tell students they can offer excuses, using the past subjunctive. Ex: **Iba a entregar el reporte, pero un cliente me pidió que lo ayudara en ese momento….** Have students exchange letters for peer editing.

4 **Una decisión difícil** Completa el párrafo con el pretérito imperfecto de subjuntivo de los verbos. **16 pts.**

aceptar	estudiar	ir
contratar	graduarse	poder
dejar	invertir	trabajar

Cuando yo tenía doce años, me gustaba mucho pintar y mi profesor de dibujo me aconsejó que (1) ___fuera___ a una escuela de arte cuando (2) ___me graduara___ de la escuela secundaria. Mis padres, por el contrario, siempre quisieron que sus hijos (3) ___trabajaran___ en la empresa familiar, y me dijeron que (4) ___dejara___ el arte y que (5) ___estudiara___ una carrera con más futuro. Ellos no querían que yo (6) ___invirtiera___ mi tiempo y mi juventud en el arte. Mi madre en particular nos sugirió a mi hermana y a mí la carrera de administración de empresas, para que los dos (7) ___pudiéramos___ ayudarlos con los negocios en el futuro. No fue fácil que mis padres (8) ___aceptaran___ mi decisión de dedicarme a la pintura, pero están muy felices de tener mis obras en su sala de reuniones.

Verbs with irregular preterites

Infinitive	Preterite form	Past subjunctive
dar	dieron	diera
decir	dijeron	dijera
estar	estuvieron	estuviera
hacer	hicieron	hiciera
ir/ser	fueron	fuera
poder	pudieron	pudiera
poner	pusieron	pusiera
querer	quisieron	quisiera
saber	supieron	supiera
tener	tuvieron	tuviera
venir	vinieron	viniera

5 **La semana de Rita** Con el futuro de los verbos, completa la descripción que hace Rita de lo que hará la semana próxima. **20 pts.**

El lunes por la mañana (1) ___llegará___ (llegar) el traje que pedí por Internet y por la tarde Luis (2) ___me invitará___ (invitar, a mí) a ir al cine. El martes mi consejero y yo (3) ___comeremos___ (comer) en La Delicia y a las cuatro (yo) (4) ___tendré___ (tener) una entrevista de trabajo en Industrias Levonox. El miércoles por la mañana (5) ___iré___ (ir) a mi clase de inglés y por la tarde (6) ___visitaré___ (visitar) a Luis. El jueves por la mañana, los gerentes de Levonox (7) ___me llamarán___ (llamar, a mí) por teléfono para decirme si conseguí el puesto. Por la tarde (yo) (8) ___cuidaré___ (cuidar) a mi sobrino Héctor. El viernes Ana y Luis (9) ___vendrán___ (venir) a casa para trabajar conmigo y el sábado por fin (yo) (10) ___descansaré___ (descansar).

6 **El futuro** Escribe al menos cinco oraciones describiendo cómo será la vida de varias personas cercanas a ti dentro de diez años. Usa tu imaginación y verbos en futuro y en futuro perfecto. **30 pts**

Answers will vary.

7 **Canción** Escribe las palabras que faltan para completar este fragmento de la canción *Lo que pidas* de Julieta Venegas. **¡4 puntos EXTRA!**

| daré | fuera | quisiera | saldré |

"Lo que más (1) ___quisiera___ pedirte
es que te quedes conmigo,
niño te (2) ___daré___ lo que pidas
sólo no te vayas nunca."

Audio: Reading

Lectura

Antes de leer

> ### Estrategia
> **Recognizing similes and metaphors**
>
> Similes and metaphors are figures of speech that are often used in literature to make descriptions more colorful and vivid.
>
> In English, a simile (**símil**) makes a comparison using the words *as* or *like*. In Spanish, the words **como** and **parece** are most often used. Example: **Estoy tan feliz como un niño con zapatos nuevos.**
>
> A metaphor (**metáfora**) is a figure of speech that identifies one thing with the attributes and qualities of another. Whereas a simile says one thing is like another, a metaphor says that one thing *is* another. In Spanish, **ser** is most often used in metaphors. Example: **La vida es sueño.** (*Life is a dream.*)

Examinar el texto

Lee el texto una vez usando las estrategias de lectura de las lecciones anteriores. ¿Qué te indican sobre el contenido de la lectura? Toma nota de las metáforas y los símiles que encuentres. ¿Qué significan? ¿Qué te dicen sobre el tema de la lectura?

¿Cómo son?

En parejas, hablen sobre las diferencias entre el **yo interior** de una persona y su **yo social**. ¿Hay muchas diferencias entre su forma de ser "privada" y su forma de ser cuando están con otras personas?

Las dos Fridas, de Frida Kahlo

A Julia de Burgos

Julia de Burgos

Julia de Burgos nació en 1914 en Carolina, Puerto Rico. Vivió también en La Habana, en Washington, D.C. y en Nueva York, donde murió en 1953. Su poesía refleja temas como la muerte, la naturaleza, el amor y la patria°. Sus tres poemarios más conocidos se titulan Poema en veinte surcos (1938), Canción de la verdad sencilla (1939) y El mar y tú (publicado póstumamente).

Después de leer

Comprensión

Responde las preguntas. Some answers may vary.

1. ¿Quiénes son las dos "Julias" presentes en el poema? Una es la persona interior y la otra es la imagen social de la escritora.
2. ¿Qué características tiene cada una? Una está limitada por su lugar en la sociedad y la otra es independiente y libre.
3. ¿Quién es la que habla de las dos? La que habla es la Julia libre, el yo interior.
4. ¿Qué piensas que ella siente por la otra Julia? A ella no le gusta cómo es la otra Julia y dice que es hipócrita y egoísta.
5. ¿Qué diferencias hay en el aspecto físico de una y otra mujer? ¿Qué simboliza esto? Una se riza el pelo y se pinta y a la otra le riza el pelo el viento y la pinta el sol.
6. ¿Cuáles son los temas más importantes del poema? la honestidad, las presiones sociales, la libertad, la individualidad

More activities

 vhlcentral   Online activities

Ya las gentes murmuran que yo soy tu enemiga
porque dicen que en verso doy al mundo tu yo.

Mienten°, Julia de Burgos. Mienten, Julia de Burgos.
5 La que se alza° en mis versos no es tu voz°: es mi voz;
porque tú eres ropaje° y la esencia soy yo;
y el más profundo abismo se tiende° entre las dos.

Tú eres fría muñeca° de mentira social,
y yo, viril destello° de la humana verdad.

10 Tú, miel° de cortesanas hipocresías; yo no;
que en todos mis poemas desnudo° el corazón.

Tú eres como tu mundo, egoísta; yo no;
que en todo me lo juego° a ser lo que soy yo.

Tú eres sólo la grave señora señorona°;
15 yo no; yo soy la vida, la fuerza°, la mujer.

Tú eres de tu marido, de tu amo°; yo no;
yo de nadie, o de todos, porque a todos, a todos,
en mi limpio sentir y en mi pensar me doy.

Tú te rizas° el pelo y te pintas°; yo no;
a mí me riza el viento; a mí me pinta el sol.

20 Tú eres dama casera°, resignada, sumisa,
atada° a los prejuicios de los hombres; yo no;
que yo soy Rocinante* corriendo desbocado°
olfateando° horizontes de justicia de Dios.

* Rocinante: El caballo de don Quijote, personaje literario
de fama universal que se relaciona con el idealismo y
el poder de la imaginación frente a la realidad.

25 Tú en ti misma no mandas°; a ti todos te mandan;
en ti mandan tu esposo, tus padres, tus parientes,
el cura°, la modista°, el teatro, el casino,
el auto, las alhajas°, el banquete, el champán,
el cielo y el infierno, y el qué dirán social°.

30 En mí no, que en mí manda mi solo corazón,
mi solo pensamiento; quien manda en mí soy yo.

Tú, flor de aristocracia; y yo la flor del pueblo.
Tú en ti lo tienes todo y a todos se lo debes,
mientras que yo, mi nada a nadie se la debo.

35 Tú, clavada° al estático dividendo ancestral°,
y yo, un uno en la cifra° del divisor social,
somos el duelo a muerte° que se acerca° fatal.

Cuando las multitudes corran alborotadas°
dejando atrás cenizas° de injusticias quemadas,
40 y cuando con la tea° de las siete virtudes,
tras los siete pecados°, corran las multitudes,
contra ti, y contra todo lo injusto y lo inhumano,
yo iré en medio de ellas con la tea en la mano.

patria *homeland* Mienten *They are lying* se alza *rises up* voz
voice ropaje *apparel* se tiende *lies* muñeca *doll* destello
sparkle miel *honey* desnudo *I uncover* me lo juego *I risk*
señorona *matronly* fuerza *strength* amo *master* te rizas *curl*
te pintas *put on makeup* dama casera *home-loving lady* atada
tied desbocado *wildly* olfateando *sniffing* no mandas *are
not the boss* cura *priest* modista *dressmaker* alhajas *jewelry*
el qué dirán social *what society would say* clavada *stuck*
ancestral *ancient* cifra *number* duelo a muerte *duel to the
death* se acerca *approaches* alborotadas *rowdy* cenizas *ashes*
tea *torch* pecados *sins*

Interpretación

Responde a las preguntas. Answers will vary.

1. ¿Qué te resulta llamativo en el título de este poema?

2. ¿Por qué crees que se repite el "tú" y el "yo" en el poema? ¿Qué función tiene este desdoblamiento?

3. ¿Cómo interpretas los versos "tú eres fría muñeca de mentira social / y yo, viril destello de la humana verdad"? ¿Qué sustantivos (*nouns*) se contraponen en estos dos versos?

4. ¿Es positivo o negativo el comentario sobre la vida social: "miel de cortesanas hipocresías"?

5. Comenta la oposición entre "señorona" y "mujer" que aparece en los versos trece y catorce. ¿Podrías decir qué personas son las que dominan a la "señorona" y qué caracteriza, en cambio, a la mujer?

Monólogo

Imagina que eres un personaje famoso de la historia, la literatura o la vida actual. Escribe un monólogo breve para presentar en clase. Debes escribirlo en segunda persona. Para la representación necesitarás un espejo. Tus compañeros/as deben adivinar quién eres. Sigue el modelo. Answers will vary.

modelo

Eres una mujer que vivió hace más de 150 años. La gente piensa que eres una gran poeta. Te gustaba escribir y pasar tiempo con tu familia y, además de poesías, escribías muchas cartas. Me gusta tu poesía porque es muy íntima y personal. (Emily Dickinson)

Escribe sobre estos temas:

▸ cómo lo/la ven las otras personas

▸ lo que te gusta y lo que no te gusta de él/ella

▸ lo que quieres o esperas que haga

Comprensión

- If students have trouble with the meaning of any word or phrase, help them identify the corresponding context clue.

- 👤↔👤 Ask students additional questions to facilitate a class conversation about the poem. Ex: **¿Los temas del poema son explícitos o implícitos? ¿Qué tono tiene el poema?**

Interpretación
Give students these questions as items 6–10:
6. ¿Qué propósito habrá tenido Julia de Burgos al escribir este poema? 7. ¿Cómo será la poeta en la vida real? 8. Cuando Julia hace referencia a "ellos" a lo largo del poema (dicen, mienten, mandan), ¿a quiénes se refiere? 9. ¿Cuál fue tu reacción la primera vez que leíste el poema? ¿Te gustó? Al leerlo una segunda vez, ¿tu impresión cambió? 10. ¿Crees que sea posible que los otros no te ven como tú te ves? ¿Es posible que los demás te conozcan de verdad?

Monólogo

- Call on a volunteer to read the model aloud.

- As a variant, give each student an index card and have them write down the name of a famous person. Then have students draw a card out of a hat and write their monologue accordingly.

TEACHING OPTIONS

Pairs 👤↔👤 Have students reread lines 24–28 of the poem. Then have them work in pairs to think about the external forces that influence their own lives. Have them rewrite the lines of the poem accordingly. Ex: **Tú en ti mismo/a no mandas; a ti todos te mandan; / en ti mandan las clases, el equipo de tenis, tus padres, los profesores…**

Cultural Comparison 👤↔👤 Have students work in pairs. For homework, ask them to relate *A Julia de Burgos* to other representations of self-portraits, such as *Las dos Fridas* by **Frida Kahlo** (page 564). How are the self-portraits similar? How are they different? Have pairs present their comparisons to the class.

Escritura

Estrategia
Using note cards

Note cards serve as valuable study aids in many different contexts. When you write, note cards can help you organize and sequence the information you wish to present.

Let's say you are going to write a personal narrative about a trip you took. You would jot down notes about each part of the trip on a different note card. Then you could easily arrange them in chronological order or use a different organization, such as the best parts and the worst parts, traveling and staying, before and after.

Here are some helpful techniques for using note cards to prepare for your writing:

▶ Label the top of each card with a general subject, such as **el avión** or **el hotel**.

▶ Number the cards in each subject category in the upper right corner to help you organize them.

▶ Use only the front side of each note card so that you can easily flip through them to find information.

Study the following example of a note card used to prepare a composition:

> 3
> *En el aeropuerto de Santo Domingo*
>
> *Cuando llegamos al aeropuerto de Santo Domingo, después de siete horas de viaje, estábamos cansados pero felices. Hacía sol y viento.*

Tema

Escribir una composición

Escribe una composición sobre tus planes profesionales y personales para el futuro. Utiliza el tiempo futuro. No te olvides de hacer planes para estas áreas de tu vida:

Lugar
▶ ¿Dónde vivirás?
▶ ¿Vivirás en la misma ciudad siempre? ¿Te mudarás mucho?

Familia
▶ ¿Te casarás? ¿Con quién?
▶ ¿Tendrás hijos? ¿Cuántos?

Empleo
▶ ¿En qué profesión trabajarás?
▶ ¿Tendrás tu propia empresa?

Finanzas
▶ ¿Ganarás mucho dinero?
▶ ¿Ahorrarás mucho? ¿Lo invertirás?

Termina tu composición con una lista de metas profesionales, utilizando el futuro perfecto.

Por ejemplo: **Para el año 2030, habré empezado mi propio negocio. Para el año 2040, habré ganado más dinero que Bill Gates.**

EVALUATION: Composición

Criteria	Scale
Content	1 2 3 4
Organization	1 2 3 4
Use of vocabulary	1 2 3 4
Accuracy and mechanics	1 2 3 4
Creativity	1 2 3 4

Scoring	
Excellent	18–20 points
Good	14–17 points
Satisfactory	10–13 points
Unsatisfactory	< 10 points

Section Goals
In **Escritura**, students will:
• learn to use note cards as a study aid
• use note cards to prepare to write a composition
• write a composition about professional and personal goals for the future

Instructional Resource
Supersite

Estrategia Explain to students that using note cards in preparation for writing a composition will help greatly in organizing the information that they may want to include. Tell them they can use note cards to prepare to write the composition about their plans for the future. Suggest that they use several note cards for each category (**lugar, familia, empleo, finanzas, metas profesionales**). Remind them to number the cards by category.

Tema Go over the directions with the class, explaining that each student will write a composition on his or her plans for the future—professional and personal. In preparation for writing about professional goals they expect to have attained, have students review the conjugation of **haber** + [*past participle*] to form the future perfect tense.

Escuchar
Antes de escuchar

Estrategia
Using background knowledge/ Listening for specific information

If you know the subject of something you are going to hear, your background knowledge will help you anticipate words and phrases you're going to hear, and will help you identify important information that you should listen for.

To practice these strategies, you will listen to a radio ad for the **Hotel El Retiro**. Before you listen, write down a list of the things you expect the ad to contain. Then make another list of important information you would listen for if you were a tourist considering staying at the hotel. After listening to the ad, look at your lists again. Did they help you anticipate the content of the ad and focus on key information? Explain your answer.

Preparación
Mira la foto. ¿De qué crees que van a hablar? Haz una lista de la información que esperas oír en este tipo de situación. Answers will vary.

Ahora escucha

Entrevista
Antes de escuchar una entrevista de trabajo, haz una lista de la información que esperas oír según tu conocimiento previo° del tema. Answers will vary.

1. _____
2. _____
3. _____
4. _____

Mientras escuchas la entrevista, llena el formulario. Si no oyes un dato° que necesitas, escribe *Buscar en el currículum*. ¿Oíste toda la información que habías anotado en tu lista?

Comprensión

Puesto solicitado contador
Nombre y apellidos del solicitante Rafael Ventura Romero
Dirección Buscar en el currículum **Tel.** Buscar en el currículum

- -

Educación Universidad Politécnica de Nicaragua
Experiencia profesional: Puesto contador
Empresa Dulces González
¿Cuánto tiempo? 3 años durante las vacaciones de la universidad

Referencias:
Nombre Héctor Cruz
Dirección Buscar en el currículum **Tel.** Buscar en el currículum
Nombre Prof. Armando Carreño
Dirección Buscar en el currículum **Tel.** Buscar en el currículum

Preguntas

1. ¿Cuántos años hace que Rafael Ventura trabaja para Dulces González? tres años, durante las vacaciones
2. ¿Cuántas referencias tiene Rafael? dos
3. ¿Cuándo se gradúa Rafael? el 15 de diciembre
4. ¿Cuál es la profesión de Armando Carreño? Es profesor.
5. ¿Cómo sabes si los resultados de la entrevista han sido positivos para Rafael Ventura?
Los resultados fueron positivos porque la jefa quiere que él empiece a trabajar antes de que se gradúe.

conocimiento previo *prior knowledge* dato *fact; piece of information*

NATIONAL communication STANDARDS

Estrategia
Script ¿Sufre usted de muchas tensiones? Con sólo una semana en el hotel El Retiro, usted podrá aliviar su estrés. Venga y disfrute de los espectaculares bosques que lo rodean, las habitaciones modernas y elegantes y las comidas sabrosas preparadas según su dieta. Además de los maravillosos baños térmicos volcánicos, se ofrecen masajes y sauna. El Retiro queda a 100 kilómetros de San José en un lugar que le traerá el descanso y la paz que usted necesita. Llame al 451-2356 para recibir más información.

Ahora escucha
Script SRA. SÁNCHEZ: Buenos días. Usted es Rafael Ventura Romero, ¿no? Soy la señora Sánchez, la jefa de esta compañía. Siéntese, por favor. RAFAEL VENTURA: Buenos días, señora. Estoy muy agradecido de tener esta oportunidad de hablar con usted hoy. S: Veo aquí que está solicitando el puesto de contador general. ¿Qué preparación tiene usted? V: En diciembre me gradúo de contador en la Universidad Politécnica de Nicaragua. Durante los últimos tres años he trabajado en Dulces González aquí en Managua como contador durante las vacaciones. Es la carrera que siempre he querido y sé que voy a tener éxito si usted me da la oportunidad. S: ¿Tiene usted algunas referencias? V: Sí, señora. El gerente de la empresa donde he trabajado, el señor Héctor Cruz, y también el profesor Armando Carreño de la Facultad de Contaduría

(Script continues at far left in the bottom panels.)

Pública y Finanzas. Los teléfonos y direcciones están apuntados en el currículum. S: Muy bien. Este puesto comienza con un salario mensual de 25.812 córdobas. Después de seis meses tiene la posibilidad de un aumento de sueldo. Ofrecemos beneficios excelentes. El horario es de 8:30 a 12:00 y de 2:00 a 6:00. ¿Está interesado? V: Estoy sumamente interesado. S: Pues, necesito unos días para comunicarme con las personas que usted ha dado de referencia. Si todo sale bien, lo llamaré antes

del viernes. ¿Cuándo está dispuesto a comenzar a trabajar? Necesito a alguien lo más pronto posible. V: No me gradúo hasta el 15 de diciembre. Pero puedo trabajar media jornada por las siguientes tres semanas hasta la graduación. S: Creo que no va a haber ningún problema con eso. Entonces hablamos en unos días. V: Muchas gracias por la entrevista, señora Sánchez. Estoy muy emocionado por la posibilidad de trabajar en esta gran empresa. ¡Que tenga muy buen día!

En pantalla Video

Ésta es la historia de un espantapájaros que trabaja en un campo de trigo°. Es un trabajo fácil, aunque muy solitario, y los días se le hacen muy largos. Para entretenerse°, mira a los pájaros, que parecen tenerle miedo. Pero ¿por qué, si él es inofensivo° y amigable°? Sin embargo, un día algo cambia en la vida del espantapájaros. Él tomará entonces una decisión que lo llevará a un final inesperado°.

Preparación

Completar

Completa cada oración con la palabra correcta de **Expresiones útiles**. Haz los cambios necesarios.

1. Me pongo una ___bufanda___ cuando estoy enfermo.
2. Como dijo Shakespeare, el amor es ___ciego___.
3. En un incendio (*fire*), todo se ___quema___ y sólo quedan las ___cenizas___.
4. El trabajo de un espantapájaros es ___asustar___ a las aves.
5. El ___cuervo___ es un pájaro muy hábil (*skillful*) para ___volar___.

¿Son buenos o son malos?

En grupos pequeños, escojan una de estas ocupaciones y conversen sobre los puntos positivos y negativos de esa área de trabajo. Answers will vary.

> **modelo**
> árbitro (*referee*)
> **Estudiante 1:** Puede conocer a jugadores famosos.
> **Estudiante 2:** Y es quien hace que las reglas del juego se obedezcan (*be obeyed*).
> **Estudiante 3:** Sí, pero si hace algo mal, todos lo odian.

• agente funerario (*mortician*)
• dentista
• ingeniero/a nuclear
• leñador(a) (*logger*)
• oficial de seguridad en un aeropuerto
• policía de tránsito (*traffic*)
• político/a
• recaudador(a) de impuestos (*tax collector*)

campo de trigo *wheat field* entretenerse *to amuse itself* inofensivo *harmless* amigable *friendly* inesperado *unexpected*

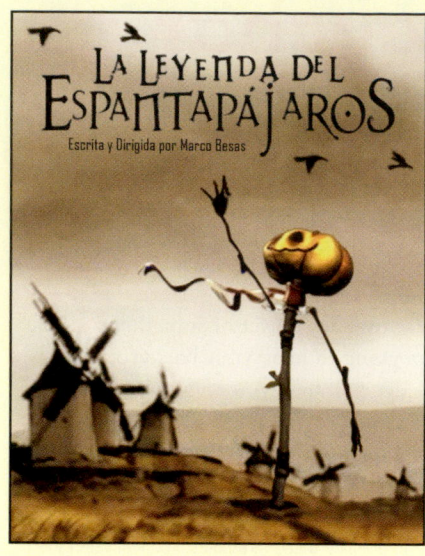

Expresiones útiles

asustar	*to scare*
la bufanda	*scarf*
las cenizas	*ashes*
ciego	*blind*
el cuervo	*crow*
érase una vez	*once upon a time*
el espantapájaros	*scarecrow*
quemar	*to burn*
salvar	*to save*
solitario/a	*lonely*
volar	*to fly*

Para hablar del corto

la calabaza	*pumpkin*
el estereotipo	*stereotype*
incomprendido/a	*misunderstood*
la leyenda	*legend*
el luto	*mourning*
el molino	*windmill*
prejuzgar	*to prejudge*

More activities

vhlcentral / Online activities

Escenas: La leyenda del espantapájaros

NARRADOR Érase una vez un espantapájaros que no tenía amigos.

NARRADOR Cada vez que [los pájaros] pasaban, él los saludaba, pero ellos nunca le respondían.

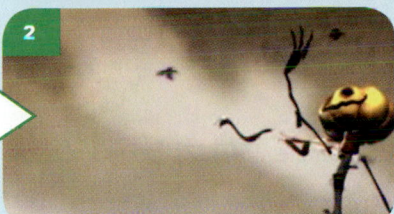

NARRADOR Y el cuervo explicó que el trabajo de los espantapájaros era asustar a los pobres pájaros que sólo querían comer.

NARRADOR Una noche fría, cayó a sus pies un cuervo ciego.

NARRADOR El espantapájaros preguntó por qué los pájaros nunca querían hacerse amigos de los espantapájaros.

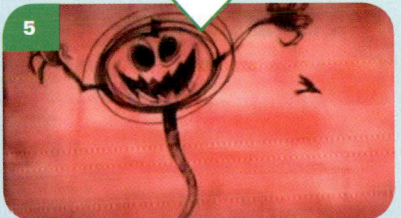

NARRADOR Esa misma noche decidió cambiar su vida.

ése era el espantapájaros bueno, el que le había salvado la vida. Conmocionados por la historia, los cuervos quisieron salvar al espantapájaros, pero era demasiado tarde y ya no podían hacer nada. [...]
N: El espantapájaros murió quemado. Los cuervos esperaron hasta el amanecer y, cuando no había llamas, se acercaron a los restos del molino, cogieron las cenizas del espantapájaros y volaron alto, muy alto; y desde lo más alto, esparcieron las cenizas por el aire. El viento

llevó las cenizas por toda la comarca... Las cenizas volaron junto con todos los pájaros, y de esta manera, el espantapájaros nunca volvió a estar solo, porque sus cenizas ahora volaban con sus nuevos amigos... Y en recuerdo de la trágica muerte del espantapájaros, el cuervo ciego y todos sus compañeros decidieron vestir de luto; y por eso, desde entonces, en memoria del espantapájaros, todos los cuervos son... negros.

La leyenda del espantapájaros Script

NARRADOR: Érase una vez un espantapájaros que no tenía amigos. Trabajaba en un campo de trigo. No era un trabajo difícil, pero sí, muy solitario. Sin nadie con quién hablar, sus días y sus noches se hacían eternas (*sic*). Lo único que podía hacer era mirar los pájaros... Cada vez que pasaban, él los saludaba. Pero ellos nunca respondían; era como si le tuviesen miedo... Un día, el espantapájaros hizo algo que estaba prohibido. Les ofreció unas semillas; pero aún así, ellos no querían saber nada. El espantapájaros se preguntaba por qué nadie quería ser su amigo.
[...]
N: Así pasó el tiempo, hasta que, una noche fría… cayó a sus pies un cuervo ciego. El cuervo estaba tiritando y hambriento. El espantapájaros decidió cuidar de él... Tras varios días, el cuervo ciego mejoró. Antes de despedirse, el espantapájaros preguntó por qué los pájaros nunca querían hacerse amigos de los espantapájaros; y el cuervo explicó que el trabajo de los espantapájaros era asustar a los pobres pájaros, que sólo querían comer; eran unos seres malvados y despreciables, unos monstruos. Ofendido, el espantapájaros le explicó que él no era malo, a pesar de ser un espantapájaros... Una vez más, el espantapájaros se quedó sin amigos.
[...]
N: Esa misma noche decidió cambiar su vida... Despertó a su amo y le dijo que quería otro oficio, que ya no quería asustar más a los pájaros.
AMO: ¡Aaaaah!
N: Aterrorizado, el amo despertó a todos los vecinos. Les contó que su espantapájaros había cobrado vida y que esto sólo podía ser obra del diablo.
[...]
N: Cerca del molino, estaba el cuervo ciego. Sus compañeros le explicaron que los vecinos de la aldea estaban quemando un molino donde se intentaba esconder un espantapájaros con una bufanda muy larga. El cuervo ciego, entonces, les explicó que

(Script continues at far left in the bottom panels.)

Comprensión

 Ordenar

Ordena las oraciones según (*as*) ocurrieron en el cortometraje.

__11__ a. Los cuervos esparcieron (*scattered*) las cenizas del espantapájaros por toda la comarca (*region*).

__5__ b. El amo (*owner*) se aterrorizó (*became terrified*) al ver que su espantapájaros hablaba.

__3__ c. El cuervo ciego supo que lo había salvado un espantapájaros.

__10__ d. El espantapájaros murió.

__2__ e. Un cuervo ciego que tiritaba (*was shivering*) y moría de hambre cayó a los pies del espantapájaros.

__12__ f. En memoria del espantapájaros, los cuervos decidieron vestirse de luto.

__8__ g. Los vecinos quemaron el lugar donde estaba el espantapájaros.

__6__ h. El amo pensó que si el espantapájaros podía hablar, era obra del diablo (*devil*).

__1__ i. El espantapájaros quiso darle semillas (*seeds*) a un pájaro, pero éste no le hizo caso (*didn't pay attention to him*).

__9__ j. Los cuervos quisieron salvar al espantapájaros.

__7__ k. El espantapájaros se escondió (*hid*).

__4__ l. El espantapájaros decidió que ya no quería trabajar asustando pájaros.

 Preguntas

En parejas, respondan a estas preguntas con oraciones completas. Luego, compartan sus respuestas con la clase. Answers will vary.

1. ¿Qué fue lo que siempre deseó el espantapájaros? ¿Por qué?

2. ¿Qué hizo el cuervo ciego al escuchar la confesión del espantapájaros? ¿Por qué?

3. Al final, ¿qué pensaron los cuervos del espantapájaros? ¿Qué cambió en su actitud (*attitude*)? ¿Por qué?

4. ¿Cómo se cumplió (*came true*) finalmente el eterno deseo (*wish*) del espantapájaros?

5. ¿Qué haces si una responsabilidad de tu trabajo va en contra de lo que tú eres, de tus principios (*principles*) o de tus deseos?

6. ¿Te has sentido víctima de los prejuicios de los demás? ¿Cómo manejas esas situaciones?

7. ¿Alguna vez has juzgado a alguien sin conocerlo/la y después descubriste que estabas equivocado/a?

8. ¿Qué haces cuando eres injusto/a con alguien? ¿Admites tu error o no le dices nada?

 Un final diferente

En parejas, escriban un final diferente para la historia del espantapájaros. Luego, compártanlo con la clase.

Answers will vary.

Vocabulario útil			
acercarse (a)	*to approach*	**la esperanza**	*hope*
las alas	*wings*	**el incendio**	*fire*
el amanecer	*dawn*	**llamar la atención**	*to call attention*
apagar (el fuego)	*to put out (the fire)*	**el monstruo**	*monster*
la armonía	*harmony*	**las plumas**	*feathers*
disfrazarse	*to disguise oneself*	**razonar**	*to reason*
escapar(se)	*to escape*	**transformarse (en)**	*to turn (into)*

Video

Viernes en la tarde, llega el esperado fin de semana… y si el lunes es día festivo°, ¡mejor aún!° En varios países hispanos, además de tener entre quince y treinta días de vacaciones pagadas, hay bastantes días festivos. Por ejemplo, Puerto Rico tiene veintiún feriados°, Colombia tiene dieciocho y Argentina, México y Chile tienen más de trece. Aunque parece que se trabaja menos, no siempre es el caso: las jornadas laborales° suelen ser más largas en Latinoamérica. Así que la gente aprovecha° los **puentes**° para descansar e incluso para hacer viajes cortos.

Vocabulario útil

el desarrollo	development
el horario	schedule
promover	to promote
las ventas	sales

Preparación

¿Trabajas? ¿Cuáles son tus metas (*goals*) profesionales?
Answers will vary.

Escoger

Escoge la opción correcta de cada par de afirmaciones.

1. a. Todos los ecuatorianos son muy felices en su trabajo.
   (b.) En Ecuador, como en todos los países del mundo, hay personas que aman su trabajo y hay otras que lo odian.
2. (a.) El objetivo principal de la agencia Klein Tours es mostrar al mundo las maravillas de Ecuador.
   b. La agencia de viajes Klein Tours quiere mostrar al mundo que tiene los empleados más fieles y profesionales de toda Latinoamérica.

día festivo *holiday* ¡mejor aún! *even better!* feriados *holidays* jornadas laborales *working days* aprovecha *make the most of* puentes *long weekends*

El mundo del trabajo

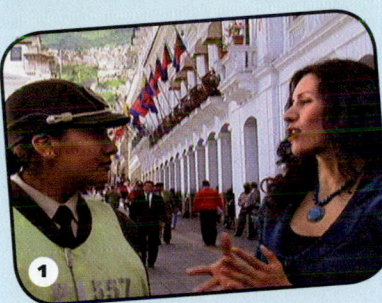

Gabriela, ¿qué es lo más difícil de ser una mujer policía?

Amo mi trabajo. Imagínate, tengo la sonrisa del mundo entre mis manos.

Nuestra principal estrategia de ventas es promover nuestra naturaleza…

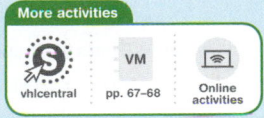

More activities

vhlcentral | VM pp. 67–68 | Online activities

Section Goals

In **Flash cultura**, students will:
- read about work and time off in the Spanish-speaking world
- watch a video about different work environments in Ecuador

Instructional Resources

Supersite: Video (*Flash cultura*); Resources (Scripts, Translations, Answer Keys)
WebSAM
Video Manual

Introduction To check comprehension, give students these true/false statements: **1. Por lo general, en los países hispanos la gente tiene treinta días de vacaciones. (Falso. Tiene entre quince y treinta días de vacaciones.) 2. Un día festivo es un día donde la gente no trabaja y tampoco recibe su sueldo. (Falso. Es un día libre pagado.) 3. Colombia celebra 18 días festivos. (Cierto.) 4. Puerto Rico tiene más feriados que Argentina. (Cierto.) 5. Un día de trabajo en un país hispano es más corto que en los Estados Unidos. (Falso. Las jornadas laborales tienden a ser más largas.)**

Antes de ver

- Have students look at the video stills, read the captions, and predict the content of the video.
- Read through **Vocabulario útil** with students and model the pronunciation.
- Explain to students that they do not need to understand every word they hear. Tell them to rely on visual cues, cognates, and words from **Vocabulario útil**.

Preparación

Even if students are working in low-wage or low-skill positions, ask them to discuss with a partner how their current jobs will help them achieve their professional goals.

Escoger

Alternatively, have students use their own words to write a brief summary of the video.

TEACHING OPTIONS

Small Groups Replay the portion of the video that features Klein Tours. In groups of three, have students role-play two interviews at the organization; one student will play the interviewer and the other two will play the applicants. Encourage the interviewers to prepare by creating a list of possible questions; have the applicants prepare résumés. Finally, ask a few of the interviewers to tell the class which person they would hire and why.

Cultural Comparison Have students research the male-female wage gap in Ecuador (or another Spanish-speaking country) and compare it to the U.S. and Canada. Then have them research and compare the salary range for a profession that interests them.

Section Goal

In **Panorama**, students will read about the geography, history, and culture of Nicaragua.

Instructional Resources

Supersite: Video (*Panorama cultural*); Resources (Scripts, Translations, Digital Image Bank, Answer Keys)
WebSAM
Workbook

Teaching Tips

• Use the **Lección 16 Panorama** digital images to assist with this presentation.

• Have students look at the map of Nicaragua and talk about the geographical features of the country. Point out the concentration of cities along the country's Pacific Coast, and note the sparse settlement in the eastern part of the country and along the Caribbean coast. Tell students that, nearly 100 years after the construction of the Panama Canal, a proposal has been made for a new interoceanic canal, utilizing the San Juan River and Lake Nicaragua.

El país en cifras Tell students that Nicaragua's national slogan is **"El país de lagos y volcanes."** After students read about the capital, ask: **Aproximadamente, ¿qué porcentaje de nicaragüenses vive en Managua? (el 15%)** Tell students that many Nicaraguans have chosen to live in the capital in part due to devastation from war and natural disasters, such as Hurricane Mitch in 1998, and earthquakes and volcanic eruptions in 1999.

Nicaragua

NATIONAL STANDARDS connections cultures

El país en cifras

▸ **Área:** 130.370 km² (50.336 millas²), *aproximadamente el área de Nueva York. Nicaragua es el país más grande de Centroamérica. Su terreno es muy variado e incluye bosques tropicales, montañas, sabanas° y marismas°, además de unos 40 volcanes.*

▸ **Población:** 6.026.000

▸ **Capital:** Managua—956.000
Managua está en una región de una notable inestabilidad geográfica, con muchos volcanes y terremotos°. En décadas recientes, los nicaragüenses han decidido que no vale la pena° construir rascacielos° porque no resisten los terremotos.

▸ **Ciudades principales:** León, Masaya, Granada

▸ **Moneda:** córdoba

▸ **Idiomas:** español (oficial); lenguas indígenas y criollas (oficiales); inglés

Bandera de Nicaragua

Nicaragüenses célebres

▸ **Rubén Darío,** poeta (1867–1916)

▸ **Violeta Barrios de Chamorro,** política y expresidenta (1929–)

▸ **Daniel Ortega,** político y presidente (1945–)

▸ **Gioconda Belli,** poeta (1948–)

▸ **Luis Enrique,** cantante y compositor (1962–)

Iglesia en León

Teatro Nacional Rubén Darío en Managua

Calle en Granada

HONDURAS
Río Coco
Cordillera Isabelia
Saslaya
Chachagón
Piu
Río Tuma
Río Grande
Cordillera Dariense
León
Sierra Madre
Lago de Managua
Managua
Lago de Nicaragua
Masaya
Granada
Océano Pacífico
Isla Zapatera
Concepción
Maderas
Isla Ometepe
Archipiélago de Solentiname
Río San Juan
COSTA RICA

Luis Enrique

ESTADOS UNIDOS
OCÉANO ATLÁNTICO
NICARAGUA
OCÉANO PACÍFICO
AMÉRICA DEL SUR

sabanas *grasslands* marismas *marshes* terremotos *earthquakes*
no vale la pena *it's not worthwhile* rascacielos *skyscrapers*

More activities
vhlcentral | WB p. 189 | Online activities

ACTIVIDADES

1 **¿Cierto o falso?** Indica si lo que dicen las oraciones es **cierto** o **falso**.

1. Nicaragua es el país más grande de Centroamérica. cierto
2. Gioconda Belli fue presidenta de Nicaragua. falso
3. En Nicaragua hay aproximadamente 40 volcanes. cierto
4. Violeta Barrios de Chamorro y Daniel Ortega son políticos. cierto
5. La moneda de Nicaragua es el dólar. falso

6. Las huellas de Acahualinca se dirigen hacia el lago de Managua. cierto
7. Ernesto Cardenal es pintor y diseñador. falso
8. El lago de Nicaragua es el lago más grande de Latinoamérica. falso
9. Ometepe es la isla más grande del mundo en un lago de agua dulce. cierto
10. Los chicheros son bandas musicales muy populares en Nicaragua. cierto

TEACHING OPTIONS

Worth Noting Managua is a city that has been destroyed and rebuilt multiple times due to wars and natural disasters. This has contributed to the unusual method used for listing street addresses in this capital city. Many places do not have an address that includes an actual building number and street name. Instead, the address includes a reference to a local landmark, and its relationship to other permanent features of the landscape, such as Lake Managua. Here is a typical Managua address: **De la Clínica Don Bosco, 2 cuadras al norte, 3 al sur.**
Extra Practice ➜🔲← Invite students to compare the romantic poetry of **Rubén Darío** to the contemporary work of **Ernesto Cardenal** and **Gioconda Belli.** Students can choose several poems to read aloud to the class, and then comment on differences in style and content.

▷ **Historia** • **Las huellas° de Acahualinca**

La región de Managua se caracteriza por tener un gran número de sitios prehistóricos. Las huellas de Acahualinca son uno de los restos° más famosos y antiguos°. Se formaron hace más de 6.000 años, a orillas° del lago de Managua. Las huellas, tanto de humanos como de animales, se dirigen° hacia una misma dirección, hacia el lago.

Artes • **Ernesto Cardenal (1925–)**

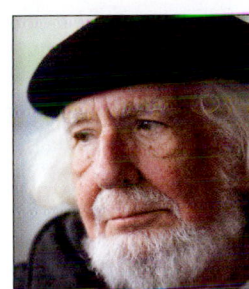

Ernesto Cardenal, poeta, escultor y sacerdote° católico, es uno de los escritores más famosos de Nicaragua, país conocido por sus grandes poetas. Ha escrito más de 35 libros y es considerado uno de los principales autores de Latinoamérica. Desde joven creyó en el poder de la poesía para mejorar la sociedad y trabajó por establecer la igualdad° y la justicia en su país. En los años 60, Cardenal estableció la comunidad artística del archipiélago de Solentiname en el lago de Nicaragua. Fue ministro de cultura del país desde 1979 hasta 1988 y participó en la fundación de Casa de los Tres Mundos, una organización creada para el intercambio cultural internacional.

Naturaleza • **El lago de Nicaragua**

El lago de Nicaragua, con un área de más de 8.000 km² (3.100 millas²), es el lago más grande de Centroamérica. Tiene más de 400 islas e islotes° de origen volcánico, entre ellas la isla Zapatera. Allí se han encontrado numerosos objetos de cerámica y estatuas prehispánicos. Se cree que la isla era un centro ceremonial indígena.

▷ **Música** • **Los chicheros**

Los chicheros son bandas musicales que animan las fiestas populares en Nicaragua. Están conformadas principalmente por instrumentos de viento y percusión, como clarinetes, tubas, trombones, trompetas, platillos° y tambores°. Los chicheros deben su nombre a una parte del pago que recibían por sus servicios: la chicha, una bebida alcohólica a base de maíz fermentado en agua azucarada.

huellas *footprints* restos *remains* antiguos *ancient* orillas *shores* se dirigen *are headed* sacerdote *priest* igualdad *equality* islotes *islets* platillos *cymbals* tambores *drums*

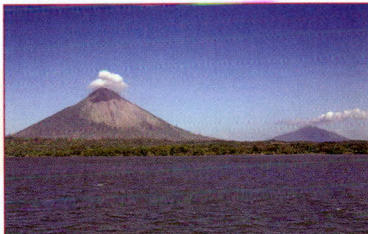

¡Increíble pero cierto!

Ometepe, que en náhuatl significa "dos montañas", es la isla más grande del mundo en un lago de agua dulce°. Surgió° en el lago de Nicaragua por la actividad de los volcanes Maderas y Concepción. Por su valor natural y arqueológico, fue nominada para las siete nuevas maravillas° del mundo en 2009.

agua dulce *fresh water* Surgió *Emerged* maravillas *wonders*

 2 **¿Qué aprendiste?** Contesta las preguntas.

1. ¿Por qué no hay muchos rascacielos en Managua?
   porque no resisten los terremotos
2. Nombra dos poetas de Nicaragua.
   Rubén Darío y Gioconda Belli/Ernesto Cardenal
3. ¿Qué significa Ometepe en náhuatl?
   "dos montañas"
4. ¿Qué cree Ernesto Cardenal acerca de la poesía?
   Cardenal cree que la poesía puede mejorar la sociedad.

 3 **Vacaciones** En parejas, imaginen que irán de vacaciones a Nicaragua y quieren tener todo preparado. Conversen sobre lo que harán en este país. Utilicen el tiempo futuro.

modelo

Estudiante 1: ¿Qué lugares visitaremos?
Estudiante 2: Visitaremos la isla Zapatera, después iremos a…

TEACHING OPTIONS

Worth Noting On July 19, 1979, the **FSLN (Frente Sandinista de Liberación Nacional)**, known as the **Sandinistas**, came to power in Nicaragua after winning a revolutionary struggle against the dictatorship of **Anastasio Somoza**. The **Sandinistas** began a program of economic and social reform that threatened the power of Nicaragua's traditional elite, leading to a civil war known as the **Contra** war. The United States became enmeshed in this conflict, illegally providing funding and arms to the **Contras**, who fought to oust the **Sandinistas**. The **Sandinistas** were voted out in 1990 but returned to power in the 2006 elections. President Daniel Ortega was reelected in 2011 and in 2016.

Las huellas de Acahualinca The **huellas de Acahualinca** consist of the prints of bison, otter, deer, lizards, and birds—as well as humans. The prints were preserved in soft mud, then covered with volcanic ash, which became petrified. You may want to play the **Panorama cultural** video for this paragraph.

Ernesto Cardenal After completing undergraduate courses in Nicaragua, **Ernesto Cardenal** studied in Mexico and in the United States, where he worked with the religious poet Thomas Merton at the Trappist seminary in Kentucky. He later studied theology in Colombia and was ordained in Nicaragua in 1965. Shortly after that, **Cardenal** founded the faith-based community of artists on the Solentiname Islands.

El lago de Nicaragua Environmental groups in Nicaragua have been concerned about the recent introduction of a variety of **tilapia** into Lake Nicaragua. Although **tilapia** are native to the lake, this variety is a more prolific species. Environmentalists are concerned that the Nicaraguan-Norwegian joint venture responsible for this initiative has not done an adequate environmental impact study, and that the delicate and unique ecology of the lake may be negatively impacted.

Los chicheros Band members are amateur musicians who've had no formal musical training; they play by ear. You may want to play the **Panorama cultural** video for this paragraph.

¡Increíble pero cierto! **Concepción** is considered an active volcano even though its last major eruption occurred in 1957. Pressure building up in the volcano caused a 6.2 earthquake in 2005.

La República Dominicana

NATIONAL connections cultures STANDARDS

El país en cifras

▶ **Área:** 48.730 km² (18.815 millas²), *el área combinada de New Hampshire y Vermont*

▶ **Población:** 10.734.000

La isla La Española, llamada así tras° el primer viaje de Cristóbal Colón, estuvo bajo el completo dominio de la corona° española hasta 1697, cuando la parte oeste de la isla pasó a ser propiedad° francesa. Hoy día está dividida políticamente en dos países, la República Dominicana en la zona este y Haití en el oeste.

▶ **Capital:** Santo Domingo—2.945.000

▶ **Ciudades principales:** Santiago de los Caballeros, La Vega, Puerto Plata, San Pedro de Macorís

▶ **Moneda:** peso dominicano

▶ **Idiomas:** español (oficial), criollo haitiano

Bandera de la República Dominicana

Dominicanos célebres

▶ **Juan Pablo Duarte,** político y padre de la patria° (1813–1876)

▶ **Celeste Woss y Gil,** pintora (1891–1985)

▶ **Juan Luis Guerra,** compositor y cantante de merengue (1957–)

▶ **Pedro Martínez,** beisbolista (1971–)

▶ **Marcos Díaz,** nadador de ultradistancia (1975–)

tras *after* corona *crown* propiedad *property*
padre de la patria *founding father*

Músicos dominicanos

Catedral de Santa María la Menor

Océano Atlántico

Isla La Española

Puerto Plata

Santiago

Pico Duarte

Río Yuna

La Vega

Bahía Escocesa

HAITÍ

Cordillera Central

Río San Juan

San Pedro de Macorís

Sierra de Neiba

Santo Domingo

Sierra de Baoruco

Bahía de Ocoa

Mar Caribe

Cultivación de arroz

ESTADOS UNIDOS

LA REPÚBLICA DOMINICANA

OCÉANO PACÍFICO

OCÉANO ATLÁNTICO

AMÉRICA DEL SUR

More activities

vhlcentral · WB p. 190 · Online activities

ACTIVIDADES

1 **¿Cierto o falso?** Indica si lo que dicen las oraciones es **cierto** o **falso**.

1. La Española recibió este nombre después del primer viaje de Colón. cierto
2. La moneda de la República Dominicana es el peso dominicano. cierto
3. Celeste Woss y Gil fue una pintora dominicana. cierto
4. La República Dominicana fue el primer país hispano que tuvo una liga de béisbol. falso
5. Marcos Díaz es un científico dominicano. falso

6. El merengue se transformó en un estilo urbano entre 1930 y 1960. cierto
7. Juan Luis Guerra es un actor dominicano. falso
8. Se dice que una de las tumbas de Colón está en Santo Domingo. cierto
9. Una de las principales actividades económicas de la República Dominicana es la minería. cierto
10. En la República Dominicana se encuentra la mina de plata más grande de Latinoamérica. falso

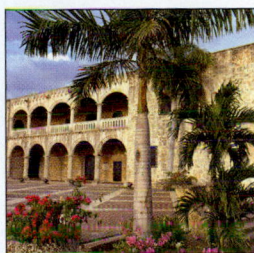

ⓘ Ciudades • Santo Domingo

La zona colonial de Santo Domingo, ciudad fundada en 1496, posee° algunas de las construcciones más antiguas del hemisferio. Gracias a las restauraciones°, la arquitectura de la ciudad es famosa no sólo por su belleza sino también por el buen estado de sus edificios. Entre sus sitios más visitados se cuentan° la Calle de las Damas, llamada así porque allí paseaban las señoras de la corte del Virrey; el Alcázar de Colón, un palacio construido entre 1510 y 1514 por Diego Colón, hijo de Cristóbal; y la Fortaleza Ozama, la más vieja de las Américas, construida entre 1502 y 1508.

Deportes • El béisbol

El béisbol es un deporte muy practicado en el Caribe. Los primeros países hispanos en tener una liga fueron Cuba y México, donde se empezó a jugar al béisbol en el siglo° XIX. Hoy día este deporte es una afición° nacional en la República Dominicana. Albert Pujols (foto, derecha), Carlos Gómez y David Ortiz son sólo tres de los muchísimos beisbolistas dominicanos que han alcanzado° enorme éxito e inmensa popularidad entre los aficionados.

ⓘ Artes • El merengue

El merengue, un ritmo originario de la República Dominicana, tiene sus raíces° en el campo. Tradicionalmente, las canciones hablaban de los problemas sociales de los campesinos°. Sus instrumentos eran la guitarra, el acordeón, el guayano° y la tambora, un tambor° característico del lugar. Entre 1930 y 1960, el merengue se popularizó en las ciudades; adoptó un tono más urbano, en el que se incorporaron instrumentos como el saxofón y el bajo°, y empezaron a formarse grandes orquestas. Uno de los cantantes y compositores de merengue más famosos es Juan Luis Guerra.

Economía • El turismo y la minería

La economía dominicana es la de mayor crecimiento° en Latinoamérica. Una de sus principales actividades es el turismo. Éste representa aproximadamente el 8% del Producto Interno Bruto (PIB)° de la República Dominicana. Este país, además, tiene una importante riqueza minera: en República Dominicana se encuentra la mina de oro° más grande de Latinoamérica. También tiene reservas de plata°, níquel, mármol°, entre otros.

posee *possesses* restauraciones *restorations* se cuentan *are included* siglo *century* afición *pastime* han alcanzado *have reached* raíces *roots* campesinos *rural people* guayano *metal scraper* tambor *drum* bajo *bass* crecimiento *growth* Producto Interno Bruto (PIB) *Gross National Product (GNP)* oro *gold* plata *silver* mármol *marble*

¡Increíble pero cierto!

Los restos° de Cristóbal Colón pasaron por varias ciudades desde su muerte en el siglo XVI hasta el siglo XIX. Por esto, se conocen dos tumbas° de este navegante°: una en la Catedral de Sevilla, España y otra en el Museo Faro a Colón en Santo Domingo, que reemplazó° la tumba inicial en la catedral de la capital dominicana.

restos *remains* tumbas *graves* navegante *sailor* reemplazó *replaced*

---

2 **¿Qué aprendiste?** Contesta las preguntas.

1. ¿Cuándo se fundó la ciudad de Santo Domingo?
en 1496
2. ¿Qué es el Alcázar de Colón?
un palacio construido entre 1510 y 1514 por Diego Colón
3. ¿De qué hablaban las canciones de merengue tradicionales?
los problemas sociales de los campesinos
4. ¿Qué instrumentos se utilizaban para tocar (*play*) el merengue?
la guitarra, el acordeón, el guayano y la tambora
5. ¿Qué cantante ha ayudado a internacionalizar el merengue?
Juan Luis Guerra

3 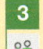 **Planear** En parejas, imaginen que el próximo año pasarán unos meses de intercambio en la República Dominicana. Hablen sobre lo que habrán hecho al final de ese viaje.

modelo

El próximo año habré visitado las construcciones más antiguas de Santo Domingo.

Instructional Resources
Supersite: Audio (Textbook & Lab MP3s); Testing Program (Tests, MP3s)
WebSAM
Lab Manual

Teaching Tip You may want to assign the **Prueba de práctica**, with its diagnostics and review activities, in the online-only **Repaso** section on the Supersite. There is also a **Repaso oral** in this section. For the Sixth Edition, a new summative vocabulary activity with speech recognition has been added to the **Repaso** section.

Las ocupaciones

el/la abogado/a	lawyer
el actor, la actriz	actor
el/la arqueólogo/a	archeologist
el/la arquitecto/a	architect
el/la bombero/a	firefighter
el/la carpintero/a	carpenter
el/la científico/a	scientist
el/la cocinero/a	cook; chef
el/la consejero/a	counselor; advisor
el/la contador(a)	accountant
el/la corredor(a) de bolsa	stockbroker
el/la diseñador(a)	designer
el/la electricista	electrician
el hombre/la mujer de negocios	businessperson
el/la maestro/a	teacher
el/la peluquero/a	hairdresser
el/la pintor(a)	painter
el/la político/a	politician
el/la psicólogo/a	psychologist
el/la reportero/a	reporter
el/la secretario/a	secretary
el/la técnico/a	technician

El mundo del trabajo

el ascenso	promotion
el aumento de sueldo	raise
la carrera	career
la compañía, la empresa	company; firm
el empleo	job; employment
el/la gerente	manager
el/la jefe/a	boss
los negocios	business; commerce
la ocupación	occupation
el oficio	trade
la profesión	profession
la reunión	meeting
el teletrabajo	telecommuting
el trabajo	job; work
la videoconferencia	videoconference
dejar	to quit; to leave behind
despedir (e:i)	to fire
invertir (e:ie)	to invest
renunciar (a)	to resign (from)
tener éxito	to be successful
comercial	commercial; business-related

La entrevista

el anuncio	advertisement
el/la aspirante	candidate; applicant
los beneficios	benefits
el currículum	résumé
la entrevista	interview
el/la entrevistador(a)	interviewer
el puesto	position; job
el salario, el sueldo	salary
la solicitud (de trabajo)	(job) application
contratar	to hire
entrevistar	to interview
ganar	to earn
obtener	to obtain; to get
solicitar	to apply (for a job)

Palabras adicionales

dentro de (diez años)	within (ten years)
próximo/a	next

Expresiones útiles	See page 547.

More activities

vhlcentral   LM p. 95

Un festival de arte

17

Communicative Goals

You will learn how to:
- Talk about and discuss the arts
- Express what you would like to do
- Express hesitation

Lesson Goals

In **Lección 17**, students will be introduced to the following:
- fine arts terms
- vocabulary for television and film
- Venezuela's **Museo de Arte Contemporáneo de Caracas**
- Colombian artist **Fernando Botero**
- conditional tense
- conditional perfect tense
- past perfect subjunctive
- analyzing author's style
- finding biographical information
- writing a composition
- listening for key words and using context
- the short film **Casting**
- a video about Madrid's Golden Triangle of museums
- cultural and geographic information about El Salvador
- cultural and geographic information about Honduras

A primera vista Here are some additional questions you can ask: **En el futuro, ¿tendrás un trabajo creativo? Explica tu respuesta. ¿Te gusta la música? ¿Quién es tu cantante favorito? ¿Te interesa el arte? ¿Quién es tu artista favorito? Para el año que viene, ¿habrás visitado algunos museos de arte? ¿Cuáles? ¿Vas mucho al cine? ¿Cuál es tu película favorita?**

Teaching Tip Look for these icons for additional communicative practice:

→●←	**Interpretive communication**
←●→	**Presentational communication**
●↔●	**Interpersonal communication**

🎧 A PRIMERA VISTA
- ¿Estará trabajando la mujer de la foto?
- ¿Es cantante o consejera?
- ¿Graba música?
- ¿Usa maquillaje?

INSTRUCTIONAL RESOURCES

Supersite (vhlcentral.com)
Video: *Fotonovela, Flash cultura, En pantalla, Panorama cultural*
Audio: Textbook and Lab MP3 Files

Activity Pack: Information Gap Activities, games, additional activity handouts
Resources: SAM Answer Key, Scripts, Translations, **Vocabulario adicional**, sample lesson plan, Grammar Presentation Slides, Digital Image Bank

Testing Program: Quizzes, Tests, Exams, MP3s
Student Activities Manual: Workbook/Video Manual/Lab Manual
WebSAM (online Student Activities Manual)

Un festival de arte

Más vocabulario

el/la compositor(a)	composer
el/la director(a)	director; (musical) conductor
el/la dramaturgo/a	playwright
el/la escritor(a)	writer
el personaje (principal)	(main) character
las bellas artes	(fine) arts
el boleto	ticket
la canción	song
la comedia	comedy; play
el cuento	short story
la cultura	culture
el drama	drama; play
el espectáculo	show
el festival	festival
la historia	history; story
la obra	work (of art, music, etc.)
la obra maestra	masterpiece
la ópera	opera
la orquesta	orchestra
aburrirse	to get bored
dirigir	to direct
presentar	to present; to put on (a performance)
publicar	to publish
artístico/a	artistic
clásico/a	classical
dramático/a	dramatic
extranjero/a	foreign
folclórico/a	folk
moderno/a	modern
musical	musical
romántico/a	romantic
talentoso/a	talented

Variación léxica

banda ⟷ grupo musical (*Esp.*)
boleto ⟷ entrada (*Esp.*)

More activities

vhlcentral | LM p. 97 | WB pp. 191–192 | Online activities

La danza

la bailarina
el bailarín
Aplaude. (aplaudir)

Aprecia. (apreciar)
el poema

La pintura

Pinta. (pintar)

La poesía
el poeta

La música

La banda da un concierto. (dar)
El músico toca un instrumento. (tocar)

la cantante
el baile

Práctica

1 Artes Escribe el número de cada oración que vas a escuchar debajo del arte correspondiente.

teatro	artesanía	poesía
1, 4, 7	5	6

música	danza
3, 8	2

2 Conversación Completa las oraciones sobre la conversación que vas a escuchar.

1. Diego y Silvia están en un ___festival de arte___.
2. La ___tragedia___ que Diego vio es *Romeo y Julieta*.
3. Silvia prefiere las ___comedias___ y los musicales.
4. Lo que más le gusta a Silvia es la ___danza___.
5. Cuando era pequeña, Silvia quería ser ___bailarina___.
6. Diego quiere ir al recital de ___poesía___.

3 ¿Cierto o falso? Indica si lo que dice cada oración es **cierto** o **falso**.

	Cierto	Falso
1. Las bellas artes incluyen la pintura, la escultura, la música, el baile y el drama.	☑	○
2. Un boleto es un tipo de instrumento musical que se usa mucho en las óperas.	○	☑
3. Un cuento es una narración corta que puede ser oral o escrita.	☑	○
4. El tejido es un tipo de música.	○	☑
5. Un compositor es el personaje principal de una obra de teatro.	○	☑
6. Publicar es la acción de hablar en público a grandes grupos.	○	☑
7. Una obra maestra es el mejor trabajo de un artista.	☑	○
8. Un músico es una persona que toca un instrumento.	☑	○

4 Artistas Indica la profesión de cada uno de estos artistas.

1. Frida Kahlo   pintora
2. Javier Bardem   actor
3. Shakira   cantante
4. Octavio Paz   poeta, escritor
5. William Shakespeare   dramaturgo, poeta, escritor
6. Miguel de Cervantes   escritor
7. Fernando Botero   pintor, escultor
8. Toni Morrison   escritora
9. Gustavo Dudamel   director
10. Fred Astaire   bailarín

Image labels (left illustration)

la estatua
Esculpe. (esculpir)
LA ESCULTURA
el escultor
LA ARTESANÍA
el tejido
la cerámica
El teatro
Hace el papel de Romeo. (hacer)
La tragedia de Romeo y Julieta
el público

---

5 **Los favoritos** En parejas, túrnense para preguntarse cuál es su película o programa favorito de cada categoría. Answers will vary.

> **modelo**
>
> película musical
> Mi *película musical favorita es La La Land.*

1. película de ciencia ficción _____
2. programa de entrevistas _____
3. telenovela _____
4. película de horror _____
5. película de acción _____
6. concurso _____
7. programa de realidad _____
8. película de aventuras _____
9. documental _____
10. programa de dibujos animados _____

El cine y la televisión

el canal	channel
el concurso	game show; contest
los dibujos animados	cartoons
el documental	documentary
la estrella (*m., f.*) de cine	movie star
el premio	prize; award
el programa de entrevistas/realidad	talk/reality show
la telenovela	soap opera
…de acción	action
…de aventuras	adventure
…de ciencia ficción	science fiction
…de horror	horror
…de vaqueros	western

6 **Completar** Completa las frases con las palabras adecuadas.

aburrirse	canal	estrella	musical
aplauden	de vaqueros	extranjera	romántica
artística	director	folclórica	talentosa

1. Una persona que puede hacer algo muy bien es una persona… talentosa.
2. Si las personas que asisten a un espectáculo lo aprecian, ellos… aplauden.
3. Una película que fue hecha en otro país es una película… extranjera.
4. Si la acción tiene lugar en el oeste de los EE.UU. durante el siglo XIX, probablemente es una película… de vaqueros.
5. Una persona que pinta, esculpe y/o hace artesanía es una persona… artística.
6. La música que refleja la cultura de una región o de un país es música… folclórica.
7. Una película que trata del amor y de las emociones es una película… romántica.
8. Una obra en la cual los actores presentan la historia por medio de (*by means of*) canciones y bailes es un drama… musical.
9. Cuando una película no tiene una buena historia, el público empieza a… aburrirse.
10. Si quieres ver otro programa de televisión, es necesario que cambies de… canal.

¡ATENCIÓN!

Apreciar means *to appreciate* only in the sense of evaluating what something is worth. Use **agradecer** to express the idea *to be thankful for.*

Ella **aprecia** la buena música.
She appreciates good music.

Le **agradezco** mucho su ayuda.
I thank you for your help.

7 **Contestar** En parejas, contesten las preguntas.

1. ¿Cómo se llama a la persona que canta en una banda? cantante
2. ¿Cuál es el opuesto de comedia? tragedia
3. ¿Cómo se llama al grupo de personas que asisten a un espectáculo? público
4. ¿Qué tipo de programa es *Los Simpson*? dibujos animados
5. ¿Cuál es el femenino de **bailarín**? bailarina
6. ¿Cómo se llama al hombre que hace estatuas? escultor
7. ¿Qué se le da a la persona que gana un concurso? premio
8. ¿Cómo se llama a la mujer que dirige una película? directora

¡LENGUA VIVA!

Remember that, in Spanish, last names do not have a plural form, although **los** may be used with a family name.

Los Simpson
The Simpsons

Teaching Tip Use information about TV programming in your area to introduce vocabulary by talking and asking questions about today's shows. Ex: **En el canal 5, la programación del día comienza con los dibujos animados. A las dos de la tarde, dan una telenovela. ¡Qué lástima que no la pueda ver! Tengo clase a esa hora. ¿Ustedes la ven?**

5 **Teaching Tip** Ask individuals each of the items. Since the answers will vary, be sure to ask more than one student to respond to each one. Express your reactions to students' opinions.

5 **Expansion** To challenge students, have them repeat the activity in another context, such as a specific era of TV and film, like Hollywood's Golden Age.

6 **Expansion** Write on the board additional vocabulary words from **Contextos** and ask pairs to write a definition, using their own words, for each one. Have them read the definitions to the class, who will guess the word.

7 **Expansion** Have students create four additional questions for a partner to answer.

TEACHING OPTIONS

Game Divide the class into two teams. Have each team list a title that fits each of the categories in **El cine y la televisión** (e.g., **dibujos animados, documental, película/programa de acción**, and so forth). The first member of team A calls out a title from his or her team's list. Ex: **la película *King Kong*.** The first member of team B must name its category. Ex: **una película de acción.** Next, the second member of team B calls out a title and the second member of team A must name its category. Continue until all titles have been mentioned. The team with the most correct answers wins.

Small Groups Have small groups think of other words that belong to the same word families as **pintura, canción, escultura, baile**, and **drama.** Ex: **pintor(a), pintar**

Comunicación

8 **Crucigrama** Su profesor(a) les va a dar un crucigrama (*crossword puzzle*) incompleto. Tú tienes las palabras que necesita tu compañero/a y él/ella tiene las palabras que tú necesitas. Sin revelar las palabras, utilicen pistas (*clues*) que les permitan adivinar las respuestas. Answers will vary.

> **modelo**
> **1 horizontal:** Fiesta popular que generalmente tiene lugar en las calles de las ciudades.
> **2 vertical:** Novelas que puedes ver en la televisión.

9 **Preguntas** Contesta estas preguntas sobre el arte en tu vida. Comparte tus respuestas con un(a) compañero/a de clase. Answers will vary.

La música

1. ¿Qué tipo de música prefieres? ¿Por qué?
2. ¿Tocas un instrumento? ¿Cuál?
3. ¿Hay algún instrumento que quisieras aprender a tocar?

El cine

4. ¿Con qué frecuencia vas al cine?
5. ¿Qué tipos de películas prefieres?

Las bellas artes

6. ¿Qué haces que se puede considerar artístico? ¿Pintas, dibujas, esculpes, haces artesanías, actúas en dramas, tocas un instrumento, cantas o escribes poemas?
7. ¿Con qué frecuencia vas a un museo de arte o asistes a conciertos, al teatro o a lecturas públicas de poesía?
8. ¿Es el arte una parte importante de tu vida? ¿Por qué?

10 **Programa** Trabajen en grupos pequeños para crear un programa de televisión o un corto (*short film*) para el canal de televisión de la universidad. Answers will vary.

> **AYUDA**
> **el género** genre
> **el propósito** purpose

▶▶ Primero decidan el género y el propósito del programa o del corto. Cada grupo debe escoger un género distinto. Algunos de los géneros posibles: documental, concurso, programa de realidad, película de acción.

▶ Después, escriban el programa o el corto y preséntenlo a la clase.

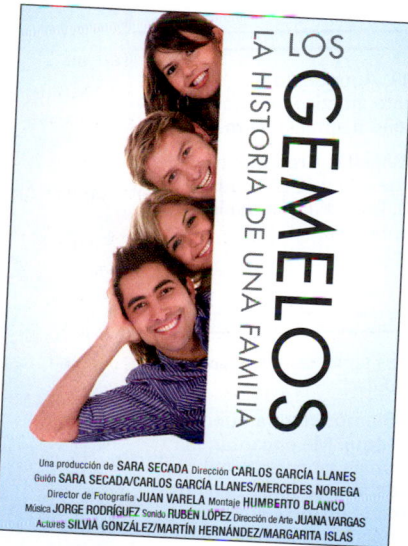

LOS GEMELOS
LA HISTORIA DE UNA FAMILIA

Una producción de SARA SECADA Dirección CARLOS GARCÍA LLANES
Guión SARA SECADA/CARLOS GARCÍA LLANES/MERCEDES NORIEGA
Director de Fotografía JUAN VARELA Montaje HUMBERTO BLANCO
Música JORGE RODRÍGUEZ Sonido RUBÉN LÓPEZ Dirección de Arte JUANA VARGAS
Actores SILVIA GONZÁLEZ/MARTÍN HERNÁNDEZ/MARGARITA ISLAS

---

8 Teaching Tip Divide the class into pairs and distribute the handouts from the Activity Pack (Activity Pack/Supersite) that correspond to this Information Gap Activity. Give students ten minutes to complete the activity. Walk around the room to make sure students are using Spanish to give the **pistas** to their partners.

8 Expansion Have pairs create four questions using answers from the crossword puzzle. Ask them to interview their classmates, asking follow-up questions when applicable.

9 Teaching Tips
• Ask students to read the questions silently and think about the answers they would give.
• Tell students to take notes on their partners' answers. Then, have students select one category and summarize the responses. Students should read the summaries to their partners to check for accuracy before sharing them with the class.

10 Teaching Tip To simplify, have groups write an outline. Then, have students divide up the scenes to be written, making sure that each one has about the same number of lines. When they have finished their drafts, students should exchange them for peer editing. Finally, the group puts all the scenes together and presents its program or film to the class.

TEACHING OPTIONS

Pairs Have pairs of students create a poster advertising an artistic event on campus or in the community, using at least six vocabulary words from **Contextos**. Hang up the posters around the classroom and have pairs circulate to view the events. They should try to convince each other to go to the events that interest them the most. Then have pairs tell the class what events they chose to attend and why.

Game Write words for various types of artists on index cards. On another set of cards, write their works. Shuffle the two sets and tape them facedown on the board. Divide the class into teams of four. Students should try to match the artists to their works. Ex: **dramaturgo / obra de teatro**. When a player makes a match, his or her team collects the cards. The team with the most cards at the end wins.

Una sorpresa para Maru

communication cultures NATIONAL STANDARDS

Miguel y Maru hacen una visita muy especial al Museo de Arte Popular. Por otra parte, Jimena y Juan Carlos hablan sobre arte.

PERSONAJES JUAN CARLOS JIMENA

 Video

1

JUAN CARLOS Cuando era niño, iba con frecuencia a espectáculos culturales con mi mamá. A ella le gustan el teatro, los conciertos, la poesía y especialmente la danza.

2

JIMENA Mi mamá hubiera querido que tocara algún instrumento. Pero la verdad es que no tengo nada de talento musical, y Felipe tampoco.

JIMENA Aunque no tengamos talento artístico, mi mamá nos enseñó a apreciar la música.

JUAN CARLOS Creo que tu mamá y la mía se llevarían bien. Tal vez algún día lleguen a conocerse.

3

(*Mientras tanto, en el Museo de Arte Popular*)

MARU Siempre había querido venir aquí. Me encantan las artesanías de cerámica y sus tejidos. El arte folclórico nos cuenta la historia de su gente y su país.

4

MARU ¿Todo bien, Miguel? ¿Qué tienes allí?

MIGUEL ¿Podría pedirte algo?

MARU Claro.

5

6

MIGUEL María Eugenia Castaño Ricaurte, ¿me harías el honor de casarte conmigo?

MIGUEL   **MARU**   **FELIPE**

7

(Juan Carlos y Jimena hablan de los espectáculos que les gustan.)

JUAN CARLOS ¿Qué clase de espectáculos te gustan?

JIMENA Me gusta la música en vivo y el teatro. Además, me encantan las películas.

8

JIMENA ¿Cuáles son tus películas favoritas?

JUAN CARLOS Las de ciencia ficción y las de terror.

9

JUAN CARLOS ¿Te gustan las películas de acción?

JIMENA Sí, me fascinan, y también los documentales.

JUAN CARLOS Bueno, podríamos ir a verlos juntos.

10

(Y... en el museo)

MARU Sí. ¡Sí acepto casarme contigo! Qué anillo tan hermoso.

Expresiones útiles

Talking about the arts

Mi mamá hubiera querido que tocara algún instrumento.
My mother would have wanted me to play some instrument.

Pero la verdad es que no tengo nada de talento musical.
But the truth is I don't have any musical talent.

Me encantan las artesanías de cerámica y los tejidos.
I love ceramic crafts and weavings.

El arte folclórico nos cuenta la historia de su gente y su país.
Folkloric art tells us the history of its people and its country.

Getting engaged

¿Podría pedirte algo?
Could I ask you for something?

¿Me harías el honor de casarte conmigo?
Would you do me the honor of marrying me?

Sí. ¡Sí acepto casarme contigo!
Yes. Yes, I'll marry you!

Qué anillo tan hermoso.
What a beautiful ring.

Additional vocabulary

(No) Estoy de acuerdo.
I (dis)agree.

More activities

vhlcentral   VM pp. 33–34   Online activities

TEACHING OPTIONS

Pairs Have students work in pairs. Ask them to write predictions about what will happen in the final **Fotonovela** episode. Then have volunteers read their predictions aloud and ask the class if they agree or disagree.

Extra Practice Ask students to imagine that they have just returned from a visit to an art museum. Have them describe the experience in a short paragraph. Students should use as many vocabulary words as possible in their paragraphs. Have them exchange their papers for peer editing.

¿Qué pasó?

1 Seleccionar Selecciona la respuesta correcta.

1. Cuando era niño, Juan Carlos iba a los ___b___ culturales.
   a. premios   b. espectáculos   c. boletos
2. Jimena dice que no tiene talento ___a___.
   a. musical   b. moderno   c. folclórico
3. A Maru le encanta ver las ___b___ en cerámica y los tejidos.
   a. bailarinas   b. artesanías   c. bellas artes
4. A Jimena le gusta escuchar música en vivo e ir al ___c___.
   a. cine   b. festival   c. teatro
5. A Juan Carlos le gustan las películas de ___c___.
   a. acción y de vaqueros   b. aventuras y de drama   c. ciencia ficción y de terror

2 Identificar Identifica quién dice estas oraciones.

1. Cuando era niño, iba con frecuencia a espectáculos culturales con mi mamá.   Juan Carlos
2. El arte folclórico nos cuenta la historia de su gente y su país.   Maru
3. Aunque no tengamos talento musical, mi mamá nos enseñó a apreciar la música.   Jimena
4. Creo que tu mamá y la mía se llevarían bien.   Juan Carlos
5. Mi mamá hubiera querido que tocara algún instrumento.   Jimena
6. Mi abuela no me daría el anillo, a menos que hubiera pedido permiso a tus padres primero.   Miguel

MARU

JIMENA

MIGUEL

JUAN CARLOS

3 Correspondencias ¿A qué eventos culturales asistirán juntos Jimena y Juan Carlos?

| una exposición de cerámica precolombina | un concierto | una ópera |
| una exposición de pintura española | una telenovela | una tragedia |

1. Escucharán música clásica y conocerán a un director muy famoso.
   un concierto
2. El público aplaudirá mucho a la señora que es soprano.
   una ópera
3. Como a Marissa le gusta la historia, la llevarán a ver esto.
   una exposición de cerámica precolombina
4. Como a Miguel le gustaría ver arte, entonces irán con él.
   una exposición de pintura española

4 El fin de semana Vas a asistir a dos eventos culturales el próximo fin de semana con un(a) compañero/a de clase. Comenten entre ustedes por qué les gustan o les disgustan algunas de las actividades que van sugiriendo. Escojan al final dos actividades que puedan realizar juntos/as.   Answers will vary.

▶ ¿Qué te gustaría ver/hacer este fin de semana?
▶ ¿Te gustaría asistir a...?
▶ ¡Me encanta(n)...!
▶ Odio..., ¿qué tal si...?

---

1 Teaching Tip
Have the class work through a few true/false items before doing this activity. Ex: **1. La familia de Jimena no aprecia el arte.** (Falso.) **2. Para Maru, las artesanías tienen valor histórico y cultural.** (Cierto.)

Nota cultural
The **Palacio de Bellas Artes** in Mexico City is an important center for dance and opera fans. Many top artists have performed there, including the famous Italian opera singer **Luciano Pavarotti.** Three times a week, the **Ballet Folklórico de México,** considered by many to be the best of its kind in the world, presents the traditional dances and music of Mexico.

2 Expansion
Give these statements to the class as items 7–9: **7. Me gusta la música en vivo y el teatro.** (Jimena) **8. Qué anillo tan hermoso.** (Maru) **9. ¿Podría pedirte algo?** (Miguel)

3 Expansion
Have students write definitions in Spanish of the words **exposición, concierto, telenovela, ópera,** and **tragedia.** Have volunteers share their definitions with the class.

4 Possible Conversation
E1: ¿Qué te gustaría hacer este fin de semana?
E2: Pues, como a mí me gusta la música, creo que me gustaría ver una ópera.
E1: ¡Uy, odio la ópera! Además, los boletos son muy caros.
E2: Ay, sí, es cierto. Bueno, ¿te gustaría asistir a un concierto de la orquesta nacional?
E1: Buena idea. Me encanta la música clásica.
E2: Y a ti, ¿qué te gustaría hacer?
E1: Bueno, como me gusta tanto el arte, me gustaría ver una exposición de arte moderno.
E2: De acuerdo.

TEACHING OPTIONS

Pairs Divide the class into pairs. Ask half the class to write a paragraph about the future of **Miguel** and **Maru's** relationship and the other half to write about **Jimena** and **Juan Carlos.** Give students time to prepare, and have a few pairs read their paragraphs to the class.
Large Groups Have students stand in a circle. Call out a statement that a famous artist could have made in his or her youth. (Ex: **Me gustaría escribir poemas sin letras mayúsculas.**) Toss a ball to

a student, who must identify the artist. (Ex: **e.e. cummings**) Then reverse the activity by naming famous artists and having students make statements.
Pairs In pairs, have students talk about what they would like to do or be in the future and why. Tell them to use **te gustaría** and **me gustaría.** Then ask a few students to summarize what their partners told them.

Ortografía

Tutorial

Las trampas ortográficas

Some of the most common spelling mistakes in Spanish occur when two or more words have very similar spellings. This section reviews some of those words.

---

compro   **compró**   **hablo**   **habló**

There is no accent mark in the **yo** form of **–ar** verbs in the present tense. There is, however, an accent mark in the **Ud./él/ella** form of **–ar** verbs in the preterite.

- - -

este (adjective)   **éste** (pronoun)   **esté** (verb)

The demonstrative adjectives **esta** and **este** do not have an accent mark. The demonstrative pronouns **ésta** and **éste** have an accent mark on the first syllable. The verb forms **está** (*present indicative*) and **esté** (*present subjunctive*) have an accent mark on the last syllable.

- - -

jo-ven   **jó-ve-nes**   **bai-la-rín**   **bai-la-ri-na**

The location of the stressed syllable in a word determines whether or not a written accent mark is needed. When a plural or feminine form has more syllables than the singular or masculine form, an accent mark must sometimes be added or deleted to maintain the correct stress.

- - -

No me gusta la ópera, sino el teatro.
No quiero ir al festival si no vienes conmigo.

The conjunction **sino** (*but rather*) should not be confused with **si no** (*if not*). Note also the difference between **mediodía** (*noon*) and **medio día** (*half a day*) and between **por qué** (*why*) and **porque** (*because*).

Práctica Completa las oraciones con las palabras adecuadas para cada ocasión.

1. Javier me explicó que _____si no_____ lo invitabas, él no iba a venir. (sino/si no)
2. Me gustan mucho las _____canciones_____ folclóricas. (canciones/canciónes)
3. Marina _____presentó_____ su espectáculo en El Salvador. (presento/presentó)
4. Yo prefiero _____éste_____. (éste/esté)

Palabras desordenadas Ordena las letras para descubrir las palabras correctas. Después, ordena las letras indicadas para descubrir la respuesta a la pregunta.

¿Adónde va Manuel?

y u n a s e d ó   ☐ Ⓞ ☐ Ⓞ ☐ ☐ ☐ ☐

q u e r o p   ☐ Ⓞ ☐ ☐ ☐ ☐

z o g a d e l a   Ⓞ ☐ ☐ Ⓞ ☐ ☐ ☐ ☐

á s e t   ☐ Ⓞ ☐ ☐

h a i t e s a b o n c i   ☐ ☐ ☐ ☐ Ⓞ ☐ ☐ Ⓞ ☐ ☐ ☐

Manuel va __ __ _____.[1]

More activities

vhlcentral   LM p. 98

Respuestas: desayunó, porque, adelgazo, está, habitaciones
[1] *Manuel va al teatro.*

Section Goal

In **Ortografía**, students will learn about Spanish words that have similar spellings.

Instructional Resources
Supersite: Audio (Lab MP3 Files); Resources (Scripts, Answer Keys)
WebSAM
Lab Manual

Teaching Tips

- Say the words **compro** and **hablo** and have volunteers write them on the board. Write the words **compró** and **habló** on the board and have volunteers pronounce them.
- Write the words **este, éste,** and **esté** on the board and have volunteers explain how the words are different. Have the class create a sentence that uses each word.
- Write the words **joven, jóve-nes, bailarín,** and **bailarina** on the board and have the class explain why a written accent is needed in **jóvenes** but not in **bailarina**.
- Write the words **sino, si no, medio día, mediodía, por qué,** and **porque** on the board. Have volunteers explain what each word means. Have the class create a sentence that uses each word.
- Point out that **Ortografía** replaces **Pronunciación** in the Student Edition for **Lecciones 10–18,** but not in the Lab Manual. The box references the **Pronunciación** sections found in all lessons of the Lab Manual.

TEACHING OPTIONS

Small Groups Working in small groups, have students write an amusing example sentence for each of the spelling rules presented on this page. Circulate around the class to verify correct spelling. Then ask a few volunteers to write their sentences on the board. **Extra Practice** → Add an auditory aspect to this **Ortografía** presentation. Read aloud a few sentences that contain words presented on this page and have students write them down.

Then write the sentences on the board so that students can check their work. Ex: **1. Si no compro la comida hoy, la compraré mañana. 2. ¿Prefieres este vestido o éste? 3. La señora Pardo no es vieja, sino joven. 4. La persona de quien hablo es el profesor que habló en la conferencia.** Ask comprehension questions as a follow-up.

Section Goals

In **Cultura**, students will:
• read about Venezuela's **Museo de Arte Contemporáneo de Caracas** and other museums in the Spanish-speaking world
• learn arts-related terms
• read about Colombian artist **Fernando Botero**
• read about Hispanic artists

Instructional Resource
Supersite

En detalle

Antes de leer

👥↔👥 Engage students in a conversation about their experiences with museums. Ex: **¿Qué museos han visitado? Describan su última visita a un museo. ¿Cómo fue? ¿Qué exponía?** Ask follow-up questions as necessary.

Lectura

• Have volunteers use the maps in the back of their textbooks to find the locations of the museums mentioned in the reading.
• ←👥→ If time and resources permit, bring in additional pictures of art and other items from the museums mentioned in the reading. Have students choose their favorite pieces and explain what they like about them, using lesson vocabulary.

Después de leer

←👥→ Ask: **¿Cuál de estos museos te gustaría visitar?** Then have students write a short paragraph explaining their answer.

1 Expansion Ask students to write two additional true/false statements. Then have them exchange papers with a classmate and complete the activity.

EN DETALLE

Museo de Arte Contemporáneo de Caracas

Una visita al Museo de Arte Contemporáneo de Caracas (MACC) es una experiencia única. Su colección permanente incluye unas 3.000 obras de artistas de todo el mundo. Además, el museo organiza exposiciones temporales° de escultura, dibujo, pintura, fotografía, cine y video. En sus salas se pueden admirar obras de artistas como Matisse, Miró, Picasso, Chagall, Tàpies y Botero.

Exposición Cuerpo plural, MACC

La lección de esquí, de Joan Miró

En 2004 el museo tuvo que cerrar a causa de un incendio°. Entonces, su valiosa° colección fue trasladada al Museo de Bellas Artes, también en Caracas. Además se realizaron exposiciones en otros lugares, incluso al aire libre, en parques y bulevares.

Cuando el MACC reabrió° sus puertas, un año después, lo hizo con nuevos conceptos e ideas. Se dio más atención a las cerámicas y fotografías de la colección. También se creó una sala multimedia dedicada a las últimas tendencias° como video-arte y *performance*.

El MACC es un importante centro cultural. Además de las salas de exposición, cuenta con° un jardín de esculturas, un auditorio y una biblioteca especializada en arte. También organiza talleres° y recibe a grupos escolares. Un viaje a Caracas no puede estar completo sin una visita a este maravilloso museo.

Otros museos importantes

Museo del Jade (San José, Costa Rica): Tiene la colección de piezas de jade más grande del mundo. La colección tiene un gran valor° y una gran importancia histórica. Incluye muchas joyas° precolombinas.

Museo de Instrumentos Musicales (La Paz, Bolivia): Muestra más de 2.500 instrumentos musicales bolivianos y de otras partes del mundo. Tiene un taller de construcción de instrumentos musicales.

Museo Nacional de Culturas Populares (Ciudad de México, México): El museo investiga y difunde° las diferentes manifestaciones culturales de México, realiza exposiciones y organiza seminarios, cursos y talleres.

Museo del Cine Pablo Ducrós Hicken (Buenos Aires, Argentina): Dedicado a la historia del cine argentino, expone películas, libros, revistas, guiones°, carteles, fotografías, cámaras y proyectores antiguos.

---

exposiciones temporales *temporary exhibitions* incendio *fire* valiosa *valuable* reabrió *reopened* tendencias *trends* cuenta con *it has* talleres *workshops* valor *value* joyas *jewelry* difunde *spreads* guiones *scripts*

ACTIVIDADES

1 **¿Cierto o falso?** Indica si lo que dice cada oración es **cierto** o **falso**. Corrige la información falsa.

1. La colección permanente del MACC tiene sólo obras de artistas venezolanos. **Falso.** Tiene obras de artistas de todo el mundo.
2. Durante el tiempo que el museo cerró a causa de un incendio, se realizaron exposiciones al aire libre. **Cierto.**
3. Cuando el museo reabrió, se dio más atención a la pintura. **Falso.** Se dio más atención a las cerámicas y a las fotografías de la colección.
4. En el jardín del museo también pueden admirarse obras de arte. **Cierto.**
5. La importancia del Museo del Jade se debe a las joyas europeas que se exponen en él. **Falso.** Se debe a las joyas precolombinas que se exponen en él.
6. En el Museo de Instrumentos Musicales de La Paz también se hacen instrumentos musicales. **Cierto.**
7. En Buenos Aires hay un museo dedicado a la historia del cine de Hollywood. **Falso.** Está dedicado al cine argentino.

TEACHING OPTIONS

Small Groups ←👥→ Have students work in small groups. Tell them to imagine that they are owners of a gallery specializing in art from Spanish-speaking countries. For homework, each student should research one piece of art on the Internet and print an image of the work for the group's gallery. In class, have each group describe the style of their artwork and what they represent to the potential buyers (the class).

Pairs ←👥→ Have students, in pairs, research an art museum in a Spanish or Latin American city that is not mentioned in **En detalle**. Ask them to create a brochure describing the museum's location, history, famous works of art, current exhibitions, and any other significant information. Have pairs present their brochures to the class.

ASÍ SE DICE

Arte y espectáculos

las caricaturas (Col., El Salv., Méx.); los dibujitos (Arg.); los muñequitos (Cuba)	los dibujos animados
el coro	*choir*
el escenario	*stage*
el estreno	*debut, premiere*
el/la guionista	*scriptwriter*

EL MUNDO HISPANO

Artistas hispanos

- **Myrna Báez** (Santurce, Puerto Rico, 1931) Innovó las técnicas de la pintura y el grabado° en Latinoamérica. En 2001, el Museo de Arte de Puerto Rico le rindió homenaje° a sus cuarenta años de carrera artística.

- **Joaquín Cortés** (Córdoba, España, 1969) Bailarín y coreógrafo. En sus espectáculos une° sus raíces gitanas° a influencias musicales de todo el mundo.

- **Tania León** (La Habana, Cuba, 1943) Compositora y directora de orquesta. Ha sido cofundadora° y directora musical del *Dance Theater of Harlem*, y ha compuesto numerosas obras.

- **Rafael Murillo Selva** (Tegucigalpa, Honduras, 1934) Dramaturgo. En su obra refleja preocupaciones sociales y la cultura hondureña.

grabado *engraving* rindió homenaje *paid homage* une *combines* raíces gitanas *gypsy roots* cofundadora *co-founder*

PERFIL

Fernando Botero: un estilo único

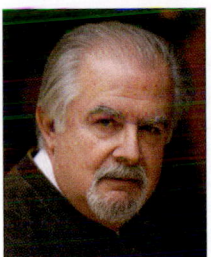

El dibujante°, pintor y escultor **Fernando Botero** es un colombiano de fama internacional. Ha expuesto sus obras en galerías y museos de las Américas, Europa y Asia.

La pintura siempre ha sido su pasión. Su estilo se caracteriza por un cierto aire ingenuo° y unas proporciones exageradas. Mucha gente dice que Botero "pinta gordos", pero esto no es correcto. En su obra no sólo las personas son exageradas; los animales y los objetos también. Botero dice que empezó a pintar personas y cosas voluminosas por intuición. Luego, estudiando la pintura de los maestros italianos, se reafirmó su interés por el volumen y comenzó a usarlo conscientemente° en sus pinturas y esculturas, muchas de las cuales se exhiben en ciudades de todo el mundo. Botero es un trabajador incansable° y es que, para él, lo más divertido del mundo es pintar y crear.

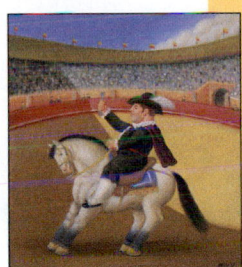

Alguacil, de **Fernando Botero**

dibujante *drawer* ingenuo *naïve* conscientemente *consciously* incansable *tireless*

CON RITMO HISPANO

Voces Universitarias de Honduras (1966–)
Lugar de origen: Tegucigalpa, Honduras

Esta agrupación cuenta la historia de Honduras a través de canciones folclóricas. Ha tenido más de doscientos integrantes.

Go to **vhlcentral.com** to find out more about **Voces Universitarias de Honduras**.

ACTIVIDADES

2 **Comprensión** Contesta las preguntas.

1. ¿Cómo se dice en español "*The scriptwriter is on stage*"?
   El/La guionista está en el escenario.
2. ¿Cuál fue la contribución de Myrna Báez al arte latinoamericano?
   Innovó las técnicas de la pintura y el grabado.
3. ¿En qué actividades artísticas trabaja Tania León?
   Es directora de orquesta y compositora.
4. ¿Qué tipo de obras realiza Fernando Botero?
   dibujo, pintura y escultura
5. ¿Cuáles son dos características del estilo de Botero?
   un aire ingenuo y unas proporciones exageradas

3 **Sus artistas favoritos** En grupos pequeños, hablen sobre sus artistas favoritos (de cualquier disciplina artística). Hablen de la obra que más les gusta de estos artistas y expliquen por qué. Answers will vary.

More activities

vhlcentral

Online activities

Section Goals

In **Estructura 17.1**, students will learn:
- to use the conditional
- to make polite requests and hypothesize about past conditions

Instructional Resources

Supersite: Audio (Lab MP3 Files); Resources (Grammar Presentation Slides, Activity Pack, Scripts, Answer Keys); Testing Program (Quizzes)
WebSAM
Workbook
Lab Manual

Teaching Tips

- 👥↔👤 Ask students to imagine they are attending an arts festival. Involve students in a conversation by asking them what they would like to do there. Ex: **¿Qué te gustaría hacer o ver en el festival de arte? A mí me gustaría ver las comedias que dan. ¿Y a ti?** Tell students that **gustaría** is a polite form of **gustar** that they already know. The conditional can be used to make polite requests.

- Ask volunteers to read the captions to the video stills and indicate which verbs are in the conditional.

- Point out that, as in the future, there is only one set of endings in the conditional.

- Check for understanding by citing an infinitive and a subject pronoun while pointing to a specific student. The student should respond with the conditional form. Ex: **decir/nosotros (diríamos); venir/tú (vendrías)**

- Ask students what the future form of **hay** is. Then ask them what they would expect the conditional form to be. **(habrá/habría)**

17.1 The conditional   Tutorial

ANTE TODO The conditional tense in Spanish expresses what you *would do* or what *would happen* under certain circumstances.

The conditional tense

		visitar	comer	aplaudir
SINGULAR FORMS	yo	visitar**ía**	comer**ía**	aplaudir**ía**
	tú	visitar**ías**	comer**ías**	aplaudir**ías**
	Ud./él/ella	visitar**ía**	comer**ía**	aplaudir**ía**
PLURAL FORMS	nosotros/as	visitar**íamos**	comer**íamos**	aplaudir**íamos**
	vosotros/as	visitar**íais**	comer**íais**	aplaudir**íais**
	Uds./ellos/ellas	visitar**ían**	comer**ían**	aplaudir**ían**

Creo que tu mamá y la mía se llevarían bien.

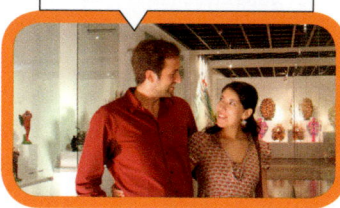

Pensé que te gustaría el Museo de Arte Popular.

▶ The conditional tense is formed much like the future tense. The endings are the same for all verbs, both regular and irregular. For regular verbs, you simply add the appropriate endings to the infinitive. **¡Atención!** All forms of the conditional have an accent mark.

▶ For irregular verbs, add the conditional endings to the irregular stems.

INFINITIVE	STEM	CONDITIONAL		INFINITIVE	STEM	CONDITIONAL
decir	dir-	dir**ía**		querer	querr-	querr**ía**
hacer	har-	har**ía**		saber	sabr-	sabr**ía**
poder	podr-	podr**ía**		salir	saldr-	saldr**ía**
poner	pondr-	pondr**ía**		tener	tendr-	tendr**ía**
haber	habr-	habr**ía**		venir	vendr-	vendr**ía**

▶ While in English the conditional is a compound verb form made up of the auxiliary verb *would* and a main verb, in Spanish it is a simple verb form that consists of one word.

Yo no me **pondría** ese vestido.
I would not put on that dress.

¿**Vivirían** ustedes en otro país?
Would you live in another country?

¡ATENCIÓN!
The polite expressions **Me gustaría...** (*I would like...*) and **Te gustaría...** (*You would like...*) are other examples of the conditional.

AYUDA
The infinitive of **hay** is **haber**, so its conditional form is **habría**.

TEACHING OPTIONS

TPR In teams of five, have students line up several feet from the board. Call out an infinitive. The first team members race to the board and write the **yo** form of the verb in the conditional, then pass the marker to the next team members, who write the **tú** form, and so on. The team that finishes first and has all the forms correct wins the round.

Extra Practice ←👤→ Ask students to write a short paragraph describing what they would do over the next six months if they could do anything their hearts desired and money and time were no object. Ex: **Yo viajaría por todo el mundo...** Call on volunteers to read their paragraphs aloud; then ask the class comprehension questions about what was said. Ex: **¿Qué harían _____ y _____?**

▶ The conditional is commonly used to make polite requests.

¿Podrías abrir la ventana, por favor?
Would you open the window, please?

¿Sería tan amable de venir a mi oficina?
Would you be so kind as to come to my office?

▶ In Spanish, as in English, the conditional expresses the future in relation to a past action or state of being. In other words, the future indicates what *will happen* whereas the conditional indicates what *would happen*.

Creo que mañana **hará** sol.
I think it will be sunny tomorrow.

Creía que hoy **haría** sol.
I thought it would be sunny today.

▶ The English *would* is often used with a verb to express the conditional, but it can also mean *used to*, in the sense of past habitual action. To express past habitual actions, Spanish uses the imperfect, not the conditional.

Íbamos al parque los sábados.
We would go to the park on Saturdays.

De adolescentes, **comíamos** mucho.
As teenagers, we used to eat a lot.

Sin ti, no sé qué haría.

Sólo tú sabes ordenar mi vida.

COMPARE & CONTRAST

In **Lección 16**, you learned the *future of probability*. Spanish also has the *conditional of probability*, which expresses conjecture or probability about a past condition, event, or action. Compare these Spanish and English sentences.

Serían las once de la noche cuando Elvira me llamó.
It must have been (It was probably) 11 p.m. when Elvira called me.

Sonó el teléfono. **¿Llamaría** Emilio para cancelar nuestra cita?
The phone rang. I wondered if it was Emilio calling to cancel our date.

Note that English conveys conjecture or probability with phrases such as *I wondered if*, *probably*, and *must have been*. In contrast, Spanish gets these same ideas across with conditional forms.

More activities

vhlcentral

LM
p. 99

WB
pp. 193–194

Online activities

¡INTÉNTALO! Indica la forma apropiada del condicional de los verbos.

1. Yo ___escucharía, leería, esculpiría___ (escuchar, leer, esculpir)
2. Tú ___apreciarías, comprenderías, compartirías___ (apreciar, comprender, compartir)
3. Ustedes ___presentarían, deberían, aplaudirían___ (presentar, deber, aplaudir)
4. Marcos ___pondría, vendría, querría___ (poner, venir, querer)
5. Nosotras ___seríamos, sabríamos, iríamos___ (ser, saber, ir)
6. Ella ___saldría, podría, haría___ (salir, poder, hacer)
7. Yo ___tendría, tocaría, me aburriría___ (tener, tocar, aburrirse)
8. Tú ___dirías, verías, publicarías___ (decir, ver, publicar)

Práctica

1

De viaje A un grupo de artistas le gustaría hacer un viaje a Honduras. Completa sus oraciones con el condicional de los verbos.

1

De viaje A un grupo de artistas le gustaría hacer un viaje a Honduras. Completa sus oraciones con el condicional de los verbos.

1. Me ___gustaría___ (gustar) llevar algunos libros de poesía de Leticia de Oyuela.
2. Ana ___querría___ (querer) ir primero a Copán para conocer las ruinas mayas.
3. Yo ___diría___ (decir) que fuéramos a Tegucigalpa primero.
4. Nosotras ___preferiríamos___ (preferir) ver una obra del Grupo Dramático de Tegucigalpa. Luego ___podríamos___ (poder) tomarnos un café.
5. Y nosotros ___veríamos___ (ver) los cuadros del pintor José Antonio Velásquez. Y tú, Luisa, ¿qué ___harías___ (hacer)?
6. Yo ___tendría___ (tener) interés en ver o comprar cerámica de José Arturo Machado. Y a ti, Carlos, ¿te ___interesaría___ (interesar) ver la arquitectura colonial?

NOTA CULTURAL

Leticia de Oyuela (1935–2008) fue una escritora hondureña. En sus obras, Oyuela combinaba la historia con la ficción y, a través de sus personajes, cuestionaba y desafiaba (*used to challenge*) las normas sociales.

2

¿Qué harías? En parejas, pregúntense qué harían en estas situaciones.   Answers will vary.

> Estás en un concierto de tu banda favorita y la persona que está sentada delante no te deja ver.

> Un amigo actor te invita a ver una película que acaba de hacer, y no te gusta nada cómo hace su papel.

> Estás invitado/a a los Premios Ariel. Es posible que te vayan a dar un premio, pero ese día estás muy enfermo/a.

> Te invitan, pagándote mucho dinero, a un programa de televisión para hablar de tu vida privada y pelearte (*to fight*) con tu novio/a durante el programa.

NOTA CULTURAL

Los Premios Ariel de México son el equivalente a los Premios Oscar en los Estados Unidos. Cada año los entrega la Academia Mexicana de Ciencias y Artes Cinematográficas. Algunas películas que han ganado un premio Ariel son *Amores perros* y *El laberinto del fauno*.

3

Sugerencias Matilde busca trabajo. Dile ocho cosas que tú harías si fueras ella. Usa el condicional. Luego compara tus sugerencias con las de un(a) compañero/a.   Answers will vary.

modelo
> *Si yo fuera tú, buscaría trabajo en la red.*

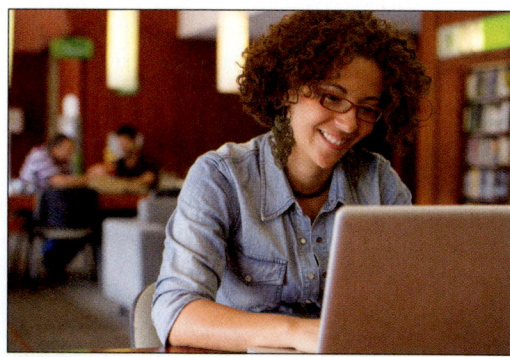

AYUDA

Here are two ways of saying *If I were you:*
Si yo fuera tú...
Yo en tu lugar...

Comunicación

4 **Conversaciones** Tu profesor(a) te dará una hoja de actividades. En ella se presentan dos listas con diferentes problemas que supuestamente tienen los estudiantes. En parejas, túrnense para explicar los problemas de su lista; uno/a cuenta lo que le pasa y el/la otro/a dice lo que haría en esa situación usando la frase "Yo en tu lugar...". Answers will vary.

> **modelo**
>
> **Estudiante 1:** ¡Qué problema! Mi novio no me habla desde el domingo.
> **Estudiante 2:** Yo en tu lugar, no le diría nada por unos días para ver qué pasa.

5 **Luces, cámara y acción** En parejas, elijan una película que les guste y después hablen sobre las cosas que harían de forma diferente si pudieran ser los directores de una secuela (*sequel*) de dicha película. Answers will vary.

Yo no contrataría a Ben Affleck para el papel de Batman.

Además, haría una película más corta.

El personaje de Lex Luthor no aparecería en mi película.

Mi película tendría un final feliz.

Síntesis

6 **Encuesta** Tu profesor(a) te dará una hoja de actividades. Circula por la clase y pregúntales a tres compañeros/as qué actividad(es) de las que se describen les gustaría realizar. Usa el condicional de los verbos. Anota las respuestas e informa a la clase los resultados de la encuesta. Answers will vary.

> **modelo**
>
> **Estudiante 1:** ¿Harías el papel de un loco en una obra de teatro?
> **Estudiante 2:** Sí, lo haría. Sería un papel muy interesante.

---

4 Teaching Tip Distribute the *Hojas de actividades* (Activity Pack/Supersite) that correspond to this activity.

4 Expansion Working as a class, name a problem from one of the lists and ask several volunteers to share the suggestions they received. Encourage other students to comment on the suggestions.

5 Expansion Ask the class for titles of additional movies and write them on the board. Ask students to imagine that they are going to produce a sequel for each one. Have them use sentences like those in the activity to describe the features that they would leave in the sequel.
Ex: **Yo contrataría otra vez a _____ para ese papel.**

6 Teaching Tip Distribute the *Hojas de actividades* (Activity Pack/Supersite) that correspond to this activity.

6 Expansion Encourage students to add two more activities to their lists. Have them select from those listed on pages 578–579.

TEACHING OPTIONS

Small Groups Divide the class into groups of four. Have each group brainstorm a list of professions, both artistic and non-artistic. Each group member then chooses a different profession. Students take turns being interviewed by a three-person board about what they would do for their community in their chosen profession. Each board member should ask the interviewee at least two questions.

Extra Practice Ask students to write a short paragraph answering this question: **¿Qué harías para cambiar tu vida?** Have students exchange papers with a classmate to check the paragraphs for accuracy.

17.2 The conditional perfect Tutorial

ANTE TODO Like other compound tenses you have learned—the present perfect, the past perfect, and the future perfect—the conditional perfect (**el condicional perfecto**) is formed with **haber** + [*past participle*].

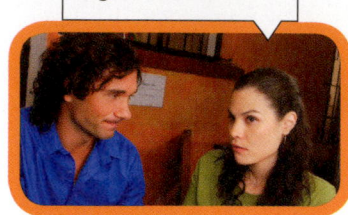

Felipe habría venido con nosotros, pero sigue molesto.

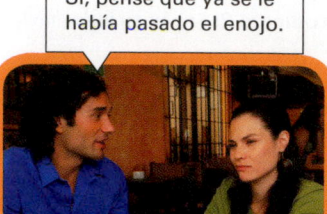

Sí, pensé que ya se le había pasado el enojo.

The conditional perfect

		pintar	**comer**	**vivir**
SINGULAR FORMS	yo	**habría** pintado	**habría** comido	**habría** vivido
	tú	**habrías** pintado	**habrías** comido	**habrías** vivido
	Ud./él/ella	**habría** pintado	**habría** comido	**habría** vivido
PLURAL FORMS	nosotros/as	**habríamos** pintado	**habríamos** comido	**habríamos** vivido
	vosotros/as	**habríais** pintado	**habríais** comido	**habríais** vivido
	Uds./ellos/ellas	**habrían** pintado	**habrían** comido	**habrían** vivido

▶ The conditional perfect is used to express an action that would have occurred, but didn't.

¿No fuiste al espectáculo?
¡Te **habrías divertido**!
You didn't go to the show?
You would have had a good time!

Sandra **habría preferido** ir a la ópera, pero Omar prefirió ir al cine.
Sandra would have preferred to go to the opera, but Omar preferred to see a movie.

🔊 **¡INTÉNTALO!** Indica las formas apropiadas del condicional perfecto de los verbos.

1. Nosotros ___habríamos hecho___ (hacer) todos los quehaceres.
2. Ellos ___habrían pintado___ (pintar) un mural.
3. Tú ___habrías apreciado___ (apreciar) mi poesía.
4. Usted ___habría tocado___ (tocar) el piano.
5. Ellas ___habrían puesto___ (poner) la mesa.
6. Yo ___habría presentado___ (presentar) el informe.
7. Silvia y Alberto ___habrían esculpido___ (esculpir) una estatua.
8. Tú y yo ___habríamos resuelto___ (resolver) los problemas.
9. Ustedes ___habrían vivido___ (vivir) en el campo.
10. Tú ___habrías abierto___ (abrir) la puerta.

More activities

vhlcentral

LM p. 100

WB p. 195

Online activities

TEACHING OPTIONS

Extra Practice ↔🧍→ Ask students to write five sentences describing how the life of their favorite writer or artist would have been different if he or she had lived in another century. Ex: **Isabel Allende habría escrito sus novelas con una pluma de ave....**

Small Groups ↔🧍→ Have students work in small groups. Give them five minutes to describe what would have happened to Cinderella had she not lost her glass slipper. Tell students that the translations for *Cinderella, prince,* and *glass slipper* in Spanish are **Cenicienta, príncipe,** and **zapato de cristal.**

Práctica

1 Completar Completa los diálogos con la forma apropiada del condicional perfecto de los verbos. Luego, en parejas, representen los diálogos.

divertirse	presentar	sentir	tocar
hacer	querer	tener	venir

1. —Tú __habrías hecho__ el papel de Aída mejor que ella. ¡Qué lástima!
   —Sí, mis padres __habrían venido__ desde California sólo para oírme cantar.
2. —Tania __habría presentado__ la comedia pero no pudo porque cerraron el teatro.
   —¡Qué lástima! Mi esposa y yo __habríamos querido__ ir a la presentación de la obra. Siempre veo tragedias y sé que __me habría divertido__.
3. —Olga, yo esperaba algo más. Con un poco de dedicación y práctica la orquesta __habría tocado__ mejor y los músicos __habrían tenido__ más éxito.
   ▶ —Menos mal que la compositora no los escuchó. Se __habría sentido__ avergonzada.

¡LENGUA VIVA!

The expression **Menos mal que…** means *It's a good thing that…* or *It's just as well that…* It is followed by a verb in the indicative.

2 Combinar En parejas, combinen elementos de cada una de las tres columnas para formar ocho oraciones usando el condicional perfecto. *Answers will vary.*

A	B	C
con talento artístico	yo	estudiar…
con más tiempo libre	tú	pintar…
en otro país	la gente	esculpir…
con más aprecio de las artes	mis compañeros y yo	viajar…
con más dinero	los artistas	escribir…
en otra película	Alejandro González Iñárritu	publicar…

NOTA CULTURAL

El director de cine **Alejandro González Iñárritu** forma parte de la nueva generación de directores mexicanos. Su película *Amores perros* fue nominada para el Oscar a la mejor película extranjera en 2001. Ganó tres Oscars por el guión, dirección y producción de la película *Birdman* (2014), y el Oscar a mejor director por *The Revenant* (2015).

3 ¿Qué habrías hecho? Estos dibujos muestran situaciones poco comunes. No sabemos qué hicieron estas personas, pero tú, ¿qué habrías hecho? Comparte tus respuestas con un(a) compañero/a. *Answers will vary.*

AYUDA

Here are some suggestions:

Habría llevado el dinero a…

Yo habría atacado al oso (*bear*) con…

Yo habría…

1.

2.

3.

4.

Concurso de Talentos

TEACHING OPTIONS

Pairs 👥↔👥 Ask students to tell their partners about their most embarrassing moment. Partners should respond to the stories by telling them what they would have done in their place. Ex: **En tu lugar, yo habría…**

Extra Practice ↔👤↔ Ask students to describe what these people would have done had they had more money: **mis padres, yo, mi mejor amigo/a, los estudiantes de la universidad, mi profesor(a) de español.** Ex: **Con más dinero, mis padres habrían comprado una casa más grande….**

1 Teaching Tip Before beginning the activity, model the use of **menos mal que…** Ex: **¿No estudiaron anoche? Menos mal que no tenemos examen hoy.**

1 Expansion

👤↔👤 Have pairs choose one of the three dialogues and write four additional lines. Call on volunteers to role-play their extended dialogues for the class.

2 Teaching Tip Have volunteers call out sentences using elements from each of the three columns. Have other volunteers act as secretaries, writing examples on the board. Ask the class to check for accurate grammar and spelling.

3 Teaching Tip

↔👤→ To simplify, begin by asking students to describe each of the drawings. Write useful vocabulary on the board, including the expressions from **Ayuda**.

Comunicación

4

Preguntas En parejas, imaginen que tienen cincuenta años y están hablando de sus años de juventud. ¿Qué habrían hecho de manera diferente? Túrnense para hacerse y contestar las preguntas. Answers will vary.

> **modelo**
>
> ¿Te (interesar) aprender a tocar un instrumento?
> **Estudiante 1:** ¿Te habría interesado aprender a tocar un instrumento?
> **Estudiante 2:** Sí, habría aprendido a tocar el piano.

1. ¿Te (gustar) viajar por Latinoamérica?
2. ¿A qué escritores (leer)?
3. ¿Qué clases (tomar)?
4. ¿Qué tipo de música (escuchar)?
5. ¿Qué tipo de amigos/as (tener)?
6. ¿A qué fiestas o viajes no (ir)?
7. ¿Con qué tipo de persona (salir)?
8. ¿Qué tipo de ropa (llevar)?

5

Pobre Mario En parejas, digan qué cosas Mario habría hecho de una manera diferente, de haber tenido la oportunidad. Answers will vary.

> **modelo**
>
> Mario no habría hecho este musical.

De:	Mario
Para:	Enrique
Asunto:	Fin de mi proyecto artístico

Enrique:

Ya llegó el último día del musical. Yo creía que nunca iba a acabar. En general, los cantantes y actores eran bastante malos, pero no tuve tiempo de buscar otros, y además los buenos ya tenían trabajo en otras obras. Ayer todo salió muy mal. Como era la última noche, yo había invitado a unos críticos a ver la obra, pero no pudieron verla. El primer problema fue la cantante principal. Ella estaba enojada conmigo porque no quise pagarle todo el dinero que quería. Dijo que tenía problemas de garganta, y no salió a cantar. Conseguí otra cantante, pero los músicos de la orquesta todavía no habían llegado. Tenían que venir todos en un autobús no muy caro que yo había alquilado, pero el autobús salió a una hora equivocada. Entonces, el bailarín se enojó conmigo porque todo iba a empezar tarde.

Quizás tenía razón mi padre. Seguramente soy mejor contador que director teatral.

Escríbeme,
Mario

¡LENGUA VIVA!

The useful expression **de haber tenido la oportunidad** means *if I/he/you/etc. had had the opportunity.* You can use this construction in similar instances, such as **De haberlo sabido ayer, te habría llamado.**

Síntesis

6

Yo en tu lugar Primero, cada estudiante hace una lista con tres errores que ha cometido o tres problemas que ha tenido en su vida. Después, en parejas, túrnense para decirse qué habrían hecho en esas situaciones. Answers will vary.

> **modelo**
>
> **Estudiante 1:** El año pasado saqué una mala nota en el examen de biología.
> **Estudiante 2:** Yo no habría sacado una mala nota. Habría estudiado más.

TEACHING OPTIONS

Pairs Have students make a list of everything they did last weekend. Then, ask students to tell their partners what they did, when they did it, and how they did it. Partners will counter with how they would have done each thing. Ex: **Bailé por cinco horas en una fiesta el sábado pasado. (Yo no habría bailado por tanto tiempo. Yo habría bailado sólo dos horas.)** Encourage students to respond to their partners' comments.

Large Groups Divide the class into three groups. Have each student answer this question: **¿Qué habrías hecho de una manera diferente este semestre?** After everyone has spoken, have the group discuss which missed opportunities would have been the most important in making a difference this semester.

17.3 The past perfect subjunctive Tutorial

CONSULTA

To review the past perfect indicative, see **Estructura 15.2**, p. 522.
To review the present perfect subjunctive, see **Estructura 15.3**, p. 525.

ANTE TODO The past perfect subjunctive (**el pluscuamperfecto de subjuntivo**), also called the pluperfect subjunctive, is formed with the past subjunctive of **haber** + [*past participle*]. Compare the following subjunctive forms.

Present subjunctive	Present perfect subjunctive
yo trabaje	yo haya trabajado

Past subjunctive	Past perfect subjunctive
yo trabajara	yo hubiera trabajado

Past perfect subjunctive

		pintar	comer	vivir
SINGULAR FORMS	yo	**hubiera** pintado	**hubiera** comido	**hubiera** vivido
	tú	**hubieras** pintado	**hubieras** comido	**hubieras** vivido
	Ud./él/ella	**hubiera** pintado	**hubiera** comido	**hubiera** vivido
PLURAL FORMS	nosotros/as	**hubiéramos** pintado	**hubiéramos** comido	**hubiéramos** vivido
	vosotros/as	**hubierais** pintado	**hubierais** comido	**hubierais** vivido
	Uds./ellos/ellas	**hubieran** pintado	**hubieran** comido	**hubieran** vivido

▶ The past perfect subjunctive is used in subordinate clauses under the same conditions that you have learned for other subjunctive forms, and in the same way the past perfect is used in English (*I had talked, you had spoken*, etc.). It refers to actions or conditions that had taken place before another action or condition in the past.

No había nadie que **hubiera dormido**.
There wasn't anyone who had slept.

Esperaba que Juan **hubiera ganado** el partido.
I hoped that Juan had won the game.

Dudaba que ellos **hubieran llegado**.
I doubted that they had arrived.

Llegué antes de que la clase **hubiera comenzado**.
I arrived before the class had begun.

¡INTÉNTALO! Indica la forma apropiada del pluscuamperfecto de subjuntivo de cada verbo.

1. Esperaba que ustedes __hubieran hecho__ (hacer) las reservaciones.
2. No creían que nosotros __hubiéramos hablado__ (hablar) con Ricardo.
3. No estaba seguro de que ellos __hubieran ido__ (ir).
4. Dudaba que tú __hubieras dicho__ (decir) eso.
5. No había nadie que __hubiera podido__ (poder) comer tanto como él.
6. No era cierto que yo __hubiera ido__ (ir) con él al concierto.
7. Me molestó que tú no me __hubieras llamado__ (llamar) antes.
8. ¿Había alguien que no __hubiera apreciado__ (apreciar) esa película?
9. No creían que nosotras __hubiéramos bailado__ (bailar) en el festival.
10. No había nadie que __hubiera visto__ (ver) el espectáculo.

Section Goal

In **Estructura 17.3**, students will learn the use of the past perfect subjunctive.

Instructional Resources
Supersite: Audio (Lab MP3 Files); Resources (Grammar Presentation Slides, Activity Pack, Scripts, Answer Keys); Testing Program (Quizzes)
WebSAM
Workbook
Lab Manual

Teaching Tips
• Briefly review the past perfect indicative and the present perfect subjunctive. Ask volunteers to identify cues that trigger the subjunctive mood in a subordinate clause (verbs of emotion; doubt, disbelief, denial; certain conjunctions; references to persons or things not known to exist, and so forth). Ask students to predict how the past perfect subjunctive is conjugated.
• Discuss the use of the past perfect subjunctive and have students examine the example sentences. Ask volunteers to identify the cue that triggered the subjunctive mood in each example. Then ask them to suggest other sentences that follow the pattern of the example sentences.
Ex: **Se sorprendió de que nadie se hubiera dormido mientras tocaba aquella banda.**
• Point out that in many parts of the Spanish-speaking world, the past perfect subjunctive is used instead of the conditional perfect.
Ex: **Maite hubiera preferido ir a la ópera, pero Álex prefirió ir al cine.**

TEACHING OPTIONS

Extra Practice Make a statement using the past perfect indicative. Then give the beginning of a reaction that calls for the subjunctive. Have students complete the reaction. Ex: **Jorge había esculpido una estatua para el festival. Fue maravilloso que…** (…**Jorge hubiera esculpido una estatua para el festival**).

TPR Make a series of statements using either the present perfect subjunctive or the past perfect subjunctive. If students hear a statement using the present perfect subjunctive, they raise one hand. If they hear one with the past perfect subjunctive, they raise both hands.

Práctica

1 Completar Completa las oraciones con el pluscuamperfecto de subjuntivo de los verbos.

1. Me molestaba que Carlos y Miguel no ___hubieran venido___ (venir) a visitarme.
2. Me alegré de que mi familia ___se hubiera ido___ (irse) de viaje.
3. Dudaba que la música que yo escuchaba ___hubiera sido___ (ser) la misma que escuchaban mis padres.
4. No creían que nosotros ___hubiéramos podido___ (poder) aprender español en un año.
5. Los músicos se alegraban de que su programa le ___hubiera gustado___ (gustar) tanto al público.
6. La profesora se sorprendió de que nosotros ___hubiéramos hecho___ (hacer) la tarea antes de venir a clase.

2 Transformar Transforma las oraciones según el modelo.

> **modelo**
>
> Me alegro de que hayan venido los padres de Micaela.
> *Me alegré de que hubieran venido los padres de Micaela.*

1. Es muy triste que haya muerto la tía de Miguel.
   Fue muy triste que hubiera muerto la tía de Miguel.
2. Dudo que Guillermo haya comprado una casa tan grande.
   Dudaba que Guillermo hubiera comprado una casa tan grande.
3. No puedo creer que nuestro equipo haya perdido el partido.
   No podía creer que nuestro equipo hubiera perdido el partido.
4. Dudo que hayan cerrado el Museo de Arte.
   Dudaba que hubieran cerrado el Museo de Arte.
5. Me molesta que el periódico no haya llegado.
   Me molestó que el periódico no hubiera llegado.
6. Me alegro de que mi novio me haya llamado.
   Me alegré de que mi novio me hubiera llamado.

3 El regreso Durante 30 años, el astronauta Emilio Hernández estuvo en el espacio sin tener noticias de la Tierra. Usa el pluscuamperfecto de subjuntivo para indicar lo que Emilio esperaba que hubiera pasado.

> **modelo**
>
> su esposa / no casarse con otro hombre
> *Esperaba que su esposa no se hubiera casado con otro hombre.*

1. su suegra / irse a vivir a El Salvador
   Esperaba que su suegra se hubiera ido a vivir a El Salvador.
2. los políticos / acabar con todas las guerras (*wars*)
   Esperaba que los políticos hubieran acabado con todas las guerras.
3. su hija Diana / conseguir ser una pintora famosa
   Esperaba que su hija Diana hubiera conseguido ser una pintora famosa.
4. su hermano Ramón / tener un empleo por más de dos meses
   Esperaba que su hermano Ramón hubiera tenido un empleo por más de dos meses.
5. todos los países / resolver sus problemas económicos
   Esperaba que todos los países hubieran resuelto sus problemas económicos.
6. su esposa / ya pagar el préstamo de la casa
   Esperaba que su esposa ya hubiera pagado el préstamo de la casa.

TEACHING OPTIONS

Pairs Have students make six statements about something that happened last year. Partners counter with statements declaring that the action had not really occurred. Ex: **El poeta Arturo Cruz se murió mientras leía su poesía. (No era cierto que Arturo Cruz se hubiera muerto mientras leía su poesía.)**

Small Groups Divide the class into small groups. Have students take turns telling their group about things they wish had happened over the course of their lives. Ex: **¡Ojalá que hubiera aprendido a tocar el piano!** Encourage students to comment on their group members' statements and ask any necessary follow-up questions.

Comunicación

4 **El robo** La semana pasada desaparecieron varias obras del museo. El detective sospechaba que los empleados del museo le estaban mintiendo. En parejas, digan qué era lo que pensaba el detective. Después, intenten descubrir qué pasó realmente. Answers will vary.

> **modelo**
> El vigilante (*security guard*) le dijo que alguien había abierto las ventanas de la sala.
> El *detective dudaba* (no creía, pensaba que no era cierto, etc.) que alguien hubiera abierto las ventanas de la sala.

1. El carpintero le dijo que ese día no había encontrado nada extraño en el museo.
2. La abogada le dijo que ella no había estado en el museo esa tarde.
3. El técnico le dijo que había comprado una casa porque había ganado la lotería.
4. La directora del museo le dijo que había visto al vigilante hablando con la abogada.
5. El vigilante dijo que la directora había dicho que esa noche no tenían que trabajar.
6. El carpintero se acordó de que la directora y el vigilante habían sido novios.

5 **Reacciones** Imagina que estos acontecimientos (*events*) ocurrieron la semana pasada. Indica cómo reaccionaste ante cada uno. Comparte tu reacción con un(a) compañero/a. Answers will vary.

> **modelo**
> Vino a visitarte tu tía de El Salvador.
> Me alegré de que hubiera venido a visitarme.

1. Perdiste tu mochila con tus tarjetas de crédito y tus documentos.
2. Tu exnovio/a se casó con tu mejor amigo/a.
3. Encontraste cincuenta mil dólares cerca del banco.
4. Tus amigos/as te hicieron una fiesta sorpresa.

Síntesis

6 **Noticias** En grupos, lean estos titulares (*headlines*) e indiquen cuáles habrían sido sus reacciones si esto les hubiera ocurrido a ustedes. Luego escriban tres titulares más y compártanlos con los demás grupos. Utilicen el pluscuamperfecto de subjuntivo. Answers will vary.

Un grupo de turistas se encuentra con Elvis en una gasolinera.
El cantante los saludó, les cantó unas canciones y después se marchó hacia las montañas, caminando tranquilamente.

Tres jóvenes estudiantes se perdieron en un bosque de Maine.
Después de estar tres horas perdidos, aparecieron en una gasolinera de un desierto de Australia.

Ayer, una joven hondureña, después de pasar tres años en coma, se despertó y descubrió que podía entender el lenguaje de los animales.
La joven, de momento, no quiere hablar con la prensa, pero una amiga suya nos dice que está deseando ir al zoológico.

---

4 Teaching Tip To simplify, before beginning the activity, have the class brainstorm expressions of doubt that trigger the subjunctive in a subordinate clause.

4 Expansion
- Ask pairs to present their theories to the class. Then have the class decide which one is the most likely and which one is the least likely. Encourage students to defend their opinions.
- Have small groups write the police report the detective submitted to his superiors.

5 Teaching Tip Have students share a few reactions to what actually happened to them last week. Ex: **Me molestó que mis padres hubieran ido de vacaciones sin mí. Me alegré de que la compañía hubiera llamado para entrevistarme. Me sorprendió que mi mejor amiga hubiera roto con su novio.**

6 Expansion Ask students to pick a fairy tale and write a five-sentence ending using the past perfect subjunctive. Ex: **No era verdad que el lobo hubiera comido a la abuela....** Write any unfamiliar vocabulary on the board for reference.

The Affective Dimension If students are feeling overwhelmed, reassure them that many tenses are made up of forms they have already learned. Encourage students to review previously learned tenses regularly.

TEACHING OPTIONS

Extra Practice Tell students to write a paragraph describing how they felt about what happened at an arts festival held last weekend. Ex: **Fue una lástima que mi cantante favorito no hubiera cantado en el festival....**

Small Groups Divide the class into groups of three. Student A picks an event, such as final exams or a concert. Student B begins a statement about the event in the past that triggers the subjunctive. Student C completes the sentence with a verb in the past perfect subjunctive. Ex: **el concierto de Shakira / No había nadie que... / ... no se hubiera divertido.**

Section Goal

In **Recapitulación**, students will review the grammar concepts from this lesson.

Instructional Resource
Supersite

Teaching Tip You may want to assign this **Recapitulación** activity on the Supersite because it has diagnostics. There is an online-only review activity for each grammar point. The Supersite also has a **Repaso de vocabulario** activity with diagnostics.

1 Teaching Tips
• Remind students that every verb form in the conditional carries an accent mark.
• Complete this activity orally as a class.

1 Expansion
• Ask students to provide the remaining forms of the verbs.
• Add **decir, tener,** and **venir** to the chart.

2 Teaching Tip To simplify, have students underline the subject for each item.

2 Expansion
• Have students compose questions about the dialogue. Ex: **¿Nidia le dijo a Omar que Jaime y ella irían al concierto?**
• To challenge students, ask them to identify which sentences from the dialogue could be replaced by **ir a** + [infinitive] in the imperfect and retain the same meaning. Ex: **1. Yo creía que iba a llover, pero hizo sol.**

Recapitulación

Completa estas actividades para repasar los conceptos de gramática que aprendiste en esta lección.

1 Completar Completa el cuadro con la forma correcta del condicional. **24 pts.**

Infinitivo	tú	nosotros	ellas
pintar	pintarías	pintaríamos	pintarían
querer	querrías	querríamos	**querrían**
poder	podrías	**podríamos**	podrían
haber	**habrías**	habríamos	habrían

2 Diálogo Completa el diálogo con la forma adecuada del condicional de los verbos. **16 pts.**

dejar	gustar	llover	sorprender
encantar	ir	poder	volver

OMAR ¿Sabes? El concierto al aire libre fue un éxito. Yo creía que (1) __lovería__ , pero hizo sol.

NIDIA Ah, me alegro. Te dije que Jaime y yo (2) __iríamos__, pero tuvimos un imprevisto (*something came up*) y no pudimos. Y a Laura, ¿la viste allí?

OMAR Sí, ella fue. Al contrario que tú, al principio me dijo que ella y su esposo no (3) __podrían__ ir, pero al final aparecieron. Necesitaba relajarse un poco; está muy estresada con su trabajo.

NIDIA A mí no me (4) __sorprendería__ que lo dejara. Yo, en su lugar, (5) __dejaría__ esa compañía y (6) __volvería__ a escribir poesía. En realidad no necesita el dinero.

OMAR Estoy de acuerdo. Oye, esta noche voy a ir al teatro. ¿(7) __Te gustaría/ Podrías__ ir conmigo? Jaime también puede acompañarnos. Es una comedia familiar.

NIDIA A nosotros (8) __nos encantaría /nos gustaría__ ir. ¿A qué hora es?

OMAR A las siete y media.

RESUMEN GRAMATICAL

17.1 The conditional   *pp. 588–589*

The conditional tense* of **aplaudir**

aplaudiría	aplaudiríamos
aplaudirías	aplaudiríais
aplaudiría	aplaudirían

*Same endings for -ar, -er, and -ir verbs.

Irregular verbs

Infinitive	Stem	Conditional
decir	**dir-**	diría
hacer	**har-**	haría
poder	**podr-**	podría
poner	**pondr-**	pondría
haber	**habr-**	habría
querer	**querr-**	querría
saber	**sabr-**	sabría
salir	**saldr-**	saldría
tener	**tendr-**	tendría
venir	**vendr-**	vendría

17.2 The conditional perfect   *p. 592*

pintar

habría pintado	**habríamos** pintado
habrías pintado	**habríais** pintado
habría pintado	**habrían** pintado

17.3 The past perfect subjunctive   *p. 595*

cantar

hubiera cantado	**hubiéramos** cantado
hubieras cantado	**hubierais** cantado
hubiera cantado	**hubieran** cantado

► To form the past perfect subjunctive, take the **Uds./ellos/ellas** form of the preterite of **haber**, drop the ending (**-ron**), and add the past subjunctive endings (**-ra, -ras, -ra, -ramos, -rais, -ran**).

► Note that the **nosotros/as** form takes an accent.

TEACHING OPTIONS

Extra Practice Tell students to imagine that they are art critics. Bring in images of artwork from the Spanish-speaking world and have them explain what changes they would make and why. Ex: **Si yo fuera el artista, cambiaría los colores del paisaje para que se viera más realista...**.
Large Groups Divide the class into two groups, **condicional** and **condicional perfecto**. Call out a sentence starter and indicate the first members of each group. The student whose group corresponds to the tense required in the second part of the sentence has five seconds to step forward and complete the sentence in a logical manner. Ex: **Si mis padres me hubieran enseñado a bailar salsa...** (Student from the **condicional perfecto** group steps forward and says: **...yo habría participado en concursos de baile.**)

3 **Fin de curso** El espectáculo de fin de curso de la escuela se canceló por falta de interés y ahora todos se arrepienten (*regret it*). Completa las oraciones con el condicional perfecto. `16 pts.`

1. La profesora de danza _habría convencido_ (convencer) a los mejores bailarines de que participaran.
2. Tú no _habrías escrito_ (escribir) en el periódico que el comité organizador era incompetente.
3. Los profesores _habrían animado_ (animar) a todos a participar.
4. Nosotros _habríamos invitado_ (invitar) a nuestros amigos y familiares.
5. Tú _habrías publicado_ (publicar) un artículo muy positivo sobre el espectáculo.
6. Los padres de los estudiantes _habrían dado_ (dar) más dinero y apoyo.
7. Mis compañeros de drama y yo _habríamos presentado_ (presentar) una comedia muy divertida.
8. El director _habría hecho_ (hacer) del espectáculo su máxima prioridad.

4 **El arte** Estos estudiantes están decepcionados (*disappointed*) con sus estudios de arte. Escribe oraciones a partir de los elementos dados. Usa el imperfecto de indicativo y el pluscuamperfecto de subjuntivo. `12 pts.`

> **modelo**
> yo / esperar / la universidad / poner / más énfasis en el arte
> Yo esperaba que la universidad hubiera puesto más énfasis en el arte.

1. Sonia / querer / el departamento de arte / ofrecer / más clases
   Sonia quería que el departamento de arte hubiera ofrecido más clases.
2. no haber nadie / oír / de ningún exalumno / con éxito en el mundo artístico
   No había nadie que hubiera oído de ningún exalumno con éxito en el mundo artístico.
3. nosotros / desear / haber / más exhibiciones de trabajos de estudiantes
   Nosotros deseábamos que hubiera habido más exhibiciones de trabajos de estudiantes.
4. ser una lástima / los profesores / no ser / más exigentes
   Era una lástima que los profesores no hubieran sido más exigentes.
5. Juanjo / dudar / nosotros / poder / escoger una universidad con menos recursos
   Juanjo dudaba que nosotros hubiéramos podido escoger una universidad con menos recursos.
6. ser increíble / la universidad / no construir / un museo más grande
   Era increíble que la universidad no hubiera construido un museo más grande.

5 **Una vida diferente** Piensa en un(a) artista famoso/a (pintor(a), cantante, actor/actriz, bailarín/bailarina, etc.) y escribe al menos cinco oraciones que describan cómo sería tu vida ahora si fueras esa persona. Usa las tres formas verbales que aprendiste en esta lección ¡y también tu imaginación! `32 pts.` Answers will vary.

6 **Adivinanza** Completa la adivinanza con la forma correcta del condicional del verbo **ser** y adivina la respuesta. `¡4 puntos EXTRA!`

“ Me puedes ver en tu piso,
y también en tu nariz;
sin mí no habría ricos
y nadie _sería_ (ser) feliz.
¿Quién soy? ”

la letra **i**

TEACHING OPTIONS

Extra Practice →👤← Prepare descriptions of fictional characters or celebrities. Write the names on the board in random order. Read each description aloud and have students match it to the appropriate name. Ex: **Si no hubiera existido tanto odio entre mi familia y la de mi esposo, me habría casado en una boda tradicional. Si mi esposo hubiera recibido mi mensaje, él no se habría tomado el veneno. Y si mi esposo no hubiera tomado el**

veneno, yo no me habría matado con un puñal. (**Julieta Capuleto**)
Small Groups 👤↔👤 Ask students, working in small groups, to imagine that they have just completed a trip to Latin America, during which they studied the region's art and artists. Have the group make a list of eight aspects that they would change about their trip. Hold a class discussion about their experiences. Ex: **El viaje habría sido más interesante si hubiéramos visitado los museos sin guía....**

3 **Expansion** Have students, in pairs, write three additional statements of regret using the conditional perfect.

4 **Teaching Tips**
- To simplify, have students circle the verb to be conjugated in the imperfect and underline the verb to be conjugated in the past perfect subjunctive.
- Remind students to use the conjunction **que** for each sentence.

4 **Expansion** Give students these cues as items 7–8:
7. Emilio y Javier / esperar / los profesores / enseñarles nuevas técnicas de pintura (Emilio y Javier esperaban que los profesores les hubieran enseñado nuevas técnicas de pintura.)
8. Piedad y yo / lamentar / los estudiantes / no poder / conocer ningún artista famoso (Piedad y yo lamentábamos que los estudiantes no hubieran podido conocer ningún artista famoso.)

5 **Expansion**
→👤← Ask volunteers to read their descriptions aloud without naming the artist. Have the class guess the person's identity.

6 **Expansion** To challenge students, have them work in pairs and create an **adivinanza** about another letter of the alphabet. Encourage them to use rhyming words and vocabulary from this lesson, if possible.

Audio: Reading

Section Goals

In **Lectura**, students will:
- analyze author's style
- read an authentic narrative in Spanish

Instructional Resource
Supersite

Estrategia Suggest that students think about the length of sentences and paragraphs, the rhythm, and the tone of the story as they analyze the author's style.

El abecedario Ask students to share their ideas with the class.

El contexto If students have trouble figuring out what the words mean, point out the context clues **exclamó**, **bebió**, **corrió**, **engulló**, and **murió**.

Teaching Tips
- Have students in groups of four each read a paragraph of the story aloud. Ask groups to comment on the rhythm of the words.
- Remind students to look for cognates as they read.
- Have students figure out the meaning of the word **decimotercera** (*thirteenth*) in the story. You may want to point out that it is a combination of two ordinals they learned in Lesson 5: **décimo/a** and **tercero/a**.

Lectura
 connections cultures / NATIONAL STANDARDS

Antes de leer

Estrategia
Analyzing author's style

Style is the way that an author uses words: word choice, sentence structure, paragraph structure, tone, etc. For example, words chosen can be formal or informal. Sentence length can vary. A story can be serious or lighthearted. An author's style conveys meaning and influences how a reader reacts to and interprets a story.

Examinar el texto

Mira el texto del cuento. ¿Cómo describirías el estilo de la autora? Considera lo siguiente: Answers will vary.
- el tono
- la elección de palabras
- la estructura de las oraciones y de los párrafos

_____
_____
_____

El abecedario

Lee el título. ¿Qué relación podría tener el abecedario con lo que pasa en el cuento? Answers will vary.

_____
_____

El contexto

Usa el contexto para descifrar el significado de estas palabras del cuento.

e	albricias	a. una bebida
a	Borgoña	b. una comida
d	carreras	c. una enfermedad
b	empanadas	d. una actividad deportiva
c	meningitis	e. una interjección

More activities

 vhlcentral / Online activities

Sobre la autora

Luisa Valenzuela nació en 1938, en Buenos Aires. Hija de una escritora y de un médico, creció rodeada de famosos escritores como Jorge Luis Borges y Ernesto Sábato. Ha trabajado como periodista, columnista y profesora en distintos países. A lo largo de su vida ha publicado más de treinta libros: novelas, cuentos y ensayos. Su obra es reconocida y estudiada por su original humor.

Después de leer

Comprensión

Indica si las oraciones sobre el protagonista del cuento son **ciertas** o **falsas**. Corrige las oraciones falsas.

1. Se despertó al mediodía el primer día de enero. **Falso**. Se despertó al alba.
2. La principal regla que decidió seguir fue respetar el abecedario. **Cierto**.
3. Comenzó su plan por la letra Z. **Falso**. Comenzó por la letra A.
4. La segunda semana besó a Beatriz. **Cierto**.
5. Al final del cuento, merendó con María. **Falso**. El protagonista murió de meningitis.

TEACHING OPTIONS

Worth Noting *Amalia* is a novel written by Argentinian José Mármol (1818–1871) while in exile. It was originally published in serial form; the first part appeared in 1851. The work was a critique of the dictator Juan Manual de Rosas (1793–1877). It was required reading in Argentinian schools until recently.

Extra Practice Have students find examples of the conditional (**actuaría**, **ajustaría**, **respetaría**) and the conditional perfect (**habría aportado**) in the story.

Teaching Tips
• Ask students why the protagonist died during the thirteenth week of his plan. Have them comment on the ending of the story.
• Read the following statement by Luisa Valenzuela to the class: **"Escribo contra aquellos que creen tener todas las respuestas."** Ask students how this could be applied to the story.

Luisa Valenzuela

El primer día de enero se despertó al alba° y ese hecho fortuito° determinó que resolviera ser metódico en su vida. En adelante° actuaría con todas las reglas° del arte. Se ajustaría a todos los códigos. Respetaría, sobre todo, el viejo y buen abecedario que, al fin y al cabo°, es la base del entendimiento humano.

Para cumplir con este plan empezó como es natural por la letra A. Por lo tanto la primera semana amó a Ana; almorzó albóndigas°, arroz con azafrán°, asado a la árabe y ananás°. Adquirió anís, aguardiente y hasta un poco de alcohol. Solamente anduvo en auto, asistió asiduamente al cine Arizona, leyó la novela *Amalia*, exclamó ¡ahijuna! y también ¡aleluya! y ¡albricias! Ascendió a un árbol, adquirió un antifaz° para asaltar un almacén y amaestró° una alondra°.

Todo iba a pedir de boca°. Y de vocabulario. Siempre respetuoso del orden de las letras la segunda semana birló° una bicicleta, besó a Beatriz, bebió Borgoña. La tercera cazó cocodrilos, corrió carreras, cortejó a Clara y cerró una cuenta. La cuarta semana se declaró a Desirée, dirigió un diario, dibujó diagramas. La quinta semana engulló° empanadas y enfermó del estómago.

Cumplía una experiencia esencial que habría aportado mucho a la humanidad de no ser por el accidente que le impidió° llegar a la Z. La decimotercera semana, sin tenerlo previsto°, murió de meningitis. ▪

alba *dawn* hecho fortuito *chance event* En adelante *From now on* reglas *rules* al fin y al cabo *after all* albóndigas *meatballs* azafrán *saffron* ananás *pineapples* antifaz *mask* amaestró *trained* alondra *lark* a pedir de boca *perfectly* birló *swiped* engulló *gobbled up* impidió *prevented* sin tenerlo previsto *without having planned it*

Interpretación

Responde a las preguntas con oraciones completas. *Answers will vary.*

1. ¿A qué crees que se refiere el protagonista cuando dice que "actuaría con todas las reglas del arte"? ¿De qué reglas se trata?

2. Un "código" puede ser un conjunto de reglas o la combinación de letras, números, etc., a la que le damos un valor determinado. ¿A cuál de estos significados crees que se refiere la autora cuando dice que "se ajustaría a todos los códigos"? Explica por qué.

3. ¿Crees que la regla de vivir la vida según el orden del alfabeto tiene lógica? ¿Por qué?

Comentar

En parejas, comenten el cuento. Usen como guía estas preguntas. *Answers will vary.*

1. ¿Creen que el alfabeto es la base de del entendimiento humano? ¿Por qué?

2. ¿Consideran que existen reglas para vivir en forma metódica que puedan ser útiles para la humanidad? ¿Cuáles, por ejemplo?

Comprensión Have students write three additional true/false statements about the story for a partner to answer.

Interpretación Tell students to consider that the word **código** could refer to one or to both meanings.

Comentar Use the questions to conduct a class discussion.

TEACHING OPTIONS

Small Groups ←👤→ Have students create their own lists of what the main character might have done in some of the weeks between D and M. Ask small groups to compile their lists to form new paragraphs of the story. Have groups present their new paragraphs of the story to the class. Comment on the activities that are the funniest, the strangest, etc.

Pairs ←👤→ Ask pairs to write a different ending for the story. For example, they could have the protagonist get to Z and then decide to live his life by some other rule. Have pairs present their ending to the class.

Escritura

Estrategia
Finding biographical information

Biographical information can be useful for a great variety of writing topics. Whether you are writing about a famous person, a period in history, or even a particular career or industry, you will be able to make your writing both more accurate and more interesting when you provide detailed information about the people who are related to your topic.

To research biographical information, you may wish to start with general reference sources, such as encyclopedias and periodicals. Additional background information on people can be found in biographies or in nonfiction books about the person's field or industry. For example, if you wanted to write about Sonia Sotomayor, you could find background information from periodicals, including magazine interviews. You might also find information in books or articles related to contemporary politics and Law.

Biographical information may also be available on the Internet, and depending on your writing topic, you may even be able to conduct interviews to get the information you need. Make sure to confirm the reliability of your sources whenever your writing includes information about other people.

You might want to look for the following kinds of information:

- date of birth
- date of death
- childhood experiences
- education
- family life
- place of residence
- life-changing events
- personal and professional accomplishments

Tema

¿A quién te gustaría conocer?

Si pudieras invitar a cinco personas famosas a cenar en tu casa, ¿a quiénes invitarías? Pueden ser de cualquier (*any*) época de la historia y de cualquier profesión. Algunas posibilidades son:

- el arte
- la música
- el cine
- las ciencias
- la religión
- la política

Escribe una composición breve sobre la cena. Explica por qué invitarías a estas personas y describe lo que harías, lo que preguntarías y lo que dirías si tuvieras la oportunidad de conocerlas. Utiliza el condicional. Answers will vary.

EVALUATION: Composición

Criteria	Scale
Content	1 2 3 4
Organization	1 2 3 4
Use of vocabulary	1 2 3 4
Grammatical accuracy	1 2 3 4
Creativity	1 2 3 4

Scoring	
Excellent	18–20 points
Good	14–17 points
Satisfactory	10–13 points
Unsatisfactory	< 10 points

Escuchar

Antes de escuchar

Estrategia

**Listening for key words/
Using the context**

The comprehension of key words is vital to understanding spoken Spanish. Use your background knowledge of the subject to help you anticipate what the key words might be. When you hear unfamiliar words, remember that you can use context to figure out their meaning.

  To practice these strategies, you will now listen to a paragraph from a letter sent to a job applicant. Jot down key words, as well as any other words you figured out from the context.

Preparación

Basándote en el dibujo, ¿qué palabras crees que usaría un crítico en una reseña (*review*) de esta película?
Answers will vary.

Ahora escucha

Reseña

 Ahora vas a escuchar la reseña de la película. Mientras escuches al crítico, recuerda que las críticas de cine son principalmente descriptivas. La primera vez que la escuches, identifica las palabras clave (*key*) y escríbelas en la columna A. Luego, escucha otra vez la reseña e identifica el significado de las palabras en la columna B mediante el contexto. *Answers will vary.*

A	B
1. _____	1. estrenar
2. _____	2. a pesar de
3. _____	3. con reservas
4. _____	4. supuestamente
5. _____	5. la trama
6. _____	6. conocimiento

Comprensión

Cierto o falso

	Cierto	Falso
1. *El fantasma del lago Enriquillo* es una película de ciencia ficción.	●	○
2. Los efectos especiales son espectaculares.	○	●
3. Generalmente se ha visto a Jorge Verdoso en comedias románticas.	●	○
4. Jaime Rebelde es un actor espectacular.	○	●

Preguntas   *Answers will vary.*

1. ¿Qué aspectos de la película le gustaron al crítico?
2. ¿Qué no le gustó al crítico de la película?
3. ¿Irías a ver esta película? ¿Por qué?
4. Para ti, ¿cuáles son los aspectos más importantes de una película? Explica tu respuesta.

Ahora ustedes

Trabajen en grupos. Escojan una película con actores muy famosos que no fue lo que esperaban. Escriban una reseña que describa el papel de los actores, la trama, los efectos especiales, la cinematografía u otros aspectos importantes de la película. *Answers will vary.*

obra que a *El fantasma del lago Enriquillo*. La trama es tan exagerada que acaba siendo una sátira. La película tiene sus momentos especiales a pesar de sus limitaciones. Las escenas que Jorge Verdoso comparte con la estrella Lourdes del Río son destacadas y fascinantes. Hay una energía fabulosa entre estos artistas. Los efectos especiales no son los que hoy día esperamos ver;

parecen ser algo de una película de hace quince años. Pero la música del gran compositor Jaime Rebelde es espectacular. Recomiendo la película pero con reservas. Los aficionados de las películas de Verdoso y del Río no se la van a querer perder. Pero vayan con el conocimiento de que algunos momentos supuestamente dramáticos son cómicos.

(Script continues at far left in the bottom panels.)

Section Goals

In **En pantalla**, students will:
• read about the short film *Casting*
• watch the short film *Casting*

Instructional Resources
Supersite: Video (**En pantalla**); Resources (Scripts, Translations)

Introduction To check comprehension, ask these questions: **1. ¿Quién dirigió la película? (Jorge Naranjo la dirigió.) 2. ¿Cuántos cortometrajes de *Casting* hay? (Hay tres.) 3. ¿Cómo se llama el personaje principal? (Se llama Javier López.)**

Antes de ver
• Have students look at the video stills, read the captions, and predict what will happen in the film.
• Explain to students that they do not need to understand every word they hear. Tell them to rely on visual cues and to listen for cognates and words from **Vocabulario útil**.

Preparación Have students share any stories they have heard about auditions.

Preguntas Have students read the questions before watching the film.

Una audición Tell students to use *Casting* as inspiration for their own auditions. Encourage them to use humor.

En pantalla  Video

Este cortometraje°, escrito y dirigido por el español Jorge Naranjo, fue el finalista de la novena edición del concurso de Jameson Notodofilmfest. Es el primero de la trilogía de cortometrajes que inspiró el largometraje *Casting, la película*, del mismo director. El protagonista de este corto, Javier López, comparte sus experiencias en el mundo de la actuación, un mundo casi impenetrable en el que los actores se lo juegan todo° en esa prueba inicial que es el casting. Con un toque° de humor e ironía, Javi nos describe lo dura que es la vida de los actores y lo absurdo y ridículo que puede llegar a ser presentarse a un casting.

Vocabulario útil

aguantando	*hanging in there*
no te atreves	*you don't dare*
no te sale	*you can't do it*
quejarse	*to complain*
representante	*agent*

Preparación

¿Alguna vez te has presentado a un casting?
¿Cómo fue la experiencia?

Preguntas

Contesta las preguntas. Answers may vary.

1. ¿Qué hace Javier en su trabajo de actor? Javier hace castings.

2. ¿Cómo está Javier al comenzar el casting? Javier está nervioso.

3. Según Javier, ¿qué es lo peor que te pueden pedir en un casting? Lo peor que te pueden pedir es llorar.

4. ¿Dónde trabaja Javier? ¿Y dónde vive?
Javier trabaja en un bar. Vive en Madrid.

Una audición

En parejas, representen una audición original ante la clase. Uno/a de ustedes es director(a) de castings, la otra persona se presenta a la prueba.

> **modelo**
> **Director(a):** *¿Podría usted representar el papel de una mosca (fly) nerviosa dentro de una botella?*

cortometraje *short film* se lo juegan todo *they risk everything* toque *touch*

Casting

Yo hago castings.

Ahora necesitamos que llores.

Eres muy bueno, buenísimo.

  More activities
vhlcentral   Online activities

TEACHING OPTIONS

Worth Noting Filmmaker Jorge Naranjo was born in Seville, Spain, in 1976. He wrote and directed the short films *Casting, Casting dos*, and *Casting tres* in 2011, as well as a feature-length version of *Casting* in 2013. In 2016 he wrote and directed another short film, *Un billete a Nunca Jamás*.

Pairs Have students work in pairs to write an epilogue to the film. Encourage them to be creative. Then have them act it out for the class.

Video

Todos los países hispanos cuentan con una gran variedad de museos, desde arte clásico o contemporáneo, hasta los que se especializan en la rica historia local que puede venir desde las antiguas° culturas prehispánicas. El museo que viste en el episodio de **Fotonovela** es el Museo de Arte Popular de la Ciudad de México y tiene como misión difundir°, preservar y continuar las técnicas tradicionales de elaborar artesanías mexicanas. Algunas de ellas son la cerámica, la joyería°, los textiles y el papel maché. A continuación vas a ver otro tipo de museos en España.

Vocabulario útil

el lienzo	*canvas*
la muestra	*exhibit*
el primer plano	*foreground*

Preparación

¿Te interesa el arte? Cuando viajas, ¿visitas los museos del lugar al que vas? ¿Cuál es, de entre todas las artes, la que más te gusta o emociona? Answers will vary.

¿Cierto o falso?

Indica si las oraciones son **ciertas** o **falsas.**

1. En Madrid, la oferta de arte es muy limitada.
   Falso. En Madrid la oferta de arte es riquísima.
2. En el Triángulo Dorado de los museos hay tres museos muy importantes de Madrid.
   Cierto.
3. En la obra *Las meninas* de Velázquez, la perspectiva es muy real.
   Cierto.
4. El Museo Reina Sofía está dedicado al arte contemporáneo y antiguo.
   Falso. Está dedicado al arte contemporáneo.
5. El lienzo *Guernica* de Picasso es pequeño.
   Falso. El lienzo del *Guernica* es enorme.
6. La colección del Museo Thyssen era privada y luego fue donada (*donated*) al Estado español.
   Cierto.
7. El Greco era español. Falso. El Greco era de Grecia, pero vivió gran parte de su vida en España.

antiguas *ancient* difundir *to spread* joyería *jewelry* aseguran *assure*

Palacios del arte

... una ciudad [...] con una riquísima y selecta oferta de hoteles, restaurantes [...] y especialmente... ¡arte!

El edificio fue [...] un hospital. Hoy en día, está dedicado al arte contemporáneo.

Muchos aseguran° que es el primer surrealista.

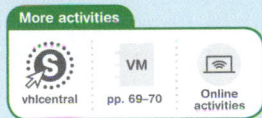

More activities

vhlcentral | VM pp. 69–70 | Online activities

Section Goals

In **Flash cultura**, students will:
• read about art museums in the Spanish-speaking world
• watch a video about Madrid's Golden Triangle of museums

Instructional Resources

Supersite: Video (*Flash cultura*); Resources (Scripts, Translations, Answer Keys)
WebSAM
Video Manual

Introduction Ask students to read the paragraph silently to themselves and then write three comprehension questions. Call on volunteers to share their questions, and then go over the answers as a class.

Antes de ver
• Read through the **Vocabulario útil** and model pronunciation.
• Assure students that they do not need to understand every Spanish word they hear in the video. Tell them to rely on visual cues and to listen for cognates and words from **Vocabulario útil**.
• Bring in a map of Madrid and help students locate the **Museo del Prado, Museo Reina Sofía,** and the **Museo Thyssen.**

Preparación Brainstorm a list of artistic movements (such as neoclassical, surrealism, cubism, realism, modernism, etc.) to help facilitate discussion.

¿Cierto o falso? Have students write three additional true/false statements for a partner to answer.

TEACHING OPTIONS

Extra Practice Have students visit your school's art museum or any other museum in your region. Have them select a few works of art and write a short essay, comparing and contrasting them with ones that they saw in the video.

Pairs Show the video again. Then have students, in pairs, discuss the different works of art. Have them explain how they would have portrayed the themes differently, using the conditional perfect. Their partner should agree or disagree.

Section Goal

In **Panorama**, students will read about the geography and culture of El Salvador.

Instructional Resources
Supersite: Video (*Panorama cultural*); Resources (Scripts, Translations, Digital Image Bank, Answer Keys)
WebSAM
Workbook

Teaching Tips
• Use the **Lección 17 Panorama** digital images to assist with this presentation.
• Have students look at the map of El Salvador.
• Draw students' attention to the number of active volcanoes in El Salvador. Tell students that because of the fertility of El Salvador's volcanic soil, the country has a strong agricultural sector. Have students look at the inset map as you point out that El Salvador is the only Central American country without coastline on the Gulf of Mexico. Look at the photos and ask volunteers to read the captions.

El país en cifras In the early 1970s, El Salvador's overpopulation, chronic economic problems, and lack of social justice resulted in social disturbances that the government put down with brutal force.

El Salvador

connections cultures NATIONAL STANDARDS

El país en cifras

▸ **Área:** 21.040 km² (8.124 millas²), *el tamaño° de Massachusetts*
▸ **Población:** 6.172.000
El Salvador es el país centroamericano más pequeño y el más densamente poblado. Su población, al igual que la de Honduras, es muy homogénea: casi el 90 por ciento es mestiza.
▸ **Capital:** San Salvador—1.098.000
▸ **Ciudades principales:** Soyapango, Santa Ana, San Miguel, Mejicanos
▸ **Moneda:** dólar estadounidense
▸ **Idiomas:** español (oficial), náhuatl, lenca

Bandera de El Salvador

Salvadoreños célebres
▸ **Óscar Romero,** arzobispo° y activista por los derechos humanos° (1917–1980)
▸ **Claribel Alegría,** poeta, novelista y cuentista (1924–2018)
▸ **Roque Dalton,** poeta, ensayista y novelista (1935–1975)
▸ **María Eugenia Brizuela,** política (1956–)
▸ **Francesca Miranda,** diseñadora (1957–)

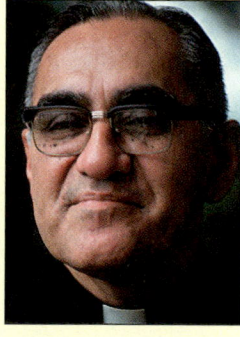

Óscar Romero

tamaño *size* **arzobispo** *archbishop* **derechos humanos** *human rights*

Ruinas de Tazumal

Catedral Metropolitana de San Salvador

GUATEMALA

Lago de Guija
Río de la Paz
Santa Ana
Río Lempa
Ilobasco
HONDURAS
Río Torola
Río Goascorán
Mejicanos
San Salvador
Volcán de San Salvador
Soyapango
Volcán de San Vicente
Río Lempa
La Libertad
Volcán de San Miguel
San Miguel
Océano Pacífico
Golfo de Fonseca

Chorros de la Calera en Juayúa

ESTADOS UNIDOS
OCÉANO ATLÁNTICO
EL SALVADOR
OCÉANO PACÍFICO
AMÉRICA DEL SUR

More activities
vhlcentral | WB p. 199 | Online activities

ACTIVIDADES

1 **¿Cierto o falso?** Indica si lo que dicen las oraciones es **cierto** o **falso.**

1. El Salvador es el país más grande de Centroamérica. falso
2. Aproximadamente el 90% de la población de El Salvador es mestiza. cierto
3. Claribel Alegría fue una famosa compositora salvadoreña. falso
4. La moneda de El Salvador es el dólar estadounidense. cierto
5. Roque Dalton fue poeta y novelista. cierto
6. La Libertad es una playa famosa en El Salvador por sus artesanías. falso
7. El Parque Nacional Montecristo se conoce también como El Trifinio. cierto
8. Las "sorpresas" de Ilobasco son canciones. falso
9. Las pupusas son tortillas de maíz o de arroz. cierto
10. La leyenda sobre la laguna de Alegría es un cuento folclórico. cierto

TEACHING OPTIONS

Worth Noting Government repression in El Salvador intensified resistance, and by the mid-1970s a civil war was being fought between government forces and the **FMLN,** an armed guerrilla movement. Among the many martyrs of the war was the Archbishop of San Salvador, **Óscar Romero.** A descendent of the privileged class in El Salvador, **Romero** came to champion the cause of peace and social justice for the poor. This position made him the target of reactionary elements. On March 24, 1980, Archbishop **Romero** was assassinated while giving mass in the Cathedral of San Salvador. His life and death became an inspiration for those seeking social justice. Still, it was only in 1991 that a cease-fire brought an end to the civil war.

Deportes • El surfing

El Salvador es uno de los destinos favoritos en Latinoamérica para la práctica del surfing. Cuenta con 300 kilómetros de costa a lo largo del océano Pacífico y sus olas° altas son ideales para quienes practican este deporte. De sus playas, La Libertad es la más visitada por surfistas de todo el mundo, gracias a que está muy cerca de la capital salvadoreña. Sin embargo, los fines de semana muchos visitantes prefieren viajar a la Costa del Bálsamo, donde se concentra menos gente.

Naturaleza • El Parque Nacional Montecristo

El Parque Nacional Montecristo se encuentra en la región norte del país. Se le conoce también como El Trifinio porque se ubica° en el punto donde se unen las fronteras de Guatemala, Honduras y El Salvador. Este bosque reúne muchas especies vegetales y animales, como orquídeas, monos araña°, pumas, quetzales y tucanes. Además, las copas° de sus enormes árboles forman una bóveda° que impide° el paso de la luz solar. Este espacio natural se encuentra a una altitud de 2.400 metros (7.900 pies) sobre el nivel del mar y recibe 200 centímetros (80 pulgadas°) de lluvia al año.

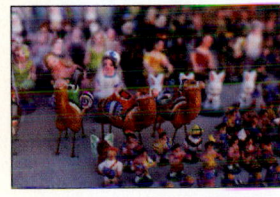

▶ Artes • La artesanía de Ilobasco

Ilobasco es un pueblo conocido por sus artesanías. En él se elaboran objetos con arcilla° y cerámica pintada a mano, como juguetes°, adornos° y utensilios de cocina. Además, son famosas sus "sorpresas", que son pequeñas piezas° de cerámica en cuyo interior se representan escenas de la vida diaria. Los turistas realizan excursiones para ver la elaboración, paso a paso°, de estos productos.

▶ Comida • Pupusas

Las pupusas son el plato nacional de El Salvador. Son tortillas hechas con masa° de maíz o de arroz, rellenas° de queso, frijoles, calabaza°, chicharrón°, pollo o pescado. Son muy parecidas a las tortillas panameñas y a las arepas venezolanas y colombianas. Desde 2005, el segundo domingo de noviembre, el gobierno salvadoreño celebra por decreto el Día Nacional de las Pupusas.

olas *waves* se ubica *it is located* monos araña *spider monkeys* copas *tops* bóveda *cap* impide *blocks* pulgadas *inches* arcilla *clay* juguetes *toys* adornos *ornaments* piezas *pieces* paso a paso *step by step* masa *dough* rellenas *stuffed* calabaza *pumpkin* chicharrón *pork rind*

¡Increíble pero cierto!

El rico folclor salvadoreño se basa sobre todo en sus extraordinarios recursos naturales. Por ejemplo, según una leyenda, las muertes que se producen en la laguna° de Alegría tienen su explicación en la existencia de una sirena° solitaria que vive en el lago y captura a los jóvenes atractivos.

laguna *lagoon* sirena *mermaid*

---

2 **¿Qué aprendiste?** Contesta las preguntas.

1. ¿Qué tienen en común las poblaciones de El Salvador y Honduras?
   son muy homogéneas
2. ¿Qué es el náhuatl?
   un idioma que se habla en El Salvador
3. ¿Quién es María Eugenia Brizuela?
   una política salvadoreña
4. ¿Cuáles son algunos de los animales y las plantas que viven en el Parque Nacional Montecristo?
   orquídeas, monos araña, pumas, quetzales y tucanes

3 **En televisión** En parejas, imaginen que van a hacer un programa de televisión sobre El Salvador. Hablen sobre lo que les gustaría mostrar en su programa. Utilicen el condicional.

modelo
Para nuestro programa de televisión me gustaría mostrar las "sorpresas" de Ilobasco.

El surfing Tell students that **La Libertad** is a relatively small town that sees a large influx of beachgoers, not just surfers, during the weekends and holidays. Black volcanic sand covers the beach of **La Libertad**. About five miles east lies Zunzal beach, which, during Holy Week (**Semana Santa**) each year, is the site of international surfing competitions.

El Parque Nacional Montecristo The Montecristo cloud forest (**bosque nuboso**) is a protected area at the point where El Salvador, Honduras, and Guatemala meet. The point, at the summit of Montecristo, is called **El Trifinio**. Visitors only have access to Montecristo between November 1st and June 1st. The rest of the year it is closed to visitors for the animals' reproductive season.

La artesanía de Ilobasco Ilobasco is a crafts village that specializes in ceramics. **Sorpresas** are one of the most famous items. They are miniscule, intricate scenes and figures inside egg-shaped shells about the size of a walnut. You may want to play the **Panorama cultural** video for this paragraph.

Pupusas This dish is usually served with a tomato **salsa** and **curtido**, a spicy slaw. You may want to play the **Panorama cultural** video for this paragraph.

¡Increíble pero cierto! In the town of Concepción de Ataco, another legend claims that on the **Cerro la Empalizada** there is a cave containing plants that disorient anyone who steps on them.

TEACHING OPTIONS

Variación léxica **Pupusa** is the name given to the Salvadoran version of the **tortilla**. In fact, **pupusas** are made by putting a filling such as red beans, onions, garlic, and cheese on one uncooked **tortilla**, laying another **tortilla** over it, and pressing the two together so they adhere, and then frying both in hot oil until the **pupusa** is golden and crunchy. Served sizzling from the fryer, **pupusas** are delicious. They are so popular that in El Salvador there are many shops, called **pupuserías**, that specialize in them. And if you visit a neighborhood in the United States where Salvadorans have settled, you will inevitably find a **pupusería**.

Honduras

El país en cifras

▸ **Área:** 112.492 km² (43.870 millas²), *un poco más grande que Tennessee*

▸ **Población:** 9.038.000
Cerca del 90 por ciento de la población de Honduras es mestiza. Todavía hay pequeños grupos indígenas como los jicaque, los misquito y los paya, que han mantenido su cultura sin influencias exteriores y que no hablan español.

▸ **Capital:** Tegucigalpa—1.123.000

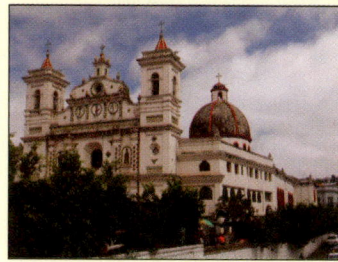
Tegucigalpa

▸ **Ciudades principales:** San Pedro Sula, El Progreso, La Ceiba

▸ **Moneda:** lempira

▸ **Idiomas:** español (oficial), lenguas indígenas, inglés

Bandera de Honduras

Hondureños célebres
▸ **José Antonio Velásquez,** pintor (1906–1983)
▸ **Argentina Díaz Lozano,** escritora (1912–1999)
▸ **Carlos Roberto Reina,** juez° y presidente del país (1926–2003)
▸ **Roberto Sosa,** escritor (1930–2011)
▸ **Salvador Moncada,** científico (1944–)

juez judge

Guacamayo
Roatán, Islas de la Bahía
Mar Caribe
Islas de la Bahía
Golfo de Honduras
GUATEMALA
La Ceiba · Santa Fe
San Pedro Sula · Río Ulúa · Sierra Rijol · Sierra de Payas · Laguna de Caratasca
Sierra Espíritu Santo
El Progreso · Río Patuca
Sierra Grita · Lago de Yojoa · Sierra Villasanta · Río Guayambre · Montañas de Colón
Tegucigalpa · Río Coco
EL SALVADOR
Río Choluteca
Océano Pacífico
NICARAGUA
Lago de Yojoa
ESTADOS UNIDOS
OCÉANO ATLÁNTICO
HONDURAS
OCÉANO PACÍFICO
AMÉRICA DEL SUR

More activities — vhlcentral | WB p. 200 | Online activities

ACTIVIDADES

1 ¿Cierto o falso? Indica si lo que dicen las oraciones es **cierto** o **falso**.

1. En Honduras hay comunidades indígenas que han mantenido su cultura y no hablan español. cierto
2. Argentina Díaz Lozano fue una escultora hondureña. falso
3. La capital de Honduras es San Pedro Sula. falso
4. Roberto Sosa fue un escritor hondureño. cierto
5. Hay edificios adornados con esculturas pintadas a mano en Copán. cierto
6. Los mayas jugaban a la pelota. cierto
7. Las obras de José Antonio Velásquez representan escenas de ciencia ficción. falso
8. La reserva de biósfera de Río Plátano es conocida como "los pulmones de Centroamérica". cierto
9. En la reserva de biósfera de Río Plátano sólo hay aves. falso
10. Los presos de la Penitenciaría Central de Tegucigalpa vendían artesanías. cierto

▷ Lugares • Copán

Copán es una zona arqueológica muy importante de Honduras. Fue construida por los mayas y se calcula que en el año 400 d. C. albergaba° a una ciudad con más de 150 edificios y una gran cantidad de plazas, patios, templos y canchas° para el juego de pelota°. Las ruinas más famosas del lugar son los edificios adornados con esculturas pintadas a mano, los cetros° ceremoniales de piedra y el templo Rosalila.

▷ Economía • Las plantaciones de bananas

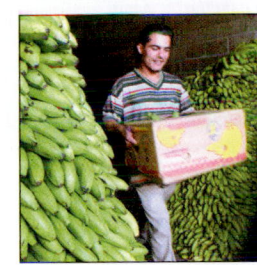

Desde hace más de cien años, las bananas son la exportación principal de Honduras y han tenido un papel fundamental en su historia. En 1899, la Standard Fruit Company empezó a exportar bananas del país centroamericano hacia Nueva Orleans. Esta fruta resultó tan popular en los Estados Unidos que generó grandes beneficios° para esta compañía y para la United Fruit Company, otra empresa norteamericana. Estas trasnacionales intervinieron muchas veces en la política hondureña debido° al enorme poder° económico que alcanzaron en la nación.

Artes • José Antonio Velásquez (1906–1983)

José Antonio Velásquez fue un famoso pintor hondureño. Es catalogado como primitivista° porque sus obras representan aspectos de la vida cotidiana. En la pintura de Velásquez es notorio el énfasis en los detalles°, la falta casi total de los juegos de perspectiva y la pureza en el uso del color. Por todo ello, el artista ha sido comparado con importantes pintores europeos del mismo género° como Paul Gauguin o Emil Nolde.

San Antonio de Oriente, 1957, José Antonio Velásquez

Naturaleza • Reserva de biósfera de Río Plátano

La reserva de biósfera de Río Plátano está ubicada en el departamento de Gracias a Dios, en la costa noroeste de Honduras. Esta área es llamada "los pulmones de Centroamérica" pues presenta la mayor riqueza ecológica y ambiental de esta parte del continente americano. En sus montañas viven cerca de 2.000 indígenas, y en sus zonas de bosque lluvioso tropical hay una gran variedad de mamíferos, aves, peces, reptiles y árboles. Fue declarada Patrimonio de la Humanidad° por la UNESCO en 1980.

albergaba *housed* canchas *courts* juego de pelota *pre-Columbian ceremonial ball game* cetros *scepters* beneficios *profits* debido a *due to* poder *power* primitivista *primitivist* detalles *details* género *genre* Patrimonio de la Humanidad *World Heritage*

¡Increíble pero cierto!

¿Irías de compras a una prisión? Hace un tiempo, cuando la Penitenciaría Central de Tegucigalpa aún funcionaba, los presos° hacían objetos de madera°, hamacas° y hasta instrumentos musicales y los vendían en una tienda dentro de la prisión. Allí, los turistas podían regatear con este especial grupo de artesanos.

presos *prisoners* madera *wood* hamacas *hammocks*

---

2 **¿Qué aprendiste?** Contesta las preguntas.

1. ¿Qué es el lempira?
   la moneda nacional de Honduras
2. ¿Por qué es famoso Copán?
   es el sitio arqueológico más importante de Honduras
3. ¿Dónde está el templo Rosalila?
   en Copán
4. ¿Cuál es la exportación principal de Honduras?
   las bananas
5. ¿Cómo es el estilo de José Antonio Velásquez?
   primitivista

3 **Yo habría...** En parejas, imaginen que fueron de excursión a Honduras y comenten qué habrían hecho en cada uno de los siguientes lugares. Utilicen el condicional perfecto.

1. Tegucigalpa
2. una plantación de bananas
3. la reserva de biósfera de Río Plátano
4. Copán

TEACHING OPTIONS

Worth Noting Honduras was among the hardest hit of the Central American nations when Hurricane Mitch struck in late October 1998. Major roadways and bridges were destroyed, entire communities were covered in mud, and an air of hopelessness and desperation pervaded the country. With one of the lowest per capita income levels and one of the highest illiteracy rates in Central America, Hondurans were already

struggling before the devastation of the hurricane. Since then, the economy has grown about 7% per year, but half of the population still remains below the poverty line.
Heritage Speakers ←🔳→ Ask heritage speakers to research one of the Honduran topics mentioned in **Panorama** and write a three-paragraph essay about it. They may then present their findings orally to the class.

Copán Recent archeological studies have focused on the abrupt disappearance of the Mayans from Copán around the ninth century C.E. Findings indicate that the Mayan dynasty suffered a sudden collapse that left the Copán valley virtually depopulated within a century. You may want to play the **Panorama cultural** video for this paragraph.

Las plantaciones de bananas When Hurricane Mitch struck Central America in October 1998, it not only wiped out much of the infrastructure of Honduras, but also destroyed 60% of the projected agricultural exports. Today's agricultural problems are due to rampant deforestation and consequent drought and soil erosion. You may want to play the **Panorama cultural** video for this paragraph.

José Antonio Velásquez The primitive style established by **José Antonio Velásquez** is now being carried on by his son, **Tulio Velásquez. Tulio**, who was taught by his father, had his first exhibition in 1959. Since then, his primitive art has been exhibited throughout the Americas, in Europe, and in Asia. Have students view works by each artist and then write a brief comparison of their styles.

Reserva de biósfera de Río Plátano This reserve is the largest protected area in Honduras. It is one of the few remaining tropical rain forests in Central America. Logging, agriculture, and illegal hunting threaten the reserve.

¡Increíble pero cierto! The case of the artisan prisoners at the **Penitenciaría Central de Tegucigalpa** is a surprising example of business ethics. All profits from the sale of the crafts went directly to the creators: the prisoners themselves.

Instructional Resources

Supersite: Audio (Textbook & Lab MP3s); Testing Program (Tests, MP3s)
WebSAM
Lab Manual

Teaching Tip You may want to assign the **Prueba de práctica**, with its diagnostics and review activities, in the online-only **Repaso** section on the Supersite. There is also a **Repaso oral** in this section. For the Sixth Edition, a new summative vocabulary activity with speech recognition has been added to the **Repaso** section.

Las bellas artes

el baile, la danza	dance
la banda	band
las bellas artes	(fine) arts
el boleto	ticket
la canción	song
la comedia	comedy; play
el concierto	concert
el cuento	short story
la cultura	culture
el drama	drama; play
la escultura	sculpture
el espectáculo	show
la estatua	statue
el festival	festival
la historia	history; story
la música	music
la obra	work (of art, music, etc.)
la obra maestra	masterpiece
la ópera	opera
la orquesta	orchestra
el personaje (principal)	(main) character
la pintura	painting
el poema	poem
la poesía	poetry
el público	audience
el teatro	theater
la tragedia	tragedy
aburrirse	to get bored
aplaudir	to applaud
apreciar	to appreciate
dirigir	to direct
esculpir	to sculpt
hacer el papel (de)	to play the role (of)
pintar	to paint
presentar	to present; to put on (a performance)
publicar	to publish
tocar (un instrumento musical)	to touch; to play (a musical instrument)
artístico/a	artistic
clásico/a	classical
dramático/a	dramatic
extranjero/a	foreign
folclórico/a	folk
moderno/a	modern
musical	musical
romántico/a	romantic
talentoso/a	talented

Los artistas

el bailarín, la bailarina	dancer
el/la cantante	singer
el/la compositor(a)	composer
el/la director(a)	director; (musical) conductor
el/la dramaturgo/a	playwright
el/la escritor(a)	writer
el/la escultor(a)	sculptor
la estrella (m., f.) de cine	movie star
el/la músico/a	musician
el/la poeta	poet

El cine y la televisión

el canal	channel
el concurso	game show; contest
los dibujos animados	cartoons
el documental	documentary
el premio	prize; award
el programa de entrevistas/realidad	talk/reality show
la telenovela	soap opera
… de acción	action
… de aventuras	adventure
… de ciencia ficción	science fiction
… de horror	horror
… de vaqueros	western

La artesanía

la artesanía	craftsmanship; crafts
la cerámica	pottery
el tejido	weaving

Expresiones útiles	See page 583.

More activities

vhlcentral | LM p. 101

Las actualidades

18

Communicative Goals

You will learn how to:

- **Discuss current events and issues**
- **Talk about and discuss the media**
- **Reflect on experiences, such as travel**

A PRIMERA VISTA

- ¿Es reportera o bailarina la mujer?
- ¿Está en el centro?
- ¿Hace entrevistas?
- ¿Tiene calor o frío?

Lesson Goals

In **Lección 18**, students will be introduced to the following:
- terms for current events, social issues, and politics
- media-related vocabulary
- social protests
- the peace process in Colombia
- **si** clauses in the subjunctive mood
- **si** clauses with verbs in the indicative mood
- review of subjunctive forms
- using the subjunctive, indicative, and infinitive in complex sentences
- recognizing chronological order
- writing strong introductions and conclusions
- writing a composition about improving the world
- recognizing genre and taking notes while listening
- a Chilean public service announcement about voting
- a video about Puerto Rican politics
- cultural and geographic information about Paraguay
- cultural and geographic information about Uruguay

A primera vista Ask these additional questions: **¿Ves mucho la tele? ¿Qué programas ves? Para obtener información, ¿visitas sitios web? ¿Harías un documental? ¿De qué?**

Teaching Tip Look for these icons for additional communicative practice:

👥→	**Interpretive communication**
👥←	**Presentational communication**
👥↔	**Interpersonal communication**

INSTRUCTIONAL RESOURCES

Supersite (vhlcentral.com)
Video: *Fotonovela, Flash cultura, En pantalla, Panorama cultural*
Audio: Textbook and Lab MP3 Files

Activity Pack: Information Gap Activities, games, additional activity handouts
Resources: SAM Answer Key, Scripts, Translations, **Vocabulario adicional**, sample lesson plan, Grammar Presentation Slides, Digital Image Bank

Testing Program: Quizzes, Tests, Exams, MP3s, Oral Testing Suggestions
Student Activities Manual: Workbook/Video Manual/Lab Manual
WebSAM (online Student Activities Manual)

Las actualidades

Más vocabulario

el acontecimiento	*event*
las actualidades	*news; current events*
el artículo	*article*
la encuesta	*poll; survey*
el informe	*report*
el/la locutor(a)	*(TV or radio) announcer*
los medios de comunicación	*media; means of communication*
las noticias	*news*
el reportaje	*report*
el desastre (natural)	*(natural) disaster*
el huracán	*hurricane*
la inundación	*flood*
el terremoto	*earthquake*
el desempleo	*unemployment*
la (des)igualdad	*(in)equality*
la discriminación	*discrimination*
la guerra	*war*
la libertad	*liberty; freedom*
la paz	*peace*
el racismo	*racism*
el sexismo	*sexism*
el SIDA	*AIDS*
anunciar	*to announce; to advertise*
comunicarse (con)	*to communicate (with)*
durar	*to last*
informar	*to inform*
luchar (por/contra)	*to fight; to struggle (for/against)*
transmitir, emitir	*to broadcast*
(inter)nacional	*(inter)national*
peligroso/a	*dangerous*

Variación léxica

informe ⟷ trabajo (*Esp.*)
noticiero ⟷ informativo (*Esp.*)

More activities
vhlcentral | LM p. 103 | WB pp. 201–202 | Online activities

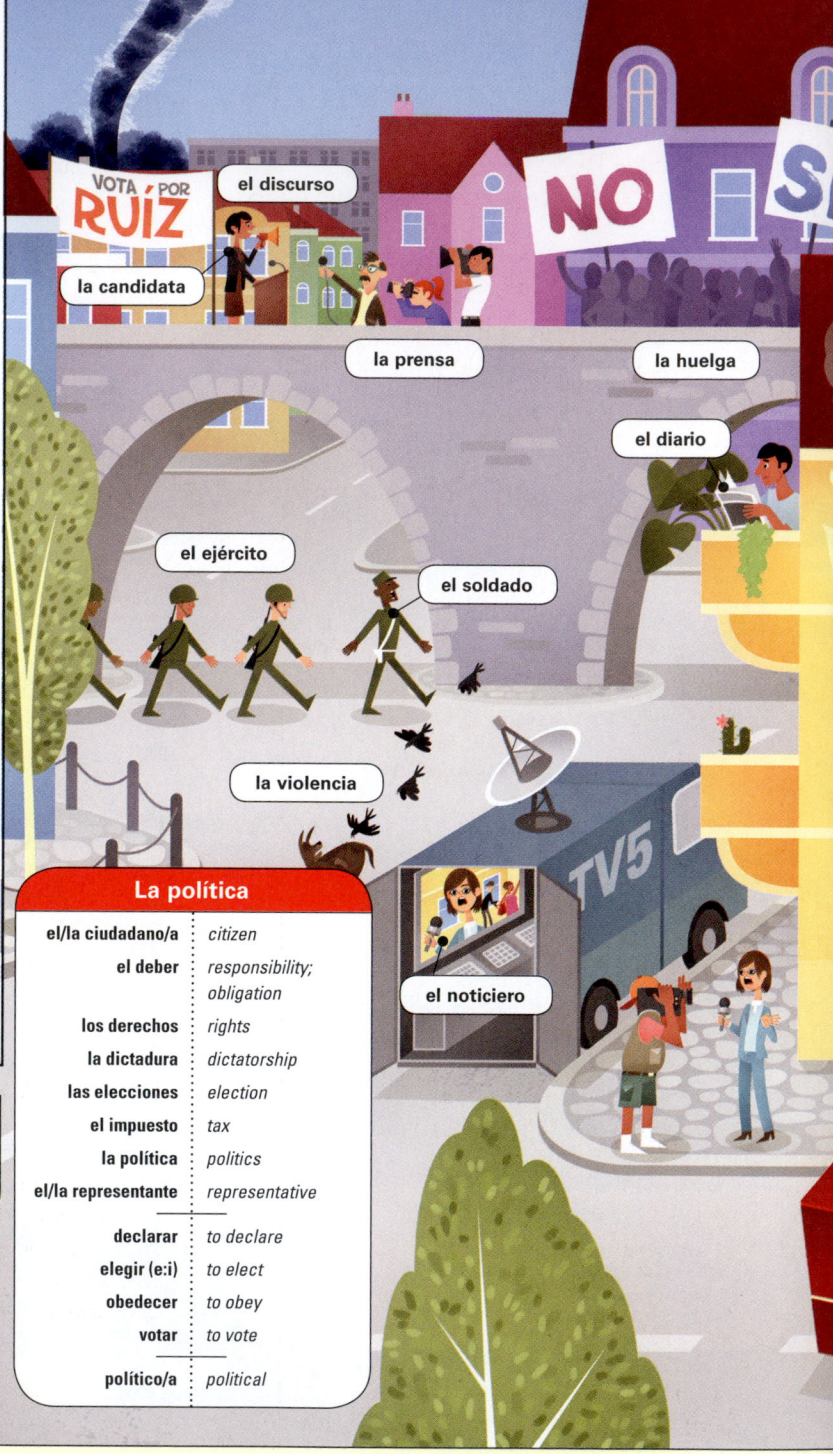

el tornado
el discurso
la candidata
la prensa
la huelga
el diario
el ejército
el soldado
la violencia
el noticiero

La política

el/la ciudadano/a	*citizen*
el deber	*responsibility; obligation*
los derechos	*rights*
la dictadura	*dictatorship*
las elecciones	*election*
el impuesto	*tax*
la política	*politics*
el/la representante	*representative*
declarar	*to declare*
elegir (e:i)	*to elect*
obedecer	*to obey*
votar	*to vote*
político/a	*political*

la tormenta

QUIZÁS

el incendio

el crimen

el choque

Práctica

1 **Buenas o malas noticias** Indica si cada una de las oraciones es una **buena** o una **mala noticia**.

1. buena noticia
2. mala noticia
3. mala noticia
4. buena noticia
5. buena noticia
6. mala noticia
7. mala noticia
8. buena noticia

2 **Contestar** Contesta las preguntas sobre las noticias.

1. ¿Qué es Notiuruguay? un noticiero
2. ¿Qué habrá en Uruguay? elecciones presidenciales
3. ¿Qué son injustos, según la encuesta? los impuestos
4. ¿Quiénes deberían asegurar la igualdad de los impuestos para todos? los candidatos
5. ¿En qué puede convertirse la tormenta? en un huracán

3 **Categorías** Indica la categoría de cada uno de estos términos. Las categorías son: **desastres naturales**, **política** y **medios de comunicación**.

1. inundación desastres naturales
2. reportaje medios de comunicación
3. incendio desastres naturales
4. candidato/a política
5. representante política
6. noticiero medios de comunicación
7. elecciones política
8. prensa medios de comunicación
9. terremoto desastres naturales
10. huracán desastres naturales

4 **Completar** Completa la noticia con los verbos adecuados para cada oración. Conjuga los verbos en el tiempo verbal correspondiente.

1. El grupo __anunció__ a todos los medios de comunicación que iba a organizar una huelga general de los trabajadores.
   a. durar   b. votar   c. anunciar
2. Los representantes les pidieron a los ciudadanos que __obedecieran__ al presidente.
   a. comer   b. obedecer   c. aburrir
3. La oposición, por otro lado, __eligió__ a un líder para promover la huelga.
   a. publicar   b. emitir   c. elegir
4. El líder de la oposición dijo que si el gobierno ignoraba sus opiniones, la huelga iba a __durar__ mucho tiempo.
   a. transmitir   b. obedecer   c. durar
5. Hoy día, el líder de la oposición declaró que los ciudadanos estaban listos para __luchar__ por sus derechos.
   a. informar   b. comunicarse   c. luchar

TEACHING OPTIONS

Pairs Ask pairs of students to categorize all the nouns using different paradigms than those given. Ex: **fenómenos del tiempo relacionados con el agua: tormenta, huracán, inundación; conceptos democráticos: huelga, elecciones, derechos.** Have each pair read their categories aloud to the class.

Extra Practice Have students complete these analogies.
1. locutora : _____ :: candidato : discurso (reportaje/noticias)
2. SIDA : salud :: _____ : libertad (dictadura)
3. pagar : impuesto :: _____ : candidato (votar)
4. lluvia : _____ :: viento : huracán (inundación/tormenta)
5. terminar : _____ :: desobedecer : obedecer (empezar/comenzar)

---

1 **Teaching Tip** You may want to do this activity as a TPR exercise. Have students give a thumbs-up for **buena noticia** and a thumbs-down for **mala noticia**.

1 **Expansion** Have students write four more statements.

1 **Script** 1. El presidente de Colombia recibió el Premio Nobel de la Paz. 2. Se acerca un huracán a la costa pacífica. 3. El próximo año subirán los impuestos un 10%. 4. El 11 de marzo se cumple otro año del fin de la dictadura. 5. Según el informe, el desempleo disminuyó durante el último año en Bolivia. 6. Esta mañana hubo otro terremoto en México. 7. Un tornado destruyó muchas casas. 8. Los colombianos celebran el fin de una guerra de más de cincuenta años.

2 **Teaching Tip** Have students read the questions before listening to the audio.

2 **Script** Ahora en Notiuruguay las noticias nacionales e internacionales… Se acercan las elecciones presidenciales en Uruguay y, según una encuesta, los ciudadanos creen que los impuestos son injustos y los candidatos tienen el deber de asegurar la igualdad de los impuestos para todos. ¡Atención! En noticias internacionales, esta noche una peligrosa tormenta se acerca a las islas del Caribe, con vientos de más de 120 kilómetros por hora. Esta tormenta se puede convertir en un huracán.

3 **Teaching Tip** Model the activity by naming a term not listed. Ex: **impuesto, diario**. Have volunteers identify the appropriate category.

4 **Expansion** Ask students to write a summary of a news event, using this activity as a model.

5 **Definiciones** Indica la palabra adecuada para cada definición.

| acontecimiento | guerra | libertad | racismo | SIDA |
| discurso | huelga | locutor(a) | sexismo | soldado |

1. conflicto entre dos ejércitos guerra
2. tipo de discriminación contra otras razas o grupos étnicos racismo
3. persona que tiene por trabajo hablar en radio o televisión locutor(a)
4. mensaje que se da de manera pública discurso
5. enfermedad infecciosa SIDA
6. evento que llama la atención acontecimiento
7. interrupción de las actividades laborales para conseguir beneficios huelga
8. persona que hace parte del ejército soldado

6 **Conversación** Completa esta conversación con las palabras adecuadas.

artículo	derechos	peligrosa
choque	dictaduras	transmitir
declarar	paz	violencia

RAÚL Oye, Agustín, ¿leíste el (1) __artículo__ del diario *El País*?

AGUSTÍN ¿Cuál? ¿El del (2) __choque__ entre dos autobuses?

RAÚL No, el otro sobre…

AGUSTÍN ¿Sobre la tormenta (3) __peligrosa__ que viene mañana?

RAÚL No, hombre, el artículo sobre política…

AGUSTÍN ¡Ay, claro! Un análisis de las peores (4) __dictaduras__ de la historia.

RAÚL ¡Agustín! Deja de interrumpir. Te quería hablar del artículo sobre la organización que lucha por los (5) __derechos__ humanos y la (6) __paz__.

AGUSTÍN Ah, no lo leí.

RAÚL Parece que te interesan más las noticias sobre la (7) __violencia__, ¿eh?

7 **La vida civil** ¿Estás de acuerdo con estas afirmaciones? Comparte tus respuestas con la clase. *Answers will vary.*

1. Los medios de comunicación nos informan bien de las noticias.
2. Los medios de comunicación nos dan una visión global del mundo.
3. Los candidatos para las elecciones deben aparecer en todos los medios de comunicación.
4. Nosotros y nuestros representantes nos comunicamos bien.
5. Es importante que todos obedezcamos las leyes.
6. Es importante luchar por los derechos.
7. Es importante mirar o escuchar un noticiero todos los días.
8. Es importante votar.
9. El deber de todos los ciudadanos es pagar impuestos.
10. La libertad de prensa debe ser protegida.

AYUDA
You may want to use these expressions:
En mi opinión…
Está claro que…
(No) Estoy de acuerdo.
Según mis padres…
Sería ideal que…

Comunicación

8 **Las actualidades** En parejas, describan lo que ven en las fotos. Luego, escriban una historia para explicar qué pasó en cada foto. Answers will vary.

9 **Un noticiero** En grupos, trabajen para presentar un noticiero de la tarde. Presenten por lo menos tres reportajes sobre espectáculos, política, crimen y temas sociales. Answers will vary.

¡LENGUA VIVA!

Here are four ways to say *to happen*:
acontecer
ocurrir
pasar
suceder

10 **Las elecciones** Trabajen en parejas para representar una entrevista entre un(a) reportero/a de la televisión y un(a) político/a que va a ser candidato/a en las próximas elecciones.

▶ Antes de la entrevista, hagan una lista de los temas de los que el/la candidato/a va a hablar y de las preguntas que el/la reportero/a le va a hacer.

▶ Durante la entrevista, la clase va a hacer el papel del público.

▶ Después de la entrevista, el/la reportero/a va a hacerle preguntas y pedirle comentarios al público.
Answers will vary.

TEACHING OPTIONS

Small Groups Divide the class into small groups for a debate on a current campus issue. Give the teams some time in class to prepare their strategy, but ask each team member to prepare his or her two-to-three minute argument as homework. Have the rest of the class judge the debate.

Game Divide the class into teams and give them five minutes to write a job announcement for one of the professions mentioned in **Contextos**. Then have them take turns reading their ads. The other teams must guess what job is being announced. Award one point for each correct guess. The team with the most points at the end wins.

---

8 **Teaching Tips**
• To simplify, give the class two minutes to note details in the photos and think of scenarios for the events.
• Ask closed-ended questions about each photo. Ex: **¿Ocurrió en la ciudad o en el campo? ¿Fue un acontecimiento político o un desastre natural? ¿Hubo muchas víctimas? ¿Es reciente el acontecimiento?**

8 **Expansion**
Ask volunteers to summarize one of their descriptions.

9 **Teaching Tip** To simplify, point out **¡Lengua viva!** and give example sentences using the four verbs. Then have groups use idea maps to brainstorm topics for their news reports.

9 **Expansion**
Ask each group to choose one report and present it to the class. Alternatively, have all groups present their news reports during the next class. Encourage them to use props and visuals to enrich their presentations.

10 **Teaching Tips**
• Name a prominent politician and ask students what questions they would ask him or her. Write their suggestions on the board.
• Record the interviews and show segments during the next class.

Section Goals

In **Fotonovela**, students will:
- receive comprehensible input from free-flowing discourse
- learn functional phrases that preview lesson grammatical structures

Instructional Resources
Supersite: Video (**Fotonovela**); Resources (Scripts, Translations, Answer Keys)
WebSAM
Video Manual

Video Recap: Lección 17
Before doing this **Fotonovela** section, review the previous episode with these questions:
1. ¿Quién llevaba a Juan Carlos a espectáculos culturales cuando era niño? (Su mamá lo llevaba.) 2. ¿Qué le encanta ver a Maru en el museo? (Le encantan las artesanías de cerámica y los tejidos.) 3. ¿Cuáles son las películas favoritas de Juan Carlos? (Le gustan las de ciencia ficción y las de terror.) 4. ¿Cuáles son las que más le gustan a Jimena? (Le gustan las películas de acción y los documentales.) 5. ¿Qué le dio Miguel a Maru? (Le dio un anillo.)

Video Synopsis
It's time for **Marissa** to go back to the U.S. **Sr. Díaz** takes her to a restaurant for a farewell meal, where the whole family and group of friends surprise her. They make plans to see each other again at **Miguel** and **Maru's** wedding.

Teaching Tips
- Have the class read the title, scan the captions for cognates, and look at the stills. Ask students to predict what the episode will be about.
- Quickly review the predictions students made. Ask a few questions to help them summarize the plot.

Hasta pronto, Marissa

Marissa debe regresar a Wisconsin y quiere despedirse de sus amigos.

PERSONAJES

 MARISSA

 SR. DÍAZ

 Video

1

MARISSA ¡Hola, don Roberto! ¿Dónde están todos?

SR. DÍAZ Todos me dijeron que te pidiera una disculpa de su parte.

MARISSA (*triste*) Ah. No hay problema. ¿Puedo poner la tele?

SR. DÍAZ Claro.

2

MAITE FUENTES Un incendio en el centro ha ocasionado daños en tres edificios. Los representantes de la policía nos informan que no hay heridos. Aunque las elecciones son en pocas semanas, las encuestas no muestran un líder definido.

(*La familia Díaz y sus amigos sorprenden a Marissa en el restaurante.*)

MARISSA No tenía ni idea. (*a Jimena*) Tu papá me hizo creer que no podría despedirme de ustedes.

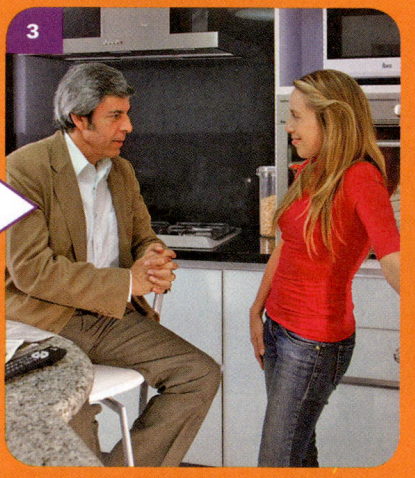

3

MARISSA Si hubiera sabido que ellos no iban a estar aquí, me habría despedido anoche.

SR. DÍAZ ¡Ánimo! No es un adiós, Marissa. Vamos a seguir en contacto. Pero, creo que tenemos algo de tiempo antes de que te vayas. Te llevo a comer tu última comida mexicana.

5

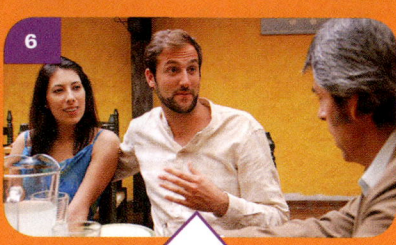

6

EMPLEADO Buenos días, señor Díaz. ¡Qué gusto verlo!

SR. DÍAZ Igualmente. Ella es Marissa. Pasó el año con nosotros. Quería que su última comida en México fuera la mejor de todas.

EMPLEADO Muy amable de su parte, señor. Su mesa está lista. Síganme, por favor.

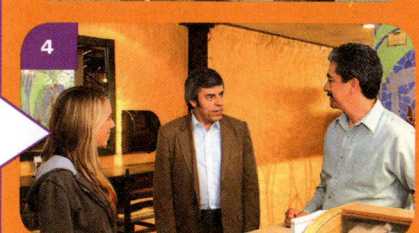

4

SR. DÍAZ Chicos, me dicen que se van a casar. Felicidades.

MIGUEL Nos casamos aquí en México el año que viene. Ojalá usted y su esposa puedan ir. (*a Marissa*) Si tú no estás harta de nosotros, nos encantaría que también vinieras.

TEACHING OPTIONS

Video Tips General suggestions for using video clips in the classroom can be found in the front matter of this Instructor's Annotated Edition.

Hasta pronto, Marissa ➜👥← Before you play the **Hasta pronto, Marissa** segment, give students a list of questions about it. (Ex: **¿Quiénes esperan en el restaurante?**) Tell them to read the questions and listen for the answers as they watch the video. After playing the segment, go over the questions with the class. If necessary, play the episode a second time.

MAITE FUENTES **DON DIEGO** **EMPLEADO** **SRA. DÍAZ** **JIMENA** **MIGUEL** **FELIPE** **MARU** **JUAN CARLOS**

7

SRA. DÍAZ Marissa, ¿cuál fue tu experiencia favorita en México?

MARISSA Bueno, si tuviera que elegir una sola experiencia, tendría que ser el Día de Muertos. Chichén Itzá fue muy emocionante también. No puedo decidirme. ¡La he pasado de película!

8

SR. DÍAZ Mi hermana Ana María me pidió que te diera esto.

MARISSA *No way!*

JUAN CARLOS ¿Qué es?

MARISSA La receta del mole de la tía.

9

FELIPE Nosotros también tenemos algo para ti.

MARISSA ¡Mi diccionario! Lo dejo contigo, Felipe. Tenías razón. No lo necesito.

SR. DÍAZ Si queremos llegar a tiempo al aeropuerto, tenemos que irnos ya.

10

FELIZ VIAJE

MARU Te veremos en nuestra boda.

MARISSA ¡Sí, seguro!

SR. DÍAZ Bueno, vámonos.

MARISSA (*a todos*) Cuídense. Gracias por todo.

More activities

vhlcentral | VM pp. 35–36 | Online activities

Expresiones útiles

Expressing delight and surprise

¡Qué gusto verlo/la!
How nice to see you! (form.)
¡Qué gusto verte!
How nice to see you! (fam.)
¡No tenía ni idea!
I had no idea!
¡Felicidades!
Congratulations!

Playing a joke on someone

Todos me dijeron que te pidiera una disculpa de su parte.
They all told me to ask you to excuse them / forgive them.
Tu papá me hizo creer que no podría despedirme de ustedes.
Your dad made me think I wouldn't be able to say goodbye to you.

Talking about past and future trips

Si tuviera que elegir una sola experiencia, tendría que ser el Día de Muertos.
If I had to pick just one experience, it would have to be the Day of the Dead.
¡La he pasado de película!
I've had an awesome time!
Ojalá usted y su esposa puedan ir.
I hope you and your wife can come.
Si tú no estás harta de nosotros, nos encantaría que también vinieras.
If you aren't sick of us, we'd love you to come, too.
Si queremos llegar a tiempo al aeropuerto, tenemos que irnos ya.
If we want to get to the airport on time, we should go now.

Additional vocabulary

despedirse
to say goodbye

Expresiones útiles Have the class locate the sentence **Si tuviera que elegir una sola experiencia, tendría que ser el Día de Muertos.** Tell students that this sentence has a **si** clause that uses the past subjunctive, followed by a clause containing a conditional form. Have the class identify the two verb forms. Then, have students look at the caption for video still 3 and find the sentence **Si hubiera sabido que ellos no iban a estar aquí, me habría despedido anoche.** Explain that this sentence has a **si** clause that uses the past perfect subjunctive, followed by a clause containing a conditional perfect form. Have the class identify the two verb forms. Tell students they will learn more about these structures in **Estructura**.

Teaching Tip
👤↔👤 Work through the **Fotonovela** by having volunteers read the various parts aloud. Ask a few students to ad-lib the episode.

The Affective Dimension
Ask students if they feel more comfortable watching the video now than when they started the course. Recommend that they view all the episodes again to help them realize how much their proficiency has increased.

TEACHING OPTIONS

Extra Practice →👤← Photocopy the **Fotonovela** Videoscript (Supersite) and white out key expressions and words in order to create a master for a cloze activity. Distribute copies of the master and, as you play the episode, have students fill in the blanks.

Small Groups 👤↔👤 Tell students to imagine that the friends have reunited at **Miguel** and **Maru's** wedding. In small groups, have them write an epilogue. Encourage humor and creativity and give them time to prepare. Then ask groups to role-play their epilogues for the class. Have the class vote for their favorite one.

¿Qué pasó?

1

¿Cierto o falso? Decide si lo que se afirma en las oraciones es **cierto** o **falso**. Corrige las oraciones falsas.

	Cierto	Falso
1. Según la reportera, las elecciones son la próxima semana. Las elecciones son en pocas semanas.	○	◉
2. Marissa dice que una de sus experiencias favoritas en México fue el Día de Muertos.	◉	○
3. La reportera dice que hay una inundación en el centro. La reportera dice que hay un incendio en el centro.	○	◉
4. La Sra. Díaz le envía la receta de los tacos a Marissa. La tía Ana María le envía la receta del mole a Marissa.	○	◉
5. Marissa le deja su diccionario a Jimena. Marissa le deja su diccionario a Felipe.	○	◉

2

Identificar Identifica quién hace estas afirmaciones.

1. Te llevo a comer tu última comida mexicana.   Sr. Díaz

2. Me da mucha tristeza no despedirme de ellos.   Marissa

3. Las encuestas no muestran un líder definido.   Maite Fuentes

4. Marissa, ¿cuál fue tu experiencia favorita en México?   Sra. Díaz

5. Te veremos en nuestra boda.   Maru

MAITE FUENTES

SR. DÍAZ

MARISSA

SRA. DÍAZ

MARU

3

Preguntas Contesta las preguntas.

1. ¿Dónde y cuándo se casarán Miguel y Maru?
 Miguel y Maru se casarán en México el año que viene.
2. ¿Por qué Marissa no imaginaba que vería a sus amigos en el restaurante?
 Porque el Sr. Díaz le hizo creer que no podría despedirse de ellos.
3. Según lo que dice Maite Fuentes, ¿qué ha ocasionado el incendio en el centro?
 El incendio en el centro ha ocasionado daños en tres edificios.
4. ¿Por qué el Sr. Díaz le dice a Marissa que tienen que irse ya?
 Porque tienen que llegar a tiempo al aeropuerto.
5. ¿Qué dice Marissa sobre la experiencia que vivió en Chichén Itzá?
 Marissa dice que la experiencia que vivió en Chichen Itzá fue muy emocionante.

4

Las experiencias de Marissa Trabajen en parejas para representar una conversación en español entre Marissa y un(a) amigo/a con quien se encuentra cuando ella acaba de regresar de México. Hablen de las experiencias buenas y malas que tuvieron durante ese tiempo.   Answers will vary.

▶ ¡Qué gusto volver a verte!
▶ Gusto de verte.
▶ Lo pasé de película/maravillosamente/muy bien.
▶ Me divertí mucho.
▶ Lo mejor fue...
▶ Lo peor fue...

NATIONAL communication STANDARDS

TEACHING OPTIONS

Extra Practice Scramble the order of these events from this **Fotonovela** episode and have the class put them in order:
1. Marissa está triste porque no puede despedirse de sus amigos. **2.** El Sr. Díaz lleva a Marissa al restaurante. **3.** Miguel invita a Marissa y a los señores Díaz a su boda. **4.** Marissa habla de sus experiencias favoritas en México. **5.** Marissa recibe unos regalos.

Extra Practice ←👤→ Have students write a short paragraph about a memorable trip, real or imaginary. Tell them to be sure to describe the best and worst parts of the trip. You may want to have students share their paragraphs with the class, along with photographs, if possible.

Ortografía
Neologismos y anglicismos

 Tutorial

As societies develop and interact, new words are needed to refer to inventions and discoveries, as well as to objects and ideas introduced by other cultures. In Spanish, many new terms have been invented to refer to such developments, and additional words have been "borrowed" from other languages.

bajar un programa *download*	**borrar** *to delete*	**correo basura** *junk mail*
en línea *online*	**enlace** *link*	**herramienta** *tool*
navegador *browser*	**pirata** *hacker*	**sistema operativo** *operating system*

Many Spanish neologisms, or "new words," refer to computers and technology. Due to the newness of these words, more than one term may be considered acceptable.

cederrón, CD-ROM	**escáner**	**fax**	**zoom**

In Spanish, many anglicisms, or words borrowed from English, refer to computers and technology. Note that the spelling of these words is often adapted to the sounds of the Spanish language.

jazz, yaz	**rap**	**rock**	**walkman**

Music and music technology are another common source of anglicisms.

gángster	**hippy, jipi**	**póquer**	**whisky, güisqui**

Other borrowed words refer to people or things that are strongly associated with another culture.

chárter	**esnob**	**estrés**	**flirtear**
gol	**hall**	**hobby**	**iceberg**
jersey	**júnior**	**récord**	**yogur**

There are many other sources of borrowed words. Over time, some anglicisms are replaced by new terms in Spanish, while others are accepted as standard usage.

Práctica Completa el diálogo usando las palabras de la lista.

borrar	correo basura	esnob
chárter	en línea	estrés

GUSTAVO Voy a leer el correo electrónico.
REBECA Bah, yo sólo recibo ___correo basura___. Lo único que hago con la computadora es ___borrar___ mensajes.
GUSTAVO Mira, cariño, hay un anuncio en Internet: un viaje barato a Punta del Este. Es un vuelo ___chárter___.
REBECA Últimamente tengo tanto ___estrés___. Sería buena idea que fuéramos de vacaciones. Pero busca un hotel muy bueno.
GUSTAVO Rebeca, no seas ___esnob___, lo importante es ir y disfrutar. Voy a comprar los boletos ahora mismo ___en línea___.

Dibujo Describe el dibujo utilizando por lo menos cinco anglicismos.
Answers will vary.

More activities
vhlcentral   LM   p. 104

Section Goals

In **Ortografía**, students will learn about:
- neologisms
- anglicisms

Instructional Resources
Supersite: Audio (Lab MP3 Files); Resources (Scripts, Answer Keys)
WebSAM
Lab Manual

Teaching Tips
- Ask the class to name some neologisms that refer to computers and technology. Then have students invent sentences that use these words. Write a few of the sentences on the board.
- Ask the class to name some anglicisms. Ask students to create sentences that use these words, and have volunteers write a few of the sentences on the board.
- Write the words **gángster, jipi, póquer, whisky, gol, yogur, récord,** and **esnob** on the board. Ask volunteers to explain what each word means and to use it in a sentence.
- Point out that **Ortografía** replaces **Pronunciación** in the Student Edition for **Lecciones 10–18**, but not in the Lab Manual. The box references the **Pronunciación** sections found in all lessons of the Lab Manual.

TEACHING OPTIONS

Small Groups In small groups, have students write a humorous paragraph using as many neologisms and anglicisms as possible. Then have a few volunteers read their paragraphs to the class.
Extra Practice Have students write questions using neologisms and/or anglicisms. Have volunteers write their questions on the board. Then work through the questions as a class.

Worth Noting New technology has long been the source of neologisms and loanwords. For example, some Spanish words of Arabic origin named innovations or new products of their day. Ex: **azúcar** (*sugar*), **zafra** (*harvest of sugarcane*), **ajedrez** (*chess*), **algodón** (*cotton*), **cero** (*zero*), **álgebra** (*algebra*), **naipes** (*playing cards*), **aduana** (*customs*).

EN DETALLE

Protestas sociales

¿Cómo reaccionas ante° una situación injusta?

¿Protestas? Las huelgas y manifestaciones° son expresiones de protesta. Mucha gente asocia las huelgas con "no trabajar", pero no siempre es así. Hay huelgas donde los empleados del gobierno aplican las regulaciones escrupulosamente, demorando° los procesos administrativos; en otras, los trabajadores aumentan la producción. En países como España, las huelgas muchas veces se anuncian con anticipación° y, en los lugares que van a ser afectados, se ponen carteles con información como: "Esta oficina cerrará el día 14 con motivo de la huelga. Disculpen las molestias°".

Las manifestaciones son otra forma de protesta: la gente sale a la calle llevando carteles con frases y eslóganes. Una forma original de manifestación son los "cacerolazos", en los cuales la gente golpea° cacerolas y sartenes°. Los primeros cacerolazos tuvieron lugar en Chile y más tarde pasaron a otros países. Otras veces, el buen humor ayuda a confrontar temas serios y los manifestantes° marchan bailando, cantando eslóganes y tocando silbatos° y tambores°.

Actualmente° se puede protestar sin salir de casa. Lo único que necesitas es tener una computadora con conexión a Internet para poder participar en manifestaciones virtuales. Y no sólo de tu país, sino de todo el mundo.

Los eslóganes

El pueblo unido jamás será vencido°. Es el primer verso° de una canción que popularizó el grupo chileno Quilapayún.

Basta ya°. Se ha usado en el País Vasco en España durante manifestaciones en contra del terrorismo.

Agua para todos. Se ha gritado en manifestaciones contra la privatización del agua en varios países hispanos.

Ni guerra que nos mate°, ni paz que nos oprima°. Surgió° en la **Movilización Nacional de Mujeres contra la Guerra,** en Colombia (2002) para expresar un no rotundo° a la guerra.

Ni un paso° atrás. Ha sido usado en muchos países, como en Argentina por las Madres de la Plaza de Mayo*.

* Las Madres de la Plaza de Mayo es un grupo de mujeres que tiene hijos o familiares que desaparecieron durante la dictadura militar en Argentina (1976–1983).

ante *in the presence of* manifestaciones *demonstrations* demorando *delaying* con anticipación *in advance* Disculpen las molestias. *We apologize for any inconvenience.* golpea *bang* cacerolas y sartenes *pots and pans* manifestantes *demonstrators* silbatos *whistles* tambores *drums* Actualmente *Currently* vencido *defeated* verso *line* Basta ya. *Enough.* mate *kills* oprima *oppresses* Surgió *It arose* rotundo *absolute* paso *step*

ACTIVIDADES

1 **¿Cierto o falso?** Indica si lo que dice cada oración es **cierto** o **falso**. Corrige la información falsa.

1. En algunas huelgas las personas trabajan más de lo normal. **Cierto.**
2. En España, las huelgas se hacen sin notificación previa. **Falso.** Se anuncian con anticipación.
3. En las manifestaciones virtuales se puede protestar sin salir de casa. **Cierto.**
4. En algunas manifestaciones la gente canta y baila. **Cierto.**
5. "Basta ya" es un eslogan que se ha usado en España en manifestaciones contra el terrorismo. **Cierto.**
6. En el año 2002 se llevó a cabo la Movilización Nacional de Mujeres contra la Guerra en Argentina. **Falso.** Se llevó a cabo en Colombia.
7. Los primeros "cacerolazos" se hicieron en Venezuela. **Falso.** Se hicieron en Chile.
8. "Agua para todos" es un eslogan del grupo Quilapayún. **Falso.** Es un eslogan contra la privatización del agua.

ASÍ SE DICE
Periodismo y política

la campaña	*campaign*
el encabezado	*headline*
la prensa amarilla	*tabloid press*
el sindicato	*(labor) union*
el suceso, el hecho	**el acontecimiento**

EL MUNDO HISPANO
Hispanos en la historia

- **Sonia Sotomayor** (Nueva York, EE.UU., 1954–) Doctora en Derecho de ascendencia puertorriqueña. Es la primera mujer hispana en ocupar el cargo de Jueza Asociada en la Corte Suprema de los Estados Unidos.

- **Che Guevara** (Rosario, Argentina, 1928–La Higuera, Bolivia, 1967) Ernesto "Che" Guevara es una de las figuras más controversiales del siglo° XX. Médico de profesión, fue uno de los líderes de la revolución cubana y participó en las revoluciones de otros países.

- **Rigoberta Menchú Tum** (Laj Chimel, Guatemala, 1959–) De origen maya, desde niña sufrió la pobreza y la represión, lo que la llevó muy pronto a luchar por los derechos humanos. En 1992 recibió el Premio Nobel de la Paz.

- **José Martí** (La Habana, Cuba, 1853–Dos Ríos, Cuba, 1895) Fue periodista, filósofo, poeta, diplomático e independentista°. Desde su juventud se opuso al régimen colonialista español. Murió luchando por la independencia de Cuba.

siglo *century* **independentista** *supporter of independence*

PERFIL
El proceso de paz en Colombia

En 2016, el diario *The Economist* eligió a Colombia como el país del año, y su presidente, Juan Manuel Santos, recibió el Premio Nobel de la Paz. Este protagonismo° del país fue resultado del histórico proceso de paz que se inició en 2012 entre el Gobierno de Colombia y las FARC (Fuerzas Armadas Revolucionarias de Colombia), con Noruega y Cuba como garantes°, y que terminó con la firma del Acuerdo para la Terminación Definitiva del Conflicto en noviembre de 2016.

El Premio Nobel, según el jurado°, quiere animar "a todos aquellos que tratan de lograr la paz, la reconciliación y la justicia en Colombia" para que "en los próximos años los colombianos recojan los frutos del proceso de paz y reconciliación en marcha".

En la ceremonia de aceptación del premio en Noruega estuvieron varias víctimas del conflicto, como la excandidata presidencial Ingrid Betancourt y la congresista Clara Rojas, secuestradas° por las FARC durante más de seis años. Santos dedicó el premio a todas las víctimas y donó el dinero obtenido.

protagonismo *limelight* **garantes** *guarantors* **jurado** *jury* **secuestradas** *kidnapped*

CON RITMO HISPANO

Jorge Drexler (1964–)
Lugar de nacimiento: Montevideo, Uruguay

Antes de dedicarse a la música, estudió y ejerció la medicina. Ha lanzado dieciséis álbumes y ha ganado dos Grammy Latinos. En 2004 ganó el premio Oscar a la mejor canción original por "Al otro lado del río".

Go to **vhlcentral.com** to find out more about **Jorge Drexler** and his music.

ACTIVIDADES

2 Comprensión Contesta las preguntas.

1. ¿Cuáles son los sinónimos de acontecimiento? *suceso y hecho*
2. ¿En qué es pionera Sonia Sotomayor? *Ella es la primera mujer hispana que ocupa un cargo en la Corte Suprema de los EE.UU.*
3. ¿Cuáles fueron las dos partes en el diálogo del proceso de paz en Colombia? *Las dos partes fueron el Gobierno de Colombia y las FARC.*
4. ¿A quiénes dedicó el Premio Nobel el presidente Santos? *El dedico el premio a las víctimas del conflicto.*

3 Líderes ¿Quién es el/la líder de tu comunidad o región que más admiras? Primero, escribe un breve párrafo explicando quién es, qué hace y por qué lo/la admiras. Luego, lee tu texto a la clase. *Answers will vary.*

More activities

vhlcentral   Online activities

TEACHING OPTIONS

Large Groups Have volunteers line up around the classroom and hold a card with a description of a person mentioned in **El mundo hispano** or **Perfil**. You might also include other influential Hispanics, such as **Evita, Hugo Chávez, Óscar Romero,** or **César Chávez.** Then have the rest of the class circulate around the room and ask questions in order to guess which historical figure the volunteer represents.

Heritage Speakers Ask heritage speakers to talk about any prominent political issues (historic or recent) in their families' home countries. Ex: Puerto Rican independence, communism in Cuba, immigrant issues in Spain. Have the class ask follow-up questions and contribute any additional information they might know about the topic.

Así se dice
- To challenge students, add these words to the list: **la calumnia, la difamación** (*slander*); **el/la editor(a), el/la redactor(a)** (*editor*).
- Ask students questions using the terms. Ex: **¿Te gusta leer la prensa amarilla? ¿Te interesaría trabajar para una campaña política?**

Perfil
- **Juan Manuel Santos** became the president of Colombia in 2010 and was reelected in 2014. Member of a wealthy and influential family in his country, he studied in the United States and England, and served as Minister of Foreign Trade and Minister of Defense before his election as president.
- It is estimated that 260,000 Colombians were killed and over eight million displaced during this 52-year conflict.

El mundo hispano Ask students if they know of any other important historic political figures from the Hispanic world.

Con ritmo hispano Point out to students that they will find supporting activities and information at **vhlcentral.com**.

2 Expansion Have students, in pairs, create three additional comprehension questions based on the reading. Then have them exchange papers with another pair and complete the activity.

3 Teaching Tip Encourage students to think beyond the world of political leaders. Ex: A teacher or business person.

3 Expansion To challenge students, have them write three questions they would like to ask their chosen figure, as well as potential answers.

Section Goals

In **Estructura 18.1**, students will learn:

- **si** clauses in the subjunctive mood
- **si** clauses with verbs in the indicative mood

Instructional Resources

Supersite: Audio (Lab MP3 Files); Resources (Grammar Presentation Slides, Activity Pack, Scripts, Answer Keys); Testing Program (Quizzes)
WebSAM
Workbook
Lab Manual

Teaching Tips

- Have volunteers read aloud the captions of the video stills. Ask them to identify the tense and the mood of the verb in the first clause and then the verb in the second clause.
- Give students a contrary-to-fact situation and make statements about it. Ex: **Si nosotros no tuviéramos clase ahora, yo iría a la playa. Si no estuviéramos en clase, yo tomaría el sol y comería un helado. Y ustedes, ¿qué harían?**
- Compare and contrast contrary-to-fact statements using the example sentences on this page. Check understanding by providing main clauses and having volunteers finish the sentence with a **si** clause. Ex: **No lo haría... (si fuera tú.) El huracán habría destruido tu casa... (si no hubieras tomado precauciones.) No lo habría hecho... (si hubiera sido tú.)**
- Continue the process with clauses that express conditions or events that are possible or likely to occur. Ex: **Iré contigo... (si vas a participar en la huelga.)**
- Add a visual aspect to this grammar presentation. Use magazine pictures to reinforce **si** clauses. Ex: **Si yo hubiera salido en esta tormenta, me habría puesto un abrigo.**

18.1 Si clauses Tutorial

ANTE TODO **Si** (*If*) clauses describe a condition or event upon which another condition or event depends. Sentences with **si** clauses consist of a **si** clause and a main (or result) clause.

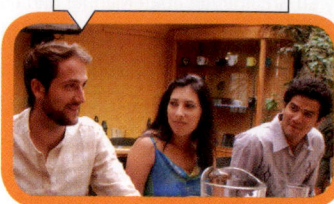

Si pudieras, ¿irías a nuestra boda?

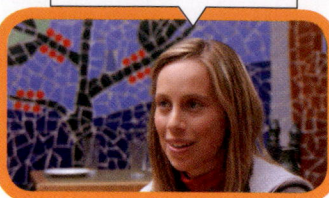

Sí, si tuviera la oportunidad, iría con mucho gusto.

▶ **Si** clauses can speculate or hypothesize about a current event or condition. They express what *would happen* if an event or condition *were to occur*. This is called a contrary-to-fact situation. In such instances, the verb in the **si** clause is in the past subjunctive while the verb in the main clause is in the conditional.

> Si **cambiaras** de empleo, **serías** más feliz.
> *If you changed jobs, you would be happier.*

> **Iría** de viaje a Suramérica si **tuviera** dinero.
> *I would travel to South America if I had money.*

▶ **Si** clauses can also describe a contrary-to-fact situation in the past. They can express what *would have happened* if an event or condition *had occurred*. In these sentences, the verb in the **si** clause is in the past perfect subjunctive while the verb in the main clause is in the conditional perfect.

> Si **hubiera sido** estrella de cine, **habría sido** rico.
> *If I had been a movie star, I would have been rich.*

> No **habrías tenido** hambre si **hubieras desayunado**.
> *You wouldn't have been hungry if you had eaten breakfast.*

▶ **Si** clauses can also express conditions or events that are possible or likely to occur. In such instances, the **si** clause is in the present indicative while the main clause uses a present, near future, future, or command form.

> Si **puedes** venir, **llámame**.
> *If you can come, call me.*

> Si **puedo** venir, **te llamo**.
> *If I can come, I'll call you.*

> Si **terminas** la tarea, **tendrás** tiempo para mirar la televisión.
> *If you finish your homework, you will have time to watch TV.*

> Si **terminas** la tarea, **vas a tener** tiempo para mirar la televisión.
> *If you finish your homework, you are going to have time to watch TV.*

¡ATENCIÓN!
Remember the difference between **si** (*if*) and **sí** (*yes*).

¡LENGUA VIVA!
Note that in Spanish the conditional is never used immediately following **si**.

TEACHING OPTIONS

Large Groups Have students stand in a circle. Say a main clause, then toss a ball to a student. He or she should suggest a **si** clause, then throw the ball back to you. Ex: **...tendría que caminar a las clases. (Si no tuviera bicicleta,...) ...hablaríamos español todo el día. (Si estuviéramos en México,...)**
Heritage Speakers Ask heritage speakers to write a composition entitled **"Si mi familia no hablara español..."** The

piece should describe how the student's life would have been different if he or she had not been born into a Spanish-speaking family. The compositions should have at least ten contrary-to-fact sentences with **si** clauses. Have students read their compositions to the class. Based on the information they hear, have the class react with **si** statements about what is likely to occur in the near future or later in the heritage speaker's life.

▶ When the **si** clause expresses habitual past conditions or events, *not* a contrary-to-fact situation, the imperfect is used in both the **si** clause and the main (or result) clause.

Si Alicia me **invitaba** a una fiesta,
yo siempre **iba**.
*If (Whenever) Alicia invited me to a party,
I would (used to) go.*

Mis padres siempre **iban** a la playa
si **hacía** buen tiempo.
*My parents always went to the beach
if the weather was good.*

▶ The **si** clause may be the first or second clause in a sentence. Note that a comma is used only when the **si** clause comes first.

Si tuviera tiempo, iría contigo.
If I had time, I would go with you.

Iría contigo **si tuviera tiempo.**
I would go with you if I had time.

Summary of si clause sequences

Condition	Si clause	Main clause
Possible or likely	**Si** + present	Present Near future (**ir a** + infinitive) Future Command
Habitual in the past	**Si** + imperfect	Imperfect
Contrary-to-fact (present)	**Si** + past (imperfect) subjunctive	Conditional
Contrary-to-fact (past)	**Si** + past perfect (pluperfect) subjunctive	Conditional perfect

 ¡INTÉNTALO! Cambia los tiempos y modos de los verbos para practicar todos los tipos de oraciones con **si** que se muestran en la tabla.

1. Si usted ___va___ (ir) a la playa, tenga cuidado con el sol.
2. Si ___hace___ (hacer) buen tiempo, voy a ir al parque.
3. Si tú ___quieres___ (querer), te preparo la merienda.
4. Si mis amigos ___iban___ (ir) de viaje, sacaban muchas fotos.
5. Si nosotros ___quisiéramos___ (querer) ir al teatro, compraríamos los boletos antes.
6. Si ella me ___llamara___ (llamar), yo la invitaría a la fiesta.
7. Si tú ___te levantaras___ (levantarse) temprano, desayunarías antes de ir a clase.
8. Si ellos ___tuvieran___ (tener) tiempo, te llamarían.
9. Si yo ___hubiera sido___ (ser) astronauta, habría ido a la Luna.
10. Si ustedes me ___hubieran dicho___ (decir) la verdad, no habríamos tenido este problema.
11. Si él ___hubiera ganado___ (ganar) un millón de dólares, habría comprado una mansión.
12. Si ellos ___hubieran trabajado___ (trabajar) más, habrían tenido más éxito.

More activities

vhlcentral

LM
p. 105

WB
pp. 203–204

Online activities

Teaching Tips
- Have students recall the latest presidential or state elections. Have them express what went wrong for the losing candidate(s), using contrary-to-fact statements about their political strategies, physical appearance, speeches, etc.
- Go over the use of the indicative in a **si** clause when it expresses habitual past conditions or events. Give additional examples.
- After going over the summary of **si** clause sequences, give students a complex sentence in the indicative, and have them, in pairs, form seven sentences using **si** clauses as per the chart. Ex: **Cuando viene un tornado, bajamos al sótano.** (Si viene un tornado, bajamos al sótano. Si viene un tornado, vamos a bajar al sótano. Si viene un tornado, bajaremos al sótano. Si viene un tornado, bajemos al sótano. Si venía…)

The Affective Dimension
If students feel intimidated by the variety of **si** clauses that can be created in Spanish, tell them that the chart on this page will help them sort out the possibilities and that they will feel more comfortable with **si** clauses with time and practice.

TEACHING OPTIONS

Pairs Ask students to reflect on the past semester(s) of studying Spanish. Then divide the class into pairs and have them write a paragraph using complex sentences to express what they wish they had done and why. Ex: **Si hubiera hablado español con mi amiga puertorriqueña, ahora podría hablar mejor....**

Extra Practice To provide oral practice, ask students to finish these sentences logically: **1. Si tomas español otra vez el próximo año, … 2. Si hubieras estudiado periodismo, … 3. Si la tormenta no pasa pronto, … 4. Si no hubiera llegado el ejército, … 5. Si quieres ser locutor(a) de televisión, …**

Práctica

1 **Emparejar** Empareja frases de las dos columnas para crear oraciones lógicas.

AYUDA

Remember these forms of **haber**:

(si) hubiera
(if) there were

habría
there would be

A		B
1. Si aquí hubiera terremotos, __e__		a. ¿se lo muestras al director?
2. Si la huelga dura más de un mes, __c__		b. habrían muerto muchos más.
3. Si te doy el informe, __a__		c. muchos van a pasar hambre.
4. Si la guerra hubiera continuado, __b__		d. podré explicar el desempleo.
5. Si me informo bien, __d__		e. no permitiríamos edificios altos.

2 **Minidiálogos** Completa los minidiálogos entre Teresa y Anita. Some answers may vary.

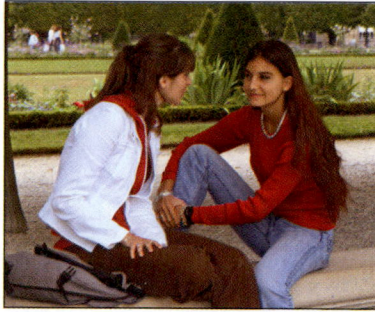

TERESA ¿Qué (1)__habrías__ hecho tú si tu papá te (2)__hubiera__ regalado un carro?
ANITA Me (3)__habría__ muerto de la felicidad.

ANITA Si (4)__viajas__ a Paraguay, ¿qué vas a hacer?
TERESA (5)__Voy__ a visitar a mis parientes.

ANITA Si tú (6)__tuvieras__ tiempo, ¿irías al cine con más frecuencia?
TERESA Sí, yo (7)__iría__ con más frecuencia si tuviera tiempo.

TERESA Si tú y tu familia (8)__tuvieran__ un millón de dólares, ¿qué comprarían?
ANITA Si nosotros tuviéramos un millón de dólares, (9)__compraríamos__ tres casas nuevas.

¡LENGUA VIVA!

Paraguay es conocido como "El Corazón de América" porque está en el centro de Suramérica. Sus lugares más visitados son la capital Asunción, que está situada a orillas (*on the banks*) del río Paraguay y la ciudad de Itauguá, en donde se producen muchos textiles.

3 **Completar** En parejas, túrnense para completar las frases de una manera lógica. Luego lean sus oraciones a la clase. Answers will vary.

1. Si tuviera un accidente de carro…
2. Me volvería loco/a (*I would go crazy*) si mi familia…
3. Me habría ido al Cuerpo de Paz (*Peace Corps*) si…
4. No volveré a ver las noticias en ese canal si…
5. Habría menos problemas si los medios de comunicación…
6. Si mis padres hubieran insistido en que fuera al ejército…
7. Si me ofrecen un viaje a la Luna…
8. Me habría enojado mucho si…
9. Si hubiera un desastre natural en mi ciudad…
10. Yo habría votado en las elecciones pasadas si…

1 Expansion Change the tense and/or mood in the **si** clauses, and have students change the main clause accordingly. Ex: **1. Si aquí hubiera habido terremotos,…** (**… no habríamos permitido edificios altos.**)

2 Teaching Tip In pairs, have one student fill in **Teresa's** answers and the other complete **Anita's**. Then have them read and correct each other's answers.

2 Expansion Ask questions about the **minidiálogos** and have students answer in complete sentences. Ex: **¿Qué haría Teresa si tuviera tiempo? (Iría al cine con más frecuencia.)**

3 Teaching Tips
• Model the activity by having three or four volunteers complete item 1 in different ways.
• Encourage students to ask their partners follow-up questions. Ex: **¿Por qué llamarías primero a tus padres si tuvieras un accidente de carro?**

TEACHING OPTIONS

Pairs Have pairs write ten sentences about what they would do to improve their community or society. First, ask them to list the problems they would solve and how they would do so. Then have them form their sentences as contrary-to-fact statements. Ex: **Si no se permitieran las contribuciones grandes a los candidatos, habría menos corrupción en el gobierno. Habría menos delincuencia si hubiera más lugares donde los jóvenes pudieran entretenerse.**

Si la universidad construyera más residencias, los alquileres no serían tan altos en nuestra comunidad.
Video Replay the **Fotonovela** to give students more input about **si** clauses. Ask students to write each one down as they hear it. Afterward, have them compare their notes in small groups.

Comunicación

4

Situaciones Trabajen en grupos para contestar las preguntas. Después deben comunicar sus respuestas a la clase. Answers will vary.

1. ¿Qué harían si fueran de vacaciones a Uruguay y al llegar no hubiera habitaciones en ningún hotel?
2. ¿Qué hacen si encuentran dinero en la calle?
3. Imaginen que estuvieron en Montevideo por tres semanas. ¿Qué habrían hecho si hubieran visto un crimen allí?
4. ¿Qué harían si fueran de viaje y las líneas aéreas estuvieran en huelga?
5. ¿Qué hacen si están en la calle y alguien les pide dinero?
6. ¿Qué harían si estuvieran en un país extranjero y un reportero los confundiera (*confused*) con unos actores o unas actrices de Hollywood?
7. ¿Qué dirían sus padres si los/las vieran ahora mismo?
8. ¿Qué haría cada uno/a de ustedes si fuera presidente/a o primer(a) ministro/a de este país?

5

¿Qué harían? En parejas, túrnense para hablar de lo que hacen, harían o habrían hecho en estas circunstancias. Answers will vary.

1. si ves a tu novio/a con otro/a en el cine
2. si hubieras ganado un viaje a Uruguay
3. si mañana tuvieras el día libre
4. si te casaras y tuvieras ocho hijos
5. si tuvieras que cuidar a tus padres cuando sean mayores
6. si no tuvieras que preocuparte por el dinero
7. si te acusaran de cometer un crimen
8. si hubieras vivido bajo una dictadura

Síntesis

6

Entrevista En grupos, preparen cinco preguntas para hacerle a un(a) candidato/a a la presidencia de su país. Luego, túrnense para hacer el papel de entrevistador(a) y de candidato/a. El/La entrevistador(a) reacciona a cada una de las respuestas del/de la candidato/a. Answers will vary.

> **modelo**
>
> **Entrevistador(a):** ¿Qué haría usted en cuanto a la obesidad infantil?
> **Candidato/a:** Pues, dudo que podamos decirles a los padres cómo alimentar a sus hijos. Creo que ellos deben preocuparse por darles comida saludable.
> **Entrevistador(a):** ¿Entonces usted no haría nada para combatir la obesidad infantil?
> **Candidato/a:** Si yo fuera presidente/a...

4 Expansion Ask groups to write a short description of what they would do if they took a group trip to Uruguay. Write a prompt on the board to get them started. Ex: **Si nosotros hiciéramos un viaje a Uruguay,...**

5 Expansion Ask students to formulate a multiple-choice survey with the sentence fragments given or with their own invented **si** clauses. Then have them survey one another and record the answers. Ex: **1. Si ves a tu novio/a con otro/a en el cine,... a. empiezas a llorar. b. haces un escándalo. c. los ignoras.**

6 Teaching Tip To simplify, begin by asking students to identify different political issues. Ex: **el crimen, el sexismo en el trabajo.** Write these issues on the board.

18.2

Summary of the uses of the subjunctive Tutorial

ANTE TODO   Since **Lección 12**, you have been learning about subjunctive verb forms and practicing their uses. The following chart summarizes the subjunctive forms you have studied. The chart on the next page summarizes the uses of the subjunctive you have seen and contrasts them with uses of the indicative and the infinitive. These charts will help you review and synthesize what you have learned about the subjunctive in this book.

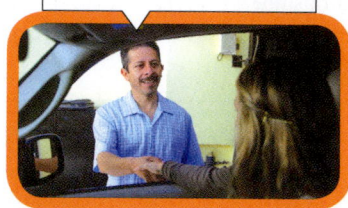

Espero que lo hayas pasado bien en México.

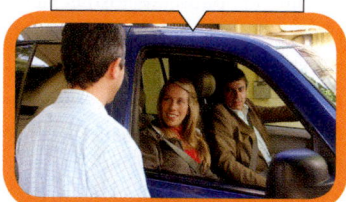

Sí, si hubiera podido, me habría quedado más tiempo.

Summary of subjunctive forms

-ar verbs		-er verbs		-ir verbs	
PRESENT SUBJUNCTIVE	PAST SUBJUNCTIVE	PRESENT SUBJUNCTIVE	PAST SUBJUNCTIVE	PRESENT SUBJUNCTIVE	PAST SUBJUNCTIVE
hable	hablara	beba	bebiera	viva	viviera
hables	hablaras	bebas	bebieras	vivas	vivieras
hable	hablara	beba	bebiera	viva	viviera
hablemos	habláramos	bebamos	bebiéramos	vivamos	viviéramos
habléis	hablarais	bebáis	bebierais	viváis	vivierais
hablen	hablaran	beban	bebieran	vivan	vivieran

PRESENT PERFECT SUBJUNCTIVE	PRESENT PERFECT SUBJUNCTIVE	PRESENT PERFECT SUBJUNCTIVE
haya hablado	haya bebido	haya vivido
hayas hablado	hayas bebido	hayas vivido
haya hablado	haya bebido	haya vivido
hayamos hablado	hayamos bebido	hayamos vivido
hayáis hablado	hayáis bebido	hayáis vivido
hayan hablado	hayan bebido	hayan vivido

PAST PERFECT SUBJUNCTIVE	PAST PERFECT SUBJUNCTIVE	PAST PERFECT SUBJUNCTIVE
hubiera hablado	hubiera bebido	hubiera vivido
hubieras hablado	hubieras bebido	hubieras vivido
hubiera hablado	hubiera bebido	hubiera vivido
hubiéramos hablado	hubiéramos bebido	hubiéramos vivido
hubierais hablado	hubierais bebido	hubierais vivido
hubieran hablado	hubieran bebido	hubieran vivido

CONSULTA

To review the subjunctive, refer to these sections:
Present subjunctive, **Estructura 12.3,** pp. 422–424.
Present perfect subjunctive, **Estructura 15.3,** p. 525.
Past subjunctive, **Estructura 16.3,** pp. 558–559.
Past perfect subjunctive, **Estructura 17.3,** p. 595.

The subjunctive is used...

1. After verbs and/or expressions of will and influence, when the subject of the subordinate clause is different from the subject of the main clause

Los ciudadanos **desean** que el candidato presidencial los **escuche.**

2. After verbs and/or expressions of emotion, when the subject of the subordinate clause is different from the subject of the main clause

Alejandra **se alegró** mucho de que le **dieran** el trabajo.

3. After verbs and/or expressions of doubt, disbelief, and denial

Dudo que **vaya** a tener problemas para encontrar su maleta.

4. After the conjunctions **a menos que, antes (de) que, con tal (de) que, en caso (de) que, para que,** and **sin que**

Cierra las ventanas **antes de que empiece** la tormenta.

5. After **cuando, después (de) que, en cuanto, hasta que,** and **tan pronto como** when they refer to future actions

Tan pronto como haga la tarea, podrá salir con sus amigos.

6. To refer to an indefinite or nonexistent antecedent mentioned in the main clause

Busco **un** empleado que **haya estudiado** computación.

7. After **si** to express something impossible, improbable, or contrary to fact

Si hubieras escuchado el noticiero, te habrías informado sobre el terremoto.

The indicative is used...

1. After verbs and/or expressions of certainty and belief

Es cierto que Uruguay **tiene** unas playas espectaculares.

2. After the conjunctions **cuando, después (de) que, en cuanto, hasta que,** and **tan pronto como** when they do not refer to future actions

Hay más violencia **cuando hay** desigualdad social.

3. To refer to a definite or specific antecedent mentioned in the main clause

Busco a **la** señora que me **informó** del crimen que ocurrió ayer.

4. After **si** to express something possible, probable, or not contrary to fact

Pronto habrá más igualdad **si luchamos** contra la discriminación.

The infinitive is used...

1. After expressions of will and influence when there is no change of subject

Martín **desea ir** a Montevideo este año.

2. After expressions of emotion when there is no change of subject

Me alegro de conocer a tu esposo.

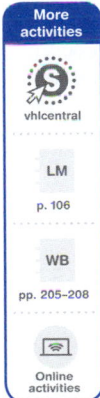

More activities

vhlcentral

LM
p. 106

WB
pp. 205–208

Online activities

Teaching Tips

- Before working through the summary of subjunctive usage, review the concepts of the indicative and subjunctive. Explain that in most discourse the verbs are in the indicative, the mood used to state facts and to express actions that the speaker considers real or definite. Then ask volunteers to tell you when the subjunctive is used. Write their statements on the board, revising them for clarity and accuracy.

- Work through the summaries of the use of the subjunctive, indicative, and infinitive comparatively. After you have worked through the comparison of the subjunctive versus the indicative with expressions of influence, emotion, doubt, and certainty, discuss cases where the infinitive is used instead of the subjunctive. Compare and contrast the use of the subjunctive and the indicative with conjunctions.

- On the computer, type up the main and subordinate clauses from the example sentences in the charts. Cut the papers into strips, with one clause per strip, and shuffle them. Distribute one clause to each student and have them circulate around the room to find the matching clause.

TEACHING OPTIONS

Large Groups ⬛↔⬛ Prepare sentences based on the example sentences from the chart. Break each sentence into two clauses or fragments and write each one on an index card. Distribute the cards and have students form sentences by finding a partner. Ex: **Me alegro mucho de que... /... hayan publicado tu artículo sobre el SIDA. Quisiera... /... visitar Montevideo algún día.**

Extra Practice To provide oral practice, create sentences that follow the pattern of the example sentences from the chart. Say the sentence, have students repeat it, then change the tense of the main clause. Have students then restate the sentence, changing the subordinate clause as necessary. Ex: **Dudo que terminemos el proyecto pronto. Dudaba que...** (**... termináramos el proyecto pronto.**)

Práctica

1 **Conversación** Completa la conversación con los tiempos verbales adecuados.

EMA Busco al reportero que (1)___publicó___ (publicar) el libro sobre la dictadura de Stroessner.

ROSA Ah, usted busca a Miguel Pérez. Ha salido.

EMA Le había dicho que yo vendría a verlo el martes, pero él me dijo que (2)___viniera___ (venir) hoy.

ROSA No creo que a Miguel se le (3)___olvidara/haya olvidado___ (olvidar) la cita. Si usted le (4)___hubiera pedido___ (pedir) una cita, él me lo habría mencionado.

EMA Pues no, no pedí cita, pero si él me hubiera dicho que era necesario, yo lo (5)___habría hecho___ (hacer).

ROSA Creo que Miguel (6)___fue___ (ir) a cubrir un incendio hace media hora. No pensaba que nadie (7)___fuera___ (ir) a venir esta tarde. Si quiere, le digo que la (8)___llame___ (llamar) tan pronto como (9)___llegue___ (llegar). A menos que usted (10)___quiera___ (querer) dejar un recado…

(*Entra Miguel.*)

EMA ¡Miguel! Amor, si hubieras llegado cinco minutos más tarde, no me (11)___habrías encontrado___ (encontrar) aquí.

MIGUEL ¡Ema! ¿Qué haces aquí?

EMA Me dijiste que viniera hoy para que (12)___pudiéramos___ (poder) pasar más tiempo juntos.

ROSA (*En voz baja*) ¿Cómo? ¿Serán novios?

2 **Escribir** Escribe uno o dos párrafos sobre tu participación en las próximas elecciones. Usa por lo menos cuatro de estas frases. *Answers will vary.*

- Votaré por… con tal de que…
- Quisiera saber…
- Si gana mi candidato/a…
- Espero que la economía…
- Estoy seguro/a de que…
- A menos que…
- Mis padres siempre me dijeron que…
- Si a la gente realmente le importara la familia…
- No habría escogido a ese/a candidato/a si…
- Si le preocuparan más los impuestos…
- Dudo que el/la otro/a candidato/a…
- En las próximas elecciones espero que…

3 **Explicar** En parejas, escriban una conversación breve sobre cada tema de la lista. Usen por lo menos un verbo en subjuntivo y otro en indicativo o en infinitivo. *Answers will vary.*

| unas elecciones | una huelga | una inundación | la prensa |
| una guerra | un incendio | la libertad | un terremoto |

modelo

un tornado
Estudiante 1: *Temo que este año haya tornados por nuestra zona.*
Estudiante 2: *No te preocupes. Creo que este año no va a haber muchos tornados.*

Comunicación

4 **Preguntas** En parejas, túrnense para hacerse estas preguntas. Answers will vary.

1. ¿Te irías a vivir a un lugar donde pudiera ocurrir un desastre natural? ¿Por qué?
2. ¿Te gustaría que tu vida fuera como la de tus padres? ¿Por qué? Y tus hijos, ¿preferirías que tuvieran experiencias diferentes a las tuyas? ¿Cuáles?
3. ¿Te parece importante que elijamos a una mujer como presidenta? ¿Por qué?
4. Si hubiera una guerra y te llamaran para entrar en el ejército, ¿obedecerías? ¿Lo considerarías tu deber? ¿Qué sentirías? ¿Qué pensarías?
5. Si sólo pudieras recibir noticias de un medio de comunicación, ¿cuál escogerías y por qué? Y si pudieras trabajar en un medio de comunicación, ¿escogerías el mismo?

5 **Consejos** En parejas, túrnense para representar los papeles de un(a) cliente/a y de un(a) agente de viajes. El/La agente le da consejos al/a la cliente/a sobre los lugares que debe visitar en Uruguay y el/la cliente/a da su opinión sobre los consejos. Answers will vary.

¡Conozca Uruguay!

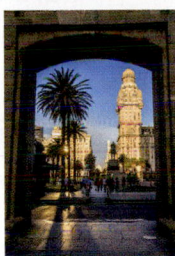

La **Plaza Independencia** en **Montevideo**, con su **Puerta de la Ciudadela**, forma el límite entre la ciudad antigua y la nueva. Si le interesan las compras, desde este lugar puede comenzar su paseo por la **Avenida 18 de Julio**, la principal arteria comercial de la capital.

No deje de ir a **Punta del Este**. Conocerá uno de los lugares turísticos más fascinantes del mundo. No se pierda las maravillosas playas, el **Museo de Arte Americano** y la **Catedral de Maldonado** (1895) con su famoso altar, obra del escultor **Antonio Veiga**.

Sin duda, querrá conocer la famosa ciudad vacacional de **Piriápolis**, con su puerto que atrae cruceros, y disfrutar de sus playas y lindos paseos.

Tampoco se debe perder la **Costa de Oro**, junto al **Río de la Plata**. Para aquéllos interesados en la historia, dos lugares favoritos son la conocida iglesia **Nuestra Señora de Lourdes** y el chalet de **Pablo Neruda**.

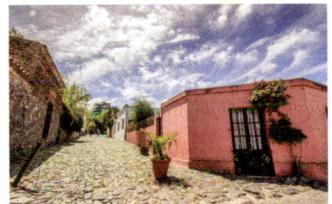

Síntesis

6 **Dos artículos** Tu profesor(a) les va a dar a ti y a tu compañero/a dos artículos. Trabajando en parejas, cada uno escoge y lee un artículo. Luego, háganse preguntas sobre los artículos. Answers will vary.

TEACHING OPTIONS

Extra Practice Have students write a news article about the end of the semester. The article should highlight the positive points of the class as well as the contributions of the students. Tell them to use the articles from **Actividad 6** as a guide.
TPR Write this cloze paragraph on the board. On separate note cards, write different forms of the verbs **ver, llegar, creer, hacer,** and **aprender**. Give each student a set of cards. As you read the paragraph aloud, have students hold up the correct form(s) of the appropriate verb.
Es difícil _____ (creer) que _____ (lleguemos/hayamos llegado) **al final del semestre. Espero que todos ustedes** _____ (hayan aprendido) **mucho, no sólo español, sino sobre el lenguaje en general. Si deciden seguir estudiando el español,** _____ (van a ver/verán) **que se** _____ (hace/hará) **más fácil con el tiempo.**

---

4 **Teaching Tip**
Tell students to take notes on what their partner says. After they complete the activity, ask questions about their responses.

4 **Expansion**
- Ask students to create two additional questions for the interview, keeping within the framework of natural disasters and sociopolitical issues.
- Facilitate a class discussion by surveying responses to find those on which there is general agreement and those on which there is not.

5 **Expansion** Have **los clientes** sit on one side of the room and **los agentes de viajes** on the other. Then ask individual students about the advice they gave or were given.
Ex: **¿Qué monumentos te aconsejó que visitaras? ¿Qué consejos le diste sobre los museos?**

6 **Teaching Tips**
- Divide the class into pairs and distribute the handouts from the Activity Pack (Activity Pack/Supersite) that correspond to this Information Gap Activity. Give students ten minutes to complete this activity.
- Go over the directions. Have partners skim the articles and choose one.

6 **Expansion** Have partners develop three more questions about each article.

Recapitulación

Completa estas actividades para repasar los conceptos de gramática que aprendiste en esta lección.

1 Condicionales Empareja las frases de las dos columnas para crear oraciones lógicas. **16 pts.**

 A   **B**

_c_ 1. Todos estaríamos mejor informados

_f_ 2. ¿Te sentirás mejor

_b_ 3. Si esos locutores no tuvieran tanta experiencia,

_h_ 4. ¿Votarías por un candidato como él

_a_ 5. Si no te gusta este noticiero,

_i_ 6. El candidato Díaz habría ganado las elecciones

_d_ 7. Si la tormenta no se va pronto,

_e_ 8. Ustedes se pueden ir

a. cambia el canal.

b. ya los habrían despedido.

c. si leyéramos el periódico todos los días.

d. la gente no podrá salir a protestar.

e. si no tienen nada más que decir.

f. si te digo que ya terminó la huelga?

g. Leopoldo fue a votar.

h. si supieras que no ha obedecido las leyes?

i. si hubiera hecho más entrevistas para la televisión.

2 Escoger Escoge la opción correcta para completar cada oración. **20 pts.**

1. Ojalá que aquí (hubiera/hay) un canal independiente.

2. Susana dudaba que (hubieras estudiado/estudias) medicina.

3. En cuanto (termine/terminé) mis estudios, buscaré trabajo.

4. Miguel me dijo que su familia nunca (veía/viera) los noticieros en la televisión.

5. Para estar bien informados, yo les recomiendo que (leen/lean) el diario *El Sol*.

6. Es terrible que en los últimos meses (haya habido/ha habido) tres desastres naturales.

7. Cuando (termine/terminé) mis estudios, encontré trabajo en un diario local.

8. El presidente no quiso (declarar/que declarara) la guerra.

9. Todos dudaban que la noticia (fuera/era) real.

10. Me sorprende que en el mundo todavía (exista/existe) la censura.

RESUMEN GRAMATICAL

18.1 Si clauses *pp. 622–623*

Summary of **si** clause sequences		
Possible or likely	**Si** + present	+ present + **ir a** + infinitive + future + command
Habitual in the past	**Si** + imperfect	+ imperfect
Contrary-to-fact (present)	**Si** + past subjunctive	+ conditional
Contrary-to-fact (past)	**Si** + past perfect subjunctive	+ conditional perfect

18.2 Summary of the uses of the subjunctive
pp. 626–627
Summary of subjunctive forms

▶ **Present:** (-ar) hable, (-er) beba, (-ir) viva

▶ **Past:** (-ar) hablara, (-er) bebiera, (-ir) viviera

▶ **Present perfect:** haya + past participle

▶ **Past perfect:** hubiera + past participle

The subjunctive is used...
1. After verbs and/or expressions of: ▶ Will and influence (when subject changes) ▶ Emotion (when subject changes) ▶ Doubt, disbelief, denial
2. After **a menos que, antes (de) que, con tal (de) que, en caso (de) que, para que, sin que**
3. After **cuando, después (de) que, en cuanto, hasta que, tan pronto como** when they refer to future actions
4. To refer to an indefinite or nonexistent antecedent
5. After **si** to express something impossible, improbable, or contrary to fact

3 **Las elecciones** Completa el diálogo con la forma correcta del verbo eligiendo entre el subjuntivo, el indicativo y el infinitivo, según el contexto. **24 pts.**

SERGIO ¿Ya has decidido por cuál candidato vas a votar en las elecciones del sábado?

MARINA No, todavía no. Es posible que no (1) _____vote_____ (yo, votar). Para mí es muy difícil (2) _____decidir_____ (decidir) quién será el mejor representante. Y tú, ¿ya has tomado una decisión?

SERGIO Sí. Mi amigo Julio nos aconsejó que (3) _____leyéramos_____ (leer) la entrevista que le hicieron al candidato Rodríguez en el diario *Tribuna*. En cuanto la (4) _____leí_____ (yo, leer), decidí votar por él.

MARINA ¿Hablas en serio? Espero que ya lo (5) _____hayas pensado_____ (tú, pensar) muy bien. El diario *Tribuna* no siempre es objetivo. Dudo que (6) _____sea_____ (ser) una fuente fiable *(reliable source)*. No vas a tener una idea clara de las habilidades de cada candidato a menos que (7) _____compares_____ (tú, comparar) información de distintas fuentes.

SERGIO Tienes razón, hoy día no hay ningún medio de comunicación que (8) _____diga_____ (decir) toda la verdad de forma independiente.

MARINA Tengo una idea. Sugiero que (9) _____vayamos_____ (nosotros, ir) esta noche a mi casa para (10) _____ver_____ (ver) juntos el debate de los candidatos por televisión. ¿Qué te parece?

SERGIO Es una buena idea, pero no creo que (11) _____tenga_____ (yo, tener) tiempo.

MARINA No te preocupes. Voy a grabarlo para que (12) _____puedas_____ (tú, poder) verlo.

4 **Escribir** Hoy día, cada vez más personas se mantienen informadas a través de Internet. Piensa cómo cambiaría tu vida diaria si no existiera este medio de comunicación. ¿Cómo te informarías de las actualidades del mundo y de las noticias locales? ¿Cómo te llegarían noticias de tus amigos si no existiera el correo electrónico ni las redes sociales en línea? Escribe al menos siete oraciones con **si**. **40 pts.** *Answers will vary.*

5 **Canción** Completa estos versos de una canción de Juan Luis Guerra con el pretérito imperfecto de subjuntivo de los verbos en la forma **nosotros/as**. **¡4 puntos EXTRA!**

❝ Y si aquí, _lucháramos_ (luchar) juntos por la sociedad y _habláramos_ (hablar) menos resolviendo más. ❞

---

3 Teaching Tip
👥↔👥 Have two volunteers role-play the dialogue for the class. Encourage them to ad-lib as they go.

3 Expansion
←👤→ To challenge students, have pairs create a dialogue between **Sergio** and **Marina** after they have watched the political debate. Tell them to use at least four examples of the subjunctive.

Nota cultural The political landscape of many Spanish-speaking countries mirrors that of the U.S. with respect to being dominated by two major political parties. However, many countries have three or more major parties. For example, in Mexico, the three parties that dominate are **PRI (Partido Revolucionario Institucional), PAN (Partido Acción Nacional),** and **PRD (Partido de la Revolución Democrática).**

4 Teaching Tip
👥↔👥 To help students get started, have the class discuss their daily news habits using these questions: **¿Cuáles son tus fuentes** *(sources)* **de información? ¿Generalmente hablas de las noticias con tus amigos?**

4 Expansion
←👤→ Have students tell anecdotes about situations in which the Internet was the only way of finding information (a weather emergency, a flight delay, research for class). Then ask: **¿Qué habrían hecho si no hubiera existido Internet?**

5 Teaching Tip Remind students that the past subjunctive **nosotros/as** form always carries a written accent mark.

Lectura

 NATIONAL communication cultures STANDARDS

Antes de leer

Estrategia
Recognizing chronological order

Recognizing the chronological order of events in a narrative is key to understanding the cause-and-effect relationship between them. When you are able to establish the chronological chain of events, you will easily be able to follow the plot. In order to be more aware of the order of events in a narrative, you may find it helpful to prepare a numbered list of the events as you read.

Examinar el texto

Lee el texto usando las estrategias de lectura que has aprendido.

▸ ¿Ves palabras nuevas o cognados? ¿Cuáles son?

▸ ¿Qué te dice el dibujo sobre el contenido?

▸ ¿Tienes algún conocimiento previo (*prior knowledge*) sobre don Quijote?

▸ ¿Cuál es el propósito (*purpose*) del texto?

▸ ¿De qué trata (*What is … about?*) la lectura?

Ordenar

Lee el texto otra vez para establecer el orden cronológico de los eventos. Luego, ordena estos eventos según la historia.

___3___ Don Quijote lucha contra los molinos de viento pensando que son gigantes.

___5___ Don Quijote y Sancho toman el camino hacia Puerto Lápice.

___2___ Don Quijote y Sancho descubren unos molinos de viento en un campo.

___4___ El primer molino da un mal golpe a don Quijote, a su lanza y a su caballo.

___1___ Don Quijote y Sancho Panza salen de su pueblo en busca de aventuras.

More activities

vhlcentral   Online activities

Don Quijote
y los molinos de viento

Miguel de Cervantes

Fragmento adaptado de
El ingenioso hidalgo don Quijote de la Mancha

Miguel de Cervantes Saavedra, el escritor más universal de la literatura española, nació en Alcalá de Henares en 1547 y murió en Madrid en 1616, tras° haber vivido una vida llena de momentos difíciles, llegando a estar en la cárcel° más de una vez. Su obra, sin embargo, ha disfrutado a través de los siglos de todo el éxito que se merece. Don Quijote representa no sólo la locura° sino también la búsqueda° del ideal. En esta ocasión presentamos el famoso episodio de los molinos de viento°.

Entonces descubrieron treinta o cuarenta molinos de viento que había en aquel campo°. Cuando don Quijote los vio, dijo a su escudero°:
—La fortuna va guiando nuestras cosas mejor de lo que deseamos; porque allí, amigo Sancho Panza, se ven treinta, o pocos más, enormes gigantes con los que pienso hacer batalla y quitarles a todos las vidas, y comenzaremos a ser ricos; que ésta es buena guerra, y es gran servicio de Dios quitar tan malos seres° de la tierra.
—¿Qué gigantes?
—Aquéllos que ves allí —respondió su amo°— de los brazos largos, que algunos normalmente los tienen de casi dos leguas°.

Después de leer

¿Realidad o fantasía?

Indica si las afirmaciones sobre la lectura pertenecen a la realidad o la fantasía.

1. Don Quijote desea matar (*to kill*) a los enemigos.   realidad

2. Su escudero no ve a ningún ser sobrenatural.   realidad

3. El caballero ataca a unas criaturas cobardes y viles.   fantasía

4. Don Quijote no ganó la batalla porque los gigantes fueron transformados en molinos de viento.   fantasía

5. El sabio Frestón transformó los gigantes en molinos de viento.   fantasía

—Mire usted —respondió Sancho— que aquéllos que allí están no son gigantes, sino molinos de viento, y lo que parecen brazos son las aspas°, que movidas por el viento, hacen andar la piedra del molino.

—Bien veo —respondió don Quijote— que no estás acostumbrado a las aventuras: ellos son gigantes; y si tienes miedo, quítate de ahí y reza° mientras yo voy a combatir con ellos en fiera° batalla.

Y diciendo esto, dio de espuelas° a su caballo Rocinante, sin oír las voces que su escudero Sancho le daba, diciéndole que, sin duda alguna, eran molinos de viento, y no gigantes, aquéllos que iba a atacar. Pero él iba tan convencido de que eran gigantes, que ni oía las voces de su escudero Sancho, ni se daba cuenta, aunque estaba ya muy cerca, de lo que eran; antes iba diciendo en voz alta:

—No huyáis°, cobardes° y viles criaturas, que sólo os ataca un caballero°.

Se levantó entonces un poco de viento, y las grandes aspas comenzaron a moverse, y cuando don Quijote vio esto, dijo:

—Pues aunque mováis más brazos que los del gigante Briareo, me lo vais a pagar.

Y diciendo esto, y encomendándose de todo corazón° a su señora Dulcinea, pidiéndole que le ayudase en esta difícil situación, bien cubierto de su rodela°, con la lanza en posición de ataque, fue a todo el galope de Rocinante y embistió° el primer molino que estaba delante: y dándole con la lanza en el aspa, el viento la giró con tanta furia, que la rompió en pequeños fragmentos, llevándose con ella al caballo y al caballero, que fue dando vueltas por el campo. Fue rápidamente Sancho Panza a ayudarle, todo lo rápido que podía correr su asno°, y cuando llegó encontró que no se podía mover: tan grande fue el golpe° que se dio con Rocinante.

—¡Por Dios! —dijo Sancho—. ¿No le dije yo que mirase bien lo que hacía, que sólo eran molinos de viento, y la única persona que podía equivocarse era alguien que tuviese otros molinos en la cabeza?

—Calla°, amigo Sancho —respondió don Quijote—, que las cosas de la guerra, más que otras, cambian continuamente; estoy pensando que aquel sabio° Frestón, que me robó el estudio y los libros, ha convertido estos gigantes en molinos por quitarme la gloria de su vencimiento°: tan grande es la enemistad que me tiene; pero al final, sus malas artes no van a poder nada contra la bondad de mi espada°.

—Dios lo haga como pueda —respondió Sancho Panza.

Y ayudándole a levantarse, volvió a subir sobre Rocinante, que medio despaldado estaba°. Y hablando de la pasada aventura, siguieron el camino del Puerto Lápice.

tras *after* **cárcel** *jail* **locura** *insanity* **búsqueda** *search* **molinos de viento** *windmills* **campo** *field* **escudero** *squire* **seres** *beings* **amo** *master* **leguas** *leagues (measure of distance)* **aspas** *sails* **reza** *pray* **fiera** *vicious* **dio de espuelas** *he spurred* **No huyáis** *Do not flee* **cobardes** *cowards* **caballero** *knight* **encomendándose de todo corazón** *entrusting himself with all his heart* **rodela** *round shield* **embistió** *charged* **asno** *donkey* **golpe** *blow (knock into)* **Calla** *Be quiet* **sabio** *magician* **vencimiento** *defeat* **espada** *sword* **que medio despaldado estaba** *whose back was half-broken*

Personajes   Answers will vary.

1. En este fragmento se mencionan estos personajes. ¿Quiénes son?
   - don Quijote
   - Rocinante
   - Dulcinea
   - Sancho Panza
   - los gigantes
   - Frestón

2. ¿Qué puedes deducir de los personajes según la información que se da en este episodio?

3. ¿Quiénes son los personajes principales?

4. ¿Cuáles son las diferencias entre don Quijote y Sancho Panza? ¿Qué tienen en común?

¿Un loco o un héroe?

En un párrafo escribe tu opinión sobre el personaje de don Quijote, basándote en la aventura de los molinos de viento. Ten en cuenta las acciones, los motivos y los sentimientos de don Quijote en su batalla contra los molinos de viento.   Answers will vary.

Una entrevista

Trabajen en grupos de tres para preparar una entrevista sobre los acontecimientos de este fragmento de la novela de Cervantes. Un(a) estudiante representará el papel del/de la entrevistador(a) y los otros dos asumirán los papeles de don Quijote y de Sancho Panza, quienes comentarán el episodio desde su punto de vista.
Answers will vary.

Escritura

Estrategia
Writing strong introductions and conclusions

Introductions and conclusions serve a similar purpose: both are intended to focus the reader's attention on the topic being covered. The introduction presents a brief preview of the topic. In addition, it informs your reader of the important points that will be covered in the body of your writing. The conclusion reaffirms those points and concisely sums up the information that has been provided. A compelling fact or statistic, a humorous anecdote, or a question directed to the reader are all interesting ways to begin or end your writing.

For example, if you were writing a biographical report on Miguel de Cervantes, you might begin your essay with the fact that his most famous work, *Don Quijote de la Mancha*, is the second most widely published book ever. The rest of your introductory paragraph would outline the areas you would cover in the body of your paper, such as Cervantes' life, his works, and the impact of *Don Quijote* on world literature. In your conclusion, you would sum up the most important information in the report and tie this information together in a way that would make your reader want to learn even more about the topic. You could write, for example: "Cervantes, with his wit and profound understanding of human nature, is without peer in the history of world literature."

Introducciones y conclusiones

Trabajen en parejas para escribir una oración de introducción y otra de conclusión sobre estos temas.

1. el episodio de los molinos de viento de *Don Quijote de la Mancha*
2. la definición de la locura
3. la realidad y la fantasía en la literatura

Tema

🔗 **Escribir una composición**

Si tuvieras la oportunidad, ¿qué harías para mejorar el mundo? Escribe una composición sobre los cambios que harías en el mundo si tuvieras el poder° y los recursos necesarios. Piensa en lo que puedes hacer ahora y en lo que podrás hacer en el futuro. Considera estas preguntas:

▶ ¿Pondrías fin a todas las guerras? ¿Cómo?

▶ ¿Protegerías el medio ambiente? ¿Cómo?

▶ ¿Promoverías° la igualdad y eliminarías el sexismo y el racismo? ¿Cómo?

▶ ¿Eliminarías la corrupción en la política? ¿Cómo?

▶ ¿Eliminarías la escasez de viviendas° y el hambre?

▶ ¿Educarías a los demás sobre el SIDA? ¿Cómo?

▶ ¿Promoverías el fin de la violencia entre seres humanos?

▶ ¿Promoverías tu causa en los medios de comunicación? ¿Cómo?

▶ ¿Te dedicarías a alguna causa específica dentro de tu comunidad? ¿Cuál?

▶ ¿Te dedicarías a solucionar problemas nacionales o internacionales? ¿Cuáles?

poder *power* Promoverías *Would you promote* escasez de viviendas *homelessness*

EVALUATION: Composición

Criteria	Scale				
Content	1	2	3	4	5
Use of vocabulary	1	2	3	4	5
Grammatical accuracy	1	2	3	4	5
Use of introductions/conclusions	1	2	3	4	5

Scoring	
Excellent	18–20 points
Good	14–17 points
Satisfactory	10–13 points
Unsatisfactory	< 10 points

Escuchar
Antes de escuchar

Estrategia
**Recognizing genre/
Taking notes as you listen**

If you know the genre or type of discourse you are going to encounter, you can use your background knowledge to write down a few notes about what you expect to hear. You can then make additions and changes to your notes as you listen.

To practice these strategies, you will now listen to a short toothpaste commercial. Before listening to the commercial, write down the information you expect it to contain. Then update your notes as you listen.

Preparación

Basándote en la foto, anticipa lo que vas a escuchar en el siguiente fragmento. Haz una lista y anota los diferentes tipos de información que crees que vas a oír. Answers will vary.

Ahora escucha

Noticiero

Revisa la lista que hiciste para **Preparación.** Luego escucha el noticiero presentado por Sonia Hernández. Mientras escuchas, apunta los tipos de información que anticipaste y los que no anticipaste.

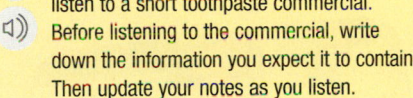

| Tipos de información que anticipaste |
1. Answers will vary.
2. _____
3. _____

| Tipos de información que no anticipaste |
1. Answers will vary.
2. _____
3. _____

Comprensión

Preguntas

1. ¿Dónde está Sonia Hernández?
   Está en una estación de televisión en Montevideo, Uruguay.

2. ¿Quién es Jaime Pantufla?
   Es un candidato presidencial.

3. ¿Dónde hubo una tormenta?
   Hubo una tormenta en las Filipinas.

4. ¿Qué tipo de música toca el grupo Dictadura de Metal?
   Toca música rock.

5. ¿Qué tipo de artista es Ugo Nespolo?
   Es un pintor.

6. Además de lo que Sonia menciona, ¿de qué piensas que va a hablar en la próxima sección del programa?
   Answers will vary.

Ahora ustedes

En parejas, usen la presentación de Sonia Hernández como modelo para escribir un breve noticiero para la comunidad donde viven. Incluyan noticias locales, nacionales e internacionales. Luego compartan el papel de locutor(a) y presenten el noticiero a la clase. Pueden grabar el noticiero si quieren. Answers will vary.

más de 17 centímetros de lluvia sobre las Filipinas ha causado desastrosas inundaciones. Reportan que aproximadamente 12.000 personas han perdido sus casas y sus bienes. Las inundaciones también han traído gran peligro de enfermedades. Seguimos con los más importantes acontecimientos de arte y cultura. Pasado mañana, el conocido grupo de rock, Dictadura de Metal, presentará un concierto en el estacionamiento del Centro Comercial Portones en Montevideo. Hoy comienza la nueva exposición de las obras del pintor Ugo Nespolo en el Museo Nacional de Artes Visuales de Montevideo. Regresamos después de unas breves noticias con el pronóstico del tiempo de Montevideo y sus alrededores.

(Script continues at far left in the bottom panels.)

En pantalla

🔄 Video

Este anuncio corresponde a la campaña para las elecciones de consejeros regionales de Chile para el período 2014 a 2018. Estas elecciones se realizaron° en noviembre de 2013, junto a las elecciones presidenciales y parlamentarias. Por primera vez en la historia de Chile, los ciudadanos pudieron elegir a sus consejeros regionales. Anteriormente, los consejeros eran elegidos por los concejales° de cada región. Los consejeros regionales componen° el Consejo Regional y desempeñan° funciones regionales, como aprobar reglamentos° y planes de desarrollo° urbano y metropolitano.

Vocabulario útil

avanza	*advances*
consejeros	*ministers*
crecer	*to grow*
voz	*voice*

Preparación

¿Votas? ¿Participas en política? ¿Crees que es necesario votar? ¿Por qué?

🔄 Preguntas

Contesta las preguntas. Answers will vary.
1. Según la campaña, ¿por qué es tan importante el voto de los ciudadanos?
2. ¿Crees que el voto de un individuo puede mejorar la calidad de vida de sus vecinos? ¿Por qué?
3. ¿A quién pueden elegir los ciudadanos por primera vez en estas elecciones? ¿Qué importancia crees que tiene este cambio?
4. ¿Cuál piensas que es el objetivo de las imágenes que se muestran de trasfondo (*background*)?
5. ¿Crees que esta campaña es efectiva? ¿Por qué?

🔄 Campaña electoral

En grupos de tres, escriban el guión de una campaña electoral para la televisión. Utilicen el subjuntivo y oraciones con **si**. Luego, representen su anuncio para la clase. La clase votará por la mejor campaña electoral. Answers will vary.

> **modelo**
> Si quieres que los precios de las viviendas bajen, vota por nuestro partido...

se **realizaron** *took place* **concejales** *councillors* **componen** *make up*
desempeñan *carry out* **reglamentos** *regulations* **desarrollo** *development*

Anuncio sobre elecciones chilenas

Tu voto puede mejorar la calidad de vida de tus vecinos.

Tu voto es tu voz.

No dejes que otros decidan por ti.

vhlcentral / Online activities
More activities

Video

Puerto Rico: ¿nación o estado?

En los años veinte, menos de 5.000 puertorriqueños vivían en Nueva York. Ahora hay un millón. Además de Nueva York, ciudades como Chicago, Philadelphia, Newark y Providence tienen grandes comunidades puertorriqueñas. Ahora cinco millones viven en todos los estados, principalmente en el noreste° del país y en el centro de Florida. Los boricuas° en los EE.UU. han creado nuevas manifestaciones de su cultura, como la música salsa en la ciudad de Nueva York y los multitudinarios° desfiles° que se realizan cada año en todo el país, una gran muestra del orgullo° y la identidad de los puertorriqueños.

Vocabulario útil

la estadidad	*statehood*
la patria	*homeland*
las relaciones exteriores	*foreign policy*
la soberanía	*sovereignty*

Preparación

¿Qué sabes de Puerto Rico? ¿Sabes qué territorios estadounidenses tienen un estatus especial? ¿En qué se diferencian de un estado normal? Answers will vary.

¿Cierto o falso?

Indica si las oraciones son **ciertas** o **falsas**.

1. Los puertorriqueños sirven en el ejército de los EE.UU.
   Cierto.
2. Puerto Rico es territorio de los EE.UU., pero el congreso estadounidense no tiene autoridad en la isla.
   Falso. El Congreso de los EE.UU. tiene autoridad en la isla.
3. En Puerto Rico se usa la misma moneda que en los EE.UU.
   Cierto.
4. El comercio de la isla está a cargo del gobernador de Puerto Rico.
   Falso. El comercio está a cargo del gobierno federal de los EE.UU.
5. La mayoría de los puertorriqueños quieren que la isla sea una nación independiente.
   Falso. Muchos también quieren que sea un estado de los EE.UU. o que permanezca como estado libre asociado.

noreste *northeast* boricuas *people from Puerto Rico*
multitudinarios *with mass participation* desfiles *parades* orgullo *pride*

Cuando estás aquí, no sabes si estás en un país latinoamericano o si estás en los EE.UU.

... todo lo relacionado a la defensa, las relaciones exteriores [...] está a cargo del gobierno federal de los EE.UU.

—¿Cuál es su preferencia política?
—Yo quiero la estadidad...

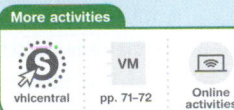

More activities

vhlcentral | VM pp. 71–72 | Online activities

Section Goals

In **Flash cultura**, students will:
- read about the Puerto Rican population in the U.S.
- watch a video about politics in Puerto Rico

Instructional Resources
Supersite: Video (*Flash cultura*); Resources (Scripts, Translations, Answer Keys)
WebSAM
Video Manual

Introduction To check comprehension, give students these true/false statements: **1. La población puertorriqueña en los EE.UU. se concentra en las áreas metropolitanas del país.** (Cierto.) **2. Hace aproximadamente 100 años, vivían más puertorriqueños en los EE.UU. que ahora.** (Falso. Antes había 5.000 en Nueva York y ahora hay un millón.) **3. Menos de un cuarto de los puertorriqueños en los EE.UU. viven en la ciudad de Nueva York.** (Cierto.) **4. Los puertorriqueños también se conocen como *multitudinarios*.** (Falso. También se conocen como *boricuas*.) **5. La influencia puertorriqueña en Nueva York se nota en la música.** (Cierto.)

Antes de ver
- Read through the **Vocabulario útil** and model pronunciation.
- Assure students that they do not need to understand every Spanish word they hear in the video. Tell them to rely on visual cues and to listen for cognates and words from **Vocabulario útil**.

Preparación Have volunteers define these words: *commonwealth*, *territory*, *state*, and *associated state*. Have the class give an example of each term.

¿Cierto o falso? Before students watch the video, have them read through the statements and predict the answers.

TEACHING OPTIONS

Large Groups Divide the class into three groups to stage a debate about the status of Puerto Rico's statehood. Each group should select a different viewpoint to research (pro-statehood, pro-commonwealth, or pro-independence) as homework and then present their position during the debate in class.
Worth Noting Puerto Ricans living on the island do not have legislative power over issues controlled by the federal government, such as citizenship, currency, and foreign affairs. Despite the plebiscites that have attempted to resolve the island's political status, no changes have been made. The pro-statehood party, **Partido Nuevo Progresista (PNP)** and the pro-commonwealth party, **Partido Popular Democrático (PPD)** enjoy equal levels of support. The pro-independence party, **Partido Independentista Puertorriqueño (PIP)**, typically gets few electoral votes.

Paraguay

NATIONAL connections cultures STANDARDS

El país en cifras

▶ **Área:** 406.750 km² (157.046 millas²), *el tamaño° de California*

▶ **Población:** 6.944.000

▶ **Capital:** Asunción—2.356.000

▶ **Ciudades principales:** Ciudad del Este, San Lorenzo, Lambaré, Fernando de la Mora

▶ **Moneda:** guaraní

▶ **Idiomas:** español (oficial), guaraní (oficial)
Las tribus indígenas que habitaban la zona antes de la llegada de los españoles hablaban guaraní. Ahora el 90% de los paraguayos habla esta lengua, que se usa con frecuencia en canciones, poemas, periódicos y libros. Varios institutos y asociaciones, como el Teatro Guaraní, se dedican a preservar la cultura y la lengua guaraníes.

Bandera de Paraguay

Paraguayos célebres

▶ **Agustín Barrios,** guitarrista y compositor (1885–1944)
▶ **Josefina Plá,** escritora y ceramista (1903–1999)
▶ **Augusto Roa Bastos,** escritor (1917–2005)
▶ **Olga Blinder,** pintora (1921–2008)
▶ **Berta Rojas,** guitarrista (1966–)

tamaño *size*

BOLIVIA

ESTADOS UNIDOS
OCÉANO PACÍFICO
OCÉANO ATLÁNTICO
AMÉRICA DEL SUR
PARAGUAY

BRASIL

Mujeres guaraníes

Río Verde
Río Negro
Río Paraguay
Concepción
Río Paraná

ARGENTINA

Asunción
Fernando de la Mora
Ciudad del Este
San Lorenzo
Lambaré
Río Iguazú
Cordillera de Caaguazú
Río Tebicuary
Río Paraná

Palacio de Gobierno en Asunción

More activities
vhlcentral   WB p. 209   Online activities

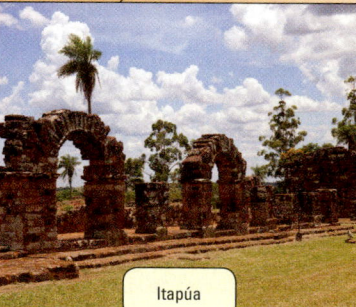
Itapúa

ACTIVIDADES

1 **¿Cierto o falso?** Indica si lo que dicen las oraciones es **cierto** o **falso**.

1. La capital de Paraguay se llama Asunción.   cierto
2. El guaraní es una lengua hablada sólo por las tribus indígenas de Paraguay.   falso
3. Josefina Plá fue una conocida escritora y ceramista paraguaya.   cierto
4. Augusto Roa Bastos fue un locutor paraguayo.   falso
5. El ñandutí es un tipo de encaje hecho a mano.   cierto
6. Itaipú se encuentra en la frontera entre Paraguay y Uruguay.   falso
7. La construcción de la represa Itaipú duró ocho años.   cierto
8. El Gran Chaco queda completamente en Paraguay.   falso
9. En Paraguay es una obligación participar en las elecciones.   cierto
10. Los ciudadanos de Paraguay tienen que pagar una multa al gobierno si no van a votar.   cierto

Artesanía • El ñandutí

La artesanía más famosa de Paraguay se llama ñandutí y es un encaje° hecho a mano originario de Itauguá. En guaraní, la palabra *ñandutí* significa telaraña°; esta pieza recibe ese nombre porque imita el trazado° que crean los arácnidos. Estos encajes suelen ser° blancos, pero también los hay de colores, con formas geométricas o florales.

Ciencias • La represa Itaipú

La represa° Itaipú es una instalación hidroeléctrica que se encuentra en la frontera entre Paraguay y Brasil. Su construcción inició en 1974 y duró ocho años. La cantidad de concreto que se utilizó durante los primeros cinco años de esta obra fue similar a la que se necesita para construir un edificio de 350 pisos. Cien mil trabajadores paraguayos participaron en el proyecto. En 1984 se puso en funcionamiento la Central Hidroeléctrica de Itaipú y, gracias a su cercanía con las famosas cataratas del Iguazú, muchos turistas la visitan diariamente.

Naturaleza • Los ríos Paraguay y Paraná

Los ríos Paraguay y Paraná sirven de frontera natural entre Argentina y Paraguay, y son las principales rutas de transporte de este último país. El Paraná tiene unos 3.200 kilómetros navegables, y por esta ruta pasan barcos de más de 5.000 toneladas, los cuales viajan desde el estuario° del Río de la Plata hasta la ciudad de Asunción. El río Paraguay divide el Gran Chaco de la meseta° Paraná, donde vive la mayoría de los paraguayos.

Geografía • El Gran Chaco

El Gran Chaco es una región geográfica que comparten Argentina, Brasil, Bolivia y Paraguay. Tiene una extensión aproximada de 1.141.000 km² (440.542 millas²), cinco veces mayor que la de Ecuador. El Chaco paraguayo o Región Occidental° representa el 60% del territorio y tan sólo el 2% de la población. A lo largo del territorio hay variaciones térmicas todos los días, aunque las lluvias son constantes en el verano y los meses de invierno son secos.

encaje *lace* telaraña *spiderweb* trazado *outline; design* suelen ser *are usually* represa *dam* estuario *estuary* meseta *plateau* Región Occidental *Western Region*

¡Increíble pero cierto!

¿Te imaginas qué pasaría si el gobierno multara° a los ciudadanos que no van a votar? En Paraguay es una obligación. Ésta es una ley nacional, que otros países también tienen, para obligar a los ciudadanos a participar en las elecciones. En Paraguay los ciudadanos que no van a votar tienen que pagar una multa al gobierno.

multara *fined*

---

 2 ¿Qué aprendiste? Contesta cada pregunta con una oración completa.

1. ¿Quién fue Augusto Roa Bastos?
   Augusto Roa Bastos fue un escritor paraguayo.
2. ¿Cómo se llama la moneda de Paraguay?
   La moneda de Paraguay se llama guaraní.
3. ¿Qué forma imita el ñandutí?
   Imita la forma de una telaraña.
4. ¿Qué países separan los ríos Paraguay y Paraná?
   Los ríos Paraguay y Paraná separan Argentina y Paraguay.

 3 Si yo... En parejas, conversen sobre lo que hacen, harían o habrían hecho si estas situaciones se presentaran durante un viaje a Paraguay. Uno de ustedes debe contradecir lo que dice su compañero/a. Utilicen cláusulas con **si**.

1. si conocieras a Berta Rosas
2. si hubieras navegado por el río Paraná
3. si vas al Gran Chaco
4. si hubieras ido al Teatro Guaraní

TEACHING OPTIONS

Worth Noting Paraguay has eight national parks, encompassing over 11,000 square miles. In addition, there are eight ecological reserves dedicated to the preservation of endangered flora and fauna. The rich diversity of plant and animal life, and the government's commitment to preserving these natural wonders, have made Paraguay a popular destination for ecotourists. The parks cover a wide spectrum of ecology. The **Parque Nacional Defensores del Chaco** and **Parque Nacional Teniente Enciso** are located in the semi-arid Chaco. Other parks, like **Parque Nacional Caaguazú** southeast of Asunción, are covered with subtropical rain forest.

El ñandutí In recent years, the number of traditional **ñandutí** makers has been in serious decline. Many artisans of Itauguá have turned to more profitable sources of income. In an effort to keep this traditional art alive, formal instruction in the skill of making **ñandutí** has been incorporated in the curriculum of local handicraft schools. You may want to play the **Panorama cultural** video for this paragraph.

La represa Itaipú The Itaipú dam project is a joint venture between Brazil and Paraguay, and has been remarkably successful. The plant supplies over 85% of Paraguay's energy and around 15% of the energy consumed in Brazil. You may want to play the **Panorama cultural** video for this paragraph.

Los ríos Paraguay y Paraná The Paraná River was a highway for the settlement of Paraguay. Along its banks, between the sixteenth and late eighteenth centuries, the Jesuits organized their **guaraní**-speaking parishioners into small, self-supporting city-states built around mission settlements, similar to the Franciscan mission system in California during the same period.

El Gran Chaco Cattle ranching has led to significant deforestation in this region.

¡Increíble pero cierto! Like Paraguay, several other Spanish-speaking countries impose fines on citizens for not voting. Ask students to research and name these countries. Ask the class if they think that such a measure should be implemented here to improve voter turnout at the polls.

Uruguay

NATIONAL STANDARDS connections cultures

El país en cifras

▸ **Área:** 176.220 km² (68.039 millas²), *el tamaño° del estado de Washington*

▸ **Población:** 3.360.000

▸ **Capital:** Montevideo—1.707.000

Casi la mitad° de la población de Uruguay vive en Montevideo. Situada en la desembocadura° del famoso Río de la Plata, esta ciudad cosmopolita e intelectual es también un destino popular para las vacaciones, debido a sus numerosas playas de arena° blanca que se extienden hasta la ciudad de Punta del Este.

▸ **Ciudades principales:** Salto, Paysandú, Las Piedras, Rivera

▸ **Moneda:** peso uruguayo

▸ **Idiomas:** español (oficial)

Bandera de Uruguay

Uruguayos célebres

▸ **Horacio Quiroga,** escritor (1878–1937)

▸ **Juana de Ibarbourou,** escritora (1892–1979)

▸ **Mario Benedetti,** escritor (1920–2009)

▸ **Cristina Peri Rossi,** escritora y profesora (1941–)

▸ **Jorge Drexler,** cantante y compositor (1964–)

tamaño *size* mitad *half* desembocadura *mouth* arena *sand*

Gauchos uruguayos

BRASIL

Río Arapey • Salto • Rivera
Río Uruguay
Cuchilla de Haedo
• Paysandú
Embalse del Río Negro
Río Negro
Río Negro
Cuchilla Grande
Río Yí
Laguna Merín
Cuchilla Grande Inferior
Colonia
Las Piedras
Río de la Plata
Montevideo ★
• Punta del Este

Entrada a la Ciudad Vieja, Colonia del Sacramento

ESTADOS UNIDOS
OCÉANO PACÍFICO
OCÉANO ATLÁNTICO
AMÉRICA DEL SUR
URUGUAY

More activities

vhlcentral | WB p. 210 | Online activities

ACTIVIDADES

1 **¿Cierto o falso?** Indica si lo que dicen las oraciones es **cierto** o **falso.**

1. Aproximadamente la mitad de la población de Uruguay vive en Punta del Este. falso

2. La moneda de Uruguay es el peso uruguayo. cierto

3. Mario Benedetti fue un soldado profesional. falso

4. Jorge Drexler es un expresidente de Uruguay. falso

5. Uno de los platos representativos de Uruguay son las pupusas. falso

6. El fútbol es el deporte nacional de los uruguayos. cierto

7. El Carnaval de Montevideo dura 40 días. cierto

8. El candombe es una danza de tradición africana. cierto

9. Juan Carlos Onetti y Eduardo Galeano fueron dramaturgos. falso

10. El ñandú es un animal pequeño pero peligroso. falso

▷ Comida • La carne y el mate

En Uruguay y Argentina, la carne es un elemento esencial de la dieta diaria. Algunos platillos representativos de estas naciones son el asado° y la parrillada°. El mate, una infusión similar al té, también es típico de la región. Esta bebida de origen indígena está muy presente en la vida social y familiar de estos países aunque, curiosamente, no se puede consumir en bares o en restaurantes.

▷ Deportes • El fútbol

El fútbol es el deporte nacional de Uruguay. El primer equipo de balompié uruguayo se formó en 1891 y en 1930 el país suramericano fue la sede° de la primera Copa Mundial de esta disciplina. El equipo nacional ha conseguido grandes éxitos a lo largo de los años: dos campeonatos olímpicos, en 1924 y 1928, y dos campeonatos mundiales, en 1930 y 1950. De hecho, para celebrar el centenario del primer torneo de la historia, Uruguay y Argentina presentaron su candidatura para ser los países anfitriones de la Copa Mundial de Fútbol de 2030. En 2017, Paraguay lanzó su propuesta para unirse a esta celebración.

Costumbres • El Carnaval

El Carnaval de Montevideo es el de mayor duración en el mundo. A lo largo de 40 días, los uruguayos disfrutan de los desfiles° y de la música que inundan las calles de su capital. La celebración más conocida es el Desfile de Llamadas, en el que participan bailarines al ritmo del candombe, una danza de tradición africana.

Literatura • Escritores

A pesar de ser el segundo país más pequeño de Latinoamérica, Uruguay ha sido cuna° de importantes escritores: Horacio Quiroga (1878–1937), Juana de Ibarbourou (1892–1979), Felisberto Hernández (1902–1964), Juan Carlos Onetti (1909–1994), Mario Benedetti (1920–2009), Eduardo Galeano (1940–2015) y Cristina Peri Rossi (1941–) han inspirado a muchos autores en el mundo. Estos escritores se han destacado en géneros literarios como la novela, el cuento, la poesía y el ensayo.

asado *barbecued beef*   **parrillada** *grilled meats*   **sede** *site*   **desfiles** *parades*   **cuna** *cradle*

¡Increíble pero cierto!

En Uruguay hay muchos animales curiosos, entre ellos el ñandú. De la misma familia del avestruz°, el ñandú es el ave no voladora° más grande del hemisferio occidental. Puede llegar a medir° dos metros. Normalmente, va en grupos de veinte o treinta y vive en el campo. Es muy cotizado° por su carne, sus plumas y sus huevos.

avestruz *ostrich*   **no voladora** *flightless*   **medir** *measure*   **cotizado** *valued*

---

2 **¿Qué aprendiste?** Contesta cada pregunta con una oración completa.

1. ¿Cuál es el elemento esencial de la dieta uruguaya?
   La carne es esencial en la dieta uruguaya.
2. ¿Qué es el ñandú?
   El ñandú es un ave no voladora que vive en Uruguay.
3. ¿Cuándo se formó el primer equipo uruguayo de fútbol?
   En 1891 se formó el primer equipo de fútbol uruguayo.
4. ¿Cuándo se celebró la primera Copa Mundial de fútbol?
   La primera Copa Mundial se celebró en 1930.

3 **Costumbres** En parejas, hablen sobre las costumbres uruguayas. Usen un verbo en subjuntivo y otro en infinitivo o en indicativo en cada caso.

> **modelo**
> Dudo que el mate me guste porque no me gusta el té.

Instructional Resources

Supersite: Audio (Textbook & Lab MP3s); Testing Program (Tests, MP3s, Oral Testing Suggestions)
WebSAM
Lab Manual

Teaching Tip You may want to assign the **Prueba de práctica**, with its diagnostics and review activities, in the online-only **Repaso** section on the Supersite. There is also a **Repaso oral** in this section. For the Sixth Edition, a new summative vocabulary activity with speech recognition has been added to the **Repaso** section.

Successful Language Learning Ask students to review all the end-of-lesson vocabulary lists at this time. Tell them to imagine how they would use each lesson's vocabulary in everyday life.

The Affective Dimension Tell students to consider their feelings about speaking Spanish at the beginning of the course and think about how they feel about speaking Spanish now. Tell them that this is a good time to consider their motivations and set new goals as they continue learning the language.

Los medios de comunicación

el acontecimiento	event
las actualidades	news; current events
el artículo	article
el diario	newspaper
el informe	report
el/la locutor(a)	(TV or radio) announcer
los medios de comunicación	media; means of communication
las noticias	news
el noticiero	newscast
la prensa	press
el reportaje	report
anunciar	to announce; to advertise
comunicarse (con)	to communicate (with)
durar	to last
informar	to inform
ocurrir	to occur; to happen
transmitir, emitir	to broadcast
(inter)nacional	(inter)national
peligroso/a	dangerous

Las noticias

el choque	collision
el crimen	crime; murder
el desastre (natural)	(natural) disaster
el desempleo	unemployment
la (des)igualdad	(in)equality
la discriminación	discrimination
el ejército	army
la guerra	war
la huelga	strike
el huracán	hurricane
el incendio	fire
la inundación	flood
la libertad	liberty; freedom
la paz	peace
el racismo	racism
el sexismo	sexism
el SIDA	AIDS
el/la soldado	soldier
el terremoto	earthquake
la tormenta	storm
el tornado	tornado
la violencia	violence

La política

el/la candidato/a	candidate
el/la ciudadano/a	citizen
el deber	responsibility; obligation
los derechos	rights
la dictadura	dictatorship
el discurso	speech
las elecciones	election
la encuesta	poll; survey
el impuesto	tax
la política	politics
el/la representante	representative
declarar	to declare
elegir (e:i)	to elect
luchar (por/contra)	to fight; to struggle (for/against)
obedecer	to obey
votar	to vote
político/a	political

Expresiones útiles	See page 617.

More activities

vhlcentral   LM p. 106

Plan de escritura

1 **Ideas y organización**

Begin by organizing your writing materials. If you prefer to write by hand, you may want to have a few spare pens and pencils on hand, as well as an eraser or correction fluid. If you prefer to use a word-processing program, make sure you know how to type Spanish accent marks, the **tilde**, and Spanish punctuation marks. Then make a list of the resources you can consult while writing. Finally, make a list of the basic ideas you want to cover. Beside each idea, jot down a few Spanish words and phrases you may want to use while writing.

2 **Primer borrador**

Write your first draft, using the resources and ideas you gathered in **Ideas y organización.**

3 **Comentario**

Exchange papers with a classmate and comment on each other's work, using these questions as a guide. Begin by mentioning what you like about your classmate's writing.

a. How can your classmate make his or her writing clearer, more logical, or more organized?

b. What suggestions do you have for making the writing more interesting or complete?

c. Do you see any spelling or grammatical errors?

4 **Redacción**

Revise your first draft, keeping in mind your classmate's comments. Also, incorporate any new information you may have. Before handing in the final version, review your work using these guidelines:

a. Make sure each verb agrees with its subject. Then check the gender and number of each article, noun, and adjective.

b. Check your spelling and punctuation.

c. Consult your **Anotaciones para mejorar la escritura** (see description below) to avoid repetition of previous errors.

5 **Evaluación y progreso**

You may want to share what you've written with a classmate, a small group, or the entire class. After your instructor has returned your paper, review the comments and corrections. On a separate sheet of paper, write the heading **Anotaciones para mejorar** (*Notes for improving*) **la escritura** and list your most common errors. Place this list and your corrected document in your writing portfolio (**Carpeta de trabajos**) and consult it from time to time to gauge your progress.

Spanish Terms for Direction Lines and Classroom Use

Below is a list of useful terms that you might hear your instructor say in class. It also includes Spanish terms that appear in the direction lines of your textbook.

En las instrucciones — *In direction lines*

Cambia/Cambien...	*Change...*
Camina/Caminen por la clase.	*Walk around the classroom.*
Ciertas o falsas	*True or false*
Cierto o falso	*True or false*
Circula/Circulen por la clase.	*Walk around the classroom.*
Completa las oraciones de una manera lógica.	*Complete the sentences logically.*
Con un(a) compañero/a...	*With a classmate...*
Contesta las preguntas.	*Answer the questions.*
Corrige las oraciones falsas.	*Correct the false statements.*
Cuenta/Cuenten...	*Tell...*
Di/Digan...	*Say...*
Discute/Discutan...	*Discuss...*
En grupos...	*In groups...*
En parejas...	*In pairs...*
Entrevista...	*Interview...*
Escúchala	*Listen to it*
Forma oraciones completas.	*Create/Make complete sentences.*
Háganse preguntas.	*Ask each other questions.*
Haz el papel de...	*Play the role of...*
Haz los cambios necesarios.	*Make the necessary changes.*
Indica/Indiquen si las oraciones...	*Indicate if the sentences...*
Intercambia/Intercambien...	*Exchange...*
Lee/Lean en voz alta.	*Read aloud.*
Pon/Pongan...	*Put...*
... que mejor completa...	*...that best completes...*
Reúnete...	*Get together...*
... se da/dan como ejemplo.	*...is/are given as a model.*
Toma nota...	*Take note...*
Tomen apuntes.	*Take notes.*
Túrnense...	*Take turns...*

Palabras útiles — *Useful words*

la adivinanza	*riddle*
el anuncio	*advertisement/ad*
los apuntes	*notes*
el borrador	*draft*
la canción	*song*
la concordancia	*agreement*
el contenido	*contents*
el cortometraje	*short film*
eficaz	*efficient; effective*
la encuesta	*survey*
el equipo	*team*
el esquema	*outline*
el folleto	*brochure*
las frases	*phrases*
la hoja de actividades	*activity sheet/handout*
la hoja de papel	*piece of paper*
la información errónea	*incorrect information*
el/la lector(a)	*reader*
la lectura	*reading*
las oraciones	*sentences*
la ortografía	*spelling*
el papel	*role*
el párrafo	*paragraph*
el paso	*step*
la(s) persona(s) descrita(s)	*the person (people) described*
la pista	*clue*
por ejemplo	*for example*
el propósito	*purpose*
los recursos	*resources*
el reportaje	*report*
los resultados	*results*
según	*according to*
siguiente	*following*
la sugerencia	*suggestion*
el sustantivo	*noun*
el tema	*topic*
último	*last*
el último recurso	*last resort*

Verbos útiles   *Useful verbs*

adivinar	*to guess*
anotar	*to jot down*
añadir	*to add*
apoyar	*to support*
averiguar	*to find out*
cambiar	*to change*
combinar	*to combine*
compartir	*to share*
comprobar (o:ue)	*to check*
contestar	*to answer*
corregir (e:i)	*to correct*
crear	*to create*
devolver (o:ue)	*to return*
doblar	*to fold*
dramatizar	*to act out*
elegir (e:i)	*to choose/select*
emparejar	*to match*
entrevistar	*to interview*
escoger	*to choose*
identificar	*to identify*
incluir	*to include*
informar	*to report*
intentar	*to try*
intercambiar	*to exchange*
investigar	*to research*
marcar	*to mark*
preguntar	*to ask*
recordar (o:ue)	*to remember*
responder	*to answer*
revisar	*to revise*
seguir (e:i)	*to follow*
seleccionar	*to select*
subrayar	*to underline*
traducir	*to translate*
tratar de	*to be about*

Expresiones útiles   *Useful expressions*

Ahora mismo.	*Right away.*
¿Cómo no?	*But of course.*
¿Cómo se dice _____ en español?	*How do you say _____ in Spanish?*
¿Cómo se escribe _____?	*How do you spell _____?*
¿Comprende(n)?	*Do you understand?*
Con gusto.	*With pleasure.*
Con permiso.	*Excuse me.*
De acuerdo.	*Okay.*
De nada.	*You're welcome.*
¿De veras?	*Really?*
¿En qué página estamos?	*What page are we on?*
¿En serio?	*Seriously?*
Enseguida.	*Right away.*
hoy día	*nowadays*
Más despacio, por favor.	*Slower, please.*
Muchas gracias.	*Thanks a lot.*
No entiendo.	*I don't understand.*
No hay de qué.	*Don't mention it.*
No importa.	*No problem./It doesn't matter.*
¡No me digas!	*You don't say!*
No sé.	*I don't know.*
¡Ojalá!	*Hopefully!*
Perdone.	*Pardon me.*
Por favor.	*Please.*
Por supuesto.	*Of course.*
¡Qué bien!	*Great!*
¡Qué gracioso!	*How funny!*
¡Qué pena!	*What a shame/pity!*
¿Qué significa _____?	*What does _____ mean?*
Repite, por favor.	*Please repeat.*
Tengo una pregunta.	*I have a question.*
¿Tiene(n) alguna pregunta?	*Do you have any questions?*
Vaya(n) a la página dos.	*Go to page 2.*

Glossary of Grammatical Terms

ADJECTIVE A word that modifies, or describes, a noun or pronoun.

muchos libros
many books

un hombre **rico**
*a **rich** man*

las mujeres **altas**
*the **tall** women*

Demonstrative adjective An adjective that specifies which noun a speaker is referring to.

esta fiesta
***this** party*

ese chico
***that** boy*

aquellas flores
***those** flowers*

Possessive adjective An adjective that indicates ownership or possession.

mi mejor vestido
***my** best dress*

Éste es **mi** hermano.
*This is **my** brother.*

Stressed possessive adjective A possessive adjective that emphasizes the owner or possessor.

Es un libro **mío**.
*It's **my** book./It's a book **of mine**.*

Es amiga **tuya**; yo no la conozco.
*She's a friend **of yours**; I don't know her.*

ADVERB A word that modifies, or describes, a verb, adjective, or other adverb.

Pancho escribe **rápidamente**.
*Pancho writes **quickly**.*

Este cuadro es **muy** bonito.
*This picture is **very** pretty.*

ARTICLE A word that points out a noun in either a specific or a non-specific way.

Definite article An article that points out a noun in a specific way.

el libro
the book

la maleta
the suitcase

los diccionarios
the dictionaries

las palabras
the words

Indefinite article An article that points out a noun in a general, non-specific way.

un lápiz
a pencil

una computadora
a computer

unos pájaros
some birds

unas escuelas
some schools

CLAUSE A group of words that contains both a conjugated verb and a subject, either expressed or implied.

Main (or Independent) clause A clause that can stand alone as a complete sentence.

Pienso ir a cenar pronto.
I plan to go to dinner soon.

Subordinate (or Dependent) clause A clause that does not express a complete thought and therefore cannot stand alone as a sentence.

Trabajo en la cafetería **porque necesito dinero para la escuela**.
*I work in the cafeteria **because I need money for school**.*

COMPARATIVE A construction used with an adjective or adverb to express a comparison between two people, places, or things.

Este programa es **más interesante** que el otro.
*This program is **more interesting than** the other one.*

Tomás no es **tan alto como** Alberto.
*Tomás is not **as tall as** Alberto.*

CONJUGATION A set of the forms of a verb for a specific tense or mood or the process by which these verb forms are presented.

Preterite conjugation of **cantar**:

cant**é**	cant**amos**
cant**aste**	cant**asteis**
cant**ó**	cant**aron**

CONJUNCTION A word used to connect words, clauses, or phrases.

Susana es de Cuba **y** Pedro es de España.
*Susana is from Cuba **and** Pedro is from Spain.*

No quiero estudiar **pero** tengo que hacerlo.
*I don't want to study, **but** I have to.*

CONTRACTION The joining of two words into one. The only contractions in Spanish are **al** and **del**.

Mi hermano fue **al** concierto ayer.
*My brother went **to the** concert yesterday.*

Saqué dinero **del** banco.
*I took money **from the** bank.*

DIRECT OBJECT A noun or pronoun that directly receives the action of the verb.

Tomás lee **el libro.**   **La** pagó ayer.
*Tomás reads **the book**.   She paid **it** yesterday.*

GENDER The grammatical categorizing of certain kinds of words, such as nouns and pronouns, as masculine, feminine, or neuter.

Masculine
articles **el, un**
pronouns **él, lo, mío, éste, ése, aquél**
adjective **simpático**

Feminine
articles **la, una**
pronouns **ella, la, mía, ésta, ésa, aquélla**
adjective **simpática**

IMPERSONAL EXPRESSION A third-person expression with no expressed or specific subject.

Es muy importante.   **Llueve** mucho.
It's very important.   It's raining hard.

Aquí **se habla** español.
*Spanish **is spoken** here.*

INDIRECT OBJECT A noun or pronoun that receives the action of the verb indirectly; the object, often a living being, to or for whom an action is performed.

Eduardo **le** dio un libro **a Linda.**
*Eduardo gave a book **to Linda**.*

La profesora **me** puso una C en el examen.
*The professor gave **me** a C on the test.*

INFINITIVE The basic form of a verb. Infinitives in Spanish end in **-ar, -er,** or **-ir.**

hablar   **correr**   **abrir**
to speak   to run   to open

INTERROGATIVE An adjective, adverb, or pronoun used to ask a question.

¿Quién habla?   **¿Cuántos** compraste?
Who is speaking?   How many did you buy?

¿Qué piensas hacer hoy?
What do you plan to do today?

INVERSION Changing the word order of a sentence, often to form a question.

Statement: Elena pagó la cuenta del restaurante.

Inversion: ¿Pagó Elena la cuenta del restaurante?

MOOD A grammatical distinction of verbs that indicates whether the verb is intended to make a statement or command or to express a doubt, emotion, or condition contrary to fact.

Imperative mood Verb forms used to make commands.

Di la verdad.   **Caminen** ustedes conmigo.
Tell the truth.   Walk with me.

¡Comamos ahora!
Let's eat now!

Indicative mood Verb forms used to state facts, actions, and states considered to be real.

Sé que **tienes** el dinero.
*I know that **you have** the money.*

Subjunctive mood Verb forms used principally in subordinate (dependent) clauses to express wishes, desires, emotions, doubts, and certain conditions, such as contrary-to-fact situations.

Prefieren que **hables** en español.
*They prefer that **you speak** in Spanish.*

Dudo que Luis **tenga** el dinero necesario.
*I doubt that Luis **has** the necessary money.*

NOUN A word that identifies people, animals, places, things, and ideas.

hombre   gato
man   *cat*

México   casa
Mexico   *house*

libertad   libro
freedom   *book*

NUMBER A grammatical term that refers to singular or plural. Nouns in Spanish and English have number. Other parts of a sentence, such as adjectives, articles, and verbs, can also have number.

Singular	Plural
una cosa	**unas** cosas
a thing	*some things*
el profesor	**los** profesores
the professor	*the professors*

NUMBERS Words that represent amounts.

Cardinal numbers Words that show specific amounts.

cinco minutos
five minutes

el año **dos mil veintitrés**
the year 2023

Ordinal numbers Words that indicate the order of a noun in a series.

el **cuarto** jugador	la **décima** hora
the fourth player	*the tenth hour*

PAST PARTICIPLE A past form of the verb used in compound tenses. The past participle may also be used as an adjective, but it must then agree in number and gender with the word it modifies.

Han **buscado** por todas partes.
They have searched everywhere.

Yo no había **estudiado** para el examen.
I hadn't studied for the exam.

Hay una **ventana abierta** en la sala.
There is an open window in the living room.

PERSON The form of the verb or pronoun that indicates the speaker, the one spoken to, or the one spoken about. In Spanish, as in English, there are three persons: first, second, and third.

Person	Singular	Plural
1st	yo *I*	nosotros/as *we*
2nd	tú, Ud. *you*	vosotros/as, Uds. *you*
3rd	él, ella *he, she*	ellos, ellas *they*

PREPOSITION A word or words that describe(s) the relationship, most often in time or space, between two other words.

Anita es **de** California.
Anita is from California.

La chaqueta está **en** el carro.
The jacket is in the car.

Marta se peinó **antes de** salir.
Marta combed her hair before going out.

PRESENT PARTICIPLE In English, a verb form that ends in *-ing*. In Spanish, the present participle ends in **-ndo,** and is often used with **estar** to form a progressive tense.

Mi hermana está **hablando** por teléfono ahora mismo.
My sister is talking on the phone right now.

PRONOUN A word that takes the place of a noun or nouns.

Demonstrative pronoun A pronoun that takes the place of a specific noun.

Quiero **ésta.**
I want this one.

¿Vas a comprar **ése?**
Are you going to buy that one?

Juan prefirió **aquéllos.**
Juan preferred those (over there).

Object pronoun A pronoun that functions as a direct or indirect object of the verb.

Te digo la verdad.
I'm telling you the truth.

Me lo trajo Juan.
Juan brought it to me.

Reflexive pronoun A pronoun that indicates that the action of a verb is performed by the subject on itself. These pronouns are often expressed in English with *-self: myself, yourself,* etc.

Yo **me** bañé antes de salir.
I bathed (myself) before going out.

Elena **se** acostó a las once y media.
Elena went to bed at eleven-thirty.

Relative pronoun A pronoun that connects a subordinate clause to a main clause.

El chico **que** nos escribió viene de visita mañana.
*The boy **who** wrote us is coming to visit tomorrow.*

Ya sé **lo que** tenemos que hacer.
*I already know **what** we have to do.*

Subject pronoun A pronoun that replaces the name or title of a person or thing, and acts as the subject of a verb.

Tú debes estudiar más.
***You** should study more.*

Él llegó primero.
***He** arrived first.*

SUBJECT A noun or pronoun that performs the action of a verb and is often implied by the verb.

María va al supermercado.
***María** goes to the supermarket.*

(Ellos) Trabajan mucho.
***They** work hard.*

Esos **libros** son muy caros.
*Those **books** are very expensive.*

SUPERLATIVE A word or construction used with an adjective or adverb to express the highest or lowest degree of a specific quality among three or more people, places, or things.

De todas mis clases, ésta es la **más interesante**.
*Of all my classes, this is the **most interesting**.*

Raúl es el **menos simpático** de los chicos.
*Raúl is the **least likeable** of the boys.*

TENSE A set of verb forms that indicates the time of an action or state: past, present, or future.

Compound tense A two-word tense made up of an auxiliary verb and a present or past participle. In Spanish, **estar** and **haber** are auxiliary verbs.

En este momento, **estoy estudiando**.
*At this time, **I am studying**.*

El paquete no **ha llegado** todavía.
*The package **has not arrived** yet.*

Simple tense A tense expressed by a single verb form.

María **estaba** enferma anoche.
*María **was** sick last night.*

Juana **hablará** con su mamá mañana.
*Juana **will speak** with her mom tomorrow.*

VERB A word that expresses actions or states of being.

Auxiliary verb A verb used with a present or past participle to form a compound tense. **Haber** is the most commonly used auxiliary verb in Spanish.

Los chicos **han** visto los elefantes.
*The children **have** seen the elephants.*

Espero que **hayas** comido.
*I hope you **have** eaten.*

Reflexive verb A verb that describes an action performed by the subject on itself and is always used with a reflexive pronoun.

Me compré un carro nuevo.
*I **bought myself** a new car.*

Pedro y Adela **se levantan** muy temprano.
*Pedro and Adela **get (themselves) up** very early.*

Spelling change verb A verb that undergoes a predictable change in spelling, in order to reflect its actual pronunciation in the various conjugations.

practicar	c→qu	practico	practiqué
dirigir	g→j	dirigí	dirijo
almorzar	z→c	almorzó	almorcé

Stem-changing verb A verb whose stem vowel undergoes one or more predictable changes in the various conjugations.

entender (e:ie)	entiendo
pedir (e:i)	piden
dormir (o:ue, u)	duermo, durmieron

Verb Conjugation Tables

The verb lists

The list of verbs below and the model-verb tables that start on page A-11 show you how to conjugate the verbs taught in **Vistas**. Each verb in the list is followed by a model verb conjugated according to the same pattern. The number in parentheses indicates where in the verb tables you can find the conjugated forms of the model verb. If you want to find out how to conjugate **divertirse**, for example, look up number 33, **sentir**, the model for verbs that follow the **e:ie** stem-change pattern.

How to use the verb tables

In the tables you will find the infinitive, present and past participles, and all the simple forms of each model verb. The formation of the compound tenses of any verb can be inferred from the table of compound tenses, pages A-11–12, either by combining the past participle of the verb with a conjugated form of **haber** or by combining the present participle with a conjugated form of **estar**.

abrazar (z:c) like cruzar (37)
abrir like vivir (3) *except* past participle is abierto
aburrir(se) like vivir (3)
acabar like hablar (1)
acampar like hablar (1)
acompañar like hablar (1)
aconsejar like hablar (1)
acordarse (o:ue) like contar (24)
acostarse (o:ue) like contar (24)
adelgazar (z:c) like cruzar (37)
afeitarse like hablar (1)
ahorrar like hablar (1)
alegrarse like hablar (1)
aliviar like hablar (1)
almorzar (o:ue) like contar (24) *except* (z:c)
alquilar like hablar (1)
andar like hablar (1) *except* preterite stem is anduv-
anunciar like hablar (1)
apagar (g:gu) like llegar (41)
aplaudir like vivir (3)
apreciar like hablar (1)
aprender like comer (2)
apurarse like hablar (1)
arrancar (c:qu) like tocar (44)
arreglar like hablar (1)
asistir like vivir (3)

aumentar like hablar (1)
ayudar(se) like hablar (1)
bailar like hablar (1)
bajar(se) like hablar (1)
bañarse like hablar (1)
barrer like comer (2)
beber like comer (2)
besar(se) like hablar (1)
borrar like hablar (1)
brindar like hablar (1)
bucear like hablar (1)
buscar (c:qu) like tocar (44)
caber (4)
caer(se) (5)
calentarse (e:ie) like pensar (30)
calzar (z:c) like cruzar (37)
cambiar like hablar (1)
caminar like hablar (1)
cantar like hablar (1)
cargar like llegar (41)
casarse like hablar (1)
cazar (z:c) like cruzar (37)
celebrar like hablar (1)
cenar like hablar (1)
cepillarse like hablar (1)
cerrar (e:ie) like pensar (30)
chatear like hablar (1)
cobrar like hablar (1)
cocinar like hablar (1)
comenzar (e:ie) (z:c) like empezar (26)
comer (2)

compartir like vivir (3)
comprar like hablar (1)
comprender like comer (2)
comprometerse like comer (2)
comunicarse (c:qu) like tocar (44)
conducir (c:zc) (6)
conectar(se) like hablar (1)
confirmar like hablar (1)
conocer (c:zc) (35)
conseguir (e:i) (g:gu) like seguir (32)
conservar like hablar (1)
consumir like vivir (3)
contaminar like hablar (1)
contar (o:ue) (24)
contestar like hablar (1)
contratar like hablar (1)
controlar like hablar (1)
conversar like hablar (1)
correr like comer (2)
costar (o:ue) like contar (24)
creer (y) (36)
cruzar (z:c) (37)
cuidar like hablar (1)
dañar like hablar (1)
dar (7)
deber like comer (2)
decidir like vivir (3)
decir (e:i) (8)

declarar like hablar (1)
dejar like hablar (1)
depositar like hablar (1)
desarrollar like hablar (1)
desayunar like hablar (1)
descansar like hablar (1)
descargar like llegar (41)
describir like vivir (3) *except* past participle is descrito
descubrir like vivir (3) *except* past participle is descubierto
desear like hablar (1)
despedir(se) (e:i) like pedir (29)
despertarse (e:ie) like pensar (30)
destruir (y) (38)
dibujar like hablar (1)
dirigir (g:j) like vivir (3) *except* (g:j)
disfrutar like hablar (1)
divertirse (e:ie) like sentir (33)
divorciarse like hablar (1)
doblar like hablar (1)
doler (o:ue) like volver (34) *except* past participle is regular
dormir(se) (o:ue) (25)
ducharse like hablar (1)
dudar like hablar (1)
durar like hablar (1)
echar like hablar (1)

elegir (e:i) like pedir (29) *except* (g:j)

emitir like vivir (3)

empezar (e:ie) (z:c) (26)

enamorarse like hablar (1)

encantar like hablar (1)

encontrar(se) (o:ue) like contar (24)

enfermarse like hablar (1)

engordar like hablar (1)

enojarse like hablar (1)

enseñar like hablar (1)

ensuciar like hablar (1)

entender (e:ie) (27)

entrenarse like hablar (1)

entrevistar like hablar (1)

enviar (envío) (39)

escalar like hablar (1)

escanear like hablar (1)

escoger (g:j) like proteger (43)

escribir like vivir (3) *except* past participle is **escrito**

escuchar like hablar (1)

esculpir like vivir (3)

esperar like hablar (1)

esquiar (esquío) like enviar (39)

establecer (c:zc) like conocer (35)

estacionar like hablar (1)

estar (9)

estornudar like hablar (1)

estudiar like hablar (1)

evitar like hablar (1)

explicar (c:qu) like tocar (44)

faltar like hablar (1)

fascinar like hablar (1)

firmar like hablar (1)

fumar like hablar (1)

funcionar like hablar (1)

ganar like hablar (1)

gastar like hablar (1)

grabar like hablar (1)

graduarse (gradúo) (40)

guardar like hablar (1)

gustar like hablar (1)

haber (hay) (10)

hablar (1)

hacer (11)

importar like hablar (1)

imprimir like vivir (3)

indicar (c:qu) like tocar (44)

informar like hablar (1)

insistir like vivir (3)

interesar like hablar (1)

invertir (e:ie) like sentir (33)

invitar like hablar (1)

ir(se) (12)

jubilarse like hablar (1)

jugar (u:ue) (g:gu) (28)

lastimarse like hablar (1)

lavar(se) like hablar (1)

leer (y) like creer (36)

levantar(se) like hablar (1)

limpiar like hablar (1)

llamar(se) like hablar (1)

llegar (g:gu) (41)

llenar like hablar (1)

llevar(se) like hablar (1)

llover (o:ue) like volver (34) *except* past participle is regular

luchar like hablar (1)

mandar like hablar (1)

manejar like hablar (1)

mantener(se) (e:ie) like tener (20)

maquillarse like hablar (1)

mejorar like hablar (1)

merendar (e:ie) like pensar (30)

mirar like hablar (1)

molestar like hablar (1)

montar like hablar (1)

morir (o:ue) like dormir (25) *except* past participle is **muerto**

mostrar (o:ue) like contar (24)

mudarse like hablar (1)

nacer (c:zc) like conocer (35)

nadar like hablar (1)

necesitar like hablar (1)

negar (e:ie) like pensar (30) *except* (g:gu)

nevar (e:ie) like pensar (30)

obedecer (c:zc) like conocer (35)

obtener (e:ie) like tener (20)

ocurrir like vivir (3)

odiar like hablar (1)

ofrecer (c:zc) like conocer (35)

oír (13)

olvidar like hablar (1)

pagar (g:gu) like llegar (41)

parar like hablar (1)

parecer (c:zc) like conocer (35)

pasar like hablar (1)

pasear like hablar (1)

patinar like hablar (1)

pedir (e:i) (29)

peinarse like hablar (1)

pensar (e:ie) (30)

perder (e:ie) like entender (27)

pescar (c:qu) like tocar (44)

pintar like hablar (1)

planchar like hablar (1)

poder (o:ue) (14)

poner(se) (15)

practicar (c:qu) like tocar (44)

preferir (e:ie) like sentir (33)

preguntar like hablar (1)

prender like comer (2)

preocuparse like hablar (1)

preparar like hablar (1)

presentar like hablar (1)

prestar like hablar (1)

probar(se) (o:ue) like contar (24)

prohibir (prohíbo) (42)

proteger (g:j) (43)

publicar (c:qu) like tocar (44)

quedar(se) like hablar (1)

querer (e:ie) (16)

quitar(se) like hablar (1)

recetar like hablar (1)

recibir like vivir (3)

reciclar like hablar (1)

recoger (g:j) like proteger (43)

recomendar (e:ie) like pensar (30)

recordar (o:ue) like contar (24)

reducir (c:zc) like conducir (6)

regalar like hablar (1)

regatear like hablar (1)

regresar like hablar (1)

reír(se) (e:i) (31)

relajarse like hablar (1)

renunciar like hablar (1)

repetir (e:i) like pedir (29)

resolver (o:ue) like volver (34)

respirar like hablar (1)

revisar like hablar (1)

rogar (o:ue) like contar (24) *except* (g:gu)

romper(se) like comer (2) *except* past participle is **roto**

saber (17)

sacar (c:qu) like tocar (44)

sacudir like vivir (3)

salir (18)

saludar(se) like hablar (1)

secar(se) (c:qu) like tocar (44)

seguir (e:i) (32)

sentarse (e:ie) like pensar (30)

sentir(se) (e:ie) (33)

separarse like hablar (1)

ser (19)

servir (e:i) like pedir (29)

solicitar like hablar (1)

sonar (o:ue) like contar (24)

sonreír (e:i) like reír(se) (31)

sorprender like comer (2)

subir like vivir (3)

sudar like hablar (1)

sufrir like vivir (3)

sugerir (e:ie) like sentir (33)

suponer like poner (15)

temer like comer (2)

tener (e:ie) (20)

terminar like hablar (1)

textear like hablar (1)

tocar (c:qu) (44)

tomar like hablar (1)

torcerse (o:ue) like volver (34) *except* (c:z) and past participle is regular; e.g., **yo tuerzo**

toser like comer (2)

trabajar like hablar (1)

traducir (c:zc) like conducir (6)

traer (21)

transmitir like vivir (3)

tratar like hablar (1)

usar like hablar (1)

vender like comer (2)

venir (e:ie) (22)

ver (23)

vestirse (e:i) like pedir (29)

viajar like hablar (1)

visitar like hablar (1)

vivir (3)

volver (o:ue) (34)

votar like hablar (1)

Regular verbs: simple tenses

Infinitive	INDICATIVE					SUBJUNCTIVE		IMPERATIVE
	Present	Imperfect	Preterite	Future	Conditional	Present	Past	
1 hablar	hablo	hablaba	hablé	hablaré	hablaría	hable	hablara	
Participles:	hablas	hablabas	hablaste	hablarás	hablarías	hables	hablaras	habla tú (no hables)
hablando	habla	hablaba	habló	hablará	hablaría	hable	hablara	hable Ud.
hablado	hablamos	hablábamos	hablamos	hablaremos	hablaríamos	hablemos	habláramos	hablemos
	habláis	hablabais	hablasteis	hablaréis	hablaríais	habléis	hablarais	hablad (no habléis)
	hablan	hablaban	hablaron	hablarán	hablarían	hablen	hablaran	hablen Uds.
2 comer	como	comía	comí	comeré	comería	coma	comiera	
Participles:	comes	comías	comiste	comerás	comerías	comas	comieras	come tú (no comas)
comiendo	come	comía	comió	comerá	comería	coma	comiera	coma Ud.
comido	comemos	comíamos	comimos	comeremos	comeríamos	comamos	comiéramos	comamos
	coméis	comíais	comisteis	comeréis	comeríais	comáis	comierais	comed (no comáis)
	comen	comían	comieron	comerán	comerían	coman	comieran	coman Uds.
3 vivir	vivo	vivía	viví	viviré	viviría	viva	viviera	
Participles:	vives	vivías	viviste	vivirás	vivirías	vivas	vivieras	vive tú (no vivas)
viviendo	vive	vivía	vivió	vivirá	viviría	viva	viviera	viva Ud.
vivido	vivimos	vivíamos	vivimos	viviremos	viviríamos	vivamos	viviéramos	vivamos
	vivís	vivíais	vivisteis	viviréis	viviríais	viváis	vivierais	vivid (no viváis)
	viven	vivían	vivieron	vivirán	vivirían	vivan	vivieran	vivan Uds.

All verbs: compound tenses

PERFECT TENSES

INDICATIVE								SUBJUNCTIVE			
Present Perfect		Past Perfect		Future Perfect		Conditional Perfect		Present Perfect		Past Perfect	
he		había		habré		habría		haya		hubiera	
has	hablado	habías	hablado	habrás	hablado	habrías	hablado	hayas	hablado	hubieras	hablado
ha	comido	había	comido	habrá	comido	habría	comido	haya	comido	hubiera	comido
hemos	vivido	habíamos	vivido	habremos	vivido	habríamos	vivido	hayamos	vivido	hubiéramos	vivido
habéis		habíais		habréis		habríais		hayáis		hubierais	
han		habían		habrán		habrían		hayan		hubieran	

PROGRESSIVE TENSES

	INDICATIVE				SUBJUNCTIVE	
Present Progressive	Past Progressive	Future Progressive	Conditional Progressive	Present Progressive	Past Progressive
estoy hablando	estaba hablando	estaré hablando	estaría hablando	esté hablando	estuviera hablando
estás comiendo	estabas comiendo	estarás comiendo	estarías comiendo	estés comiendo	estuvieras comiendo
está viviendo	estaba viviendo	estará viviendo	estaría viviendo	esté viviendo	estuviera viviendo
estamos	estábamos	estaremos	estaríamos	estemos	estuviéramos
estáis	estabais	estaréis	estaríais	estéis	estuvierais
están	estaban	estarán	estarían	estén	estuvieran

Irregular verbs

Infinitive	INDICATIVE					SUBJUNCTIVE		IMPERATIVE
	Present	Imperfect	Preterite	Future	Conditional	Present	Past	
4 caber	**quepo**	cabía	**cupe**	**cabré**	**cabría**	**quepa**	**cupiera**	
	cabes	cabías	**cupiste**	**cabrás**	**cabrías**	**quepas**	**cupieras**	cabe tú (no **quepas**)
	cabe	cabía	**cupo**	**cabrá**	**cabría**	**quepa**	**cupiera**	**quepa** Ud.
Participles:	cabemos	cabíamos	**cupimos**	**cabremos**	**cabríamos**	**quepamos**	**cupiéramos**	**quepamos**
cabiendo	cabéis	cabíais	**cupisteis**	**cabréis**	**cabríais**	**quepáis**	**cupierais**	cabed (no **quepáis**)
cabido	caben	cabían	**cupieron**	**cabrán**	**cabrían**	**quepan**	**cupieran**	**quepan** Uds.
5 caer(se)	**caigo**	caía	caí	caeré	caería	**caiga**	**cayera**	
	caes	caías	**caíste**	caerás	caerías	**caigas**	**cayeras**	cae tú (no **caigas**)
	cae	caía	**cayó**	caerá	caería	**caiga**	**cayera**	**caiga** Ud.
Participles:	caemos	caíamos	**caímos**	caeremos	caeríamos	**caigamos**	**cayéramos**	**caigamos**
cayendo	caéis	caíais	**caísteis**	caeréis	caeríais	**caigáis**	**cayerais**	caed (no **caigáis**)
caído	caen	caían	**cayeron**	caerán	caerían	**caigan**	**cayeran**	**caigan** Uds.
6 conducir (c:zc)	**conduzco**	conducía	**conduje**	conduciré	conduciría	**conduzca**	**condujera**	
	conduces	conducías	**condujiste**	conducirás	conducirías	**conduzcas**	**condujeras**	conduce tú (no **conduzcas**)
	conduce	conducía	**condujo**	conducirá	conduciría	**conduzca**	**condujera**	**conduzca** Ud.
Participles:	conducimos	conducíamos	**condujimos**	conduciremos	conduciríamos	**conduzcamos**	**condujéramos**	**conduzcamos**
conduciendo	conducís	conducíais	**condujisteis**	conduciréis	conduciríais	**conduzcáis**	**condujerais**	conducid (no **conduzcáis**)
conducido	conducen	conducían	**condujeron**	conducirán	conducirían	**conduzcan**	**condujeran**	**conduzcan** Uds.

Infinitive	INDICATIVE Present	Imperfect	Preterite	Future	Conditional	SUBJUNCTIVE Present	Past	IMPERATIVE
7 dar	doy	daba	di	daré	daría	dé	diera	
Participles:	das	dabas	diste	darás	darías	des	dieras	da tú (no des)
dando	da	daba	dio	dará	daría	dé	diera	dé Ud.
dado	damos	dábamos	dimos	daremos	daríamos	demos	diéramos	demos
	dais	dabais	disteis	daréis	daríais	deis	dierais	dad (no deis)
	dan	daban	dieron	darán	darían	den	dieran	den Uds.
8 decir (e:i)	digo	decía	dije	diré	diría	diga	dijera	
Participles:	dices	decías	dijiste	dirás	dirías	digas	dijeras	di tú (no digas)
diciendo	dice	decía	dijo	dirá	diría	diga	dijera	diga Ud.
dicho	decimos	decíamos	dijimos	diremos	diríamos	digamos	dijéramos	digamos
	decís	decíais	dijisteis	diréis	diríais	digáis	dijerais	decid (no digáis)
	dicen	decían	dijeron	dirán	dirían	digan	dijeran	digan Uds.
9 estar	estoy	estaba	estuve	estaré	estaría	esté	estuviera	
Participles:	estás	estabas	estuviste	estarás	estarías	estés	estuvieras	está tú (no estés)
estando	está	estaba	estuvo	estará	estaría	esté	estuviera	esté Ud.
estado	estamos	estábamos	estuvimos	estaremos	estaríamos	estemos	estuviéramos	estemos
	estáis	estabais	estuvisteis	estaréis	estaríais	estéis	estuvierais	estad (no estéis)
	están	estaban	estuvieron	estarán	estarían	estén	estuvieran	estén Uds.
10 haber	he	había	hube	habré	habría	haya	hubiera	
Participles:	has	habías	hubiste	habrás	habrías	hayas	hubieras	
habiendo	ha	había	hubo	habrá	habría	haya	hubiera	
habido	hemos	habíamos	hubimos	habremos	habríamos	hayamos	hubiéramos	
	habéis	habíais	hubisteis	habréis	habríais	hayáis	hubierais	
	han	habían	hubieron	habrán	habrían	hayan	hubieran	
11 hacer	hago	hacía	hice	haré	haría	haga	hiciera	
Participles:	haces	hacías	hiciste	harás	harías	hagas	hicieras	haz tú (no hagas)
haciendo	hace	hacía	hizo	hará	haría	haga	hiciera	haga Ud.
hecho	hacemos	hacíamos	hicimos	haremos	haríamos	hagamos	hiciéramos	hagamos
	hacéis	hacíais	hicisteis	haréis	haríais	hagáis	hicierais	haced (no hagáis)
	hacen	hacían	hicieron	harán	harían	hagan	hicieran	hagan Uds.
12 ir	voy	iba	fui	iré	iría	vaya	fuera	
Participles:	vas	ibas	fuiste	irás	irías	vayas	fueras	ve tú (no vayas)
yendo	va	iba	fue	irá	iría	vaya	fuera	vaya Ud.
ido	vamos	íbamos	fuimos	iremos	iríamos	vayamos	fuéramos	vamos
	vais	ibais	fuisteis	iréis	iríais	vayáis	fuerais	id (no vayáis)
	van	iban	fueron	irán	irían	vayan	fueran	vayan Uds.
13 oír (y)	oigo	oía	oí	oiré	oiría	oiga	oyera	
Participles:	oyes	oías	oíste	oirás	oirías	oigas	oyeras	oye tú (no oigas)
oyendo	oye	oía	oyó	oirá	oiría	oiga	oyera	oiga Ud.
oído	oímos	oíamos	oímos	oiremos	oiríamos	oigamos	oyéramos	oigamos
	oís	oíais	oísteis	oiréis	oiríais	oigáis	oyerais	oíd (no oigáis)
	oyen	oían	oyeron	oirán	oirían	oigan	oyeran	oigan Uds.

14. poder (o:ue) — Participles: pudiendo, podido

	INDICATIVE					SUBJUNCTIVE		IMPERATIVE
	Present	Imperfect	Preterite	Future	Conditional	Present	Past	
	puedo	podía	pude	podré	podría	pueda	pudiera	
	puedes	podías	pudiste	podrás	podrías	puedas	pudieras	puede tú (no puedas)
	puede	podía	pudo	podrá	podría	pueda	pudiera	pueda Ud.
	podemos	podíamos	pudimos	podremos	podríamos	podamos	pudiéramos	podamos
	podéis	podíais	pudisteis	podréis	podríais	podáis	pudierais	poded (no podáis)
	pueden	podían	pudieron	podrán	podrían	puedan	pudieran	puedan Uds.

15. poner — Participles: poniendo, puesto

	INDICATIVE					SUBJUNCTIVE		IMPERATIVE
	Present	Imperfect	Preterite	Future	Conditional	Present	Past	
	pongo	ponía	puse	pondré	pondría	ponga	pusiera	
	pones	ponías	pusiste	pondrás	pondrías	pongas	pusieras	pon tú (no pongas)
	pone	ponía	puso	pondrá	pondría	ponga	pusiera	ponga Ud.
	ponemos	poníamos	pusimos	pondremos	pondríamos	pongamos	pusiéramos	pongamos
	ponéis	poníais	pusisteis	pondréis	pondríais	pongáis	pusierais	poned (no pongáis)
	ponen	ponían	pusieron	pondrán	pondrían	pongan	pusieran	pongan Uds.

16. querer (e:ie) — Participles: queriendo, querido

	INDICATIVE					SUBJUNCTIVE		IMPERATIVE
	Present	Imperfect	Preterite	Future	Conditional	Present	Past	
	quiero	quería	quise	querré	querría	quiera	quisiera	
	quieres	querías	quisiste	querrás	querrías	quieras	quisieras	quiere tú (no quieras)
	quiere	quería	quiso	querrá	querría	quiera	quisiera	quiera Ud.
	queremos	queríamos	quisimos	querremos	querríamos	queramos	quisiéramos	queramos
	queréis	queríais	quisisteis	querréis	querríais	queráis	quisierais	quered (no queráis)
	quieren	querían	quisieron	querrán	querrían	quieran	quisieran	quieran Uds.

17. saber — Participles: sabiendo, sabido

	INDICATIVE					SUBJUNCTIVE		IMPERATIVE
	Present	Imperfect	Preterite	Future	Conditional	Present	Past	
	sé	sabía	supe	sabré	sabría	sepa	supiera	
	sabes	sabías	supiste	sabrás	sabrías	sepas	supieras	sabe tú (no sepas)
	sabe	sabía	supo	sabrá	sabría	sepa	supiera	sepa Ud.
	sabemos	sabíamos	supimos	sabremos	sabríamos	sepamos	supiéramos	sepamos
	sabéis	sabíais	supisteis	sabréis	sabríais	sepáis	supierais	sabed (no sepáis)
	saben	sabían	supieron	sabrán	sabrían	sepan	supieran	sepan Uds.

18. salir — Participles: saliendo, salido

	INDICATIVE					SUBJUNCTIVE		IMPERATIVE
	Present	Imperfect	Preterite	Future	Conditional	Present	Past	
	salgo	salía	salí	saldré	saldría	salga	saliera	
	sales	salías	saliste	saldrás	saldrías	salgas	salieras	sal tú (no salgas)
	sale	salía	salió	saldrá	saldría	salga	saliera	salga Ud.
	salimos	salíamos	salimos	saldremos	saldríamos	salgamos	saliéramos	salgamos
	salís	salíais	salisteis	saldréis	saldríais	salgáis	salierais	salid (no salgáis)
	salen	salían	salieron	saldrán	saldrían	salgan	salieran	salgan Uds.

19. ser — Participles: siendo, sido

	INDICATIVE					SUBJUNCTIVE		IMPERATIVE
	Present	Imperfect	Preterite	Future	Conditional	Present	Past	
	soy	era	fui	seré	sería	sea	fuera	
	eres	eras	fuiste	serás	serías	seas	fueras	sé tú (no seas)
	es	era	fue	será	sería	sea	fuera	sea Ud.
	somos	éramos	fuimos	seremos	seríamos	seamos	fuéramos	seamos
	sois	erais	fuisteis	seréis	seríais	seáis	fuerais	sed (no seáis)
	son	eran	fueron	serán	serían	sean	fueran	sean Uds.

20. tener (e:ie) — Participles: teniendo, tenido

	INDICATIVE					SUBJUNCTIVE		IMPERATIVE
	Present	Imperfect	Preterite	Future	Conditional	Present	Past	
	tengo	tenía	tuve	tendré	tendría	tenga	tuviera	
	tienes	tenías	tuviste	tendrás	tendrías	tengas	tuvieras	ten tú (no tengas)
	tiene	tenía	tuvo	tendrá	tendría	tenga	tuviera	tenga Ud.
	tenemos	teníamos	tuvimos	tendremos	tendríamos	tengamos	tuviéramos	tengamos
	tenéis	teníais	tuvisteis	tendréis	tendríais	tengáis	tuvierais	tened (no tengáis)
	tienen	tenían	tuvieron	tendrán	tendrían	tengan	tuvieran	tengan Uds.

21 traer — Participles: trayendo, traído

Infinitive	INDICATIVE					SUBJUNCTIVE		IMPERATIVE
	Present	Imperfect	Preterite	Future	Conditional	Present	Past	
traer	traigo	traía	traje	traeré	traería	traiga	trajera	
	traes	traías	trajiste	traerás	traerías	traigas	trajeras	trae tú (no traigas)
Participles:	trae	traía	trajo	traerá	traería	traiga	trajera	traiga Ud.
trayendo	traemos	traíamos	trajimos	traeremos	traeríamos	traigamos	trajéramos	traigamos
traído	traéis	traíais	trajisteis	traeréis	traeríais	traigáis	trajerais	traed (no traigáis)
	traen	traían	trajeron	traerán	traerían	traigan	trajeran	traigan Uds.

22 venir (e:ie) — Participles: viniendo, venido

Infinitive	INDICATIVE					SUBJUNCTIVE		IMPERATIVE
	Present	Imperfect	Preterite	Future	Conditional	Present	Past	
venir (e:ie)	vengo	venía	vine	vendré	vendría	venga	viniera	
	vienes	venías	viniste	vendrás	vendrías	vengas	vinieras	ven tú (no vengas)
	viene	venía	vino	vendrá	vendría	venga	viniera	venga Ud.
Participles:	venimos	veníamos	vinimos	vendremos	vendríamos	vengamos	viniéramos	vengamos
viniendo	venís	veníais	vinisteis	vendréis	vendríais	vengáis	vinierais	venid (no vengáis)
venido	vienen	venían	vinieron	vendrán	vendrían	vengan	vinieran	vengan Uds.

23 ver — Participles: viendo, visto

Infinitive	INDICATIVE					SUBJUNCTIVE		IMPERATIVE
	Present	Imperfect	Preterite	Future	Conditional	Present	Past	
ver	veo	veía	vi	veré	vería	vea	viera	
	ves	veías	viste	verás	verías	veas	vieras	ve tú (no veas)
	ve	veía	vio	verá	vería	vea	viera	vea Ud.
Participles:	vemos	veíamos	vimos	veremos	veríamos	veamos	viéramos	veamos
viendo	veis	veíais	visteis	veréis	veríais	veáis	vierais	ved (no veáis)
visto	ven	veían	vieron	verán	verían	vean	vieran	vean Uds.

Stem-changing verbs

24 contar (o:ue) — Participles: contando, contado

Infinitive	INDICATIVE					SUBJUNCTIVE		IMPERATIVE
	Present	Imperfect	Preterite	Future	Conditional	Present	Past	
contar (o:ue)	cuento	contaba	conté	contaré	contaría	cuente	contara	
	cuentas	contabas	contaste	contarás	contarías	cuentes	contaras	cuenta tú (no cuentes)
	cuenta	contaba	contó	contará	contaría	cuente	contara	cuente Ud.
Participles:	contamos	contábamos	contamos	contaremos	contaríamos	contemos	contáramos	contemos
contando	contáis	contabais	contasteis	contaréis	contaríais	contéis	contarais	contad (no contéis)
contado	cuentan	contaban	contaron	contarán	contarían	cuenten	contaran	cuenten Uds.

25 dormir (o:ue) — Participles: durmiendo, dormido

Infinitive	INDICATIVE					SUBJUNCTIVE		IMPERATIVE
	Present	Imperfect	Preterite	Future	Conditional	Present	Past	
dormir (o:ue)	duermo	dormía	dormí	dormiré	dormiría	duerma	durmiera	
	duermes	dormías	dormiste	dormirás	dormirías	duermas	durmieras	duerme tú (no duermas)
	duerme	dormía	durmió	dormirá	dormiría	duerma	durmiera	duerma Ud.
Participles:	dormimos	dormíamos	dormimos	dormiremos	dormiríamos	durmamos	durmiéramos	durmamos
durmiendo	dormís	dormíais	dormisteis	dormiréis	dormiríais	durmáis	durmierais	dormid (no durmáis)
dormido	duermen	dormían	durmieron	dormirán	dormirían	duerman	durmieran	duerman Uds.

26 empezar (e:ie) (z:c) — Participles: empezando, empezado

Infinitive	INDICATIVE					SUBJUNCTIVE		IMPERATIVE
	Present	Imperfect	Preterite	Future	Conditional	Present	Past	
empezar	empiezo	empezaba	empecé	empezaré	empezaría	empiece	empezara	
(e:ie) (z:c)	empiezas	empezabas	empezaste	empezarás	empezarías	empieces	empezaras	empieza tú (no empieces)
	empieza	empezaba	empezó	empezará	empezaría	empiece	empezara	empiece Ud.
Participles:	empezamos	empezábamos	empezamos	empezaremos	empezaríamos	empecemos	empezáramos	empecemos
empezando	empezáis	empezabais	empezasteis	empezaréis	empezaríais	empecéis	empezarais	empezad (no empecéis)
empezado	empiezan	empezaban	empezaron	empezarán	empezarían	empiecen	empezaran	empiecen Uds.

27. entender (e:ie) — Participles: entendiendo, entendido

	INDICATIVE					SUBJUNCTIVE		IMPERATIVE
	Present	Imperfect	Preterite	Future	Conditional	Present	Past	
	entiendo	entendía	entendí	entenderé	entendería	entienda	entendiera	
	entiendes	entendías	entendiste	entenderás	entenderías	entiendas	entendieras	entiende tú (no entiendas)
	entiende	entendía	entendió	entenderá	entendería	entienda	entendiera	entienda Ud.
	entendemos	entendíamos	entendimos	entenderemos	entenderíamos	entendamos	entendiéramos	entendamos
	entendéis	entendíais	entendisteis	entenderéis	entenderíais	entendáis	entendierais	entended (no entendáis)
	entienden	entendían	entendieron	entenderán	entenderían	entiendan	entendieran	entiendan Uds.

28. jugar (u:ue) (g:gu) — Participles: jugando, jugado

	INDICATIVE					SUBJUNCTIVE		IMPERATIVE
	Present	Imperfect	Preterite	Future	Conditional	Present	Past	
	juego	jugaba	jugué	jugaré	jugaría	juegue	jugara	
	juegas	jugabas	jugaste	jugarás	jugarías	juegues	jugaras	juega tú (no juegues)
	juega	jugaba	jugó	jugará	jugaría	juegue	jugara	juegue Ud.
	jugamos	jugábamos	jugamos	jugaremos	jugaríamos	juguemos	jugáramos	juguemos
	jugáis	jugabais	jugasteis	jugaréis	jugaríais	juguéis	jugarais	jugad (no juguéis)
	juegan	jugaban	jugaron	jugarán	jugarían	jueguen	jugaran	jueguen Uds.

29. pedir (e:i) — Participles: pidiendo, pedido

	INDICATIVE					SUBJUNCTIVE		IMPERATIVE
	Present	Imperfect	Preterite	Future	Conditional	Present	Past	
	pido	pedía	pedí	pediré	pediría	pida	pidiera	
	pides	pedías	pediste	pedirás	pedirías	pidas	pidieras	pide tú (no pidas)
	pide	pedía	pidió	pedirá	pediría	pida	pidiera	pida Ud.
	pedimos	pedíamos	pedimos	pediremos	pediríamos	pidamos	pidiéramos	pidamos
	pedís	pedíais	pedisteis	pediréis	pediríais	pidáis	pidierais	pedid (no pidáis)
	piden	pedían	pidieron	pedirán	pedirían	pidan	pidieran	pidan Uds.

30. pensar (e:ie) — Participles: pensando, pensado

	INDICATIVE					SUBJUNCTIVE		IMPERATIVE
	Present	Imperfect	Preterite	Future	Conditional	Present	Past	
	pienso	pensaba	pensé	pensaré	pensaría	piense	pensara	
	piensas	pensabas	pensaste	pensarás	pensarías	pienses	pensaras	piensa tú (no pienses)
	piensa	pensaba	pensó	pensará	pensaría	piense	pensara	piense Ud.
	pensamos	pensábamos	pensamos	pensaremos	pensaríamos	pensemos	pensáramos	pensemos
	pensáis	pensabais	pensasteis	pensaréis	pensaríais	penséis	pensarais	pensad (no penséis)
	piensan	pensaban	pensaron	pensarán	pensarían	piensen	pensaran	piensen Uds.

31. reír(se) (e:i) — Participles: riendo, reído

	INDICATIVE					SUBJUNCTIVE		IMPERATIVE
	Present	Imperfect	Preterite	Future	Conditional	Present	Past	
	río	reía	reí	reiré	reiría	ría	riera	
	ríes	reías	reíste	reirás	reirías	rías	rieras	ríe tú (no rías)
	ríe	reía	rio	reirá	reiría	ría	riera	ría Ud.
	reímos	reíamos	reímos	reiremos	reiríamos	riamos	riéramos	riamos
	reís	reíais	reísteis	reiréis	reiríais	riáis	rierais	reíd (no riáis)
	ríen	reían	rieron	reirán	reirían	rían	rieran	rían Uds.

32. seguir (e:i) (gu:g) — Participles: siguiendo, seguido

	INDICATIVE					SUBJUNCTIVE		IMPERATIVE
	Present	Imperfect	Preterite	Future	Conditional	Present	Past	
	sigo	seguía	seguí	seguiré	seguiría	siga	siguiera	
	sigues	seguías	seguiste	seguirás	seguirías	sigas	siguieras	sigue tú (no sigas)
	sigue	seguía	siguió	seguirá	seguiría	siga	siguiera	siga Ud.
	seguimos	seguíamos	seguimos	seguiremos	seguiríamos	sigamos	siguiéramos	sigamos
	seguís	seguíais	seguisteis	seguiréis	seguiríais	sigáis	siguierais	seguid (no sigáis)
	siguen	seguían	siguieron	seguirán	seguirían	sigan	siguieran	sigan Uds.

33. sentir (e:ie) — Participles: sintiendo, sentido

	INDICATIVE					SUBJUNCTIVE		IMPERATIVE
	Present	Imperfect	Preterite	Future	Conditional	Present	Past	
	siento	sentía	sentí	sentiré	sentiría	sienta	sintiera	
	sientes	sentías	sentiste	sentirás	sentirías	sientas	sintieras	siente tú (no sientas)
	siente	sentía	sintió	sentirá	sentiría	sienta	sintiera	sienta Ud.
	sentimos	sentíamos	sentimos	sentiremos	sentiríamos	sintamos	sintiéramos	sintamos
	sentís	sentíais	sentisteis	sentiréis	sentiríais	sintáis	sintierais	sentid (no sintáis)
	sienten	sentían	sintieron	sentirán	sentirían	sientan	sintieran	sientan Uds.

34

Infinitive	INDICATIVE					SUBJUNCTIVE		IMPERATIVE
	Present	Imperfect	Preterite	Future	Conditional	Present	Past	
volver (o:ue)	vuelvo	volvía	volví	volveré	volvería	vuelva	volviera	
	vuelves	volvías	volviste	volverás	volverías	vuelvas	volvieras	vuelve tú (no vuelvas)
Participles:	vuelve	volvía	volvió	volverá	volvería	vuelva	volviera	vuelva Ud.
volviendo	volvemos	volvíamos	volvimos	volveremos	volveríamos	volvamos	volviéramos	volvamos
vuelto	volvéis	volvíais	volvisteis	volveréis	volveríais	volváis	volvierais	volved (no volváis)
	vuelven	volvían	volvieron	volverán	volverían	vuelvan	volvieran	vuelvan Uds.

Verbs with spelling changes only

Infinitive	INDICATIVE					SUBJUNCTIVE		IMPERATIVE
	Present	Imperfect	Preterite	Future	Conditional	Present	Past	

35

Infinitive	Present	Imperfect	Preterite	Future	Conditional	Present	Past	Imperative
conocer (c:zc)	conozco	conocía	conocí	conoceré	conocería	conozca	conociera	
	conoces	conocías	conociste	conocerás	conocerías	conozcas	conocieras	conoce tú (no conozcas)
Participles:	conoce	conocía	conoció	conocerá	conocería	conozca	conociera	conozca Ud.
conociendo	conocemos	conocíamos	conocimos	conoceremos	conoceríamos	conozcamos	conociéramos	conozcamos
conocido	conocéis	conocíais	conocisteis	conoceréis	conoceríais	conozcáis	conocierais	conoced (no conozcáis)
	conocen	conocían	conocieron	conocerán	conocerían	conozcan	conocieran	conozcan Uds.

36

Infinitive	Present	Imperfect	Preterite	Future	Conditional	Present	Past	Imperative
creer (y)	creo	creía	creí	creeré	creería	crea	creyera	
	crees	creías	creíste	creerás	creerías	creas	creyeras	cree tú (no creas)
Participles:	cree	creía	creyó	creerá	creería	crea	creyera	crea Ud.
creyendo	creemos	creíamos	creímos	creeremos	creeríamos	creamos	creyéramos	creamos
creído	creéis	creíais	creísteis	creeréis	creeríais	creáis	creyerais	creed (no creáis)
	creen	creían	creyeron	creerán	creerían	crean	creyeran	crean Uds.

37

Infinitive	Present	Imperfect	Preterite	Future	Conditional	Present	Past	Imperative
cruzar (z:c)	cruzo	cruzaba	crucé	cruzaré	cruzaría	cruce	cruzara	
	cruzas	cruzabas	cruzaste	cruzarás	cruzarías	cruces	cruzaras	cruza tú (no cruces)
Participles:	cruza	cruzaba	cruzó	cruzará	cruzaría	cruce	cruzara	cruce Ud.
cruzando	cruzamos	cruzábamos	cruzamos	cruzaremos	cruzaríamos	crucemos	cruzáramos	crucemos
cruzado	cruzáis	cruzabais	cruzasteis	cruzaréis	cruzaríais	crucéis	cruzarais	cruzad (no crucéis)
	cruzan	cruzaban	cruzaron	cruzarán	cruzarían	crucen	cruzaran	crucen Uds.

38

Infinitive	Present	Imperfect	Preterite	Future	Conditional	Present	Past	Imperative
destruir (y)	destruyo	destruía	destruí	destruiré	destruiría	destruya	destruyera	
	destruyes	destruías	destruiste	destruirás	destruirías	destruyas	destruyeras	destruye tú (no destruyas)
Participles:	destruye	destruía	destruyó	destruirá	destruiría	destruya	destruyera	destruya Ud.
destruyendo	destruimos	destruíamos	destruimos	destruiremos	destruiríamos	destruyamos	destruyéramos	destruyamos
destruido	destruís	destruíais	destruisteis	destruiréis	destruiríais	destruyáis	destruyerais	destruid (no destruyáis)
	destruyen	destruían	destruyeron	destruirán	destruirían	destruyan	destruyeran	destruyan Uds.

39

Infinitive	Present	Imperfect	Preterite	Future	Conditional	Present	Past	Imperative
enviar (envío)	envío	enviaba	envié	enviaré	enviaría	envíe	enviara	
	envías	enviabas	enviaste	enviarás	enviarías	envíes	enviaras	envía tú (no envíes)
Participles:	envía	enviaba	envió	enviará	enviaría	envíe	enviara	envíe Ud.
enviando	enviamos	enviábamos	enviamos	enviaremos	enviaríamos	enviemos	enviáramos	enviemos
enviado	enviáis	enviabais	enviasteis	enviaréis	enviaríais	enviéis	enviarais	enviad (no enviéis)
	envían	enviaban	enviaron	enviarán	enviarían	envíen	enviaran	envíen Uds.

| Infinitive | INDICATIVE | | | | | SUBJUNCTIVE | | IMPERATIVE |
	Present	Imperfect	Preterite	Future	Conditional	Present	Past	
40 graduarse (gradúo)	gradúo	graduaba	gradué	graduaré	graduaría	gradúe	graduara	
	gradúas	graduabas	graduaste	graduarás	graduarías	gradúes	graduaras	gradúa tú (no gradúes)
	gradúa	graduaba	graduó	graduará	graduaría	gradúe	graduara	gradúe Ud.
Participles:	graduamos	graduábamos	graduamos	graduaremos	graduaríamos	graduemos	graduáramos	graduemos
graduando	graduáis	graduabais	graduasteis	graduaréis	graduaríais	graduéis	graduarais	graduad (no graduéis)
graduado	gradúan	graduaban	graduaron	graduarán	graduarían	gradúen	graduaran	gradúen Uds.
41 llegar (g:gu)	llego	llegaba	llegué	llegaré	llegaría	llegue	llegara	
	llegas	llegabas	llegaste	llegarás	llegarías	llegues	llegaras	llega tú (no llegues)
	llega	llegaba	llegó	llegará	llegaría	llegue	llegara	llegue Ud.
Participles:	llegamos	llegábamos	llegamos	llegaremos	llegaríamos	lleguemos	llegáramos	lleguemos
llegando	llegáis	llegabais	llegasteis	llegaréis	llegaríais	lleguéis	llegarais	llegad (no lleguéis)
llegado	llegan	llegaban	llegaron	llegarán	llegarían	lleguen	llegaran	lleguen Uds.
42 prohibir (prohíbo)	prohíbo	prohibía	prohibí	prohibiré	prohibiría	prohíba	prohibiera	
	prohíbes	prohibías	prohibiste	prohibirás	prohibirías	prohíbas	prohibieras	prohíbe tú (no prohíbas)
	prohíbe	prohibía	prohibió	prohibirá	prohibiría	prohíba	prohibiera	prohíba Ud.
Participles:	prohibimos	prohibíamos	prohibimos	prohibiremos	prohibiríamos	prohibamos	prohibiéramos	prohibamos
prohibiendo	prohibís	prohibíais	prohibisteis	prohibiréis	prohibiríais	prohibáis	prohibierais	prohibid (no prohibáis)
prohibido	prohíben	prohibían	prohibieron	prohibirán	prohibirían	prohíban	prohibieran	prohíban Uds.
43 proteger (g:j)	protejo	protegía	protegí	protegeré	protegería	proteja	protegiera	
	proteges	protegías	protegiste	protegerás	protegerías	protejas	protegieras	protege tú (no protejas)
	protege	protegía	protegió	protegerá	protegería	proteja	protegiera	proteja Ud.
Participles:	protegemos	protegíamos	protegimos	protegeremos	protegeríamos	protejamos	protegiéramos	protejamos
protegiendo	protegéis	protegíais	protegisteis	protegeréis	protegeríais	protejáis	protegierais	proteged (no protejáis)
protegido	protegen	protegían	protegieron	protegerán	protegerían	protejan	protegieran	protejan Uds.
44 tocar (c:qu)	toco	tocaba	toqué	tocaré	tocaría	toque	tocara	
	tocas	tocabas	tocaste	tocarás	tocarías	toques	tocaras	toca tú (no toques)
	toca	tocaba	tocó	tocará	tocaría	toque	tocara	toque Ud.
Participles:	tocamos	tocábamos	tocamos	tocaremos	tocaríamos	toquemos	tocáramos	toquemos
tocando	tocáis	tocabais	tocasteis	tocaréis	tocaríais	toquéis	tocarais	tocad (no toquéis)
tocado	tocan	tocaban	tocaron	tocarán	tocarían	toquen	tocaran	toquen Uds.

Guide to Vocabulary

Note on alphabetization

For purposes of alphabetization, **ch** and **ll** are not treated as separate letters, but **ñ** follows **n**. Therefore, in this glossary you will find that **año**, for example, appears after **anuncio.**

Abbreviations used in this glossary

adj.	adjective	*form.*	formal	*pl.*	plural
adv.	adverb	*indef.*	indefinite	*poss.*	possessive
art.	article	*interj.*	interjection	*prep.*	preposition
conj.	conjunction	*i.o.*	indirect object	*pron.*	pronoun
def.	definite	*m.*	masculine	*ref.*	reflexive
d.o.	direct object	*n.*	noun	*sing.*	singular
f.	feminine	*obj.*	object	*sub.*	subject
fam.	familiar	*p.p.*	past participle	*v.*	verb

Spanish-English

A

a *prep.* at; to 1
   ¿A qué hora...? At what time...? 1
   a bordo aboard
   a dieta on a diet 15
   a la derecha de to the right of 2
   a la izquierda de to the left of 2
   a la plancha grilled 8
   a la(s) + *time* at + *time* 1
   a menos que *conj.* unless 13
   a menudo *adv.* often 10
   a nombre de in the name of 5
   a plazos in installments 14
   A sus órdenes. At your service.
   a tiempo *adv.* on time 10
   a veces *adv.* sometimes 10
   a ver let's see
abeja *f.* bee
abierto/a *adj.* open 5, 14
abogado/a *m., f.* lawyer 16
abrazar(se) *v.* to hug; to embrace (each other) 11
abrazo *m.* hug
abrigo *m.* coat 6
abril *m.* April 5
abrir *v.* to open 3
abuelo/a *m., f.* grandfather/ grandmother 3
abuelos *pl.* grandparents 3
aburrido/a *adj.* bored; boring 5
aburrir *v.* to bore 7
aburrirse *v.* to get bored 17
acabar de (+ *inf.*) *v.* to have just done something 6
acampar *v.* to camp 5
accidente *m.* accident 10
acción *f.* action 17
   de acción action (genre) 17

aceite *m.* oil 8
aceptar: ¡Acepto casarme contigo! I'll marry you! 17
acompañar *v.* to accompany 14
aconsejar *v.* to advise 12
acontecimiento *m.* event 18
acordarse (de) (o:ue) *v.* to remember 7
acostarse (o:ue) *v.* to go to bed 7
activo/a *adj.* active 15
actor *m.* actor 16
actriz *f.* actress 16
actualidades *f., pl.* news; current events 18
adelgazar *v.* to lose weight; to slim down 15
además (de) *adv.* furthermore; besides 10
adicional *adj.* additional
adiós *m.* goodbye 1
adjetivo *m.* adjective
administración de empresas *f.* business administration 2
adolescencia *f.* adolescence 9
¿adónde? *adv.* where (to)? (destination) 2
aduana *f.* customs
aeróbico/a *adj.* aerobic 15
aeropuerto *m.* airport 5
afectado/a *adj.* affected 13
afeitarse *v.* to shave 7
aficionado/a *m., f.* fan 4
afirmativo/a *adj.* affirmative
afuera *adv.* outside 5
afueras *f., pl.* suburbs; outskirts 12
agencia de viajes *f.* travel agency
agente de viajes *m., f.* travel agent
agosto *m.* August 5
agradable *adj.* pleasant **agua** *f.* water 8
   agua mineral mineral water 8

aguantar *v.* to endure, to hold up 14
ahora *adv.* now 2
   ahora mismo right now 5
ahorrar *v.* to save (money) 14
ahorros *m., pl.* savings 14
aire *m.* air 13
ajo *m.* garlic 8
al (*contraction of* **a** + **el**) 4
   al aire libre open-air 6
   al contado in cash 14
   (al) este (to the) east 14
   al lado de next to; beside 2
   (al) norte (to the) north 14
   (al) oeste (to the) west 14
   (al) sur (to the) south 14
alcoba *f.* bedroom
alcohol *m.* alcohol 15
alcohólico/a *adj.* alcoholic 15
alegrarse (de) *v.* to be happy 13
alegre *adj.* happy 5
alegría *f.* happiness 9
alemán, alemana *adj.* German 3
alérgico/a *adj.* allergic 10
alfombra *f.* carpet; rug 12
algo *pron.* something; anything 7
algodón *m.* cotton 6
alguien *pron.* someone; somebody; anyone 7
algún, alguno/a(s) *adj.* any; some 7
alimentación *f.* diet
alimento *m.* food
aliviar *v.* to reduce 15
   aliviar el estrés/la tensión to reduce stress/tension 15
allá *adv.* over there 2
allí *adv.* there 2
alma *f.* soul 9
almacén *m.* department store 6
   almohada *f.* pillow 12
almorzar (o:ue) *v.* to have lunch 4

almuerzo *m.* lunch 4, 8
aló *interj.* hello (*on the telephone*) 11
alquilar *v.* to rent 12
alquiler *m.* rent (payment) 12
altar *m.* altar 9
altillo *m.* attic 12
alto/a *adj.* tall 3
aluminio *m.* aluminum 13
amo/a de casa *m., f.* homemaker 12
amable *adj.* nice; friendly 5
amarillo/a *adj.* yellow 6
amigo/a *m., f.* friend 3
amistad *f.* friendship 9
amor *m.* love 9
   amor a primera vista love at first sight 9
anaranjado/a *adj.* orange 6
ándale *interj.* come on 14
andar *v.* **en patineta** to skateboard 4
ángel *m.* angel 9
anillo *m.* ring 17
animal *m.* animal 13
aniversario (de bodas) *m.* (wedding) anniversary 9
anoche *adv.* last night 6
anteayer *adv.* the day before yesterday 6
antes *adv.* before 7
   antes de *prep.* before 7
   antes (de) que *conj.* before 13
antibiótico *m.* antibiotic 10
antipático/a *adj.* unpleasant 3
anunciar *v.* to announce; to advertise 18
anuncio *m.* advertisement 16
año *m.* year 5
   año pasado last year 6
apagar *v.* to turn off 11
aparato *m.* appliance
apartamento *m.* apartment 12
apellido *m.* last name 3
apenas *adv.* hardly; scarcely 10
aplaudir *v.* to applaud 17
aplicación *f.* app 11
apreciar *v.* to appreciate 17
aprender (a + *inf.*) *v.* to learn 3
apurarse *v.* to hurry; to rush 15
aquel, aquella *adj.* that (over there) 6
aquél, aquélla *pron.* that (over there) 6
aquello *neuter, pron.* that; that thing; that fact 6
aquellos/as *pl. adj.* those (over there) 6
aquéllos/as *pl. pron.* those (ones) (over there) 6
aquí *adv.* here 1
   Aquí está(n)... Here is/are... 5
árbol *m.* tree 13 **archivo** *m.* file 11
arete *m.* earring 6
argentino/a *adj.* Argentine 3
armario *m.* closet 12
arqueología *f.* archeology 2

arqueólogo/a *m., f.* archeologist 16
arquitecto/a *m., f.* architect 16
arrancar *v.* to start (*a car*) 11
arreglar *v.* to fix; to arrange 11; to straighten up 12
arreglarse *v.* to get ready 7; to fix oneself (*clothes, hair, etc. to go out*) 7
arroba *f.* @ symbol 11
arroz *m.* rice 8
arte *m.* art 2
artes *f., pl.* arts 17
artesanía *f.* craftsmanship; crafts 17
artículo *m.* article 18
artista *m., f.* artist 3
artístico/a *adj.* artistic 17
arveja *f.* pea 8
asado/a *adj.* roast 8
ascenso *m.* promotion 16
ascensor *m.* elevator 5
así *adv.* like this; so (*in such a way*) 10
asistir (a) *v.* to attend 3
aspiradora *f.* vacuum cleaner 12
aspirante *m., f.* candidate; applicant 16
aspirina *f.* aspirin 10
atún *m.* tuna 8
aumentar *v.* to grow; to get bigger 13
aumentar *v.* **de peso** to gain weight 15
aumento *m.* increase
   aumento de sueldo pay raise 16
aunque although
autobús *m.* bus 1
automático/a *adj.* automatic
auto(móvil) *m.* car 5
autopista *f.* highway 11
ave *f.* bird 13
avenida *f.* avenue
aventura *f.* adventure 17
   de aventuras adventure (genre) 17
avergonzado/a *adj.* embarrassed 5
avión *m.* airplane 5
¡Ay! *interj.* Oh!
   ¡Ay, qué dolor! Oh, what pain!
ayer *adv.* yesterday 6
ayudar(se) *v.* to help (each other) 11
azúcar *m.* sugar 8
azul *adj. m., f.* blue 6

B

bailar *v.* to dance 2
bailarín/bailarina *m., f.* dancer 17
baile *m.* dance 17
bajar(se) de *v.* to get off of/out of (a vehicle) 11

bajo/a *adj.* short (*in height*) 3
balcón *m.* balcony 12
balde *m.* bucket 5
ballena *f.* whale 13
baloncesto *m.* basketball 4
banana *f.* banana 8
banco *m.* bank 14
banda *f.* band 17
bandera *f.* flag
bañarse *v.* to take a bath 7
baño *m.* bathroom 7
barato/a *adj.* cheap 6
barco *m.* boat 5
barrer *v.* to sweep 12
   barrer el suelo *v.* to sweep the floor 12
barrio *m.* neighborhood 12
bastante *adv.* enough; rather 10
basura *f.* trash 12
batería *f.* battery 11
baúl *m.* trunk 11
beber *v.* to drink 3
bebida *f.* drink 8
   bebida alcohólica *f.* alcoholic beverage 15
béisbol *m.* baseball 4
bellas artes *f., pl.* fine arts 17
belleza *f.* beauty 14
beneficio *m.* benefit 16
besar(se) *v.* to kiss (each other) 11
beso *m.* kiss 9
biblioteca *f.* library 2
bicicleta *f.* bicycle 4
bien *adv.* well 1
bienestar *m.* well-being 15
bienvenido(s)/a(s) *adj.* welcome 1
billete *m.* paper money; ticket
billón *m.* trillion
biología *f.* biology 2
bisabuelo/a *m., f.* great-grandfather/great-grandmother 3
bistec *m.* steak 8
blanco/a *adj.* white 6
blog *m.* blog 11
(blue)jeans *m., pl.* jeans 6
blusa *f.* blouse 6
boca *f.* mouth 10
boda *f.* wedding 9
boleto *m.* ticket 2, 17
bolsa *f.* purse, bag 6
bombero/a *m., f.* firefighter 16
bonito/a *adj.* pretty 3
borrador *m.* eraser 2
borrar *v.* to erase 11
bosque *m.* forest 13
   bosque tropical tropical forest; rain forest 13
bota *f.* boot 6
botella *f.* bottle 9
   botella de vino bottle of wine 9
botones *m., f. sing.* bellhop 5
brazo *m.* arm 10
brindar *v.* to toast (*drink*) 9
bucear *v.* to scuba dive 4

buen, bueno/a *adj.* good 3, 6
  buena forma good shape
    (*physical*) 15
  Buenas noches. Good evening;
    Good night. 1
  Buenas tardes. Good
    afternoon. 1
  Bueno. Hello. (*on telephone*)
    11
  Buenos días. Good morning. 1
bulevar *m.* boulevard
buscador *m.* browser 11
buscar *v.* to look for 2
buzón *m.* mailbox 14

C

caballero *m.* gentleman, sir 8
caballo *m.* horse 5
cabe: no cabe duda de there's
  no doubt 13
cabeza *f.* head 10
cada *adj. m., f.* each 6
caerse *v.* to fall (down) 10
café *m.* café 4; *adj. m., f.*
  brown 6; *m.* coffee 8
cafeína *f.* caffeine 15
cafetera *f.* coffee maker 12
cafetería *f.* cafeteria 2
caído/a *p.p.* fallen 14
caja *f.* cash register 6
cajero/a *m., f.* cashier
  cajero automático *m.* ATM 14
calavera de azúcar *f.* skull made
  out of sugar 9
calcetín (calcetines) *m.*
  sock(s) 6
calculadora *f.* calculator 2
calentamiento global *m.* global
  warming 13
calentarse (e:ie) *v.* to warm
  up 15
calidad *f.* quality 6
calle *f.* street 11
calor *m.* heat
caloría *f.* calorie 15
calzar *v.* to take size... shoes 6
cama *f.* bed 5
cámara digital *f.* digital camera 11
camarero/a *m., f.* waiter/
  waitress 8
camarón *m.* shrimp 8
cambiar (de) *v.* to change 9
cambio: de cambio in change 2
cambio *m.* **climático** climate
  change 13
cambio *m.* **de moneda** currency
  exchange
caminar *v.* to walk 2
camino *m.* road
camión *m.* truck; bus
camisa *f.* shirt 6
camiseta *f.* t-shirt 6
campo *m.* countryside 5
canadiense *adj.* Canadian 3
canal *m.* (TV) channel 11; 17

canción *f.* song 17
candidato/a *m., f.* candidate 18
canela *f.* cinnamon 10
cansado/a *adj.* tired 5
cantante *m., f.* singer 17
cantar *v.* to sing 2
capital *f.* capital city
capó *m.* hood 11
cara *f.* face 7
caramelo *m.* caramel 9
cargador *m.* charger 11
cargar *v.* to charge; to upload 11
carne *f.* meat 8
  carne de res *f.* beef 8
carnicería *f.* butcher shop 14
caro/a *adj.* expensive 6
carpintero/a *m., f.* carpenter 16
carrera *f.* career 16
carretera *f.* highway; (main)
  road 11
carro *m.* car 11
carta *f.* letter 4; (playing) card 5
cartel *m.* poster 12
cartera *f.* wallet 4, 6
cartero *m.* mail carrier 14
casa *f.* house; home 2
casado/a *adj.* married 9
casarse (con) *v.* to get married
  (to) 9
casi *adv.* almost 10
catorce fourteen 1
cazar *v.* to hunt 13
cebolla *f.* onion 8
celebrar *v.* to celebrate 9
cementerio *m.* cemetery 9
cena *f.* dinner 8
cenar *v.* to have dinner 2
centro *m.* downtown 4
  centro comercial shopping
    mall 6
cepillarse los dientes/el pelo *v.*
  to brush one's teeth/one's hair 7
cerámica *f.* pottery 17
cerca de *prep.* near 2
cerdo *m.* pork 8
cereales *m., pl.* cereal; grains 8
cero *m.* zero 1
cerrado/a *adj.* closed 5
cerrar (e:ie) *v.* to close 4
cerveza *f.* beer 8
césped *m.* grass
ceviche *m.* marinated fish dish 8
  ceviche de camarón *m.*
    lemon-marinated shrimp 8
chaleco *m.* vest
champán *m.* champagne 9
champiñón *m.* mushroom 8
champú *m.* shampoo 7
chaqueta *f.* jacket 6
chatear *v.* to chat 11
chau *fam. interj.* bye 1
cheque *m.* (bank) check 14
chévere *adj., fam.* terrific
chico/a *m., f.* boy/girl 1
chino/a *adj.* Chinese 3
chocar (con) *v.* to run into
chocolate *m.* chocolate 9

choque *m.* collision 18
chuleta *f.* chop (food) 8
  chuleta de cerdo *f.* pork
    chop 8
ciclismo *m.* cycling 4
cielo *m.* sky 13
cien(to) one hundred 2
ciencias *f., pl.* sciences 2
  ciencias ambientales
    environmental science 2
  de ciencia ficción *f.* science
    fiction (genre) 17
científico/a *m., f.* scientist 16
cierto/a *adj.* certain 13
  es cierto it's certain 13
  no es cierto it's not certain 13
cima *f.* top, peak 15
cinco five 1
cincuenta fifty 2
cine *m.* movie theater 4
cinta caminadora *f.* treadmill 15
cinturón *m.* belt 6
circulación *f.* traffic 11
cita *f.* date; appointment 9
ciudad *f.* city
ciudadano/a *m., f.* citizen 18
Claro (que sí). *fam.* Of course.
clase *f.* class 2
  clase de ejercicios aeróbicos
    f. aerobics class 15
clásico/a *adj.* classical 17
cliente/a *m., f.* customer 6
clínica *f.* clinic 10
cobrar *v.* to cash (a check) 14
coche *m.* car 11
cocina *f.* kitchen; stove 9, 12
cocinar *v.* to cook 12
cocinero/a *m., f.* cook, chef 16
cofre *m.* hood 14
cola *f.* line 14
colesterol *m.* cholesterol 15
color *m.* color 6
comedia *f.* comedy; play 17
comedor *m.* dining room 12
comenzar (e:ie) *v.* to begin 4
comer *v.* to eat 3
comercial *adj.* commercial;
  business-related 16
comida *f.* food; meal 4, 8
como like; as 8
¿cómo? what?; how? 1, 2
  ¿Cómo es...? What's... like?
  ¿Cómo está usted? *form.*
    How are you? 1
  ¿Cómo estás? *fam.* How are
    you? 1
  ¿Cómo se llama usted?
    form. What's your name? 1
  ¿Cómo te llamas? *fam.*
    What's your name? 1
cómoda *f.* chest of drawers 12
cómodo/a *adj.* comfortable 5
compañero/a de clase *m., f.*
  classmate 2
compañero/a de cuarto *m., f.*
  roommate 2
compañía *f.* company; firm 16

compartir *v.* to share 3
compositor(a) *m., f.* composer 17
comprar *v.* to buy 2
   comprar en línea to buy
    online 6
compras *f., pl.* purchases
   ir de compras to go shopping 5
comprender *v.* to understand 3
comprobar *v.* to check
comprometerse (con) *v.* to get
   engaged (to) 9
computación *f.* computer science 2
computadora *f.* computer 1
computadora portátil *f.* portable
   computer; laptop 11
comunicación *f.* communication 18
comunicarse (con) *v.* to
   communicate (with) 18
comunidad *f.* community 1
con *prep.* with 2
   Con él/ella habla. Speaking.
    (*on telephone*) 11
   con frecuencia *adv.* frequently 10
   Con permiso. Pardon me;
    Excuse me. 1
   con tal (de) que *conj.* provided
    (that) 13
concierto *m.* concert 17
concordar *v.* to agree
concurso *m.* game show; contest 17
conducir *v.* to drive 6, 11
conductor(a) *m., f.* driver 1
conectarse *v.* **a Internet** to get
   connected to the Internet 11
conexión *f.* **inalámbrica** wireless
   connection 11
confirmar *v.* to confirm 5
confirmar *v.* **una reservación** *f.*
   to confirm a reservation 5
confundido/a *adj.* confused 5
congelador *m.* freezer 12
congestionado/a *adj.* congested 10
conmigo *pron.* with me 4, 9
conocer *v.* to know; to be
   acquainted with 6
conocido/a *adj.; p.p.* known
conseguir (e:i) *v.* to get; to obtain 4
consejero/a *m., f.* counselor;
   advisor 16
consejo *m.* advice
conservación *f.* conservation 13
conservar *v.* to conserve 13
construir *v.* to build
consultorio *m.* doctor's office 10
consumir *v.* to consume 15
contabilidad *f.* accounting 2
contador(a) *m., f.* accountant 16
contaminación *f.* pollution 13
   contaminación del aire/del
    agua air/water pollution 13
contaminado/a *adj.* polluted 13
contaminar *v.* to pollute 13
contar (o:ue) *v.* to count; to tell 4
contento/a *adj.* content 5
contestar *v.* to answer 2
contigo *fam. pron.* with you 5, 9
contraseña *f.* password 11

contratar *v.* to hire 16
control *m.* **remoto** remote
   control 11
controlar *v.* to control 13
conversación *f.* conversation 1
conversar *v.* to converse, to chat 2
copa *f.* wineglass 12
corazón *m.* heart 10
corbata *f.* tie 6
corredor(a) *m., f.* **de bolsa**
   stockbroker 16
correo *m.* mail; post office 14
   correo de voz *m.* voice mail 11
   correo electrónico *m.* e-mail 4
correr *v.* to run 3
cortesía *f.* courtesy
cortinas *f., pl.* curtains 12
corto/a *adj.* short (*in length*) 6
cosa *f.* thing 1
costar (o:ue) *v.* to cost 6
costarricense *adj.* Costa Rican 3
cráter *m.* crater 13
creer *v.* to believe 3, 13
   creer (en) *v.* to believe (in) 3
   no creer *v.* not to believe 13
creído/a *adj., p.p.* believed 14
crema de afeitar *f.* shaving
   cream 5, 7
crimen *m.* crime; murder 18
cruzar *v.* to cross 14
cuaderno *m.* notebook 1
cuadra *f.* (city) block 14
¿cuál(es)? which?; which one(s)? 2
   ¿Cuál es la fecha de hoy?
    What is today's date? 5
cuadro *m.* picture 12
cuando *conj.* when 7; 13
¿cuándo? when? 2
¿cuánto(s)/a(s)? how much/how
   many? 1, 2
   ¿Cuánto cuesta...? How
    much does... cost? 6
   ¿Cuántos años tienes? How
    old are you?
cuarenta forty 2
cuarto *m.* room 2; 7
   cuarto de baño *m.* bathroom 7
cuarto/a *adj.* fourth 5
   menos cuarto quarter to
    (time) 1
   y cuarto quarter after (time) 1
cuatro four 1
cuatrocientos/as four hundred 2
cubano/a *adj.* Cuban 3
cubiertos *m., pl.* silverware
cubierto/a *p.p.* covered
cubrir *v.* to cover
cuchara *f.* (table or large) spoon 12
cuchillo *m.* knife 12
cuello *m.* neck 10
cuenta *f.* bill 8; account 14
   cuenta corriente *f.* checking
    account 14
   cuenta de ahorros *f.* savings
    account 14
cuento *m.* short story 17
cuerpo *m.* body 10

cuidado *m.* care
cuidar *v.* to take care of 13
cultura *f.* culture 2, 17
cumpleaños *m., sing.* birthday 9
cumplir años *v.* to have a birthday
cuñado/a *m., f.* brother-in-law/
   sister-in-law 3
currículum *m.* résumé 16
curso *m.* course 2

<hr>

D

danza *f.* dance 17
dañar *v.* to damage; to break
   down 10
dar *v.* to give 6
   dar un consejo *v.* to give advice
   darse con *v.* to bump into; to
    run into (something) 10
   darse prisa *v.* to hurry; to rush
    15
de *prep.* of; from 1
   ¿De dónde eres? *fam.*
    Where are you from? 1
   ¿De dónde es usted? *form.*
    Where are you from? 1
   ¿De parte de quién? Who is
    speaking/calling? (*on telephone*)
    11
   ¿de quién...? whose...? (*sing.*) 1
   ¿de quiénes...? whose...? (*pl.*) 1
   de algodón (made) of cotton 6
   de aluminio (made) of
    aluminum 13
   de buen humor in a good
    mood 5
   de compras shopping 5
   de cuadros plaid 6
   de excursión hiking 4
   de hecho in fact
   de ida y vuelta roundtrip 5
   de la mañana in the morning;
    A.M. 1
   de la noche in the evening; at
    night; P.M. 1
   de la tarde in the afternoon; in
    the early evening; P.M. 1
   de lana (made) of wool 6
   de lunares polka-dotted 6
   de mal humor in a bad mood 5
   de moda in fashion 6
   De nada. You're welcome. 1
   de niño/a as a child 10
   de parte de on behalf of 11
   de plástico (made) of plastic 13
   de rayas striped 6
   de repente suddenly 6
   de seda (made) of silk 6
   de vaqueros western (genre) 17
   de vez en cuando from
    time to time 10
   de vidrio (made) of glass 13
debajo de *prep.* below; under 2
deber (+ inf.) *v.* should; must;
   ought to 3

deber *m.* responsibility; obligation 18

debido a due to (the fact that)

débil *adj.* weak 15

decidir (+ *inf.*) *v.* to decide 3

décimo/a *adj.* tenth 5

decir (e:i) *v.* **(que)** to say (that); to tell (that) 4

   decir la respuesta to say the answer 4

   decir la verdad to tell the truth 4

   decir mentiras to tell lies 4

declarar *v.* to declare 18

dedo *m.* finger 10

dedo del pie *m.* toe 10

deforestación *f.* deforestation 13

dejar *v.* to let; to quit; to leave behind 16

   dejar de (+ *inf.*) *v.* to stop (*doing something*) 13

   dejar una propina *v.* to leave a tip

del (*contraction of* **de** + **el**) of the; from the 1

delante de *prep.* in front of 2

delgado/a *adj.* thin 3

delicioso/a *adj.* delicious 8

demás *adj.* the rest

demasiado *adv.* too much 6

dentista *m., f.* dentist 10

dentro de (diez años) within (ten years) 16; inside

dependiente/a *m., f.* clerk 6

deporte *m.* sport 4

deportista *m.* sports person

deportivo/a *adj.* sports-related 4

depositar *v.* to deposit 14

derecha *f.* right 2

   a la derecha de to the right of 2

derecho *adv.* straight (ahead) 14

derechos *m., pl.* rights 18

desarrollar *v.* to develop 13

desastre (natural) *m.* (natural) disaster 18

desayunar *v.* to have breakfast 2

desayuno *m.* breakfast 8

descafeinado/a *adj.* decaffeinated 15

descansar *v.* to rest 2

descargar *v.* to download 11

descompuesto/a *adj.* not working; out of order 11

describir *v.* to describe 3

descrito/a *p.p.* described 14

descubierto/a *p.p.* discovered 14

descubrir *v.* to discover 13

desde *prep.* from 6

desear *v.* to wish; to desire 2

desempleo *m.* unemployment 18

desierto *m.* desert 13

desigualdad *f.* inequality 18

desordenado/a *adj.* disorderly 5

despacio *adv.* slowly 10

despedida *f.* farewell; goodbye

despedir (e:i) *v.* to fire 16

despedirse (de) (e:i) *v.* to say goodbye (to) 18

despejado/a *adj.* clear (*weather*)

despertador *m.* alarm clock 7

despertarse (e:ie) *v.* to wake up 7

después *adv.* afterward; then 7

   después de *prep.* after 7

   después de que *conj.* after 13

destruir *v.* to destroy 13

detrás de *prep.* behind 2

día *m.* day 1

   día de fiesta holiday 9

diario *m.* diary 1; newspaper 18

diario/a *adj.* daily 7

dibujar *v.* to draw 2

dibujo *m.* drawing

   dibujos animados *m., pl.* cartoons 17

diccionario *m.* dictionary 1

dicho/a *p.p.* said 14

diciembre *m.* December 5

dictadura *f.* dictatorship 18

diecinueve nineteen 1

dieciocho eighteen 1

dieciséis sixteen 1

diecisiete seventeen 1

diente *m.* tooth 7

dieta *f.* diet 15

   comer una dieta equilibrada to eat a balanced diet 15

diez ten 1

difícil *adj.* difficult 3

Diga. Hello. (*on telephone*) 11

diligencia *f.* errand 14

dinero *m.* money 6

dirección *f.* address 14

   dirección electrónica *f.* e-mail address 11

director(a) *m., f.* director; (*musical*) conductor 17

dirigir *v.* to direct 17

discriminación *f.* discrimination 18

discurso *m.* speech 18

diseñador(a) *m., f.* designer 16

diseño *m.* design

disfraz *m.* costume 9

disfrutar (de) *v.* to enjoy; to reap the benefits (of) 15

disminuir *v.* to reduce 16

diversión *f.* fun activity; entertainment; recreation 4

divertido/a *adj.* fun

divertirse (e:ie) *v.* to have fun 9

divorciado/a *adj.* divorced 9

divorciarse (de) *v.* to get divorced (from) 9

divorcio *m.* divorce 9

doblar *v.* to turn 14

doble *adj.* double 5

doce twelve 1

doctor(a) *m., f.* doctor 3; 10

documental *m.* documentary 17

documentos de viaje *m., pl.* travel documents

doler (o:ue) *v.* to hurt 10

dolor *m.* ache; pain 10

dolor de cabeza *m.* headache 10

doméstico/a *adj.* domestic 12

domingo *m.* Sunday 2

don *m.* Mr.; sir 1

doña *f.* Mrs.; ma'am 1

donde *adv.* where

   ¿Dónde está...? Where is...? 2

   ¿dónde? where? 1, 2

dormir (o:ue) *v.* to sleep 4

dormirse (o:ue) *v.* to go to sleep; to fall asleep 7

dormitorio *m.* bedroom 12

dos two 1

   dos veces *f.* twice 6

doscientos/as two hundred 2

drama *m.* drama; play 17

dramático/a *adj.* dramatic 17

dramaturgo/a *m., f.* playwright 17

droga *f.* drug 15

drogadicto/a *m., f.* drug addict 15

ducha *f.* shower 7

ducharse *v.* to take a shower 7

duda *f.* doubt 13

dudar *v.* to doubt 13

   no dudar *v.* not to doubt 13

dueño/a *m., f.* owner 8

dulces *m., pl.* sweets; candy 9

durante *prep.* during 7

durar *v.* to last 18

E

e *conj.* (*used instead of* **y** *before words beginning with* **i** *and* **hi**) and

echar *v.* to throw

   echar (una carta) al buzón *v.* to put (a letter) in the mailbox; to mail 14

ecología *f.* ecology 13

ecológico/a *adj.* ecological 13

ecologista *m., f.* ecologist 13

economía *f.* economics 2

ecoturismo *m.* ecotourism 13

ecuatoriano/a *adj.* Ecuadorian 3

edad *f.* age 9

edificio *m.* building 12

   edificio de apartamentos apartment building 12

(en) efectivo *m.* cash 6

ejercer *v.* to practice/exercise (a degree/profession) 16

ejercicio *m.* exercise 15

   ejercicios aeróbicos aerobic exercises 15

   ejercicios de estiramiento stretching exercises 15

ejército *m.* army 18

el *m., sing., def. art.* the 1

él *sub. pron.* he 1; *obj. pron.* him

elecciones *f., pl.* election 18

electricista *m., f.* electrician 16

electrodoméstico *m.* electric appliance 12

elegante *adj. m., f.* elegant 6
elegir (e:i) *v.* to elect 18
ella *sub. pron.* she 1; *obj. pron.* her
ellos/as *sub. pron.* they 1;
　obj. pron. them
embarazada *adj.* pregnant 10
emergencia *f.* emergency 10
emitir *v.* to broadcast 18
emocionante *adj. m., f.* exciting
empezar (e:ie) *v.* to begin 4
empleado/a *m., f.* employee 5
empleo *m.* job; employment 16
empresa *f.* company; firm 16
en *prep.* in; on 2
　en casa at home
　en caso (de) que *conj.* in case
　　(that) 13
　en cuanto *conj.* as soon as 13
　en efectivo in cash 14
　en exceso in excess; too
　　much 15
　en línea online 6
　en punto on the dot; exactly;
　　sharp (*time*) 1
　en qué in what; how
　¿En qué puedo servirles?
　　How can I help you? 5
　en vivo live 7
enamorado/a (de) *adj.* in love
　(with) 5
enamorarse (de) *v.* to fall in love
　(with) 9
encantado/a *adj.* delighted;
　pleased to meet you 1
encantar *v.* to like very much; to
　love (*inanimate objects*) 7
encima de *prep.* on top of 2
encontrar (o:ue) *v.* to find 4
encontrar(se) (o:ue) *v.* to meet
　(each other); to run into (each
　other) 11
　encontrarse con to meet up
　　with 7
encuesta *f.* poll; survey 18
energía *f.* energy 13
　energía nuclear nuclear
　　energy 13
　energía solar solar energy 13
enero *m.* January 5
enfermarse *v.* to get sick 10
enfermedad *f.* illness 10
enfermero/a *m., f.* nurse 10
enfermo/a *adj.* sick 10
enfrente de *adv.* opposite; facing 14
engordar *v.* to gain weight 15
enojado/a *adj.* angry 5
enojarse (con) *v.* to get angry
　(with) 7
ensalada *f.* salad 8
ensayo *m.* essay 3
enseguida *adv.* right away
enseñar *v.* to teach 2
ensuciar *v.* to get (something)
　dirty 12
entender (e:ie) *v.* to understand 4
enterarse *v.* to find out 16
entonces *adv.* so, then 5, 7

entrada *f.* entrance 12; ticket
entre *prep.* between; among 2
entregar *v.* to hand in 11
entremeses *m., pl.* appetizers 8
entrenador(a) *m., f.* trainer 15
entrenarse *v.* to train 15
entrevista *f.* interview 16
entrevistador(a) *m., f.*
　interviewer 16
entrevistar *v.* to interview 16
envase *m.* container 13
enviar *v.* to send; to mail 14
equilibrado/a *adj.* balanced 15
equipaje *m.* luggage 5
equipo *m.* team 4
equivocado/a *adj.* wrong 5
eres *fam.* you are 1
es he/she/it is 1
　Es bueno que… It's good
　　that… 12
　es cierto it's certain 13
　es extraño it's strange 13
　es igual it's the same 5
　Es importante que… It's
　　important that… 12
　es imposible it's impossible 13
　es improbable it's
　　improbable 13
　Es malo que… It's bad
　　that… 12
　Es mejor que… It's better
　　that… 12
　Es necesario que… It's
　　necessary that… 12
　es obvio it's obvious 13
　es posible it's possible 13
　es probable it's probable 13
　es ridículo it's ridiculous 13
　es seguro it's certain 13
　es terrible it's terrible 13
　es triste it's sad 13
　Es urgente que… It's urgent
　　that… 12
　Es la una. It's one o'clock. 1
　es una lástima it's a shame 13
　es verdad it's true 13
esa(s) *f., adj.* that; those 6
ésa(s) *f., pron.* that (one);
　those (ones) 6
escalar *v.* to climb 4
　escalar montañas to climb
　　mountains 4
escalera *f.* stairs 12
escalón *m.* step 15
escanear *v.* to scan 11
escoger *v.* to choose 8
escribir *v.* to write 3
　escribir un mensaje
　　electrónico to write an
　　e-mail 4
　escribir una carta to write a
　　letter 4
escrito/a *p.p.* written 14
escritor(a) *m., f.* writer 17
escritorio *m.* desk 2
escuchar *v.* to listen (to) 2
　escuchar la radio to listen to

　the radio 2
　escuchar música to listen to
　　music 2
escuela *f.* school 1
esculpir *v.* to sculpt 17
escultor(a) *m., f.* sculptor 17
escultura *f.* sculpture 17
ese *m., sing., adj.* that 6
ése *m., sing., pron.* that one 6
eso *neuter, pron.* that;
　that thing 6
esos *m., pl., adj.* those 6
ésos *m., pl., pron.* those (ones) 6
España *f.* Spain
español *m.* Spanish (*language*) 2
español(a) *adj. m., f.* Spanish 3
espárragos *m., pl.* asparagus 8
especialidad: las especialidades
　del día today's specials 8
especialización *f.* major 2
espectacular *adj.* spectacular
espectáculo *m.* show 17
espejo *m.* mirror 7
esperar *v.* to hope; to wish 13
　esperar (+ *inf.*) *v.* to wait
　　(for); to hope 2
esposo/a *m., f.* husband/wife;
　spouse 3
esquí (acuático) *m.* (water)
　skiing 4
esquiar *v.* to ski 4
esquina *f.* corner 14
está he/she/it is, you are 1
　Está bien. That's fine.
　Está (muy) despejado. It's
　　(very) clear. (*weather*)
　Está lloviendo. It's raining. 5
　Está nevando. It's snowing. 5
　Está (muy) nublado. It's
　　(very) cloudy. (*weather*) 5
esta(s) *f., adj.* this; these 6
　esta noche tonight
ésta(s) *f., pron.* this (one); these
　(ones) 6
establecer *v.* to establish 16
estación *f.* station; season 5
　estación de autobuses
　　bus station 5
　estación del metro subway
　　station 5
　estación de tren train
　　station 5
estacionamiento *m.* parking
　lot 14
estacionar *v.* to park 11
estadio *m.* stadium 2
estado civil *m.* marital status 9
Estados Unidos *m., pl.* (EE.UU.;
　E.U.) United States
estadounidense *adj. m., f.* from
　the United States 3
estampilla *f.* stamp 14
estante *m.* bookcase;
　bookshelves 12
estar *v.* to be 2
　estar a dieta to be on a diet 15

estar aburrido/a to be bored 5   **estar**
afectado/a (por) to be affected (by) 13
estar cansado/a to be tired 5
estar contaminado/a to be polluted 13
estar de acuerdo to agree 17
  Estoy de acuerdo. I agree. 17
  No estoy de acuerdo. I don't agree. 17
estar de moda to be in fashion 6
estar de vacaciones *f., pl.* to be on vacation 5
estar en buena forma to be in good shape 15
estar enfermo/a to be sick 10
estar harto/a de... to be sick of... 18
estar listo/a to be ready 5
estar perdido/a to be lost 14
estar roto/a to be broken
estar seguro/a to be sure 5
estar torcido/a to be twisted; to be sprained 10
  No está nada mal. It's not bad at all. 5
estatua *f.* statue 17
este *m.* east 14
este *m., sing., adj.* this 6
éste *m., sing., pron.* this (one) 6
estéreo *m.* stereo
estilo *m.* style
estiramiento *m.* stretching 15
esto *neuter pron.* this; this thing 6
estómago *m.* stomach 10
estornudar *v.* to sneeze 10
estos *m., pl., adj.* these 6
éstos *m., pl., pron.* these (ones) 6
estrella *f.* star 13
  estrella de cine *m., f.* movie star 17
estrés *m.* stress 15
estudiante *m., f.* student 1, 2
estudiantil *adj. m., f.* student 2
estudiar *v.* to study 2
estufa *f.* stove 12
estupendo/a *adj.* stupendous 5
etapa *f.* stage 9
evitar *v.* to avoid 13
examen *m.* test; exam 2
  examen médico physical exam 10
excelente *adj. m., f.* excellent 5
exceso *m.* excess 15
excursión *f.* hike; tour; excursion 4
excursionista *m., f.* hiker
éxito *m.* success
experiencia *f.* experience
explicar *v.* to explain 2
explorar *v.* to explore
expresión *f.* expression
extinción *f.* extinction 13
extranjero/a *adj.* foreign 17

extrañar *v.* to miss 16
extraño/a *adj.* strange 13

F

fábrica *f.* factory 13
fabuloso/a *adj.* fabulous 5
fácil *adj.* easy 3
falda *f.* skirt 6
faltar *v.* to lack; to need 7
familia *f.* family 3
famoso/a *adj.* famous
farmacia *f.* pharmacy 10
fascinar *v.* to fascinate 7
favorito/a *adj.* favorite 4
febrero *m.* February 5
fecha *f.* date 5
¡Felicidades! Congratulations! 9
¡Felicitaciones! Congratulations! 9
feliz *adj.* happy 5
  ¡Feliz cumpleaños! Happy birthday! 9
fenomenal *adj.* great, phenomenal 5
feo/a *adj.* ugly 3
festival *m.* festival 17
fiebre *f.* fever 10
fiesta *f.* party 9
fijo/a *adj.* fixed, set 6
fin *m.* end 4
  fin de semana weekend 4
finalmente *adv.* finally
firmar *v.* to sign (*a document*) 14
física *f.* physics 2
flan (de caramelo) *m.* baked (caramel) custard 9
flexible *adj.* flexible 15
flor *f.* flower 13
folclórico/a *adj.* folk; folkloric 17
folleto *m.* brochure
forma *f.* shape 15
formulario *m.* form 14
foto(grafía) *f.* photograph 1
francés, francesa *adj. m., f.* French 3
frecuentemente *adv.* frequently
frenos *m., pl.* brakes
frente (frío) *m.* (cold) front 5
fresco/a *adj.* cool
frijoles *m., pl.* beans 8
frío/a *adj.* cold
frito/a *adj.* fried 8
fruta *f.* fruit 8
frutería *f.* fruit store 14
fuera *adv.* outside
fuerte *adj. m., f.* strong 15
fumar *v.* to smoke 15
  (no) fumar *v.* (not) to smoke 15
funcionar *v.* to work 11; to function
fútbol *m.* soccer 4
fútbol americano *m.* football 4
futuro/a *adj.* future
  en el futuro in the future

G

gafas (de sol) *f., pl.* (sun)glasses 6
gafas (oscuras) *f., pl.* (sun)glasses
galleta *f.* cookie 9
ganar *v.* to win 4; to earn (money) 16
ganga *f.* bargain 6
garaje *m.* garage; (mechanic's) repair shop 11; garage (*in a house*) 12
garganta *f.* throat 10
gasolina *f.* gasoline 11
gasolinera *f.* gas station 11
gastar *v.* to spend (*money*) 6
gato *m.* cat 13
gemelo/a *m., f.* twin 3
genial *adj.* great 16
gente *f.* people 3
geografía *f.* geography 2
gerente *m., f.* manager 8, 16
gimnasio *m.* gymnasium 4
gobierno *m.* government 13
golf *m.* golf 4
gordo/a *adj.* fat 3
grabar *v.* to record 11
gracias *f., pl.* thank you; thanks 1
  Gracias por invitarme. Thanks for inviting me. 9
graduarse (de/en) *v.* to graduate (from/in) 9
grande *adj.* big; large 3
grasa *f.* fat 15
gratis *adj. m., f.* free of charge 14
grave *adj.* grave; serious 10
gripe *f.* flu 10
gris *adj. m., f.* gray 6
gritar *v.* to scream, to shout
grito *m.* scream 5
guantes *m., pl.* gloves 6
guapo/a *adj.* good-looking 3
guardar *v.* to save (on a computer) 11
guerra *f.* war 18
guía *m., f.* guide
gustar *v.* to be pleasing to; to like 2
  Me gustaría... I would like...
gusto *m.* pleasure 1
  El gusto es mío. The pleasure is mine. 1
  Mucho gusto. Pleased to meet you. 1
  ¡Qué gusto verlo/la! *form.* How nice to see you! 18
  ¡Qué gusto verte! *fam.* How nice to see you! 18

H

haber *(auxiliar) v.* to have (done something) 15
habitación *f.* room 5
  habitación doble double room 5
  habitación individual single room 5

hablar *v.* to talk; to speak 2
hacer *v.* to do; to make 4
  Hace buen tiempo. The weather is good. 5
  Hace (mucho) calor. It's (very) hot. (*weather*) 5
  Hace fresco. It's cool. (*weather*) 5
  Hace (mucho) frío. It's (very) cold. (*weather*) 5
  Hace mal tiempo. The weather is bad. 5
  Hace (mucho) sol. It's (very) sunny. (*weather*) 5
  Hace (mucho) viento. It's (very) windy. (*weather*) 5
  hacer cola to stand in line 14
  hacer diligencias to run errands 14
  hacer ejercicio to exercise 15
  hacer ejercicios aeróbicos to do aerobics 15
  hacer ejercicios de estiramiento to do stretching exercises 15
  hacer el papel (de) to play the role (of) 17
  hacer gimnasia to work out 15
  hacer juego (con) to match (with) 6
  hacer la cama to make the bed 12
  hacer las maletas to pack (one's) suitcases 5
  hacer quehaceres domésticos to do household chores 12
  hacer (wind)surf to (wind)surf 5
  hacer turismo to go sightseeing
  hacer un viaje to take a trip 5
  ¿Me harías el honor de casarte conmigo? Would you do me the honor of marrying me? 17
hacia *prep.* toward 14
hambre *f.* hunger
hamburguesa *f.* hamburger 8
hasta *prep.* until 6; toward
  Hasta la vista. See you later. 1
  Hasta luego. See you later. 1
  Hasta mañana. See you tomorrow. 1
  Hasta pronto. See you soon. 1
  hasta que *conj.* until 13
hay there is; there are 1
  Hay (mucha) niebla. It's (very) foggy.
  Hay que It is necessary that
  No hay de qué. You're welcome. 1
  No hay duda de There's no doubt 13
hecho/a *p.p.* done 14
heladería *f.* ice cream shop 14
helado *m.* ice cream 9
helado/a *adj.* iced 8
hermanastro/a *m., f.* stepbrother/ stepsister 3

hermano/a *m., f.* brother/sister 3
hermano/a mayor/menor *m., f.* older/younger brother/sister 3
hermanos *m., pl.* siblings (brothers and sisters) 3
hermoso/a *adj.* beautiful 6
hierba *f.* grass 13
hijastro/a *m., f.* stepson/ stepdaughter 3
hijo/a *m., f.* son/daughter 3
  hijo/a único/a *m., f.* only child 3
  hijos *m., pl.* children 3
híjole *interj.* wow 6
historia *f.* history 2; story 17
hockey *m.* hockey 4
hola *interj.* hi 1
hombre *m.* man 1
  hombre de negocios *m.* businessman 16
hora *f.* hour 1; the time
horario *m.* schedule 2
horno *m.* oven 12
  horno de microondas *m.* microwave oven 12
horror *m.* horror 17
  de horror horror (genre) 17
hospital *m.* hospital 10
hotel *m.* hotel 5
hoy *adv.* today 2
  hoy día *adv.* nowadays
  Hoy es... Today is... 2
hueco *m.* hole 4
huelga *f.* strike (*labor*) 18
hueso *m.* bone 10
huésped *m., f.* guest 5
huevo *m.* egg 8
humanidades *f., pl.* humanities 2
huracán *m.* hurricane 18

<hr>

I

ida *f.* one way (*travel*)
idea *f.* idea 18
iglesia *f.* church 4
igualdad *f.* equality 18
igualmente *adv.* likewise 1
impermeable *m.* raincoat 6
importante *adj. m., f.* important 3
importar *v.* to be important to; to matter 7
imposible *adj. m., f.* impossible 13
impresora *f.* printer 11
imprimir *v.* to print 11
improbable *adj. m., f.* improbable 13
impuesto *m.* tax 18
incendio *m.* fire 18
increíble *adj. m., f.* incredible 5
indicar cómo llegar *v.* to give directions 14
individual *adj.* single (*room*) 5
infección *f.* infection 10
informar *v.* to inform 18
informe *m.* report 18

ingeniero/a *m., f.* engineer 3
inglés *m.* English (*language*) 2
inglés, inglesa *adj.* English 3
inodoro *m.* toilet 7
insistir (en) *v.* to insist (on) 12
inspector(a) de aduanas *m., f.* customs inspector 5
inteligente *adj. m., f.* intelligent 3
intento *m.* attempt 11
intercambiar *v.* to exchange
interesante *adj. m., f.* interesting 3
interesar *v.* to be interesting to; to interest 7
internacional *adj. m., f.* international 18
Internet Internet 11
inundación *f.* flood 18
invertir (e:ie) *v.* to invest 16
invierno *m.* winter 5
invitado/a *m., f.* guest 9
invitar *v.* to invite 9
inyección *f.* injection 10
ir *v.* to go 4
  ir a (+ *inf.*) to be going to do something 4
  ir de compras to go shopping 5
  ir de excursión (a las montañas) to go on a hike (in the mountains) 4
  ir de pesca to go fishing
  ir de vacaciones to go on vacation 5
  ir en autobús to go by bus 5
  ir en auto(móvil) to go by car 5
  ir en avión to go by plane 5
  ir en barco to go by boat 5
  ir en metro to go by subway
  ir en moto(cicleta) to go by motorcycle 5
  ir en taxi to go by taxi 5
  ir en tren to go by train
irse *v.* to go away; to leave 7
italiano/a *adj.* Italian 3
izquierda *f.* left 2
  a la izquierda de to the left of 2

<hr>

J

jabón *m.* soap 7
jamás *adv.* never; not ever 7
jamón *m.* ham 8
japonés, japonesa *adj.* Japanese 3
jardín *m.* garden; yard 12
jefe, jefa *m., f.* boss 16
jengibre *m.* ginger 10
joven *adj. m., f., sing.* (**jóvenes** *pl.*) young 3
joven *m., f., sing.* (**jóvenes** *pl.*) young person 1
joyería *f.* jewelry store 14
jubilarse *v.* to retire (*from work*) 9
juego *m.* game
jueves *m., sing.* Thursday 2
jugador(a) *m., f.* player 4

jugar (u:ue) *v.* to play 4
  jugar a las cartas *f., pl.* to play cards 5
jugo *m.* juice 8
  jugo de fruta *m.* fruit juice 8
julio *m.* July 5
jungla *f.* jungle 13
junio *m.* June 5
juntos/as *adj.* together 9
juventud *f.* youth 9

K

kilómetro *m.* kilometer 11

L

la *f., sing., def. art.* the 1; *f., sing., d.o. pron.* her, it, *form.* you 5
laboratorio *m.* laboratory 2
lago *m.* lake 13
lámpara *f.* lamp 12
lana *f.* wool 6
langosta *f.* lobster 8
lápiz *m.* pencil 1
largo/a *adj.* long 6
las *f., pl., def. art.* the 1; *f., pl., d.o. pron.* them; you 5
lástima *f.* shame 13
lastimarse *v.* to injure oneself 10
  lastimarse el pie to injure one's foot 10
lata *f.* (*tin*) can 13
lavabo *m.* sink 7
lavadora *f.* washing machine 12
lavandería *f.* laundromat 14
lavaplatos *m., sing.* dishwasher 12
lavar *v.* to wash 12
  lavar (el suelo, los platos) to wash (the floor, the dishes) 12
lavarse *v.* to wash oneself 7
  lavarse la cara to wash one's face 7
  lavarse las manos to wash one's hands 7
le *sing., i.o. pron.* to/for him, her, *form.* you 6
  Le presento a... *form.* I would like to introduce you to (name). 1
lección *f.* lesson 1
leche *f.* milk 8
lechuga *f.* lettuce 8
leer *v.* to read 3
  leer el correo electrónico to read e-mail 4
  leer un periódico to read a newspaper 4
  leer una revista to read a magazine 4
leído/a *p.p.* read 14
lejos de *prep.* far from 2
lengua *f.* language 2
  lenguas extranjeras *f., pl.* foreign languages 2

lentes de contacto *m., pl.* contact lenses
  lentes (de sol) (sun)glasses
lento/a *adj.* slow 11
les *pl., i.o. pron.* to/for them, you 6
letrero *m.* sign 14
levantar *v.* to lift 15
  levantar pesas to lift weights 15
levantarse *v.* to get up 7
ley *f.* law 13
libertad *f.* liberty; freedom 18
libre *adj. m., f.* free 4
librería *f.* bookstore 2
libro *m.* book 2
licencia de conducir *f.* driver's license 11
limón *m.* lemon 8
limpiar *v.* to clean 12
  limpiar la casa *v.* to clean the house 12
limpio/a *adj.* clean 5
línea *f.* line 4
listo/a *adj.* ready; smart 5
literatura *f.* literature 2
llamar *v.* to call 11
  llamar por teléfono to call on the phone
llamarse *v.* to be called; to be named 7
llanta *f.* tire 11
llave *f.* key 5; wrench 11
llegada *f.* arrival 5
llegar *v.* to arrive 2
llenar *v.* to fill 11, 14
  llenar el tanque to fill the tank 11
  llenar (un formulario) to fill out (a form) 14
lleno/a *adj.* full 11
llevar *v.* to carry 2; to wear; to take 6
  llevar una vida sana to lead a healthy lifestyle 15
  llevarse bien/mal (con) to get along well/badly (with) 9
llorar *v.* to cry 15
llover (o:ue) *v.* to rain 5
  Llueve. It's raining. 5
lluvia *f.* rain
lo *m., sing. d.o. pron.* him, it, *form.* you 5
  ¡Lo he pasado de película! I've had a fantastic time! 18
  lo mejor the best (thing)
  lo que that which; what 12
  Lo siento. I'm sorry. 1
loco/a *adj.* crazy 6
locutor(a) *m., f.* (TV or radio) announcer 18
lodo *m.* mud
los *m., pl., def. art.* the 1; *m. pl., d.o. pron.* them, you 5
luchar (contra/por) *v.* to fight; to struggle (against/for) 18

luego *adv.* then 7; later 1
lugar *m.* place 2, 4
luna *f.* moon 13
lunares *m.* polka dots
lunes *m., sing.* Monday 2
luz *f.* light; electricity 12

M

madrastra *f.* stepmother 3
madre *f.* mother 3
madurez *f.* maturity; middle age 9
maestro/a *m., f.* teacher 16
magnífico/a *adj.* magnificent 5
maíz *m.* corn 8
mal, malo/a *adj.* bad 3
maleta *f.* suitcase 1
mamá *f.* mom
mandar *v.* to order 12; to send; to mail 14
manejar *v.* to drive 11
manera *f.* way
mano *f.* hand 1
manta *f.* blanket 12
mantener *v.* to maintain 15
  mantenerse en forma to stay in shape 15
mantequilla *f.* butter 8
manzana *f.* apple 8
mañana *f.* morning, a.m. 1; tomorrow 1
mapa *m.* map 1, 2
maquillaje *m.* makeup 7
maquillarse *v.* to put on makeup 7
mar *m.* sea 5
maravilloso/a *adj.* marvelous 5
marcador *m.* marker 2
mareado/a *adj.* dizzy; nauseated 10
margarina *f.* margarine 8
mariscos *m., pl.* shellfish 8
marrón *adj. m., f.* brown 6
martes *m., sing.* Tuesday 2
marzo *m.* March 5
más *adv.* more 2
  más de (+ *number***)** more than 8
  más tarde later (on) 7
  más... que more... than 8
masaje *m.* massage 15
matemáticas *f., pl.* mathematics 2
materia *f.* course 2
matrimonio *m.* marriage 9
máximo/a *adj.* maximum 11
mayo *m.* May 5
mayonesa *f.* mayonnaise 8
mayor *adj.* older 3
  el/la mayor *adj.* oldest 8
me *sing., d.o. pron.* me 5; *sing. i.o. pron.* to/for me 6
  Me gusta... I like... 2
  Me gustaría(n)... I would like... 15
  Me llamo... My name is... 1

Me muero por... I'm dying to (for)...
mecánico/a *m., f.* mechanic 11
mediano/a *adj.* medium
medianoche *f.* midnight 1
medias *f., pl.* pantyhose, stockings 6
medicamento *m.* medication 10
medicina *f.* medicine 10
médico/a *m., f.* doctor 3; *adj.* medical 10
medio/a *adj.* half 3
  medio ambiente *m.* environment 13
  medio/a hermano/a *m., f.* half-brother/half-sister 3
  mediodía *m.* noon 1
  medios de comunicación *m., pl.* means of communication; media 18
  y media thirty minutes past the hour (time) 1
mejor *adj.* better 8
  el/la mejor *m., f.* the best 8
mejorar *v.* to improve 13
melocotón *m.* peach 8
menor *adj.* younger 3
  el/la menor *m., f.* youngest 8
menos *adv.* less 10
  menos cuarto..., menos quince... quarter to... (time) 1
  menos de (+ number) fewer than 8
  menos... que less... than 8
mensaje *m.* **de texto** text message 11
mensaje electrónico *m.* e-mail message 4
mentira *f.* lie 4
menú *m.* menu 8
mercado *m.* market 6
  mercado al aire libre open-air market 6
merendar (e:ie) *v.* to snack 8; to have an afternoon snack
merienda *f.* afternoon snack 15
mes *m.* month 5
mesa *f.* table 2
mesita *f.* end table 12
  mesita de noche night stand 12
meterse en problemas *v.* to get into trouble 13
metro *m.* subway 5
mexicano/a *adj.* Mexican 3
mí *pron., obj. of prep.* me 9
mi(s) *poss. adj.* my 3
microonda *f.* microwave 12
  horno de microondas *m.* microwave oven 12
miedo *m.* fear
miel *f.* honey 10
mientras *conj.* while 10
miércoles *m., sing.* Wednesday 2
mil *m.* one thousand 2
  mil millones billion
milla *f.* mile
millón *m.* million 2

millones (de) *m.* millions (of)
mineral *m.* mineral 15
minuto *m.* minute
mío(s)/a(s) *poss.* my; (of) mine 11
mirar *v.* to look (at); to watch 2
  mirar (la) televisión to watch television 2
mismo/a *adj.* same 3
mochila *f.* backpack 2
moda *f.* fashion 6
moderno/a *adj.* modern 17
molestar *v.* to bother; to annoy 7
mono *m.* monkey 13
montaña *f.* mountain 4
montar *v.* **a caballo** to ride a horse 5
montón: un montón de a lot of 4
monumento *m.* monument 4
morado/a *adj.* purple 6
moreno/a *adj.* brunet(te) 3
morir (o:ue) *v.* to die 8
mostrar (o:ue) *v.* to show 4
moto(cicleta) *f.* motorcycle 5
motor *m.* motor
muchacho/a *m., f.* boy/girl 3
mucho/a *adj.,* a lot of; much; many 3
  (Muchas) gracias. Thank you (very much); Thanks (a lot). 1
  muchas veces *adv.* a lot; many times 10
  Mucho gusto. Pleased to meet you. 1
mudarse *v.* to move (from one house to another) 12
muebles *m., pl.* furniture 12
muerte *f.* death 9
muerto/a *p.p.* died 14
mujer *f.* woman 1
  mujer de negocios *f.* business woman 16
  mujer policía *f.* female police officer
multa *f.* fine
mundial *adj. m., f.* worldwide
mundo *m.* world 8
muro *m.* wall 15
músculo *m.* muscle 15
museo *m.* museum 4
música *f.* music 2, 17
musical *adj. m., f.* musical 17
músico/a *m., f.* musician 17
muy *adv.* very 1
  (Muy) bien, gracias. (Very) well, thanks. 1

N

nacer *v.* to be born 9
nacimiento *m.* birth 9
nacional *adj. m., f.* national 18
nacionalidad *f.* nationality 1
nada nothing 1; not anything 7
  nada mal not bad at all 5
nadar *v.* to swim 4
nadie *pron.* no one, nobody, not anyone 7

naranja *f.* orange 8
nariz *f.* nose 10
natación *f.* swimming 4
natural *adj. m., f.* natural 13
naturaleza *f.* nature 13
navegador *m.* **GPS** GPS 11
Navidad *f.* Christmas 9
necesario/a *adj.* necessary 12
necesitar (+ inf.) *v.* to need 2
negar (e:ie) *v.* to deny 13
  no negar (e:ie) *v.* not to deny 13
negocios *m., pl.* business; commerce 16
negro/a *adj.* black 6
nervioso/a *adj.* nervous 5
nevar (e:ie) *v.* to snow 5
  Nieva. It's snowing. 5
ni...ni neither... nor 7
niebla *f.* fog
nieto/a *m., f.* grandson/ granddaughter 3
nieve *f.* snow
ningún, ninguno/a(s) *adj.* no; none; not any 7
niñez *f.* childhood 9
niño/a *m., f.* child 3
no no; not 1
  ¿no? right? 1
  no cabe duda de there is no doubt 13
  no es seguro it's not certain 13
  no es verdad it's not true 13
  No está nada mal. It's not bad at all. 5
  no estar de acuerdo to disagree
  No estoy seguro. I'm not sure.
  no hay there is not; there are not 1
  No hay de qué. You're welcome. 1
  no hay duda de there is no doubt 13
  ¡No me diga(s)! You don't say!
  No me gustan nada. I don't like them at all. 2
  no muy bien not very well 1
  No quiero. I don't want to. 4
  No sé. I don't know.
  No te preocupes. *fam.* Don't worry. 7
  no tener razón to be wrong 3
noche *f.* night 1
nombre *m.* name 1
norte *m.* north 14
norteamericano/a *adj.* (North) American 3
nos *pl., d.o. pron.* us 5; *pl., i.o. pron.* to/for us 6
  Nos vemos. See you. 1
nosotros/as *sub. pron.* we 1; *obj. pron.* us
noticia *f.* news 11
noticias *f., pl.* news 18
noticiero *m.* newscast 18

novecientos/as nine hundred 2
noveno/a *adj.* ninth 5
noventa ninety 2
noviembre *m.* November 5
novio/a *m., f.* boyfriend/ girlfriend 3
nube *f.* cloud 13
nublado/a *adj.* cloudy 5
   Está (muy) nublado. It's very cloudy. 5
nuclear *adj. m., f.* nuclear 13
nuera *f.* daughter-in-law 3
nuestro(s)/a(s) *poss. adj.* our 3; our, (of) ours 11
nueve nine 1
nuevo/a *adj.* new 6
número *m.* number 1; (shoe) size 6
nunca *adv.* never; not ever 7
nutrición *f.* nutrition 15
nutricionista *m., f.* nutritionist 15

O

o or 7
o... o ; either... or 7
obedecer *v.* to obey 18
obra *f.* work (*of art, literature, music, etc.*) 17
   obra maestra *f.* masterpiece 17
obtener *v.* to obtain; to get 16
obvio/a *adj.* obvious 13
océano *m.* ocean
ochenta eighty 2
ocho eight 1
ochocientos/as eight hundred 2
octavo/a *adj.* eighth 5
octubre *m.* October 5
ocupación *f.* occupation 16
ocupado/a *adj.* busy 5
ocurrir *v.* to occur; to happen 18
odiar *v.* to hate 9
oeste *m.* west 14
oferta *f.* offer
oficina *f.* office 12
oficio *m.* trade 16
ofrecer *v.* to offer 6
oído *m.* (sense of) hearing; inner ear 10
oído/a *p.p.* heard 14
oír *v.* to hear 4
ojalá (que) *interj.* I hope (that); I wish (that) 13
ojo *m.* eye 10
olvidar *v.* to forget 10
once eleven 1
ópera *f.* opera 17
operación *f.* operation 10
ordenado/a *adj.* orderly 5
ordinal *adj.* ordinal (*number*)
oreja *f.* (outer) ear 10
organizarse *v.* to organize oneself 12
orquesta *f.* orchestra 17

ortografía *f.* spelling
ortográfico/a *adj.* spelling
os *fam., pl. d.o. pron.* you 5; *fam., pl. i.o. pron.* to/for you 6
otoño *m.* autumn 5
otro/a *adj.* other; another 6
   otra vez again

P

paciente *m., f.* patient 10
padrastro *m.* stepfather 3
padre *m.* father 3
padres *m., pl.* parents 3
pagar *v.* to pay 6
   pagar a plazos to pay in installments 14
   pagar al contado to pay in cash 14
   pagar en efectivo to pay in cash 14
   pagar la cuenta to pay the bill
página *f.* page 11
   página principal *f.* home page 11
país *m.* country 1
paisaje *m.* landscape 5
pájaro *m.* bird 13
palabra *f.* word 1
paleta helada *f.* popsicle 4
pálido/a *adj.* pale 14
pan *m.* bread 8
   pan tostado *m.* toasted bread 8
panadería *f.* bakery 14
pantalla *f.* screen 11
   pantalla táctil *f.* touch screen
pantalones *m., pl.* pants 6
   pantalones cortos *m., pl.* shorts 6
pantuflas *f., pl.* slippers 7
papa *f.* potato 8
   papas fritas *f., pl.* fried potatoes; French fries 8
papá *m.* dad
   papás *m., pl.* parents
papel *m.* paper 2; role 17
papelera *f.* wastebasket 2
paquete *m.* package 14
par *m.* pair 6
   par de zapatos pair of shoes 6
para *prep.* for; in order to; by; used for; considering 11
   para que *conj.* so that 13
parabrisas *m., sing.* windshield 11
parar *v.* to stop 11
parecer *v.* to seem 6
pared *f.* wall 12
pareja *f.* (married) couple; partner 9
parientes *m., pl.* relatives 3
parque *m.* park 4
párrafo *m.* paragraph
parte: de parte de on behalf of 11
partido *m.* game; match (*sports*) 4
pasado/a *adj.* last; past 6
   pasado *p.p.* passed

pasaje *m.* ticket 5
   pasaje de ida y vuelta *m.* roundtrip ticket 5
pasajero/a *m., f.* passenger 1
pasaporte *m.* passport 5
pasar *v.* to go through
   pasar la aspiradora to vacuum 12
   pasar por la aduana to go through customs
   pasar tiempo to spend time
   pasarlo bien/mal to have a good/bad time 9
pasatiempo *m.* pastime; hobby 4
pasear *v.* to take a walk; to stroll 4
   pasear en bicicleta to ride a bicycle 4
   pasear por to walk around
pasillo *m.* hallway 12
pasta *f.* **de dientes** toothpaste 7
pastel *m.* cake; pie 9
   pastel de chocolate *m.* chocolate cake 9
   pastel de cumpleaños *m.* birthday cake
pastelería *f.* pastry shop 14
pastilla *f.* pill 10
patata *f.* potato 8
   patatas fritas *f., pl.* fried potatoes; French fries 8
patinar *v.* to skate 4
patineta *f.* skateboard 4
patio *m.* patio; yard 12
pavo *m.* turkey 8
paz *f.* peace 18
pedir (e:i) *v.* to ask for; to request 4; to order (*food*) 8
   pedir prestado *v.* to borrow 14
   pedir un préstamo *v.* to apply for a loan 14
peinarse *v.* to comb one's hair 7
película *f.* movie 4
peligro *m.* danger 13
peligroso/a *adj.* dangerous 18
pelirrojo/a *adj.* red-haired 3
pelo *m.* hair 7
pelota *f.* ball 4
peluquería *f.* beauty salon 14
peluquero/a *m., f.* hairdresser 16
penicilina *f.* penicillin
pensar (e:ie) *v.* to think 4
   pensar (+ inf.) *v.* to intend to; to plan to (*do something*) 4
   pensar en *v.* to think about 4
peor *adj.* worse 8
   el/la peor *adj.* the worst 8
pequeño/a *adj.* small 3
pera *f.* pear 8
perder (e:ie) *v.* to lose; to miss 4
perdido/a *adj.* lost 13, 14
Perdón. Pardon me.; Excuse me. 1
perezoso/a *adj.* lazy
perfecto/a *adj.* perfect 5
perfil *m.* profile 11
periódico *m.* newspaper 4
periodismo *m.* journalism 2

periodista *m., f.* journalist 3
permiso *m.* permission
pero *conj.* but 2
perro *m.* dog 13
persona *f.* person 3
personaje *m.* character 17
   personaje principal *m.*
     main character 17
pesas *f. pl.* weights 15
pesca *f.* fishing
pescadería *f.* fish market 14
pescado *m.* fish (*cooked*) 8
pescar *v.* to fish 5
peso *m.* weight 15
pez *m., sing.* (**peces** *pl.*) fish (*live*) 13
pie *m.* foot 10
piedra *f.* stone 13
pierna *f.* leg 10
pimienta *f.* black pepper 8
pintar *v.* to paint 17
pintor(a) *m., f.* painter 16
pintura *f.* painting; picture 12, 17
piña *f.* pineapple
piscina *f.* swimming pool 4
piso *m.* floor (*of a building*) 5
pizarra *f.* whiteboard 2
placer *m.* pleasure
planchar la ropa *v.* to iron the
   clothes 12
planes *m., pl.* plans
planta *f.* plant 13
   planta baja *f.* ground floor 5
plástico *m.* plastic 13
plato *m.* dish (*in a meal*) 8; *m.*
   plate 12
   plato principal *m.* main dish 8
playa *f.* beach 5
plaza *f.* city or town square 4
plazos *m., pl.* periods; time 14
pluma *f.* pen 2
plumero *m.* duster 12
población *f.* population 13
pobre *adj. m., f.* poor 6
pobrecito/a *adj.* poor thing 3
pobreza *f.* poverty
poco *adv.* little 5, 10
poder (o:ue) *v.* to be able to; can 4
   ¿Podría pedirte algo? Could I
     ask you something? 17
   ¿Puedo dejar un recado?
     May I leave a message? 11
poema *m.* poem 17
poesía *f.* poetry 17
poeta *m., f.* poet 17
policía *f.* police (force) 11
política *f.* politics 18
político/a *m., f.* politician 16; *adj.*
   political 18
pollo *m.* chicken 8
   pollo asado *m.* roast chicken 8
poner *v.* to put; to place 4; to turn
   on (*electrical appliances*) 11
   poner la mesa to set the
     table 12
   poner una inyección to give
     an injection 10
   ponerle el nombre to name
   someone/something 9

ponerse (+ *adj.*) *v.* to become
   (+ *adj.*) 7; to put on 7
por *prep.* in exchange for; for;
   by; in; through; around; along;
   during; because of; on account
   of; on behalf of; in search of;
   by way of; by means of 11
   por aquí around here 11
   por ejemplo for example 11
   por eso that's why;
     therefore 11
   por favor please 1
   por fin finally 11
   por la mañana in the
     morning 7
   por la noche at night 7
   por la tarde in the afternoon 7
   por lo menos *adv.* at least 10
   ¿por qué? why? 2
   Por supuesto. Of course.
   por teléfono by phone; on the
     phone
   por último finally 7
porque *conj.* because 2
portátil *adj.* portable 11
portero/a *m., f.* doorman/
   doorwoman 1
porvenir *m.* future 16
   por el porvenir for/to the
     future 16
posesivo/a *adj.* possessive
posible *adj.* possible 13
   es posible it's possible 13
   no es posible it's not
     possible 13
postal *f.* postcard
postre *m.* dessert 9
practicar *v.* to practice 2
   practicar deportes *m., pl.* to
     play sports 4
precio (fijo) *m.* (fixed; set)
   price 6
preferir (e:ie) *v.* to prefer 4
pregunta *f.* question
preguntar *v.* to ask (*a question*) 2
premio *m.* prize; award 17
prender *v.* to turn on 11
prensa *f.* press 18
preocupado/a (por) *adj.* worried
   (about) 5
preocuparse (por) *v.* to worry
   (about) 7
preparar *v.* to prepare 2
preposición *f.* preposition
presentación *f.* introduction
presentar *v.* to introduce; to
   present 17; to put on (*a
   performance*) 17
   Le presento a… I would like
     to introduce you to (name).
     form. 1
   Te presento a… I would like
     to introduce you to (name).
     fam. 1
presiones *f., pl.* pressures 15
prestado/a *adj.* borrowed
préstamo *m.* loan 14

prestar *v.* to lend; to loan 6
primavera *f.* spring 5
primer, primero/a *adj.* first 5
primero *adv.* first 2
primo/a *m., f.* cousin 3
principal *adj. m., f.* main 8
prisa *f.* haste
   darse prisa *v.* to hurry;
     to rush 15
probable *adj. m., f.* probable 13
   es probable it's probable 13
   no es probable it's not
     probable 13
probar (o:ue) *v.* to taste; to try 8
probarse (o:ue) *v.* to try on 7
problema *m.* problem 1
profesión *f.* profession 3; 16
profesor(a) *m., f.* teacher 1, 2
programa *m.* program 1
   programa de computación
     m. software 11
   programa de entrevistas *m.*
     talk show 17
   programa de realidad *m.*
     reality show 17
programador(a) *m., f.* computer
   programmer 3
prohibir *v.* to prohibit 10;
   to forbid
pronombre *m.* pronoun
pronto *adv.* soon 10
propina *f.* tip 8
propio/a *adj.* own
proteger *v.* to protect 13
proteína *f.* protein 15
próximo/a *adj.* next 3, 16
proyecto *m.* project 11
prueba *f.* test; quiz 2
psicología *f.* psychology 2
psicólogo/a *m., f.*
   psychologist 16
publicar *v.* to publish 17
público *m.* audience 17
pueblo *m.* town
puerta *f.* door 2
puertorriqueño/a *adj.* Puerto
   Rican 3
pues *conj.* well
puesto *m.* position; job 16
puesto/a *p.p.* put 14
puro/a *adj.* pure 13

Q

que *pron.* that; which; who 12
   ¿En qué…? In which…?
   ¡Qué…! How…!
   ¡Qué dolor! What pain!
   ¡Qué ropa más bonita!
     What pretty clothes! 6
   ¡Qué sorpresa! What a
     surprise!
   ¿qué? what? 1, 2
   ¿Qué día es hoy? What day is
     it? 2

¿Qué hay de nuevo? What's new? 1
¿Qué hora es? What time is it? 1
¿Qué les parece? What do you (*pl.*) think?
¿Qué onda? What's up? 14
¿Qué pasa? What's happening? What's going on? 1
¿Qué pasó? What happened?
¿Qué precio tiene? What is the price?
¿Qué tal...? How are you?; How is it going? 1
¿Qué talla lleva/usa? What size do you wear? 6
¿Qué tiempo hace? How's the weather? 5
quedar *v.* to be left over; to fit (*clothing*) 7; to be located 14
quedarse *v.* to stay; to remain 7
quehaceres domésticos *m., pl.* household chores 12
querer (e:ie) *v.* to want; to love 4
queso *m.* cheese 8
quien(es) *pron.* who; whom; that 12
¿quién(es)? who?; whom? 1, 2
  ¿Quién es...? Who is...? 1
  ¿Quién habla? Who is speaking/calling? (*telephone*) 11
química *f.* chemistry 2
quince fifteen 1
  menos quince quarter to (time) 1
  y quince quarter after (time) 1
quinceañera *f.* young woman celebrating her fifteenth birthday 9
quinientos/as five hundred 2
quinto/a *adj.* fifth 5
quisiera *v.* I would like
quitar el polvo *v.* to dust 12
quitar la mesa *v.* to clear the table 12
quitarse *v.* to take off 7
quizás *adv.* maybe 5

racismo *m.* racism 18
radio *f.* radio (*medium*) 2; *m.* radio (set) 11
radiografía *f.* X-ray 10
rápido *adv.* quickly 10
ratón *m.* mouse 11
ratos libres *m., pl.* spare (free) time 4
raya *f.* stripe
razón *f.* reason
rebaja *f.* sale 6
receta *f.* prescription 10
recetar *v.* to prescribe 10
recibir *v.* to receive 3
reciclaje *m.* recycling 13
reciclar *v.* to recycle 13
recién casado/a *m., f.* newly-wed 9

recoger *v.* to pick up 13
recomendar (e:ie) *v.* to recommend 8, 12
recordar (o:ue) *v.* to remember 4
recorrer *v.* to tour an area
recorrido *m.* tour 13
recuperar *v.* to recover 11
recurso *m.* resource 13
  recurso natural *m.* natural resource 13
red *f.* network; Web 11
reducir *v.* to reduce 13
refresco *m.* soft drink 8
refrigerador *m.* refrigerator 12
regalar *v.* to give (a gift) 9
regalo *m.* gift 6
regatear *v.* to bargain 6
región *f.* region; area
regresar *v.* to return 2
regular *adv.* so-so; OK 1
reído *p.p.* laughed 14
reírse (e:i) *v.* to laugh 9
relaciones *f., pl.* relationships
relajarse *v.* to relax 9
reloj *m.* clock; watch 2
renovable *adj.* renewable 13
renunciar (a) *v.* to resign (from) 16
repetir (e:i) *v.* to repeat 4
reportaje *m.* report 18
reportero/a *m., f.* reporter 16
representante *m., f.* representative 18
resfriado *m.* cold (*illness*) 10
residencia estudiantil *f.* dormitory 2
resolver (o:ue) *v.* to resolve; to solve 13
respirar *v.* to breathe 13
responsable *adj.* responsible 8
respuesta *f.* answer
restaurante *m.* restaurant 4
resuelto/a *p.p.* resolved 14
reunión *f.* meeting 16
revisar *v.* to check 11
  revisar el aceite *v.* to check the oil 11
revista *f.* magazine 4
rico/a *adj.* rich 6; *adj.* tasty; delicious 8
ridículo/a *adj.* ridiculous 13
río *m.* river 13
rodilla *f.* knee 10
rogar (o:ue) *v.* to beg 12
rojo/a *adj.* red 6
romántico/a *adj.* romantic 17
romper *v.* to break 10
  romper (con) *v.* to break up (with) 9
  romperse la pierna *v.* to break one's leg 10
ropa *f.* clothing; clothes 6
  ropa interior *f.* underwear 6
rosado/a *adj.* pink 6
roto/a *adj.* broken 14
rubio/a *adj.* blond(e) 3
ruso/a *adj.* Russian 3
rutina *f.* routine 7
  rutina diaria *f.* daily routine 7

sábado *m.* Saturday 2
saber *v.* to know; to know how 6
  saber a to taste like 8
sabrosísimo/a *adj.* extremely delicious 8
sabroso/a *adj.* tasty; delicious 8
sacar *v.* to take out
  sacar buenas notas to get good grades 2
  sacar fotos to take photos 5
  sacar la basura to take out the trash 12
  sacar(se) un diente to have a tooth removed 10
sacudir *v.* to dust 12
  sacudir los muebles to dust the furniture 12
sal *f.* salt 8
sala *f.* living room 12; room
  sala de emergencia(s) emergency room 10
salario *m.* salary 16
salchicha *f.* sausage 8
salida *f.* departure; exit 5
salir *v.* to leave 4; to go out
  salir con to go out with; to date 4, 9
  salir de to leave from 4
  salir para to leave for (*a place*) 4
salmón *m.* salmon 8
salón de belleza *m.* beauty salon 14
salud *f.* health 10
saludable *adj.* healthy 10
saludar(se) *v.* to greet (each other) 11
saludo *m.* greeting 1
  saludos a... greetings to... 1
sandalia *f.* sandal 6
sandía *f.* watermelon
sándwich *m.* sandwich 8
sano/a *adj.* healthy 10
se *ref. pron.* himself, herself, itself, *form.* yourself, themselves, yourselves 7
se *impersonal* one 10
  Se hizo... He/she/it became...
secadora *f.* clothes dryer 12
secarse *v.* to dry (oneself) 7
sección de (no) fumar *f.* (non) smoking section 8
secretario/a *m., f.* secretary 16
secuencia *f.* sequence
sed *f.* thirst
seda *f.* silk 6
sedentario/a *adj.* sedentary 15
seguir (e:i) *v.* to follow; to continue 4
según according to
segundo/a *adj.* second 5
seguro/a *adj.* sure; safe; confident 5
seis six 1
seiscientos/as six hundred 2
sello *m.* stamp 14
selva *f.* jungle 13

semáforo *m.* traffic light 14
semana *f.* week 2
   fin *m.* **de semana** weekend 4
   semana *f.* **pasada** last week 6
semestre *m.* semester 2
sendero *m.* trail; path 13
sentarse (e:ie) *v.* to sit down 7
sentir (e:ie) *v.* to be sorry; to
   regret 13
sentirse (e:ie) *v.* to feel 7
señor (Sr.); don *m.* Mr.; sir 1
señora (Sra.); doña *f.* Mrs.;
   ma'am 1
señorita (Srta.) *f.* Miss 1
separado/a *adj.* separated 9
separarse (de) *v.* to separate
   (from) 9
septiembre *m.* September 5
séptimo/a *adj.* seventh 5
ser *v.* to be 1
   ser aficionado/a (a) to be a
     fan (of)
   ser alérgico/a (a) to be allergic
     (to) 10
   ser gratis to be free of
     charge 14
serio/a *adj.* serious
servicio *m.* service 15
servilleta *f.* napkin 12
servir (e:i) *v.* to serve 8; to help 5
sesenta sixty 2
setecientos/as seven hundred 2
setenta seventy 2
sexismo *m.* sexism 18
sexto/a *adj.* sixth 5
sí *adv.* yes 1
si *conj.* if 4
SIDA *m.* AIDS 18
siempre *adv.* always 7
siete seven 1
silla *f.* seat 2
sillón *m.* armchair 12
similar *adj. m., f.* similar
simpático/a *adj.* nice; likeable 3
sin *prep.* without 13
   sin duda without a doubt
   sin embargo however
   sin que *conj.* without 13
sino but (rather) 7
síntoma *m.* symptom 10
sitio *m.* place 3
sitio *m.* **web** website 11
situado/a *p.p.* located
sobre *m.* envelope 14; *prep.*
   on; over 2
   sobre todo above all 13
(sobre)población *f.*
   (over)population 13
sobrino/a *m., f.* nephew/niece 3
sociología *f.* sociology 2
sofá *m.* couch; sofa 12
sol *m.* sun 13
solar *adj. m., f.* solar 13
soldado *m., f.* soldier 18
soleado/a *adj.* sunny
solicitar *v.* to apply (*for a job*) 16
solicitud (de trabajo) *f.* (job)
   application 16

sólo *adv.* only 6
solo/a *adj.* alone
soltero/a *adj.* single 9
solución *f.* solution 13
sombrero *m.* hat 6
Son las dos. It's two o'clock. 1
sonar (o:ue) *v.* to ring 11
sonreído *p.p.* smiled 14
sonreír (e:i) *v.* to smile 9
sopa *f.* soup 8
sorprender *v.* to surprise 9
sorpresa *f.* surprise 9
sótano *m.* basement 12
soy I am 1
   Soy de... I'm from... 1
su(s) *poss. adj.* his; her; its; *form.*
   your; their 3
subir(se) a *v.* to get on/into
   (*a vehicle*) 11
sucio/a *adj.* dirty 5
sudar *v.* to sweat 15
suegro/a *m., f.* father-in-law/
   mother-in-law 3
sueldo *m.* salary 16
suelo *m.* floor 12
sueño *m.* sleep
suerte *f.* luck
suéter *m.* sweater 6
sufrir *v.* to suffer 10
   sufrir muchas presiones to
     be under a lot of pressure 15
   sufrir una enfermedad to
     suffer an illness 10
sugerir (e:ie) *v.* to suggest 12
supermercado *m.* supermarket 14
suponer *v.* to suppose 4
sur *m.* south 14
sustantivo *m.* noun
suyo(s)/a(s) *poss.* (of) his/her; (of)
   hers; its; *form.* your, (of) yours,
   (of) theirs, their 11

T

tabla de (wind)surf *f.* surf
   board/sailboard 5
tableta *f.* tablet (computer) 11
tal vez *adv.* maybe 5
talentoso/a *adj.* talented 17
talla *f.* size 6
   talla grande *f.* large
taller *m.* **mecánico** garage;
   mechanic's repair shop 11
también *adv.* also; too 2; 7
tampoco *adv.* neither; not
   either 7
tan *adv.* so 5
   tan... como as... as 8
   tan pronto como *conj.* as
     soon as 13
tanque *m.* tank 11
tanto *adv.* so much
   tanto... como as much... as 8
tantos/as... como as many...
   as 8
tarde *adv.* late 7; *f.* afternoon;
   evening; P.M. 1
tarea *f.* homework 2

tarjeta *f.* (post) card
tarjeta de crédito *f.* credit card 6
tarjeta de débito *f.* debit card 6
tarjeta postal *f.* postcard
taxi *m.* taxi 5
taza *f.* cup 12
te *sing., fam., d.o. pron.* you 5;
   sing., fam., i.o. pron. to/for
   you 6
   Te presento a... *fam.* I would
     like to introduce you to (name). 1
   ¿Te gustaría? Would you like
     to?
   ¿Te gusta(n)...? Do you
     like...? 2
té *m.* tea 8
   té helado *m.* iced tea 8
teatro *m.* theater 17
teclado *m.* keyboard 11
técnico/a *m., f.* technician 16
tejido *m.* weaving 17
teleadicto/a *m., f.* couch
   potato 15
(teléfono) celular *m.* (cell)
   phone 11
telenovela *f.* soap opera 17
teletrabajo *m.* telecommuting 16
televisión *f.* television 2
televisor *m.* television set 11
temer *v.* to fear; to be afraid 13
temperatura *f.* temperature 10
temporada *f.* period of time 5
temprano *adv.* early 7
tenedor *m.* fork 12
tener *v.* to have 3
   tener... años to be... years
     old 3
   tener (mucho) calor to be
     (very) hot 3
   tener (mucho) cuidado to be
     (very) careful 3
   tener dolor to have pain 10
   tener éxito to be successful 16
   tener fiebre to have a fever 10
   tener (mucho) frío to be (very)
     cold 3
   tener ganas de (+ inf.) to feel
     like (*doing something*) 3
   tener (mucha) hambre *f.* to
     be (very) hungry 3
   tener (mucho) miedo (de) to
     be (very) afraid (of); to be
     (very) scared (of) 3
   tener miedo (de) que to be
     afraid that
   tener planes *m., pl.* to have
     plans
   tener (mucha) prisa to be in a
     (big) hurry 3
   tener que (+ inf.) *v.* to have
     to (*do something*) 3
   tener razón *f.* to be right 3
   tener (mucha) sed *f.* to be
     (very) thirsty 3
   tener (mucho) sueño to be
     (very) sleepy 3
   tener (mucha) suerte to be
     (very) lucky 3
   tener tiempo to have time 14

tener una cita to have a date; to have an appointment 9
tenis *m.* tennis 4
tensión *f.* tension 15
tercer, tercero/a *adj.* third 5
terco/a *adj.* stubborn 10
terminar *v.* to end; to finish 2
  terminar de (+ inf.) *v.* to finish (*doing something*)
terremoto *m.* earthquake 18
terrible *adj. m., f.* terrible 13
textear *v.* to text 11
ti *obj. of prep., sing., fam.* you 9
tiempo *m.* time 14; weather 5
  tiempo libre free time
tienda *f.* store 6
tierra *f.* land; soil 13
tinto/a *adj.* red (wine) 8
tío/a *m., f.* uncle/aunt 3
tíos *m., pl.* aunts and uncles 3
título *m.* title 16
tiza *f.* chalk
toalla *f.* towel 7
tobillo *m.* ankle 10
tocar *v.* to play (*a musical instrument*) 17; to touch 17
todavía *adv.* yet; still 3, 5
todo *m.* everything 5
todo(s)/a(s) *adj.* all
todos *m., pl.* all of us; *m., pl.* everybody; everyone
todos los días *adv.* every day 10
tomar *v.* to take; to drink 2
  tomar clases *f., pl.* to take classes 2
  tomar el sol to sunbathe 4
  tomar en cuenta to take into account
  tomar fotos *f., pl.* to take photos 5
  tomar la temperatura to take someone's temperature 10
  tomar una decisión to make a decision 15
tomate *m.* tomato 8
tonto/a *adj.* foolish 3
torcerse (o:ue) (el tobillo) *v.* to sprain (one's ankle) 10
tormenta *f.* storm 18
tornado *m.* tornado 18
tortuga (marina) *f.* (sea) turtle 13
tos *f., sing.* cough 10
toser *v.* to cough 10
tostado/a *adj.* toasted 8
tostadora *f.* toaster 12
trabajador(a) *adj.* hard-working 3
trabajar *v.* to work 2
trabajo *m.* job; work 16
traducir *v.* to translate 6
traer *v.* to bring 4
tráfico *m.* traffic 11
tragedia *f.* tragedy 17
traído/a *p.p.* brought 14
traje *m.* suit 6
  traje de baño *m.* bathing suit 6
trajinera *f.* type of barge 3
tranquilo/a *adj.* calm; quiet 15

Tranquilo/a. Relax. 7
Tranquilo/a, cariño. Relax, sweetie. 11
transmitir *v.* to broadcast 18
tratar de (+ inf.) *v.* to try (*to do something*) 15
trece thirteen 1
treinta thirty 1, 2
  y treinta thirty minutes past the hour (time) 1
tren *m.* train 5
tres three 1
trescientos/as three hundred 2
trimestre *m.* trimester; quarter 2
triste *adj.* sad 5
tú *sing., fam. sub. pron.* you 1
tu(s) *fam. poss. adj.* your 3
turismo *m.* tourism
turista *m., f.* tourist 1
turístico/a *adj.* touristic
tuyo(s)/a(s) *fam. poss. pron.* your; (of) yours 11

U

Ud. *form. sing.* you 1
Uds. *pl.* you 1
último/a *adj.* last 7
  la última vez the last time 7
un, uno/a *indef. art.* a; one 1
  a la una at one o'clock 1
  una vez once 6
  una vez más one more time
uno one 1
único/a *adj.* only 3; unique 9
universidad *f.* university; college 2
unos/as *m., f., pl. indef. art.* some 1
urgente *adj.* urgent 12
usar *v.* to wear; to use 6
usted (Ud.) *form. sing.* you 1
ustedes (Uds.) *pl.* you 1
útil *adj.* useful
uva *f.* grape 8

V

vaca *f.* cow 13
vacaciones *f. pl.* vacation 5
valle *m.* valley 13
vamos let's go 4
vaquero *m.* cowboy 17
  de vaqueros *m., pl.* western (genre) 17
varios/as *adj. m. f., pl.* various; several
vaso *m.* glass 12
veces *f., pl.* times 6
vecino/a *m., f.* neighbor 12
veinte twenty 1
veinticinco twenty-five 1
veinticuatro twenty-four 1
veintidós twenty-two 1
veintinueve twenty-nine 1
veintiocho twenty-eight 1

veintiséis twenty-six 1
veintisiete twenty-seven 1
veintitrés twenty-three 1
veintiún, veintiuno/a *adj.* twenty-one 1
veintiuno twenty-one 1
vejez *f.* old age 9
velocidad *f.* speed 11
  velocidad máxima *f.* speed limit 11
vencer *v.* to expire 14
vendedor(a) *m., f.* salesperson 6
vender *v.* to sell 6
venir *v.* to come 3
ventana *f.* window 2
ver *v.* to see 4
  a ver *v.* let's see
  ver películas *f., pl.* to see movies 4
verano *m.* summer 5
verbo *m.* verb
verdad *f.* truth 4
  (no) es verdad it's (not) true 13
  ¿verdad? right? 1
verde *adj., m. f.* green 6
verduras *pl., f.* vegetables 8
vestido *m.* dress 6
vestirse (e:i) *v.* to get dressed 7
vez *f.* time 6
viajar *v.* to travel 2
viaje *m.* trip 5
viajero/a *m., f.* traveler 5
vida *f.* life 9
video *m.* video 1
videoconferencia *f.* videoconference 16
videojuego *m.* video game 4
vidrio *m.* glass 13
viejo/a *adj.* old 3
viento *m.* wind
viernes *m., sing.* Friday 2
vinagre *m.* vinegar 8
vino *m.* wine 8
  vino blanco *m.* white wine 8
  vino tinto *m.* red wine 8
violencia *f.* violence 18
visitar *v.* to visit 4
  visitar monumentos *m., pl.* to visit monuments 4
visto/a *p.p.* seen 14
vitamina *f.* vitamin 15
viudo/a *adj.* widower/widow 9
vivienda *f.* housing 12
vivir *v.* to live 3
vivo/a *adj.* clever; living
volante *m.* steering wheel 11
volcán *m.* volcano 13
vóleibol *m.* volleyball 4
volver (o:ue) *v.* to return 4
volver a ver(te, lo, la) *v.* to see (you, him, her) again
vos *pron.* you
vosotros/as *fam., pl.* you 1
votar *v.* to vote 18
vuelta *f.* return trip

vuelto/a *p.p.* returned 14
vuestro(s)/a(s) *poss. adj.* your 3;
   your, (of) yours *fam., pl.* 11

Y

y *conj.* and 1
   y cuarto quarter after (time) 1
   y media half-past (time) 1
   y quince quarter after (time) 1
   y treinta thirty (minutes past
      the hour) 1
   ¿Y tú? *fam.* And you? 1
   ¿Y usted? *form.* And you? 1
ya *adv.* already 6
yerno *m.* son-in-law 3
yo *sub. pron.* I 1
yogur *m.* yogurt 8

Z

zanahoria *f.* carrot 8
zapatería *f.* shoe store 14
zapatos de tenis *m., pl.* tennis
   shoes, sneakers 6

English-Spanish

A

a **un/a** *m., f., sing.; indef. art.* 1
@ (*symbol*) **arroba** *f.* 11
a.m. **de la mañana** *f.* 1
able: be able to **poder (o:ue)** *v.* 4
aboard **a bordo**
above all **sobre todo** 13
accident **accidente** *m.* 10
accompany **acompañar** *v.* 14
account **cuenta** *f.* 14
   on account of **por** *prep.* 11
accountant **contador(a)** *m., f.* 16
accounting **contabilidad** *f.* 2
ache **dolor** *m.* 10
acquainted: be acquainted with
   conocer *v.* 6
action (genre) **de acción** *f.* 17
active **activo/a** *adj.* 15
actor **actor** *m.*, **actriz** *f.* 16
addict (*drug*) **drogadicto/a**
   m., f. 15
additional **adicional** *adj.*
address **dirección** *f.* 14
adjective **adjetivo** *m.*
adolescence **adolescencia** *f.* 9
adventure (genre) **de aventuras**
   f. 17
advertise **anunciar** *v.* 18
advertisement **anuncio** *m.* 16
advice **consejo** *m.*
   give advice **dar consejos** 6
advise **aconsejar** *v.* 12
advisor **consejero/a** *m., f.* 16
aerobic **aeróbico/a** *adj.* 15
   aerobics class **clase de**
      ejercicios aeróbicos 15
   to do aerobics **hacer ejercicios**
      aeróbicos 15
affected **afectado/a** *adj.* 13
   be affected (by) **estar** *v.*
      afectado/a (por) 13
affirmative **afirmativo/a** *adj.*
afraid: be (very) afraid (of) **tener**
   (mucho) miedo (de) 3
   be afraid that **tener miedo**
      (de) que
after **después de** *prep.* 7;
   después de que *conj.* 13
afternoon **tarde** *f.* 1
afterward **después** *adv.* 7
again **otra vez**
age **edad** *f.* 9
agree **estar** *v.* **de acuerdo** 17
   I agree. **Estoy de acuerdo.** 17
   I don't agree. **No estoy de**
      acuerdo. 17
agreement **acuerdo** *m.*
AIDS **SIDA** *m.* 18
air **aire** *m.* 13
   air pollution **contaminación**
      del aire 13
airplane **avión** *m.* 5
airport **aeropuerto** *m.* 5
alarm clock **despertador** *m.* 7

alcohol **alcohol** *m.* 15
   to consume alcohol **consumir**
      alcohol 15
alcoholic **alcohólico/a** *adj.* 15
all **todo(s)/a(s)** *adj.*
   all of us **todos**
allergic **alérgico/a** *adj.* 10
   be allergic (to) **ser alérgico/a**
      (a) 10
alleviate **aliviar** *v.*
almost **casi** *adv.* 10
alone **solo/a** *adj.*
along **por** *prep.* 11
already **ya** *adv.* 6
also **también** *adv.* 2; 7
altar **altar** *m.* 9
aluminum **aluminio** *m.* 13
   (made) of aluminum **de**
      aluminio 13
always **siempre** *adv.* 7
American (*North*)
   norteamericano/a *adj.* 3
among **entre** *prep.* 2
amusement **diversión** *f.*
and **y** 1, **e** (*before words beginning*
   with i or hi)
   And you? **¿Y tú?** *fam.* 1;
      ¿Y usted? *form.* 1
angel **ángel** *m.* 9
angry **enojado/a** *adj.* 5
   get angry (with) **enojarse** *v.*
      (con) 7
animal **animal** *m.* 13
ankle **tobillo** *m.* 10
anniversary **aniversario** *m.* 9
   (wedding) anniversary
      aniversario *m.* **(de bodas)** 9
announce **anunciar** *v.* 18
announcer (*TV/radio*) **locutor(a)**
   m., f. 18
annoy **molestar** *v.* 7
another **otro/a** *adj.* 6
answer **contestar** *v.* 2;
   respuesta *f.*
antibiotic **antibiótico** *m.* 10
any **algún, alguno/a(s)** *adj.* 7
anyone **alguien** *pron.* 7
anything **algo** *pron.* 7
apartment **apartamento** *m.* 12
apartment building **edificio de**
   apartamentos 12
app **aplicación** *f.* 11
appear **parecer** *v.*
appetizers **entremeses** *m., pl.* 8
applaud **aplaudir** *v.* 17
apple **manzana** *f.* 8
appliance (electric)
   electrodoméstico *m.* 12
applicant **aspirante** *m., f.* 16
application **solicitud** *f.* 16
   job application **solicitud de**
      trabajo 16
apply (*for a job*) **solicitar** *v.* 16
   apply for a loan **pedir (e:i)** *v.*
      un préstamo 14
appointment **cita** *f.* 9
   have an appointment **tener** *v.*
      una cita 9
appreciate **apreciar** *v.* 17

April **abril** *m.* 5
archeologist **arqueólogo/a**
   m., f. 16
archeology **arqueología** *f.* 2
architect **arquitecto/a** *m., f.* 16
area **región** *f.*
Argentine **argentino/a** *adj.* 3
arm **brazo** *m.* 10
armchair **sillón** *m.* 12
army **ejército** *m.* 18
around **por** *prep.*
   around here **por aquí** 11
arrange **arreglar** *v.* 11
arrival **llegada** *f.* 5
arrive **llegar** *v.* 2
art **arte** *m.* 2
   (fine) arts **bellas artes** *f., pl.* 17
article **artículo** *m.* 18
artist **artista** *m., f.* 3
artistic **artístico/a** *adj.* 17
arts **artes** *f., pl.* 17
as **como** 8
   as a child **de niño/a** 10
   as... as **tan... como** 8
   as many... as **tantos/as...**
      como 8
   as much... as **tanto...**
      como 8
   as soon as **en cuanto** *conj.* 13;
      tan pronto como *conj.* 13
ask (*a question*) **preguntar** *v.* 2
   ask for **pedir (e:i)** *v.* 4
asparagus **espárragos** *m., pl.* 8
aspirin **aspirina** *f.* 10
at **a** *prep.* 1; **en** *prep.* 2
   at + time **a la(s)** + time 1
   at home **en casa**
   at least **por lo menos** 10
   at night **por la noche** 7
   At what time...? **¿A qué**
      hora...? 1
   At your service. **A sus**
      órdenes.
ATM **cajero automático** *m.* 14
attempt **intento** *m.* 11
attend **asistir (a)** *v.* 3
attic **altillo** *m.* 12
audience **público** *m.* 17
August **agosto** *m.* 5
aunt **tía** *f.* 3
   aunts and uncles **tíos** *m., pl.* 3
autumn **otoño** *m.* 5
avenue **avenida** *f.*
avoid **evitar** *v.* 13
award **premio** *m.* 17

B

backpack **mochila** *f.* 2
bad **mal, malo/a** *adj.* 3
   It's bad that... **Es malo**
      que... 12
   It's not bad at all. **No está**
      nada mal. 5
bag **bolsa** *f.* 6
bakery **panadería** *f.* 14

balanced **equilibrado/a** *adj.* 15
  to eat a balanced diet **comer una dieta equilibrada** 15
balcony **balcón** *m.* 12
ball **pelota** *f.* 4
banana **banana** *f.* 8
band **banda** *f.* 17
bank **banco** *m.* 14
bargain **ganga** *f.* 6; **regatear** *v.* 6
baseball (*game*) **béisbol** *m.* 4
basement **sótano** *m.* 12
basketball (*game*) **baloncesto** *m.* 4
bath: take a bath **bañarse** *v.* 7
bathing suit **traje** *m.* **de baño** 6
bathroom **baño** *m.* 7; **cuarto de baño** *m.* 7
battery **batería** *f.* 11
be **ser** *v.* 1; **estar** *v.* 2
  be... years old **tener... años** 3
  be sick of... **estar harto/a de...** 18
beach **playa** *f.* 5
beans **frijoles** *m., pl.* 8
beautiful **hermoso/a** *adj.* 6
beauty **belleza** *f.* 14
  beauty salon **peluquería** *f.* 14; **salón** *m.* **de belleza** 14
because **porque** *conj.* 2
  because of **por** *prep.* 11
become (+ *adj.*) **ponerse (+ adj.)** 7; **convertirse** *v.*
bed **cama** *f.* 5
  go to bed **acostarse (o:ue)** *v.* 7
bedroom **alcoba** *f.*, **recámara** *f.*; **dormitorio** *m.* 12
beef **carne de res** *f.* 8
beer **cerveza** *f.* 8
before **antes** *adv.* 7; **antes de** *prep.* 7; **antes (de) que** *conj.* 13
beg **rogar (o:ue)** *v.* 12
begin **comenzar (e:ie)** *v.* 4; **empezar (e:ie)** *v.* 4
behalf: on behalf of **de parte de** 11
behind **detrás de** *prep.* 2
believe (in) **creer** *v.* **(en)** 3; **creer** *v.* 13
  not to believe **no creer** 13
believed **creído/a** *p.p.* 14
bellhop **botones** *m., f. sing.* 5
below **debajo de** *prep.* 2
belt **cinturón** *m.* 6
benefit **beneficio** *m.* 16
beside **al lado de** *prep.* 2
besides **además (de)** *adv.* 10
best **mejor** *adj.*
  the best **el/la mejor** *m., f.* 8
  lo mejor *neuter*
better **mejor** *adj.* 8
  It's better that... **Es mejor que...** 12
between **entre** *prep.* 2
beverage **bebida** *f.* 8
  alcoholic beverage **bebida alcohólica** *f.* 15
bicycle **bicicleta** *f.* 4

big **grande** *adj.* 3
bill **cuenta** *f.* 8
billion **mil millones**
biology **biología** *f.* 2
bird **ave** *f.* 13; **pájaro** *m.* 13
birth **nacimiento** *m.* 9
birthday **cumpleaños** *m., sing.* 9
  have a birthday **cumplir** *v.* **años**
black **negro/a** *adj.* 6
blanket **manta** *f.* 12
block (city) **cuadra** *f.* 14
blog **blog** *m.* 11
blond(e) **rubio/a** *adj.* 3
blouse **blusa** *f.* 6
blue **azul** *adj. m., f.* 6
boat **barco** *m.* 5
body **cuerpo** *m.* 10
bone **hueso** *m.* 10
book **libro** *m.* 2
bookcase **estante** *m.* 12
bookshelves **estante** *m.* 12
bookstore **librería** *f.* 2
boot **bota** *f.* 6
bore **aburrir** *v.* 7
bored **aburrido/a** *adj.* 5
  be bored **estar** *v.* **aburrido/a** 5
  get bored **aburrirse** *v.* 17
boring **aburrido/a** *adj.* 5
born: be born **nacer** *v.* 9
borrow **pedir (e:i)** *v.* **prestado** 14
borrowed **prestado/a** *adj.*
boss **jefe** *m.*, **jefa** *f.* 16
bother **molestar** *v.* 7
bottle **botella** *f.* 9
  bottle of wine **botella de vino** 9
bottom **fondo** *m.*
boulevard **bulevar** *m.*
boy **chico** *m.* 1; **muchacho** *m.* 3
boyfriend **novio** *m.* 3
brakes **frenos** *m., pl.*
bread **pan** *m.* 8
break **romper** *v.* 10
  break (one's leg) **romperse (la pierna)** 10
  break down **dañar** *v.* 10
  break up (with) **romper** *v.* **(con)** 9
breakfast **desayuno** *m.* 8
  have breakfast **desayunar** *v.* 2
breathe **respirar** *v.* 13
bring **traer** *v.* 4
broadcast **transmitir** *v.* 18; **emitir** *v.* 18
brochure **folleto** *m.*
broken **roto/a** *adj.* 14
  be broken **estar roto/a**
brother **hermano** *m.* 3
brother-in-law **cuñado** *m.* 3
brothers and sisters **hermanos** *m., pl.* 3
brought **traído/a** *p.p.* 14
brown **café** *adj.* 6; **marrón** *adj.* 6
brunet(te) **moreno/a** *adj.* 3

brush **cepillar(se)** *v.* 7
  brush one's hair **cepillarse el pelo** 7
  brush one's teeth **cepillarse los dientes** 7
bucket **balde** *m.* 5
build **construir** *v.*
building **edificio** *m.* 12
bump into (*something accidentally*) **darse con** 10; (*someone*) **encontrarse** *v.* 11
bus **autobús** *m.* 1
  bus station **estación** *f.* **de autobuses** 5
business **negocios** *m. pl.* 16
  business administration **administración** *f.* **de empresas** 2
  business-related **comercial** *adj.* 16
businessperson **hombre** *m.* **/ mujer** *f.* **de negocios** 16
busy **ocupado/a** *adj.* 5
but **pero** *conj.* 2; (*rather*) **sino** *conj.* (*in negative sentences*) 7
butcher shop **carnicería** *f.* 14
butter **mantequilla** *f.* 8
buy **comprar** *v.* 2
  buy online **comprar en línea** 6
by **por** *prep.* 11; **para** *prep.* 11
  by means of **por** *prep.* 11
  by phone **por teléfono**
  by way of **por** *prep.* 11
bye **chau** *interj. fam.* 1

C

café **café** *m.* 4
cafeteria **cafetería** *f.* 2
caffeine **cafeína** *f.* 15
cake **pastel** *m.* 9
  chocolate cake **pastel de chocolate** *m.* 9
calculator **calculadora** *f.* 2
call **llamar** *v.* 11
  be called **llamarse** *v.* 7
  call on the phone **llamar por teléfono**
calm **tranquilo/a** *adj.* 15
calorie **caloría** *f.* 15
camera **cámara** *f.* 11
camp **acampar** *v.* 5
can (*tin*) **lata** *f.* 13
can **poder (o:ue)** *v.* 4
  Could I ask you something? **¿Podría pedirte algo?** 17
Canadian **canadiense** *adj.* 3
candidate **aspirante** *m., f.* 16; **candidato/a** *m., f.* 18
candy **dulces** *m., pl.* 9
capital city **capital** *f.*
car **coche** *m.* 11; **carro** *m.* 11; **auto(móvil)** *m.* 5
caramel **caramelo** *m.* 9
card **tarjeta** *f.*; (*playing*) **carta** *f.* 5

care **cuidado** *m.*
  take care of **cuidar** *v.* 13
career **carrera** *f.* 16
careful: be (very) careful **tener** *v.*
  (mucho) cuidado 3
carpenter **carpintero/a** *m., f.* 16
carpet **alfombra** *f.* 12
carrot **zanahoria** *f.* 8
carry **llevar** *v.* 2
cartoons **dibujos** *m., pl.*
  animados 17
case: in case (that) **en caso (de)**
  que 13
cash (a check) **cobrar** *v.* 14;
  cash **(en) efectivo** 6
  cash register **caja** *f.* 6
  pay in cash **pagar** *v.* **al contado**
    14; **pagar en efectivo** 14
cashier **cajero/a** *m., f.*
cat **gato** *m.* 13
celebrate **celebrar** *v.* 9
celebration **celebración** *f.*
(cell) phone **(teléfono)**
  celular *m.* 11
cemetery **cementerio** *m.* 9
cereal **cereales** *m., pl.* 8
certain **cierto/a** *adj.*; **seguro/a**
  adj. 13
  it's (not) certain **(no) es**
    cierto/seguro 13
chalk **tiza** *f.*
champagne **champán** *m.* 9
change **cambiar** *v.* **(de)** 9
change: in change **de cambio** 2
channel (*TV*) **canal** *m.* 11; 17
character (*fictional*) **personaje**
  m. 17
  (main) character *m.* **personaje**
    (principal) 17
charge **cargar** *v.* 11
charger **cargador** *m.* 11
chat **conversar** *v.* 2; **chatear** *v.* 11
cheap **barato/a** *adj.* 6
check **comprobar (o:ue)** *v.*;
  revisar *v.* 11; (*bank*) **cheque**
    m. 14
  check the oil **revisar el aceite** 11
checking account **cuenta** *f.*
  corriente 14
cheese **queso** *m.* 8
chef **cocinero/a** *m., f.* 16
chemistry **química** *f.* 2
chest of drawers **cómoda** *f.* 12
chicken **pollo** *m.* 8
child **niño/a** *m., f.* 3
childhood **niñez** *f.* 9
children **hijos** *m., pl.* 3
Chinese **chino/a** *adj.* 3
chocolate **chocolate** *m.* 9
  chocolate cake **pastel** *m.* **de**
    chocolate 9
cholesterol **colesterol** *m.* 15
choose **escoger** *v.* 8
chop (*food*) **chuleta** *f.* 8
Christmas **Navidad** *f.* 9
church **iglesia** *f.* 4
cinnamon **canela** *f.* 10
citizen **ciudadano/a** *m., f.* 18
city **ciudad** *f.*

class **clase** *f.* 2
  take classes **tomar clases** 2
classical **clásico/a** *adj.* 17
classmate **compañero/a** *m., f.* **de**
  clase 2
clean **limpio/a** *adj.* 5;
  limpiar *v.* 12
  clean the house *v.* **limpiar la**
    casa 12
clear (*weather*) **despejado/a** *adj.*
  clear the table **quitar la**
    mesa 12
  It's (very) clear. (*weather*)
    Está (muy) despejado.
clerk **dependiente/a** *m., f.* 6
climate change **cambio climático**
  m. 13
climb **escalar** *v.* 4
  climb mountains **escalar**
    montañas 4
clinic **clínica** *f.* 10
clock **reloj** *m.* 2
close **cerrar (e:ie)** *v.* 4
closed **cerrado/a** *adj.* 5
closet **armario** *m.* 12
clothes **ropa** *f.* 6
  clothes dryer **secadora** *f.* 12
clothing **ropa** *f.* 6
cloud **nube** *f.* 13
cloudy **nublado/a** *adj.* 5
  It's (very) cloudy. **Está (muy)**
    nublado. 5
coat **abrigo** *m.* 6
coffee **café** *m.* 8
  coffee maker **cafetera** *f.* 12
cold **frío** *m.* 5;
  (*illness*) **resfriado** *m.* 10
  be (feel) (very) cold **tener**
    (mucho) frío 3
  It's (very) cold. (*weather*) **Hace**
    (mucho) frío. 5
college **universidad** *f.* 2
collision **choque** *m.* 18
color **color** *m.* 6
comb one's hair **peinarse** *v.* 7
come **venir** *v.* 3
come on **ándale** *interj.* 14
comedy **comedia** *f.* 17
comfortable **cómodo/a** *adj.* 5
commerce **negocios** *m., pl.* 16
commercial **comercial** *adj.* 16
communicate (with) **comunicarse**
  v. **(con)** 18
communication **comunicación**
  f. 18
  means of communication
    medios *m. pl.* **de**
      comunicación 18
community **comunidad** *f.* 1
company **compañía** *f.* 16;
  empresa *f.* 16
comparison **comparación** *f.*
composer **compositor(a)** *m., f.* 17
computer **computadora** *f.* 1
  computer programmer
    programador(a) *m., f.* 3
  computer science **computación**
    f. 2
concert **concierto** *m.* 17

conductor (*musical*) **director(a)**
  m., f. 17
confident **seguro/a** *adj.* 5
confirm **confirmar** *v.* 5
  confirm a reservation **confirmar**
    una reservación 5
confused **confundido/a** *adj.* 5
congested **congestionado/a**
  adj. 10
Congratulations! **¡Felicidades!**;
  ¡Felicitaciones! *f., pl.* 9
conservation **conservación** *f.* 13
conserve **conservar** *v.* 13
considering **para** *prep.* 11
consume **consumir** *v.* 15
container **envase** *m.* 13
contamination **contaminación** *f.*
content **contento/a** *adj.* 5
contest **concurso** *m.* 17
continue **seguir (e:i)** *v.* 4
control **control** *m.*; **controlar** *v.* 13
conversation **conversación** *f.* 1
converse **conversar** *v.* 2
cook **cocinar** *v.* 12; **cocinero/a**
  m., f. 16
cookie **galleta** *f.* 9
cool **fresco/a** *adj.* 5
  It's cool. (*weather*) **Hace**
    fresco. 5
corn **maíz** *m.* 8
corner **esquina** *f.* 14
cost **costar (o:ue)** *v.* 6
Costa Rican **costarricense** *adj.* 3
costume **disfraz** *m.* 9
cotton **algodón** *f.* 6
  (made of) cotton **de algodón** 6
couch **sofá** *m.* 12
couch potato **teleadicto/a**
  m., f. 15
cough **tos** *f.* 10; **toser** *v.* 10
counselor **consejero/a** *m., f.* 16
count **contar (o:ue)** *v.* 4
country (*nation*) **país** *m.* 1
countryside **campo** *m.* 5
(married) couple **pareja** *f.* 9
course **curso** *m.* 2; **materia** *f.* 2
courtesy **cortesía** *f.*
cousin **primo/a** *m., f.* 3
cover **cubrir** *v.*
covered **cubierto/a** *p.p.*
cow **vaca** *f.* 13
crafts **artesanía** *f.* 17
craftsmanship **artesanía** *f.* 17
crater **cráter** *m.* 13
crazy **loco/a** *adj.* 6
create **crear** *v.*
credit **crédito** *m.* 6
  credit card **tarjeta** *f.* **de**
    crédito 6
crime **crimen** *m.* 18
cross **cruzar** *v.* 14
cry **llorar** *v.* 15
Cuban **cubano/a** *adj.* 3
culture **cultura** *f.* 2, 17
cup **taza** *f.* 12
currency exchange **cambio** *m.* **de**
  moneda
current events **actualidades** *f.,*
  pl. 18

curtains **cortinas** *f., pl.* 12
custard (*baked*) **flan** *m.* 9
custom **costumbre** *f.*
customer **cliente/a** *m., f.* 6
customs **aduana** *f.*
   customs inspector **inspector(a)**
    m., f. **de aduanas** 5
cycling **ciclismo** *m.* 4

D

dad **papá** *m.*
daily **diario/a** *adj.* 7
   daily routine **rutina** *f.* **diaria** 7
damage **dañar** *v.* 10
dance **bailar** *v.* 2; **danza** *f.* 17;
   baile *m.* 17
dancer **bailarín/bailarina** *m.,*
   f. 17
danger **peligro** *m.* 13
dangerous **peligroso/a** *adj.* 18
date (*appointment*) **cita** *f.* 9;
   (*calendar*) **fecha** *f.* 5; (*someone*)
   salir *v.* **con (alguien)** 9
   have a date **tener una cita** 9
daughter **hija** *f.* 3
daughter-in-law **nuera** *f.* 3
day **día** *m.* 1
   day before yesterday
    anteayer *adv.* 6
death **muerte** *f.* 9
debit card **tarjeta** *f.* **de débito** 6
decaffeinated **descafeinado/a**
   adj. 15
December **diciembre** *m.* 5
decide **decidir** *v.* (**+** *inf.*) 3
declare **declarar** *v.* 18
deforestation **deforestación** *f.* 13
delicious **delicioso/a** *adj.* 8;
   rico/a *adj.* 8; **sabroso/a** *adj.* 8
delighted **encantado/a** *adj.* 1
dentist **dentista** *m., f.* 10
deny **negar (e:ie)** *v.* 13
   not to deny **no negar** 13
department store **almacén** *m.* 6
departure **salida** *f.* 5
deposit **depositar** *v.* 14
describe **describir** *v.* 3
described **descrito/a** *p.p.* 14
desert **desierto** *m.* 13
design **diseño** *m.*
designer **diseñador(a)** *m., f.* 16
desire **desear** *v.* 2
desk **escritorio** *m.* 2
dessert **postre** *m.* 9
destroy **destruir** *v.* 13
develop **desarrollar** *v.* 13
diary **diario** *m.* 1
dictatorship **dictadura** *f.* 18
dictionary **diccionario** *m.* 1
die **morir (o:ue)** *v.* 8
died **muerto/a** *p.p.* 14
diet **dieta** *f.* 15; **alimentación**
   balanced diet **dieta**
    equilibrada 15
   be on a diet **estar a dieta** 15
difficult **difícil** *adj. m., f.* 3

digital camera **cámara** *f.*
   digital 11
dining room **comedor** *m.* 12
dinner **cena** *f.* 8
   have dinner **cenar** *v.* 2
direct **dirigir** *v.* 17
director **director(a)** *m., f.* 17
dirty **ensuciar** *v.*; **sucio/a** *adj.* 5
   get (something) dirty **ensuciar**
    v. 12
disagree **no estar de acuerdo**
disaster **desastre** *m.* 18
discover **descubrir** *v.* 13
discovered **descubierto/a** *p.p.* 14
discrimination **discriminación**
   f. 18
dish **plato** *m.* 8, 12
   main dish *m.* **plato principal** 8
dishwasher **lavaplatos** *m.,*
   sing. 12
disorderly **desordenado/a** *adj.* 5
divorce **divorcio** *m.* 9
divorced **divorciado/a** *adj.* 9
   get divorced (from) **divorciarse**
    v. (**de**) 9
dizzy **mareado/a** *adj.* 10
do **hacer** *v.* 4
   do aerobics **hacer ejercicios**
    aeróbicos 15
   do household chores **hacer**
    quehaceres domésticos 12
   do stretching exercises **hacer**
    ejercicios de estiramiento 15
   (I) don't want to. **No quiero.** 4
doctor **doctor(a)** *m., f.* 3; 10;
   médico/a *m., f.* 3
documentary (*film*) **documental**
   m. 17
dog **perro** *m.* 13
domestic **doméstico/a** *adj.*
   domestic appliance
    electrodoméstico *m.*
done **hecho/a** *p.p.* 14
door **puerta** *f.* 2
doorman/doorwoman **portero/a**
   m., f. 1
dormitory **residencia** *f.*
   estudiantil 2
double **doble** *adj.* 5
   double room **habitación** *f.*
    doble 5
doubt **duda** *f.* 13; **dudar** *v.* 13
   not to doubt **no dudar** 13
   there is no doubt that
    no cabe duda de 13;
    no hay duda de 13
download **descargar** *v.* 11
downtown **centro** *m.* 4
drama **drama** *m.* 17
dramatic **dramático/a** *adj.* 17
draw **dibujar** *v.* 2
drawing **dibujo** *m.*
dress **vestido** *m.* 6
   get dressed **vestirse (e:i)** *v.* 7
drink **beber** *v.* 3; **bebida** *f.* 8;
   tomar *v.* 2
drive **conducir** *v.* 6; **manejar**
   v. 11
driver **conductor(a)** *m., f.* 1

drug **droga** *f.* 15
   drug addict **drogadicto/a**
    m., f. 15
dry (oneself) **secarse** *v.* 7
during **durante** *prep.* 7; **por**
   prep. 11
dust **sacudir** *v.* 12;
   quitar *v.* **el polvo** 12
dust the furniture **sacudir los**
   muebles 12
duster **plumero** *m.* 12

E

each **cada** *adj.* 6
ear (outer) **oreja** *f.* 10
early **temprano** *adv.* 7
earn **ganar** *v.* 16
earring **arete** *m.* 6
earthquake **terremoto** *m.* 18
ease **aliviar** *v.*
east **este** *m.* 14
   to the east **al este** 14
easy **fácil** *adj. m., f.* 3
eat **comer** *v.* 3
ecological **ecológico/a** *adj.* 13
ecologist **ecologista** *m., f.* 13
ecology **ecología** *f.* 13
economics **economía** *f.* 2
ecotourism **ecoturismo** *m.* 13
Ecuadorian **ecuatoriano/a** *adj.* 3
effective **eficaz** *adj. m., f.*
egg **huevo** *m.* 8
eight **ocho** 1
eight hundred **ochocientos/as** 2
eighteen **dieciocho** 1
eighth **octavo/a** 5
eighty **ochenta** 2
either… or **o… o** *conj.* 7
elect **elegir (e:i)** *v.* 18
election **elecciones** *f. pl.* 18
electric appliance
   electrodoméstico *m.* 12
electrician **electricista** *m., f.* 16
electricity **luz** *f.* 12
elegant **elegante** *adj. m., f.* 6
elevator **ascensor** *m.* 5
eleven **once** 1
e-mail **correo** *m.* **electrónico** 4
   e-mail address **dirección** *f.*
    electrónica 11
   e-mail message **mensaje** *m.*
    electrónico 4
   read e-mail **leer** *v.* **el correo**
    electrónico 4
embarrassed **avergonzado/a**
   adj. 5
embrace (each other) **abrazar(se)**
   v. 11
emergency **emergencia** *f.* 10
   emergency room **sala** *f.* **de**
    emergencia(s) 10
employee **empleado/a** *m., f.* 5
employment **empleo** *m.* 16
end **fin** *m.* 4; **terminar** *v.* 2
   end table **mesita** *f.* 12
endure **aguantar** *v.* 14
energy **energía** *f.* 13
engaged: get engaged (to)
   comprometerse *v.* (**con**) 9

engineer **ingeniero/a** *m., f.* 3
English (*language*) **inglés** *m.* 2; **inglés, inglesa** *adj.* 3
enjoy **disfrutar** *v.* (**de**) 15
enough **bastante** *adv.* 10
entertainment **diversión** *f.* 4
entrance **entrada** *f.* 12
envelope **sobre** *m.* 14
environment **medio ambiente** *m.* 13
environmental science **ciencias ambientales** 2
equality **igualdad** *f.* 18
erase **borrar** *v.* 11
eraser **borrador** *m.* 2
errand **diligencia** *f.* 14
essay **ensayo** *m.* 3
establish **establecer** *v.* 16
evening **tarde** *f.* 1
event **acontecimiento** *m.* 18
every day **todos los días** 10
everything **todo** *m.* 5
exactly **en punto** 1
exam **examen** *m.* 2
excellent **excelente** *adj.* 5
excess **exceso** *m.* 15
in excess **en exceso** 15
exchange **intercambiar** *v.*
in exchange for **por** 11
exciting **emocionante** *adj. m., f.*
excursion **excursión** *f.*
excuse **disculpar** *v.*
Excuse me. (*May I?*) **Con permiso.** 1; (*I beg your pardon.*) **Perdón.** 1
exercise **ejercicio** *m.* 15; **hacer** *v.* **ejercicio** 15; (*a degree/profession*) **ejercer** *v.* 16
exit **salida** *f.* 5
expensive **caro/a** *adj.* 6
experience **experiencia** *f.*
expire **vencer** *v.* 14
explain **explicar** *v.* 2
explore **explorar** *v.*
expression **expresión** *f.*
extinction **extinción** *f.* 13
eye **ojo** *m.* 10

F

fabulous **fabuloso/a** *adj.* 5
face **cara** *f.* 7
facing **enfrente de** *prep.* 14
fact: in fact **de hecho**
factory **fábrica** *f.* 13
fall (*down*) **caerse** *v.* 10
fall asleep **dormirse (o:ue)** *v.* 7
fall in love (*with*) **enamorarse** *v.* (**de**) 9
fall (*season*) **otoño** *m.* 5
fallen **caído/a** *p.p.* 14
family **familia** *f.* 3
famous **famoso/a** *adj.*
fan **aficionado/a** *m., f.* 4
be a fan (*of*) **ser aficionado/a (a)**
far from **lejos de** *prep.* 2
farewell **despedida** *f.*

fascinate **fascinar** *v.* 7
fashion **moda** *f.* 6
be in fashion **estar de moda** 6
fast **rápido/a** *adj.*
fat **gordo/a** *adj.* 3; **grasa** *f.* 15
father **padre** *m.* 3
father-in-law **suegro** *m.* 3
favorite **favorito/a** *adj.* 4
fear **miedo** *m.*; **temer** *v.* 13
February **febrero** *m.* 5
feel **sentir(se) (e:ie)** *v.* 7
feel like (*doing something*) **tener ganas de (+ inf.)** 3
festival **festival** *m.* 17
fever **fiebre** *f.* 10
have a fever **tener** *v.* **fiebre** 10
few **pocos/as** *adj. pl.*
fewer than **menos de (+ number)** 8
fifteen **quince** 1
fifteen-year-old girl celebrating her birthday **quinceañera** *f.* 9
fifth **quinto/a** 5
fifty **cincuenta** 2
fight (*for/against*) **luchar** *v.* (**por/contra**) 18
figure (*number*) **cifra** *f.*
file **archivo** *m.* 11
fill **llenar** *v.* 11
fill out (*a form*) **llenar (un formulario)** 14
fill the tank **llenar el tanque** 11
finally **finalmente** *adv.*; **por último** 7; **por fin** 11
find **encontrar (o:ue)** *v.* 4
find (*each other*) **encontrar(se)**
find out **enterarse** *v.* 16
fine **multa** *f.*
(*fine*) arts **bellas artes** *f., pl.* 17
finger **dedo** *m.* 10
finish **terminar** *v.* 2
finish (*doing something*) **terminar** *v.* **de (+ inf.)**
fire **incendio** *m.* 18; **despedir (e:i)** *v.* 16
firefighter **bombero/a** *m., f.* 16
firm **compañía** *f.* 16; **empresa** *f.* 16
first **primer, primero/a** 2, 5
fish (*food*) **pescado** *m.* 8; **pescar** *v.* 5; (*live*) **pez** *m., sing.* (**peces** *pl.*) 13
fish market **pescadería** *f.* 14
fishing **pesca** *f.*
fit (*clothing*) **quedar** *v.* 7
five **cinco** 1
five hundred **quinientos/as** 2
fix (*put in working order*) **arreglar** *v.* 11; (*clothes, hair, etc. to go out*) **arreglarse** *v.* 7
fixed **fijo/a** *adj.* 6
flag **bandera** *f.*
flexible **flexible** *adj.* 15
flood **inundación** *f.* 18

floor (*of a building*) **piso** *m.* 5; **suelo** *m.* 12
ground floor **planta baja** *f.* 5
top floor **planta** *f.* **alta**
flower **flor** *f.* 13
flu **gripe** *f.* 10
fog **niebla** *f.*
folk **folclórico/a** *adj.* 17
follow **seguir (e:i)** *v.* 4
food **comida** *f.* 4, 8
foolish **tonto/a** *adj.* 3
foot **pie** *m.* 10
football **fútbol** *m.* **americano** 4
for **para** *prep.* 11; **por** *prep.* 11
for example **por ejemplo** 11
for me **para mí** 8
forbid **prohibir** *v.*
foreign **extranjero/a** *adj.* 17
foreign languages **lenguas** *f., pl.* **extranjeras** 2
forest **bosque** *m.* 13
forget **olvidar** *v.* 10
fork **tenedor** *m.* 12
form **formulario** *m.* 14
forty **cuarenta** 2
four **cuatro** 1
four hundred **cuatrocientos/as** 2
fourteen **catorce** 1
fourth **cuarto/a** *m., f.* 5
free **libre** *adj. m., f.* 4
be free (*of charge*) **ser gratis** 14
free time **tiempo libre**; spare (*free*) time **ratos libres** 4
freedom **libertad** *f.* 18
freezer **congelador** *m.* 12
French **francés, francesa** *adj.* 3
French fries **papas** *f., pl.* **fritas** 8; **patatas** *f., pl.* **fritas** 8
frequently **frecuentemente** *adv.*; **con frecuencia** *adv.* 10
Friday **viernes** *m., sing.* 2
fried **frito/a** *adj.* 8
fried potatoes **papas** *f., pl.* **fritas** 8; **patatas** *f., pl.* **fritas** 8
friend **amigo/a** *m., f.* 3
friendly **amable** *adj. m., f.* 5
friendship **amistad** *f.* 9
from **de** *prep.* 1; **desde** *prep.* 6
from the United States **estadounidense** *m., f.* *adj.* 3
from time to time **de vez en cuando** 10
I'm from… **Soy de…** 1
front: (*cold*) front **frente (frío)** *m.* 5
fruit **fruta** *f.* 8
fruit juice **jugo** *m.* **de fruta** 8
fruit store **frutería** *f.* 14
full **lleno/a** *adj.* 11
fun **divertido/a** *adj.*
fun activity **diversión** *f.* 4
have fun **divertirse (e:ie)** *v.* 9

function **funcionar** *v.*
furniture **muebles** *m., pl.* 12
furthermore **además (de)** *adv.* 10
future **porvenir** *m.* 16
   for/to the future **por el porvenir** 16
   in the future **en el futuro**

G

gain weight **aumentar** *v.* **de peso** 15; **engordar** *v.* 15
game **juego** *m.*; (*match*) **partido** *m.* 4
   game show **concurso** *m.* 17
garage (*in a house*) **garaje** *m.* 12; **garaje** *m.* 11; **taller (mecánico)** 11
garden **jardín** *m.* 12
garlic **ajo** *m.* 8
gas station **gasolinera** *f.* 11
gasoline **gasolina** *f.* 11
gentleman **caballero** *m.* 8
geography **geografía** *f.* 2
German **alemán, alemana** *adj.* 3
get **conseguir (e:i)** *v.* 4; **obtener** *v.* 16
   get along well/badly (with) **llevarse bien/mal (con)** 9
   get bigger **aumentar** *v.* 13
   get bored **aburrirse** *v.* 17
   get connected to the Internet **conectarse** *v.* **a Internet** 11
   get good grades **sacar buenas notas** 2
   get into trouble **meterse en problemas** *v.* 13
   get off of (a vehicle) **bajar(se)** *v.* **de** 11
   get on/into (a vehicle) **subir(se)** *v.* **a** 11
   get out of (a vehicle) **bajar(se)** *v.* **de** 11
   get ready **arreglarse** *v.* 7
   get up **levantarse** *v.* 7
gift **regalo** *m.* 6
ginger **jengibre** *m.* 10
girl **chica** *f.* 1; **muchacha** *f.* 3
girlfriend **novia** *f.* 3
give **dar** *v.* 6; (*as a gift*) **regalar** 9
   give directions **indicar cómo llegar** 14
glass (*drinking*) **vaso** *m.* 12; **vidrio** *m.* 13
   (made) of glass **de vidrio** 13
glasses **gafas** *f., pl.* 6
   sunglasses **gafas** *f., pl.* **de sol** 6
global warming **calentamiento global** *m.* 13
gloves **guantes** *m., pl.* 6
go **ir** *v.* 4
   go away **irse** 7
   go by boat **ir en barco** 5

go by bus **ir en autobús** 5
go by car **ir en auto(móvil)** 5
go by motorcycle **ir en moto(cicleta)** 5
go by plane **ir en avión** 5
go by taxi **ir en taxi** 5
go down **bajar(se)** *v.*
go on a hike **ir de excursión** 4
go out (with) **salir** *v.* **(con)** 9
go up **subir** *v.*
Let's go. **Vamos.** 4
going to: be going to (*do something*) **ir a (+ inf.)** 4
golf **golf** *m.* 4
good **buen, bueno/a** *adj.* 3, 6
   Good afternoon. **Buenas tardes.** 1
   Good evening. **Buenas noches.** 1
   Good morning. **Buenos días.** 1
   Good night. **Buenas noches.** 1
   It's good that… **Es bueno que…** 12
goodbye **adiós** *m.* 1
   say goodbye (to) **despedirse** *v.* **(de) (e:i)** 18
good-looking **guapo/a** *adj.* 3
government **gobierno** *m.* 13
GPS **navegador GPS** *m.* 11
graduate (from/in) **graduarse** *v.* **(de/en)** 9
grains **cereales** *m., pl.* 8
granddaughter **nieta** *f.* 3
grandfather **abuelo** *m.* 3
grandmother **abuela** *f.* 3
grandparents **abuelos** *m., pl.* 3
grandson **nieto** *m.* 3
grape **uva** *f.* 8
grass **hierba** *f.* 13
grave **grave** *adj.* 10
gray **gris** *adj. m., f.* 6
great **fenomenal** *adj. m., f.* 5; **genial** *adj.* 16
great-grandfather **bisabuelo** *m.* 3
great-grandmother **bisabuela** *f.* 3
green **verde** *adj. m., f.* 6
greet (each other) **saludar(se)** *v.* 11
greeting **saludo** *m.* 1
   Greetings to… **Saludos a…** 1
grilled **a la plancha** 8
ground floor **planta baja** *f.* 5
grow **aumentar** *v.* 13
guest (*at a house/hotel*) **huésped** *m., f.* 5 (*invited to a function*) **invitado/a** *m., f.* 9
guide **guía** *m., f.*
gymnasium **gimnasio** *m.* 4

H

hair **pelo** *m.* 7
hairdresser **peluquero/a** *m., f.* 16

half **medio/a** *adj.* 3
   half-brother **medio hermano** *m.* 3
   half-past… (*time*) **…y media** 1
   half-sister **media hermana** *f.* 3
hallway **pasillo** *m.* 12
ham **jamón** *m.* 8
hamburger **hamburguesa** *f.* 8
hand **mano** *f.* 1
hand in **entregar** *v.* 11
handsome **guapo/a** *adj.* 3
happen **ocurrir** *v.* 18
happiness **alegría** *v.* 9
happy **alegre** *adj.* 5; **contento/a** *adj.* 5; **feliz** *adj. m., f.* 5 be happy **alegrarse** *v.* **(de)** 13
   Happy birthday! **¡Feliz cumpleaños!** 9
hard **difícil** *adj. m., f.* 3
hard-working **trabajador(a)** *adj.* 3
hardly **apenas** *adv.* 10
hat **sombrero** *m.* 6
hate **odiar** *v.* 9
have **tener** *v.* 3
   have time **tener tiempo** 14
   have to (*do something*) **tener que (+ inf.)**
   have a tooth removed **sacar(se) un diente** 10
he **él** 1
head **cabeza** *f.* 10
headache **dolor** *m.* **de cabeza** 10
health **salud** *f.* 10
healthy **saludable** *adj. m., f.* 10; **sano/a** *adj.* 10
   lead a healthy lifestyle **llevar** *v.* **una vida sana** 15
hear **oír** *v.* 4
heard **oído/a** *p.p.* 14
hearing: sense of hearing **oído** *m.* 10
heart **corazón** *m.* 10
heat **calor** *m.*
Hello. (*on the telephone*) **Aló.** 11; **Bueno.** 11; **Diga.** 11
help **ayudar** *v.*; **servir (e:i)** *v.* 5
   help each other **ayudarse** *v.* 11
her **su(s)** *poss. adj.* 3; (of) hers **suyo(s)/a(s)** *poss. pron.* 11
   her **la** *f., sing., d.o. pron.* 5
   to/for her **le** *f., sing., i.o. pron.* 6
here **aquí** *adv.* 1
   Here is/are… **Aquí está(n)…** 5
Hi. **Hola.** 1
highway **autopista** *f.* 11; **carretera** *f.* 11
hike **excursión** *f.* 4
   go on a hike **ir de excursión** 4
hiker **excursionista** *m., f.*
hiking **de excursión** 4
him *m., sing., d.o. pron.* **lo** 5; to/for him **le** *m., sing., i.o. pron.* 6
hire **contratar** *v.* 16

his **su(s)** *poss. adj.* 3; (of) his
  suyo(s)/a(s) *poss. pron.* 11
history **historia** *f.* 2; 17
hobby **pasatiempo** *m.* 4
hockey **hockey** *m.* 4
hold up **aguantar** *v.* 14
hole **hueco** *m.* 4
holiday **día** *m.* **de fiesta** 9
home **casa** *f.* 2
  home page **página** *f.*
    principal 11
homemaker **amo/a** *m.*,
  f. **de casa** 12
homework **tarea** *f.* 2
honey **miel** *f.* 10
hood **capó** *m.* 11; **cofre** *m.* 11
hope **esperar** *v.* (+ *inf.*) 2;
  esperar *v.* 13
  I hope (that) **ojalá (que)** 13
horror (genre) **de horror** *m.* 17
horse **caballo** *m.* 5
hospital **hospital** *m.* 10
hot: be (*feel*) (very) hot **tener**
  (mucho) calor 3
  It's (very) hot. **Hace (mucho)**
    calor. 5
hotel **hotel** *m.* 5
hour **hora** *f.* 1
house **casa** *f.* 2
household chores **quehaceres** *m.*
  pl. **domésticos** 12
housing **vivienda** *f.* 12
How…! **¡Qué…!**
  how **¿cómo?** *adv.* 1, 2
  How are you? **¿Qué tal?** 1
  How are you?**¿Cómo estás?**
    fam. 1
  How are you?**¿Cómo está**
    usted? *form.* 1
  How can I help you? **¿En qué**
    puedo servirles? 5
  How is it going? **¿Qué tal?** 1
  How is the weather? **¿Qué**
    tiempo hace? 5
  How much/many?
    ¿Cuánto(s)/a(s)? 1
  How much does… cost?
    ¿Cuánto cuesta…? 6
  How old are you? **¿Cuántos**
    años tienes? *fam.*
however **sin embargo**
hug (each other) **abrazar(se)**
  v. 11
humanities **humanidades** *f., pl.* 2
hundred **cien, ciento** 2
hunger **hambre** *f.*
hungry: be (very) hungry **tener** *v.*
  (mucha) hambre 3
hunt **cazar** *v.* 13
hurricane **huracán** *m.* 18
hurry **apurarse** *v.* 15; **darse prisa**
  v. 15
  be in a (big) hurry **tener** *v.*
    (mucha) prisa 3
hurt **doler (o:ue)** *v.* 10
husband **esposo** *m.* 3

I

I **yo** 1
  I hope (that) **Ojalá (que)**
    interj. 13
  I wish (that) **Ojalá (que)**
    interj. 13
ice cream **helado** *m.* 9
  ice cream shop **heladería** *f.* 14
iced **helado/a** *adj.* 8
  iced tea **té** *m.* **helado** 8
idea **idea** *f.* 18
if **si** *conj.* 4
illness **enfermedad** *f.* 10
important **importante** *adj.* 3
  be important to **importar** *v.* 7
  It's important that… **Es**
    importante que… 12
impossible **imposible** *adj.* 13
  it's impossible **es imposible** 13
improbable **improbable** *adj.* 13
  it's improbable **es**
    improbable 13
improve **mejorar** *v.* 13
in **en** *prep.* 2; **por** *prep.* 11
  in the afternoon **de la tarde** 1;
    por la tarde 7
  in a bad mood **de mal humor** 5
  in the direction of **para** *prep.* 11
  in the early evening **de la tarde** 1
  in the evening **de la noche** 1;
    por la tarde 7
  in a good mood **de buen**
    humor 5
  in the morning **de la**
    mañana 1; **por la**
    mañana 7
  in love (with)
    enamorado/a (de) 5
  in search of **por** *prep.* 11
in front of **delante de** *prep.* 2
increase **aumento** *m.*
incredible **increíble** *adj.* 5
inequality **desigualdad** *f.* 18
infection **infección** *f.* 10
inform **informar** *v.* 18
injection **inyección** *f.* 10
  give an injection *v.* **poner una**
    inyección 10
injure (oneself) **lastimarse** 10
  injure (one's foot) **lastimarse** *v.*
    (el pie) 10
inner ear **oído** *m.* 10
inside **dentro** *adv.*
insist (on) **insistir** *v.* **(en)** 12
installments: pay in installments
  pagar *v.* **a plazos** 14
intelligent **inteligente** *adj.* 3
intend to **pensar** *v.* (+ *inf.*) 4
interest **interesar** *v.* 7
interesting **interesante** *adj.* 3
  be interesting to **interesar** *v.* 7
international **internacional**
  adj. m., f. 18

Internet **Internet** 11
  get connected to the Internet
    conectarse *v.* **a Internet** 11
interview **entrevista** *f.* 16;
  entrevistar *v.* 16
interviewer **entrevistador(a)** *m.,*
  f. 16
introduction **presentación** *f.*
  I would like to introduce you to
    (name). **Le presento a…**
    form. 1; **Te presento a…**
    fam. 1
invest **invertir (e:ie)** *v.* 16
invite **invitar** *v.* 9
iron (clothes) **planchar** *v.* **la**
  ropa 12
it **lo/la** *sing., d.o., pron.* 5
Italian **italiano/a** *adj.* 3
its **su(s)** *poss. adj.* 3;
  suyo(s)/a(s) *poss. pron.* 11
it's the same **es igual** 5

J

jacket **chaqueta** *f.* 6
January **enero** *m.* 5
Japanese **japonés, japonesa**
  adj. 3
jeans **(blue)jeans** *m., pl.* 6
jewelry store **joyería** *f.* 14
job **empleo** *m.* 16; **puesto**
  m. 16; **trabajo** *m.* 16
  job application **solicitud** *f.* **de**
    trabajo 16
jog **correr** *v.*
journalism **periodismo** *m.* 2
journalist **periodista** *m., f.* 3
joy **alegría** *f.* 9
juice **jugo** *m.* 8
July **julio** *m.* 5
June **junio** *m.* 5
jungle **selva, jungla** *f.* 13
just **apenas** *adv.*
  have just done something
    acabar de (+ *inf.*) 6

K

key **llave** *f.* 5
keyboard **teclado** *m.* 11
kilometer **kilómetro** *m.* 11
kiss **beso** *m.* 9
  kiss each other **besarse** *v.* 11
kitchen **cocina** *f.* 9, 12
knee **rodilla** *f.* 10
knife **cuchillo** *m.* 12
know **saber** *v.* 6; **conocer** *v.* 6
know how **saber** *v.* 6

L

laboratory **laboratorio** *m.* 2
lack **faltar** *v.* 7
lake **lago** *m.* 13

lamp **lámpara** *f.* 12
land **tierra** *f.* 13
landscape **paisaje** *m.* 5
language **lengua** *f.* 2
laptop (computer) **computadora**
     f. **portátil** 11
large **grande** *adj.* 3
large (*clothing size*) **talla**
     grande
last **durar** *v.* 18; **pasado/a**
     adj. 6; **último/a** *adj.* 7
     last name **apellido** *m.* 3
     last night **anoche** *adv.* 6
     last week **semana** *f.* **pasada** 6
     last year **año** *m.* **pasado** 6
     the last time **la última vez** 7
late **tarde** *adv.* 7
later (on) **más tarde** 7
     See you later. **Hasta la vista.** 1;
     Hasta luego. 1
laugh **reírse (e:i)** *v.* 9
laughed **reído** *p.p.* 14
laundromat **lavandería** *f.* 14
law **ley** *f.* 13
lawyer **abogado/a** *m., f.* 16
lazy **perezoso/a** *adj.*
learn **aprender** *v.* (**a** + *inf.*) 3
least, at **por lo menos** *adv.* 10
leave **salir** *v.* 4; **irse** *v.* 7
     leave a tip **dejar una**
         propina
     leave behind **dejar** *v.* 16
     leave for (*a place*) **salir para**
     leave from **salir de**
left **izquierda** *f.* 2
     be left over **quedar** *v.* 7
     to the left of **a la izquierda de** 2
leg **pierna** *f.* 10
lemon **limón** *m.* 8
lend **prestar** *v.* 6
less **menos** *adv.* 10
     less... than **menos... que** 8
     less than **menos de** (+ *number*)
lesson **lección** *f.* 1
let **dejar** *v.*
let's see **a ver**
letter **carta** *f.* 4, 14
lettuce **lechuga** *f.* 8
liberty **libertad** *f.* 18
library **biblioteca** *f.* 2
license (*driver's*) **licencia** *f.* **de**
     conducir 11
lie **mentira** *f.* 4
life **vida** *f.* 9
lifestyle: lead a healthy lifestyle
     llevar una vida sana 15
lift **levantar** *v.* 15
     lift weights **levantar pesas** 15
light **luz** *f.* 12
like **como** *prep.* 8; **gustar** *v.* 2
     I like... **Me gusta(n)...** 2
     like this **así** *adv.* 10
     like very much **encantar** *v.*;
         fascinar *v.* 7
     Do you like...? **¿Te**
         gusta(n)...? 2
likeable **simpático/a** *adj.* 3
likewise **igualmente** *adv.* 1

line **línea** *f.* 4; **cola** (*queue*) *f.* 14
     listen (to) **escuchar** *v.* 2
     listen to music **escuchar**
         música 2
     listen to the radio **escuchar la**
         radio 2
literature **literatura** *f.* 2
little (*quantity*) **poco** *adv.* 10
live **vivir** *v.* 3; **en vivo** *adj.* 7
living room **sala** *f.* 12
loan **préstamo** *m.* 14; **prestar**
     v. 6, 14
lobster **langosta** *f.* 8
located **situado/a** *adj.*
     be located **quedar** *v.* 14
long **largo/a** *adj.* 6
look (at) **mirar** *v.* 2
look for **buscar** *v.* 2
lose **perder (e:ie)** *v.* 4
     lose weight **adelgazar** *v.* 15
lost **perdido/a** *adj.* 13, 14
     be lost **estar perdido/a** 14
lot, a **muchas veces** *adv.* 10
lot of, a **mucho/a** *adj.* 3; **un**
     montón de 4
love (*another person*) **querer**
     (e:ie) *v.* 4; (*inanimate objects*)
     encantar *v.* 7; **amor** *m.* 9
     in love **enamorado/a** *adj.* 5
     love at first sight **amor a**
     primera vista 9
luck **suerte** *f.*
lucky: be (very) lucky **tener**
     (mucha) suerte 3
luggage **equipaje** *m.* 5
lunch **almuerzo** *m.* 4, 8
     have lunch **almorzar (o:ue)**
     v. 4

M

ma'am **señora (Sra.); doña** *f.* 1
mad **enojado/a** *adj.* 5
magazine **revista** *f.* 4
magnificent **magnífico/a** *adj.* 5
mail **correo** *m.* 14; **enviar** *v.*,
     mandar *v.* 14; **echar (una**
     carta) al buzón 14
     mail carrier **cartero** *m.* 14
mailbox **buzón** *m.* 14
main **principal** *adj. m., f.* 8
maintain **mantener** *v.* 15
major **especialización** *f.* 2
make **hacer** *v.* 4
     make a decision **tomar una**
     decisión 15
     make the bed **hacer la**
     cama 12
makeup **maquillaje** *m.* 7
     put on makeup **maquillarse** *v.* 7
man **hombre** *m.* 1
manager **gerente** *m., f.* 8, 16
many **mucho/a** *adj.* 3
     many times **muchas veces** 10
map **mapa** *m.* 1, 2
March **marzo** *m.* 5
margarine **margarina** *f.* 8

marinated fish **ceviche** *m.* 8
     lemon-marinated shrimp
         ceviche *m.* **de camarón** 8
marital status **estado** *m.* **civil** 9
marker **marcador** *m.* 2
market **mercado** *m.* 6
     open-air market **mercado al**
         aire libre 6
marriage **matrimonio** *m.* 9
married **casado/a** *adj.* 9
     get married (to) **casarse** *v.*
         (con) 9
     I'll marry you! **¡Acepto**
         casarme contigo! 17
marvelous **maravilloso/a** *adj.* 5
massage **masaje** *m.* 15
masterpiece **obra maestra** *f.* 17
match (*sports*) **partido** *m.* 4
match (with) **hacer** *v.*
     juego (con) 6
mathematics **matemáticas**
     f., pl. 2
matter **importar** *v.* 7
maturity **madurez** *f.* 9
maximum **máximo/a** *adj.* 11
May **mayo** *m.* 5
May I leave a message? **¿Puedo**
     dejar un recado? 11
maybe **tal vez** 5; **quizás** 5
mayonnaise **mayonesa** *f.* 8
me **me** *sing., d.o. pron.* 5
     to/for me **me** *sing., i.o. pron.* 6
meal **comida** *f.* 8
means of communication **medios**
     m., pl. **de comunicación** 18
meat **carne** *f.* 8
mechanic **mecánico/a** *m., f.* 11
     mechanic's repair shop **taller**
         mecánico 11
media **medios** *m., pl.* **de**
     comunicación 18
medical **médico/a** *adj.* 10
medication **medicamento** *m.* 10
medicine **medicina** *f.* 10
medium **mediano/a** *adj.*
meet (each other) **encontrar(se)**
     v. 11; **conocer(se)** *v.* 8
     meet up with **encontrarse con** 7
meeting **reunión** *f.* 16
menu **menú** *m.* 8
message **mensaje** *m.*
Mexican **mexicano/a** *adj.* 3
microwave **microonda** *f.* 12
     microwave oven **horno** *m.* **de**
     microondas 12
middle age **madurez** *f.* 9
midnight **medianoche** *f.* 1
mile **milla** *f.*
milk **leche** *f.* 8
million **millón** *m.* 2
     million of **millón de** 2
mine **mío(s)/a(s)** *poss.* 11
mineral **mineral** *m.* 15
     mineral water **agua** *f.*
     mineral 8

minute **minuto** *m.*
mirror **espejo** *m.* 7
Miss **señorita (Srta.)** *f.* 1
miss **perder (e:ie)** *v.* 4; **extrañar**
   v. 16
mistaken **equivocado/a** *adj.*
modern **moderno/a** *adj.* 17
mom **mamá** *f.*
Monday **lunes** *m., sing.* 2
money **dinero** *m.* 6
monkey **mono** *m.* 13
month **mes** *m.* 5
monument **monumento** *m.* 4
moon **luna** *f.* 13
more **más** 2
   more... than **más... que** 8
   more than **más de** (+
      number) 8
morning **mañana** *f.* 1
mother **madre** *f.* 3
mother-in-law **suegra** *f.* 3
motor **motor** *m.*
motorcycle **moto(cicleta)** *f.* 5
mountain **montaña** *f.* 4
mouse **ratón** *m.* 11
mouth **boca** *f.* 10
move (*from one house to another)*
   mudarse *v.* 12
movie **película** *f.* 4
   movie star **estrella** *f.*
      de cine 17
   movie theater **cine** *m.* 4
Mr. **señor (Sr.); don** *m.* 1
Mrs. **señora (Sra.); doña** *f.* 1
much **mucho/a** *adj.* 3
mud **lodo** *m.*
murder **crimen** *m.* 18
muscle **músculo** *m.* 15
museum **museo** *m.* 4
mushroom **champiñón** *m.* 8
music **música** *f.* 2, 17
musical **musical** *adj., m., f.* 17
musician **músico/a** *m., f.* 17
must **deber** *v.* (+ *inf.*) 3
my **mi(s)** *poss. adj.* 3; **mío(s)/a(s)**
   poss. pron. 11

N

name **nombre** *m.* 1
   be named **llamarse** *v.* 7
   in the name of **a nombre de** 5
   last name **apellido** *m.* 3
   My name is... **Me llamo...** 1
   name someone/something
      ponerle el nombre 9
napkin **servilleta** *f.* 12
national **nacional** *adj. m., f.* 18
nationality **nacionalidad** *f.* 1
natural **natural** *adj. m., f.* 13
   natural disaster **desastre** *m.*
      natural 18
   natural resource **recurso** *m.*
      natural 13

nature **naturaleza** *f.* 13
nauseated **mareado/a** *adj.* 10
near **cerca de** *prep.* 2
necessary **necesario/a** *adj.* 12
   It is necessary that... **Es**
      necesario que... 12
neck **cuello** *m.* 10
need **faltar** *v.* 7; **necesitar** *v.* (+
   inf.) 2
neighbor **vecino/a** *m., f.* 12
neighborhood **barrio** *m.* 12
neither **tampoco** *adv.* 7
neither... nor **ni... ni** *conj.* 7
nephew **sobrino** *m.* 3
nervous **nervioso/a** *adj.* 5
network **red** *f.* 11
never **nunca** *adj.* 7; **jamás** 7
new **nuevo/a** *adj.* 6
newlywed **recién casado/a**
   m., f. 9
news **noticias** *f., pl.* 18;
   actualidades *f., pl.* 18; **noticia**
   f. 11
newscast **noticiero** *m.* 18
newspaper **periódico** 4; **diario**
   m. 18
next **próximo/a** *adj.* 3, 16
   next to **al lado de** *prep.* 2
nice **simpático/a** *adj.* 3; **amable**
   adj. 5
niece **sobrina** *f.* 3
night **noche** *f.* 1
   night stand **mesita** *f.* **de**
      noche 12
nine **nueve** 1
nine hundred **novecientos/as** 2
nineteen **diecinueve** 1
ninety **noventa** 2
ninth **noveno/a** 5
no **no** 1; **ningún, ninguno/a(s)**
   adj. 7
   no one **nadie** *pron.* 7
nobody **nadie** 7
none **ningún, ninguno/a(s)**
   adj. 7
noon **mediodía** *m.* 1
nor **ni** *conj.* 7
north **norte** *m.* 14
   to the north **al norte** 14
nose **nariz** *f.* 10
not **no** 1
   not any **ningún, ninguno/a(s)**
      adj. 7
   not anyone **nadie** *pron.* 7
   not anything **nada** *pron.* 7
   not bad at all **nada mal** 5
   not either **tampoco** *adv.* 7
   not ever **nunca** *adv.* 7; **jamás**
      adv. 7
   not very well **no muy bien** 1
   not working **descompuesto/a**
      adj. 11
notebook **cuaderno** *m.* 1
nothing **nada** 1; 7
noun **sustantivo** *m.*
November **noviembre** *m.* 5

now **ahora** *adv.* 2
nowadays **hoy día** *adv.*
nuclear **nuclear** *adj. m., f.* 13
   nuclear energy **energía**
      nuclear 13
number **número** *m.* 1
nurse **enfermero/a** *m., f.* 10
nutrition **nutrición** *f.* 15
nutritionist **nutricionista** *m.,*
   f. 15

O

o'clock: It's... o'clock. **Son**
   las... 1
   It's one o'clock. **Es la una.** 1
obey **obedecer** *v.* 18
obligation **deber** *m.* 18
obtain **conseguir (e:i)** *v.* 4;
   obtener *v.* 16
obvious **obvio/a** *adj.* 13
   it's obvious **es obvio** 13
occupation **ocupación** *f.* 16
occur **ocurrir** *v.* 18
October **octubre** *m.* 5
of **de** *prep.* 1
   Of course. **Claro que sí.;**
      Por supuesto.
offer **oferta** *f.*; **ofrecer (c:zc)** *v.* 6
office **oficina** *f.* 12
   doctor's office **consultorio** *m.*
      10
often **a menudo** *adv.* 10
Oh! **¡Ay!**
oil **aceite** *m.* 8
OK **regular** *adj.* 1
old **viejo/a** *adj.* 3
old age **vejez** *f.* 9
older **mayor** *adj. m., f.* 3
   older brother, sister **hermano/a**
      mayor *m., f.* 3
oldest **el/la mayor** 8
on **en** *prep.* 2; **sobre** *prep.* 2
   on behalf of **por** *prep.* 11
   on the dot **en punto** 1
   on time **a tiempo** 10
   on top of **encima de** 2
once **una vez** 6
one **uno** 1
   one hundred **cien(to)** 2
   one million **un millón** *m.* 2
   one more time **una vez más**
   one thousand **mil** 2
onion **cebolla** *f.* 8
online: to buy online **comprar** *v.*
   en línea 6
only **sólo** *adv.* 6; **único/a** *adj.* 3
   only child **hijo/a único/a**
      m., f. 3
open **abierto/a** *adj.* 5, 14;
   abrir *v.* 3
open-air **al aire libre** 6
opera **ópera** *f.* 17
operation **operación** *f.* 10
opposite **enfrente de** *prep.* 14
or **o** *conj.* 7

orange **anaranjado/a** *adj.* 6;
  naranja *f.* 8
orchestra **orquesta** *f.* 17
order **mandar** 12; (*food*) **pedir
  (e:i)** *v.* 8
  in order to **para** *prep.* 11
orderly **ordenado/a** *adj.* 5
ordinal (*numbers*) **ordinal** *adj.*
organize oneself **organizarse** *v.* 12
other **otro/a** *adj.* 6
ought to **deber** *v.* (+ *inf.*) *adj.* 3
our **nuestro(s)/a(s)** *poss. adj.* 3;
  poss. pron. 11
out of order **descompuesto/a**
  adj. 11
outside **afuera** *adv.* 5
outskirts **afueras** *f., pl.* 12
oven **horno** *m.* 12
over **sobre** *prep.* 2
(over)population
  (sobre)población *f.* 13
over there **allá** *adv.* 2
own **propio/a** *adj.*
owner **dueño/a** *m., f.* 8

P

p.m. **de la tarde, de la noche** *f.* 1
pack (one's suitcases) **hacer** *v.* **las
  maletas** 5
package **paquete** *m.* 14
page **página** *f.* 11
pain **dolor** *m.* 10
  have pain **tener** *v.* **dolor** 10
paint **pintar** *v.* 17
painter **pintor(a)** *m., f.* 16
painting **pintura** *f.* 12, 17
pair **par** *m.* 6
  pair of shoes **par** *m.* **de
  zapatos** 6
pale **pálido/a** *adj.* 14
pants **pantalones** *m., pl.* 6
pantyhose **medias** *f., pl.* 6
paper **papel** *m.* 2
Pardon me. (*May I?*) **Con
  permiso.** 1; (*Excuse me.*)
  Pardon me. **Perdón.** 1
parents **padres** *m., pl.* 3; **papás**
  m., pl.
park **estacionar** *v.* 11; **parque**
  m. 4
parking lot **estacionamiento**
  m. 14
partner (*one of a married couple*)
  pareja *f.* 9
party **fiesta** *f.* 9
passed **pasado/a** *p.p.*
passenger **pasajero/a** *m., f.* 1
passport **pasaporte** *m.* 5
password **contraseña** *f.* 11
past **pasado/a** *adj.* 6
pastime **pasatiempo** *m.* 4
pastry shop **pastelería** *f.* 14
path **sendero** *m.* 13
patient **paciente** *m., f.* 10
patio **patio** *m.* 12

pay **pagar** *v.* 6
  pay in cash **pagar** *v.* **al contado;
  pagar en efectivo** 14
  pay in installments **pagar** *v.* **a
  plazos** 14
  pay the bill **pagar la cuenta**
pea **arveja** *m.* 8
peace **paz** *f.* 18
peach **melocotón** *m.* 8
peak **cima** *f.* 15
pear **pera** *f.* 8
pen **pluma** *f.* 2
pencil **lápiz** *m.* 1
penicillin **penicilina** *f.*
people **gente** *f.* 3
pepper (*black*) **pimienta** *f.* 8
per **por** *prep.* 11
perfect **perfecto/a** *adj.* 5
period of time **temporada** *f.* 5
person **persona** *f.* 3
pharmacy **farmacia** *f.* 10
phenomenal **fenomenal** *adj.* 5
photograph **foto(grafía)** *f.* 1
physical (exam) **examen** *m.*
  médico 10
physician **doctor(a), médico/a**
  m., f. 3
physics **física** *f. sing.* 2
pick up **recoger** *v.* 13
picture **cuadro** *m.* 12;
  pintura *f.* 12
pie **pastel** *m.* 9
pill (*tablet*) **pastilla** *f.* 10
pillow **almohada** *f.* 12
pineapple **piña** *f.*
pink **rosado/a** *adj.* 6
place **lugar** *m.* 2, 4; **sitio** *m.* 3;
  poner *v.* 4
plaid **de cuadros** 6
plans **planes** *m., pl.*
  have plans **tener planes**
plant **planta** *f.* 13
plastic **plástico** *m.* 13
  (made) of plastic **de
  plástico** 13
plate **plato** *m.* 12
play **drama** *m.* 17; **comedia** *f.* 17
  jugar (u:ue) *v.* 4; (*a musical
  instrument*) **tocar** *v.* 17; (*a role*)
  hacer el papel de 17; (*cards*)
  jugar a (las cartas) 5; (*sports*)
  practicar deportes 4
player **jugador(a)** *m., f.* 4
playwright **dramaturgo/a**
  m., f. 17
pleasant **agradable** *adj.*
please **por favor** 1
Pleased to meet you. **Mucho
  gusto.** 1; **Encantado/a.** *adj.* 1
pleasing: be pleasing to **gustar**
  v. 7
pleasure **gusto** *m.* 1; **placer** *m.*
  The pleasure is mine. **El gusto
  es mío.** 1
poem **poema** *m.* 17
poet **poeta** *m., f.* 17
poetry **poesía** *f.* 17
police (force) **policía** *f.* 11

political **político/a** *adj.* 18
politician **político/a** *m., f.* 16
politics **política** *f.* 18
polka-dotted **de lunares** 6
poll **encuesta** *f.* 18
pollute **contaminar** *v.* 13
polluted **contaminado/a** *m., f.* 13
  be polluted **estar
  contaminado/a** 13
pollution **contaminación** *f.* 13
pool **piscina** *f.* 4
poor **pobre** *adj., m., f.* 6
  poor thing **pobrecito/a** *adj.* 3
popsicle **paleta helada** *f.* 4
population **población** *f.* 13
pork **cerdo** *m.* 8
  pork chop **chuleta** *f.* **de
  cerdo** 8
portable **portátil** *adj.* 11
  portable computer
  computadora *f.*
  portátil 11
position **puesto** *m.* 16
possessive **posesivo/a** *adj.*
possible **posible** *adj.* 13
  it's (not) possible **(no) es
  posible** 13
post office **correo** *m.* 14
postcard **postal** *f.*
poster **cartel** *m.* 12
potato **papa** *f.* 8; **patata** *f.* 8
pottery **cerámica** *f.* 17
practice **practicar** *v.* 2; (*a degree/
  profession*) **ejercer** *v.* 16
prefer **preferir (e:ie)** *v.* 4
pregnant **embarazada** *adj. f.* 10
prepare **preparar** *v.* 2
preposition **preposición** *f.*
prescribe (*medicine*) **recetar** *v.* 10
prescription **receta** *f.* 10
present **regalo** *m.*; **presentar** *v.* 17
press **prensa** *f.* 18
pressure **presión** *f.*
  be under a lot of pressure **sufrir
  muchas presiones** 15
pretty **bonito/a** *adj.* 3
price **precio** *m.* 6
  (fixed, set) price **precio** *m.* **fijo** 6
print **imprimir** *v.* 11
printer **impresora** *f.* 11
prize **premio** *m.* 17
probable **probable** *adj.* 13
  it's (not) probable **(no) es
  probable** 13
problem **problema** *m.* 1
profession **profesión** *f.* 3; 16
professor **profesor(a)** *m., f.*
profile **perfil** *m.* 11
program **programa** *m.* 1
programmer **programador(a)**
  m., f. 3
prohibit **prohibir** *v.* 10
project **proyecto** *m.* 11
promotion (*career*)
  ascenso *m.* 16
pronoun **pronombre** *m.*
protect **proteger** *v.* 13
protein **proteína** *f.* 15

provided (that) **con tal (de) que** *conj.* 13
psychologist **psicólogo/a** *m., f.* 16
psychology **psicología** *f.* 2
publish **publicar** *v.* 17
Puerto Rican **puertorriqueño/a** *adj.* 3
purchases **compras** *f., pl.*
pure **puro/a** *adj.* 13
purple **morado/a** *adj.* 6
purse **bolsa** *f.* 6
put **poner** *v.* 4; **puesto/a** *p.p.* 14
    put (a letter) in the mailbox **echar (una carta) al buzón** 14
    put on (*a performance*) **presentar** *v.* 17
    put on (*clothing*) **ponerse** *v.* 7
    put on makeup **maquillarse** *v.* 7

Q

quality **calidad** *f.* 6
quarter (*academic*) **trimestre** *m.* 2
    quarter after (*time*) **y cuarto** 1; **y quince** 1
    quarter to (*time*) **menos cuarto** 1; **menos quince** 1
question **pregunta** *f.*
quickly **rápido** *adv.* 10
quiet **tranquilo/a** *adj.* 15
quit **dejar** *v.* 16
quiz **prueba** *f.* 2

R

racism **racismo** *m.* 18
radio (*medium*) **radio** *f.* 2
    radio (set) **radio** *m.* 11
rain **llover (o:ue)** *v.* 5; **lluvia** *f.*
    It's raining. **Llueve.** 5; **Está lloviendo.** 5
raincoat **impermeable** *m.* 6
rain forest **bosque** *m.* **tropical** 13
raise (*salary*) **aumento** *m.* **de sueldo** 16
rather **bastante** *adv.* 10
read **leer** *v.* 3; **leído/a** *p.p.* 14
    read e-mail **leer el correo electrónico** 4
    read a magazine **leer una revista** 4
    read a newspaper **leer un periódico** 4
ready **listo/a** *adj.* 5
reality show **programa de realidad** *m.* 17
reap the benefits (of) *v.* **disfrutar** *v.* **(de)** 15
receive **recibir** *v.* 3
recommend **recomendar (e:ie)** *v.* 8; 12
record **grabar** *v.* 11

recover **recuperar** *v.* 11
recreation **diversión** *f.* 4
recycle **reciclar** *v.* 13
recycling **reciclaje** *m.* 13
red **rojo/a** *adj.* 6
red-haired **pelirrojo/a** *adj.* 3
reduce **reducir** *v.* 13; **disminuir** *v.* 16
    reduce stress/tension **aliviar el estrés/la tensión** 15
refrigerator **refrigerador** *m.* 12
region **región** *f.*
regret **sentir (e:ie)** *v.* 13
relatives **parientes** *m., pl.* 3
relax **relajarse** *v.* 9
    Relax. **Tranquilo/a.** 7
    Relax, sweetie. **Tranquilo/a, cariño.** 11
remain **quedarse** *v.* 7
remember **acordarse (o:ue)** *v.* **(de)** 7; **recordar (o:ue)** *v.* 4
remote control **control remoto** *m.* 11
renewable **renovable** *adj.* 13
rent **alquilar** *v.* 12; (payment) **alquiler** *m.* 12
repeat **repetir (e:i)** *v.* 4
report **informe** *m.* 18; **reportaje** *m.* 18
reporter **reportero/a** *m., f.* 16
representative **representante** *m., f.* 18
request **pedir (e:i)** *v.* 4
reservation **reservación** *f.* 5
resign (from) **renunciar (a)** *v.* 16
resolve **resolver (o:ue)** *v.* 13
resolved **resuelto/a** *p.p.* 14
resource **recurso** *m.* 13
responsibility **deber** *m.* 18; **responsabilidad** *f.*
responsible **responsable** *adj.* 8
rest **descansar** *v.* 2
restaurant **restaurante** *m.* 4
résumé **currículum** *m.* 16
retire (from work) **jubilarse** *v.* 9
return **regresar** *v.* 2; **volver (o:ue)** *v.* 4
returned **vuelto/a** *p.p.* 14
rice **arroz** *m.* 8
rich **rico/a** *adj.* 6
ride a bicycle **pasear** *v.* **en bicicleta** 4
ride a horse **montar** *v.* **a caballo** 5
ridiculous **ridículo/a** *adj.* 13
    it's ridiculous **es ridículo** 13
right **derecha** *f.* 2
    be right **tener razón** 3
    right? (*question tag*) **¿no?** 1; **¿verdad?** 1
    right away **enseguida** *adv.*
    right now **ahora mismo** 5
    to the right of **a la derecha de** 2
rights **derechos** *m., pl.* 18
ring **anillo** *m.* 17

ring **sonar (o:ue)** *v.* 11
river **río** *m.* 13
road **carretera** *f.* 11; **camino** *m.*
roast **asado/a** *adj.* 8
roast chicken **pollo** *m.* **asado** 8
romantic **romántico/a** *adj.* 17
room **habitación** *f.* 5; **cuarto** *m.* 2; 7
    living room **sala** *f.* 12
roommate **compañero/a** *m., f.* **de cuarto** 2
roundtrip **de ida y vuelta** 5
    roundtrip ticket **pasaje** *m.* **de ida y vuelta** 5
routine **rutina** *f.* 7
rug **alfombra** *f.* 12
run **correr** *v.* 3
    run errands **hacer diligencias** 14
    run into (*have an accident*) **chocar (con)** *v.*; (*meet accidentally*) **encontrar(se) (o:ue)** *v.* 11; (*run into something*) **darse (con)** 10
    run into (each other) **encontrar(se) (o:ue)** *v.* 11
rush **apurarse, darse prisa** *v.* 15
Russian **ruso/a** *adj.* 3

S

sad **triste** *adj.* 5; 13
    it's sad **es triste** 13
safe **seguro/a** *adj.* 5
said **dicho/a** *p.p.* 14
sailboard **tabla de windsurf** *f.* 5
salad **ensalada** *f.* 8
salary **salario** *m.* 16; **sueldo** *m.* 16
sale **rebaja** *f.* 6
salesperson **vendedor(a)** *m., f.* 6
salmon **salmón** *m.* 8
salt **sal** *f.* 8
same **mismo/a** *adj.* 3
sandal **sandalia** *f.* 6
sandwich **sándwich** *m.* 8
Saturday **sábado** *m.* 2
sausage **salchicha** *f.* 8
save (*on a computer*) **guardar** *v.* 11; save (money) **ahorrar** *v.* 14
savings **ahorros** *m.* 14
    savings account **cuenta** *f.* **de ahorros** 14
say **decir** *v.* 4;
    say (that) **decir (que)** *v.* 4
    say the answer **decir la respuesta** 4
scan **escanear** *v.* 11
scarcely **apenas** *adv.* 10
scared: be (very) scared (of) **tener (mucho) miedo (de)** 3
schedule **horario** *m.* 2
school **escuela** *f.* 1
sciences **ciencias** *f., pl.* 2
science fiction (genre) **de ciencia ficción** *f.* 17

scientist **científico/a** *m., f.* 16
scream **grito** *m.* 5; **gritar** *v.*
screen **pantalla** *f.* 11
scuba dive **bucear** *v.* 4
sculpt **esculpir** *v.* 17
sculptor **escultor(a)** *m., f.* 17
sculpture **escultura** *f.* 17
sea **mar** *m.* 5
  (sea) turtle **tortuga (marina)**
    f. 13
season **estación** *f.* 5
seat **silla** *f.* 2
second **segundo/a** 5
secretary **secretario/a** *m., f.* 16
sedentary **sedentario/a** *adj.* 15
see **ver** *v.* 4
  see (you, him, her) again **volver**
    a ver(te, lo, la)
  see movies **ver películas** 4
  See you. **Nos vemos.** 1
  See you later. **Hasta la vista.** 1;
    Hasta luego. 1
  See you soon. **Hasta pronto.** 1
  See you tomorrow. **Hasta**
    mañana. 1
seem **parecer** *v.* 6
seen **visto/a** *p.p.* 14
sell **vender** *v.* 6
semester **semestre** *m.* 2
send **enviar; mandar** *v.* 14
separate (from) **separarse** *v.*
  (de) 9
separated **separado/a** *adj.* 9
September **septiembre** *m.* 5
sequence **secuencia** *f.*
serious **grave** *adj.* 10
serve **servir (e:i)** *v.* 8
service **servicio** *m.* 15
set (*fixed*) **fijo/a** *adj.* 6
  set the table **poner la mesa** 12
seven **siete** 1
seven hundred **setecientos/as** 2
seventeen **diecisiete** 1
seventh **séptimo/a** 5
seventy **setenta** 2
several **varios/as** *adj. pl.*
sexism **sexismo** *m.* 18
shame **lástima** *f.* 13
  it's a shame **es una lástima** 13
shampoo **champú** *m.* 7
shape **forma** *f.* 15
  be in good shape **estar en**
    buena forma 15
  stay in shape **mantenerse en**
    forma 15
share **compartir** *v.* 3
sharp (*time*) **en punto** 1
shave **afeitarse** *v.* 7
shaving cream **crema** *f.* **de**
  afeitar 5, 7
she **ella** 1
shellfish **mariscos** *m., pl.* 8
ship **barco** *m.*
shirt **camisa** *f.* 6
shoe **zapato** *m.* 6
  shoe size **número** *m.* 6
  shoe store **zapatería** *f.* 14
    tennis shoes **zapatos** *m., pl.*
      de tenis 6

shop **tienda** *f.* 6
shopping, to go **ir de compras** 5
  shopping mall **centro**
    comercial *m.* 6
short (*in height*) **bajo/a** *adj.* 3; (*in*
  length) **corto/a** *adj.* 6
short story **cuento** *m.* 17
shorts **pantalones cortos**
  m., pl. 6
should (*do something*) **deber** *v.*
  (+ inf.) 3
shout **gritar** *v.*
show **espectáculo** *m.* 17;
  mostrar (o:ue) *v.* 4
  game show **concurso** *m.* 17
shower **ducha** *f.* 7
shrimp **camarón** *m.* 8
siblings **hermanos/as** *pl.* 3
sick **enfermo/a** *adj.* 10
  be sick **estar enfermo/a** 10
  get sick **enfermarse** *v.* 10
sign **firmar** *v.* 14; **letrero** *m.* 14
silk **seda** *f.* 6
  (made of) silk **de seda** 6
since **desde** *prep.*
sing **cantar** *v.* 2
singer **cantante** *m., f.* 17
single **soltero/a** *adj.* 9
  single room **habitación** *f.*
    individual 5
sink **lavabo** *m.* 7
sir **señor (Sr.), don** *m.* 1;
  caballero *m.* 8
sister **hermana** *f.* 3
sister-in-law **cuñada** *f.* 3
sit down **sentarse (e:ie)** *v.* 7
six **seis** 1
six hundred **seiscientos/as** 2
sixteen **dieciséis** 1
sixth **sexto/a** 5
sixty **sesenta** 2
size **talla** *f.* 6
  shoe size *m.* **número** 6
skate **patinar** 4
skateboard **andar en patineta**
  v. 4
ski **esquiar** *v.* 4
skiing **esquí** *m.* 4
  water-skiing **esquí** *m.*
    acuático 4
skirt **falda** *f.* 6
skull made out of sugar **calavera**
  de azúcar *f.* 9
sky **cielo** *m.* 13
sleep **dormir (o:ue)** *v.* 4; **sueño** *m.*
  go to sleep **dormirse**
    (o:ue) *v.* 7
sleepy: be (very) sleepy **tener**
  (mucho) sueño 3
slender **delgado/a** *adj.* 3
slim down **adelgazar** *v.* 15
slippers **pantuflas** *f., pl.* 7
slow **lento/a** *adj.* 11
slowly **despacio** *adv.* 10
small **pequeño/a** *adj.* 3
smart **listo/a** *adj.* 5
smile **sonreír (e:i)** *v.* 9
smiled **sonreído** *p.p.* 14
smoke **fumar** *v.* 15
  (not) to smoke **(no) fumar** 15

smoking section **sección** *f.* **de**
  fumar 8
  (non) smoking section *f.* **sección**
    de (no) fumar 8
snack **merendar (e:ie)** *v.* 8
  afternoon snack **merienda**
    f. 15
  have a snack **merendar** *v.* 8
sneakers **zapatos** *m., pl.*
  de tenis 6
sneeze **estornudar** *v.* 10
snow **nevar (e:ie)** *v.* 5; **nieve** *f.*
snowing: It's snowing. **Nieva.** 5;
  Está nevando. 5
so (*in such a way*) **así** *adv.* 10;
  tan *adv.* 5
  so much **tanto** *adv.*
  so-so **regular** 1
  so that **para que** *conj.* 13
soap **jabón** *m.* 7
soap opera **telenovela** *f.* 17
soccer **fútbol** *m.* 4
sociology **sociología** *f.* 2
sock(s) **calcetín (calcetines)** *m.* 6
sofa **sofá** *m.* 12
soft drink **refresco** *m.* 8
software **programa** *m.* **de**
  computación 11
soil **tierra** *f.* 13
solar **solar** *adj., m., f.* 13
  solar energy **energía solar** 13
soldier **soldado** *m., f.* 18
solution **solución** *f.* 13
solve **resolver (o:ue)** *v.* 13
some **algún, alguno/a(s)** *adj.* 7;
  unos/as *indef. art.* 1
somebody **alguien** *pron.* 7
someone **alguien** *pron.* 7
something **algo** *pron.* 7
sometimes **a veces** *adv.* 10
son **hijo** *m.* 3
song **canción** *f.* 17
son-in-law **yerno** *m.* 3
soon **pronto** *adv.* 10
  See you soon. **Hasta pronto.** 1
sorry: be sorry **sentir (e:ie)** *v.* 13
  I'm sorry. **Lo siento.** 1
soul **alma** *f.* 9
soup **sopa** *f.* 8
south **sur** *m.* 14
  to the south **al sur** 14
Spain **España** *f.*
Spanish (*language*) **español** *m.* 2;
  español(a) *adj.* 3
spare (free) time **ratos libres** 4
speak **hablar** *v.* 2
  Speaking. (*on the telephone*)
    Con él/ella habla. 11
special: today's specials **las**
  especialidades del día 8
spectacular **espectacular** *adj.*
  m., f.
speech **discurso** *m.* 18
speed **velocidad** *f.* 11
  speed limit **velocidad** *f.*
    máxima 11
spelling **ortografía** *f.*,
  ortográfico/a *adj.*

spend (*money*) **gastar** *v.* 6
spoon (*table or large*) **cuchara**
 f. 12
sport **deporte** *m.* 4
 sports-related **deportivo/a**
  adj. 4
spouse **esposo/a** *m., f.* 3
sprain (*one's ankle*) **torcerse**
 (o:ue) *v.* **(el tobillo)** 10
spring **primavera** *f.* 5
(*city or town*) square **plaza** *f.* 4
stadium **estadio** *m.* 2
stage **etapa** *f.* 9
stairs **escalera** *f.* 12
stamp **estampilla** *f.* 14; **sello**
 m. 14
stand in line **hacer** *v.* **cola** 14
star **estrella** *f.* 13
start (*a vehicle*) **arrancar** *v.* 11
station **estación** *f.* 5
statue **estatua** *f.* 17
status: marital status **estado** *m.*
 civil 9
stay **quedarse** *v.* 7
 stay in shape **mantenerse en**
  forma 15
steak **bistec** *m.* 8
steering wheel **volante** *m.* 11
step **escalón** *m.* 15
stepbrother **hermanastro** *m.* 3
stepdaughter **hijastra** *f.* 3
stepfather **padrastro** *m.* 3
stepmother **madrastra** *f.* 3
stepsister **hermanastra** *f.* 3
stepson **hijastro** *m.* 3
stereo **estéreo** *m.*
still **todavía** *adv.* 5
stockbroker **corredor(a)** *m., f.* **de**
 bolsa 16
stockings **medias** *f., pl.* 6
stomach **estómago** *m.* 10
stone **piedra** *f.* 13
stop **parar** *v.* 11
 stop (*doing something*) **dejar de**
 (+ inf.) 13
store **tienda** *f.* 6
storm **tormenta** *f.* 18
story **cuento** *m.* 17; **historia**
 f. 17
stove **cocina, estufa** *f.* 12
straight **derecho** *adv.* 14
 straight (*ahead*) **derecho** 14
straighten up **arreglar** *v.* 12
strange **extraño/a** *adj.* 13
 it's strange **es extraño** 13
street **calle** *f.* 11
stress **estrés** *m.* 15
stretching **estiramiento** *m.* 15
  do stretching exercises **hacer**
   ejercicios *m. pl.* **de**
   estiramiento 15
strike (*labor*) **huelga** *f.* 18
striped **de rayas** 6
stroll **pasear** *v.* 4
strong **fuerte** *adj. m., f.* 15
struggle (*for/against*) **luchar** *v.*
 (por/contra) 18

student **estudiante** *m., f.* 1; 2;
 estudiantil *adj.* 2
study **estudiar** *v.* 2
stupendous **estupendo/a** *adj.* 5
style **estilo** *m.*
suburbs **afueras** *f., pl.* 12
subway **metro** *m.* 5
 subway station **estación** *f.*
  del metro 5
success **éxito** *m.*
successful: be successful **tener**
 éxito 16
such as **tales como**
suddenly **de repente** *adv.* 6
suffer **sufrir** *v.* 10
 suffer an illness **sufrir una**
  enfermedad 10
sugar **azúcar** *m.* 8
suggest **sugerir (e:ie)** *v.* 12
suit **traje** *m.* 6
suitcase **maleta** *f.* 1
summer **verano** *m.* 5
sun **sol** *m.* 13
sunbathe **tomar** *v.* **el sol** 4
Sunday **domingo** *m.* 2
(sun)glasses **gafas** *f., pl.*
 (de sol) 6
sunny: It's (very) sunny. **Hace**
 (mucho) sol. 5
supermarket **supermercado**
 m. 14
suppose **suponer** *v.* 4
sure **seguro/a** *adj.* 5
 be sure **estar seguro/a** 5
surf **hacer** *v.* **surf** 5
surfboard **tabla de surf** *f.* 5
surprise **sorprender** *v.* 9;
 sorpresa *f.* 9
survey **encuesta** *f.* 18
sweat **sudar** *v.* 15
sweater **suéter** *m.* 6
sweep the floor **barrer el suelo** 12
sweets **dulces** *m., pl.* 9
swim **nadar** *v.* 4
swimming **natación** *f.* 4
 swimming pool **piscina** *f.* 4
symptom **síntoma** *m.* 10

T

table **mesa** *f.* 2
tablespoon **cuchara** *f.* 12
tablet (*computer*) **tableta** *f.* 11
take **tomar** *v.* 2; **llevar** *v.* 6
 take care of **cuidar** *v.* 13
 take someone's temperature
  tomar *v.* **la temperatura** 10
 take (*wear*) a shoe size
  calzar *v.* 6
 take a bath **bañarse** *v.* 7
 take a shower **ducharse** *v.* 7
 take off **quitarse** *v.* 7
 take out the trash **sacar** *v.* **la**
  basura 12
 take photos **tomar** *v.* **fotos** 5;
  sacar *v.* **fotos** 5

talented **talentoso/a** *adj.* 17
talk **hablar** *v.* 2
 talk show **programa** *m.* **de**
  entrevistas 17
tall **alto/a** *adj.* 3
tank **tanque** *m.* 11
taste **probar (o:ue)** *v.* 8
 taste like **saber a** 8
tasty **rico/a** *adj.* 8; **sabroso/a**
 adj. 8
tax **impuesto** *m.* 18
taxi **taxi** *m.* 5
tea **té** *m.* 8
teach **enseñar** *v.* 2
teacher **profesor(a)** *m., f.* 1, 2;
 maestro/a *m., f.* 16
team **equipo** *m.* 4
technician **técnico/a** *m., f.* 16
telecommuting **teletrabajo** *m.* 16
telephone **teléfono** 11
television **televisión** *f.* 2
 television set **televisor** *m.* 11
tell **contar** *v.* 4; **decir** *v.* 4
 tell (*that*) **decir** *v.* **(que)** 4
 tell lies **decir mentiras** 4
 tell the truth **decir la verdad** 4
temperature **temperatura** *f.* 10
ten **diez** 1
tennis **tenis** *m.* 4
 tennis shoes **zapatos** *m., pl.* **de**
  tenis 6
tension **tensión** *f.* 15
tent **tienda** *f.* **de campaña**
tenth **décimo/a** 5
terrible **terrible** *adj. m., f.* 13
 it's terrible **es terrible** 13
terrific **chévere** *adj.*
test **prueba** *f.* 2; **examen** *m.* 2
text **textear** *v.* 11
text message **mensaje** *m.* **de**
 texto 11
Thank you. **Gracias.** *f., pl.* 1
 Thank you (very much).
  (Muchas) gracias. 1
 Thanks (a lot). **(Muchas)**
  gracias. 1
 Thanks for inviting me. **Gracias**
  por invitarme. 9
that **que, quien(es)** *pron.* 12
 that (one) **ése, ésa, eso**
  pron. 6; **ese, esa,** *adj.* 6
 that (*over there*) **aquél,**
  aquélla, aquello *pron.* 6;
  aquel, aquella *adj.* 6
 that which **lo que** 12
 that's why **por eso** 11
the **el** *m.,* **la** *f. sing.,* **los** *m.,*
 las *f., pl.* 1
theater **teatro** *m.* 17
their **su(s)** *poss. adj.* 3;
 suyo(s)/a(s) *poss. pron.* 11
them **los/las** *pl., d.o. pron.* 5
 to/for them **les** *pl., i.o. pron.* 6
then (*afterward*) **después** *adv.* 7;
 (*as a result*) **entonces** *adv.* 5, 7;
 (*next*) **luego** *adv.* 7
there **allí** *adv.* 2
 There is/are… **Hay…** 1
 There is/are not… **No hay…** 1

therefore **por eso** 11
these **éstos, éstas** *pron.* 6;
  estos, estas *adj.* 6
they **ellos** *m.*, **ellas** *f. pron.* 1
thin **delgado/a** *adj.* 3
thing **cosa** *f.* 1
think **pensar (e:ie)** *v.* 4; (believe)
  creer *v.*
  think about **pensar en** *v.* 4
third **tercero/a** 5
thirst **sed** *f.*
thirsty: be (very) thirsty **tener**
  (mucha) sed 3
thirteen **trece** 1
thirty **treinta** 1; thirty (*minutes*
  past the hour) **y treinta; y**
  media 1
this **este, esta** *adj.*; **éste, ésta,**
  esto *pron.* 6
those **ésos, ésas** *pron.* 6; **esos,**
  esas *adj.* 6
those (over there) **aquéllos,**
  aquéllas *pron.* 6; **aquellos,**
  aquellas *adj.* 6
thousand **mil** *m.* 2
three **tres** 1
three hundred **trescientos/as** 2
throat **garganta** *f.* 10
through **por** *prep.* 11
Thursday **jueves** *m., sing.* 2
thus (*in such a way*) **así** *adv.*
ticket **boleto** *m.* 2, 17; **pasaje** *m.* 5
tie **corbata** *f.* 6
time **vez** *f.* 6; **tiempo** *m.* 14
  have a good/bad time **pasarlo**
    bien/mal 9
  I've had a fantastic time. **Lo**
    he pasado de película. 18
  What time is it? **¿Qué hora**
    es? 1
  (At) What time…? **¿A qué**
    hora…? 1
times **veces** *f., pl.* 6
  many times **muchas veces** 10
tip **propina** *f.* 8
tire **llanta** *f.* 11
tired **cansado/a** *adj.* 5
  be tired **estar cansado/a** 5
title **título** *m.* 16
to **a** *prep.* 1
toast (*drink*) **brindar** *v.* 9
  toast **pan** *m.* **tostado** 8
toasted **tostado/a** *adj.* 8
  toasted bread **pan tostado** *m.* 8
toaster **tostadora** *f.* 12
today **hoy** *adv.* 2
  Today is… **Hoy es…** 2
toe **dedo** *m.* **del pie** 10
together **juntos/as** *adj.* 9
toilet **inodoro** *m.* 7
tomato **tomate** *m.* 8
tomorrow **mañana** *f.* 1
  See you tomorrow. **Hasta**
    mañana. 1
tonight **esta noche** *adv.*
too **también** *adv.* 2; 7
  too much **demasiado** *adv.* 6;
    en exceso 15

tooth **diente** *m.* 7
toothpaste **pasta** *f.* **de dientes** 7
top **cima** *f.* 15
tornado **tornado** *m.* 18
touch **tocar** *v.* 17
touch screen **pantalla táctil** *f.*
tour **excursión** *f.* 4; **recorrido**
  m. 13
tour an area **recorrer** *v.*
tourism **turismo** *m.*
tourist **turista** *m., f.* 1;
  turístico/a *adj.*
toward **hacia** *prep.* 14;
  para *prep.* 11
towel **toalla** *f.* 7
town **pueblo** *m.*
trade **oficio** *m.* 16
traffic **circulación** *f.* 11; **tráfico**
  m. 11
  traffic light **semáforo** *m.* 14
tragedy **tragedia** *f.* 17
trail **sendero** *m.* 13
train **entrenarse** *v.* 15; **tren** *m.* 5
  train station **estación** *f.* **de**
    tren *m.* 5
trainer **entrenador(a)** *m., f.* 15
translate **traducir** *v.* 6
trash **basura** *f.* 12
travel **viajar** *v.* 2
  travel agency **agencia** *f.*
    de viajes
  travel agent **agente** *m., f.*
    de viajes
traveler **viajero/a** *m., f.* 5
treadmill **cinta caminadora** *f.* 15
tree **árbol** *m.* 13
trillion **billón** *m.*
trimester **trimestre** *m.* 2
trip **viaje** *m.* 5
  take a trip **hacer un viaje** 5
tropical forest **bosque** *m.*
  tropical 13
true: it's (not) true **(no) es**
  verdad 13
trunk **baúl** *m.* 11
truth **verdad** *f.* 4
try **intentar** *v.*; **probar (o:ue)** *v.* 8
  try (*to do something*) **tratar de**
    (+ inf.) 15
  try on **probarse (o:ue)** *v.* 7
t-shirt **camiseta** *f.* 6
Tuesday **martes** *m., sing.* 2
tuna **atún** *m.* 8
turkey **pavo** *m.* 8
turn **doblar** *v.* 14
  turn off (*electricity/appliance*)
    apagar *v.* 11
  turn on (*electricity/appliance*)
    poner *v.* 11; **prender** *v.* 11
twelve **doce** 1
twenty **veinte** 1
twenty-eight **veintiocho** 1
twenty-five **veinticinco** 1
twenty-four **veinticuatro** 1
twenty-nine **veintinueve** 1
twenty-one **veintiuno** 1;
  veintiún, veintiuno/a *adj.* 1

twenty-seven **veintisiete** 1
twenty-six **veintiséis** 1
twenty-three **veintitrés** 1
twenty-two **veintidós** 1
twice **dos veces** 6
twin **gemelo/a** *m., f.* 3
two **dos** 1
  two hundred **doscientos/as** 2

U

ugly **feo/a** *adj.* 3
uncle **tío** *m.* 3
under **debajo de** *prep.* 2
understand **comprender** *v.* 3;
  entender (e:ie) *v.* 4
underwear **ropa interior** 6
unemployment **desempleo** *m.* 18
unique **único/a** *adj.* 9
United States **Estados Unidos**
  (EE.UU.) *m. pl.*
university **universidad** *f.* 2
unless **a menos que** *conj.* 13
unmarried **soltero/a** *adj.* 9
unpleasant **antipático/a** *adj.* 3
until **hasta** *prep.* 6; **hasta que**
  conj. 13
upload **cargar** *v.* 11
urgent **urgente** *adj.* 12
  It's urgent that… **Es urgente**
    que… 12
us **nos** *pl., d.o. pron.* 5
  to/for us **nos** *pl., i.o. pron.* 6
use **usar** *v.* 6
used for **para** *prep.* 11
useful **útil** *adj. m., f.*

V

vacation **vacaciones** *f., pl.* 5
  be on vacation **estar de**
    vacaciones 5
  go on vacation **ir de**
    vacaciones 5
vacuum **pasar** *v.* **la aspiradora** 12
  vacuum cleaner **aspiradora** *f.* 12
valley **valle** *m.* 13
various **varios/as** *adj. m., f. pl.*
vegetables **verduras** *pl., f.* 8
verb **verbo** *m.*
very **muy** *adv.* 1
  (Very) well, thank you. **(Muy)**
    bien, gracias. 1
video **video** *m.* 1
  video game **videojuego** *m.* 4
videoconference
  videoconferencia *f.* 16
vinegar **vinagre** *m.* 8
violence **violencia** *f.* 18
visit **visitar** *v.* 4
  visit monuments **visitar**
    monumentos 4

vitamin **vitamina** *f.* 15
voice mail **correo de voz** *m.* 11
volcano **volcán** *m.* 13
volleyball **vóleibol** *m.* 4
vote **votar** *v.* 18

W

wait (for) **esperar** *v.* (+ *inf.*) 2
waiter/waitress **camarero/a**
   m., f. 8
wake up **despertarse (e:ie)** *v.* 7
walk **caminar** *v.* 2
   take a walk **pasear** *v.* 4
   walk around **pasear por** 4
wall **pared** *f.* 12; **muro** *m.* 15
wallet **cartera** *f.* 4, 6
want **querer (e:ie)** *v.* 4
war **guerra** *f.* 18
warm up **calentarse (e:ie)** *v.* 15
wash **lavar** *v.* 12
   wash one's face/hands **lavarse**
     la cara/las manos 7
   wash (the floor, the dishes)
     lavar (el suelo, los
     platos) 12
   wash oneself **lavarse** *v.* 7
washing machine **lavadora** *f.* 12
wastebasket **papelera** *f.* 2
watch **mirar** *v.* 2; **reloj** *m.* 2
   watch television **mirar (la)**
     televisión 2
water **agua** *f.* 8
   water pollution **contaminación**
     del agua 13
   water-skiing **esquí** *m.*
     acuático 4
way **manera** *f.*
we **nosotros(as)** *m., f.* 1
weak **débil** *adj. m., f.* 15
wear **llevar** *v.* 6; **usar** *v.* 6
weather **tiempo** *m.*
   The weather is bad. **Hace mal**
     tiempo. 5
   The weather is good. **Hace**
     buen tiempo. 5
weaving **tejido** *m.* 17
Web **red** *f.* 11
website **sitio** *m.* **web** 11
wedding **boda** *f.* 9
Wednesday **miércoles** *m., sing.* 2
week **semana** *f.* 2
weekend **fin** *m.* **de semana** 4
weight **peso** *m.* 15
   lift weights **levantar** *v.* **pesas**
     f., pl. 15
welcome **bienvenido(s)/a(s)**
   adj. 1
well: (Very) well, thanks. **(Muy)**
   bien, gracias. 1
well-being **bienestar** *m.* 15
well organized **ordenado/a** *adj.* 5

west **oeste** *m.* 14
   to the west **al oeste** 14 western
   (genre) **de vaqueros** 17
whale **ballena** *f.* 13
what **lo que** *pron.* 12
what? **¿qué?** 1
   At what time…? **¿A qué**
     hora…? 1
   What a pleasure to…! **¡Qué**
     gusto (+ inf.)…! 18
   What day is it? **¿Qué día es**
     hoy? 2
   What do you guys think? **¿Qué**
     les parece?
   What happened? **¿Qué**
     pasó?
   What is today's date? **¿Cuál**
     es la fecha de hoy? 5
   What nice clothes! **¡Qué ropa**
     más bonita! 6
   What size do you wear? **¿Qué**
     talla lleva (usa)? 6
   What time is it? **¿Qué hora**
     es? 1
   What's going on? **¿Qué pasa?** 1
   What's happening? **¿Qué**
     pasa? 1
   What's… like? **¿Cómo es…?**
   What's new? **¿Qué hay de**
     nuevo? 1
   What's the weather like? **¿Qué**
     tiempo hace? 5
   What's up? **¿Qué onda?** 14
   What's wrong? **¿Qué pasó?**
   What's your name? **¿Cómo se**
     llama usted? *form.* 1;
     ¿Cómo te llamas (tú)? *fam.* 1
when **cuando** *conj.* 7; 13
When? **¿Cuándo?** 2
where **donde**
where (to)? (*destination*)
   ¿adónde? 2; (*location*)
   ¿dónde? 1, 2
   Where are you from? **¿De**
     dónde eres (tú)? *fam.* 1;
     ¿De dónde es (usted)?
     form. 1
   Where is…? **¿Dónde está…?** 2
which **que** *pron.*, **lo que** *pron.* 12
which? **¿cuál?** 2; **¿qué?** 2
   In which…? **¿En qué…?**
   which one(s)? **¿cuál(es)?** 2
while **mientras** *conj.* 10
white **blanco/a** *adj.* 6
   white wine **vino blanco** 8
whiteboard **pizarra** *f.* 2
who **que** *pron.* 12; **quien(es)**
   pron. 12
who? **¿quién(es)?** 1, 2
   Who is…? **¿Quién es…?** 1
   Who is speaking? (*on telephone*)
     ¿Quién habla? 11
   Who is speaking/calling?
     (*on telephone*) **¿De parte**
     de quién? 11

whole **todo/a** *adj.*
whom **quien(es)** *pron.* 12
whose? **¿de quién(es)?** 1
why? **¿por qué?** 2 widower/
   widow **viudo/a** *adj.* 9
wife **esposa** *f.* 3
win **ganar** *v.* 4
wind **viento** *m.*
window **ventana** *f.* 2
windshield **parabrisas** *m.,*
   sing. 11
windsurf **hacer** *v.* **windsurf** 5
windy: It's (very) windy. **Hace**
   (mucho) viento. 5
wine **vino** *m.* 8
   red wine **vino tinto** 8
   white wine **vino blanco** 8
wineglass **copa** *f.* 12
winter **invierno** *m.* 5
wireless connection **conexión**
   inalámbrica *f.* 11
wish **desear** *v.* 2; **esperar** *v.* 13
   I wish (that) **ojalá (que)** 13
with **con** *prep.* 2
   with me **conmigo** 4; 9
   with you **contigo** *fam.* 5, 9
within (ten years) **dentro de (diez**
   años) *prep.* 16
without **sin** *prep.* 2; **sin que**
   conj. 13
woman **mujer** *f.* 1
wool **lana** *f.* 6
   (made of) wool **de lana** 6
word **palabra** *f.* 1
work **trabajar** *v.* 2; **funcionar**
   v. 11; **trabajo** *m.* 16
   work (of art, literature, music,
     etc.) **obra** *f.* 17
   work out **hacer gimnasia** 15
world **mundo** *m.* 8
worldwide **mundial** *adj. m., f.*
worried (about) **preocupado/a**
   (por) *adj.* 5
worry (about) **preocuparse** *v.*
   (por) 7
   Don't worry. **No te preocupes.**
     fam. 7
worse **peor** *adj. m., f.* 8
worst **el/la peor** 8
Would you like to…? **¿Te**
   gustaría…? *fam.*
Would you do me the honor of
   marrying me? **¿Me harías**
     el honor de casarte
     conmigo? 17
wow **híjole** *interj.* 6
wrench **llave** *f.* 11
write **escribir** *v.* 3
   write a letter/an e-mail
     escribir una carta/un
     mensaje electrónico 4
writer **escritor(a)** *m., f* 17
written **escrito/a** *p.p.* 14
wrong **equivocado/a** *adj.* 5
   be wrong **no tener razón** 3

X

X-ray **radiografía** *f.* 10

Y

yard **jardín** *m.* 12; **patio** *m.* 12
year **año** *m.* 5
  be… years old **tener…
    años** 3
yellow **amarillo/a** *adj.* 6
yes **sí** *interj.* 1
yesterday **ayer** *adv.* 6
yet **todavía** *adv.* 5
yogurt **yogur** *m.* 8
you **tú** *fam.* **usted (Ud.)** *form.*
  sing. **vosotros/as** *m., f. fam. pl.*
  ustedes (Uds.) *pl.* 1; (to, for)
  you *fam. sing.* **te** *pl.* **os** 6; *form.*
  sing. **le** *pl.* **les** 6
  you **te** *fam., sing.,* **lo/la** *form.,*
    sing., **os** *fam., pl.,* **los/las**
    pl., d.o. pron. 5
You don't say! **¡No me digas!**
  fam.; **¡No me diga!** *form.*
You're welcome. **De nada.** 1; **No
  hay de qué.** 1

young **joven** *adj., sing.* (**jóvenes**
  pl.) 3
  young person **joven** *m., f., sing.*
  (**jóvenes** *pl.*) 1
  young woman **señorita
    (Srta.)** *f.*
younger **menor** *adj. m., f.* 3
younger: younger brother, sister *m.,*
  f. **hermano/a menor** 3
youngest **el/la menor** *m., f.* 8
your **su(s)** *poss. adj. form.* 3;
  tu(s) *poss. adj. fam. sing.* 3;
  vuestro/a(s) *poss. adj. fam.*
  pl. 3
your(s) *form.* **suyo(s)/a(s)** *poss.*
  pron. form. 11; **tuyo(s)/a(s)**
  poss. fam. sing. 11; **vuestro(s)**
  /a(s) *poss. fam.* 11
youth *f.* **juventud** 9

Z

zero **cero** *m.* 1

Comics

31 © Joaquin Salvador Lavado (QUINO) Toda Mafalda - Ediciones de La Flor, 1993.

394-395 TUTE.

Literature

499 © Fundación mario Benedetti c/o Schavelzon Graham Agencia Literaria www.schavelzongraham.com

531 Cecilia de Menéndez Leal

565 de Burgos, Julia. "Julia de Burgos: yo misma fui mi ruta" from Song of the Simple Truth: The Complete Poems of Julia de Burgos. Willimantic: Curbstone Press, 1995.

601 Courtesy of Luisa Valenzuela.

Short Films

146 Courtesy of FeelSales/ContentLine.

534-535 Courtesy of Instituto Mexicano de Cinematografía (IMCINE).

568-569 Courtesy of Elemental Films.

604 By Jorge Naranjo and Nana Films (http://vimeo.com/35170814).

TV Clips

34 Courtesy of Edgardo Tettamanti.

72 © Cencosud Supermercados

110 Courtesy of Banco Galicia.

184 Courtesy of Visit Panama.

220 Courtesy of Juguettos.

256 Courtesy of Asepxia, Genommalab and Kepel & Mata.

294 Courtesy of Andres Felipe Roa.

326 Courtesy of Javier Ugarte (director).

362 Courtesy of Getting Better Creative Studio.

398 Courtesy of Popularlibros.com

436 Courtesy of Conforama España

470 Courtesy of Entropic Films.

502 Courtesy of Ogilvy & Mathers Honduras.

636 By permission of Subdirector de la Secretaria de Comunicaciones, Gobierno de Chile.

Photography Credits

Cover: Anna Gorin/Getty Images; (sky) Eric Lowenbach/Getty Images.

Front Matter (SE): iii: Andres Rodriguez/Shutterstock.

Front Matter (IAE): IAE-36: Rido/123RF.

Lesson 1: 1: Lumi Images/Alamy; **2:** John Henley/Getty Images; **3:** Martín Bernetti; **10:** (l) Rachel Distler; (r) Ali Burafi; **11:** (t) Hans Georg Roth/Getty Images; (ml) Elisabetta A. Villa/Getty Images; (mr) Paola Rios; (b) Chelsea Lauren/Variety/REX/Shutterstock; **12:** (l) Janet Dracksdorf; (r) Tom Grill/Corbis, **16:** (l) José Girarte/iStockphoto; (r) Blend Images/Alamy, **19:** (l) Goodluz/Shutterstock; (m) Anne Loubet; (r) Digi4tal Vision/Getty Images; **28:** (all) Martín Bernetti; **31:** (tl) Ana Cabezas Martín; (tml) Martín Bernetti; (tmr) Shvadchak Vasyl/123RF; (tr) Vanessa Bertozzi; (bl) Jan Pietruszka/Deposit Photos; (bm) Sanek70974/Fotolia; (br) Ramiro Isaza/Fotocolombia; **32:** Carolina Zapata; **33:** Paula Díez; **36:** (t) Robert Huberman/Alamy; (b) Photogal/Shutterstock; **37:** (tl) Timolina/Deposit Photos; (tr) Sean Drakes/Alamy; (ml) Stocksnapper/123RF; (mr) Toronto-Images.Com/Shutterstock; (b) Andres R/Shutterstock.

Lesson 2: 39: Radius Images/MaXx Images; **48:** (l) Martin Bernetti; (r) Pablo Corral/Getty Images; **49:** (t) Murle/Alamy; (m) Paul Almasy/Getty Images; (b) S Bukley/Shutterstock; **57:** Stephen Coburn/Shutterstock; **59:** (l) Paola Rios-Schaaf; (r) Image Source/Corbis; **68:** Jose Blanco; **69:** PNC/Media Bakery; **70:** (t) Martín Bernetti; (b) Aspen Photo/Shutterstock; **71:** Nora y Susana/Fotocolombia; **74:** (tl) Jose Blanco; (tr) Jose Blanco; (bl) Jose Tandem/Deposit Photos; (br) Iconotec/Fotosearch; **75:** (tl) Jacquelyn Martin/AP/REX/Shutterstock; (tr) Jose Blanco; (ml) Jose Blanco; (mr) Pete Goding/SIME/eStockphoto; (b) David Ramos/Getty Images.

Lesson 3: 77: Paul Bradbury/AGE Fotostock; **80:** (tl) Anne Loubet; (tr) Elena Kouptsova-Vasic/Shutterstock; (ml) Ana Cabezas Martin; (mr) Blend Images/Alamy; (bl) Martín Bernetti; (br) Bikerider London/Shutterstock; **86:** (tl) David Cantor/AP Images; (tr) Rafael Perez/Reuters; (b) Jeff Vespa/WireImage/Getty Images; **87:** (t) Chelsea Lauren/REX/Shutterstock; (ml) Marc Piasecki/Getty Images; (m) Eamonn McCormack/WireImage/Getty Images; (mr) Carlos Alvarez/Getty Images; (b) PG/Splash News/Newscom; **90:** (l) VaLiza/Shutterstock; (r) Fotoluminate/123RF; **92:** Andres Rodriguez/Alamy; **97:** (l) Tyler Olsen/Fotolia; (r) Blend Images/Alamy; **98:** Aldo Murillo/iStockphoto; **102:** (tl) Shakzu/Fotolia; (tm) Mihailomilovanovic/iStockphoto; (tr) Rosa Images/Media Bakery; (bl) Onoky/Fotolia; (bm) Jamie Grill/Getty Images; (br) Paula Diez; **106:** (t) Glow Images/AGE Fotostock; (m) Hill Street Studios/Media Bakery; (b) GM Visuals/AGE Fotostock; **107:** (t) Nora y Susana/Fotocolombia; (m) Chuck Savage/Getty Images; (b) Antonio Diaz/Shutterstock; **108:** Janet Dracksdorf; **109:** ASIFE/Alamy; **112:** (t) Wildlife GmbH/Alamy; (ml) John Beatty/Getty Images; (mr) Ecuadorpostales/Shutterstock; (bl) Onairda/Getty Images; (br) Lauren Krolick; **113:** (tl) Michael S. Nolan/AGE Fotostock; (tr) Pablo Corral/Getty Images; (ml) Marin Stefani; (mr) Fotos593/Shutterstock; (b) Patricio Hidalgo/Alamy.

Lesson 4: 115: Manu Prats/Offset; **117:** George Shelley/Getty Images; **119:** Nora y Susana/Fotocolombia; **124:** (l) Javier Soriano/AFP/Getty Images; (r) Fernando Bustamante/AP Images; **125:** (t) Photoworks/Shutterstock; (m) Zuma Press/Alamy; (b) RB/Bauer-Griffin/Getty Images; **127:** (t) Radu Bercan/Shutterstock; (ml) Fotomicar/Shutterstock; (mm) David R. Frazier Photolibrary/Alamy; (mr) Iakov Filimonov/123RF; (bl) Henn Photography/Getty Images; (bm) Sigrid Olsson/AGE Fotostock; (br) Janet Dracksdorf; **135:** Warner Bros Pictures/Everett Collection; **139:** Anne Loubet; **141:** Agan/Shutterstock; **142:** Jolopes/Fotolia; **143:** Fernando Llano/AP Images; **144:** Paula Diez; **145:** Rick Gomez/Getty Images; **148:** (tl) Randy Miramontez/Shutterstock; (tr) Self-Portrait with Thorn Necklace and Hummingbird, 1940 (oil on canvas), Kahlo, Frida (1907-54)/ Harry Ransom Center, University of Texas at Austin, Austin, USA / Leemage / Bridgeman Images; (bl) Ruben Varela; (br) Carolina Zapata; **149:** (tl) Radius Images/Alamy; (tr) Bettmann/Getty Images; (mt) Corel/Corbis; (mb) David R. Frazier Photolibrary/Alamy; (b) Diego Grandi/Alamy.

Lesson 5: 151: Gemma Ferrando/Offset; **162:** (l) Emporarcosar/Shutterstock; (r) Efrain Padro/Alamy; **163:** (t) AFP/Getty Images; (m) Pierre-Yves Babelon/123RF; (b) Neilson Barnard/Getty Images; **165:** (tl) Nenetus/Fotolia; (tr) Hart Creations/iStockphoto; (bl) Fotografixx/iStockphoto; (br) Mediaphotos/iStockphoto; **167:** Ronnie Kaufman/Getty Images; **180:** Janet Dracksdorf; **181:** (tl) Corel/Corbis; (tr) Dudarev Mikhail/Shutterstock; (m) Epicstockmedia/123RF; (b) Volodymyr Goinyk/Shutterstock; **182:** Carolina Zapata; **186:** (tl) Eddie Toro/123RF; (tr) Jose Blanco; (bl) Israel Pabon/Shutterstock; (br) Capricornis Photographic/Shutterstock; **187:** (tl) Jose Blanco; (tr) Lawrence Manning/Getty Images; (ml) Michele Falzone/Getty Images; (mr) Daniel Alvarez/123RF; (b) Ricardo Arduengo/Getty Images.

Lesson 6: 189: Antonio Diaz/Shutterstock; **198:** (l) Jose Caballero Digital Press Photos/Newscom; (r) Janet Dracksdorf; **199:** (t) Carlos Alvarez/Getty Images; (ml) Guiseppe Carace/Getty Images; (mr) Mark Mainz/Getty Images; (b) John Parra/Getty Images; **201:** Jack Hollingsworth/Corbis; **204:** (all) Pascal Pernix; **209:** (tl) Mauro Grigollo/AGE Fotostock; (tr) Syda Productions/AGE Fotostock; (bl) James Carman/AGE Fotostock; (br) Ben Welsh/AGE Fotostock; **210:** (all) Paula Díez; **211:** Paula Díez; **216-217:** (collage) Paula Díez; Karkas/Shutterstock; Elnur/Shutterstock; Paul Buturlimov/Shutterstock; Sergey Peterman/Shutterstock; Andrey Armyagov/Shutterstock; Polryaz/Shutterstock; Paula Díez; Paula Díez; Vladyslav Starozhylov/Shutterstock; Fadedink.net/Shutterstock; V.S. Anandhakrishna/Shutterstock; Sagir/Shutterstock, **218:** Noam/Fotolia; **219:** Martín Bernetti; **222:** (all) Pascal Pernix; **223:** (tl) Don Emmert/AFP/Getty Images; (tr) Pascal Pernix; (ml) Pascal Pernix; (mr) Road Movie Prods/Kobal/REX/Shutterstock; (b) James Bloor Griffiths/Shutterstock.

Lesson 7: 225: Media Bakery; **228:** (tl) PhotoAlto/Alamy; (tr) Radnatt/Fotolia; (tml) Bernd Vogel/Getty Images; (tmr) Blend Images/Media Bakery; (bml) Kemler/iStockphoto; (bmr) Paula Diez; (bl) Zeljkosantrac/iStockphoto; (br) Paula Diez; **234:** Stewart Cohen/Blend Images/Corbis; **235:** (t) Ali Burafi (m) Janet Dracksdorf; (b) Tommy Lindholm/Alamy; **237:** (l) Paula Diez; (r) PeopleImages/Getty Images; **239:** (l) Paula Diez; (r) Igor Mojzes/123RF; **242:** Jose Blanco; **243:** Anya Berkut/Fotolia; **252-253:** Didem Hizar/Fotolia; **254:** I Love Images/Alamy; **255:** Hill Street Studios/Getty Images; **258:** (t) Christian Vinces/Shutterstock; (ml) Reiner Elsen/Alamy; (mr) Ian Wood/Alamy; (bl) Juan Manuel Serrano Arce/Getty Images; (br) Oscar Espinosa/123RF; **259:** (tl) Martín Bernetti; (tr) Nicolamargaret/Getty Images; (ml) Manual Romaris/Getty Images; (mr) Marshall Bruce/iStockphoto; (b) Jarno Gonzalez Zarraonandia/Shutterstock.

Lesson 8: 261: Terry Vine/Media Bakery; **265:** Lauren Krolick; **267:** (l) Monkey Business/Shutterstock; (r) Anne Loubet; **272:** (t) Rachel Distler; (b) Greg Elms/Lonely Planet Images/Getty Images; **273:** (t) Pablo Cuadra/Getty Images; (ml) Rafael Rios; (mr) Studio Bonisolli/Stockfood; (b) Gerardo Mora/Getty Images; **275:** (t) Vanessa Bertozzi; (ml) Annie Pickert Fuller; (mm) Martin Bernetti; (mr) Margouillat Photo/Shutterstock; (bl) Susan Schmitz/Shutterstock; (bm) Nitr/Shutterstock; (br) Adlife Marketing/iStockphoto; **276:** Paula Diez; **278:** (l) Pixtal/AGE Fotostock; (r) Jose Blanco; **282:** (l) Andresr/Shutterstock; (r) Jose Blanco; **283:** (l) Jose Blanco; (r) Monkey Business/Shutterstock; **292:** Vanessa Bertozzi; **293:** Jack Hollingsworth/Getty Images; **296:** (t) Henryk Sadura/Shutterstock; (m) Martin Engelmann/Media Bakery; (b) Henryk Sadura/Shutterstock; **297:** (tl) Jenkedco/Shutterstock; (tr) Robert Matton AB/Alamy; (ml) Vladimir Korostyshevskiy/Shutterstock; (mr) Tom Salyer/Alamy; (b) Phil Clarke Hill/In Pictures/Getty Images.

Lesson 9: 299: Jupiter Images/Getty Images; **303:** Cathy Yeulet/123RF; **308:** (l) Javier Larrea/AGE Fotostock; (r) PictureNet/Getty Images; **309:** (t) GDA/El Mercurio/Chile/El Mercurio de Chile/Newscom; (m) GDA/El Mercurio/Chile/El Mercurio de Chile/Newscom; (b) Tim Mosenfelder/Getty Images; **322:** (t) Katrina Brown/123RF; (b) Digital Vision/Media Bakery; **323:** Carlos Hernandez/Media Bakery; **324:** Blend Images/Alamy; **328:** (tl) Lauren Krolick; (tr) Lauren Krolick; (ml) Kathryn Alena-Korf; (mr) Lauren Krolick; (bl) Bettmann/Getty Images; (br) Martin Bernetti/AFP/Getty Images; **329:** (tl) Lars Rosen Gunnilstam; (tr) Lauren Krolick; (ml) Nikolay Starchenko/Shutterstock; (mr) Lauren Krolick; (b) Bruce R. Korf.

Lesson 10: 331: Custom Medical Stock Photo/Alamy; **340:** (t) Ali Burafi; (b) Andresr/Shutterstock; **341:** (t) Courtesy of Arizona State University Hispanic Research Center; (ml) Phootlicensors International AG/Alamy; (mr) AFP/Getty Images; (b) Jealex Photo/Getty Images; **345:** ISO K Photography/Fotolia; **349:** Oscar Artavia Solano; **355:** Martin Bernetti; **358:** Dream Pictures/Getty Images; **359:** Danita Delimont/Newscom; **360:** Anthony Redpath/Masterfile; **361:** Paula Diez; **364:** (tl) Oscar Artavia Solano; (tr) Oscar Artavia Solano; (ml) Timothy A. Clary/AFP/Getty Images; (mm) Oscar Artavia Solano; (mr) Oscar Artavia Solano; **365:** (tl) Nik Wheeler/Alamy; (tr) Atlantide Phototravel/Getty Images; (tml) Jacques M. Chenet/Corbis; (tmr) Megapress/Alamy; (m) Oscar Artavia Solano; (b) E. Rojas/Shutterstock.

Lesson 11: 367: Stefan Dahl Langstrup/Alamy; **376:** (l) GM Visuals/AGE Fotostock; (r) Quka/Shutterstock; **377:** (t) Zsolt Nyulaszi/Shutterstock; (bl) M. Timothy O'Keefe/Alamy; (br) Difusion/El Comercio de Peru/Newscom; **381:** LdF/iStockphoto; **385:** Katie Wade; **386:** (all) Paula Diez; **387:** (tl) AGE Fotostock; (tr) Ali Burafi; (bl) JGI/Jamie Grill/Getty Images; (br) Paula Diez; **390:** (t) Gmnicholas/iStockphoto; (ml) Elen 418/Shutterstock; (mm) Aleksandr Kurganov/Shutterstock; (mr) Liliana Bobadilla; (bl) LdF/iStockphoto; (bm) Auris/iStockphoto; (br) Scanrail1/Shutterstock; **396:** Chad Johnson/Masterfile; **397:** Morchella/Fotolia; **400:** (t) Ali Burafi; (ml) María Eugenia Corbo; (mr) Ali Burafi; (bl) F. Neukirchen/AGE Fotostock; (br) Lauren Krolick; **401:** (tl) María Eugenia Corbo; (tr) Ali Burafi; (ml) Ali Burafi; (mr) Rocharibeiro/Shutterstock; (b) Ali Burafi.

Lesson 12: 403: Gravity Images/Getty Images; **407:** (t) Terry J/iStockphoto; (b) Harry Neave/Fotolia; **412:** (l) Dusko Despotovic; (r) Martín Bernetti; **413:** (tl) Fran Fernandez; (tr) Rafal Cichaway/123RF; (b) AB1/Adriana M. Barraza/WENN/Newscom; **415:** (l) JGI/Tom Grill/Media Bakery; (r) Anne Loubet; **416:** Blend Images/Alamy; **432:** Wilmar Photography/Alamy; **434:** Dragon Images/Shutterstock; **435:** Jolanda Van Den Oudenalder/123RF; **438:** (tl) Sergi Reboredo/Alamy; (tr) Melba/AGE Fotostock; (m) Claudio Lovo/Shutterstock; (b) Hernan H. Hernandez/Shutterstock; **439:** (tl) Galina Savina/Shutterstock; (tr) Danny Lehman/Corbis; (bl) Courtesy of www.Tahiti-Tourisme.com; (br) Jupiter Images/Getty Images.

Lesson 13: 441: Blend Images/Alamy; **443:** (tl) Gaccworship/Big Stock; (tr) Goodshoot/Alamy; (bl) National Geographic Singles 65/Inmagine; (br) Les Cunliffe/123RF; **450:** (t) Lauren Krolick; (b) Digital Vision/Fotosearch; **451:** (t) Oscar Garces/AGE Fotostock; (m) David South/Alamy; (bl) David Liittschwager/Getty Images; (br) Agencia el Universal GDA Photo Service/Newscom; **454:** Andy Shchekalev/123RF; **459:** (all) Courtesy of Mary Axtmann; **466:** (l) Apisit Sorin/EyeEm/Getty Images; **466-467:** (t) Borja Andreu/Shutterstock; (b) Yeryomina Anastassiya/Shutterstock; **467:** (r) Kitzzeh/Shutterstock; **468:** Frederic Prochassen/123RF; **472:** (tl) Andrey Gontarev/Shutterstock; (tr) Foto593/Shutterstock; (m) Jose Blanco; (b) Santiago Saldarriaga GDA Photo Service/Newscom; **473:** (tl) Ulf Andersen/Getty Images; (tr) Monica Maria Gonzalez; (ml) Jeremy Horner/Getty Images; (mr) Jess Kraft/Shutterstock; (b) Ardea.com/Mary Evans/Renato Granieri/AGE Fotostock.

Lesson 14: 475: Hilary Jane Morgan/AGE Fotostock; **484:** (l) Stuwdamdorp/Alamy; (r) David Wall/Alamy; **485:** (t) John Mitchell/Alamy; (m) Courtesy of the Barragan Foundation; (b) GV Cruz/WireImage/Alamy; **491:** Paula Diez; **498-499:** Filo/Getty Images; **500:** Masterfile RF; **501:** Paula Diez; **504:** (t) Janne Hamalainen/Shutterstock; (m) Alexander Chaikin/Shutterstock; (b) F. Neukirchen/AGE Fotostock; **505:** (tl) Julio Etchart/Alamy; (tr) Daniel Romero/VW Pics/Getty Images; (ml) Ken Welsh/Alamy; (mr) Nehophoto/Shutterstock; (b) Vladimir Melnik/Shutterstock.

Lesson 15: 507: Henglein and Steets/AGE Fotostock; **511:** Javier Larrea/AGE Fotostock; **516:** (l) Posztos/Shutterstock; (r) Oscar Artavia Solano; **517:** (t) David Mercado/Reuters/Newscom; (m) Stockcreations/Shutterstock; (b) Courtesy of Chila Jatun; **524:** Diego Cervo/iStockphoto; **530-531:** Michael Klippfeld/Getty Images; **532:** Martin Bernetti; **533:** Javier Larrea/AGE Fotostock; **538:** (tl) Elzbieta Sekowska/Shutterstock; (tr) Massimo Borchi/SIME/eStock Photo; (b) Peter Langer/AGE Fotostock; **539:** (tl) Daniel Wiedmann/Shutterstock; (tr) Anders Ryman/Alamy; (ml) VHL; (mr) Ben Pipe/SIME/eStockphoto; (b) Jess Kraft/Shutterstock.

Lesson 16: 541: Caiaimage/Lukasz Olek/Getty Images; **545:** (t) Orange Line Media/Shutterstock; (b)Paula Diez; **550:** PhotoAlto sas/Alamy; **551:** (t) VHL; (m) Galen Rowell/Getty Images; (b) Courtesy of Eterno Fotoarte; **560:** Pezography/Bigstock; **561:** RJ Lerich/Bigstock; **564:** (t) Courtesy of María Consuelo Sáez de Burgos; (b) Frida Khalo. Las dos Fridas. 1939. 2014 Banco de Mexico Diego Rivera Frida Kahlo Museums Trust, Mexico, D.F./Artists Rights Society (ARS), New York. Photo credit: Schalkwijk/Art Resource, NY; **566:** Martin Bernetti; **567:** Paula Diez; **572:** (tl) Endless Traveller/Shutterstock; (tr) RJ Lerich/Shutterstock; (m) Tobe_dw/Shutterstock; (b) Johnny Louis/FilmMagic/Getty Images; **573:** (tl) Grigory Kubatyan/Shutterstock; (tr) Dennis Drenner/Washington Post/Getty Images; (ml) Holdeneye/Shutterstock; (mr) Thornton Cohen/Alamy; (b) Scott B. Rosen/Alamy; **574:** (tl) Salim October/Shutterstock; (tr) Daniel Indiana/Shutterstock; (b) Werner Otto/Alamy; **575:** (tl) Alvaro Leiva/Alamy; (tr) Aspen Photo/Shutterstock; (ml) Lucas Vallecillos/AGE Fotostock; (mr) Evannovostro/Shutterstock; (b) AKG-Images/The Image Works.

Lesson 17: 577: Dragon Images/Shutterstock; **581:** Andres Rodriguez/Fotolia; **586:** (l) Exposicion Cuerpo Plural, Museo de Arte Contemporaneo Caracas, Venezuela, Octubre 2005 (Sala1). Fotografia Morella Munox-Tebar. Archivo Mac; (r) Art Resource, NY; **587:** (t) Eric Roberts/VIP Productions/Getty Images; (m) Museo de Antioquia; (b) Courtesy of Ángel Lopez; **590:** GM Visuals/Media Bakery; **591:** DC Comics/DC Entertainment/Album/Newscom; **600-601:** (background) Bro Studio/Shutterstock; (foreground) Juanmonino/Getty Images; **602:** Lichtmaster/Shutterstock; **606:** (tl) John Coletti/Getty Images; (tr) L. Kragt Bakker/Shutterstock; (bl) Leif Skogfors/Getty Images; (br) Andre Nantel/Shutterstock; **607:** (tl) Edfuentesg/iStockphoto; (tr) Ondrej Prosicky/Shutterstock; (ml) Jose Cabezas/Reuters/Newscom; (mr) Sheridan Stancliff/Exactostock-1491/Superstock; (b) Corbis; **608:** (tl) B & T Media Group Inc/Shutterstock; (tr) Philippe Turpin/AGE Fotostock; (bl) Sandra A. Dunlap/Shutterstock; (br) Christian Kober/Alamy; **609:** (tl) Vik Vojtech/AGE Fotostock; (tr) Elmer Martinez/Stringer/Getty Images; (ml) Jose Antonio Velasquez. San Antonio de Oriente. 1957. Collection OAS AMA/Art Museum of Americas; (mr) B Trapp/AGE Fotostock; (b) Martin Bernetti.

Lesson 18: 611: Nano Calvo/AGE Fotostock; **615:** (t) Robert Paul Van Beets/Shutterstock; (b) VHL; **620:** (l) Jose Blanco; (r) TravelStockCollection - Homer Sykes/Alamy; **621:** (t) Haakon Mosvold LarsenAFP/Getty Images; (b) Juan Aguado/Redferns/Getty Images; **624:** Anne Loubet; **629:** (l) John Dambik/Alamy; (r) Globe Guide Media/Shutterstock; **634:** Joel Nito/Stringer/Getty Images; **635:** Dream Pictures/Getty Images; **638:** (t) Julian Peters Photography/Getty Images; (bl) Ian Trower/Getty Images; (br) VHL; **639:** (tl) De Agostini/G. Kiner/Getty Images; (tr) Christian Rizzi/AFP/Getty Images; (ml) Hugh Percival/Fotolia; (mr) Thomas Vinke/Getty Images; (b) Jorge Saenz/AP Images; **640:** (tl) Peter Groenendijk/Robert Harding/Media Bakery; (b) Hans Neleman/Getty Images; (b) Maria Eugenia Corbo; **641:** (tl) Janet Dracksdorf; (tr) Jonathon Larsen/Diadem Images/Alamy; (ml) Richard I'Anson/Getty Images; (mr) JMN/Cover/Getty Images; (b) Maria Eugenia Corbo.

Back Cover: Demaerre/iStockphoto.

About the Authors

José A. Blanco founded Vista Higher Learning in 1998. A native of Barranquilla, Colombia, Mr. Blanco holds a B.A. in Literature from the University of California, Santa Cruz, and a M.A. in Hispanic Studies from Brown University. He has worked as a writer, editor, and translator for Houghton Mifflin and D.C. Heath and Company and has taught Spanish at the secondary and university levels. Mr. Blanco is also the co-author of several other Vista Higher Learning programs: **Panorama, Aventuras,** and **¡Viva!** at the introductory level; **Enlaces, Facetas, Enfoques, Imagina,** and **Sueña** at the intermediate level; and **Revista** at the advanced conversation level.

Philip Redwine Donley received his M.A. in Hispanic Literature from the University of Texas at Austin in 1986 and his Ph.D. in Foreign Language Education from the University of Texas at Austin in 1997. Dr. Donley taught Spanish at Austin Community College, Southwestern University, and the University of Texas at Austin. He published articles and conducted workshops about language anxiety management, and the development of critical thinking skills, and was involved in research about teaching languages to the visually impaired. Dr. Donley was also the co-author of **Aventuras** and **Panorama,** two other introductory college Spanish textbook programs published by Vista Higher Learning.

Estados Unidos

Golfo de México

Honduras

Belice

Guatemala

El Salvador

Cancún

Mérida

YUCATÁN

Campeche

Bahía de Campeche

Villahermosa

ISTMO DE
TEHUANTEPEC

Matamoros

Reynosa

Tampico

Jalapa

Veracruz

México, D.F.

Puebla

Oaxaca

Cuernavaca

Nuevo Laredo

Monterrey

San Luis Potosí

Ciudad Victoria

Saltillo

León

Guanajuato

Zacatecas

R. Balsas

Aguascalientes

Morelia

Uruapan

Acapulco

México

Sierra Madre Oriental

Río Grande

Río Bravo del Norte

R. Conchos

Guadalajara

Mazatlán

Puerto Vallarta

Ciudad Juárez

Chihuahua

Sierra Madre Occidental

La Paz

Nogales

Hermosillo

Golfo de California

Océano Pacífico

BAJA CALIFORNIA

R. Colorado

Mexicali

Tijuana

N E
O S

México

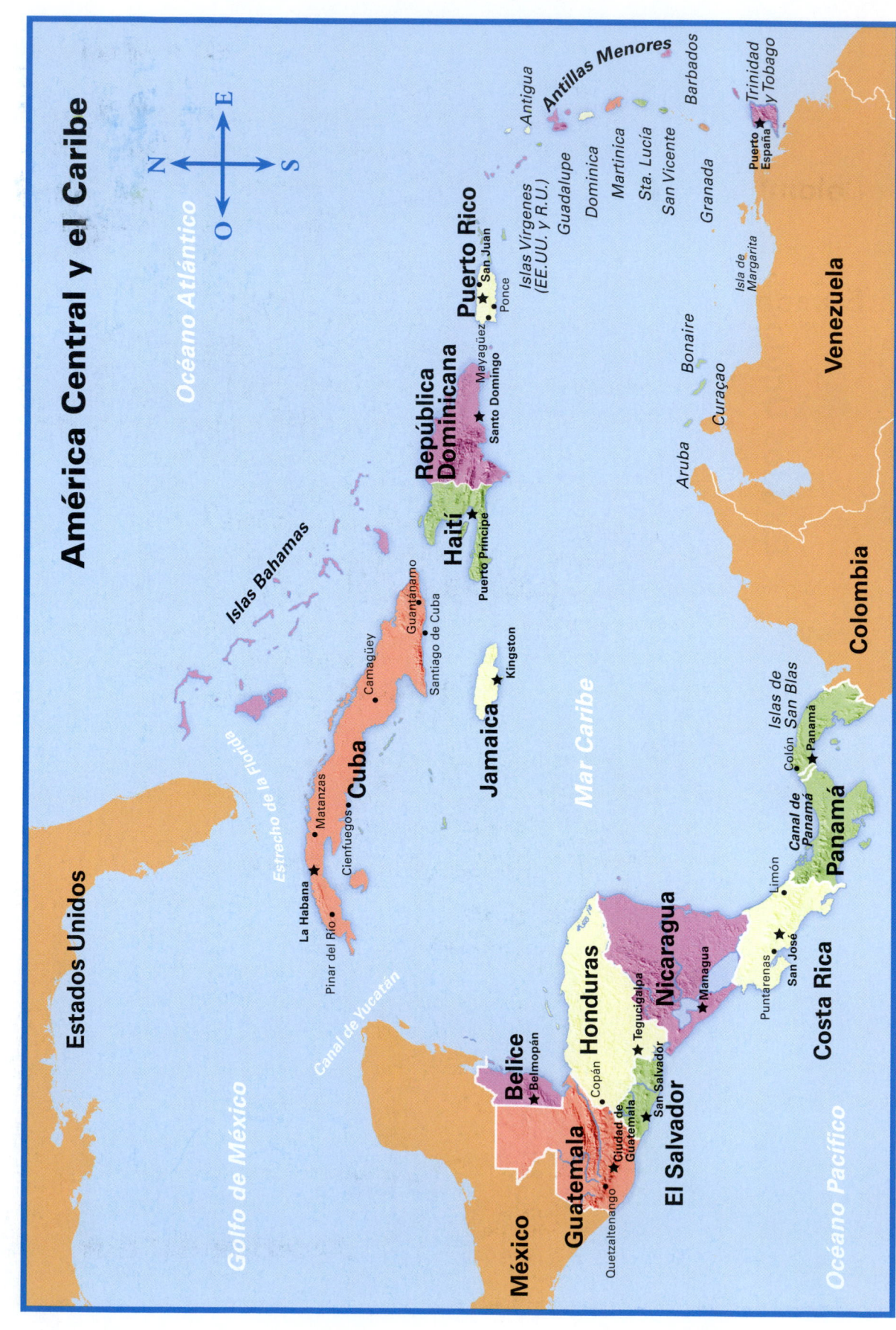

América Central y el Caribe

N E S O

Océano Atlántico

Golfo de México

Estados Unidos

México

Islas Bahamas

Estrecho de la Florida

Canal de Yucatán

La Habana
Pinar del Río
Matanzas
Cienfuegos
Cuba
Camagüey
Santiago de Cuba
Guantánamo

Jamaica
Kingston

Mar Caribe

Belice
Belmopán
Copán
Honduras
Tegucigalpa
Guatemala
Ciudad de Guatemala
Quetzaltenango
San Salvador
El Salvador
Nicaragua
Managua

Costa Rica
Puntarenas
San José
Limón

Haití
Puerto Príncipe
República Dominicana
Santo Domingo

Puerto Rico
Mayagüez
San Juan
Ponce

Islas Vírgenes
(EE.UU. y R.U.)

Antillas Menores
Antigua
Guadalupe
Dominica
Martinica
Sta. Lucía
San Vicente
Granada
Barbados
Trinidad y Tobago
Puerto España

Isla de Margarita

Aruba
Curaçao
Bonaire

Islas de San Blas
Colón
Panamá
Panamá
Canal de Panamá

Colombia

Venezuela

Océano Pacífico

Mar Caribe

Barranquilla • Maracaibo
Caracas • Puerto España
Trinidad y Tobago

Venezuela

Colombia
Medellín •
Bogotá ★
• Cali
R. Orinoco
Georgetown ★
Guyana
Paramaribo ★
Surinam
Cayena •
Guayana Francesa

Pasto •
★ Quito
Ecuador
Guayaquil •

R. Negro
R. Amazonas
Manaus •
Belém •

• Iquitos

Perú
R. Madeira

Recife •

Lima ★
• Cuzco
Brasil
Salvador •

Lago Titicaca
Arequipa •
★ La Paz
Bolivia
★ Brasilia •

Arica •
Sucre ★
• Belo Horizonte

Iquique •
R. Paraguay

Antofagasta •
R. Paraná
São Paulo •
• Río de Janeiro
Santos •

• Salta
Paraguay

Chile
Asunción ★
R. Uruguay

Córdoba •
R. Paraná
Porto Alegre •

Valparaíso •
Mendoza •
• Rosario
Uruguay

★ Santiago
Buenos Aires ★
Montevideo •

Concepción •
Argentina

• Bahía Blanca

Puerto Montt •

Estrecho de Magallanes
Punta Arenas •
Islas Malvinas

Tierra del Fuego

América del Sur

Cordillera de los Andes

Océano Pacífico

Océano Atlántico

N
O — E
S

Islas Galápagos

Océano Pacífico

Isla Pinta
Isla Marchena
Isla Genovesa

Isla Isabela

Línea Ecuatorial
Volcán Darwin
Isla Santiago (San Salvador)

Isla Fernandina
Puerto Ayora
Isla San Cristóbal

Santo Tomás
Isla Santa Cruz
Puerto Barquerizo Moreno

Isla Santa María
Isla Española

ECUADOR

Francia

Andorra

CATALUÑA

Gerona

Menorca

Palma de Mallorca

Mallorca

Mar Mediterráneo

Islas Canarias

Lanzarote

Arrecife

Puerto del Rosario

Fuerteventura

Marruecos

Pirineos

Tarragona

Barcelona

Ibiza

Formentera

Islas Baleares

La Palma

Santa Cruz de la Palma

Tenerife

Santa Cruz de Tenerife

Las Palmas de Gran Canaria

Océano Atlántico

Lérida

NAVARRA

Zaragoza

ARAGÓN

Valencia

COMUNIDAD VALENCIANA

Gomera

Hierro

Gran Canaria

PAÍS VASCO

Pamplona

España

Alicante

San Sebastián

LA RIOJA

Madrid

CASTILLA-LA MANCHA

Albacete

Murcia

Cartagena

Bilbao

Mar Cantábrico

CANTABRIA

Santander

Burgos

CASTILLA-LEÓN

Segovia

Toledo

Sierra Nevada

Almería

Melilla (Esp.)

ASTURIAS

Oviedo

Gijón

Avilés

Valladolid

Salamanca

Ávila

Sierra Morena

Jaén

ANDALUCÍA

Granada

Málaga

Córdoba

Palencia

Zamora

Gibraltar (R.U.)

Ceuta (Esp.)

La Coruña

GALICIA

Pontevedra

Cáceres

EXTREMADURA

Mérida

Badajoz

Sevilla

Huelva

Cádiz

Algeciras

Marruecos

Vigo

Braga

Coimbra

Serra da Estrela

Setúbal

Estrecho de Gibraltar

Oporto

Portugal

Lisboa

Océano Atlántico

N

O

E

S